CONTEMPORARY MONEY, BANKING, AND FINANCIAL MARKETS

THEORY AND PRACTICE

Michael G Hadjimichalakis
Karma G. Hadjimichalakis
University of Washington

The McGraw-Hill Companies, Inc.
Primis Custom Publishing

New York St. Louis San Francisco Auckland Bogota
Caracas Lisbon London Madrid Mexico Milan Montreal
New Delhi Paris San Juan Singapore Sydney Tokyo Toronto

McGraw-Hill Higher Education

A Division of The McGraw·Hill Companies

ISBN-13: 978-0-07-245781-0
ISBN-10: 0-07-245781-3

Custom Editor: Lynn Nordbrock
Printer/Binder: Quebecor World, Dubuque, Iowa

CONTEMPORARY MONEY, BANKING, AND FINANCIAL MARKETS

Theory and Practice

THE IRWIN SERIES IN ECONOMICS

Appleyard and Field
International Economics
Second Edition

Appleyard and Field
**International Economics: Trade
Theory and Policy**
Second Edition

Appleyard and Field
**International Economics: Payments,
Exchange Rates, and Macro Policy**
Second Edition

Baily and Friedman
**Macroeconomics, Financial Markets,
and the International Sector**
Second Edition

Barron and Lynch
Economics
Third Edition

Baye and Beil
**Managerial Economics and Business
Strategy**

Blair
Urban and Regional Economics

Bornstein
**Comparative Economic Systems:
Models and Cases**
Seventh Edition

Brown and Moore
**Readings, Issues and Problems in
Public Finance**
Fourth Edition

Colander
Economics
Second Edition

Colander
Microeconomics
Second Edition

Colander
Macroeconomics
Second Edition

Denzau
**Microeconomic Analysis: Markets and
Dynamics**

Fisher
State and Local Government Finance

Hadjimichalakis & Hadjimichalakis
**Contemporary Money, Banking, and
Financial Markets: Theory and
Practice**

Hyman
Economics
Third Edition

Hyman
Microeconomics
Third Edition

Hyman
Macroeconomics
Third Edition

Hyman
**Modern Microeconomics: Analysis
and Applications**
Third Edition

Katz and Rosen
Microeconomics
Second Edition

Lehmann
**Real World Economic Applications:
The Wall Street Journal Workbook**
Third Edition

Lindert
International Economics
Ninth Edition

Maurice and Phillips
**Economic Analysis: Theory and
Application**
Sixth Edition

Maurice and Thomas
**Managerial Economics: Applied
Microeconomics for Decision Making**
Fifth Edition

O'Sullivan
Urban Economics
Second Edition

O'Sullivan
Essentials of Urban Economics

Prager
**Applied Microeconomics: An
Intermediate Approach**

Rima
Development of Economic Analysis
Fifth Edition

Roger and Daniel
**Principles of Economics Software
Simulation**

Rosen
Public Finance
Fourth Edition

Schwarz and Van Dyken
**Manager: Managerial Economics
Software**

Seo
**Managerial Economics: Text, Short
Cases**
Seventh Edition

Sharp, Register, and Leftwich
Economics of Social Issues
Eleventh Edition

Shepherd
Public Policies Toward Business
Eight Edition

Shughart
The Organization of Industry

Slavin
Microeconomics
Third Edition

Slavin
Macroeconomics
Third Edition

Streifford
Economic Perspective

Walton and Wykoff
Understanding Economics Today
Fourth Edition

Why write a textbook on money, banking, and financial markets? As we set out on this project, we envisioned a book that would be different and, we believed, better than those available in the market: a book that (1) would deal with the real-life financial system and the real-life conduct of monetary policy, (2) would be based on a coherent, recognizable, economic framework, and (3) would be accessible to anybody who has completed an introductory course on the principles of economics.

Accessibility is crucial. Why write a book if it cannot be read by those it addresses? But sacrificing substance for accessibility would be a hollow success. A substantive approach to money, banking, and financial markets requires an analytical framework that permits one to tackle important issues rather than to skirt them, especially during a period of great change and even upheaval in financial markets, as the past 15 years have been.

Learning about money, banking, and financial markets and their links to the rest of the economy has been exciting and challenging in recent years. During the past 15 years, deposit rates paid by U.S. banks and other depository institutions have been deregulated for the first time since the 1930s. Restrictions on permissible activities of financial institutions have been relaxed and, in some cases, removed. As we write this preface, President Clinton has signed into law the Riegle–Neal Interstate Banking and Branching Efficiency Act of 1994. This law permits nationwide banking by allowing banks to set up branches across state lines, thereby removing a restriction on banks dating back to the 1920s. The last decade also witnessed the failure of banks and thrifts at rates unseen for 60 years. Moreover, in the early 1990s a credit crunch, in which banks became less willing and able to lend, hampered the recovery of the U.S. economy.

We have both been involved in studying and teaching these developments. First, from 1980 to 1982, as economists at the Board of Governors of the Federal Reserve System in Washington, D.C., we witnessed and wrote about the quantum leap the financial system took toward the new financial environment with the passage of the Depository Institutions Deregulation and Monetary Control Act of 1980 and the challenges the new financial environment created for the conduct of monetary policy. Since our return to the University of Washington in 1982, we have been teaching money, banking, and financial markets—one of us in the economics department, the other in the business school. In our teaching we have tried to bring to the classroom the excitement of exploring these issues. Our approach has been to establish a theoretical framework to examine today's monetary and financial system and to connect theory with practice. The enthusiastic response of our students convinced us to write this book.

THE TWO-PILLAR FRAMEWORK

The framework that we have worked on and refined over the past 14 years and that we develop in this book is simple and powerful. It is based on (1) the rational behavior of participants in the economy and (2) their interaction in the marketplace. How participants make decisions and how markets work are, what we call, the two pillars of economics. These two pillars embody our approach to money, banking, and financial markets. We use this two-pillar framework to describe the contemporary monetary and financial system; to build a theoretical model to understand and analyze the workings of that system and its links to the rest of the economy; and to connect theory with practice, such as assessing the practices of the Federal Reserve in its conduct of monetary policy, the activities of banks, and the workings of financial markets.

The most immediate payoff of the two-pillar framework is to make teaching and learning money, banking, and financial markets easier. Students with a principles of economics background are familiar with the two pillars of economics, especially in the form of profit-maximizing decisions, on the one hand, and the forces of supply and demand, on the other. The message of even a beginning course is that economics is about incentives and purposeful behavior and about market forces. Students feel at home when instructors explain money, banking, and financial markets in these terms, because they see the exposition as a natural application of concepts they already know. Learning money, banking and financial markets in this way is a lot easier and more fruitful than memorizing disjointed material. Beyond the final exam, students have a framework they can continue to apply to understand and analyze current issues.

The two-pillar framework also simplifies the exposition by enabling us to present the material in self-contained but not disjointed chapters. Most chapters can be read by themselves, and yet, all chapters are unified in a coherent framework. With a unified framework it is easy to incorporate important new concepts of economic theory, such as asymmetric information, as we do beginning in Chapter 2. Moreover, existing theories can be extended to incorporate new practices. For example, ours is the only textbook that develops a theory of the deposit-rate setting behavior of banks in the new financial environment and incorporates this theory into traditional models of money demand. The resulting contemporary theory of money demand is essential for understanding and analyzing the portfolio decisions of the public and the policy decisions of the Federal Reserve, such as the Fed's decision in July 1993 to downgrade the role of monetary aggregates in the policy process.

Now that we have finished writing this book, we believe that we have achieved all three goals we set out to accomplish. But we are not impartial observers. The students and professors who use this book must be the ultimate judges.

AN INTEGRATED APPROACH TO INTERNATIONAL TOPICS

The U.S. economy is connected to the rest of the world through trade in goods and services and trade in financial and real assets. Because the international linkages are a key part of the economic system, we incorporate them in our framework from the start, beginning with Chapter 2, in which the foreign sector is one of the six participants. The last two chapters of the book present more detailed treatments of international issues. These chapters are designed so that they may be introduced earlier. For example, instructors who want a full-blown treatment of the balance of payments accounts and the foreign exchange market early in their course may introduce Chapter 29 after Chapter 9 or Chapter 10.

PEDAGOGICAL FEATURES

The book has a variety of learning tools:

- **Part Openers** list the chapters in each part and explain briefly how they fit into the two-pillar framework.
- **Chapter Previews** typically begin with a vignette to introduce key issues and then explain how the chapter is organized.
- **"Watch" Boxes** connect theory with practice by using real-world data, policy reports of the Federal Reserve, excerpts from *The Wall Street Journal*, and interesting anecdotes to illuminate concepts developed in each chapter. The four types of watch boxes are tied to the two-pillar framework.

    SectorWatch examines the behavior of the participants, which is the subject of the first pillar of economics. There are six categories of participants: households, firms, financial intermediaries, the government, the Federal Reserve, and foreign participants. All the participants in one category are often referred to as a "sector," such as the household sector.

    MarketWatch examines the behavior of participants in the marketplace, which is the subject of the second pillar of economics.

    FedWatch follows and explains the actions of the Federal Reserve, as professional Fedwatchers do. Because of the importance of the Federal Reserve in the economy, the Fed is assigned its own watch box.

    GlobalWatch presents the international perspective by explaining the behavior of foreign participants and also by explaining how the domestic economy is linked to foreign economies through the markets for goods and services and financial assets.

- **Schematic Explanations** in the text and in summary tables help students understand and remember the basic logic behind important economic relations.
- **Try-It-Out Exercises** are workstations for students that appear within most chapters. They are tools to check and reinforce student understanding. Answers to the try-it-out exercises are at the end of the book.
- **End-of-Chapter Questions and Problems** consist of a variety of review questions and analytical and quantitative problems. Our approach of connecting theory with practice extends to this end-of-chapter material. Questions identified by The Wall Street Journal ask students to interpret quotations and data from *The Wall Street Journal*.
- **Key Terms and Concepts** appear in boldface when they are defined in a chapter. They are also listed at the end of each chapter.
- **A Glossary** at the end of the book provides definitions of all the key terms and concepts.
- **End-of-Chapter Summaries** present concise reviews of the main points in each chapter.
- **A short, annotated list of readings** ends each chapter. The readings were chosen to be accessible and interesting to a student audience.

OVERVIEW AND ORGANIZATION OF TOPICS

For a bird's-eye view of the entire book, we present a brief summary of each of the eight parts of the book.

Part 1: Introduction (Chapter 1)   This introductory chapter explains the importance of money in the economy by looking at its functions and definitions and by previewing the relation between money and the economy. It also introduces the two-pillar framework that is the foundation of our approach to money, banking, and financial markets.

Part 2: The U.S. Financial System: *The Participants, the Instruments, and the Environment* **(Chapters 2–5)**   Money is a key financial asset, but it is not the only asset in the financial system. Part 2 describes the entire financial system by introducing the participants, the financial instruments they issue and acquire, and the environment in which they operate.

Chapter 2 poses two questions. Who are the participants in the financial system? And why do they issue and acquire financial instruments? In answering these questions, the chapter explains the linkages between the domestic economy and foreign economies and introduces the concepts of direct and indirect finance and asymmetric information. Chapter 3 explains six characteristics of financial instruments: maturity, marketability, rate of return, risk, liquidity, and divisibility. Chapter 4 describes the basic instruments in the financial system in terms of these characteristics and puts the financial instruments into the participants' balance sheets. There are six participants: households, firms, financial intermediaries, the government, the Federal Reserve, and foreign participants. The balance sheets of these participants are profiles of their financial condition. Bringing the balance sheets to life to describe the purposeful behavior of the participants is the subject of one of the two pillars of economics that will occupy us throughout the book. Chapter 5 surveys the evolution from the old financial environment to the new financial environment in which participants operate. A key characteristic of the new financial environment that emerged in the 1980s is that the interest paid on bank deposits is market determined. By contrast, in the old financial environment regulators set the deposit rate. The chapter begins by explaining the market forces that made the rise of the new financial environment inevitable and ends by examining how that environment functioned under a crisis and a crunch: the thrift crisis of the 1980s and the credit crunch of the early 1990s.

Part 3: Money, Interest Rates, and Prices (Chapters 6–10)   Part 3 uses the two-pillar framework to explain the portfolio choice of the participants, the interaction of participants in financial markets, and the connection between the markets for domestic financial instruments, foreign exchange, and goods and services.

Chapter 6 develops five laws of asset demand by explaining the portfolio choice of the public (households and firms) in terms of the characteristics of assets introduced in Chapter 3. Chapter 7 first develops a theory of the deposit-rate setting behavior of banks and applies the theory to explain movements in deposit rates in the early 1990s. Then it combines the theory of deposit-rate determination with the laws of asset demand to develop a contemporary theory of money demand. Chapter 8 uses the balance sheets of the Fed, banks, and the public to develop and apply a simple and realistic explanation of the money supply process based on the concepts of nonborrowed reserves, borrowed reserves, required reserves, and excess reserves. An appendix presents the monetary base approach to the money supply. Chapter 9 moves to the markets to explain interest rate determination by using the money market (the liquidity preference theory) and the bonds market (the loanable funds theory). The chapter connects theory with practice to explain the behavior of the Fed after the stock market crash of 1987 and to compare the monetary policies of the Fed and the Bundesbank in the early 1990s. Chapter 10 completes the framework of the economy by adding the foreign exchange market and the market for goods and services to the model. The chapter develops the aggregate demand-aggregate supply model in a simple way to explore the effects of policy and other shocks on interest rates, prices, and output. Emphasis is on the four effects of a change in the money supply on interest rates: the liquidity effect, the real income effect, the price level effect, and the expected inflation effect. The chapter connects theory with practice by using the model to assess and compare the conduct of policy in the United States and Japan in the early 1990s.

Chapters 6 through 10 present comprehensive but concise explanations of the behavior of the participants and their interaction in markets. Each of the remaining parts gives fuller treatments of these topics. Instructors can tailor the order in which they cover these parts to suit the needs of their class.

Part 4: The Federal Reserve and Its Behavior (Chapters 11–16)   Part 4 combines real-world data and policy reports of the Federal Reserve with an analytical framework that helps one to understand and assess past, present, and future policy decisions of the Federal Reserve. The up-to-date analysis includes an explanation of why the Fed downgraded the monetary aggregates in July 1993 and put greater reliance on judgment and discretion in its policy process in 1994.

Chapter 11 lays out the structure and functions of the entire Federal Reserve System and explores political issues that arise from that structure, such as the ongoing debate about the independence of the Fed and about reducing secrecy. Chapter 12 explains in detail the operations of the 12 district Federal Reserve banks, such as their role as banker to banks, banker to the U.S. government, and examiner and supervisor of banks. Chapter 13 introduces a three-stage process that links the instruments, the operating targets, the intermediate targets, and the ultimate goals of monetary policy. It uses this framework to analyze past and current policies of the Fed, including the Fed's downgrading of the role of money as an intermediate target in July 1993. The chapter ends with a discussion of how the Fed used short-term real interest rates as an indicator in its search for a neutral monetary policy between February and August 1994. Chapter 14 explains how the Trading Desk of the Federal Reserve Bank of New York decides on the amount of securities to buy or sell in the open market, how Fedwatchers have traditionally followed the daily open market operations to detect shifts in the stance of monetary policy, and how the Fed began to announce these shifts in 1994 rather than filtering the information through Fedwatchers. It then uses an actual statistical release of the Federal Reserve System to explain all the factors that affect reserves in the banking system. Chapter 15 examines in detail the relation between reserves and the money supply. The chapter begins with a "bouncing ball" metaphor followed by balance sheets of the Fed and banks to explain the mechanics of deposit creation. Next it links the mechanics of deposit creation to the money supply process introduced in Chapter 8 and presents a full discussion of all the factors affecting the money supply, including the interest rate. Finally, Chapter 16 combines the quantity theory of money with the Fed's monetary policy reports and actual data from the 1980s and 1990s to explain the Fed's conduct of monetary policy. The chapter explains the challenges posed by deregulation and uses data to show that since the mid-1980s the Fed has acted as if it were targeting velocity-indexed money growth, which equals the growth of nominal gross domestic product. Placed in this perspective, we see the downgrading of the monetary aggregates in 1993 as the culmination of a move away from monetary targeting that began in 1982.

Part 5: Financial Institutions: *Structure, Regulation, and Behavior* (Chapters 17–19)   Part 5 examines the structure of financial institutions, the regulatory and supervisory environment in which they operate, and the strategies they use to maximize profits.

After presenting a roadmap for examining the organization and structure of all financial institutions, Chapter 17 concentrates on the structure, regulation, and supervision of banks and thrifts. The chapter assesses the changes that arose from the Financial Institutions Reform, Recovery and Enforcement Act (FIRREA) of 1989—passed in response to the thrift crisis—and the Federal Deposit Insurance Corporation Improvement Act (FDICIA) of 1991. The chapter also examines current debates on consolidating regulatory agencies and reforming deposit insurance. Chapter 18 develops a profit-maximizing model to explain the behavior of banks. To set the stage, the chapter begins with actual income statements and balance sheets of U.S. commercial banks and applies the concepts of adverse selection and moral hazard, which are related to the concept of asymmetric information introduced in Chapter 2. The chapter brings the balance sheet of banks to life by explaining how the choice of each item in a simplified balance sheet can be explained as the result of a profit-maximizing exercise. The chapter connects theory with practice by using the profit-maximizing model to explain the credit crunch of the 1990s. Finally, Chapter 19 explains the structure, regulation, and decisionmaking of nondepository institutions, such as finance companies, mutual funds, insurance companies, and pension funds.

Part 6: Financial Markets, Interest Rates, and the Conduct of Monetary Policy (Chapters 20–23)   Part 6 expands the analysis of financial markets introduced in Chapter 9. The chapters in this part examine the deposit market and the money market in more detail and add more financial markets and, hence, more rates of return to the picture.

Chapter 20 derives the laws of money demand in a way that shows how the theory has evolved over the past 100 years. Emphasis is on modern treatments of the transactions motive and the speculative motive. Chapter 21, by exploring the workings of the deposit market, extends the analysis introduced in Chapter 7 of factors affecting the deposit rate. Following the approach of Chapter 7, the deposit rate relation distilled from the deposit market is incorporated into the money demand relation to arrive at a complete theory of money demand. The chapter connects theory with practice to explain why banks bid less aggressively for deposits in the early 1990s and how deregulation affected the stability of money demand in the 1980s and early 1990s. Chapter 22 explores the workings of the money market to explain how the actions of the Fed, the public, and banks, as well as changes in the price level and in the level of real economic activity, affect the interest rate, the quantity of money, and the deposit rate. The chapter also uses the model of the money market to examine alternative practices of the Fed, under which the Fed targets either the quantity of money or the interest rate. Chapter 23 disaggregates the model of the financial system to explain factors that affect a spectrum of interest rates on debt securities and rates of return on equity securities. First the chapter examines the term structure of interest rates. It connects theory with practice by examining the debate about whether a shortening of the maturity structure of government debt can reduce long-term interest rates. Next, the chapter examines the risk structure of interest rates. Finally, the chapter uses a four-asset model that includes the stock market to examine how monetary policy affects interest rates on open-market debt securities, bank loan rates, deposit rates, and the rate of return on equity securities.

Part 7: The Integration of the Financial and Real Sectors (Chapters 24–28)
Part 7 expands the discussion introduced in Chapter 10 of the connection between the financial sector and the real sector. The chapters in this part paint a more detailed picture of the factors that affect interest rates, output, and prices. They also explain the theoretical underpinnings of controversies about the conduct of monetary and fiscal policy and use economic history to show how these controversies have played out in practice.

To keep our early discussion of the linkages between the financial sector and the real sector as simple as possible, Chapter 10 bypassed the IS-LM model and went straight to the AD-AS model. In contrast, this part begins with the IS-LM model. Chapter 24 develops a modern version of the IS-LM model that includes the international linkages and a credit channel. Chapter 25 applies the model to examine the effects on the interest rate and output of changes in monetary and fiscal policy and changes in the behavior of the private sector. The chapter connects theory with practice to explain the twin deficits in the United States in the 1980s and in Germany in the 1990s. It also explains the shocks, dubbed headwinds, that buffeted the U.S. economy in the early 1990s. Finally, the chapter uses the model to examine the Fed's choice of an intermediate target for the conduct of monetary policy. Chapter 26 combines the IS-LM model with the markets for inputs to derive and apply the AD-AS model, which explains the factors affecting interest rates, output, and the price level. Chapter 27 examines in more detail the most controversial part of the macroeconomic model: the theoretical underpinnings of the aggregate supply relation. The chapter develops the concept of rational expectations and explains how new classicists combine this concept with the assumption of continuous clearance of the labor market whereas new Keynesians combine it with the assumption of slow clearance of the labor market. The chapter then examines differences in the policy prescriptions of Keynesians, classicists, new classicists, and new Keynesians. Chapter 28 uses the AD-AS model and the Phillips curve model to examine the relation between inflation and unemployment. The chapter connects theory with practice by examining the effects on inflation, output, unemployment, and interest rates of wars, supply-side shocks, stock-market crashes, and revolutions in economic policymaking.

Part 8: International Finance (Chapters 29–30)   This last part of the book extends the analysis of international trade and finance that appears throughout the book.

Chapter 29 begins with the U.S. balance of payments accounts and then brings the accounts to life by connecting them to the foreign exchange market. The chapter explains the workings of the foreign exchange market under flexible and fixed exchange rate systems and explains and applies the concepts of interest rate parity and purchasing power parity. Finally, the chapter explains the evolution of the existing international payments system, which is a mix of fixed and floating exchange rates. Chapter 30 extends the discussion of the international dimensions of economic policy by building and applying the IS-LM-BP model, where BP stands for the balance of payments. This model is well suited to explaining the differences in the effects of economic policy under fixed and flexible exchange rates. The chapter connects theory with practice to explain crises in the European Monetary System in 1992 and 1993.

FLEXIBILITY

The preceding summary highlights the main points of each chapter in the order in which the chapters appear in the book. The book, however, is designed to be flexible. There are numerous alternative ways to arrange the chapters. Most courses will use the first nine or ten chapters, which are the core of the book. Below are illustrations of sequences of chapters that can be used in four types of courses. *The Instructors' Manual* provides more details.

General Course on Money, Banking, and Financial Markets	Chapters 1–10, 11, 13, 15–16, 17–19, 22–23
Course with an Emphasis on Financial Institutions and Markets	Chapters 1–9, 23, 29, 11–14, 17–19
Course with an Emphasis on Monetary Policy	Chapters 1–10, 11–16, 17, 24–25, 29–30
Course with an Emphasis on Monetary Theory and Macroeconomics	Chapters 1–9, 11, 13, 20–30

SUPPLEMENTARY MATERIALS

In order to make the instructor's transition to our book smooth, we've prepared an *Instructor's Manual* that makes good use of our teaching experience with this text. It includes lecture outlines and teaching tips, as well as solutions to the end-of-chapter questions.

Also for the instructor, *Computest 4* (as well as a bound version of the *Test Bank*), has been prepared for this text by Marvin S. Margolis, of Millersville University of Pennsylvania. The testing material consists of multiple-choice and essay questions which range both in type (analytical vs. definitional) and level of difficulty.

The *Study Guide* by Frederick L. Joutz, of George Washington University, and Jane de Winter, completes the learning package. We think it's important for students to know how to read (and to understand what they read in) *The Wall Street Journal*—that's why it's a fundamental part of the text. The study guide extends this concept. In addition to "drill and review" questions, this problem-solving manual also includes at least two articles from the popular press per chapter—in particular from the *Journal*. These articles encourage students to apply the text material to what they read in the papers.

A Wall Street Journal edition of our book is also available. For those of you unfamiliar with this uniquely Irwin product, an order form (along with a few pages of instruction) is bound into the edition. Students mail in the order form and shortly thereafter they will begin to receive their 10-week subscription. For an additional $4, there's no better way to get *The Wall Street Journal* into your classroom. Instructors will receive a year-long complimentary subscription to the *Journal*. Also, a fax newsletter is under development and will be made available to all instructors using our book.

ACKNOWLEDGMENTS

In writing this book, we have benefited from the comments, advice, and suggestions of students, colleagues, reviewers, and editors. We have both class-tested the book, in manuscript form and in galley pages. The detailed comments of our students helped us to keep in mind the student perspective as we revised each chapter. We have also benefited from numerous discussions with our colleagues. We are especially grateful to William W. Alberts, Kaz Miyagiwa, Richard Startz, and Stephen J. Turnovsky, who read and commented on specific chapters.

We thank Richard D. Irwin, Inc., for assembling a panel of reviewers whose comments and insights helped us to avoid pitfalls and to improve the content and exposition of this book. We are grateful to all of them.

Christine Amsler	Michigan State University
Scott Bloom	North Dakota State University
Robert Carpenter	Emory University
Mitch Charkiewicz	Central Connecticut State University
Kristine Chase	St. Mary's College of California
Ivan Cohen	University of North Carolina
Gary Dymski	University of California/Riverside
David Findlay	University of Illinois
James Gerber	San Diego State University
Morgan Lynge	University of Illinois
Marvin S. Margolis	Millersville University of Pennsylvania
Donald Mullineaux	University of Kentucky
Thomas Odegaard	Baylor University
Alfred Parker	University of New Mexico
Douglas Pearce	North Carolina State University
Ronnie J. Phillips	Colorado State University
John Scadding	California Public Utilities Commission
Calvin Siebert	University of Iowa
Charles Staley	SUNY Stony Brook

Robert Tokle	Idaho State University
Mark Vaughan	The Federal Reserve Bank of St. Louis
D. H. Vrooman	St. Lawrence University
Donald Wells	Memphis State University
Mark Wohar	University of Nebraska/Omaha

We have been fortunate to work with a group of outstanding professionals at Richard D. Irwin, Inc. Our greatest debt is to Gary Nelson, senior sponsoring editor, for his confidence and support over several years. In the early stages of this book, we benefited from the developmental work of the late Joan Hopkins. We are especially grateful to developmental editor Ellen Cleary, whose work over the past 2½ years was crucial in bringing this project to fruition. Without her gentle but firm prodding, this book would still be unfinished. Special thanks to project editor Ethel Shiell whose dedication to quality was crucial in the final stages of the production process. We extend our thanks to the following Irwin people as well: production supervisor Laurie Kersch, interior designer Maureen McCutcheon, cover designer Heidi Baughman, editorial coordinator Tia Schultz, adminstrative assistant Elois Mason, and senior marketing manager Ron Bloecher. We are also indebted to Michael O'Neal and the people at Elm Street Publishing Services for numerous editorial suggestions that greatly improved the clarity and exposition of this book. We also thank Dollmarvelene Flood Pardi for helping us with the editing in the early stages of this project, as she has done so often in the past, and Mark Albright for assistance with collecting data and constructing charts and tables. Finally, we thank Frederick L. Joutz, Jane de Winter, and Marvin S. Margolis, who prepared the supplements that are an important part of the entire package.

Michael G. Hadjimichalakis
Karma G. Hadjimichalakis

BRIEF CONTENTS

PART 1

INTRODUCTION · 1

CHAPTER 1

The Importance of Money 2

PART 2

THE U.S. FINANCIAL SYSTEM:
*The Participants, the Instruments, and
the Environment* 19

CHAPTER 2

Introducing the Participants 20

CHAPTER 3

A Framework for Understanding
Financial Instruments 42

CHAPTER 4

The Basic Financial Instruments 67

CHAPTER 5

The Evolution to the New Financial
Environment 92

PART 3

MONEY, INTEREST RATES,
AND PRICES 117

CHAPTER 6

The Public's Portfolio Choice: *The
Laws of Asset Demand* 118

CHAPTER 7

Deposit Rate Deregulation and Money
Demand 131

CHAPTER 8

The Basics of the Money Supply 147

CHAPTER 9

Two Tales of Determining the Interest
Rate 172

CHAPTER 10

A Framework for the Economy: *The
Real and the Financial Sectors* 191

PART 4

THE FEDERAL RESERVE AND
ITS BEHAVIOR 221

CHAPTER 11

The Federal Reserve System: *Form
and Function* 222

CHAPTER 12

Functions of Federal Reserve Banks:
The Details 248

CHAPTER 13

Instruments, Targets, and Goals of the
Federal Reserve 267

CHAPTER 14

Open Market Operations and
Movements in Reserves 291

CHAPTER 15

Deposit Creation and the Money
Supply 310

CHAPTER 16

Targeting Monetary Aggregates:
Theory and Experience 329

PART 5

FINANCIAL INSTITUTIONS:
Structure, Regulation, and Behavior   353

CHAPTER 17

The Structure, Regulation, and
Supervision of U.S. Depository
Institutions   354

CHAPTER 18

The Profit-Maximizing Banking Firm   382

CHAPTER 19

Nondepository Financial Institutions   411

PART 6

FINANCIAL MARKETS,
INTEREST RATES, AND THE
CONDUCT OF MONETARY
POLICY   429

CHAPTER 20

The Theory of Money Demand   430

CHAPTER 21

The Deposit Market and Money
Demand   448

CHAPTER 22

The Money Market   472

CHAPTER 23

The Structure of Rates of Return   496

PART 7

THE INTEGRATION OF THE
FINANCIAL AND REAL
SECTORS   521

CHAPTER 24

Determining the Interest Rate and
Real Income: *The IS-LM Model*   522

CHAPTER 25

Monetary and Fiscal Policy in the
IS-LM Model   547

CHAPTER 26

The Price Level and Real Income: *The
Aggregate Demand-Aggregate Supply
Model*   572

CHAPTER 27

Aggregate Supply, Expectations, and
Policy   604

CHAPTER 28

Inflation, Unemployment, and
Economic Policy: *History and Theory*   630

PART 8

INTERNATIONAL FINANCE   663

CHAPTER 29

International Payments and the
Foreign Exchange Market   664

CHAPTER 30

Economic Policy in an Open Economy   696

Glossary   G-1

Answers to Try-It-Out Exercises   A-1

Index   I-1

CONTENTS

PART 1

INTRODUCTION   1

CHAPTER 1

The Importance of Money   2

Chapter Preview 2

The Mystery of Money 3

The Functions of Money 3

  Medium of Exchange 3

  Unit of Account 5

  Store of Value 5

Measurements of Money throughout History 6

  From Unminted to Minted Gold 6

  Fractionally Backed Paper Money 6

  Fiat Money (Paper and Coins) and Checking
  Accounts 7

  Controlling the Quantity of Money 8

Current Measures of Money 9

Money and the Economy: A Preview 11

FedWatch 1.1: Tracking the Monetary Aggregates 12

  Money, Financial Markets, and Rates of Return 12

  Nominal GDP, Real GDP, and the Price Level 13

  Money, Economic Activity, and Prices 13

GlobalWatch 1.2: Plummeting Purchasing Power of the
Russian Ruble 15

Looking Ahead: The Two-Pillar Framework 15

Summary 16

Key Terms and Concepts 17

Questions and Problems 17

Suggested Readings 18

PART 2

THE U.S. FINANCIAL SYSTEM:
*The Participants, the Instruments, and
the Environment*   19

CHAPTER 2

Introducing the Participants   20

Chapter Preview 20

Who Are the Participants? 21

  Households 21

  Nonfinancial Firms 22

  Financial Intermediaries 22

  Government 23

  The Federal Reserve 23

  Foreign Participants 24

  A Word on Stocks and Flows 24

Why Do the Participants Issue and Acquire Financial
Instruments? 25

  The Role of Surplus and Deficit Units 25

GlobalWatch 2.1: Is Foreign Borrowing Bad 32

  The Role of Financial Go-Betweens 33

SectorWatch 2.2: A Web of Bank Regulators 38

  The Role of Monetary Policymaker 39

Looking Ahead 39

Summary 40

Key Terms and Concepts 40

Questions and Problems 41

Suggested Readings 41

CHAPTER 3

A Framework for Understanding
Financial Instruments   42

Chapter Preview 42

Maturity 43

Marketability 44

  Primary and Secondary Markets 44

  Money and Capital Markets 45

  Spot and Futures Markets 45

Rate of Return: The Most Watched Characteristic 45

  Approximating the Rate of Return 46

MarketWatch 3.1: Is Gold a Good Investment? 48

Timing of Receipts and Expenditures 48

Calculating Present and Future Values 49

The Rate of Return 50

The Language and Mechanics of Notes and Bonds 51

Try It Out 3.1 53

MarketWatch 3.2: Tracking Rates on Treasury Notes and Bonds 54

Risk 55

Market Risk, or Interest Rate Risk 55

Default Risk 56

Risk of Inflation 57

MarketWatch 3.3: The Rise, Fall, and Rise of Junk Bonds 58

Liquidity 58

Divisibility 60

More Details on Calculating Interest Rates: Zero Coupon Securities 60

A "Zoo of Zeros" 61

Coupon Equivalent Yield on Zero Coupon Notes and Bonds 61

Coupon Equivalent Yield on Treasury Bills 62

Yield on a Discount Basis 63

MarketWatch 3.4: Tracking Treasury Bill Rates 64

Summary 64

Key Terms and Concepts 64

Questions and Problems 65

Suggested Readings 66

CHAPTER 4

The Basic Financial Instruments   67

Chapter Preview 67

Classifying Domestic Financial Instruments 68

Government Debt 68

U.S. Treasury Securities 68

Federal Agency Securities 70

SectorWatch 4.1: Will Sallie Mae Survive? 71

Municipal Securities 72

Why Hold U.S. Government Debt? 72

Open Market Debt and Equity of Firms 72

Corporate Bonds 72

GlobalWatch 4.2: The Foreign Presence in the U.S. Financial System 73

GlobalWatch 4.3: A Surge in Convertible Bonds in Japan 74

Commercial Paper 74

Bankers' Acceptances 75

Corporate Stock 76

The Debt of Households and Firms to Banks: Bank Loans 78

MarketWatch 4.4: Debt Hangover in the 1990s 79

The Debt of Banks: Bank Deposits 80

The Federal Reserve's Debt 82

Currency in Circulation 82

Total Reserves 82

Federal Funds 82

Try It Out 4.1 83

Placing the Financial Instruments into the Participants' Balance Sheets 84

What's in a Balance Sheet? 84

The Balance Sheet of Households 85

The Balance Sheet of Firms 85

SectorWatch 4.5: National Balance Sheet Distress 86

The Balance Sheet of Banks 86

The Balance Sheet of the U.S. Government 87

The Balance Sheet of the Fed 87

The External Balance Sheet 88

Two Key Questions and the Two Pillars 88

Summary 89

Key Terms and Concepts 89

Questions and Problems 90

Suggested Readings 91

CHAPTER 5

The Evolution to the New Financial Environment   92

Chapter Preview 92

The Rise and Fall of the Old Financial Environment 93

Financial Innovations and the Public 95

Cash Management Practices of Nonfinancial Firms 95

Cash Management Practices of Households 97

Financial Innovations and Banks 98

Financial Innovations in Bank Liabilities 98

Financial Innovations in Bank Assets 103

MarketWatch 5.1: The Essence of an Interest Rate Swap 108

Technological Progress and Financial Innovations 109

Market*Watch* 5.2: Will Debt Cards Replace Cash and Checks? 110

Financial Innovations and the Federal Reserve 111

A Crisis and a Crunch in the New Financial Environment 112

The Thrift Crisis of the 1980s 112

The Credit Crisis of the 1990s 113

Looking Ahead 114

Summary 114

Key Terms and Concepts 115

Questions and Problems 115

Suggested Readings 116

P A R T   3

MONEY, INTEREST RATES, AND PRICES   117

C H A P T E R   6

The Public's Portfolio Choice: *The Laws of Asset Demand*   118

Chapter Preview 118

The Balance Sheet Equation 119

Try It Out 6.1 121

Asset Choice: Risk and Rate of Return 121

Sector*Watch* 6.1: Explaining Portfolio Choice to the Press 122

Factors Affecting Asset Demand 123

The Laws of Asset Demand 124

Looking Ahead 129

Summary 129

Key Terms and Concepts 129

Questions and Problems 130

Suggested Readings 130

C H A P T E R   7

Deposit Rate Deregulation and Money Demand   131

Chapter Preview 131

The Laws of Deposit Demand 132

The Opportunity Cost of Deposits 132

A Theory of Deposit Rate Determination 134

The Deposit Rate Curve 135

Market*Watch* 7.1: Historical Movements in the M2 Deposit Rate 137

Ultimate Factors Affecting Deposit Demand 139

Movements along the D^d Curve 139

Market*Watch* 7.2: Falling Deposit Rates in the 1990s 140

Shifts in the D^d Curve 140

Factors Affecting the Demand for Money 142

Try It Out 7.1 143

Looking Ahead 143

Summary 144

Key Terms and Concepts 145

Questions and Problems 145

Suggested Readings 146

C H A P T E R   8

The Basics of the Money Supply   147

Chapter Preview 147

Six Steps to Derive the Money Supply 148

Supply of Reserves 148

Changes in the Supply of Total Reserves 150

Demand for Reserves 153

From the Reserves Constraint to Deposits 154

The Reserves Constraint 154

Deposits Supported by Reserves 155

Fed*Watch* 8.1: Tracking the Reserves Constraint 156

Try It Out 8.1 157

The Money Supply Equation 157

Factors that Affect the Money Supply 158

Nonborrowed Reserves 158

Borrowed Reserves 158

Excess Reserves 159

Currency in Circulation 159

Try It Out 8.2 159

Reserve Requirement Ratio 159

Interest Sensitivity of the Money Supply 160

Money Supply Curve 160

The Equations for M1 and M2 162

The M1 Equation 162

The M2 Equation 163

Illustration of the Two Equations 164

Looking Ahead 164

Summary 165

Key Terms and Concepts 165

Questions and Problems 166

Suggested Readings 167

Appendix: The Monetary Base Multiplier 168

Key Terms and Concepts 171

CHAPTER 9

Two Tales of Determining the Interest
Rate   172

Chapter Preview 172

The Second Pillar: How Markets Work 173

The Money Market: Liquidity Preference Theory 173

Determining the Interest Rate and the Quantity of
Money 174

The Deposit Rate 175

Factors Affecting Rates and Money 176

Try It Out 9.1 177

Global*Watch* 9.1: Fed and Bundesbank Push Rates in
Opposite Directions 180

Fed*Watch* 9.2: The Fed Responds to the Stock Market
Crash of 1987 182

The Securities Market: Loanable Funds Theory 182

The Demand for Securities 182

The Supply of Securities 184

The Interest Rate 185

Factors Affecting the Interest Rate 186

Try It Out 9.2 188

Looking Ahead 188

Summary 189

Key Terms and Concepts 189

Questions and Problems 189

Suggested Readings 190

CHAPTER 10

A Framework for the Economy: *The
Real and the Financial Sectors*   191

Chapter Preview 191

The Real-Sector Framework and Foreign Exchange 192

The Real Sector 192

Foreign Exchange 197

Linkages between the Financial Sector and the Real
Sector 198

From the Financial Sector to the Real Sector 198

From the Real Sector to the Financial Sector 200

Try It Out 10.1 204

The Aggregate Demand–Aggregate Supply Model 204

The Aggregate Demand Curve 204

Try It Out 10.2 205

The Aggregate Supply Curve 205

Determination of P and Y 206

Demand-Side Shocks 206

Money, Interest, and Prices: Putting the Pieces
Together 208

Liquidity Effect 208

Income Effect and Price-Level Effect 209

Neutrality of Money 210

Expected Inflation Effect 211

Fed*Watch* 10.1: The Fed, Inflation, and Interest Rates:
1979–1982 214

Economic Policy in the United States and Japan: The
1990s 214

The U.S. Economy 215

The Japanese Economy 217

Summary 218

Key Terms and Concepts 219

Questions and Problems 219

Suggested Readings 220

PART   4

THE FEDERAL RESERVE AND
ITS BEHAVIOR   221

CHAPTER 11

The Federal Reserve System: *Form
and Function*   222

Chapter Preview 222

A Brief History of the Federal Reserve 223

Global*Watch* 11.1: Historical Tidbits on Foreign Central
Banks 224

The Board of Governors of the Federal Reserve
System 225

An Overview of the Functions of the Board 226

Fed*Watch* 11.2: Backgrounds of Board Members 227

Financing the Activities of the Board 229

Federal Reserve Banks 229

The Organization and Control of the Reserve
Banks 230

An Overview of the Functions of the Reserve
Banks 231

The Earnings of the Reserve Banks 231

The Federal Open Market Committee 232

Composition of the FOMC 232

FOMC Meetings and Deliberations 233

Policy Directives 233

Member Banks 235

Independence and Accountability of the Fed 236

Financial Independence 236

Accountability to Congress 236

Reform versus the Status Quo 237

Independence and Central Bank Performance 241

Political Pressures 242

Global Watch 11.3: Comparing the Performance of Central
Banks 243

Looking Ahead 245

Summary 245

Key Terms and Concepts 246

Questions and Problems 246

Suggested Readings 247

CHAPTER 12

Functions of Federal Reserve Banks:
The Details 248

Chapter Preview 248

Banker to Banks 249

Check Collecting and Clearing 249

Try It Out 12.1 251

Bookkeeping Services 253

Discount Window Loans 253

FedWatch 12.1: Discounting, Rediscounting, and Discount
Window Loans 254

Distribution of Coin and Currency 257

Banker to the U.S. Government 258

The U.S. Treasury's Checking Account 258

Brokerage Services 259

Management of Foreign Exchange Reserves 259

Banker to Foreign Organizations 260

Examiner and Supervisor of Member Banks 260

Participant in the Design of U.S. Monetary Policy 261

FedWatch 12.2: Tug of War between the Board and
Federal Reserve Banks 262

Economic Researcher 263

The Consolidated Balance Sheet of All Reserve
Banks 263

Summary 265

Key Terms and Concepts 265

Questions and Problems 266

Suggested Readings 266

CHAPTER 13

Instruments, Targets, and Goals of the
Federal Reserve 267

Chapter Preview 267

From Instruments to Ultimate Goals 268

From Intermediate Targets to Ultimate Goals 270

The Long-Run Interest Rate as the Intermediate
Target 271

The Quantity of Money as the Intermediate Target 271

FedWatch 13.1: The Growth of M2 and the Economy in
1992 275

From Operating Targets to Intermediate Targets 276

Federal Funds Rate Operating Target 277

Reserves Operating Targets 278

FedWatch 13.2: Interpreting the Cryptic Domestic Policy
Directives 285

Back to a Federal Funds Rate Target 286

The Change in Policy in 1993 287

From Instruments to Operating Targets 287

Summary 287

FedWatch 13.3: Searching for a Neutral Policy Stance in
1994 288

Key Terms and Concepts 289

Questions and Problems 289

Suggested Readings 290

CHAPTER 14

Open Market Operations and
Movements in Reserves 291

Chapter Preview 291

The Trading Desk 292

A Day of Fedwatching 294

    Scenario 1: A Defensive Open Market Operation 295

    Scenario 2: A Dynamic Open Market Operation 295

    Scenario 3: A Hybrid Open Market Operation 295

    The Euthanasia of Fedwatchers 295

Fed*Watch* 14.1: Fedwatchers Blunder 296

    Policy Shifts 297

Sources and Uses of Reserves Statement 297

    A Simplified Statement 298

    An Actual Statement: The H.4.1 Statistical
Release 300

Try It Out 14.1 301

    The Individual Technical Factors 303

Looking Ahead 307

Summary 307

Key Terms and Concepts 308

Questions and Problems 308

Suggested Readings 309

CHAPTER 15

**Deposit Creation and the Money
Supply**   **310**

Chapter Preview 310

The Bouncing Ball of Deposit Creation 311

Open Market Operations and Multiple Deposit
Creation 312

    Step 1: An Open Market Purchase of Securities 313

    Step 2: Bank A 314

    Step 3: Group B Banks 316

    The Process at a Glance 317

Try It Out 15.1 319

    Deposit Contraction 319

Determinants of the Money Supply 319

    Deposits Supported by Reserves 320

    M1: The Narrow Measure of Money 321

    M2: The Broad Measure of Money 323

Summary 326

Key Terms and Concepts 327

Questions and Problems 327

Suggested Readings 328

CHAPTER 16

**Targeting Monetary Aggregates:
*Theory and Experience***   **329**

Chapter Preview 329

Definitions of Velocity, Velocity-Indexed Money, and
Related Concepts 330

    The Definition of Velocity and the Cambridge k 330

    The Equation of Exchange 331

    The Cambridge Equation 332

    Recent History of Velocity 332

Theories of Velocity and Velocity-Indexed Money 332

    Velocity as a Behavioral Relation 333

    The Quantity Theory of Money 335

Quantity Theory and Monetary Aggregate Targeting 336

    The Quantity Theory Equation Expressed in Rates of
Change 336

    Long-Run Monetary Aggregate Targeting 337

    Short-Run Monetary Aggregate Targeting 338

    Pragmatic versus Rigid Monetary Aggregate
Targeting 339

The U.S. Experience in the 1980s 341

    M1: The Narrow Monetary Aggregate 341

    M2: A Broad Monetary Aggregate 344

The U.S. Experience in the 1990s 346

Summary 349

Key Terms and Concepts 350

Questions and Problems 350

Suggested Readings 351

P A R T   5

**FINANCIAL INSTITUTIONS:
*Structure, Regulation, and Behavior***   **353**

CHAPTER 17

**The Structure, Regulation, and
Supervision of U.S. Depository
Institutions**   **354**

Chapter Preview 354

Financial Firms: An Overview 355

    Financial versus Industrial Firms 355

    Depositories versus Nondepositories 355

    Commercial Banks versus Thrifts 357

National Banks versus State Banks: Dual Banking 357

Bank Holding Companies 357

The Structure of Commercial Banks 358

Geographic Restrictions 358

Pros and Cons of Branching 359

Introduction of Nationwide Branching 360

The Supervision and Regulation of Banks 360

Reasons for Bank Regulation 360

Multiple and Overlapping Regulatory and Supervisory Jurisdictions 361

Streamlining Regulatory Agencies 362

Details of Bank Supervision 363

FedWatch 17.1: Two Views on Centralizing Bank Regulation 364

CAMEL Rating 365

Capital Adequacy 365

Prompt Corrective Action 368

The FDIC and Deposit Insurance 368

Resolving Bank Failures 369

Keeping Banks Open 369

GlobalWatch 17.2: Deposit Insurance Systems around the World 370

Arguments For and Against the Too-Big-to-Fail Policy 371

Pros and Cons of Deposit Insurance 372

Reforming Deposit Insurance 373

The Structure and Regulation of Thrifts 375

Saving and Loan Associations (S&Ls) 375

Savings Banks 377

Credit Unions 378

Summary 378

Key Terms and Concepts 380

Questions and Problems 380

Suggested Readings 381

CHAPTER 18

The Profit-Maximizing Banking Firm   382

Chapter Preview 382

The Balance Sheet of U.S. Banks 383

The Income Statement of Banks: Revenue, Cost, and Profit 385

Revenue 386

Expenses 386

Banking and Information 386

Assessing and Pricing Risk on Loans 386

SectorWatch 18.1: Accounting for Troubled Loans 387

Preventing Adverse Selection: Screening 388

Coping with Moral Hazard 389

Bringing the Balance Sheet to Life 390

The Structure and Functions of the ALCO 390

The Simplifed Balance Sheet 391

Profit Maximization 391

The Supply of Deposits 392

The Net Marginal Revenue from Supplying Deposits 392

The Marginal Cost of Supplying Deposits 393

The Supply of Deposits Curve 394

Shifts in the Supply of Deposits Curve 395

Try It Out 18.1 397

Reserve Management 397

Borrowed Reserves 398

Excess Reserves 401

The Demand for Loans and Securities 403

The Determinants of Demand for Loans and Securities 403

The Credit Crunch of the 1990s: Connecting Theory with Practice 405

Summary 407

Key Terms and Concepts 408

Questions and Problems 408

Suggested Readings 410

CHAPTER 19

Nondepository Financial Institutions   411

Chapter Preview 411

Finance Companies 412

Early Finance Companies 412

Anatomy of Today's Finance Companies 412

Operation of Finance Companies 414

Regulation of Finance Companies 415

Mutual Funds 415

Types of Mutual Funds 416

SectorWatch 19.1: Banks and Mutual Funds 417

Regulation of Mutual Funds 418

Money Market Mutual Funds 418

Insurance Companies 419

Some Fundamentals of Insurance 420

Life Insurance Companies 420

Property/Casualty Insurance Companies 423

Pension Funds 423

Types of Pension Funds 424

Size and Assets of Pension Funds 424

Regulation of Pension Funds 424

Investment Banks, Brokers, and Dealers 425

Summary 426

Key Terms and Concepts 427

Questions and Problems 427

Suggested Readings 428

PART   6

FINANCIAL MARKETS,
INTEREST RATES, AND THE
CONDUCT OF MONETARY
POLICY   429

CHAPTER 20

The Theory of Money Demand   430

Chapter Preview 430

The Early Quantity Theory Approach 431

The Keynesian Approach 433

Modern Treatment of the Transactions Demand 435

Tobin's Explanation 435

Try It Out 20.1 438

Baumol's Explanation 438

Sector*Watch* 20.1: Illustrating Baumol's Money Demand
Equation 441

A Word on the Precautionary Demand 442

Modern Treatment of Speculative Demand 442

Modern Treatment of the Quantity Theory 444

Stability of Money Demand 445

Summary 446

Key Terms and Concepts 446

Questions and Problems 447

Suggested Readings 447

CHAPTER 21

The Deposit Market and Money
Demand   448

Chapter Preview 448

The Deposit Market 449

The Demand Curve for Deposits 449

The Supply Curve for Deposits 449

Equilibrium in the Deposit Market 449

The Interest Rate and the Deposit Market 452

The Interest Rate, the Deposit Rate, and the Quantity
of Deposits 452

The Equilibrium Relations 454

A Numerical Illustration 456

Try It Out 21.1 457

Other Factors Affecting the Deposit Market 458

A Change in Real Income 458

A Change in the Collective Variable 459

A Change in the Technology and Regulatory
Index 459

Market*Watch* 21.1: Banks Bid Less Aggressively for
Deposits 461

A Change in the Reserve Requirement Ratio 461

Summary 461

Money Demand 462

The Old Financial Environment: A Special Case 463

Empirical Studies of Money Demand 466

Shifts in the Demand Curve for M1: The Case of
"Missing Money" 466

Shifts in and Tilts of the Demand Curve for M1: The
Case of "Too Much Money" 467

Deregulation of the Deposit Rate and Interest
Sensitivity of Demand for M2 468

The Case of Missing M2 468

Summary 469

Key Terms and Concepts 469

Questions and Problems 470

Suggested Readings 471

CHAPTER 22

The Money Market   472

Chapter Preview 472

Determinants of Money Market Equilibrium 473

Factors Affecting Money Demand 473

Factors Affecting Money Supply 474

Grouping the Factors 475

Changes in the Instruments of Monetary Policy 476

Open Market Operations 476

Discount Window Operations 477

Changes in the Reserve Requirement Ratio 479

Changes in the Behavior of the Public and Banks 480

Money Demand Shocks 480

Money Supply Shocks 482

Global*Watch* 22.1: Shocks to the Japanese Money Market in 1993 483

Try It Out 22.1 484

Changes in Real-Sector Variables 485

Changes in the Price Level 485

Changes in Real Income 486

Targeting Money versus Targeting the Interest Rate or Doing Nothing 486

A Numerical Example 487

Uncertain Money Demand 490

One Rule for All Reasons? 491

Summary 493

Key Terms and Concepts 494

Questions and Problems 494

Suggested Readings 495

CHAPTER 23

The Structure of Rates of Return   496

Chapter Preview 496

The Term Structure of Interest Rates 497

The Yield Curve 497

Market*Watch* 23.1: Tracking the Yield Curve in *The Wall Street Journal* 498

Forward Rates and the Term Structure 499

Try It Out 23.1 499

The Pure Expectations Hypothesis of the Term Structure 499

The Liquidity Preference Hypothesis and the Liquidity Premium 502

The Preferred Habitat Hypothesis 503

Market*Watch* 23.2: Reducing the Supply of T-Bonds 504

The Segmented-Markets Hypothesis 505

The Default Risk Structure of Interest Rates 506

Default Risk, the Default Risk Premium, and Interest Rates 506

The State of the Economy and Default Risk 507

Liquidity, Marketability, and Default Risk 507

Market*Watch* 23.3: Tracking Default Risk Premiums 508

Tax Features and Interest Rates 509

Equity Capital in a Four-Asset Model 509

The Model 510

Effects of Monetary Policy on Rates of Return 511

Try It Out 23.2 513

The *Q*-Ratio, the Stock Market, and Investment Demand 514

Market*Watch* 23.4: Tobin on *Q* 516

Summary 517

Key Terms and Concepts 518

Questions and Problems 518

Suggested Readings 519

PART   7

THE INTEGRATION OF THE FINANCIAL AND REAL SECTORS   521

CHAPTER 24

Determing the Interest Rate and Real Income: *The* IS-LM *Model*   522

Chapter Preview 522

Genesis of the Modern Theory of Income Determination 523

Determining National Income: The Market for Goods and Services 524

Endogenous and Exogenous Changes in Aggregate Demand 526

The Effect on Real Income of Exogenous Changes in Aggregate Demand 528

Changes in Fiscal Policy and Other Shocks: The Details 530

Sector*Watch* 24.1: Aggregate Demand and the Recession of 1990–1991 531

The Simple Algebra of Income Determination 535

Try It Out 24.1 536

Goods Market Equilibrium: The *IS* Curve 536

Investment Demand 536

Derivation of the *IS* Curve 539

Adding the International Linkages 539

Money Market Equilibrium: The *LM* Curve 540

The *IS-LM* Model 540

    Determining the Interest Rate and Real Income: The *IS-LM* Graph 541

    Shifts of the *IS* and *LM* Curves 541

Summary 543

Key Terms and Concepts 544

Questions and Problems 544

Suggested Readings 546

C H A P T E R 25

Monetary and Fiscal Policy in the *IS-LM* Model   547

Chapter Preview 547

Monetary Policy 548

    Open Market Operations 548

    Adding the International Linkages 550

    Discount Window Operations 550

Fiscal Policy 551

    Effects of an Increase in Government Spending 552

    The Crowding Out of Net Exports 554

    Effects of a Reduction in Taxes 554

    Financing the Budget Deficit 555

Global*Watch* 25.1: The Twin Deficits: The United States and Germany 557

Other Shocks: Changes in the Behavior of the Public and Banks 558

    LM Sector Shocks 558

    IS Sector Shocks 561

The Choice of an Intermediate Target for the Conduct of Monetary Policy 561

Fed*Watch* 25.2: Headwinds 562

    Targeting the Quantity of Money and the Slope of the *LM* Curve 563

    Targeting the Quantity of Money versus Targeting the Interest Rate 564

    Variability in Real Income versus Variability in the Interest Rate 567

Fed*Watch* 25.3: Downgrading Money in 1993 569

Summary 569

Key Terms and Concepts 570

Questions and Problems 570

Suggested Readings 571

C H A P T E R 26

The Price Level and Real Income: *The Aggregate Demand-Aggregate Supply Model*   572

Chapter Preview 572

Looking Backward and Forward 573

Aggregate Demand 573

    The Schematics of the *AD* Curve 573

    The Graphics 574

    Shifts of the Aggregate Demand Curve 576

The Aggregate Supply 579

    The Keynesian Fixed-Price Aggregate Supply Curve 580

    The Classical Aggregate Supply Curve 581

    The Keynesian Short-Run Aggregate Supply Curve 582

    Combining the Keynesian Short Run with the Classical Long Run 586

The Effects of Policy and Shocks in the Keynesian Short Run and the Classical Long Run 590

    The Keynesian Short Run 590

Try It Out 26.1 592

Market*Watch* 26.1: The Oil Shock of 1990 596

    The Classical Long Run 597

Economic Policy and Schools of Thought 600

Looking Ahead 601

Summary 601

Key Terms and Concepts 602

Questions and Problems 602

Suggested Readings 603

C H A P T E R 27

Aggregate Supply, Expectations, and Policy   604

Chapter Preview 604

Evolution of the Theory 605

The Lucas Aggregate Supply Curve 606

    Continuous Clearance of the Labor Market 606

    Rational Expectations 609

    Two Approaches to the Lucas Supply Curve 610

The Policy Ineffectiveness Proposition of the New Classicists 614

    Painless Disinflation 615

Empirical Investigations of the Policy Ineffectiveness Proposition 616

Other New Classical Results 616

Theoretical Challenges to Policy Ineffectiveness and the Emergence of the New Keynesians 617

Imperfect Information 617

Market*Watch* 27.1: Are Tax Cuts Effective? 618

Rigidity in Nominal Wages 619

Rigidity in Real Wages 620

Rigidity in Prices 621

The Role of Policy: Keynesians, Classicists, New Classicists, and New Keynesians 622

An Inward Shift in Aggregate Demand 622

The Consequences of an Anti-Inflationary Policy 624

The Legacy of Rational Expectations 625

Global*Watch* 27.2: Credibility of Monetary Policy: The United States and Japan 626

Summary 627

Key Terms and Concepts 628

Questions and Problems 628

Suggested Readings 629

CHAPTER 28

Inflation, Unemployment, and Economic Policy: *History and Theory*   630

Chapter Preview 630

Demand-Pull versus Cost-Push Inflation 631

Demand-Pull Inflation 631

Cost-Push Inflation 633

Of Wars, Peace, Stock Market Crashes, and Other Economic Shocks 635

Economic Performance during Wars 635

Supply-Side Shocks of the 1970s 637

Deliberate and Inadvertent Shocks to the Monetary Sector: 1981–1982 639

Two Stock Market Crashes: 1929 and 1987 639

Headwinds and Economic Policy in the 1990s 642

Revolutions in Economic Policy: Kennedy and Reagan 645

The Kennedy Years 645

The Reagan Years 646

Comparison of Revolutions 647

Inflation and Unemployment: The Phillips Curve 648

A Simple Derivation of the Phillips Curve 649

The Vertical Long-Run Phillips Curve 652

Try It Out 28.1 656

Costs of Inflation 657

Unexpected Inflation 657

Fully Expected Inflation 659

Summary 660

Key Terms and Concepts 661

Questions and Problems 661

Suggested Readings 662

PART 8

INTERNATIONAL FINANCE   663

CHAPTER 29

International Payments and the Foreign Exchange Market   664

Chapter Preview 664

Balance of Payments Accounts 665

Anatomy of the Current Account 665

Anatomy of the Capital Account 666

The Foreign Exchange Market 668

The Mechanics of Exchange Rates 668

Market*Watch* 29.1: Tracking Exchange Rates in *The Wall Street Journal* 669

Try It Out 29.1 670

The Demand for Foreign Exchange 670

The Supply of Foreign Exchange 671

Flexible Exchange Rates 672

Fixed Exchange Rates 674

A Hybrid System 675

Market*Watch* 29.2: An Ineffective Intervention in 1994 676

Factors Affecting Exchange Rates 676

Foreign and Domestic Interest Rates 676

Expectations of Currency Appreciation or Depreciation 677

Interest Rate Parity 678

Foreign and Domestic Incomes 679

Foreign and Domestic Prices 680

The Real Exchange Rate 682

The Mechanics of the Real Exchange Rate 682

Try It Out 29.2 682

Purchasing Power Parity 683

Real Interest Rate Parity 685

The Exchange Rate Mountains of the 1980s 687

A Brief History of the International System of Payments 687

The Gold Standard 687

The Bretton Woods System 688

Managed, or Dirty, Float 689

The Fiftieth Anniversary of Bretton Woods 690

The European Monetary System 691

Summary 692

Key Terms and Concepts 693

Questions and Problems 693

Suggested Readings 695

CHAPTER 30

Economic Policy in an Open Economy 696

Chapter Preview 696

A Model of the Open Economy 697

The *IS-LM-BP* Graph 697

The *IS* Curve in the Open Economy 697

The *LM* Curve in the Open Economy 698

The *BP* Curve 699

Perfect and Imperfect Capital Mobility 701

Equilibrium in the *IS-LM-BP* Model 703

Monetary Policy under Fixed and Flexible Exchange Rates 703

Flexible Exchange Rates 703

Fixed Exchange Rates 704

Fiscal Policy under Fixed and Flexible Exchange Rates 705

Flexible Exchange Rates 706

Investment, National Savings, and Capital Inflows 707

Fixed Exchange Rates 709

Summary of the Effects of Policy 710

Shocks from the Foreign Exchange Market 711

A Rise in Foreign Interest Rates 711

Crises in the European Monetary System 713

Expected Currency Appreciation or Depreciation 713

Fed*Watch* 30.1: How to Respond to a Falling Dollar 714

Summary 714

Key Terms and Concepts 715

Questions and Problems 716

Suggested Readings 716

Glossary   G-1

Answers to Try-It-Out Exercises   A-1

Index   I-1

P A R T   1

INTRODUCTION

1   The Importance of Money

Money is the first key word in the title of the book. Part 1 surveys the role of money in the economy and introduces the two-pillar framework that is the foundation of our approach to money, banking, and financial markets.

THE IMPORTANCE OF MONEY

CHAPTER PREVIEW

We start with the title. This is a book about money, banking, and financial markets. Our approach is contemporary: both in theory and in practice.

One of our goals is to describe today's monetary and financial system. Another, more important, goal is to build a theoretical framework for understanding and analyzing contemporary money, banking, and financial markets. But how does one deal with the maze of details that characterize the monetary and financial system? We are guided in our approach by the advice of Albert Einstein, a master builder of models: "Make everything as simple as possible, but not simpler." That is, we shall simplify, but in doing so, we take care not to make our analysis irrelevant. Relevance is necessary for our third goal: to connect theory with practice. In connecting theory with practice throughout the book, we shall answer questions, such as these, about the domestic and global economy:

- Why did U.S. interest rates hit record highs in the late 1970s and early 1980s and quarter-century lows in 1993?
- What was the role of monetary policy in the recession of 1981–82, which was the worst slowdown in the U.S. economy since the Great Depression?
- Why wasn't there a recession after the stock market crash of 1987, contrary to the predictions of many economists at the time?
- How did deposit insurance, coupled with deregulation, contribute to the thrift crisis of the 1980s, in which an immense number of savings and loan associations failed?
- What is a bubble economy and what happened to burst the bubble in Japan in the 1990s?

- Why did the decision of German policymakers to reduce money growth in the early 1990s create a crisis in England?

- Why did the rate of inflation in Russia skyrocket in 1992 and 1993?

- How will the growth of money and credit this year affect your job prospects next year?

This chapter explores the concept of money by looking at its functions and definitions. By tracing the measures of money through history, we see how modern banking practices evolved. We also preview the relations among money, financial markets, and rate of return and among money, interest, and prices. These relations will occupy a major portion of this book.

THE MYSTERY OF MONEY

Money is commonplace, yet mysterious. Exploring its mysteries has fascinated and confounded great thinkers as well as cranks. Even common usage of the word often indicates confusion between *money* and *income,* and *money* and *wealth.*[1] For example, when we say "she makes a lot of money," we may mean "she earns a high annual income from her job as an attorney." On the other hand, when we say "he has a lot of money," we may mean that "he has a lot of accumulated savings, or wealth." What makes it more confusing to noneconomists is that money is related to economywide income; that is, money influences national income. Money is also one form in which we keep our wealth.

One common misconception restricts the concept of money to currency, that is, to paper notes and coins. Currency, however, is only a small fraction of the actual quantity of money. Deposits in bank accounts make up the largest part of the quantity of money. To understand money as a concept, we first need to examine the functions of money.

THE FUNCTIONS OF MONEY

Money serves as (1) a medium of exchange, (2) a unit of account, and (3) a store of value. We examine each of these functions, beginning with medium of exchange.

Medium of Exchange

A **medium of exchange**, or a transactions medium, is anything generally acceptable as a means of payment in the exchange of goods and services, in repaying debts, and in the exchange of assets, such as shares of common stock. To understand the importance of a medium of exchange, consider what happens when one does not exist.

---

[1] In a 1968 paper, Nobel laureate Milton Friedman pointed out the confusion resulting from the different ways we use the term *money* in everyday language. More recently, he discusses this issue in *Money Mischief: Episodes in Monetary History* (New York: Harcourt Brace Jovanovich, 1992), Chapter 2, "The Mystery of Money," 8–50.

Imagine the simple case of a carpenter who makes a chair and goes to the marketplace, where he puts up a sign announcing that he wants to exchange the chair for grain, cookware, fish, and clothing. Suppose that a producer and supplier of one of the items the carpenter wants to purchase—say, grain—wants to purchase a chair. The carpenter sells the chair and receives its value in grain. He sets aside the amount of grain he needs, then puts up another sign announcing that he wants to sell grain for cookware, fish and clothing. Now he must search for a supplier of one or more of these items who is interested in buying grain. The process will go on until the carpenter purchases all the items on his shopping list. It may take the entire day or even several days.

One can imagine even more-complicated cases. What if the only person who needs a chair is the fisherman? Will the carpenter exchange his chair for an equivalent amount of fish and become a seller of fish? Will the fish remain fresh until he purchases all the items on his list? Alternatively, what will happen if no supplier of the items on his list needs a chair? In this case, he must buy an item he does not need but that a larger number of others may need so that he can have a better chance of finding people who may want to pay him in the goods he wants.

From this simple exercise, the carpenter learns several lessons. Let us begin with the most important. The absence of a medium of exchange forces him to spend a long time making his purchases because there must be a *double coincidence of wants*: The carpenter must find someone who wants his chair and who has an item he wants. Money eliminates the need for the double coincidence of wants and thus reduces transactions costs—the time the carpenter spends searching for an individual to trade with, time he could use to make more chairs. Thus, money makes the economy more efficient.

A second lesson the carpenter learns is this: The more desired and, hence, the more acceptable the item he possesses (the grain that he bought in exchange for his chair), the faster he can complete his shopping list. Thus, on his next shopping trip, he may choose to exchange his chairs for an item such as grain that is in great demand. He may also want to choose an item that is not only in wide demand but also can be divided into smaller lots and is nonperishable.

From these lessons, born of experience, societies began to designate as media of exchange those commodities that were nonperishable, divisible, and widely demanded. Because barter is inefficient, societies have always developed media of exchange that would economize on the resources used to facilitate transactions. Throughout history, the medium of exchange has taken many forms: from commodities, to precious metals, to paper, to mere entries in ledgers (accounts). In its early, almost prehistoric, phase the medium of exchange was commodities such as feathers, livestock, grain, stones, and a variety of metals. Soon, however, these items were replaced by precious metals such as silver and gold. The precious-metal phase was lengthy, lasting in various forms until the twentieth century.

The prolonged use of precious metals suggests some characteristics that a commodity must have to become a medium of exchange: It must be scarce, divisible, transportable, and storable (nonperishable). While the importance of the last two characteristics is obvious, divisibility is also vital if a commodity is to be used for small and large purchases. Perhaps the most important property is scarcity; a commodity that is too plentiful may become worthless. Primarily because of their scarcity, precious metals, especially gold, were the commodities of choice as money throughout history. The eventual demise of gold is attributable, in part, to limited supply, for excessive scarcity hinders payments and economic growth. To satisfy the requirements of a growing economy, the monetary authority must be able to increase the quantity of the medium of exchange at will. This is why governments devised new forms of money, especially paper money, whose supply they could increase easily and inexpensively.

Unit of Account

The second function of money is to serve as a unit of account. A **unit of account** is a yardstick for measuring prices and values and a benchmark for comparing them. In principle, any commodity can serve as a unit of account. Having chosen the good, we can express the price of each of the rest of the goods in units of that good. Historically, societies designated a single item to serve as the unit of account, say, a kilogram of wheat. In this way, each good could be priced at so many kilograms of wheat per unit.

In modern times, paper money is the unit of account. For example, the dollar is the unit of account in the United States. Knowing that a pound of peaches costs two dollars and a pound of apples costs one dollar enables us to compare their value. Thus, money becomes a standard of value.

Normally, the same item serves as the unit of account and the medium of exchange: the dollar in the United States; the yen in Japan; the mark in Germany. In abnormal times, however, societies divorce the two functions of money, often unofficially. For example, although the ruble is the unit of account in Russia, in 1992 and 1993 some Russians were using foreign currencies, such as the dollar and the mark, as the unofficial medium of exchange. Many Russians, without access to foreign currencies, resorted to barter. Invariably, the reason for the divorce of the medium of exchange from the unit of account is a deterioration of the currency as a store of value, which takes us to the third function of money.

Store of Value

A **store of value** is a reservoir of future purchasing power. Money is both a temporary and a permanent store of purchasing power.

The function of money as a temporary store of purchasing power is an outgrowth of its function as a medium of exchange. If an item is to serve as a medium of exchange, people must hold that item to carry out their transactions. For example, consider an individual who earns $700 a week but plans to spend $560 on goods and services and save $140 every week. Usually this individual will not spend the entire $560 on payday. Instead, he may spend $90 on payday and hold $470 in the form of money to be spent over the course of the week. This $470 held in money is a temporary store of purchasing power.

People, however, hold more money than they need to carry out their transactions. Why? The answer is that money can also serve as a permanent store of purchasing power. Individuals who save forgo present consumption to have higher future consumption. The wealth of individuals is their accumulated savings. Money is one form in which individuals may keep their wealth; stocks, bonds, and real estate are other forms. Of course, when wealth is held in money, in the future it will not need to be exchanged to buy goods and services.

The ability of money to serve as a store of value depends on its capacity to retain its purchasing power. When the purchasing power of money plummets, that is, when the prices of goods and services rise rapidly, the public does not want to hold money as a permanent store of value. Even more ominous, the public shortens the amount of time it holds money as a medium of exchange. The rapid decrease in the purchasing power of the Russian ruble in 1992 and 1993 sparked the unofficial use of foreign currencies as the medium of exchange in Russia. By the end of this chapter, you will understand why the purchasing power of the Russian ruble was eroding.

MEASUREMENTS OF MONEY THROUGHOUT HISTORY

To understand the current measures of money, it is instructive to trace the evolution of the monetary system. In early history any commodity that traders considered important, such as feathers, stones, grain, or tobacco, could be and was used as money. Most societies, however, moved quickly to employ precious metals, especially gold and silver, for this purpose.

From Unminted to Minted Gold

Soon after people began using gold as a means of payment, they realized that transactions would be facilitated if some authority certified the weight and purity of the precious metal. The obvious choice was the government, which minted coins from gold or silver. For example, in the democracy of ancient Athens the government minted silver drachma coins and certified their authenticity by the emblem of the city of Athens, the owl. In monarchies, such as England, the sovereign—the king or queen—minted coins from gold and certified the purity of each coin with the royal stamp. The gold pound minted in England was even called the *sovereign*.

The sovereign leader of each country minted gold coins out of the royal inventory each time money was needed to pay soldiers or other government employees or to purchase government supplies. This was one method of increasing the money supply and putting money into circulation. The money supply also increased when the public discovered new gold, which it took to the royal mint to be made into coins. (The sovereign would charge a fee for this service, that is, a certain amount of gold for each coin minted.) The payment system that used gold as the unit of account became known as the **gold standard**.

With this system the quantity of money in circulation could also increase either by the discovery of gold or by the reduction of the gold content of each coin. If, for example, the gold content were reduced from one-tenth to one-twentieth of an ounce, the quantity of money could be doubled with the same quantity of gold. All that was needed was for the public to turn in their coins to be melted and reminted, receiving two new one-pound coins for each old one-pound coin. This approach to increasing the quantity of money by debasing it was introduced to satisfy the needs of a growing economy when gold discoveries did not keep pace with the growth or with the state's need to finance major endeavors, especially wars.

Fractionally Backed Paper Money

The next step in the evolutionary process was the creation of paper currency used simultaneously with coins. Because the public found it difficult to carry large quantities of coins, governments issued paper currency, or notes, that could be exchanged on demand for the denominated number of gold coins. The public routinely accepted these notes in transactions because they were "as good as gold."

Initially all notes were as good as gold because they were fully backed by unminted or minted gold in the national treasury. Later, however, governments realized that they did not need to hold an equal amount of gold to support the notes. Only a small fraction of the notes were turned in for gold coins, suggesting that only a fraction of the gold would suffice. Thus, governments began to print "fractionally backed" paper money.

This approach was also used by private issuers of paper money, such as goldsmiths and other trusted business establishments, with whom the public would leave (deposit) its gold coins for safekeeping. In exchange, depositors (the public) received receipts, or notes, that were promises to pay gold coins on demand. Eventually, these notes were themselves accepted in transactions.

In a manner akin to modern banking practices, a depository kept only a fraction of the deposited gold coins in its safe and lent the rest to households and businesses that needed funds. The borrowers then deposited these coins with their depositories for safekeeping and received, as a receipt from the depositories, paper notes that could be used more conveniently in transactions. Depositories in this second group did the same as those in the first; they kept only a fraction of the deposited coins and lent the rest to other borrowers. The process went on, creating a total number of notes equal to a multiple of the deposited coins, or, conversely, notes that were only fractionally backed by gold (coins). These depositories were the forerunners of modern depository institutions, comprising banks and thrift institutions, such as savings and loan associations, mutual savings banks, and credit unions, that accept deposits and make loans and provide the medium of exchange. (Chapter 2 explains the difference between banks and thrifts.)

Fiat Money (Paper and Coins) and Checking Accounts

The introduction of two more innovations essentially led to today's payments system. First, banks began giving depositors an apparatus to write their own notes: a book of sheets of formed paper, called *checks,* which, when correctly filled out, order the bank to pay the bearer the amount specified by the depositor. These checks were more convenient and safer to use in transactions than currency. In addition, unlike the use of currency, payment by check provided a record of transactions. Checks are usually, but not always, accepted by recipients as payment. To this day, however, recipients are not obligated by law to accept a check as payment.

A second important development was the severance of the link between money and gold. Governments, or authorized agencies, began to issue notes that were not backed by gold or by any commodity. These notes are called **fiat money**, which means that they are created by government order or decree. The paper notes are, however, accepted for payments because the recipient is obligated by law to accept them; the notes are **legal tender**.

The move to fiat money—paper and coins—developed for two reasons. First commodity money, especially in the form of precious metals, is costly to produce, while paper or copper and nickel coins can by comparison be produced almost costlessly. Second, the quantity of precious metals cannot be varied easily, whereas the amount of paper money can be increased or decreased almost instantly.

Because transactions accounts (checking accounts) were not and still are not legal tender, governments have found other ways to make them more acceptable. A principal method is to insure the deposits of the public in case the depository (bank or thrift) closes down. **Deposit insurance** is a commitment by the government to pay depositors in currency (legal tender) if the depository institution goes bankrupt. This commitment makes checking accounts virtually indistinguishable from currency. In addition, stiff penalties discourage people from writing checks not supported by sufficient funds in their accounts.

Similarly, severe restrictions are imposed on a variety of bank activities to reduce the likelihood that the bank loans backing the deposits will lose value or become worthless. In the United States a number of government agencies evaluate whether banks follow prudent lending practices and obey banking regulations. The goal of bank regulation and supervision is to ensure the smooth functioning of the payments system.

In modern monetary systems, therefore, one measure of the quantity of money is the sum of paper notes and coins held by the public, called **currency in circulation**, and checkable deposit accounts. Today the usual access to checking accounts is by writing a check. Recent advances in computer technology, however, have increased the potential for the electronic transfer of funds to replace checks at the retail level. (Chapter 5 explains the mechanics of the electronic transfer of funds using point-of-sale terminals.) Electronic banking, which is likely to become more widespread with improvements in computer technology, changes the method and the speed of the transfer of funds between deposit accounts, but it does not change the salient fact that checking accounts are money.

Controlling the Quantity of Money

As long as the government can control the quantity of currency (paper notes and coins) and can affect the volume of checkable deposit accounts in banks, it can influence the total quantity of money and, ultimately, the level of economic activity. The **central bank** is the national institution that controls the growth of money. In the United States, the central bank is called the Federal Reserve System, or Fed for short. According to current practice, the Federal Reserve provides the amounts of paper notes and coins demanded by the public to conduct transactions. This means that the public, not the Fed, dictates the amount of fiat money outstanding. Thus, the Fed's ability to control the quantity of money rests with its ability to control the quantity of checkable deposits.

Checkable deposit accounts are controlled primarily by requiring banks (and other depository institutions) to hold a portion of their deposits in the form of cash in their vaults or cash in the form of accounts with their banker, the central bank. Cash that banks have in their vaults, as well as in their tills and their ATMs (automatic teller machines), is naturally called **vault cash**; accounts that banks have with the Fed are called **reserve balances with the Fed**. The sum of vault cash and reserve balances with the Fed is **reserves,** which are the Fed's obligations to banks. Because banks must hold a fraction of their deposits in the form of reserves, bank deposits are, in effect, fractionally backed by reserves, in a manner akin to the earlier system under which bank notes were fractionally backed by gold. Of course, the remaining fraction of deposits is backed by the bank loans funded by these deposits.

The central bank can engineer an increase in the amount of checkable deposits by increasing the reserves available to support deposits. Conversely, by reducing reserves, the central bank can engineer a reduction in checkable deposits. Until the 1920s in the United States, and later in other countries, the principal method by which central banks increased reserves was by lending reserves to banks. By varying the amount of these loans of reserves, central banks were able to vary the amount of checkable deposits and, hence, the quantity of money.

In the 1920s, the Fed began to use a second method of providing reserves to the banking system. With the method, the central bank buys government securities in the open market by creating reserves, which find their way into the reserve accounts of banks. Purchases and sales of government securities in the open market by the central bank are called **open market operations**. In countries such as the United States, with fully developed financial markets and large quantities of outstanding government debt, open market operations have now become the primary instrument of **monetary policy**, which we define as the art and science that a central bank pursues to influence a nation's money supply, level of interest rates, and, ultimately, inflation and growth.

CURRENT MEASURES OF MONEY

Today the standard measures of money in all developed countries include the volume of currency and the volume of deposits at a point in time. Usually there are narrow and broad measures, distinguished by the type of deposits included in the definition of money. In the United States, the central bank tracks and reports on three measures of money, M1, M2, and M3.

Table 1–1 briefly describes the components of M1, M2, and M3. It also shows the relation among the three measures of money, and reports the size of each measure and its components in December 1993. The numbers in the table for M1, M2, M3, and their components are seasonally adjusted, which means that temporary changes arising from seasonal variations in the need for money by the public, such as at Christmas, have been removed. (Chapter 5 discusses the individual components of the monetary aggregates in detail.)

The narrowest measure of money, **M1**, consists of currency, traveler's checks, non-interest-bearing checking accounts (called *demand deposits*), and interest-bearing checking accounts (called *other checkable deposits*).[2] All the components of M1 are funds that are generally acceptable immediately for transactions and are naturally referred to by the Fed as **transactions balances**. They are pure media of exchange; in other words, M1 consists of perfectly liquid assets. The term **liquidity** refers to the ease and convenience with which an asset can be converted to a medium of exchange. Currency and checking accounts do not need to be converted to anything else to be used as a medium of exchange. They are already the medium of exchange.

A broader measure of money is **M2**, which consists of M1 plus savings deposits, small-denomination time deposits, (private) money market mutual funds (MMMFs), money market deposit accounts, and two smaller items used primarily by businesses: overnight repurchase agreements and overnight Eurodollars. All the non-M1 components of M2, called **nontransactions balances**, can be used for payments but usually with some delay. Certainly that is the case with savings and time deposits. Funds in other accounts, such as the money market deposit accounts and money market mutual funds, can be transfered by

---

[2]   Only traveler's checks issued by nonbank institutions, such as American Express, are included in the category of traveler's checks. The Fed lumps traveler's checks issued by banks together with demand deposits.

TABLE 1-1
M1, M2, M3, and
Their Components:
Definitions and
Amount Outstanding
in December 1993
($ Billions)

M1 and Its Components

M1	$1,131.2

=

Currency in circulation	321.5

Coins and paper notes outside of the Fed, the U.S. Treasury, and depository institutions.

+

Traveler's checks of nonbank issuers	8.0

Generally accepted means of payment that is enhanced currency because the issuer of the check gives a refund to the holder if the checks are lost.

+

Demand Deposits	386.1

Non-interest-bearing checking accounts at banks.

+

Other checkable deposits	415.7

Interest-bearing checking accounts consisting of NOW accounts (negotiable order of withdrawal), super-NOW accounts, ATS (automatic transfer from savings), and credit union share drafts.

M2 and Its Components

M2*	$3,551.7

=

M1	1,131.2

+

Savings deposits and money market deposit accounts	1,218.6

Savings deposits are interest-bearing accounts at depository institutions from which funds cannot be transferred by check; traditionally deposits and withdrawals were recorded in passbooks held by the depositor.

Money market deposit accounts are interest-bearing accounts at depository institutions on which a limited number of checks may be written per month.

+

Small time deposits	783.5

Interest-bearing deposits of less than $100,000 at depository institutions; funds can be withdrawn from these accounts without penalty only after a specified date.

+

Money market mutual fund shares	336.4

Interest-bearing shares in pools of funds accumulated by investment companies and invested in short-term obligations of the government, firms, and banks; funds may be transferred by check, subject to a small minimum denomination (excludes shares held by institutions.)

+

Overnight repurchase agreements (RPs) and overnight Eurodollars	84.7

Overnight RPs are overnight borrowing by a bank or thrift from a depositor; the bank or thrift sells some of its holdings of Treasury securities to the customer and agrees to buy them back the next day at a specified price above the selling price.

Overnight Eurodollars are interest-bearing dollar-denominated deposits in foreign branches of U.S. banks worldwide; deposits mature (funds may be obtained) the next day.

TABLE 1–1
(*concluded*)

M3 and Its Components	
M3*	**$4,207.7**
=	
M2	3,551.7
+	
Large time deposits	331.5
Time deposits of more than $100,000.	
+	
Term repurchase agreements	95.3
RPs with a longer term than overnight.	
+	
Term Eurodollar deposits	47.8
Eurodollar deposits with a term longer than overnight at U.S. branches of foreign banks worldwide and at all banking offices in the United Kingdom and Canada.	
+	
Money market mutual fund shares held by institutions	198.8

*The number given for M2 and M3 differ from the sum of their components for two reasons. One is the techniques used to seasonally adjust the data. The other is adjustments made to the sum of the components to avoid double counting. For example, in calculating M3 the amount of overnight repurchase agreements and overnight Eurodollars held by institution-only money market mutual funds is subtracted from the sum of the components to avoid counting RPs and Eurodollars twice.
Source: *Economic Report of the President, 1994*, Tables B-68 and B-69.

check, but there are limits on either the number or the size of checks that can be written against these accounts. Typically very few checks are written on these accounts, and the checks that are written are for major payments. Thus, the broader measure emphasizes the store-of-wealth (value) function more than the medium-of-exchange function.

Finally, **M3** equals M2 plus balances of less-liquid accounts that are even less likely to be used for payments. These balances are large-denomination time deposits and institutional money market mutual funds as well as term Eurodollars and term repurchase agreements.

The Federal Reserve System is the agency responsible for gathering and releasing the U.S. data for the measures of money, also called the **monetary aggregates**, or the *Ms*. FedWatch 1.1 explains how to track these data in the financial press. In addition to the Ms, the Fed also gathers data on a broader concept of liquidity. This broad measure of liquidity, called **L**, consists of M3 plus banker's acceptances, commercial paper, savings bonds issued by the U.S. government, and short-term Treasury obligations. Chapter 4 explains the non-M3 components of *L* in detail. For now we simply note that bankers' acceptances are financial instruments used to finance international trade and that commercial paper is a short-term obligation of firms. In December 1993 the size of *L* was $5,131.8 billion.

MONEY AND THE ECONOMY: A PREVIEW

What is the relationship between money and the economy? The function of money as a permanent store of purchasing power connects money with rates of return on assets, which, in turn, are connected with spending on goods and services and, hence, with

GlobalWatch 1.1
Tracking the Monetary Aggregates

Every Thursday at 4:30 PM the Federal Reserve makes available a statistical release, titled "Money Stock, Liquid Assets, and Debt Measures." This release (about ten pages long) reports weekly, monthly, quarterly, and annual data on M1, M2, M3, *L*, and debt. Professional Fedwatchers follow the release closely. For others with a more casual interest in tracking measures of money, the financial press reports key data from the release on Friday.

The Wall Street Journal publishes weekly and monthly data on M1, M2, and M3 as part of a table titled "Federal Reserve Data" that appears every Friday. The relevant part of the table appearing on Friday, October 23, 1993, is reproduced below. We see that there are two sets of numbers: one seasonally adjusted (sa), the other not seasonally adjusted (nsa). In analyz-

ing the relation between money and the economy, economists use the seasonally adjusted numbers because seasonal movements do not have a lasting effect on the economy.

FEDERAL RESERVE DATA

MONETARY AGGREGATES
(daily averages in billions)

	One week ended:	
	Oct. 11	Oct. 4
Money supply (M1) sa	1113.1	1113.5
Money supply (M1) nsa	1117.0	1110.3
Money supply (M2) sa	3537.4	3539.2
Money supply (M2) nsa	3542.1	3529.5
Money supply (M3) sa	4186.3	4190.7
Money supply (M3) nsa	4187.5	4165.9
	Four weeks ended:	
	Oct. 11	Sep. 13
Money supply (M1) sa	1112.9	1100.0
Money supply (M1) nsa	1101.0	1109.4
Money supply (M2) sa	3537.4	3527.4
Money supply (M2) nsa	3519.8	3520.1
Money supply (M3) sa	4186.9	4171.9
Money supply (M3) nsa	4165.3	4169.5
	Month	
	Sep.	Aug.
Money supply (M1) sa	1107.6	1094.8
Money supply (M2) sa	3534.5	3521.9
Money supply (M3) sa	4180.7	4167.9

nsa-Not seasonally adjusted. sa-Seasonally adjusted

economic activity and prices. The effect of a change in the quantity of money on rates of return is direct and immediate. The effect on economic activity and prices, however, is indirect and takes time. These relations will be examined extensively throughout the book. Here we take a first look at how the process works.

Money, Financial Markets, and Rates of Return

As a permanent store of purchasing power, money competes with other assets for a place in the portfolio of the public. **Assets** are what individuals, firms, and other participants in the economy own. **Real assets**, also called **tangible assets**, are lasting physical objects, such as houses, cars, and office buildings. **Financial assets** do not have physical characteristics. Instead, they are claims to immediate or future cash payments and include bank deposits, bonds, and shares of common stock. Other terms for financial assets are **financial instruments** *or* **securities**.

People hold their wealth in various assets depending on the characteristics of the assets, especially their rewards, or rates of return. The rates of return on all assets depend on the assets' relative scarcity. A change in the quantity of money alters the scarcity of other assets relative to money, thereby affecting their rates of return. How an increase or decrease in the quantity of money affects financial markets and influences the rates of return will occupy a major portion of this book. Here we note that an increase in the quantity of money makes bonds relatively more scarce, reducing the interest rate, which is the rate of return on bonds. Conversely, a reduction in the quantity of money makes bonds relatively more plentiful, thereby increasing the interest rate.

Nominal GDP, Real GDP, and the Price Level

Before we examine the connections among money, prices, and economic activity, we need to define three key concepts and explain their relationships. They are nominal GDP, real GDP, and the price level.

Gross domestic product (GDP) is the value of total goods and services produced inside a country in a given period, usually a year. There are two ways to measure GDP. One is at current prices. To find GDP at current prices, also called **nominal GDP**, we multiply the quantity of each final good and service produced in a given year by its dollar price that year. Then we add all the results to get one number for total output. For example, nominal GDP for the United States in 1993 was $6,374.0 billion.

Because prices as well as quantities of goods and services change from year to year, we want to know how much of a change in nominal GDP comes from a change in prices and how much from a change in quantities. **Real GDP** solves this problem by measuring output at fixed prices: the prices of a base year. In the United States, which currently uses 1987 as the base year, the value of real GDP in 1993 was $5,132.7 billion (that is, if 1993 production were valued in 1987 prices, the total would be $5,132.7 billion).

The **price level**, which is the collective price of goods and services, is calculated by dividing nominal GDP by real GDP:

$$P = \text{Nominal GDP/Real GDP} \tag{1–1}$$

In the base year, P is always equal to 1, because, by definition, nominal GDP equals real GDP in the base year. Now let us look at another year. Applying Equation 1–1, we find that the price level in 1993 was 1.242: $6,374.0 billion/$5,132.7 billion = 1.242. A price level of 1.242 means that the price level in 1993 was 1.242 times the price level in 1987 (the base year); that is, prices rose by 24.2 percent between 1987 and 1993.

By rearranging Equation 1–1, we find the relationship among nominal GDP, the price level, and real GDP:

$$\text{Nominal GDP} = P \times \text{Real GDP} \tag{1–2}$$

We see from Equation 1–2 that the level of nominal GDP equals the price level multiplied by the level of real GDP. The usual symbol in economics for real GDP is Y. Hence,

$$\text{Nominal GDP} = P \times Y \tag{1–3}$$

Now we are ready to examine the relation among money, economic activity, and prices.

Money, Economic Activity, and Prices

We have seen that a change in the quantity of money affects the interest rate. An increase in the quantity of money lowers the interest rate, and a reduction in the quantity of money raises it. Because the interest rate is the cost of borrowing, there will be additional repercussions. The lower the cost of borrowing, the more households and businesses borrow to spend on goods and services. Businesses borrow to enlarge or renovate their plant and equipment, and households borrow to buy new homes, remodel their existing homes, and to buy new cars and furniture. Hence, a fall in the interest rate, brought about by an increase in the quantity of money, increases nominal GDP, and vice versa.

FIGURE 1–1
The Quantity of
Money (M2) and
Nominal GDP:
1970–1993

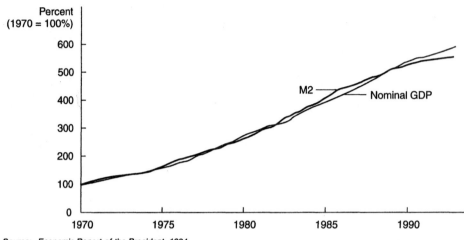

Source: *Economic Report of the President, 1994.*

In sum, a change in the quantity of money (*M*) works through the financial sector to change the interest rate (*i*), which, in turn, affects aggregate demand for goods and services (*AD*) and the level of nominal GDP (denoted by *PY*). Schematically, we have:

$$M\uparrow \rightarrow i\downarrow \rightarrow AD\uparrow \rightarrow PY\uparrow$$

and

$$M\downarrow \rightarrow i\uparrow \rightarrow AD\downarrow \rightarrow PY\downarrow$$

This is the approach we shall follow in most of this book. There is, however, a long tradition behind an alternative approach that concentrates on the endpoints of the process. An increase in the quantity of money will lead to an increase in nominal GDP, and a decrease in the quantity of money to a decrease in nominal GDP.

$$M\uparrow \rightarrow PY\uparrow \text{ and } M\downarrow \rightarrow PY\downarrow$$

We shall also explain this approach and relate it to the Federal Reserve's practices, especially in Chapter 16.

Figure 1–1 examines the history of nominal GDP and M2 from 1970 to 1993. The solid line traces the history of M2 as a fraction of its 1970 level of 100 percent. Similarly, the dashed line shows the history of nominal GDP, also as a fraction of its 1970 level. The graph shows that an increase in the quantity of money was accompanied by an increase in nominal GDP.

We have established that an increase in the quantity of money increases nominal GDP. But how is this increase in nominal GDP apportioned between an increase in prices, *P*, and an increase in real output, *Y*? The answer depends on the state of the economy, that is, on conditions of supply.

GlobalWatch 1.2
Plummeting Purchasing Power of the Russian Ruble

In January 1993 the price level in Russia rose 28 percent; in February it rose 25 percent; and in March, 17 percent. In other words, the purchasing power of the Russian ruble fell about 25 percent *per month* in the first quarter of 1993. By contrast, in 1993 the purchasing power of the U.S. dollar fell by less than 3 percent for the entire year.

What was the cause of the plummeting purchasing power of the ruble? In April 1993 Jeffrey Sachs, a pro-

fessor of economics at Harvard University and an economic adviser to the Russian government, explained it this way:

The Russian Central Bank, controlled by the parliament, has quadrupled the money supply in eight months, fueling a galloping inflation. As John Maynard Keynes sagely observed, the irresponsible increase of domestic currency is devastating because it "engages all the hidden forces of economic law on the side of destruction, and it does it in a manner which not one man in a million is able to diagnose." The Washington Post National Weekly Edition, *April 5–11, 1993: 24.*

An increase in the quantity of money increases spending on (demand for) goods and services. If there is slack in the economy in the form of unemployed labor and unused plant and equipment, the supply of output increases to meet the demand. The price of output also rises. If the economy is operating at full capacity, any attempt to increase production results only in higher costs and higher prices. In either case, any increase in spending fueled by an increase in the quantity of money results in a higher price level. On the other hand, a decrease in the quantity of money results in a lower price level.

$$M\uparrow \Rightarrow P\uparrow \text{ and } M\downarrow \Rightarrow P\downarrow$$

We can use this relation to link the quantity of money with its purchasing power. If a one-pound loaf of bread costs two dollars, the purchasing power of each dollar is one-half of a loaf of bread. In general, the **purchasing power of money,** *or* **value of money**, is $1/P$; it is the amount of goods and services that each dollar can purchase. It is clear, then, that the higher the U.S. price level, the lower the purchasing power of the dollar. Thus, the relation between money and prices is also a relation between money and its purchasing power. The greater the quantity of money, the smaller its purchasing power, and the smaller the quantity of money, the greater its purchasing power.

When prices are continually rising, the purchasing power of a country's currency is being eroded. Continually rising prices means there is inflation. The **inflation rate** is the rate of increase in the price level. Because inflation is the rate at which the purchasing power of money is eroded, it receives a lot of attention from the press, policymakers, and the public. GlobalWatch 1.2 looks at an extreme case: the plummeting purchasing power of the Russian currency (the ruble) in 1993.

LOOKING AHEAD: THE TWO-PILLAR FRAMEWORK

This chapter has focused on money. Money is a key financial asset, but it is not the only asset in the financial system. Beginning in Part 2, we build and analyze a framework of the contemporary U.S. financial system. Both the design and analysis of this framework

FIGURE 1–2
The Two-Pillar
Framework

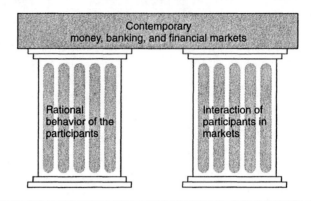

rely on the two pillars of economics depicted in Figure 1–2: (1) the rational behavior of participants in the financial system, and (2) their interaction in the marketplace. How participants make their decisions and how markets work will be the recurring themes of this book.

SUMMARY

· Money serves three functions: a medium of exchange, a unit of account, and a store of value.

· A medium of exchange is anything generally acceptable as a means of payment.

· A unit of account is a yardstick for measuring prices and values and a benchmark for comparing them.

· A store of value is a temporary and permanent reservoir of future purchasing power.

· Historically, commodities, especially gold and silver, were used as money. In modern monetary systems, money consists of paper notes and coins and accounts with depository institutions.

· In the United States depository institutions are required to hold a fraction of their checkable deposits in the form of reserves. Reserves consist of cash that depository institution have on hand, called *vault cash,* and accounts with the Federal Reserve, called *reserve balances with the Fed.*

· By controlling the quantity of reserves, the Federal Reserve influences the quantity of money. Open market operations, which are purchases and sales of government securities by the Fed in the open market, are the primary way the Fed controls reserves.

· The Federal Reserve tracks and reports on one narrow measure of money, M1, and two broad measures, M2 and M3. M1 consists of currency, traveler's checks, and interest-bearing and non-interest-bearing checking accounts. The broader measures add less-liquid accounts, such as savings deposits, time deposits, and money market mutual funds.

· Money is one of several assets in which individuals hold their wealth. A change in the quantity of money alters the scarcity of money relative to other assets, thereby affecting the rate of return on all assets. In particular, a change in the quantity of money changes the interest rate, which is the rate of return on bonds.

· The interest rate links money to nominal GDP, which is economywide output measured in current dollars. An increase in the quantity of money lowers the interest rate, inducing households and businesses to increase their spending on goods and services, which increases the level of nominal GDP.

· How an increase in nominal GDP is apportioned between a change in the price level and a change in real GDP depends on the amount of slack in the economy.

KEY TERMS AND CONCEPTS

medium of exchange	reserves	assets
unit of account	open market operations	real assets/tangible assets
store of value	monetary policy	financial assets/financial instruments/securities
gold standard	M1	
fiat money	transactions balances	gross domestic product (GDP)
legal tender	liquidity	nominal GDP
deposit insurance	M2	real GDP
currency in circulation	nontransactions balances	price level
central bank	M3	purchasing power of money/value of money
vault cash	monetary aggregates	
reserve balances with the Fed	*L*	inflation rate

QUESTIONS AND PROBLEMS

1. Why is wheat better suited to serve as money than Chevys are? Why is paper currency better suited than wheat?

2. The scarcity of gold contributed to its demise as money. Would its fate have been different if it were as plentiful as the soil in your backyard?

The Wall Street Journal

3. The following statement is from the "World Wire" column of the July 1, 1993, issue of *The Wall Street Journal:* "Brazil will print new banknotes of 1 million and 5 million cruzeiro denominations. . . . The largest bill now circulating is 500,000 cruzeiros ($9.70). Prices last year rose 1,150%." Explain Brazil's action in terms of the medium of exchange function of money.

4. For centuries a nation's quantity of money was fully or fractionally backed by precious metals such as gold. In modern times most money is bank deposits, that is, obligations of banks to the public. What, if anything, backs this part of the quantity of money? What, if anything, backs the rest of money, that is, currency?

5. What are reserves? What is the relation between deposits and reserves?

6. Which of the following two statements is true?

   a. "The Federal Reserve and the law require banks to keep a fraction of their deposits in reserves—vault cash and deposits with the Fed—in order to protect the public's deposits."

   b. "The requirement that banks hold a fraction of their deposits as reserves provides the Fed with instruments to control the volume of deposits and, hence, of money."

7. Suppose you transfer $1,000 from your money market mutual fund to your checking account. What will be the effect on M1? On M2?

8. Suppose that you sell a corporate bond for $5,000 and deposit the funds in your checking account. What will be the effect on M1? On M2?

The Wall Street Journal

9. Every Monday, forecasts of the coming week's change in M1, M2, and M3 appear on page A2 of *The Wall Street Journal* as part of a table, "Statistics to Be Released This Week." The accompanying table from the Monday, June 28, 1993, issue shows that the forecast is: M1 will rise, M2 will remain unchanged, and M3 will fall. Use the definitions of M1, M2, and M3 to explain how this prediction could come true.

Statistics to Be Released This Week

ECONOMIC INDICATOR	PERIOD	RELEASE DATE	PREVIOUS ACTUAL	TECHNICAL DATA CONSENSUS FORECAST
Consumer Confidence Index	June	June 29	61.5	**62.5**
Leading Indicators	May	June 29	+0.1%	**−0.1%**
New-Home Sales	May	June 29	+22.7%	**−10.0%**
Factory Orders	May	June 30	−0.1%	**−0.8%**
Construction Spending	May	July 1	−0.4%	**+0.7%**
Initial Jobless Claims	Week to June 26	July 1	353.000	**349.000**
→ **Money Supply: M1**	Week to June 21	July 1	−$2.1 billion	**+$3.7 billion** ←
→ **Money Supply: M2**	Week to June 21	July 1	−$2.3 billion	**No change** ←
→ **Money Supply: M3**	Week to June 21	July 1	−$2.5 billion	**−$2.4 billion** ←
Purchasing Mgrs. Survey	June	July 1	51.1%	**50.0%**
Nonfarm Payrolls	June	July 2	+209.000	**+140.000**
Unemployment Rate	June	July 2	6.9%	**7.0%**

10. Rank the three measures of money according to their liquidity.

11. The Fed calls M1 transactions balances and non-M1 components of M2 or M3 nontransactions balances. What is the theoretical basis for this distinction?

12. Explain the mechanism by which a decrease in the quantity of money is transmitted into a change in nominal GDP.

13. "An increase in the quantity of money always increases real GDP." True, false, or uncertain? Explain.

14. In the mid-1980s the rate of inflation in Bolivia reached 20,000 percent. How good a store of value was the Bolivian péso?

15. Since ancient times it has been observed that during wartime the public is reluctant to hold money for long. "It burns holes in their pockets." Why?

SUGGESTED READINGS

Brunner, Karl, and Allan H. Meltzer. "The Uses of Money: Money in the Theory of an Exchange Economy." *American Economic Review* 61, no. 5 (December 1971): 784–905.

An examination of the economic forces that produced the current monetary system.

Friedman, Milton. *Money Mischief: Episodes in Monetary History.* New York: Harcourt Brace Jovanovich, 1992.

An examination in layperson's language of monetary systems throughout history.

Friedman, Milton, and Anna J. Schwartz. *Monetary Statistics of the United States.* New York: National Bureau of Economic Research, 1970, Chapters 2–5, pp. 89–198.

A detailed examination of the theoretical and empirical importance of the various measures of money.

Simpson, Thomas D. "The Redefined Monetary Aggregates." *Federal Reserve Bulletin* 66, no. 2 (February 1980): 97–114.

A rationale for the current measures of money in the United States.

Tobin, James. "Financial Innovation and Deregulation in Perspective." *Bank of Japan Monetary and Economic Studies* 3, no. 2 (September 1985): 19–29; reprinted in James Tobin, *Policies for Prosperity: Essays in a Keynesian Mode.* Cambridge, Mass.: The MIT Press, 1987, pp. 255–64.

A concise treatment of the functions of money and a glimpse of the monetary system of the future.

Tobin, James. "Monetary Policies and the Economy: The Transmission Mechanism," *Southern Economic Journal* 44, no. 3 (January 1978): 421–31; reprinted in James Tobin, *Essays in Economics.* Cambridge, Mass.: The MIT Press, 1982, pp. 3–13.

An analysis of the process by which a change in monetary policy is transmitted to a change in nominal GDP.

THE U.S. FINANCIAL SYSTEM

The Participants, the Instruments, and the Environment

2   Introducing the Participants
3   A Framework for Understanding Financial Instruments
4   The Basic Financial Instruments
5   The Evolution to the New Financial Environment

Part 2 introduces the participants, the financial instruments they issue and acquire, and the environment in which they operate, thus laying the financial foundation on which we apply the two-pillar framework in the remainder of the book.

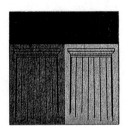

CHAPTER 2

INTRODUCING THE PARTICIPANTS

CHAPTER PREVIEW

As individuals, we often take for granted how intimately involved we are with the U.S. financial system. Imagine the following scenarios:

- Jack Burns runs a small printing company. At a recent printing show he discovered a technologically advanced press that could help him increase his business significantly. He'll need a $70,000 loan to purchase the press.

- Yoshio Eguchi, an electronics worker in Osaka, Japan, saved the yen equivalent of $10,000 this year. Because interest rates are higher in the United States than in Japan, he put $5,000 in high-quality U.S. corporate bonds.

- Alex Palos is a young loan officer at a newly opened First Chicago branch. He's out to impress his vice-president by aggressively pursuing companies that will enhance his bank's loan portfolio.

- Amanda Sharp, who heads a biotechnology company, had a very good year. She saved $200,000, most of which she invested in the stock market.

Though they will not meet, individuals like these will all be connecting and helping each other through the U.S. financial system.

The term **financial system** describes collectively the financial markets, the participants in the markets, and the instruments that are traded. The function of the financial system is to channel funds between savers and borrowers, provide a medium of exchange, provide a mechanism for risk sharing, and provide a conduit through which the Federal Reserve can influence the economy.

In this chapter we introduce the participants. They make up the first pillar of our two-pillar framework. The discussion revolves around two questions. First, *who are the participants?* What are their needs and motives, their similarities and differences? One characteristic the participants share is that they issue and acquire financial instruments. This brings us to the second question: *Why do they issue and acquire financial instruments?* The next chapter answers a third question: *What are the characteristics of financial instruments?* The answers to these questions will help us understand the contemporary U.S. financial system and set the stage for the rest of the book.

WHO ARE THE PARTICIPANTS?

The participants in the financial system fall into six categories, or sectors: (1) households, also known as consumers; (2) nonfinancial firms, or simply firms; (3) financial intermediaries, of which banks are the most important subgroup; (4) the government; (5) the Federal Reserve System, the central bank of the United States; and (6) foreign participants. The Federal Reserve systematically maintains data on these six participants. Because we want to pattern our analysis after the actual U.S. system, we will use the same classifications. The rationale for this classification is that entities within each category exhibit similar behavior. We often use the term **sector** when we refer to all participants in one category; for example, the "household sector" refers to all households.

Households

Households, or what economists often call *consumers*, share certain characteristics and behaviors. Generally, they receive income, two-thirds of which typically comes from wages paid by firms. This income is then saved or spent on goods and services. **Gross savings** refers to the difference between current income and current expenditures.

If the goods and services on which consumers spend their income are consumed within the current period (typically a year), as hamburgers, notebooks, or haircuts are, they are called **nondurable consumer goods**. If the goods provide use beyond the current period, as automobiles or refrigerators do, they are called **durable consumer goods**. (Economic activity is usually measured and assessed annually. The standard definition of consumer durables, however, is that they are consumption goods with a life of three or more years. The assumption is that all consumer goods with shorter lives are used up in the year in which they are purchased. Hence, these goods are classified as nondurables.) Residential structures (homes) are classified separately.

Households generally follow similar funding patterns. Typically they pay for nondurable goods and services from current income. On the other hand, they often borrow to finance the purchase of consumer durables, such as stoves or cars, as well as to finance houses.

Nonfinancial Firms

Nonfinancial firms, or **firms**, produce goods and services for both households and other firms. In addition to consumer goods and services like hamburgers and haircuts, firms also provide **producer durable goods**. These are goods used in the production process over many years, that is, new plants, additions to existing plants, or new equipment.

In producing goods and services for households and businesses, firms combine inputs of labor and raw materials with the use of plant and equipment; hence, they incur expenses. Firms also receive revenue from selling goods or services. For a firm to be profitable, revenue must exceed operating expenses, or costs, such as those for labor, raw materials, and rent. Whether firms are profitable in a particular year or not, they frequently need to invest in machinery or equipment and often borrow to fund these purchases.

Defining Some Terms   In our discussion of the financial system we distinguish between consumption goods and capital goods. **Capital goods** are lasting physical objects, while **consumption goods** are used up in the year in which they are purchased. According to this definition, nondurable consumer goods and services are consumption goods, while consumer durables, producer durables, and residential structures are capital goods.[1]

Financial Intermediaries

Financial intermediaries are financial institutions that channel funds to other participants and in the process issue their own financial instruments. Other financial institutions, called **market specialists**, help move funds through financial markets but do not issue their own financial instruments. (We will discuss market specialists in greater detail in the discussion of direct finance later in the chapter.) The goal of all financial institutions, whether intermediaries or others, is to make a profit by providing financial services.

Financial intermediaries encompass all **depository institutions**: commercial banks, savings and loans associations, mutual savings banks, and credit unions. The common feature of these institutions is that they issue (attract) deposits and make loans. At the end of 1993, there were approximately 26,000 depository institutions in the United States, of which about 11,000 were **commercial banks**. Traditionally commercial banks were the only depository institutions allowed by law to offer transactions services by providing a financial instrument—demand deposits (better known as checking accounts)—that serves as a medium of exchange. **Thrifts**, the collective name for S&Ls, mutual savings banks, and credit unions, specialized in issuing savings deposits, that is, nontransactions deposits, and in financing home mortgages or, in the case of credit unions, consumer loans.

In the 1980s, however, deregulation blurred the distinction between commercial banks and thrifts. Today thrifts issue checkable deposits and thus, like commercial banks, provide transactions services. They also finance business loans within limits prescribed by law.

Financial intermediaries also include **nondepository institutions**, such as pension funds, life insurance companies, mutual funds, and finance companies. The financial instruments issued by nondepository institutions generally differ from the deposits issued

---

[1] This classification of consumption goods and capital goods follows the Flow of Funds Accounts, a national statistical system developed by the Federal Reserve to measure the financial activity of the different sectors of the U.S. economy and their interrelationships.

TABLE 2–1
Types of U.S.
Financial
Intermediaries and
Their Asset Size:
1993

	Assets ($ billions)
Depository institutions	
Commercial banks	$3,868.9
Savings and loan associations and mutual savings banks	1,033.3
Credit unions	280.7
Nondepository institutions	
Life insurance companies	$1,792.0
Other insurance companies	636.7
Private pension funds	2,336.1
State and local government retirement funds	1,065.2
Mutual funds	1,426.8
Money market mutual funds	559.1
Finance companies	658.2

Source: Federal Reserve Flow of Funds Accounts.

by banks and thrifts. Pension funds and insurance companies issue contracts for future payments under specified conditions. Mutual funds, on the other hand, issue shares in a portfolio of securities, that is, a selection, or "basket," of financial instruments. Mutual funds vary according to the types of securities they purchase for their portfolios. In the case of money market mutual funds, the shares can be withdrawn by check and thus have transactions characteristics. Finally, finance companies raise funds to lend to households and firms by selling marketable securities and by borrowing from banks. Table 2–1 lists the types of financial intermediaries and their size in 1993.

Government

By **government** we mean local, state, and federal governments. This category includes the U.S. Treasury and certain other federal agencies. The **U.S. Treasury** is the department of the federal government that collects tax revenues and makes expenditures appropriated by Congress and approved by the president. It also issues financial instruments to finance the gap between government expenditures and tax revenues.

The Federal Reserve

The **Federal Reserve System**, or simply the **Fed**, is the central bank of the United States, mandated to oversee the health of the national financial system and of the economy. Chapters 11 and 12 discuss the form and function of the Federal Reserve System in detail. Here we get a glimpse of the workings of the Fed.

The Fed plays several roles, including "banker" to banks, regulator of banks, and monetary policymaker. As banker to banks, the Fed provides various services to banks, such as helping them collect and clear checks and loaning them funds. As a lender to banks and one of the regulators of banks, the Fed specifically oversees the health of the banking system. Finally, as the U.S. monetary policymaker, the Fed monitors the health of the national economy.

The Fed has three basic components: a seven-member Board of Governors and its staff, headquartered in Washington, D.C.;[2] 12 Federal Reserve Banks and their branches, dispersed throughout the United States; and member commercial banks. A fourth component, the Federal Open Market Committee (FOMC), draws its 12 members from the Board of Governors and the Reserve Banks.[3]

When we refer to the Fed, we usually mean the Board, the FOMC, and the Reserve Banks. The Board itself and the FOMC are the policy-making bodies within the Federal Reserve System. There is, however, another component of the Federal Reserve System, namely member banks. At the end of 1993, 39 percent of all commercial banks were members of the Federal Reserve System. Nothing special, however, in the economic analysis of member banks distinguishes them from nonmember banks. Since the passage of the Monetary Control Act of 1980, the monetary policy reach of the Fed extends directly to all depository institutions—member banks, nonmember banks, and thrifts. All of these institutions are required by law to hold reserves with the Fed.

Foreign Participants

Finally, **foreign participants** make up the foreign sector. This sector consists of all the participants from the rest of the world: households, nonfinancial firms, governments, and central banks. Goods and services and financial instruments are exchanged across national borders as well as within those borders. As international trade and finance loom larger in the U.S. economy, the role of foreign participants has become more important.

A Word on Stocks and Flows

Before we proceed with our discussion of how the production and spending decisions of the various sectors interact with their financial decisions, we need to distinguish between stocks and flows. The classic visual illustration of stocks and flows is a bathtub filling with water. The rate at which the water enters the tub, say, 10 gallons per minute, is a flow. The amount of water in the tub at a given time, say, 40 gallons, is a stock. In general, a **flow** is expressed as a quantity per period of time. A **stock** on the other hand, is a quantity existing at a point in time.

In financial terms, consider the following hypothetical example. Suppose that when Tom Rice enrolled as a freshman at Allstate University on September 3, 1992, he had no debt; his stock of outstanding IOUs was zero. Suppose, however, that during his freshman year he borrowed $2,000 from his relatives. This $2,000 per year is a flow.

To derive a stock at a point in time, we must find the sum of all the flows up to that point. Thus, the stock of Tom Rice's outstanding debt on September 3, 1993, is $2,000, that is, 0 + $2,000. Further, suppose that Tom borrows $2,500 during his sophomore year. Adding the two flows, we find that on September 3, 1993, the stock of his outstanding debt is $4,500.

So far we have seen how to convert flows to stocks. But how do we convert stocks to flows? Simply put, we measure the stock of an item at two difference points in time and

---

[2] The seven members of the Board of Governors are appointed by the president and confirmed by the U.S. Senate.

[3] The FOMC consists of the seven members of the Board of Governors plus five presidents of the Reserve Banks, one of whom must be the president of the Federal Reserve Bank of New York. The remaining four members are selected on a rotating basis from among the remaining 11 presidents of the Reserve Banks.

take the difference between the two stocks. Thus, the difference between Tom Rice's (stock of) debt on September 3, 1993, and September 3, 1992, is a flow: $4,500 − $2,000 = $2,500 for that year.

Now armed with the concept of stock and flows, we can proceed with our discussion of why participants issue and acquire financial instruments.

WHY DO THE PARTICIPANTS ISSUE AND ACQUIRE FINANCIAL INSTRUMENTS?

All participants in the financial system interact by issuing and acquiring financial instruments. The underlying reasons for their behavior, however, are based on the different roles the participants play in the financial system. *Each of the six participants falls into one of three roles:*

1. **The role of surplus or deficit units** (defined below): Households, firms, government, and the foreign sector fall into this category.
2. **The role of financial go-betweens,** or financial intermediaries, which channel funds between surplus and deficit units. In this category, depository institutions are unique among financial intermediaries because they also provide the medium of exchange (by issuing checking accounts).
3. **The role of monetary policymakers,** whose broad function is to protect the health of the economy. The Federal Reserve is the only participant with this function.

The Role of Surplus and Deficit Units

Some participants in the financial system are "savers" and therefore can lend out excess funds. In other words, they are lenders. Other participants are primarily "spenders" and often need to borrow. They are borrowers. The more precise economic terms for these concepts are *surplus units* and *deficit units,* respectively.

A **surplus unit** is a participant for whom current gross savings exceed current expenditures on capital goods.[4] The surplus funds of such a unit are the excess of its current gross savings over its current capital expenditures (i.e., its investment in real assets). Surplus funds are a flow concept because current gross savings and current capital expenditures are savings and expenditures per unit of time, typically per year.

Consider, for example, a household that earns $25,000 in after-tax income this year. Assume it spends $20,000 on consumption goods such as food, heat, and a family vacation. The household also spends $2,000 on new furniture, a capital expenditure on real assets. The household has $5,000 of gross savings, the difference between its current income and its current consumption expenditures. Its gross savings exceed its capital expenditures by $3,000. Thus, our hypothetical household is a surplus unit this year. The extra (surplus) funds may be used to pay off (retire) existing debt (e.g., credit card bills) or to finance the deficits of other participants.

A **deficit unit** is a participant whose current gross savings fall short of its current expenditures on capital goods. The funding gap (a flow concept) of a deficit unit reflects

---

[4] The designation of savings as "gross savings" means that no deduction has been made for depreciation, which is the amount by which real assets wear out each year. Net savings equal gross savings minus depreciation.

its current financing needs. The funding gap equals the participant's current expenditures on capital goods minus its current savings. For example, a business firm builds a new plant for $1 million this year. Retained profits of $100,000 for the year—the gross savings of the firm—leave the firm with a funding gap of $900,000.

A deficit unit can finance its funding gap in two ways. If the deficit unit holds real or financial assets, it can sell some of those assets (which includes reducing money holdings). Let's say the firm referred to previously has government bonds valued at $500,000 and sells the bonds to close part of the funding gap. In this case, existing financial assets change hands. Alternatively, the deficit unit can sell new issues of financial securities. These securities may be either debt or equity securities. When a deficit unit borrows funds from a surplus unit or a financial intermediary, it issues an IOU called a **debt security**, which is a promise by the issuing unit to make fixed payments at specified dates in the future. The surplus unit or the financial intermediary that acquires the debt security is a lender.

Another way a deficit unit may obtain funds from a surplus unit is by bringing the surplus unit into the enterprise as a co-owner. In this case, the deficit unit issues a certificate of partial ownership, an **equity security**. Shares of common stock are an example of an equity security.

Let us now apply the concept of deficit and surplus units to our participants. We find that some sectors are usually surplus units while others are usually deficit units.

Households   As we saw in our earlier example, the current gross savings of an individual household equal current income minus current consumption. A household whose current income exceeds its current consumption has positive gross savings. On the other hand, a household whose current income falls short of its current consumption has negative gross savings; it dissaves. Many college students are dissavers because they borrow to finance current consumption. On the other hand, later in life they usually borrow to finance big-ticket items like cars or houses; that is, they invest in real assets.

Consider a household whose only capital expenditure this year is for a house. If the purchase price of the house exceeds the household's gross savings, the household is a deficit unit for the year; its current capital expenditures exceed its current gross savings. Such deficit households typically finance their funding gaps by selling an existing house, by selling some existing financial assets, by borrowing from financial intermediaries, or by using a combination of the three alternatives. Households that borrow from financial intermediaries issue IOUs called mortgages, which are assets for the financial intermediaries that acquire them.

Only a small percentage of the U.S. population, however, buy a house in a year. A greater percentage buy durable goods: furniture, automobiles, appliances, and personal computers. If expenditures on consumer durables are greater than a household's gross savings, the household is again a deficit unit and must finance its funding gap by borrowing or by selling existing assets.

Other households may borrow to finance big-ticket items even though their gross savings exceed their expenditures on these items. In the end, however, these households count as surplus units because their lending (gross savings) is greater than their borrowing. Still other households borrow because their expenditures outpace their income at certain times of the year, perhaps at Christmas or during summer vacations. Such households, however, may also be a net surplus unit for the entire year.

FIGURE 2-1
The Surplus Funds
of Households:
Gross Savings –
Capital
Expenditures

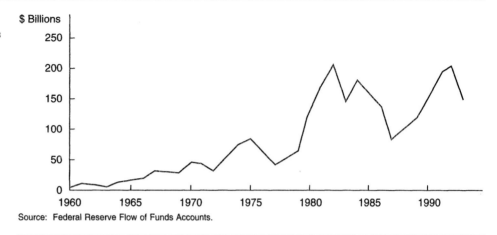

Source: Federal Reserve Flow of Funds Accounts.

Although individual households run deficits, households, considered as a sector, are usually a surplus unit in the United States. Each year the aggregate gross savings of all households usually exceed their investment in new houses and new durable goods, as shown in Figure 2–1.[5] These funds can and do find outlets in the deficits of other sectors.

Nonfinancial Firms   Every year in the United States, as in other developed capitalist economies, firms invest in real assets by building new plants, expanding existing ones, acquiring new equipment, and adding to their inventories of finished goods and raw materials.

Gross retained profits (for the period, say, a year) are the business sector's gross savings. They are the internal funds available to firms to finance investment in real assets. Gross profits are calculated by subtracting operating expenses and taxes from receipts. Retained profits are undistributed profits; that is, the profits have not been distributed to shareholders. Hence, the amount of gross retained profits for firms equals receipts from the sale of output minus operating expenses, taxes, and dividends. For example, a toy manufacturer had revenue of $200,000 last year, and operating expenses totaled $150,000, taxes totaled $5,000, and dividends were $30,000. Therefore, subtracting $185,000 from $200,000, we find that gross retained profits for the year equaled $15,000.

Operating expenses do not include costs of replacing worn-out plant and equipment, that is, depreciation. Depreciation of existing capital appears in profits, making profits appear larger, which accounts for the term *gross profits*. In our example, a $10,000 annual depreciation allowance on the toy manufacturer's plant and equipment means that net retained profits (gross retained profits minus depreciation) were $5,000. The typical firm has both the accounting expertise and the tax incentive to earmark part of gross retained

---

[5] At the sector level, only the purchase of new real assets matters in determining the sector's net need for funds. For example, for every household that buys an existing house, there is another household that sells it—assuming that all houses are traded within the household sector.

FIGURE 2–2
Funding Gap of
Firms: *Capital
Expenditures –
Gross Savings*

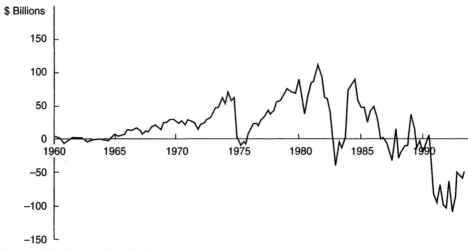

Source: Federal Reserve Flow of Funds Accounts.

profits as depreciation allowances. For the business sector, the annual dollar amount of these allowances is usually greater than the dollar amount of net retained profits.

An individual firm may be a deficit unit in one period and a surplus unit in another. Sometimes a firm needs funds to finance investment in plant and equipment. A firm often needs funds for reasons other than financing investment in real assets. Even a profitable firm sometimes finds itself short of cash at certain times of the year when operating expenses temporarily outpace receipts from the sale of output. For example, the bulk of our toy manufacturer's sales are made during the Christmas season. Although the company was profitable last year, by August it ran low on funds and needed to borrow on its line of credit to pay employees and suppliers. Other times the firm has surplus funds to lend to other firms or to households and governments.

While the circumstances of individual firms vary from year to year, nonfinancial firms as a group typically are a deficit sector. Figure 2–2 shows the difference between capital expenditures and internal funds (gross retained profits) for firms from 1960 on. The graph shows that unlike most previous years, in the early 1990s capital expenditures were less than gross savings. What was the reason? Investment by firms was low because of a weak U.S. economy and diminished business confidence.

Because the business sector's investment in (new) real assets often exceeds its gross retained profits, firms persistently need funds. They are major issuers of debt and equity securities.[6]

---

[6] At the level of the individual firm, we do not distinguish between new plant and equipment and existing plant and equipment in defining a deficit unit. At the sector level, however, only the purchase of new real assets matters in determining the sector's net need for funds. For every firm that sells an existing factory, there is another firm that buys it, so purchases and sales of existing factories cancel out. If one of the firms is a foreign firm, there is an effect on the foreign sector.

FIGURE 2–3
**Federal Budget
Deficits:**
*Government
Expenditures – Tax
Receipts*

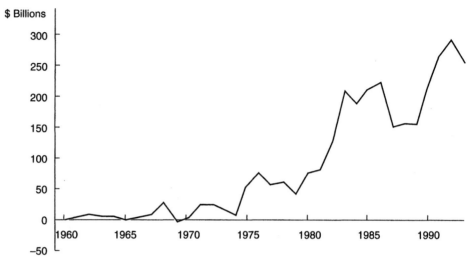

Source: *Economic Report of the President, 1994*, Table B-77.

Government   Although the consolidated government sector consists of local, state, and federal governments, we focus on the federal government here. The government budget does not distinguish between capital expenditures and current consumption expenditures of the U.S. government. Government expenditures on paper clips, civilian and military employees, computers, roads, space stations, and medical research are treated similarly in the budget: as current consumption expenditures. So the status of the federal government as a surplus unit or a deficit unit depends solely on whether the government saves or dissaves in any given period.

Government outlays consist of expenditures not only for goods and services but also for **transfer payments**. With these payments, the government transfers income to recipients, but no goods or services are produced in return. Unemployment compensation, Social Security payments, and interest payments on existing government debt are examples of transfer payments. In the early 1990s transfer payments accounted for about two-thirds of all government spending. The remaining one-third consisted of government expenditures on final goods and services, including military expenditures.

Government receipts come primarily from taxes. When current government expenditures exceed current receipts, the government is a dissaver, or deficit unit. The magnitude of the government funding gap, called the **budget deficit**, is the amount by which expenditures exceed receipts. On the other hand, when receipts exceed expenditures, the government is a saver, or surplus unit. The magnitude of the **budget surplus** is the amount by which receipts exceed expenditures. Finally, when expenditures equal receipts, the government has a balanced budget.

Figure 2–3 shows the annual federal budget from 1960 on. Increases in the budget deficit in the mid-1970s, early 1980s, and early 1990s stand out. In the mid-1970s, the

U.S. economy was in a severe recession. With income levels depressed nationwide, tax receipts, linked automatically to income, fell. On the other hand, expenditures on transfer payments, such as unemployment compensation and welfare payments, automatically rose as more households qualified for benefits under existing programs. Thus, the increase in the deficit was an automatic increase that normally accompanies a recession.

A short recession in 1980 and a severe one in 1982 again increased the deficit. Other factors, however, also were at work. Tax cuts enacted in the early 1980s, increases in military spending, and increases in transfer payments (which include interest paid on the outstanding government debt) all contributed to the budget deficits of the 1980s. In 1991 a recession again increased the deficit. In addition, payments by the government to bail out the thrift industry contributed to the high deficits in the early 1990s. (The thrift bailout is discussed in Chapter 5.) A deficit reduction law passed in the summer of 1993 raises taxes and cuts expenditures. The Clinton administration estimates that the tax increases and expenditure cuts will reduce the deficit by a total of about $500 billion between 1994 and 1998.

Part 7 examines the effects of deficits on the economy. Here we merely explore why the government issues financial instruments. The answer is that deficits must be financed whether they result from automatic changes in tax receipts and expenditures within the structure of existing policy, from changes in tax and spending policy, or from special circumstances such as the thrift bailout. The government finances federal deficits by issuing interest-bearing debt that is an IOU of the federal government. Deficits, which are a flow, increase the stock of outstanding government debt. Surpluses, another flow, reduce the stock of that debt.[7] At the end of 1980 the nominal value of the total amount of debt outstanding was $906.4 billion. By the end of 1993, the nominal value had more than quadrupled to $4,408.6 billion.

Foreign Participants   Finally, we need to examine the role of the rest of the world in the U.S. economic system. The United States sells financial instruments to the rest of the world if it has a gap in its international trade in goods and services and its international transfers. In contrast, it acquires financial instruments from the rest of the world if it has surplus funds in these accounts. Let's look at the specifics.

The accounts of U.S. transactions with the rest of the world do not distinguish between consumption goods and capital goods. Exporting (selling to foreigners) goods such as grain, computers, and airplanes generates receipts for the United States, as does exporting services. In records of international transactions, receipts from services include receipts from true services, such as travel and transportation. They also include investment income in the form of interest, dividends, and profits on American-owned assets abroad. Unilateral transfers from abroad, in the form of gifts and grants from foreign governments, firms, and households, also generate receipts for the United States. Payments to the rest of the world arise from importing (buying) foreign goods and services and from unilateral transfers to foreigners. Payments for services include interest, dividends, and profits paid on foreign-owned assets in the United States.

---

[7] The effects of budget deficits on the economy are discussed at length in Chapters 25 and 28.

FIGURE 2–4
U.S. Current
Account Balance
with the Rest of the
World: *A Positive*
Number Means a
Surplus.

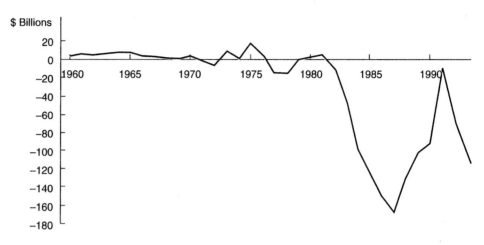

Source: *Economic Report of the President, 1994*, Table B-103.

When payments for imports and unilateral transfers exceed receipts from exports and unilateral transfers, the United States has a funding gap in its international trade in goods and services (and international transfers). This funding gap, called a **current account deficit**, is the excess of payments for imports and transfers over receipts from imports and transfers.[8]

Current account deficits with the rest of the world are financed by selling financial instruments to foreign participants, including foreign governments. The direct sale of real assets to foreign participants is another option. For foreign participants, the purchase of U.S. government bonds, corporate bonds, or corporate stock are example of financial, or portfolio, investment. On the other hand, building a new factory in the United States or buying an existing factory represents direct investment. Current account deficits increase the amount of foreign financial and direct investment in the United States. For example, Yoshio Eguchi, whom we met in the preview, is helping to finance the current account deficit by purchasing U.S. corporate bonds.

A **current account surplus** exists when receipts from exports and transfers exceed payments for imports and transfers. Surplus funds on current account find outlets in funding foreign deficits.

Figure 2–4 shows the U.S. current account balance with the rest of the world. From 1960 to the mid-1970s the United States regularly ran surpluses or maintained near balance in its current account. Current account surpluses (and deficits) are flows. As a result of the string of surpluses, Americans built up a stock of assets abroad that exceeded the stock of assets in the United States held by foreigners. In other words,

---

[8] Typically, U.S. payments for transfers exceed receipts from transfers, but net transfers are small compared with payments for imports.

GlobalWatch 2.1
Is Foreign Borrowing Bad?

If the United States were a closed economy, Americans could buy only what they themselves produced and spend only what they earned. To cast the same issue in terms of deficit and surplus units, domestic households, firms, or government units that were running deficits would be limited to borrowing only from other domestic households, firms, or government units with surplus funds to lend. By contrast, in an open economy, a country can be a net borrower. When domestic households, firms, and the government together spend more than the national income, they run a current account deficit; they finance the deficit by borrowing from the rest of the world. The United States did this in the 1980s and continues to do so, though at a diminished rate, in the 1990s.

The debt to foreigners accumulated by the United States in the 1980s means the United States financed spending in those years that would not have occurred without the annual deficits. In those years American households financed more vacations, new cars, college educations, primary residences, and summer homes;

American firms financed more plant and equipment purchases; the government financed more outlays on defense, infrastructure (such as bridges and highways), education, and transfers to the poor, elderly, and unemployed without needing to raise taxes.

As with an individual debtor, the future prospects of a debtor nation depend on how it has spent the funds it borrowed. For example, if you borrowed from relatives to pay for your current expenses in college this year, your future prospects would be different than if you had borrowed to spend the year on the beach in Hawaii.

The main concern about the U.S. current account deficits and foreign borrowing is that Americans spent too much of the borrowed funds on current consumption, such as vacations, and on consumer durables, such as cars and furniture, and not enough on "investing" in education (human capital), plant and equipment, and infrastructure, which contribute to future growth and increased standards of living. If future growth is meager, Americans may have to reduce their standard of living to pay interest on their debt to foreigners. On the other hand, if future growth is robust, Americans will be able to service that debt and enjoy a higher standard of living.

the United States was a **net creditor nation**: a net lender of funds to the rest of the world.

As Figure 2–4 illustrates, the current account moved from a surplus in the mid-1970s to a deficit in the late 1970s, then back to a surplus in 1980 and 1981. A series of subsequent current account deficits followed. By 1988, seven years of current account deficits had turned the United States from a net creditor nation to a **net debtor nation**. For the first time in 60 years, the stock of foreign-owned American assets (financial and real) exceeded the stock of American-owned foreign assets. If direct investment is measured at market value, the size of the U.S. net debtor position was minus $38 billion dollars in 1988.

Since the late 1980s, the United States has been accumulating debt at a diminished rate: The annual current account deficits decreased in the late 1980s and early 1990s, as shown in Figure 2–4. In 1991, the current account deficit was negligible because of unilateral transfers to the United States from foreign governments to help finance Operation Desert Storm. At the end of 1992, the country's net debtor position stood at $611.5 billion.

Parts 7 and 8 examine the causes and effects of the current account deficits of the United States. In GlobalWatch 2.1 we take a first look at the effects by asking whether foreign borrowing is bad.

FIGURE 2–5
Direct and Indirect
Finance: *The Flow
of Funds and
Securities*

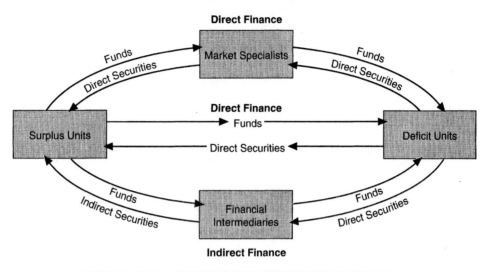

The Role of Financial Go-Betweens

We have seen that deficit and surplus units issue and acquire financial instruments because of their needs as consumers, producers, and government units. Financial intermediaries, on the other hand, issue and acquire financial instruments as a function of their goal to make a profit. (They accomplish their goal of profitability by lending funds at a higher interest rate than they pay to borrow them.)

To better understand the special role of financial intermediaries in channeling funds between deficit and surplus units and to distinguish financial intermediaries from the other financial institutions called *market specialists*, we need to discuss the concepts of direct versus indirect finance.

Direct versus Indirect Finance   Figure 2–5 depicts the flow of funds and financial instruments between surplus units and deficit units. Only indirect finance—depicted in green—involves financial intermediaries. To understand the operation of indirect finance, we first have to examine direct finance—depicted in black.

Direct Finance   The distinguishing characteristic of **direct finance** is that the security acquired by the surplus unit is the same security, which we will call a **direct security**, issued by the deficit unit. In general, a direct security is a financial instrument a deficit unit issues and sells to a surplus unit with or without the help of a market specialist. Let us illustrate by considering the case of Jack Burns, introduced in the preview.

Jack needs a $70,000 loan to expand his printing business. In his search for funds, he finds friends and relatives who give him that amount in exchange for his IOU—a direct security. The middle line of Figure 2–5 shows this method of direct finance. Direct securities flow from Jack (a deficit unit) to his friends and relatives (surplus units), and funds flow in the opposite direction.

Like Jack Burns's small business, major corporations that want to start new businesses or expand existing ones could also search for surplus units to buy their securities. Usually, however, they employ market specialists to conduct the search on their behalf. These market specialists are investment banks and brokers that help design and move direct securities through financial markets. Some of these financial institutions, such as Merrill Lynch, are household names.

Investment banks advise clients such as nonfinancial firms and state and local governments on the timing and pricing of new issues of securities. In addition to giving advice on the origination of securities, investment banks also underwrite the new issues either by purchasing them outright or by guaranteeing their sale at an agreed price. Finally, investment banks sell the securities to investors in the open market. By underwriting securities, investment banks take on the risk of bringing the securities to market. If market prices of securities are lower than the prices they guarantee to their clients, investment banks incur a loss; in the opposite case, they earn a profit. Unlike investment bankers, **brokers** do not buy or sell securities themselves. They simply bring surplus and deficit units together and earn a commission for their services. Often the same financial institution, such as Merrill Lynch, provides both brokerage and investment banking services.

Amanda Sharp and Yoshio Eguchi, introduced in the preview, are surplus units in need of a broker: Amanda to buy stocks, and Yoshio to buy U.S. corporate bonds. Yoshio's purchase of bonds is a cross-border transaction involving foreign exchange, which in this case is U.S. dollars. Yoshio can leave the purchase of dollars to his broker and pay for the bonds in his domestic currency, Japanese yen. For example, he may buy the bonds from Nomura Securities Co., a Japanese financial institution that is the largest brokerage firm in the world, with subsidiaries in other countries including the United States.

Direct securities such as stocks and bonds that are sold in the open market through market specialists are also referred to as **open market securities**. The upper loop of Figure 2–5 shows these direct securities flowing from deficit units through market specialists to surplus units, and funds flowing in the opposite direction.

Direct finance is the method typically used by big deficit units such as large corporations. There are two reasons. One is economies of scale, which make this method of finance cost effective to large firms. The other is name recognition, which makes their securities desirable to surplus units.

Large fixed costs of issuing securities in the open market are the reason for economies of scale. Large firms reap economies of scale because they raise vast amounts of funds, making the per dollar cost small and this method of financing affordable. In contrast, the per dollar cost for small firms is prohibitive.

Investors are more likely to buy securities issued by a firm about which they have information than from an unknown firm. Established firms have an advantage over newly established firms, which either must use other forms of financing, or must offer a higher rate to the investor. (Bonds issued by newly established firms are part of the "junk bonds" market that emerged in the 1980s, as we shall see in Chapter 3.)

Indirect Finance   Now we come to **indirect finance** and the special role of financial intermediaries. To illustrate, let us return to the example of Jack Burns and his printing business. The high fixed cost of floating debt or equity puts the open market out of reach of small borrowers like Jack. Also, suppose Jack's friends and relatives are unwilling (they do not want any more of his IOUs) to finance a new printing press. After looking around, however, he finds a bank that is willing. He gives the bank an IOU (a direct security), and the bank gives him $70,000. The bank obtains the funds that it lends Jack from surplus units who deposit some of their surplus funds in the bank. In exchange, the bank gives the surplus units IOUs of the bank, such as certificates of deposits (CDs). CDs are an example of indirect securities.

Now we can generalize our example. The distinguishing characteristic of *indirect finance* is that the financial security acquired by the surplus unit is different from the security issued by the deficit unit. Herein lies the special role of financial intermediaries. In channeling funds between surplus and deficit units, a financial intermediary acquires direct securities from deficit units and issues its own securities, called **indirect securities**.

A crucial function of all financial intermediaries is to transform direct securities into indirect securities to make a profit. The lower loop of Figure 2–5 depicts this transformation. Direct securities flow from deficit units into financial intermediaries, and indirect securities flow out of financial intermediaries to surplus units. Funds, of course, flow in the opposite direction.

Asymmetric Information: The "Lemons Problem" Indirect finance, or financial intermediation, is a natural consequence of **asymmetric information**, where one party to a transaction has more information than the other party. George Akerloff[9] introduced the concept of asymmetric information in 1970 in the context of the used car market. The seller of a used car knows whether the car is good, but the buyer does not. Because of unequal, or asymmetric, information in the used car market, direct sales between buyer and seller are relatively few. Most sales take place through a used car dealer, an intermediary who has the expertise to determine whether or not the car is a lemon. Since the publication of Akerloff's seminal work, economists refer to problems arising from asymmetric information as the "lemons problem." Let's see how the concept has been used to explain the special role of financial intermediaries, especially commercial banks.

In assessing the attractiveness of a loan, the lender—whether a surplus unit or a financial intermediary—must gather information. For example, in deciding whether lending to Jack Burns is a good investment, a potential lender will have to answer several questions. What is Jack's reputation? Does he have a good credit history? Are his estimates of how much the new press will increase his revenue and profit realistic? Is his business healthy enough to withstand a downturn in the economy? Ultimately, how risky is lending to Jack Burns? Answering these and similar questions is costly in time and money, and involves a lot of guesswork. What complicates the assessment is the lender's disadvantage in one crucial respect: The prospective borrower has more information than the lender, and he has an incentive to be "economical" with the information (and the truth) he provides the lender. For example, Jack, who has the most information about his

---

9 George Akerloff, "The Market for 'Lemons': Quality, Uncertainty and the Market Mechanism," *Quarterly Journal of Economics* 84 (August 1970): 488–500.

TABLE 2–2
Advantages of
Intermediation

To Lenders	To Borrowers	To Economy
1. Higher rate of return	1. Lower cost of borrowing	1. Provision of credit
2. Greater access to investments	2. Greater access to credit	2. Provision of medium of exchange—liquidity
3. Greater flexibility— broader menu of investments	3. Greater flexibility— custom-made loans	
4. Reduced risk		
5. Liquidity		

credit history and business prospects, has an incentive to put a rosy spin on this information because he wants the loan. This is an example of asymmetric information: The borrower (the deficit unit) has more information than the lender (the surplus unit).

The Advantages of Intermediation   Overcoming the disadvantage of asymmetric information requires considerable expertise and involves substantial costs. Individual surplus units, except for a few large ones, do not possess this expertise. Even if they did, the cost of gathering information would be exorbitant, greatly reducing the net return on their loans. These high costs might even make the net return negative. Individual savers can earn a higher net rate of return by lending to a financial intermediary.

Financial intermediaries, in general, and banks, in particular, specialize in information gathering. They are better prepared to weed out lemons than are individual savers. They employ experts to assess the risk of lending by evaluating a borrower's prospects for success *before* they make a loan. These experts also monitor a borrower's compliance with the terms of a loan *after* it has been made. They also establish long-term customer relations that enable them to assess the risk of lending and monitor a customer's compliance better than individual surplus units.

Because banks pool the surplus funds of many savers, they spread their fixed cost over many loans, thereby lowering the per unit cost of lending. The lower costs enable banks to offer a higher rate to depositors and a lower rate to businesses and households who borrow from them. In addition, because they work with large sums, banks diversify their loan portfolio by making loans to a variety of businesses. By not putting all their eggs in one basket, banks reduce their exposure to the potential losses of an individual customer. In this way, the risk of losses to individual depositors is substantially less than if they lent directly to an individual deficit unit.

There is another important benefit to surplus units if the financial intermediary is a bank. Lenders to banks, that is, depositors, can withdraw their funds *on demand,* by simply writing a check. This increases liquidity, which is the ability to convert claims to cash. In contrast, loans to individual deficit units are difficult to convert to cash; they are illiquid.

Table 2–2 breaks down the advantages of intermediation into categories: to lenders, to borrowers, and to the economy. Let's begin with the lenders.

Benefits to Lenders   First, financial intermediaries provide a *higher rate of return,* as we have explained. Second, they provide *greater access* to individual investors. Financial intermediaries can pool funds in small denominations and accumulate enough of them to buy open market instruments that are inaccessible to an individual investor. Thus, "small-potatoes" investors have access to investments that would otherwise be accessible only to "big guys."

Third, intermediaries provide *greater flexibility* to individual investors: They offer indirect securities with a different mix of characteristics than direct securities. In particular, open market securities may have limitations on size, maturity, or risk that make them unattractive to a surplus unit with a small amount of funds or a special need (Chapter 3 examines the characteristics of securities in detail.)

Fourth, financial intermediaries provide *reduced risk* to individual investors for two reasons. First, because funds are continually coming in while other funds are maturing and going out, a financial intermediary is fairly safe. Second, because financial intermediaries can diversify their portfolios better than most individual investors, lending to intermediaries is safer.

And fifth, financial intermediaries provide *liquidity* to investors. Investors can convert the indirect securities issued by the intermediary to cash with greater ease than if they made a loan to an individual borrower. If the indirect security is a demand deposit or similar instrument, it is the medium of exchange.

Benefits to Borrowers   For borrowers, financial intermediaries provide a *lower cost of borrowing,* as explained earlier. Second, they provide *greater acccess to credit.* Many households or small businesses are unable to find individual surplus units willing to lend to them. Or deficit units may be unable, because of their small size, to raise funds in the open market by issuing stocks or bonds. For all these deficit units, financial intermediaries provide the *only access.*

And, third, financial intermediaries also provide deficit units with *greater flexibility.* Some businesses' borrowing needs can be satisfied only by a "custom-made" loan, and it is here that that financial intermediaries have always excelled. For this reason alone, even business giants sometimes borrow from banks rather than resort to the open markets.

Benefits to the Economy   Finally we move beyond the individual participants to look at the benefits of intermediation to the economy as a whole. Financial intermediaries fulfill two broad functions. The first function of all financial intermediaries is to provide *credit* to participants in the economy by taking in funds from surplus units and making loans to deficit units. The second function, unique to depository institutions (typically commercial banks) is to provide the *medium of exchange.* [10]

These two functions underscore the importance of banks. Provision of credit to businesses is essential to economic growth. To see why, let's suppose that fewer loans are available to commercial and industrial businesses. Investment in plant and equipment will be lower. Thus, national output will be lower. National output will also be lower if there

---

[10] A third function is a consequence of these two functions. Financial intermediaries are major repositories of the public's wealth.

SectorWatch 2.2
A Web of Bank Regulators

Banks are highly regulated and supervised to ensure sound banking practices and protect the safety of deposited funds. A host of regulatory agencies conduct on-site examinations of banks, administer laws, and issue rules and decisions that affect the size of banks and their permissible activities. The underlying reason is that if banks fail, depositors lose money, borrowing and lending activities suffer, and the payments mechanism is handicapped. Consequently, the production of goods and services suffers.

The most vivid example of the costs of bank failures occurred in the 1930s, when the collapse of thousands of U.S. banks contributed to the Great Depression. In fact, this painful experience was the catalyst for much of the regulatory system still in place today. Many of the regulations were introduced by legislation enacted in the 1930s, at the beginning of Franklin D. Roosevelt's presidency. The regulatory picture is further complicated by the fact that banks can be chartered (licensed) on either the national or the state level. Thus, a "dual banking system" is in place in the United States.

Following are some strands of the tangled web of regulators that oversee the U.S. financial system:

- The Fed, created in 1913, is charged with the responsibility of overseeing the health of the economy and the health of banks. To carry out this responsibility, the Federal Reserve Act of 1913 and subsequent legislation empowered the Fed to supervise and regulate member banks. Note that the Fed is not only a regulator of the system but also a participant.

- The Federal Deposit Insurance Corporation (FDIC), created in 1933, insures bank deposits and pays depositors from its insurance fund when banks fail. For this reason, the FDIC supervises and regulates insured depository institutions.

- The Office of the Comptroller of the Currency (OCC), an agency of the U.S. Treasury, charters national banks and has been regulating banks since 1863.

- Fifty separate state banking commissions charter state banks. Some of these state regulatory agencies date back to the 1700s.

- To reduce the cost and burden of bank regulation, in November 1993 the Clinton administration proposed to consolidate the regulatory and supervisory functions of the Fed, the FDIC, and the OCC into one federal banking agency. As Chapter 17 discusses, the Fed is likely to maintain some regulatory functions under any new arrangements.

is an insufficient quantity of the medium of exchange, which will hamper the payments system. Resources that could be used for production must be diverted to facilitate the payments mechanism.

Because the health of banks, businesses, and the economy are closely intertwined, let's return to the credit function. The essence of entrepreneurship is to undertake risk. Credit to businesses by banks and other financial intermediaries encourages enterpreneurship and economic growth. If the financial system in general, or banks in particular, are impaired, credit will be reduced. Risk taking by businesses and the fruits of enterpreneurship—economic growth—suffer. For example, many economists believe that the slow growth of the U.S. economy in the early 1990s was partly attributable to an increased inability and unwillingness of banks to lend, even to creditworthy customers. Chapter 5 explores the reason for this "credit crunch."

Because of their role in the provision of credit and in the payments system and because they are repositories of a major portion of the public's wealth, banks are highly regulated. SectorWatch 2.2 introduces the complex network of bank regulators.[11] A regulator is different from a participant; a regulator generally does not issue or acquire securities as part of its regulatory function. The Fed, however, wears two hats: one as a regulator and another as a participant. We turn to the role of the Fed as a participant next.

The Role of Monetary Policymaker

The ultimate goal of a monetary policymaker is to protect the health of the economy by seeking price stability, full employment, and maximum sustainable economic growth. In the United States the Federal Reserve fulfills that role; that is why the Fed issues and acquires financial instruments. More specifically, the Fed provides raw material for the financial system in the form of the **monetary base**, which consists of currency held by the public plus reserves held by depository institutions. Currency held by the public, called currency in circulation, consists of the public's holdings of coins and paper currency.[12]

Typically, currency in circulation accounts for at least three-fourths of the total monetary base. For example, in December 1993 the (average) level of the monetary base was $386.07 billion, of which $325.54 billion consisted of currency in circulation and $60.53 billion of reserves.

According to existing law, all depository institutions must hold reserves against certain types of deposits. The **reserve requirement ratio** is the fraction of deposits that must be held in the form of reserves. Deposits with unlimited checking privileges, such as demand deposits, NOW accounts, and super-NOW accounts, are currently the only deposits subject to reserves, with the reserve requirement ratio set at 10 percent. A 10 percent reserve requirement ratio on checkable deposits means that for every $1 of these deposits, depository institutions must hold 10 cents in reserves. Inverting the relationship, we can say that a 10 percent reserve requirement ratio means that every $1 of reserves can support $10 of checkable deposits. We confirm this by observing that 10 percent of $10 is $1. In general, with a reserve requirement ratio less than 1, every dollar of reserves can support a multiple amount of deposits.

By using the monetary policy tools at its disposal, the Fed can increase or decrease the amount of currency and reserves in the financial system. Changes in policy change the monetary base and, hence, M1, and eventually interest rates and other macroeconomic variables. In this sense, the base can be thought of as "raw material."

Changes in money, debt, and interest rates, in turn, affect the level of expenditure on goods and services and, hence, the general level of economic activity and prices in the United States. This is a bird's-eye view of how the Fed seeks to achieve its ultimate goals of price stability, full employment, and maximum sustainable economic growth.

LOOKING AHEAD

In the chapter we have answered two key questions about the U.S. financial system: Who are the participants? And why do they issue and acquire financial instruments? In the next chapter, we ask a third question: What are the characteristics of financial instruments?

---

[11] Chapter 17 examines depository institutions and their regulators in more detail. Chapter 19 examines nondepository institutions and their regulators.

[12] The bulk of paper currency is in the form of Federal Reserve notes, which are issued by the Fed. All coins and a small amount of paper currency are issued by the Treasury. Therefore, strictly speaking, a small portion of the monetary base is issued by the U.S. Treasury.

SUMMARY

- The financial system consists of six sectors, or participants, who interact by issuing and acquiring financial instruments in the various financial markets: (1) households, (2) nonfinancial firms, (3) financial intermediaries, especially banks, (4) the government, (5) the Federal Reserve System, and (6) the foreign sector. The Federal Reserve collects and regularly publishes data on these sectors.

- In a given period some participants issue securities and others acquire securities, depending on whether they are deficit units or surplus units, respectively. A deficit unit is a participant whose gross savings fall short of its expenditure on capital goods. To finance this gap, the participant issues securities. Nonfinancial firms and the U.S. government are typically deficit units.

- A surplus unit is a participant whose gross savings exceed its expenditure on capital goods. The participant uses these excess funds to acquire securities issued by other participants. Households are usually a surplus sector. Foreign participants have also been a surplus sector in the 1980s and 1990s.

- A financial intermediary both issues and acquires securities to make a profit by channeling funds between surplus and deficit units. An intermediary acquires direct securities, such as mortgages, and transforms them into indirect securities, such as deposit accounts.

- Surplus funds can reach deficit units either directly or indirectly, via intermediaries. With direct finance, the surplus unit receives a promise of future payments from the deficit unit. With indirect finance, the surplus unit receives a promise from a financial intermediary, which, in turn, receives a promise from the deficit unit.

- Direct finance is the method used by big deficit units, such as large corporations. They sell their securities directly in the open market without resorting to financial intermediaries. There are economies of scale that enable large deficit units to bypass the intermediary and finance their needs at lower costs by issuing and selling securities in the open market. Smaller businesses and households finance their needs primarily via intermediaries, such as banks.

- Information about whether the deficit unit will keep its promises is important to the lender (surplus unit.) Asymmetric information means that the borrower has more information than the lender.

- Information about large companies is more plentiful and, therefore, surplus units are more willing to finance the needs of large established corporations. Information about small firms and households is difficult and costly for the typical surplus unit to acquire. Banks excel in information gathering and can ascertain and monitor the condition of borrowers more efficiently than small savers. This explains why most financing is indirect, via banks.

- Among financial intermediaries, banks perform a dual role. In addition to providing credit to deficit units, banks also provide the medium of exchange.

- The Federal Reserve, the central bank of the United States, acts as both a participant and regulator of the financial system. As the national monetary policymaker, it issues the monetary base, consisting of currency in circulation and reserves. As a regulator, the Fed protects the health of depository institutions. As a banker to banks, the Fed provides special services to the U.S. banking system, such as assistance in check clearing.

KEY TERMS AND CONCEPTS

financial system
sector
households
gross savings
nondurable consumer goods
durable consumer goods
firms
producer durable goods
capital goods

consumption goods
financial intermediaries
market specialists
depository institutions
commercial banks
thrifts
nondepository institutions
government

U.S. Treasury
Federal Reserve System, or Fed
foreign participants
flow
stock
surplus unit
deficit unit
debt security

equity security	net creditor nation	open market securities
transfer payments	net debtor nation	indirect finance
budget deficit	direct finance	indirect securities
budget surplus	direct security	asymmetric information
current account deficit	investment banks	monetary base
current account surplus	brokers	reserve requirement ratio

QUESTIONS AND PROBLEMS

1. Suppose that in the first year after graduation you earn $40,000. You spend $25,000 on living expenses, $5,000 to repay student loans, and $10,000 to buy a new car. Are you a surplus or a deficit unit? By how much?

2. "A saver is always a surplus unit." True or false? Explain.

3. Which sectors of the U.S. financial system are typically deficit units? Explain how each of these participants finances its deficits.

4. Which sectors of the U.S. financial system are surplus units? How do they dispose of their surplus funds?

5. "Nations that run large budget deficits, by definition, must borrow from the rest of the world to finance these budget deficits." True or false? Explain.

6. Classify the following concepts as stocks or flows.
   a. Budget deficit
   b. National debt
   c. Current account deficit
   d. Net debtor nation

7. "A deficit unit is a burden to the economy." True, false, or uncertain? Explain.

8. Explain the difference between direct and indirect finance and the role played by deficit/surplus units and financial intermediaries in each method of finance.

9. Which financial institutions does the term *financial intermediaries* encompass?

10. "Financial intermediaries are parasites. They do not contribute to the economy. They merely shuffle funds from one participant to another." True or false? Explain your answer.

11. Suppose that IBM considers expanding its plant and equipment. Which of the following methods of finance is it least likely to use? Explain.
    a. Issuing bonds
    b. Issuing new stock
    c. Borrowing from a bank

12. "An individual, as opposed to a corporation, has access only to indirect finance." True or false? Explain.

13. "By offering both credit services (bank loans) and transactions services (checking accounts) to their customers, banks are in a better position to cope with asymmetric information than other lenders." Do you agree or disagree? Explain.

14. Why might you be willing to lend your funds to a bank that paid a deposit rate of only 3 percent if you knew that the bank loaned your funds to others at 8 percent?

15. Why might you be willing to borrow from a bank at 8 percent if you knew that the bank borrowed those funds at 3 percent?

16. The Fed is both a regulator of and participant in the financial system. Explain the difference.

SUGGESTED READINGS

Bernanke, Ben S. "Credit in the Macroeconomy." *Quarterly Review* (Federal Reserve Bank of New York) 18, no. 1 (Spring 1993): 50–70.
   Discusses the role of credit, information, and intermediation.
Board of Governors of the Federal Reserve System. *Introduction to the Flow of Funds Accounts.* Washington, D.C.: U.S. Government Printing Office, 1975.
   A primer on the flow-of-funds system of social accounting.
Board of Governors of the Federal Reserve System. "Flow of Funds Accounts: Flows and Outstandings." *Z1 Statistical Release.* Published quarterly.
   A major source of data on the U.S. Financial system.
Van Horne, James C. *Financial Market Rates and Flows,* 3rd ed. Englewood Cliffs, N.J.: Prentice Hall, 1990.
   A small book about financial markets and interest rates that has become a classic. Chapter 1 discusses the function of financial markets, and Chapter 2 discusses the flow of funds system.

CHAPTER 3

A FRAMEWORK FOR UNDERSTANDING FINANCIAL INSTRUMENTS

CHAPTER PREVIEW

If you find yourself visiting San Francisco, you may choose where to dine based on the advice of a friend or food critic. Or you may scour guidebooks to restaurants in the San Francisco Bay area to make your choice. In any case, the characteristics of restaurants—type of food, prices, location, service—will influence your choice. For example, Chez Panisse offers innovative food and excellent service, but its location in Berkeley and high prices might cause you to consider instead Fior d'Italia, which offers Italian food at moderate prices and is located in the city.

In the same manner, if you plan to buy a security (financial instrument), you ask: What are its characteristics? For example, can you get your funds back on demand? If not, can you sell the security to a third party? And how easily? What is the rate of return? And how predictable is that return?

This chapter explores the characteristics of securities, providing a framework for understanding existing financial instruments. Knowing these characteristics also prepares us to understand all the unknown new securities that will be developed in the future. We begin with maturity and marketability, then take a detailed look at rate of return, the most watched characteristic. In explaining how to calculate the rate of return, we start with an easy-to-compute approximation, then introduce the equation for the precise rate of return. These equations can be used to calculate the rate of return on any financial instrument, such as a bond or shares of common stock. They can even be used to calculate the rate of return on a tangible asset, such as an apartment building or gold. Finally, to help you understand the mechanics of financial markets and the financial press, we apply these equations to explain different measures of the interest rate on debt securities.

The other characteristics of securities examined in this chapter are risk, liquidity, and divisibility. These characteristics, as well as maturity and marketability, are important on their own and also because they ultimately affect the structure of rates of return on securities.

Chapter 4 uses these six characteristics—maturity, marketability, rate of return, risk, liquidity, and divisibility—to describe the wide variety of securities in the U.S. financial system. Chapter 6 then examines how these characteristics guide decisions to buy securities.

MATURITY

Our discussion of the characteristics of securities begins with the concept of maturity. Suppose that on January 21, 1989, you purchased a bond newly issued by General Electric Corporation. Suppose too that the funds are due for repayment on January 20, 2029. The initial term to maturity of this bond is 30 years, which is the length of time between the date the issuer (General Electric) acquired funds from the purchaser (you) and the date the issuer must repay the funds.

After the issuing date, **maturity** is often specified simply by the end point of the security, the date the funds must be repaid. We can then calculate the remaining term to maturity. For example, the GE bond maturing on January 20, 2029, has 20 years left to maturity on January 21, 1999. If this bond had a call provision, General Electric could repay you before January 21, 2029. A **call provision**, a common feature of corporate bonds, gives the issuer the right to buy the bond back at a set price after a specified number of years, thereby making the maturity of the security uncertain.

The maturity of securities ranges from immediate to infinite, as shown in Table 3–1. Immediate maturity means the issuer must repay the funds on demand by the holder. Checking accounts—demand deposits, NOW accounts, and super-NOW accounts—and passbook savings accounts are examples of securities with immediate maturity.

TABLE 3–1
The Maturity of
Securities

Classification	Length of Time to Maturity	Example
Immediate	Funds must be repaid on demand	Checking accounts issued by banks
Short term	Overnight to one year	26-week Treasury bills issued by the U.S. government
Intermediate term	More than one year, to ten years	5-year Treasury notes issued by the U.S. government
Long term	More than ten years upward	30-year Treasury bonds issued by the U.S. government
Infinite	Never matures	Shares of common stock issued by corporations

On the other hand, a security with infinite maturity never matures. Equity securities, such as shares of common stock, are an example. Unless a firm buys back some of its outstanding common stock, the stock remains in the market forever. Among debt securities, a particular type of bond, called a *consol* also has infinite maturity. Consols are promises to pay interest indefinitely. They never, however, repay the principal. The British government first introduced consols in the mid-eighteenth century. By the early twentieth century, most of the British national debt was in consols, but today they account for only a very small part of that debt.

Between securities with immediate maturity and those with infinite maturity are short-term, intermediate-term, and long-term securities. The length of time to maturity on **short-term securities** ranges from overnight to one year; on **intermediate-term securities** from more than one year to ten years; and on **long-term securities** from more than ten years upward.

MARKETABILITY

A second important characteristic of securities is **marketability**. Marketability refers to whether an existing security can be sold before maturity to another market participant, a third party. Some securities, such as bank CDs in denominations of less than $100,000, are not marketable. Nonmarketable securities can be redeemed only with the issuer at maturity and at a prescribed price; if the contract so specifies, they can be redeemed at an earlier date but subject to some penalty. Marketable securities, in contrast, can be sold to a third party before maturity with varying degrees of ease and convenience.

Primary and Secondary Markets

New issues of securities are sold in what is termed the **primary market** and so are known as *primary securities*.[1] Some examples are a deposit in a checking account, a new issue of a Treasury bond, and a new issue of shares of corporate stock. Existing securities, which is what this discussion focuses on, are sold in the **secondary market** and are thus known as *secondary securities*. Secondary markets increase the liquidity of financial instruments. For example, investors who buy Treasury bonds can sell them in the secondary market before maturity.

Absence of a secondary market may or may not diminish a security's attractiveness. Although demand deposits and passbook savings accounts are not marketable, they are still attractive to investors because of their immediate maturity. On the other hand, absence of marketability is a drawback for a security such as a time deposit that does not have immediate maturity. The creation of a secondary market for negotiable certificates of deposit (time deposits of $100,000 or more) in the early 1960s was heralded as a landmark in financial innovation.

Brokers and dealers in existing securities bring together buyers and sellers in the secondary market. Like brokers in primary securities, brokers in existing securities do not

---

[1] In Chapter 2, when discussing direct and indirect finance, we used the term *direct securities* to describe new issues of securities sold by deficit units to surplus units with or without the help of market specialists. These securities are primary securities.

take a position in those securities. Dealers in secondary securities, however, do buy and sell existing securities for their own accounts. Thus, they function as the secondary market's counterpart to investment bankers.

The size of the secondary market dwarfs that of the primary market. The two markets are closely interrelated, however, because primary securities and secondary securities are substitutes for each other in the portfolios of investors. For example, if the interest rate of an existing bond is 10 percent, no one will buy a new bond with comparable characteristics unless it too pays at least 10 percent. On the other hand, issuers of new bonds will not offer an 11 percent rate of interest if the going rate on comparable existing bonds is 10 percent.

Money and Capital Markets

There are other ways of classifying securities and their associated markets besides primary and secondary. One important classification is the money market/capital market distinction, based on length of time to maturity. **Money market securities** are marketable debt securities with maturities of a year or less, and the *money markets* are the markets in which these securities are traded. **Capital market securities** include marketable debt securities with maturities of a year or more and equity securities. The associated markets are naturally called *capital markets*. Treasury bills are an example of money market securities, while Treasury bonds are capital market securities. (Other money market and capital market securities are introduced in Chapter 4, where we compile a list of basic securities in the U.S. system and describe their characteristics.)

Spot and Futures Markets

Another classification is the distinction between spot and futures markets. A **spot market** is a market for the immediate delivery of an item, from grain and cattle to Treasury bonds and notes. In contrast, a **futures market** is a market in which the parties trade an agreement, called a *futures contract,* to exchange an item at a specified time in the future for a specified price. When the contract calls for the delivery of a financial instrument such as Treasury notes or Treasury bonds, it is called a *financial futures contract.*

The Chicago Board of Trade, the most prominent exchange for all kinds of futures contracts, started trading futures in commodities such as grain in 1848. Financial futures are a recent development, having made their appearance in the mid-1970s. Chapter 5 discusses how participants in financial markets may use financial futures contracts to transfer risk.

RATE OF RETURN: THE MOST WATCHED CHARACTERISTIC

The rate of return is the most visible and widely mentioned characteristic of securities. The return on an asset (whether financial or real) is the reward to the asset holder. This reward comes from two sources. One is annual receipts, which can be interest, dividends, or rent, depending on whether the asset is a bond, shares of common stock, or an apartment building. The other source is a one-time capital gain or loss if the holder sells the asset (or cashes it in at maturity) at a price greater than or less than the purchase price. The annual rate of return on an asset is the annual reward expressed as a fraction of the purchase price of the asset.

Figure 3–1 will help us understand how to calculate the rate of return on an asset. It depicts a cash-flow chart for a hypothetical asset. Let us suppose that today, period 0, we

FIGURE 3–1
Cash-Flow Chart
for a Hypothetical
Five-Year Asset

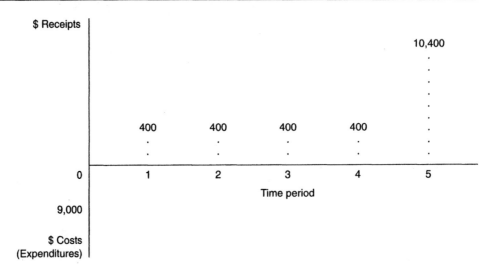

Note: By convention, a cash-flow chart depicts receipts as positive entries—above the axis—and expenditures as negative entries.

pay $9,000 to buy an asset that we plan to hold for five years. This asset yields expected annual receipts of $400 for each of the five years. At the end of the fifth year we also expect to receive $10,000 from the redemption of the asset. We want to know how to calculate our annual rate of return, and we begin by using a simple equation that approximates the rate of return. As we shall see, the approximated rate of return is close to the precise rate of return.

Approximating the Rate of Return

Our method for approximating the annual rate of return breaks the return into two components: an annual yield, called the *current yield,* and an average annual capital gains rate.

The current yield comes from the yearly payments that the issuer of a financial asset or the renter of a real asset makes to the asset holder. For the asset holder, these yearly payments are, of course, receipts. If the asset is shares of common stock, periodic receipts take the form of dividend payments by the issuer of the stock. If the asset is a bond, receipts come from interest payments by the issuer of the bond. If the asset is an apartment building, receipts come from rent, net of any maintenance and other costs incurred during the period. For our hypothetical security we assumed fixed and identical annual receipts, a pattern typical of bonds rather than stocks, whose dividends are neither fixed nor known in advance. In any case, the **current yield** is calculated as the year's (net) receipts (R) expressed as a percentage of the current purchase price of the asset (P_a).[2]

---

[2] Be careful not to confuse P_a, which represents the price of an asset, with P, which is the symbol to represent the collective price of goods and services.

$$\text{Current yield} = \frac{\text{Annual receipts}}{\text{Purchase price}} \tag{3-1}$$

$$= \frac{R}{P_a}$$

$$= \frac{\$400}{\$9,000}$$

$$= 0.044, \text{ or } 4.4 \text{ percent}$$

Now we turn to (expected) capital gains or losses. **Total capital gains** are the difference between the redemption price (F) and the current purchase price of the security (P_a). If the investor plans to sell the security before maturity, the redemption price is not known with certainty, but it is the price at which the investor expects to sell the security in the secondary market. On the other hand, if the investor plans to hold the security until maturity, the redemption price is the amount that will be paid by the issuer of the security at maturity, called the **face value**. Dividing the total capital gains by the purchase price, we determine the total capital gains rate, that is, the total capital gains as a percentage of the purchase price. To find the **average annual capital gains rate**, we divide the total capital gains rate by the number of years (n) that the investor holds the security; in other words, we multiply the total capital gains rate by ($1/n$).

$$\begin{matrix}\text{Average annual} \\ \text{capital gains rate}\end{matrix} = \frac{\text{Redemption price} - \text{purchase price}}{\text{Purchase price}} \times \frac{1}{\text{No. of Yr. held}} \tag{3-2}$$

$$= \frac{F - P_a}{P_a} \times \frac{1}{n}$$

$$= \frac{\$10,000 - \$9,000}{\$9,000} \times \frac{1}{5}$$

$$= 0.022, \text{ or } 2.2 \text{ percent}$$

Finally, adding the average annual capital gains rate to the current yield, we arrive at the **approximation of the annual rate of return**, r_{approx}.

$$r_{\text{approx}} = \text{Current yield} + \text{Average annual capital gains rate} \tag{3-3}$$

$$= 0.044 \qquad + 0.022$$

$$= 0.066, \text{ or } 6.6 \text{ percent}$$

Not all assets earn both a periodic return and a capital gain. For example, assets with immediate maturity, such as demand deposits, have no capital gain. On the other hand, some tangible assets, such as gold, do not pay periodic returns, as explained in MarketWatch 3.1.

Equation 3–3 approximates the rate of return before taxes. After-tax rates of return vary according to the tax bracket of the investor. Special tax features are themselves important characteristics of securities. For example, the interest payments on most debt securities issued by state and local governments are exempt from federal income taxes. Also, prior to 1986 the federal government taxed income from capital gains at a lower rate than other income, such as income from wages, rent, interest payments, and dividends. The Tax Reform Act of 1986 eliminated the capital gains differential. The deficit reduction law passed in 1993 raised the top marginal individual income tax rate to 39.6

Market*Watch* 3.1
Is Gold a Good Investment?

Unlike bonds or common stock, gold does not pay a periodic return. The rate of return comes solely from capital gains or losses. Investors enjoy capital gains or suffer losses depending on whether the price of gold is rising or falling. An increase in world tensions or in ex-pected inflation often causes a flight to gold, which boosts its price. Gold prices also rise when commercial demand from jewelers and industrial users rises relative to the supply.

Let's see how someone who bought gold on April 20, 1992, fared one year later. Information on the price of commodities, including gold, is available every day on page C1 of *The Wall Street Journal,* as part of the "Markets Diary." The following excerpt is from April 21, 1993.

MARKETS DIARY   4/21/93

COMMODITY	CLOSE	CHANGE	TUES	YR AGO	12-MO HIGH — AT CLOSE —	12-MO LOW — AT CLOSE —
Gold (Comex spot), troy oz.	$339.50	$– 0.40	$339.90	$339.30	$359.30	$326.30
Oil (W. Tex. int. crude), bbl.	20.00	+ 0.15	19.85	19.90	23.15	18.35
Wheat (#2 hard KC), bu.	3.54	– 0.05	3.59	4.06	4.22	3.11
Steers (Tex.-Okla. choice), 100 lb.	81.50	– 0.25	81.75	76.25	84.75	72.00

The first column of the first row shows that the (spot) price of gold on the Commodity Exchange (Comex) on April 20, 1993, was $339.50 per ounce, and the fourth column shows that the price one year earlier was $339.30. Therefore, the total capital gain for the year was a mere 20 cents. Obviously, the capital gains rate was almost nil. We find this rate by dividing the total capital gain of $0.20 by the purchase price of $339.30, then multiplying the result by 100 to express the rate as a percentage. Carrying out the arith-metic, we find that the annual rate of return on gold was only 6/100 of 1 percent, or six basis points. (A basis point is one 1/100 of a percentage point.) By comparison, the rate of return on a one-year Treasury bill in the same period was about 4 percent. Therefore, the op-portunity cost of gold, that is, the difference between the T-bill rate and the rate on gold, was 3.94 percent-age points. Moreover, we have not accounted for sales and storage fees, which can be considerable for gold but not for Treasury securities.

percent, but kept the top capital gains tax rate unchanged at 28 percent, thereby introduc-ing a differential between the two tax rates once again.

Timing of Receipts and Expenditures

Equation 3–3 for calculating the rate of return gives us only an approximation of the true, or precise, rate of return. This is because of the timing of receipts (and expendi-tures.) A $400 receipt at the end of the third period is not the same as a $400 receipt at the end of the first, or any other, period. A receipt of $400 at the end of the first period can be reinvested for the second and third periods and, thus, will yield more than $400 at the end of the third period. So, $400 received at the end of the first period is worth more than $400 received at the end of the third period. Similarly, $10,000 at the end of the fifth period is not the same as $10,000 today or $10,000 divided equally over five years.

Adding receipts from different periods is like adding apples and oranges. The only way to add different units is first to convert them to identical units—in this case, dollars of the same period. We can convert all receipts to dollars today, when the decision to invest is made. The sum of all the receipts converted to today's dollars is called the **present value** of the stream of receipts. Alternatively, we can convert all receipts to dollars of a future period, such as at the end of the stream of receipts. The sum of all the receipts converted to tomorrow's dollars is called the *future value of the stream of receipts.*

Calculating Present and Future Values

To find the present value of a stream of future receipts, we must find what each item is worth in today's dollars and add them up. However, to see how we can find the present value of a single item available in the future requires some digression. We first determine how to find the future value of a given amount of money today. Then we work backwards to show how to go from a known future value to an unknown present value.

Suppose that we invest $1,000 today at the rate of return r. At the end of the year our asset will be worth:

$$\$1,000 + \$1,000r = \$1,000(1+r)$$

In the second year, we will earn a return not only on our original investment of $1,000 but also on our first year's return of $1,000r$. Therefore, at the end of the second year our asset will be worth what it was at the end of the first year, $1000(1 + r)$, plus the return in the second year, $1000(1 + r)r$:

$$\$1,000(1 + r) + \$1,000(1 + r)r = \$1,000(1 + r)(1 + r)$$
$$= \$1,000(1 + r)^2$$

Continuing in this manner, we find that in general, at the end of period n, the asset will be worth:

$$\$1,000(1 + r)^n$$

For illustration, we arbitrarily chose $1,000 as the given amount of money invested today. Of course, our result applies to any number of dollars invested today. Suppose we denote the present value of our investment, that is, the amount of our investment in today's dollars, by PV, and the future value by FV. We can then express the relationship between present value and future value as follows:

$$FV = PV(1 + r)^n \tag{3-4}$$

According to Equation 3–4, to find the future value of a given amount of money today invested for n years at the annual rate of return r, we multiply the present value of our investment by $(1 + r)^n$. For example, if we put $1,000 in the bank today and the bank pays us 4 percent a year for the next five years, we will have $1,217 at the end of five years. The future value of our $1,000 deposit is $1,217.

Now we can work backwards and solve Equation 3–4 for PV:

$$PV = \frac{FV}{(1 + r)^n} \tag{3-5}$$

According to Equation 3–5, to find the present value of a given number of dollars receivable in the future, we divide the given future value by $(1 + r)^n$. When the rate of return is 4 percent, $1,217 received at the end of five years is worth only $1,000 today. This process of finding the value today of a future receipt is called **discounting** because a dollar tomorrow is worth less than a dollar today.

In general, to find the present value for any stream of receipts, we use Equation 3–6:

$$PV = \frac{R_1}{(1 + r)} + \frac{R_2}{(1 + r)^2} + \frac{R_3}{(1 + r)^3} + \cdots + \frac{R_n}{(1 + r)^n} + \frac{F}{(1 + r)^n} \qquad (3\text{–}6)$$

where the Rs denote periodic receipts; that is, R_1 denotes receipts at the end of the first year; R_2, receipts at the end of the second year; R_n, receipts at the end of nth year, F denotes the redemption price of the asset at the end of the nth year.

The Rate of Return

Now that we know how to determine the present value of a given stream of receipts, we can give a precise definition of the rate of return. The **rate of return** on an asset is the rate, r, that makes the present value of the stream of receipts equal to the current purchase price of the asset, P_a. The terms *rate of return, yield to maturity,* and *interest rate* are all synonyms, as we shall see.

Why must the price of an asset equal its present value? To answer, let's see what happens if the price is not equal to the present value. If the price is lower than the present value, profit-seeking investors rush to buy the asset, thereby pushing the price up. On the other hand, if the price is higher than the present value, no one buys the asset, forcing the price down. Therefore, the price of an asset must equal its present value.

To calculate the rate of return, we must set PV equal to P_a in Equation 3–6 and solve the resulting equation for r, the rate of return. Let's write out that equation explicitly:

$$P_a = \frac{R_1}{(1 + r)} + \frac{R_2}{(1 + r)^2} + \cdots + \frac{R_n}{(1 + r)^n} + \frac{F}{(1 + r)^n} \qquad (3\text{–}7)$$

If we substitute the price and receipts for our hypothetical security into Equation 3–7, we get Equation 3–8:

$$\$9,000 = \frac{\$400}{(1 + r)} + \frac{\$400}{(1 + r)^2} + \frac{\$400}{(1 + r)^3} + \frac{\$400}{(1 + r)^4} + \frac{\$400}{(1 + r)^5} + \frac{\$10,000}{(1 + r)^5} \qquad (3\text{–}8)$$

Equations of this type are difficult to solve, but many modern calculators are programmed to solve them. Solutions can also be calculated by using present value tables. For bonds the solutions have been worked out and tabulated in bond tables. The solution here is $r = 0.064$. Thus, the rate of return on our hypothetical asset is 6.4 percent. Remember that our method for approximating the rate of return gave us a rate of 6.6 percent. Thus, our approximation, which was easy to calculate, overestimated the true rate of return by 20 basis points.[3] A **basis point** is $\frac{1}{100}$ of a percentage point. In other words, 100 basis points make up 1 percentage point.

---

[3] The approximation will be even closer to the precise rate if we use an average of the purchase price and the redemption price, instead of simply the purchase price, in the denominator of the equations for the current yield and the capital gains rate. To keep the concepts as simple as possible, we used merely the purchase price.

The Language and Mechanics of Notes and Bonds

So far our discussion of the rate of return has been general enough to apply to both real assets and financial assets, which include equity and debt securities. Now we focus on interest-bearing debt securities, in particular, notes and bonds, that are liabilities of deficit units. The difference between bonds and notes lies in the initial length of time to maturity; notes are intermediate-term securities, and bonds are long-term securities.[4]

Before we explain the language and mechanics of notes and bonds, let us be more specific about the example in Figure 3–1. Suppose that our hypothetical asset is an existing Treasury bond with only five years left to maturity. We have assumed that this bond sells in the market for $9,000 today and can be redeemed at maturity for $10,000. Using this example as a springboard, we introduce and illustrate terms and details that are important in understanding the mechanics of financial markets and the financial pages of newspapers.

Face Value   Each bond or note bears a face value, also called the *par value,* which is the amount that will be paid by the issuer at maturity. The face value on our hypothetical security is $10,000.

Coupon   The **coupon** is the fixed periodic dollar payments, also referred to as *interest payments,* to holders of bonds and notes. Usually, coupon payments are identical amounts, made twice a year. In our example, we assumed for simplicity only one annual coupon payment of $400.

Coupon Rate   The **coupon rate** is the ratio between the fixed annual coupon payment and the face value of the security, multiplied by 100 to express it in percentage units. The coupon rate on our hypothetical Treasury bond is ($400/$10,000), or 4 percent. The coupon rate on a bond never changes because the coupon payment and the face value never change.

Current Yield   This rate is the ratio between the fixed annual coupon payment and the current purchase price of the security, again multiplied by 100 to express it in percentage units. The current yield on our hypothetical Treasury bond is $400/$9,000, or 4.44 percent. In this case, the current yield is higher than the coupon rate because the purchase price of the bond is less than its face value.

Yield to Maturity   The **yield to maturity** is the rate of return that makes the present discounted value of the fixed coupon payments and the final payment of the face value equal to the current purchase price of the security. In other words, the yield to maturity is the rate of return to maturity, at which time the redemption price equals the face value of the security. To find the precise yield to maturity on a security, we solve Equation 3–7 for r, where n is the number of years to maturity, the Rs are the coupon payments, and F is the face value.

For our hypothetical bond with five years to maturity, the rate of return of 6.4 percent is the precise yield to maturity. The yield to maturity is approximated by the sum of the current yield and the average annual capital gains rate (to maturity).

---

[4] We postpone a discussion of calculating rates on bills until the end of the chapter.

TABLE 3–2
Inverse Relationship between the Interest Rate and the Price of a Bond: *A Bond with Five Years to Maturity, Annual Coupon of $400, and a Face Value of $10,000*

r %	Pₐ in $*	r %	Pₐ in $*
3.0	**10,458**	8.5	8,227
3.5	10,226	9.0	8,056
4.0	**10,000**	9.5	7,889
4.5	9,781	10.0	7,726
5.0	**9,567**	10.5	7,568
5.5	9,360	11.0	7,414
6.0	9,158	12.0	7,117
6.40	**9,000**	13.0	6,836
6.5	8,962	14.0	6,568
6.67	8,897	15.0	6,314
7.0	8,770	16.0	6,072
7.5	8,585	21.15	5,000
8.0	8,404		

Note: Items referred to in the text are in boldface.
*P_a is calculated from Equation 3–9.

Interest Rate   By **interest rate** we usually mean the yield to maturity rather than the coupon rate or the current yield. For a new or existing bond sold at face value, the three rates are equal. The coupon rate equals the current yield because the current purchase price equals the face value of the security. Furthermore, the yield to maturity equals the current yield because the capital gain on such a bond is zero if held to maturity. Financial analysts sometimes use the current yield as a proxy for the yield to maturity. The smaller the average annual capital gains rate on an asset, the closer the current yield is to the yield to maturity.

Inverse Relation between Interest Rate and Price   There is an inverse relationship between the price of a debt security such as a bond and its interest rate. The higher the interest rate on a bond, the lower the price of the bond. Conversely, the higher the price, the lower the interest rate. Table 3–2 illustrates this important inverse relationship for our hypothetical bond by presenting different combinations of r and P_a that satisfy Equation 3–9, where r now stands for the interest rate, or yield to maturity:

$$P_a = \frac{\$400}{(1 + r)} + \frac{\$400}{(1 + r)^2} + \frac{\$400}{(1 + r)^3} + \frac{\$400}{(1 + r)^4} + \frac{\$10,400}{(1 + r)^5} \tag{3–9}$$

For example, if we set the interest rate at 3 percent in Equation 3–9, we find that the price of the bond is $10,458. If the rate is higher, say 4 percent, the price is $10,000; that is, the price is lower. And if the interest rate is 5 percent, the price of $9,567 is even lower. This example illustrates two results. First, *there is an inverse relation between the market interest rate and the price of bonds.* Second, if the interest rate is above the coupon rate (4 percent), the bond *sells at a discount,* which means the price of the bond is less than its face value. On the other hand, if the interest rate is below the coupon rate, the bond *sells at a premium,* which means its price is greater than its face value.

What is the reason behind the inverse relation? At the mechanical, mathematical level, the explanation is that the interest rate, *r*, is in the denominator of each item in the stream of funds in Equation 3–9. Hence, the higher *r*, the more drastically each item is discounted, resulting in a smaller present value of all these terms. Because price equals present value, a lower present value implies a lower price of the bond. What, however, is the economic reasoning behind the negative relation? Why does a rise in the market rate of interest reduce the price of bonds? The answer is simple. New bonds and old bonds are close to perfect substitutes. If the rates available on new instruments rise, demand for old instruments will fall. As a result, their price will fall until the yield to maturity matches the rate available on new instruments.

Holding-Period Yield   We have seen that the interest rate is the rate of return, or yield, to maturity, at which time the final payment is the face value of the debt security. Of course, an investor may sell a security before maturity. The actual return to that investor, called the **holding-period yield**, will be equal to the yield to maturity only if the sale price of the security equals its face value.

To calculate the holding-period yield on a security, we must solve Equation 3–7 for *r*, where *n* is the number of years the investor actually holds the security, *F* is the sale price at the end of *n* years, and P_a is the price the investor paid to buy the security. (Equation 3–3 gives an approximation of the holding-period yield.) When we purchase a security, we can always calculate the yield to maturity because we know the face value. However, we can merely forecast the sale price before maturity and the associated holding-period yield. Only when we sell a security do we know the holding-period yield with certainty, and that yield may be greater or less than the yield to maturity (i.e., the interest rate). It may even be negative. If the sale price falls below the purchase price, the capital gains rate will be negative and may outweigh a positive annual yield.

To solidify your understanding of the different measures of the interest rate on debt securities and their relation to each other and to the actual rate of return (holding-period yield), work through the "Try It Out" exercise. Then read MarketWatch 3.2, which explains how to track rates and prices on Treasury bonds and notes in *The Wall Street Journal* every day.

TRY IT OUT 3.1

1. *a.* Suppose that you buy today a newly issued ten-year corporate bond with a purchase price of $9,800, annual coupon payments of $1,000, and a face value of $10,000. Calculate the coupon rate, the current yield, and the initial yield to maturity. (Use Equation 3–3 to find the approximation of the yield to maturity.)

   b. Suppose that you sell the bond after five years for only $4,000 because the credit rating of the issuing corporation has fallen drastically. Calculate your actual rate of return, that is, your holding-period yield. (Use Equation 3–3 for the approximation of the holding-period yield.)

   c. Suppose that the individual who buys the bond from you plans to hold it to maturity in the expectation that the issuing firm will make all promised payments. What interest rate (yield to maturity) does this individual expect to earn?

2. Suppose that the U.S. Treasury issues today a ten-year bond with annual coupon payments of $100, a face value of $1,000, and a current purchase price of $1,000. Consider also an existing 20-year Treasury bond with ten years left to maturity, annual coupon payments of $90, and a face value of $1,000. Suppose that the original purchase price of this bond when it was newly issued ten years ago was $1,000. For an investor to be willing to buy this existing Treasury bond in the secondary market today, what must its market price be? Why?

Market*Watch* 3.2
Tracking Rates on Treasury Notes and Bonds

A table titled "Treasury Bonds, Notes, and Bills" appears every day in section C of *The Wall Street Journal.*

Let's see how we can track rates and prices on Treasury bonds and notes by looking at an excerpt from the table that appeared in the April 22, 1993, issue.

We begin with the security listed in the first row. The rate of 8 ⅞ in the first column is the coupon rate on this security, which never changes. From the second col-

TREASURY BONDS, NOTES & BILLS

GOVT. BONDS & NOTES

Rate	Maturity Mo/Yr	Bid	Asked	Chg.	Ask Yld.
8⅞	Nov 98n	117:14	117:16	+ 4	5.21
6⅜	Jan 99n	105:12	105:14	+ 4	5.26
8⅞	Feb 99n	117:22	117:24	+ 3	5.29
7	Apr 99n	108:15	108:17	+ 3	5.32
8½	May 94-99	105:07	105:15	− 1	3.22
9⅛	May 99n	119:11	119:13	+ 4	5.34
6⅜	Jul 99n	105:07	105:09	+ 4	5.37

umn, we learn that this security is a Treasury note that matures in November 98. We know the security is a note because the letter *n* follows the maturity date. If the security were a bond, there would be no letter designation after the date.

The "bid" and "asked" columns give information about the price at which investors could sell and buy this note, respectively, on the previous day, April 21. Prices are expressed per $100 of face value. Moreover, the numbers after the colons in the prices represent 32nds. It follows that a *bid price* of 117:14 in the third column means investors could sell the note to a dealer for $117 ¹⁴/₃₂ for every $100 of face value. An *asked price* of 117:16 in the fourth column means they could buy the note from a dealer for $117 ¹⁶/₃₂ for every $100 of face value. The difference between the bid and asked price, called the *spread*, is the profit to the dealer. The fifth column gives the change in the asked price, measured in 32nds, from the previous day: +4 means +⁴/₃₂nds.

Finally, the last column gives the yield to maturity, calculated from the asked price. At 5.21 percent, the yield to maturity is more than 3 percentage points below the coupon rate. We confirm this relationship by noting that the asked price in column 4 is above 100, which means that the purchase price is greater than the face value of the note—the note is selling at a premium.

TRY IT OUT

Test your understanding of the information in the table by explaining the entries in the other rows. Note that there are two years to describe the bond in the fifth row: May 94–99. This means the bond is callable, with the first year being the year of the first call and the second the year of maturity. The yield in the last column is calculated to the call year.

RISK

The rate of return is the most visible characteristic of securities. Another important characteristic is **risk**, which is the predictability of the return. Because returns are uncertain, investors may suffer losses as well as enjoy gains. On average, investors are risk averse, which means they are willing to take on additional risk only if they expect to be compensated by higher returns.

Holders of securities face three major types of risk: market risk, also called interest rate risk; default risk; and risk of inflation.[5]

Market Risk, or Interest Rate Risk

When an investor purchases a security, he or she is uncertain of the sale price of the security at all future dates except the maturity date. Uncertainty breeds risk. **Market risk** refers to the likelihood that the market price of a security will fall (rise) between the time the security is purchased and sold, resulting in capital losses (capital gains) for the holder of the security. The greater the potential change in the price of an asset, the riskier the asset is. In other words, the greater the potential for capital gains or losses on an asset, the greater the market risk.

We have already established that security prices fall when interest rates rise, and security prices rise when interest rates fall. Therefore, market risk is also called **interest rate risk**. It is the risk that the interest rate may rise, thereby lowering the price of a security and, hence, inflicting capital losses on the holder.

Market risk, or interest rate risk, depends on the strength of the inverse relationship between security prices and interest rates. The strength of the relationship between interest rates and security prices depends on the maturity of a security: **The decrease (increase) in the price of a debt security because of a given rise (fall) in the interest rate is greater the longer the maturity of the security.**

To illustrate this principle, compare two U.S. Treasury securities, one with ten years to maturity, the other with five years to maturity. In all other respects the two securities are identical: Each has annual coupons of $400 and a face value of $10,000. Furthermore, we assume that both securities were originally issued five years earlier at a purchase price of $10,000. Thus, the interest rate on both of these securities five years ago was 4 percent.

Table 3–3 gives the price today of these two securities for alternative interest rates. If the interest rate today on both securities is still 4 percent, the market price of both securities will be $10,000. Suppose, instead, that interest rates have risen from 4 percent to 5 percent. The security with ten years to maturity will sell for $9,228 today, while the security with five years to maturity will sell for $9,567. A rise in the interest rate by 1 percentage point causes a fall of $772 ($9,228 − $10,000) in the market price of the ten-year security, but a fall of only $433 ($9,567 − $10,000) in the market price of the five-year security. We observe this pattern at all levels of interest rates. **The capital losses (gains) associated with a given rise (fall) in interest rates are greater the longer the maturity of an asset. Therefore, interest rate risk is greater the longer the maturity of any asset.**

---

[5] Foreign securities are also subject to exchange rate risk. If the price of the foreign currency falls with respect to the dollar, the dollar-denominated return on foreign securities also falls.

TABLE 3–3
Ten-Year Bond versus Five-Year
Note: *Each with $400 Coupon and $10,000 Face Value*

r %	Price of Ten-Year Asset*	Price of Five-Year Asset*
3.0	$10,853	$10,458
3.5	10,416	10,226
4.0	**10,000**	**10,000**
4.5	9,604	9,781
5.0	**9,228**	**9,567**
5.5	8,870	9,360
6.0	8,528	9,158
6.5	8,203	8,962
7.0	7,893	8,770
7.5	7,598	8,585
8.0	7,716	8,404
8.5	7,048	8,227
9.0	6,792	8,056
9.5	6,547	7,889
10.0	6,314	7,726
10.5	6,091	7,568
11.0	5,878	7,414
12.0	5,480	7,117
13.0	5,117	6,836
14.0	4,785	6,568
15.0	4,480	6,314

Note: Items referred to in the text are in boldface.
*Calculated from Equation 3–7.

Interest rate risk by itself implies that long-term rates will be higher than short-term rates, because investors will demand a premium to compensate them for greater interest rate risk on long-term securities. However, interest rate risk is not the only factor affecting the relation, called the **term structure of interest rates**, between short-term rates and long-term rates on comparable debt securities. In Chapter 23, we will see that most economists believe that two factors affect the term structure of interest rates: expectations of future interest rates and interest rate risk. Once we bring expectations into our story, long-term rates can be lower than short-term rates. This will occur if expectations of falling interest rates in the future overwhelm the risk premium. For now, we merely note that usually long-term rates are higher than short-term rates.

Default Risk

A second type of risk is **default risk**, which applies only to debt securities, and, thus, is also called *credit risk*. It is the risk that the issuer of a debt security may not pay all of the specified interest payments or may not repay fully the face value at maturity.

Debt securities issued by the U.S. government, such as Treasury notes and bonds, are default free. The U.S. government can always raise funds to repay its debt because it has the power to levy taxes and to "print money" (in conjunction with the Federal Reserve).

TABLE 3–4
Bond Ratings

Moody's	Standard & Poor's	Explanation
Investment grade		
Aaa	AAA	Highest quality; lowest default risk
Aa	AA	High quality
A	A	High-medium quality
Baa	BBB	Medium quality
Below investment grade		
Ba	BB	Low-medium quality
B	B	Speculative quality
Caa	CCC	Poor quality
Ca	CC	High speculative quality
C	C	Lowest quality; highest default risk
—	DDD	In default
—	DD	
—	D	

Therefore, U.S. government debt is the benchmark to which other debt is compared for risk of default. Other things being equal, the difference between the interest rate on a U.S. Treasury debt security and a corporate debt security of the same maturity is called the **default risk premium**. In general, the higher the credit risk, the higher the risk premium and, therefore, the higher the interest rate. In other words, buyers of debt securities demand and receive in the marketplace a higher interest rate to compensate them for higher default risk, other things being equal.

Several private rating services rate newly issued and existing debt securities for credit risk as a guide for potential investors. Table 3–4 explains the bond ratings used by Moody's Investor Service and Standard & Poor's Corporation, the two most prominent rating services. Each rating service distinguishes about ten rating categories. In addition, they divide bonds into two broad categories: investment-grade bonds and below-investment-grade bonds. MarketWatch 3.3 looks at below-investment-grade bonds, called **junk bonds**.

Risk of Inflation

Inflation risk on a debt security is the risk to the holder that the periodic income or the ultimate redemption of the principal may be in inflation-cheapened dollars. Inflation risk is related to interest rate risk, because increases in the inflation rate are generally accompanied by increases in the interest rate. As anticipated inflation rises, borrowers expect to repay their debt in inflation-cheapened dollars and, thus, are willing to pay a higher interest rate. Lenders demand a higher interest rate to compensate them for the expected loss of purchasing power from inflation.

Chapter 10 examines the relation between expected inflation and interest rates in more detail. For now we merely note that the concept of expected inflation leads us to the important distinction between the **nominal interest rate** and the *real interest rate*. Nominal interest rates are the observed rates. The **expected real interest rate**, also called the

MarketWatch 3.3
The Rise, Fall, and Rise of Junk Bonds

Traditionally, only firms with investment-grade ratings on their bonds had access to open markets. Established firms with less than top-quality creditworthiness and newly established firms with no credit history had to resort to bank financing or to private placement of their IOUs. The late 1970s, however, witnessed the development of a market for newly issued, below-investment-grade bonds. These high-risk bonds became known as junk bonds.

Throughout the 1980s lesser-known firms issued junk bonds to finance expansion, and large well-known firms issued junk bonds to finance takeovers of other firms. The investment banking firm of Drexel Burnham Lambert, Inc., created and dominated the market for junk bonds, which grew to almost $200 billion by the end of the 1980s. At that time, however, a series of shocks hit the junk bond market. Michael R. Milken, the head of Drexel's junk bond department, was indicted on charges of racketeering, insider trading, and fraud. Some major issuers of junk bonds defaulted, and others had their credit ratings downgraded. Then Drexel itself declared bankruptcy on February 13, 1990. Investors in junk bonds rushed to sell their holdings, but buyers were scarce, and the junk bond market collapsed. At the time, many experts predicted that a slimmed down junk bond market would eventually emerge.

Interest rates fell in December 1991, and the junk bond market rose from the dead in 1992. Unlike earlier junk bonds issued predominantly to finance takeovers, these newer issues carried ratings at the high end of the below-investment-grade scale, such as Standard & Poor's BB (Moody's Ba) rating. Risk premiums on junk bonds typically range from 4 to 5 percent for the "best quality junk" (BB rating) to 12 percent or more for lower quality (CCC and below).

ex ante real rate, is an implied rate, derived from the nominal rate after subtracting expected inflation. In other words, the real interest rate, i_r, on a debt security equals the nominal interest rate, i, on that security minus the expected rate of inflation, $(\Delta P/P)^{exp}$:

$$i_r = i - (\Delta P/P)^{exp}$$

The **actual real interest rate**, also called the *ex post real rate,* is the nominal rate minus the actual rate of inflation. Figure 3–2 depicts the nominal and actual real rates of interest on short-term debt in the United States, Japan, Germany, and Britain from the mid-1980s through 1993.

LIQUIDITY

Liquidity, another important characteristic of securities, was introduced in Chapter 1. The everyday use of the term originates in the verb *liquidate*, which means to convert an asset to cash. This everyday usage, of course, does not fully capture the economic meaning of the term. You can always and almost immediately find someone to buy your shiny one-year-old Corvette for $500, but this does not mean that your automobile is a liquid asset. It is not simply converting an asset to cash that matters but converting the asset to its maximum cash value. Realizing the maximum cash value of an asset depends on such characteristics as marketability, maturity, and risk, which are themselves interrelated. Thus, liquidity is a derivative characteristic of an asset.

FIGURE 3–2
Nominal and Real
Interest Rates
across Countries

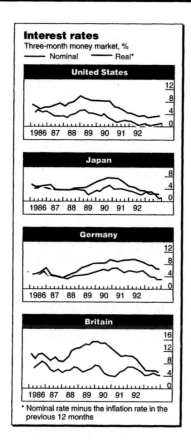

The nominal rate of interest minus the actual rate of inflation equals the actual real rate of interest. In 1993, short-term real rates were near zero in the United States and Japan, but higher in Germany and Britain.

Source: *The Economist,* 329, no. 7841 (December 11, 1993): 116.

The following three statements summarize the relationship between liquidity and marketability, maturity, and risk:

1. The more marketable an asset, the more liquid the asset is.
2. The shorter the maturity of an asset, the more liquid the asset is.
3. The riskier an asset, the less liquid the asset is.

You cannot convert an asset to cash unless a secondary market exists for it—provided the asset itself is not a cash item, that is, an item with immediate maturity. As in any other market, there are costs, called *transactions costs,* of bringing together buyers and sellers in the secondary market. Brokerage fees are one example of transactions costs. The spread between a dealer's **asked price** and **bid price** is another. A third is the cost of the investor's own time spent in arranging for the sale of the asset. The more efficient a market is, the lower the transactions costs and, thus, the higher the realized cash value for the seller, other things being equal. In other words, the more efficient the market for an asset is, the more liquid the asset is. The market for Treasury securities, where the fees for trading are minimal, is much more liquid than the market for art, where the fees to sell a painting typically range from 10 to 20 percent.

Of course, the realized cash value of an asset depends on other factors besides transactions costs, which are known in advance. The value depends primarily on the market price of the asset at the time the investor sells it, which is not generally known in advance. We have seen that market risk is greater the longer the maturity of an asset: Market prices of long-term securities fluctuate more than market prices of short-term securities when interest rates change. This greater market risk is reflected in the liquidity of an asset. In general, the shorter the maturity of an asset, the more liquid the asset is. In addition to market risk, some assets may be subject to default risk. A negative relationship also exists between default risk and liquidity. For example, when the rating services downgrade a company's bonds, the bonds become more difficult to sell. Therefore, their liquidity suffers.

DIVISIBILITY

Divisibility of a financial or real asset is another characteristic that influences the decisions of investors. It refers to the smallest unit, called the *minimum denomination,* in which the asset is available.

An instrument such as money that is available in units as small as a penny possesses perfect divisibility: One can hold money in any quantity. At the other extreme, the Empire State Building in New York is indivisible. There is only one Empire State Building. In between, there are various degrees of divisibility. For example, the minimum denomination of a 26-week Treasury bill is $10,000, while that of a negotiable certificate of deposit is $100,000.

In practice, transactions costs such as brokerage fees restrict the divisibility of assets. For example, the minimum fee for buying shares of common stock through a broker may be $50 whether you buy one share or 20 shares. If the price of each share of XYZ Corporation is $40, acquiring just one share will cost $90, making it too costly and, hence, out of reach.

Divisibility of an asset is desirable. For this reason, there is an incentive to improve the divisibility of assets, as there are incentives to improve other properties. For example, a standard method for improving the divisibility of stock whose price has risen is by splitting the shares: two new shares for one old share, say, of Boeing stock. The proliferation of mutual funds since the 1970s has increased the divisibility of a wide range of securities. Investment firms collect the funds of small savers into large pools, thereby bypassing the hurdle of large minimum denominations. Money market mutual funds, for example, invest the collected funds in short-term financial instruments such as Treasury bills; growth mutual funds invest in riskier assets with more potential for capital gains, such as long-term bonds and stocks.

MORE DETAILS ON CALCULATING INTEREST RATES: ZERO COUPON SECURITIES

In explaining how to calculate interest rates earlier in this chapter, we concentrated exclusively on debt securities with explict coupon payments, that is, on interest-bearing securities. In contrast, **zero coupon securities**, as the name suggests, have no coupon payments. They only have face value.

Zero coupon securities *sell at a discount,* which means their purchase price is less than their face value. This difference between their purchase price and their face value is the sole source of their return. The 13-week, 26-week, and 52-week Treasury bills are by design zero coupon, or discount, paper. The U.S. government does not issue zero coupon bonds or notes. Nevertheless, they do exist. Financial institutions buy coupon-bearing government bonds and notes and transform them into zero coupon securities of various maturities. Let's see how this is done.

A "Zoo of Zeros"

Financial institutions may strip bonds and notes of their coupons and sell the individual coupons and the principal payment (face value) separately. For example, a ten-year Treasury note makes 20 semiannual coupon payments and 1 principal payment. By stripping this note, a financial institution may create 21 zero coupon securities. The securities created from the principal and the last coupon each have a maturity of ten years. Maturities of the other 19 securities range from 6 months to 9 years and 6 months.

In practice, financial institutions do not sell the actual stripped coupons and stripped bonds and notes. Instead, they sell their own securities in amounts and maturities corresponding to their stripped counterparts, and keep the actual bond in a custody account to serve as collateral. Merrill Lynch and Salomon Brothers started the practice of stripping securities in 1982. As a marketing device, they gave them names with catchy acronymns. Merrill Lynch's securities are called TIGRs, short for "Treasury Income Growth Receipts," and Salomon Brothers' securities are called CATS, for "Certificates of Accrual on Treasury Securities." In the "zoo of zeros," we also find securities named DOGS and LIONS.

The U.S. Treasury initially was hostile to bond stripping. In 1985, however, the Treasury created its own program, appropriately named STRIPS (for "Separate Trading of Registered Interest and Principal of Securities"), to facilitate stripping of U.S. Treasury securities. Now most strips are sold through the Treasury's program, leaving the TIGRs and CATS far behind. These stripped securities are a favorite instrument for investors seeking to make provisions for anticipated future expenditures, such as the college education of their children.

In the remainder of this chapter, we explain how to calculate the yield to maturity, called the **coupon equivalent yield**, on zero coupon bonds, notes, and bills. We also explain a second measure of the yield on Treasury bills, called the *yield on a discount basis.* It is useful to know two methods of calculating the yield on a Treasury bill because both measures are used by financial practitioners and reported in the financial press, as we shall see.

Coupon Equivalent Yield on Zero Coupon Notes and Bonds

We can calculate the yield to maturity on a zero coupon bond or note in the same way we calculate the yield to maturity on a coupon security. With a zero coupon bond or note, however, the only future receipt is the face value of the security.

To find the coupon equivalent yield, we must adapt Equation 3–7 to fit the facts of a zero coupon security. The result is Equation 3–10, where P_a is the purchase price, F is the face value, n is the number of years to maturity, and r is the coupon equivalent yield.

$$P_a = \frac{F}{(1 + r)^n} \tag{3–10}$$

FIGURE 3–3
Cash-Flow Chart
for a Hypothetical
26-Week Treasury
Bill

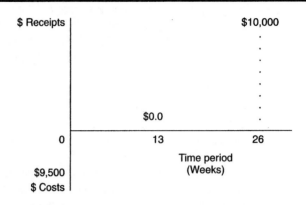

Coupon Equivalent Yield on Treasury Bills

A Treasury bill is a zero coupon security issued by the U.S. Treasury with a maturity of a year or less. For a one-year security, the coupon equivalent yield is equal to the capital gains rate, which we show by setting n equal to 1 in Equation 3–10 and solving for r:

$$P_a = \frac{F}{(1 + r)}$$

$$r = \frac{(F - P_a)}{P_a}$$

We now turn to a Treasury bill with a maturity of less than one year. Figure 3–3 depicts the cash flow chart for a hypothetical, newly issued 26-week Treasury bill with a purchase price of $9,500 and a face value of $10,000.

The total capital gains on this bill is $500, the difference between the face value of $10,000 and the purchase price of $9,500. The capital gains rate is found by dividing $500 by the purchase price, $9,500:

$$\frac{(\$10,000 - \$9,500)}{\$9,500} = 0.0526, \text{ or } 5.26 \text{ percent}$$

This rate is for only 26 weeks, that is, one-half of one year. To annualize, we multiply by two and get 10.52 percent. Actually, 26 weeks are slightly less than one-half of a year. There are only 182 days in 26 weeks. In a normal year there are 365 days. Hence, 26 weeks are 182/365, or 0.49863 of a year, the inverse of which equals 2.005495. Thus, we must multiply the capital gains rate of 0.0526 by 2.005495 to determine the annual rate of return. Incorporating this information into our calculation, we have:

$$\frac{(\$10,000 - \$9,500)}{\$9,500} \times 2.005495 = 0.1056$$

or an annual rate of 10.56 percent, four basis points greater than 10.52 percent.

In general, the coupon equivalent yield, r, on a Treasury bill is found by applying the following formula:

$$r = \frac{(F - P_a)}{P_a} \times T \tag{3–11}$$

Where

$$T = \frac{365}{\text{Number of days to maturity}}$$

Equation 3–11 applies not only to Treasury bills but also to any other zero coupon security with a maturity of a year or less.

Yield on a Discount Basis

Modification of Equation 3–11 for the coupon equivalent yield gives us a formula for calculating the **yield on a discount basis**, or the discounted rate. To calculate the yield on a discount basis, we use the following formula:

$$\text{Discounted rate} = \frac{F - P_a}{F} \times \frac{360}{\text{Number of days to maturity}} \tag{3–12}$$

Market*Watch* 3.4
Tracking Treasury Bill Rates

In MarketWatch 3.2 we learned how to track rates on Treasury bonds and notes in *The Wall Street Journal*. Now we look at another part of the same table, "Treasury Bonds, Notes, and Bills," to track the rates on bills. Again, the excerpt is from April 22, 1993.

Let's look at the Treasury bill in the first row. From the first column, we see that this bill matures on April 29, 1993, and from the second column, that there are six days left to maturity.

The third and fourth column give rates. The rate of 2.56 percent in the "bid" column is the discounted yield, calculated from the bid price on April 21, and the rate of 2.46 percent in the "asked" column is the discounted yield, calculated from the asked price on April 21. The

TREASURY BONDS, NOTES & BILLS

Wednesday, April 21, 1993

TREASURY BILLS

Maturity	Days to Mat.	Bid	Asked	Chg.	Ask Yld.
Apr 29 '93	6	2.56	2.46	−0.04	2.50
May 06 '93	13	2.77	2.67	−0.04	2.71
May 13 '93	20	2.75	2.65	....	2.69
May 20 '93	27	2.75	2.71	+0.01	2.75
May 27 '93	34	2.74	2.70	+0.01	2.74
Jun 03 '93	41	2.77	2.73	....	2.78
Jun 10 '93	48	2.77	2.73	+0.02	2.78
Jun 17 '93	55	2.78	2.73	+0.02	2.79

"Chg" column gives the change in the bid yield from the previous day.

Finally, the rate of 2.50 percent in the last column is the coupon equivalent yield, calculated from the asked price. This yield is four basis points higher than the comparable discounted yield in the fourth column. By com-parable, we mean that both yields are calculated using the asked price.

TRY IT OUT

Explain the entries in the other rows of the table.

The coupon equivalent yield is the true rate of return. The discounted rate differs from the coupon equivalent yield in two respects, both of which make the discounted rate understate the true rate. First, it assumes that a year consists of 12 30-day months, or 360 days. This rough method, introduced many years ago, was presumably used for ease in calculations when they were carried out by hand. Second, the discounted rate is expressed as a percentage of the face value rather than as a percentage of the purchase price. Perhaps the origins of this approach also can be found in simplicity; it is easier to hand-calculate when dividing by a number ending with several zeros. Bowing to tradition, financial practitioners and the financial press still quote rates on Treasury bills and similar discount paper on a discount basis, as illustrated in MarketWatch 3.4.

SUMMARY

- This chapter builds a framework for understanding financial instruments by examining their characteristics: maturity, marketability, rate of return, risk, liquidity, and divisibility.
- The term to maturity on a debt security is the length of time until the funds must be repaid. The term to maturity ranges from immediate on checkable deposits to infinite on equity securities.
- Marketability refers to whether an existing security can be sold before maturity. Many securities are marketable, but not all. Nonmarketable securities can be redeemed only by the issuer at maturity. Marketable securities are traded in the secondary market.
- A security's rate of return is the rate that makes the present value of all future receipts accruing to the owner of the security equal to the security's purchase price. The rate of return is approximated by the sum of the current yield and the average annual capital gains rate.
- The interest rate on a debt security is the rate of return to maturity, or yield to maturity, at which time the redemption price is the face value of the security.
- There is a negative relation between the interest rate and the price of a debt security. The strength of this relation is greater the longer the maturity. In particular, the longer the maturity, the greater the fall in the market price in response to a given increase in the interest rate.
- Risk arises from the uncertainty of returns. Holders of securities face three kinds of risk: interest rate risk, or market risk; default risk; and inflation risk.
- Interest rate risk is the risk that the interest rate may rise and, thus, reduce the price of the security, thereby inflicting capital losses on the holder of the security. Interest rate risk is greater the longer the maturity of the security.
- Default risk is the risk that the issuer may not make all the periodic payments or may not repay the full face value of the security.
- Inflation risk is the risk that the inflation rate may rise and, hence, repayment may be in cheaper dollars than originally anticipated.
- Liquidity is the ease and convenience with which a security can be converted to cash. Liquidity is greater the more marketable a security, liquidity is greater the shorter the maturity of a security, and liquidity is greater the less risky a security.
- Divisibility refers to the minimum denomination (smallest unit) in which a security is available.

KEY TERMS AND CONCEPTS

maturity

call provision

short-term securities/intermediate-
  term securities/long-term securities

marketability

primary market

secondary market

money market securities

capital market securities

spot market

futures market

current yield

total capital gains

face value

average annual capital gains rate

approximation of the annual rate of return

present value

discounting

rate of return

basis point

coupon

coupon rate

yield to maturity

interest rate

holding-period yield

risk

market risk

interest rate risk

term structure of interest rates

default risk

default risk premium

junk bonds

inflation risk

nominal interest rate

expected real interest rate

actual real interest rate

liquidity

asked price

bid price

divisibility

zero coupon securities

coupon equivalent yield

yield on a discount basis

QUESTIONS AND PROBLEMS

1. Why is a marketable security more desirable than a nonmarketable security of the same maturity, other things being equal?

The Wall Street Journal

2. The following title appeared on the "Credit Markets" column in the June 29, 1993, issue of *The Wall Street Journal:* "Treasury Prices Continue Rising as Yield on Long Bond Falls to Lowest Point in 16 Years." Use the concept of present value to explain this title.

3. Suppose you are told that the coupon rate, current yield, and yield to maturity on a Treasury note are all 6 percent. What does this information tell you about the purchase price of the security compared with its face value? Explain.

4. You are considering buying a bond with a face value of $1,000, three years left to maturity, and three annual coupon payments of $100.
   a. If the interest rate is 8 percent, how much will you be willing to pay for this bond?
   b. Suppose that you buy the bond at the price determined in your answer to question *a* and then the interest rate falls to 7 percent. Will you gain or lose? How much?

The Wall Street Journal

5. Calculate the annual rate of return on gold by using the data in the "Markets Diary" column on page C1 of a recent issue of *The Wall Street Journal.*

6. "U.S. Treasury securities are risk free." True or false? Explain.

The Wall Street Journal

7. The following statement appeared in the "Credit Markets" column of the July 1, 1993, issue of *The Wall Street Journal:* "U.S. corporations sold more than $1 billion of new notes and bonds yesterday, including a pair of . . . issues from USAir Group and Turner Broadcasting System Inc., that met very strong investor demand. . . . The issue from USAir Group, parent of the airline USAir, was greeted with enough demand to merit an increase in its size to $300 million from a planned $150 million. The ten-year notes were priced to yield 10%, more than four percentage points above the Treasury's ten-year note." What kind of notes were these? Explain.

8. "The creation of a secondary market for a security will increase the liquidity of that security." Comment.

9. If you expect that interest rates will soon fall, will you buy or sell bonds now?

10. If you expect that interest rates will soon fall, will you prefer to buy bonds with shorter or longer maturities at the present time?

11. If you expect that in the near future the rate of inflation will fall, what do you expect to happen to the value of your bond holdings? Would you want to hold fewer or more bonds?

12. Consider a one-year Treasury bill that has a face value of $1,000 and that currently sells for $950. What is its coupon equivalent yield?

13. Suppose that you want to make sure that in ten years you will have $25,000 to pay for your education. You are advised to buy now a zero coupon U.S. Treasury

security with a ten-year maturity and a face value of $25,000. If the ten-year interest rate is 8 percent, how much will this zero coupon bond cost you?

The Wall Street Journal

14. To answer this question, refer to the table "Treasury Bonds, Notes, and Bills" in section C of a recent issue of *The Wall Street Journal*.

a. Compare the "asked yield" on U.S. Treasury notes maturing in any month of 1998 with the "asked yield" on U.S. Treasury strips maturing in the same month of 1998.

b. What is the difference between these two securities? How does this difference affect the way their yields are calculated?

SUGGESTED READINGS

Becketti, Sean. "The Truth about Junk Bonds." *Economic Review* (Federal Reserve Bank of Kansas City), July–August 1990, 45–54.
> Examines whether junk bonds have special characteristics that disrupt financial markets.

Jones, Frank J. *Macrofinance: The Financial System and the Economy*. Cambridge, Mass.: Winthrop Publishers, 1978.
> Although this small book is out of print, it is worth looking up in the library because of its concise and lucid explanation of financial instruments and markets.

Lehmann, Michael B. *The Business One Irwin Guide to Using The Wall Street Journal*, 4th ed. Homewood, IL: Business One Irwin, 1993.
> A handbook that will help you understand and use the wealth of financial data in *The Wall Street Journal*.

Weiner, Stuart E. "Why Are So Few Financial Assets Indexed to Inflation?" *Economic Review* (Federal Reserve Bank of Kansas City), May 1983, 3–18.
> Examines the near absence of inflation-indexed financial instruments in the United States.

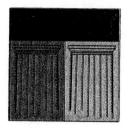

THE BASIC FINANCIAL INSTRUMENTS

CHAPTER PREVIEW

Chapter 2 introduced the participants in the financial system and explained why they issue and acquire financial instruments. Chapter 3 introduced a framework for understanding financial instruments based on their characteristics. This chapter applies that framework to describe the basic instruments in the U.S. financial system. In particular, it explains who issues each instrument, who holds it, what the source of its rate of return is, and what its market risk, credit risk, marketability, liquidity, and divisibility are.

After describing the basic instruments, we place them into the balance sheets of the six participants. The six balance sheets are profiles of the financial condition of the participants. The balance sheets are a launching pad for explaining the purposeful behavior of the participants throughout the remainder of the book.

CLASSIFYING DOMESTIC FINANCIAL INSTRUMENTS

To keep our discussion of the U.S. financial system as simple as possible, we distinguish six broad categories of domestic financial instruments:

- · U.S. Treasury securities and other securities issued by the federal, state, and local governments and by federal agencies and federally sponsored agencies
- · Open market debt issued by firms
- · Corporate stock issued by firms
- · Bank loans issued by firms and households
- · Deposits issued by banks (depository institutions)
- · Currency and reserves issued by the Fed.

In the sections that follow, we examine the securities in each category and explain their characteristics. Although we concentrate on the U.S. financial system, the same types of financial instruments exist in all major industrial countries.

GOVERNMENT DEBT

Our discussion of government debt begins with U.S. Treasury securities, which are familiar from Chapters 2 and 3. Then we consider types of IOUs issued by other federal agencies and state and local governments.

U.S. Treasury Securities

Treasury securities are an obligation of the issuing participant, the U.S. government. All the other participants—the household sector, the banking sector, the Federal Reserve, and foreign participants—hold them. The Treasury issues securities throughout the year to finance recurring deficits of the U.S. government. Table 4–1 shows that the great bulk of Treasury securities are marketable, meaning there is a secondary market for them. Out-

TABLE 4–1
Outstanding
Government Debt:
*Billions of Dollars,
Year-End 1993*

Interest-bearing debt of U.S. Treasury	4,532.3
Marketable debt	2,989.5
T-bills	714.6
T-notes	1,764.0
T-bonds	495.9
Nonmarketable debt	1,542.9
Savings bonds	169.4
Other	1,373.5
Debt of federal and federally sponsored credit agencies	570.7
Federal agencies	45.2
Federally sponsored agencies	525.5
Debt of state and local governments	1,056.9
Tax-exempt	1,047.6
Other	9.3

Source: *Federal Reserve Bulletin* and Federal Reserve Flow of Funds Accounts.

standing issues of T-bills, T-notes, and T-bonds are sold in the most active secondary market in the world, through market specialists, brokers, and dealers.

The Treasury sells new issues of T-bills, T-notes, and T-bonds at preannounced auctions in which the Fed acts as the broker between the Treasury and prospective purchasers, mostly large institutional investors. Participants in the auction submit bids to one of the 12 district Federal Reserve banks, stating the amount they want to buy and the yield they are willing to accept (or the price they are willing to pay). At the end of the day, the Fed determines the successful bidders and the average interest rate established at the auction. "Small-potatoes" investors submit noncompetitive bids, which guarantees them securities at this average rate.

The length of time to maturity on marketable Treasury securities ranges from a few months to 30 years.[1] **Treasury bills, *or* T-bills**, have a maturity of a year or less. T-bills do not pay explicit interest but instead are sold at a discount, with the minimum denomination being a face value of $10,000. Intermediate-term Treasury securities, with a maturity of one to ten years, are called **Treasury notes, *or* T-notes**. Finally, long-term Treasury securities, with a maturity of more than ten years, are called **Treasury bonds, *or* T-bonds**. T-notes and T-bonds both pay interest semiannually and are sold at or near face value. Minimum denominations are $5,000 on two-year and three-year notes and $1,000 on five-year to ten-year notes and on bonds. The rates of return on these securities are called, respectively, the T-bill rate, the T-note rate, and the T-bond rate; Chapter 3 explained the various techniques used to compute these rates. Finally, T-bills, T-notes, and T-bonds are all free of default risk but not interest rate risk. T-bonds have greater interest rate risk than T-bills because for a given change in the yield to maturity, the longer the time to maturity of the bond, the larger the price change.

Figure 4–1 shows the average term to maturity of marketable interest-bearing Treasury securities held by private investors. The length of time to maturity has crept upward, from 2.58 years (two years and seven months) in 1976 to just under six years in 1992. In January 1992 the U.S. Treasury Department, under President George Bush, was actively considering reducing the issuance of 30-year bonds. On January 6, 1992, *The Wall Street Journal* quoted Nobel laureate James Tobin as saying "it is foolish for the government to issue long-term bonds at rates that are as much as 3½ percentage points higher than short-term rates."

In May 1993 the Treasury under the Clinton administration announced plans to reduce the maturity of its marketable debt by cutting the annual issuance of 30-year bonds by about 40 percent and by eliminating seven-year Treasury notes. One of the goals was to reduce interest payments on government debt by shifting from long-term to short-term debt. At the time of the announcement, interest rates on 30-year Treasury bonds were just under 7 percent, and interest rates on three-month Treasury bills were just under 3 percent. Whether the Treasury will actually save on interest payments is a hotly debated issue among academics, government economists, and Wall Street bond dealers. Chapter 23 discusses this debate.

---

[1] The Treasury has not issued 40-year bonds since 1955.

FIGURE 4–1   Average Maturity of Marketable U.S. Treasury Securities

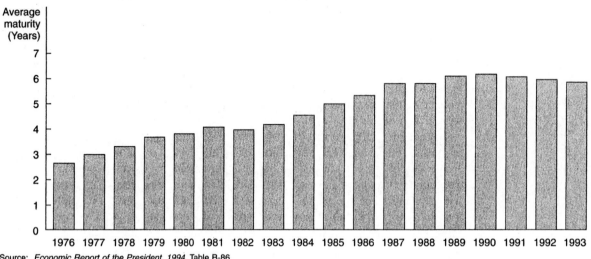

Source: *Economic Report of the President, 1994,* Table B-86.

Table 4–1 shows that in addition to marketable debt, the Treasury also issues interest-bearing nonmarketable debt, such as *U.S. savings bonds and notes.* These notes and bonds do not pay explicit interest; instead, they are sold to the public at a discount. Savings bonds are attractive to small savers because they are available in denominations as low as $50. Savings bonds account for about 10 percent of the outstanding non-marketable debt of the U.S. Treasury. Most of the other nonmarketable debt in Table 4–1 is held by U.S. government agencies such as the Social Security Administration and other such trust funds and by state, local, and foreign governments.

Federal Agency Securities

The U.S. Treasury is the fiscal agent of the U.S. government, which means it collects tax revenues and makes expenditures. Its securities are issued to finance the federal budget deficit. Other federal agencies and federally sponsored agencies, however, perform specific federal functions, financial or otherwise. Federal agencies are bona fide government bodies. Federally sponsored agencies, on the other hand, are privately owned bodies that were originally promoted by or were part of the federal government. These federal agencies and federally sponsored agencies finance their activities by issuing notes and bonds of varying maturities, collectively called **federal agency securities**.

Most of these agencies are financial intermediaries created by Congress to aid the flow of credit to targeted sectors of the economy, for example, housing, agriculture, foreign trade, and education. They issue their own indirect securities and with the funds thus collected acquire securities from other participants, especially financial intermediaries. An example of a federal agency is the Government National Mortgage Association, often referred to by its nickname, Ginnie Mae. Ginnie Mae channels funds to the mortgage market by issuing its own liabilities and using the funds to acquire mortgages held by

Sector*Watch* 4.1
Will Sallie Mae Survive?

Sallie Mae, the nickname for Student Loan Marketing Association, was created by Congress in 1972 to facilitate the provision of student loans by banks, thereby supporting higher education. Sallie Mae is a private corporation owned by private-sector shareholders. Under current arrangements, private banks that participate in the Federal Guaranteed Student Loan Program and other smaller student assistance programs make loans to students. While students are in college, the federal government makes the interest payments on the students' behalf. When students graduate and begin repaying their loans, Sallie Mae buys the loans from banks and begins collecting repayments. Sallie Mae keeps part of the loans in its portfolio as assets; the remainder it repackages and sells to private investors to hold in their portfolios.

Sallie Mae finances its purchases of student loans by issuing bonds and notes in the open market. Unlike U.S. Treasury securities, Sallie Mae Securities are not free of credit risk. However, they are nearly risk free because it is presumed the federal government will not permit the default of an intermediary it sponsors. For these reasons, the interest rate on Sallie Mae's debt is only slightly greater than that on U.S. Treasury securities of the same maturity.

By creating Sallie Mae, Congress sponsored the creation of two secondary markets for student loans. In the first Sallie Mae is the demander for student loans, and banks are the suppliers. In the other Sallie Mae is the supplier of repackaged student loans, and the investing public are the demanders. These secondary markets have increased liquidity in the financial system.

The significance of the student loan program is underscored by its numbers: about 5 million student loans annually, which translates to almost 40 percent of college students in the United States. Perhaps because of the magnitude of the student loan program, in 1994 the Clinton administration began phasing in a program to reduce and possibly eliminate the intermediation of banks and Sallie Mae. Under the Clinton program, the government itself, through the Department of Education, makes loans to students and collects payments from graduates, thereby saving students and the general public the "cut" taken by banks and Sallie Mae. By 1998 the government will directly finance about 60 percent of all student loans. The administration estimates that the savings will be $4.3 billion between 1994 and 1998.

Critics of the Clinton program doubt that the government will be more efficient than the market system and capable of saving the estimated amount. Supporters of the program point to the default rate of about 12 percent that Sallie Mae absorbs. They argue that the administration's program has features that provide for better performance in the repayment of student loans. These features include a repayment schedule tailored to fit the borrower's income.

The future of Sallie Mae after 1998 is uncertain. Sallie Mae's management believes that it can survive as a totally private institution without any links to the government. Even if Sallie Mae does survive, it may have only a minor role to play in financing student loans.

---

depository institutions. The Federal National Mortgage Association (Fannie Mae) and the Federal Home Loan Mortgage Corporation (Freddie Mac) are also federally sponsored agencies of this type. SectorWatch 4.1 discusses the uncertain future of Sallie Mae, another federally sponsored agency.

Table 4–1 shows that at the end of 1993 the outstanding debt of the federally sponsored agencies was more than 10 times that of the federal agencies. Significantly, the Fed conducts open market operations in federal agency securities and, hence, is a holder of these securities. In addition, these federal agency securities are also held by the public and financial intermediaries. Agency notes and bonds pay explicit interest, and new issues are sold in the market at face value through dealers. A relatively active secondary market exists for agency securities. As with all securities, market risk on agency securities varies inversely with the term to maturity. Credit risk, on the other hand, is very low. Although the bulk of agency securities are not direct obligations of the federal government, they do have the implicit backing of the government. It is unlikely that the federal government would let a federally sponsored agency default on its IOUs.

Municipal Securities

State and local governmental bodies that need intermediate-term and long-term funding issue notes and bonds, called **municipal securities,** *or* **munis** for short. New and existing issues are sold through dealers and brokers. Like federal agency securities, municipal securities are not free of default risk, although typically that risk is low. Munis, however, have some special characteristics that distinguish them from federal agency securities. First, the interest payments on most municipal securities are exempt from federal income taxes. Second, because the Fed does not conduct open market operations in municipal securities, it does not purchase them. Munis are especially attractive to high-income households, who hold them to reduce their taxes.

Why Hold U.S. Government Debt?

To answer this question, it is helpful to classify the participants according to their motives for holding these securities. Households, firms, and banks in the United States and in the rest of the world hold U.S. Treasury and agency securities for the same reason they hold other securities: to earn a rate of return, with due consideration given to other characteristics such as risk, marketability, divisibility, and liquidity.

However, the Federal Reserve, the other holder of U.S. Treasury and agency securities, is not attempting to profit by investing in these securities. In its role as the overseer of the health of the U.S. economy, the Fed acquires these securities and pays for them by creating Federal Reserve debt, which we examine later in this chapter. The Fed acquires or sells these securities via open market operations; that is, it buys or sells existing U.S. Treasury securities from or to security dealers in the secondary market. Foreign official authorities, primarily central banks, hold U.S. assets for the same reason the Fed holds foreign assets: for intervention in the foreign exchange markets. GlobalWatch 4.2 looks at the foreign presence in U.S. financial markets.

OPEN MARKET DEBT AND EQUITY OF FIRMS

Next we turn to business firms, which are also deficit units. Chapter 2 noted that nonfinancial businesses issue securities to finance long-term and short-term funding gaps. **Open market debt of firms** consists of all the IOUs firms issue and sell in the open market through market specialists or through direct placement. It includes long-term debt such as corporate bonds and short-term debt such as commercial paper and bankers' acceptances. However, funds borrowed from banks are included in a separate category because they are indirectly financed IOUs, that is, financed through financial intermediaries.

Corporate Bonds

Corporate bonds are interest-bearing, long-term debt issued by well-known corporations. Maturities typically range from 10 to 40 years. In 1993, however, the Boeing Company, Conrail, and Texaco issued 50-year bonds. Fifty-year bonds were common

GlobalWatch 4.2
The Foreign Presence in the U.S. Financial System

How big is the foreign presence in U.S. financial markets? To answer this question, we look at foreign holdings of U.S. government debt, corporate bonds, and corporate stocks.

First we examine the percentage of marketable U.S. Treasury securities held by foreigners from 1978 to 1991. This ratio fell from 27 percent in 1978 to 19 percent in 1991. These numbers, however, do not reveal the entire story. There are two components of foreign-held U.S. Treasury securities: (1) official holdings, which are the amounts held by foreign central banks and governments, mostly for intervention in foreign exchange

markets; and (2) private holdings for investment purposes. If we concentrate only on the percentage of privately held marketable U.S. Treasury securities, we find that it rose drastically, from 1.84 percent in 1978 to 6.47 percent in 1991—an increase of 352 percent.

To a varying degree, a similar pattern of foreign participation in the markets for private U.S. debt and equity emerges. The percentage of U.S. corporate bonds held by the foreign public rose from 5.49 percent in 1978 to 14.31 percent in 1991, an increase of 261 percent. The percentage of corporate stock held by foreigners increased the least, although still substantially, from 4.28 percent to 6.81 percent. Of course, the greater participation of foreigners in U.S. financial markets is a manifestation of the change in the U.S. status from a net creditor nation to a net debtor nation.

more than a century ago, but they have been rare in recent times. They reappeared in 1993 because long-term interest rates were at their lowest level in nearly 20 years and firms were eager to enjoy favorable borrowing terms as long as possible. Walt Disney Co. and Coca-Cola extended the maturity spectrum even further by issuing 100-year bonds in mid-1993.

A fixed dollar amount of interest paid out twice a year and a relatively low par value, usually $1,000, are standard features on many bonds. Special features on some issues, such as callability or convertibility, add diversity for both buyers and sellers. A callable bond gives the seller the option of paying off the loan and retiring the bond before maturity under prespecified terms. For example, the 50-year bonds issued by Texaco are callable after 20 years, and the 100-year bonds issued by Walt Disney are callable after 30 years. A convertible bond gives the buyer the option of exchanging the bond for common stock of the issuing corporation under prespecified terms. GlobalWatch 4.3 explains why convertibles were popular in Japan in 1993.

Businesses rely on the services of market specialists to sell new and existing issues of corporate bonds. Investment banks underwrite new issues, and brokers and dealers assist in selling existing issues in an active secondary market. The rate of return to maturity on corporate bonds is called the *corporate bond rate*. As we saw in Chapter 3, rating services such as Moody's and Standard & Poor's evaluate and rate new and existing issues for credit risk and, thus, help buyers make informed decisions. Finally, ownership of long-term, private-sector debt, like long-term government debt, carries substantial interest rate risk because of the term to maturity.

The first row of Table 4–2 shows the total amount of corporate bonds outstanding at the end of 1993. Households, who hold about one-fifth of the value of existing issues, are a major player in this market. Foreign participants are also a major holder of corporate

Global*Watch* 4.3
A Surge in Convertible Bonds in Japan

What securities were hot in the Japanese primary markets in mid-1993? Convertible bonds, according to a report in *The Wall Street Journal*.* The volume of new issues of convertible bonds rose from 30 billion yen ($0.28 billion) in January 1993 to 300 billion yen ($2.8 billion) in June.

Investors in convertible bonds have the right to exchange them in the future at a preset conversion ratio. Thus, they have a foot in the door of the stock market. If the stock market rises, investors gain because they can convert the bonds to stock at a discount. Because of this feature, convertible bonds pay a lower yield to investors than "plain-vanilla" bonds. To find the reason for their popularity in Japan in 1993, we must look at the advantages convertible bonds offered to investors and to issuing corporations against the background of economic and financial conditions in Japan.

Between 1989 and 1992, the Nikkei average of stock market prices in Japan fell by more than 50 percent. Stocks rallied between January and June 1993 but started to fall again at midyear because of political uncertainty. Moreover, economic growth was weak at the time. In this climate, convertibles offered investors

greater safety than stocks and standard bonds because the issuing corporations were those with the highest credit ratings. Thus, the move of investors to convertible bonds can be viewed as a flight to quality and safety. Also, in a weak economy convertibles usually outperform stocks because, unlike stocks, they pay interest. Finally, if the stock market does start to rise again, investors in convertibles gain because of the right to convert their bonds to stocks at a preset conversion ratio. According to analysts quoted in *The Wall Street Journal* report, the willingness of investors to buy convertibles boded well for the stock market because it suggested that they expected the stock market to rise.

What were the advantages to the issuing corporations? The higher the credit rating of a corporation, the lower the interest it must pay on convertible bonds. Therefore, the switch to convertibles from other forms of raising funds such as issuing stock can be seen as a move by creditworthy corporations to capitalize on their high credit ratings. Other corporations, which may have preferred to issue equities instead, were discouraged by the low prices they could fetch in the stock market. Furthermore, the Japanese Ministry of Finance was actively discouraging corporations from further depressing the stock market by issuing additional shares of stock. The final advantage of convertibles to businesses came by default. Even creditworthy corporations could not rely on Japanese banks, weakened by a huge amount of bad debt from falling property prices and by losses on their holdings of corporate stock, to finance their needs. (Unlike American banks, Japanese banks hold corporate stock.)

* "Wary Japanese Bet on Convertible Bonds," *The Wall Street Journal*, June 28, 1993, p. C1.

---

bonds. In GlobalWatch 4.2 we saw that the percentage of U.S. corporate bonds held by foreigners has increased since the 1970s. Nonbank financial intermediaries, such as life insurance companies and pension and retirement funds, are the largest holders of corporate bonds. Banks, on the other hand, do not hold a large amount of corporate bonds. Instead, bankers use their expertise to assess firm-specific risk and to provide tailor-made loans to nonfinancial firms. Other firms may also hold some of these bonds.

Commercial Paper

Like its long-term counterpart, the corporate bond, **commercial paper** is an IOU issued by well-known, creditworthy corporations. Commercial paper is sold at a discount, either through dealers or through direct placement by the issuing firm. Its maturity ranges from one to nine months. The rate of return implied by the discount and the

TABLE 4–2
Outstanding Open Market Debt of Nonfinancial Firms: *Billions of Dollars, Year-End 1993*

Corporate bonds	1,225.7
Commercial paper	117.8
Banker's acceptances	17.1

Source: Federal Reserve Flow of Funds Accounts.

FIGURE 4–2
Commercial Paper Issued by Nonfinancial Firms

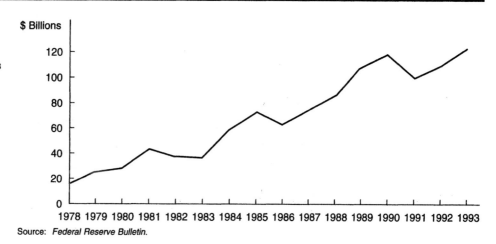

Source: *Federal Reserve Bulletin.*

length of time to maturity is called the *commercial paper rate.* The secondary market is limited, with many investors holding commercial paper until maturity. Market risk is relatively small for those who do sell existing issues in the secondary market because of the short term to maturity. The same services that rate corporate bonds for credit risk also rate commercial paper. Creditworthy nonfinancial firms typically substitute commercial paper for bank loans when financing short-term needs such as building up inventories. Figure 4–2 shows the explosion of commercial paper issued by nonfinancial firms in the 1980s.[2]

Who holds this debt instrument as an asset? Other nonfinancial businesses can and do hold some. Foreign participants also hold (U.S.-issued) commercial paper. The bulk of commercial paper, however, is held by nonbank financial intermediaries.

Bankers' Acceptances

Bankers' acceptances often arise from and facilitate international trade. A **banker's acceptance** is a guarantee to a foreign exporter of goods, usually made between the time the goods are ordered and the time they are shipped, that the importer will indeed pay for

---

[2] Business firms are not the only issuers of commercial paper. In fact, they issue only about 25 percent of all commercial paper. The remainder is issued by financial institutions.

the goods at a specified future date, such as when the goods are unloaded at the point of entry or a few months thereafter. The exporter may be reluctant to take an IOU from the importer, especially if the importing firm is small and unknown. However, the exporter may welcome an IOU from the importer's bank. Let's look at how this is done.

At the time of the agreement, the exporter "draws a time draft" on the importer's bank. This means that the exporter sends a document to the importer's bank that orders the bank to pay a given amount at a specified future date. The bank accepts the draft by signing it and returning it to the exporter. From the moment the bank accepts the draft, the acceptance becomes the bank's liability. By substituting its own credit-worthiness for that of the importer, the bank effectively becomes a surrogate borrower for the importer. (It is similar to your arranging for a wealthy relative to borrow on your behalf.) The bank charges the importer a fee for this service, usually one-half of 1 percent of the accepted funds. The length of time between the date the bank accepts the draft and the specified payment date is the maturity of the acceptance, usually 30 to 180 days.

The exporter, who is now more certain of payment by having the bank rather than the importer as its debtor, may decide to hold this draft until it matures. At maturity, the bank will pay the exporter the full face value of the acceptance and simultaneously receive payment from the importer. More often, however, the exporting firm prefers immediate payment for its goods, so it sells the acceptance at a discount in the open market through a dealer. The return on the acceptance to an investor comes from the difference between the discounted value and the face value, if held to maturity. The banker's acceptance rate is the implied rate of return to maturity.

Who Holds Bankers' Acceptances?   About one-third of the total volume is held by commercial banks, especially the ones that accepted the drafts in the first place. Pension funds, insurance companies, and other financial firms, such as money market mutual funds, are also major investors; so are foreigners, especially foreign central banks. For these participants, the attractions of bankers' acceptances lies not only in their rate of return but also in their high degree of liquidity and relatively small credit risk. The credit risk on bankers' acceptances is small because they are liabilities of commercial banks rather than of the originating firms. Their high degree of liquidity stems from a very active secondary market and a short term to maturity. Because investors consider bankers' acceptances superior to commercial paper in terms of credit risk and liquidity, they are willing to hold them at rates slightly lower than those of commercial paper. Finally, the Federal Reserve used to be an active participant in this market, buying and selling bankers' acceptances in its open market operations. From 1977 to 1984, however, the Fed used this market sparingly, and in 1984 it ceased even this minimal involvement.

Corporate Stock

In addition to debt securities, corporations issue equity securities to finance their long-term needs. Equity securities, or shares of **corporate stock**, are certificates (titles) of ownership in the corporations that issue them. For example, a holder of 100 shares in a corporation that has issued 100,000 shares owns 1/1,000 of that corporation. Unlike debt securities, equity securities have no face value and no maturity. Unless a firm buys back outstanding issues of corporate stock, the stock remains in the market forever.

Holders of corporate stock may receive periodic payments in the form of dividends. Unlike coupon payments on bonds, dividend payments are neither fixed in dollar value nor guaranteed. In general, there are two types of equities: common stock and preferred stock. The owner of the latter has some special privileges, the most important of which is being ahead of common stockholders if the corporation's assets are liquidated: that is, the preferred stockholder is first in line among stockholders but always behind creditors.

Most new issues of stock are offered to the public through underwriters, although some are placed directly. The secondary market (for existing issues), however, dwarfs the primary market. Existing issues of stock are bought and sold in organized exchanges and in over-the-telephone (over-the-counter) markets. Stocks of well-established and well-regarded corporations are listed and exchanged on the New York Stock Exchange (NYSE), the most prestigious of the exchanges, followed closely by the American Stock Exchange (AMEX). Other stocks are listed in 11 regional exchanges. Nearly all the rest are traded over the counter by dealers who are members of the National Association of Security Dealers (NASD). Both the organized and the unlisted exchanges provide up-to-the-minute information about volume of trade and prices of the securities under their jurisdiction.

As we saw in Chapter 2, the total rate of return on equity consists of two components: a dividend yield component and a capital gains component. An investor does not know either component with certainty at the time of purchase and therefore must predict them. Of course, the actual dividend may deviate from the expected dividend, and the actual price from the expected price. The substantial market risk of holding corporate stock stems from these deviations.

New issues and existing stock are held as assets by the public, primarily households, and by nonbank financial intermediaries, such as mutual funds specializing in capital market instruments, pension funds, and the like. Banks, on the other hand, have been prohibited by law since the 1930s from stock ownership.

Buyouts in the 1980s   The market value of stock outstanding at the end of 1989 was $4,368.2 billion. Very little of this stock was issued in the 1980s, however. Even more remarkable is that from 1984 to 1989 the net issuance of corporate stock was negative because firms bought back more stock than they issued, as shown in Figure 4–3. This decrease resulted from the wave of corporate buyouts in the 1980s as well as from defensive measures corporations took to prevent them.

A **buyout** is the purchase of controlling interest in a company either by another company or by a group of investors. Usually the new owners finance the purchase of company stock by issuing debt. Defensive measures to prevent takeovers also involve borrowing—in this case, a company borrowing to buy its own stock. The end result is a reduction in corporate stock outstanding in the market and an increase in debt outstanding—both open market debt and bank loans. For example, from 1984 to 1989 the cumulative net issuance of corporate stock fell by $640 billion, while total debt of corporations rose by $1,050 billion. Of this $1,050 billion in new debt, $650 billion consisted of open

FIGURE 4–3   **Net Equity Issuance by U.S. Nonfinancial Corporations**

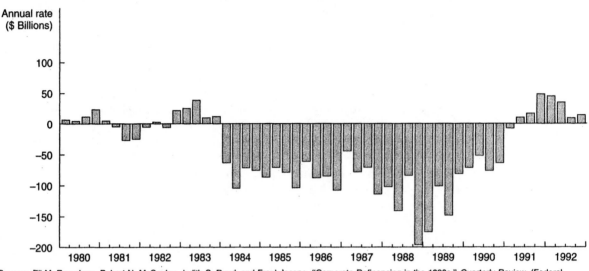

Source: Eli M. Remolona, Robert N. McCauley, Judith S. Ruud, and Frank Iacono, "Corporate Refinancing in the 1990s," *Quarterly Review* (Federal Reserve Bank of New York) 17, no. 4 (Winter 1992–93): 6.

market debt, including high-risk (junk) bonds; $400 billion consisted of loans from banks and other intermediaries.[3]

Figure 4–3 shows that the net issuance of corporate stock turned positive in 1991. This increase in stock issuance coincided with a reduction in corporate buyouts and a reduction in debt in response to the debt hangover explained in MarketWatch 4.4.

THE DEBT OF HOUSEHOLDS AND FIRMS TO BANKS: BANK LOANS

Bank loans are an obligation of households and firms, who are the borrowers, to banks, who are the lenders. Bank loans come with a wide variety of characteristics tailored to the needs and circumstances of borrowers.

Households borrow to finance the purchase of homes; these long-term loans are called *home mortgages*. Households also borrow for shorter terms to finance the purchase of automobiles and other consumer goods; these loans are called *consumer loans*. Traditionally, firms have borrowed from banks for short and intermediate terms to finance a host of business expenses associated with building up inventories, meeting payrolls, purchasing new equipment, and carrying out other business activities; these loans are called *commercial and industrial* (C&I) *loans*.

---

[3] Considerable controversy still exists about the benefits and costs of the buyouts of the 1980s. Proponents argue that they increased efficiency; critics claim that they mainly redistributed income. Paul Krugman summarizes the debate and puts forth a compromise position in *The Age of Diminished Expectations: U.S. Economic Policy in the 1990s* (Cambridge, Mass.: The MIT Press, 1990), Chapter 13, "Corporate Finance," pp. 153–68.

MarketWatch 4.4
Debt Hangover in the 1990s

What was ailing the U.S. economy in the early 1990s? Edward J. Frydl, vice-president of the Federal Reserve Bank of New York, has diagnosed the ailment as a "debt hangover."

The data in the table show the debt binge of the 1980s that resulted in a hangover in the 1990s. The first column shows the growth rate of nominal GDP, which equals the rate of inflation plus the rate of growth of real GDP. The second column shows the growth rate of private debt, consisting of funds borrowed by households and firms in the open market and from banks. The third column records the difference.

The third column shows that between 1960 and 1979, growth of private debt exceeded growth of nominal GDP by less than 1 percentage point. The difference was also less than 1 percentage point in the 1980 to 1982 period, which included the most severe slowdown in real economic activity since the Great Depression: Real GDP fell by 2.2 percent in 1982. When the economy recovered beginning in 1983, the excess of growth in private debt over growth in nominal GDP was high by historical standards: 3.1 percentage points in the 1983 to 1985 period and 3.3 percentage points from 1986 to 1988.

What was the reason for the debt binge between 1983 and 1988? There is no consensus among economists. Among the many factors they cite are optimism about the economy; expectations of continued high in-

flation and of high prices of tangible assets, such as real estate; changing attitudes about debt; easier availability of credit because of the emergence of the junk bond market, financial deregulation, and financial innovations*; and tax advantages resulting from reforms in 1981 that provided incentives to invest in commercial real estate.

As households and firms accumulated debt in the 1980s, some economists expressed concern about the future. They argued that heightened financial stress caused by the increase in private debt relative to nominal GDP would show up when the economy turned down and that this stress could exacerbate the downturn. Their fears seem to have been realized. The eight-year expansion of real GDP in the United States came to an end in the summer of 1990 when real GDP grew by a paltry 0.8 percent in 1990 and by *minus* 1.2 percent in 1991. Firms and households began to have difficulty meeting interest payments because of the reduced earnings and incomes that naturally accompany a downturn. Defaults on corporate bonds increased, and the volume of problem loans and loan losses mounted at banks. Responding to this debt hangover, households and firms began to reduce their debt, and banks became more prudent in their lending practices. The last row of the table shows that from 1989 to 1991, the excess of private debt over nominal GDP fell to less than 1 percentage point.

_____

* Deregulation and innovations are examined in Chapter 5 on the evolution of the new financial environment.

Growth of Private Debt Compared with Growth of Nominal GDP

	Average Growth Rates (percent)		
Period	Nominal GDP (1)	Private Debt (2)	Nominal GDP Less Private Debt (3) = (1) − (2)
1960–1979	8.8	9.4	−0.6
1980–1982	7.6	8.3	−0.7
1983–1985	9.1	12.2	−3.1
1986–1988	6.8	10.1	−3.3
1989–1991	4.5	5.2	−0.7

Source: Richard Cantor and John Wenninger, "Perspective on the Credit Slowdown," *Quarterly Review* (Federal Reserve Bank of New York) 18, no. 1 (Spring 1993): 9.

FIGURE 4–4
Real Estate versus
Commercial and
Industrial Loans by
Banks

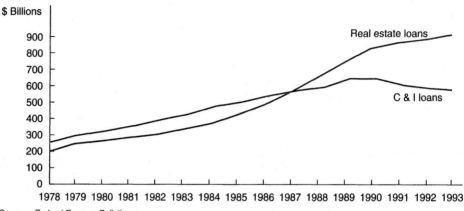

Source: *Federal Reserve Bulletin.*

In the 1980s the most creditworthy corporate customers of banks switched from issuing C&I loans to issuing commercial paper because commercial paper rates were below bank loan rates. To fill the void, banks began to make loans to real estate developers to finance shopping malls, office buildings, and apartment buildings and to "corporate raiders" to finance buyouts. Figure 4–4 shows that by 1987 the volume of real estate loans made by banks had surpassed that of C&I loans.

Banks have traditionally held all these loans until maturity, at which time the borrower repays the funds. In recent years, however, active secondary markets for bank loans, especially home mortgages, have sprung up. They usually involve arrangements under which a bank packages a group of loans and sells the package to investors, often through a third party. The process of transforming bank loans into marketable assets is called **securitization**.[4]

The cost of borrowing associated with each type of loan is different. Some of these borrowing rates are fixed for the duration of the loan. Other rates, called *floating rates,* change over the term of the loan, typically following market rates of interest up or down. The **prime rate**, an oft-quoted floating rate, is a base rate on bank loans to businesses, applying today primarily to loans to small and medium-sized businesses. Large creditworthy corporations, whose access to the commercial paper market is an indicator of lower default risk, frequently borrow at below-prime rates. Many banks also use the prime rate as a base rate, or reference rate as it is sometimes called, on consumer loans.

THE DEBT OF BANKS: BANK DEPOSITS

For years the **demand deposit** was the standard indirect security with immediate maturity issued by commercial banks and held by the public. Traditional demand deposits, which still exist, have been prohibited by law from paying interest since the 1930s. The funds in

---

[4] Securitization is discussed further in Chapter 5.

these deposit accounts can be withdrawn upon demand, either in person or by writing a check, without any restrictions. Another form of checkable deposits called **NOW accounts** and **Super-NOW accounts** were introduced nationwide in the early 1980s. These accounts not only have unlimited checking privileges but also pay interest. Furthermore, the deposit rates on NOWs and Super-NOWs are nonregulated, as rate ceilings on these accounts were fully phased out in 1986.[5] Finally, deposits with unrestricted checking privileges, whether demand deposits, NOWs, or Super-NOWs, are all subject to reserve requirements, currently 10 percent; that is, depository institutions must hold 10 percent of the value of those accounts, above a specified minimum level, in the form of reserves.

Unlike demand deposits, **time deposits**, as their name indicates, have a fixed maturity. The **negotiable CD**, or large time deposit, was introduced in 1961 and was the forerunner of a wide variety of current time deposits that earn a nonregulated interest rate. The negotiable CD rate was deregulated completely by 1973. Rate ceilings on small time deposits began to be lifted in the late 1970s and were fully eliminated in 1983. Negotiable CDs, however, differ from small time deposits because of two special features: their minimum denomination requirements and their marketability. Negotiable CDs are issued in minimum denominations of $100,000, and $1 million units are common. An active secondary market exists for these deposits, whose typical maturities range from one to six months. They are usually traded in $1 million lots and sold at par, with interest paid at maturity. These arrangements, however, do vary. Like their checkable counterparts, negotiable CDs are potentially subject to reserve requirements, but the reserve requirement ratio is lower. The law allows the Fed to set the reserve requirement on negotiable CDs between 0 and 3 percent. In December 1990 the Fed reduced the reserve requirement ratio on CDs from 3 percent to 0. For reserve purposes, these CDs fall under the category of *nonpersonal time deposits*: any time deposit or account that is transferable or held by a party other than a private individual (i.e., a household).

Households, nonfinancial firms, and foreign participants hold checkable deposits and time deposits as assets. Deposits with unlimited checking privileges have perfect liquidity—that is, their full cash value can be realized immediately. These deposits form a benchmark for liquidity to which all other deposits and assets held by the public are compared. Time deposits, of course, are less liquid. The existence of a secondary market enhances the liquidity of negotiable CDs in comparison with other time deposits, but they are still less liquid than unrestricted checkable deposits. Furthermore, negotiable CDs are not insured against default risk, because deposits in excess of $100,000 are not covered by the insuring agencies.

The main reason the public holds checkable deposits is to carry out transactions. Portfolio considerations also enter their decision to hold all types of deposits. In other words, the more attractive the deposit rate compared with the rate on other securities, the more deposits these participants want to hold. The $100,000 minimum on negotiable CDs precludes most households from holding this instrument. Thus, firms are the major holder, but financial institutions such as money market mutual funds also hold these CDs as an alternative to commercial paper and bankers' acceptances.

---

[5] The particulars as well as the importance of these interest-bearing checkable deposits are explained in detail in Chapter 5.

As we shall see in detail in Chapter 5, depository institutions issue a wide variety of indirect securities. Some resemble interest-bearing checkable deposits; some resemble negotiable CDs; and others are hybrids. For now, it is sufficient to note that the item called *deposits* is a catchall term for all deposit-type securities issued by depository institutions and held by households and nonfinancial firms. The **deposit rate** is the representative (average) rate of interest paid on these deposit securities.

THE FEDERAL RESERVE'S DEBT

The last domestic financial instrument is the **monetary base**, which is the debt of the Federal Reserve. The monetary base has two components: currency in circulation and total reserves.

Currency in Circulation

Currency in circulation is the Fed's obligation to the public (households and firms). This currency consists of the coins and paper currency in the hands of households and firms, who hold it for use in the payments system. Currency, of course, pays no interest. It is a perfectly liquid asset and bears no credit risk. Currency is not, however, immune from the risk of inflation, for an increase in the price level reduces the purchasing power of currency.

Total Reserves

Reserves, consisting of vault cash and banks' reserve accounts with the Fed, are the Fed's obligation to banks. Reserve accounts with the Fed and vault cash have immediate maturity and no credit risk. They are perfectly liquid assets for the banks that hold them. The Fed does not pay interest on reserves.

Banks use the reserves they hold as required reserves or excess reserves. **Required reserves** are nondiscretionary reserves, and banks are currently required to hold 10 percent of their checkable deposits in the form of reserves. Also, many banks hold reserves in excess of legal minimum reserve requirements. Banks hold discretionary reserves, or **excess reserves**, as a buffer against an unexpected need.

Banks that find themselves short of reserves may try to borrow from their banker, the Federal Reserve. Loans to banks by the Fed are called **discount window loans**, and the **discount rate**, the only interest rate set by the Fed, is the rate the Fed charges banks to borrow. Borrowing from the Fed is a privilege and not a right. Hence, banks may be turned down for a discount window loan and forced to go elsewhere, such as to the federal funds market.

Federal Funds

The Fed does not pay interest on required reserves or on excess reserves. Banks have periodically lobbied and petitioned the U.S. Congress for legislation to force the Fed to pay interest on required reserve balances, but so far, they have not been successful. A bank can, however, earn interest on its unwanted excess reserves by lending the funds to another bank in the interbank loan market. The market for interbank loans is called the **federal funds market** because funds deposited in a bank's reserve account are referred to as federal funds. Most loans in the federal funds market are very short term loans, usually overnight. Term loans with maturities greater than one business day do exist, but they are much less common than overnight loans. There are no secondary markets for federal funds of any maturity.

One reason banks borrow in the federal funds market is to fund a reserve deficiency. Banks whose reserve balances fall short of the required amount borrow from banks with excess reserves. Such loans are an alternative to discount window loans. The **federal funds rate** is the cost of borrowing funds in this market. Financial analysts monitor this rate closely because changes in the federal funds rate are a key indicator of the stance of Federal Reserve monetary policy. An increase in the federal funds rate indicates a scarcity in the supply of reserves relative to demand, and a decrease indicates an abundance of supply relative to demand.

TRY IT OUT 4.1: Characteristics of U.S. Financial Instruments

Reinforce your understanding of the key characteristics of individual financial instruments by completing the following table. See the note at the end of the table for a guide to filling in columns 4 through 7.

Financial Instrument	Issuer (1)	Holder (2)	Typical Maturity (3)	Marketability (4)	Source of Return to Holder (5)	Market Risk (6)	Credit Risk (7)
Treasury bills							
Treasury notes							
Treasury bonds							
Federal agency securities							
Municipal securities							
Reserve balances with Fed and vault cash							
Currency in circulation							
Federal funds							
Commercial paper							
Bankers' acceptances							
Corporate bonds							
Corporate stock							
Bank loans							
Demand deposits							
NOW & Super-NOW accounts							
Negotiable CDs							

Note: Use the following illustrations as a guide for filling in columns 4 through 7:
(4) Marketability: active secondary market, no secondary market, not applicable because of immediate maturity, etc.
(5) Source of return to holder: sold at a discount, interest payments plus capital gain/loss if sold before maturity, interest payments alone, etc.
(6) Market risk: high, moderate, low, varies, zero
(7) Credit risk: high, moderate, low, varies, zero

PLACING THE FINANCIAL INSTRUMENTS INTO THE PARTICIPANTS' BALANCE SHEETS

Having described the basic instruments in the U.S. financial system, we now use them to construct financial profiles of our six participants. These profiles are called *balance sheets*. Before we place the instruments into the participants' balance sheets, however, we must present some basic information about balance sheets.

What's in a Balance Sheet?

A **balance sheet** is a snapshot of the financial condition of a participant at a moment in time. The balance sheet of each participant shows what the participant owns—its **assets**, both financial and tangible. The balance sheet also shows what the participant owes—its obligations, or **liabilities**. Finally, the balance sheet shows the difference, called **net worth**, between the participant's assets and liabilities. Another term for net worth is *wealth*.

Denoting assets by *A*, liabilities by *L,* and net worth by *NW*, we can write the accounting relation between assets, liabilities, and net worth as:

$$A - L = NW$$

We can rearrange the relationship to get:

$$A = L + NW$$

This last equation is the basis of the T-account, the usual device for presenting a balance sheet. The left side shows assets, and the right side shows liabilities plus net worth.

Table 4–3 presents a hypothetical numerical illustration of the balance sheet of a college graduate one year after graduation. She has financial assets of $3,200 and tangible assets of $10,000 for a total of $13,200 of assets; on the liability side are two loans totaling $11,500. Because assets exceed liabilities, her net worth is positive: $1,700.

The balance sheet in Table 4–3 is a hypothetical account for one individual. By adding the accounts of all individuals in one sector such as all households, we find the balance sheet of that sector. The Flow of Funds Accounts of the Federal Reserve publishes data on the actual balance sheets of our six sectors (participants). The data consist of both year-end positions (stocks) and quarterly and annual changes (flows).

TABLE 4–3
The Balance Sheet of a College Graduate One Year after Graduation: *June 12, 1994*

Assets		Liabilities plus Net Worth	
ASSETS (*A*)	$13,200	LIABILITIES (*L*)	$11,500
Financial assets:		Loans from bank	7,000
Currency	100	Loans from relative	4,500
Checking account	600	NET WORTH (*NW = A − L*)	1,700
Mutual funds	2,500		
Tangible assets:			
Automobile	6,000		
Furniture and other consumer			
durables	4,000		

TABLE 4–4
The Balance Sheet
of Households

Assets	Liabilities plus Net Worth
(1) Currency	(8) Bank loans
(2) Bank deposits	(9) Net worth
(3) U.S. Treasury securities and other government securities	
(4) Open market debt of firms	
(5) Corporate stock (Equity in business)	
(6) Foreign assets	
(7) Real estate and other tangible assets	

TABLE 4–5
The Balance Sheet
of Firms

Assets	Liabilities plus Net Worth
(1) Currency	(6) Open market debt
(2) Bank deposits	(7) Bank loans
(3) U.S. Treasury securities and other government securities	(8) Corporate stock
(4) Foreign assets	(9) Retained earnings
(5) Plant and equipment and other tangible assets	Note: (8) + (9) = Net Worth

We present simplified balance sheets, without numbers, for the six participants by placing into these balance sheets the six basic types of financial instruments described in this chapter: U.S. Treasury securities and other government securities, open market debt issued by firms, corporate stock, bank loans, bank deposits, and currency and reserves. Foreign participants also issue financial instruments held by domestic participants, which we lump together and identify as foreign assets.

The Balance Sheet of Households

Table 4–4 shows that all six types of domestic financial instruments appear in the balance sheet of households. Bank loans are a liability of households, while the other five financial instruments are assets. (For simplicity, we identify all equity in business as corporate stock.) In addition, households hold foreign assets and tangible assets.

The Balance Sheet of Firms

Table 4–5 presents the balance sheet of firms. On the asset side are three domestic financial instruments: currency, bank deposits, and U.S. Treasury and other government securities. In addition, firms hold foreign assets and tangible assets. Open market debt is a liability of firms. Some of this debt may actually be held by other firms, but this possibility is not shown explicitly in Table 4–5. This is because open market debt on the liability side of the balance sheet represents the *net* amount of such debt issued, that is, open market debt issued by firms minus open market debt held by firms. Finally, the amount of

SectorWatch 4.5
National Balance Sheet Distress

The chairman of the Board of Governors of the Federal Reserve System appears often to testify before congressional committees on the state of the economy. When asked during testimony at the end of 1991 why U.S. economic growth was so sluggish, Chairman Alan Greenspan cited "national balance sheet distress" as the culprit. In the Federal Reserve lexicon, national balance sheet distress is a synonym for the term *debt hangover* introduced by Ed Frydl of the Federal Reserve Bank of New York. Let's see why.

Between 1980 and 1989, the net worth of U.S. corporations, measured as a fraction of gross national output (GNP)*, fell 25.4 percent. This reduction in net worth resulted from an 11.2 percent increase in liabilities, a

13.5 percent decrease in tangible assets, and a 0.7 percent decrease in financial assets, all measured as percentages of GNP. How could firms borrow more and yet buy fewer tangible and financial assets? The answer is that the increase in corporate debt financed stock repurchases rather than plant and equipment.

During the same period, the liabilities of households rose by 14.2 percent of GNP, their financial assets rose by 26.6 percent of GNP, and their tangible assets fell by 3.9 percent. As a result, the net worth of households increased slightly. Between 1980 and 1989, their net worth rose by 8.5 percent of GNP.†

The balance sheet distress from increased debt emerged in the 1990s when the economy turned downward and firms and households began to have difficulty meeting interest payments on their debt. In response, they began to restructure their balance sheets by reducing their debt burdens, as MarketWatch 4.4 shows.

---

* Gross national product is the output of final goods and services produced by a country's labor and capital, some of which may be located abroad.

† The data on changes in the balance sheets of households and firms are from Benjamin M. Friedman, "Views on the Likelihood of Financial Crisis," in *The Risk of Economic Crisis*, ed. Martin Feldstein (University of Chicago Press, 1991), 27.

TABLE 4–6
The Balance Sheet of Banks

Assets	Liabilities plus Net Worth
(1) Total reserves	(6) Deposits of households and firms (domestic and foreign)
(2) U.S. Treasury securities and other government securities	(7) Discount window loans of reserves
(3) Bank loans to households and firms	(8) Net worth
(4) Foreign assets	
(5) Tangible assets	

corporate stock outstanding plus the accumulated retained earnings of firms is the net worth of the business sector, which equals the assets of firms minus their liabilities. SectorWatch 4.5 uses actual data from the balance sheets of households and firms to relate the concept of debt hangover to that of national balance sheet distress.

The Balance Sheet of Banks

The next balance sheet is that of banks, shown in Table 4–6. The first item on the asset side is total reserves, that is, the vault cash and reserve accounts that banks hold with the Fed. The other domestic financial instruments on the asset side of banks' balance sheets

TABLE 4–7
The Balance Sheet
of the U.S.
Government

Assets	Liabilities plus Net Worth
(1) Tangible assets (capital stock of the U.S. government)	(2) U.S. Treasury securities and other government securities
	(3) Net worth

TABLE 4–8
The Balance Sheet
of the Fed

Assets	Liabilities plus Net Worth
(1) U.S. Treasury securities	(4) Currency in circulation
(2) Discount window loans	(5) Total reserves (reserve balances with the Fed + vault cash)
(3) Other assets	(6) Other liabilities + net worth
	Note: (4) + (5) = Total monetary base

are U.S. Treasury and other government securities and IOUs from households and firms, that is, bank loans. Banks are prohibited by law from owning corporate stock. Moreover, they do not hold a large amount of open market debt of firms. Therefore, we simplify their balance sheet in Table 4–6 by omitting open market debt of firms from the asset side. On the liability side are bank deposits, which are obligations of banks to households and firms, and discount window loans, which are obligations of banks to the Fed.

Note that the simplified balance sheet of banks does not include federal funds. Federal funds loaned are an asset in the balance sheet of the lending bank and a liability in the balance sheet of the borrowing bank. For the banking sector as a whole, federal funds loaned are equal to federal funds sold. Table 4–6 presents a net form of the balance sheet of banks by not including federal funds on either side.

The Balance Sheet of the U.S. Government

Table 4–7 presents the simplified balance sheet of the U.S. government. On the asset side are tangible assets, such as bridges, highways, schools, and prisons, and on the liability side, U.S. Treasury securities and other government securities.

The Balance Sheet of the Fed

The last domestic participant is the Federal Reserve, whose simplified balance sheet is shown in Table 4–8. On the liability side, currency and reserves are obligations of the Fed to the public and to banks, respectively. On the asset side, the Fed holds IOUs of the U.S. Treasury and IOUs of banks, that is, U.S. Treasury securities and discount window loans, respectively. The other two items in the Fed's balance sheet are catchall items, called *other assets* and *other liabilities plus net worth*. These other assets and other liabilities originate in the Fed's role as the banker to banks, the banker to the U.S. government, and the banker to international institutions. For example, included in other liabilities are

TABLE 4–9
External Balance
Sheet: U.S.
Investment Position
with the Rest of the
World

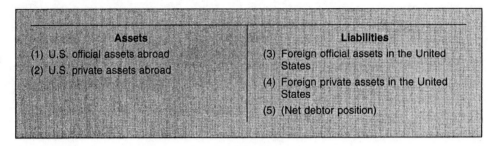

Assets	Liabilities
(1) U.S. official assets abroad (2) U.S. private assets abroad	(3) Foreign official assets in the United States (4) Foreign private assets in the United States (5) (Net debtor position)

accounts that the U.S. government has with the Fed. Included in other assets are the official U.S. holdings of foreign currencies.[6]

The External
Balance Sheet

Finally, we turn to the financial links between the United States and the rest of the world, represented by the external balance sheet in Table 4–9. In the external balance sheet, U.S. official assets abroad, item 1, refers to the foreign securities, foreign currencies, and other foreign assets the Fed holds as the agent for the U.S. Treasury. On the other hand, foreign securities and foreign currencies all other domestic participants hold are lumped together and designated as U.S. private assets abroad, item 2. Similarly, the rest of the world holds securities and dollars issued in the United States. The U.S. Treasury securities and the U.S. dollars foreign central banks hold make up foreign official assets in the United States, item 3. Finally, foreign private assets in the United States, item 4, consist of the American-issued securities and dollars held by the foreign private sector.

The difference between the total American-owned foreign assets (1 + 2) and the total foreign-owned American assets (3 + 4) is the net creditor position of the United States, item 5. As we saw in Chapter 2, this difference is currently negative, which accounts for the term *net debtor position* in the external balance sheet.

TWO KEY QUESTIONS AND THE TWO PILLARS

The balance sheets in Tables 4–4 to 4–9 are a springboard for raising two key questions. *First, why do the participants choose a particular menu of assets and liabilities?* That is, what factors determine the amount of each financial instrument that a participant wants to hold, the participant's demand? And what factors determine the amount that a participant wants to issue, the participant's supply? In answering these questions for each participant, we bring the entries of the balance sheets to life by analyzing the behavior of the participant. In our two-pillar framework, this is the subject of the first pillar: the rational behavior of participants.

Second, how does the interaction of the participants in the marketplace make their plans for holding and issuing financial instruments match? This, of course, is the subject of the second pillar: the interaction of participants in markets. In answering this question,

---

[6] Chapter 14 examines the details behind the other assets and the other liabilities.

we examine the economic forces, namely, the movements in interest rates, that make the quantity demanded equal to the quantity supplied of each instrument.

Chapters 6 to 9 address these two questions. First, however, in Chapter 5 we look at how the financial environment has changed in recent years.

SUMMARY

- The six broad categories of domestic securities include U.S. Treasury securities and other securities issued by the federal, state, and local governments and by federal agencies and federally sponsored agencies; open market debt issued by firms; corporate stock issued by firms; bank loans issued by firms and households; deposits issued by banks; and currency and reserves issued by the Fed.

- Government debt consists of U.S. Treasury securities issued to finance the federal deficit; federal agency securities issued by federal agencies (other than the U.S. Treasury) and federally sponsored agencies to collect and channel funds to targeted sectors of the economy, such as housing; and municipal securities issued by state and local governments. All other participants hold government securities. The Fed holds Treasury and agency securities but not municipal securities.

- Corporations finance their long-term needs, such as investing in plant and equipment, by issuing shares of stock and by issuing bonds. Shares of stock represent ownership of the issuing corporation, while bonds are IOUs. Domestic households, domestic private nonbank financial intermediaries, and foreign participants are the major holders of stocks and bonds.

- Corporations finance their short-term needs by issuing commercial paper and bankers' acceptances. Bankers' acceptances ultimately become the liability of the sponsoring banks, which finance the needs of firms engaging in international commerce. Banks and nonbank financial intermediaries hold the bulk of commercial paper and bankers' acceptances.

- Corporate bonds, commercial paper, and bankers' acceptances fall under the category of open market debt of

firms, which is sold in the market through specialists or placed directly. Firms also borrow from banks.

- The wave of buyouts in the 1980s resulted in a major shift by corporations from equity financing to debt financing.

- Bank loans consist of a wide variety of IOUs issued by households and firms and held as assets by banks. In the 1980s banks increased their holdings of commercial and residential real estate loans much faster than their holdings of traditional commercial and industrial loans.

- Deposits consist of a variety of checking and savings accounts issued by banks and held as assets by households, firms, and foreign participants. These participants hold checking accounts mainly to carry out transactions, but they hold time deposits as investment vehicles.

- Currency in circulation and reserves are liabilities issued by the Federal Reserve. Households and firms hold currency to carry out transactions. Banks hold reserves to satisfy fractional reserve requirements and to provide a buffer against an unexpected need for funds. The sum of currency and reserves is called the *monetary base*.

- The Fed does not pay interest on reserves held by banks. Banks with excess reserves can earn interest by lending them to other banks in the interbank loan market, called the *federal funds market*.

- A balance sheet is a statement of the financial condition of a participant. It shows the participant's assets, liabilities, and net worth, which equals assets minus liabilities.

- By placing the six types of financial instruments into the balance sheets of the participants, we construct financial profiles of the six participants.

KEY TERMS AND CONCEPTS

Treasury securities	Treasury bonds, or T-bonds	open market debt of firms
Treasury bills, or T-bills	federal agency securities	corporate bonds
Treasury notes, or T-notes	municipal securities, or munis	commercial paper

banker's acceptance

corporate stock

buyout

bank loans

securitization

prime rate

demand deposit

NOW accounts and Super-NOW
  accounts

time deposits

negotiable CD

deposit rate

monetary base

currency in circulation

reserves

required reserves

excess reserves

discount window loans

discount rate

federal funds market

federal funds rate

balance sheet

assets

liabilities

net worth

QUESTIONS AND PROBLEMS

1. "Every financial instrument is the liability of some sector." Explain this statement by examining the six basic financial instruments and identifying their issuers.

2. "All financial instruments are assets of some sector(s)." Explain for each instrument.

3. "In contrast to financial assets, tangible assets are not an obligation of any sector." True or false?

4. The U.S. Treasury issues both marketable and nonmarketable debt instruments. Identify one of each.

5. Classify government debt instruments by interest rate risk.

6. In 1993 the U.S. Treasury began reducing the maturity of government debt by reducing the annual issuance of 30-year Treasury bonds.
   a. Did this increase or decrease liquidity?
   b. Did this increase or decrease interest rate risk?
   c. Did this make government debt more or less desirable?

7. What characteristic(s) do Treasury bills, commercial paper, and federal funds have in common? What characteristics are different?

The Wall Street Journal

8. A graph of short-term interest rates appears every Thursday as a regular feature in the "Credit Markets" column in section C of *The Wall Street Journal*. The accompanying graph is reproduced from the April 14, 1994, issue.

   What characteristic of securities explains why the three-month commercial paper rate is uniformly above the three-month Treasury bill rate? The federal funds rate is often below the T-bill rate. What difference in their characteristics could account for this?

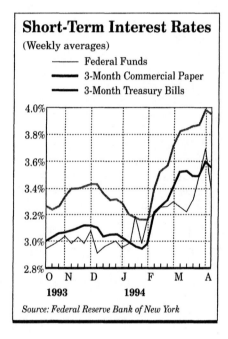

Short-Term Interest Rates
(Weekly averages)
—— Federal Funds
—— 3-Month Commercial Paper
—— 3-Month Treasury Bills

Source: Federal Reserve Bank of New York

9. Explain the similarities and differences between corporate bonds and commercial paper.

10. What distinguishes preferred stock from common stock?

11. Who issues bankers' acceptances and who holds them?

12. "The prime rate is the interest rate banks charge their best customers." True or false?

13. The public holds most of the debt issued by the Fed, but it cannot have an account with the Fed. Explain and identify the participant(s) that can have such an account with the Fed.

14. Whose obligation is the $10 bill?

15. "Discount window loans are loans from banks to good customers who deserve a discount." True or false?

16. Who participates in the federal funds market?

17. Classify each of the following securities as money market or capital market securities: Treasury bills, Treasury notes, Treasury bonds, commercial paper, corporate bonds, bankers' acceptances, and federal funds.

18. What is a balance sheet? Illustrate by listing the items in your personal balance sheet.

19. Explain the link between the concept of debt hangover and the concept of national balance sheet distress.

SUGGESTED READINGS

Fabozzi, Frank J., and Franco Modigliani. *Capital Markets: Institutions and Instruments.* Englewood Cliffs, N.J.: Prentice Hall, 1991.

A text on capital markets that combines theory with practice.

Frydl, Edward J. "Overhangs and Hangovers: Coping with the Imbalances of the 1980s," *Federal Reserve Bank of New York Annual Report,* 1991, pp. 5–30.

Introduces and examines the concept of the debt hangover.

Meulendyke, Anne-Marie. *U.S. Monetary Policy and Financial Markets.* New York: Federal Reserve Bank of New York, 1989, Chapter 4, "The Financial Markets," pp. 66–105.

An overview of U.S. financial instruments and markets.

Stigum, Marcia. *The Money Market,* 3rd ed. Homewood, Ill: Dow Jones–Irwin, 1990.

A handbook on money markets for both the practitioner and the novice.

THE EVOLUTION TO THE NEW FINANCIAL ENVIRONMENT

CHAPTER PREVIEW

Until the mid-1970s, a joke in the banking community was that to succeed in banking one needed simply to know the "3-6-3 rule": Borrow from depositors at 3 percent, lend at 6 percent, and close at 3:00 PM. The truth behind the joke was that legal and regulatory restrictions not only severely constrained bankers' actions but also freed bankers from some of the burden of decision making. Bankers did not have to decide at what level to set deposit rates to attract deposits, for that decision was made for them by laws and by regulators. They found, however, that they could still influence the volume of their deposits by giving "free" gifts, such as toasters or transistor radios, or free services, such as use of safe deposit boxes. That led to a second rule of banking: A successful banker must know what free merchandise or free services are most likely to attract depositors.

Thrift institutions, prohibited from issuing checking accounts and making loans to businesses, were even more constrained than banks. We call the environment in which regulators placed ceilings on deposit rates and imposed severe restrictions on the portfolios of depository institutions, especially thrifts, the **old financial environment (OFE)**.

The old financial environment, which dates back to 1933, began to unravel in the mid-1970s when the increase in market rates of interest that accompanied high and rising rates of inflation clashed with the existing regulatory structure. A **new financial environment (NFE)**, characterized by market-determined, or deregulated, rates on the assets and liabilities of financial intermediaries and by greater homogeneity among financial institutions, emerged in the 1980s. This chapter examines the avalanche of financial innovations that led to the new financial environment. As the words themselves suggest, **financial innovations** are new practices and products introduced into the financial system. These novelties sprang from changes in laws, regulations, institutional arrangements, and the state of financial technology.

First, we examine briefly the rise and fall of the old financial environment. Then we turn to the participants and their incentives for innovation. Many financial innovations emerged from attempts by households, firms, and banks to circumvent existing regulations to maximize their wealth or profit. The Fed, in contrast, is not a wealth maximizer or a profit maximizer. Instead, the Fed's attitude to financial innovations is guided by its goal of protecting the health of the economy and of the financial industry.

THE RISE AND FALL OF THE OLD FINANCIAL ENVIRONMENT

The old financial environment had its origin in the Great Depression of the 1930s. From 1930 to 1933, an average of 2,250 banks failed per year. The consequent loss of deposits hindered the payments mechanism, further aggravating the depressed economy. By 1933 the unemployment rate had risen to 25 percent of the labor force.

At the time, two factors were widely believed to be behind the massive failure of banks: (1) excessive competition between banks in providing intermediation and transactions services and (2) excessive risk taking arising from the involvement of commercial banks in investment banking activities, especially underwriting stocks and bonds issued by corporate clients to whom they also provided banking services.[1] The **Banking Act of 1933** (better known as the **Glass-Steagall Act**) addressed these two issues.

First, the 1933 act deprived banks of the ability to compete for deposits by raising deposit rates. In particular, it prohibited banks from paying interest on demand deposits, and it gave the Fed the authority to impose ceilings on interest paid by member banks (of the Federal Reserve System) on savings and time deposits. The Fed carried out this authority through an internal regulation called **Regulation Q**. Second, the act prohibited commercial banks from providing investment banking services, a prohibition still in effect today. In addition, the act provided a safety net for depositors by creating the Federal Deposit Insurance Corporation (FDIC) to insure bank deposits up to $2,500 per deposit.[2] The **Banking Act of 1935** gave the FDIC the authority to extend Regulation Q to rate ceilings on savings and time deposits issued by insured banks that were not members of the Federal Reserve System.

---

[1] In a path-breaking book published in 1963, Friedman and Schwartz strongly disagree with these reasons for the bank failures. They argue that the Fed brought on the widespread collapse of banks during the 1930s by not providing sufficient reserves to the banking system. See Milton Friedman and Anna J. Schwartz, *A Monetary History of the United States, 1867–1960* (Princeton, N. J.: Princeton University Press, 1963), Chapter 7. See also Chapter 28 of this book.

[2] The limit on insured deposits was raised to $5,000 in 1934.

FIGURE 5–1
The 3-Month T-Bill
Rate versus the
Passbook Savings
Rate: *OFE*

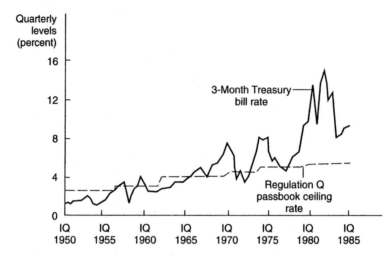

Source: Alfred Broaddus, "Financial Innovation in the United States—Background, Current Status, and Prospects," *Economic Review*, Federal Reserve Bank of Richmond, January/February 1985.

The system of regulated deposit rates imposed in the 1930s was the hallmark of the old financial environment in banking. This system functioned without major disruptions in the climate of low inflation and low interest rates throughout the 1950s and early 1960s. Banks made loans to firms and to households and also purchased government securities. The loans to households were subject to interest rate ceilings imposed by state usury laws. Banks funded the purchase of all these assets by issuing deposits with regulated rates. Up to a limit, these deposits were covered by deposit insurance.[3]

The unraveling of the old financial environment began in the 1970s. The proximate cause for the demise of regulated deposit rates was the high and still rising rate of inflation of the late 1960s, the 1970s, and the early 1980s. Inflation rose from 4.7 percent in 1972 to 9.7 percent in 1981. As inflation accelerated and came to be expected, the inflation premium embedded in market interest rates rose. Lenders demanded this premium to compensate them for the loss of purchasing power from expected inflation, and borrowers, expecting to repay the loans in inflation-cheapened dollars, were willing to pay the premium.

Figure 5–1 shows that market rates of interest increased while the regulated deposit rates either remained fixed or were changed infrequently and by small magnitudes; as a result, the spread between the two rates widened. In response, wealthy households and firms withdrew their funds from the regulated-rate accounts at depository institutions and placed them in instruments such as Treasury bills that paid market-determined rates. (Minimum denominations placed these instruments out of the reach of small savers.) The

---

[3] The limit on insured deposits was increased from $5,000 to $10,000 in 1950; to $15,000 in 1966; to $25,000 in 1969; and to $40,000 in 1974. A $100,000 limit was added in 1980.

outflow of funds from financial intermediaries is called **disintermediation**. As interest rates moved steadily upward, disintermediation soared and plagued depository institutions, especially the thrifts. Furthermore, aided by the new financial technology, the public and banks sought ways to circumvent the existing regulatory structure. Participants increasingly devoted resources to evading existing regulations, and the old regulatory structure became less and less effective.

In 1980 Congress and the president bowed to market forces by passing the **Depository Institutions Deregulation and Monetary Control Act of 1980 (DID&MCA)**. This banking and financial legislation revolutionized the financial structure in the United States. Among the many provisions of this act, two key ones brought the old financial environment to an end. The first authorized banks and thrifts, beginning December 31, 1980, to issue interest-bearing checking accounts (NOW accounts), subject to a rate ceiling of 5.25 percent. The second provided for the gradual phasing out of interest rate ceilings on all deposits by 1986. Two years later, Congress enacted the **Garn–St Germain Depository Institutions Act of 1982**, which was designed to aid the thrift industry by extending considerably the permissible menu of assets held and liabilities issued. The Garn–St Germain Act did not, however, prevent the subsequent failure of several hundred savings and loan associations, as we shall see. Later we introduce more details about these two key acts as we consider the participants and their incentives for innovation, especially banks and thrifts.

FINANCIAL INNOVATIONS AND THE PUBLIC

The sector called the *public* consists of households and nonfinancial firms. In most cases we assume that a household is driven by its desire to maximize utility and that a nonfinancial firm is driven by its desire to maximize profit. Hence, the public responds favorably to a financial innovation that increases its utility or its profit.

To carry out transactions, the public must hold money in its portfolio. Holding money, however, deprives the public of the opportunity to hold another asset, say a security, that pays a higher rate of return. The difference between the two returns is the **opportunity cost of money**, that is, the interest forgone by holding money needed for transactions. Financial innovations that permit the public to carry out its transactions and yet hold less money—or to hold the same amount of money but for a shorter period of time—are called **innovations in cash management practices**. As the opportunity cost of holding money increased in the 1970s, nonfinancial firms and households became more interested in cash management techniques.

Cash Management Practices of Nonfinancial Firms

Among the techniques that became available to firms seeking to economize on their demand deposits were cash concentration systems, lockboxes, and repurchase agreements.[4] Let's see how they work.

---

[4] For a detailed discussion of the cash management practices of nonfinancial firms, see Thomas D. Simpson, "The Market for Federal Funds and Repurchase Agreements," Board of Governors of the Federal Reserve System Staff Study 106, July 1979; and Ralph C. Kimball, "Wire Transfer and the Demand for Money," *New England Economic Review*, Federal Reserve Bank of Boston, March/April 1980, 5–20.

Cash Concentration Systems   A **cash concentration system** is a mechanism used by corporations that maintain demand deposit accounts with several banks, usually in different parts of the country. Under this system, funds from bank accounts around the country are electronically transferred to one or more central accounts from which all payments are made. All regional deposit accounts have a zero (or minimum) balance until a check is presented for collection against one of those accounts. At that moment, the central account wires the exact amount to the bank to cover the check. In this way, a corporation economizes on the total amount of funds that it holds in demand deposits nationwide. The firm can then invest the released funds in interest-bearing securities.

Fedwire   Cash concentration accounts would not be possible without an electronic system that transfers funds between banks. In its role as the banker to banks, the Fed operates **Fedwire**, a computer network connecting banks and the Fed. Fedwire permits banks and other depository institutions that hold reserve accounts with the Fed to transfer funds between each other on the same day on their own behalf or on behalf of their customers. Consider the following hypothetical illustration: Suppose that Seafair Corporation wants to transfer $1 million immediately from its demand deposit account at Bay Bank in San Francisco to its demand deposit account at Empire Bank in New York. Seafair gives instructions to Bay Bank to carry out the transaction. With Fedwire, the entire transaction is executed in a matter of minutes. The Federal Reserve System debits the reserve account of Bay Bank $1 million and credits the reserve account of Empire Bank $1 million. In turn, Bay Bank debits the deposit account of Seafair $1 million, and Empire Bank credits the deposit account of Seafair $1 million. By comparison, transferring the funds by check would take several days.

Lockboxes   The use of **lockboxes** is another cash management technique nonfinancial firms use. Lockboxes are post office boxes banks operate to speed up the collection of checks for their customers. For example, your dentist may use one lockbox in the city where he or she practices. All mail containing payments is sent to the dentist's lockbox address rather than being routed initially to the dentist's office and then to the bank. The bank collects the mail from the lockbox and deposits the checks into the dentist's account. Large national firms may have lockboxes in several cities to receive local payments. The receiving bank collects the checks and transfers the funds by Fedwire to the firm's main account.

In sum, lockboxes and cash concentration accounts are examples of cash management practices that permit firms to carry out the same volume of transactions with fewer demand deposits. With advances in computer and communications technology, cash management techniques tailored to the needs of businesses are continually evolving.

Repurchase Agreements   **Repurchase agreements (RPs)** also allow firms to economize on their demand deposits but for a different reason. Overnight RPs are a highly liquid financial instrument and, hence, are a substitute for demand deposits. Under an overnight repurchase agreement between a bank and a firm, the bank sells Treasury securities or federal agency securities in its portfolio to the firm, with the understanding that the bank will repurchase the securities the next morning at a prescribed (higher) price. The interest rate the firm earns is the difference between the purchase price and the sale price of the securities. The next morning the funds the firm receives are placed in its demand deposit account on which it can draw checks until the close of the business day. In effect, overnight RPs are checking accounts that earn interest on the balance at the end of the day.

The minimum denomination of RPs usually exceeds $100,000, and the minimum size of most RP transactions exceeds $1 million. Because of their size, RPs compete with negotiable CDs, commercial paper, and Treasury bills for a place in the portfolios of nonfinancial firms. On the other hand, because of their short maturity, overnight RPs are a closer substitute for demand deposits than are these other financial instruments. As market rates of interest increased in the 1970s, nonfinancial firms acquired more overnight RPs. Outstanding RPs increased a thousand percent between 1970 and 1980: from about $2 billion in 1970 to about $20 billion in 1980.

Cash Management Practices of Households

Households and small businesses also made more use of cash management practices in the 1970s and 1980s. For households, money market mutual funds and cash management accounts were the tools for more effective cash management.

Money Market Mutual Funds   Because of their large denominations, RPs are better suited for nonfinancial firms than for households. On the other hand, **money market mutual funds (MMMFs)** were designed as an outlet for small and intermediate investors, such as households and small businesses. When MMMFs were first introduced in the early 1970s, their minimum denomination was usually $5,000, but gradually it fell to $1,000 or less. MMMFs pool funds from many participants and invest the total in a variety of short-term marketable securities, called money market securities, such as commercial paper, negotiable CDs, and Treasury bills. Because the financial instruments in which MMMFs invest pay market-determined interest rates, the shares owned by participants in the fund also earn these rates. MMMFs have one additional attraction: Funds can be withdrawn by check, although typically the amount of the check must exceed a minimum amount, which can be as low as $100. Thus, they are substitutes for demand deposits, thereby allowing the public to economize on demand balances.

MMMFs, with their market rates, small minimum denomination, and their checkability, became increasingly attractive as market rates of interest increased. In 1975, there was less than $5 billion in MMMFs. By January 1979, the amount had increased to $12 billion and by January 1982 had skyrocketed to $187 billion. By comparison, at the beginning of 1982 the size of M1, consisting of currency, demand deposits, and interest-bearing checking accounts, was about $450 billion.

Cash Management Accounts   In 1977 a major brokerage house, Merrill Lynch, combined the MMMF with additional financial services by introducing the **cash management account (CMA)**, which was soon imitated by other brokerage firms. The CMA brings under one umbrella a money market mutual fund, a securities account, and a credit line. In effect, the CMA is an MMMF in which deposited funds can be used to purchase securities or can be withdrawn by check or credit card. A $20,000 minimum balance is required on the Merrill Lynch account, but there are no restrictions on the number of checks or the size of each check. The unlimited checkability and the money market interest rate make the CMA a substitute for demand deposits and other checkable deposits. Realistically, however, the funds in CMAs are not to be used for daily transactions, as are typical checking account balances; CMAs are closer substitutes for CDs and time deposits. Empirical research shows that the turnover of funds in CMAs is substantially lower than the turnover of funds in demand deposits. Even so, the CMA reduces the holdings of demand deposits and other checkable deposits, thereby releasing funds to be held in securities.

Credit Cards   The first cash management tool was the credit card. Although credit cards have existed since the 1950s, they proliferated in the 1970s, when advances in computer technology made it profitable for banks to mass-market them. Today they are a popular method of payment. Credit card holders routinely use the same card to purchase a restaurant meal in London and a bicycle in Boston. In addition to the convenience in transacting, a credit card allows the holder to defer payments on expenditures charged to the credit card account until the receipt of a monthly bill. About 40 percent of credit card holders pay their balances in full each month, thus, avoiding interest charges on their accounts.

FINANCIAL INNOVATIONS AND BANKS

Next, we turn to banks, which have been a key player in changing the financial environment. As Chapter 2 noted, a bank is an intermediary between borrowers and lenders. It pools the public's deposited funds and invests these funds in assets that are inaccessible to the individual investor or, if accessible, at inferior terms. In other words, a bank manages its liabilities (sources of bank funds) and its assets (uses of bank funds) to minimize its costs, or to maximize its profits. Banks also provide the economy and the public with transaction services; that is, they provide the medium of exchange. Obviously, banks strive to find innovations that help them acquire and use funds as well as innovations that reduce the cost of intermediation (the cost of transforming sources of funds into uses of funds) and of providing transactions services.

Financial innovations used by banks fall into three categories based on the definition of a banking firm:

1. Novel liability instruments, that is, instruments designed to attract deposits, such as repurchase agreements and money market deposit accounts.
2. New asset instruments, such as floating-rate loans.
3. Technological advances that induce banks to provide new transaction services and reduce the cost of intermediation and of offering transaction services.

Financial Innovations in Bank Liabilities   Innovations in liabilities were a response to regulatory restrictions and outside competition. The two most notable restrictions on the borrowing activities of banks were the prohibition of interest on demand deposits and the Regulation Q ceilings on interest paid on savings and time deposits. Naturally, profit-maximizing depository institutions attempted to introduce liabilities that would circumvent ceilings on deposit rates, especially during periods of high interest rates. In so doing, they invented substitutes for demand deposits and for traditional savings and time deposits that between 1970 and 1986 led to

TABLE 5–1
A Brief
Chronology of the
Deregulation of
Deposit Rates

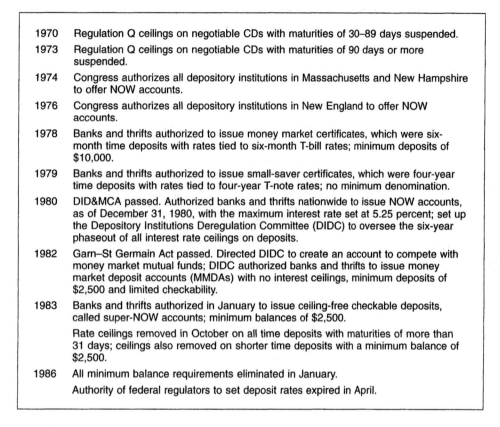

1970	Regulation Q ceilings on negotiable CDs with maturities of 30–89 days suspended.
1973	Regulation Q ceilings on negotiable CDs with maturities of 90 days or more suspended.
1974	Congress authorizes all depository institutions in Massachusetts and New Hampshire to offer NOW accounts.
1976	Congress authorizes all depository institutions in New England to offer NOW accounts.
1978	Banks and thrifts authorized to issue money market certificates, which were six-month time deposits with rates tied to six-month T-bill rates; minimum deposits of $10,000.
1979	Banks and thrifts authorized to issue small-saver certificates, which were four-year time deposits with rates tied to four-year T-note rates; no minimum denomination.
1980	DID&MCA passed. Authorized banks and thrifts nationwide to issue NOW accounts, as of December 31, 1980, with the maximum interest rate set at 5.25 percent; set up the Depository Institutions Deregulation Committee (DIDC) to oversee the six-year phaseout of all interest rate ceilings on deposits.
1982	Garn–St Germain Act passed. Directed DIDC to create an account to compete with money market mutual funds; DIDC authorized banks and thrifts to issue money market deposit accounts (MMDAs) with no interest ceilings, minimum deposits of $2,500 and limited checkability.
1983	Banks and thrifts authorized in January to issue ceiling-free checkable deposits, called super-NOW accounts; minimum balances of $2,500.
	Rate ceilings removed in October on all time deposits with maturities of more than 31 days; ceilings also removed on shorter time deposits with a minimum balance of $2,500.
1986	All minimum balance requirements eliminated in January.
	Authority of federal regulators to set deposit rates expired in April.

the gradual removal of interest rate ceilings on deposits. Table 5–1 presents a brief chronology of the deregulation of deposit rates.

Substitutes for Demand Deposits   In prohibiting the payment of interest on demand deposits beginning in 1933, the U.S. government sought to reduce bank costs and thereby protect the safety and stability of banks (and their depositors' funds). Although the logic of this prohibition was simple, it was correct only up to a point. Other things being equal, a reduction in the deposit rate (e.g., from a positive rate to zero) does reduce the cost of acquiring funds and, thus, does increase the profit on each dollar of deposits. However, other things do not remain equal. In particular, banks may not be able to attract deposits, and obviously they cannot attract unlimited quantities of deposits. At the low deposit rate (which is zero if payment of interest is prohibited), banks want to attract more deposits than the public wants to hold. These deposits are assets in the balance sheets of households and firms, who are the demanders, and liabilities in the balance sheets of banks, who are the suppliers. When the deposit rate ceiling is set at zero, the suppliers of deposits, the banks, want to issue more deposits than the public wants to hold. Thus, at the zero rate for deposits there is an excess supply of deposits.

If the law of supply and demand were allowed to operate directly, competition between banks would eliminate this excess supply. The most direct and most effective competition would be pecuniary: The explicit deposit rate would be raised, inducing the public to hold more of their net worth in deposits. But because banks were not allowed to compete by offering higher explicit interest, they offered higher nonpecuniary interest, or interest in kind. This implicit interest was paid as "free" financial services: checks, safe deposit boxes, and even transistor radios, toasters, and similar innovative payments in kind.

Realizing that these in-kind payments were neither perfect substitutes for explicit interest payments nor as cost effective, banks became more innovative in circumventing the law that prohibits interest on demand deposits. They invented schemes whereby they could offer explicit interest on deposits that were essentially demand deposits and yet not violate the letter of the law.

Other Checkable Deposits   The first interest-bearing checking accounts to appear were *NOW accounts*. The concept of a NOW account was born in 1970 when a mutual savings bank in Massachusetts permitted its depositors to withdraw their savings deposits by using a negotiable draft, that is, by writing a check rather than going to the bank. The Massachusetts banking commissioner ruled against such a practice, but in May 1972 the state supreme court overturned the commissioner's ruling and established the right of state-chartered financial institutions to offer NOW accounts.

After congressional authorization, NOW accounts proliferated in New England. By 1979 they were introduced in the states of New York and New Jersey. Nationwide introduction of NOW accounts was authorized as of December 31, 1980, by DID&MCA. This act also authorized the nationwide introduction of credit union share drafts, which permit withdrawal of deposits by a negotiable draft (i.e., by a check). These accounts made their debut in 1974.

However, DID&MCA placed severe restrictions on NOW accounts. First, it regulated the deposit rate through a special committee, the Depository Institutions Deregulation Committee (DIDC). DIDC was a temporary committee created by the 1980 act to oversee the orderly phasing out, by 1986, of interest rate ceilings on deposits.[5] Second, it allowed only consumers to have NOW accounts; business and governmental agencies were not allowed to open such accounts. The passage of the Garn–St Germain Act of 1982 accelerated the deregulation process. Of particular importance were Super-NOW accounts, which the DIDC authorized in January 1983. For accounts opened with a minimum of $2,500 and maintained at that level, Super-NOWs offered unregulated deposit rates. Thus, the key characteristic of the new financial environment emerged three years ahead of schedule.

NOWs, Super-NOWs, and credit union share drafts are the backbone of what the Fed calls **other checkable deposits**, as we saw in Chapter 1. The term presumably distinguishes them from demand deposits proper, which cannot pay explicit interest

---

[5] The voting members of the committee were the secretary of the Treasury, the chairman of the Federal Reserve Board, the chairman of the FDIC, the chairman of the Federal Home Loan Bank Board (the regulator of savings and loan associations), and the chairman of the National Credit Union Administration Board.

FIGURE 5–2
History of Demand
Deposits Compared
with Other
Checkable Deposits

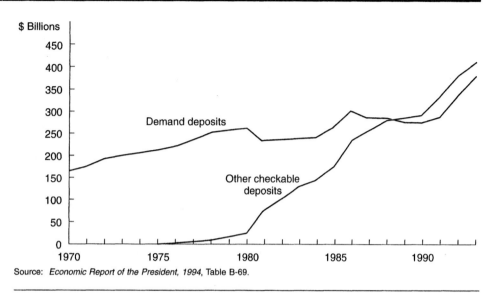

Source: *Economic Report of the President, 1994*, Table B-69.

because the provision of the Glass-Steagall Act that prohibits interest on demand deposits has not been repealed. Another item in the category of other checkables is the *automatic transfer service (ATS) account*, which DID&MCA authorized nationwide and permanently. ATS came into existence in 1978 when banks were authorized to offer their customers automatic transfers from their savings accounts to their checking accounts when payments were needed. Thus, deposit holders were able to earn interest (the passbook savings rate) on essentially demand deposits because, by design, a zero balance is always in the customer's checking account until the moment when funds are needed to cover a check; at that point the funds are transferred from the savings account to the checking account.

As Chapter 1 noted, the Fed classifies demand deposits and other checkable deposits as transactions deposits because of their unlimited checking privileges. All are included in M1 and are subject to the highest reserve requirement ratio, currently 10 percent. Figure 5–2 traces the history of demand deposits compared with other checkable deposits from 1970 through 1993. It shows that the dollar amount of other checkable deposits surpassed the dollar amount of demand deposits in 1989. Significantly, DID&MCA of 1980 prohibited businesses from holding interest-bearing checking accounts. Banks pay businesses implicit interest on demand deposits by offering businesses services below cost to compensate them for holding demand deposits.

Substitutes for Traditional Savings and Time Deposits   Instruments designed to circumvent Regulation Q ceilings on savings and time deposits and to alleviate the burden of reserve requirements include negotiable certificates of deposits (CDs), money market certificates, small-saver certificates, term RPs, and, in part, money market deposit accounts (MMDAs). Of these instruments, the negotiable CD was as effective in eventually abolishing Regulation Q ceilings for savings and time deposits as NOW accounts were in abolishing the interest prohibition on demand deposits.

The Negotiable CD: A Forerunner   The *negotiable CD* was born in 1961 when the First National City Bank of New York introduced this instrument and the Discount Corporation of New York, a major securities dealer, simultaneously created a secondary market for it. The negotiability, or marketability, of the CD in the secondary market is crucial; without this secondary market the CD would be the same as any other time deposit in a large denomination. The CD was created by the financial industry (and accepted by its regulators) as a concession to large investors, such as businesses, non-profit organizations, and wealthy individuals, who led the disintermediation march in periods of rising interest rates.

Before 1973 even negotiable CDs were subject to regulatory ceilings, but the ceilings were usually not binding. Regulators set the ceiling above the prevailing level of market interest rates so that negotiable CDs could pay a market-based rate of interest. In 1969, however, the ceiling did become binding, which resulted in the expected outflow of funds from negotiable CDs. In response, some large U.S. banks turned to their foreign branches to raise funds in the Eurodollar market. These **Eurodollar deposits** are dollar-denominated deposits in banks located outside the United States. Although the origins of Eurodollar deposits predate World War II, these deposits did not take off until the 1950s, when the dollar began to replace the British pound as the key currency in international trade and finance. Before 1966 the typical Eurodollar deposit was a nonnegotiable time deposit with a maturity of less than one year. The Eurodollar market developed further in the 1960s as market rates of interest rose and Regulation Q ceilings threatened to become binding. In 1966 foreign branches of U.S. banks (and to a lesser extent foreign-owned banks) began issuing negotiable Eurodollar CDs: dollar-denominated, negotiable, large time deposits in banks outside the United States. The attraction of these CDs for U.S. banks was that they were not subject to interest rate ceilings or reserve requirements. Because of these two features, banks could pay a higher interest rate on negotiable Eurodollar CDs than on their domestic counterparts and, thus, were able to replace funds lost through disintermediation from domestic CDs.

In 1970 the Fed removed the regulatory ceilings on domestic negotiable CDs with maturities of less than three months. In 1973 they removed the ceilings on all other negotiable CDs. As full-fledged deregulated deposit accounts, CDs were no longer threatened by disintermediation.

Money Market Certificates and Small-Saver Certificates   In the mid-1970s there were no small time deposits (i.e., time deposits with minimum balances of less than $100,000) with market-based rates for small investors. Depository institutions, especially the thrifts, were hit hard by disintermediation in the 1970s, as was the housing industry to which most of the thrift deposits were traditionally channeled. Therefore, new sources of funds designed to attract small savers were created. As Table 5–1 shows, small time deposits, called *money market certificates*, and *small-saver certificates*, with rates tied to Treasury bill and Treasury note rates, respectively, were introduced in 1978 and 1979. By October 1983 the DIDC had removed many of the interest rate ceilings on small time deposits.

Thus, Regulation Q ceilings on deposit rates were in effect eliminated, before they were officially abolished in 1986.

Hybrid Accounts: RPs and MMDAs   So far we have examined checking accounts, which are transactions deposits, and time deposits, which are nontransactions deposits. Repurchase agreements (RPs) and money market deposit accounts (MMDAs), however, are hybrid accounts with characteristics that resemble both transactions and nontransactions deposits.[6] Overnight RPs remain popular with the business sector, in part because businesses are prohibited from holding interest-bearing NOW accounts. RPs are also popular with financial institutions as a source of funds. In addition to being free of interest rate ceilings, the accounts are not subject to reserve requirements—as long as the collateral is government securities. Depository institutions also issue *term RPs,* which have a maturity greater than one day. The difference between overnight RPs and term RPs mirrors the difference between demand deposits and time deposits. Term RPs were one way to circumvent the interest rate ceilings on time deposits.

Money market deposit accounts, on the other hand, were introduced to give depository institutions an instrument to compete with money market mutual funds. The popularity of MMMFs posed a threat to the financial security and therefore the viability of depository institutions. MMMFs are not administered by banks and thrifts. If they were, they would not cause disintermediation; the particular source of funds for banks and thrifts would change, but not the total.

Legislators decided to help the threatened depository institutions by enacting legislation allowing them to issue a similar financial instrument. A provision of the Garn–St Germain Act of 1982 instructed DIDC to authorize a deposit "directly equivalent to and competitive with money market mutual funds." Thus, DIDC authorized the **money market deposit account (MMDA)** as of December 14, 1982. MMDAs pay unregulated deposit rates and are federally insured. There are, however, restrictions on the maximum number of checks written per month and on initial and maintained balances.

The MMDA was indeed competitive with the MMMF, whose growth was retarded, as Figure 5–3 shows. The figure also shows that the situation changed in the late 1980s. As open market rates of interest rose in the late 1980s, banks increased the rate on MMDAs more slowly than the rate of MMMFs increased. As a result, MMMFs became more attractive, and their volume increased at the expense of MMDAs.

Financial Innovations in Bank Assets

Financial innovations have not been confined to the liability side of the bank's balance sheet. There have also been important innovations in bank assets. These innovations were introduced mostly to reduce exposure to interest rate risk and to stem outside competition.

Portfolio Imbalances and Interest Rate Risk   Two types of imbalances in the portfolios of banks and thrifts expose them to interest rate risk. One arises because the maturity of bank (and thrift) assets has historically been longer than the maturity of their liabilities. This mismatch arises from the nature of intermediation: In catering to the

---

[6] Remember from Chapter 1 that overnight RPs and MMDAs are in M2.

FIGURE 5–3
History of MMMFs
Compared with
MMDAs

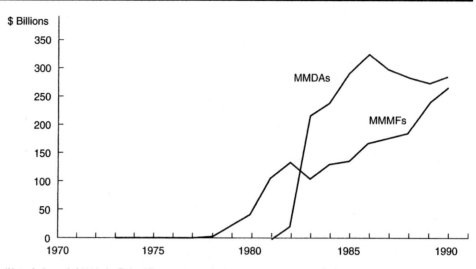

*Note: At the end of 1991, the Federal Reserve stopped publishing separate data on MMDAs. Since then, aggregate data on savings deposits include MMDAs.

Source: *Economic Report of the President, 1991,* Table B-68.

needs of their customers, banks issue short-term deposits to customers who desire liquidity and use the proceeds to fund longer term loans desired by other customers. When the average maturity of a bank's assets is greater than the average maturity of its liabilities, an increase in the interest rate will reduce the bank's net worth, because the value (price) of the bank's assets will fall by more than the value of its liabilities. Similarly, a reduction in the interest rate will increase net worth by increasing the value of assets by more than the value of liabilities.

A second type of imbalance arises from a mismatch between the volume of assets with variable (or adjustable) interest rates and the volume of liabilities with variable rates. A **variable-rate asset or liability** is one whose rate of return moves up or down with market rates of interest. If the volume of variable-rate assets is not equal to the volume of variable-rate liabilities, a gap exists in the portfolio of the depository institution. Suppose that there is a negative gap in the portfolio of a bank; that is, the volume of variable-rate assets is less than the volume of variable-rate liabilities. If interest rates rise, the increase in the revenue from the bank's assets will be less than the increase in the cost of the bank's liabilities. The bank will therefore experience a reduction in profits or an actual increase in losses. On the other hand, a reduction in interest rates will increase the profits of a bank with a negative gap. We can see, then, that when a gap exists in a bank's portfolio, the profits and losses of the bank vary with changes in interest rates. The variability of profits and losses caused by changes in the interest rate is a second kind of interest rate risk.

The interest sensitivity of the cost of funds for large commercial banks started to rise in the 1960s when large banks relied increasingly on liabilities with variable rates, such

FIGURE 5–4
Interest Rate
Volatility

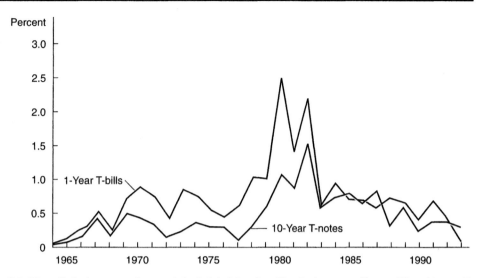

Note: The vertical axis measures the annual standard deviation of monthly rates for one-year Treasury bills and ten-year T-notes. The standard deviation is the average divergence of the interest rate from its mean and, therefore, is a measure of the volatility of rates.
Source: Federal Reserve Board.

as negotiable CDs. Deregulation made the cost of funds for all banks and thrifts vary with market rates of interest. In 1978, less than 5 percent of the financial instruments making up the non-M1 component of M2 paid market-related or market-determined rates of return. By mid-1982, the proportion had risen to 60 percent. Naturally, then, banks sought ways to increase the interest variability of their assets.

The Art of Managing Interest Rate Risk   Figure 5–4 shows that the volatility of short-term and long-term interest rates in the United States started to increase in the early 1970s, then rose drastically after October 1979. The increase in the volatility of interest rates between 1979 and 1982 was the result of the procedures used by the Fed to reduce money growth to reduce inflation.[7] After 1982 the volatility of interest rates decreased to pre-1979 levels.

Interest rate risk rises when the volatility of interest rates increases and falls when the volatility of interest rates decreases. Hence, interest rate risk is usually measured by the volatility in interest rates themselves. As the volatility of interest rates increased in the 1970s, banks intensified their efforts to manage interest rate risk. They shortened the maturity of assets in their portfolios; they increasingly switched from fixed-rate loans to variable-rate loans; they began to **hedge** in the futures and options markets, that is, to take actions to reduce their exposure to losses from interest rate risk; and finally, they adopted the newest technique, interest rate swaps. These techniques were all aimed at

---

[7] Fed procedures are discussed in Chapter 13.

FIGURE 5–5
The Prime Rate
versus the
Commercial
Paper Rate

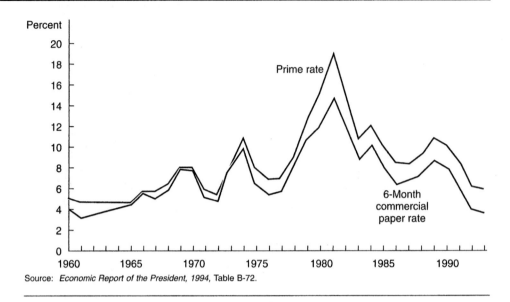

Source: *Economic Report of the President, 1994,* Table B-72.

shifting risk. By shortening the maturity of its assets or switching to variable-rate loans, a bank shifts interest rate risk to its customers, the borrowers. By hedging in the futures and options markets and by using interest rate swaps, a bank shifts that risk to other market participants who are willing to assume it.

From Fixed to Floating Rates on Loans   Early in the 1970s banks introduced floating rates (another term for variable rates) on short-term loans to nonfinancial businesses by tying the prime rate formally or informally to short-term market rates such as the commercial paper rate, as shown in Figure 5–5. In turn, they tied other loan rates to this variable prime rate. In 1981 the comptroller of the currency authorized national banks to offer adjustable-rate mortgages (ARMs). Because repricing of the interest rate on adjustable-rate long-term loans is done periodically, this approach effectively shortens the maturity and increases the interest variability of assets.

Commercial banks had more freedom in choosing the composition of their portfolios, while the thrift institutions were relegated to financing the housing industry and to managing a portfolio that was almost exclusively mortgages at long-term fixed rates. Before 1980, state usury laws set ceilings on the interest rates that banks and thrifts could charge on home mortgages. In 1980, DID&MCA overrode existing state usury laws but gave states the right to pass new usury laws until April 1983. Moreover, depending on state laws and regulations, some state-chartered thrifts were allowed to offer adjustable-rate mortgages and some were not. Even the federally chartered thrifts could not offer adjustable-rate mortgages until 1979 and 1980. The Garn–St Germain Act of 1982 authorized all state-chartered thrifts to offer adjustable-rate mortgages.

This approach of shifting interest rate risk from the lender (the depository institution) to the borrower has been only partly successful. Some consumers still resist variable-rate loans, such as variable-rate mortgages. Fearing that other lenders may compete by offering fixed-rate loans to these dissatisfied potential customers, most banks offer both fixed- and adjustable-rate mortgages. Moreover, for depository institutions variable-rate loans have drawbacks because of the trade-off between interest rate risk and credit risk on these loans. As market rates of interest rise, the rates on these assets also rise, but the quality of the assets falls as more borrowers fail to meet their commitments. Finally, all of the Treasury securities held by depository institutions are fixed-income securities (because the U.S. Treasury issues only fixed-income securities). Hence, banks adopted or even introduced new methods to reduce their interest rate risk. Two techniques are now common. The first is to hedge in the futures and options markets. The second and newest method is to enter into interest rate swaps.

Futures Markets, Options Markets, and Interest Rate Swaps   We begin by describing the essence of hedging in the futures market. Suppose that a bank fears that the interest rate will rise and, hence, that the value of its assets will fall. To protect itself against losses, the bank agrees to deliver an asset in the future at a predetermined price, say, today's price. If the price falls, the bank can buy the asset in the spot market at a lower price and deliver it at the agreed-upon higher price, gaining exactly as much as the value of its portfolio would fall. Thus, the risk disappears. If the bank simply wants the right (option), but not the obligation, to sell and deliver the assets, it participates in the **options market**, which followed the introduction of financial futures in the mid-1970s.

A more recent development is the introduction of **interest rate swaps**, one purpose of which is to transfer interest rate risk. A variety of participants may enter into interest rate swaps. For example, swaps can be arranged between depository institutions, for example, between a bank and a thrift, or between depository institutions and insurance companies, between banks and nonfinancial firms, or even between nonfinancial firms. MarketWatch 5.1 illustrates the essence of interest rate swaps with a story of two neighbors. Here we consider a bank and a pension fund.

The bank's problem is that it has primarily fixed-rate long-term assets (loans) that it finances with variable short-term liabilities (deposits.) To correct this imbalance, it finds another institution such as a pension fund that has fixed liabilities (future pensions) but variable-rate assets. They enter into a swap, with the pension fund agreeing to exchange its future variable returns on its assets with the bank's future fixed receipts on its loans. The swap has, in effect, transformed the pension fund's variable-rate assets into fixed-rate assets and done the opposite for the bank's assets.

This example illustrates asset swaps. In general, an asset swap is an agreement between two parties to exchange the returns (receipts) of each other's assets (of the same principal, of course). The owner of the fixed-rate asset pays the other party the fixed return. The owner of the variable-rate asset gives the other the variable receipts. In effect, then, the asset swap transforms fixed-rate assets into variable-rate assets and vice versa. On the other hand, a liability swap is an agreement in which two parties make each other's interest payments. The party with the fixed-rate liability makes the variable-rate payments, and the party with the variable-rate liability makes the fixed-rate payments. It is as if they swapped liabilities. In fact, they swapped only the payments, not the principal. The example in MarketWatch 5.1 is an illustration of a liability swap.

Market*Watch* 5.1
The Essence of an Interest Rate Swap

Suppose you and your childhood friend decide to buy identical homes, side by side, in a new development. Naturally, the price is identical, say $100,000. Where you differ is in the type of mortgage you obtain. You prefer the certainty of a fixed-rate mortgage; your neighbor opts for an adjustable-rate mortgage. Soon after you sign the contracts and move into your respective houses, you begin envying your neighbor. Expecting that the economy will turn soft, you think that interest rates will fall. You wish that you could undo your mortgage contract with your bank. Surprisingly, your neighbor begins envying you. He believes that interest rates will rise and that he will soon be required to make higher mortgage payments each month. Suddenly, you are struck by an idea that you propose to your neighbor: "Let's swap our interest payments by agreeing to make each other's mortgage payments. We shall, in effect, undo our contracts."

This simple illustration is the essence of an interest rate swap. In this case, because the parties swap payments on liabilities, the agreement is called a *liability swap*. Of course our example is merely an anecdote. In reality, it is unlikely that two parties will have identical liabilities or even know each other. That is why intermediaries enter the picture to bring the parties together—for a fee, of course. The intermediaries are usually commercial banks or investment banks.

Banks are involved in interest rate swaps both as participants (that is, counterparties) and as intermediaries bringing counterparties together for a fee. Often a bank is both—one of the parties and the intermediary receiving the fee. Acting in interest rate swaps as a counterparty or an intermediary is one of the off-balance-sheet activities of modern banks, as we shall soon see.

Increased Competition   In the late 1970s banks had to cope not only with higher interest rate risk but also with more-intense competition. They faced increased domestic competition from nonbanks on the liability side of their balance sheet. Banks also had to deal both with increased domestic competition on the asset side and with increased foreign competition on both sides of their balance sheet.

Securitization   The expansion of the market for commercial paper and the emergence of the market for junk bonds examined in Chapters 3 and 4 are symptomatic of a worldwide trend in finance: a shift from indirect to direct finance, a process that falls under the general heading of securitization. Advances in electronic technology that ease the burden of recordkeeping and changes in regulations that ease the burden of issuing securities have given long-standing bank customers increased access to open markets. As a result, these customers increasingly bypass banks altogether. Banks themselves are making more use of markets by transforming bank loans into marketable securities, another aspect of securitization that occurs at a later stage of the loan process.

Today loan-backed securities are created from mortgages, automobile loans, and even credit card loans. The oldest and most popular loan-backed securities are mortgage-backed securities created from pools of mortgages that are packaged and sold to investors, often with the help of a federal agency such as Ginnie Mae. The percentage of securitized mortgages rose from about 10 percent of the mortgages originated in the 1970s to almost 50 percent of those originated in the 1980s. The original and still most common type of mortgage-backed security is the pass-through security. Investors in pass-through securities own a fraction of the underlying mortgages in the pool. The banks that originated the mortgages collect monthly payments of interest and principal, which they pass on to the ultimate investors. Securitization benefits the economy because it increases marketability of assets and, hence, liquidity.

The Spread of Off-Balance-Sheet Activities   As securitization erodes the traditional role of banks in intermediation, banks are turning to more specialized lines of business. These new endeavors increasingly involve **off-balance-sheet activities** that do not show up either as assets or as liabilities on the balance sheet of banks. Instead, the banks provide services for a fee.

We have already seen one group of off-balance-sheet bank activities: futures, options, and interest rate swaps. Here are some other examples. When a bank securitizes mortgages in its portfolio, the underlying mortgages and the associated interest payments no longer belong to the bank. Instead, the bank receives a fee for originating the mortgages behind mortgage-backed securities and for passing the interest and principal on to the ultimate investors. Banks also receive fees for providing *standby letters of credit* that guarantee the creditworthiness of commercial paper issued by lesser known businesses. Because of their long-standing role in providing bank loans to nonfinancial firms, bankers traditionally evaluate the risk of IOUs issued by these firms. In helping their corporate customers originate open market securities, banks provide investment banking services. As long as the Banking Act of 1933 remains in effect, however, they must stop short of underwriting those securities. In addition to standby letters of credit, banks also make *loan commitments*, which generate fee income. These commitments are agreements to lend customers a specified amount for a stated purpose, usually at an agreed upon interest rate.

Globalization   Deregulation and securitization are global phenomena. More and more countries have changed their laws and regulations to permit variable rates on assets and liabilities of depository institutions while simultaneously expanding their markets for direct finance. For example, Canada, Italy, and the United Kingdom have no interest rate ceilings on deposits. In 1994 Japan completed its program of deposit rate deregulation begun in 1985. Moreover, since 1979, Japan has expanded its markets for government bonds and commercial paper, created futures and options markets, and permitted securitization of mortgages. As a result, financial instruments issued in different countries are more homogeneous than in the past.

Deregulation has also lifted barriers prohibiting foreign entry into the banking business. Today U.S. banks and securities firms have branches throughout the world, and foreign commercial and investment banks operate in the United States. For example, in 1990 the share of U.S. banking assets held by foreign-owned commercial banks was about 22 percent, with about 10 percent held by Japanese banks. This internationalization of banking operations has further increased competition between banks.

Technological Progress and Financial Innovations

Although regulations and regulatory changes spurred financial innovations in bank assets and liabilities, technological progress in computers and electronic communication has also contributed to these innovations. But the role of technology has not been confined to broadening the menu of bank assets and liabilities. Advances in computer and electronic

Market*Watch* 5.2
Will Debit Cards Replace Cash and Checks?

Point-of-sale terminals are computer terminals located in retail stores. They are most often found in supermarkets, fast-food restaurants, and convenience stores, where customers typically pay for their purchases with cash or checks rather than credit cards. Each computer terminal links a retail store to a bank so that customers can automatically pay for purchases from the store. Usually a debit card, which takes the place of a check, activates the payments process. A debit card looks like a credit card, but it serves a different function. While a credit card is a method of deferred payment, a debit card is a method of immediate payment.

The debit card activates the payments process by identifying the cardholder to the computer system. The computer immediately debits (charges) the bank account of the cardholder by the amount of the purchase and credits the bank account of the store by the same amount. In this way, the retailer can conduct its business with fewer money balances—both cash and demand deposits. Furthermore, with less cash on hand, the retailer reduces potential loss from robberies.

The debit card holder, the consumer, also benefits by not having the burden of carrying excess cash. Even consumers who usually pay for their purchases by check avoid the inconvenience of having to handwrite a check and present identification. On the other hand, there are also disadvantages. Typically the check-collection process takes a few days. In the meantime, consumers have use of funds against which they have written checks. Point-of-sale terminals eliminate this temporary source of funds, called *checkbook float.*

Until advances in technology significantly reduce float by speeding up the check-collecting process, debit cards at the point of sale are not likely to replace checks. Today, these cards account for less than 0.3 percent of payments made in the United States.

communication have also revolutionized transaction services and lowered costs in the banking business.

Innovations in Transaction Services   One of the functions of a bank is to provide transaction services that smooth the functioning of the payments system. Traditionally, this function has been performed with the cooperation and supervision of the Fed. Banks provided the demand deposits that the public needed for its transactions, and the Federal Reserve assisted in collecting and clearing the checks. Technological progress has introduced new techniques that speed up the payments process and help households and firms economize on transactions balances.

This chapter has already described the introduction of devices such as cash concentration accounts designed to speed up the payments process for (primarily) large nonfinancial firms. New technology has also led to the introduction of analogous devices at the retail level. These devices help households avoid trips to the bank and shorten their waiting time at the bank; some of these devices also permit households to economize on cash. Equally important, they enable retail businesses to be paid faster and thereby to hold fewer transactions balances.

One example of these devices is *automatic teller machines (ATMs)*, which are located on bank premises and in shopping areas. ATMs enable bank customers to receive routine banking services, such as depositing or withdrawing funds and transferring funds between accounts, 24 hours a day. Point-of-sale terminals, explained in MarketWatch 5.2, are another example. Finally, the widespread ownership of personal computers has naturally led to the next step, home banking, which is still in its infancy. Customers can simply use their personal computers, equipped with the appropriate software, to access their accounts from home and transfer funds or pay bills. In sum, a whole new financial services industry has developed during the 1980s, one that will no doubt continue to expand.

Innovations in the Cost of Banking   Like any other business, the banking business generates revenues and incurs costs. The aim is to maximize profits or, what amounts to the same thing, minimize costs.

A banking firm's costs consist of two components: interest payments on its liabilities and noninterest payments. The bulk of a bank's noninterest costs are variable costs. These costs involve the bank's highly trained work force, who gather information about assets and liabilities, use the information in decision making, and transmit that information and their decisions quickly throughout the world. Technological advances in data gathering, data processing, and transmitting information have enlarged the menu of transaction services and have made them more affordable by reducing their costs. Technological advances have also lowered the cost of intermediation.

The term **cost-reducing financial innovations** refers to technological advances that reduce the cost of banking. In the early 1900s technological advances in manufacturing automobiles lowered the price of automobiles and increased their quantity. Therefore, it should not surprise us that more than a half century later technological advances in banking affected the price and the quantity of banking services. Chapter 7 explains that in the new financial environment, cost-reducing financial innovations enable banks to offer higher deposit rates, ultimately affecting open market interest rates, the quantity of money, and the level of real GDP and prices.

FINANCIAL INNOVATIONS AND THE FEDERAL RESERVE

Having examined the public and banks and their incentives for innovation, we turn to the Federal Reserve. The main concern of the Federal Reserve is the health of the entire economy and of the financial industry. Therefore, the Fed is likely to accept or even to introduce innovations that it believes will contribute to better monetary policy or the smoother functioning of the financial system. As banks began actively to circumvent reserve requirements and the restrictions on deposit rates in the 1970s, the Fed raised objections. In particular, the Fed maintained that the circumvention of the reserve requirement ratio—accomplished either by inventing liabilities not subject to these requirements or by abandoning the Federal Reserve System—was detrimental to the Fed's ability to control the quantity of money.[8] For the same reason, the Fed objected to market-determined deposit rates on demand deposits; originally, the Fed objected to regulated, but positive, deposit rates. The Fed also objected to the infiltration of nonbanks into the field of banking.

---

[8] The 1913 act that created the Federal Reserve System requires national banks to be members of the system. Because state banks are not required to be members of the Federal Reserve System, national banks may leave the system by switching from a national charter to a state charter.

The Fed challenged these intrusions in the courts and in Congress but consistently lost the judicial and the legislative decisions. More important, the fight against deregulation was being lost in the market as market-led innovations aimed at circumventing regulations proliferated. The Fed eventually abandoned its objections and became an active participant in shaping legislation for the new financial environment and in overseeing the deregulation process.

We know that the letters MCA in DID&MCA stand for Monetary Control Act. Key provisions of this part of the act were designed to improve the Fed's ability to control money by introducing "uniform and universal reserve requirements," universal provision and pricing of Fed services, and new data-reporting requirements. As noted earlier, until the 1980 act only member banks were required to hold a percentage of their deposits as reserves. The DID&MCA imposed reserve requirements according to the type of deposit rather than the type of institution. The permissible range for the reserve requirement ratio on transactions deposits is 6 to 14 percent; the range for nonpersonal time deposits is 0 to 9 percent; personal time deposits are not subject to reserve requirements. The 1980 act also opened up the discount window to nonmember banks and thrifts by making any institution subject to reserve requirements on its deposits eligible to borrow at the discount window.

A CRISIS AND A CRUNCH IN THE NEW FINANCIAL ENVIRONMENT

Since the advent of the new financial environment, the U.S. financial system has experienced a crisis in the thrift industry and a crunch in banking. These two shocks to the financial system give a glimpse of the workings of the new financial environment under stress.

The Thrift Crisis of the 1980s

Between 1980 and 1989 more than 1,000 savings and loan associations nationwide were declared insolvent and were forced to either close their doors or merge with healthy institutions. Among the 2,900 that remained, as many as 1,000 were not healthy. Not since the Great Depression have so many financial institutions failed or been on the brink of failure.

In some headline-grabbing cases, the S&L failures arose from outright fraud by management. Fraud, however, was not the major cause of the **thrift crisis**. Many S&Ls suffered losses in the first half of the 1980s because of overexposure to interest rate risk. In search of high returns to offset those losses, some institutions took on excessive credit risk. The structure of federal deposit insurance gave thrifts an incentive to take excessive risks, and deregulation gave them the opportunity to exploit these incentives. Finally, oversight by regulatory agencies was inadequate.

Deregulation of deposit rates permitted thrifts to bid for deposits by varying the deposit rate, and relaxed menu-of-asset restrictions gave them the opportunity to invest in a wider variety of assets. For example, DID&MCA authorized federal savings and loan associations to issue credit cards and to invest up to 20 percent of their assets in consumer loans, commercial paper, and corporate debt securities. In 1982, the Garn–St Germain Act extended the ability of federal S&Ls to diversify by increasing the limit on consumer loans and commercial mortgages to 30 percent and 40 percent of assets, respectively, and by permitting them to invest in commercial loans up to 10 percent of their assets. Subsequent decisions by regulatory bodies, at both the federal and state level, authorized additional lending in riskier assets, such as junk bonds.

The high-risk institutions bid aggressively for deposits by offering high deposit rates and invested the funds in assets with high returns and high risk of default, such as junk bonds and real estate ventures. When real estate prices plunged in some regions of the country and the prices of junk bonds fell, these institutions suffered heavy losses. Deposit insurance, however, insulated depositors from the high-risk strategy of management. Significantly, DID&MCA had increased the amount of deposit insurance coverage from $40,000 per deposit to $100,000 per deposit, so depositors with insured accounts were protected from the risk of default and were not concerned about the safety of their deposits. Thus, deposit insurance distorted or removed the normal incentives for depositors to monitor and control risk taking. Furthermore, thrifts actually had an incentive to take on excessive risk because the premiums on federal deposit insurance were not risk based. Thrifts paid the same flat-rate insurance premium on their deposits, regardless of the quality of their assets. In addition, their sources of funds were almost exclusively deposits. Very little of the net worth, or capital, of the owners was at stake. The less capitalized an institution, the smaller the stakes of its owners and, hence, the greater the incentive for high-risk loans and investments.

In sum, neither the thrifts nor their customers had the proper incentives to control these financial institutions' risk taking. Finally, the regulatory authorities did not close failed institutions in a timely manner. Instead, they allowed them to continue operating in the hope that they would eventually grow out of their difficulties. The result was that many of the unhealthy thrifts built up bigger and bigger losses that only added to the cost of the thrift bailout. Chapter 17 describes how two laws, the Financial Institutions Reform, Recovery and Enforcement Act (FIRREA) of 1989 and the Federal Deposit Insurance Corporation Improvement Act (FDICIA) of 1991, addressed both short-run and long-run maladies of the thrift industry. Now we turn to the credit crunch of the 1990s, which, in part, was an outgrowth of the thrift crisis.

The Credit Crunch of the 1990s

Credit crunch is the term used when banks are less willing and able to lend to creditworthy customers. In the old financial environment, credit crunches were usually associated with high and rising market rates of interest, which led to an outflow of funds from depository institutions constrained by Regulation Q from raising deposit rates. In response, deposit-strapped banks tightened their lending standards. By contrast, in the early 1990s, the first credit crunch of the new financial environment occurred when market rates of interest and bank deposit rates were falling.

Economists attribute this credit crunch to two broad factors: (1) tighter capital requirements on banks at a time when bank capital was falling; and (2) tighter regulatory standards. A bank's capital is its net worth. The higher a bank's capital-asset ratio, that is, the higher its capital relative to its assets, the healthier the bank. A healthy bank is less likely to fail when faced with adverse economic conditions. For this reason, bank regulators set minimum capital-asset ratios for banks.

In 1988 representatives of 12 industrial nations met in Basle, Switzerland, and agreed to implement uniform capital requirements by 1992. For the United States, the *Basle Agreement* meant higher capital requirements. At the time these new requirements were being phased in, increased losses on loans were reducing banks' capital. The loan losses stemmed from a weaker economy and deteriorating real estate and junk bond markets. Because of the Basle agreement and the loan losses, U.S. banks had to increase their capital-asset ratios.

Banks had two choices: They either could raise more capital by issuing stocks or they could reduce their assets by cutting back on loans. Because banks had difficulty raising capital in the stock market, they had to shed some of their assets. They also had to deal with tougher scrutiny by bank regulators eager to avoid a thrift-type debacle in the banking industry. Against this background, banks became less willing and able to lend, even to long-standing, creditworthy customers in some cases. Therefore, they bid less aggressively for deposits. Depositors, seeking higher rates, shifted their funds from bank deposits, such as small time deposits, to competing financial instruments, especially bond and stock mutual funds. Large firms that can borrow in the open market had access to these funds. Small firms without access to the open market bore the brunt of the tighter credit conditions, or credit crunch. Chapter 18 examines the credit crunch more extensively by looking at the behavior of banks and bank regulators in the context of a profit-maximizing banking firm. Our aim here has been to point out that while the new financial environment has changed the character of credit crunches, it has not eliminated them.

LOOKING AHEAD

The new financial environment is not static. It will continue to evolve as new laws to reform the banking system are enacted and as new technology enhances the choices of the public and depository institutions. Part 5 examines financial institutions and their behavior in more detail. There we consider reforms that would allow banks to enter new lines of business, permit them to set up branches nationwide without restrictions, consolidate regulatory agencies, and more. No matter how reform proceeds in these and other areas, the key characteristic of the new financial environment is here to stay: market-determined deposit rates. Therefore, a theory of the determination of the deposit rate is an essential ingredient of a contemporary approach to money, banking, and financial markets. Part 3 develops this theory.

SUMMARY

- In the current financial environment the assets and liabilities in the balance sheets of financial institutions pay market-determined rates of return. Moreover, these institutions are more homogeneous than they were in the past. Under the old financial environment regulators placed ceilings on deposit rates and on some lending rates and imposed more severe restrictions on the portfolios of depository institutions, especially thrifts.

- The old financial environment began unraveling with the high and rising inflation rates and interest rates of the late 1970s. As the spread between market rates of interest and regulated deposit rates rose, the participants (especially depository institutions) explored new avenues for attracting and using funds.

- A multitude of financial innovations brought about the new financial environment. These novelties in the financial system came from changes in laws, regulations, and institutional arrangements and from changes in the state of financial technology.

- Two new banking acts—the Depository Institutions Deregulation and Monetary Control Act of 1980 and the Garn–St Germain Act of 1982—ushered in the regulatory climate for the new financial environment.

- The incentives for financial innovation vary according to the goals of the participant. Households and nonfinancial firms embrace financial innovations that increase their utility or profit. Depository institutions are usually the initiators of financial innovations. Their criterion also is profit maximization. The Federal Reserve is likely to accept or even to introduce an innovation that contributes to better monetary policy or more-effective regulation of depository institutions.

· Financial innovations in cash management practices enable nonfinancial firms and households to pare down their transaction balances and to invest the released funds in assets with higher rates of return.

· In the 1970s banks introduced novelties to circumvent the interest rate ceilings imposed on their borrowing activities. They invented substitutes for demand deposits and for traditional savings and time deposits. These innovations made the restrictions on bank liabilities less effective and convinced regulators to lift those restrictions in the 1980s.

· Faced with an increase in interest rate risk in the 1970s, banks shifted that risk to borrowers by shortening the maturity of their assets to better match that of their liabilities and by introducing floating-rate loans. They also used futures contracts, options contracts, and interest rate swaps to shift risk to others willing to assume it.

· Technological progress in gathering, processing, and transmitting information was essential for the development of many of the financial innovations in the assets and liabilities of financial institutions. Technological progress also gave rise to innovations in transaction services and to innovations in the cost of intermediation itself.

· In the late 1980s, hundreds of savings and loan associations failed. The thrift crisis was a result of (1) overexposure to interest rate risk, (2) deregulation, (3) deposit insurance practices, and (4) lax supervision by regulators.

· The first credit crunch of the new financial environment occurred in the early 1990s against the background of falling real estate prices and more intense scrutiny by bank regulators in the wake of the thrift crisis. Banks became less willing to lend and therefore bid less aggressively for deposits.

KEY TERMS AND CONCEPTS

old financial environment (OFE)

new financial environment (NFE)

financial innovations

Banking Act of 1933, or Glass-Steagall Act

Regulation Q

Banking Act of 1935

disintermediation

Depository Institutions Deregulation and Monetary Control Act of 1980 (DID&MCA)

Garn–St Germain Depository Institutions Act of 1982

opportunity cost of money

innovations in cash management practices

cash concentration system

Fedwire

lockboxes

repurchase agreements (RPs)

money market mutual funds (MMMFs)

cash management account (CMA)

other checkable deposits

Eurodollar deposits

money market deposit account (MMDA)

variable-rate asset or liability

hedge

options market

interest rate swap

off-balance-sheet activities

cost-reducing financial innovations

thrift crisis

credit crunch

QUESTIONS AND PROBLEMS

1. Use the concept of the opportunity cost of money to explain how inflation contributed to the demise of the old financial environment.

2. Why did banks offer free services in the old financial environment? What is the alternative to free services in the new financial environment? As a bank customer, which do you prefer? Why?

3. Why would you have both a credit card and a debit card? Under which circumstances are you most likely to use each one?

4. What financial innovations were introduced to circumvent the prohibition of paying interest on demand deposits?

5. What financial innovations were introduced to circumvent the restriction imposed by Regulation Q ceilings?

6. Some financial innovations had their origin in the reaction of banks to the reserve requirement ratio. Explain this reaction.

7. What are money market deposit accounts (MMDAs)? When and why were they introduced?

The Wall Street Journal

8. The graph in column two of "Yields for Consumers" from March through June 1993 appeared in *The Wall Street Journal* on July 2, 1993. What feature of MMDAs can explain why their yield was less than that of money market mutual funds?

9. A mismatch in the maturities of bank assets and bank liabilities is inherent in banking. Explain how banks have reacted to the consequent risk.

10. Explain the technological advances in the provision of transaction services that played a role in the emergence of the new financial environment.

11. Would the thrift crisis have occurred if deposit rates had not been deregulated?

Yields for Consumers

Averages compounded yields in percent: money market funds' yield is 7-day average; CD yields are for deposits of $50,000 or less at major banks.

Money Market Funds **2.67%**

3-Month Bank CDs **2.47%**

Bank Money Mkt. Accounts **2.35%**

Sources: Banxquote Money Markets; Money Fund Report

12. "High and rising interest rates did not play a role in the credit crunch in banking in the early 1990s." True, false, or uncertain? Explain.

SUGGESTED READINGS

Barth, James R. *The Great Savings and Loan Debacle*. Washington, D.C.: American Enterprise Institute, 1991.

> An analysis of the thrift crisis by a former chief economist of the Federal Home Loan Bank Board and the Office of Thrift Supervision.

Broaddus, Alfred. "Financial Innovation in the United States—Background, Current Status, and Prospects." *Economic Review* (Federal Reserve Bank of Richmond), January/February 1985, 2–21.

> An overview of the transition from the old to the new financial environment.

Burns, Arthur F. *The Ongoing Revolution in American Banking*. Washington, D.C.: American Enterprise Institute, 1987.

> A concise and authoritative examination of changes in the American banking system by a former chairman of the Federal Reserve Board.

Cantor, Richard, and John Wenninger. "Perspective on the Credit Slowdown." *Quarterly Review* (Federal Reserve Bank of New York) 18, no. 1 (Spring 1993): 3–36.

> Analyzes the credit crunch of the 1990s and places it in historical perspective.

Fraser, Donald R., and Peter S. Rose, eds. *Financial Institutions and Markets in a Changing World*. 3rd ed. Plano, Tex.: Business Publications, 1987, Part Seven, "Financial Innovations."

> A collection of articles on financial innovations and deregulation in the United States and foreign countries; interest rate swaps; futures and options; and electronic banking.

Hadjimichalakis, Michael G. *Monetary Policy and Modern Money Markets* Lexington, Mass.: D. C. Heath, 1982, Chapter 2, "The New Financial Environment," pp. 17–42

> An examination of the new financial environment as it was unfolding.

Tobin, James. "Deposit Insurance Must Go." *The Wall Street Journal*," November 22, 1989, A12.

> An op-ed piece on the causes of the thrift crisis and recommendations for reform.

PART 3

MONEY, INTEREST RATES, AND PRICES

6   The Public's Portfolio Choice: *The Laws of Asset Demand*

7   Deposit Rate Deregulation and Money Demand

8   The Basics of the Money Supply

9   Two Tales of Determining the Interest Rate

10 A Framework for the Economy: *The Real and the Financial Sectors*

Part 3 applies the two-pillar framework to explain how money, interest rates, prices, and output are determined and why they change. Chapters 6, 7, and 8 examine the financial and monetary decisions of the participants. Chapter 9 examines the interaction of the participants in financial markets, and Chapter 10 combines the financial markets with the markets for foreign exchange, goods and services, and factors of production.

THE PUBLIC'S PORTFOLIO CHOICE

The Laws of Asset Demand

CHAPTER PREVIEW

Suppose that because of your interest in economics and finance, you obtain an internship with a local firm of financial advisers. Your first assignment is to acquaint yourself with the portfolio of Jessica Nichols, one of the firm's clients. Reading her file, you notice that in August last year she held a greater percentage of her net worth in money and a lower percentage in stocks and bonds than she did in July. What may be the reason for this difference?

One possibility is that the rates of return on stocks and bonds fell, making them less desirable than money. A second possibility is that in August the stock and bond markets became more volatile, with prices moving wildly up and down. Concerned about the risk of capital losses, Jessica put more of her net worth in money. A third possibility is that a change in her circumstances increased her need for liquidity. She may have been planning to take a trip around the world, buy a house, or enroll in an executive education program in September, so she needed to convert stocks and bonds into money.

This chapter brings the balance sheet of the public to life by systematically examining the factors that affect the public's portfolio choice. Therefore, it belongs in the first pillar of economics: the rational, purposeful behavior of participants. The participants here are households and firms, or, collectively, the public.

The chapter begins by examining the relation between risk and return and explaining the benefits of not putting all your eggs in one basket, that is, the benefits of diversifying. Then it identifies all the factors that affect portfolio choice and groups them into five categories: own rate of return, rate of return on competing assets, income, wealth, and a collective variable that includes other factors such as risk, liquidity, and the circumstances and attitudes of the public.

Next, the chapter examines how a change in any of these factors affects the composition or size of the portfolio. These relationships are called the *laws of asset demand*. Knowledge of these laws will help you make your own investment decisions and understand and analyze those of others.

THE BALANCE SHEET EQUATION

Since the public is a collective participant consisting of households and nonfinancial firms, we must combine their balance sheets. Tables 6–1 and 6–2 reproduce the balance sheets of households and firms examined in Chapter 4. We derive the balance sheet of the public shown in Table 6–3 by adding identical items on each side of the balance sheets in Tables 6–1 and 6–2. Most of the items on these balance sheets are identical. On the asset side, the quantity of currency held by the public is the sum of currency held by households and firms; similarly, the amount of bank deposits, U.S. Treasury securities, foreign assets, and real assets held by the public is the sum of the amounts held by households

TABLE 6–1
Balance Sheet of Households

Assets	Liabilities plus Net Worth
Currency	Bank loans
Bank deposits	
Open market debt of firms	
U.S. Treasury securities	
Foreign assets	
Corporate stock (Equity in business)	
Real assets	**Net Worth**

TABLE 6–2
Balance Sheet of Nonfinancial Firms

Assets	Liabilities plus Net Worth
Currency	Open market debt
Bank deposits	Bank loans
U.S. Treasury securities	Corporate stock
Foreign assets	Accumulated retained profits
Real assets	

Note: Corporate stock plus Accumulated retained profits = **Net Worth**

TABLE 6–3
Balance Sheet of
the Public

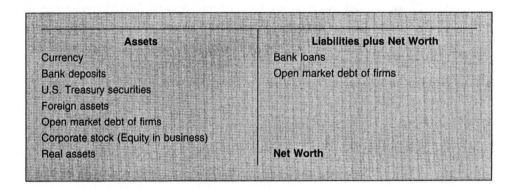

Assets	Liabilities plus Net Worth
Currency	Bank loans
Bank deposits	Open market debt of firms
U.S. Treasury securities	
Foreign assets	
Open market debt of firms	
Corporate stock (Equity in business)	
Real assets	**Net Worth**

and firms. On the liability plus net worth side, we add bank loans of households and firms and, separately, we add net worth. Firms issue open market debt, which appears as a liability in their balance sheet; it also appears as an asset in the balance sheet of the public because households hold some of this debt.

The public's balance sheet, like that of any participant, says that the sector's net worth, augmented by borrowing, is held in a variety of assets. It is an accounting identity that can be written in equation form:

$$\text{Net worth} + \text{Bank loans} + \text{Open market debt of firms} =$$
$$\text{Currency} + \text{Bank deposits} + \text{U.S. Treasury securities} + \text{Foreign assets} + \qquad (6\text{–}1)$$
$$\text{Open market debt of firms} + \text{Corporate stock} + \text{Real assets}$$

Table 6–3 and Equation 6–1 display all the assets and liabilities of the public. However, we do not always need this much detail. To simplify, we can aggregate similar assets and liabilities. We begin the process of simplifying on the asset side of the public's balance sheet by adding U.S. Treasury securities and open market debt of firms to find debt securities held by the public. Similarly, on the liability side, adding bank loans and open market debt of firms gives us debt securities issued by the public. If we make these substitutions in Equation 6–1 and rearrange terms, the balance sheet equation of the public becomes:

$$\text{Net worth of the public} = (\text{Currency} + \text{Deposits}) + (\text{Debt securities held}$$
$$- \text{Debt securities issued}) + \text{Corporate stock} + \text{Foreign assets} + \text{Real assets} \qquad (6\text{–}2)$$

The sum of currency plus deposits equals the quantity of money held by the public. The difference between debt securities held by the public and debt securities issued by the public is net debt securities held by the public. We can further simplify the balance sheet by incorporating foreign assets into net debt securities, corporate stock, and real assets, that is, by assuming that these items include foreign as well as domestic assets. Making these substitutions in Equation 6–2, we get:

$$\text{Net worth} = \text{Money} + \text{Net debt securities} + \text{Corporate stock} + \text{Real assets} \qquad (6\text{–}3)$$

According to Equation 6–3, the public holds its net worth, or wealth, in four assets: money, debt securities, equity securities (that is, corporate stock), and real assets. By aggregating net debt securities and equity securities and calling them simply *securities*, we can reduce the balance sheet equation to three assets, as shown in Equation 6–4:

$$\text{Net worth} = \text{Money} + \text{Securities} + \text{Real assets} \tag{6–4}$$

All the balance sheet equations highlight a key principle: The public holds several assets—that is, it diversifies its portfolio. Given that these assets earn different rates of return, it is natural to ask why the public is willing to hold an asset that has a lower rate of return than another. To answer this question we must go beyond the balance sheet equations and appeal to theory. First, however, let's insert some numbers into these balance sheets to test your understanding.

TRY IT OUT 6.1

The following are hypothetical balance sheets for households and firms:

Households

Assets		Liabilities plus Net Worth	
Currency	100	Bank loans	400
Bank deposits	200	**Net Worth**	1,100
Open market debt of firms	200		
U.S. Treasury securities	350		
Corporate stock (Equity in business)	200		
Real assets	450		
Total	**1,500**		**1,500**

Firms

Assets		Liabilities plus Net Worth	
Currency	50	Open market debt of firms	200
Bank deposits	150	Bank loans	100
U.S. Treasury securities	250	**Net Worth**	350
Real assets	200		
Total	**650**		**650**

1. Illustrate the balance sheet of the public in numbers by combining the balance sheets of households and firms.
2. Illustrate balance sheet Equation 6–1 using the numbers in these tables.
3. Illustrate balance sheet Equation 6–4 in numbers by aggregating the appropriate assets and liabilities.

ASSET CHOICE: RISK AND RATE OF RETURN

The balance sheet equations are accounting identities that merely list the actual mix of assets in which the public keeps its wealth. The **theory of asset choice,** or **portfolio choice**, goes a step farther by explaining the factors that affect how the public decides to allocate its wealth among those assets.

SectorWatch 6–1
Explaining Portfolio Choice to the Press

In awarding the Nobel Prize in economics to James Tobin in 1981, the Nobel committee cited his work on portfolio theory as one of his contributions to economics. In the words of the committee, this work provided "a basis for understanding how subjects actually behave when they acquire different assets and incur debts." In the following excerpt from an autobiographical essay, Tobin recounts his attempt to explain diversification to the press:

When my prize was announced in Stockholm in 1981, the first reports that reached this country mentioned portfolio theory. This caught the interest of the reporters who faced me at a hastily arranged press conference at Yale. They wanted to know what it was, so I did my best to explain it in lay language, after which they said, "Oh no, please explain it in lay language." That's when I referred to the benefits of diversification: "You know, don't put all your eggs in one basket" (emphasis added). And that is why headlines throughout the world said, "Yale economist wins Nobel for 'Don't put all your eggs . . . ,' " and why a friend of mine sent me a cartoon he had clipped, which followed that headline with a sketch of next year's winner in medicine explaining how his award was for "An apple a day keeps the doctor away."

Source: William Breit and Roger W. Spencer, eds., Lives of the Laureates: Seven Nobel Economists (Cambridge, Mass.: The MIT Press, 1986), 127.

The most prominent characteristic of an asset is its rate of return. It is natural to expect that the higher an asset's rate of return, the more funds the asset will attract. If it were not for the other characteristics of assets, such as their level of risk, and for each investor's circumstances and attitudes, there would be only a single, very simple investment rule: Always choose only one asset, the one with the highest rate of return. Other factors, however, may lead an investor to diversify his or her portfolio by holding two or more assets with different rates of return.

The public chooses the most preferred, or optimal, combination of assets by trying to maximize the rate of return on its portfolio. But assets are not safe, making returns uncertain. Hence, investing is risky. The public, therefore, tries to maximize the expected return of its portfolio of assets consistent with its tolerance of risk. In other words, the public tries to minimize risk for each targeted rate of return.

On average, investors are **risk averse**, which means they dislike losses more than they like gains. By losses, we mean a return lower than expected (the average), and by gains a return higher than expected (the average). Risk-averse investors reduce risk by **diversifying**, that is, by holding several assets or groups of assets, each with a different possibility of loss. It is easy to identify the reason why holding assets with different possibilities of gains or losses reduces risk: The ups and downs of dissimilar assets do not coincide. Therefore, in any given period, assets that do well (above average) offset those that do poorly (below average), thereby moderating the swings in the overall return to the portfolio. The risk of the portfolio is the variability of its overall rate of return. Thus, holding dissimilar assets reduces risk. This would not be the case if the swings coincided, that is, if the portfolio's assets were similar. For an even more nontechnical explanation of diversification, see SectorWatch 6–1.

The risk that can be reduced through diversification is called **diversifiable risk**, illustrated by the following example from the computer industry. Between 1987 and 1992 IBM stock fell by more than 60 percent as corporate customers switched from buying all-purpose mainframe computers and built-in software—IBM's primary business—to buying desktop computers and specialized software. Companies such as Apple, Compaq, Microsoft, and Sun Microsystems were the beneficiaries of this switch in customer tastes. A diversified portfolio, one that included shares of Apple, Compaq, Microsoft, and Sun Microsystems in addition to shares of the "blue-chip" IBM, was less vulnerable to the misfortunes of IBM.

Not all risk, however, is diversifiable. What is left of total risk after diversification is called **nondiversifiable risk**. Suppose, for example, that you hold a portfolio of all traded securities, that is, an index of the entire U.S. stock market. Your portfolio of U.S. stock is perfectly diversified. Yet the risk has not entirely disappeared. If, for example, the Fed embarks on a restrictive monetary policy, raising interest rates, the entire market will suffer, and so will your portfolio. Similarly, if the business cycle enters a downward phase, profits fall. Again, the entire market, and your portfolio, will suffer.

Nondiversifiable risk within a country may be reduced by expanding the reach of a portfolio. For example, returns in the United States may be low because the U.S. economy is in a slump, while returns in Asian countries such as Thailand, Hong Kong, Malaysia, and Indonesia are high because their economies are booming. In addition to differences in economic conditions, foreign companies may specialize in different products than U.S. companies. Adding foreign stocks to a portfolio of U.S. stocks further diversifies a portfolio.

Diversification within a country and across countries cannot eliminate risk entirely. By assuming that investors choose an optimal portfolio, we also assume that the only remaining risk is nondiversifiable risk, for which they must be compensated. The nature of this compensation can be expressed in three ways:

1. The higher the nondiversifiable risk, the greater the rate of return investors demand.
2. *For a given rate of return*, the higher the nondiversifiable risk, the lower the demand for an asset.
3. *For the same nondiversifiable risk*, the public prefers the asset(s) to generate a higher rate of return.

Thus, the demand for an asset is positively related to its own rate of return and negatively to its risk. Of course, when we refer to an increase or decrease in an asset's rate of return, we mean an increase or decrease *relative to the return of other assets*. Similarly, when we refer to an increase or decrease in an asset's risk, we mean an increase or decrease *relative to the risk of other assets*.

FACTORS AFFECTING ASSET DEMAND

Having examined how relative returns and relative risk affect asset choice, we are now ready to explain systematically the factors that affect asset demand.[1] Table 6–4 groups these factors into two broad categories: characteristics of assets and circumstances of the investor.

---

[1] We have benefited from James Tobin's unpublished manuscript on financial markets, Chapter II, "Property of Assets," and Chapter III, "Theory of Portfolio Selection," Yale University, 1959

The first column of the table lists the five characteristics of assets (securities) introduced in Chapter 3. In addition to the relative rate of return and relative risk are the asset's maturity, liquidity, and marketability. These characteristics are expressed in relative terms, which means they are compared with the same characteristic of competing assets. The four factors in the second column—current income, uncertainty of future income, wealth, and the state of cash management technology—are **circumstances of the investor**, which are factors constraining an investor's behavior.

Table 6–5 groups the factors of Table 6–4 in a way that helps explain the laws of demand. In addition to changing the order of the factors, we unbundle the concept of "relative rate of return" into two separate factors, the "own rate of return" and the "rate of return on competing assets," and list them as factors 1 and 2. For example, when we look at debt securities, the nominal interest rate paid on a debt security is the "own rate." Deposits compete with debt securities for a place in the portfolio of the public, so in this case the deposit rate is an example of the rate of return on a competing asset.

The Laws of Asset Demand

Let us now examine how each of the factors in Table 6–5 affects asset demand, with an eye toward eventually concentrating on money demand. A **law of asset demand** describes how the demand for an asset changes when one of the factors affecting asset demand changes (in a particular direction) *while all the other factors remain unchanged,*

TABLE 6–4
Factors Affecting Asset Demand:
The General Categories

Characteristics of Assets	Circumstances of the Investor
Relative rate of return	Current income
Relative risk	Uncertainty of future income
Relative maturity	Wealth
Relative marketability	State of cash management technology
Relative liquidity	

TABLE 6–5
Detailed List of Factors Affecting Asset Demand

1. Own rate of return
2. Rate of return on competing assets
3. Current income (current expenditures)
4. Wealth (of investors)
5. Cash management technology
6. (Degree of) uncertainty of future income
7. Relative risk of asset
8. Relative maturity of asset
9. Relative marketability of asset
10. Relative liquidity of asset

or, in standard economic terminology, *other things equal.* Working with ten factors is cumbersome, because there would be ten laws of asset demand. The usual practice is to keep the own rate of return, the rate(s) of return on competing assets, income, and wealth distinct because of their importance in the economy. These are the first four factors in Table 6–5. To keep the analysis simple, however, we lump the remaining factors (5 through 10) together into a single **collective factor** (variable), which we denote by the symbol script $\mathcal{C}$. These six factors form a group because a change in any one of them changes the collective factor and, in turn, the demand for assets.

This technique enables us to reduce the list of factors that influence the demand for assets to five: (1) the asset's own rate of return, (2) the rate of return on competing assets, (3) income, (4) wealth, and (5) the collective factor, $\mathcal{C}$. Corresponding to these factors are five laws of asset demand, to which we now turn.

Own Rate of Return The average individual stores wealth in an asset primarily for the return it earns. If all other factors remain the same, an individual wants to hold more of an asset whose rate of return has risen. Other things equal, the demand for an asset rises when its own rate of return rises and falls when its own rate falls. Note that the rate of return on competing assets is one of the other factors held constant. The positive relation between the demand for an asset and its own rate of return is the first law of asset demand, listed in the first row of Table 6–6.

As an example of the first law, the public will want to hold more debt securities when the rate of return (interest rate) on debt securities rises, other things equal.[2] The assumption that other things remain equal means that the level of wealth does not change. Where then do the funds to buy debt securities come from? Factor 2 and the corresponding second law of asset demand provide the answer.

Rate of Return on Competing Assets An increase in the rate of return on one asset makes competing assets less desirable, inducing investors to withdraw funds from those competing assets. These funds are directed toward the asset whose rate has risen. The negative relation between the demand for an asset and the rate of return on another asset is the second law of asset demand. The second law states that other things equal, the demand for an asset falls when the rate of return on a competing asset rises, and rises when the rate of return on a competing asset falls. This relation is listed in the second row of Table 6–6.

Current Expenditures (Current Income) To carry out their transactions, individuals must have readily available funds that are accepted as a means of payment. The greater an individual's intended expenditures, the greater the funds that must be set aside. On average, expenditures are strongly correlated with income. Therefore, the higher the level of current income, the higher the demand for liquid funds, that is, the higher the demand for money. In this analysis we are examining the effect of an increase in expendi-

---

[2] Net demand for securities rises because the public increases its demand for securities and decreases its supply (i.e., the amount issued by firms) when the rate on securities rises.

TABLE 6–6
The Five Laws of
Asset Demand

1. Own Rate of Return	Other things equal, the demand for an asset rises when its own rate of return rises and falls when its rate falls.
2. Return on Competing Assets	Other things equal, the demand for an asset falls when the rate on a competing asset rises and rises when the rate of return on a competing asset falls.
3. National Income	Other things equal, an increase in national income increases the demand for money and reduces the demand for securities and real assets together; a decrease in national income reduces the demand for money and increases the demand for securities and real assets together.
4. Wealth	Other things equal, an increase in wealth increases the demand for all assets; a decrease in wealth reduces the demand for all assets.
5. The Rest (Collective Factor)	Other things equal, the demand for money rises and the demand for securities and real assets together falls if ℓ rises; analogously, the demand for money falls and the demand for securities and real assets rises when ℓ falls. ℓ falls if:
	a. Improvements in cash management technology are introduced.
	b. The uncertainty of future income is reduced.
	c. The relative risk of securities and real assets falls.
	d. The relative maturity of securities falls.
	e. The relative marketability of securities and real assets rises.
	f. The relative liquidity of securities and real assets rises.
	ℓ rises when any of these variables move in the opposite direction.

tures (income) on the demand for money, *assuming all the other factors, including wealth, remain the same.* The funds that are directed toward money must come from liquidating other assets. Therefore, other things equal, an increase in economywide income, called *national income,* increases the demand for money and *reduces* the demand for other securities and real assets. This result is recorded as the third law of asset demand in Table 6–6.

Wealth   The major determinant of asset demand is the investor's wealth. The greater the level of wealth, the greater the size of the investor's portfolio and, hence, the greater the demand for each item in the portfolio. The relation between wealth and asset demand is the fourth law of asset demand in Table 6–6. Of course, when wealth increases by a certain amount, the total increase in the demand for assets must equal that amount.

A simple rule of thumb financial advisers use in the real world of investments is that investors within a given wealth bracket should allocate their wealth, and any increase in wealth, in a manner that keeps constant the fraction of wealth invested in each asset. An adviser may recommend, for example, that if the net worth of a client is in the $500,000 to $1 million bracket, it should be allocated as follows: 5 percent in currency and demand deposits, 10 percent in short-term debt securities, 20 percent in long-term debt securities, 25 percent in equity securities, and the remaining 40 percent in real estate—typically the client's own residence. To maintain this allocation, the investor should also allocate any increase in wealth to these assets by the same percentages. Although we shall not restrict our analysis to this simple case, it is reassuring to know that rules of thumb commonly used by practitioners are consistent with our analysis.

The Collective Factor　　The fifth law of asset demand as shown in Table 6–6 states that an increase in the collective variable will increase the demand for money (deposits) and reduce the demand for securities and real assets together, and a decrease in the collective factor will reduce the demand for money and increase the demand for securities and real assets. Two of the determinants of $\mathcal{C}$, the state of cash management technology and the uncertainty of future income, affect money demand directly. The other components of the collective variable exert their influence through the demand for securities and real assets. To develop the fifth law of demand, we must look at the components of the collective variable.

Cash Management Technology　　The public must hold some wealth in the form of money to be used at the time of a transaction. The form in which funds are held just prior to a transaction, however, depends on the state of cash management technology. As Chapter 5 noted, advancements in computer technology in the past two decades have enabled financial institutions to offer their customers a variety of cash management techniques. The essence of these techniques is to transfer funds from (higher) interest-paying securities to checking accounts from which payments can be made. In other words, the more advanced a nation's cash management technology, the fewer the funds the public must hold in the form of money for prolonged periods.

According to the rule for the collective factor, $\mathcal{C}$, any item that reduces money demand is represented by a decrease in $\mathcal{C}$. Improvements in cash management technology reduce money demand. Therefore, they result in a decrease in $\mathcal{C}$. Several studies of money demand by economists at the Fed and in academia have shown that U.S. money demand fell in the second half of the 1970s because of new cash management techniques in the United States.[3] These improvements enable the public to hold less of its wealth in money (deposits) and to use the released funds to demand more securities and real assets.

Degree of Uncertainty of Future Income (Employment)　　For most individuals, wages from employment are the main source of income. In periods of increasing unemployment, wage earners become less certain that they will hold on to their jobs. When the uncertainty of employment increases, individuals increase their demand for liquid assets, such as money, and decrease their demand for less-liquid assets, such as long-term debt securities or equity securities. In other words, they cash in some of the securities they hold to support themselves if the need arises.

---

[3] Chapter 21 examines these empirical studies.

In 1982 the U.S. economy experienced the worst downturn since the Great Depression, and the public's demand for money was greater than could be explained by changes in rates of return, current income, and wealth. Economists at the Fed attributed the higher demand for money to an increase in the uncertainty of income caused by the recession. An increase in the uncertainty of future (employment and) income can be seen as an increase in the collective factor, $\mathcal{C}$. This increase in the collective variable increases the demand for money and reduces the demand for securities and real assets.

Relative Risk of the Asset   We have already seen that the riskiness of assets combined with the average investor's risk aversion is a major reason investors diversify. When investors perceive that the riskiness of an asset has increased, they move funds away from this asset toward other assets, which are now relatively less risky. In a system with money, securities, and real assets, an increase in the risk of securities and real assets diverts funds toward money, referred to as a *flight to quality.* For example, in the aftermath of Black Monday (October 19, 1987), when the stock market lost about 20 percent of its value in one day, there was a flight to money by asset holders. Applying our rule for the collective factor, an increase in the relative risk of securities is an increase in $\mathcal{C}$, and a decrease in the relative risk of securities is a decrease in $\mathcal{C}$.

Relative Maturity of the Asset   For many investors, securities with shorter maturities are more desirable than those with longer maturities. The appetite for securities with shorter maturities stems from the greater risk of capital loss that securities with longer maturities have. Furthermore, securities with relatively short maturities are attractive because they are more liquid. The shorter the maturity of an asset, the greater its liquidity and, hence, the greater its appeal to the average investor. Thus, the shorter the maturity of securities (a reduction in $\mathcal{C}$), the greater the demand for them and the smaller the demand for money (assuming no change in the demand for real assets).

Relative Marketability of the Asset   Investors want an asset that can be sold when the need or occasion arises. However, there are various degrees of marketability. For example, compared with bonds, a house is not very marketable. Most bonds can be sold with a phone call to a broker, but houses are not as homogeneous as bonds, the housing market is geographically fragmented, and the total transaction costs are far greater than those of the bond market. This difference in relative marketability of assets shows up as a difference in their relative liquidity. As Chapter 3 explained, the more marketable an asset, the more liquid and, other things equal, the more desirable the asset.

Many of the financial innovations in the past two decades have created new asset markets or transformed nonmarketable assets into marketable ones. The securitization of bank loans discussed in Chapter 5 is an example of the latter. The development of a market for an asset increases the demand for that asset, other things equal. Therefore, an increase in the marketability of securities reduces $\mathcal{C}$, reduces money demand, and increases the demand for securities and real assets.

Relative Liquidity of the Asset   As Chapter 3 discussed, the liquidity of an asset refers to the ease, speed, and cost of converting the asset to cash. Liquidity depends on the asset's other properties, namely, its marketability, maturity, and risk. Therefore, we do not have to list liquidity separately as a determinant of asset demand. Liquidity is such an important property, however, that we want to highlight its effect on asset demand: The greater the relative liquidity of an asset, the greater its demand, other things equal. Conversely, the less liquid the asset, the smaller its demand. In terms of the simple model of money, securities, and real assets, an increase in the liquidity of securities and real assets can be seen as a fall in the collective variable.

LOOKING AHEAD

In this chapter we have learned about the importance of diversification and about the determinants of the components of an optimal portfolio. This knowledge will guide us as we progress through the book, with an immediate payoff in the next chapter.

SUMMARY

- The public is a collective participant that consists of households and firms. The public diversifies its portfolio, which means that it holds wealth in several assets with different possibilities of loss.

- We can group the public's assets into three categories: (1) money, consisting of currency plus deposits; (2) securities; and (3) tangible, or real, assets.

- The major reason for asset diversification is to minimize the risk of loss. The public as a whole is risk averse. To reduce its exposure to risk, the public diversifies its portfolio.

- Not all risk is diversifiable. The public must be compensated for nondiversifiable risk, which is endemic to the market.

- The higher the nondiversifiable risk, the greater the rate of return the public requires from an asset. This also suggests that for a given risk, the higher the rate of return, the higher the public's demand for an asset. By "higher return" we mean higher relative to the return on a competing asset, and by "higher risk" we mean higher relative to the risk of a competing asset.

- In general, the demand for assets by the public depends on the characteristics of assets and the circumstances of the investors (public). Relative return and relative risk are two characteristics. The others are relative maturity, relative marketability, and relative liquidity. The circumstances of investors refers to current income, uncertainty of future income, wealth, and the state of cash management technology.

- By rearranging the characteristics of assets and circumstances of investors, we develop five laws of asset demand. Each law denotes the response of demand to a change in one of the factors while all other factors are assumed unchanged. The five laws are (1) the demand for an asset rises when the rate of return on the asset rises, (2) the demand for an asset falls when the rate of return on a competing asset rises, (3) an increase in national income increases the demand for money and reduces the demand for securities and real assets, (4) an increase in wealth increases the demand for all assets, and (5) an increase in the collective variable increases the demand for money and reduces the demand for securities and real assets.

- The factors that make up the collective variable are (1) the state of cash management technology, (2) uncertainty of future income, (3) risk of securities and real assets, (4) maturity of securities, (5) marketability of securities and real assets, and (6) liquidity of securities and real assets.

KEY TERMS AND CONCEPTS

theory of asset choice, or portfolio choice

risk averse

diversifying

diversifiable risk

nondiversifiable risk

circumstances of the investor

law of asset demand

collective factor

QUESTIONS AND PROBLEMS

1. The cofounder of Microsoft, Bill Gates, has become the richest person in the United States because of the stellar performance of his company. If you were his financial adviser, would you recommend that he keep all of his wealth in Microsoft stock?

2. "An optimal portfolio is one with no risk." True or false? Explain.

3. Suppose that, other things equal, the deposit rate rises. Would this affect your demand for six-month T-bills? Explain, indicating the law of asset demand that would guide your decision.

4. Suppose that, other things equal, the rate on six-month T-bills falls.
   a. Would you want to hold more or fewer six-month T-bills?
   b. Would you want to hold more or fewer two-year T-notes?
   c. Would you be more willing to hold deposits?
   d. Would you be more or less willing to hold IBM shares?

   In your explanations identify the laws of asset demand that are involved in your decision.

5. Suppose that the prices of securities rise. Explain whether:
   a. Other things equal, the demand for securities will rise or fall.

   b. Other things equal, the demand for demand deposits will rise or fall.

6. Suppose you inherited $500,000.
   a. How would you allocate this sum among deposits, securities, and tangible assets? What law(s) of asset demand would guide your decision?
   b. Suppose that the rate of return on real estate subsequently rises. How would your holdings of securities be affected?

7. Suppose that prices of bonds and stock become more volatile.
   a. Will you want to invest more or less in securities?
   b. Will you want to increase or decrease your checking account balances?

8. Suppose that the downsizing of the defense industry and the restructuring of U.S. corporations cause many American workers to be concerned that they may lose their jobs and their income. Other things equal, what would be the effect on the nation's demand for money? For securities?

9. Suppose that brokers increase their commission for trading stocks but not for bonds. What will happen to the relative liquidity of bonds and stocks? What will happen to their demand?

SUGGESTED READINGS

Fabozzi, Frank J., and Franco Modigliani. *Capital Markets: Institutions and Instruments*. Englewood Cliffs, N.J.: Prentice Hall, 1992, Chapter 5, "Risk/Return and Asset Pricing Models," 119–58.
   A more detailed treatment of risk and return.

"Schools Brief: Risk and Return," *The Economist*, February 2, 1991, 72–73.
   A concise statement of the work on risk and return of three Nobel laureates: Harry Markowitz (cowinner in 1990), William Sharpe (1990), and James Tobin (1981).

C H A P T E R 7

DEPOSIT RATE DEREGULATION AND MONEY DEMAND

CHAPTER PREVIEW

In the early 1980s, when deposit rates were first deregulated, depositors could earn 15 percent on bank CDs. A decade later, CD rates were 10 percentage points lower. This chapter develops a theory of the determination of the deposit rate that is useful not only for understanding movements in the deposit rate, but also for understanding and analyzing money demand in the new financial environment.

The laws of asset demand discussed in general terms in Chapter 6 apply to all assets—bonds, stocks, money, and even houses. These assets are all a store of value. Only money, however, is also a unit of account (standard of value) and a medium of exchange. Because of the importance of money in the economy, this chapter focuses on money demand.

The demand for money is the sum of the demand for currency and the demand for deposits. The deposit rate is one factor affecting the demand for deposits. In the old financial environment regulators set the deposit rate. In contrast, in the new financial environment the deposit rate moves up or down in response to market forces. *The main message of this chapter is that the theory of the determination of the deposit rate is an integral part of a contemporary theory of money demand.*

To find the ultimate factors that affect deposit demand in the new financial environment, we combine the five laws of demand from Chapter 6 with a theory of the determination of the deposit rate. Then we add the demand for currency to the demand for deposits to find all the factors affecting money demand.

How does this chapter fit into our two-pillar framework? It belongs in both pillars, because it combines the behavior of the public as demanders of currency and deposits with the determination of the deposit rate by market forces. Chapter 8 discusses the factors that affect money supply. Then Chapter 9 combines money demand with money supply to determine the interest rate.

THE LAWS OF DEPOSIT DEMAND

Applying the five laws of asset demand from Chapter 6 to deposits, we can write the demand-for-deposits relation in functional form as follows:

$$D^d = D^d(r_D, \; i, \; Y, \; W, \; \mathcal{C}) \qquad\qquad (7\text{--}1)$$
$$ +\;\; -\;\; +\;\; +\;\; +$$

The variables inside the parentheses in Equation 7–1 are the factors that affect the demand for deposits: the deposit rate, r_D; the rate of interest, i, on competing assets; national income, Y; wealth, W; and the collective factor, $\mathcal{C}$. The sign under each factor indicates whether deposit demand varies positively or negatively with that factor. The positive sign under r_D means that the demand for deposits varies positively with the deposit rate, reflecting the first law of asset demand. The negative sign under i means that the demand for deposits varies inversely with the rate on competing assets, reflecting the second law of asset demand. These competing assets consist of securities and real assets. For simplicity, however, we ignore real assets (or assume that the rate on real assets moves in the same direction as i). Therefore, i represents the interest rate on securities. Finally, the positive signs under Y, W, and $\mathcal{C}$ represent the third, fourth, and fifth laws of demand, respectively.

The Opportunity Cost of Deposits

A concept that is useful in combining the first and seconds laws is that of opportunity cost. As Chapter 5 noted, the opportunity cost of holding an asset is the difference between the rate of return on an alternative asset and the rate of return on the asset under consideration.[1] Therefore, the **opportunity cost of deposits** is the difference between the interest rate on securities, i, and the rate on deposits, r_D; that is, the opportunity cost of holding deposits is equal to $(i - r_D)$. Using this concept, we write the demand-for-deposit relation as:

$$D^d = D^d[(i{-}r_D), \; Y, \; W, \; \mathcal{C}] \qquad\qquad (7\text{--}2)$$
$$ -\qquad +\;\; +\;\; +$$

The negative sign under $i - r_D$ in Equation 7–2 means that the demand for deposits is a decreasing function of the opportunity cost, which captures both the first and second laws of asset demand.

---

[1] Obviously, the size of the opportunity cost of holding an asset depends on which asset the investor forgoes. In a two-asset world, there is no ambiguity; the concept of opportunity cost is precise because there is only one alternative asset.

FIGURE 7–1
The Demand for
Deposits

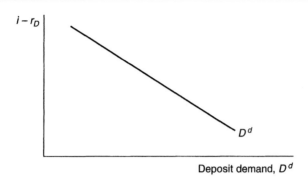

With $i - r_D$ measured on the vertical axis, a downward-sloping demand curve means that the demand for deposits varies inversely with the opportunity cost of holding deposits.

Deposit demand, D^d

To demonstrate this relationship, consider a numerical example. If the interest rate is 8 percent and the deposit rate is 5 percent, the opportunity cost of holding deposits is 8 percent minus 5 percent, or 3 percent. The investor forgoes a return of 3 percent by holding deposits rather than securities. If the interest rate remains at 8 percent and the deposit rate rises to 6 percent, the opportunity cost of holding deposits falls to 2 percent, thereby inducing investors to hold more deposits, as the first law prescribes.

Alternatively, assume again an initial opportunity cost of 3 percent. Next, suppose that the interest rate rises from 8 percent to 9 percent, while the deposit rate remains at 5 percent. The opportunity cost of holding deposits rises from 3 percent to 4 percent, which induces investors to hold fewer deposits, as the second law of demand asserts.

Figure 7–1 illustrates both laws graphically. The vertical axis measures the opportunity cost of deposits, and the horizontal axis measures deposit demand. The downward-sloping demand curve indicates the negative relation between the opportunity cost of holding deposits and the demand for deposits.

Old versus New Financial Environment   In the old financial environment (OFE), r_D was fixed either by law or by the regulators. Therefore, an increase in the interest rate, i, would increase the opportunity cost of holding deposits, $i - r_D$, by the same amount. To illustrate, suppose the interest rate is 10 percent, and the deposit rate is 4 percent; the opportunity cost is therefore 6 percent. If the interest rate rises by 2 percentage points to 12 percent and the regulated deposit rate is kept at 4 percent, the opportunity cost also rises by 2 percentage points to 8 percent. In general, under the OFE, the change in the opportunity cost is the same as the change in the interest rate. Because of this property, the D^d curve in the old financial environment would have the same slope if i were measured on the vertical axis in Figure 7–1 instead of $i - r_D$.

The situation is different if the deposit rate is allowed to change when the market interest rate changes, as it is in the new financial environment (NFE). In the NFE, a change in i will induce a change in r_D in the same direction. For example, an increase in i will increase r_D, thereby muting the increase in the opportunity cost. In other words, with deposit rate deregulation, the change in the opportunity cost is smaller than the change in the interest rate.

FIGURE 7–2
The Demand for
Deposits in the Old
and New Financial
Environments

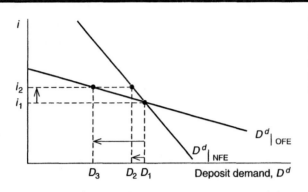

The demand curve in the new financial environment is steeper than in the old financial environment, meaning that a change in the interest rate changes the quantity of deposits demanded by less in the NFE than in the OFE.

Continuing our example, suppose that when the interest rate rises from 10 percent to 12 percent, the deposit rate increases from 4 percent to 5.25 percent. Under these circumstances, the opportunity cost would be $(12 - 5.25)$ percent, or, 6.75 percent. Thus, in the NFE the opportunity cost rises by 0.75 percent compared with 2 percent in the OFE.

Of course, an increase in the opportunity cost of holding deposits by only 0.75 percent will reduce the demand for deposits by a lot less than an increase of 2 percent. Thus, under the NFE, the demand for deposits is less sensitive to changes in the interest rate, as shown in Figure 7–2, where i is measured on the vertical axis. The demand curve in the new financial environment $(D^d|_{NFE})$ is steeper than the demand curve in the old financial environment $(D^d|_{OFE})$. The result of this change in the demand curve is that an increase in the interest rate from i_1 to i_2 reduces the quantity of deposits demanded by the amount D_1D_3 in the OFE but by only D_1D_2 in the NFE.

A THEORY OF DEPOSIT RATE DETERMINATION

The discussion to this point has shown that the deposit rate rises when the interest rate rises and that it falls when the interest rate falls. Our examples have also implied that the change (increase or decrease) in the deposit rate is smaller than the change in the interest rate. The next step is to back up these assertions.

The interest rate, i, is the rate that banks charge their customers to borrow funds. It is natural to expect that when the interest rate rises, banks will pass some of the increase on to depositors to attract more deposits. Will this come about from the generosity of bankers? The answer is no. Instead, market forces will oblige banks to raise the deposit rate. For if the interest rate rises, but banks do not raise the deposit rate, the opportunity cost of holding deposits will rise and the public will want to hold fewer, not more, deposits. Instead of gaining deposits, banks would lose deposits—at the very time that it would be profitable for them to attract *more* deposits to lend at the higher interest rate. Thus, banks are obliged to raise their deposit rate.[2]

---

[2] We shall see that banks will still lose some deposits, but less than if they were not allowed to raise the deposit rate.

By how much should banks increase the deposit rate they offer depositors when the interest rate they charge rises? Should they raise the deposit rate by the same amount as the increase in the interest rate? To answer these questions, we must first explore the decision-making process of banks.

To attract one more dollar of deposits, a bank must pay the deposit rate r_D. It cannot lend the entire dollar, however, because the Federal Reserve requires banks to keep a fraction of each deposited dollar in the form of required reserves. We denote the reserve requirement ratio by rr. Thus, the bank will receive a (gross) return of $(1 - rr)i$ for each additional dollar of deposits it attracts. When the out-of-pocket expense of r_D is subtracted, the result is the net pecuniary return per additional dollar of deposits, or the **net marginal revenue of deposits**, $[(1 - rr)i - r_D]$. This marginal revenue must equal the marginal cost, which is the operating cost, not including r_D. *A profit-maximizing bank strives to equate the net marginal revenue it receives from an extra dollar of deposits to the marginal cost of attracting this extra dollar of deposits.* (Notice that the equality *MR=MC*, discussed in economics, applies to banks as well as to steel mills!)

Other things equal, an increase in the interest rate will increase the net marginal revenue above the marginal cost, making it profitable for the bank to attract more deposits by raising the deposit rate. The bank, however, will suffer losses if it raises the deposit rate by the same amount, because it cannot lend out every dollar it takes in. To illustrate, suppose that the reserve requirement ratio, rr, is 0.10 and that the interest rate, i, rises by 1 percentage point, that is, 100 basis points. The bank can lend 90 cents on each dollar it attracts, or 0.9 of one dollar. Lending that amount at an extra 100 basis points (1 percent), the bank will earn 90 basis points on each dollar of additional deposits it attracts and lends. If it pays depositors 100 more basis points, the bank will lose 10 basis points on each additional dollar of deposits. Thus, the increase in the interest rate will lead to a smaller increase in the deposit rate.

We can capture the relation between the deposit rate and the interest rate succinctly by an equation:

$$r_D = r_D(i, \ldots), \text{ where } 0 < \Delta r_D / \Delta i < 1 \tag{7–3}$$

Equation 7–3, called the **deposit rate relation**, says that the market deposit rate is a function of the market interest rate, i, which is the variable inside the parentheses. The dots inside the parentheses are placeholders for additional determinants to be specified later. The stipulation in Equation 7–3 that $0 < \Delta r_D / \Delta i < 1$ means that when the interest rate rises (falls) the deposit rate also rises (falls) but by less.

The Deposit Rate Curve

The **deposit rate curve**, labeled $r_D(i)$ in Figure 7–3a, incorporates the properties of Equation 7–3. Movements along the curve show how the deposit rate changes when the interest rate changes. The curve is upward sloping to indicate the positive relation between the two. It lies entirely below the 45-degree line to indicate that the deposit rate is always lower than the interest rate. It is flatter than the 45-degree line to indicate that when the interest rate rises, the deposit rate rises by less.[3]

---

[3] These results follow from the geometric property that at any point on the 45-degree line, the coordinates—the interest rate and the deposit rate—are equal. This, in turn, implies that along the 45-degree line the change in

FIGURE 7–3
The Deposit Rate
Curve in the New
and Old Financial
Environments

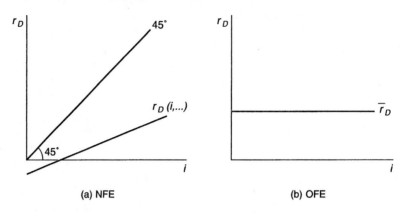

(a) NFE

The deposit rate, r_D, is always lower
than the interest rate, i; an increase in
the market rate of interest increases the
deposit rate by less.

(b) OFE

A change in the market rate of interest
does not change the deposit rate, which
is fixed by regulators.

For easy visual comparison, Figure 7–3b depicts the deposit rate curve under a regime
of fixed deposit rates. The horizontal line at the fixed rate $\bar{r}_D$ indicates that changes in the
market interest rate do not change the deposit rate. When regulators raise the deposit rate,
the horizontal line in Figure 7–3b shifts upward; of course, when they lower it, the line
shifts downward. MarketWatch 7.1 looks at actual movements in the M2 deposit rate
compared with the Treasury bill rate in the OFE and the NFE.

Shifts in the Deposit Rate Curve   Figure 7–3a shows that movements along the
deposit rate curve depict the effects of changes in the interest rate on the deposit rate. A
change in any other factor that affects the deposit rate will not result in a movement *along*
the curve, but will shift the entire curve. Factors that lower the deposit rate banks are
willing to pay *at each level of the interest rate* shift the curve downward, and factors that
raise the deposit rate *at each level of the interest rate* shift the curve upward. Figure 7–4
depicts a downward shift in the r_D curve. As a general rule, any factor that affects the
decision of banks to attract deposits or the decision of the public to hold them at any
interest rate level will affect the deposit rate. The paragraphs that follow examine some of
these factors.

The Reserve Requirement Ratio   We begin the discussion of factors that shift the deposit
rate curve with banks. Since profit-maximizing banks decide how many deposits they
want to attract by the rule that "marginal cost equals net marginal revenue," any factor
that influences the net marginal revenue or the marginal cost of deposits will also influence the deposit rate. The reserve requirement is one of those factors.

r_D equals the change in i or that its slope equals 1. Because the deposit relation is flatter than the 45-degree
line, it follows that its slope is less than 1.

MarketW*atch* 7.1
Historical Movements in the M2 Deposit Rate

In the 1960s and 1970s banks nationwide were prohibited from paying interest on checkable deposits. Although interest was paid on savings deposits and time deposits, these rates were subject to Regulation Q. The following graph shows that as open market rates trended upward during the 1960s and 1970s, regulators did adjust the level of the regulated rates upward. The graph also shows a pronounced change in the interest sensitivity of deposit rates after deposit rate deregulation began in mid-1978. Since then, the rate on M2 deposits has generally responded more systematically to the fluctuations in open market rates. Recall that demand deposits, NOW accounts, super-NOW accounts, savings and time deposits, and money market mutual funds are all part of M2. The M2 deposit rate is the average rate paid on the deposits that make up M2.

The Historical Relationship between the M2 Deposit Rate and the Treasury Bill Rate

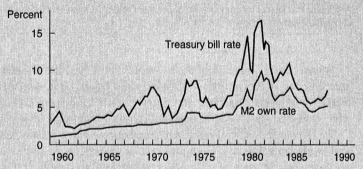

Source: David H. Small and Richard D. Porter, "Understanding the Behavior of M2 and V2," *Federal Reserve Bulletin*, Board of Governors of the Federal Reserve System 75, no. 4 (April 1989): 245.

The Federal Reserve may change the reserve requirement ratio, rr, within limits prescribed by law. If the Fed (or a new law) increases the reserve requirement ratio, the net marginal revenue, $[(1 - rr)i - r_D]$, falls. The marginal revenue falls below the original marginal cost, forcing profit-maximizing banks to reduce the amount of deposits they want to attract. With banks less eager to attract deposits, the public has to accept a lower deposit rate. Thus, other things equal, the deposit rate falls. Among the other things assumed equal is the interest rate. Hence, we have established that at each interest rate level, the deposit rate will be lower, which means the r_D curve shifts downward, as in Figure 7–4.

Technological and Regulatory Climate   Changes in the technological and regulatory climate that alter the marginal cost of banking also shift the deposit rate curve. For example, technological progress that reduces the marginal cost of banking for each level of attracted and placed funds makes marginal revenue greater than marginal cost. Deposits are thus more profitable for banks. To attract more deposits, banks are forced in the marketplace to raise the deposit rate. In this case, the r_D curve will shift upward: At each level of i, banks are willing to pay a higher deposit rate.

FIGURE 7–4
Shifts of Deposit
Rate Curve

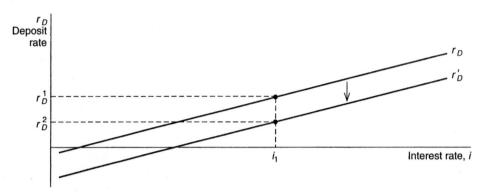

Any factor that lowers the deposit rate banks want to pay at each level of the interest rate shifts the
deposit rate curve downward, and vice versa.

Improvements in the regulatory climate that reduce the marginal cost of banking will also shift the r_D curve upward. One example would be a reduction in reporting requirements by regulatory agencies that reduces staff time spent compiling information. Another would be reductions in deposit insurance premiums levied by the FDIC.

We denote the technological and regulatory climate facing banks by the **technology and regulatory index**, $\Im\Re$. For purposes of discussion, an increase in $\Im\Re$ will represent a cost-increasing change in technology or regulations; a reduction in this index will represent a cost-reducing change in technology or regulations. Thus, an increase in $\Im\Re$ lowers the deposit rate at each level of the interest rate, thereby shifting the deposit rate curve downward; a reduction in $\Im\Re$ raises the deposit rate at each level of the interest rate, thereby shifting the deposit rate curve upward.

The Collective Variable and National Income   Three factors affect the public's willingness to hold deposits. Two are the collective factor and national income. An increase in $\mathcal{C}$, caused, say, by increased uncertainty about future employment, increases the desire to hold deposits, thereby making the public willing to accept a lower deposit rate from bankers who naturally oblige or even instigate the change in r_D. Thus, an increase in $\mathcal{C}$ will shift the deposit rate curve down. The same reasoning also applies to the second factor affecting the public's demand for deposits. An increase in national income, Y, will also make deposits more desirable, leading to a fall in the deposit rate at each level of the interest rate and, hence, to a downward shift of the curve.

Wealth   The third factor affecting the public's demand for deposits is wealth. An increase in wealth increases the demand for deposits, permitting banks to lower the deposit rate.

Table 7–1 summarizes the properties of the deposit rate relation. The first row indicates movements along the deposit rate curve: An increase in the market interest rate increases the market deposit rate. The other rows specify how the r_D curve shifts when a determinant other than the interest rate rises.

TABLE 7–1
Factors Affecting
the Deposit Rate,
r_D

Change in Factor	Change in r_D
Interest rate, $i \uparrow$	$\uparrow$
Reserve requirement ratio, $rr \uparrow$	$\downarrow$
Technology and regulatory index, $\mathfrak{R} \uparrow$	$\downarrow$
Collective factor, $\mathcal{C} \uparrow$	$\downarrow$
National income, $Y \uparrow$	$\downarrow$
Wealth, $W \uparrow$	$\downarrow$

Finally, Equation 7–4 replaces the dots that were placeholders in Equation 7–3 with the shift factors in Table 7–1:

$$r_D = r_D(i, \ rr, \ \mathfrak{R}, \ \mathcal{C}, \ Y, \ W) \qquad\qquad (7\text{–}4)$$
$$+ \ - \ - \ - \ - \ -$$

The signs under each of the six determinants of the deposit rate indicate how the deposit rate changes when the indicated determinant rises. These signs correspond to the arrows in Table 7–1. MarketWatch 7.2 applies Equation 7–4 to explain the fall in deposit rates in the early 1990s.

ULTIMATE FACTORS AFFECTING DEPOSIT DEMAND

Now we are ready to find all the factors affecting D^d in the new financial environment. The demand for deposits depends on the opportunity cost of deposits, which is the difference between the interest rate and the deposit rate. Therefore, to find the ultimate factors that affect the demand for deposits in the new financial environment, we must incorporate the factors that affect the deposit rate into our analysis. Symbolically, we substitute Equation 7–4 (the deposit rate relation) into Equation 7–2 (the demand function) to get:

$$D^d = D^d[i - r_D \, (i, \ rr, \ \mathfrak{R}, \ \mathcal{C}, \ Y, \ W), \ Y, \ W, \ \mathcal{C}] \qquad\qquad (7\text{–}5)$$

Some factors—i, Y, W, and $\mathcal{C}$—appear twice in the demand function. These factors affect the demand for deposits through two channels: a direct effect that is independent of the deposit rate and an indirect effect that works through the deposit rate. In contrast, the reserve requirement ratio, rr, and the technology and regulatory index, $\mathfrak{R}$, have only an indirect effect on the demand for deposits because their influence comes only through the deposit rate. Let us examine each of these factors and their effects on the demand for deposits.

Movements
along the D^d
Curve

We have already discussed the two effects of a change in i. Because of the importance of the relation between the demand for deposits and the interest rate, let us review that discussion. For a given r_D, an increase, say, in i increases the opportunity cost of holding deposits, which reduces the demand for deposits. This is the direct effect of an increase in i. In the new financial environment, however, the deposit rate rises when the interest rate

MarketWatch 7.2
Falling Deposit Rates in the 1990s

From 1990 to 1993, deposit rates were on the move downward. The first four rows of the accompanying table show that rates fell on NOW accounts, savings deposits, and time deposits of varying maturities. To understand why, we apply the theory of deposit rate determination.

Type of Financial Instrument	1990	1991	1992	1993
NOW accounts	4.89	3.76	2.33	1.86
Savings deposits (includes MMDAs)	5.84	4.30	2.88	2.46
Small time deposits (183 days to 1 year)	7.33	4.59	3.37	3.14
Small time deposits (more than 2½ years)	7.53	5.52	4.77	4.29
One-year Treasury bills	7.89	5.86	3.89	3.43
Ten-year Treasury notes	8.55	7.86	7.01	5.87

Deposit Rates and Interest Rates (Annual Effective Yields)

Source: *Federal Reserve Bulletin*, various issues.

Falling interest rates, shown in the last two rows of the table, were one reason for the drop in deposit rates. Falling interest rates reduced the net marginal revenue from attracting deposits, thereby inducing banks to lower deposit rates. Another reason was a tougher regulatory climate, which increased the marginal cost of attracting deposits, thereby inducing banks to lower deposit rates even more. One part of the increase in marginal costs was explicit, in the form of higher deposit insurance premiums and capital requirements. Another part was implicit, in the form of tougher scrutiny by bank regulators eager to avoid an S&L-type debacle in the banking industry.

The Fed helped banks to offset partially these increases in cost by lowering reserve requirement ratios. In December 1990 it reduced the reserve requirement ratio on nonpersonal time deposits and Eurodollar deposits from 3 percent to zero. Then in April 1992 it lowered the reserve requirement ratio on checkable deposits from 12 percent to 10 percent. A lower reserve requirement ratio means that banks can lend out a greater fraction of every dollar they take in and thus earn a higher net marginal revenue. Without the reductions in the reserve requirement ratios, deposit rates would have fallen even more.

rises. The rise in the deposit rate, by itself, increases the demand for deposits. This is the indirect effect of an increase in i. Because the increase in i is greater than the increase in r_D, the opportunity cost rises and the demand for deposits falls. Hence, the D^d curve is downward sloping on a graph where the vertical axis measures the interest rate and the horizontal axis measures the quantity of deposits, as in Figure 7–5. (We know that without the indirect effect, the D^d curve would be flatter, as in the OFE depicted in Figure 7–2.)

Shifts in the D^d Curve

A change in any of the other factors affecting the demand for deposits shifts the D^d curve. One of those factors is national income, Y. Figure 7–6 shows the direct, indirect, and net effects of an increase in Y on D^d. Other things equal, in particular, given i and r_D, an increase in Y increases the demand for deposits because the need for transaction balances increases. This is the direct effect shown in Figure 7–6 by a movement from point A to point B at the interest rate i_1. But there is also an indirect effect that works through r_D. Given i equals i_1, an increase in Y lowers the deposit rate, because when the demand for deposits increases banks do not have to pay as high a rate to attract depositors. The fall in

FIGURE 7–5
The Demand for
Deposits Again

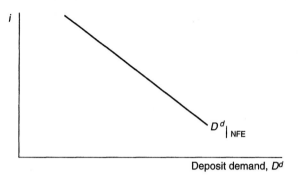

A downward-sloping demand curve for
deposits means a reduction in the
interest rate increases the quantity of
deposits demanded.

Deposit demand, D^d

FIGURE 7–6
The Effect of an
Increase in Income
on Deposit
Demand

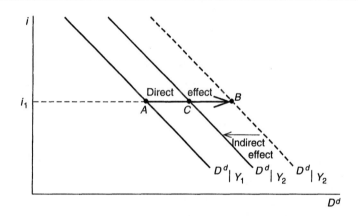

An increase in income, Y, has a direct effect which increases D^d, and an
indirect effect, working through the deposit rate, which reduces D^d. On net,
deposit demand rises by AC.

the deposit rate raises the opportunity cost, which reduces deposit demand from its
increased level, shown by the movement from point B to point C. On net, at the interest
rate i_1, the demand for deposits increases by an amount equal to the distance between
point A and point C.[4] We can establish this pattern at all levels of interest rates, so that the
demand curve for deposits shifts to the right when Y increases, as shown in Figure 7–6.

An increase in the collective factor, $\mathcal{C}$, has the same qualitative effects: a positive direct
effect and a negative indirect effect. On net, the demand for deposits rises. The same
explanation applies to wealth, W. An increase in wealth increases deposit demand because the public has more funds to hold in the form of deposits. The consequent reduction

----

[4] The increase in demand in the NFE is smaller than in the OFE. The reason is that with a regulated deposit
rate there is no indirect effect.

TABLE 7–2
Factors Affecting
Deposit Demand in
the New Financial
Environment

Change in Factor	Change in Deposit Demand, D^d
Interest rate, i ↑	↓
Income, Y ↑	↑
Collective factor, $\mathcal{C}$ ↑	↑
Wealth, W ↑	↑
Reserve requirement ratio, rr ↑	↓
Technology and regulatory index, $\mathfrak{TR}$ ↑	↓

in the deposit rate, however, increases the opportunity cost, which indirectly reduces deposit demand from its higher level.

The remaining two factors, rr and $\mathfrak{TR}$, work only through the deposit rate and, hence, are unique to the new financial environment. Other things equal, an increase in the reserve requirement ratio, rr, reduces the market-determined deposit rate, thereby increasing the opportunity cost of deposits and inducing the public to reduce its demand. The demand curve (not shown) shifts to the left in this case. In contrast, a cost-reducing change in technology or regulations, indicated by a decrease in $\mathfrak{TR}$, raises the deposit rate, lowers the opportunity cost, and increases the demand for deposits, shifting the D^d curve to the right. The factors affecting deposit demand in the new financial environment, along with their effects, appear in Table 7–2.

FACTORS AFFECTING THE DEMAND FOR MONEY

The final goal of this chapter is to explain money demand and its determinants. Since money is the sum of deposits and currency, **money demand** is the sum of deposit demand and currency demand (Cur^d).

$$M^d = D^d + Cur^d$$

Therefore, the factors affecting money demand, M^d, are the same as the factors affecting deposit demand, D^d, plus any factors affecting currency demand, Cur^d.

The major determinant of a nation's demand for currency is the volume of payments that must be undertaken. A good measure of the volume of payments, in turn, is the level of national income, Y: The higher the level of income, the greater the need for currency and, hence, the greater the demand for currency. An increase in Y also increases deposit demand. Thus, both components of money contribute to the increase in money demand when national income, Y, increases.

The demand for currency may also be affected by the interest rates paid on securities and deposits. For simplicity, however, we ignore these effects.

Another determinant of the demand for money is the payment habits of the nation. Demand for currency is high in countries where the public pays for its purchases of goods and services in currency or where firms pay wages and salaries in currency. In contrast, demand for currency is low in countries that rely more on checks, credit cards, and debit cards. Other factors, such as the volume of illegal activities, also affect the demand for

TABLE 7–3
Factors Affecting
Money Demand in
the NFE

Change in Factor	Change in Money Demand, M^d
Interest rate, i ↑	↓
Income, Y ↑	↑
Wealth, W ↑	↑
Collective factor, $\mathcal{C}$ ↑	↑ .
Reserve requirement ratio, rr ↑	↓
Technology and regulatory index, $\mathfrak{IR}$ ↑	↓

currency. Drug dealers and tax evaders are part of the underground economy, where transactions are in currency. A change in the payment habits that substitutes deposits for currency (or currency for deposits) affects the composition of money demand but not the size. Therefore, payment habits are not included in the list of factors affecting money demand in Table 7–3.

Figure 7–7 depicts the negative relation between money demand and the interest rate by a downward-sloping curve. The curve will shift to the right if Y, W, or $\mathcal{C}$ increase or if rr or $\mathfrak{IR}$ fall. On the other hand, it will shift to the left if Y, W, or $\mathcal{C}$ fall or if rr or $\mathfrak{IR}$ rise. An application of this theory to the demand for M2 in 1990 follows.

TRY IT OUT 7.1

In 1990, the M2 measure of money increased by 3.9 percent in the face of the following changes in factors affecting money demand: (1) interest rates on open market instruments, such as Treasury bills, fell; (2) a recession developed after midyear, which means Y fell; (3) in December, the Fed reduced the reserve requirement ratio on nonpersonal time deposits and Eurodollar deposits from 3 percent to zero; (4) banks faced the prospect of adjusting to higher capital requirements and tougher scrutiny by bank regulators; and (5) there was a large increase in the demand for currency, the bulk of which came from foreigners (in Eastern Europe, Latin America, and the Middle East) wanting to hold U.S. dollars during troubled political and economic times in their countries.

Explain the effect of each of these factors on the demand for M2. In each case, indicate whether there is a movement along the money demand curve or a shift of the curve, and in what direction the curve will shift.

LOOKING AHEAD

This chapter has shown that the deposit rate-setting behavior of banks is an integral part of a contemporary theory of money demand. Part 4—especially Chapter 16—applies this theory to the M1 and M2 measures of money to analyze the problems and practices of the Fed since deposit rates were deregulated in the 1980s. The next chapter, however, discusses the money supply process.

FIGURE 7–7
The Money
Demand Curve

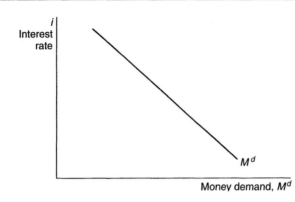

The downward-sloping money demand curve means that the demand for money varies inversely with the interest rate, other things equal. The factors that are held fixed along the curve are the other factors listed in Table 7–3 that affect money demand. A change in any of these factors will shift the curve.

SUMMARY

- Applying the five laws of asset demand to deposits, we derive these principles: (1) the higher the deposit rate, the higher the deposit demand; (2) the higher the interest rate (on securities), the lower the deposit demand; (3) the higher the national income, the higher the deposit demand; (4) the higher the national wealth, the higher the deposit demand; and (5) the higher the collective variable, the higher the deposit demand.

- If r_D is the deposit rate and i the interest rate on securities, the opportunity cost of holding deposits is the difference, $i - r_D$. The statement that the demand for deposits is a decreasing function of the opportunity cost of deposits captures both the first law and the second law of deposit demand.

- Under the old financial environment (OFE), the deposit rate, r_D, was fixed by regulation. Therefore, an increase in the interest rate, i, increased the opportunity cost by the same amount. Under the new financial environment (NFE), the deposit rate also increases when the interest rate rises, but by less than the increase in the interest rate. Hence, an increase in i increases the opportunity cost $i - r_D$ by less in the NFE. It follows that an increase in the interest rate reduces deposit demand by less in the NFE than the OFE.

- The deposit rate curve depicts the positive relation between the deposit rate and the market rate of interest. The curve is not only upward sloping but also has a slope less than 1 because an increase in the market rate of interest increases the deposit rate by less.

- Other factors besides the interest rate affect the deposit rate. An increase in the reserve requirement ratio reduces bank profit per dollar of attracted deposits, thereby inducing banks to reduce the deposit rate. Similarly, an increase in the marginal cost of servicing deposits also reduces bank profitability, inducing banks to lower the deposit rate. In both cases, the deposit rate curve shifts downward.

- Any factor that increases the public's demand for deposits also reduces the market deposit rate and shifts the deposit rate curve downward. The increased willingness of the public to hold deposits permits banks to reduce the deposit rate. Thus, an increase in national income, wealth, or the collective factor reduces the deposit rate at each level of the interest rate.

- The interest rate, income, wealth, and the collective factor affect the demand for deposits through two channels: a direct effect that is independent of the deposit rate and an indirect effect that works through the deposit rate. The indirect effects mitigate but do not offset the direct effects.

- The reserve requirement ratio and the technology and regulatory index affect the demand for deposits through only one channel: They affect the deposit rate that banks are willing to pay. Hence, these factors are unique to the new financial environment.

· Money is the sum of currency plus deposits. Hence, the demand for money is the sum of currency demand and deposit demand. It follows that the factors affecting currency demand must be included in the list of factors affecting the demand for money. The major factors that affect currency demand are, first, the size of payments, represented by the national income; and, second, the payment habits of the nation. Changes in payment habits usually shift funds between currency and deposits, affecting the composition but not the size of money demand.

KEY TERMS AND CONCEPTS

opportunity cost of deposits	deposit rate relation	technology and regulatory index
net marginal revenue of deposits	deposit rate curve	money demand

QUESTIONS AND PROBLEMS

1. Suppose that deposit demand, D^d, (in $ billions) is described by the following equation:

   $$D^d = -10 - 3(i - r_D) + 0.10Y + 0.02W + 0.2\mathcal{C}$$

   Confirm that the above equation illustrates all five laws of asset demand as applied to deposits. (Hint: Use the sign in front of each variable to answer this question.)

2. Suppose that the interest rate banks charge rises by 200 basis points. Which of the following (one or more) responses by a bank can definitely be excluded?
   a. The bank will increase the rate it pays depositors (the deposit rate) by 170 basis points.
   b. The bank will reduce the deposit rate by 100 basis points.
   c. The bank will increase the deposit rate by 200 basis points.
   d. The bank will increase the deposit rate by 100 basis points.

3. Suppose that the interest rate rises by 200 basis points. Which of the following (one or more) results can definitely be excluded?
   a. The opportunity cost (of holding deposits) will rise by 100 basis points.
   b. The opportunity cost will rise by 200 basis points.
   c. The opportunity cost will fall by 100 basis points.
   d. The opportunity cost will remain unchanged.

4. Why do banks raise the deposit rate when the market interest rate rises?

5. Suppose that the market interest rate is 10 percent, the reserve requirement ratio is 0.10, and a bank sets the deposit rate at 5 percent. What must the bank's marginal cost of attracting deposits be?

The Wall Street Journal

6. The following statement is from "FDIC's Forecast for Bank Failures Is Sharply Lowered." *The Wall Street Journal*, June 25, 1993: "The Federal Deposit Insurance Corporation sharply lowered its projections for bank failures this year and next, suggesting that banks will win a reduction in their deposit insurance premiums more quickly than expected." Illustrate graphically the effect that a reduction in the deposit insurance premium will have on the deposit rate curve and the deposit demand curve.

7. "An increase in national income shifts the deposit rate curve upward." True or false? Explain.

8. Suppose that deposit demand (in $ billions) is described by the following equation:

   $$D^d = -10 - 3(i - r_D) + 0.10Y + 0.02W + 0.2\mathcal{C}$$

   Where
   $Y = $5,500$ billion per year
   $W = $15,000$ billion
   $\mathcal{C} = 100$ points

   a. Express deposit demand, D^d, as a function of i and r_D.
   b. Suppose that the deposit rate is set by regulators at the level $\bar{r}_D = 4$ percent. Show that there is an inverse relation between D^d and i by deriving the deposit demand equation as a function of i. (In your

calculations, $r_D = 4$ percent should be written as 4 and not as .04.)

c. Suppose, instead, that the deposit rate relation is given by

$$r_D = -6.3043 + 0.913i$$

Show that deposit demand is much less sensitive to the interest rate in this case than in the case in which the deposit rate is fixed by regulators.

9. Suppose that the demand for currency is given by

$$Cur^d = 152 + 0.01Y$$

a. Use your answers to questions 8a and 8c to find the relation between money demand and the interest rate.

b. If $i = 10$ percent, what would the deposit rate, r_D, be? What would money demand, M^d, be? How would money demand be apportioned between currency and deposits?

10. Illustrate graphically and explain the effect that an improvement in cash management techniques will have on the money demand curve in the new financial environment.

11. "An increase in the reserve requirement ratio affects the money demand curve whether deposit rates are regulated or market determined." True, false, or uncertain? Explain.

12. "Some changes in the deposit rate are captured by movements along the money demand curve, and others by a shift of the money demand curve." True, false, or uncertain? Explain.

13. Suppose that prices of bonds and stocks become more volatile.
    a. What will happen to the deposit rate relation?
    b. What will happen to money demand?

14. Suppose that because of downsizing in the defense industry and the restructuring of the U.S. economy, American workers are concerned that they may lose their jobs and their incomes.
    a. What will happen to the deposit rate relation?
    b. What will happen to money demand?

SUGGESTED READINGS

Hadjimichalakis, Michael G. *Monetary Policy and Modern Money Markets: Fixed versus Market-Determined Deposit Rates.* Lexington, Mass.: D. C. Heath, 1982.

Develops a model of the new financial environment and contrasts its implications with those of the old financial environment; exposition is mostly mathematical.

Hadjimichalakis, Michael G. *The Federal Reserve, Money, and Interest Rates: The Volcker Years and Beyond.* New York: Praeger, 1984.

Uses a framework of the new financial environment to analyze the conduct of monetary policy; exposition is verbal and graphical.

Small, David H., and Richard D. Porter. "Understanding the Behavior of M2 and V2." *Federal Reserve Bulletin* 75, no. 4 (April 1989): 244–55.

An empirical examination of the deposit rate relation, demand for the M2 measure of money, and the related concept of velocity in the new financial environment.

Wenninger, John. "Responsiveness of Interest Rate Spreads and Deposit Flows to Changes in Market Rates." *Quarterly Review,* Federal Reserve Bank of New York 11, no. 3 (Autumn 1986): 1–10.

An empirical examination of changes in the opportunity cost of different types of deposits in the new financial environment.

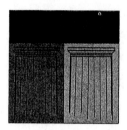

THE BASICS OF THE MONEY SUPPLY

CHAPTER PREVIEW

Money consists of currency plus deposits. Because we all hold currency and bank deposits, we can relate the laws of money demand explained in Chapter 7 to our own experience.

In contrast, the factors affecting the money supply are mysterious to most people. To understand the money supply process, we must learn how the Fed creates reserves and how banks use them. But what are reserves? We already know that they are the Fed's obligations to banks. Although the vault cash that banks have on hand is one component of reserves, the bulk of reserves consists of accounts that banks have with the Fed. These accounts are bookkeeping entries that are part of the daily lives of bankers and central bankers but not of the general public.

The aim of this chapter is to explain the basics of the money supply process by the behavior of the Fed, banks, and the public. Therefore, the chapter fits into the first pillar of our two-pillar framework. We can think of the money supply as the output and reserves as the input in the process of money creation. By focusing on the Fed's actions as the supplier of reserves and banks as demanders, this chapter explains the money supply and establishes the factors that influence it.

In addition to the Fed and banks, the public also plays a role in the money supply process. Currency held by the public, called *currency in circulation,* is one component of the money supply. Moreover, there is a relation between currency in circulation and reserves, for whenever individuals withdraw cash from their checking accounts by writing a check or by using an automatic teller machine, vault cash falls, which means reserves in the banking system go down.

TABLE 8–1
Simplified Balance Sheet of the Fed

Assets	Liabilities
(1) U.S. Treasury securities held by the Fed, (B_F)	(4) Currency in circulation (*Cur*)
(2) Discount window loans (*DWL*)	**(5) Total reserves issued by Fed (TR^s)** **(Bank reserve balances + Bank vault cash)**
(3) Other assets (*OA*)	(6) Other liabilities (*OL*)

SIX STEPS TO DERIVE THE MONEY SUPPLY

We begin by mapping a six-step plan for deriving the money supply and establishing the factors that influence it. This plan helps us to derive the money supply easily. It also highlights the role of each participant in the money supply process. Beginning with the Fed, we make use of the balance sheets introduced in Chapter 4.

1. From the balance sheet of the Fed, we determine the supply of reserves.
2. From the balance sheet of banks, we determine the demand for reserves.
3. Next, we set the demand for reserves equal to the supply. We call the requirement that the demand for reserves be equal to the supply the *reserves constraint.* From this constraint, we find the amount of reserves that can be used as required reserves, that is, the reserves that support deposits. Because the reserve requirement ratio is a fraction (substantially) smaller than 1, deposits are a multiple of required reserves.
4. By adding to this quantity of deposits the amount of currency the public wants to hold (and the Fed makes available), we determine the money supply.
5. Next, we examine the effect of a change in each of the factors that affect the money supply and depict the results graphically.
6. Finally, we refine our equation for the money supply to distinguish between M1 and M2, and we illustrate the M1 and M2 equations using actual data.

SUPPLY OF RESERVES

The Fed is a key player in the money supply process. We begin with its role. The supply of reserves is derived from the balance sheet of the Fed. Table 8–1 depicts the simplified balance sheet of the Fed introduced in Chapter 4. Total reserves are a liability (item 5) of the Fed. To find how the Fed creates, or supplies, reserves, we must look at the remaining entries in its balance sheet.

First, let us introduce some abbreviations for simplicity. On the asset side, we denote item 1, the Treasury securities held by the Fed, by B_F. B is the symbol for securities (bills, notes, bonds), and the subscript F denotes the Fed. We denote item 2, discount window loans, by *DWL*; and item 3, other assets, by *OA*.

On the liability side, we denote item, 4, currency in circulation, by *Cur*; item 5, the total reserves issued (or supplied) by the Fed, by TR^s[1]; and item 6, other liabilities, by *OL*.

---

[1] Note that TR^s consists of reserve balances with the Fed, which are accounts of banks with the Fed, and vault cash, which is currency held by banks.

Remember from previous chapters that the items called *other assets* and *other liabilities* consist of the assets the Fed acquires or liabilities it incurs in its functions as a banker to banks and a banker to the U.S. government, to foreign governments, and to international organizations. The other assets, other liabilities, and currency in circulation are all called **technical factors affecting reserves,** *or* **noncontrolled factors**, because they are outside the decision-making power of the Fed.[2]

As with any balance sheet, the amount of the Fed's total liabilities must equal its total assets. Therefore, we can write the balance sheet relationship as an equation:

Sum of the Fed's liabilities = Sum of the Fed's assets

$$Cur + TR^s + OL \quad = B_F \; + DWL + OA \qquad\qquad (8\text{--}1)$$
$$(4) \; + (5) \; + (6) \qquad = (1) \; + (2) \; + (3)$$

Rearranging terms in Equation 8–1 produces Equation 8–2 for the **supply of total reserves**:

$$TR^s = B_F + DWL + (OA - OL - Cur) \qquad\qquad (8\text{--}2)$$

Equation 8–2 shows that the supply of total reserves has its origin in three factors: the U.S. Treasury securities the Fed has purchased in the open market; the discount window loans it has made to banks; and the **net technical factors,** that is, $(OA - OL - Cur)$. When any of these factors increase, the supply of total reserves increases, and when any decrease, the supply decreases.

Equation 8–2 is often expressed in a more compact way as the sum of nonborrowed reserves and borrowed reserves. Introducing these concepts will help us track the supply of total reserves in *The Wall Street Journal* after we present the demand for reserves in the next section.

The reserves that originate from discount window loans are naturally called **borrowed reserves** because banks are borrowing these reserve funds from the Fed. In other words, borrowed reserves (*BR*) equal discount window loans:

$$BR = DWL \qquad\qquad (8\text{--}3)$$

There are three types of discount window loans, all of which are included in borrowed reserves:

1. Very short term loans to help depository institutions meet a temporary need for funds are called **adjustment borrowings**. The maturity of these loans typically ranges from overnight to a few days.
2. The Fed also makes longer term loans of reserves—up to several months—for seasonal purposes. **Seasonal credit** often goes to small banks in farm areas whose needs vary with the agricultural cycle.
3. Finally, banks in trouble, such as those with liquidity problems from a large amount of bad loans, may be permitted to borrow from the Fed for even longer periods. Such discount window loans are appropriately referred to as **extended credit**.

The reserves that originate from all sources other than discount window loans are called **nonborrowed reserves (*NBR*)**. These originate from the Treasury securities that the Fed holds and from the net technical factors. Putting this definition in symbols, we have

---

[2] Chapter 14 examines the details of "other assets" and "other liabilities."

FIGURE 8–1
Total Reserves
Supplied and
Components

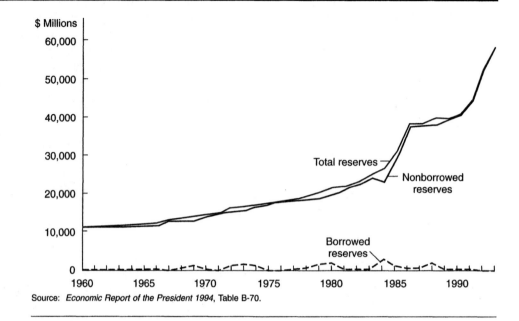

Source: *Economic Report of the President 1994*, Table B-70.

$$NBR = B_F + (OA - OL - Cur) \tag{8–4}$$

Substituting Equations 8–3 and 8–4 into Equation 8–2, gives the supply of total reserves as the sum of nonborrowed reserves and borrowed reserves:

$$TR^s = \underbrace{B_F + (OA - OL - Cur)}_{NBR} + DWL \tag{8–2}$$

$$TR^s = \qquad\qquad NBR \qquad\quad + BR \tag{8–5}$$

Figure 8–1 shows the history of the supply of total reserves and its components, nonborrowed reserves and borrowed reserves. As can be seen, the magnitude of borrowed reserves is uniformly small compared with nonborrowed reserves. By changing the scale of the vertical axis, Figure 8–2 provides a better look at changes in borrowed reserves.

The large increase in borrowed reserves in 1984 stands out in Figure 8–2. In that year, the Fed provided a large amount of extended credit to Continental Illinois—at the time, the nation's seventh largest bank—which was in danger of failing because of losses on energy loans. A look back at Figure 8–1 finds that the Fed reduced the amount of nonborrowed reserves supplied in 1984 so that the total amount of reserves would not be more than the Fed wanted to supply.

Changes in the
Supply of Total
Reserves

Before we go to the next step, let's look into the story behind changes in nonborrowed reserves and borrowed reserves, for later this will help us understand how changes in these factors affect the money supply. We begin with borrowed reserves because the explanation is more intuitive.

FIGURE 8–2
Borrowed Reserves

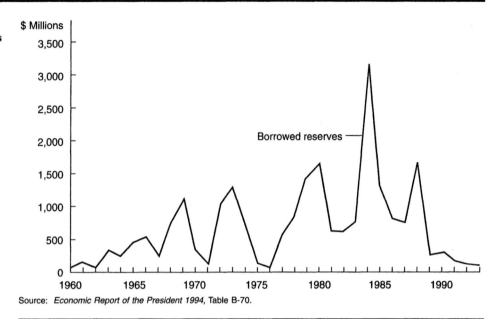

Source: *Economic Report of the President 1994*, Table B-70.

Borrowed Reserves   Just as you may borrow from your bank and give it an IOU, so may a bank borrow from its banker, the Fed, and give it an IOU. That IOU is an asset, identified as discount window loans, item 2 in the Fed's balance sheet in Table 8–1. The Fed, in turn, credits the bank's reserve account with the Fed by the amount of the loan. Reserves, of course, are a liability in the Fed's balance sheet. Hence, when the Fed makes more loans to banks at the discount window, it creates more total reserves. Item 2 on the asset side of the Fed's balance sheet and item 5 on the liability side increase by an equal amount, as do the corresponding items, *DWL* and *TR^s* in Equation 8–2.

Nonborrowed Reserves   More than one item affects the magnitude of the nonborrowed component of total reserves. First we examine an open market purchase of Treasury securities. Then we examine a change in one technical factor, namely, an increase in currency in circulation. We highlight this technical factor because currency in circulation is also a component of the money supply and thus, appears again in step 4, in the discussion of the money supply equation.

Open Market Operations   The Fed creates reserves primarily by buying Treasury securities in the open market. The Fed buys these securities from a selected group of 39 security dealers, called **primary dealers**. Some of these dealers are commercial banks, such as Bank of America and Citibank. Others are securities firms, such as Salomon Brothers and Merrill Lynch. Whether the dealer is a commercial bank or a securities firm, the effect on the supply of reserves is the same.

TABLE 8–2
Effect of an Open Market Operation on the Balance Sheet of the Fed
($ Billions)

Before				After			
Assets		**Liabilities**		**Assets**		**Liabilities**	
B_F	202	Cur	150	B_F	204	Cur	150
DWL	5	TR^s	63	DWL	5	TR^s	65
OA	8	OL	2	OA	8	OL	2
Total	215	Total	215	Total	217	Total	217

When the Fed buys Treasury securities from a commercial bank, it pays for them by crediting the bank's reserve account with the Fed. In other words, the Fed pays for the Treasury securities by creating reserves. As a result of this open market operation, Treasury securities held by the Fed (item 1 on the asset side of its balance sheet) and total reserves issued by the Fed (item 5 on the liability side of its balance sheet) increase by the same amount, as do the corresponding amounts B_F and TR^s in Equation 8–2. In effect, what the Fed does is to take the IOUs of the U.S. Treasury out of the system and replace them with its own IOUs.

When the securities dealer is not a commercial bank, the Fed gives the dealer a check written on the Fed. After the dealer deposits this check in its bank, the bank sends the check back to the Fed, which credits the bank's reserve account with the Fed. Again, the supply of total reserves increases by the amount of the open market purchase of securities.[3]

To illustrate the effect of open market operations on the balance sheet of the Fed, let's demonstrate these changes in two hypothetical balance sheets, shown in Table 8–2. The one on the left shows the initial situation: There are $63 billion of total reserves, which originate in $202 billion of Treasury securities held by the Fed, $5 billion of discount window loans, and *minus* $144 billion of net technical factors (i.e., $OA - OL - Cur = 8 - 2 - 150 = -\$144$).

Suppose that the Fed buys $2 billion of U.S. Treasury bills in the open market. The balance sheet on the right shows that the Treasury securities held by the Fed increase by $2 billion, as does the quantity of the supply of total reserves, TR^s.

Currency in Circulation   Unlike open market operations, which the Fed initiates, a change in currency in circulation originates with the public. To find the effect of an increase in currency in circulation on the supply of reserves, let's go back to Equation 8–2. A minus sign in front of *Cur* in Equation 8–2 means that when the amount of currency the public holds increases, total reserves supplied fall, as the following example illustrates:

Suppose that before you leave for spring break you withdraw $200 from your checking account; that is, you reduce the amount of bank deposits you hold by $200 and increase the amount of currency you hold by the same amount. You accomplish this redistribution of your money by withdrawing funds from an ATM or by writing a check.

---

[3] The notion of a check moving through the system is only an explanatory device. Nowadays, the Fed settles its accounts electronically.

TABLE 8–3
Balance Sheet of
Banks

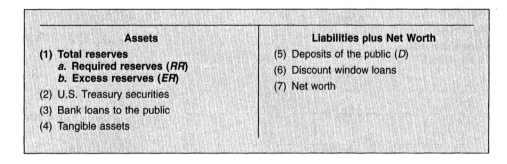

Assets	Liabilities plus Net Worth

(1) **Total reserves**
   a. **Required reserves (*RR*)**
   b. **Excess reserves (*ER*)**
(2) U.S. Treasury securities
(3) Bank loans to the public
(4) Tangible assets
	(5) Deposits of the public (*D*)
	(6) Discount window loans
	(7) Net worth

In either case, the bank pays you $200 out of vault cash and reduces your deposits with the bank by $200. If the bank needs to replenish its supply of vault cash, it orders $200 more currency from the Fed. The Fed ships the currency to the bank and debits (charges) the bank's reserve account with the Fed. In the end, total reserves supplied by the Fed fall because either vault cash or reserve balances with the Fed go down by the amount that currency in circulation rises.[4]

DEMAND FOR RESERVES

Now that we have seen how the supply of reserves increases or decreases, the next step is to find the demand for reserves. This story is much shorter than that of supply: The demand comes from banks. Table 8–3, which reproduces the balance sheets of banks from Chapter 4, shows that reserves are an asset in the balance sheet of banks.

The major portion of the total reserves banks hold are required reserves (*RR*). By definition, required reserves are equal to the reserve requirement ratio (*rr*) multiplied by bank deposits (*D*), which is item 5 on the liability side of the balance sheet of banks; that is, $RR = rrD$. For example, if *rr* is 0.10 and *D* is $780 billion, then *RR* is $78 billion. The other component of total reserves held by banks is excess reserves (*ER*), which are a discretionary item for banks.

Excess reserves serve as a buffer to a bank when unanticipated deposit withdrawals lead to an unexpected loss of reserves. In uncertain (unusually risky) environments, a bank may also choose to hold excess reserves instead of committing funds to loans or to Treasury securities.

The **demand for total reserves (*TR^d*)** is the sum of these two uses:

$$TR^d = RR + ER \tag{8–6}$$

Figure 8–3 shows the history of total reserves demanded and its components: required reserves and excess reserves. We see that excess reserves are tiny in comparison with required reserves. Figure 8–4 changes the scale of the vertical axis to show the changes in excess reserves more clearly.

---

[4] The Fed can negate the effect on reserves of an increase in currency in circulation by an offsetting open market purchase of Treasury securities. We examine these offsetting open market operations in Chapter 14, where we look at all the factors in detail.

FIGURE 8–3
Total Reserves
Demanded and
Components

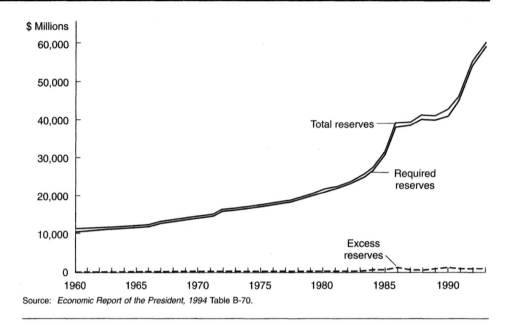

Source: *Economic Report of the President, 1994* Table B-70.

Figure 8–4 shows that the quantity of excess reserves has increased drastically since the early 1980s. The reason is increased uncertainty about a bank's need for reserves since February 1984. At that time, the Fed changed the accounting procedure banks must use to calculate their required reserves. Before 1984, under a lagged reserve accounting procedure, the required reserves a bank needed to maintain in the current week were based on its deposits two weeks earlier. Under the contemporaneous accounting procedure introduced in February 1984, a bank's required reserves are based on its current deposits.[5] As a result, banks are more uncertain about their need for reserves and, hence, hold more excess reserves.

FROM THE RESERVES CONSTRAINT TO DEPOSITS

In the third step, we find the deposit component of the money supply. We go from setting the demand for total reserves equal to the supply to finding the amount of deposits that can be supported by reserves.

The Reserves
Constraint

The requirement that the demand for total reserves must equal the supply is the **reserves constraint**. This constraint is written as Equation 8–7:

---

[5] Actually, the current accounting system is *nearly* contemporaneous. In February 1984 the Fed lengthened the periods on which reserves are calculated and maintained to two weeks. Under the current system, the reserves a bank needs to maintain in the current 2-week period are based on deposits in the 2-week period ending two days earlier.

FIGURE 8–4
Excess Reserves

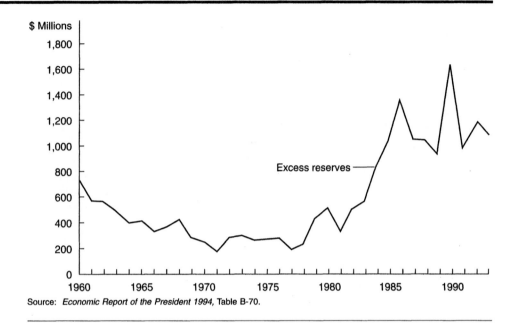

Source: *Economic Report of the President 1994*, Table B-70.

$$TR^d = TR^s \tag{8–7}$$

Substituting the right side of Equation 8–6 for the demand and the right side of Equation 8–5 for the supply, we can rewrite the reserves constraint equation as:

$$RR + ER = NBR + BR \tag{8–8}$$

FedWatch 8.1 illustrates the reserve constraint using actual data published in *The Wall Street Journal*.

Deposits Supported by Reserves

We can rewrite the reserves constraint in a way that will permit us to find the volume of deposits that satisfy the constraint. First, we solve Equation 8–8 for *RR*:

$$RR = NBR + BR - ER \tag{8–9}$$

The right side of Equation 8–9 is the amount of total reserves supplied that can be used as required reserves after we subtract the amount that is siphoned off as excess reserves held by banks. We call this amount **effective reserves**.

We know that by definition the quantity of required reserves is the product of the reserve requirement ratio, *rr*, and the volume of deposits, *D*:

$$RR = rrD$$

It follows (by definition) that the volume of deposits equals the inverse of the reserve requirement ratio multiplied by required reserves; that is:

FedWatch 8.1
Tracking the Reserves Constraint

TR^d	=	TR^s
$RR + ER$	=	$NBR + BR$
53,847 + 1,298	=	55,047 + 98
55,145	=	55,145

Every Thursday at 4:30 PM Eastern time the Federal Reserve issues the H.3 statistical release, "Aggregate Reserves of Depository Institutions and the Monetary Base," with data on several measures of reserves and the base. *The Wall Street Journal* reports the data on Friday in a table titled "Federal Reserve Data." The illustration below is from Friday, April 2, 1993.

RESERVE AGGREGATES
(daily average in millions)

	Two weeks ended:	
	Mar. 31	Mar. 17
Total Reserves (sa)	55,145	55,320
Nonborrowed Reserves (sa)	55,047	55,227
Required Reserves (sa)	53,847	54,033
Excess Reserves (nsa)	1,298	1,287
Borrowing from Fed (nsa)-a	98	93
Free Reserves (nsa)	1,200	1,194
Monetary Base (sa)	359,382	357,858

a-Excluding extended credit. nsa-Not seasonally adjusted. sa-Seasonally adjusted.

These numbers illustrate the reserves constraint: The sum of required reserves and excess reserves demanded by banks equals the sum of nonborrowed reserves and borrowed reserves supplied by the Fed.

In the first column, the quantity of total reserves is $55,145 million. This number is both the demand and the supply. Adding the two components of demand, $53,847 million of required reserves and $1,298 million of excess reserves, we find a total of $55,145 million. Similarly, adding the components of supply, $55,047 million of nonborrowed reserves and $98 million of borrowed reserves, we arrive at the same number: $55,145 million.

Displaying these results in the form of an equation, we have:

Footnote a alerts us to the possibility that nonborrowed reserves and borrowed reserves may not *seem* to add up to total reserves. The reason is that "borrowings from the Fed" as reported in *The Wall Street Journal* do not include extended credit. For the two sides to be equal, we must add extended credit to borrowed reserves (and hence to the supply side). Of course, we can compute borrowed reserves, including extended credit, from the given information by subtracting the quantity of nonborrowed reserves from the quantity of total reserves. Thus, by subtracting $55,047 million from $55,145 million, we find that borrowed reserves, including extended credit, were $98 million, which means that extended credit was zero.

Another measure of reserves given in the table is free reserves, which are excess reserves minus borrowed reserves. For March 31, if $98 million of borrowed reserves is subtracted from the $1,298 million of excess reserves, the quantity of free reserves was $1,200 million. Finally, currency in circulation was $304,237 million for the period ending March 31. How do we know this from the given information? (Hint: Use the monetary base.)

TRY IT OUT

Use the numbers in the second column to illustrate the reserves constraint for the two weeks ending March 17 and to find the magnitude of currency in circulation.

$$D = \frac{1}{rr} \times RR \qquad (8\text{–}10)$$

Substituting the right side of Equation 8–9 for *RR* in Equation 8–10 and denoting the volume of deposits that can be supported by effective reserves by D_R instead of simply *D*, we get Equation 8–11:

$$D_R = \frac{1}{rr} \times (NBR + BR - ER) \tag{8-11}$$

Because the reserve requirement ratio, rr, is a (small) fraction, its inverse, $(1/rr)$, is a number (substantially) greater than 1. For example, if $rr = 0.10$, $(1/rr)$ is 10. Therefore, the volume of deposits that can be supported by reserves is a multiple of effective reserves. The number $(1/rr)$ is called the **simple deposits multiplier.**

Recapping the story behind Equation 8–11, we start with the amount of nonborrowed reserves provided from the Treasury securities held by the Fed and from the net technical factors. When we add borrowed reserves provided at the discount window to nonborrowed reserves, we find the supply of total reserves. Subtracting the amount of reserves that banks hold as excess reserves from the supply of total reserves, we find effective reserves, which equal required reserves. Multiplying effective reserves by the inverse of the reserve requirement ratio, we find the amount of deposits that can be supported by reserves.

TRY IT OUT 8.1

Given the following hypothetical numbers, work through Questions 1–5 to find the amount of deposits that can be supported by reserves.

B_F = \$202 billion
DWL = \$5 billion
Cur = \$150 billion
OA = \$20 billion
OL = \$14 billion
ER = \$5 billion
rr = 0.10

1. Find nonborrowed reserves, NBR.
2. Find borrowed reserves, BR.
3. Find effective reserves.
4. Find the simple deposits multiplier.
5. Find the amount of deposits, D_R, that can be supported by reserves.

THE MONEY SUPPLY EQUATION

The fourth step is short and simple. To find the **money supply**, M^s, we merely add currency in circulation to the amount of deposits that can be supported by reserves:

$$M^s = Cur + D_R \tag{8-12}$$

$$M^s = Cur + \frac{1}{rr} \times \underbrace{(NBR + BR - ER)}_{\text{Effective Reserves}}$$

(Carry Try It Out 8.1 to its logical conclusion by finding the value of M^s.)

FACTORS THAT AFFECT THE MONEY SUPPLY

Equation 8–12 shows that five immediate factors affect the money supply: nonborrowed reserves, borrowed reserves, excess reserves, currency in circulation, and the reserve requirement ratio. Equation 8–12 is the key to understanding the effect of an increase in each of the factors on the money supply.

Nonborrowed Reserves

Other things equal, an increase in nonborrowed reserves increases effective reserves by an equal amount. As a result, the deposits that can be supported by effective reserves increase by a multiple amount. The increase in the money supply is equal to the increase in the deposit component.

What causes nonborrowed reserves to rise? Equation 8–4 shows that nonborrowed reserves increase when the Fed buys more Treasury securities in the open market or when the net technical factors ($OA - OL - Cur$) rise. Currency is one of the four factors assumed fixed in this exercise. Let's assume that the other technical factors, OA and OL, are also fixed and look into the process by which an open market purchase of Treasury securities results in an increase in deposits.

When the Fed supplies more reserves to the banking system through an open market operation, banks, of course, hold more reserves. Suppose that banks had all the required reserves they needed to support existing deposits before this open market operation. Then, the additional reserves supplied by the Fed show up as excess reserves in the banks' balance sheets.

Excess reserves, however, earn no interest. If banks do not want to hold additional idle excess reserves, they put them to work by making more loans (or by buying Treasury securities). When banks make more loans, they credit the amount of the loans to new or existing checking accounts of their loan customers. For example, if you borrow $1,000 from your local bank next week, your bank will increase the balances in your checking account by $1,000. In this way, bank deposits increase.

As deposits rise, the demand for required reserves by banks also rises. Now we see how this process works: Banks can make more loans and create more deposits until every dollar of additional reserves supplied by the Fed has been turned into a dollar of required reserves. That happens when deposits increase by ($1/rr$) times the increase in nonborrowed reserves, which confirms our results using Equation 8–12.[6]

Borrowed Reserves

Other things equal, an increase in discount window loans to banks by the Fed also increases effective reserves by an equal amount. In this case the borrowed reserves component of effective reserves increases. Of course, deposits that can be supported by reserves increase by a multiple amount. Again, the increase in the money supply is equal to the increase in the deposit component.

---

[6] Our explanation goes straight to the result for the entire banking system. Chapter 15 provides more details on the mechanics of deposit expansion. It explains how, in a system of more than 11,000 banks, reserves may bounce from bank to bank as individuals write checks against their accounts and how the deposits created by all banks together add up to the simple deposits multiplier times the change in nonborrowed reserves. That chapter may be read after this one.

Excess Reserves

Now we turn to an increase in the demand for reserves. Other things equal, an increase in banks' demand for excess reserves reduces effective reserves by an equal amount and deposits by a multiple amount.

Among the other factors held constant in this case are nonborrowed reserves and borrowed reserves. With the supply of total reserves given, if banks want to hold more excess reserves, they have to reduce their need for required reserves, which means they must reduce their deposits. To accomplish this, banks reduce their loans or their holdings of Treasury securities.

Currency in Circulation

Among the five factors that affect the money supply, an increase in currency in circulation is unique because it affects both the currency component and the deposit component. An increase in currency in circulation increases the currency component of the money supply by an equal amount. However, because currency is a technical factor that drains reserves from the banking system, an increase in currency in circulation reduces nonborrowed reserves by an equal amount. Thus, effective reserves fall by an equal amount. In other words, a smaller amount of reserves is available to be used as required reserves to support deposits. When we multiply the fall in effective reserves by the multiplier, $(1/rr)$, we find that deposits that can be supported by reserves fall by a multiple of the increase in demand for currency. Thus, the money supply falls because the deposit component falls more than the currency component rises.

TRY IT OUT 8.2

To solidify your understanding of the effects of a change in currency, work through the following hypothetical numerical example, which builds on Try It Out 8.1 (identified as the initial case). In the new case, the demand for currency increases by $2 billion.

Initial Case		New Case	
B_F	= $202 billion	B_F	= $202 billion
DWL	= $5 billion	*DWL*	= $5 billion
Cur	= $150 billion	*Cur*	= $152 billion
OA	= $20 billion	*OA*	= $20 billion
OL	= $14 billion	*OL*	= $14 billion
ER	= $5 billion	*ER*	= $5 billion
rr	= 0.10	*rr*	= 0.10

1. Find the change in nonborrowed reserves.
2. Find the change in effective reserves.
3. Find the change in the quantity of deposits that can be supported by reserves.
4. Find the change in the money supply.

Reserve Requirement Ratio

Finally, an increase in the reserve requirement ratio reduces the simple deposits multiplier, $(1/rr)$. As a result, effective reserves support fewer deposits, so the deposit component of the money supply falls.

TABLE 8–4
Immediate Factors
that Affect the
Money Supply

Change in Factor	Effect on M^s
$NBR\uparrow$	$M^s\uparrow$
$BR\uparrow$	$M^s\uparrow$
$Cur\uparrow$	$M^s\downarrow$
$ER\uparrow$	$M^s\downarrow$
$rr\uparrow$	$M^s\downarrow$

Table 8–4 summarizes schematically the effects of a change in each of these five factors on the money supply.

Interest Sensitivity of the Money Supply

Of the five immediate factors that affect the money supply, only two factors depend on the interest rate: borrowed reserves and excess reserves. Both are affected by decisions banks make.

The discount rate is the rate the Fed charges banks to borrow at the discount window.[7] The spread between the interest rate, i, on debt securities, and the discount rate, d, signifies the return to the bank from borrowing at the discount window. Other things equal, the higher the spread, $i - d$, the more profit-maximizing banks want to borrow at the discount window.[8] In contrast, the higher the spread, the fewer noninterest-bearing excess reserves that banks want to hold.

For a given discount rate, an increase in the interest rate affects the money supply by increasing the spread between the interest rate and the discount rate, which, in turn induces banks to increase their borrowed reserves and reduce their excess reserves. Such a response by banks increases the quantity of reserves available to be used as required reserves. That is, effective reserves rise. As a result, the amount of deposits that can be supported by reserves rises. Thus, an increase in the interest rate increases the money supply. We can represent schematically the linkages between a rise in the interest rate, i, and a rise in the money supply, M^s, as follows:

$$i \uparrow \Rightarrow \{BR \uparrow \text{ and } ER \downarrow\} \Rightarrow [NBR + BR - ER] \uparrow \Rightarrow D_R \uparrow \Rightarrow M^s \uparrow$$

Money Supply Curve

We have established that the money supply is positively related to the interest rate: The money supply increases when the interest rate increases, and it falls when the interest rate falls; that is, $i \uparrow \Rightarrow M^s \uparrow$, as we see by connecting the end points of the schematic. This relation is illustrated by an upward-sloping curve in Figure 8–5, where the interest rate is measured on the vertical axis and the quantity of money on the horizontal axis.

---

[7] The basic discount rate is the rate charged for adjustment borrowings. The Fed adds surcharges for seasonal credit and extended credit.

[8] Borrowing at the discount window is a privilege and not a right for banks. Chapter 12 explains the Fed's operation of the discount window in detail. Chapter 18 derives the borrowed reserves relation and the excess reserves relation from the profit-maximizing behavior of banks.

FIGURE 8–5
The Money Supply
Curve

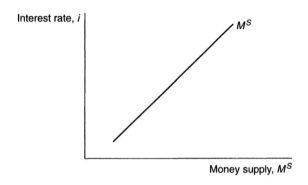

The money supply is positively related
to the interest rate. An increase in the
interest rate increases the money
supply, and a decrease in the interest
rate reduces the money supply.

FIGURE 8–6
Open Market
Operations and the
Money Supply
Curve

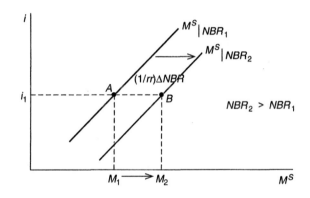

At the given interest rate, i_1, an open
market purchase of Treasury securities
by the amount ΔB_F increases
nonborrowed reserves by the same
amount. The money supply increases
by the multiple amount $(1/rr)\,\Delta NBR$,
which is equal to the horizontal
distance between point A and point B.
Repeating the exercise for every level
of i and connecting the corresponding
points, we see that the money supply
curve shifts to the right by the amount
$(1/rr)\Delta NBR$.

Shifts in the Money Supply Curve   A change in any factor that affects the money
supply other than the interest rate shifts the curve. This chapter concentrates on open
market operations and discount rate policy, the two major tools of monetary policy.
Chapter 15 examines the other factors affecting the money supply process in more detail.

Open Market Operations   An increase in the supply of reserves from a purchase of U.S.
Treasury securities in the open market by the amount ΔB_F increases nonborrowed reserves by the same amount. According to the multiplier relation, the money supply
increases by a multiple amount: $\Delta M^s = (1/rr)\,\Delta NBR$, other things equal. Among the other
things assumed equal is the interest rate, i. The horizontal distance between the curves in
Figure 8–6 depicts this increase in the money supply at the interest rate i_1. If we repeat
this process for each level of the interest rate, we see that the money supply curve shifts
to the right by the amount $(1/rr)\,\Delta NBR$.

Changes in the Discount Rate   Other things equal, a reduction in the discount rate also
shifts the money supply curve to the right. Such a reduction in the discount rate, d,

FIGURE 8–7
An Increase in the
Discount Rate and
the Money Supply
Curve

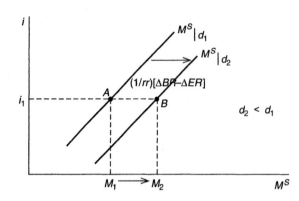

A reduction in the discount rate from d_1 to d_2, given the interest rate, i_1, increases borrowed reserves, and reduces excess reserves. Effective reserves increase by the difference between the change in borrowed and excess reserves. The money supply increases by a multiple of the change in effective reserves, which is the distance by which the money supply curve shifts to the right.

increases the spread, $i - d$, inducing an increase in borrowed reserves, BR, and a reduction in excess reserves, ER, thereby increasing effective reserves. As a result, given the interest rate, the money supply increases by a multiple of the increase in effective reserves, that is, by the amount $(1/rr)[\Delta BR - \Delta ER]$. Graphically, the money supply curve shifts to the right by this distance, as shown in Figure 8–7.

THE EQUATIONS FOR M1 AND M2

There are narrow and broad measures of money. In deriving the money supply relation, we have not distinguished between the supply of the narrow measure of money, M1, and the supply of the broad measure, M2. Under the current structure of reserve requirements, Equation 8–12 represents the supply of M1 because banks must hold reserves against all of the deposits in M1. The equation for the supply of M2 has the same form, but the deposit multiplier is different.

Remember that M1 consists mainly of currency in circulation and checkable deposits, also called *transactions deposits,* which we denote by $D1$. The M2 measure consists of M1 plus other deposits, called *nontransactions deposits,* such as savings deposits, small time deposits, and money market mutual funds. We denote nontransactions deposits by $D2$; they are the deposits that are in M2 but not in M1. It follows that:

$$M1 = Cur + D1 \qquad (8\text{–}13)$$
$$M2 = Cur + D1 + D2 \qquad (8\text{–}14)$$

To find the equations for the supply of M1 and M2, we need to know the reserve requirement ratios for each category of deposits. Under the current structure, the reserve requirement ratio, rr, is 10 percent on checkable deposits ($D1$) and zero percent on all other deposits ($D2$).

The M1
Equation

To find the equation for the supply of M1, as earlier, we equate the demand and supply of total reserves.

$$rr\underbrace{D1}_{RR} + ER = NBR + BR$$

Solving for $D1$, we have:

$$D1 = (1/rr) \times (NBR + BR - ER) \tag{8–15}$$

Finally, adding currency in circulation to $D1$ gives the equation for the supply of M1, which is the same as Equation 8–12:

$$M1^s = Cur + (1/rr) \times (NBR + BR - ER). [9] \tag{8–16}$$

The M2 Equation

Next, to find the equation for the supply of M2, we begin by expressing $D2$ deposits as a fraction of $D1$ deposits:

$$D2 = d2 \times D1 \tag{8–17}$$

where $d2 = D2/D1$, the ratio of $D2$ deposits to $D1$ deposits.

Substituting Equation 8–17 for $D2$ in Equation 8–14, we get:

$$M2 = Cur + D1 + (d2 \times D1)$$

or,

$$M2 = Cur + (1 + d2) \times D1$$

Finally, substituting for $D1$, that is, substituting the right side of Equation 8–15 for $D1$, we arrive at the equation for the supply of M2:

$$M2^s = Cur + [(1 + d2)/rr] \times (NBR + BR - ER) \tag{8–18}$$

Comparing Equation 8–18 with Equation 8–16, we see that the deposit multipliers are different. To find the deposit component of M1, we multiply effective reserves by the simple deposits multiplier, $1/rr$. In contrast, to find the deposit component of M2, we multiply effective reserves by $(1 + d2)/rr$, which is the **deposit multiplier for M2**.

Because $d2$ is positive, the multiplier for M2 is greater than the multiplier for M1. Moreover, the greater the value of $d2$, the greater the supply of M2. The reason is simple: Banks are not required to hold reserves against $D2$ deposits, such as small time deposits and money market deposit accounts. Therefore, the greater the ratio of $D2$ deposits to $D1$ deposits, the greater the quantity of total deposits that will be supported by reserves, and the smaller this ratio, the smaller the quantity of deposits that will be supported by reserves.

---

[9] To ease the burden of reserve requirements on small depository institutions, a small amount of deposits at all institutions are exempt from reserve requirements, and an additional amount is subject to a reserve requirement ratio below the top rate, currently 10 percent. Existing law requires that the Fed adjust these amounts annually to reflect the growth of deposits. Equation 8–14 can be adapted to incorporate these details. For simplicity, however, we do not introduce them here.

Illustration of the Two Equations

Next we illustrate the difference between the two multipliers by plugging actual data into Equations 8–16 and 8–18 and solving for the multipliers. We begin with Equation 8–16 for M1. All the numbers are in billions of dollars and are averages of daily figures for December 1993.[10]

$$M1^s \quad = Cur \quad + (1/rr) \times (NBR + BR - ER)$$
$$1{,}128.50 = 329.30 + (1/rr) \times (60.45 + 0.09 - 1.07) \tag{8–16}$$

Subtracting *Cur* from both sides of Equation 8–16 we find the equation for *D*1:

$$D1 = (1/rr) \times \text{Effective reserves}$$
$$1{,}128.50 - 329.30 = (1/rr) \times (60.45 + 0.09 - 1.07)$$
$$799.20 = (1/rr) \times (59.47)$$

Finally, solving for $(1/rr)$, we find that $(1/rr)$ equals 13.44 and *rr* equals 0.074.

In sum, the average reserve requirement ratio on checkable deposits (*D*1) was 0.074, or 7.4 percent, in December 1993. This ratio was less than 10 percent because some checkable deposits are exempt from reserve requirements. Inverting the reserve requirement ratio, we find that the value of the deposit multiplier for M1 was 13.44: Every dollar of effective reserves supported $13.44 of checkable deposits.

Next, to find the size of the multiplier for M2 deposits in December 1993, we plug the relevant data into Equation 8–18:

$$M2^s \quad = Cur \quad + [(1 + d2)/rr] \times (NBR + BR - ER)$$
$$3{,}565.80 = 329.30 + [(1 + d2)/rr] \times (60.45 + 0.09 - 1.07) \tag{8–18}$$

Subtracting *Cur* from both sides of Equation 8–18, we find the equation for all M2 deposits, that is, for *D*1 + *D*2:

$$D1 + D2 = [(1 + d2)/rr] \times \text{Effective reserves}$$
$$3{,}565.80 - 329.30 = [(1 + d2)/rr] \times (60.45 + 0.09 - 1.07)$$
$$3{,}236.50 = [(1 + d2)/rr] \times (59.47)$$

Of course, we know that *rr* was 0.074 in December 1993. Substituting this value for *rr* into the above equation and solving for *d*2, we find that *d*2 = 3.03: There were $3.03 of nontransactions deposits for every dollar of checkable deposits in December 1993. Finally, we determine the value of the multiplier for M2 deposits:

$$(1 + d2)/rr = (1 + 3.03)/0.074 = 54.46$$

In sum, every dollar of effective reserves supported $54.46 of M2 deposits but only $13.44 of M1 deposits.[11]

LOOKING AHEAD

Our goal in this chapter has been to present the basics of the money supply process. Chapter 15 looks at more details about the money supply. In the next chapter, we move to the second pillar by combining money supply and money demand to determine the interest rate.

---

[10] The data for both equations are from the *Federal Reserve Bulletin*, April 1994, A13 and A14.

[11] The results of these calculations may vary slightly because of rounding errors in each step.

SUMMARY

- This chapter takes a first look at money creation. Money creation is a process in which the money supply is the output and the total reserves are the input.

- The balance sheet of the Fed shows that the supply of total reserves comes from three factors: the Treasury securities the Fed has purchased in the open market; the discount window loans it has made to banks; and the other assets, other liabilities, and currency in circulation, which are called *technical factors*.

- That portion of total reserves originating from discount window loans is naturally called *borrowed reserves*. The remaining portion, called *nonborrowed reserves*, originate from the Treasury securities held by the Fed and from the technical factors. Hence, the supply of total reserves equals nonborrowed reserves plus borrowed reserves.

- The Fed increases the supply of total reserves by purchasing Treasury securities in the open market and by making additional loans to banks at the discount window.

- The demand for total reserves comes from banks that use them as required reserves to fractionally back deposits or as excess reserves.

- The demand for reserves by banks must equal the supply. This relation is called the *reserves constraint*.

- From the reserves constraint, we can find the quantity of the reserves that can be used by banks as required reserves. We call this quantity *effective reserves*, which are what remain of total reserves supplied by the Fed after the amount banks hold as excess reserves is subtracted.

- The quantity of deposits is a multiple of effective reserves, where the multiplier is the inverse of the reserve requirement ratio. Deposits are the major component of money supply. The other component is currency in circulation.

- Five immediate factors affect the money supply: nonborrowed reserves, borrowed reserves, excess reserves, currency in circulation, and the reserve requirement ratio. The money supply rises when nonborrowed reserves or borrowed reserves go up; it falls when excess reserves, currency in circulation, or the reserve requirement ratio go up.

- Borrowed reserves and excess reserves depend on the interest rate. Other things equal, an increase in the interest rate increases effective reserves because borrowed reserves rise and excess reserves fall. Hence, an increase in the interest rate increases the money supply. We depict this relation graphically by an upward-sloping curve in a graph with the interest rate on the vertical axis and quantity of money on the horizontal axis.

- Open market operations and changes in the discount rate shift the money supply curve. Open market purchases of securities and decreases in the discount rate shift the money supply curve to the right. Other factors, such as exogenous changes in borrowed and excess reserves and changes in currency, also shift the money supply curve, as do changes in the reserve requirement ratio.

- Under the current structure of reserve requirements, banks are required to hold reserves on the checkable deposits that make up M1 but not on the non-M1 component of M2. Therefore, the multiplier for M2 is greater than the multiplier for M1.

KEY TERMS AND CONCEPTS

technical factors affecting reserves, or noncontrolled factors

supply of total reserves

net technical factors

borrowed reserves

adjustment borrowings

seasonal credit

extended credit

nonborrowed reserves

primary dealers

demand for total reserves

reserves constraint

effective reserves

simple deposits multiplier

money supply

deposit multiplier for M2

QUESTIONS AND PROBLEMS

1. Use the numbers in the accompanying hypothetical balance sheet of the Fed to find the amount of total reserves supplied, the amount of nonborrowed reserves, and the amount of borrowed reserves.

Hypothetical Balance Sheet of the Fed
($ Billions)

Assets		Liabilities	
Treasury securities held by the Fed	335	Currency in circulation	294
Discount window loans	2	Total reserves supplied	
Other assets	16	Other liabilities	4

2. Assume the initial balance sheet of the Fed is that given in Question 1. Now suppose that the Fed sells $3 billion of Treasury securities in the open market. By how much will the supply of total reserves change? By how much will nonborrowed and borrowed reserves change?

3. Suppose that discount window loans fall because banks become more reluctant to borrow from the Fed. Will the supply of total reserves rise, fall, or remain unchanged? Nonborrowed reserves?

4. Suppose that currency in circulation rises because of an increase in illegal activities. What will happen to the supply of total reserves? Nonborrowed reserves?

The Wall Street Journal

5. Illustrate the reserve constraint for the two weeks ended July 7, 1993, by using the accompanying data from the July 9, 1993, issue of *The Wall Street Journal*.

RESERVE AGGREGATES
(daily average in millions)

	Two weeks ended:	
	July 7	June 23
Total Reserves (sa)	57,568	56,915
Nonborrowed Reserves (sa)	57,257	56,758
Required Reserves (sa)	56,324	56,154
Excess Reserves (nsa)	1,244	761
Borrowing from Fed (nsa)-a	311	158
Free Reserves (nsa)	933	603
Monetary Base (sa)	369,893	368,253

a-Excluding extended credit. nsa-Not seasonally adjusted. sa-Seasonally adjusted.

6. Explain the difference between total reserves and effective reserves.

7. Why does a dollar of effective reserves support more than a dollar of deposits?

8. Use the following hypothetical numbers (in $ billions) to find the quantity of the money supply:

$$B_F = 335$$
$$DWL = 2$$
$$OA = 16$$
$$OL = 4$$
$$Cur = 294$$
$$ER = 4$$
$$rr = 0.075$$

9. Assume your answer to Question 8 represents the initial situation. Now suppose that the demand for currency in circulation rises to $296 billion because of an increase in illegal activities.
   a. Assuming no change in the Fed's behavior, find the change in the money supply.
   b. Suppose that concurrently the Fed buys $2 billion of Treasury securities in the open market. Find the change, if any, in the money supply.

10. The Fed, the banks, and the public are all participants in determining the money supply. With the help of the money supply equation, explain the role of each of these participants in the money supply process.

11. Derive the money supply as an equation from the following hypothetical data describing the behavior of the participants in the money supply process:

   $B_F = \$335$ billion securities held by Fed
   $OA = \$16$ billion other assets held by Fed
   $OL = \$4$ billion other liabilities of Fed
   $DWL = 1.5 + 0.2(i - d)$ discount window loans
   $ER = 3.5 - 0.2(i - d)$ excess reserves
   $Cur = \$294$ billion currency in circulation
   $d = 4.00$ percent discount rate
   $rr = 0.075$ reserve requirement ratio

   (Write all numbers as they appear here; for example a 4 percent discount rate means $d = 4$.)

12. Explain the difference between movements along and shifts of the money supply curve.

13. Explain what happens to free reserves (that is, excess reserves minus borrowed reserves) as we move from left to right along a money supply curve.

14. Evaluate the following statement: "It is easier for the Fed to control the M1 measure of money than the M2 measure."

15. Use the following actual data for money and reserves in March 1993 to find the reserve requirement ratio, the simple deposits multiplier (for M1), and the deposits multiplier for M2.

$M1 = \$1,034.9$ billion

$M2 = \$3,471.7$ billion

$TR = \$55.17$ billion

$NBR = \$55.08$ billion

$ER = \$1.22$ billion

$Cur = \$303.21$ billion

SUGGESTED READINGS

Axilrod, Stephen H., and Henry C. Wallich. "Open Market Operations." In *The New Palgrave: Money*, ed. John Eatwell, Murray Milgate, and Peter Newman. New York: W. W. Norton, 1989, 288–94.

An essay on open market operations by a former Fed official and a former Fed governor, respectively.

Brunner, Karl. "Money Supply." In *The New Palgrave: Money*, ed. John Eatwell, Murray Milgate, and Peter Newman. New York: W. W. Norton, 1989, 263–67.

An essay on the relation between the monetary base and the money supply. The appendix to this chapter explains this approach.

Feinman, Joshua N. "Reserve Requirements: History, Current Practice, and Potential Reform." *Federal Reserve Bulletin* 79, no. 6 (June 1993): 569–89.

A Fed economist examines the role of reserve requirements.

THE MONETARY BASE MULTIPLIER

In the body of this chapter we derived and applied the following money supply equation:

$$M^s = Cur + (1/rr) \times (NBR + BR - ER) \tag{8--12}$$

Keeping the quantities of currency, nonborrowed reserves, borrowed reserves, and excess reserves separate in the money supply equation helps us to explain simply how the behavior of the public and banks affects the money supply. More important, this approach fits with the Fed's practices and with its statistical releases, which report data on nonborrowed reserves, borrowed reserves, excess reserves, and currency in circulation.

An alternative approach that has a long and venerable history presents the money supply equation in more compact form as the product of a **money multiplier (m)** and the total monetary base supplied by the Fed (TMB^s):

$$M^s = m \times TMB^s \tag{A8--1}$$

Within the Federal Reserve System, economists at the Federal Reserve Bank of St. Louis—one of the 12 district banks—have done extensive research on this approach.[12] Moreover, the Federal Reserve Bank of St. Louis regularly publishes historical data on $m1$ and $m2$, the money multipliers for M1 and M2, respectively. To understand m and its relation to the simple deposit multiplier ($1/rr$), we must look into the derivation of Equation A8--1.

We start with the **total monetary base supplied**, which is a liability of the Fed. It is the sum of currency and total reserves issued by the Fed. We know that currency in circulation is a technical factor affecting reserves: An increase in currency in circulation drains reserves from the banking system. It has no effect, however, on the supply of the total monetary base because the fall in total reserves supplied offsets the increase in currency. Similarly, a decrease in currency increases reserves but leaves the monetary base unchanged.

What does affect the supply of the total monetary base? The answer is, all of the assets and the "other liabilities" in the Fed's balance sheet. It follows that the total monetary base supplied by the Fed originates in three items: Treasury securities held by the Fed, discount window loans, and "other assets" minus "other liabilities," which are the **net technical factors affecting the monetary base**. An increase in any of these factors increases the total monetary base supplied by the Fed, and a decrease in any factors decreases the monetary base.

On the demand side, the **total monetary base demanded (TMB^d)** equals currency demanded by the public (i.e., currency in circulation) plus total reserves demanded by

---

[12] See Albert E. Burger, *The Money Supply Process* (Belmont Calif.: Wadsworth, 1971).

banks. Because the demand for total reserves is the sum of required reserves and excess reserves, we can express the demand for the total monetary base as:

$$TMB^d = Cur + RR + ER \qquad\qquad\qquad (A8\text{–}2)$$

The **monetary base constraint**, which is a variation of the reserves constraint, requires that the total monetary base demanded by the public and banks equal the total monetary base supplied by the Fed:

$$TMB^d = TMB^s \qquad\qquad\qquad (A8\text{–}3)$$

(To derive the monetary base constraint from the reserves constraint, we merely add currency to both sides of the equation, $TR^d = TR^s$.)

Next, substituting the right side of Equation A8–2 for TMB^d in Equation A8–3, we get:

$$Cur + RR + ER = TMB^s \qquad\qquad\qquad (A8\text{–}4)$$

We know that by definition,

$$RR = rr \times D \qquad\qquad\qquad (A8\text{–}5)$$

We can also express currency and excess reserves as a ratio multiplied by deposits if we divide and multiply each item by D:

$$Cur = cur \times D \qquad\qquad\qquad (A8\text{–}6)$$

where cur is the currency-to-deposits ratio, Cur/D; and

$$ER = er \times D \qquad\qquad\qquad (A8\text{–}7)$$

where er is the excess-reserves-to-deposits ratio, ER/D.

Next, substituting Equations A8–5 for RR, A8–6 for Cur, and A8–7 for ER in Equation A8–4 and collecting terms, we get:

$$(cur + rr + er) \times D = TMB^s$$

It follows that deposits equal the inverse of $(cur + rr + er)$ multiplied by the total monetary base supplied:

$$D = [1/(cur + rr + er)] \times TMB^s \qquad\qquad\qquad (A8\text{–}8)$$

According to Equation A8–8, deposits are a multiple of the total monetary base, where the multiplier is $[1/(cur + rr + er)]$. The multiplier rises if the currency-to-deposits ratio, the reserve requirement ratio, or the excess-reserves-to-deposits ratio falls, and the multiplier falls if any of these ratios rise.

Deposits, of course, are only one component of the money supply. To find the money multiplier, m, we must add currency to deposits:

$$M^s = Cur + D \qquad\qquad\qquad (A8\text{–}9)$$

Substituting $cur \times D$ for Cur in Equation A8–9 and combining terms, we get:

$$\begin{aligned} M^s &= cur \times D + D \\ &= (1 + cur) \times D \end{aligned} \qquad\qquad\qquad (A8\text{–}10)$$

Finally, substituting Equation A8–8 for *D* in Equation A8–10, we find the value of the money multiplier, *m*:[13]

$$M^s = [(1 + cur)/(cur + rr + er)] \times TMB^s \tag{A8–11}$$

which means that

$$m = (1 + cur)/(cur + rr + er) \tag{A8–12}$$

Despite the difference in their appearance, the two money supply equations, that is, Equation 8–12 in the main text and Equation A8–11 in this appendix, are the same. This is easy to show for the special case in which excess reserves and currency are zero. In this case, Equation 8–12 simplifies to Equation 8–12′, and Equation A8–11 to Equation A8–11′:

$$M^s = (1/rr) \times (NBR + BR) \tag{8–12′}$$
$$M^s = (1/rr) \times (TMB)^s \tag{A8–11′}$$

We know, however, that

$$\begin{aligned} TMB^s &= TR^s + Cur \\ &= NBR + BR + Cur \end{aligned}$$

By setting *Cur* equal to zero, TMB^s reduces to TR^s, that is, $NBR + BR$, which is the same as Equation 8–12′, proving that the two equations are the same in this special case. We can also prove that the two money supply equations are identical in the general case, but we shall spare you the extensive algebra.

Having derived the money multiplier, *m,* we see that Equation A8–1 is not as simple as it appears because it lumps the reserve requirement ratio together with the behavior of the public and banks. Unlike the simple deposits multiplier, (1/*rr*), the money multiplier is not a constant determined by the Fed. The reason is that the currency-to-deposits ratio and the excess-reserves-to-deposits ratio are behavioral relations determined by the decision making of the public and of banks, respectively.

By plugging data for TMB^s and M1 into Equation 8–1, we can illustrate the size of *m*1 in a particular period. We use data from December 1993, the same period we used to illustrate Equation 8–12 in the body of this chapter.

$$M1^s = m1 \times TMB^s$$
$$\$1,128.50 \text{ billion} = m1 \times \$385.90 \text{ billion}$$

It follows that *m*1 = 2.92. Remember that we found that the value of (1/*rr*), the simple deposits multiplier for M1 deposits, was 13.44 in the same period.

The main reason that *m*1 is much smaller than (1/*rr*) is that *m*1 incorporates the effect of currency in circulation, which dilutes the money-making power of the monetary base: Every dollar increase in the monetary base can support a multiple increase in deposits, but only $1 of currency in circulation. In addition, *m*1 also includes the effect of excess reserves, which also reduces the money-making power of the monetary base.

---

[13] Because we have assumed that all deposits are subject to reserve requirements, the money multiplier in Equation A8–10 is *m*1, the M1 multiplier.

What about the size of the M2 money multiplier, $m2$? Even without deriving the expression for $m2$,[14] we know that $m2$ will be greater than $m1$. The reason is that banks are not required to hold reserves on the savings deposits, time deposits, and other deposits that are in M2 but not in M1. Therefore, any given amount of the monetary base will support a larger amount of M2 than of M1. To illustrate that $m2$ is greater than $m1$, we use actual data to find the value of $m2$ in December 1993:

$$M2^s = m2 \times TMB^s$$
$$\$3,565.80 \text{ billion} = m2 \times \$385.90 \text{ billion}$$

It follows that $m2 = 9.24$.

---

[14] We note that $m2 = (1 + cur + d2)/(cur + rr + er)$, where $d2 = D2/D1$. To derive this expression, we start with the definition of M2, that is, $M2 = Cur + D1 + D2$. Next, we rewrite Cur and $D2$ as $cur \times D1$ and $d2D1$, respectively. Substituting these expressions for Cur and $D2$ into the definition of M2 and substituting Equation A8–8 for $D1$, we find $m2$.

KEY TERMS AND CONCEPTS

money multiplier	net technical factors affecting the monetary base	total monetary base demanded
total monetary base supplied		monetary base constraint

TWO TALES OF DETERMINING THE INTEREST RATE

CHAPTER PREVIEW

How is the interest rate on debt securities determined? In the financial world, practitioners usually say that it is determined by demand and supply in the debt securities market. This approach is called the *loanable funds theory of interest rate determination*. Monetary policymakers and many academic economists, when they focus on monetary policy, usually employ another approach, called the *liquidity preference theory of interest rate determination*. According to this theory, the interest rate on debt securities is determined in the money market by the interaction of money demand and money supply. This chapter shows how both theories determine the interest rate. It uses a simple model with two assets, money and securities, more specifically, debt securities. We will see that in this model the one theory is equivalent to the other.

Having established the principles of money demand in Chapter 7 and money supply in Chapter 8, Chapter 9 begins with the liquidity preference theory. One advantage of the liquidity preference theory is that with one graph it displays both the interest rate on debt securities and the quantity of money—two variables at the heart of money and banking. This chapter uses it to examine the effects of changes in monetary policy and of inadvertent shocks. In particular, two changes in monetary policy that shift the money suppy curve are considered: an open market operation and a change in the discount rate. The chapter also examines the effects on the interest rate and the quantity of money when the public restructures its portfolio, thereby shifting the money demand curve. Moreover, by employing the relation, introduced in Chapter 7, between the deposit rate and the interest rate, we see how the deposit rate changes in each case. Finally, we see that we get the same results by using the loanable funds theory instead of liquidity preference theory. The chapter connects both theories with practice by examining

behavior of the public and the Fed after the stock market crash of 1987 and also by

ning monetary policy in the early 1990s.

THE   : HOW MARKETS WORK

This chapter fits into the second pillar of economics: how markets work. To understand the workings of the markets for money and debt securities, it is necessary to consider some concepts that are fundamental to understanding and analyzing markets in general.

The market for any item—a good, a service, or an asset—is in **equilibrium** when the plans of demanders match the plans of suppliers; that is, when the quantity demanded equals the quantity supplied. Another term for equilibrium is **market clearance**.

When the quantity demanded exceeds the quantity supplied, the market is out of equilibrium. In this case, the market for that item registers **excess demand**. In the opposite case, when the quantity demanded falls short of the quantity supplied, the market registers **excess supply**. The **principles of excess demand and excess supply** describe the economic forces that bring the market to equilibrium; that is, they indicate how prices or rates of return change to restore equilibrium.

The apples market, an example that is most likely familiar to you from your principles of economics course, provides a good illustration. The price of apples is determined at the level that makes the quantity of apples demanded equal to the quantity supplied. At a higher price, the market registers excess supply, because when the price of apples rises, consumers reduce the quantity of apples they demand and producers increase the quantity they supply. By the principle of excess supply, the price of apples falls, inducing consumers to demand more and producers to supply less, until the quantity demanded matches the quantity supplied. On the other hand, if the price of apples is lower than its equilibrium level, the quantity demanded exceeds the quantity supplied, and, by the principle of excess demand, the price of apples rises until the two quantities are equal.

We now proceed to apply this general theory of markets to the market for money and the market for debt securities. These markets deal with assets, the demand for which depends on rates of return, as Chapters 6 and 7 explained.

THE MONEY MARKET: LIQUIDITY PREFERENCE THEORY

The **liquidity preference theory of interest rate determination** stipulates that the interest rate is determined in the money market at the point where the demand for money equals the supply of money:

$$M^d = M^s \qquad\qquad (9\text{--}1)$$

Determining the Interest Rate and the Quantity of Money

Chapter 7 explains that money demand depends negatively on the interest rate; Chapter 8, that money supply depends positively on the interest rate. Putting the downward-sloping money demand curve and the upward-sloping money supply curve in the same graph, we illustrate the money market. The intersection of the two curves, the *equilibrium point in the money market*, determines the interest rate and the quantity of money. Herein lies the appeal of the liquidity preference theory of interest, for one graph displays both the interest rate and the quantity of money—two variables of extreme importance in monetary economics.

Figure 9–1 depicts the liquidity preference theory. The interest rate is determined at that level where the demand for money equals the supply, shown by point E. Thus, the equilibrium level of the interest rate is i_1, and the equilibrium level of the quantity of money is M_1. The graph, however, says more than that: If the interest rate is lower, say, at i_2, the quantity of money demanded will be greater than the quantity of money supplied, which means there is *excess demand for money (EDM)*. Applying the principle of excess demand to the money market, the interest rate will rise. The rising interest rate induces the public to switch from money to securities, thereby reducing the quantity of money demanded, shown by the movement from point D to point E along the money demand curve in Figure 9–1. On the supply side, the rising interest rate increases the quantity of money supplied, because borrowed reserves rise and excess reserves fall when the interest rates rise. The movement along the supply curve from point C to point E shows the increase in the quantity of money supplied. The interest rate rises until the market clears at point E.

On the other hand, if the interest rate is above i_1, say, at i_3, the quantity of money demanded will be less than the quantity of money supplied, which means there is *excess*

FIGURE 9–1
Liquidity
Preference Theory

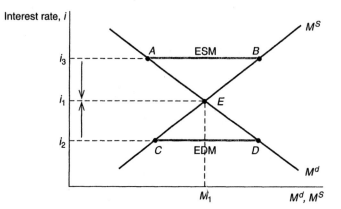

If $i < i_1$, $M^d > M^s$; there is EDM $\Rightarrow$ $i \uparrow$.
If $i = i_1$, $M^d = M^s$; there is equilibrium in the money market and i does not change.
If $i > i_1$, $M^d < M^s$; there is ESM $\Rightarrow$ $i \downarrow$.

supply of money (ESM) equal to *AB* in Figure 9–1. Applying the principle of excess supply to the money market, the interest rate will fall to clear the market. The falling interest rate increases the quantity of money demanded and reduces the quantity of money supplied until the two equal. This is how market forces determine the interest rate according to the liquidity preference theory.

The notion that the interest rate is determined in the money market by supply and demand is relatively new. It was introduced in the 1930s by John Maynard Keynes, who at the same time also introduced the concept of money demand. Because Keynes used the term *liquidity preference* for money demand, the theory that asserts that the demand for money and the supply of money determine the interest rate became known as the liquidity preference theory of interest rate determination.

In addition to the interest rate, the liquidity preference theory also determines the quantity of money, M_1 in the graph. An alternative to the graphical method of finding the equilibrium quantity of money is using either the money demand or the money supply equation. Because the equilibrium point lies on both the demand and the supply curves, we can calculate the quantity of money by simply substituting the equilibrium value of the interest rate, i_1, in either relation. Let us see how this is done using the money supply relation, where included in the notation is the property that borrowed reserves and excess reserves depend on the spread, $(i - d)$:

$$M^s = Cur + (1/rr) \times \underbrace{\{NBR + BR(i - d) - ER(i - d)\}}_{\text{Effective reserves}}$$

(9–2)

Substituting in Equation 9–2 the equilibrium level of the interest rate, i_1, in addition to the specific values of *NBR, d, rr,* and *Cur,* we can determine *M.*

The Deposit Rate

The quantity of money is not the only variable that depends on the interest rate. Figure 9–2 depicts the upward-sloping deposit rate curve introduced in Chapter 7. This graph shows that there is a different deposit rate for each interest rate. Having determined that

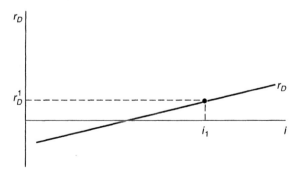

FIGURE 9–2
The Deposit Rate Relation and the Deposit Rate

When the interest rate is i_1, the deposit rate is r_D^1

the equilibrium interest rate is i_1, we find the equilibrium level of the deposit rate: r_D^1 in Figure 9–2.

Factors Affecting Rates and Money

We are now ready to examine changes in the interest rate, the deposit rate, and the quantity of money. Factors that affect rates and money are naturally divided into two categories: those that shift the money supply curve and those that shift the money demand curve.

Shifts in Money Supply   The money supply curve can shift because of changes in the behavior of the Fed, banks, or the public. We concentrate here on the Fed.

Open Market Operations   Open market operations (OMO) are the primary instrument of monetary policy. Figure 9–3 shows the effects of an open market purchase of securities equal to ΔB_F. The money market is initially in equilibrium at point 1, with the interest rate at i_1 and the quantity of money at M_1. An open market purchase of securities equal to ΔB_F increases nonborrowed reserves by the same amount: $\Delta B_F = \Delta NBR$. At the initial interest rate, i_1, this is the only change in effective reserves because borrowed reserves and excess reserves remain unchanged. Therefore, according to Equation 9–2, the money supply increases by a multiple of the open market purchase, that is by $(1/rr) \times \Delta NBR$, which equals the distance between point 1 and point 1′. In other words, the open market purchase of securities shifts the money supply curve to the right by the amount $(1/rr) \times \Delta NBR$.

At the original interest rate, i_1, money demand is unchanged. Therefore, the money market exhibits excess supply, equal to the distance between point 1 and point 1′. This excess supply is eliminated only when the interest rate falls to i_2, the interest rate at point 2. The effect of the lower interest rate on the quantity of money supplied is shown by a movement along the new money supply curve from point 1′ to point 2. The quantity of money supplied falls because banks want to borrow fewer reserves from the Fed and to

FIGURE 9–3
The Effects of an Open Market Purchase of Securities on the Interest Rate and the Quantity of Money

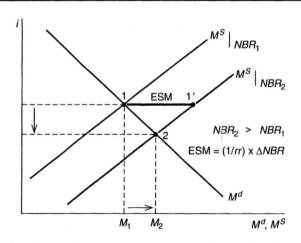

An open market purchase of securities by the Fed increases the quantity of reserves available to be used as required reserves and, hence, the supply of money. As a result, there is excess supply of money at the interest rate i_1, which causes the equilibrium level of the interest rate to fall. The equilibrium level of the quantity of money rises.

FIGURE 9–4
The Effect of an
Open Market
Purchase of
Securities on the
Deposit Rate

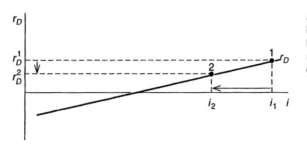

An open market purchase of securities by the Fed reduces the equilibrium level of the interest rate, which, in turn, reduces the equilibrium level of the deposit rate.

hold more excess reserves as the interest rate falls, thereby lowering effective reserves. This fall in effective reserves mitigates but does not offset the original increase from the Fed's purchase of Treasury securities. Therefore, in the end, the equilibrium level of the quantity of money rises to M_2, shown by point 2 in the graph. In sum, an open market purchase of securities by the Fed lowers the interest rate and increases the quantity of money.

Finally, having determined that an open market purchase of securities by the Fed reduces the interest rate, we use the relationship between the deposit rate and the interest rate to find the new deposit rate. Figure 9–4 shows that when the interest rate falls from i_1 to i_2, banks lower the deposit rate from r_D^1 to r_D^2, shown by the movement from point 1 to point 2. The fall in the deposit rate is less than the fall in the interest rate because the slope of the deposit rate curve is less than 1.

TRY IT OUT 9.1

Suppose that the Fed sells $100 million of Treasury securities in the open market and that the reserve requirement ratio is 0.10. With the help of a graph of the money market, explain why the M^s curve will shift to the left by $1,000 million but the equilibrium value of the quantity of money will fall by less than $1,000 million.

Discount Rate Policy   Changes in the discount rate by the Fed also shift the money supply curve. Suppose that the Fed reduces the discount rate from d_1 to d_2. Figure 9–5 depicts this case, where point 1 is the initial equilibrium. For a given value of i, a reduction in d increases the spread, $(i - d)$, which induces banks to increase the amount of reserves they borrow from the Fed and to reduce the amount of excess reserves they hold, thereby leaving more reserves to support deposits. That is, other things equal, the effective reserves increase by the amount $(\Delta BR - \Delta ER)$. Further, the money supply rises by the multiple amount, $(1/rr) \times (\Delta BR - \Delta ER)$. Thus, at the original interest rate, i_1, the money supply curve shifts to the right by this multiple amount, as illustrated in Figure 9–5, where point 1′ shows the new quantity of money supplied at the interest rate i_1. There is excess supply of money equal to the distance between point 1 and point 1′. As a result, the interest rate falls. Point 2 depicts the new equilibrium. The interest rate at point

FIGURE 9–5
The Effects of a Reduction in the Discount Rate on the Interest Rate and the Quantity of Money

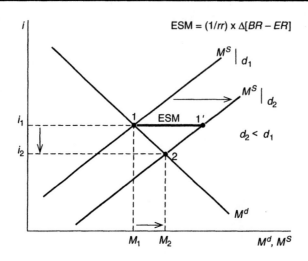

A reduction by the Fed of the discount rate from d_1 to d_2 increases the quantity of reserves available to be used as required reserves and, hence, the supply of money. As a result, there is excess supply of money at the interest rate i_1, which causes the equilibrium level of the interest rate to fall. The equilibrium level of the quantity of money rises.

TABLE 9–1
Reductions in the U.S. Discount Rate: *1990–1992*

Effective Date		Discount Rate
1990	December 19	6.5%
1991	February 4	6.0
	May 2	5.5
	September 17	5.0
	November 7	4.5
	December 24	3.5
1992	July 7	3.0

Source: *Federal Reserve Bulletin.*

2 is lower, and the quantity of money higher, than at point 1. The deposit rate also falls. The graph of the deposit rate looks like Figure 9–4.

In the early 1990s the Fed used discount rate policy often. Table 9–1 shows that the Fed lowered the discount rate from 6.5 percent to 3 percent in six steps between December 1990 and July 1992.

The discount rate, however, is only a secondary instrument of monetary policy. The Fed combined reductions in the discount rate with numerous open market purchases of securities. As a result of these changes in the primary and secondary instruments of monetary policy, the Fed brought down short-term market rates of interest by about 4 percentage points from the end of 1990 to mid-1992, as shown in Figure 9–6.

FIGURE 9–6
The Discount Rate
and Short-Term
Market Rates of
Interest

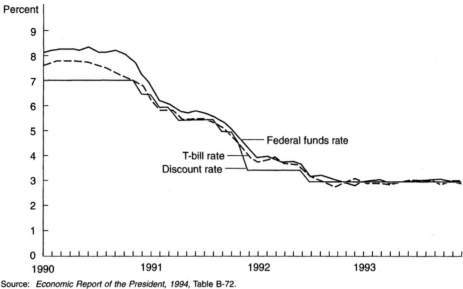

Source: *Economic Report of the President, 1994,* Table B-72.

GlobalWatch 9.1 explains why policymakers in Germany and the United States were pushing interest rates in opposite directions in 1991 and 1992.

General Principle   Open market operations and changes in the discount rate are two factors that affect rates and the quantity of money by shifting the money supply curve. This curve also shifts if the Fed changes the reserve requirement ratio.[1] Moreover, the money supply curve can shift without any change in Federal Reserve policy. For example, banks may change their behavior by deciding to hold fewer excess reserves at any given spread between the interest rate and the discount rate. As a result, effective reserves rise and the money supply increases at each value of the interest rate.

In general, any factor that increases the supply of money will reduce the equilibrium level of the interest rate and will increase the equilibrium level of the quantity of deposits and the money supply. The opposite holds for any factor that decreases the money supply.

Shifts in Money Demand   Another group of factors affects rates and money by shifting the money demand curve. As an example, we examine one of those factors— cash management techniques—before stating the general principle.

---

[1] In the new financial environment, a change in the reserve ratio also shifts the money demand curve because the deposit rate varies with this ratio. We consider the details in Chapter 22.

Global*Watch* 9.1

Fed and Bundesbank Push Rates in Opposite Directions

On January 31, 1991, the Bundesbank (the central bank of Germany) raised the discount rate in Germany from 6.0 to 6.5 percent. A few days later, the Federal Reserve lowered the U.S. discount rate from 6.0 to 5.5 percent. As a result, short-term market rates of interest rose in Germany and fell in the United States.

Why were monetary policymakers in Germany and the United States trying to push interest rates in opposite directions? The answer is they were reacting to different domestic economic conditions. In Germany, the pressures of reunification had ratcheted up the inflation rate to 3 percent, which was high by German standards. Further, rapid money growth was signaling further increases in inflation. To dampen demand for goods and services and quell rising prices, the Bundesbank raised the discount rate. In contrast, the Fed confronted a weak U.S. economy, with real GDP falling and house-holds, firms, and banks suffering from balance sheet distress. Therefore, the Fed was pushing rates down to stimulate demand for goods and services.

Because of divergent domestic conditions, the Fed and the Bundesbank continued to move their discount rates in opposite directions throughout 1991 and 1992, as shown in the first two columns of the table. The third column shows that the Bank of Japan (the Japanese central bank) lowered its discount rate in 1991 and 1992. Why? The Japanese economy was in a slump, with growth of real GDP falling along with property prices and the stock market.

Discount Rate (end of year)

	United States	Germany	Japan
1990	6.5%	6.0%	6.0%
1991	3.5	8.0	4.5
1992	3.0	8.25	3.25

Source: *Bank of Japan Quarterly Bulletin.*

Improvements in Cash Management Techniques   As Chapter 6 discussed, an improvement in cash management techniques, represented by a reduction of the collective variable, $\mathcal{C}$, induces the public to reduce its demand for deposits (money) and, with the released funds, to increase its demand for securities. The switch from deposits to securities reduces the demand for money at each level of the interest rate. As a result, the money demand curve shifts to the left in Figure 9–7, where point 1 is the initial equilibrium. At the original level of the interest rate, i_1, there is now excess supply of money equal to the distance between point 1 and point 1′. By the principle of excess supply, the interest rate falls to the new equilibrium level, i_2, depicted by point 2. With a lower interest rate, a smaller amount of money is supported by reserves because borrowed reserves fall and excess reserves rise; that is, the effective reserves fall. The horizontal axis of Figure 9–7 shows that the equilibrium level of the quantity of money falls to M_2.

Finally, what happens to the deposit rate? In this case there are two effects on the r_D curve: a shift of the curve and a movement along the new curve. Chapter 7 explains that a change in $\mathcal{C}$ shifts the r_D curve at each value of the interest rate. Given i, a fall in $\mathcal{C}$ reduces the amount of deposits the public wants to hold, thereby inducing banks to raise the deposit rate to try to keep their customers. As a result, the r_D curve shifts upward, as shown in Figure 9–8 by the movement from point 1 to point 1′. On the other hand, the lower equilibrium value of the interest rate lowers the deposit rate, as shown by a

FIGURE 9–7
The Effects of an
Improvement in
Cash Management
on the Interest
Rate and the
Quantity of Money

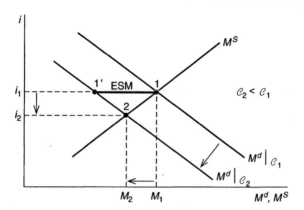

A decrease in the demand for money by the public creates excess supply of money. As a result, the equilibrium level of the interest rate falls. The equilibrium level of the quantity of money also falls.

FIGURE 9–8
The Effect of an
Improvement in
Cash Management
on the Deposit
Rate

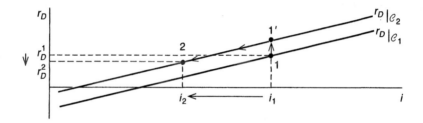

A decrease in the demand for money has two effects on the deposit rate: The deposit rate curve shifts upward at each interest rate as banks try to keep their customers, and there is a movement down the new curve because the interest rate falls. The deposit rate may rise, fall, or remain unchanged. The graph shows a lower deposit rate.

movement down the new r_D curve in Figure 9–8 from point $1'$ to point 2. Whether the deposit rate falls enough to negate the initial rise is an empirical issue.

The General Principle   The money demand curve also shifts due to other causes, such as changes in the level of national income, the risk structure of securities, or the uncertainty surrounding future employment. At this point, our interest is in establishing the general principle: **Any factor that reduces the demand for deposits and increases the demand for securities will reduce the equilibrium level of the interest rate, the equilibrium level of the quantity of deposits, and the equilibrium level of the quantity of money. The opposite holds for any factor that increases the demand for deposits and reduces the demand for securities.**

So far we have examined shifts of the money supply and demand curves separately. FedWatch 9.2 explains why both curves shifted after the stock market crash of 1987.

FedWatch 9.2

The Fed Responds to the Stock Market Crash of 1987

On Monday, October 19, 1987, the Dow Jones Industrial Average fell 22.6 percent. In the aftermath of this crash, there was a flight to quality. Concerned about the increased risk of holding securities, asset holders diverted funds from securities to money. If the Fed had not acted, this rise in money demand would have increased the interest rate, and the higher cost of borrowing would have slowed the U.S. economy.

The Fed, however, did respond immediately. The immediate concern of the Fed was to provide liquidity to the financial system to prevent a financial collapse. It poured reserves into the banking system through open market operations. The resulting increase in the supply of money accommodated the increase in money demand and kept interest rates from rising, as illustrated in the graph. As a result, the slowdown in economic activity that was widely predicted at the time never materialized.

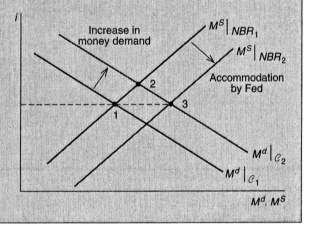

THE SECURITIES MARKET: LOANABLE FUNDS THEORY

Having examined the liquidity preference theory, we turn now to the loanable funds theory of interest rate determination. This commonsense theory says that the interest rate on securities is determined in the securities market by the demand for securities and the supply of securities. The demanders of securities are lenders. For example, if you buy a Treasury bill, you make a loan to the U.S. government. The suppliers of debt securities, such as the U.S. Treasury, are borrowers. This is the reason this theory is called the *loanable funds theory*.

The Demand for Securities

The **demand for securities** (B^d) is the sum of the demand by the public, the demand by the banks, and the demand by the Fed.[2] We begin by considering how the demand by each of these participants responds to a change in the interest rate.

Other things equal, the public's demand for securities increases when the interest rate (on securities) increases. This is a direct consequence of the first law of asset demand. Similarly, other things equal, the demand by banks also increases when the interest rate increases. We add the two demands together and illustrate them graphically by the upward-sloping curve $B_P^d + B_B^d$ in Figure 9–9. You may have never seen an upward-sloping demand curve before. Remember that there is an inverse relation between the price of securities and the interest rate on securities. Therefore, the demand curve for

---

[2]   The demand for securities is the quantity demanded at a point in time. Therefore, like the demand for money, the demand for securities is a stock.

FIGURE 9–9
The Demand for
Securities by the
Public and Banks

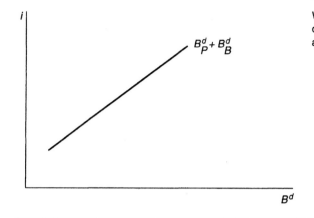

When the interest rate rises, the
demand for securities by the public
and by banks increases.

FIGURE 9–10
The Demand
for Securities by
the Fed

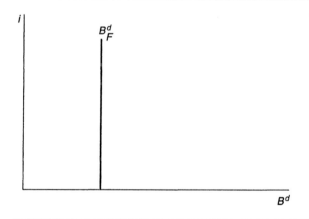

The demand for securities by the Fed
is independent of the interest rate.

securities would be downward sloping if the vertical axis in Figure 9–9 depicted the price
of securities instead of the interest rate on securities.

The Fed, too, buys securities—not, however, to earn interest, but rather for policy
purposes. In other words, the demand for securities by the Fed is a policy decision,
independent of the interest rate. The vertical demand curve in Figure 9–10 depicts the
Fed's demand.

Finally, to determine the demand for securities, we merely add the fixed demand by
the Fed to the demand by the public and by banks $B^d = B_p^d + B_B^d + B_F^d$. Graphically, we find
the demand curve by adding horizontally the two curves in Figure 9–9 and 9–10. The
result is an upward-sloping curve, such as the one in Figure 9–11, which establishes that,
other things equal, the demand for securities increases when the interest rate increases.
Note that this curve has the same slope as the curve in Figure 9–9. The reason is that in

FIGURE 9–11
The Demand for
Securities

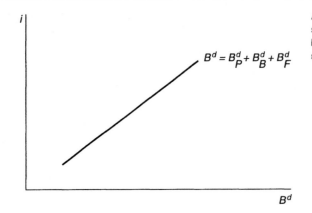

Adding horizontally the demand for
securities by the public and banks and
by the Fed, we derive the demand for
securities.

$$B^d = B^d_P + B^d_B + B^d_F$$

FIGURE 9–12
The Supply of
Securities and its
Components

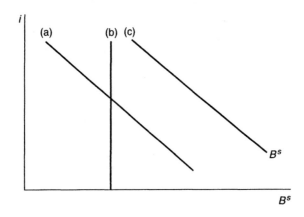

Curve (a) illustrates the public's supply
of securities: the higher the interest
rate, the smaller the supply. The U.S.
Treasury's supply of securities is
illustrated by the vertical line (b) to
signify that the Treasury's supply of
securities is independent of the interest
rate. Adding the two curves
horizontally, we derive the supply of
securities, curve (c).

deriving the curve in Figure 9–11, we add the Fed's demand for debt securities, which
has a zero slope, to the curve in Figure 9–9.

The Supply of Securities

To determine the interest rate, we also need to ascertain the supply of securities. The
supply of securities (B^s) consists of the supply by the public plus the supply by the U.S.
Treasury at a moment in time. When firms supply securities, they borrow funds. Borrowing increases when the cost of borrowing falls, that is, when the interest rate falls. Thus,
the public's supply of securities is related negatively to the interest rate, as illustrated by
the downward-sloping curve designated (a) in Figure 9–12.[3] On the other hand, the

---

[3] If the vertical axis in Figure 9–12 depicted the price of securities instead of the interest rate on securities, the
public's supply curve would be upward sloping.

supply of securities by the U.S. Treasury is represented by the vertical line (b) in the same graph. The vertical supply curve means that the supply is independent of the interest rate. Why? At any moment in time, this supply is fixed from the past. The U.S. Treasury borrows to finance the national debt no matter what the level of the interest rate. Adding the two curves horizontally, we derive the supply of securities, the downward-sloping curve (c).

The Interest Rate

The **loanable funds theory of interest rate determination** stipulates that the interest rate is determined in the securities market at the point where the demand for securities equals the supply of securities:

$$B^d = B^s \tag{9–3}$$

Figure 9–13 depicts the graphical solution to Equation 9–3. At point E, the *equilibrium point in the securities market*, the demand curve and the supply curve intersect. The equilibrium level of the interest rate is i_1, and the equilibrium level of the quantity of securities is B_1.

To say that the interest rate is determined in the securities market also means that the interest rate moves to clear the securities market when the market is out of equilibrium. For example, in Figure 9–13, at the interest rate i_3 there is *excess demand for securities (EDB)*: The quantity demanded of securities exceeds the quantity supplied by the amount AB. Applying the principle of excess demand to the securities market, the interest rate falls. Remember that the price of a security and the interest rate on a security move in opposite directions. With demand outstripping supply at the existing interest rate, market participants bid up the price of securities. Thus, the interest rate falls. A fall in the interest rate reduces the quantity demanded of securities, shown by a movement down the demand curve from point B to point E, and increases the quantity supplied, shown by a movement down the supply curve from point A to point E. The interest rate falls until the excess demand is eliminated, at point E.

FIGURE 9–13
Loanable Funds Theory

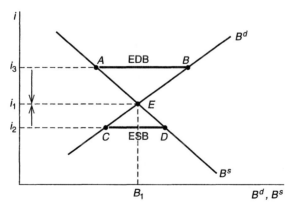

If $i > i_1$, $B^d > B^s$, there is EDB $\Rightarrow i\downarrow$.
If $i = i_1$, $B^d = B^s$, there is equilibrium in the securities market and i will not change.
If $i < i_1$, $B^d < B^s$, there is ESB $\Rightarrow i\uparrow$.

On the other hand, at interest rates below the equilibrium, such as i_2, there is *excess supply of securities (ESB)*: The quantity of securities supplied exceeds the quantity demanded by the amount CD. Applying the principle of excess supply to the securities market, the price of securities will fall, and the interest rate will rise. The consequent rise in the interest rate increases the quantity demanded and reduces the quantity supplied of securities, thereby eleminating the excess supply.

The graph in Figure 9–13 determines the interest rate, i, but not the quantity of money, M. To determine the quantity of money, we use the money supply equation. Finally, we determine the deposit rate by using the relation between the deposit rate and the interest rate, as we did with the liquidity preference theory.

Factors Affecting the Interest Rate

We are now ready to find the effects on the interest rate of open market operations, discount rate policy, and a change in cash management techniques. The analysis shows that the loanable funds theory gives the same results as the liquidity preference theory.

Open Market Operations   An open market purchase of securities by the Fed is an increase in its demand for securities, B_F. Thus, at the original interest rate, there is an excess demand for securities. By the principle of excess demand, the price of securities will rise and the interest rate will fall.

Graphically, the Fed's vertical demand curve in Figure 9–14(a) shifts to the right by a horizontal distance equal to the amount of the purchased securities. As a consequence, in Figure 9–14(b) the aggregate demand for securities will shift to the right by the same horizontal distance. The resulting excess demand for securities forces the interest rate down to i_2. Let's see this in more detail. At the initial interest rate, i_1, there is now excess demand

FIGURE 9–14
The Effects of an
Open Market
Purchase of
Securities on the
Interest Rate and
the Quantity of
Securities

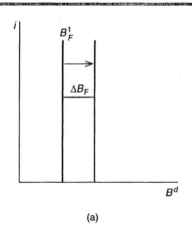

(a)

An open market purchase of securities
shifts the Fed's demand for securities.

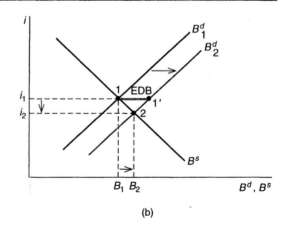

(b)

An open market purchase of securities causes excess
demand for securities, which reduces the equilibrium level
of the interest rate. The equilibrium level of the quantity of
securities rises.

for securities equal to the distance between point 1 and point 1'. By the principle of excess demand, the interest rate on debt securities falls, as demanders who cannot buy securities at the original interest rate accept a lower rate, and suppliers (borrowers) oblige.

Discount Rate Policy   Now consider the effect of a reduction in the discount rate, d. Such a reduction increases the spread, $i - d$, which is the measure of the marginal revenue of borrowing from the Fed as well as the opportunity cost of holding excess reserves. As a consequence, the banking system as a whole increases its borrowing from the Fed. Typically, banks are allowed to borrow from the Fed only when they have a reserve deficiency and not to make investments. However, the entire banking system will have a greater quantity of available funds, which can ultimately be used for lending. In addition, of course, funds that are released from their role as excess reserves can also be used for loans and investments.

The combination of increased borrowed reserves and reduced excess reserves makes an equal amount of funds available for buying securities depicted by the distance between point 1 and point 1' in Figure 9–15. The increased demand for securities by banks causes excess demand for securities, thereby forcing the interest rate to fall to i_2, reestablishing equilibrium at point 2 as Figure 9–15 shows. Thus, the effect of a reduction in the discount rate on the interest rate is identical to the effect predicted by the liquidity preference theory.

Improvements in Cash Management Techniques   As earlier, suppose that the collective variable, $\mathcal{C}$, falls because of, say, the introduction of new cash management techniques. The public needs a smaller amount of money to carry out its transactions. Thus, the public has more funds that it can use to invest in securities. The increase in the

FIGURE 9–15
The Effects of a Reduction in the Discount Rate on the Interest Rate and the Quantity of Securities

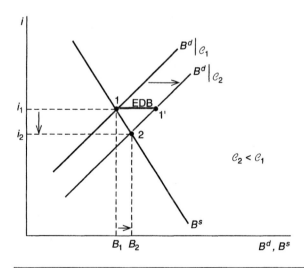

A reduction in the discount rate, d, increases the banking system's available funds, thereby increasing the demand for securities and reducing the interest rate. The equilibrium level of the quantity of securities rises.

FIGURE 9–16
The Effects of
Improvements in
Cash Management
Techniques on the
Interest Rate and
the Quantity of
Securities

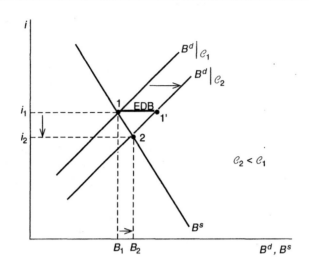

Improvements in cash management
techniques reduce the public's need
for money, releasing funds to be
invested in securities. The consequent
excess demand reduces the interest
rate. The equilibrium level of the
quantity of securities rises.

public's demand for securities creates an excess demand for securities, depicted by the distance between point 1 and point 1′ in Figure 9–16. By the principle of excess demand, the interest rate falls, just as the liquidity preference theory predicts.

TRY IT OUT 9.2

In FedWatch 9.2, we saw that the flight to quality by the public after the stock market crash of 1987 increased the demand for money. The Fed's response of purchasing Treasury securities increased the supply of money, thereby keeping the interest rate unchanged. In the following situations, illustrate these results using the loanable funds theory.

1. Use the loanable funds theory of interest rate determination to illustrate the effect on the interest rate of a decrease in the demand for securities and an increase in the demand for money.

2. Next, show how open market purchases by the Fed could offset the effect on the interest rate of the flight from securities to money.

LOOKING AHEAD

This chapter has examined the effect on the interest rate of changes in monetary policy and in the behavior of the public. The next chapter explains how changes in real income and in the price level also affect the interest rate by shifting the money demand curve or the money supply curve. Moreover, by connecting the money market to the market for goods and services, the chapter shows that a change in monetary policy has more than one effect on the interest rate.

SUMMARY

- According to the liquidity preference theory of interest rate determination, the interest rate is determined in the money market by the demand for money and the supply of money. If there is excess demand for money, the interest rate rises, if there is excess supply, the interest rate falls, and if demand equals supply, the interest rate is at its equilibrium level.

- To find the deposit rate, we use the relation between the deposit rate and the interest rate.

- Changes in the policy instruments of the Federal Reserve or in the behavior of banks or the public will change the equilibrium levels of the interest rate, the deposit rate, and the quantity of money. We gain insight into these applications by examining two factors that affect the supply of money and one that affects the demand.

- An increase in the supply of money brought about by an open market purchase of securities by the Fed reduces the interest rate and the deposit rate and increases the quantity of money. A reduction in the discount rate has the same effects.

- A decrease in the demand for money and a corresponding increase in the demand for securities brought about by new or improved cash management techniques reduces the interest rate and the quantity of money. The deposit rate, however, may rise, fall, or remain unchanged.

- The loanable funds theory is an alternative theory of interest rate determination. According to this theory, the interest rate is determined in the securities market by the demand for securities and the supply of securities.

- The demand for securities varies positively with the interest rate. It consists of the demand by the public, banks, and the Fed.

- The supply of securities varies inversely with the interest rate. It consists of the supply by the public and by the Treasury.

- According to the loanable funds theory, if there is excess demand for securities, the price of securities rises and the interest rate falls; if there is excess supply, the price of securities falls and the interest rate rises, and if supply equals demand, neither the price nor the interest rate changes.

- The effects on the interest rate of changes in Fed policy or in the behavior of the public can be examined using the loanable funds theory. The results are the same as with the liquidity preference theory.

- An open market purchase by the Fed increases the Fed's demand for Treasury securities, which creates excess demand for securities, forcing the price of securities to rise and the interest rate to fall.

- A decrease in the discount rate raises the demand for securities by banks, again causing the interest rate to fall.

- A reduction in money demand and an increase in demand for securities by the public also cause the interest rate to fall.

KEY TERMS AND CONCEPTS

equilibrium

market clearance

excess demand

excess supply

principles of excess demand and excess supply

liquidity preference theory of interest rate determination

demand for securities

supply of securities

loanable funds theory of interest rate determination

QUESTIONS AND PROBLEMS

The Wall Street Journal

1. The following quotation is from "Money Supply Weakness Could Bring Rates Down," *The Wall Street Journal*, September 20, 1991. " 'If the rate of growth in money and credit doesn't accelerate quickly, the Fed may not wait long to nudge rates down again, predicts Fed watcher Robert Chandross at Lloyd's Bank in New

York." Explain the primary way that the Fed "nudges rates down." Also explain how this action by the Fed increases the money supply.

2. Suppose that banks become more prudent: At any given value of the spread, $(i - d)$, they want to hold more excess reserves and make fewer loans and investments, that is, to buy fewer securities.

   a. Use the liquidity preference theory of interest rate determination to explain and illustrate the effect of this change in bank behavior on the interest rate.

   b. Confirm your answer to *a* by using the loanable funds theory of interest rate determination.

   c. Also explain what will happen to the deposit rate.

3. Suppose that the Fed increases the discount rate. Explain and illustrate graphically what will happen to the deposit rate.

4. Suppose that the Fed uses open market operations to keep the quantity of money unchanged no matter what else happens in the economy. With the help of a money demand–money supply diagram, show how the Fed will react if increased uncertainty about the economy increases the demand for money. What will be the effect on the interest rate?

5. Suppose that the Fed uses open market operations to keep the interest rate fixed no matter what else happens in the economy. With the help of a money demand–money supply diagram, show how the Fed will react if increased uncertainty about the economy increases the demand for money. What will be the effect on the quantity of money?

6. Depict the demand and supply of securities as a function of the price of securities by drawing a graph with the price on the vertical axis and the quantity of securities on the horizontal axis. On your graph, identify a securities price at which there is excess demand and a price at which there is excess supply. Explain how the price of securities and the interest rate change in each case.

7. Suppose that banks become more reluctant to approach the Fed for a discount window loan: At any given value of the spread, $(i - d)$, they want to borrow less from the Fed and to buy fewer securities. Use the loanable funds theory of interest rate determination to show what will happen to the interest rate. Confirm the result by using the liquidity preference theory.

8. Suppose that the money supply process is based on the following hypothetical data:

   $NBR = \$53$ billion

   $Cur = \$294$ billion

   $BR = 1.5 + 0.2(i - d)$ \$ billions

   $ER = 3.5 - 0.2(i - d)$ \$ billions

   $d = 4$ percent

   $rr = 0.075$

   Also suppose that money demand is given by:

   $M^d = 973 - 0.25i + 0.2\mathcal{C}$

   Where

   $\mathcal{C} = 100$

   Find the equilibrium values of the interest rate, i, and the quantity of money, M.

9. Suppose your answer to Question 8 is the initial equilibrium. Next, suppose the Fed purchases $1 billion worth of Treasury securities in the open market. Find the new equilibrium values of the interest rate and the quantity of money. Illustrate your results graphically.

10. Again, start with your answer to Question 8. Now suppose the Fed reduces the discount rate to 3 percent. Find the new equilibrium values of i and M.

11. Starting from your answer to Question 8, find the effects on i and M of an increase in the collective variable, $\mathcal{C}$, from 100 to 120.

SUGGESTED READINGS

Keynes, John Maynard. *The General Theory of Employment, Interest, and Money.* New York: Harcourt Brace Jovanovich, 1936, Chapter 13, "The General Theory of the Rate of Interest."

   The original statement of the liquidity preference theory.

Tsiang, S. C. "Loanable Funds." In *The New Palgrave: Money,* ed. John Eatwell, Murray Milgate, and Peter Newman. New York: W. W. Norton, 1989, 190–94.

   An essay on loanable funds versus liquidity preference theories of interest rate determination.

A FRAMEWORK FOR THE ECONOMY:
The Real and the Financial Sectors

CHAPTER PREVIEW

Why did nominal interest rates in the United States hit record highs in the late 1970s and early 1980s, and quarter-century lows in 1993? How did monetary policy in Japan help create a "bubble economy" in the 1980s, and how was it used to burst the bubble in 1990? To answer these questions, we must complete the macroeconomic framework of the entire economy by linking the real sector, augmented by foreign exchange, to the financial sector examined in Chapter 9. This chapter is the epitome of the second pillar of economics, because it includes all the markets in the economy.

The real sector consists of the market for economywide output and the markets for two factors of production: labor and physical capital. The foreign exchange market consists of the market for foreign currency. After describing the real-sector variables and foreign exchange, this chapter examines the linkages between the real sector and the financial sector.

The links from the financial sector to the real sector work mainly through the interest rate. Key components of aggregate demand for goods and services depend on the interest rate. In the case of domestic demand, the connection is direct. In the case of exports and imports, however, the linkage works through the foreign exchange market. Effects are also felt in the opposite direction. Real-sector variables, such as the price level and real income, affect the demand for money or the supply of money and, hence, the interest rate.

Next, the chapter continues the discussion by introducing the aggregate demand–aggregate supply model. This model shows how the price level and real GDP are determined and how they change with economic policy. Emphasis is on monetary policy. Chapter 9 examined the money market in isolation and derived an inverse relation between changes in the money supply and changes in the interest rate, other things equal. But other things will not remain equal. By connecting the money market with the rest of the economic system, primarily with the market for goods and services, we see that a change in monetary policy has more than one effect on the interest rate. It sets in motion a chain of events that may change the price level, the level of output, and expected inflation; these changes, in turn, affect the interest rate. This chapter also examines how fiscal policy affects the price level, output, and the interest rate.

The chapter ends by connecting theory with practice. This chapter's analysis of the economic framework illuminates the conduct of economic policy in the United States and Japan in the 1990s.

THE REAL-SECTOR FRAMEWORK AND FOREIGN EXCHANGE

In modeling the real sector of the economy, we continue to follow Einstein's advice to make everything as simple as possible. Table 10–1 summarizes the simplified facts of the real sector augmented by foreign exchange. We begin with the real sector, represented in the first three rows of the table.

The Real Sector

The real sector consists of one output, the nation's annual output of final goods and services, and two inputs, labor and capital, the nation's productive resources. The annual output, called **gross domestic product (GDP)**, is produced by the nation's factors of

TABLE 10–1   Real Sector Augmented by Foreign Exchange

Goods and Services, Factors of Production, or Foreign Exchange	Demanders	Suppliers	Price, or Reward	Quantity
Real sector				
Goods and services	Households, firms, government, foreigners	Firms	Price level, P	Real GDP
Labor	Firms	Households	Real wage, W/P	Employed labor, N
Physical capital (plant and equipment)	Firms	Firms	Profit rate	Capital stock, K
Foreign exchange	U.S. public and financial institutions, Fed and foreign central banks	Foreign public and financial institutions, Fed and foreign central banks	Exchange rate, e	Foreign exchange, FE

production, labor and capital. By physical capital, or the **capital stock**, we mean the quantity of the nation's plant and equipment.

The Output of Goods and Services: Nominal GDP and Real GDP In our examination of the economy as a whole, we are interested in the collective experience of all markets for goods and services rather than the individual fortunes of specific markets. The most common models for an entire economy treat all final goods and services produced in a given year as a single collective good, as in Table 10–1. The focus is on *final* goods and services to avoid double counting. For example, we do not want to count both a loaf of bread and the wheat that goes into producing the loaf of bread. In this example, the wheat is an intermediate good used in the production of bread.

The goal is to examine how to add the components that make up the physical output of a nation—that is, to obtain a single measure of the quantity of final goods and services produced in a country in a given year. First, we multiply the quantity of each final good and service produced in a given year by its dollar price that year. Then we add all the results to get one number for total output. Chapter 1 explains that this sum is called *nominal GDP*. It also explains that *real GDP* is national output measured at fixed prices: the prices prevailing in a year designated as the base year, currently 1987.

A Note on GNP The Office of Business Economics of the Department of Commerce publishes quarterly and annual data on U.S. output and income in a set of tables called the National Income and Product Accounts. Before 1991, the main measure of U.S. output published by the Department of Commerce was **gross national product (GNP)**. At the end of 1991, the Commerce Department switched to GDP, which is the measure of output reported by most industrial countries. The difference is that GDP is the output of final goods and services produced *within* a country while GNP is the output of final goods and services produced by the country's residents and by domestically owned capital, whether that output is produced at home or abroad. For the United States, the difference between GNP and GDP is small. For example, in 1992 real GDP was ³⁄₁₀ of 1 percent smaller than real GNP.

The Price Level The price level, *P*, is an index that represents the collective dollar price of goods and services. The **consumer price index (CPI)** and the **GDP price deflator** are two alternative measures of the price level used in the United States. The Bureau of Labor Statistics compiles the consumer price index by pricing items in a fixed basket of goods and services, which represents the consumption of a typical urban family. The GDP price deflator, on the other hand, is constructed from a basket that includes all goods and services produced in the economy. The GDP price deflator is the measure of the price level that we introduced in Chapter 1 without giving it a name. It is calculated by dividing nominal GDP by real GDP.

P = GDP price deflator = (Nominal GDP/Real GDP)　　　　　　　　(10–1)

Remember that the value of the price level is 1 in the base year.

Rearranging Equation 10–1 highlights the following relationships among nominal GDP, the price level, and real GDP:

$$\text{Nominal GDP} = \text{Price level} \times \text{Real GDP} = PY \qquad (10\text{-}2)$$
$$\text{Real GDP} = \text{Nominal GDP}/P \qquad (10\text{-}3)$$

In general, the price level transforms the real value of a variable into its nominal value, and vice versa. Given the real value of any variable, we multiply by P to get the nominal value of the same variable. Conversely, given the nominal value of any variable, we divide by P, that is, deflate by P, to get the real value. Hence, P is called the *price deflator*. Of course, dividing a nominal value by the price level is the same as multiplying that nominal value by $(1/P)$; $(1/P)$ is the purchasing power of money, which represents the amount of output that a dollar can buy. Figure 10-1 shows the purchasing power of the U.S. dollar between 1960 and 1993, using 1987 as the base year. (Note that in 1987 the purchasing power is 1.)

The National Product Identity   In addition to the price and the quantity of goods and services, the first row of Table 10-1 identifies the demanders and suppliers of goods and services. On the demand side, households, firms, the government, and foreigners purchase the nation's domestic product. On the supply side, firms produce this product, known as Y. By definition, the product purchased by households, firms, the government, and foreigners together equals the domestic product, Y, produced and sold by firms. This relationship, expressed in equation form, is called the **national product identity**:[1]

FIGURE 10-1
The Domestic
Purchasing Power
of the Dollar

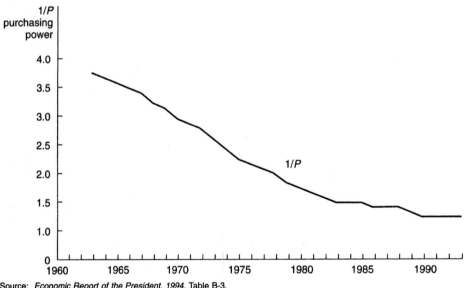

Source: *Economic Report of the President, 1994*, Table B-3.

---

[1] The term *national product identity* is used whether Y refers to gross domestic product or gross national product.

$$C + I + G + NX = Y \qquad\qquad (10\text{--}4)$$

Where:

C = Consumption

I = Investment

G = Government purchases

NX = net exports

Y = Domestic product

and C, I, G, NX, and Y are all in real terms.

In the National Income and Product Accounts, **consumption** is defined as expenditures by households on final goods and services, including nondurable and durable consumption goods.[2] **Investment** consists of expenditures by firms on plant, equipment, and inventories, and expenditures by households on new houses. **Government purchases** consist of government expenditures on final goods and services. They are not broken down into a consumption component and an investment component. Neither are **net exports**, which equal exports of goods and services minus imports of goods and services. The symbol X denotes exports and Q denotes imports. Therefore, $NX = X - Q$.

From the U.S. perspective, exports are expenditures by residents of foreign countries on final goods and services produced in the United States. They must be added to domestic expenditures to determine total expenditure on domestically produced goods. Imports are subtracted because some of the expenditures included in C, I, and G are for goods produced in foreign countries. For example, C includes purchases of clothing made both in the United States and in the rest of the world; I includes business equipment made both in the United States and in the rest of the world. In other words, there is an import content to C, I, and G that must be netted out to arrive at total expenditures on domestically produced goods.

Table 10–2 illustrates the national product identity for 1993. The table also illustrates the difference between gross domestic product (GDP) and **net domestic product (NDP)**. The distinction depends on whether the investment component of the equation refers to gross investment or net investment. Gross investment counts as investment all additions to the stock of plant, equipment, and houses, including the replacement of worn-out capital. Net investment, on the other hand, equals gross investment minus depreciation. If the investment measure on the left side of Equation 10–4 is gross investment, then the measure of national product, Y, on the right side is GDP. On the other hand, if I represents net investment, then Y represents NDP, which equals GDP minus depreciation.

Equation 10–4 is an identity devoid of theoretical connotation. It simply says that the *actual* quantity of GDP (or NDP) bought is always equal to the *actual* quantity of GDP (or NDP) produced and sold. Business inventories, which are a component of investment,

---

[2] The National Income and Product Accounts assume that households use up consumer durables in the year in which they purchase them. Therefore, these accounts include consumer durables in consumption. The Flow of Funds Accounts published by the Federal Reserve treat consumer durables differently. They include consumer durables in investment and, therefore, calculate the amount by which these goods wear out each year.

TABLE 10–2
The National
Product Identity:
1993 (In Billions
of Dollars, at
1987 Prices)

Consumption (C)	3,452.5
+	+
Investment (I)	820.9
+	+
Government purchases (G)	938.6
+	+
Net exports (NX)	−79.3
=	=
Gross domestic product (GDP)	5,132.7
−	−
Depreciation	598.6
=	=
Net domestic product (NDP)	4,534.1

Source: *Economic Report of the President, 1994,* Tables B–2 and B–18.

make the two sides of the identity balance. For example, suppose that at the existing level of output firms cannot sell all the goods they planned to sell. The unsold output is included in investment as a part of inventory accumulation. In this case, firms have unplanned investment in the form of unplanned accumulation of inventories. Conversely, suppose that at the existing level of output, firms sell more goods than they planned to sell. As a result, they have unplanned disinvestment in the form of an unplanned running down of inventories. Later in this chapter, we will see that when the market for goods and services is in equilibrium, the plans of all the participants are fulfilled. There is no *unplanned* running down or building up of inventories by firms. Instead, actual investment equals planned investment.

National Product and Income   One way of measuring the value of final goods and services produced in a given year is to add up all expenditures on that output. That sum is called *national product,* or *domestic product.* Alternatively, the value of final goods and services produced in a given year is the sum of the payments to all the factors of production that produce that output. In the accounts published by the Department of Commerce, factor payments are divided into wages, proprietors' income, rent, interest, and profits. The sum of factor payments is called the **national income**. National product and national income must be equal because they measure the same flow of final goods and services, but from different angles. We can therefore use the two terms interchangeably.

In the simplified framework in Table 10–1, the inputs, or factors of production, that produce the national product are divided into two categories: labor and physical capital, a catchall category that includes all other inputs used to produce GDP. Physical capital includes plant and equipment, land, and natural resources. It is often called, somewhat narrowly, *plant and equipment.* With this classification of the factors of production, there are only two types of factor payments: wages and profits.

Wages are the total return to labor. Under labor in Table 10–1, N represents the quantity of employed labor as measured, say, by the number of hours worked. W/P represents the real wage, the remuneration of a unit of labor in terms of purchasing power, where W is the nominal (dollar) wage per hour and P is the price level. Thus, total wages, in real terms, equal $(W/P) \times N$.

Profits are the total return to capital. In our simplified framework, we can think of profits as encompassing proprietors' income, rent, and interest. Under physical capital in Table 10–1 K denotes the quantity of physical capital. When profit is expressed as a percentage of the physical capital, it is called the *rate of profit.* Total profits equal the rate of profit multiplied by K. Total wages plus total profits equal national income in our simplified two-factor framework.

Foreign Exchange

The last category of Table 10–1 is foreign exchange. When Americans buy domestic goods and services and domestic financial assets, they pay for their purchases in U.S. dollars, the home country currency. On the other hand, when they buy foreign goods and services or foreign financial assets, they need foreign currencies, such as British pounds (£), German marks (DM), and Japanese yen (¥).

The quantity of foreign currency is denoted by FE, and the dollar price of a unit of foreign currency by e, which is called the **exchange rate**. There is a different exchange rate, or dollar price, for each foreign currency that can be exchanged with the dollar. For example, on April 29, 1993, the price of one British pound was $1.57; the price of one German mark was $0.63; and the price of one Japanese yen was $0.009 (nine-tenths of a cent). The inverse of the exchange rate, $1/e$, is the foreign exchange price of the dollar. It follows that to buy a dollar on April 29 it took 0.64 British pounds, 1.59 German marks, and 111.11 Japanese yen.

As in any market, there are demanders (buyers) of foreign exchange and suppliers (sellers) of foreign exchange. American importers of goods and services enter the foreign exchange market as demanders, as do Americans who purchase foreign assets. The supply of foreign exchange comes from foreigners who want to buy American goods and services and American assets. To obtain the dollars needed for their purchasers, foreigners supply their home country currencies. Finally, both the Federal Reserve and foreign central banks can participate in the foreign exchange market, either as demanders or suppliers.

Under a **flexible exchange rate system**, the interaction of the demand for and the supply of foreign exchange determines the exchange rate. Such a regime is also referred to as a **floating exchange rate system**. With a **clean float**, central banks do not intervene to influence the foreign exchange market. At the other extreme, in a **fixed exchange rate system**, the exchange rate is set by government fiat and is not allowed to fluctuate in response to excess demand or supply in the foreign exchange market. A commitment to a fixed exchange rate requires central banks to intervene in the foreign exchange market to mop up any excess supply of foreign exchange or to accommodate any excess demand.

The hybrid system in existence today is referred to as a **managed**, or **dirty, float**. Under this system, demand and supply in the foreign exchange market determine the exchange rate, but central banks sometimes participate in the market to influence the level of the exchange rate. The market for foreign exchange is not located in one place. Demanders and suppliers trade foreign exchange through commercial banks and brokerage firms linked by a worldwide communications network.

LINKAGES BETWEEN THE FINANCIAL SECTOR AND THE REAL SECTOR

Now that we have described the real sector and the foreign exchange market, the next step is to connect them with the financial sector. Chapter 9 distilled all the information about the financial sector into two markets: the market for money and the market for debt securities. Table 10–3 displays this information. It shows that the interest rate on debt securities may be determined in the money market (the liquidity preference theory) or the debt securities market (the loanable funds theory). For brevity, the debt securities market is often referred to simply as the *bonds market.*

The next step is to see how changes in the interest rate that originate in the financial sector affect real-sector variables and how these changes feed back to the financial sector. Similarly, we examine how changes that originate in the real sector affect the financial sector and how they feed back to the real sector. Our analysis uses the liquidity preference theory of interest rate determination, that is, the market for money, because we want to emphasize the effects of a change in the quantity of money on the economy.

From the Financial Sector to the Real Sector

The transmission mechanism from the financial sector to the real sector works through the effect of the interest rate on the **aggregate demand for goods and services**, which is the sum of planned consumption, planned investment, planned government purchases, and planned net exports. The overall aggregate demand for goods and services depends on all the factors that affect its components. One of these factors is the interest rate, which is determined in the money market.

Linkage via the Interest Rate   Several components of the aggregate demand for goods and services depend on the interest rate. These components are the demand for fixed investment in the form of plant and equipment, the demand for new housing, the demand for consumer durables, and the demand for net exports. A negative relation exists between these components of aggregate demand and the interest rate: When the interest rate rises, these components of aggregate demand fall, and when the interest rate falls, these components rise. Let's see why.

TABLE 10–3
The Financial Sector

Market	Equilibrium Condition	Interest Rate
Money	$M^d = M^s$ determines	
	or	i
Bonds	$B^d = B^s$ determines	

The linkage between the interest rate and demand for fixed investment, new houses, and consumer durables is direct. The interest rate is the cost of borrowing, that is, the cost of financing the purchase of new structures, new equipment, and consumer durables. Other things equal, when the cost of borrowing rises, these components of aggregate demand fall, and when the cost of borrowing falls, these components rise. In brief:

$$i\uparrow \rightarrow C \text{ and } I\downarrow$$

Note that the relevant interest rate that affects consumption and investment is the expected real rate of interest, not the nominal rate. The two differ by the rate of inflation that is expected at the repayment of the loan. Reserving the symbol i for the nominal interest rate, and denoting the expected rate of inflation by $(\Delta P/P)^{exp}$, we can write the expected real interest rate, i_r, as:

$$i_r = i - (\Delta P/P)^{exp} \tag{10–5}$$

Of course, if no inflation is expected, the nominal rate is also the real rate. We follow this simplified approach until we examine issues of inflation at the end of the chapter.

The other component of aggregate demand that depends on the interest rate is net exports. For net exports, the connection to the interest rate is indirect, operating through the foreign exchange market. An increase in the domestic interest rate, i, relative to foreign interest rates, i_f, increases the demand for U.S. securities by foreigners.[3] To buy American securities, however, the rest of the world needs dollars, which they obtain by offering their own currencies for sale in the foreign exchange market. As a result, there is excess supply of foreign exchange, which forces the exchange rate, e, to fall. In brief:

Given i_f, if $i \uparrow \rightarrow$ Demand for American securities by foreigners $\uparrow \rightarrow$
Supply of foreign exchange $\uparrow \rightarrow$ Excess supply of foreign exchange $\rightarrow e \downarrow$

Now we can find how imports and exports change. Other things equal, when the dollar price of foreign currency, e, falls, the dollar price of foreign goods and services also falls. In response, Americans increase their demand for foreign goods and services; that is, American imports rise. For example, if the dollar price of a British pound is $2/£1, Americans must pay $40 to buy a British sweater that costs £20. If the price of a pound falls from $2/£1 to $1.50/£/1, the dollar price of the same sweater will be only $30. Other things equal, Americans will buy more British sweaters at this lower dollar price.

A change in e also affects American exports. A decrease in e, the number of dollars it takes to buy a unit of foreign currency, implies an increase in $1/e$, the number of units of foreign currency that it takes to buy a dollar. In other words, the international price of the dollar rises. Other things equal, American goods now become more expensive to foreigners, who must pay more of their home currency to buy these goods. In response, the demand for American goods by the rest of the world falls; that is, American exports fall.

---

[3] Chapter 29 shows that the expected rate of change in the exchange rate also matters. We ignore this complication here.

In sum, an increase in the domestic interest rate relative to foreign interest rates reduces the exchange rate, which reduces exports and increases imports, so net exports fall. In terms of a simple schematic:

$$i\uparrow \rightarrow e\downarrow \rightarrow NX\downarrow$$

By combining the effects of a rise in the interest rate on all the components of aggregate demand, we find an inverse relation between the interest rate and aggregate demand, as shown by Schema 10–6a:

$$i\uparrow \rightarrow C \text{ and } I\downarrow \rightarrow AD\downarrow$$
$$\searrow e\downarrow \rightarrow NX\downarrow \rightarrow AD\downarrow \tag{10-6a}$$

Schema 10–6b reverses these results to show how a decrease in the interest rate increases aggregate demand for goods and services:

$$i\downarrow \rightarrow C \text{ and } I\uparrow \rightarrow AD\uparrow$$
$$\searrow e\uparrow \rightarrow NX\uparrow \rightarrow AD\uparrow \tag{10-6b}$$

Bank Credit Channel   Another link between the financial sector and the real sector that has received renewed attention recently works through the quantity of bank credit.[4] Proponents of the view that bank credit provides an independent link with aggregate demand argue that the interest rate is not always a reliable indicator of economic activity. The modern view utilizes the concept of asymmetric information and adverse selection to show that banks ration credit to borrowers.[5]

Asymmetric information, discussed in Chapter 2, means that borrowers have better information about their prospects of success than lenders, that is, banks. Adverse selection means that customers who are willing or anxious to pay a higher interest rate are the ones most likely to default. Thus, banks prefer not to charge the interest rate that the market can bear. This practice leaves a group of unsatisfied customers at the margin, thereby enabling banks to weed out the lemons (the bad risks) by rationing credit. It follows that to gauge the strength of economic activity, one must look beyond the going interest rate and also consider the quantity of bank credit. Even at the same interest rate, an increase in bank credit will increase aggregate demand, and a decrease in bank credit will decrease aggregate demand. Schematically,

$$\text{Bank credit}\uparrow \rightarrow C \text{ and } I\uparrow \rightarrow AD\uparrow$$
$$\text{Bank credit}\downarrow \rightarrow C \text{ and } I\downarrow \rightarrow AD\downarrow$$

From the Real Sector to the Financial Sector

The connection between the financial sector and the real sector also runs in the other direction, for real-sector variables, notably real income and the price level, affect the financial sector. In examining the laws of asset demand in Chapter 6, we did not distin-

---

[4] For early, influential work on the role of bank credit, see Benjamin Friedman, "The Roles of Money and Credit in Macroeconomic Analysis," in *Macroeconomics, Prices and Quantities: Essays in Memory of Arthur M. Okun*, ed. James Tobin (Washington, D.C.: Brookings Institution, 1983).

[5] For an early, influential paper on this view, see Joseph E. Stiglitz and Andrew Weiss, "Credit Rationing to Markets with Imperfect Information," *American Economic Review* 71 (June 1981), 393–410.

guish between real magnitudes and nominal magnitudes, nor did we mention the price level as one of the determinants of asset demand. On the other hand, we included income as one of the five factors affecting asset demand. Now, it is time to be more explicit about nominal and real values.

Following most economic literature, we specify all markets in real terms. Thus, for example, the demand for money is the demand for *real* money balances. We want to see how changes in the level of real income, Y, and in the price level, P, affect the demand for or the supply of money and, ultimately, the interest rate.

Linkage via Real Income   The **demand for real money balances** is the quantity of money, measured in terms of the prices of a base year, that the public wants to hold. This demand depends on the level of **real income**, which is national income measured in the prices of a base year. Because real income is identical to real output, we denote them by the same symbol, Y. Other things equal, when the level of real income rises, the public wants to hold more money, and when the level of real income falls, the public wants to hold less money.

Suppose that the money market is initially in equilibrium at point 1 in Figure 10–2. Next suppose that the level of real income rises. As a result, the demand for money rises. At the initial equilibrium level of the interest rate, i_1, the demand for money now exceeds the supply of money; there is excess demand for money equal to the distance between point 1 and point 1'. In response, the interest rate rises to i_2.[6] Conversely, a decrease in the level of real income reduces the demand for money and the money market–clearing level of the interest rate. Schema 10–7 sums up the linkages between a change in the level of real income and a change in the level of the interest rate; the positive relation between changes in real income and the interest rate is called the **real income effect on the interest rate**.

$$Y\uparrow \rightarrow M^d\uparrow \rightarrow \text{EDM} \rightarrow i\uparrow$$
and   (10–7)
$$Y\downarrow \rightarrow M^d\downarrow \rightarrow \text{ESM} \rightarrow i\downarrow$$

Linkage via the Price Level   A change in the price level does not affect the demand for real money balances, but it does affect the supply of real money balances.

Money Demand   On the demand side, the standard assumption is that the utility-maximizing public is interested in the purchasing power of its money holdings. Thus, the public makes plans about how much money to hold in real terms. As we saw earlier, the demand for real money balances depends on real income, Y, which equals real output. A change in the price level does not affect real output, because it is measured at constant prices, that is, in terms of the prices of a base year. Neither does it affect the demand for money measured in terms of the prices of a base year.

---

[6] A rise in real income increases money demand because demand for both currency and deposits rises. But a rise in currency also reduces the money supply. We simplify here by ignoring the effect on currency and hence on the money supply. Note, however, that i will rise even more when the money supply effect is incorporated.

FIGURE 10–2
The Real Income
Effect on the
Interest Rate

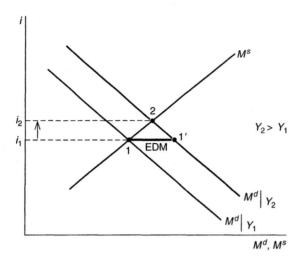

An increase in real income, *Y*,
increases the demand for real money
balances, thereby creating excess
demand for money. In response, the
interest rate rises.

We note the demand for real money balances by M^d. It follows that the demand for nominal money balances equals $P \times M^d$. An increase in P increases the nominal demand for money but not the real demand.

Money Supply   On the supply side, the **supply of real money balances** is the quantity of money, measured in real terms, that can be supported by reserves. The real supply of money, denoted by M^s, depends on the behavior of the Fed, the banks, and the public, as indicated in Equation 10–8.

$$M^s = Cur + \frac{1}{rr} \times \left(\frac{NBR}{P} + BR - ER\right)$$ (10–8)

Note that in Equation 10–8 we divide *NBR* by *P,* but we do not divide *Cur, BR,* or *ER* by *P.* Let's see why.

The public decides on the quantity of currency that it wants to hold, and banks decide on the quantity of excess reserves they want to hold and the quantity of reserves they want to borrow from the Fed. (Although the Fed provides borrowed reserves through discount window loans, it is the banks, based on their needs, that initiate the borrowing process.) The usual assumption is that profit-maximizing banks, like the utility-maximizing public, make their plans in real terms. Thus, *ER, BR, and Cur* are all in real terms.

The Fed, on the other hand, is not a profit maximizer. The ultimate goals of the Fed are to foster price stability, full employment, and maximum sustainable economic growth. In pursuit of these goals the Fed buys and sells Treasury securities in the open market, which increases or decreases the *nominal* quantity of nonborrowed reserves, *NBR*. To find the *real* value of nonborrowed reserves, we must divide *NBR* by *P.* In Equation 10–8 all other variables are in real terms, so nonborrowed reserves must also be in real terms, which accounts for *NBR/P* in the equation.

Note that Equation 10–8 is the same as Equation 8–12 in Chapter 8, except that Equation 8–12 does not include *P*. In Chapter 8, we had not introduced the price level or the effects of changes in the price level. Hence, we suppressed the issue by assuming that *P* was 1, as it is in the base year.

A Word on Notation   In economics, we often denote the nominal money supply by *M*. The real money supply is then denoted by *M/P* because the real value of any variable equals its nominal value divided by the price level. We can fit this notation into our model, where M^s denotes the real money supply, simply by setting M^s equal to *M/P*:

$$M^s = \frac{M}{P}$$

It follows that the nominal money supply, *M*, equals the real money supply, M^s, multiplied by the price level, *P*. The fact that the real money supply equals *M/P* becomes crucial later in this chapter when we discuss the neutrality of money. First, we examine the effect of an increase in the price level.

The Price-Level Effect   Equation 10–8 shows that, other things equal, an increase in the price level reduces the real supply of money. In particular, an increase in *P* reduces the real value of nonborrowed reserves, *NBR/P*. As a result, the real value of the quantity of reserves available for use as required reserves falls. So does the real value of the quantity of deposits supported by reserves and, hence, the real value of the money supply.

Figure 10–3 depicts the effect of an increase in the price level on the interest rate. An increase in *P*, from P_1 to P_2, shifts the (real) money supply curve to the left. At the initial equilibrium level of the interest rate, i_1, there is excess demand for money equal to the distance between point 1 and point 1′. In response, the interest rate rises to clear the money market. The positive relation between changes in the price level and the interest rate is called the **price-level effect on the interest rate**, which is shown compactly by Schema 10–9:

FIGURE 10–3
The Price-Level
Effect on the
Interest Rate

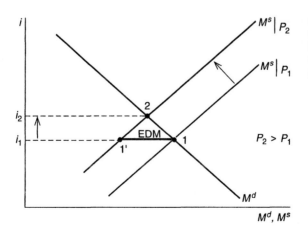

An increase in the price level, *P*, decreases the supply of real money balances, thereby creating excess demand for money. In response, the interest rate rises.

$$P\uparrow \rightarrow (NBR/P)\downarrow \rightarrow M^s\downarrow \rightarrow EDM \rightarrow i\uparrow$$
and
$$P\downarrow \rightarrow (NBR/P)\uparrow \rightarrow M^s\uparrow \rightarrow ESM \rightarrow i\downarrow$$

(10–9)

TRY IT OUT 10.1

Suppose the price level and the level of real income fall. Using only one graph, illustrate the effect on the equilibrium level of the interest rate and explain the result.

THE AGGREGATE DEMAND–AGGREGATE SUPPLY MODEL

All the pieces of the framework come together in the aggregate demand–aggregate supply model, or *AD–AS* model for short. The name comes from the graphical depiction of the model in the (P,Y) plane as a demand curve and a supply curve.

The Aggregate Demand Curve

The macroeconomic demand curve, called the **aggregate demand (AD) curve**, depicts a negative relation between the demand for economywide output (Y) and the price of output (P), as shown in Figure 10–4. In this way, it seems to resemble a microeconomic demand curve, which shows a negative relation between the quantity demanded of a good and the price of that good. Unlike its micro counterpart, however, the macro *AD* curve incorporates influences of the money market and the foreign exchange market. Let's see how the relation works.

In a closed economy, the influence of a change in the price level on aggregate demand comes mainly from the money market. We represent this influence schematically as follows:

$$P\uparrow \rightarrow (NBR/P)\downarrow \rightarrow M^s\downarrow \rightarrow EDM \rightarrow i\uparrow \rightarrow (C + I)\downarrow \rightarrow AD\downarrow$$

(10–10)

Thus, an increase in P reduces $AD,$ and a fall in P increases $AD.$[7]

FIGURE 10–4
The Aggregate Demand Curve

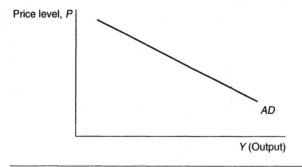

Price level, P

As the price level falls, the aggregate demand for economywide output rises.

AD

Y (Output)

---

[7] A change in the price level can also influence consumption directly through the wealth effect. A rise in the price level reduces real wealth, which reduces planned consumption. The wealth effect is also called the

FIGURE 10–5
The Aggregate
Supply Curve

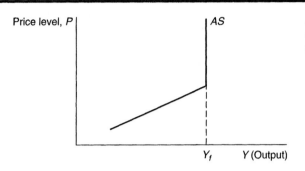

As the price level rises, the supply of
output rises, up to the full-employment
point, Y_f. After that, further increases in
P have no effect on Y.

When we include the international linkages, there are two additional reasons for the negative relation between P and AD. First, as we noted earlier, the increase in i will increase the supply of foreign exchange and thereby reduce the exchange rate e. This fall in e makes foreign goods more desirable and U.S. goods less so, thereby reducing NX. Schematically, we have:

$$P \uparrow \to (NBR/P)\downarrow \to M^s\downarrow \to \text{EDM} \to i\uparrow \to e\downarrow \to NX\downarrow \to AD\downarrow \qquad (10\text{–}11)$$

In addition, the rise in P has a direct effect on NX. At a given exchange rate and a given foreign price level, when P rises American goods become relatively more expensive. As a result, foreigners demand fewer American goods (exports), and Americans demand more foreign goods (imports), thereby reducing NX. This direct link between P and the NX component of aggregate demand is an application of standard demand analysis to international trade: A rise in the price of one good relative to that of another reduces the demand for the good whose price has risen and increases the demand for the competing good. In this case the competing good is foreign goods.

TRY IT OUT 10.2

Explain how a fall in P increases aggregate demand by reversing Schemas 10–10 and 10–11.

The Aggregate Supply Curve

To determine the actual price level and the actual level of output that will come out of the system, we must examine the capacity of the economy to produce output, which takes us to the **aggregate supply (AS) curve**. This curve, depicted in Figure 10–5, shows the amount of real GDP that firms are willing to produce at each price level.

Economists disagree about the theoretical underpinnings of the AS curve. We examine these controversies in Chapters 26 and 27. Here we merely describe the AS curve in the simplest way. Along the upward-sloping portion of the AS curve, there is slack, or excess

Pigou effect in honor of the late A. C. Pigou, a British economist who, in the 1940s, introduced the link between consumption and real wealth.

capacity, in the economy in the form of unemployed labor or idle plant and equipment. Therefore, firms are able to produce additional output, but they incur higher costs. Because price has to cover (marginal) costs, the higher the price level, the more output firms can produce and supply.

On the other hand, when all slack is exhausted, the economy reaches the **full-employment level of output**, denoted by Y_f. Because there is no additional excess capacity, attempts to produce more output lead to higher costs and prices with no perceptible increase in output. The vertical section of the supply curve depicts this situation.

Determination of P and Y

The equilibrium price level and the associated equilibrium level of output are determined at the point where the AD curve intersects the AS curve, at point E in Figure 10–6. Point E says more, however. In deriving the AD curve, we have used the determination of the interest rate in the money market and the determination of the exchange rate in the foreign exchange market. Thus, point E denotes a **full equilibrium**: The demand for goods and services equals the supply, the demand for money equals its supply, and the demand for foreign exchange equals the supply. We can write these equilibrium relations in equation form:

$$AD = AS$$
$$M^d = M^s \qquad\qquad\qquad (10\text{–}12)$$
$$FE^d = FE^s$$

Figure 10–6 displays only the first relation explicitly; the others are implicit in the AD curve, although they could be shown explicitly in graphs of the money market and the foreign exchange market.

Demand-Side Shocks

To explain why prices, output, interest rates, and exchange rates change, we must inquire about shifts of the AD curve or the AS curve. Shocks to the economy that shift the AD curve can originate in any of the markets from which the curve is derived: the goods and services market, the money market, or the foreign exchange market. When these shocks arise from deliberate changes in policy parameters, they are called **demand management policies**. Policies that shift the demand curve to the right are called *expansionary demand*

**FIGURE 10–6
Full Equilibrium:
The Price Level
and Output**

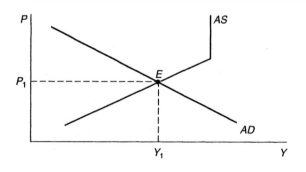

The equilibrium values of the price level and output are determined at the intersection of aggregate demand and aggregate supply.

management policies, and policies that shift the curve to the left are called *contractionary demand management policies.*

Any policy that shifts the *AD* curve to the right increases nominal income, *PY.* Along the upward-sloping portion of the *AS* curve, both *P* and *Y* increase. Along the vertical portion, however, only *P* rises. The two panels of Figure 10–7 illustrate these two cases. In general, the steeper the slope of the *AS* curve, the smaller the increase in *Y* and the greater the increase in *P* for any given shift of the *AD* curve to the right; the flatter the slope of the *AS* curve, the greater the increase in *Y* and the smaller the increase in *P*.

The two basic types of demand management policies are fiscal and monetary. Expansionary or contractionary fiscal and monetary policies have similar effects on *P* and *Y,* but different effects on the interest rate.

Fiscal Policy   Fiscal policy refers to government expenditure and taxation policy. A rise in government expenditures on final goods and services increases the aggregate demand for goods and services. (So does a reduction in income tax rates, which increases the consumption component of aggregate demand.) For each level of *P,* the level of aggregate demand is greater, so the *AD* curve shifts to the right.

As a consequence of an increase in government expenditures, the equilibrium levels of *P* and *Y* rise when the *AS* curve is upward sloping. The interest rate also rises because of the price-level effect and the real income effect on the interest rate. This rise in the interest rate reduces the demand for consumer durables, investment, and net exports. Economists refer to this reduction in consumption, investment, and net exports as **crowding out**; government expenditure crowds out private expenditures. With an

FIGURE 10–7
Expansionary
Demand
Management
Policies

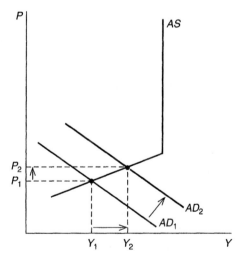

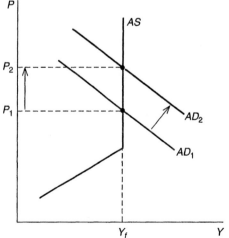

With an upward-sloping *AS* curve, policies that increase *AD* result in an increase in both *P* and *Y.*

With a vertical *AS* curve, the same increase in *AD* results in a larger increase in *P* and no change in *Y.*

upward-sloping supply curve, crowding out is incomplete. How can we tell? We know that Y rises, which means that AD has also risen for the goods market to be in equilibrium. In contrast, with a vertical supply curve the crowding out is complete. The fall in $(C + I + NX)$ offsets the rise in G, so there is no change in AD and Y.

Monetary Policy   Expansionary monetary policy, such as an increase in nonborrowed reserves through open market operations, also shifts the AD curve to the right. The effects of expansionary monetary policy on P and Y are the same as the effects of expansionary fiscal policy: P and Y both increase with an upward-sloping AS curve, but only P increases with a vertical curve.

The difference between fiscal and monetary policy lies in the effects on the interest rate. In the case of monetary policy, the increase in NBR increases the money supply, which causes the interest rate to fall. This fall in the interest rate then engineers the increase in aggregate demand and, hence, the rise in P and Y. The rise in P and Y, however, increases the interest rate from its lower level. The increase in P reduces the real money supply, and the increase in Y increases money demand. The consequent excess demand for money raises the interest rate. The next section examines whether the interest rate will settle at a lower level as a result of the increase in nonborrowed reserves.

MONEY, INTEREST, AND PRICES: PUTTING THE PIECES TOGETHER

The final step in examining the framework of the economy is to examine the total effect of monetary policy—for example, of an increase in the money supply through open market operations—on the interest rate. Nearly a quarter of a century ago, Nobel laureate Milton Friedman distinguished four effects of an increase in the money supply on the interest rate: the liquidity effect, the real income effect, the price-level effect, and the expected inflation effect.[8] Let us see how to incorporate these four effects into the AD–AS framework.

Liquidity Effect   The **liquidity effect** is the inverse relation between a change in the money supply and the interest rate, holding real income, the price level, and expected inflation constant. For example, an increase in the money supply brought about by an open market purchase of government securities causes excess supply of money at the current interest rate, thereby forcing the interest rate down. The excess supply of money is a measure of the increased liquidity in the economy, which accounts for the term *liquidity effect* on the interest rate.

Chapter 9 examined this effect without giving it a name. The schematic representation of the liquidity effect is:

$$NBR\uparrow \rightarrow M^s\uparrow \rightarrow \text{ESM} \rightarrow i\downarrow$$

The left panel of Figure 10–8 illustrates the liquidity effect. Starting from position 1, the increase in NBR shifts the M^s curve to the right, forcing the equilibrium level of the interest rate to fall to i_2, as shown by point 2.

---

[8] See Milton Friedman, "Factors Affecting Interest Rates," in *Money and Finance: Readings in Theory, Policy, and Institutions,* ed. D. Carson (New York: John Wiley & Sons, 1972), 319–30.

FIGURE 10-8
Effects of an
Increase in Money
Supply

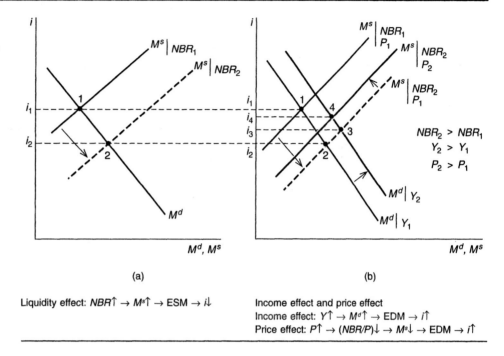

(a)

Liquidity effect: $NBR\uparrow \rightarrow M^s\uparrow \rightarrow ESM \rightarrow i\downarrow$

(b)

Income effect and price effect
Income effect: $Y\uparrow \rightarrow M^d\uparrow \rightarrow EDM \rightarrow i\uparrow$
Price effect: $P\uparrow \rightarrow (NBR/P)\downarrow \rightarrow M^s\downarrow \rightarrow EDM \rightarrow i\uparrow$

Empirical work by Milton Friedman and Anna Schwartz has shown that in the absence of inflationary expectations, the interest rate falls almost immediately and remains at a lower level for about six to nine months after an open market operation.[9] This result has been observed in many countries, including the United States, Japan, and Great Britain.

Income Effect and Price-Level Effect

The fall in the interest rate from the liquidity effect increases aggregate demand for goods and services. Firms find they can sell more than they planned to, so they experience an unplanned decrease of inventories. They hire more labor to produce more output, but at increased costs. Hence, the price level, P, increases as output, Y, increases. Friedman and Schwartz show that (real) output typically starts to rise about six to nine months after the Fed adds reserves to the banking system, but prices usually do not begin to rise until 18 to 24 months after the open market operation.

The *income effect* by itself is shown in Figure 10-8b as a movement from point 2 to point 3. The increase in output and real income increases the demand for real money balances, and the resulting excess demand forces the interest rate to rise. The *price-level effect* by itself is shown in Figure 10-8b as a movement from point 3 to point 4. The increase in the price level reduces the real quantity of nonborrowed reserves, NBR/P, and reduces the real supply of money. The consequent excess demand increases the interest rate.

---

[9] See Milton Friedman and Anna Schwartz, *Monetary Trends in the United States and the United Kingdom* (University of Chicago Press, 1982).

The combined effects of the rise in the price level and in real income are shown as a movement from point 2 to point 4, which takes considerably more than a year to run its course. In the graph the combined positive effect is not sufficient to erase the negative liquidity effect. Thus, the interest rate ended up lower than its original level, i_1. This is not a mirage caused by the arbitrary way we drew the graph. Actually, the graph depicts the correct result: that the interest rate will end up lower when the *AS* curve is upward sloping. We know this from the fact that real income rose, which means that aggregate demand for goods and services also rose. However, aggregate demand could not have risen without a fall in the interest rate. This discussion opens our eyes to the possibility that there are circumstances in which the interest rate will end up at its initial level, a possibility to which we now turn.

Neutrality of Money

The preceding analysis assumed that the economy was at a point on the upward-sloping portion of the *AS* curve, which is the consequence of excess capacity in the economy. Suppose, instead, that the economy was at full employment, that is, on the vertical portion of *AS*. In this case, the liquidity effect would not have an impact on output. The attempt by firms to increase production by hiring labor (from other firms) would only increase costs and prices without an increase in *Y*. With no increase in output, the entire impact of the increase in *NBR* and M^s will be felt as an increase in prices. As we shall see, the percentage increase in the price level will equal the percentage increase in *NBR*, and the interest rate will end up at its initial level, i_1.

First, consider the effects on the interest rate. Because aggregate supply remains the same, at Y_f, the equilibrium level of aggregate demand cannot change. Aggregate demand will be unchanged, however, only if the interest rate, on which *AD* depends, returns to its initial level. Hence, the interest rate first falls by the liquidity effect, then rises by the price effect, settling at its initial level. Figure 10–9 illustrates this case.

Having ascertained that the increase in the price level moves the interest rate back to its initial level, we ask the next question: By how much must the price level rise to keep

FIGURE 10–9
The Neutrality of Money

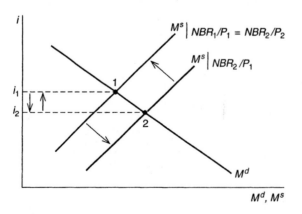

An increase in *NBR* first increases M^s and lowers the interest rate. Then it increases the price level by the same percentage, forcing the money supply back to its initial position and restoring the interest rate to its initial level.

the interest rate unchanged? We know that with Y also unchanged at Y_f, real money demand is unchanged. Therefore, real money supply must be unchanged for the interest rate to stay at its initial level. But nominal nonborrowed reserves (*NBR*) have risen. The money supply Equation 10–8,

$$M^s = Cur + \frac{1}{rr} \times \left(\frac{NBR}{P} + BR - ER\right) \tag{10–8}$$

shows that if the price level rises by the same percentage as nominal nonborrowed reserves, the real value of nonborrowed reserves, *NBR/P*, does not change; neither does the real value of the money supply, M^s. Therefore, the interest rate must not have changed, as required. In brief, the interest rate will be unchanged if the rate of inflation equals the rate of growth of nominal nonborrowed reserves:

$$\frac{\Delta P}{P} = \frac{\Delta NBR}{NBR}$$

The result that the rate of inflation equals the rate of growth of nominal nonborrowed reserves is called the *neutrality of money.*

The neutrality of money is often stated in terms of nominal money growth instead of the growth of nominal *NBR*: The percentage increase in the price level equals the percentage increase in the nominal money supply, *M*. To see that this result also follows from our analysis, we simply note that $M^s = M/P$. Although the real money supply, M^s, must remain unchanged when the price level rises by $\Delta P/P$ percent, this can happen only if the nominal money supply, *M*, rises by the same percentage. Hence, **neutrality of money** means that:

$$\frac{\Delta P}{P} = \frac{\Delta NBR}{NBR} = \frac{\Delta M}{M}$$

The neutrality result holds *only* under the assumption of a vertical aggregate supply curve, which means that output is at its full-employment level.

Expected Inflation Effect

Our results so far have assumed a one-time increase in nonborrowed reserves. There will be additional repercussions if the Fed increases nonborrowed reserves *continuously* at the rate $\Delta NBR/NBR$, say, at a 5 percent annual rate. The given annual rate of growth of *NBR* will appear as an equal percentage increase in the price level, that is, an equal inflation rate. Inflation means a sustained and continuous increase in the price level. Eventually the public will expect such inflation, which will be factored into its decisions to borrow. At this point, the distinction between real and nominal interest rates comes into play.

As noted earlier, the public decides how much to borrow on the basis of the real interest rate, i_r, which equals the nominal rate of interest, i, minus expected inflation, $(\Delta P/P)^{exp}$. At any given level of i, a rise in expected inflation reduces the expected real interest rate, which is the true expected cost of borrowing. Hence, households will demand more consumer durables and more housing, and firms will increase their demand for plant and equipment, thereby increasing *AD*. We can summarize these linkages schematically. Given i,

$$\left(\frac{\Delta P}{P}\right)^{exp} \uparrow \rightarrow i_r \downarrow \rightarrow AD \uparrow$$

As a result of the rise in expected inflation, the *AD* curve shifts further to the right, raising the price level. The higher price level, in turn, reduces real nonborrowed reserves and the real supply of money, raising the interest rate above its initial level instead of merely restoring it. The rise in the interest rate triggered by an increase in expected inflation is Friedman's fourth effect: the **expected inflation effect** of changes in the money supply on the interest rate.

Two questions arise from this discussion. The first is about the magnitude of the expected inflation effect; the second is about its timing. Consider magnitude first. In a fully employed economy, a one-shot increase in the money supply eventually leaves the interest rate at its initial level. In contrast, a rise in inflationary expectations stemming from an equal increase in the rate of growth of the nominal money supply increases the nominal interest rate. By how much? The answer is clear-cut when the economy is at full employment. At each level of the nominal interest rate, an increase in expected inflation reduces the expected real interest rate, thereby increasing planned aggregate demand. Because aggregate supply is fixed at Y_f, aggregate demand cannot increase. Since *AD* depends on the real interest rate, the real interest rate must remain unchanged when expected inflation increases. The real interest rate remains unchanged, however, only if the nominal interest rate rises by the full increase in expected inflation.

We have shown that in a fully employed economy an increase in inflation brought about by an equal increase in money growth increases the nominal interest rate by the same rate, thereby leaving the real interest rate unchanged. This result is called the **Fisher effect** in recognition of the seminal work on money, interest, and prices of the American economist Irving Fisher (1867–1947). The Fisher effect can be stated succinctly as follows:

$$\begin{array}{c} \text{Rate of change in} \\ \text{money growth} \end{array} = \begin{array}{c} \text{Rate of change in} \\ \text{actual inflation} \end{array} = \begin{array}{c} \text{Rate of change in} \\ \text{expected inflation} \end{array} = \begin{array}{c} \text{Change in nominal} \\ \text{interest rate} \end{array}$$

For example, an increase in money growth by 2 percent will increase actual and expected inflation by 2 percent, increasing the nominal interest rate by 2 percent.

The real-world explanation of the Fisher effect is straightforward: As expected inflation rises, firms and households that borrow to add to their plant and equipment or to buy homes and consumer durables anticipate repaying their debt in inflation-cheapened dollars. Because the reduction in purchasing power equals the inflation rate, the public is willing to pay a higher interest rate, which, of course, lenders will demand.

The Fisher effect can also be explained in terms of the public's portfolio choice. When asset holders anticipate a higher rate of inflation, they consider long-term bonds less desirable. Acting on their expectations, they switch their wealth away from long-term bonds to assets that are less vulnerable to inflation, such as short-term debt securities, equity securities, and real estate. The reduction in the demand for bonds leads to a fall in the price of bonds and, hence, a rise in the interest rate on bonds.

The Fisher effect is usually written in the form of an equation, called the **Fisher equation**:

$$i = i_r + \left(\frac{\Delta P}{P}\right)^{exp} \qquad\qquad (10\text{–}13)$$

Equation 10–13 shows that, other things equal, an increase in expected inflation increases the nominal interest rate by the magnitude of the increased expected inflation. There is only one "other thing" in this equation, the real interest rate, i_r. Therefore, if the real interest rate remains unchanged, an increase in expected inflation will be fully reflected in the nominal rate of interest. We know that the real rate of interest is unchanged when the economy is at full employment, that is, when the economy operates on the vertical portion of the *AS* curve. Thus, the following conclusion is inescapable: If the economy is at full employment, a given increase in the rate of growth of the nominal money supply increases the inflation rate and the nominal interest rate by the same percentage. On the other hand, if the economy is not at full employment, this exact form of the Fisher theorem will not apply. The nominal interest rate increases, but not by the full increase in inflation. The Fisher equation can be expressed in terms of money growth simply by substituting $\Delta M/M$ for $(\Delta P/P)^{exp}$ in Equation 10–13 to get:

$$i = i_r + \frac{\Delta M}{M} \qquad\qquad (10\text{–}14)$$

Financiers rely on Equation 10–14 to explain why they expect a higher interest rate and, hence, a fall in the price of bonds when the Fed raises its targets for the rate of money growth. Of course, there is a one-to-one relationship between increases in money growth and increases in nominal interest rates only at full employment.

The second question concerns the appearance and timing of the expected inflation effect. In their empirical work, Friedman and Schwartz found that in the climate of low inflation in the United States and the United Kingdom before 1960, expected inflation had no significant effect on interest rates. Their work shows, however, that since then the relation between an increase in the rate of money growth and an increase in nominal interest rates has been "very clear and very prompt," with interest rates starting to rise above their initial level about 18 months after an increase in the rate of money growth. By contrast, in countries with high and volatile inflation, such as some South American countries, increases in money growth are reflected in higher interest rates more quickly.

In the late 1970s, the inflation rate approached 10 percent in the United States. As our theory predicts, high actual and expected inflation led to high nominal interest rates. The high rate of inflation was the consequence of shocks to the aggregate demand and aggregate supply curves and to accommodating monetary policy in earlier years. Soon after the appointment of Paul A. Volcker to the chairmanship of the Federal Reserve Board in 1979, the Fed embarked on a single-minded effort to disinflate the economy. FedWatch 10.1 explains this episode by applying our theory of money, interest, and prices. (We explain this case in greater detail in Part 4.)

FedWatch 10.1
The Fed, Inflation, and Interest Rates: 1979–1982

With the rate of inflation at 9 percent and interest rates high and rising, on October 6, 1979, the Federal Reserve embarked on a policy to reduce money growth to reduce inflation. The three-year ride was a bumpy one. The average rate of money growth fell, but its volatility increased. Interest rates and economic activity also fluctuated widely.

The U.S. economy suffered a short but sharp recession in the first half of 1980. Falling income brought interest rates down, as the accompanying graph shows. The economy recovered in the second half of the year, and

inflation and interest rates ratcheted upward. With interest rates at a record high in 1981, the public, the press, and even picketers outside the Federal Reserve building in Washington, D.C., called on the Fed "to do something about interest rates." In public statements, Federal Reserve officials repeatedly responded that they *were* doing something. Reductions in money growth, they explained, would reduce actual inflation, expected inflation, and the inflation premium embedded in interest rates.

By 1982, the restrictive monetary policy had reduced inflation to about 6 percent, and interest rates fell, as the graph shows. The policy was not benign, however. The U.S. economy suffered the worst recession since the Great Depression in 1982. Real GDP fell by 2.2 percent that year, contributing to falling interest rates.

U.S. Interest Rates: *1978–1982*

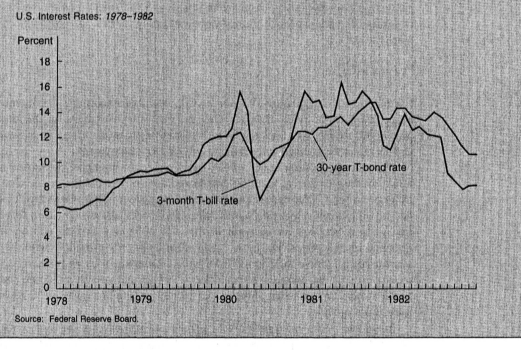

Source: Federal Reserve Board.

ECONOMIC POLICY IN THE UNITED STATES AND JAPAN: THE 1990s

Our analysis can account for the conduct of policy, especially monetary policy, in the United States and Japan in the 1990s. Both countries experienced downturns in their economies, to which their central banks responded by easing monetary policy. Moreover, in both cases balance sheet distress of households, firms, and banks complicated the response of the economy to monetary policy. Both countries were also reluctant to apply fiscal stimulus, despite drastic differences in their fiscal conditions.

The U.S. Economy

To set the stage for examining U.S. economic policy in the 1990s, we begin in 1988. The inflation rate was 3.9 percent and the unemployment rate was 5.5 percent, considered close to (or even below) the full-employment rate of unemployment. How did the U.S. economy get to this position from the severe recession of 1982? The Fed applied expansionary monetary policy, and the Reagan administration and Congress applied expansionary fiscal policy, especially tax cuts.

In 1988 the Fed adopted a strategy "to achieve a soft landing of the economy," that is, to reduce the growth of M2 in order to reduce inflation without creating negative growth of real GDP. To achieve its goal, the Fed began pushing up interest rates. Between the beginning of 1988 and mid-1989, contractionary open market operations, coupled with two increases in the discount rate, pushed up nominal short-term rates, as shown by the three-month T-bill rate in Figure 10–10.[10]

In response to bad employment numbers in mid-1989, the Fed began gradually to ease monetary policy through open market operations. An adverse supply shock in August 1990 complicated the conduct of monetary policy. The shock came from the Iraqi invasion of Kuwait, which temporarily raised the price of oil, thereby raising the cost of

**FIGURE 10–10
U.S. Interest
Rates: *1987–1993***

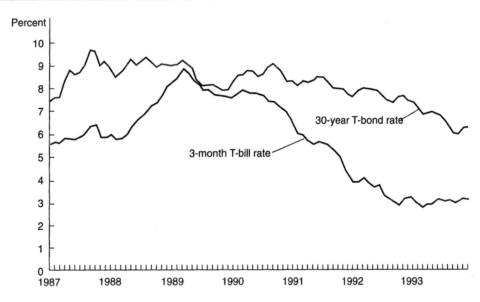

Source: Federal Reserve Board.

---

[10] Chapter 16 takes a detailed look at the behavior of the monetary aggregates during this period.

supplying output and shifting the aggregate supply curve up and to the left. Such a shift of the supply curve raises the price level and reduces output.

Conventional wisdom at the time held that this supply shock was responsible for tipping the U.S. economy into a recession in the summer of 1990, and that without the supply shock the Fed would have achieved its soft landing. Subsequently, however, the data showed that real GDP turned negative in July 1990, one month before Iraq invaded Kuwait.

To foster an economic recovery, between December 1990 and December 1992 the Fed used all three tools of monetary policy. It used open market operations to add more reserves to the banking system and lower interest rates. It also lowered the discount rate, from 6.5 to 3 percent, in several steps and took the unusual step of lowering reserve requirement ratios, as discussed in Chapters 7 and 9.

The recession ended in the spring of 1991, but the recovery was weak by historical standards. Many analysts, including the Fed itself, cited balance sheet distress, the debt hangover, and the credit crunch as the reason for the weak recovery. As Chapters 4 and 5 discussed, the downturn in the economy exposed the debt overhang of many households and firms who had trouble meeting their interest payments and responded by working to reduce their debt burdens. Banks, struggling to deal with loans losses, especially on real estate loans, and to meet new capital requirements, became less willing and able to lend, even to longstanding creditworthy customers in some cases. In 1991 and 1992 banks actually reduced the loans in their portfolio and increased their holdings of Treasury securities, thereby creating a credit crunch, especially for small firms without access to open markets.

Critics of the Fed's monetary policy argued that Fed was too timid. It had been injecting small doses of monetary stimulus into the economy over a long duration, when, critics argued, what the economy needed was a more potent medicine: larger doses of stimulus over a shorter duration. Responding to its critics, the Fed argued that a more expansionary monetary policy would have ignited inflationary expectations, which would have raised long-term interest rates. To buttress its argument, the Fed noted that although nominal short-term interest rates had fallen by about 4 percentage points from 1990 to 1992, nominal long-term interest rates had fallen by less than 2 percentage points, as Figure 10–10 shows.

Monetary policy, of course, is not the only policy. There also is fiscal policy. In 1990, however, fiscal policy focused on deficit reduction. In October, Congress and the Bush administration reached an agreement on new targets and procedures to bring down the budget deficit over the next five years. Facing a sluggish recovery, the administration proposed some fiscal stimulus measures in 1992. The president and Congress, however, became entangled in a disagreement over tax cuts versus increases in government expenditures and failed to pass any stimulus package.

At the start of his new administration, President Clinton proposed a small ($13 billion) fiscal stimulus, to be followed by deficit reduction. The stimulus package failed to pass Congress. The president then opted for deficit reduction, signing into law in the summer of 1993 a program of future tax increases and expenditure cuts, as noted in Chapter 4. The indirect effects of deficit reduction are expansionary because they lower interest rates, but the direct effects of tax increases and expenditure cuts are contractionary.

Between November 1992 and November 1993, nominal interest rates on 30-year Treasury bonds fell by about 150 basis points. The administration argued that the prospect of future deficit reduction accounted for most of this reduction: If the public expects that deficit reduction will lower interest rates, it will try to lock in higher rates by purchasing long-term securities today, thereby pushing their prices up and their rates down. Low actual and expected inflation and the government's decision to cut the supply of 30-year Treasury bonds also played a role in lowering long-term interest rates. There is no consensus among economists about the relative importance of each of these factors in bringing down long-term rates.

By the fourth quarter of 1993, the economy began to grow robustly as interest-sensitive sectors economy finally began to respond to the lowest nominal short-term and long-term interest rates in more than 20 years. Expenditures on consumer durables, business equipment, and home building rose.[11] Exports, on the other hand, were weak because of sluggish economies overseas, especially in Europe and Japan. While pursuing deficit reduction at home, the Clinton administration was encouraging Japan to cut taxes to stimulate the Japanese economy.

The Japanese Economy

To understand the Japanese economy in the 1990s, we must go back to the 1980s. Between the end of 1986 and 1989, partly at the urging of the United States and other Western countries, the Bank of Japan (BOJ) followed an easy monetary policy. By 1988 the BOJ had reduced the discount rate to a record low 2.5 percent, and from early 1987 to early 1988 the growth of Japan's broad measure of money (M2 + CDs) reached a record high of 12 percent. The impact of loose monetary policy was reflected primarily in asset inflation. The Nikkei average of stock prices rose 300 percent during that period, and the price of land in major urban areas also rose at about that rate. By one estimate, Japanese land prices were so high in 1990 that the grounds of the Imperial Palace in Tokyo were worth more than all the land in California.[12] Because of these inflated asset prices, the Japanese economy was called a **bubble economy**, a term usually associated with excessive speculation, which pushes asset prices substantially above their long-run equilibrium values. On the other hand, the annual rate of inflation—the rate of change in the price of goods and services—was only about 3 percent. The concern, however, was that high asset prices inflated wealth which, in turn, foretold higher future inflation.

With the appointment of Yasushi Mieno as governor of the Bank of Japan in late 1989, the BOJ embarked on a relentless tight money policy. It more than doubled the discount rate to 6 percent, and reduced money growth to 2 percent. As expected, asset prices fell dramatically. Stock prices fell more than 50 percent and land prices more than 30 percent. Of course, lower asset prices meant higher rates of return and higher interest rates. As our analysis predicts, the Japanese economy slowed down in 1991, and real GDP actually fell in the last three quarters of 1992. In 1993, the growth rate was zero. The weak economy led the Bank of Japan to reverse its tight monetary policy at the end of 1991. By the end of 1993, the BOJ had lowered its discount rate to 1.75 percent.

---

[11] In Part 4 we shall see that the Fed, concerned about prospective inflation, pushed up short-term interest rates in 1994. This was the first increase by the Fed in five years.

[12] This statistic is from "Turning Point: A Survey of Japan," *The Economist*, March 6, 1993, 5.

Despite the lowest interest rates in Japan's history, households and firms were reluctant to borrow and spend. Falling land and stock prices had reduced the wealth of households and firms. The balance sheet distress was even more severe than in the United States a few years earlier. Moreover, banks in Japan, like their U.S. counterparts, suffered from loan losses brought on by the weakened condition of their borrowers. They also incurred losses from the falling stock market, because Japanese banks are allowed to hold stock for their own portfolio. Needing to rebuild their capital positions, banks in Japan became less willing and able to lend.

Although monetary conditions in the United States and Japan were similar, fiscal conditions were different. Beginning in the late 1970s, the Ministry of Finance (MOF) had weaned the Japanese economy away from budget deficits to a decade of budget surpluses. The first attempts in the early 1990s to stimulate the Japanese economy by increasing government expenditure were insufficient because of the MOF's reluctance to run budget deficits. The Clinton administration and many American economists urged Japan to cut taxes on the grounds that Japan was the one country in the world that could afford the luxury of a large fiscal stimulus. At the end of 1993, as an emergency measure, the MOF proposed an income tax cut. It also proposed, however, that the tax cut be followed by an increase in consumption taxes a few years later to make up for lost revenue. Its critics argued that this was a weak measure that would not invigorate the Japanese economy.

SUMMARY

- In the standard macroeconomic framework of an entire economy, the real sector consists of one output and two inputs, labor and physical capital.

- National output, Y, is the sum of four broad categories of expenditures: consumption, C; investment, I; government purchases, G; and net exports, NX.

- National output is equal to national income, which is the sum of the payments to labor and capital. These produce national output.

- When transactions take place across national boundaries, foreign currencies are needed. The exchange rate, e, is the dollar price of a unit of foreign currency.

- For a complete view of the national economy, we attach the real-sector framework, augmented by foreign exchange, to the financial sector framework presented in Chapter 9.

- The transmission mechanism from the financial sector to the real sector works through the effect of the interest rate on the aggregate demand for goods and services. Other things equal, an increase in the interest rate reduces the aggregate demand for goods and services. The effect on consumption and investment is direct; the effect on net exports works through the exchange rate.

- The linkages also run from the real sector to the financial sector. An increase in the level of national income increases the demand for real money balances. Hence, the interest rate rises. An increase in the price level decreases the supply of real money balances. Again, the interest rate rises.

- The AD–AS apparatus pulls the pieces of the macroeconomic framework together into one model, which is illustrated graphically in the (P, Y) plane.

- The AD curve depicts a negative relation between the demand for economywide output, Y, and the price of output, P. The AD curve is downward sloping because a decrease in the price level reduces the interest rate, which, in turn, increases the aggregate demand for goods and services.

- For each price level, the AS curve shows the corresponding level of output that firms want to supply. If firms produce output under conditions of increasing costs and if there is slack in the economy, the AS curve is upward sloping. On the other hand, at capacity, or at the full-employment level of output, the AS curve becomes vertical, meaning that further attempts to increase output merely result in higher prices and virtually no increase in output.

- The intersection of the *AD* and *AS* curves determines the full-equilibrium values of *P* and *Y*. Using these values, we can backtrack and determine the full-equilibrium values of the remaining real-sector and financial-sector variables.

- Fiscal policy and monetary policy are called *demand management policies* because they affect the position of the *AD* curve. An increase in money supply, brought about by an open market purchase of securities, increases aggregate demand; so does an increase in government expenditures or a reduction in taxes.

- When output is below the full-employment level, an increase in money supply increases both output and the price level. When the economy operates at full capacity, money is neutral, which means that an increase in the nominal money supply by a given percentage will increase the price level by the same percentage and leave output unchanged.

- In the absence of expected inflation, an increase in the money supply has three effects on the interest rate. The liquidity effect is the fall in the interest rate caused by the excess supply of money, given real income and the price level. The income effect is the rise in the interest rate resulting from the higher income. The price effect is the higher interest rate resulting from the higher price level. If the economy is below full employment, on net, the interest rate will fall.

- When the economy is at full employment, an increase in money supply has only two effects: the liquidity effect and an equal price effect. The interest rate first falls, then returns to its initial level.

- When the rate of growth of the money supply is increased, the rate of inflation rises and becomes expected. If the economy is at full employment, the nominal interest rate rises above its initial level by the amount that the rate of inflation increases.

KEY TERMS AND CONCEPTS

gross domestic product (GDP)

capital stock

gross national product (GNP)

consumer price index

GDP price deflator

national product identity

consumption

investment

government purchases

net exports

net domestic product (NDP)

national income

wages

profits

exchange rate

flexible exchange rate system

floating exchange rate system

clean float

fixed exchange rate system

managed, or dirty, float

aggregate demand for goods and services

real income

demand for real money balances

real income effect on the interest rate

supply of real money balances

price-level effect on the interest rate

aggregate demand (*AD*) curve

aggregate supply (*AS*) curve

full-employment level of output

full equilibrium

demand management policies

fiscal policy

crowding out

liquidity effect

neutrality of money

expected inflation effect

Fisher effect

Fisher equation

bubble economy

QUESTIONS AND PROBLEMS

1. Given the following data for the U.S. economy in 1991, find net exports (all variables are in billions of 1987 dollars): $C = 3,240.8$; $I = 670.4$; $G = 941.0$; $Y = 4,821.0$.

The Wall Street Journal

2. Explain the following statement from "Germany Lifts Discount Rate to 8.75%, Putting Squeeze on Already

Weak Dollar," *The Wall Street Journal*, July 17, 1992, p. A2: "The German Bundesbank raised its highly visible discount rate to the highest level since 1931 to underscore its inflation-fighting resolve, a move that had ripple effects throughout Europe and pushed down the already weak dollar."

3. Explain the difference between the nominal money supply and the real money supply.

4. Explain why a change in the price level affects the real supply of money but not the real demand for money.

5. Explain the following statement: Money market equilibrium and foreign exchange market equilibrium are embedded in the macroeconomic demand curve (that is, the *AD* curve).

6. Explain the following statement: If the Fed increases the money supply, interest rates will first move in one direction and then the other.

7. With an upward-sloping *AS* curve, expansionary monetary and fiscal policies both increase *P* and *Y*. Is there any difference between them?

8. Expansionary demand management policies always increase nominal GDP but not real GDP. Why not?

9. Use the *AD–AS* model to explain the effects of the downsizing of the U.S. military on the economy.

10. Explain how an increase in government expenditure crowds out net exports.

The Wall Street Journal

11. Use the *AD–AS* model to explain the following statement from "Your Money Matters," *The Wall Street Journal*, February 4, 1991, p. C1: "If money and credit grow too slowly, that can choke the economy and lead to a recession, or even a depression. But if the money supply expands too rapidly, it can lead to inflation and higher interest rates. . . ."

The Wall Street Journal

12. Explain the following quotation from George Melloan, "Don't Write Off Deflation Quite Yet," *The Wall Street Journal*, July 19, 1993, p. A11: "As to the inflation outlook generally, former Fed Chairman Paul Volcker has a point of view. He told Forbes magazine a few weeks ago that businessmen may have to adjust their thinking to a low-inflation era. 'You can't expect inflationary rates of return in low inflationary times.' "

13. Explain the difference between the price-level effect and the expected inflation effect on the interest rate.

The Wall Street Journal

14. Explain the following quotation from Milton Friedman, "Too Tight for a Strong Recovery," *The Wall Street Journal*, October 23, 1992, p. A12: "Declining or low interest rates may at times correspond to easy money, but so may rising or high interest rates."

SUGGESTED READINGS

Friedman, Milton. "Monetarism in Rhetoric and in Practice." In *Monetary Policy in Our Times*, ed. Albert Ando, Hideakazu Eguchi, Roger Farmer, and Yoshio Suzuki. Cambridge, Mass.: The MIT Press, 1985, 15–28.

   One of two keynote addresses at a conference in Tokyo on June 22–24, 1983, in commemoration of the centenary of the Bank of Japan.

Schultze, Charles L. *Memos to the President: A Guide through Macroeconomics for the Busy Policymaker*. Washington, D.C.: The Brookings Institution, 1992.

   A former chairman of the Council of Economic Advisors explains macroeconomic principles and their applications through a series of imaginary memos to a president.

Stein, Herbert, and Murray Foss. *An Illustrated Guide to the American Economy: A Hundred Key Issues*. Washington, D.C.: The AEI Press, 1992.

   An introduction to the American economy through a series of charts and brief narratives by a former chairman of the Council of Economic Advisors and a former staff member, respectively.

Tobin, James. "Monetary Policy in an Uncertain World." In *Monetary Policy in Our Times*, ed. Albert Ando, Hideakazu Eguchi, Roger Farmer, and Yoshio Suzuki. Cambridge, Mass.: The MIT Press, 1985, 29–44.

   The other keynote address at the Bank of Japan conference.

"Turning Point: A Survey of the Japanese Economy." *The Economist*, March 1993, 3–18.

   A look at the Japanese economy after the bubble.

P A R T 4

THE FEDERAL RESERVE AND ITS BEHAVIOR

11   The Federal Reserve System: *Form and Function*

12   Functions of Federal Reserve Banks: *The Details*

13   Instruments, Targets, and Goals of the Federal Reserve

14   Open Market Operations and Movements in Reserves

15   Deposit Creation and the Money Supply

16   Targeting Monetary Aggregates: *Theory and Experience*

Part 4 examines the Federal Reserve, its policies, and its record. The chapters in this part fit into the first pillar of our framework because they explain the purposeful behavior of the Fed. They also fit into the second pillar because they show how the Fed interacts with other participants in the marketplace.

THE FEDERAL RESERVE SYSTEM
Form and Function

CHAPTER PREVIEW

The Federal Reserve describes itself as *independent within the government* rather than independent *of* it. This choice of words reveals that the structure of the Fed is unusual. The president nominates and the Senate confirms the seven members of the Fed's Board of Governors, including the chair. Like the heads of other government agencies, the Fed chair testifies before Congress on the Fed's activities. Unlike other government agencies, however, the Fed does not rely on congressional appropriations for its budget. Moreover, commercial banks that are members of the Federal Reserve System own stock in the Federal Reserve bank of their district and help select its board of directors, who choose the reserve bank's president. Because reserve bank presidents participate in the design of the Fed's monetary policy, populists—traditionally mistrustful of bankers—often question the motives of Fed policies. Other critics consider a central bank outside the control of elected officials as undemocratic.

The purpose of this section of the book is to examine the Federal Reserve, its policies, and its record. This chapter looks at the form and function of the four components of the system: the Board of Governors, the 12 district banks, the Federal Open Market Committee, and member banks. Armed with this information, we are in a position to examine the pros and cons of the existing structure of the Federal Reserve System.

A BRIEF HISTORY OF THE FEDERAL RESERVE

The authority to create and regulate money rests with Congress, which is empowered, according to Article 1, Section 8, Clause 5, of the U.S. Constitution, "to coin money [and to] regulate the value thereof." By enacting the Federal Reserve Act in 1913, Congress, in turn, created the Federal Reserve System and authorized it to create money and regulate its value. In designing the Federal Reserve System, Congress benefited from the experience of other countries' central banks. GlobalWatch 11.1 presents some interesting facts from a study that Congress commissioned at the time.

By the time the Federal Reserve was founded in 1913, the phrase "regulate the value" had acquired an interpretation broader than mere regulation of the purchasing power of money. The Federal Reserve Act came in the aftermath of several financial panics, which were accompanied by the failure of many banks and nonfinancial businesses and by the disruption of commerce and general economic activity. In response, the act was specifically designed to provide the country with enough liquidity, to provide facilities for discounting commercial credit, and to improve the supervision of the banking system. Thus, from the beginning, the Federal Reserve Act mandated the functions of the Fed: (1) to provide enough money and credit to facilitate economic activity and (2) to supervise banks. In other words, *safeguarding the health of the economy and the health of the financial system itself were the dual ultimate goals of the Federal Reserve.*

By working toward these goals, the Fed hoped to prevent bankruptcies of financial and nonfinancial businesses and disruptions in economic activity. It failed, however, to avert the Great Depression of the 1930s, when thousands of banks and even more nonfinancial businesses failed. The level of economic activity became so weak that it could support only a shockingly small proportion of the labor force. Unemployment soared.

In the aftermath of the Great Depression, the Banking Acts of 1933 and 1935 amended the form and functions of the Federal Reserve. In addition to giving the Fed power to regulate rates on savings and time deposits, the 1933 act established the Federal Open Market Committee (FOMC), the third component of the Federal Reserve System. The 1935 act restructured both the Board and the FOMC by removing the secretary of the Treasury and the comptroller of the currency from these two bodies, thereby making the Fed more independent. The next major amendment came with the Depository Institutions Deregulation and Monetary Control Act of 1980 (DID&MCA). As Chapter 5 points out, this act deregulated deposit rates and subjected all depository institutions to reserve requirements.

These three acts—the Banking Act of 1933, the Banking Act of 1935, and DID&MCA of 1980—were concerned with the Fed's role as a regulator both of the banking industry and of economic activity. Two additional acts focused primarily on the Fed's role as a regulator of economic activity. The Full Employment Act of 1946 directed the government to promote "maximum employment, production, and purchasing power." The term *government* was interpreted to include the Federal Reserve. The goals of monetary policy were further refined by the 1978 Full Employment and Balanced Growth Act, commonly called the Humphrey-Hawkins Act in honor of its prime sponsors, the late senator Hubert Humphrey and Congressman Augustus Hawkins. The preceding 15 years had been characterized by high and rising inflation rates. The Humphrey-Hawkins Act instructs the Fed

GlobalWatch 11.1

Historical Tidbits on Foreign Central Banks

Before drafting and passing the Federal Reserve Act of 1913, Congress appointed the National Monetary Commission to prepare studies on the establishment, organization, and functions of existing foreign central banks. The following are some interesting historical tidbits based primarily on a detailed study of the commission's papers by a former British central banker, Charles Goodhart.*

- The early functions of central banks were to issue currency and to finance government activities. These functions gradually evolved to include regulating and supervising banks and providing banks with services such as check clearing and discount window lending.
- The Swedish *Riksbank,* founded in 1668, was the world's first central bank; the Bank of England followed in 1694. The Bank of England was a private commercial bank, although it was nationalized in 1945, while the Swedish Riksbank was created, owned, and supervised by Parliament. Both banks issued notes and engaged in commercial banking activities.
- Some central banks, following the British model, evolved from private, profit-maximizing banks to nonprofit central banks. Others were established as public, nonprofit institutions from the outset. Whatever their origin, the banks that evolved into central banks were those that governments favored with the right to issue currency and to be their bankers.
- To the general public, Napoleon is best known for his military exploits. Less well known is that he founded the *Banque de France* in 1800. Although it initially was a privately owned bank, by 1806 the government appointed the governor and two deputy governors. Besides issuing currency, the

Banque de France was mandated to stabilize interest rates by stabilizing the discount rate. Goodhart notes that the French discount rate remained unchanged for the next 30 years. The government nationalized the Banque de France in 1945.

- The Danish National Bank was founded in 1736 as a private bank with the right to issue notes. The government took over the bank in 1773. Three episodes in the history of the Danish National Bank are unique:
  1. It is the only state-owned central bank that ever went bankrupt. This happened in 1813 after it issued too many notes not backed by gold.
  2. Following its reopening in 1814, Danish notes were backed, not by gold, but by real estate taxes on wealthy real estate owners.
  3. The real estate owners whose taxes backed the notes eventually became stockholders of the central bank, transforming it from a state bank to a private bank.
- The central bank of Belgium (the National Bank of Belgium) was established in 1850 as a private bank, but the law explicitly restricted its commercial banking activities. The stockholders chose the directors, but the king appointed the governor.
- The Bank of Japan, founded in 1882, was patterned after the National Bank of Belgium. Unlike its Belgian counterpart, however, the Bank of Japan was part of the government, under the immediate supervision of the Ministry of Finance. It quickly developed the function of banker to banks, which helped Japanese banks to flourish: About 2,355 banks operated in Japan at the turn of the century.
- The German *Reichsbank* was founded in 1875 and patterned after the Austro-Hungarian Bank, founded in 1816. From the beginning the *Reichsbank,* renamed the *Bundesbank* in 1957, was designed as a nonprofit state bank with government responsibilities.
- The *Banca d'Italia,* established in its present form in 1893, traces its origins to the regional central banks of the 1840s that existed before Italy was unified.
- The Swiss National Bank was established (in its present form) in 1905 by referendum.

---

* Charles Goodhart, *The Evolution of Central Banks* (Cambridge, Mass.: The MIT Press, 1988).

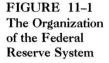

FIGURE 11-1
The Organization
of the Federal
Reserve System

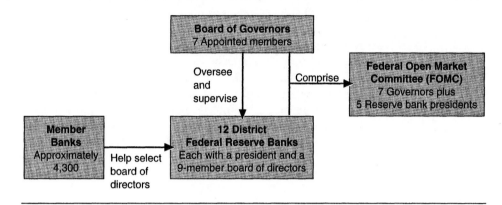

to pay attention not only to the rate of unemployment and the rate of growth of real GDP but also to the rate of inflation. It also requires the Fed to report semiannually to Congress about its outlook on economic activity and inflation and to relate this outlook for the economy to that set down by the administration in the annual *Economic Report of the President.* Additionally, the Humphrey-Hawkins Act requires the Fed to set and report on targets for money growth. The requirements of the Humphrey-Hawkins Act reflected not only the public's awareness and concern about inflation but also the ascendancy of monetarism, a school of thought whose basic tenet is that inflation is caused by excessive growth of monetary aggregates.

To date, none of the laws mandates a rigid set of practices to which the Fed must adhere regardless of economic conditions. The practices that the Fed has pursued in striving to achieve its twin goals of safeguarding the health of the economy and the health of the financial system have changed over time, as the Fed has adapted to the economic and political realities of the day. The instruments, targets, and goals of monetary policy are the subject of Chapter 13.

Figure 11-1 shows the organization of the Federal Reserve System. We begin our examination of the Federal Reserve System with the Board of Governors at the top of the chart. Then we consider the 12 Federal Reserve banks that serve as the operating arms of the Federal Reserve System. Next, we examine the Federal Open Market Committee, an important policy-making body composed of the seven members of the Board of Governors and five presidents of the reserve banks. Finally, we examine the role of member banks. We shall see that the system was originally given its unusual structure to disperse authority but that authority has become increasingly centralized over the decades.

THE BOARD OF GOVERNORS OF THE FEDERAL RESERVE SYSTEM

The headquarters of the Federal Reverse System is in Washington, D.C., where the offices of the Board of Governors are located. Today the Board of Governors, or simply the Board, is by far the strongest component of the Federal Reserve System. The term **Board of Governors of the Federal Reserve System** is used to denote both the agency located in Washington, D.C., and the group of governors. The latter consists of seven members appointed by the president of the United States and confirmed by the U.S. Senate.

The full term of a governor is 14 years, and no governor can be reappointed after serving a full term. The seven terms are staggered so that one term expires every even-numbered year. If a member resigns, a new member is appointed, but only for the remainder of the term. (That member, however, can be reappointed for another term.) The president selects the chair and the vice-chair of the Board from among the seven members, and the Senate confirms the nominees, who serve for a term of four years. The chair and vice-chair may be redesignated and reconfirmed by the Senate, provided that their terms as governors have not expired. A further restriction states that no two governors may be from the same reserve district. FedWatch 11.2 looks at the backgrounds of recent governors and chairs.

An Overview of the Functions of the Board

Table 11–1 summarizes the functions of the Board. These functions range from formulating and carrying out monetary policy to providing services for public interest. We examine the first four functions listed in Table 11–1 in turn.

Formulates and Conducts Monetary Policy   The first item in the table, the formulation and conduct of U.S. monetary policy, is the primary function of the Board. The three tools it uses to conduct monetary policy are open market operations, the discount rate and general administration of the discount window, and the reserve requirement ratios. The Board has either exclusive authority or controlling authority in the use of all three tools, each of which we examine in turn.

Open Market Operations   The most important and most widely used instrument of monetary policy is open market operations: the buying and selling of government securities by the Federal Reserve agent, the New York Fed, in the open market. As Chapter 8 notes, by buying and selling Treasury securities in the open market, the Federal Reserve controls the quantity of nonborrowed reserves, which are the raw material out of which money is created. As the effects of this buying and selling diffuse throughout financial markets, the structure of interest rates is also affected. Although the FOMC has the authority to direct these open market operations, the 7 members of the Board of Governors constitute the majority of the 12-member FOMC. Of course, this does not mean that the Board votes as a block; far from it, as the record of the 1980s and 1990s reminds us. It merely means that the Board has the majority of the votes, whereas each reserve bank has at most one vote.

Discount Window Loans   The second most frequently used instrument of monetary policy is the discount window—called that because at one time banks literally stood in line at a teller "window" in their district Federal Reserve bank to obtain a loan. Manipulation of the discount rate is one of the two methods the Federal Reserve employs to influence the quantity of reserves lent to depository institutions. Each district reserve bank, by a decision of its board of directors, establishes its discount rate "subject to review and determination by the Board of Governors." Therefore, the Board is the final arbiter of the discount rate.

The designers of the Federal Reserve System originally intended for the discount rate to vary across reserve districts in response to the specific needs of banks in that district; these needs would reflect regional economic conditions. In modern times, however, financial

FedWatch 11.2
Backgrounds of Board Members

Every Monday morning the seven members of the Board of Governors gather around an oval-shaped table in the board room of the Federal Reserve building in Washington, D.C., to be briefed by senior staff on national and international economic conditions. The staff members who prepare the briefing materials are professionally trained economists. But who are the board members themselves?

The table shows that most of the governors appointed since the Carter years have been economists. Three of the four noneconomists (Schultz, Kelley, and LaWare) came from the financial industry. The most unusual appointment was that of G. William Miller as chairman in 1978. Miller came from the business world, where he was the chairman of Textron, Inc. Reportedly he had little interest in the details of monetary policy-making or in the traditional role of the chair as a consensus builder on the Board. For example, the Board votes on changes in the discount rate recommended by the reserve banks. Miller

was the only chair in Fed history to be on the losing side of a vote to change (in this case, increase) the discount rate. Not surprisingly, he did not last long at the Fed. In 1979 Miller resigned to become secretary of the Treasury, and President Carter appointed Paul A. Volcker as chairman.

Volcker was not only a professional economist but also the consummate insider. Prior to assuming the chairmanship, Volcker had been assistant secretary of the Treasury for monetary affairs and, more important, president of the Federal Reserve Bank of New York. President Reagan appointed Volcker to a second term as chairman in 1983. Alan Greenspan succeeded Volcker in 1987 and was reappointed by President Bush in 1992. A professional economist, Greenspan had been chairman of the Council of Economic Advisors under President Ford (1974–1977) and the head of a private economic consulting firm. Greenspan reportedly has a voracious appetite for economic data and a reputation as a consensus builder on the Board. Greenspan's term as chairman runs until March 1996, when President Clinton will appoint a Fed chairman. Greenspan is eligible to be reappointed because his term as a governor does not expire until 2006.

Appointments to the Board of Governors

Appointing President	Economist	Noneconomist
Carter	Nancy Teeters	G. William Miller, chairman: 1978–1979
	Emmett Rice	Frederick Schultz
	Paul Volcker, chairman: 1979–1987	
	Lyle Gramley	
Reagan (first term)	Preston Martin	
	Martha Seger	
Reagan (second term)	Wayne Angell	Edward Kelley*
	Manuel Johnson	John LaWare*
	H. Robert Heller	
	Alan Greenspan,* chairman: 1987–	
Bush	David Mullins	
	Lawrence Lindsey*	
	Susan Phillips*	
Clinton	Alan Blinder*	
	Janet Yellen*	

*Board member in 1994.

Source: Adapted from Thomas Havrilesky, *The Pressures on American Monetary Policy* (Boston: Kluwer Academic Publishers, 1993).

TABLE 11–1
Functions of the Board of Governors

1. Formulates and conducts U.S. monetary policy.
   a. Manipulates, via the FOMC, in which it has majority membership, open market operations (OMO), the primary instrument of monetary control.
   b. Sets or has final authority over the secondary instruments of monetary control; approves or disapproves the discount rate suggested by the reserve banks and sets the reserve requirement ratios.
2. Supervises and regulates member banks and bank holding companies, either directly or via the reserve banks.
3. Oversees and supervises the functions of its operating arm, the Federal Reserve banks, including salaries and construction of buildings.
4. Gathers data and conducts extensive economic research.
5. Provides services for public interest, for example, by implementing key federal laws governing consumer lending, such as the Truth in Lending Act, the Equal Credit Opportunity Act, and the Home Mortgage Disclosure Act.

markets are not segmented by region; markets are linked nationally and internationally. Because market rates of interest do not differ regionally, it would not be practical, and could even be counterproductive, for the Board to permit the discount rate to differ across reserve districts. Hence, the Board pursues a policy of a uniform discount rate.

Manipulation of the discount rate is one way the Fed rations discount window loans. A second method is the use of direct quantity controls, or what is called the *administration of the discount window.* Because loans of reserves are made through the reserve banks, the administration of the discount window is discussed at length in the next chapter, where reserve bank functions are discussed in detail.

Reserve Requirement Ratio   The third, and least frequently used, tool is the reserve requirement ratio, which, since the enactment of DID&MCA of 1980, is uniform among institutions for the same kind of deposits. The Board of Governors alone has the authority to vary reserve requirement ratios according to the needs of monetary policy and within the ranges prescribed by law. Since the passage of DID&MCA, the Board has changed reserve requirement ratios only twice. In December 1990 it reduced the reserve requirement on nonpersonal time deposits from 3 percent to zero; in 1992 it reduced the ratio on transactions deposits from 12 percent to 10 percent.

Supervises and Regulates Member Banks   A second function of the Board is to supervise and regulate member banks and bank holding companies, either directly or through its operating arm, the reserve banks. The Board retains for itself the authority to supervise bank holding companies, international banking facilities in the United States, and foreign activities of member banks. It also retains regulatory authority over these institutions.

Oversees Federal Reserve Banks   The Federal Reserve Board oversees all other activities of the reserve banks. Of particular importance are what are called the activities of a banker's bank: services provided by reserve banks to depository institutions such as check collecting and clearing. Moreover, certain expenditures at reserve banks, including the salaries of key officers and the construction or substantial alteration of reserve bank buildings, require the explicit approval of the Board.

Gathers Data and Conducts Research   The Division of Research and Statistics and the Division of Monetary Affairs of the Federal Reserve Board are the official gatherers and keepers of U.S. financial data. The Board disseminates data on reserves, monetary aggregates, and interest rates weekly in its statistical releases and monthly in the *Federal Reserve Bulletin.* The bulletin also publishes international financial data and real-sector data collected by the Commerce Department. Economists in the academic and business world as well as at the Board use these data in their research.

The Board has a large staff of economists whose research is an important part of the Board's work. Staff research ranges from position papers for immediate use in designing and implementing current monetary policy to more lasting contributions on almost every aspect of economic theory and policy. Research on current policy uses two basic econometric models. The **Quarterly Model** is a detailed model of the entire economy, that is, of both the financial and the real sectors. The Quarterly Model is also known as the "Federal Reserve, MIT, Research Council, Pennsylvania" model, or, simply, the FMRP model, because of the original affiliation of its designers. The other model, called the **Monthly Money Market Model**, is a model of only the financial sector. The staff uses both models to prepare briefing books that guide the FOMC in its deliberations.

Financing the Activities of the Board

Although the Board is an agency of the U.S. government, it does not depend on the federal budget to finance its operations. Who pays its expenses? The Board simply imposes a levy on each Federal Reserve bank. For example, in 1993 the total levy for the Board's expenses was $140 million. The collective earnings of reserve banks total billions of dollars, and they emanate primarily from their portfolio of U.S. government securities. This independent source of earnings was part of the design for an independent Fed, one free to achieve its primary goals: to safeguard the health of the U.S. economy and that of the financial industry. Thus, the Board appears to be independent of the administration, which otherwise would have the authority to include the Fed's expenditures in the annual budget, and from the U.S. Congress, which would vote on appropriations of funds for the Fed. We examine the issue of the Fed's independence in greater detail at the end of the chapter. At that point, we will have examined the composition and role of the Federal Open Market Committee, the primary policy-making arm of the Federal Reserve, and the functions of the Federal Reserve banks.

FEDERAL RESERVE BANKS

The second major component of the Federal Reserve System is the **district Federal Reserve banks**. There are 12 Federal Reserve districts, numbered 1 through 12, and 12 Federal Reserve banks, each named after the city in which it is located. The boundaries of the 12 districts are shown in Figure 11–2. The district headquarters are located in (1) Boston, (2) New York, (3) Philadelphia, (4) Cleveland, (5) Richmond, (6) Atlanta, (7) Chicago, (8) St. Louis, (9) Minneapolis, (10) Kansas City, (11) Dallas, and (12) San

FIGURE 11–2   The Federal Reserve System: *Boundaries of Federal Reserve Districts and Their Branch Territories*

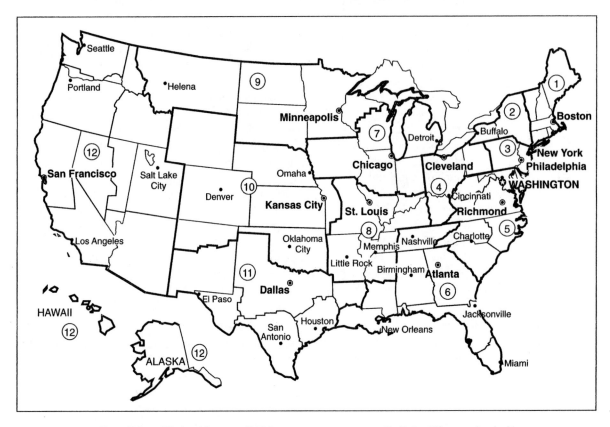

—   Boundaries of Federal Reserve districts
—   Boundaries of Federal Reserve branch territories
◎   Board of Governors of the Federal Reserve System

◉   Federal Reserve bank cities
•   Federal Reserve branch cities
·   Federal Reserve bank facility

Source: *Federal Reserve Bulletin.*

Francisco. Most of the reserve banks have several branches that assist in carrying out some of the responsibilities of the reserve bank.

The Organization and Control of the Reserve Banks

Each reserve bank has a nine-member board—a board of directors, not "governors." Three of the directors are class A directors, elected by and representing member banks within each district. Another three are class B directors, also elected by the member banks but representing the public; they must not be officers, directors, or employees of a bank but instead must represent commerce, industry, and agriculture. The remaining three are class C directors, appointed by the Board of Governors. Class C directors must also represent the public; in fact, they may not even hold stock in a bank, let alone be officers,

TABLE 11–2
The Functions of
Federal Reserve
Banks

1. Banker to banks
2. Banker to the U.S. government and to federal agencies
3. Banker to foreign organizations, such as central banks, International Monetary Fund (IMF), and World Bank
4. Examiner and supervisor of member banks
5. Participant in the making of U.S. monetary policy
   a. Proposing the discount rate
   b. Participating in the FOMC
6. Researcher and data gatherer

directors, or employees of a bank. One class C director is appointed by the Board of Governors to be the chair and another to be the deputy chair of the board. The board of directors appoints the president and vice-president of the reserve bank and recommends their salaries. Each branch of the reserve bank has its own board of directors, composed of three or five directors. The majority of these directors are appointed by the board of directors of the reserve bank and the rest by the Board of Governors.

An Overview of the Functions of the Reserve Banks

It is tempting to consider each reserve bank as the central bank of the states in its district, and the Federal Reserve Board as the central bank of the entire nation. Under this scenario, a district bank would deal with regional economic policy, and the Federal Reserve Board would deal with national economic policy. This interpretation is especially tempting, given the federal form of the U.S. government, with state governments handling regional issues and the federal government assuming responsibility for national issues. Evidence suggests that this was the original intent of the designers of the Federal Reserve System, but it is not an accurate description of the system today, that is, as it has evolved over time. Given the exigencies of modern economies, the Board has emerged as the senior partner, by far. Although the reserve banks do have an important role in the structure of the U.S. central banking system, their functions have turned out to be different from those originally planned.

Reserve banks play a major role in the formulation and implementation of a *national* monetary policy. The role of each bank in designing and implementing a regional policy is, at most, minor. However, as the guardian of the good health of depository institutions, including the role of supervisor and provider of services to depository institutions in its region, the reserve bank is paramount. This preeminence emerges primarily from a key role of reserve banks, namely, that they are *the operating arms of the Federal Reserve System.*

Because we devote an entire chapter to a detailed examination of the functions of the Federal Reserve banks, in this overview we provide only a summary of these functions in Table 11–2.

The Earnings of the Reserve Banks

The bulk of the system's assets is, as we have seen, the portfolio of government securities acquired through open market operations. Hence, the bulk of the system's interest earnings is the interest accrued on these government securities. Each Federal Reserve bank receives a share of the return on the system's asset holdings. Each also receives earnings from the system's holdings of foreign securities, interest (that is, the discount rate) on loans of reserves to depository institutions, and fees for services rendered to financial institutions. Charges for services rendered are a recent phenomenon, mandated by DID&MCA of 1980. Before 1980, the Fed provided services free to member banks, which were the only institutions eligible for Fed services. Today, fees constitute a very small portion of a reserve bank's net earnings because these services are priced at levels close to cost. In 1993, for example, income from services was $945.1 million and costs were $906.8 million.

Judging from the magnitude of total net earnings of Federal Reserve banks, their business must be very profitable. In 1992, for example, the net earnings of Federal Reserve banks totaled $18.8 billion; in 1993, they were $17.3 billion. To appreciate how the unique position of the Fed as the central bank of the United States generates its high earnings, it helps to examine what managing a portfolio of securities means.

Managing a portfolio of securities means allocating a given amount of wealth to an array of assets. This allocation depends on two important factors: first, a given, fixed amount of wealth; and second, a criterion of choice, which in turn requires a method for ranking potential "baskets," or "portfolios," of assets. Because open market operations are conducted exclusively in government and agency securities, usually T-bills, the high earnings of reserve banks cannot be attributed to their wise selection of assets. This leaves the other alternative, namely, the size of the wealth to be allocated. It is here that the Fed holds an ace, for it is not limited to a given size of wealth. Through open market operations, the Fed can buy any amount of securities it chooses by creating reserves.

The Fed's huge net earnings result from its ability to buy interest-bearing IOUs of the U.S. Treasury and replace them with its own non-interest-bearing IOUs. Member banks, however, are not allowed to profit from the unique position of the Fed. Each member bank is required to buy stock in its district Federal Reserve bank. However, the law imposes a cap of 6 percent on the dividends that a member bank can earn as a stockholder in its reserve bank. Moreover, what remains of the Fed's net earnings after expenses are subtracted are given back to the U.S. Treasury.

According to the *80th Annual Report* of the Board of Governors of the Federal Reserve System, the system's total net earnings in 1993 amounted to $17.3 billion, of which the Fed returned $16.5 billion to the U.S. Treasury. That is, the Fed returned more than 96 percent of its net earnings to the U.S. Treasury. Since its inception, the Fed has returned to the U.S. Treasury about 95 percent of all its total net earnings.

THE FEDERAL OPEN MARKET COMMITTEE

As we have already seen, U.S. monetary policy is conducted by two governing bodies of the Federal Reserve System, the FOMC and the Board itself. The Board alone sets the reserve requirement ratio and, with some input from individual reserve banks, establishes the discount rate and the stringency in the administration of the discount window. However, the primary instrument of monetary policy, open market operations, is under the jurisdiction of the FOMC.

Composition of the FOMC

The **Federal Open Market Committee (FOMC)** consists of the seven members of the Board of Governors plus five presidents of reserve banks, one of whom must be the president of the Federal Reserve Bank of New York. The remaining 4 members of the FOMC are selected on a rotating basis from among the remaining 11 presidents of the reserve banks. The rotation follows an established geographical grouping of the 11 reserve banks: One group is composed of the 4th and the 7th reserve districts; another of the 9th, the 10th, and the 12th; another of the 1st, the 3rd, and the 5th; and one of the 6th, the 8th, and the 11th districts. Every year one president is selected on a rotating basis from each of these four groups. In this way all reserve districts can be voting members of the FOMC. We did not say "participants" because all reserve bank presidents participate in the FOMC meetings and do indeed air their views and concerns. By tradition, the chair of the Board of Governors serves as the chair and the president of the New York Fed serves as the vice-chair of the FOMC.

FOMC Meetings and Deliberations

The FOMC determines annually the number and the schedule of its meetings, usually eight per year. At those meetings, members decide primarily whether to provide or withdraw reserves from depository institutions through open market operations. The committee makes these decisions about both near-term and longer-term operations; that is, the timing and size of open market operations may cover the interim between meetings of the FOMC, about six weeks, or extend to as long as a year.

In making decisions about future open market operations, the FOMC relies on a variety of reports prepared by the staff of the Board and the reserve banks. Two briefing books prepared by the Board staff are of particular importance. One of the briefing books, called the Green Book because of the color of its cover, presents a snapshot of current economic and financial conditions and their prospects for the immediate future. By "economic conditions" the Fed means the real-sector variables, that is, the rate of inflation, the rates of growth of real and nominal GDP, and the unemployment rate. By "financial conditions" the Fed means collectively both interest rates and the growth rates of the various monetary and credit aggregates.

The other briefing book, called the Blue Book, offers a range of possibilities for growth in money and credit and the associated movements in reserves and the federal funds rate. The briefing books prepared for the February and July FOMC meetings are most important. In February the FOMC sets its targets for money and credit for the entire year. In July it conducts a midyear review of those targets and sets preliminary targets for the following year.

For every FOMC meeting, the Board staff also prepares reports on conditions in foreign exchange markets and in foreign economies. Finally, the staffs of the Federal Reserve banks prepare reports about regional economic conditions in the United States.

Policy Directives

At the end of each meeting the FOMC decides on the pattern of open market operations that will be pursued until the next FOMC meeting. If the need arises, however, FOMC members may consult by telephone in the interim. The FOMC also decides on the pattern of foreign currency operations that will be pursued.

These decisions are drafted into two directives—one for domestic open market operations and one for foreign currency operations—to the Federal Reserve Bank of New York, which is authorized and instructed to execute the directives in these areas of operations.

The Domestic Policy Directive

A few days after each FOMC meeting, the Fed makes public the **domestic policy directive** from the previous meeting in a release called the "Record of Policy Actions of the Federal Open Market Committee." Thus, each new domestic policy directive is kept secret from the public for about six weeks.

A domestic policy directive is usually about five or six paragraphs long. The key paragraph for short-run implementation of monetary policy gives operating instructions to the manager for domestic operations at the Federal Reserve Bank of New York, as illustrated by the following excerpt from the FOMC meeting held on July 7, 1993:

> In the implementation of policy for the immediate future, the Committee seeks to maintain the existing degree of pressure on reserve positions. In the context of the committee's long-run objectives for price stability and sustainable economic growth, and giving careful consideration to economic, financial, and monetary developments, slightly greater reserve restraint would or slightly less restraint might be acceptable in the intermeeting period. The contemplated reserve conditions are expected to be consistent with modest growth in the broader monetary aggregates over the third quarter. [*Federal Reserve Bulletin* 79, no. 10 (October 1993): 947]

The preceding paragraph illustrates that even after its release the directive is not helpful to readers unless they can decipher its cryptic language. Chapter 13, which discusses the instruments, targets, and goals of monetary policy, provides a framework for analyzing the directive. Here we consider the meaning of the words *would* and *might* in the directive. The directive stated that slightly greater reserve restraint *would* be acceptable or slightly lesser restraint *might be* acceptable. Because *would* is stronger than *might,* this statement means that the Fed was more likely to reduce rather than to increase the supply of reserves between FOMC meetings. It is an example of a *biased, or asymmetric, directive.* In this case, the tilt was toward tightening monetary policy in the intermeeting period.

The other four or five paragraphs of the directive, not illustrated here, summarize existing economic conditions and reasons behind the committee's instructions to the manager for domestic operations. The directive ends with a record of the votes of individual members of the FOMC. If a member dissents, the reasons for the dissent are given. A four or five page summary of the FOMC's discussion of policy and evaluation of conditions in the real and financial sectors accompanies the actual directive.

The Foreign Currency Directive   During the last two or more decades, the Federal Reserve, in cooperation with the U.S. Treasury, has periodically intervened in the foreign exchange market(s) in an effort to stabilize the foreign value of the dollar. However, the Fed and the Treasury do not always agree on the need for intervention. In the early 1980s, for example, Fed Chairman Volcker tried unsuccessfully to persuade the staunchly anti-interventionist secretary of the Treasury, Donald Regan, to intervene more often in the foreign exchange market to try to hold down the skyrocketing value of the dollar. A decade later the situation was reversed, with the Treasury more enthusiastic about intervention than the Fed. In the case of disagreements, the Treasury has the final say. The Fed acts as an adviser to the Treasury and as the Treasury's broker in executing the transactions. The **foreign currency directive** issued by the FOMC instructs the system manager for foreign operations on how to carry out the day-to-day purchases and sales of foreign currencies, again in a language that would be cryptic for the general reader.

MEMBER BANKS

Approximately 40 percent of commercial banks are members of the Federal Reserve System, but this small percentage issues nearly 70 percent of all commercial bank deposits. The new financial environment, however, has made the distinction between **member banks** and nonmember banks practically irrelevant. According to provisions of DID&MCA of 1980, all depository institutions—whether member banks or nonmember banks, commercial banks or thrift institutions—are subject to the same reserve requirements for identical deposit liabilities. In addition, any depository institution with deposit liabilities that are subject to reserve requirements has access to the discount window. Finally, as long as it is eligible for federal deposit insurance, any depository institution may have access to all Federal Reserve services, such as check clearing and collection, discount window borrowing, and acquisition of coin and currency.

These provisions of DID&MCA were designed to improve the precision of monetary control by either stemming the flight of commercial banks from membership with the Fed or, failing that, by making nonmember banks indistinguishable from member banks for monetary control purposes. At the heart of the issue is the concept of *dual banking:* Commercial banks may be chartered at either the state or national level. If chartered at the national level by the comptroller of the currency, a commercial bank must be a member of the Federal Reserve System. If a bank receives its charter at the state level, however, then it may choose membership or nonmembership in the Federal Reserve. In deciding whether to be a member, or whether to remain a member, a commercial bank makes a cost-benefit analysis; that is, it weighs the cost and benefits of membership.

Before the enactment of the MCA, the "costs" of membership included (1) obligatory ownership of the stock of the district reserve bank, which yields a statutory maximum dividend of 6 percent, without any real control over this stock; (2) higher (by comparison with nonmember banks) reserve requirements on its liabilities; and (3) stricter regulations and supervision. On the benefit side was exclusive access to Federal Reserve services, especially discount window borrowing and check collecting and clearing. To this list of benefits we must add the member bank's influence on the design of national and regional monetary policy; that influence originates in the right of member banks to elect six of the nine directors on the board of the district bank.

As Chapter 5 explained, DID&MCA of 1980 removed item (2) on the cost side. The same reserve requirements apply to member and nonmember banks. Banks can thus no longer escape higher reserve requirements by choosing nonmembership. That leaves item (3) as the distinguishing factor. In the future, therefore, the flight of commercial banks from membership may or may not be stemmed, depending on how banks compare federal regulation and supervision with that exercised by the relevant state authorities. Such disparity in regulation and the consequent overlapping authority for examination and supervision are topics of constant concern among banking system observers. Chapter 17 examines these issues, pointing out that calls for new legislation that standardizes regulation have been heard more often since the thrift crisis.

INDEPENDENCE AND ACCOUNTABILITY OF THE FED

The independence of the Fed is an issue that continues to provoke controversy. Although this issue covers the entire Federal Reserve System, it applies mostly to the policy-making bodies, that is, to the Board of Governors and the FOMC. It is primarily to the Board and the FOMC that we refer in the following pages when we examine the independence of the Fed. Although the Fed is financially independent, it is still accountable to Congress, and some legislators want to see that accountability increased.

Financial Independence

Of all federal agencies, only the Federal Reserve Board does not rely on Congress for funds. Thus, the Fed is financially independent in all its operations, from carrying out monetary policy to performing more mundane activities such as paying its personnel, buying supplies, and maintaining the "Marble Palace," the twin Board buildings on each side of 21st Street, N.W., between Constitution and Virginia Avenues, in Washington, D.C. This independent source of funding gives the Fed a certain measure of freedom from the executive and legislative branches. The Fed does not rely on the administration to submit its budget to the Congress for appropriation of funds. Additional independence is provided by the tenure of the governors. Each serves for a single, 14-year term and cannot be dismissed except for misconduct in office.

Accountability to Congress

The financial independence and the tenure of its governors give the Federal Reserve some measure of autonomy, but the Board is still accountable for its actions. The ultimate test of accountability lies in the U.S. Constitution and stems from the fact that the Federal Reserve System is the creation of the U.S. Congress. Congress can impose restrictions on the entire Fed or even repeal the Federal Reserve Act of 1913! But short of repealing or revising the act and the more recent legislation that governs the Federal Reserve System, what sort of supervision does Congress exercise over the Fed?

It is remarkable that until the end of World War II, the Fed had no formal, regular supervision by Congress. Of course, an occasional legislator, concerned about the plight of his constituency, would make noises about imposing restraints on the Fed; Congress would pass an occasional "Sense of Congress Resolution"—nonbinding, of course—expressing the "concern" of the Congress about some aspects of Federal Reserve policies. By and large, however, the Federal Reserve easily withstood this pressure.

In 1946, however, the Full Employment Act mandated that the Fed pursue the goal of full employment. This mandate however, was couched in terms that gave the Fed almost unlimited discretion. It was not until the mid-1970s that Congress required the Fed to report in detail on its pursuit of economic goals and to sharpen the goals themselves. Of considerable importance was the passage of the 1978 Full Employment and Balanced Growth Act (Humphrey-Hawkins Act), which requires the Fed to pursue full employment and "reasonable" price stability. More important, the act mandates extensive periodic reports.

According to the requirements of the Humphrey-Hawkins Act, the Board must prepare in February and July a report, addressed to the Senate and the House of Representatives and presented in person by the chair with accompanying testimony to the House Committee on Banking, Housing, and Urban Affairs and the Senate Banking Committee. As

Chapter 13 explains in greater detail, these reports present the FOMC's predictions of inflation, growth of real GDP, and unemployment, and compare them to the predictions of the administration. The reports also announce the targets for monetary and credit aggregates that the Board will pursue for the year, presumably to achieve those projections of real-sector variables. It is noteworthy that even here the Fed has latitude in its actions: It is required merely to announce its monetary targets, not to achieve them. The reports are the only means by which the Fed demonstrates, on a regular and formal basis, its accountability to the executive and the legislative branches of government.

Reform versus the Status Quo

Over the years proposals for reforming the Fed have proliferated. Most of the proposals, however, die before reaching the legislative stage. The few that are formulated into an actual congressional bill rarely get voted into law because a quasi-independent Fed suits both the legislative and executive branches of government. It allows elected officials to distance themselves from unpopular monetary policies, usually disinflationary (contractionary) policies that raise interest rates and reduce output in the short run.

Most of the proposals for reforming the Fed focus on the FOMC, the chief policy-making body within the Federal Reserve System. Some reformers want to standardize the selection process for all members of the FOMC; others want to formalize the FOMC's relationship with the administration or to reduce the secrecy surrounding the domestic policy directive; and still others want to strip the FOMC of all discretionary power.

Changing the Selection Process for Reserve Bank Presidents

Under the existing system the public has no say, via its elected officials, in the selection of reserve bank presidents. As we have seen, the president of each reserve bank is nominated by the bank's board of directors, six of whom are chosen by member commercial banks and three of whom represent those banks. The Board of Governors confirms the nominations. This undemocratic selection process has made the FOMC a favorite target of populist legislators and reformers, who argue that the reserve bank presidents represent the interests of bankers rather than the interests of the public. The attacks usually increase when contractionary monetary policy causes interest rates to rise. (It is not clear that rising interest rates benefit commercial banks.)

Although interest rates were neither high nor rising at the beginning of 1993, some members of Congress were not satisfied with monetary policy. They had been pressing the Fed for a more stimulative monetary policy for more than a year because of the unusually slow recovery from the 1990–91 recession. In March 1993, the Senate Committee on Banking, Housing, and Urban Affairs summoned all 12 reserve bank presidents to testify on economic and monetary conditions before the committee. The chair of the Federal Reserve Board regularly testifies about the state of the economy and the conduct of monetary policy before congressional committees; other governors also appear before these committees to testify on issues about which they have special expertise. Occasionally, a reserve bank president, especially the president of the New York Fed, is called to testify. However, to summon all 12 reserve bank presidents to appear together was highly unusual. Although the senators were not particularly hostile in their questioning of the reserve bank presidents, merely by holding the session the committee sent a signal to the Fed about the power of Congress to alter its charter.

At the time, Senator Paul Sarbanes, a Democrat from Maryland, and Congressman Lee Hamilton, a Democrat from Indiana, were sponsoring legislation to remove reserve bank presidents from the FOMC, while congressman Henry Gonzalez, a Texas Democrat and chairman of the House Banking Committee, was sponsoring legislation to subject reserve bank presidents to the same confirmation process as governors. Proponents of the Gonzalez proposal argue that it would strengthen public confidence in the FOMC. Opponents, on the other hand, argue that it would reduce the Fed's independence from political pressures. In a letter to Congressman Gonzalez on September 20, 1993, President Clinton supported the status quo: "Changing the way bank presidents are elected at this time runs the risk of undermining market confidence in the Fed." He also said: "There is virtue in having the Federal Open Market Committee input (and votes) that truly comes from outside Washington, D.C." With the president on its side, the Fed withstood the attempt by some members of Congress to alter the role of reserve bank presidents in the FOMC.

Formalizing the Links between the Administration and the FOMC   In 1935, when Congress established the FOMC in its present form, it removed the secretary of the Treasury as a nonvoting member. Since then the relation between the administration and the Fed has been informal. Staff members from the Fed and the Treasury meet regularly to discuss economic policy and the economy. Meetings also take place at higher levels, usually between the Fed chair and the secretary of the Treasury.

In 1989, two representatives, Byron Dorgan and Lee Hamilton, introduced legislation to reestablish a formal relationship between the administration and the FOMC. The Dorgan-Hamilton bill would have required the FOMC to meet formally three times a year with the secretary of the Treasury, the director of the Office of Management and Budget, and the Council of Economic Advisors, all of whom advise the president on economic policy. Although the bill died in Congress, it reopened the public debate about the role of elected officials in formulating monetary policy. Supporters of the Dorgan-Hamilton bill argued that reestablishing formal links between the FOMC and the administration would lead to more effective coordination of monetary and fiscal policy and would increase the accountability and responsibility of the president for economic policy. Critics argued that elected officials, if given more influence in the process of creating money, would be tempted to solve current and future deficit problems by opening up the monetary spigot, thereby creating inflation.

Reducing Secrecy   Historically the Fed has shown reluctance to disclose information about the policy intentions of the FOMC. Until the late 1960s the Fed released the domestic policy directives and accompanying summaries of FOMC meetings only once a year, in the publication of its annual report about six months after the end of the year. In 1967, the Board began to publish the directive in the *Federal Reserve Bulletin* with a three-month lag. They gradually shortened the lag for the release of the directive to about six weeks. The Dorgan-Hamilton bill would have required the Fed to disclose the information immediately. The issue came up again in 1993 in the Gonzalez bill, which would require the Fed to release the directive within seven days after the FOMC meeting.

Immediate disclosure has wide support among academics and market professionals. Supporters argue that the freer flow of information would improve market efficiency and Fed credibility because market participants would not have to waste time and resources trying to divine the policy intentions of the Fed. The Fed, however, has traditionally been against immediate disclosure. The Fed's argument has been that immediate release of the policy directive would create unnecessary volatility in financial markets.

To illustrate the Fed's argument, let's consider again the July 1993 directive. In that directive the FOMC expressed a bias toward greater reserve restraint, which means it was tilting toward pushing up interest rates in the intermeeting period. As the period unfolded, however, the Fed did not push up rates. Instead, it maintained the status quo because the economic and financial conditions for tightening did not develop. Fed officials argue that if they were to release such a directive immediately after an FOMC meeting, market participants would take for granted that the Fed would implement the tighter policy. Acting to protect their financial interests, these participants would cause market rates of interest to rise. If the Fed did not tighten, eventually interest rates would come back down. The result, according to the Fed, would be unnecessary volatility in interest rates.

The Fed has objected not only to immediate disclosure but also to full disclosure of FOMC proceedings. The Fed argues that full disclosure would (1) inhibit wide-ranging discussion of alternative views at FOMC meetings and (2) compromise confidential information, especially about foreign exchange operations. The Fed's critics counter that the Fed merely wants to avoid accountability. Until 1976 the Fed did release detailed nonverbatim minutes (after deleting sensitive information) of FOMC meetings with a five-year lag. When it discontinued the practice in 1976, the Fed stated that it would no longer keep complete minutes of FOMC meetings.

The bill introduced by Congressman Gonzalez in 1993 would require the Fed not only to release directives within 7 days but also to release complete transcripts of meetings within 60 days. As a result of congressional hearings on the Gonzalez bill in October 1993, it was revealed that FOMC meetings are tape recorded and that more than 20,000 pages of unedited transcripts of meetings dating back to 1976 are kept in locked file cabinets in the Board building. Even most FOMC members were not aware of this. The revelation that the Fed has continued to keep transcripts of FOMC meetings for 17 years after it claimed to have abandoned the practice undermined the credibility of the Fed's argument against full disclosure and strengthened the argument of its critics that the Fed wants to avoid accountability.

In the face of mounting criticism, the Fed made two concessions. First, it reverted to its pre-1976 practice of releasing lightly edited transcripts of FOMC meetings to the public with a five-year lag. This action resulted in the immediate release of transcripts of meetings between 1976 and 1988. The Fed's second concession was more important, because it dealt with the release of information on current policy.

In February 1994, the Fed broke with tradition by announcing at the conclusion of the FOMC meeting that the FOMC had decided to "increase slightly the degree of pressure on reserve positions," and that the action was expected "to be associated with a small increase in short-term money market interest rates." In the past, the Fed provided this information to the public indirectly through the Fedwatchers of large banks and brokerage houses. These Fedwatchers followed the Fed's actions in the open market to detect changes in the stance of monetary policy. Occasionally, however, they would err, as we shall see in Chapter 14. Announcements by the Fed are a more straightforward way of providing information about changes in interest rates.

At the time of the first announcement, the Fed did not commit itself to continue the practice. Instead, the Fed said it was making the announcement "to avoid any misunderstanding of the Committee's purpose," given the fact that this was the first rate increase by the FOMC since 1989. While still calling the practice provisional, the Fed announced increases in pressure on reserve positions following FOMC meetings in March, May, and August. It also announced an intermeeting increase in April. In some of these announcements, the Fed provided a brief (one or two sentences) explanation of the reason for the increase, as we shall see in Chapter 13. Such explanations help to communicate the Fed's goals to the public in a way that signaling changes in the stance of policy through Fedwatchers cannot. The Fed is unlikely to discontinue the practice of announcing changes in the stance of policy, because it would be inviting an attack by its critics. In 1994, however, the Fed continued to resist pressure from its critics to make the *entire* directive available on a more timely basis.

Mandating a Monetary Policy Rule   Some economists have recommended radical changes in the conduct of monetary policy that, if adopted, would make irrelevant the organizational and institutional reforms we have examined so far. Prominent monetarists such as Milton Friedman, Alan Meltzer, and the late Karl Brunner have repeatedly argued in favor of stripping the Fed of its discretionary power. They want Congress to mandate that the Fed follow a policy rule regardless of the state of the economy. The rule suggested most often is that the central bank be required to expand the monetary base or some specified measure of money, such as M2, at a fixed annual rate. Moreover, proponents of rules want the enabling legislation to have teeth. For example, the **Shadow Open Market Committee**, a group of private economists, has recommended that the law require members of the FOMC to resign if they miss the stipulated target. This private group of economists, mostly of the monetarist persuasion, meets twice a year to analyze monetary policy and the economy and to offer policy recommendations.

Some allowances would have to be made however, for errors. As we have seen, the Fed can completely control neither the monetary base nor the monetary aggregates. These are determined by the interaction of decisions made by the Fed, the banks, and the public. The only item in the Fed's balance sheet that it can completely control is its portfolio of Treasury securities. No one has suggested that the FOMC should simply let the Treasury securities in the Fed's portfolio grow at a constant rate because Treasury securities are not the only factor in the Fed's balance sheet that affects reserves in the banking system.

The subject of rules versus discretion in the conduct of monetary (and fiscal) policy is a controversial one that sharply divides economists. The pros and cons of the various positions are examined in Chapter 27. Here we merely point out that legislation has never been introduced in Congress that would require the Fed to follow a prescribed rule for a financial or a real-sector variable. In 1989, however, Congressman Stephen L. Neal did introduce a bill directing the Fed to reduce inflation to zero in five years. The legislation had no bite, however; it did not spell out any policies for eliminating inflation or impose any penalties on policymakers for failing to do so. Unlike the Dorgan-Hamilton bill, the Neal bill was supported by the Fed, but it too died in Congress. From the Fed's perspective, the bill would have helped it deflect criticism in its inflation-fighting efforts without imposing any new constraints on the central bank.

Independence and Central Bank Performance

Price stability is a goal of all central banks, not only of the Fed. Therefore, we would expect that central banks, if left to themselves, would be inflation fighters. That is, the more independent the central bank, the better it is at fighting inflation. There is theoretical argreement on this issue for two principal reasons.

The first is political. Independence makes it politically easier for a central bank to reduce inflation once it has taken hold. When inflation becomes entrenched, it takes contractionary monetary policies to wring out that inflation and the inflation premium embedded in interest rates. Unfortunately, these favorable long-term effects of contractionary monetary policy often do not show up until after the next election. In the short run, disinflationary monetary policies raise interest rates, reduce output, and increase unemployment, making it difficult for elected officials to support publicly such policies. Between 1979 and 1982, for example, the Volcker-led Fed pursued a disinflationary monetary policy that drove short-term interest rates up to 15 percent and the unemployment rate up to 10.8 percent. The president and members of Congress pointed to the independent Fed as the culprit. Many of the same elected officials, however, embraced the significantly lower inflation rates and interest rates that persisted for the remainder of the decade.

So far, we have emphasized political independence. Economists also measure independence by the degree to which the central bank does not have to participate in financing government deficits by buying securities and issuing reserves. This is referred to as *economic independence*. During World War II and through the beginning of the Korean War, the Fed was obligated to support the financing of the deficit. Thus, the Fed had little economic independence. At the end of 1952, however, the Eisenhower administration relieved the Fed of that burden; since then, the Fed has been free from the obligation to help the U.S. Treasury finance the deficit.

This separation of the responsibilities for fiscal and monetary policies is a major reason for the Fed's independence and for its greater ability to combat inflation. To see why, suppose that the U.S. Treasury is faced with financing a deficit and, thus, with selling a given amount of new securities. If the Fed is not obligated to buy an equal amount of securities in the open market, there will be excess supply of securities in the market. As a result, the price of securities will fall and interest rates will rise. The higher interest rates will dampen, or crowd out, aggregate demand and, hence, reduce the price level. If, on the other hand, the Fed is obligated to finance the deficit, it must buy an equal amount of securities in the open market. In this case, there will be no excess supply of securities and therefore no change in the interest rate. As a result, neither aggregate demand nor the price level will fall, and the price level will be higher than when the Fed does not have to finance the deficit.

In summary, economic independence in the form of freedom from the responsibility to help finance the deficit gives a central bank the *ability* to fight inflation. Political independence gives the central bank the *will* to do so by insulating it from explicit or implicit pressures. A central bank needs the political courage (reinforced by this insulation) to pursue a policy designed to achieve a universally considered good thing—a lower rate of inflation—because of the potential side effects of its actions on the economy. Economists do not agree, however, about these side effects. Economists on one side argue that in the short run an attempt to reduce inflation through a tighter monetary policy reduces aggregate demand, which leads to a higher unemployment rate and lower real GDP growth.

Thus, this side argues that an independent central bank achieves a lower inflation rate at the price of lower real growth and higher unemployment.

Economists on the other side argue that rather than causing inferior real-sector performance, an independent central bank improves that performance. One line of argument points to the predictability of economic policy that results from independence. Such predictability improves the business environment and, in turn, promotes growth.[1] Another line of argument points to the lower inflation associated with an independent central bank. Lower inflation creates fewer economic distortions, thereby promoting growth. GlobalWatch 11.3 summarizes recent empirical work that relates central bank independence to inflation, economic growth, and unemployment.

Political Pressures

Independent central banks, such as the Federal Reserve System in the United States, are more likely to be inflation fighters. This does not mean that the Fed is not political—that it does not read the newspapers to see who wins the election, to learn the latest utterances of members of Congress, or to learn the public utterances of named and unnamed "high administration officials." Administration officials also jawbone the Fed in private, but the public utterances are intended to put maximum political pressure on the Fed.

In a recent book, Thomas Havrilesky introduces an index called the *SAFER index* (Signaling from the Administration to the Federal Reserve) to measure the overt pressure put on the Fed by the administration.[2] Havrilesky constructs the index for the period from 1953 to 1991 from articles in *The Wall Street Journal* in which administration officials express a desire for a tighter or looser monetary policy. His results show that signaling took place in every administration from Eisenhower to Bush. Using data from 1964 through 1991, he finds, however, that signaling affected the outcome of monetary policy in only two periods: from 1970 to 1974 under the chairmanship of Arthur Burns, and from 1980 to 1984 under the chairmanship of Paul Volcker. Burns responded to signals from the Nixon administration for an easier monetary policy, and Volcker to signals first from Carter and then from Reagan (in his first term) for a tighter monetary policy. In both periods, the Fed was under close scrutiny from Congress, which posed a threat to the power of the Fed. Havrilesky argues that to prevent Congress from tampering with its power, the Fed needed to ally itself with the administration by responding to its signaling.

What has been the record under the Clinton administration? Initially, the relationship was cordial, as the following quotation in the *New York Times* on August 16, 1993, indicates: " 'They're doing what we want them to do on short-term rates and we're doing what they want us to do about the deficit,' said Alan Blinder, a member of the President's Council of Economic Advisers, referring to the rate the Fed charges for overnight loans. 'And as long as we're doing what the other wants, things will be hunky-dory.' "[3]

---

[1] This argument rests on the theory of the political business cycle, which maintains that a dependent bank may either manipulate monetary policy before elections to help the party in power politically or to reward the constituency of a party after the election.

[2] Thomas Havrilesky, *The Pressures on American Monetary Policy* (Boston: Kluwer Academic Publishers, 1993).

[3] President Clinton appointed Blinder vice chairman of the Federal Reserve Board in 1994.

GlobalWatch 11.3
Comparing the Performance of Central Banks

Is the Fed's independence good for the economy? To answer this question, several recent papers have compared the economic performance of central banks around the world. The most recent of this growing literature is the work of two Harvard professors, Alberto Alesina and Lawrence H. Summers.*

Alesina and Summers first rank the central banks of 16 industrial countries by their independence. Criteria include "the institutional relationship between the central bank and the executive [branch], the procedure to nominate and dismiss the head of the central bank, the role of government officials on the central bank board, and the frequency of contacts between the executive and the bank." Another basis for ranking is "how easy it is for the government to finance its deficit by direct access to credit from the central bank." The least independent bank is given an index of 1.0 and the most independent a 4.0. Of the 16 banks, two are "totally independent," meriting a 4.0: Germany's *Bundesbank* and the Swiss National Bank. At the other end, the central bank of New Zealand ranks last for the period examined (but not currently), with 1.0, followed closely by the banks of Spain and Italy with, respectively, 1.5 and 1.75. The Federal Reserve stands near the top, according to the study, with an index of 3.5. All other central banks fall in the 2 to 2.5 range.

Alesina and Summers proceed to relate central bank independence to inflation in these countries from 1955 through 1988. The first graph, reproduced from their paper, illustrates their results. The authors confirm earlier results by Alesina and other economists that the more independent a country's central bank, the lower the country's inflation. For example, Germany and Switzerland registered the lowest average inflation rates—3.0 and 3.2 percent, respectively, followed by the United States with a 4.1 percent rate. At the other extreme, the two countries with the least independent banks, Spain and New Zealand, had the highest inflation, 8.5 and 7.6 percent, respectively.

If the sole purpose of the central bank were to minimize inflation, independence would indeed be a good thing. Other things equal, a permanently lower inflation rate is better than a higher one. Suppose, however, that other things are not equal. Suppose, for example, that a permanently lower inflation rate is achieved at the expense of real GDP growth and greater unemployment. Alesina and Summers investigate this issue and find no relation between central bank independence and economic performance measured by real GDP growth or the unemployment rate.

In the same spirit, and using the Alesina-Summers data, we examine both issues simultaneously by relat-

---

* Alberto Alesina and Lawrence H. Summers, "Central Bank Independence and Macroeconomic Performance," *Journal of Money, Credit And Banking* 25, no. 2 (May 1993): 151–62.

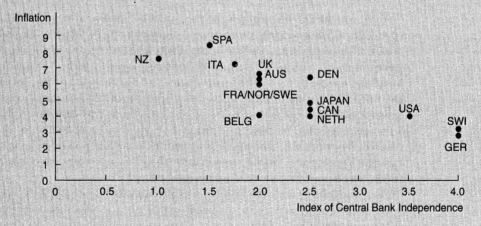

continued

GlobalWatch 11.3
Comparing the Performance of Central Banks (concluded)

ing independence to the sum of the inflation rate and the unemployment rate, called the *misery index* by the late Arthur Okun. There are data for only 13 of the countries examined by Alesina and Summers. Relating central bank independence and the misery index, we see in the second graph that Germany, with the most independent bank, scores the best, with the lowest misery index of 6.6 percent; Italy, with the least independent bank in this

sample, scores the worst, with a misery index of 14.3 percent. Unfortunately, we cannot conclude that central bank independence is superior. Japan, the one country that is nearly tied with Germany for the best misery index, has a central bank that is not very independent. In addition, countries with central banks that possess little independence—Norway and Sweden—perform very well, with an index of 8.2.

Where does the United States rate in the misery department? With a misery index of 10.1, it ranks close to countries with central banks that have little independence—France, Australia, and the United Kingdom.

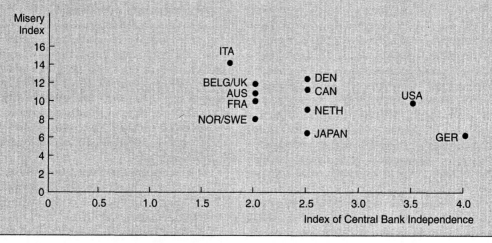

What was the Fed doing about short-term rates? Nothing; it was pushing them neither up nor down. What was the administration doing about the deficit? A few days earlier the president had signed into law a five-year, $500 billion deficit reduction program. Expectations of deficit reduction were one of the factors that had pushed long-term rates down more than one percentage point since Clinton had been elected in November 1992. This happened because market participants, expecting lower long-term rates as a result of deficit reduction, attempted to lock in higher rates by increasing their purchases of long-term securities; this increase in demand raised the price of long-term securities and lowered their rate. The Clinton administration was counting on lower long-term rates to stimulate the economy. Therefore, it was satisfied with the status quo on short-term rates, which are the rates that the Fed affects most.

By the fourth quarter of 1993, real GDP increased at the robust rate of 7 percent, as the lower long-term interest rates stimulated spending on residential construction and consumer and producer durables. Convinced that the recovery was firmly underway and concerned that the economy was in danger of overheating, the Fed pushed up short-term interest rates a total of 175 basis points between February and August 1994. Some members of Congress and some academic economists criticized the Fed's preemptive strike against inflation as a premature move that threatened the recovery. The response from the Clinton administration, however, was muted, with the president's economic advisors pointing out that some increase in interest rates was built into the administration's forecast. Because monetary policy affects the economy with lags of nine months or more, the administration may have preferred to take its contractionary medicine in 1994, with the hope that additional dosages would not be needed in 1995—one year before the presidential elections.

LOOKING AHEAD

Although the Clinton administration did not want to tamper with the structure of the FOMC, it did have plans to reduce the role of the Fed as a regulator of banks. In November 1993, it announced a plan to consolidate the regulatory functions of the Federal Reserve, the Comptroller of the Currency, the FDIC, and the Office of Thrift Supervision into one Federal Banking Commission. Chapter 17, which examines the structure and regulation of banks and thrifts, explains the administration's plan and the Fed's objections.

SUMMARY

- The primary twin functions of the Fed are safeguarding the health of financial institutions and the health of the U.S. economy itself. These goals evolved from the U.S. Constitution, which empowered Congress to create the Federal Reserve System.

- The Federal Reserve System consists of four basic components: the Board of Governors, often referred to as the Board; the 12 Federal Reserve banks; member commercial banks; and the Federal Open Market Committee (FOMC), which draws its membership from the seven governors and 5 of the 12 presidents of the reserve banks.

- The dominant component of the Federal Reserve System is the Board. The Board, located in Washington, D.C., consists of seven governors, each appointed for a single 14-year term.

- To foster the health of the U.S. economy, the Board participates in FOMC decisions about open market operations, the primary instrument of monetary policy. The Board, often at the initiative of district banks, also changes the secondary instrument of monetary policy, the discount rate. The Board alone occasionally changes the reserve requirement ratio(s).

- To foster the health of financial institutions, the Board oversees and supervises member banks, via its operating arm, the 12 reserve banks.

- The Board also supervises all other functions of the reserve banks, conducts extensive research on the state of the economy and on the role of monetary policy, and provides services of public interest.

- The Federal Reserve banks are the banker to banks, the banker to the U.S. government, and the banker to foreign governments and international organizations. Second only to their role as a banker to banks is their role as examiner and supervisor of member banks. Reserve banks also participate in the making of monetary policy by proposing discount rate changes and by providing 5 of the 12 voting members of the FOMC.

- Reserve banks return to the Board their profits from holding U.S. government securities and from making discount window loans. After subtracting its own expenses, the Board returns the remainder to the U.S. Treasury.

- The FOMC is the chief policy-making body in the Federal Reserve System. It meets 8 to 10 times a year to draw up annual and intermeeting plans for open market operations. After each meeting, the FOMC issues a domestic policy directive addressed to the Federal Reserve Bank of New York, the FOMC's agent for open market operations.

- The law requires nationally chartered banks to be members of the Federal Reserve System. State-chartered banks decide on membership after evaluating the costs and benefits of being a member.

- The financing of the Fed independently of the budget of the federal government and the single 14-year tenure of its governors give the Fed a measure of independence.

- The Fed's independence has been the subject of controversy since its inception. Critics range from populist legislators to experts on central banking. A major criticism is that an independent Fed has insufficient accountability, which is considered an anomaly in a democratic society.

- Proponents of the current arrangements argue that independent central banks are greater inflation fighters than central banks that are part of the executive branch.

- Recommendations for reform include changing the selection process of the reserve bank presidents, establishing formal rather than informal links with the executive branch, releasing the domestic policy directive immediately after the FOMC meeting, and mandating a monetary policy rule.

- In 1994 the Fed initiated the practice of announcing changes in the degree of reserve pressure, and accompanying changes in interest rates, directly to the public instead of filtering the information through Fedwatchers.

KEY TERMS AND CONCEPTS

Board of Governors of the Federal Reserve System
Quarterly Model
Monthly Money Market Model

district Federal Reserve banks
Federal Open Market Committee (FOMC)
domestic policy directive

foreign currency directive
member banks
Shadow Open Market Committee

QUESTIONS AND PROBLEMS

1. What law requires the Fed to set targets for money growth and to report those targets to Congress? What is the penalty for the Fed if it fails to meet its targets?

The Wall Street Journal

2. The following statement is from "Fed Officials, Meeting Next Week, Are Facing Policy Confrontation," which appeared in *The Wall Street Journal* on Friday, June 26, 1992: "Of the 12 Fed officials who will vote at the FOMC meeting, at least three seem prepared to cut rates and at least four lean against. The views of the remaining five aren't discernible. The most significant unknown is Mr. Greenspan."

   a. What positions do the 12 individuals who vote in the FOMC hold in the Federal Reserve System?

   b. The same article identified David Mullins, Lawrence Lindsey, and Susan Phillips as the three officials "said to be ready to push rates down again." What do they have in common?

3. If the law required the Federal Reserve to follow a policy rule, such as a constant rate of growth of the monetary base, would there be a need for the FOMC? Explain.

4. "The seven members of the Board of Governors have the authority to set reserve requirement ratios at any level they deem appropriate." True, false, or uncertain? Explain.

5. The FOMC decides on open market operations and the discount rate. True or false? Explain.

6. Member banks of the Federal Reserve System have a financial incentive to promote higher interest rates because higher interest rates mean higher Fed earnings, which result in higher dividends paid to member banks. True or false? Explain.

7. Why do you think that six of the nine directors of each district Federal Reserve bank may not be officers, directors, or employees of a bank?

8. Because governors serve for 14 years, not every president of the United States appoints a chair of the Board

of Governors of the Federal Reserve System. True or false? Explain.

9. Bank of America is a nationally chartered bank. Can it choose whether to be a member of the Federal Reserve System?

10. How can the president try to influence monetary policy?

11. Explain the difference between political independence and economic independence of a central bank.

The Wall Street Journal

12. Explain why you agree or disagree with the following statement by Alan Greenspan that appeared in "The Federal Reserve: A Very Easy Target," *The Wall Street Journal*, February 8, 1993: "A significant retrenchment in the independence of the institution [that is, the Fed] . . . would not serve the American people."

SUGGESTED READINGS

Board of Governors of the Federal Reserve System. *Annual Report.*
Published every spring, this report contains summaries of economic conditions during the preceding year, the monetary policy reports to the Congress, a record of policy actions of the Board of Governors and the FOMC, and other information on operations and organization of the Federal Reserve System.

Board of Governors of the Federal Reserve System, *Federal Reserve Bulletin.*
Published monthly, this journal contains articles on the economy, speeches by the Fed chairman and other governors, legal developments, and financial and business statistics.

Board of Governors of the Federal Reserve System. *The Federal Reserve System: Purposes and Functions,* 1984.
An official overview of the Federal Reserve System.

Friedman, Milton, and Anna J. Schwartz. "A Tale of Fed Transcripts." *The Wall Street Journal,* December 20, 1993, A12.
An op-ed piece on the history of the Fed's disclosure of FOMC deliberations.

Greider, William. *Secrets of the Temple: How the Federal Reserve Runs the Country.* New York: Simon & Schuster, 1987.

An investigative reporter with a populist outlook peeks inside the Federal Reserve System.

Havrilesky, Thomas. *The Pressures on American Monetary Policy.* Boston: Kluwer Academic Publishers, 1993.
A Duke University professor of economics examines the relationship between politics and economics in the making of monetary policy.

Jones, David M. *The Politics of Money: The Fed under Alan Greenspan.* New York: New York Institute of Finance, 1991.
A Wall Street economist and former economist at the Federal Reserve Bank of New York looks at the Fed under the leadership of Alan Greenspan.

Melton, William C. *Inside the Fed: Making Monetary Policy.* Homewood, Ill.: Dow Jones-Irwin, 1985.
A private-sector economist and former official of the Federal Reserve Bank of New York examines monetary policy in the 1980s.

"Statements to the Congress." *Federal Reserve Bulletin* 79, no. 12 (December 1993): 1100–1126.
The governors and the reserve bank presidents provide views on legislation dealing with disclosure of FOMC deliberations.

FUNCTIONS OF FEDERAL RESERVE BANKS

The Details

CHAPTER PREVIEW

Do you ever wonder how the check you sent to a bookstore in New York came back to you? Or consider the following: When you need cash, you borrow from your banker. But where do bankers go when they need cash? And when you need to make a payment, you write a check drawn on your checking account with your bank. On what checking account does the federal government draw the checks used to pay federal employees such as military personnel? To answer such questions as these, we must look into the role of the district Federal Reserve banks.

The 12 Federal Reserve banks are the operating arms of the Federal Reserve System. They provide services necessary for the smooth functioning of the payments system, and they support and monitor the health of depository institutions in their districts. In addition, reserve banks participate in the formation of national monetary policy. This chapter examines the five major functions of district banks:

1. Banker to banks

2. Banker to the U.S. government

3. Banker to foreign governments and international organizations

4. Examiner and supervisor of banks

5. Participant in the design and execution of U.S. monetary policy.

BANKER TO BANKS

The primary function of a reserve bank is to act as a banker's bank, that is, to provide services to commercial banks and other depository institutions in its district. The most important of these services are collecting and clearing checks, transferring funds by wire, and distributing (wrapping and transporting) coin and currency. According to provisions of the Depository Institutions Deregulation and Monetary Control Act (DID&MCA) of 1980, these services must be provided to all depository institutions, members and non-members alike, at a fee that covers costs.

To ensure the smooth functioning of depository institutions, reserve banks also provide loans to them at the established discount rate. Depository institutions, however, are supposed to explore alternative sources of funding before approaching the discount window. In this section, we examine three important "banker's bank" functions. After examining check collecting and clearing, we examine the criteria reserve banks use in making discount window loans. Then we explain how reserve banks distribute coins and currency.

Check Collecting and Clearing

The role of a reserve bank as the banker for a bank in its district is best exemplified by the services of check collecting and clearing. Each bank has a reserve account with its banker, the Federal Reserve bank for its district. It is these reserve accounts that the reserve banks credit and debit to settle claims between banks.

An Example   Let us illustrate the process of **check collecting and clearing** with a typical example. Suppose that Ann from Buffalo writes a $100 check, drawn on Bufbank and payable to George in Seattle. She mails the check to George, who deposits it with his bank, Seabank, in Seattle. In effect, George wants Seabank to collect the $100 for him and to credit his account.

Figure 12–1 shows how the check-collecting process works. The left column shows the check moving through the system. So far the check has gone from Ann to George to Seabank. Next, Seabank sends the check to its bank, the Federal Reserve Bank of San Francisco, and asks it to collect the $100 from Bufbank. Because Bufbank is not in the San Francisco Reserve District, the Federal Reserve Bank of San Francisco must send the check to Bufbank's reserve bank, the Federal Reserve of New York, which then sends the check to Bufbank. Upon receiving the check, Bufbank debits Ann's account $100 and, at the end of the month, sends Ann the canceled check along with the statement of her deposit account. The check has reached the end of the line. However, what has happened to George's deposit account with Seabank? Seabank's reserve account with the San Francisco Fed? Bufbank's reserve account with the New York Fed?

The second column in Figure 12–1 shows the bookkeeping changes made by Bufbank, Seabank, and the Federal Reserve banks in this transaction. As we just saw, Bufbank, upon receiving the check, debits Ann's deposit account $100. On the same day that Bufbank receives Ann's check, the Federal Reserve Bank of New York debits Bufbank's reserve account $100. Bufbank therefore loses reserves with the Fed. These reserves are transferred to Seabank, whose reserve account with the Federal Reserve Bank of San Francisco is credited $100. Seabank may actually gain the $100 in reserves before Bufbank loses them because the receiving bank's reserve account with the Fed is credited on a preset schedule, not to exceed two days. Seabank, of course, credits $100 to

FIGURE 12–1
The Check-
Collecting and
Clearing Process

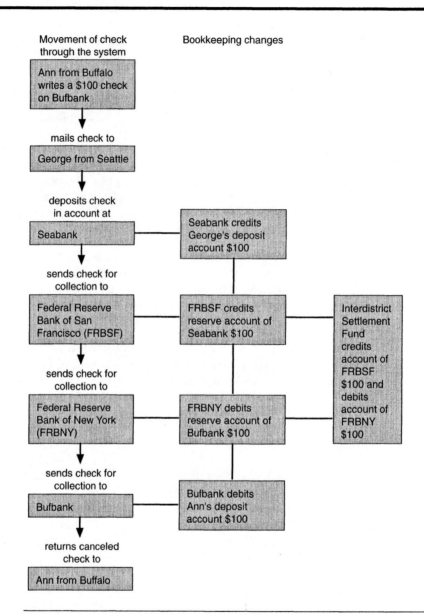

George's deposit account. To allow time for the check to be collected, most banks make the funds deposited by check available to the deposit holder only after a few days.

The only loose end in this example is the position of each of the reserve banks, shown in the third column in Figure 12–1. The New York Reserve Bank owes $100 to the San Francisco Reserve Bank, the amount that the latter paid Seabank on behalf of the New York Reserve Bank. How is this debt settled? Each Federal Reserve Bank has an account with the Interdistrict Settlement Fund, managed by the Federal Reserve Board in Washington, D.C. just for that purpose. The Board credits the account of the San Francisco Fed and debits the account of the New York Fed. Of course, there is no change in total reserves supplied by the Fed in this case. In a sense, the Board is the banker, or rather the bookkeeper, for the reserve banks. In fact, the same fund settles other transfers of funds such as wire transfers between reserve banks.

TRY IT OUT 12.1

Show the changes in the T-accounts of Ann, George, Bufbank, Seabank, and the Fed that result from the example in Figure 12–1 by inserting the number +100 or –100 in the blank spaces in the following T-accounts. Note that there is only one T-account for the entire Federal Reserve System; this account is the sum of the accounts of all the Federal Reserve banks.

Ann		George	
Deposits with Bufbank _____	Net Worth _____	Deposits with Seabank _____	Net Worth _____

Bufbank		Seabank	
Reserves with Fed _____	Deposits _____	Reserves with Fed _____	Deposits _____

Fed	
	Reserve Account of Bufbank _____
	Reserve Account of Seabank _____

Complications in the Process   The preceding example assumes that the check-clearing process has proceeded smoothly. Several things, however, can go wrong in this example. For one thing, if Ann does not have enough funds in her checking account with Bufbank, Bufbank will refuse to pay. It will send the check marked "insufficient funds," back to George so that he can try to collect on his own. Another problem may arise if Bufbank itself has insufficient funds with the New York Federal Reserve Bank. In this case, Bufbank will get the notification "adverse clearing balances" from its banker, the New York Fed. Bufbank must come up with the balances. In this case, however, special provisions prevent the process from being reversed and George from losing his deposit with Seabank.

Another, more typical, complication causes problems for the Fed itself. Suppose that the plane scheduled to carry Ann's check from Seattle to Buffalo for collection cannot take off because of bad weather, even after the Seattle branch of the San Francisco District Bank has credited Seabank with the $100. Under these circumstances, not only does Ann's deposit account get a temporary reprieve (from paying) but also Seabank gets a free ride; that is, it gets reserves from the San Francisco Reserve Bank. This is because after a maximum of two days, Seabank's reserve account is credited by the San Francisco

Reserve Bank, even though Bufbank's account with the New York Reserve Bank has not been debited. In other words, the Federal Reserve System, which paid reserves to Seabank, has not yet been paid by Bufbank. Reserves "float" temporarily in the system because one of the technical factors affecting reserves changes. If the Fed does not want reserves in the banking system to change, it must neutralize the increase by an offsetting open market operation, as Chapter 14 explains.

More Details   Thousands of checks move through the payments system each day. In practice, each reserve bank transfers only the net funds for checks that move between reserve districts each day. Suppose, for example, that on the same day that George deposits in Seabank the check of Ann from Buffalo, Joyce deposits in her bank in Rochester a check for $40 received from Peter and drawn on another Seattle bank. The San Francisco Fed would then debit this Seattle bank for $40. Rochester and Buffalo are both in the New York District, in fact, in the same branch of that district. Therefore, instead of crediting the New York Reserve Bank with $40 for Peter's check and separately debiting the New York Reserve Bank for $100 for Ann's check, the San Francisco Reserve Bank credits or debits the New York Fed for only the net outcome. In this example, the San Francisco Reserve Bank debits the New York Reserve Bank $60, or $100 − $40. Thus, "clearing" means netting the credits and debits.

Of course, clearing is done not only between reserve banks but also within districts, even within cities or banks. The latter movement can be illustrated as follows: Suppose that George deposits in his bank, Seabank, a check from Andrew, also drawn on Seabank. In this case, Seabank clears these transactions by itself. It credits George's account and debits Andrew's account by the same amount. The San Francisco Fed or other reserve banks do not have to intervene. On the other hand, if the check that George deposited in Seabank were drawn on a different Seattle bank, say, Mt. Rainier Bank, the San Francisco Fed would be involved. At the end of the day, Mt. Rainier Bank would have to give Seabank a check drawn on Mt. Rainier's account with the San Francisco Fed. At the same time, the Reserve Bank of San Francisco would credit Seabank and debit Mt. Rainier an equal amount. Of course, a multitude of these combinations are involved in the U.S. payments system.

Wire Transfer of Funds   In our description of check collecting we noted that the checks were transferred by airplane. Of course, private citizens or corporations sometimes need immediate transfers of funds. Using Fedwire, the Fed's electronic transfer system, Ann can send George $100 without the round-trip journey for her check.

Ann first asks her bank to debit her account by $100, plus an appropriate fee. She signs a check for this amount, drawn on Bufbank, which, in turn, wires $100 to its banker, the Federal Reserve Bank of New York. The New York Fed charges Bufbank's reserve account and wires $100 to the Federal Reserve Bank of San Francisco, which, in turn, wires $100 to Seabank (and credits Seabank's reserve account). Finally, Seabank credits George's account, and the transfer is accomplished. Of course, the Federal Reserve banks charge for this service. Also, the Board's Interdistrict Settlement Fund gets involved as the bookkeeper for the reserve banks, debiting the New York Fed and crediting the San Francisco Fed.

Bookkeeping Services

It is clear from our description of the check-processing services provided to banks that Federal Reserve banks also provide substantial bookkeeping services to these institutions. The bookkeeping is an outgrowth of the reserve account that each depository institution must have with the reserve bank of its district. In this account the reserve bank records, as credits, all transfers of reserves to the financial institution from other financial institutions, as well as reserves that the financial institution borrows from its Federal Reserve bank. Of course, these items enter as liabilities of the reserve bank on the reserve bank's own balance sheet. After all, reserves, whether borrowed from the Fed or created by the Fed because of a purchase of securities, are IOUs, or liabilities, of the Federal Reserve. Similarly, a reduction in the asset reserves of a financial institution is also a reduction in the liability of the Federal Reserve.

Discount Window Loans

In its role as a banker's bank, each Reserve Bank provides not only check-clearing and bookkeeping services but also credit (loans) to depository institutions in its district. To ensure the smooth functioning of depository institutions and ultimately of the economy, the Fed is the *lender of last resort* to banks. At one level, the term **lender of last resort** means that any bank is supposed to explore alternative sources of funding before approaching the discount window. At a more fundamental level, however, the term means that the Fed is the ultimate line of defense against the danger of financial panics and collapse of the monetary system. On such occasions, the Fed uses open market operations in addition to discount window loans to prevent a financial collapse, as it did after the stock market crash in October 1987.

After the creation of the Federal Reserve in 1913, lending to banks via the discount window was the primary method both for helping member banks in need and for conducting monetary policy. FedWatch 12.1 explains how these loans were made in the early years after the Federal Reserve was created.

With the passage of time, access to discount window borrowing has remained a primary service of the Federal Reserve to financial institutions. Now, however, these operations are only a secondary instrument of monetary policy; since the late 1930s they have been displaced by open market operations as the primary instrument of monetary policy.

As noted earlier, until the enactment of DID&MCA of 1980, only member banks had regular access to discount window borrowing. Title I of that act, however, opened the discount window to any financial institution that accepts reservable deposits, whether the institution is a member commercial bank or a nonmember bank, a bank or a thrift, a domestic institution, or a U.S. branch or an agency of a foreign bank.

General guidelines for access to the discount window are set forth in **Regulation A** of the Board of Governors of the Federal Reserve System.[1] Implementation of Regulation A, that is, administration of the discount window, is left to lending officers of the reserve banks, while the Board of Governors is a supervisor and coordinator. According to Regulation A, borrowing at the discount window of a reserve bank is a *privilege, not a right,* of a financial institution. This, of course, gives a particular district reserve bank and

---

[1] One should note the importance that the Fed assigned to discount window borrowing. Its first regulation dealt with the administrative details of discount window borrowing.

Fed*Watch* 12.1
Discounting, Rediscounting, and Discount Window Loans

The interest rate Federal Reserve banks charge on loans to banks in their district is called the *discount rate*. The facility, or division, through which these loans are provided is called the *discount window*, and the loans are called *discount window loans*. The least mysterious of these terms is the *window*, referring to the actual window where at one time Fed tellers made loans to banks. But why the term *discount*? What is discounted? Today, nothing is discounted; discount loans are merely loans of reserve funds to banks in need of reserves.

The Federal Reserve Act of 1913, which created the Federal Reserve System, provided for the Fed to make loans to banks. Actually, the act provided for "rediscounting commercial paper." All of these terms have their origins in the early history of central bank practices, especially in Europe and Japan, on which the Fed's practices were patterned.

To understand discounting and rediscounting, let us imagine ourselves back at the early years of the Fed's life. (This also permits us to use the present rather than the past tense.) Imagine a retailer in Raincity, Washington, who places an order with a manufacturer in New York for 100 umbrellas to be delivered in three months, in time for the coming rainy season. He signs and gives to the manufacturer an IOU, or "bill of exchange," of $1,000, which promises payment of that amount at the time of delivery. The New York manufacturer, however, wants to be paid at once. He takes the bill to his bank, NYBank, which "discounts" the paper. That is, NYBank pays the manufacturer the present value of the three-month $1,000 bill, which, of course, is less than $1,000; hence, the term *discounting*. The two parties agree that in calculating the present value NYBank uses the current three-month interest rate. The bank now has in its portfolio the bill signed by the Raincity retailer. In effect, NYBank has made a three-month loan to the retailer at the market interest rate.

Next, suppose that on the same day NYBank realizes that it needs more liquidity and decides to sell this IOU by endorsing it to another bank, Streetbank. The buying bank discounts it, that is, pays the present value of the $1,000 face value. Of course, if Streetbank uses the same interest rate in the calculation, the selling price would be exactly what NYBank paid the manufacturer. NYBank can also sell the paper at the discount window of its banker, the New York Fed. In this case, the New York Fed "rediscounts" the paper. If the discount window officer uses today's three-month market interest rate to calculate the paper's present value, NYBank will be paid the same price that it would have received from Streetbank. The Fed would merely provide NYBank liquidity. This service would be especially valuable to banks in areas with limited access to financial markets.

If the discount window officer calculates the present value using a discount rate lower than the market interest rate, the price that NYBank receives will be higher. In this case, the Fed's service to the bank is more than merely providing liquidity. It is a source of profit for the bank. The difference between the price the bank paid to acquire the IOU and the price it receives at the discount window is a result of the difference between the interest rate on the paper and the discount rate the Fed used. In effect, NYBank borrows from the Fed at a lower rate (the discount rate) than the rate it charges the retailer.

Central banks, including the Fed, learned early on that by changing the discount rate, they could affect the profitability of borrowing from the Fed and thus affect the amount of credit in the economy. Until the 1930s, discount rate policy was the principal, if not the only, instrument of monetary policy.

In modern times, the Fed does not make loans to banks by rediscounting paper in their possession. The Fed simply makes outright loans, called *advances*. Perhaps to underscore the history of discounting or to keep up appearances, the Fed normally requires borrowing banks to post supporting collateral paper, even though "borrowers in good financial condition who seek short-term adjustment credit may be permitted to hold their own collateral appropriately earmarked."

FIGURE 12–2
Discount Window
Borrowing by Type:
*Not Seasonally
Adjusted*

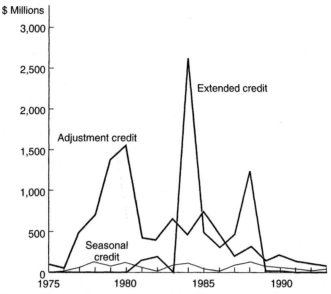

Source: *Economic Report of the President, 1994,* Table B-70.

its discount window officer considerable discretion, although the Board, in its role as coordinator, strives to minimize differences in implementation across reserve banks.

Borrowing from the discount window is divided into three categories: adjustment credit, seasonal credit, and extended credit. Adjustment credit is for a short period of time, often overnight, and historically accounts for most discount window borrowing. Seasonal credit and extended credit are for longer periods of time. Figure 12–2 shows discount window borrowing, by type, since 1975.

Adjustment Credit   Adjustment credit is designed to help depository institutions satisfy unexpected, temporary needs for (reserve) funds to satisfy reserve requirements. The need may arise either from an unexpected drain in the sources of funds, or from an unexpected increase in the demand for loans from depository institutions by the public. (Fed credit for this second reason is extended only in "some circumstances.") A drain in reserves can happen with an unexpected withdrawal of checkable deposits. To illustrate, suppose that the public withdraws $1 million more than the bank expected. The bank loses to other banks $1 million of reserves. With a 10 percent reserve requirement ratio, the bank kept $100,000 in reserves that are not now required. Subtracting this amount from the $1 million, the bank's net deficiency of reserves is $900,000. The bank may cover this deficiency by liquidating assets and by borrowing in the market for federal funds. If the bank cannot reasonably get the entire $900,000 from these sources, it may approach the Fed's discount window. The Fed considers an unexpected withdrawal of deposits an *appropriate reason* for granting adjustment credit. Such a loan by the Federal

Reserve is a true service to a depository institution, one that also increases the supply of total reserves and the money supply. Providing adjustment credit for the second appropriate reason, an unexpected increase in loan demand, also increases total reserves and the money supply.

On the list of *inappropriate reasons* for adjustment credit, the Fed includes financing "speculative loans and investment, substituting Federal Reserve credit for the borrowing institution's capital, financing lending in the federal funds market, acquiring securities or other money market paper at a profit, refinancing existing indebtedness to private lenders at a lower rate, or avoiding relatively expensive money market funding."[2] The lists of appropriate and inappropriate reasons for adjustment credit leaves much room for discretionary, and subjective, decisions. The Fed's usual practice of setting the discount rate below short-term market rates of interest heightens the need for discretion because it makes borrowing at the discount window profitable to banks.[3] Therefore, it is advantageous for financial institutions to borrow frequently large amounts of reserve funds from their "friendly" discount window officer (unless, of course, the discount window officer is not that friendly).

Herein lies the reason for quantitive controls, or "rationing," of Fed loans to banks. Rationing is administered by the discount window officers of the reserve banks according to preset criteria. Using these criteria, the officers decide whether a financial institution's request for adjustment credit is appropriate or inappropriate, that is, whether the financial institution is abusing its privilege. The criteria include "the institution's indebtedness in relation to its total deposits, the frequency and duration of its past borrowing, any special circumstances affecting its current position, and efforts it has made to obtain funds from other reasonably available sources."[4] Occasionally, for the health of financial institutions or of the entire economy, the Federal Reserve may want to tighten or loosen these quantitative controls; that is, at the existing discount rate, the Fed can tighten or loosen the administration of the discount window.

Of course, administrative control of the discount window is not the only means the Fed uses to allocate discount window loans. It also rations indirectly through price; that is, it manipulates the basic discount rate, the interest rate it charges on adjustment borrowings. Discount window loans rise with an increase in the spread between market interest rates and the discount rate. Therefore, other things equal, discount window loans rise with a fall in the discount rate because the spread increases; and other things equal, discount window loans fall with an increase in the discount rate because the spread decreases.

Changes in the discount rate are proposed by reserve banks and are subject to approval by the Board of Governors. As discussed earlier, the Board pursues a policy of a uniform discount rate across districts. Hence, differences in adjustment borrowings based on regional considerations, if they exist at all, must be reflected in the administration of the

[2] Board of Govenors of the Federal Reserve System, *The Federal Reserve System: Purposes and Functions* (Washington, D.C., 1984), 60.

[3] Figure 9–6 in Chapter 9 compares the discount rate with short-term market rates of interest in the 1990s.

[4] Board of Governors of the Federal Reserve System, *The Federal Reserve System: Purposes and Functions* (Washington, D.C., 1984), p. 60.

discount window, rather than in the discount rate. Regional exigencies are addressed more directly in the other two categories of discount window loans, namely, seasonal credit and extended credit.

Seasonal Credit   Credit for seasonal purposes assists financial institutions that face (recurring) seasonal changes either in their deposits or their loans. Usually, these are small financial institutions with limited access to major money markets. The seasonal loans are usually for several months, until the next phase of the seasonal cycle. Financial institutions in farm areas are the typical users of this form of assistance from their banker, the Federal Reserve bank of their district.

Extended Credit   Extended credit is usually offered to financial institutions that face bankruptcy. In this case the Fed is truly the lender of last resort. The Fed provides liquidity either to restore, eventually and in a timely manner, the health of the financial institution or to temporarily sustain it until it merges with a healthier financial institution that is acceptable to the Fed. The 1980s are replete with instances of this type of assistance given to commercial banks. Figure 12–2, for example, shows a sharp rise in extended credit in 1984. This credit was part of a multimillion-dollar assistance package put together by the Fed, the FDIC, and a group of commercial banks to prevent the collapse of Continental Illinois, the nation's seventh largest bank at the time.[5] Decisions to attempt to restore these institutions to health or to facilitate their demise through a merger are made by the Board of Govenors. Implementation, however, especially the provision of extended credit, is the responsibility of the reserve bank in the district where the financial institution is located.

Extended credit is for prolonged periods of time, so the Federal Reserve treats it differently than other forms of credit to banks. Extended credit is reported separately in the statistical releases because in its effects on the economy, it is indistinguishable from nonborrowed reserves. In fact, the Federal Reserve compensates for this similarity by subtracting an equal amount from the volume of reserves the Fed had originally decided to create through open market operations. Finally, the interest rate charged by the Fed on these loans may be higher than the basic discount rate.

Distribution of Coin and Currency   Another important service Federal Reserve banks extend to banks and, ultimately, to the public is the distribution of coin and currency. The U.S. Treasury issues coin, which, of course, is its liability. On the other hand, most paper currency, which consists of Federal Reserve notes, is a liability of the Federal Reserve. Only a small amount of paper currency is a liability of the Treasury. The reserve banks put all currency into circulation through the depository institutions, in the manner described in Chapter 8 for Federal Reserve notes. Note that both coin and currency are produced by the U.S. Treasury, the former by the Bureau of the Mint and the latter by the Bureau of Engraving and Printing. Putting coin and currency into circulation entails wrapping and transporting them to financial institutions,

---

[5] At the time, Continental Illinois had more than 15 percent of its assets in energy loans. When oil prices collapsed in the early 1980s, the bank suffered large losses. In response, there was a massive outflow of funds from the bank's deposits.

which is a service to these institutions. The institutions then pay the Federal Reserve a fee for this service, according to current provisions of DID&MCA of 1980.

BANKER TO THE U.S. GOVERNMENT

In addition to acting as banker to banks, the reserve banks fulfill a second major function: banker to the federal government. Like business firms, or even households, the U.S. government requires certain banking services. Receipts come in and payments continually go out, mostly in checks, and the two are rarely synchronized perfectly. At times, receipts exceed payments, and the surplus must be invested. More often, payments must be made before receipts come in, or payments exceed expected receipts, and the shortages must be financed for short or long periods. The Federal Reserve assists either directly or indirectly with these and similar needs of the U.S. government and with some needs of federal agencies.

The U.S. Treasury's Checking Account

As banker to the federal government, the 12 Federal Reserve banks and their branches handle the Treasury's "checking account," that is, they handle the Treasury's tax receipts and expenditures. The most straightforward way to handle this account would be for the U.S. Treasury to deposit in the Federal Reserve banks all tax checks from the public and to have the Treasury pay all the expenditures of the U.S. government with Federal Reserve checks, that is, checks drawn against the U.S. Treasury's account with the Federal Reserve banks.

Actually, only the second part of this proposition is what really happens: All payments by the U.S. government are made with Federal Reserve checks (paper or electronic). The funds for these checks, however, are in commercial banks and other depository institutions, where they stay until needed to support the checks drawn against the Federal Reserve account. At that time the funds are transferred from these depository institutions to the reserve bank against which the check is drawn. In other words, all government funds are deposited with private institutions, which benefit from this arrangement, and not with the federal government's federal bank.

Some might conclude that this beneficial arrangement for banks is the result of lobbying by the powerful banking industry. Actually, there is no sinister motive; this symbiotic relationship between the public and private sectors actually improves the conduct of monetary policy because it gives the Fed better control over nonborrowed reserves. As a matter of fact, until recently, tax receipts were deposited with reserve banks, and the Treasury's expenditures were made by drawing checks on those accounts at the reserve banks. This procedure, however, caused problems for the Fed. Treasury deposits with the Fed are one of the "other liabilities" in the Fed's balance sheet and, hence, are a technical factor affecting reserves. Like currency, these deposits are a competing use of reserves, or a factor absorbing reserve funds. As a result, increases in Treasury deposits drain reserves from the banking system, reserves that could otherwise be used to support deposits.

Suppose, for example, that on April 15, George pays the IRS (that is, the U.S. Treasury) his "Tax Due the IRS," with a check of $1,000, drawn on Seabank. If the IRS deposits this check with the San Francisco Federal Reserve Bank, the reserve account of

Seabank will be debited by $1,000 of reserves. These changes are shown in T-accounts as follows:

George				Seabank		
Deposits	−1,000	Net Worth	−1,000	Reserves with Fed −1,000		Deposits	−1,000

Fed	
	Gov't (IRS) Deposits +1,000
	Reserves of Seabank −1,000

The analysis of the multiplier relationship for the money supply in Chapter 8 shows that such a reduction of reserves in the banking system causes a multiple contraction in the money supply. To offset this reduction in reserves and in the money supply, the Fed must engage in "defensive" open market operations. Namely, it must buy government securities equal to $1,000, thereby creating $1,000 of reserves to replenish the ones Seabank "lost" on George's check. If, on the other hand, the IRS deposits George's check with another commercial bank—the procedure currently followed—there is no net reduction of reserves. This other commercial bank gains whatever reserves Seabank loses, and, hence, the Fed does not need to carry out defensive open market operations. For this reason the Treasury began depositing IRS revenues into private financial institutions, not for sinister reasons but to tighten the Fed's control over the reserves available to the banking system.

Brokerage Services

In addition to handling the government's checking account, the Fed, through the reserve banks, helps the U.S. government borrow funds. The simplest analogy to the services that banks provide to private clients would be if the Fed loaned funds directly to the U.S. government, that is, contributed directly in financing the budget deficit. However, the Fed directly provides only "brokerage" services in the process of financing the budget deficit. That is, the Fed brings together the borrower—the U.S. government—and the lenders, including households, nonfinancial firms, and financial firms. In this process, the Federal Reserve banks provide information on new issues of marketable Treasury securities, accept tenders from customers, collect payments, credit the Treasury's account for the proceeds, maintain records of buyers on their computers, and handle the subsequent payment of interest and principal on behalf of the Treasury.

As Chapter 11 explains, however, the Fed itself does not lend directly to the federal government; that is, the Fed does not buy new issues of debt securities from the U.S. Treasury. In the end, however, the Fed does finance part of the deficit by buying existing securities in the open market from security dealers. Federal Reserve banks play a role in this decision through their participation in the FOMC.

Management of Foreign Exchange Reserves

So far we have focused on the banking services the Fed provides to the U.S. Treasury in conjunction with the federal budget and in support of the Treasury's role as manager of domestic fiscal policy. However, the Treasury is also involved with issues of international finance because it is responsible for the overall management of U.S. international reserves. In that capacity, the Treasury occasionally intervenes in the foreign exchange market to counter disorderly conditions there.

What is the scope of such foreign exchange interventions? During periods when the value of the dollar is falling, the Fed, in order to support the dollar, may purchase dollars, that is, sell foreign currency. The Fed thereby increases the demand for dollars and, hence, the dollar's international value. Conversely, during periods of upward pressure on the international value of the dollar, the Fed may sell dollars, that is, buy foreign currencies.

Because the intervention is usually carried out in the New York foreign exchange market, only the Federal Reserve Bank of New York is directly involved. The manager for foreign operations at the New York Federal Reserve Bank acts as the agent for the U.S. Treasury and the FOMC. The FOMC is involved because the interests of the FOMC are at stake. Intervention in the foreign exchange market involves an increase or decrease of the "other assets" entry in the Fed's balance sheet, and hence, a decrease or an increase of reserves; such a change may interfere with the reserve targets already set by the FOMC. In such circumstances, the need may arise for offsetting, or "sterilizing," open market operations, that is, buying or selling securities to thwart the potential change in reserves; the FOMC is responsible for those open market operations.

BANKER TO FOREIGN ORGANIZATIONS

Our discussion of the role of the Federal Reserve as the agent for the U.S. Treasury in foreign exchange operations leads us to the third major function of the reserve banks, which arises from the considerable interaction that occurs among the Fed, foreign central banks, and several international organizations. Because of the size of the U.S. economy and the function of the dollar as an internationally accepted currency, and because most activity in international financial markets is centered in New York, the Federal Reserve Bank of New York acts as the banker for other central banks and other international organizations. These central banks and international organizations have "checking" and other accounts with the Reserve Bank of New York to conduct their own international activities.

The most important services rendered regularly by the Reserve Bank of New York to official foreign accounts are to pay and receive funds in dollars. In addition, foreign central banks conduct their foreign exchange interventions in New York by using their account with the New York Fed. The New York Fed, using these accounts, buys and sells foreign exchange on behalf of these central banks. Besides conducting these and other functions, foreign central banks buy and sell securities and gold, for which the New York Fed provides custodial services.

EXAMINER AND SUPERVISOR OF MEMBER BANKS

One of the purposes of the Federal Reserve System, as stated in the Banking Act of 1913, was to provide an "elastic currency," aimed at sustaining the good health of the economy. Of course, that goal presupposes the good health of the banking industry itself, and brings us to the fourth major function of reserve banks: "to establish a more effective supervision of banking," according to the Banking Act of 1913. Inadequate supervision of banks was considered one of the reasons for the many bank failures at the time the act was established. Additionally, financial institutions are depositories of the public's wealth, and the protection of that wealth was an underlying purpose of the Banking Act.

The term *bank supervision* is usually connected with the term *bank regulation*, as in the phrase "supervisory and regulatory functions of the Federal Reserve." The Federal Reserve shares the functions of supervision and regulation of depository institutions with the Office of the Comptroller of the Currrency, the FDIC, the Office of Thrift Supervision, and the National Credit Union Administration. Within the Federal Reserve System itself, the regulatory and supervisory functions are divided between the Board and the reserve banks.

Bank regulation, the domain of the Board, involves drafting and issuing a set of rules and regulations, within the strictures of existing laws, to which banks must adhere in the interests of a safe and sound banking system. **Bank supervision**, on the other hand, involves the actual oversight and examination of individual banks to ensure that each bank is safe and sound. Although the Fed has oversight over all member banks, bank examiners from the reserve banks actually examine only the state-chartered banks in their district. The Office of the Comptroller of the Currency examines nationally chartered banks and files reports on these banks with the Fed. The Fed, however, examines the activities of all bank holding companies, the parent companies of banks.

The involvement of the Federal Reserve as an examiner and supervisor of member banks would diminish under a plan proposed by the Clinton administration in late 1993 to streamline bank regulation by consolidating under one banking commission the regulatory function of existing agencies. The Bush administration tried unsuccessfully to streamline regulatory agencies to alleviate the burden to banks caused by multiple and overlapping regulators. Chapter 17 examines these plans. Both plans encountered objections from the Fed, which argues that because of its role of lender of last resort, it needs firsthand information that comes only from direct involvement in examining banks.

Bank examiners check the overall solvency of the bank, the soundness of its assets and its internal operations, the adequacy of its capital and its liquidity, its exposure to interest rate risk, and its compliance with existing laws and regulations. When Federal Reserve examiners find that a bank is deficient, the Board usually administers corrective action, which is tailored to the severity of the bank's problems. In critical cases, the Board can approve an acquisition of a member bank by a bank holding company or a state member bank; occasionally, the reserve bank may help tide the troubled bank over with a discount window loan until the acquisition is arranged. In such cases, the Fed truly is the lender of last resort.

PARTICIPANT IN THE DESIGN OF U.S. MONETARY POLICY

The final major role of Federal Reserve banks is to act as partners in the design of national monetary policy. Of the three instruments of monetary policy, the reserve requirement ratios are totally outside a reserve bank's influence, so reserve banks play no role in setting them. However, as we have seen repeatedly, reserve banks do play a role in setting the discount rate, which is uniform across reserve districts, although their role is secondary to that of the Board. Their primary role is in the conduct of open

FedWatch 12.2
Tug of War between the Board and Federal Reserve Banks

In the early years of the Fed's existence, reserve bank presidents, then called governors, engaged in a power struggle with the Board for dominance of the Federal Reserve System.* At the time, the Board resented the power of the Federal Reserve Bank of New York. That power emanated from two factors: First, New York was the center of financial activity. The Board, located in Washington, D.C., had no easy access to financial markets and had to rely on the New York Reserve Bank. Even the New York Fed's research department was stronger than that of the Board. The second reason for the New York Fed's power was that its governor, Benjamin Strong, was a capable economist and a forceful personality who did not hesitate to challenge the Board at every chance.

Within a year of the selection of the "governors" of the 12 reserve banks, Strong helped organize them into a "Governors Conference," which began to make policy statements and even to criticize Board decisions. The Board retaliated in January 1916 by not approving travel expenses of reserve bank governors and expenses for the salary of the secretary of the conference. The Board also ordered the conference to meet in Washington, D.C., at a time of the Board's choosing.

In May 1922, the Conference of Governors met, with the approval of the Board. At the time, manipulating the discount rate was the primary tool of monetary policy; open market operations were not yet considered a policy tool, and individual reserve banks were allowed to purchase securities at their own discretion. The original reason for these purchases was to support the U.S. effort in World War I. Another reason was that individual reserve banks could reap revenues from such purchases. At the May meeting, the Governors Conference set up a committee to coordinate the open market purchases of securities by individual reserve banks. This action infuriated the Board, which considered coordination of the activities of the reserve banks to be its turf.

In March 1923, while Strong was recuperating from tuberculosis in Colorado, the Board disbanded the conference's committee on open market operations and created its own committee, called the Open Market Investment Committee. The Board also constrained the ability of individual reserve banks to engage in open market operations. The Banking Act of 1935 sealed the Board's dominance by officially prohibiting individual reserve banks from engaging in open market operations and giving the authority for conducting those operations to the newly established FOMC, on which the Board has majority representation.

The Governors Conference survives today in two forms: the "Conference of Presidents" and the "Conference of Chairmen" of Federal Reserve banks. Both meet periodically in Washington to discuss issues concerning the reserve banks and to consult with and advise the Board of Governors.

---

* For a summary of the extensive literature on the early history of the Federal Reserve System, see Sayre Ellen Dykes and Michael A. Whitehouse, "The Establishment and Evolution of the Federal Reserve Board: 1913–23," *Federal Reserve Bulletin* 75, no. 4 (April 1989): 227–43.

---

market operations through their participation in the FOMC. It is interesting to note that open market operations originated with reserve banks, which bought U.S. Treasury securities on their own account and for their own profit. FedWatch 12.2 recounts the struggle for power between the Board and the district banks that led to the creation of the FOMC.

As Chapter 11 describes, today 5 of the 12 members of the FOMC come from reserve banks, including the vice-chair of the FOMC, who is the president of the Federal Reserve Bank of New York. In the deliberations of the FOMC, a reserve bank, through its president, expresses the wishes of its district about monetary policy. In formulating a position, the president of a reserve bank relies on reports about national and regional economic conditions prepared by staff economists at the bank.

The Federal Reserve Bank of New York plays a special role in implementing the policy decisions of the FOMC. The trading desk, which carries out open market operations, is part of the New York Fed. We examine the workings of the trading desk in Chapter 14.

ECONOMIC RESEARCHER

Although not a major "official" function, the reserve banks' role in economic research is critical. Each reserve bank collects economic and financial data that the bank's staff of economists uses in its research on the regional economy. Each bank publishes a periodic review with articles on the regional economy as well as the national and international economy. Reserve banks also publish a wealth of other material, including weekly letters and special reports that are used from the board room to the classroom.

Some reserve banks are known for distinct points of view or methodologies. For example, the Federal Reserve Bank of St. Louis pays special attention to the monetary base. It regularly publishes data on the monetary base and the monetary base multiplier. Over the years, its researchers have often recommended that the Fed set targets for the monetary base. Chapter 13 points out that while the Fed has set targets for nonborrowed reserves and borrowed reserves, which are components of the base, it never has targeted the monetary base.

Most important, each reserve bank contributes to the Beige Book, a compilation of reports prepared for each FOMC meeting on economic conditions in the 12 reserve districts. The Beige Book is one of three briefing books prepared for members of the FOMC to study before each FOMC meeting. As we have seen, the staff of the Federal Reserve Board prepares the other two books, also referred to by the color of their covers. The Beige Book, however, is the only one of the three books that is released to the public at the time of each FOMC meeting. The other two books are not generally released to the public at all, although researchers may request old copies from the Board.

THE CONSOLIDATED BALANCE SHEET OF ALL RESERVE BANKS

Table 12–1 introduces the consolidated balance sheet of all 12 Federal Reserve banks, which summarizes the functions of these banks. Several items on the balance sheet have a direct bearing on the role of reserve banks.

- Items 1 and 2 originate with the U.S. Treasury's role as the manager of U.S. international reserves and represent the extent to which these reserves have been "monetized," that is, the quantity of domestic reserves that have been created in their place.
- Items 3 and 8 are obviously references to the distribution of coin and currency to the banks (and the public). Item 3, coin, is that quantity of coins sold to the Fed by the Treasury for distribution to depository institutions in exchange for a credit to the U.S. Treasury's account, item 9*b*. On the other hand, item 8 is the Federal Reserve notes outside of the Fed, which includes vault cash held by depository institutions and by the Treasury and currently held by the public.

TABLE 12–1
Consolidated Statement of Condition (Balance Sheet) of All Federal Reserve Banks: *Wednesday, December 29, 1993 (millions)*

Assets	
1. Gold Certificate Account	11,053
2. Special Drawing Rights Certificate Account	8,018
3. Coin	358
4. Loans	47
5. Securities	
a. Bought outright	337,541
b. Held under repurchase agreement	12,303
6. Cash Items in Process of Collection (CIPC)	5,607
7. Other Assets	33,652
Total Assets	408,579
Liabilities	
8. Federal Reserve Notes	345,878
9. Deposits	
a. Depository institutions	42,097
b. U.S. Treasury, general account	5,407
c. Foreign Official accounts	286
d. Other	245
10. Deferred Availability Cash Items	5,048
11. Other Liabilities and Accrued Dividends	2,533
Capital Accounts	
12. Capital Paid In	3,377
13. Surplus	3,054
14. Other Capital Accounts	652
Total Liabilities and Capital Accounts	408,577*

*The total assets differ slightly from the total liabilities and capital accounts because of rounding.
Source: *Federal Reserve Bulletin,* April 1994, Table 1.18, A11.

- Item 4 represents discount window loans to depository institutions and has its counterpart in part of item 9*a.* That is, when a reserve bank makes a discount window loan to a depository institution, the asset loans (item 4) of the reserve bank increases; so does its liability, the reserve balances of depository institutions (item 9*a*).
- Item 5, securities, and item 9*a*, deposits of depository institutions, are manifestations of the use of the primary instrument of monetary policy. When the Federal Reserve buys securities in the open market, its asset securities (item 5) increases; so does item 9*a*, the reserve balances of depository institutions.
- Items 6 and 10, in conjunction with item 9*a*, are involved in the check-collecting and -clearing process and in the bookkeeping services provided to depository institutions. The wire transfer of funds and securities is also included in 9*a*.
- We have already mentioned item 9*b* in U.S. Treasury functions, namely, the management of international reserves and the production of coin. However, most of the responsibility for that item lies with the Federal Reserve banks as the banker, the

"fiscal agent," of the U.S. Treasury. Funds are transferred into this account just before they are paid to those who provide goods and services to the U.S. government.

Our aim here has been to summarize the functions of the reserve banks by associating those functions with the entries in the consolidated balance sheet of the district banks. Chapter 14 scrutinizes the Fed's balance sheet more closely. Our aim in that chapter will be to paint a complete picture of the factors supplying reserves to the banking system and the factors absorbing reserves from the system. There we augment the Fed's balance sheet with the monetary accounts of the Treasury.

SUMMARY

- In its role as a banker's bank, each Federal Reserve bank provides services to commercial banks and to other depository institutions. Important services are collecting and clearing checks and associated bookkeeping, transferring funds by wire, and distributing coin and currency. These services contribute to the smooth functioning of the U.S. payments system.

- Another key service is lending to depository institutions. As a lender of last resort, each reserve bank provides loans via its discount window. There are three types of discount window loans: adjustment borrowing (credit), seasonal credit, and extended credit. Adjustment credit is for short-run needs, often for a day or two. Seasonal credit is provided for longer periods to smaller financial institutions, usually in rural areas, that demonstrate a need arising from a recurrirng pattern of movements in their deposits and loans. Extended credit is for banks in trouble that need funds for longer periods.

- Because the discount rate is usually set below short-term market rates of interest, reserve banks ration discount window loans by quantity as well as by price.

- As a "fiscal agent," that is, as a banker to the U.S. government, the reserve banks handle the U.S. government's checking account, from which all federal payments are made. The reserve bank also act as a broker for the U.S. government when the Treasury issues securities.

- The Federal Reserve Bank of New York manages the U.S. government's international reserves (gold and foreign currencies), as well as those of foreign governments. The reserve banks also provide similar services to international organizations, such as the International Monetary Fund (IMF) and the World Bank.

- Federal Reserve banks participate in the design of U.S. monetary policy. They propose changes in the discount rate, which are approved by the Board and are uniform across districts. More important, reserve banks contribute 5 of the 12 members of the FOMC, including its permanent vice-chair, the president of the New York Fed. All 12 presidents of the reserve banks participate in the deliberations of the FOMC, even though only five vote on a rotating basis. The Federal Reserve Bank of New York acts as the FOMC's agent in carrying out open market operations.

- In addition to preparing the Beige Book on regional economic conditions for FOMC meetings, reserve banks conduct and publish economic studies that are useful to financial institutions and the general public.

- The consolidated balance sheet of all 12 Federal Reserve banks is an accounting statement of the monetary and financial activities of the reserve banks.

KEY TERMS AND CONCEPTS

check collecting and clearing	Regulation A	bank supervision
lender of last resort	bank regulation	

QUESTIONS AND PROBLEMS

1. Suppose that Hillary from Hawaii writes a check for $2,000, drawn on First Hawaiian Bank and payable to Murray from Massachusetts, who deposits the check in Massachusetts National Bank. Use T-accounts to show the changes in the balance sheets of Hillary, Murray, First Hawaiian Bank, and Massachusetts National Bank as a result of this transaction. By how much do reserves in the banking system change as a result of this transaction?

2. Suppose that the Fed eliminated reserve requirements. Would banks hold any reserves with their Federal Reserve district bank? Why or why not?

3. "In the first decade of the Federal Reserve System's existence all 12 reserve banks conducted and profited from open market operations. Now, only the Federal Reserve Bank of New York is authorized to conduct open market operations and profit from them." True or false? Explain.

4. Which participants of the U.S. financial system can borrow from Federal Reserve banks?

5. "Borrowing from their district bank is a privilege, not a right, for depository institutions." What is meant by this statement?

6. "Changes in the discount rate are the sole province of Federal Reserve banks." True or false? Explain.

7. Federal Reserve banks provide banking services to the U.S. government. Identify these services.

8. The discount rate that reserve banks charge is the same in all districts. How, then, can reserve banks address through the discount window financial needs unique to the banks in their districts?

9. What is the role of all 12 reserve banks in designing U.S. monetary policy?

10. What is the role of the New York Fed in designing U.S. monetary policy? What is its role in implementing monetary policy?

SUGGESTED READINGS

Federal Reserve Bank of New York. *Quarterly Review.*
    Published quarterly by the Research and Statistics Group of the Federal Reserve Bank of New York and available free of charge. Because the Trading Desk is located at the Federal Reserve Bank of New York, many articles on the conduct of monetary policy appear in this review.

Tootell, Geoffrey M. B. "Are District Presidents More Conservative than Board Governors?" *New England Economic Review,* September–October 1991, 3–12.
    The author uses FOMC voting records to test the hypothesis that compared with governors, reserve bank presidents prefer policies that result in lower inflation and higher unemployment.

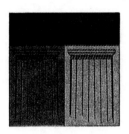

INSTRUMENTS, TARGETS, AND GOALS OF THE FEDERAL RESERVE

CHAPTER PREVIEW

In ancient times whenever an important person such as a king was embarking on a war or a similar risky endeavor, he would send an emissary to Delphi, Greece, for a forecast of the outcome. There, in the Temple of Apollo, through smoke coming from leaves of burning laurel, the Delphic oracle would utter its forecast, always with more than one, and often with conflicting, interpretations.

In modern times, the Fed chair plays the role of an economic oracle. Every February and July, the chair appears before the appropriate committees of the Senate and House of Representatives to announce the Fed's forecasts of inflation and GDP growth and to explain the monetary policy designed to achieve those forecasts. Although no laurel is burned, these utterances, too, are subject to conflicting interpretations.

The ultimate goal of U.S. monetary policy is the welfare of the American people. The rate of inflation, the rate of growth of real GDP, and the unemployment rate are standard macroeconomic measures of economic welfare. In its semiannual report to Congress on monetary policy, the Fed provides numerical projections, or forecasts, for these variables. The Fed prefers, however, to describe its **ultimate goals** in broad qualitative terms rather than in precise numbers. Price stability, full employment, and maximum sustainable economic growth are the persistent goals of monetary policy. Conditions in the nation's international accounts and in foreign exchange markets are also important.

The Fed has no buttons to press to achieve its ultimate goals or forecasts. Instead, it has three **monetary policy instruments** that directly affect the availability or the cost of reserves: open market operations (OMO), the discount rate, and the reserve requirement ratio(s). Because the link between the instruments and the ultimate goals is neither immediate nor direct, the Fed sets targets, called **intermediate targets**, for financial variables that are linked to economic activity and, hence, to the ultimate goals. The Fed hopes that by hitting the intermediate targets, it can achieve its ultimate goals. The intermediate targets, however, are usually not directly influenced by the Fed's instruments. Therefore, as a short-run guide for achieving the intermediate targets, the Fed employs variables, called **operating targets**, that are closely linked to the intermediate targets. Finally, the Fed manipulates the policy instruments to achieve its operating targets.

This chapter uses the three-stage linkage between the instruments and the operating target, the operating target and the intermediate target, and the intermediate target and the ultimate goals as an organizing framework to analyze the conduct of U.S. monetary policy since 1970. For economic and political reasons the Fed has changed operating targets several times since then. And even though some measure of money has served informally or formally as the intermediate target since 1970, the Fed has set the target and then often ignored it. In other words, judgment and discretion have traditionally been an important part of the Fed's policymaking process. In this chapter we shall see that the Fed downgraded the monetary aggregates and upgraded judgment and discretion in the summer of 1993.

FROM INSTRUMENTS TO ULTIMATE GOALS

Before we look at the three individual linkages, let's survey the big picture, which is that the Fed tries to achieve its ultimate goals by manipulating the policy instruments at its disposal. The Humphrey-Hawkins Act requires the Fed to report to Congress in February and July of each year its projections of the rate of inflation, the rate of growth of real GDP, and the unemployment rate for the current year. Like a modern-day version of the Delphic oracle, the chair of the Federal Reserve Board must appear before a designated committee of each of the houses of Congress to issue the Fed's forecasts for these real-sector variables and to state how the Fed will achieve them. The Fed states its ultimate goals for the real sector in broad qualitative terms rather than as precise numerical goals. Thus, the Fed refers to the numbers that the chair provides as *projections,* or *forecasts,* for inflation, real GDP growth, and unemployment, rather than targets or goals for these variables. The annual *Economic Report of the President,* published a few weeks before the testimony of the Fed chair in February, also includes forecasts for these three variables.

To achieve its ultimate goals or forecasts for the real sector, the Fed sets and manipulates three key policy instruments, as illustrated by the following schematic:

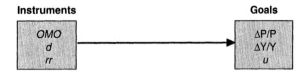

Where:

OMO = Open market operations

d = Discount rate

rr = Reserve requirement ratio

$\Delta P/P$ = Rate of inflation

$\Delta Y/Y$ = Rate of Growth of real GDP

u = Unemployment rate

This schematic illustrates the relationship between the Fed's three policy instruments and the goals it wants to achieve: controlling inflation, spurring sustainable economic growth, and curbing unemployment. The primary instrument of monetary policy is open market operations. The Fed enters the market as often as several times a week as a buyer or seller of government securities. Other things equal, when the Fed buys government securities, it creates reserves, and when it sells government securities, it destroys reserves. These reserves are called *nonborrowed reserves,* which, you recall, are all reserves that have not been borrowed by banks at the discount window. Other things, however, do not always remain equal. Changes in the technical factors affecting reserves, including currency in circulation and the other assets and liabilities in the Fed's balance sheet, also change the quantity of nonborrowed reserves in the banking system.

Hence, open market operations are of two types. Most of the Fed's open market operations are *defensive open market operations* designed to offset the effect of changes in the technical factors. In contrast, open market operations aimed at achieving changes in the quantity of nonborrowed reserves are called *dynamic open market operations.*

Secondary instruments of monetary policy include both the discount rate and the reserve requirement ratios. The Fed changes the discount rate, on average, only a few times per year, if at all. Even though it is authorized to manipulate reserve requirement ratios within predetermined limits, the Fed rarely changes these ratios in conducting monetary policy. It does change them, however, primarily to facilitate reforms in the financial system. Therefore, it is significant that the Fed reduced the reserve requirement ratio twice in the early 1990s. In December 1990, the Board eliminated the 3 percent reserve requirement ratio on nonpersonal time deposits and Eurodollar liabilities. Then in April 1992, it reduced the ratio on transactions deposits from 12 percent to 10 percent. The reserve requirement ratio acts like a tax on banks that equals the interest they forgo by holding non-interest-bearing reserve balances. By reducing these ratios, the Fed reduced the reserve tax on banks in an effort to encourage them to increase lending. At the time banks were under financial strain, in part because of the debt hangover of the 1980s.

In calibrating its instruments to achieve its goals, the Fed recognizes that the link between instruments and goals is neither immediate nor direct. The instruments exert

FIGURE 13–1
The Three-Stage
Transmission
Process of
Monetary Policy

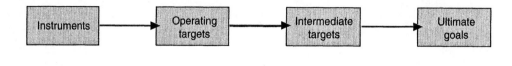

their influence on the ultimate goals through the financial markets. For example, open market purchases of securities reduce the federal funds rate because they provide banks with additional reserves that banks can turn into earning assets by lending them to other banks in the interbank loan market. Then, through a chain of substitution among financial assets, other interest rates on short-term and long-term debt instruments also fall. In turn, the reduction in interest rates affects real-sector variables by increasing the aggregate demand for goods and services.

Because the process takes time, the Fed relies on a variety of **financial indicators**, such as reserves, money, credit, and interest rates, for guidance while conducting monetary policy. These indicators help the Fed judge how loose or tight monetary policy is. The Fed uses some of these indicators themselves as targets, which means it sets numerical objectives for these measures and assigns them a special role in the policymaking process. It distinguishes, however, between intermediate targets and operating targets. Figure 13–1 shows how the instruments influence the ultimate goals: from the instruments to the operating targets; from the operating targets to the intermediate targets; and from the intermediate targets to the ultimate goals.

This schematic captures the purposeful behavior of the Fed and, therefore, fits in the first pillar of our two-pillar framework. It also fits in the second pillar because analysis of the links will show how the Fed interacts with other participants in the marketplace. As we examine each link in the process, we shall consider potential transmission problems.

FROM INTERMEDIATE TARGETS TO ULTIMATE GOALS

Our examination of the three links of the transmission process begins at the end, with the link between the intermediate targets and the ultimate goals. From there we will back up to discuss operating targets and instruments.

There are three important criteria for choosing intermediate targets. First, the Fed must be able to hit the target consistently; that is, the variable must be *controllable*. Second, the link between the intermediate target and the real sector (the ultimate goals) must be *predictable* and *stable*. Third, the variable must be *measurable,* with information available frequently, preferably weekly. In practice, there is no perfect variable to serve as the intermediate target. Moreover, circumstances change so that a target that performs reasonably well in one period may not in another. Since the Full Employment Act of 1946, the Fed has used either the long-term interest rate or the quantity of money as the intermediate target. We shall see that the Fed has had problems with each of them.

The Long-Term Interest Rate as the Intermediate Target

Until the early 1970s, the Fed tried to manipulate the long-term interest rate to influence real-sector variables and, hence, to achieve its ultimate goals. The interest rate affects the real sector through its effect on aggregate demand, especially the investment component of aggregate demand. As Chapter 10 discusses, other things equal, the higher the interest rate, the lower the aggregate demand for goods and services, and the lower the interest rate, the higher the aggregate demand.

Information on the long-term interest rate is available daily, but the Fed cannot easily control this rate. Although it is the *long-term* interest rate that affects aggregate demand, the Fed can influence this rate only indirectly, by influencing the *short-term* interest rate. For example, a reduction in short-term interest rates through open market operations makes long-term securities more attractive to investors, who increase their demand for them. Excess demand in the market for long-term securities pushes their price up and their interest rate down.

A second problem is that it is not simply the long-term interest rate but the *ex ante (expected) real* long-term interest rate that influences aggregate demand. Market participants infer this rate by subtracting an estimate of expected inflation from the nominal, observed interest rate. When firms and households do not anticipate inflation, targeting the observed, nominal interest rate poses no problem for the Fed. In periods of inflation and inflationary expectations, however, nominal interest rates are a poor indicator of the strength or weakness of aggregate demand. In other words, the link between the nominal, observed long-term interest rate and aggregate demand is neither stable nor predictable in inflationary periods such as the 1970s.

To these problems we must add a third, a political problem. Congress is authorized by the Constitution to conduct monetary policy. Congress has delegated to the Fed the authority to conduct monetary policy, but it can also alter or even revoke that authority. If the public perceives that the Fed is responsible for high interest rates, it may pressure the Fed, through Congress, to lower interest rates.

The Quantity of Money as the Intermediate Target

Because of these three problems with using long-term interest rates as a target, in the early 1970s the Fed itself informally switched its target to the quantity of money. For years monetarist economists, led by Milton Friedman, had been urging the Fed to target some measure of the quantity of money. A central tenet of **monetarism** is that inflation is always a monetary phenomenon and that inflation can be controlled by controlling the growth of money. The high and rising rates of inflation in the early 1970s combined with the ascending prominence of monetarism in academic and political circles were the catalysts for the change in policy.

The switch to using the quantity of money as an intermediate target became official when the Full Employment and Balanced Growth Act, also called the Humphrey-Hawkins Act, became law in 1978. This act requires the Federal Reserve to set target ranges for the rate of growth of money and to report these targets to Congress twice yearly, along with its projections of inflation, real GDP growth, and the unemployment rate.

TABLE 13–1
Economic
Projections for
1993 and 1994

1993		Range	Central Tendency
Percentage change, fourth quarter to fourth quarter:	Nominal GDP	4¾ to 6¼	5 to 5¾
	Real GDP	2 to 3½	2¼ to 2¾
	Consumer price index	3 to 3½	3 to 3¼
Average level in the fourth quarter, percent:	Civilian unemployment rate	6½ to 7	6¾

1994		Range	Central Tendency
Percentage change, fourth quarter to fourth quarter:	Nominal GDP	4½ to 6¾	5 to 6½
	Real GDP	2 to 3¼	2½ to 3¼
	Consumer price index	2 to 4¼	3 to 3½
Average level in the fourth quarter, percent:	Civilian unemployment rate	6¼ to 7	6½ to 6¾

Source: Board of Governors of the Federal Reserve System, *Monetary Policy Report to the Congress Pursuant to the Full Employment and Balanced Growth Act of 1978,* July 20, 1993, 3–4.

    A Humphrey-Hawkins report typically includes two tables. One gives the Fed's projections, or forecasts, of inflation, growth of nominal and real GDP, and unemployment.[1] The other gives the Fed's target ranges for M2 and M3 growth. Tables 13–1 and 13–2 are the actual tables from the July 1993 *Monetary Policy Report to Congress.* As these tables show, the July report provides targets and projections not only for the current year but also for the next year. Table 13–2 also shows that in 1993 the Fed lowered its target range for M2 growth at midyear.

    The content of Table 13–2 has changed over the years. The Humphrey-Hawkins Act does not specify which measures of money the Fed must target, nor does it require the Fed to hit its targets for money. Using its discretion, the Fed began by setting target ranges for the growth of all three measures of money: M1, M2, and M3. In 1983, it added a monitoring range for **total domestic nonfinancial debt**, a measure of debt consisting of the borrowing of households, firms, and federal, state and local governments.[2] The Fed, however, stopped setting targets for M1 in February 1987 because of the erratic behavior of this aggregate after the deregulation of deposit rates. It continues, however, to target

---

[1]   In February the table also gives the administration's projections of these variables.

[2]   By establishing a numerical range for debt, the Fed elevated the importance of this financial indicator, but not to the same status as a target. That is why the range is called a *monitoring range* instead of a target range.

TABLE 13–2
Ranges for Growth
of Monetary and
Credit Aggregates:
Percentage Change,
Fourth Quarter to
Fourth Quarter

	1992	1993 (As of February)	1993 (As of July)	1994
M2	2½ to 6½	2 to 6	1 to 5	1 to 5
M3	1 to 5	½ to 4½	0 to 4	0 to 4
Debt	4½ to 8½	4½ to 8½	4 to 8	4 to 8

Source: Board of Governors of the Federal Reserve System, *Monetary Policy Report to the Congress Pursuant to the Full Employment and Balanced Growth Act of 1978*, July 20, 1993, 3–4.

M2 and M3 growth. Of course, the Fed still collects and publishes data on all three measures of money. Data on M1 are available weekly. Although data on many components of M2 and M3 are also available weekly, complete data on these measures are available only monthly.

To understand the relation between Tables 13–1 and 13–2, we need to examine how the quantity of money affects economic activity, concentrating on the relation between money and nominal GDP. The quantity theory of money provides a compact way to view this relation.

The Quantity Theory of Money   According to the quantity theory, the link between the quantity of money, *M,* and aggregate demand for goods and services measured in current dollars is the **velocity of circulation, V.** Velocity is the number of times per period (year) that each dollar turns over to buy final goods and services. For example, suppose that for a given year velocity is equal to six. This means that each dollar is used, on average, six times a year to buy final goods and services. Suppose, too, that the average quantity of money, *M,* is $1,000 billion. Multiplying *M* by *V,* we find that expenditures on final goods and services over the year equal $6,000 billion in current dollars, which is the nominal value of aggregate demand for goods and services. Because the nominal value of aggregate demand determines the level of nominal GDP, denoted by *PY,* the **quantity theory of money** is usually expressed in the following form:

$$MV = PY \tag{13–1}$$

Equation 13–1 relates the *level* of the quantity of money to the *level* of the quantity of nominal GDP. The Fed, however, presents its targets and forecasts in terms of *growth rates,* as Tables 13–1 and 13–2 show. By applying to Equation 13–1 the rule that the percentage change in the product of two variables is the sum of the percentage change in each of the variables, we can express the quantity theory equation in terms of growth rates:

$$\Delta M/M + \Delta V/V = \Delta P/P + \Delta Y/Y \tag{13–2}$$

We call the sum of money growth and velocity growth on the left side of Equation 13–2 **velocity-indexed money growth**. The sum of the rate of inflation and the rate of growth of real GDP on the right side of Equation 13–2 is the rate of growth of nominal GDP.

Therefore, according to Equation 13–2, **velocity-indexed money growth equals the growth of nominal GDP.**

For the quantity of money to be an effective intermediate target, the Fed must be able to control the growth of money. In addition, the rate of change in the velocity of circulation of money, the link with the real sector, must be predictable, or stable. If the Fed hits its targets for money growth and correctly predicts velocity growth, actual growth in nominal GDP will equal forecasted growth.

Chapter 16 examines the factors affecting velocity and its rate of growth. Here we merely point out that velocity is inversely related to money demand, so that the factors that affect money demand also affect velocity. No sooner had *M* been chosen as the intermediate target than the Fed encountered problems because velocity began to behave in unpredictable ways. This anomaly first occurred from 1974 to 1975, when the economy was emerging from a severe recession and velocity was growing at a rate substantially above its historical trend. The Fed responded by adjusting its monetary target downward.

Downgrading the Monetary Aggregates   By the end of the 1970s when targeting the quantity of money was mandated by law, the Fed began having difficulties controlling the intermediate target, *M*, as we shall see later in this chapter. Eventually some of the problems were ironed out. However, velocity, especially the velocity of M1, was not well behaved, mainly because of disinflation, deregulation, and financial innovations in the 1980s. As a result, in the first half of the 1980s, the Fed was continually adjusting or ignoring its M1 target, which led it eventually to abandon an M1 target.

Since 1987, the Fed has continued to set targets for M2 and M3, but it uses its discretion about whether to achieve the targets or not, as permitted by law. Since the mid-1980s domestic policy directives have routinely stated that the growth of the monetary aggregates will be evaluated in light of other factors such as progress toward price stability, movements in the velocities of the monetary aggregates, and developments in the economy, in financial markets, and in foreign exchange markets. We can conclude from these policy statements that the Fed targets the real sector as well as the quantity of money. Research inside and outside the Fed confirms that the Fed has been acting as if it were targeting nominal GDP growth. FedWatch 13.1 illustrates how the Fed's behavior in 1992 can be explained in this way.

The Emergence of Real Interest Rates as an Indicator   In the middle of 1993, the Fed began to rely on an additional variable, ex ante real interest rates, to guide monetary policy. The real interest rate is linked directly to the real sector. Chapter 10 explains this link, pointing out that the higher the ex ante real rate, the lower aggregate demand, and the lower the rate, the higher demand. Of course, the ex ante real interest rate, that is, the nominal rate minus expected inflation, is not observable. It must be estimated by estimating expected inflation and subtracting this from the observed nominal rate.

Chairman Greenspan announced the change in the Fed's procedure when he appeared before Congress in July 1993 to present the Humphrey-Hawkins report.[3] Greenspan

---

[3] Greenspan's statement to Congress is published in the *Federal Reserve Bulletin,* September 1993, 849–55. The "Monetary Report to Congress" is published in the same issue, pp. 827–45.

FedWatch 13.1
The Growth of M2 and the Economy in 1992

In 1992 the Fed set a target range of 2.5 percent to 6.5 percent for M2 growth, and it forecasted that growth in nominal GDP would range from 4 percent to 6 percent. Actual growth of M2 turned out to be a scant 1.8 percent, yet actual growth of nominal GDP, at 5.7 percent, was at the upper end of the Fed's forecasting range. To see how this happened, let's apply the equation that velocity-indexed money growth equals growth in nominal GDP:

$$\Delta M/M + \Delta V/V = \Delta P/P + \Delta Y/Y$$

We start by plugging the Fed's 1992 targets for money growth and its forecasts for growth in nominal GDP into this equation and solving for predicted velocity growth:

Lower end of target range		Predicted growth of velocity		Lower end of forecasting range	
$\Delta M/M$	+	$\Delta V/V$	=	$(\Delta P/P + \Delta Y/Y)$	
2.5%	+	1.5%	=	4%	(1)

The right side of Equation 1 shows that the lower end of the Fed's forecasting range for nominal GDP growth was 4 percent. The left side shows that the lower end of its target range for M2 growth was 2.5 percent. Solving for $\Delta V/V$, we find that at this end of the range predicted velocity growth was 1.5 percent.

Next, we repeat this exercise for the upper ends of the forecasting and target ranges:

Upper end of target range		Predicted growth of velocity		Upper end of forecasting range	
$\Delta M/M$	+	$\Delta V/V$	=	$(\Delta P/P + \Delta Y/Y)$	
6.5%	+	(−0.5%)	=	6%	(2)

Equation 2 shows that at the upper end of the target and forecasting ranges, the predicted growth of velocity was −0.5 percent.

In sum, in setting its targets for M2 growth in February 1992, the Fed predicted that velocity growth would range from a high of 1.5 percent to a low of −0.5 percent.

Actual experience in 1992 is represented by the following equation:

$\Delta M/M$	+	$\Delta V/V$	=	$(\Delta P/P + \Delta Y/Y)$	
1.8%	+	3.9%	=	5.7%	(3)

The right side of Equation 3 shows that actual growth in nominal GDP was 5.7 percent; the left side shows that actual growth in M2 was 1.8 percent. Solving for velocity growth, we find that actual growth of M2 velocity was 3.9 percent in 1992.

How did the Fed do in 1992? Money growth was below target. However, velocity growth, at 3.9 percent, was above the upper end of the Fed's predicted range.* As a result, growth in nominal GDP was at the high end of the forecasting range despite the scant money growth.

One interpretation of these results is that the Fed was targeting the growth of nominal GDP, which equals velocity-indexed money growth. Therefore, over the course of the year, as actual velocity came in higher than predicted velocity, the Fed allowed M2 to grow at rates below the original target range. With this interpretation, monetary policy was successful even though money growth was below the Fed's target range.

Of course, "success" here is defined as achieving the Fed's "target" for growth in nominal GDP. Many of the Fed's critics in Congress and academia, however, argued that this target was too low to achieve sufficient growth in *real GDP* for a satisfactory recovery from the 1990–91 recession. As it turned out, after a weak first half, growth of real GDP picked up in the second half of 1992. For the year, real GDP grew by 3.2 percent, the highest rate since 1988, but low compared with previous recoveries. Growth of real GDP fell to 1.3 percent in the first half of 1993, however, when growth of M2 was barely above zero.

---

* The main reason for the rise in velocity in 1992 is that the public shifted funds out of low-yielding bank CDs into higher-yielding stock and bond mutual funds, which are not in M_2. This shift lowered the demand for M_2 and raised its velocity, as Chapter 16 explains in more detail.

explained that to guide monetary policy, the Fed would rely not just on the monetary aggregates but also on the real interest rate, specifically on the current value of the ex ante real rate of interest in relation to the **equilibrium real interest rate**. The Fed defined the equilibrium real rate as "the real rate level that, if maintained, would keep the economy at its production potential over time."[4] Thus, if the current real rate is above the equilibrium rate, it signals a slowdown; if it is below the equilibrium real rate, it signals inflationary pressures. Although Greenspan was not explicit, he implied that in the former case the Fed would increase the quantity of money and in the latter case it would decrease the quantity of money, even though doing so might move the monetary aggregates outside the announced target ranges.

The Fed recognizes that the imaginary equilibrium real rate is not a fixed number and that it cannot estimate this rate "with a great deal of confidence." Despite this uncertainty, or perhaps because of it, the Fed intends to use the real rate in relation to its equilibrium level as a "longer-term policy guide." Such longer-term policy guides and aims give the Fed as much latitude in conducting monetary policy as it desires. Accordingly, the Fed also announced that "at least for the time being, M2 has been downgraded as a reliable indicator of financial conditions in the economy, and no single variable has yet been identified to take its place." Thus, in July 1993, while resetting its 1993 targets for M2 and M3 and announcing its preliminary monetary targets for 1994, the Fed was also cautioning that it did not expect to stay within the targeted ranges. In Greenspan's words, "The behavior of the aggregates relative to their annual ranges will likely be of limited use in guiding policy over the next eighteen months."

The official demotion of M2 in 1993 was not an abrupt change in policy regimes. Instead it was the culmination of a process, initiated in 1982, away from the monetary aggregates and toward a broad array of indicators of monetary policy. The inclusion of real interest rates in that array gave the Fed not only a new "long-term policy guide" but also an answer to its growing number of critics. These critics argued that monetary policy was too tight, as evidenced by low growth of M2 in 1992 and the first half of 1993. The Fed countered by pointing to low real rates. Figure 13–2 depicts estimated short-term and long-term real interest rates from 1981 to 1993. The graph shows that in mid-1993, when Chairman Greenspan announced the change in the Fed's approach to policy, short-term real interest rates were at their lowest level in more than a decade—near zero. Long-term real interest rates, at slightly more than 2 percent, were near their 1987 low.

FROM OPERATING TARGETS TO INTERMEDIATE TARGETS

Now that we have identified intermediate targets, we are in a position to back up one more step and examine the relation between operating targets and intermediate targets. Because intermediate targets are not directly influenced by the Fed's instruments, the Fed chooses another set of variables to aim for, called *operating targets*. Since 1970, the Fed has relied at different times on three alternative operating targets, variables that are linked to the intermediate target, *M,* and that the Fed monitors on a daily basis. In the 1970s, the

---

[4] The *potential level of production* is another term for the full-employment level of output introduced in Chapter 10.

FIGURE 13–2
Real Interest Rates
on Treasury
Securities

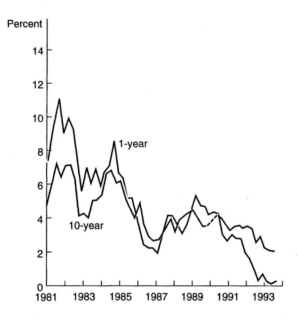

One-year rate is the spread between the one-year Treasury bill yield and one-year inflation expectations as measured by the University of Michigan's Survey of Consumers. Ten-year rate is the spread between the ten-year Treasury note yield and ten-year inflation expectations as measured by the Barclays de Zoete Wedd, Inc., survey from the first quarter of 1981 to the fourth quarter of 1989 and by the University of Michigan's Survey of Consumers from the second quarter of 1990 to the third quarter of 1993. (Data are unavailable for the first quarter of 1990 on the ten-year rate.)

Source: Federal Reserve Bank of Cleveland, *Economic Trends*, October 1993, 4.

federal funds rate was the operating target. The Fed switched to a nonborrowed reserves target in 1979, then to a borrowed reserves target in 1982. By 1987 the Fed had come full circle, back to a federal funds target. These changes in operating targets coincided with the changing importance of money as an intermediate target.

Federal Funds Rate Operating Target

Until October 1979 the federal funds rate served as the operating target. According to the second law of money demand, there is an inverse relation between the demand for money and short-term interest rates. Short-term interest rates can be represented by the federal funds rate. If this money demand relationship is predictable, the Fed can use it in conjunction with a federal funds rate as the operating target to achieve its target for the quantity of money, as illustrated in Figure 13–3.

Suppose, for example, that the Fed aims at achieving a quantity of money equal to M^1. The money demand curve in Figure 13–3 shows that the Fed must set a federal funds rate target equal to i_1. (For economy of notation, we have not introduced a different symbol here for the short-term interest rate.) Then the Fed must provide the quantity of nonborrowed and borrowed reserves that is consistent with a federal funds rate target of i_1. If the Fed wants to increase the quantity of money, say to M^2, it must reduce its target for the federal funds rate to i_2. To hit its target for the funds rate, the Fed must determine how many additional reserves to provide to the banking system so that the funds rate falls to i_2. If the Fed's estimate of the money demand curve turns out to be correct, and if it can achieve its targets for the federal funds rate, the Fed will hit its targets for the quantity of

FIGURE 13–3
Money Demand
and a Federal
Funds Operating
Target

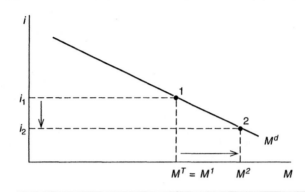

According to the money demand relation, if the intermediate target for money is M^1, the operating target for the federal funds rate must be set at i_1. If the Fed increases the intermediate target to M^2, it must reduce the operating target to i_2.

money. On the other hand, the Fed will make errors if it fails to predict a shift in money demand.

To illustrate, suppose money demand increases because of a change in one of the factors that we grouped under the collective factor $\mathscr{C}$ in Chapter 6. Recall that the factors that make up the collective variable are the state of cash management technology, the uncertainty of future income, and the risk, maturity, marketability, and liquidity of securitires. Suppose, for example, that because of increased uncertainty about future income, the public increases its demand for money, as Figure 13–4 illustrates. Also suppose that the Fed, not realizing that money demand has shifted, sets a federal funds target of i_1 to hit a money target of M_1. The actual level of the quantity of money will be above target, as shown by the horizontal distance between points 1 and 2 in Figure 13–4. At interest rate i_1, individuals want to hold a quantity of money equal to M^2 rather than M^1. To reach its unchanged target for the quantity of money after the increase in money demand, the Fed must set a higher target for the federal funds rate, namely, i_2, as shown by point 3 in Figure 13–4.

In 1977 and again in 1978 the actual rate of growth of the narrow measure of money, M1, was above the Fed's target range, although the federal funds rate consistently fell within the narrow ranges set by the Fed, as shown in Figure 13–5. (Note that until the end of 1979 the ranges for the federal funds rate were usually 50 to 75 basis points wide.) The Fed attributed its poor performance to shifts in money demand that were uneven over time and difficult to predict. Critics, however, argued that the Fed's problems were largely self-inflicted. They claimed that the Fed, motivated by its traditional (and misplaced) concern with holding down the level and volatility of interest rates, was setting targets for the federal funds rate that were too low.

Reserves
Operating
Targets

The 1979 switch from the federal funds rate to a reserves operating target took the Fed out of the business of targeting interest rates and shifted the operational focus from the money demand relation to the money supply relation. The move was important politically because the goal of monetary policy from 1979 to 1982 was to reduce the growth of money to reduce inflation. Achieving this goal required a reduction in reserves to the

FIGURE 13–4
Missing the Target
for *M: A Shift in
Money Demand*

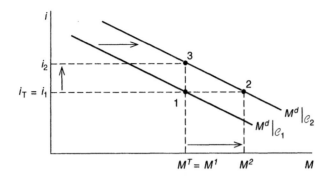

If the Fed does not predict the outward shift in money demand, it will incorrectly set a federal funds rate target of i_1 to reach a money target of M^1. At i_1, the actual quantity of money, M^2, will be above the targeted quantity. To reach the target for M, the federal funds rate must be set at i_2.

banking system and an increase in interest rates. By targeting reserves rather than the federal funds rate, the Fed could distance itself from the rise in rates.

The Fed's decision to change policy procedures came at a rare Saturday meeting of the FOMC on October 6, 1979. It announced the change in procedures with uncharacteristic fanfare, designed to draw public attention to the Fed's commitment to controlling the growth of money to control inflation. To achieve its monetary targets, the Fed announced it would henceforth use the money supply relationship between the quantity of reserves and the quantity of money.

The multiplier relationship between the quantity of total reserves and the quantity of money is represented by Equation 13–3 and illustrated by the upward-sloping money supply curve in Figure 13–6, where the quantity of money is measured on the horizontal axis and the quantity of total reserves on the vertical axis.

$$M^s = Cur + (1/rr) \times (TR^s - ER) \tag{13–3}$$

Where:

Cur = Currency in circulation

rr = Reserve requirement ratio

TR^s = Total reserves supplied

ER = Excess reserves

To achieve a target for the quantity of money that is equal, say, to M^1 in Figure 13–6, the Fed must create, via open market operations and discount window loans, a quantity of total reserves equal to TR_1. The Fed, however, has never used a total reserves target, although many monetarists have recommended a total reserves or a total monetary base target. Instead, in October 1979 the Fed adopted nonborrowed reserves as the operating target. To understand how this operating procedure works, we must examine the relationship between nonborrowed reserves and total reserves.

FIGURE 13–5
Short-Run
Tolerance Ranges
and Actual Levels
for Federal Funds
Rate: + *Denotes*
Average Federal
Funds Rate

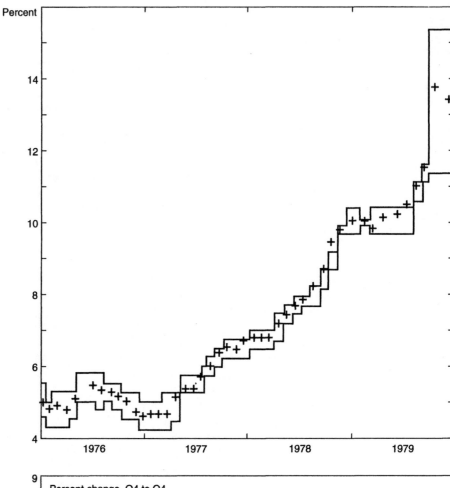

Target Ranges and
Actual Growth
Rates for M1*

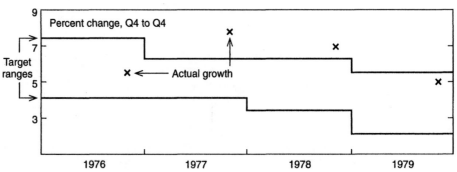

*M1 defined as currency and demand deposits.
Source: Federal Reserve Board.

FIGURE 13–6
The Money Supply
Relation between
Total Reserves and
the Quantity of
Money

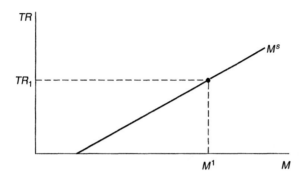

Other things equal, to achieve a
money target of M^1, the Fed must set
a target for total reserves equal to TR_1.

FIGURE 13–7
The Nonborrowed
Reserves–Total
Reserves Relation

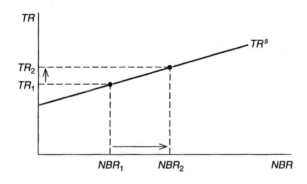

Every dollar increase in nonborrowed
reserves increases total reserves by
less than a dollar because of an
indirect reduction in borrowed
reserves.

Nonborrowed Reserves Operating Target   Figure 13–7 depicts the relationship between the operating target—nonborrowed reserves—and total reserves, which equals the sum of nonborrowed reserves (NBR) and borrowed reserves (BR):

$$TR^s = NBR + BR$$

The slope of the total reserves curve is less than 1 because every dollar increase in nonborrowed reserves increases total reserves by less than a dollar. This is because a change in nonborrowed reserves affects the quantity of borrowed reserves in the opposite direction. For example, an increase in the quantity of nonborrowed reserves brought about by an open market purchase of government securities reduces the interest rate. A lower interest rate, in turn, reduces the profitability of borrowing from the discount window. Banks, therefore, reduce their borrowed reserves. We can represent this relation schematically as follows:

| Open market purchase of securities | ⇒ | Rise in nonborrowed reserves | ⇒ | Fall in the interest rate | ⇒ | Decrease in borrowed reserves |

FIGURE 13–8
Monthly History of
M1 and M2
Growth Rates from
1975 to 1984:
Seasonally Adjusted,
Annual Rates

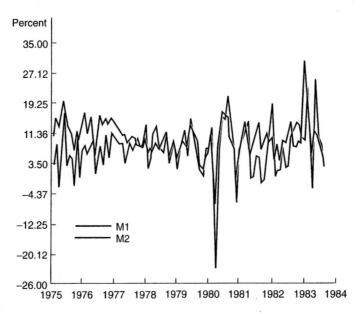

Source: Federal Reserve Board.

The reduction in borrowed reserves does not outweigh the direct effect of increasing the quantity of nonborrowed reserves, but it does prevent the quantity of total reserves from increasing as much as nonborrowed reserves, so the slope of the curve in Figure 13–7 is less than 1. Conversely, of course, an open market sale of securities reduces nonborrowed reserves and increases the interest rate. As a result, borrowed reserves rise, but total reserves fall.

The Fed can successfully use nonborrowed reserves as an operating target only if it can take into account the effect of its own open market operations on the quantity of borrowed reserves. During the first year of the new operating procedures, the Fed overshot the upper bounds of its target ranges for M1 and M2 growth primarily because it did not account for the effect on borrowed reserves.[5] In 1980 actual growth of M1 was 7.3 percent, while the target range was 4 percent to 6½ percent; actual growth of M2 was 9.8 percent, while the target range was 6 percent to 9 percent. Moreover, between 1979 and 1982 the volatility of M1 and M2 increased substantially, which was not expected. Figure 13–8 traces the history of M1 and M2 growth from 1975 to 1984. The increased volatility in the growth of the monetary aggregates is seen easily on the graph, with its sharp peaks and valleys. In its attempts to control the growth of money, the Fed wound up increasing its volatility.

---

[5] Errors may also occur because the Fed may not accurately predict other components of the money supply relationship. For example, the Fed may underestimate or overestimate the quantity of reserves that financial institutions decide to hold as excess reserves or the amount of currency that the public wants to hold.

The spotty record of the Fed between 1979 and 1982 led prominent monetarists such as Milton Friedman to disavow any connection between the Fed's policies and the doctrine of monetarism, which called for steady growth in the money supply. By 1982, however, the Fed had ironed out its problems with the new operating procedures. It is ironic, then, that no sooner had the Fed mastered the art of recognizing the effects of nonborrowed reserves on borrowed reserves than it decided to abandon nonborrowed reserves as an operating target in favor of the quantity of borrowed reserves itself. With this approach, the Fed uses open market operations to achieve a given level of discount window borrowing. Let's see how the procedure works.

Borrowed Reserves Operating Target   Borrowed reserves are linked to the quantity of money through the money supply equation:

$$M^s = Cur + (1/rr) \times (NBR + BR - ER)$$

Once the Fed has set its target for borrowed reserves based on its target for money, it must provide nonborrowed reserves via open market operations to induce financial institutions to borrow the targeted quantity. Profit-maximizing depository institutions borrow reserves up to the point at which their marginal revenue from borrowing equals the marginal cost of borrowing. The marginal revenue is the spread between the interest rate, i, that banks can charge and the discount rate, d, they pay the Fed to borrow. The marginal cost of borrowing is primarily the cost of being turned down for future loans at the discount window and having to go to the open market for funds, perhaps under unfavorable circumstances. Other things equal, an increase in the spread between the interest rate and the discount rate increases the marginal revenue from borrowing and induces banks to increase their borrowings from the Fed, as shown by the upward-sloping curve for borrowed reserves in Figure 13–9.

Figure 13–9 shows that to achieve its target for borrowed reserves, a target equal to, say, BR_T, the Fed must induce a spread equal to $(i - d)_1$. Because the Fed fixes the discount rate, it follows that to achieve its target for borrowed reserves the Fed must achieve the appropriate level of the interest rate, i_1, through open market operations. In other words, the Fed must provide nonborrowed reserves to the banking system until the federal funds rate reaches the level i_1 and borrowed reserves reach the level BR_T.

FIGURE 13–9
The Borrowed
Reserves Relation

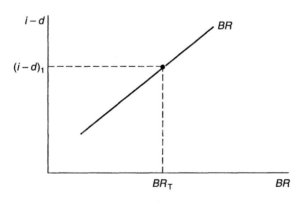

According to the borrowed reserves relation, if the operating target for borrowed reserves is BR_T, the spread between the interest rate and the discount rate must be $(i{-}d)_1$.

FIGURE 13–10
A Shift in the
Borrowed Reserves
Relation

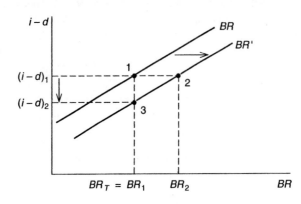

With an unchanged federal funds rate target and a given discount rate, the quantity of borrowed reserves increases from BR_1 to BR_2 in response to a rightward shift in the borrowed reserves relation. On the other hand, with an unchanged borrowed reserves target and a given discount rate, the federal funds rate would have to fall.

So far, then, targeting borrowed reserves is tantamount to targeting the interest (federal funds) rate. If a shift occurs in the borrowed reserve relationship, however, the two procedures will diverge. Suppose, for instance, that banks change their behavior: At any given spread between the interest rate and the discount rate, they want to borrow more reserves, as shown by the shift of the borrowed reserves curve from BR to BR' in Figure 13–10. Under an interest rate target, the Fed would increase the amount of borrowed reserves provided through discount window loans from BR_1 to BR_2, shown by the movement from point 1 to point 2 in Figure 13–10. On the other hand, with an unchanged borrowed reserves target and a given discount rate, the Fed would allow the interest rate to fall so that the spread would fall from $(i-d)_1$ to $(i-d)_2$, as shown by the movement from point 1 to point 3 in the same graph. In other words, the Fed would buy Treasury securities and supply nonborrowed reserves until the interest rate fell sufficiently to keep the quantity of borrowed reserves unchanged.

When the Fed switched to a borrowed reserves target, it insisted that this was not simply a guise for targeting the federal funds rate. The gist of the Fed's argument was that in the short run there is enough "looseness" in the relationship between borrowed reserves and the spread between the interest rate and the discount rate to make the two operating procedures different.

The evidence indicates that the borrowed reserves procedure was a hybrid approach that the Fed used to reduce the level and volatility of interest rates without the constraint of overtly targeting interest rates. When the Fed switched from a federal funds rate target to a nonborrowed reserves target in 1979, the volatility of the federal funds rate increased fourfold. On the other hand, when the Fed switched from nonborrowed reserves to borrowed reserves in 1982, the volatility of the federal funds rate fell, but it was still about twice as great as it was under the funds rate target.[6]

---

[6] For a conceptual and empirical analysis of the Fed's operating procedures in the 1980s by two former officials of the Federal Reserve, see William C. Melton and V. Vance Roley, "Federal Reserve Behavior Since 1980: A Financial-Market Perspective," *The Political Economy of American Monetary Policy,* ed. Thomas Mayer (New York: Cambridge University Press, 1990), 65–82.

FedWatch 13.2

Interpreting the Cryptic Domestic Policy Directives

To the uninitiated, the instructions in the domestic policy directive to the Federal Reserve Bank of New York seem incomprehensible. Even to the specialist, the message is cryptic. Here we look at how major changes in policy brought small but key changes in the language of the directive.

From the mid-1970s until the directive of October 6, 1979, the standard paragraph was similar to the following, taken from the FOMC meeting of September 18, 1979, the last one before the Fed switched from a federal funds operating target to a nonborrowed reserves operating target:

In the short-run, the Committee seeks to achieve bank reserve and money market conditions *that are broadly consistent with the longer-run ranges for monetary aggregates cited above, while giving due regard to developing conditions in foreign exchange and domestic financial markets.* Early in the period before the next regular meeting, System open market operations are to be directed at attaining a weekly average federal funds rate slightly above the current level. Subsequently, operations shall be directed at maintaining the weekly average federal funds rate within the range of 11¼ to 11¾ percent. *In deciding on the specific objective for the federal funds rate the Manager for Domestic Operations shall be guided mainly by the relationship between the* latest estimates of annual rates of growth in the September–October period of M-1 and M-2 and the following ranges of tolerance: 3 to 8 percent for M-1 and 6½ to 10½ percent for M-2. *If rates of growth of M-1 and M-2, given approximately equal weight, appear to be close to or beyond the upper or lower limits of the indicated ranges, the objective for the funds rate is to be raised or lowered in an orderly fashion within the range.*

If the rates of growth in the aggregates appear to be beyond the upper or lower limits of the indicated ranges at a time when the objective for the funds rate has already been moved to the corresponding limit of its range, the Manager shall promptly notify the Chairman, who will then decide whether the situation calls for supplementary instructions from the Committee (Board of Governors of the Federal Reserve System, *Annual Report 1979*, 197–98, emphasis added)

In contrast, the comparable paragraph in the directive of October 6, 1979, (and the ones that followed up to October 1982) read more like this:

In the short-run the Committee seeks to restrain expansion of reserve aggregates to a pace consistent with deceleration in growth of M-1, M-2, and M-3 *in the fourth quarter of 1979 to rates that would hold growth of these monetary aggregates over the whole period from the fourth quarter of 1978 to the fourth quarter of 1979 within the Committee's longer-run ranges,* provided that in the period before the next regular meeting, the weekly average federal funds rate remains within a range of 11½ to 15½ percent. *The Committee will consider the*

continued

The Fed's abandonment of nonborrowed reserves as the operating target was part of a retreat from its commitment to keep money growth within prespecified target ranges, regardless of other developments in the economy. By 1982, three years of reduction in money growth, although uneven, had succeeded in reducing the rate of inflation to about 6 percent. Contractionary monetary policy had also created the most severe recession since the Great Depression. In the spring of 1982, the Fed was faced with above-target M1 growth and a deteriorating economy. In October 1982, when it adopted a borrowed reserves target, the Fed began an increasingly eclectic monetary policy to provide reserves to the banking system in light of movements in a wide spectrum of financial and real-sector variables, including interest rates, exchange rates, monetary and credit aggregates, the price level, output, and unemployment. FedWatch 13.2 looks at how the FOMC modified the instructions in its domestic policy directives with each new operating target.

FedWatch 13.2
Interpreting the Cryptic Domestic Policy *(concluded)*

need for supplementary instructions if it appears that operations to restrain expansion of reserve aggregates would maintain the federal funds rate near the upper limit of its range. (Board of Governors of the Federal Reserve System, *Annual Report 1979*, 205, emphasis added)

In the first sentence we see the demotion of "money market conditions," that is, of the federal funds interest rate, which is not mentioned with reserves; changes in the quantity of reserves are the only means of achieving the targeted growth rates in M1, M2, and M3. Interest rates are further downgraded by widening their ranges of tolerance from 50 basis points to 400 basis points, an eightfold increase in the range.

After October 1982, when the Fed abandoned a nonborrowed reserves target in favor of a borrowed reserves target, additional changes in the policy directive evolved, as illustrated in the following one dated August 18, 1987:

In the implementation of policy for the immediate future, the Committee seeks to maintain the existing degree of pressure on reserve positions. Somewhat greater reserve restraint would, or slightly lesser reserve restraint might, be acceptable depending on indications of inflationary pressures, the strength of the business expansion, developments in foreign exchange markets, as well as the behavior of the aggregates. *This approach is expected to be consistent with growth in M2 and M3 over the period from June through September at annual rates of around 5 percent. Growth in M1, while picking up from recent levels, is expected to remain well below its pace during 1986.* The Chairman may call for Committee consultation if it appears to the Manager for Domestic Operations that reserve conditions during the period before the next meeting are likely to be associated with a federal funds rate persistently outside a range of 4 to 8 percent. (Board of Governors of the Federal Reserve System, *Federal Reserve Bulletin* 73, no. 10, 868, emphasis added)

In this directive, monetary aggregates, which are not mentioned in the first sentence, are downgraded. Opening instructions are now expressed in terms of the "degree of pressure on reserve positions," which replaces instructions about "expansion of reserve aggregates." In the second sentence, growth in the monetary aggregates is only one factor by which pressure on reserve positions will be judged. This particular directive mentions real-sector factors—inflationary pressures and the strength of the business expansion—and conditions in foreign exchange markets before the monetary aggregates. Numerical targets are given for M2 and M3, but not for M1, which is still mentioned, however. (The Fed stopped setting targets for M1 in 1987 and stopped referring to M1 in the directive in 1988.) Finally, the tolerance range for the federal funds rate remains 400 basis points wide.

Back to a Federal Funds Rate Target

The Fed modified the borrowed reserves approach after the precipitous decline in the stock market on Black Monday, October 19, 1987. At that time the Fed rushed to provide reserves to the banking system to support the expected increase in demand for liquid assets and to stabilize the funds rate within a narrow range. Because later downward shifts in borrowed reserves made the Fed unwilling to rely fully on borrowed reserves as its target, it continued to target the federal funds rate. Thus, the Fed had come full circle, back to its pre-1979 operating target.

The Fed, however, did not return to the pre-October 1979 practice of announcing a narrow tolerance range for the federal funds rate in the domestic policy directive. As we saw in FedWatch 13.2, when the Fed switched to a nonborrowed reserves target in October 1979, it set a range of 400 basis points for the federal funds rate in the domestic policy directive. The Fed insisted that the range was merely a "consultation range," meaning that a movement of the funds rate out of the range would trigger further consultation among FOMC members. They continued the practice of announcing a wide range for the federal funds rate in the policy directive until the end of 1990. At the FOMC meeting on November 13, 1990, the committee decided to drop the sentence about the consultation range because it served no real operational purpose. Ironically, although the federal funds rate continues to serve as the operating target, it is not mentioned in the policy directive at all. Instead, directives continue to refer to the "degree of pressure on reserve positions."

The Change in Policy in 1993

We have already seen that in 1993 the Fed downgraded the role of money as an intermediate target and added real interest rates to its array of indicators of the stance of monetary policy. So what does the Fed do? It has an operating target for the federal funds rate, forecasts of the real sector, and a broad array of policy indicators, including short-term real interest rates. Guided by the indicators, the Fed attempts to manipulate the operating target to achieve its real-sector forecasts. FedWatch 13.3 explains how the Fed implemented this approach in the first half of 1994.

FROM INSTRUMENTS TO OPERATING TARGETS

The final link we consider is that between open market operations, the primary instrument of monetary policy, and the operating target. Through open market operations the Fed directly affects the supply of nonborrowed reserves. When nonborrowed reserves themselves are the operating target, the Trading Desk of the Federal Reserve Bank of New York conducts open market operations to reach that target. Even when nonborrowed reserves are not the operating target, the Desk establishes an objective for nonborrowed reserves. For instance, with a borrowed reserves operating target, the Desk determines the quantity of nonborrowed reserves that is consistent with the FOMC's borrowed reserves target; then it conducts open market operations to achieve the needed level of nonborrowed reserves. With a federal funds operating target the Desk also has an objective for nonborrowed reserves. In this case the Desk aims at providing the quantity of nonborrowed reserves needed to maintain the funds rate at the desired level.

Once the Desk has an objective for nonborrowed reserves, however, it must still forecast the technical factors affecting reserves in order to set its program for open market operations. The next chapter explains how the technical factors affecting reserves affect the actions of the Trading Desk.

Fed*Watch* 13.3
Searching for a Neutral Policy Stance in 1994

At the beginning of 1994 the nominal federal funds rate stood at 3 percent and the estimated real rate at zero. In February the Fed raised its target for the nominal rate from 3 to 3¼ percent. In March it raised the target to 3½ percent, and in April to 3¾ percent.

After a 7 percent rate of growth of real GDP in the fourth quarter of 1993 and a 3½ percent growth rate in the first quarter of 1994, the Fed was groping its way toward a neutral monetary policy. A neutral policy is one that would allow the economy to grow at its sustainable, noninflationary rate, estimated to be between 2½ to 3 percent. The associated neutral level of the real interest rate, however, is uncertain, as the accompanying excerpt from the April 19, 1994 issue of *The Wall Street Journal* explains:

Fed Chairman Alan Greenspan has said the Fed had been holding short-term interest rates, adjusted for inflation, near zero to stimulate a sluggish economy that was restrained by a widespread determination to reduce debt. But with the economy now growing at a robust pace, he has said, the Fed has concluded that it is time to take the foot off the accelerator and put monetary policy into a "neutral" stance.

*   *   *   *   *

. . . Mr. Greenspan has noted that, adjusted for inflation, short-term interest rates were close to zero. After the latest Fed move (in April), the rates are now roughly ¾ percent. Mr. Greenspan won't say how much further rates will have to rise to reach "neutral."

Robert Reischauer, director of the Congressional Budget Office, said neutral probably means inflation-adjusted rates of somewhere between ¾ percent and 1½ percent. But chief White House economist Laura

Tyson has said that—excluding the anomalous 1980s—inflation-adjusted interest rates "have always been below 1 percent." Internal Fed estimates are higher. One Fed policymaker puts the relevant historic average at between 1 percent and 1½ percent. That suggests the federal funds rate may rise to 4 percent or 4½ percent before the Fed rests.*

In May, the Fed pushed the federal funds rate into the estimated neutral zone by raising its target from 3¾ percent to 4¼ percent. It also raised the discount rate from 3 percent to 3½ percent. In announcing the changes in a press release on May 17, the Fed said: "The Board approved an increase in the discount rate from 3 percent to 3½ percent, effectively immediately, and the Federal Open Market Committee agreed that this increase should be allowed to show through completely into interest rates in reserve markets. These actions, combined with the three adjustments initiated earlier this year by the FOMC, *substantially* [italics added] remove the degree of monetary accomodation which prevailed throughout 1993." The word substantially indicated to Fedwatchers that the FOMC would not rest for long if it saw signs of a pickup in inflation.

And the Fed did not rest. With unemployment running at 6.1 percent—close to what many economists consider the full-employment level—and factories running at their highest level of capacity utilization in nearly five years, in August 1994 the Fed raised its target for the federal funds rate from 4¼ to 4¾ percent and also raised the discount rate from 3½ percent to 4 percent. In announcing the increases, the Fed said: "these actions are expected to be sufficient, at least for a time, *to meet the objective of sustained, noninflationary growth* [italics added]." This statement indicates that the Fed thought it had reached a neutral stance, for the time being.

· David Wessel, "Fed Boosts Short-Term Rates ¼ Point," *The Wall Street Journal*, April 19, 1994, A2 and A10.

SUMMARY

· The ultimate goals of monetary policy are price stability, full employment, maximum sustainable economic growth, and viability in international accounts. In its semiannual report to Congress on monetary policy, the Fed provides numerical forecasts for the annual rate of inflation, the annual rate of growth of real GDP, and the annual rate of unemployment.

- To achieve its ultimate goals and forecasts, the Fed uses three policy instruments: open market operations, the discount rate, and the reserve requirement ratio(s).

- Because the transmission mechanism from the instruments to the ultimate goals and forecasts is neither immediate nor direct, the Fed divides the process into three steps: the link from the instruments to the operating target; the link from the operating target to the intermediate target; and the link from the intermediate target to the ultimate goals.

- Until the early 1970s the Fed employed the (nominal) long-term interest rate as the intermediate target. The inverse relation between the interest rate and aggregate demand links the intermediate target to the real sector.

- Since the early 1970s, the Fed has used various measures of money as the intermediate target. According to the quantity theory of money, the velocity of circulation of money is the link between the quantity of money and the real sector.

- The velocity of circulation is the number of times per year that each dollar turns over to buy final goods and services. In the early 1980s velocity began to behave erratically. In the fall of 1982 the Fed retreated from its commitment to keep money growth within prespecified ranges, regardless of other developments in the economy.

- In 1987 the Fed stopped setting targets for M1. In 1993, it downgraded its reliance on M2 and M3, although it continues to set targets for these two measures. At the same time, the Fed introduced the real interest rate as an indicator to guide the conduct of monetary policy.

- To achieve its intermediate target, the Fed sets a short-run target, called an *operating target,* for a financial variable that is linked to the intermediate target and that can be directly affected by the policy instruments.

- From the early 1970s until 1979, the Fed used the federal funds rate as the operating target by exploiting the relation between this rate and the demand for money.

- On October 6, 1979, the Fed switched to a nonborrowed reserves operating target. In implementing the new procedure, the Fed used the money supply relation between the quantity of nonborrowed reserves and the quantity of money.

- In the fall of 1982, the Fed switched to a borrowed reserves operating target. One interpretation of this procedure is that the Fed employed the money supply relation between borrowed reserves and the quantity of money. Another interpretation is that the Fed was in essence targeting the federal funds rate, because the Fed must exploit the relation between borrowed reserves and the federal funds rate (net of the discount rate) to achieve its target for borrowed reserves.

- After the stock market crash of 1987, the Fed returned to a federal funds rate operating target.

- Since 1993 the Fed has used more judgment and discretion in manipulating its operating target to achieve its real-sector forecasts.

- Open market operations, which directly affect the supply of nonborrowed reserves, are the primary instrument of monetary policy. With a federal funds rate target, the Fed aims at providing the quantity of nonborrowed reserves needed to maintain the funds rate within the desired range. With a nonborrowed reserves target, the Fed buys or sells government securities to achieve the desired change in nonborrowed reserves. With a borrowed reserves target, the Fed aims at providing the quantity of nonborrowed reserves consistent with its borrowed reserves target.

KEY TERMS AND CONCEPTS

ultimate goals	financial indicators	quantity theory of money
monetary policy instruments	monetarism	velocity-indexed money growth
intermediate targets	total domestic nonfinancial debt	equilibrium real interest rate
operating targets	velocity of circulation, V	

QUESTIONS AND PROBLEMS

1. What is the difference between the ultimate goals of monetary policy and the projections the Fed provides in its semiannual "Monetary Policy Report to Congress"?

2. What is the difference between an intermediate target and a financial indicator of monetary policy?

3. Explain the difference between using the nominal long-term interest rate and the quantity of money as an intermediate target.

The Wall Street Journal

4. Evaluate the following statement from "The Federal Reserve: A Very Easy Target," *The Wall Street Journal,* February 8, 1993:

> Newly converted to monetarism, Democratic Senators Paul Sarbanes of Maryland and James Sasser of Tennessee regularly trot out charts showing that the money supply has grown more slowly than the Fed wanted. Congress produces big-name economists from Democrats such as MIT's Paul Samuelson and Yale's James Tobin to Republicans such as Harvard's Martin Feldstein and University of Michigan's Paul McCracken to complain that the Fed has been and still is too stingy with credit. . . . Mr. Greenspan argues that the senators' money-supply charts aren't that important, and he may be correct.

5. What variables have been used as operating targets of monetary policy in the United States?

6. What problems may arise with the use of the federal funds rate as an operating target when money is the intermediate target?

7. What problems may arise with the use of nonborrowed reserves as an operating target when money is the intermediate target?

8. Suppose that the Fed sells $1 billion of Treasury securities in the open market. Will the quantity of total reserves rise or fall? Will the change in total reserves be greater than, equal to, or less than $1 billion?

9. Answer the following questions with the help of a money demand diagram: Suppose that the Fed uses the federal funds rate as the operating target and the quantity of money as the intermediate target. Suppose, too, that, unknown to the Fed, the public considers investing in securities to be less risky than before. Will the quantity of money be greater than, equal to, or less than the Fed's target for money? What, if anything, should the Fed do to achieve its target for money?

10. Suppose that real income (i.e., real GDP) rises above the level projected by the Fed. Will the Fed achieve its target for money if it uses the federal funds rate as the operating target? Will it achieve its monetary target if, instead, it uses the quantity of nonborrowed reserves as the operating target?

11. What are the similarities and differences between a borrowed reserves operating target and a federal funds operating target?

12. Is the federal funds rate the operating target today? Is it mentioned in the policy directive? Has the funds rate ever been mentioned in the directive during periods when it was not the operating target? If so, why?

13. Why did the Fed add short-term real interest rates to its array of policy indicators in 1993? How did the Fed use these rates in its policymaking decisions in 1994?

SUGGESTED READINGS

Federal Reserve Bank of New York. *Intermediate Targets and Indicators for Monetary Policy: A Critical Survey.* New York: Federal Reserve Bank of New York, 1990.
    A collection of articles on the pros and cons of alternative financial measures as intermediate targets or indicators.

Feinman, Joshua N. "Reserve Requirements: History, Current Practice, and Potential Reform." *Federal Reserve Bulletin* 79, no. 6 (June 1993): 569–89.
    A Federal Reserve Board economist examines the roles of reserve requirements in the United States and other industrialized countries.

Feldstein, Martin. "The Recent Failure of U.S. Monetary Policy," National Bureau of Economic Research, Working Paper 4236, December 1992.

    A critical evaluation of U.S. monetary policy in the early 1990s.

Friedman, Benjamin. "The Role of Judgment and Discretion in the Conduct of Monetary Policy: Consequences of Changing Financial Markets," National Bureau of Economic Research, Working Paper 4599, December 1993.
    Makes the case for the use of multiple, information-based indicators to guide monetary policy.

Hadjimichalakis, Michael. *The Federal Reserve, Money, and Interest Rates: The Volcker Years and Beyond.* New York: Praeger, 1984.
    Chapters 2 and 3 derive the theoretical implications of a switch from a federal funds rate operating target to a nonborrowed reserves operating target and use the results to evaluate the U.S. experience from 1979 to 1982.

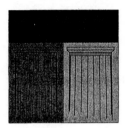

OPEN MARKET OPERATIONS AND MOVEMENTS IN RESERVES

CHAPTER PREVIEW

At the conclusion of the FOMC meeting on July 6, 1994, the Fed issued a press release stating that: "The meeting of the Federal Open Market Committee ended at 12:35 PM and there will be no further announcement." The announcement that it had no announcement was the Fed's way of saying that the FOMC decided not to change its target for the federal funds rate for the time being. After the meetings in February, March, and May of 1994, the Fed had announced increases in its target for the funds rate. It also had announced an intermeeting increase in the target in April. But July was the first time the Fed had ever announced an FOMC decision not to change rates.

Prior to 1994, the Fed signaled the FOMC's policy decisions indirectly through major banks and brokerage houses, whose Fedwatchers interpreted the Fed's daily action, or inaction, in the open market to detect changes in the degree of reserve pressure and accompanying changes in the federal funds rate. Occasionally, however, the Fedwatchers would misinterpret the Fed's actions, as we shall see in this chapter. With the practice adopted in 1994, the Fed provides the information directly rather than filtering it through Fedwatchers. As Chapter 11 discusses, this new practice emerged as a result of Congressional pressure on the Fed to reduce secrecy.

This chapter begins with a brief description of the decision-making process that culminates in the Fed's action, or inaction, in the open market on any given day. Then it explains the implications of those open market operations for movements in reserves. Most open market operations are defensive open market operations designed to offset changes in the technical factors affecting reserves rather than dynamic operations aimed at changing reserves in the banking system. The Fed's new practice of announcing policy shifts means that Fedwatchers do not need to read the tea leaves of open market operations to detect changes in the stance of monetary policy.

The main analytical tool introduced in this chapter for understanding movements in reserves is a *sources and uses of reserves statement,* which is an accounting statement of the "factors supplying reserves and the factors absorbing reserves." The statement is the consolidated balance sheet of the 12 Federal Reserve banks, augmented by the monetary accounts of the Treasury. By examining an actual set of accounts, we identify all the technical factors affecting reserves and gain an appreciation of their size and scope.

THE TRADING DESK

The Federal Reserve Bank of New York is the FOMC's agent for open market operations. The unit of the New York Fed that oversees and undertakes the operations is called the **Trading Desk**, or simply the **Desk.** The Desk has formal, established relations with 39 government security dealers, called **primary dealers,** through which it buys and sells securities for the Fed's portfolio. Both banks and nonbank securities firms are primary dealers.

The Desk itself does not make monetary policy; it merely implements the policy decisions of the FOMC. As we have seen, the FOMC meets about eight times a year to set the intermeeting guidelines for open market operations, against the background of its annual targets and goals set forth in the semiannual "Monetary Policy Report to Congress" in February and July. After each meeting the decisions of the FOMC are summarized in the domestic policy directive.

The statement of the instructions in the directive varies with the operating targets of the Fed. As we saw in Chapter 13, currently the federal funds rate is the operating target, and the FOMC frames its instructions in terms of the **degree of reserve pressure**: to increase reserve pressure, to reduce reserve pressure, or to maintain current reserve pressure, with possible additional refinements about "bias."

When the FOMC increases reserve pressure, this means there will be insufficient reserves in the system relative to the demand by banks for required and excess reserves, forcing some banks to borrow reserves in the federal funds market to fulfill their reserve requirements. This increased demand creates pressure in the federal funds market, which results in a higher federal funds rate. Conversely, when the FOMC reduces reserve pressure, this means there will be more reserves in the system relative to the demand by banks, reducing pressure in the federal funds market and lowering the federal funds rate. This is the reason that targeting the degree of reserve pressure means targeting the federal funds rate and that the current operating target is the federal funds rate.

No matter what the operating target, the Board staff and the Desk staff must translate the directive into a plan for open market operations—the primary instrument for changing

**TABLE 14–1
A Day at the
Trading Desk**

8:30 AM	Watching the market react to data
9:00 AM	Discussing market developments with securities dealers
10:30 AM	Consulting the Treasury by phone about its balances at the Federal Reserve banks
10:45 AM	Developing a plan of action for the day
11:15 AM	The daily conference call with FOMC representatives
11:40 AM	Contacting dealers to announce an open market operation
5:00 PM	Reviewing how the day turned out

Source: Ann-Marie Meulendyke, *U.S. Monetary Policy and Financial Markets* (New York: Federal Reserve Bank of New York, December 1989), 160–61.

reserves—for various time frames: the period of five to eight weeks between FOMC meetings; the shorter reserves maintenance period of two weeks;[1] and day to day.

In deciding whether to increase or decrease reserves, the Board and the Desk forecast anticipated reserve pressure for the next one to three maintenance periods and compare it to the reserve pressure mandated in the directive. If the forecasted pressure is less than desired, the Desk must raise the pressure by reducing the supply of reserves, and if the pressure is more than desired, the Desk must lower the pressure. The expected reserve needs of banks and the expected technical factors supplying reserves are two key elements of the Desk's forecast of pressure.

Table 14–1 shows a typical day's activities at the Trading Desk. Let's examine that day in more detail. Given the Desk's estimate of the need for reserves in the banking system, the manager of the System Open Market Account for Domestic Operations at the Trading Desk and the Desk staff prepare the daily program for open market operations after discussing the market with dealers; after reviewing the previous day's financial data, especially the level of nonborrowed reserves, borrowed reserves, and the fund's rate; and after assessing the technical factors affecting reserves, including the Treasury's balances with Federal Reserve banks. The manager then reviews and confirms the plan with other Fed officials in "the call," which is a daily conference call, at 11:15 AM, among the manager of the Trading Desk, senior staff at the Board of Governors in Washington, D.C., and 1 of the 12 reserve bank presidents who is a current voting member of the FOMC. The established game plan is conveyed to all voting members of the FOMC and to the nonvoting reserve bank presidents on the same day. Finally, the Desk staff executes the program.

On a day when the Fed has decided to buy government securities in the open market, the Desk staff contacts the primary securities dealers for offers, that is, the prices at which the dealers are willing to sell securities and the quantities they are willing to sell. The staff then ranks the offers, and the traders execute the purchases, beginning with the lowest priced offers, until the desired quantities are purchased. The Desk may buy securi-

---

[1] On average, banks must satisfy their reserve requirements over a two-week period, called the *reserves maintenance period.*

ties outright or through a repurchase agreement. Chapter 5 looked at repurchase agreements between depository institutions and nonfinancial firms. With a **Federal Reserve repurchase agreement**, the nature of the agreement is the same, but the parties are different. In this case, the Desk buys securities from primary dealers and agrees to sell them back at a specified price and date, usually within a week.

On the other hand, when the plan calls for the sale of securities, the Desk contacts dealers for bids, that is, for the price at which they are willing to buy securities and the quantities they are willing to buy. Again, the staff ranks the bids and subsequently executes the sales, beginning with the highest bids. The sale may be an outright sale or a **matched sale-purchase transaction**, which is a reverse repurchase agreement. In this type of transaction, the Desk sells securities to primary dealers and agrees to buy them back at a specified date and price.

Once the Fed executes the purchases or sales of securities through the dealers, the open market operations of that day are public information. What, then, can the observer conclude from this information? That every purchase of government securities by the Desk indicates a planned increase in the supply of reserves, and every sale a planned decrease? The answer is no, as we can see by considering alternative scenarios consistent with a hypothetical open market operation.

A DAY OF FEDWATCHING

Suppose that we observe that at 11:45 AM on a Tuesday the Desk purchased $1,000 million dollars of Treasury bills from government securities dealers in the open market through a seven-day repurchase agreement. Now we come face-to-face with our question: Why does every purchase of securities in the open market not indicate a planned increased in nonborrowed reserves, and every sale a planned decrease? The answer is that not all purchases and sales of securities are **dynamic open market operations** designed to increase or decrease the supply of nonborrowed reserves. Instead, some open market operations are **defensive open market operations** designed to offset expected changes in the technical factors affecting nonborrowed reserves.[2] These technical factors affecting reserves arise from the financial activities of the public, depository institutions, the Treasury, and foreign central banks and institutions, as well as from the operating and service functions of the Fed itself. For example, currency in circulation is a technical factor affecting reserves. When the public increases its currency holdings, reserves in the banking system fall, as Chapter 8 explains. Because the Fed does not control the technical factors affecting reserves and does not know with certainty how they will change, the staff must forecast them. Economists at the Federal Reserve Bank of New York and at the Federal Reserve Board in Washington, D.C., prepare forecasts for changes in the technical factors to guide the Desk in its open market operations.[3]

Depending on the expected behavior of the technical factors affecting reserves, the observed $1,000 million purchase of Treasury securities could be part of a Fed plan to

---

[2] Robert V. Roosa, a former official of the Federal Reserve Bank of New York, introduced the distinction between defensive and dynamic open market operations in 1956.

[3] The Fed does not make its forecasts available to the public.

maintain the existing level of nonborrowed reserves in the banking system, to increase nonborrowed reserves, or even to decrease nonborrowed reserves, as the following three scenarios illustrate.

Scenario 1: A Defensive Open Market Operation

Suppose the staff economists forecast that on this Tuesday the technical factors will drain $1,000 million of reserves from the banking system. Suppose, too, that the Desk's plan for the day is to maintain the existing level of nonborrowed reserves in the system. The Desk must thus buy $1,000 million of securities in the open market to compensate for the forecasted decrease in reserves from the technical factors. According to this scenario, the open market operations on Tuesday are purely defensive.

Scenario 2: A Dynamic Open Market Operation

Suppose, instead, staff economists at the Fed forecast that on Tuesday the technical factors affecting reserves will not change. With this scenario, the $1,000 million purchase of Treasury securities is a purely dynamic open market operation, designed to increase the supply of nonborrowed reserves by $1,000 million.

Scenario 3: A Hybrid Open Market Operation

Our last scenario is a hybrid open market operation, partly defensive and partly dynamic. Suppose the staff forecasts a $1,500 million decrease in nonborrowed reserves on Tuesday because of technical factors, while the desired change in reserves is a $500 million decrease in reserve balances. Then the Desk will buy $1,000 million of securities, which will provide $1,000 million of nonborrowed reserves to the system. This purchase will leave a planned net reduction of $500 million in nonborrowed reserves.

The Euthanasia of Fedwatchers?

Large banks and brokerage firms have traditionally employed Fedwatchers to detect shifts in Fed policy and accompanying changes in interest rates. Prior to 1994, some of these Fedwatchers specialized in interpreting the Fed's action, or inaction, in the open market on a daily basis by relying on their own forecasts of the technical factors affecting reserves. Several of them learned their trade while forecasting at the Fed. The closer their forecasts were to those of their counterparts at the Fed, the more accurate their daily assessments of open market operations were. For example, suppose that in our hypothetical case the Fed's game plan for the Tuesday in question was scenario 1. If Fedwatchers also forecasted a $1,000 million decrease in the technical factors affecting reserves, they would correctly assess that the purchase of securities was not meant to increase reserves in the banking system and to lower interest rates. In other words, the Fed was not shifting to an easier monetary policy.

FedWatch 14.1 looks at a famous 1989 case in which Fedwatchers blundered by mistaking a defensive open market operation for a shift to an easier policy. Fedwatchers erred in 1989 even though the Fed used a repurchase agreement, which it commonly uses for defensive open market operations. Following that incident the Fed tried to make it easier for Fedwatchers to discern policy shifts, culminating in its decision in 1994 to announce them.

The Fed's practice of announcing changes in its target for the federal funds rate means that financial firms do not need Fedwatchers to detect these policy changes from current open market operations. This does not, however, imply the euthanasia of Fedwatchers. Financial firms have always used Fedwatchers to predict changes in policy before these

FedWatch 14.1
Fedwatchers Blunder

Wednesday, November 22, 1989, was the day before Thanksgiving. Just before noon, the Trading Desk of the Federal Reserve Bank of New York entered the market and bought $2.8 billion of Treasury securities, and the federal funds rate fell from 8½ percent to 8¼ percent.

For weeks, many Fedwatchers had been predicting that the Fed would ease monetary policy and had advised their own firms and their clients to buy securities in anticipation of that easing. Was this the dynamic open market operation Fedwatchers were expecting? Or was it merely a defensive open market operation to offset a drainage of reserves caused by a change in the technical factors? If it were a dynamic operation, Fedwatchers and their clients stood to gain on their earlier purchases, and they could gain even more by buying more securities. As we see in the following excerpt from the "Credit Markets" column in *The Wall Street Journal* on November 24, the majority opinion, reflected in the title of the column, was that the Fed had indeed eased.

Bond Prices Firm, Short-Term Rates Fall on Perceived Easing of Fed Credit Policy

NEW YORK—Bond prices firmed and short-term rates fell ahead of the Thanksgiving holiday on widespread perceptions that the Federal Reserve has once again eased credit policy.

"The Fed was in the holiday spirit," said F. Ward McCarthy Jr., a managing director at Stone & McCarthy Research Associates. "That made what was an otherwise boring day kind of interesting."

Speculation that the Fed wants interest rates to move lower started soon after the nation's central bank executed five-day system repurchase agreements during its normal prenoon intervention period. That is a trading operation designed to add reserves to the banking system.

The Fed doesn't explain the intent of its open market activity, but government officials confirmed that the move was designed to reduce the key federal funds rate. Economists believe the rate was reduced by about ¼ percentage point to 8¼%. The federal funds rate—the

rate banks charge each other on overnight loans—is closely watched because the Fed often uses it to signal credit policy changes. When the Fed executed the repurchase agreements, the rate was about 8⁷⁄₁₆% but drifted as low as 8⅛% after the Fed's action. "On a morning where the consensus was for little or no action by the Fed, this seems like a fairly clear-cut signal," said Mr. McCarthy.

Maria Fiorini Ramirez, managing director and money market economist at Drexel Burnham Lambert Inc., said Wednesday's move "paves the way for broader base declines in other rates," such as the prime rate and various consumer lending rates. The prime, or base lending rate, is about 10.5% at most commercial banks. Several small banks reduced their prime lending rate to 10% several weeks ago when the Fed eased rates, but the major banks didn't follow.

Some economists expect commercial banks to reduce the prime as early as today.

Trading activity was extremely light on Wednesday, in part because of the approaching Thanksgiving holiday and because some credit market analysts reacted cautiously to the Fed's move.

These skeptics thought that technical and seasonal factors likely forced the Fed to provide reserves to the banking system. They pointed to a large rise in the amount of currency in circulation, which typically begins to surge shortly before Thanksgiving and drains reserves from the banking system. The rise in currency, related to Christmas spending, should continue through New Year's Day. Economists will focus on fed funds today and Monday to see whether the rate stays around 8¼%, which would support the easing view, or moves back to 8½, which would signal the Fed hasn't changed policy.

In any case, the market reacted as if the Fed eased, even though trading activity was light during the holiday-shortened session. Most government securities dealers closed shop at 3 p.m. EST on the recommendations of the Public Securities Association.

---

* Constance Mitchell and Laurence Bauman, *The Wall Street Journal*, November 24, 1989, C15.

continued

FedWatch 14.1
Fedwatchers Blunder
(concluded)

Despite the reporters' reference to unnamed government officials who confirmed that the Fed was easing monetary policy, the skeptics mentioned in the column turned out to be right. The purchase of securities was nothing more than the usual defensive open market operation to offset the effect on reserves of increases in the demand for currency around the Thanksgiving holiday.

To send a clear message that it was not easing, the Fed sold securities on Friday and Monday after Thanksgiving, pushing the federal funds rate above 8½ percent. When it became apparent that the Fed had not eased, the interest rates on other securities shot up, bringing their prices down and inflicting heavy capital losses on those who held them. It was a Thanksgiving week that Fedwatchers would not soon forget.

changes showed up in open market operations. With the new practices, they try to predict changes in policy before the day of the Fed's announcement. Fedwatchers who specialized in reading the tea leaves of open market operations will have to branch out to this broader type of Fedwatching if they want to remain in the business.

Policy Shifts

We have seen that not every open market purchase or sale of securities by the Fed is meant to change nonborrowed reserves. Now we must emphasize that not every change in nonborrowed reserves is meant to change the stance of monetary policy. A change in nonborrowed reserves clearly changes the degree of reserve pressure only if other things are equal, in particular, if the demand for reserves by banks is unchanged. If the demand is not the same, an increase in nonborrowed reserves can mean a looser policy, a tighter policy, or even an unchanged policy.

To decide whether an increase in nonborrowed reserves implies an easing in reserve pressure, we must compare it with banks' demand for reserves. Suppose, for example, the public shifts funds out of bank CDs into NOW accounts because of a fall in the deposit rate on CDs relative to the rate on NOW accounts. This shift increases the need for required reserves by banks, which must hold reserves against NOW accounts but not against CDs. In this case, if the Fed does not increase the supply of nonborrowed reserves, the degree of reserve pressure will rise. If the Fed wants the degree of reserve pressure and, hence, the federal funds rate to remain unchanged, it must increase nonborrowed reserves to satisfy the increased need for reserves by banks. This was the case in 1993 when shifts from nontransactions to transactions deposits increased the amount of required reserves that banks needed. The Fed increased the supply of nonborrowed reserves by 10.2 percent in 1993, while holding its target for the federal funds rate at 3 percent for the entire year.

SOURCES AND USES OF RESERVES STATEMENT

The three hypothetical scenarios in the preceding section were a convenient device for explaining the role of defensive and dynamic open market operations in the conduct of monetary policy. To understand fully all the factors that affect the supply of reserves in

TABLE 14–2
A Simplified
Sources and Uses
of Reserves
Statement

Sources of Reserves	Uses of Reserves
(1) Federal Reserve's portfolio of securities (B_F)	(4) Currency in circulation + Other uses ($Cur + OU$)
(2) Discount window loans (DWL)	(5) Total Reserves (TR^S)
(3) Other sources (OS)	(a) Total reserve balances with Fed
	(b) Vault cash

TABLE 14–3
A Simplified
Balance Sheet of
the Federal
Reserve System

Assets	Liabilities
(1) Federal Reserve's portfolio of securities	(4) Federal Reserve notes + Other liabilities
(2) Discount window loans	(5) Total reserves
(3) Other assets	(a) Total reserve balances with Fed
	(b) Vault cash

the banking system, we must move beyond these three scenarios to a **sources and uses of reserves statement,** which is an accounting statement of all the factors supplying reserves and absorbing reserves. We begin with an aggregate version of the statement, from which we derive equations for the supply of total reserves and nonborrowed reserves. Then we look at an actual statistical release of the Federal Reserve to identify all the technical factors affecting reserves. Familiarity with the numbers in the release give us an appreciation of the size and scope of the technical factors affecting reserves. Because reserves are the raw material out of which money is created, a change in a technical factor, other things equal, will affect the money supply. Of course, other things do not remain equal. The Fed uses defensive open market operations to prevent changes in technical factors from having unwanted effects on the supply of reserves.

A Simplified Statement

Table 14–2 presents an aggregated, simplified version of the sources and uses statement. The sources of reserves on the left side of the statement are the factors supplying reserves. The first two entries are the Fed's portfolio of Treasury securities and discount window loans. The third factor supplying reserves is a catchall category called "other sources," which are the technical factors supplying reserves. The uses of reserves on the right side of the statement consist of total reserves themselves and all the technical factors that absorb reserves, that is, currency in circulation and "other uses" of reserves.

The simplified sources and uses of reserves statement is essentially the simplified balance sheet of the Fed introduced earlier, reproduced here as Table 14–3. Essentially, but not exactly, for we must augment the Fed's balance sheet by the monetary accounts of the Treasury to get a complete statement of all the factors supplying reserves or absorbing reserves.

Items (1) and (2) are the same in both tables. Thus, if we could rename "other assets" in the Fed's balance sheet as "other sources," rename "Federal Reserve notes" as "currency in circulation," and rename "other liabilities" as "other uses," we would end up with the sources and uses of reserves statement in Table 14–2. Going from the Fed's balance sheet to the sources and uses statement, however, involves more than a mere change in terminology. All "other assets" in the Fed's balance sheet are included in *but do not exhaust* the "other sources" in the sources and uses statement. Similarly, all "other liabilities" in Table 14–3 are included in but do not exhaust the "other uses" in Table 14–2. On the other hand, not all Federal Reserve notes, a component of item (4) in the Fed's balance sheet, are part of currency in circulation. Some are held in the vaults of the U.S. Treasury or the vaults of banks. Moreover, not all currency in circulation consists of Federal Reserve notes. All coins and a small amount of paper currency are obligations of the Treasury.

To move from the Fed's balance sheet to the complete sources and uses of reserves statement, we must make the appropriate additions and regroup the terms. All the adjustments concern two relatively minor monetary accounts of the U.S. Treasury that can potentially add or absorb reserves and that are not reflected in the Fed's balance sheet because they do not involve direct transactions between the Treasury and the Fed. They must be added to the Fed's balance sheet to obtain a complete sources and uses of reserves statement. These two items are a small part of the Treasury's gold stock and coins and paper currency issued by the Treasury and held outside the vaults of the Federal Reserve. In other words, a sources and uses of reserves statement consists of the balance sheet of the Fed augmented by the monetary accounts of the Treasury. We shall consider the details later in this chapter. First, let us derive equations for the supply of total reserves and the supply of nonborrowed reserves from Table 14–2.

The Supply of Reserves The information in the sources and uses of reserves statement can be written in equation form, namely, that the sum of the sources of reserves equals the sum of the uses of reserves:

$$B_F + DWL + OS = Cur + OU + TR^S \tag{14–1}$$

Next, we can rearrange Equation 14–1 so that the level of total reserves is on one side of the equation and all the factors that affect the level of total reserves are on the other side. The result is Equation 14–2, the supply of total reserves.[4]

$$TR^S = B_F + DWL + (OS - OU - Cur) \tag{14–2}$$

Equation 14–2 shows that three types of factors affect the supply of total reserves. The first factor is the Federal Reserve's portfolio of securities, B_F. Via an open market pur-

---

4 This equation is similar to Equation 8–2 in Chapter 8: $TR^S = B_F + DWL + (OA - OL - Cur)$. The difference is that "other sources" (OS) replaces "other assets" (OA) and "other uses" replaces "other liabilities" (OL).

TABLE 14–4
Factors Affecting
Supply of Total
Reserves

$$B_F \uparrow \;\Rightarrow\; TR^s \uparrow$$
$$DWL \uparrow \;\Rightarrow\; TR^s \uparrow$$
$$(OS - OU - Cur) \uparrow \;\Rightarrow\; TR^s \uparrow$$
$$OS \uparrow \;\Rightarrow\; TR^s \uparrow$$
$$OU \uparrow \;\Rightarrow\; TR^s \downarrow$$
$$Cur \uparrow \;\Rightarrow\; TR^s \downarrow$$

chase or a sale of government securities, the Fed increases or decreases, respectively, the level of total reserves. The Federal Reserve's portfolio of securities is the one factor under the Fed's complete control because the Fed initiates open market operations.

The next factor, discount window loans, is also associated with Federal Reserve policy. When the Fed makes more loans to depository institutions through the discount window, the borrowed component of total reserves increases, and when the Fed makes fewer loans, the borrowed component decreases. The Fed exercises control over discount window loans both through its control of the discount rate and through its administrative control of such loans. Nevertheless, discount window loans are not under the complete control of the Fed because depository institutions initiate the action to borrow from the Fed.

The last category, the **net technical factors affecting reserves**, consists of the other sources of reserves minus the other uses of reserves, minus currency in circulation. These net technical factors affecting reserves are the technical, or noncontrolled, factors affecting reserves. Other things equal, an increase in the net technical factors raises total reserves, and a decrease in the net technical factors lowers total reserves. Thus, for example, if currency in circulation rises, the net technical factors go down and reserves go down. Table 14–4 sums up these relations by listing the types of factors affecting total reserves and showing how a change in each of these factors affects reserves.

Finally, we can derive an equation for the supply of nonborrowed reserves (*NBR*) by subtracting the level of discount window loans from both sides of Equation 14–2. Discount window loans are the source of borrowed reserves, and total reserves minus borrowed reserves are equal to nonborrowed reserves.

$$NBR = B_F + (OS - OU - Cur) \tag{14–3}$$

According to Equation 14–3, nonborrowed reserves are the sum of two items: the Fed's portfolio of securities, B_F; and the net technical factors, $(OS - OU - Cur)$. In Try It Out 14.1 in the next section, you will use actual accounts to illustrate this equation numerically.

An Actual
Statement: The
H.4.1 Statistical
Release

Every Thursday afternoon, the Fed publishes a complete accounting statement of the *actual* magnitudes of all of the factors affecting reserves on a weekly basis. The statistical release is entitled "Factors Affecting Reserves of Depository Institutions and Condition Statement of Federal Reserve Banks." The Fed staff and Fedwatchers refer to the release as "the H.4.1," after the Fed's identification code of the release. The

H.4.1 reports the average level of all the factors affecting reserves for the week ending the Wednesday before the release. It also reports the changes in these factors from one week earlier, two weeks earlier, and a year earlier. The key accounting statement from the release is published in *The Wall Street Journal* on Friday under the heading "Federal Reserve Data."

Table 14–5 reproduces the first page of the H.4.1 release of May 26, 1994. The only modification is that the categories are numbered 1 through 5. The numbers will help you compare the entries in the H.4.1 with the corresponding entries in the aggregated statement in Table 14–2.

Entries 1 through 3 are the factors supplying reserves. All the items under entry 1 make up the Fed's portfolio of securities. This includes U.S. government securities and federal agency securities bought outright and under repurchase agreements. Entry 2 is total discount window loans, composed of adjustment credit, seasonal credit, and extended credit.

The items under entry 3, that is, (*a*) through (*e*), are other sources of reserves. Entry 4, in contrast, consists of the factors absorbing reserves: Item (4*a*) is currency in circulation and (4*b*), (4*c*), and (4*d*) are the other uses of reserves. The remaining item is entry 5, reserve balances with the Fed.[5] By working through the Try It Out exercise, you can put the numbers in Table 14–5 in the form of the aggregated sources and uses of reserves statement in Table 14–2 to gain an appreciation of the magnitude of each of the categories.

TRY IT OUT 14.1

1. Use the numbers from the first column of the H.4.1 in Table 14–5 to fill in the blanks in the aggregate sources and uses of reserves statement below.

Sources and Uses of Reserves: *Week Ended May 26, 1994 (millions of dollars)*

Sources of Reserves	Uses of Reserves
(1) Federal Reserve portfolio of securities ____	(4) Currency in circulation + Other uses of reserves _____
(2) Discount window loans _____	(5) Total reserve balances with the Fed _____
(3) Other sources of reserves _____	

2. Find the magnitude of the net technical factors affecting reserves. Is it larger or smaller than the size of the Fed's portfolio of securities?
3. Use your answers to *1* and *2* to illustrate numerically Equation 14–3 for the supply of nonborrowed reserves.

---

[5] The H.4.1 reports total reserve balances with the Fed—as reflected in the title of the release—instead of total reserves. Under its present accounting procedures, the Fed does not add current vault cash to current reserve balances with the Fed to determine the current level of total reserves. Instead, the Fed treats current vault cash as part of currency in circulation; it adds lagged vault cash, that is, vault cash held two weeks earlier, to current reserve balances to determine total reserves.

TABLE 14–5   The H.4.1 Statistical Release

FEDERAL RESERVE

These data are scheduled for release each Thursday. The exact time of each release will be announced, when the information is available, on (202) 452-3206.

H.4.1

Factors Affecting Reserve Balances of Depository Institutions and Condition Statement of F.R. Banks

May 26, 1994

Millions of dollars

Reserve balances of depository institutions at F.R. Banks, Reserve Bank credit, and related items	Averages of daily figures			Wednesday May 25, 1994
	Week ended May 25, 1994	Change from week ended		
		May 18, 1994	May 26, 1993	
Reserve Bank credit[1][2] *(Sum of 1, 2, 3a, and 3b)*	382,516	+ 249	+ 33,650	383,834
1. U.S. government securities				
Bought outright--system account	344,147	+ 729	+ 38,200	346,899
Held under repurchase agreements	1,716	+ 267	- 3,970	375
Federal agency obligations				
Bought outright	4,016	- 6	- 1,068	3,977
Held under repurchase agreements	942	+ 806	+ 552	725
Acceptances	0	0	0	0
2. Loans to depository institutions				
Adjustment credit	30	- 91	+ 10	35
Seasonal credit	148	+ 15	+ 55	165
Extended credit	0	0	0	0
3. a. Float	17	- 425	- 144	37
b. Other F.R. assets	31,500	- 1,045	+ 15	31,622
c. Gold stock	11,052	0	- 2	11,053
d. Special drawing rights certificate account	8,018	0	0	8,018
e. Treasury currency outstanding	22,400	+ 14	+ 737	22,400
Total factors supplying reserve funds	423,986	+ 263	+ 34,385	425,304
4. a. Currency in circulation*	374,016	- 16	+ 35,422	375,694
b. Treasury cash holdings*	373	- 2	- 115	361
c. Deposits, other than reserve balances, with F.R. Banks				
Treasury	5,287	- 711	- 823	5,594
Foreign	215	+ 10	+ 19	222
Service-related balances and adjustments[3]	6,017	- 44	- 307	6,017
Other	282	- 36	- 30	297
d. Other F.R. liabilities and capital	10,489	+ 49	+ 1,222	10,291
Total factors, other than reserve balances, absorbing reserve funds	396,678	- 750	+ 35,388	398,475
5. Reserve balances with F.R. Banks[4]	27,308	+ 1,013	- 1,003	26,829

On   May 25, 1994, marketable U.S. government securities held in custody by the Federal Reserve Banks for foreign official and international accounts were $ 365,291 million, a change of + $ 1,306 million for the week.
1 Net of $ 6,152 million, daily average, matched sale-purchase transactions outstanding during the latest statement week, of which a net of $ 6,152 million was with foreign official and international accounts. Includes securities loaned--fully secured by U.S. government securities.
2 Net of $ 3,569 million matched sale-purchase transactions outstanding at the end of the latest statement week, of which a net of $ 3,569 million was with foreign official and international accounts. Includes $ 475 million securities loaned--fully secured U.S. government securities.
3 Consists of required clearing balances of $ 5,917 million and adjustments of $ 100 million to compensate for float.
4 Excludes required clearing balances and adjustments to compensate for float.

* Estimated (Treasury's figures).
Components may not add to totals due to rounding.

The Individual Technical Factors

Now that we have examined the sources and uses of reserves statement, we can turn to the individual technical factors affecting reserves. Equation 14–4 identifies the components of the net technical factors affecting reserves from the H.4.1:

$$\text{Net technical factors} = \left(\begin{array}{c} \text{Other sources} \\ \text{of reserves} \end{array}\right) - \left(\begin{array}{c} \text{Currency in circulation +} \\ \text{Other uses of reserves} \end{array}\right) \quad (14\text{--}4)$$

$$\left(\begin{array}{c}\text{Net technical} \\ \text{factors}\end{array}\right) = \left\{\begin{array}{l}\text{Float} \\ + \\ \text{Gold stock} \\ + \\ \text{SDR certificates} \\ + \\ \text{U.S. Treasury currency} \\ \text{outstanding} \\ + \\ \text{Other (miscellaneous)} \\ \text{F. R. assets}\end{array}\right\} - \left\{\begin{array}{l}\text{Currency in circulation} \\ + \\ \text{U.S. Treasury} \\ \text{cash holdings} \\ + \\ \text{Deposits with Fed} \\ \text{other than reserve} \\ \text{balances} \\ + \\ \text{Other F. R. liabilities} \\ \text{and capital accounts}\end{array}\right\}$$

As we explain each factor, keep in mind one basic principle: *Other things equal, an increase in any of the other sources of reserves increases nonborrowed and total reserve balances with the Fed; on the other hand, other things equal, an increase in currency in circulation or in any of the other uses of reserves decreases nonborrowed and total reserve balances with the Fed.* We begin with currency in circulation, the factor most familiar to us from previous discussion and personal experience.

Currency in Circulation   Currency in circulation consists of all the paper currency and coins held by the public. Most of the paper currency is Federal Reserve notes, which are liabilities of the Fed, though a small amount of paper currency and all coins are liabilities of the U.S. Treasury. Currency is a use of reserves. For example, at Christmas time, when people need more currency, they write checks against their deposit accounts, and reserves in the banking system fall by an equal amount. After Christmas, when the need for currency falls, the public deposits the currency back in its bank accounts, and reserves rise.

We saw in Table 14–5 that currency in circulation is by far the largest technical factor affecting reserves. Figure 14–1 shows that currency in circulation trends upward over the long run. The reason is the higher the level of economic activity, the greater the demand for currency.

Treasury Cash Holdings   Not all currency outside of bank vaults is held by the public. Some is held by the U.S. Treasury and appears on the "uses" side of the H.4.1. Suppose that the U.S. Treasury were to reduce its cash holdings by making a payment of $500 to a private citizen. Five hundred dollars moves out of the vaults of the U.S. Treasury into the hands of the public. In this way it becomes a part of currency in circulation; currency held by the U.S. Treasury has fallen and currency in circulation has increased. Next, suppose that the individual who receives the $500 from the U.S. Treasury does not want to hold any more currency. He therefore deposits the currency in his

FIGURE 14–1
Currency in
Circulation

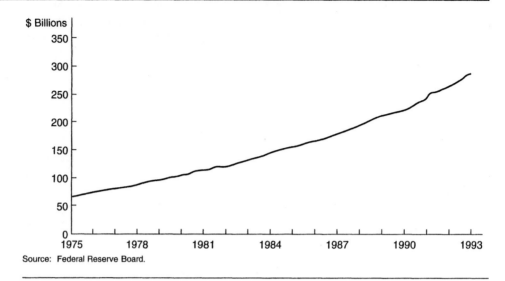

Source: Federal Reserve Board.

bank account. As a result, currency in circulation returns to its original level, and reserves in the banking system rise by $500.

The U.S. Treasury, of course, does not pay for most government expenditures in cash. Instead, it pays with checks drawn on its account with the Fed, which takes us to the next factor affecting reserves.

Deposits with the Fed Other Than Reserve Balances   Depository institutions are not the only institutions that have accounts with the Fed. Other accounts include *general accounts of the U.S. Treasury,* from which it makes payments for goods and services purchased by the federal government; *foreign official accounts* held by foreign central banks and governments and used for international settlements; *service-related balances* of small banks that satisfy reserve requirements out of vault cash and therefore hold theses accounts for check clearing; and *"other" accounts*, which include those of international agencies such as the World Bank and accounts of U.S. government agencies. Other things equal, a decrease in any of these accounts increases reserve balances with the Fed.

Suppose, for example, that the Treasury writes checks on its general accounts with the Fed for a total of $1 million to pay for repairs to interstate highways nationwide. The construction companies across the country that receive these checks deposit them with their local banks, which, in turn, present the checks to the Fed for collection. The end result is that the reserve accounts of banks increase by $1 million and the general account of the U.S. Treasury decreases by $1 million.

On the other hand, the U.S. Treasury can also build up its accounts with the Fed in anticipation of expenditures. The Treasury initially deposits tax receipts and proceeds from the sale of U.S. government securities into "tax and loan" accounts with commercial banks. However, the Treasury makes payments for federal expenditures from its general accounts with the Fed. The Treasury can build up its accounts with the Fed by $1 million by reducing its tax and loan accounts by that amount. In this case, the Fed reduces the reserve accounts of the depository institutions that lose the Treasury accounts by $1 million and increases the Treasury's accounts by $1 million.

Other Federal Reserve Liabilities and Capital Accounts   The last item on the "uses" side includes all other liabilities of the Fed and its net worth.

Now that we have examined "currency in circulation" and "other uses of reserves" from Equation 14–4, we turn to the other term of that equation, "other sources of reserves."

Float   Federal Reserve **float** is a temporary source of reserves created when the check collection process takes longer than the time set by the Fed for crediting the reserve account of the bank presenting the check for collection. As Chapter 12 discusses, when a commercial bank sends a check to its reserve bank for collection, the reserve bank does not necessarily credit the reserve account of the receiving bank immediately. The Fed has a schedule by which it automatically credits the accounts of receiving banks. The schedule is based on normal amounts of time for out-of-town checks to be processed and sent to the paying bank. The maximum amount of time allowed for the completion of the check collection process is two days. On the other hand, the Fed does not actually debit the reserve account of the paying bank until it completes the check collection process. If this takes longer than the prearranged time, there is a permissible double-counting of reserves reflected in the creation of Federal Reserve float. Float and the corresponding reserve balances automatically disappear when the Fed completes the check collection process.

Historically, float has been one of the most volatile technical factors affecting reserves. Figure 14–2 shows that the level and volatility of float decreased after 1980. The Monetary Control Act of 1980 required the Fed to begin levying service charges for float. The pricing of float (begun in 1983) and the use of alternative check-clearing services by depository institutions were responsible for the reduction in float.

Gold Stock   The U.S. gold stock is an asset of the U.S. Treasury. Most of the gold stock, however, has been "monetized." Monetizing gold means the U.S. Treasury issues warehouse receipts, called **gold certificates,** to the Fed and receives in exchange deposits with the Fed. These certificates are one of the "other assets" in the Fed's balance sheet, and the deposits are one of the "other liabilities." No change in reserves results from monetizing the gold stock because the Fed's "other assets" and "other liabilities" increase by equal amounts. Subsequent expenditures from the Treasury's account, however, do increase reserve balances, precisely in the manner explained earlier for any decrease in Treasury deposits with the Fed.

A small amount of the gold stock has not been monetized by the Treasury and, therefore, does not appear in the Fed's balance sheet. It is a potential source of reserves, however, because it can be monetized. Unmonetized gold is one of the two items added

FIGURE 14–2
Federal Reserve
Float

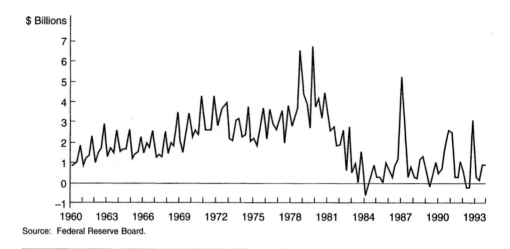

Source: Federal Reserve Board.

to both sides of the Fed's balance sheet to get the sources and uses of reserves statement. It appears on the "sources" side as a part of the gold stock. On the "uses" side, unmonetized gold is included in Treasury cash holdings.

Special Drawing Rights   **Special drawing rights (SDRs)** are sometimes called *paper gold.* They are international monetary reserves created by the International Monetary Fund and allocated to fund members according to specific quotas. They can be used to settle debts to other nations or to the IMF. In the United States the SDRs are allocated to the Treasury for its exchange stabilization fund. Like gold certificates, special drawing rights certificates enter the Fed's balance sheet because of institutional arrangements between the Fed and the Treasury. When the Treasury monetizes special drawing rights, as it does occasionally, it issues to the Fed special drawing rights certificates, which appear on the asset side on the Fed's balance sheet. The Fed, in turn, increases its liabilities by an equal amount with a credit to the deposit accounts of the Treasury. As with the monetization of gold, the monetization of SDRs by itself does not change reserve balances. When the Treasury spends the funds in its accounts, however, reserve balances with the Fed rise.

U.S. Treasury Currency Outstanding   U.S. Treasury currency and coin outstanding consists of coins and paper currency issued by the Treasury and held by the Fed, by the public, by banks, or by the Treasury itself. Only the amount held by the Fed in its vaults appears in the Fed's balance sheet—as an asset, of course. Treasury currency and coin held by the public, banks, and the Treasury is the second small item that we add to both sides of the Fed's balance sheet to derive the complete sources and uses statement. Treasury currency and coin outstanding is a potential source of reserves. Some will be held in bank vaults and therefore actually be used as reserves. Some, however finds its way into competing uses, as currency in circulation or Treasury cash holdings. Other things equal, when Treasury currency and coin outstanding increases, reserves rise, and when currency and coin decrease, reserves decrease.

Other (Miscellaneous) Federal Reserve Assets   The remaining item is miscellaneous Federal Reserve assets not included elsewhere. They consist of the value of the Federal Reserve bank properties, interest accrued on the Fed's portfolio of securities, and holdings of foreign currency.

LOOKING AHEAD

Reserves are the raw material out of which money is created. Now that we know all the factors that affect reserves in the banking system, we move to the next step, which is to explain the mechanics of deposit creation and the money supply process.

SUMMARY

- The Trading Desk of the Federal Reserve Bank of New York prepares the Fed's daily game plan for open market operations based on the instructions in the directive about the desired degree of reserve pressure and the associated target for the federal funds rate. No matter what the operating target of the Fed, the Desk must make a plan for nonborrowed reserves.

- Both the Fed's portfolio of government securities and the technical factors affecting reserves supply nonborrowed reserves to the banking system. The Fed controls its portfolio of securities through open market operations. The Fed, however, does not control the technical factors.

- The change in nonborrowed reserves equals the size of open market operations plus the change in the net technical factors affecting reserves.

- Economists at the Board and at the Desk provide the Desk with forecasts of changes in the technical factors affecting reserves.

- Defensive open market operations are purchases or sales of government securities by the Desk to offset expected changes in the technical factors. Dynamic open market operations are purchases or sales of government securities to change the quantity of nonborrowed reserves in the banking system.

- In 1994, the Fed initiated the practice of announcing changes in the desired degree of reserve pressure and, thus, in its target for the federal funds rate, rather than signaling these changes through large financial institutions whose Fedwatchers made their own forecasts of the tech-

nical factors affecting reserves to detect shifts in the stance of monetary policy.

- If the need for reserves by banks is unchanged, an increase in the supply of reserves reduces the degree of reserve pressure.

- A sources and uses of reserves statement is an accounting statement of the factors supplying reserves and the factors absorbing reserves. It is the balance sheet of the Fed augmented by those monetary accounts of the Treasury that are not included in the Fed's balance sheet. The Fed publishes a weekly sources and uses of reserves statement every Thursday afternoon in its H.4.1 statistical release.

- From the H.4.1. we obtain a complete list of the technical factors affecting reserves. The technical factors supplying reserves, called *other sources of reserves,* are float, the gold stock, special drawing rights certificates, Treasury currency outstanding, and miscellaneous Federal Reserve assets. Other things equal, an increase in any one of the other sources of reserves increases reserve balances with the Fed, and a decrease in one of the other sources decreases reserve balances.

- The technical factors absorbing reserves, called *other uses of reserves,* are currency in circulation, Treasury cash holdings, deposits with the Fed other than reserve balances, and other Federal Reserve liabilities and capital accounts. Other things equal, an increase in any one of the other uses of reserves decreases reserve balances with the Fed, and a decrease in one of the other uses increases reserve balances.

KEY TERMS AND CONCEPTS

Trading Desk, or Desk

primary dealers

degree of reserve pressure

Federal Reserve repurchase
 agreement

matched sale-purchase transaction

dynamic open market operations

defensive open market operations

sources and uses of reserves
 statement

net technical factors affecting
 reserves

float

gold certificates

special drawing rights

QUESTIONS AND PROBLEMS

1. Explain the relation between the concept of the "degree of reserve pressure" that the Federal Reserve refers to in its domestic policy directive and the federal funds rate.

2. Explain the difference between defensive and dynamic open market operations.

3. Suppose that at 11:45 AM Eastern time today the Trading Desk buys securities in the open market. Could this be consistent with a plan by the Fed to reduce nonborrowed reserves in the banking system? Explain why or why not.

4. Explain the relation between the Fed's balance sheet and a sources and uses of reserves statement.

5. *a.* Use a simplified sources and uses of reserves statement to derive an equation for the supply of total reserves.
   b. By definition, the supply of the total monetary base is the sum of currency in circulation and the supply of total reserves. Use your answer to (*a*) to derive an equation for the supply of the total monetary base.

6. Suppose that the public wants to hold more currency and fewer bank deposits. Will there be an effect on the supply of the total monetary base? Explain your answer.

The Wall Street Journal

7. Every Friday *The Wall Street Journal* publishes data from the H.4.1. statistical release on the sources and uses of reserves. This set of data appears in the weekly table of "Federal Reserve Data" under the title "Member Bank Reserve Changes." The following data are from the table in the October 29, 1993, issue. Use the data in the first column to do the following:

FEDERAL RESERVE DATA

MEMBER BANK RESERVE CHANGES

Changes in weekly averages of reserves and related items during the week and year ended October 27, 1993 were as follows (in millions of dollars)

	Oct. 27, 1993	Chg fm wk end Oct. 20, 1993	Oct. 28, 1992
Reserve bank credit:			
U.S. Gov't securities:			
Bought outright	321,263	+ 697	+ 39,357
Held under repurch agreemt	2,621	− 1,074	+ 1,475
Federal agency issues:			
Bought outright	4,754	− 41	− 780
Held under repurch agreemt	323	− 212	+ 245
Acceptances			
Borrowings from Fed:			
Adjustment credit	12	− 6	− 25
Seasonal borrowings	176	− 26	+ 90
Extended credit	....	....	
Float	630	+ 63	+ 627
Other Federal Reserve Assets	33,612	+ 49	+ 1,546
Total Reserve Bank Credit	363,391	− 550	+ 42,536
Gold Stock	11,056	.... −	4
SDR certificates	8,018	.... −	2,000
Treasury currency			
outstanding	21,920	+ 14	+ 549
Total	404,384	− 536	+ 41,082
Currency in circulation	352,894	− 1,190	+ 32,953
Treasury cash holdings	383	− 4	− 126
Treasury dpts with F.R. Bnks	5,130	− 625	− 61
Foreign dpts with F.R. Bnks	406	+ 135	+ 4
Other dpts with F.R. Bnks	268	− 35	+ 3

a. Find the magnitude of the other sources of reserves.

b. Find the magnitude of the other uses of reserves.

c. Find the magnitude of the net technical factors affecting reserves. Which technical factor is the largest?

d. Find the magnitude of reserve balances with the Fed.

The Wall Street Journal

8. Use the data in the second column of the table in Question 7 to do the following:
   a. Find the change in reserve balances between October 20, 1993, and October 27, 1993.
   b. Compare the size of the change in government securities with the size of the change in the net technical factors.

9. Explain the difference between an outright sale of Treasury bills by the Fed and a matched sale-purchase transaction.

10. Suppose that the Federal Reserve sells Japanese yen in the foreign exchange market to try to push down the value of the yen. What will be the effect on the supply of total reserves in the United States?

11. Suppose that because of a winter storm checks drawn on Illinois banks and presented to the Federal Reserve Bank of New York for collection do not reach the Federal Reserve Bank of Chicago until four days after being received by the New York Fed. What will be the effect on the supply of reserves? How can the Fed offset this effect?

12. Do you think that it is common for the Fed to sell Treasury securities in the open market after Christmas? Explain.

13. Explain how monetizing gold affects the U.S. Treasury's deposits with the Fed.

SUGGESTED READINGS

Board of Governors of the Federal Reserve System. *The Federal Reserve System: Purposes and Functions.* Washington, D.C., 1984, Chapter 5.
   A detailed explanation of the Fed's balance sheet and the sources and uses of reserves statement.
Jones, David. *The Politics of Money: The Fed under Alan Greenspan.* New York: New York Institute of Finance, 1991, Chapter 5, 103–10.

An assessment of the Thanksgiving 1989 blunder by Fedwatchers.
Meulendyke, Ann-Marie. *U.S. Monetary Policy and Financial Markets.* New York: Federal Reserve Bank of New York, 1989, Chapters 6 and 7, 124–77.
   An inside view of the operations of the Trading Desk.

CHAPTER 15

DEPOSIT CREATION AND THE MONEY SUPPLY

CHAPTER PREVIEW

If you ask a banker to explain the banking business, he will say that banks attract deposits, which they use to make loans. The more deposits they attract, the more loans they can make. Thus, the banker's view is that deposits create loans. If, on the other hand, you ask an economist about the relation of deposits to loans, she will explain the economist's view that loans create deposits. Who is right, the banker or the economist? This chapter will show that both are right.

If it is true that bankers create deposits, does it not follow that banks can increase or decrease the quantity of money at will? The answer is no. Banks can increase checkable deposits only if more reserves are injected into the financial system. If no new reserves enter the system, banks merely reshuffle existing deposits. What one bank gains in deposited funds, another bank loses as withdrawn funds.

To explain these issues, this chapter begins by tracing the additions to deposits that the Fed engineers when it injects new reserves into the system through an open market purchase of securities, described in Chapter 14. We shall see that successive additions to deposits become smaller and smaller, but when the process ends, the sum of these additions is a multiple of the original injections.

Next, this chapter links the multiple creation of deposits to the money supply equations derived in Chapter 8, and examines all the factors that affect the narrow and broad measures of money. Then we connect theory with practice to explain the robust growth of M1 and the meager growth of M2 in the early 1990s.

THE BOUNCING BALL OF DEPOSIT CREATION

We can envision the process of deposit creation in the U.S. banking system as a bouncing ball. Figure 15–1 shows that the Fed sets the ball in motion with the purchase of $1,000 million of securities. Suppose the Fed buys these securities from a nonbank security dealer, who deposits the check from the Fed in its bank, Bank A. This is the first and highest bounce of the ball. Bank A has $1,000 million of new deposits and $1,000 million of reserves. Where did the reserves come from? The Fed created them to pay for the securities it bought from the dealer.

With a reserve requirement ratio of 10 percent on checking accounts, Bank A needs to hold $100 million of additional required reserves. The remaining $900 million of reserves are excess reserves. Let's assume that Bank A does not want to hold additional excess reserves. Bank A runs down these **unwanted excess reserves** by making $900 million of new loans, say, to real estate developers, home owners, small businesses, and college students. [Note that $900 = (1 - rr) \times \Delta B_F = (1 - 0.10) \times 1,000$.] In making these loans, the bank credits the checking accounts of the borrowers by the amount of the loan. Thus, deposits rise by an additional $900 million.

Of course, Bank A's customers did not borrow to keep the money sitting in their checking accounts. They borrowed to spend it! The ball bounces a second time as these borrowers write checks on their accounts with Bank A, and the recipients deposit the checks in their banks, say, Group B banks. Group B banks take in $900 million of new deposits through check clearing, so the second bounce is not quite as high as the first one.

Group B banks also have $900 million of additional reserves because check clearing transfers deposits and an equal amount of reserves. However, Group B banks need to hold only $90 million of required reserves, so they have $810 million of excess reserves, which we assume are all unwanted. Therefore, they make $810 million of loans and create $810 million of deposits. Note that $810 = (1 - rr) \times (1 - rr) \times \Delta B_F$.

The ball bounces a third time as the borrowers from Group B banks write checks against their deposits and the recipients deposit the checks in their banks, Group C banks.

FIGURE 15–1
The Bouncing Ball of Deposit Creation

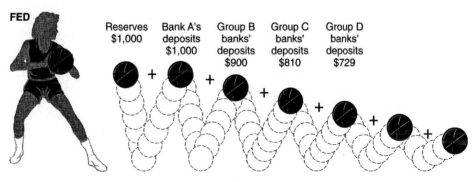

Cumulative increase in deposits: $1,000 + $900 + $810 + 729 + . . . = $10,000
Reserve requirement ratio: rr = .10

How high is this third bounce? $810 million. And what will Group C banks do? They will hold $81 million of required reserves and lend the remaining $729 million.

The ball keeps bouncing until banks wring all the unwanted excess reserves out of the system by making loans and creating deposits. When the ball stops bouncing, $10,000 million of additional deposits will be in the banking system:

$$1,000 + 900 + 810 + 729 + \ldots = 10,000 \tag{15-1}$$

The first term in Equation 15–1 is the deposits that Bank A acquired when the dealer deposited the receipts of the sale of $1,000 million securities to the Fed. That is, the first term is the amount of securities that the Fed added to its portfolio, ΔB_F. The second term is the deposits that Group B banks acquired, which equal the loans that Bank A made: $(1 - rr) \times \Delta B_F = 0.9 \times 1,000 = 900$. The third term is the deposits acquired by Group C banks, which equal the loans made by Group B banks: $(1 - rr)(1 - rr) \times \Delta B_F = 0.9 \times 0.9 \times 1,000 = 810$. Similarly, the fourth term is the deposits acquired by Group D banks, $(1 - rr)^3 \times \Delta B_F$, and so on. Adding up the terms, we have the change in deposits:

$$\Delta D = \Delta B_F + (1 - rr)\Delta B_F + (1 - rr)^2 \Delta B_F + (1 - rr)^3 \Delta B_F + \ldots$$
$$\Delta D = (1/rr)\Delta B_F^1 \tag{15-2}$$

According to Equation 15–2, the change in deposits equals the simple deposits multiplier times the change in the Fed's portfolio of securities, other things equal. The other things held equal here are all the other factors that affect the volume of deposits that can be supported by reserves: the interest rate, the discount rate, the attitudes of bankers about excess reserves and borrowed reserves, and the net technical factors affecting reserves.

OPEN MARKET OPERATIONS AND MULTIPLE DEPOSIT CREATION

The metaphor of the bouncing ball introduces the process of **multiple deposit creation.** To explain the process more fully, let's look at the changes that take place in the balance sheets of the Fed and banks.

Table 15–1 depicts the initial simplified balance sheet, or the T-account, of Bank A. It shows that Bank A has $20,000 million of deposits and $2,000 million of reserves, all of which are required reserves (*RR*).

---

[1] We can derive this result as follows:

 (1) $\Delta D = \Delta B_F + (1 - rr)\Delta B_F + (1 - rr)^2 \Delta B_F + (1 - rr)^3 \Delta B_F + \ldots$

Multiply both sides of (1) by $(1 - rr)$ to get:

 (2) $(1 - rr)\Delta D = (1 - rr)\Delta B_F + (1 - rr)^2 \Delta B_F + (1 - rr)^3 \Delta B_F + \ldots$

Subtracting each side of (2) from the corresponding side of (1), and canceling terms, we get:

 $\Delta D - (1 - rr)\Delta D = \Delta B_F$

Finally, collecting terms and solving, we have:

 $\Delta D = (1/rr)\Delta B_F$

TABLE 15–1
Initial Balance Sheet of Bank A: *In Millions of Dollars*

Assets		Liabilities plus Net Worth	
Reserves	2,000	Deposits	20,000
Loans and investments	19,000	Loans from Fed	0
		Net worth	1,000
Memo:			
$rr = 0.10$			
$RR = 2,000$			
$ER = 0$			
Total assets	21,000	Total liabilities + Net worth	21,000

TABLE 15–2
An Open Market Purchase of Securities: *The Changes in the Balance Sheets of the Participants (in Millions of Dollars)*

Federal Reserve System

Assets		Liabilities	
U.S. Treasury securities	+1,000	Reserves (Bank A)	+1,000

Security Dealer

Assets		Liabilities	
Securities	−1,000		
Deposits	+1,000		

Bank A

Assets		Liabilities	
Reserve balances with Fed	+1,000	(Dealer's) deposits	+1,000
Memo:			
$RR = +100$			
$ER = +900$			

Step 1: An Open Market Purchase of Securities

Next, the Trading Desk enters the market and buys $1,000 million of securities from a dealer, who deposits the check from the Fed in Bank A. (Of course, Bank A actually represents many banks in the real world because the Desk purchases government securities from many dealers.) Table 15–2 shows the initial changes in the T-accounts of all participants in the open market operation.

The balance sheet of the Fed records a $1,000 million increase in its holdings of T-bills and a $1,000 million increase in reserves provided to the banking system. The balance sheet of the dealer records a reallocation of funds on the asset side: a $1,000 million reduction in holdings of T-bills and an equal increase in deposits at Bank A. Similarly, the balance sheet of Bank A records an increase of $1,000 million in deposits matched by an equal increase in reserves. With an increase in deposits of $1,000 million,

TABLE 15-3
Balance Sheet of
Bank A after Open
Market Operation:
*In Millions of
Dollars*

Assets		Liabilities plus Net Worth	
Reserves	3,000	Deposits	21,000
Loans and investments	19,000	Loans from Fed	0
Memo:			
$rr = 0.10$		Net worth	1,000
$RR = 2,100$			
$ER = 900$			
Total assets	22,000	Total liabilities + Net worth	22,000

TABLE 15-4
An Increase in
Loans and Loan-
Generated Deposits
by Bank A: *In
Millions of Dollars*

Assets		Liabilities	
Loans and investments	+900	Deposits	+900
Memo:			
$RR = +90$			
$ER = -90$			

the required reserves of Bank A increase by only $100 million. The remaining $900 million of reserves are unwanted excess reserves.

Step 2: Bank A   Table 15–2 records only the *changes* in the balance sheets. In Table 15–3, however, we show the complete balance sheet of Bank A after the open market operation. Bank A now has $3,000 million of reserves, of which $2,100 million are required reserves and $900 million are excess reserves. We assume, though, that Bank A does not want to hold any excess reserves.

To wring out its unwanted excess reserves, Bank A makes loans and investments. In making new loans and in buying open market securities such as T-bills, the bank creates deposits, called **loan-generated deposits**.

When banks make more loans to the public, they open checking accounts for the borrowers or credit an existing account by the amount of the loan. Alternatively, the bank may buy securities from the public or dealers, again crediting their deposit accounts. In this way Bank A creates $900 million of additional deposits. Table 15–4 shows the *changes* in Bank A's balance sheet as a result of loan expansion: Loans and investments increase by $900 million, and deposits increase by the same amount.

In a system of thousands of independent depository institutions, Bank A can expect to lose its loan-generated deposits to other banks when the depositors write checks on these accounts with Bank A and the recipients deposit them with other banks. Because we are interested only in the collective behavior of the receiving banks, we simply identify them

TABLE 15–5
Deposits and
Reserves Lost by
Bank A in Check
Clearing with
Group B Banks: *In
Millions of Dollars*

Assets		Liabilities	
Reserves	–900	Deposits	–900
Memo:			
RR = –90			
ER = –810			

TABLE 15–6
Bank A's Balance
Sheet after Loan
Expansion and
Check Clearing: *In
Millions of Dollars*

Assets		Liabilities and Net Worth	
Reserves	2,100	Deposits	21,000
Loans and investments	19,900	Loans from Fed	0
		Net worth	1,000
Memo:			
RR = 2,100			
ER = 0			
Total assets	22,000	Total liabilities + Net worth	22,000

as Group B banks. Of course, Bank A itself can be one of the Group B banks. The recipients of checks written on Bank A may redeposit them in Bank A, or the borrowers from Bank A may not run down their deposits by the full $900 million. This does not affect the outcome, because all banks behave the same way in our simple scenario.

Once the recipients deposit the $900 million of checks written on Bank A into their accounts at Group B banks, the check-clearing process begins. As Chapter 12 notes, check clearing is one of the services provided by the Fed. The reserve accounts that banks have with the Fed are used for interbank settlements. In transferring reserves from one account to the other, the Fed is acting only as a bookkeeper.

The Fed credits (increases) the reserve accounts of Group B banks, the receiving banks, $900 million, and it debits (decreases) the reserve account of Bank A, the paying bank, $900 million. Correspondingly, Bank A debits (reduces) the accounts of its depositors $900 million, and Group B banks credit (increase) the accounts of their depositors by $900 million. Table 15–5 shows the changes in the balance sheet of Bank A as a result of check clearing with Group B banks.

Table 15–6 shows the balance sheet of Bank A after loan expansion and after check clearing with Group B banks. Bank A has $2,100 million of reserves, which are just sufficient to cover reserve requirements against its deposit accounts of $21,000 million.

Compared with its initial balance sheet in Table 15–1, Bank A's deposits have increased by $1,000 million, which is the amount received by the security dealer from the sale of securities to the Trading Desk. On the asset side, reserve balances of Bank A have risen by $100 million; loans and investments have risen by $900 million.

TABLE 15–7
Reserves and
Deposits Received
by Group B Banks
in Check Clearing
with Bank A: *In
Millions of Dollars*

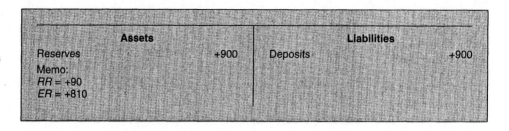

Assets		Liabilities	
Reserves	+900	Deposits	+900
Memo:			
$RR = +90$			
$ER = +810$			

TABLE 15–8
The Increase in
Loans and In
Loan-Generated
Deposits by Group
B Banks: *In
Millions of Dollars*

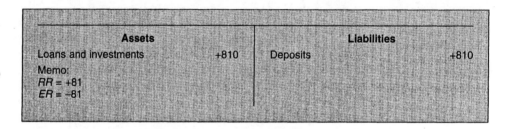

Assets		Liabilities	
Loans and investments	+810	Deposits	+810
Memo:			
$RR = +81$			
$ER = -81$			

**Step 3: Group
B Banks**

From here on, we shall examine only *changes* in the balance sheets of banks. Table 15–7 shows the changes in the balance sheet of Group B banks that result from check clearing with Bank A. Check clearing does not destroy any deposits; they become deposits with other banks.

Of the $900 million of reserves that it lost, Bank A was using $90 million to satisfy reserve requirements. The remaining $810 million were unwanted excess reserve balances. Of the $900 million of reserves that they gain, Group B banks must keep $90 million to satisfy reserve requirements against the $900 million of deposits transferred from Bank A. The remaining $810 million of reserves are unwanted excess reserve balances. Hence, check clearing transfers the unwanted excess reserves to Group B banks.

Group B banks now increase their loans and investments by the amount of the increase in their excess reserve balances, that is, by $810 million. They also increase their loan-generated deposits by the same amount. Table 15–8 shows the changes in the aggregate balance sheet of Group B banks as a result of loan expansion.

By creating $810 million of deposits, Group B banks transform $81 million of excess reserves into required reserves. That leaves $729 million of unwanted excess reserves in the system: $810 million – $81 million. For the moment, these unwanted excess reserves reside in the reserve accounts of Group B banks. As in step 2, however, they will be transferred to other banks, along with $81 million of required reserves, when the borrowers from Group B banks write checks on their loan-generated deposits and when the recipients deposit the checks into their banks, Group C banks. Table 15–9 shows the changes in the balance sheet of Group B banks as a result of check clearing with Group C banks.

Finally, Table 15–10 shows the net change in the balance sheet of Group B banks after receiving deposits and reserves from Bank A, after increasing their loans and loan-generated deposits by the amount of their unwanted excess reserve balances, and after

TABLE 15–9
Reserves and
Deposits Lost by
Group B Banks in
Check Clearing
with Group C
Banks: *In Millions
of Dollars*

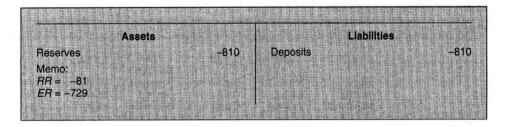

Assets		Liabilities	
Reserves	–810	Deposits	–810
Memo:			
RR = –81			
ER = –729			

TABLE 15–10
Net Change in the
Balance Sheet of
Group B Banks
after Loan
Expansion and
Check Clearing: *In
Millions of Dollars*

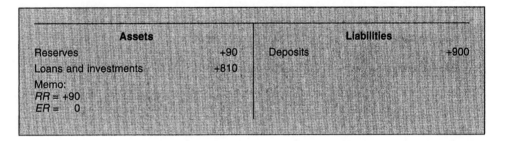

Assets		Liabilities	
Reserves	+90	Deposits	+900
Loans and investments	+810		
Memo:			
RR = +90			
ER = 0			

losing their loan-generated deposits and an equal amount of reserves to Group C banks. On the liability side of their balance sheet, deposit accounts are up $900 million, the amount of deposits that they received from Bank A in check clearing. On the asset side, the $900 million increase in assets is split between a $90 million increase in required reserves and an $810 million increase in loans and investments. As we know, Group B banks' loan-generated deposits and an equal amount of reserves have been lost to Group C banks in check clearing.

The Process at a Glance

Now that we have seen how the T-accounts change in each step, let's consolidate the results by putting all the steps in a table. Table 15–11 assigns each step in the deposit creation process a row. The column entries record the changes in reserves, loans, and deposits. The last row records the total effects, the end result of the process of deposit creation.

Step 1 is split in two to show the role of the Fed and Bank A in open market operations. The Fed starts the ball bouncing by purchasing $1,000 million of securities (column 1) from a nonbank security dealer with a deposit account at Bank A. This purchase of securities increases reserves (column 2) and deposits (column 3) at Bank A by $1,000 million.

In step 2, after setting aside $100 million for required reserves (column 4) against its new deposits, Bank A finds itself with $900 million of unwanted excess reserves (column 5). Bank A increases its loans and loan-generated deposits by $900 million (column 6). Finally, Bank A loses these deposits and an equal amount of reserves in check clearing (column 7) as borrowers spend the funds in their loan-generated deposit accounts. This takes us to step 3.

TABLE 15–11   The Multistep Process of Deposit Creation: *The Running Down of Unwanted Excess Reserves (in Millions of Dollars)*

	(1) Open Market Purchase	(2) Reserves Gained in Clearing	(3) Deposits Gained in Clearing	(4) Required Reserves against Deposits	(5) Unwanted Excess Reserves	(6) Loan- Generated Deposits	(7) Reserves and Deposits Transferred
Step 1							
Fed	1,000						
Bank A		1,000	1,000				
Step 2							
Bank A				100	900	900	900
Step 3							
Group B banks		900	900	90	810	810	810
Step 4							
Group C banks		810	810	81	729	729	729
•		•	•	•	•	•	•
•		•	•	•	•	•	•
•		•	•	•	•	•	•
Final step		•	•	•	0	0	0
Total	1,000		10,000	1,000	0	9,000	

* The format of this table is adapted from a similar table in Thomas M. Havrilesky and John T. Boorman, *Monetary Macroeconomics* (Arlington Heights, Ill.: AHM Publishing, 1978), 14. Our exposition of deposit creation has also benefited from the lucid presentation of Havrilesky and Boorman in Chapter 1, pp. 8–15.

Step 3 illustrates the banker's view that a bank takes in deposits and makes loans. The process begins for Group B banks when they take in $900 million of reserves (column 2) and deposits (column 3) from Bank A in check clearing. After setting aside $90 million for required reserves, they increase their loans and investments by $810 million. The $810 million stays in checking accounts at Group B banks only for a fleeting moment before being spent and transferred to Group C banks. That ends the process from the perspective of Group B bankers, but not from the economist's perspective.

To see the economist's view, we turn to the last row of the table, which records the cumulative changes. The first column shows that the open market operation injects $1,000 million of (nonborrowed) reserves into the banking system. The fourth and fifth columns show that banks ultimately use all the additional reserves as required reserves. All the unwanted excess reserves have been wrung out of the system, and banks now hold the level of excess reserves they want to hold, which is zero by assumption.

How many deposits have been created? According to column 6, loan-generated deposits increase by $9,000 million: The sum of $900 million + $810 million + $729 million + ... The total increase in deposits is $10,000 million: $1,000 million of deposits created by the open market operation itself and $9,000 million of loan-generated deposits.

TRY IT OUT 15.1

Explain why Bank A does not undertake by itself the entire multiple expansion in deposits by pumping up its deposits by 10 times its unwanted excess reserves.

Deposit Contraction

The multiplier process summarized in Table 15–11 works both ways: Deposits expand when the Fed buys Treasury securities and contract when the Fed sells Treasury securities. With a sale of $1,000 million of Treasury securities, the numbers would be the same, but the column headings would change to the following:

(1) Open Market Sale	(2) Reserves Lost in Clearing	(3) Deposits Extinguished in Clearing	(4) Reduction in Required Reserves	(5) Reserve Deficiency	(6) Decrease in Loans and Investments	(7) Reserves Gained in Clearing

The process of deposit contraction begins when the Fed sells $1,000 million of Treasury bills to a nonbank securities dealer, who pays the Fed with a check written on Bank A, and the Fed reduces the reserve account of Bank A by $1,000 million. The reduction in deposits at Bank A also reduces the need for required reserves by $100 million. Therefore, Bank A has a reserve deficiency of $900 million. Suppose Bank A sells $900 million of short-term securities in its portfolio to security dealers or to individuals who bank with Group B banks. When the exchange of assets is completed, Bank A has $900 million fewer loans and investments, and $900 million of checks written against Group B banks. Bank A sends the checks to the Fed for collection, and the Fed credits Bank A's reserve account $900 million. Bank A is no longer reserve deficient. The result would be the same if Bank A called in loans, which were paid with checks drawn on Group B banks. Group B banks, of course, now have a reserve deficiency of $810 million. They lose $900 million of reserves, but their need for required reserves falls by only $90 million. And so the process continues until deposits in the system fall by $10,000 million and the need for required reserves falls by $1,000 million, the amount of the Fed's open market sale of securities.

DETERMINANTS OF THE MONEY SUPPLY

The multistep process of multiple deposit expansion and contraction described in this chapter is closely related to the explanation of the money supply process in Chapter 8. In Chapter 8 we also derived a formula for the multiple expansion of deposits. Then we added currency to deposits to find the formula for money supply. Our purpose here is to expand on that discussion by explaining the connections between the multistep process and the money supply equation introduced in Chapter 8.

First, we will show how the information in Table 15–11 fits into the equation for deposits derived in Chapter 8. We will see that the multistep process of deposit creation applies whether the injection of reserves originates in open market operations or in a change in borrowed reserves, excess reserves, or the technical factors affecting reserves.

Then we will establish the ultimate factors that affect the narrow and broad measures of the money supply, some of which were only implicit in Chapter 8.

Deposits Supported by Reserves

We begin by reviewing the equation for the quantity of deposits that can be supported by reserves that we derived in Chapter 8. In that chapter, we used the reserves constraint, $TR^d = TR^s$, to find that the quantity of deposits that can be supported by reserves is a multiple of **effective reserves**, $(NBR + BR - ER)$; that is,

$$D_R = (1/rr) \times \underbrace{(NBR + BR - ER)}_{\text{Effective reserves}} \tag{15–3}$$

Effective reserves equal required reserves. The reason is that the sum of nonborrowed reserves and borrowed reserves equals total reserves supplied by the Fed. Subtracting excess reserves from total reserves supplied, we are left with the amount of reserves available to be used as required reserves to support deposits. When we multiply required reserves by the inverse of the reserve requirement ratio, we find the amount of deposits these reserves support (D_R).

We also know that nonborrowed reserves equal the Fed's holdings of Treasury securities (B_F) plus the net technical factors affecting reserves, $(OS - OU - Cur)$:

$$NBR = B_F + (OS - OU - Cur) \tag{15–4}$$

Substituting Equation 15–4 into Equation 15–3, we get:

$$D_R = (1/rr) \times \underbrace{[B_F + (OS - OU - Cur) + BR - ER]}_{\text{Effective reserves}} \tag{15–5}$$

If we assume that borrowed reserves, excess reserves, and the net technical factors affecting reserves do not change—as we have so far in this chapter—it follows from Equation 15–5 that an increase in the Fed's portfolio of securities through open market operations will increase the quantity of deposits by a multiple; that is:

$$\Delta D_R = (1/rr) \times \Delta B_F$$

In other words, the amount of deposit expansion or contraction is exactly the amount we found in this chapter. What we have done here is to explain in more detail the process of deposit creation and, hence, the money supply process. The D_R equation and its companion, the M^S equation, merely concentrate on the final, cumulative result: the economist's view.

Our description of the multistep process is general enough to explain an injection or a withdrawal of reserves for any reason. For example, suppose that the Fed had provided $1,000 million of additional reserves through the discount window instead of open market operations. In this case, ΔBR equals $1,000 million. The numbers in Table 15–11 would remain the same. The only change would be in the title of column 1, which would read "increase in borrowed reserves" instead of "open market purchase." The table could be similarly modified to accommodate a change in the desired amount of excess reserves held by banks, in the quantity of currency desired by the public, or in the other sources and other uses of reserves.

FIGURE 15–2
The Money Supply
Curve

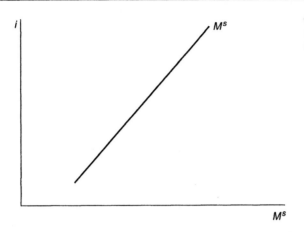

Other things equal, as the interest rate rises, the quantity of money supplied increases.

M1: The Narrow Measure of Money

Only checkable deposits are subject to reserve requirements. Hence, the explanation of multiple deposit creation refers to checkable deposits, $D1$, which are the deposit component of the narrow supply of money, M1. Adding currency to the amount of checkable deposits that can be supported by reserves ($D1_R$), we find the formula for $M1^S$.

$$M1^S = Cur + \qquad\qquad D1_R$$
$$= Cur + (1/rr) \times [B_F + (OS - OU - Cur) + BR - ER] \qquad (15\text{–}6)$$

Chapter 8 established that money supply increases with the interest rate, so that the money suply curve is upward sloping. It also showed how this curve shifts when the Fed engages in open market operations or changes the discount rate. In that same spirit, we shall use Equation 15–6 to look at the five types of factors that affect the money supply:

1. The interest rate, i
2. Policy instruments of the Fed
3. Attitudes of banks about borrowed reserves and excess reserves
4. Demand for currency by the public
5. Other sources and other uses of reserves

The Interest Rate   The interest rate affects the money supply through borrowed reserves and excess reserves, which depend on the spread between the interest rate and the discount rate. Other things equal, an increase in the interest rate increases the spread between the interest rate and the discount rate. As a result, profit-maximizing banks want to borrow more reserves from the Fed and to hold fewer excess reserves, which means that both effective reserves and (checkable) deposits that can be supported by reserves rise, as does the narrow money supply:

$$i \uparrow \rightarrow (i - d) \uparrow \rightarrow BR \uparrow \text{ and } ER \downarrow \rightarrow \text{Effective reserves} \uparrow \rightarrow D1_R \uparrow \rightarrow M1^S \uparrow$$

A movement along the upward-sloping money supply curve in Figure 15–2 depicts this positive relation between the interest rate and the money supply. It follows that a change in any of the other factors affecting the money supply will shift the curve. The curve shifts to the right if the money supply increases at each level of the interest rate, and to the left if the money supply decreases at each level of the interest rate.

Policy Instruments of the Fed   The Fed is an important participant in the money supply process. In addition to buying or selling Treasury securities or changing the discount rate, the Fed may tighten or loosen the volume of discount window loans it makes at any discount rate. Also, it may change the reserve requirement ratio.

Open Market Operations   The effects of buying or selling securities have already been fully described. Therefore, we can merely show the effect of an open market purchase of Treasury securities in symbols.

$$B_F \uparrow \rightarrow \text{Effective reserves} \uparrow \rightarrow D1_R \uparrow \rightarrow M1^S \uparrow$$

Discount Rate   An increase in the discount rate reduces the amount of reserves banks want to borrow from the Fed and increases the amount of excess reserves they want to hold. This is because the spread between the interest rate on earning assets and the discount rate falls. As a result, effective reserves, deposits that can be supported by reserves, and the money supply all fall.

$$d \uparrow \rightarrow (i - d) \downarrow \rightarrow BR \downarrow \text{ and } ER \uparrow \rightarrow \text{Effective reserves} \downarrow \rightarrow D1_R \downarrow \rightarrow M1^S \downarrow$$

Administration of the Discount Window   Because the discount rate is usually equal to or lower than market rates of interest, the Fed rations discount window loans not only by rate but also by quantity. As Chapter 12 notes, borrowing from the discount window is a privilege, not a right. Suppose that the Fed decides to pursue a kinder, gentler discount window policy: At any given discount rate, it allows banks to borrow more. Provided that banks do want to increase their borrowings, effective reserves will rise, as will deposits and the money supply.

A loosening in the administration of the discount window $\rightarrow BR\uparrow \rightarrow$ Effective reserves $\uparrow \rightarrow D1_R \uparrow \rightarrow M1^S \uparrow$

Reserve Requirement Ratio   This last policy instrument is the one the Fed uses the least. Other things equal, an increase in the reserve requirement ratio reduces the multiplier so that deposits that can be supported by reserves and the money supply fall.

$$rr \uparrow \rightarrow (1/rr) \downarrow \rightarrow D1_R \downarrow \rightarrow M1^S \downarrow$$

Attitudes of Banks   Borrowed or excess reserves may change even without a change in the interest rate or in Fed policy. Banks themselves may change their behavior, based on their attitudes toward borrowed and excess reserves.

Attitude about Borrowed Reserves   At any given spread between the interest rate and the discount rate, banks may become more or less reluctant to borrow from the discount window. Suppose they become more reluctant, which means they want to borrow less from the Fed, other things equal. Expressing the result in symbols, we have:

Reluctance to borrow at the discount window $\uparrow \rightarrow BR\downarrow \rightarrow$ Effective reserves $\downarrow \rightarrow D1_R\downarrow \rightarrow M1^S\downarrow$

Attitude about Excess Reserves   At any given spread between the interest rate and the discount rate, banks may decide to hold more or less excess reserves. Suppose that banks become more prudent, that is, other things equal, they want to hold more idle excess reserves and make fewer loans and investments. Of course, effective reserves fall because banks use the reserves supplied by the Fed less intensively than before. As a result, checkable deposits and the money supply also fall.

Prudence of banks $\uparrow \rightarrow ER \uparrow \rightarrow$ Effective reserves $\downarrow \rightarrow D1_R \downarrow M1^S \downarrow$

The Public's Demand for Currency   The public is also a player in the money supply process because currency in circulation is demand determined. When you go to a bank to cash a check, the bank never turns you down if you have funds in your account.

A reduction in the demand for currency by the public injects more reserves into the system because currency is one of the technical factors affecting reserves. As soon as you deposit currency in your bank, it becomes part of vault cash and, hence, part of reserves. As a result, effective reserves rise, and deposits that can be supported by reserves rise by a multiple amount. The increase in the money supply, however, is less than the increase in deposits because the currency component of the money supply falls. In general,

$$\Delta Cur \rightarrow \Delta M^S = \Delta Cur - (1/rr) \times \Delta Cur$$

What factors affect the demand for currency by the public? One is the payments habits of society, which themselves are affected by other factors, such as the state of financial technology and the size of underground activity. Improvements in financial technology reduce the demand for currency, while an increase in illegal activities increases the demand for currency. Another factor that affects the demand for currency is the level of economic activity, represented by the size of national income, Y. Other things equal, an increase in national income increases the demand for currency, and a decrease in national income decreases the demand for currency.

Other Sources and Other Uses of Reserves   This last item includes all the technical factors affecting reserves other than currency in circulation. We can show the effects of changes in the other sources and other uses of reserves in symbols as follows:

$$(OS - OU) \uparrow \rightarrow \text{Net technical factors} \uparrow \rightarrow \text{Effective reserves} \uparrow \rightarrow D1_R \uparrow \rightarrow M1^S \uparrow$$

What are some examples of changes in other sources and other uses? Chapter 14 shows that other sources rise when float increases or when the Fed buys foreign currency in the foreign exchange market. On the other hand, other uses decrease when the U.S. Treasury pays for government expenditures by writing checks on its accounts with the Fed.

M2: The Broad Measure of Money

By adding nontransactions deposits ($D2$) to the M1 measure of money, we get the broad measure of money, M2:

$$M2 = M1 + D2$$
$$M2 = Cur + D1 + D2 \tag{15-7}$$

Transactions deposits are checkable deposits. The nontransactions deposits in M2 are savings and small time deposits, money market deposit accounts, money market mutual funds shares, and overnight repurchase agreements and Eurodollars. The Fed currently does not require banks to hold reserves on nontransactions deposits.

In Chapter 8, we manipulated the definitions of M2 and M1 to derive a relation between M2 and currency in circulation and effective reserves. As expected, we found that the M2 deposit multiplier is larger than that of M1 because the same quantity of effective reserves can support a much larger quantity of total deposits. Let's briefly review those results.

First, we define $d2$ as the ratio of $D2$ deposits to $D1$ deposits:

$$d2 = \frac{D2}{D1}$$

It follows that:

$$D2 = d2 \times D1 \tag{15-8}$$

Substituting Equation 15–8 into Equation 15–7 and combining terms, we get:

$$M2 = Cur + (1 + d2)D1 \tag{15-9}$$

Finally, we can substitute Equation 15–5 for $D1$ in Equation 15–9:

$$M2^s = Cur + \frac{1 + d2}{rr} \times (\text{Effective reserves}) \tag{15-10}$$

Where:

$$\text{Effective reserves} = NBR + BR - ER$$
$$= [B_F + (OS - OU - Cur) + BR - ER]$$

All the factors that affect M1 also affect M2. In addition, M2 depends on $d2$, the ratio of nontranactions deposits to transactions deposits. For a given level of effective reserves, the larger $d2$, the greater the supply of M2, and the smaller $d2$, the smaller the supply of M2.

Meager M2 Growth in the 1990s   The three panels of Figure 15–3 show the recent history of transactions deposits (checkable deposits), nontransactions deposits, and their ratio. We see that between 1991 and 1993 transactions deposits were rising and nontransactions deposits were falling or stable. Consequently, the ratio of nontransactions to transactions deposits fell, as shown in the graph. To understand why, we must look at the deposit rate–setting behavior of banks.

In several of its monetary policy reports to Congress between 1991 and 1993, the Fed pointed out that banks were bidding less aggressively for deposits, especially higher cost deposits such as time deposits. Why? First, market rates of interest were falling, thereby reducing the marginal revenue from issuing deposits. In addition, higher explicit and implicit regulatory costs were increasing the marginal cost of issuing deposits. Both these factors made these deposits less profitable for banks and led to falling deposit rates. Third, the downsizing of the thrift industry resulted in a smaller amount of financial

FIGURE 15–3
Recent History of
Deposits

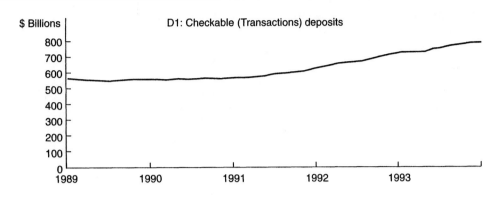

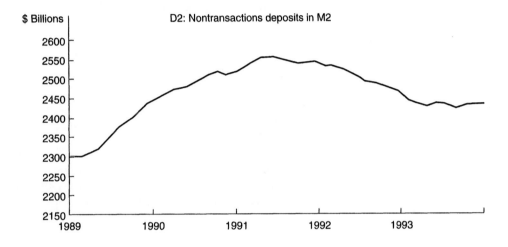

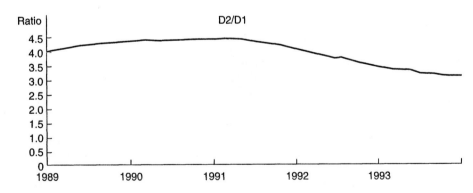

Source: Federal Reserve Board.

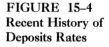

**FIGURE 15–4
Recent History of
Deposits Rates**

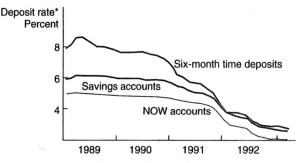

* Retail deposit rates at all commercial banks; savings accounts
include money market deposit accounts.

Source: Allan D. Brunner and William B. English, "Profits and Balance Sheet
Developments at U.S. Commercial Banks in 1992," *Federal Reserve Bulletin*
79, no. 7 (July 1993): 656.

intermediation and more reliance on direct finance, which also contributed to lower deposit rates.

Figure 15–4 shows falling rates on all categories of deposits. It also shows that the spread between the rates on savings and time deposits and NOW accounts fell considerably in 1991.

In 1992 total reserves grew by a robust 20.2 percent and M1 by 14.3 percent. M2, on the other hand, grew by a meager 2.8 percent because of the falling $d2$. The next chapter shows how changing interest rates and deposit rates in the 1990s affected the growth of the velocity of circulation of money, which links money growth to growth of nominal GDP.

SUMMARY

- When the Fed purchases securities in the open market from a nonbank securities dealer, reserves and deposits initially increase by the amount of the open market operation. If the reserve requirement ratio is 10 percent, 90 percent of the reserves added by the open market operation will be excess reserves.

- If banks do not want to hold additional excess reserves, they increase their loans and investments to eliminate the unwanted excess reserves. When banks make additional loans and investments, they create deposits, called *loan-generated deposits.*

- In a multiunit banking system, a single bank can increase its loans and investments only up to the amount of reserve

balances that it can afford to lose in check clearing with other banks. Thus, each bank will increase its earning assets by the amount of its unwanted excess reserves.

- The multistep process of creating loans and deposits ends when banks wring out the unwanted excess reserves by transforming them into required reserves. Total deposits increase by a multiple of the change in required reserves. The multiplier is the inverse of the reserve requirement ratio. Because the reserve requirement ratio is 1/10 in our example, the multiplier is 10.

- Deposit contraction is symmetric to deposit expansion. An open market sale of Treasury securities by the Fed creates a reserve deficiency, forcing banks to contract.

When banks reduce loans and investments, they extinguish deposits. Thus, the need for required reserves falls. The process continues until banks eliminate the reserve deficiency. Deposits decrease by a multiple of the decrease in reserves.

- Multiple expansion or contraction occurs whether the injection or withdrawal of reserves originates in open market operations or in a change in borrowed reserves, excess reserves, or the technical factors affecting reserves. Therefore, the story of multiple deposit creation fits into the equations for the supply of M1 derived in Chapter 8.

- Five types of factors ultimately affect the narrow measure of money, M1: the interest rate, the policy instruments of the Fed, the attitudes of banks about borrowed reserves and excess reserves, the public's demand for currency, and the other sources and other uses of reserves. The broad measure of money, M2, depends on all the factors that affect M1 plus the ratio of nontransactions to transactions deposits.

- In the early 1990s, M1 growth was robust while M2 growth was meager. The ratio of nontransactions deposits to transactions deposits fell as market interest rates fell and the cost of intermediation rose.

KEY TERMS AND CONCEPTS

unwanted excess reserves	loan-generated deposits	effective reserves
multiple deposit creation		

QUESTIONS AND PROBLEMS

1. Suppose the Fed sells $5 million of T-bills to Merrill Lynch, which pays for the securities by writing a check on its account with Citibank.
   a. Show the changes in the T-accounts of Merrill Lynch, Citibank, and the Fed as a result of this sale.
   b. Do Citibank's reserves with the Fed increase or decrease as a result of this sale? By how much?
   c. Do the banking system's reserves with the Fed increase, decrease, or remain unchanged? Why?

2. Suppose the Fed lends Riverside Bank $1 million. Show the changes in the T-accounts of Riverside Bank and the Fed.

3. "For the banking system to create additional checkable deposits, there must be unwanted excess reserves in the banking system." True or false? Explain.

4. "Only the Fed can inject additional reserves into the banking system." True or false? Explain.

5. Do you agree or disagree with the following statement? "Loan-generated deposits bounce from bank to bank but do not disappear from the banking system." Explain the reasons for your agreement or disagreement and state any key assumptions you make.

6. Explain why an increase in unwanted excess reserves leads to an increase in the amount of checkable deposits in the banking system, but an increase in desired excess reserves leads to a decrease in the amount of checkable deposits.

The Wall Street Journal

7. What are the components of effective reserves? Calculate effective reserves by using the information in the "Federal Reserve Data" table in this Friday's issue of *The Wall Street Journal.*

8. A change in borrowed reserves may result in a movement along the money supply curve or a shift of the curve. Explain the difference.

9. Suppose that the Fed buys $1 million of Treasury securities in the open market and the demand for excess reserves by banks also increases by $1 million. What will be the effect on the money supply?

10. Suppose the reserve requirement ratio on checkable deposits is 12 percent. Also, suppose that the demand for currency falls by $1 billion because of a reduction in the level of economic activity. Will the money supply curve shift to the left or the right? By how much?

11. Suppose you deposit your paycheck of $1,000, drawn on your employer's checking account at National Bank, into your checking account at Metropolitan Bank.
    a. Show the changes in the T-accounts of National Bank and Metropolitan Bank.
    b. Will there be any change in the need for required reserves in this case?
    c. Suppose that instead of depositing your paycheck into your checking account, you deposit it into your money market deposit account at National Bank.

Will there be any change in the need for required reserves in this case?

12. Explain why for any given level of M2, the need for required reserves may be high or low.

13. Suppose that the public shifts its funds from NOW accounts to savings and time deposits because the deposit rates on savings and time deposits are rising faster than the rate on NOW accounts. What will be the effect on the M2 deposit multiplier?

SUGGESTED READINGS

Board of Governors of the Federal Reserve System. "Monetary Policy and Financial Markets in 1992." *79th Annual Report 1992.* Washington, D.C., April 16, 1993, 21-34.

A detailed explanation of the behavior of M1 and M2 in 1992. Nichols, Dorothy. *Modern Money Mechanics: A Workbook on Deposits, Currency, and Bank Reserves.* Federal Reserve Bank of Chicago, 1982.

First published in 1961, this 31-page workbook has become a standard tool for introducing money creation to students.

TARGETING MONETARY AGGREGATES

Theory and Experience

CHAPTER PREVIEW

Chapter 13 explains that the Humphrey-Hawkins Act of 1978 requires the Fed to report regularly on the state of the economy. Twice a year, the Fed chair must report to Congress the FOMC's predictions of inflation, real GDP growth, and nominal GDP growth for the current calendar year. The chair also announces the FOMC's annual targets of money growth that purport to bring about the forecasted inflation and output growth.

This chapter examines the quantity theory of money, which provides the theoretical underpinnings for using money as an intermediate target. According to the quantity theory, the link between the nominal quantity of money and nominal GDP is the velocity of circulation, V. To apply this theory, we must find the determinants of velocity and relate them to the determinants of the demand for money.

After establishing the determinants of velocity, we explain the market forces that make nominal GDP (PY) equal to the velocity-indexed money supply (MV). The theory that explains velocity and the market forces that bring about the equality of MV and PY is called the *quantity theory of money*. We connect theory with practice by using the quantity theory to see how the Fed sets its targets for money growth. Moreover, we develop the analysis in a way that will enable the reader to understand the Fed's monetary policy reports to Congress. Finally, we use the quantity theory to evaluate the performance of the Fed in the 1980s and 1990s and to explain the demotion of the monetary aggregates in the Fed's decision-making process.

Our examination of monetary policy in the 1980s shows that the severe recession of 1982 was not intended, or at least not predicted, by the Fed. After its midyear policy review in 1982, the Fed began acting as a pragmatic monetary targeter by adjusting its targets for money growth in response to new information on velocity growth. In 1987 the Fed stopped setting targets for M1 because of difficulties in predicting the velocity of M1 in an environment of deregulation and disinflation. It continued, however, to set targets for M2. In 1988 the Fed widened the target range for M2 growth from 3 to 4 percentage points. But in 1992 and the first half of 1993, money growth fell outside even these wider ranges, because of shifts of funds by the public out of low-yielding bank deposits into higher-yielding stock and bond mutual funds. In July 1993, the Fed further downgraded the monetary aggregates by announcing that its monetary targets probably would not be useful guides to monetary policy for the next 18 months.

Our examination of the Fed's behavior in this chapter shows that since 1982 the Fed has acted as if it were targeting velocity-indexed money growth, which equals the growth of nominal GDP. Our analysis also shows that by design and by serendipity actual growth of nominal GDP fell within the Fed's forecasting range almost every year between 1983 and 1993.

DEFINITIONS OF VELOCITY, VELOCITY-INDEXED MONEY, AND RELATED CONCEPTS

The Fed's success in setting intermediate targets to reach ultimate goals depends on the stability and predictability of the link between the target variable and aggregate demand for goods and services. In the case of the monetary aggregates, the link is the velocity of circulation, and the underlying theory is the quantity theory of money. To understand the role of velocity and the quantity theory in setting intermediate targets for monetary aggregates, we must distinguish between identities and theories. *Identities* are tautologies, or definitions. *Theories* are explanations of behavior of participants or markets.

The Definition of Velocity and the Cambridge *k*

We begin with the definitions of two related variables. First, **velocity of circulation** is the number of times (per period, say, per year) that each dollar circulates to buy final goods and services. To calculate velocity, we divide the annual dollar expenditure on goods and services by the quantity of money; that is, we divide nominal income, *PY*, by the nominal quantity of money, *M*:

$$V \equiv \frac{PY}{M} \tag{16-1}$$

The identity sign ($\equiv$) means that the relation is true by definition. It does not explain economic behavior.

On the other hand, if we divide the quantity of money by nominal income, we determine the second variable, the **Cambridge k,** which is the fraction of nominal income held in the form of money:[1]

$$k \equiv \frac{M}{PY} \equiv \frac{1}{V} \tag{16–2}$$

The Cambridge k, of course, is the inverse of velocity. Velocity is a frequency, and the inverse of frequency is a period of time. Thus, k has the dimension of a unit of time; it is the period of time that the average dollar "rests" in the pockets or checking accounts of the public. Velocity measures how hard money works, while the Cambridge k measures how long it rests.

To illustrate V and k, suppose that the average level of the quantity of money, M, is $600 billion and that nominal GDP—that is, expenditure on final goods and services—is $3,600 billion per year. The income velocity of circulation is thus six times per year, the result of the following calculation:

$$V \equiv \frac{\$3,600 \text{ billion per year}}{\$600 \text{ billion}} \equiv 6 \text{ times per year}$$

The same data imply that the Cambridge k is one-sixth of a year. On average, the public holds one-sixth of its annual income in the form of money; put differently, a dollar rests in the pockets or checkbooks of the public for one-sixth of a year.

$$k \equiv \frac{\$600 \text{ billion}}{\$3,600 \text{ billion per year}} \equiv \frac{1}{6} \text{ year}$$

If nominal GDP were $2,400 billion instead of $3,600 billion, with the same money stock of $600 billion, velocity would be only four times per year; each dollar would turn over fewer times in buying final goods and services. On the other hand, the Cambridge k would be one-fourth of a year, which means that the public would hold a larger fraction of its annual income, one-fourth, in the form of money.

The Equation of Exchange

Now that we have defined velocity, we can use it to calculate expenditures and, thus, nominal GDP. Any equation derived by manipulating the definition of velocity is also a definition, or identity. Thus, multiplying each side of Equation 16–1 by M, we get Equation 16–3, referred to as the **equation of exchange:**

$$MV \equiv PY \tag{16–3}$$

For example,

$600 billion × 6 times per year ≡ $3,600 billion per year
$3,600 billion per year   ≡ $3,600 billion per year

---

[1] The appellation *Cambridge* was given because k was the notation used by three famous Cambridge University professors, Alfred Marshall (1842–1924) and his prize pupils, A. C. Pigou (1877–1959) and John Maynard Keynes (1883–1946).

The left side of Equation 16–3, *MV,* measures expenditure on final goods and services in a given period (year). If, as in our example, *M* equals $600 billion and each dollar turns over six times a year to buy goods and services, the quantity of money achieves a total expenditure of $3,600 billion per year. To highlight that it is not only what the quantity of money is but also how hard each dollar works (in making expenditures), we call *MV velocity-adjusted supply of money,* or **velocity-indexed supply of money.** In this book we shall use the term *velocity-indexed*[2] when we refer to Equation 16–3.

The right side of the equation of exchange is the nominal value of output, that is, nominal GDP. Thus, the equation $MV \equiv PY$ says that total expenditure on goods and services equals nominal GDP. Alternatively, we can use our terminology to say that *velocity-indexed money supply equals nominal GDP.*

The Cambridge Equation

Just as we used the definition of velocity to generate the equation of exchange, we can use the definition of the Cambridge *k* to generate the Cambridge equation. Multiplying each side of Equation 16–2 by *PY,* we get Equation 16–4, referred to as the **Cambridge equation:**

$$kPY \equiv M \tag{16–4}$$

For example,

$$1/6 \text{ year} \times \$3,600 \text{ billion per year} \equiv \$600 \text{ billion}$$
$$\$600 \text{ billion} \qquad\qquad \equiv \$600 \text{ billion}$$

According to the Cambridge equation, the quantity of money held by the public, *kPY,* is always equal to the existing quantity of money, *M.* Note that *kPY* is a stock, because *PY* is a flow and *k* a time period.

Recent History of Velocity

Figure 16–1 depicts the history of velocity for the last 30 years. We track two measures of velocity, one for M1 and another for M2. To calculate *V1,* the velocity of M1, we divide nominal GDP by the nominal value of M1; and to calculate *V2,* we divide nominal GDP by the nominal value of M2. The graph shows that both *V1* and *V2* fell in the first half of the 1980s. However, their paths diverged in the late 1980s and early 1990s: *V1* rose in the late 1980s, then started falling again in the 1990s; *V2* also rose in the late 1980s, and after a small dip, continued climbing in the early 1990s. Of course, Equation 16–1 cannot tell us why *V1* and *V2* behaved in this way, because it is merely a definition. To explain the behavior of velocity, we need a theory.

THEORIES OF VELOCITY AND VELOCITY-INDEXED MONEY

As definitions, or accounting identities, Equations 16–1 through 16–4 are useful in data gathering. These equations, however, can be used more fruitfully as something more than mere definitions. Their usefulness lies with helping economists evaluate the way monetary policy is conducted.

---

[2] James Tobin coined the term *velocity-adjusted quantity of money.* Our term, *velocity-indexed quantity of money,* is inspired by that of Tobin.

FIGURE 16–1
The History of the
Velocity of M1 and
M2

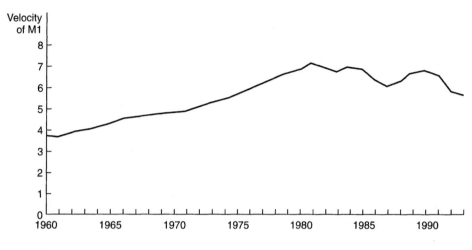

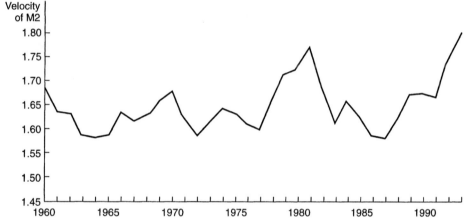

Source: Federal Reserve Board.

First, we examine velocity as a behavioral relation; that is, we specify the factors affecting velocity. Only then can we address the issue of the stability and predictability of velocity. Second, we consider the relation $MV = PY$ as an equilibrium relation. To understand the meaning of this equilibrium relation, we must examine the market forces that bring about the equality. This inquiry leads us to the Fisher-Friedman version of the quantity theory of money.

**Velocity as a
Behavioral
Relation**

Actual velocity, V^a, is the number of times each dollar turns over in buying final goods and services. On the other hand, **planned, or estimated, velocity** is the number of times the public *wants* each dollar to turn over in buying goods and services. We denote planned, or estimated, velocity by V^e.[3] To compute V^e, we divide nominal income by the quantity of nominal money balances that the public *wants* to hold. Remember that M^d denotes the quantity of real money balances that the public wants to hold. Therefore, PM^d is the nominal demand for money. Thus, to compute V^e, we divide PY by PM^d. The result is that planned velocity is equal to the ratio of real income and (real) money demand:

$$V^e = \frac{PY}{PM^d}$$
$$V^e = \frac{Y}{M^d} \tag{16-5}$$

Equation 16–5 presents velocity of circulation as a theory of money demand, exactly as Milton Friedman demonstrated 35 years ago.[4] Because money demand is in the denominator of the right side in Equation 16–5, it follows that **reductions in money demand are tantamount to increases in velocity, and increases in money demand to reductions in velocity.**

Factors Affecting Velocity   To determine the factors affecting velocity, we must identify the factors affecting money demand. The signs under each factor in the money demand function in Equation 16–6 indicate the laws of money demand: A plus sign means a positive relation and a minus sign an inverse relation. Similarly, the signs under the velocity function indicate the relation between planned velocity and the factors that affect it. Using the definition of planned velocity and the laws of money demand, we establish these relations.

$$V^e = \frac{Y}{M^d(i - r_D, Y; \mathcal{C})} = V^e(i - r_D; Y, \mathcal{C}) = V^e(i, r_D, Y; \mathcal{C}) \tag{16-6}$$
$$\quad\quad\quad - \;\; + + \quad\quad + \;\; ? - \quad\quad +, - \; ? -$$

1. Other things equal, an increase in the opportunity cost of holding money, $(i - r_D)$, decreases money demand and, hence, increases velocity. The more it costs to hold idle money, the stronger the incentive to make money balances circulate faster:

   $$(i - r_D)\!\uparrow \;\rightarrow\; M^d\!\downarrow \;\rightarrow\; V^e\!\uparrow$$

   This result implies the next two results as corollaries.

2. Other things equal, an increase in the interest rate increases the opportunity cost of holding money, which reduces money demand and increases velocity.

   $$i\!\uparrow \;\rightarrow\; M^d\!\downarrow \;\rightarrow\; V^e\!\uparrow$$

3. Other things equal, an increase in the deposit rate reduces the opportunity cost of holding money, which increases money demand and reduces velocity.

   $$r_D\!\uparrow \;\rightarrow\; M^d\!\uparrow \;\rightarrow\; V^e\!\downarrow$$

---

[3] We introduce the superscripts here to explain the difference between actual and planned velocity. Later, when the context makes clear the velocity we use, we shall drop this more complicated notation.

[4] See Milton Friedman, "The Quantity Theory of Money—A Restatement," in *Studies in the Quantity Theory of Money,* ed. M. Friedman (University of Chicago Press, 1956), 3–21.

4. Other things equal, a negative shift in money demand increases velocity. That is, a fall in $\mathcal{C}$ reduces M^d and, thereby, increases velocity:

$$\mathcal{C}\downarrow \rightarrow M^d\downarrow \rightarrow V^e\uparrow$$

For example, improvements in cash management technology make money rest less and, hence, increase velocity.

5. Other things equal, the effect of an increase in real income on velocity is indeterminate, because an increase in Y increases both the numerator and the denominator in Equation 16–6.

$$Y\uparrow \rightarrow \text{Numerator of } V^e\uparrow \rightarrow V^e\uparrow$$
$$Y\uparrow \rightarrow M^d\uparrow \rightarrow \text{Denominator of } V^e\uparrow \rightarrow V^e\downarrow$$

The effect on velocity depends on how responsive money demand is to a change in Y. We measure this responsiveness by the *income elasticity of money demand*, defined as the percentage change in money demand divided by the percentage change in real income. If this elasticity is smaller than 1, the percentage increase in the denominator of Equation 16–6 is less than the percentage increase in the numerator, thereby increasing velocity. The opposite is true when the elasiticy is greater than 1. Of course, if income elasticity is equal to 1, the increase in the denominator is equal to the increase in the numerator, thereby leaving velocity unchanged. Empirical studies show that the income elasticity of money demand is less than 1.

Velocity in Equation Form   We can capture the determinants of velocity in a simple linear equation,

$$V^e = v_0 - v_1 r_D + v_2 i \pm v_3 Y - v_4 \mathcal{C} \qquad (16\text{–}7)$$

where all coefficients—v_0, v_1, v_2, v_3, and v_4—are positive numbers. The positive sign in front of i depicts result 2 in the factors affecting velocity. Other things equal, an increase in i increases V^e by v_2 times the change in i. Similarly, the negative sign before r_D depicts result 3, and the negative sign before $\mathcal{C}$, result 4. The ambivalent effect of a change in income, Y, is shown by the indeterminate sign in front of $v_3 Y$. Guided by the empirical evidence, however, we will put a plus sign in front of Y from now on.

The Quantity Theory of Money

Now that velocity has been expanded from a definition in Equation 16–1 to a theory in Equation 16–6, we turn to formulating the theory for the equation of exchange. The replacement of the identity sign in Equation 16–3 with an equality sign changes the meaning of the equation. Equation 16–8 is the quantity theory equation:

$$MV = PY \qquad (16\text{–}8)$$

According to this equation, the velocity-indexed supply of money equals nominal GDP only at equilibrium. Multiplying M by the number of times individuals want money to turn over in buying goods and services (that is, by planned velocity) gives us planned expenditure on final goods and services. In equilibrium, planned expenditure on final goods and services equals nominal GDP.

Market Forces behind the Quantity Theory   The transformation of the equation of exchange into an equilibrium condition raises two questions. First, which variable does this market equilibrium condition determine? The **quantity theory of money** stipulates that the equality of MV and PY determines nominal GDP, that is, PY. This theory was introduced by Irving Fisher of Yale in the early 1900s and was restated and extended by Milton Friedman of the University of Chicago in the 1950s.[5] The second question is: How does nominal GDP move to establish equilibrium? According to the quantity theory, if MV is less than PY, the nominal GDP falls, because planned expenditure on final goods and services falls short of nominal GDP. On the other hand, if MV is greater than PY, planned expenditure outstrips nominal GDP, so nominal GDP rises.

We can put this mechanism in schematic form as follows:

$$\left.\begin{array}{l} MV < PY \Rightarrow PY\downarrow \\ MV > PY \Rightarrow PY\uparrow \\ MV = PY \Rightarrow PY \text{ unchanged} \end{array}\right\} \tag{16–9}$$

Connecting the theory of velocity with the market mechanism behind the quantity theory, we see that the quantity theory has two key features. First, it is a statement about the determinants of velocity, which are the same as the determinants of money demand, as we have seen. Second, the quantity theory is a statement about the determination of nominal GDP.

Now, let's see what happens when an increase in M disturbs the equality between MV and PY. A rise in M increases MV, so that planned expenditure on final goods and services (MV) is greater than nominal GDP. As a result PY rises. Chapter 10 also notes that an increase in M leads to an increase in PY. In that chapter we used the AD–AS framework, where a change in M works its effects through the money market: An increase in M reduces the interest rate, which increases aggregate demand for goods and services, leading to an increase in nominal GDP. The end result of the two approaches is the same. One difference is that the AD–AS model takes us through the interaction between the financial sector and the real sector, while the quantity theory goes straight to the end result. Another difference is that the AD–AS model tells us how any change in nominal GDP will be divided between a change in the price level and a change in real GDP, depending on the slope of the AS curve.

QUANTITY THEORY AND MONETARY AGGREGATE TARGETING

Now that we know the factors that affect velocity and the relation between changes in M and changes in PY, we are ready to examine the issue of targeting the monetary aggregates. As Chapter 13 explains, the Fed states its targets for money and its projections of prices and real GDP in terms of rates of change rather than in terms of levels of these variables. Therefore, we want to express the quantity theory equations in terms of rates of change.

The Quantity Theory Equation Expressed in Rates of Change

Because the *level* of velocity-indexed money supply is equal to the *level* of nominal GDP, it must also be true that the *percentage change* in velocity-indexed money supply must be equal to the percentage change in nominal GDP. By applying to Equation 16–8 the

---

[5] Irving Fisher, *The Purchasing Power of Money* (New York: Macmillan, 1911); Milton Friedman, "The Quantity Theory of Money—A Restatement," in *Studies in the Quantity Theory of Money*, ed. M. Friedman (University of Chicago Press, 1956), 3–21; and Milton Friedman, "A Monetary Theory of Nominal Income," *Journal of Political Economy* 79 (March/April 1971): 323–37.

algebraic rule that the percentage change in the product of two variables is the sum of the percentage change in each of the variables, we obtain Equation 16–10:

$$\frac{\Delta M}{M} + \frac{\Delta V}{V} = \frac{\Delta P}{P} + \frac{\Delta Y}{Y} \tag{16–10}$$

The sum of the rate of growth of money and the rate of growth of velocity on the left side of Equation 16–10 is velocity-indexed money growth. And the sum of the rate of inflation and the rate of growth of real GDP on the right side is the rate of growth of nominal GDP. Thus, Equation 16–10 says that **velocity-indexed money growth equals nominal GDP growth.**

Quantity theory Equation 16–10 is the foundation for various proposals to target the monetary aggregates. There is no disagreement among economists over the statement that, in the long run, velocity-indexed money growth is equal to nominal GDP growth. Disagreements arise, however, over the use of this equation as a formula to conduct economic policy. The basic problem is that Equation 16–10 is one equation in four unknowns. Targeting the rate of growth of the money stock, $\Delta M/M$, does not necessarily tell us what the inflation rate will be, if this is the ultimate target of monetary policy. Setting a target for money growth does not even tell us what nominal GDP growth will be, unless we also know the magnitude of velocity growth, the remaining variable in the equation.

Long-Run Monetary Aggregate Targeting

To extract from Equation 16–10 a rule for money growth to achieve a target for inflation, we need to know both real GDP growth and velocity growth. If we concentrate on the long run—the *very* long run—we can rely on some known theoretical and empirical regularities that may help us solve our problem. In particular, a well-established result is that in the (very) long run, real GDP grows at its natural rate, which is equal to the rate of growth of the labor force plus the rate of growth of technological knowledge. Historically, the magnitude of the natural rate of growth of real GDP has been between 3 and 4 percent. Also, between 1950 and 1980 the average rate of growth of the velocity of M1 was about 3 percent.[6] Thus, in the long run the difference between velocity growth and real GDP growth can be considered a constant whose magnitude is close to zero.

Let us now see how we can use this information to devise a monetary rule to achieve a given (ultimate) target for the inflation rate. Rearranging Equation 16–10, we get:

$$\frac{\Delta P}{P} = \frac{\Delta M}{M} + \frac{\Delta V}{V} - \frac{\Delta Y}{Y} \tag{16–11}$$

$$\frac{\Delta P}{P} = \frac{\Delta M}{M} + cons\tan t \tag{16–12}$$

$$\frac{\Delta P}{P} = \frac{\Delta M}{M} \text{ if the constant is zero} \tag{16–13}$$

---

[6] In a study published in 1963, Milton Friedman and Anna J. Schwartz found that velocity growth had been stable over a long period of time, staying at a rate of between 2 and 3 percent. See Milton Friedman and Anna Jacobson Schwartz, *A Monetary History of the United States, 1867–1960* (Princeton, N.J.: Princeton University Press for the National Bureau of Economic Research, 1963.)

These equations can be used as a guide for long-run inflation. For example, if policymakers aim at a long-run annual inflation rate of 5 percent, the nominal money stock should be rising at an annual rate of 5 percent. (If the value of the constant were minus 1 rather than zero, the target for money growth should be 6 percent instead of 5 percent). On the other hand, if they want to reduce inflation, say, from 5 percent to 3 percent, nominal money growth should be reduced from 5 percent to 3 percent. In other words, to reduce inflation by 2 percentage points, policymakers must reduce nominal money growth by 2 percentage points. These examples can be generalized as follows:

1. **The long-run rate of inflation is equal to the rate of growth of the nominal money stock plus a constant. The magnitude of the constant equals the difference between the long-run growth rate of velocity and the long-run growth rate of real GDP.**

2. **An increase (decrease) in the growth rate of the nominal money supply results in an equal increase (decrease) in inflation in the long run.**

Actual inflation, of course, may deviate from targeted inflation. Discrepancies occur if the actual value of the constant term in Equation 16–12 differs from its trend value or if actual money growth differs from the targeted value. Suppose, for example, that real GDP growth deviates from its trend value, other things equal. If real GDP growth is above its trend, the constant term in Equation 16–12 will be less than expected, actual inflation will be below target, and monetary policy will be less inflationary than intended. On the other hand, if real GDP growth is below its trend, monetary policy will be more inflationary than intended. Similar results can be derived when actual velocity growth deviates from its trend value. The case for setting long-run targets for money growth is not seriously impaired, however, if we recognize that, on average, these discrepancies cancel out in the long run. Therefore, in the long run nominal money growth determines the inflation rate. Monetarists, such as Milton Friedman, who favor a rule for money growth base their analysis on the long run.

Short-Run Monetary Aggregate Targeting

Using Equation 16–10 for short-run monetary targeting poses a variety of problems.

$$\frac{\Delta M}{M} + \frac{\Delta V}{V} = \frac{\Delta P}{P} + \frac{\Delta Y}{Y} \tag{16–10}$$

Velocity-indexed money growth on the left side of the equation determines the size of nominal GDP growth. However, the distribution of the total percentage change in nominal GDP between inflation ($\Delta P/P$) and real GDP growth, ($\Delta Y/Y$), depends on additional assumptions about, and characteristics of, the economy. For example, at high rates of employment of the labor force and high rates of capacity utilization, a given rate of growth in nominal GDP growth would be achieved primarily with high rates of inflation and relatively low rates of real GDP growth. On the other hand, when the economy is experiencing low employment rates and low rates of capacity utilization, the same rate of growth in nominal GDP would be apportioned more heavily in favor of real GDP growth and less heavily to inflation. It is clear, then, that targeting a specific mix of inflation and real GDP growth requires additional assumptions or additional theorizing. A substantial portion of modern macroeconomics is devoted to analyzing this issue.

Many economists have argued that the Fed should set an ultimate goal, or target, for nominal GDP growth ($\Delta P/P + \Delta Y/Y$) rather than for inflation ($\Delta P/P$) alone. Some economists, such as Robert Hall, explicitly prescribe nominal GDP targets, while others suggest them implicitly. For example, James Tobin has suggested that if the Fed wants to target money growth, it should target velocity-adjusted money growth.

Setting an ultimate goal for nominal GDP growth means that policy decisions do not have to be made about the mix of the right side of Equation 16–10. But the same target rate of growth for nominal GDP can be achieved with an infinity of combinations of nominal money growth ($\Delta M/M$) and velocity growth ($\Delta V/V$) on the left side of the equation. This brings us to the heart of the problem of short-run (activist) monetary aggregate targeting. Short-run targeting requires an estimate of velocity growth. The Fed determines the desired size of velocity-indexed money growth from its target, or forecast, of nominal GDP growth. However, to set a target for nonindexed money growth ($\Delta M/M$), the Fed must estimate the index; that is, the Fed must estimate velocity growth.

If the Fed's forecast of velocity growth turns out to be accurate and if the Fed hits its target for (nonindexed) money growth, it will achieve its ultimate target (or projection) of nominal GDP growth. On the other hand, if there is an error in the Fed's estimate of velocity growth, the nominal GDP target will not be reached if the Fed sticks with its original target for nonindexed money growth.

Estimating velocity growth brings us back to velocity as a behavioral relation and to Equation 16–7 for estimated velocity:

$$V^e = v_0 - v_1 r_D + v_2 i + v_3 Y - v_4 \mathcal{C} \qquad (16\text{–}7)$$

We see from this equation that for a given level of Y and the factors represented by $\mathcal{C}$, the Fed must predict the interest rate, i, and the deposit rate, r_D, in order to predict the level of velocity. (Predicting velocity amounts to predicting money demand.) Also, to predict the rate of velocity growth, the Fed must predict changes in these interest rates.

Of course, actual velocity growth may deviate from predicted velocity growth because of errors in forecasting interest rates. More important, errors in predicted changes in velocity may occur even if predicted changes in interest rates and predicted changes in income materialize. Such errors in prediction may be attributable to changes in the financial environment that cause shifts in money demand (changes that are incorporated in $\mathcal{C}$).

Pragmatic versus Rigid Monetary Aggregate Targeting

Errors in predicting velocity growth lie at the heart of the operational difference between rigid monetary aggregate targeting and pragmatic monetary aggregate targeting. The distinction centers on how the Fed should react if it finds out that actual velocity growth is deviating from estimated velocity growth.

1. **Pragmatic monetary targeters** are willing to forecast velocity growth by forecasting the factors affecting velocity growth. They are also willing to revise the monetary targets if new information shows that actual velocity growth is turning out to be different from predicted velocity growth.

2. In contrast, **rigid monetary targeters** object to basing monetary targets on continuous, regular forecasting of velocity growth; they prefer that the Fed use the trend in velocity growth as its forecast. Second, they argue that the Fed should not change its monetary targets every time there is a discrepancy between observed

velocity growth and its trend. They argue that the Fed should focus on the long run, when errors in predicting velocity growth disappear. Even if the errors do not cancel out, however, these economists are against revising the original targets. They believe that the damage that would occur in the form of unintended inflation (or deflation) is smaller than the harmful destablizing effects caused by the Fed's continuous changing of its targets for monetary growth. Moreover, rigid targeters contend that frequent revisions of the targets undermine the credibility of those targets and the credibility of the Fed itself.

We can illustrate the difference between pragmatic and rigid monetary aggregate targeting with a numerical example. Suppose the Fed predicts that the rate of growth of nominal GDP this year will be 7 percent, with inflation at 3 percent and real GDP growth at 4 percent. Suppose, too, they forecast that velocity growth will be equal to its trend of 3 percent, so they set a target of 4 percent for money growth. Now suppose that actual velocity growth turns out to be 5 percent instead of the predicted 3 percent. If the Fed sticks with and achieves its monetary target of 4 percent, actual velocity-indexed money growth will be 9 percent; and actual growth of nominal GDP will be 9 percent, which is 2 percentage points above the Fed's forecast. To prevent the economy from overheating in the short run, pragmatic targeters would be willing to reduce the target for monetary growth by 2 percentage points offset the error in velocity growth. Rigid targeters, however, would argue that the higher-than-forecasted growth in nominal GDP was merely a temporary bulge that will eventually be reversed, and they would also contend that the Fed's reputation for sticking to its commitment of fixed money growth is more important to the economy than the temporary overheating of the economy.

Finally, we can generalize the results in our numerical example by looking at the difference between actual velocity-indexed money growth and planned velocity-indexed money growth. **Actual velocity-indexed money growth** (VIMG) equals the sum of actual money growth and actual velocity growth:

$$\text{Actual VIMG} = \left(\frac{\Delta M}{M}\right)^a + \left(\frac{\Delta V}{V}\right)^a \tag{16-14}$$

Planned velocity-indexed money growth equals the sum of targeted money growth and estimated velocity growth:

$$\text{Planned VIMG} = \left(\frac{\Delta M}{M}\right)^t + \left(\frac{\Delta V}{V}\right)^e \tag{16-15}$$

The difference between the two is:

$$\text{Actual VIMG} - \text{Planned VIMG} = \left(\frac{\Delta M}{M}\right)^a + \left(\frac{\Delta V}{V}\right)^a - \left(\frac{\Delta M}{M}\right)^t - \left(\frac{\Delta V}{V}\right)^e$$

or,

$$\text{Actual VIMG} - \text{Planned VIMG} = \left[\left(\frac{\Delta M}{M}\right)^a - \left(\frac{\Delta M}{M}\right)^t\right] + \left[\left(\frac{\Delta V}{V}\right)^a - \left(\frac{\Delta V}{V}\right)^e\right] \tag{16-16}$$

Equation 16–16 shows that actual velocity-indexed money growth can differ from planned velocity-indexed money growth for two reasons: One, actual money growth differs from targeted money growth, or two, actual velocity growth differs from estimated velocity growth. The difference between actual and planned velocity-indexed money

TABLE 16-1
The Quantity
Theory Equation:
*Actual Experience of
M1 in the 1980s (in
Percents)*

Year	(1) Actual Rate of Change in M1	+	(2) Actual Rate of Change in V1	=	(3) Actual Inflation Rate	+	(4) Actual Rate of Change in Real GNP	=	(5) Actual Rate of Change in Nominal GNP*
	$\Delta M1/M1$	+	$\Delta V1/V1$	=	$\Delta P/P$	+	$\Delta Y/Y$	=	$(\Delta P/P + \Delta Y/Y)$
1980	7.4	+	1.4	=	9.0	−	0.2	=	8.8
1981	5.4	+	6.2	=	9.7	+	1.9	=	11.6
	(2.3)†		(9.3)						
1982	8.8	−	4.9	=	6.4	−	2.5	=	3.9
1983	10.4	−	2.9	=	3.9	+	3.6	=	7.5
1984	5.4	+	5.1	=	3.7	+	6.8	=	10.5
1985	12.0	−	5.6	=	3.0	+	3.4	=	6.4
1986	15.5	−	10.2	=	2.6	+	2.7	=	5.3
1987	6.3	+	0.6	=	3.2	+	3.7	=	6.9
1988	4.3	+	3.4	=	3.3	+	4.4	=	7.7
1989	0.6	+	6.4	=	4.1	+	2.9	=	7.0

*Before 1992, the main measure of output reported by the Department of Commerce was gross national product. Therefore, the Fed used GNP in its monetary policy reports. Since 1992, it uses GDP.
†Actual M1 figures in parentheses are adjusted for shifts in NOW accounts in 1981.
Source: Federal Reserve Board and *Economic Report of the President,* 1981 to 1990.

growth is equal to the difference between actual and predicted growth in nominal GDP. Pragmatic monetary targeters are willing to alter targets for money growth in response to velocity errors to prevent actual growth in nominal GDP from deviating from planned growth; rigid monetary targeters are not.

In practice there are shades of pragmatic and rigid monetary aggregate targeting. By and large, however, the Fed has acted as a pragmatic targeter, as we shall see by examining the U.S. experience with targeting monetary aggregates in the 1980s and 1990s.

THE U.S. EXPERIENCE IN THE 1980s

To evaluate the conduct of monetary policy in the 1980s, we shall use quantity theory Equation 16–10 in three ways: to interpret the setting of targets and forecasts by the FOMC in February of each year; to interpret the actual outcome of monetary policy each year; and to compare the FOMC's policy intentions with the actual outcomes. We shall look at the experience with M1 and M2 targets between 1980 and 1989.

M1: The Narrow Monetary Aggregate

When applied to the actual outcome of monetary policy each year, quantity theory Equation 16–10 says that actual money growth plus actual velocity growth must equal the actual growth in nominal GNP (or GDP). In Table 16–1, we solve Equation 16–10 for the actual annual rate of change in V1, given the actual rate of change in M1, *P*, and *Y* for the years from 1980 to 1989. The numbers in column 2 of the table show the erratic behavior

TABLE 16–2
The Quantity
Theory Equation:
*M1 Target Ranges
and Associated
Predictions in the
1980s (in Percents)*

Year	(1) Target Range for M1 Growth ΔM1/M1	+	(2) Estimated Range for *V*1 Growth Δ*V*1/*V*1	=	(3) Predicted Range for Growth of Nominal GNP (Δ*P*/*P* + Δ*Y*/*Y*)
1980	4 to 6 1/2		3 1/2 to 4 1/2		7 1/2 to 11
1981	6 to 8 1/2		3 to 3 1/2		9 to 12
	(3 1/2 to 6)*		(5 1/2 to 6)		
1982	2 1/2 to 5 1/2		5 1/2 to 5		8 to 10 1/2
1983	4 to 8		3 1/4		7 1/4 to 11 1/4
1984	4 to 8		4 to 2 1/2		8 to 10 1/2
1985	4 to 7		3 to 1 1/2		7 to 8 1/2
1986	3 to 8		2 to 1/2		5 to 8 1/2
1987	No target				4 1/2 to 7 1/2
1988	No target				5 1/2 to 8 1/2
1989	No target				5 1/2 to 8 1/2

*M1 target ranges in parentheses are adjusted for shifts in NOW accounts.

Source: Federal Reserve Board, *Monetary Policy Report to the Congress* in February of each year.

of *V*1 in the 1980s. In 1982, growth in *V*1 turned negative and was negative again in 1983, 1985, and 1986.

Were these negative growth rates predicted by the Fed? To answer this question, in Table 16–2 we use the quantity theory equation to compute the ranges for the estimated growth of *V*1, given the FOMC's annual target ranges for M1 growth and its prediction ranges for growth in nominal GNP. When applied to the decision making of the FOMC, Equation 16–10 says that the targeted rate of growth of M1 plus the estimated rate of growth of *V*1 must equal the predicted rate of growth in nominal GNP.

The second column of Table 16–2 reveals that the Fed never predicted a negative growth rate of *V*1, that its lowest prediction of *V*1 growth was *plus* 1/2 percent in 1986, and that the midpoint of the range of predictions of *V*1 growth was close to the historical norm of 3 percent most years. Comparing the second columns of Table 16–1 and 16–2, we see that velocity growth was outside the predicted ranges every year between 1980 and 1986.

How did the Fed react to these velocity errors? By comparing the first column in the two tables, we see that actual M1 growth was outside the target ranges every year between 1980 and 1986, except 1984. In 1980 and 1981 the deviation between actual and targeted money growth most likely reflected the Fed's difficulty in controlling money growth under the nonborrowed reserves operating procedures. From 1982 on, however, the monetary policy reports to Congress show that the Fed was acting as a pragmatic monetary targeter; it allowed M1 to grow outside the preestablished target ranges to compensate for velocity errors. Actual growth in nominal GNP was within the predicted range in five of the seven years, as shown by a comparison of the last column in the two tables.

The year 1982 was a turning point for the Fed. By the time of the midyear policy review, it was evident to the Fed that monetary policy was more contractionary than intended. Thus, the FOMC allowed M1 growth to exceed the upper end of its target range. The additional 3 percent growth in M1, however, was not enough to offset the decline in velocity, and the growth in nominal GNP was about 4 percentage points less than the Fed had predicted in February of 1982. We also note that although real GNP fell by 2.5 percent, this decline was not intended, or at least not predicted, by the Fed. In its monetary policy report to Congress in February 1982, the Fed predicted that real GNP growth would range from 1/2 to 3 percent in 1982 (not shown in Table 16–2).

In 1983 and in 1985, velocity growth was again unexpectedly negative. In response, the Fed rebased and widened the target ranges for M1 at midyear and then let M1 grow above its revised target ranges. Thus, actual growth in nominal GNP was close to or within the predicted ranges in each of those years. In 1986, the Fed allowed M1 growth to soar to 15.5 percent to offset a postwar record decline in $V1$ of 10.2 percent. Finally in 1987, the Fed stopped setting targets for M1.

Why Was $V1$ Falling?   Beginning in the mid-1970s, more intensive use of cash management techniques by nonfinancial firms and by households led to an unexpected decrease in the demand for M1 and, thus, an unexpected increase in $V1$. By 1982, however, the situation changed; $V1$ began to decline. To investigate why $V1$ was falling, we round up the obvious suspects: i, r_D, Y, and C, which are the factors affecting velocity in Equation 16-7.

- First, real GNP fell by 2.5 percent in 1982 as the United States suffered the worst recession since the Great Depression. A decrease in Y induces a decrease in velocity if the income elasticity of money demand is less than 1.
- Second, in 1982 interest rates began to fall in response to a weak economy, a decline in inflation, and a more expansionary monetary policy. As a result, demand for M1 increased and $V1$ fell.
- Third, the nationwide introduction of NOW accounts in 1981 increased the M1 deposit rate, with the ceiling temporarily set at 5 1/4 percent. As a result, the spread between the interest rate and the M1 deposit rate decreased, thereby increasing the demand for M1 deposits vis-à-vis marketable securities.
- Fourth are the other factors grouped under the collective variable, C. For example, the Fed argued that increased uncertainty caused by the recession was depressing the velocity of M1 by increasing the demand for liquid money balances. On the other hand, monetarist critics of the Fed contended that the Fed's own erratic monetary policy was the source of the increased uncertainty that was increasing money demand.

Against the backdrop of deregulation and falling interest rates, the Fed continued to have problems predicting velocity growth, as we have seen. Because the behavior of $V1$ was far from historical norms and because the Fed was not able to predict the new behavior, it stopped setting targets for M1 after 1986. The Fed, however, did provide an explanation for the new behavior of money demand by applying to the laws of asset demand the observed rate-setting practices of banks under the new financial environment. Several Humphrey-Hawkins reports in the 1980s argued that the *short-run* interest responsiveness of M1 had increased because of these new rate-setting practices. Let us see why.

According to the laws of asset demand, the demand for M1 varies inversely with the spread between the interest rate on substitutes for M1 deposits and the interest rate on M1 deposits. Marketable securities and non-M1 deposits are both substitutes for M1 deposits. In the old financial environment, the M1 deposit rate and the non-M1 deposit rate were fixed by regulation, as was the spread between the two rates. In the new financial environment, these rates are free to move in response to market forces. Until 1986 the rate on NOW accounts was fixed, but the rates on Super-NOW accounts and on the bulk of non-M1 deposits were free to move. With the rate-setting practices of banks that have emerged since the advent of the new financial environment, the deposit rate on checkable deposits moves more sluggishly in response to changes in market interest rates than does the deposit rate on non-M1 deposits.

With the current behavior of banks, the speed of adjustment in deposit rates generally varies inversely with the liquidity of deposit accounts. The more liquid the deposit, the slower the speed of adjustment. Hence, when market rates of interest fall, the spread between the non-M1 deposit rate and the M1 deposit rate falls. In response, the public moves funds out of time deposits, money market mutual funds, and other M2 deposits into interest-bearing M1 deposits whose rates have not yet fallen. This shift in funds from the broad to the narrow monetary aggregate is in addition to the traditional shift in funds from marketable securities into M1 deposits when market rates of interest decline. Similarly, when market rates of interest rise, the public moves funds out of M1 deposits into marketable securities and into other deposit categories whose rates rise faster than the M1 deposit rate. Thus, the short-run interest responsiveness of M1 increases, as does the short-run interest responsiveness of $V1$.

Because of the uncertainties surrounding the behavior of $V1$, especially its short-run interest responsiveness, the Fed has not resumed the practice of setting targets for M1. Note, however, that in 1987 $V1$ growth did turn positive as market rates of interest rose.

M2: A Broad Monetary Aggregate

Tables 16–3 and 16–4 apply quantity theory Equation 16–10 to M2. Table 16–3 records the actual experience, and Table 16–4 the targets and predictions. Table 16–3 shows that the rate of change in $V2$, like the rate of change in $V1$, was negative in 1982, 1983, 1985, and 1986. Some of the same factors affecting M1 were also affecting the non-M1 components of M2 and, thus, $V2$. For example, a deteriorating economy in 1982 decreased $V2$. Also, the availability of new deposit instruments that paid market-related rates drew funds from Treasury securities and other marketable securities into M2 deposits, thereby decreasing $V2$. However, the prediction problems with $V2$ were not as acute as those with $V1$.

The errors in predicting velocity growth were smaller for $V2$ than for $V1$ in 1982, 1985, and 1986; in 1983 the errors were equal. Let us carry out the calculations for 1986, the year when the difference between the size of the $V1$ error and the $V2$ error was greatest.

By definition, the error in predicting velocity growth equals actual velocity growth minus predicted velocity growth. For $V1$, actual velocity growth was minus 10.2 percent in 1986. On the other hand, the Fed predicted that the growth rate of $V1$ would range from 0.5 percent of 2 percent, which means that the midpoint of the prediction range was 1.25 percent. Using the midpoint for the predicted rate of growth of $V1$ in our calculation,

TABLE 16–3
The Quantity
Theory Equation:
Actual Experience of
M2 in the 1980s (in
Percents)

Year	(1) Actual Rate of Change in M2 $\Delta M2/M2$	+	(2) Actual Rate of Change in V2 $\Delta V2/V2$	=	(3) Actual Rate of Change in Nominal GNP $(\Delta P/P + \Delta Y/Y)$
1980	8.9	−	0.1	=	8.8
1981	9.3	+	2.3	=	11.6
1982	9.1	−	5.2	=	3.9
1983	12.2	−	4.7	=	7.5
1984	7.9	+	2.6	=	10.5
1985	8.9	−	2.5	=	6.4
1986	9.3	−	4.0	=	5.3
1987	4.3	+	2.6	=	6.9
1988	5.2	+	2.5	=	7.7
1989	4.5	+	2.5	=	7.0

Source: Federal Reserve Board and *Economic Report of the President,* 1981 to 1990.

we find that the prediction error for $V1$ in 1986 was minus 11.45 percent: − 10.2 percent − 1.25 percent = −11.45 percent. This means that the actual growth rate of $V1$ was about 11 percentage points below the Fed's prediction. On the other hand, the error in predicting $V2$ growth was only minus 3.25 percent: the difference between minus 4 percent, the actual growth rate of $V1$, and minus 0.75 percent, the midpoint of the Fed's prediction range.

One reason for the smaller errors in predicting $V2$ growth is that the decline in $V2$ was not as far from its historical experience as was the decline in $V1$. The average rate of growth of $V1$ was plus 3.8 percent for the period from 1972 to 1981, but minus 0.9 percent for the period from 1982 to 1989. By comparison, the average rate of growth of $V2$ was plus 0.9 percent for the period from 1972 to 1981 and minus 0.7 percent for the period from 1982 to 1989. Furthermore, some problems associated with predicting the demand for M1 balances do not affect the demand for M2 balances. In particular, shifts between NOW accounts and the non-M1 component of M2, in response to changes in the spread between deposit rates, are internalized within M2. Of course, this does not mean that deregulation has not affected the interest responsiveness of the demand for M2. As Chapter 7 notes, deregulation has reduced the long-run interest responsiveness of M2. Economists at the Fed estimate that it currently takes about a year and a half for the M2 deposit rate to adjust fully to a change in the market rate of interest. For periods of a year or less, demand for M2 retains considerable interest responsivenss.

The Fed did not abandon M2 targets along with M1 targets in 1987. In 1988, however, it widened the M2 target range from 3 to 4 percentage points. It also began a strategy to achieve a soft landing of the economy, that is, to reduce inflation without creating negative growth in real output. In line with this strategy, in 1989 the Fed lowered the target range for M2 growth from 4 to 8 percent to 3 to 7 percent.

TABLE 16–4
The Quantity Theory Equation: *M2 Target Ranges and Associated Predictions in the 1980s (in Percents)*

Year	(1) Target Range for M2 Growth $\Delta M2/M2$	+	(2) Estimated Range for *V2* Growth $\Delta V2/V2$	=	(3) Predicted Range for Growth in Nominal GNP $(\Delta P/P + \Delta Y/Y)$
1980	6 to 9		1 1/2 to 2 1/2		7 1/2 to 11 1/2
1981	6 to 9		3		9 to 12
1982	6 to 9		2 to 1 1/2		8 to 10 1/2
1983	7 to 10		1/4 to 1 1/4		7 1/4 to 11 1/4
1984	6 to 9		2 to 1 1/2		8 to 10 1/2
1985	6 to 9		1 to –1/2		7 to 8 1/2
1986	6 to 9		–1 to –1/2		5 to 8 1/2
1987	5 1/2 to 8 1/2		–1		4 1/2 to 7 1/2
1988	4 to 8		1 1/2 to 1/2		5 1/2 to 8 1/2
1989	3 to 7		2 1/2 to 1 1/2		5 1/2 to 8 1/2

Source: Federal Reserve Board, *Monetary Policy Report to the Congress* in February of each year.

THE U.S. EXPERIENCE IN THE 1990s

Tables 16–5 and 16–6 illustrate the quantity theory equation from 1990 through the first half of 1993. Table 16–5 shows the actual experience, and Table 16–6 the Fed's targets and predictions. If we compare these tables with Tables 16–3 and 16–4, we see that actual and predicted growth of nominal GNP (or GDP) were lower in the 1990s than in the late 1980s. So were actual and targeted growth of M2.

In the second half of 1990, growth in real GDP (not shown in the tables) was negative. The Fed did not achieve its soft landing. Tighter monetary policy in the late 1980s coupled with temporarily higher oil prices in the aftermath of the Iraqi invasion of Kuwait in the summer of 1990, caused the slowdown in economic activity.[7]

In setting its monetary targets in February 1991, the FOMC again lowered the target ranges: from 3 to 7 percent to 2 1/2 to 6 1/2 percent. The *Monetary Policy Report to the Congress,* however, explicitly noted that the FOMC was seeking money growth at least in the middle of the range: "While acknowledging some uncertainty about developing velocity relationships, Committee members stress that M2 expansion noticeably above the lower end of the range likely woud be needed to foster a satisfactory performance of the economy in 1991." Actual growth in M2, however, came in near the lower end of the target range, at

---

[7] The rise in oil prices was an adverse supply-side shock that increased the cost of supplying output, resulting in an increase in the price level. As a result, the interest rate rose and aggregate demand for goods and services fell.

TABLE 16–5
The Quantity
Theory Equation:
Actual Experience of
M2 in the 1990s

Year	(1) Actual Rate of Change in M2 ΔM2/M2	+	(2) Actual Rate of Change in V2 ΔV2/V2	=	(3) Actual Rate of Change in Nominal GNP (or GDP)* $(\Delta P/P + \Delta Y/Y)$
1990	4.0	+	1.2	=	5.2
1991	2.9	+	−0.2	=	2.7
1992	1.8	+	3.6	=	5.4
1993	1.6	+	4.2	=	5.8

*Nominal GDP is the measure of output used after 1991.
Source: Federal Reserve Board and *Economic Report of the President* 1991–1994.

TABLE 16–6
The Quantity
Theory Equation:
M2 Target Ranges
and Associated
Predictions in the
1990s

Year	(1) Target Range of M2 Growth ΔM2/M2	+	(2) Estimated Range of V2 Growth ΔV2/V2	=	(3) Predicted Range for Growth of Nominal GNP (or GDP) $(\Delta P/P + \Delta Y/Y)$
1990	3 to 7		1 to 0		4 to 7
1991	2 1/2 to 6 1/2		1 to −1		3 1/2 to 5 1/2
1992	2 1/2 to 6 1/2		1 1/2 to −1/2		4 to 6
1993	2 to 6		3 1/4 to 1/4		5 1/4 to 6 1/4

Source: Federal Reserve Board and *Economic Report of the President,* 1991–1994.

2.9 percent, and nominal GDP growth fell below the lower end of the predicted range, as shown in Tables 16–5 and 16–6.

In 1992 and 1993, M2 growth slowed, but velocity growth spurted above the upper end of the Fed's prediction ranges, so that nominal GDP growth fell within the Fed's prediction ranges. What was the reason for the increase in *V2*?

At the time, market rates of interest and deposit rates were both falling to levels not seen since the 1960s. We know that velocity varies positively with i and inversely with r_D; that is:

$$i\downarrow \to M^d\uparrow \to V\downarrow$$

and

$$r_D\downarrow \to M^d\downarrow \to V\uparrow$$

FIGURE 16–2
M2 Velocity and
Opportunity Cost

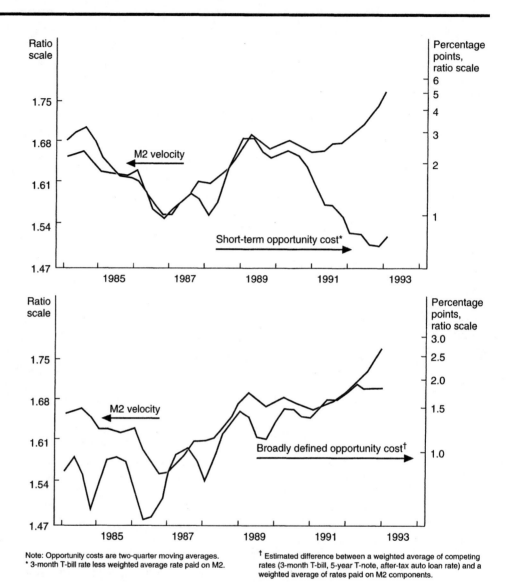

Note: Opportunity costs are two-quarter moving averages.
* 3-month T-bill rate less weighted average rate paid on M2.

† Estimated difference between a weighted average of competing rates (3-month T-bill, 5-year T-note, after-tax auto loan rate) and a weighted average of rates paid on M2 components.

Source: *Monetary Policy Report to the Congress,* July 1993, 24.

We also know from Equation 16–6 that for falling rates to explain rising velocity, the opportunity cost of deposits must rise. This, in turn, requires that deposit rates fall by a greater amount than market rates of interest. Was the opportunity cost of M2 deposits rising in 1992 and 1993? To answer this question, let's look at Figure 16–2, which is from the Fed's *Monetary Policy Report to the Congress* in July 1993.

The upper panel shows *V*2 and the traditional short-run opportunity cost of M2 deposits: the difference between the three-month T-bill rate and a weighted average of rates paid on components of M2. This measure of the opportunity cost fell steeply in 1992 and 1993 and therefore cannot explain the rise in *V*2. The lower panel of the graph shows that a broader measure of the opportunity cost explains the behavior of *V*2 better, although not perfectly. This broader measure of the opportunity cost rose in the first part of 1992, then dipped down, and later leveled out.

The market interest rates the Fed used to construct the broader measure are the three-month T-bill rate, the five-year T-note rate, and after-tax rates on auto loans. Longer term interest rates did not fall as much as short-term interest rates. In search of rates higher than the paltry 3 to 4 percent banks were paying on small time deposits, the public moved out of these deposits in droves. Small time deposits issued by commercial banks fell by almost 30 percent in 1992. These funds went into longer term debt and equity securities and into mutual funds that buy these securities, none of which are included in the monetary aggregates, and into transactions deposits, whose rates had not fallen as much as the rates on nontransactions deposits.

Why did the Fed also include auto loans in its broad measure of the opportunity cost of deposits? The reason is that repaying debt is an alternative to holding bank deposits. With deposit rates low compared with bank loan rates, many households took the opportunity to repay some of the debt that had built up in the 1980s and thereby reduced their balance sheet stress.

Because of the difficulty in forecasting velocity growth in this environment, Fed Chairman Alan Greenspan announced in July 1993 that "the behavior of the aggregates relative to their annual ranges will likely be of limited use in guiding policy over the next eighteen months." (The Fed also reduced the target range for growth of M2 from 2 to 6 percent to 1 to 5 percent for the second half of 1993.) It also elevated the status of real interest rates as an indicator of monetary policy, as Chapter 13 explaines. The Fed does not, however, announce numerical objectives for real interest rates. That leaves the Fed's forecasts of nominal GDP. Despite the Fed's reluctance to call this variable a target, this chapter has shown that the Fed acts as if it were targeting growth of nominal GDP. At the time of Greenspan's announcement in mid-1993, growth of nominal GDP was below the Fed's forecasting range. For the entire year, however, the nominal GDP growth, at 5.8 percent, fell within the forecasting range, as Tables 16–5 and 16–6 show. Moreover, inflation was in check at 2.9 percent.

SUMMARY

- As an identity, the velocity of circulation is the number of times per period that each dollar circulates to buy final goods and services. To calculate *V*, we divide nominal GDP by the stock of money. The inverse of velocity is the Cambridge *k*, calculated by dividing the nominal quantity of money by nominal GDP. It is the fraction of income that the public holds as money.

- Multiplying each side of the definition of velocity by the quantity of money, *M*, we end up with the identity $MV \equiv PY$, called the *equation of exchange*. This identity states that the velocity-indexed quantity of money is equal to nominal GDP.

- As a behavioral relation, velocity is the number of times per period that the public wants each dollar to circulate in buying final goods and services. Thus, planned velocity is the ratio between GDP and the demand for money. Planned velocity depends on GDP and on the determinants of money demand.

- We make the equation of exchange a theory by specifying the economic variable that moves to establish the equation. According to the quantity theory of money, nominal GDP is determined at the point that velocity-indexed money equals nominal GDP. If velocity-indexed money is greater than nominal GDP, nominal GDP rises, and if velocity-indexed money is less than nominal GDP, nominal GDP falls.

- Rewriting the quantity theory equation $MV = PY$ in percentage form, we obtain the statement that velocity-indexed money growth equals the rate of growth in nominal GDP, which is equal to the sum of the rate of inflation and the rate of growth of real GDP.

- Assuming that, in the long run, velocity growth and real GDP growth are constant, we have a one-to-one relation between (nonindexed) nominal money growth and inflation. There is no debate about this relation as a long-run guide to monetary policy.

- Controversy arises when the equality of velocity-indexed money growth and nominal GDP growth is used as the basis for short-run, activist, monetary policy. Rigid monetary targeters recommend a constant rate of (nonindexed) growth of the quantity of money. Pragmatic monetary targeters argue in favor of varying the targets for money growth in view of new information about actual velocity growth and even new information about the mix of inflation and real GDP growth.

- Deregulation and disinflation in the 1980s caused velocity growth to deviate from its historical norm. The deviations were greatest for $V1$. The Fed found it difficult to predict the new behavior of $V1$. Thus, beginning in 1982, it began acting as a pragmatic monetary targeter by letting M1 growth move outside the preestablished target ranges to offset velocity errors. In 1987 the Fed stopped setting targets for M1 altogether, and in 1988 it widened the target range for M2 from 3 to 4 percentage points.

- In 1992 and 1993, M2 growth fell below the lower end of the Fed's wider target ranges, while $V2$ growth was above the upper end of its estimated range. In July 1993, the Fed downgraded M2 as a guide to monetary policy.

- Since 1982 the Fed has acted as if it were targeting nominal GDP growth.

KEY TERMS AND CONCEPTS

velocity of circulation

Cambridge k

equation of exchange

velocity-indexed supply of money

Cambridge equation

planned, or estimated, velocity

quantity theory of money

pragmatic monetary targeters

rigid monetary targeters

actual velocity-indexed money growth

planned velocity-indexed money growth

QUESTIONS AND PROBLEMS

1. Use the following data for 1991 to calculate $V1$ and $V2$: M1 = \$898.1 billion; M2 = \$3,439.8 billion; PY = \$5,677.5 billion/year.

2. Use the data in Question 1 to calculate the Cambridge k for the M1 and M2 measures of money.

3. Use the data in Tables B-1 and B-65 of the most recent *Economic Report of the President* to calculate the values of $V1$ and $V2$ last year.

4. Explain the following statement: The equation of exchange is about money moving while the Cambridge equation is about money resting.

5. What is the difference between actual and planned velocity?

6. What is the difference between the equation of exchange and the quantity theory of money?

7. Suppose that interest rates and deposit rates both rise, but interest rates rise more than deposit rates. What will be the effect on planned velocity?

8. Suppose the public wants to hold more securities and less money because of an improvement in financial technology that increases the liquidity of securities.
   a. What will be the effect on planned velocity?
   b. According to the quantity theory of money, what will be the effect on nominal GDP?

9. The AD–AS model developed in Chapter 10 and the quantity theory model both give the result that an increase in *M* will increase nominal GDP. What are the differences between the models?

10. In 1992, the growth of the broad measure of money (M2 + CDs) in Japan was 0.6 percent, the rate of inflation was 1.8 percent, and the rate of growth of real GNP was 0.5 percent. Find the actual growth of velocity.

11. Use the information in Tables 16–5 and 16–6 to find the difference between actual and planned velocity-indexed money growth in the United States in 1991. (Use the midpoints of the ranges in calculating planned velocity-indexed money growth.) Was monetary policy more or less expansionary than predicted in 1991?

The Wall Street Journal

12. Use the concepts of rigid and pragmatic monetary aggregate targeting to analyze the following statement by Milton Friedman, "Too Tight for a Strong Recovery," *The Wall Street Journal,* October 23, 1992:

> Continuation of M2 growth at 2% per year would imply actual deflation, not negligible inflation. Given its departure from its own policy, the Fed now needs to speed up sharply monetary growth to bring M2 back into its target range and then hold it there. If it continues with its present excessively tight monetary policy it will set the stage, if it has not already done so, for an economic situation that will produce irresistable pressure to go from one extreme to the other, as it has so often done in the past. And if that happens, and the Fed reacts too strongly, it would produce another inflationary bubble.

13. With long-run monetary aggregate targeting, under what conditions will actual inflation deviate from targeted inflation?

14. Would you characterize the Fed as a rigid monetary targeter or a pragmatic monetary targeter in the 1980s and 1990s? What evidence supports your answer?

15. Why did the Fed stop setting targets for M1 in 1987?

16. Suppose that in February of next year the Fed predicts that the annual rate of growth of nominal GDP will be 6 percent, with inflation at 2.5 precent and real GDP growth at 3.5 percent. Suppose, too, that the Fed forecasts growth of *V2* equal to 2 percent and, thus, sets a target of 4 percent for M2 growth. (Assume that all forecasts and targets are midpoints of the respective ranges.) Suppose, finally, that at midyear the Fed revises its forecast of annual velocity growth downward from 2 percent to 0.5 percent. What would the Fed do if it were a rigid monetary targeter? A pragmatic monetary targeter?

17. What is the "broad opportunity cost" of M2 deposits? What is its relevance to monetary policy in 1992 and 1993?

SUGGESTED READINGS

Feinman, Joshua, and Richard D. Porter. "The Continuous Weakness in M2." Board of Governors of the Federal Reserve System, Finance and Economic Discussion Series no. 209, September 1992.
   A theoretical and empirical analysis of the factors responsible for weak M2 demand in the early 1990s.
Friedman, Benjamin M. "Lessons on Monetary Policy from the 1980s." *Journal of Economic Perspectives* 2, no. 3 (Summer 1988): 51–72.
   An analysis of the conduct of monetary policy in the 1980s.
Friedman, Milton. "Quantity Theory of Money." In *The New Palgrave: Money,* ed. John Eatwell, Murray Milgate, and Peter Newman. New York: W. W. Norton, 1989, 1–40.

A concise statement of the intellectual foundations of the quantity theory of money and its policy implications. Contains an extensive bibliography.
Poole, William. "Monetary Policy Lessons of Recent Inflation and Disinflation," *Journal of Economic Perspectives* 2, no. 3 (Summer 1988): 73–100.
   An analysis of the conduct of monetary policy in the 1980s.
Tobin, James. "Monetary Policy: Rules, Targets, and Shocks." *Journal of Money, Credit and Banking,* November 1983, 506–18.
   The "Journal of Money, Credit, and Banking Lecture" in which Tobin sketched a multistage framework for the conduct of monetary policy based on discretion rather than rules.

Wenninger, John, and John Partlan. "Small Time Deposits and Recent Weakness in M2." *Quarterly Review* (Federal Reserve Bank of New York) 17, no. 1 (Spring 1992): 21–35.

Examines the factors that contributed to the decline of small time deposits in 1992 and considers whether M2 should be redefined to exclude small time deposits.

P A R T 5

FINANCIAL INSTITUTIONS
Structure, Regulation, and Behavior

17   The Structure, Regulation, and Supervision of U.S. Depository Institutions

18   The Profit-Maximizing Banking Firm

19   Nondepository Financial Institutions

Part 5 examines the regulatory environment in which financial institutions operate and the strategies they pursue to maximize profits. Therefore, it fits into the first pillar of our two-pillar framework.

THE STRUCTURE, REGULATION, AND SUPERVISION OF U.S. DEPOSITORY INSTITUTIONS

CHAPTER PREVIEW

From 1945 to 1980 there were, on average, fewer than five bank failures per year in the United States. The number started to rise after that, peaking at 206 in 1989. In the 1980s, thrift institutions were failing by even larger numbers, as Chapter 5 discusses. Even after this decrease in the number of banks and thrifts, approximately 26,000 depository institutions still operated in the United States in 1993. Of this number, about 11,000 were commercial banks, compared with only about 1,500 commercial banks in Great Britain, France, Germany, and Japan together.

This chapter begins with a road map of the U.S. financial system. After surveying this road map, it examines how banks and thrifts are organized and regulated. The regulatory structure for depository institutions grew out of the need to stem the collapse of thousands of banks and restore confidence in the banking system after the Great Depression. Measured by the number of bank failures, the regulatory structure worked reasonably well until the late 1970s, when the health of thrifts, and later banks, weakened. There were several culprits: declining levels of capital, a nonrisk-based system of deposit insurance, insufficient supervision, geographic restrictions, increased competition from nondepositories, and even fraud in some cases.

The *Financial Institutions Reform, Recovery and Enforcement Act (FIRREA) of 1989* attempted to address the causes of the thrift crisis by providing new regulatory and insurance environments for savings and loan associations and by strengthening capital requirements. FIRREA also mandated the U.S. Treasury to organize a study of deposit insurance. As an outgrowth of that study, in 1991 the Bush administration proposed a bank reform plan that would permit interstate banking, consolidate regulatory agencies, reform deposit insurance, allow industrial companies to own commercial banks, and allow banks to sell and underwrite securities and to sell insurance policies.

In 1991 Congress did pass new banking legislation, but in the aftermath of the thrift crisis, it was in no mood to give banks broad new powers. The *Federal Deposit Insurance Corporation Improvement Act (FDICIA) of 1991* mandated supervisory and regulatory reforms and expanded the borrowing authority of the FDIC, but did not expand the power of banks to diversify through nationwide branching or through entering new lines of business. Neither did it consolidate regulatory agencies. In 1994, however, Congress passed legislation allowing banks to branch nationwide. Moreover, regulators have been allowing banks to enter new lines of business within the framework of existing regulations. And in November 1993, the Clinton administration put forth a plan to consolidate regulatory agencies, as this chapter explains.

FINANCIAL FIRMS: AN OVERVIEW

Figure 17–1 will serve as our road map for examining the organization and regulatory structure of financial institutions in this part of the book. It shows how various kinds of financial firms fit into the U.S. economy.

Financial versus Industrial Firms

The apex of Figure 17–1 shows the separation, dating back to the 1930s, of financial and nonfinancial businesses in the United States. The Banking Act of 1933 (usually referred to as the Glass-Steagall Act) prevents banks from owning stock of nonfinancial (industrial) firms; a variety of other laws prohibit industrial firms from owning banks. These laws separating finance from commerce in the United States evolved from traditional populist mistrust of banks, combined with real concerns for potential abuses and conflicts of interest. For example, one concern is that an industrial firm in financial trouble might use the deposits of a bank it owns to finance its own risky or unprofitable endeavors. The intent of the 1933 act and related laws was to erect a wall between industrial firms and banks to prevent such abuses and their detrimental effects on the financial system. The Bush administration recommended the elimination of this wall. The proposed reform, which did not pass in Congress, would have permitted industrial firms to have controlling interests in banks and, conversely, would have permitted banks to own stock of industrial corporations.

Depositories versus Nondepositories

Financial institutions fall into two categories: depository and nondepository institutions. The difference between the two stems from their sources of funds: Depository institutions obtain funds by issuing deposits, while nondepositories, such as insurance companies and pension funds, issue contracts that are not deposits. Investment banks are also nonde-

FIGURE 17–1
Financial and
Nonfinancial Firms
in the U.S.
Economy

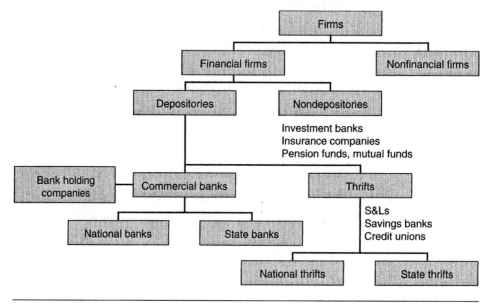

positories that underwrite new issues of securities and generally assist clients in buying or selling securities, as we saw in Chapter 2.

The Banking Act of 1933 also formalized the separation between depositories and nondepositories, especially between commercial banks and investment banks. This act not only prohibits banks from holding corporate stock, but also from underwriting such stock and, in general, from engaging in investment banking. Conversely, the act prohibits nondepositories from engaging in commercial banking activities, defined as the twin activities of accepting demand deposits and making commercial loans.

Financial innovations that exploited loopholes in the law have gradually eroded the distinction between commercial banks and investment banks, as Chapter 5 shows. Of primary importance is the ability of investment banks and brokerage houses to issue accounts, called *money market mutual funds,* against which checks may be written. Even though they issue checkable deposits, brokerage houses do not violate the letter of the law that prohibits them from engaging in commercial banking because they abstain from making commercial loans. The intrusion of nondepositories onto the turf of banks raises issues of fairness: If investment banks are allowed to engage in commercial banking, shouldn't commercial banks be permitted to engage in investment banking, say, to under-write stocks and to provide investment advice? Since 1989, on a case-by-case basis, the Fed has allowed commercial banks to set up separate affiliates to underwrite a limited amount of corporate bonds and stocks. Moreover, from the mid-1980s to the late 1980s the Fed and the comptroller of the currency extended the power of banks to offer broker-age services. It was not until 1992, however, that the Fed simplified the lengthy applica-tion process, thereby opening the door for more bank holding companies to offer brokerage services.

Commercial Banks versus Thrifts

Figure 17–1 shows that depository institutions are either commercial banks or thrifts. The names stem from the traditional purpose of each institution. Historically, commercial banks have catered to the financial needs of commerce by providing a substantial portion of short-term credit to nonfinancial businesses; they have also provided the bulk of the money in the form of checkable deposits. Thrifts, on the other hand, have specialized in the savings and credit needs of households.

There are three categories of traditional thrifts: savings and loan associations (S&Ls), savings banks, and credit unions. Each of these financial institutions pools the savings of households and places them (lends them) to satisfy particular credit needs of the public. The S&Ls and savings banks have primarily provided long-term credit in the form of mortgages to home buyers. Credit unions have provided short-term credit to their members, usually households.

National Banks versus State Banks: Dual Banking

To set up a commercial bank, the prospective owners must obtain a license, called a **charter**, that gives them the authority to operate. Banks chartered by the federal government are called **national banks**, and those chartered by state governments are called **state banks.**

The National Bank Act of 1863 established the **Office of the Comptroller of the Currency (OCC)**, a federal agency within the U.S. Treasury, to charter national banks. The act also set forth a procedure for chartering and supervising these banks. The chartering and supervision of state banks, on the other hand, were relegated to state banking commissions or departments. Thus, the 1863 act created a **dual banking system**, a system of national banks existing side by side with state banks.

Bank Holding Companies

Since the 1960s, another form of financial firm, called a **bank holding company**, has flourished in the United States. A bank holding company is a corporation that owns stock in one or more banks. One-bank holding companies own only one bank, while multiple-bank holding companies own two or more banks. One-bank holding companies came into prominence with the Bank Holding Act of 1956, which exempted them from registering with the Fed and, thus, placed them outside the regulatory reach of the Fed. As a result, many banks formed one-bank holding companies to avoid restrictions placed directly on the activities of banks. In 1970, amendments to the Bank Holding Act extended the supervisory and regulatory reach of the Fed to one-bank holding companies.

The Fed regulates banks primarily through bank holding companies. As of December 31, 1993, there were 6,111 bank holding companies, which controlled about 8,100 commercial banks—72 percent of all commercial banks. Because bank holding companies control the largest commercial banks, they also control the majority of bank assets—90 percent on December 31, 1993.

Having surveyed the road map, we turn to a detailed examination of the structure, regulation, and supervision of commercial banks and then thrifts. The next chapter examines the behavior of banks as profit-maximizing financial firms. Finally, Chapter 19 examines the structure, regulation, and supervision of nondepository institutions.

FIGURE 17–2
The Structure of
Commercial Banks:
December 1993

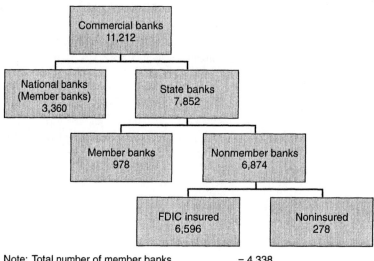

Note: Total number of member banks   = 4,338
      Total number of branches of members banks = 35,564
      Average number of branches per member   = 8.2

Source: Board of Governors of the Federal Reserve System, 80th Annual Report, 1993.

THE STRUCTURE OF COMMERCIAL BANKS

By the structure of banking we mean the number or size of banks at the national, state, or local level. Figure 17–2 shows that as of December 31, 1993, there were 11,212 commercial banks, of which 3,360 were national banks and 7,852 state banks.

The act that created the Federal Reserve System in 1913 requires that national banks be members of the system. State banks, however, are given a choice. They may become members if they satisfy some stringent requirements. By becoming a member bank, a state commercial bank is subject to supervision and regulation by the Federal Reserve. Only a small fraction of state banks, however, have chosen to be members of the Federal Reserve System. As of December 31, 1993, only 978 out of 7,852 state banks were members. Nonmember state banks outnumber member banks by eight to one. All banks that are members of the Federal Reserve System must have their deposits insured by the FDIC. Most nonmember state banks are also insured. As of December 31, 1993, only 278 out of 6,874 nonmember (state) banks were uninsured.

GEOGRAPHIC RESTRICTIONS

Laws that affect branching by banks within states and across state lines also affect the structure of the banking system. A unique feature of the U.S. banking system is the array of geographic restrictions placed on banks since the 1860s. These are the outgrowth of the dual banking system and the traditional populist hostility toward large banks, especially in rural areas.

Four laws are primarily responsible for the geographic restrictions. First, the National Banking Act of 1863 gave each state the right to control branching within its borders. By **branching** we mean the operation of a bank in more than one office. In 1927 the **McFadden Act** prohibited branching across state lines by national banks. It allowed, however, a national bank to open branches in the same city where its main office is located, provided that state banks are allowed the same privilege. The Banking Act of 1933 extended this privilege by allowing national banks to open branches in the same state, not simply the same city, provided that state banks also were allowed the same privilege. As of December 1992, the average member bank of the Federal Reserve system had 8.2 branches, a miniscule number compared with foreign banks.

Although the McFadden Act prevents a bank from setting up a unified branch network across state lines, neither it nor the Banking Act of 1933 prevent bank holding companies from chartering or acquiring banks in other states. As a result, the bank holding company became a popular device to avoid restrictions on interstate banking. In 1956 the Douglas Amendment to the Bank Holding Company Act introduced restrictions on bank holding companies. This amendment prohibited bank holding companies from chartering or acquiring a bank in another state, *unless explicitly permitted by state law.*

In sum, interstate banking by national banks had to be done by acquiring and owning a bank across state lines via a subsidiary of a bank holding company. To use this method a bank needed the explicit authorization of the state where the subsidiary would be located. While there were practically no authorizations between 1956 (the year of the passage of the Douglas Amendment) and 1979, the situation changed during the 1980s. By 1990 all but four states had permitted some sort of interstate banking via the use of a bank holding company. Thus, interstate banking was a reality, but a costly one. The costs of setting up a legally separate subsidiary in another state outweigh the costs of setting up branches of the same national bank. As part of its proposal to reform the banking system, in 1991 the U.S. Treasury recommended that nationwide branching by national banks be allowed in three years. This provision, however, did not pass the Congress.

Pros and Cons of Branching

Economists agree that nationwide branching would be beneficial not only to the economy as a whole, but also to small communities whose banks have resisted branching at any level—local, state, or national. Arguments against branching are advanced by community banks that want to protect their monopolistic advantages. Opponents of branching argue that large urban banks, through their branches, will siphon off the deposits from a small community bank to the big money-center banks, thereby depriving the community of funds for local loans. Reason and experience, however, suggest otherwise.

All banks, whether large ones with many branches or small community banks, want to make loans and investments that will be the most profitable. The prohibition of branching in a particular town or state will not prevent the bank from investing elsewhere, usually via a larger bank, if local lending opportunities are not profitable. Other things equal, the search for profits has the same effect on lending patterns as if the small bank were truly a branch of the larger bank. But other things are not equal. If the local community that is served by a single bank experiences an economic slowdown, the small bank that depends solely on its investments in this community will suffer losses. If these losses are severe, the bank may have to reduce lending even to creditworthy customers and may ultimately have to close its doors. As a result, the local community suffers. On the other hand, if the bank is a branch of a larger bank, the losses of this branch would be only a small part of a well-diversified portfolio and would not affect its ability to lend to good customers in the community.

The issue of diversification brings us to the most important reason why branching is desirable: Interstate branching will enable banks to achieve geographic diversification of their loan portfolios and, thus, make them less prone to insolvency in case of adverse economic conditions. In other words, removal of geographic restrictions promotes sound and safe banking. Without branching, diversification is limited, and banks are more likely to fail when adverse economic conditions hit the regional economy. Experience confirms this reasoning. Insolvencies and bank runs have been more widespread in states with limited statewide branching, notably Texas and Oklahoma.

Moreover, requiring bank holding companies to set up separately chartered and managed banks in different states raises costs and fosters inefficiency. Higher costs result in higher loan rates for the communities they serve, as compared with those served by branches of larger banks. Similarly, interstate branching is more likely to permit healthy competition in attracting funds and making loans.

Introduction of Nationwide Branching

In January 1994, the Office of the Comptroller of the Currency gave nationwide branching a boost by permitting First Fidelity Bancorp to consolidate its branches in New Jersey and Pennsylvania. The OCC's decision was based on its opinion that existing law allowed a bank operating on both sides of a state line to operate as a single bank. More important than this piecemeal approach, however, was the passage in September 1994 of the **Riegle-Neal Interstate Banking and Branching Efficiency Act**, which allows Banks to operate branches across the nation. The movement is toward a truly nationwide banking system with fewer banks. In such a system there will be large banks with nationwide branching and small unit banks capable of exploiting their superior knowledge of the small communities they serve. These small banks will rely on their efficiency rather than on monopoly power given to them by the McFadden Act.

THE SUPERVISION AND REGULATION OF BANKS

All banks are supervised and regulated. **Bank supervision** deals with ensuring the soundness and safety of banks. Examination of bank practices falls under the function of supervision. On the other hand, **bank regulation** consists of the administration of laws in the form of rules and regulations that affect the structure of the banking industry and the conduct of banking. Decisions about whether to approve a state bank as a new member of the Federal Reserve System, to approve a merger or acquisition involving a bank and another institution, or to approve a new activity by a bank would fall under the function of bank regulation.

Reasons for Bank Regulation

Banks are regulated and supervised to ensure that they remain healthy by following prudent practices. Healthy banks are important because:

· They are providers of credit.
· They are an outlet for small savers.
· They are providers of the medium of exchange.

First, because banks are the major source of credit to households and small businesses, the quantity of credit falls and the economy suffers when banks fail. Thus, banks are regulated to ensure that lending to households and firms is not disrupted. Second, because banks are major repositories of the public's wealth, they are regulated to protect the public. Third, because banks are the major source of the medium of exchange, the payments system is impaired and the economy suffers when banks fail.

The problem of ascertaining the health of banks is complicated because the bulk of their assets consists of loans to businesses and households. The quality of these loans, however, is the bank's privileged information. Depositors are unsure of that quality. Thus, depositors are influenced by rumors about the quality of a bank's assets and, hence, the bank's health. With the slightest rumor that a bank is unhealthy, depositors run to the bank to withdraw their deposits. A run on even a healthy bank will cause problems because loans are illiquid. There will be few buyers and only at substantially discounted prices. Therefore, the bank will not be able to sell enough loans to meet the withdrawals and may be forced to close.

Multiple and Overlapping Regulatory and Supervisory Jurisdictions

As we have seen, the Office of the Comptroller of the Currency issues charters to national banks. At the state level, the banking commission of the state in which the proposed bank will be located issues the charter. These authorities have supervisory jurisdiction over the banks they charter; the OCC supervises national banks, and the 50 state banking commissions supervise state banks. But two other authorities are also interested parties. The Federal Reserve has an interest because banks issue money in the form of deposits and because the Fed is the lender of last resort to the banking system. According to the law, the Fed is responsible for the nation's monetary policy as well as safeguarding the health of (member) banks. Also, the **Federal Deposit Insurance Corporation (FDIC)** insures the deposits issued by banks.

Figure 17–3 shows the four regulatory and supervisory agencies and their jurisdictions. State banking commissions are the oldest of the four agencies. They existed before the Banking Act of 1863, which formalized the authority of these state commissions and created the Office of the Comptroller of the Currency. The Federal Reserve System was created, as we saw in Chapter 11, by the Federal Reserve Act of 1913. Finally, the FDIC was created by the Glass-Steagall Act of 1933, and its authority strengthened by FIRREA (1989).

Most banks have multiple regulatory and supervisory agencies, as shown in Figure 17–3. For example, in principle, the OCC, the Fed, and the FDIC may supervise national banks; the Fed and the FDIC may supervise state member banks; and state banking commissions and the FDIC may supervise insured state banks that are not members of the Federal Reserve System. In practice, however, the agencies make arrangements to reduce duplication of supervision. The OCC has principal supervisory responsibility for national banks; the Federal Reserve for all bank holding companies and state member banks; and the FDIC for insured nonmember state banks. The Fed exercises its supervisory responsibilities over state member banks and bank holding companies through the 12 Federal Reserve District banks and through state banking agencies. Also, an agency fulfills its supervisory responsibility by reading reports prepared by banks and by their primary supervisory agency. Another common arrangement is for examiners from the Fed and from state banking commissions to alternate their annual on-site examinations.

FIGURE 17–3
The Four Bank
Regulatory and
Supervisory
Agencies and Their
Jurisdictions

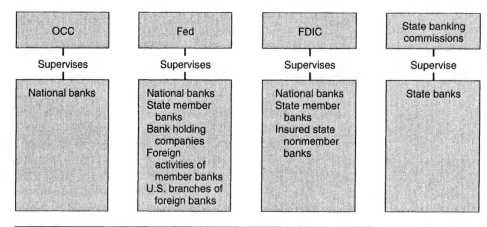

In addition to these four agencies, banks and bank holding companies are governed by laws. The Federal Reserve Board is responsible for administering key laws that affect bank holding companies. The Bank Holding Company Act of 1956 empowered the Fed to approve the formation of new bank holding companies and the acquisition of financial or nonfinancial firms by bank holding companies. The Merger Act of 1960 authorized the Fed to decide on the merger of a bank holding company with another firm. And according to the Change in Bank Control Act, the Fed must also approve any change in the control of a bank. To reach its decision, the Fed inquires about the financial condition, competence, experience, and integrity of the prospective owners. In recent years, the Fed has approved acquisitions by bank holding companies of corporations that are only remotely related to banking or to the financial industry. In this way, the Fed has allowed the separation between commercial banking and investment banking imposed by the Glass-Steagall Act gradually to erode.

The Fed also makes regulatory decisions about banking structure that affect state members banks. Of primary consideration is the decision to approve or disapprove the opening of new domestic branches. The members of the Board of Governors of the Federal Reserve System usually delegate these decisions to the Federal Reserve Bank in whose district the applying bank is located or to the Division of Banking Supervision and Regulation within the Board itself.

Streamlining
Regulatory
Agencies

As part of its reform plan, in 1991 the U.S. Treasury sought to reduce the cost and the burden of federal bank regulation by consolidating regulatory agencies. To achieve this goal, the Treasury proposed to reduce the number of federal banking regulators from three (OCC, Fed, and FDIC) to two: the Federal Reserve and a new agency, to be called the Federal Banking Agency, under the U.S. Treasury. Under the plan, the Federal Reserve would have supervised all state-chartered banks and their bank holding companies. The new agency would have supervised all national banks and their bank holding companies. The new agency would also have taken over all the duties of the OCC.

Finally, the FDIC would have been stripped of all regulatory and supervisory authority and be left to concentrate exclusively on insurance and resolution of failed depository institutions.

The Fed and the FDIC objected to the plan. Critics accused them of merely wanting to protect their turf. The Fed argued, however, that direct contact with banks through regulation and supervision was essential for it to carry out monetary policy and to safeguard the health of the financial system. The debate was a short one. This part of the reform plan never made it out of the subcommittee on financial institutions of the House Banking Committee. The issue came up again as part of the Clinton administration's drive to increase the efficiency and reduce the cost of government. In November 1993, the Treasury proposed to take the Fed and the FDIC out of the business of supervising and regulating banks. Under the proposed plan

- The regulatory functions of the Fed, the OCC, and the FDIC would be merged into a new independent federal regulatory agency governed by a five-member board. The Treasury and the Fed would each choose one member and the president would nominate and the Senate confirm the other three.
- The Office of the Comptroller of the Currency would be eliminated.
- The FDIC would continue to insure banks.
- The Federal Reserve would continue to determine monetary policy.

The Fed immediately objected to the plan. FedWatch 17.1 gives an overview of the Fed's arguments against the plan and counterarguments by a former FDIC chairman. This time, however, the Fed went beyond merely criticizing the Treasury's proposal. It offered a counterproposal, which ironically was similar to the 1991 proposal of the Bush administration. The Fed proposed that it regulate and supervise all state banks and that a new federal agency regulate and supervise national banks. The Fed's proposal gives banks regulatory choice. Banks that want to be regulated by the Fed would choose a state charter, while banks that want to be regulated by the new federal agency would choose a national charter. In addition, according to the Fed plan, the Fed would supervise and regulate bank holding companies.

As the public battle between the Fed and the Treasury intensified in March 1994, they were holding informal meetings to try to reach a compromise, with the Council of Economic Advisers trying to serve as an intermediary. In May 1994, the Fed and the Treasury put their negotiations on hold. They agreed that there was not enough time to resolve their differences and enact new legislation in 1994. In any future consolidation arrangement, the Fed is likely to retain a significant role as a regulator, especially because banks want to preserve regulatory choice.

DETAILS OF BANK SUPERVISION

Having looked at what agencies regulate banks and why, now let's see what an examination entails. All agencies usually follow the same general principles when conducting bank examinations. Agencies at the federal level have a standing committee that makes continuous efforts toward uniformity.

Fed*Watch* 17.1
Two Views on Centralizing Bank Regulation

In November 1993, the U.S. Treasury proposed to centralize bank regulation by creating a new federal agency to take over the regulatory and supervisory roles of the OCC, the Fed, and the FDIC, The proposal drew an immediate and unusually public response from Fed Chairman Alan Greenspan in an op-ed piece in *The Wall Street Journal** on December 15, 1993. In February 1994, in another op-ed piece in *The Wall Street Journal*,† William Seidman, the head of the FDIC from 1985 to 1991, refuted Greenspan's arguments against the Treasury's proposal. The following points and counterpoints are excerpts from the two op-ed pieces.

Greenspan:

While a single regulator would deal with duplication, inconsistency and overlap, it would also have important and exceptionally severe drawbacks: First, it would remove the Federal Reserve from direct, hands-on involvement in supervision and regulation, with bad effects on public policy in a number of areas, most especially in our ability to anticipate and cope with potential systemic financial problems.

Seidman:

What about the argument that the Fed would be unable to handle a crisis in the system without supervisory and regulatory authority? . . . Under the administration's proposal, the Federal Reserve will be part of the regulatory authority as a board member, and no doubt most of its current examiners will transfer to, and work for, the new consolidated agency. Further, all information related to the entire banking industry by law will be instantly available in one place *on a fully coordinated*

basis for the Fed's use. Such information is not available to the Fed or anyone else today.

Greenspan:

Second, a monolithic regulator would be less effective than two or more regulators in providing a necessary set of checks and balances to the oversight of depository institutions.

Seidman:

With regard to the argument that two or more regulators are necessary as "checks and balances," do we need two SECs or two FCCs for balance, or to provide regulatory shopping? The answer is no, clearly. No one would even suggest such a thing.

Greenspan:

While crises arise only sporadically, the Federal Reserve is involved in monetary policy continuously. In this area, too, the insights derived from our supervision and regulation are important inputs to the policy process. Certainly, a major factor in our decision to ease interest rates from 1989 on was our increasing awareness, importantly gained through the examination process, that banks were rapidly tightening their lending terms and standards. We were never able to offset fully the lending trauma that led to the "credit crunch" of the early 1990s, but we clearly contained its deleterious effects in a significant way. Without our hands-on bank supervisory activities, we might not have been aware of the seriousness of this problem until later.

Seidman:

Mr. Greenspan's statement to the effect that sound monetary policy requires supervisory authority has not been supported by the experience of other central banks, particularly the German Bundesbank, which many consider the pre-eminent monetary operator in Europe and perhaps the world. The Bundesbank has no regulatory duties, nor do about two-thirds of the central banks in the countries of the Organization for Economic Cooperation and Development.

---

* Alan Greenspan, "No Single Regulator for Banks," *The Wall Street Journal,* December 15, 1993, A16.
† William L. Seidman, "A New Way to Govern Banks," *The Wall Street Journal,* February 3, 1994, A14.

CAMEL Rating

Bank examiners from the primary supervisory authority make regular on-site reviews of the operations of a bank to appraise the quality of the bank's assets and evaluate the quality of its management. The examination culminates in a **CAMEL rating**:

C = Capital adequacy

A = Asset quality

M = Management

E = Earnings

L = Liquidity

The CAMEL rating is comprehensive, on a scale of one to five, with one signifying the best rating and five the worst.

This rating system is designed to provide an early warning signal to prevent a collapse. A CAMEL rating of three suggests that the bank deserves more supervisory attention. A bank with a rating of four or five is a *problem bank*. Past experience suggests that a substantial percentage of banks with ratings of five fail within one to three years. Banks with a rating of four have a better record of survival.

If examiners conclude that the overall CAMEL rating is unsatisfactory or even a particular component of CAMEL, say, the quality of management, is unsatisfactory, they recommend corrective actions. These recommendations range from informal (but written) agreements of understanding about the necessary steps to be taken by the bank to formal actions. Informal agreements are usually made if the problems are not too serious and the regulators have confidence in the ability and integrity of the bank's management. In more serious cases, including the failure of the management to abide by the agreed-upon informal measures, regulators resort to formal actions, such as cease-and-desist orders to the management, suspension or removal of the management, prohibition of certain activities, provision of loans via the Fed's discount window, and imposition of monetary fines. In 1993, for example, the Fed took 138 separate actions in 65 cases. Of particular note was the headline-grabbing case involving fraud by a foreign bank, the Bank of Credit and Commerce International (BCCI). The Fed assessed BCCI more than $45 million in fines and ordered restitution of an additional $188 million. More typical is the year 1990 when the Fed imposed a total of $3.1 million in fines.

Eventually, the decision to close or reorganize an insolvent bank may be necessary. The key player for reaching the decision and for implementing the closure itself is the FDIC, to which we shall turn shortly. First, however, we examine capital adequacy, a key indicator of the health of a bank.

Capital Adequacy

The capital, or, net worth, of a bank is the difference between the value of the bank's assets and its liabilities. Capital adequacy is the first term in the acronym CAMEL because it is the first item that bank supervisors examine. **Capital adequacy** refers to the extent to which net worth is satisfactory for a safe and sound operation.

Bank regulators consider the size of a bank's capital important for a variety of reasons:

1. The higher a bank's capital, the better the prospect for the bank's survival in case of adverse conditions. Capital provides a cushion against unexpected losses. Better-capitalized banks simply fail less often.

2. In case of a bank failure, the capital of the bank serves as an insurance "deductible," because the owner's capital must be exhausted before the FDIC pays depositors. The better capitalized the bank, the lower the cost of the bank's failure to the insurer, the FDIC, and, ultimately, to the taxpayers.

3. Perhaps more important, the better capitalized the bank, the greater the stakes of its owners and, hence, the greater the incentive for sounder, safer lending practices. Banks with little capital of their own to lose may have an incentive to invest in high-yield, high risk securities, especially when the FDIC insures their source of funds (deposits) at flat rates, which means they pay the same insurance premium no matter how risky their portfolio of assets. If their ventures succeed, they keep the spoils; if they fail, they send the bill to the FDIC and the taxpayers.

Deposit insurance combined with low capital requirements encourages depository institutions to pursue greater risk. This is referred to as **moral hazard** in insurance parlance. To reduce moral hazard regulators began imposing minimum capital standards on depository institutions. In practice, these standards also serve as indicators of the health of banks. Why, then, must banks be coaxed into holding more capital to be healthier? The reason is that given the level of bank profits, the higher the capital, the lower profit per unit of capital from banking. It is more profitable to borrow and lend than to lend the owner's capital. For example, consider a bank with assets of $1 billion and net return of $10 million. If the bank's equity capital (net worth) is $100 million, its rate of return on equity would be 10/100, or 10 percent. If, on the other hand, its net worth is only $50 million, while everything else is the same, its rate of return would be 10/50, or 20 percent.

The Capital-Asset Ratio   A bank's capital adequacy is determined by the lending activities of the bank, that is, by the assets held. Thus, regulators examine the ratio of capital to assets, *K/A,* as an indicator of sound banking practices, or as a summary index of a bank's strength (health). The higher a bank's capital-asset ratio, the sounder, or the healthier, the bank. Until 1981, there were no explicit capital requirements. Regulators examined a bank's capital-asset ratio, and if they considered it too small, they used "moral suasion" to induce the bank to increase the ratio. In 1981 the Office of the Comptroller of the Currency and the Federal Reserve, joined later by the FDIC, imposed formal minimum capital-ratio requirements on the banks under their supervision in order to introduce greater uniformity in the supervisory process and to deal with the long-term decline in the capital ratios of banks.

Risk-Based Capital-Asset Ratios   Even after modification and streamlining in 1985, these formal minimum ratios were indiscriminate in the sense that they did not account for the quality, or riskiness, of assets held by a bank. The riskiness of a bank's operation was addressed separately in the second element of the CAMEL test: asset quality. If examiners found excessive risk in a bank's assets, they pressured the bank to increase its capital ratio above the minimum requirement.

As Chapters 4 and 5 discuss, the 1980s witnessed a substantial shift of bank portfolios toward riskier assets and to risky off-balance-sheet activities, such as loan commitments. Hence, the simple formal capital-asset ratio was not a good indicator of the riskiness of a

FIGURE 17–4
Bank Failures:
1980–1993

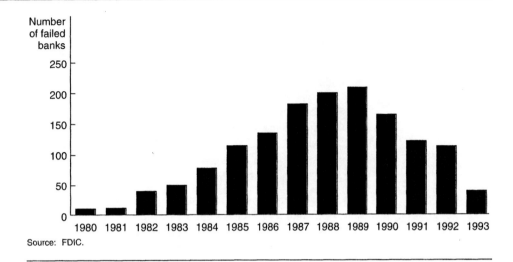

Source: FDIC.

bank's position and its health. Research at the Fed showed that even though the actual asset-capital ratio of banks increased during the 1980s, the increased riskiness of bank assets more than offset the higher ratios, thereby increasing the riskiness of banking. The increased number of bank failures in the 1980s, shown in Figure 17–4, attests to this increase in risk.

As a result, the three federal regulators—the OCC, the Federal Reserve, and the FDIC—began to consider imposing risk-based, minimum capital-asset ratios. At the same time, representatives of banking authorities from 12 industrialized nations, including the United States, were negotiating for international uniformity in standards for capital adequacy. They reached an agreement on July 11, 1988, in Basle, Switzerland, to phase in uniform, risk-based capital-asset ratios by December 31, 1992.

This agreement, known as the **Basle Agreement**, ties capital requirements to the risk of assets and the risk of off-balance-sheet items of each bank. In a sense, the new requirements customize capital-asset ratios, depending on the individual bank's portfolio of assets and off-balance-sheet commitments. The denominator of the required capital-asset ratio is a weighted average of all assets and off-balance-sheet items. To calculate this weighted average, assets and off-balance-sheet items are grouped into four risk categories, in ascending order from riskless to riskiest, with corresponding weights of 0, 20, 50, and 100 percent. For example, U.S. Treasury securities have a zero weight; banks do not have to hold any capital against Treasury securities. In contrast, home mortgages have a 50 percent weight, while most commercial loans have a 100 percent weight, which means banks must hold twice as much capital against commercial loans as against mortgages. Dividing a bank's capital by its risk-weighted assets, bank examiners determine the bank's risk-weighted, capital-asset ratio. Since the new requirements were fully phased in at the end of 1992, this ratio must be at least 8 percent.

TABLE 17–1
Capital Adequacy
Categories for
Banks

Categories	Risk-Based Capital-to-Asset Ratio (*K/A*)	Number of Banks as of September 1992
Well capitalized	$K/A \geq 10\%$	11,100
Adequately capitalized	$8\% \leq K/A < 10\%$	550
Undercapitalized	$6\% \leq K/A < 8\%$	150
Significantly undercapitalized	$2\% < K/A < 6\%$	50
Critically undercapitalized	Unadjusted $K/A \leq 2\%$	50

Source: Adapted from "Fed Votes Capital Adequacy," *The American Banker,* September 15, 1992.

Critics of the Basle Agreement argue that the risk-based capital requirements are indiscriminate. For example, most commercial loans have a 100 percent weighting regardless of the credit rating of the borrower. Moreover, the agreement ignores other types of risk, such as interest rate risk and liquidity risk. To account for these risks, examiners must determine the remaining components of the CAMEL rating. In 1993 regulatory authorities in the United States initiated a process of refining capital requirements to account for interest rate risk.

Prompt
Corrective
Action

Risk-based capital-to-asset ratios provide the underpinnings for the more stringent supervisory and regulatory regime mandated by the **Federal Deposit Insurance Corporation Improvement Act (FDICIA) of 1991**. The act links bank supervision to five categories of capitalization, ranging from well capitalized to severely undercapitalized, as defined in Table 17–1. Banks that meet the Basle Agreement's requirement of 8 percent are classified as adequately capitalized. As a bank's risk-based capital-to-asset ratio declines below the adequately capitalized level, regulators must take "prompt corrective action," by imposing sanctions such as limits on growth, reduction in dividends and salaries, and management changes. Regulators are required to close down a severely undercapitalized bank or merge it with a healthier one. The last column of the table shows that when the new regime was implemented in September 1992, only 50 banks were severely undercapitalized and more than 11,000 were well capitalized, according to the FDIC's measurements. As the agency that insures deposits, the FDIC is always at the center of the decision to close or reorganize a bank.

THE FDIC AND DEPOSIT INSURANCE

The FDIC sprang from hard economic times in the 1930s. Over 20 percent of the labor force was unemployed and bank failures ran in the thousands during the Great Depression. About 9,000 banks failed from 1930 to 1933—an average of 2,250 bank failures per year. In 1933 alone, a record 4,000 American banks failed.

Franklin D. Roosevelt was sworn in as president of the United States on March 4, 1933. Soon after his inauguration, he declared a national bank holiday to begin on March 6 and last four days. The administration drafted legislation to resolve the bank crisis;

Congress, with uncharacteristic speed, passed the Banking Act of 1933, which was signed by President Roosevelt on June 16, 1933.

A key provision of the 1933 act created the FDIC and established a temporary system of deposit insurance, which became the permanent insurance fund with the passage of the Banking Act of 1935. In the meantime, the National Housing Act of 1934 created a parallel authority, the *Federal Savings and Loans Insurance Corporation (FSLIC)*, to insure S&Ls.

One function of deposit insurance is to guarantee that depositors will be able to withdraw their deposits up to some specified amount if a bank fails. That amount was gradually increased from $5,000 per account in 1933 to $100,000 per account in 1980, as Chapter 5 notes. Another function of deposit insurance is to reduce disruptions to the economy caused by bank failures. The revenue for the insurance funds comes from assessing premiums on banks and S&Ls as well as from liquidating the assets of failed depository institutions. In addition, the insurance funds may also borrow from the U.S. Treasury, which they did to finance the S&L bailout, as we shall see. FIRREA of 1989, passed in response to the thrift crisis, disbanded the FSLIC and placed the FDIC in charge of insuring both commercial banks and thrifts under two separate funds: the **Bank Insurance Fund (BIF)** for banks, and the **Savings Association Insurance Fund (SAIF)** for S&Ls. GlobalWatch 17.2 compares the U.S. system of deposit insurance with those of other countries.

Resolving Bank Failures

The FDIC uses two basic methods for handling failed banks. The first, authorized by the Glass-Steagall Act itself, is called the **payoff method**. With this method the FDIC allows the bank to fail and then pays off insured deposits from its insurance fund. The FDIC subsequently sells the assets of the failed bank and pays off part of the claims of the uninsured depositors and other creditors. The payoff method has been used in only 21 percent of the cases over the last two decades and, most recently, in a *modified payout* form. The modification involves a partial payment to uninsured depositors and other creditors to avoid disruptions to the local economy during the period when the FDIC is engaged in selling the assets and ascertaining how much is left for uninsured creditors.

With the second method, called the **purchase and assumption (P&A) method**, the FDIC closes the failing bank and then allows new owners to purchase it, usually in a bidding process. The P&A method is the most common approach to handling failed banks. During the last two decades, 73 percent of bank closures by the FDIC used this method.

In 1987 Congress authorized temporary banks, called **bridge banks**, to help the FDIC handle difficult cases. A bridge bank absorbs a failed bank via a P&A action. In this way the failed bank continues to operate until it is purchased by a healthy institution. The FDIC used bridge banks only 5 times between 1987 and 1989, but 21 times in 1992, as it gained more experience with this tool for handling failed banks.

Keeping Banks Open

So far we have examined the methods the FDIC uses to close failed banks. In contrast, with an approach called **open bank assistance** regulators use a variety of methods to help banks remain open. There have been 80 cases of open bank assistance since 1934: 5 from 1934 to 1980, and 75 from 1981 to 1992.

GlobalWatch 17.2
Deposit Insurance Systems around the World

The FDIC, created in response to massive bank failures during the Great Depression, was the first formal system of deposit insurance in the world. The deposit insurance systems operating in most other major industrial countries also sprang from some financial crisis.

In 1966 Germany was the first European country to introduce a system of deposit insurance, which it extended in 1974 after the failure of a major German bank. The British introduced a system in 1982, again after a major bank crisis in the 1970s. Before that, Britain had not experienced a major bank failure for two centuries. Until 1980, the Bank of England relied on a combination of careful bank supervision and a willingness to intervene as a lender of last resort to prevent bank failures. The French introduced an insurance system in 1980, and the Italians in 1987, after a major bank failure that extended to many foreign subsidiaries of a bank in Milan. The Japanese system was introduced by law in 1965, after large losses by three major securities firms. The Japanese system relies on the Bank of Japan to intervene and arrange assistance to troubled banks and securities firms.

Today deposit insurance systems are in place in all industrialized countries. There are similarities among these systems, but there are also important differences in the way the systems are sponsored and funded. Three methods of sponsoring deposit insurance programs are in use. The systems in the United States, Canada, the United Kingdom, Belgium, and Switzerland are all sponsored (and administered) by an official government agency. In contrast, most of the continental European systems—the German, Austrian, French, Italian, Swiss, and Finnish—are sponsored and administered by the banking industry itself. Still other systems combine both features: They are operated jointly by government and industry. The systems in Japan, the Netherlands, and Norway are of this type.

There are two methods of funding insurance programs. One assesses regular premiums on banks to maintain a fund that handles all losses. The systems in the United States, Japan, Germany, and the United Kingdom use this method of funding. With the second method, the insurance authority does not assess any premiums and does not even maintain an insurance fund. Instead, the authority imposes a levy after a bank failure. The insurance programs in France, Austria, Switzerland, Italy, and the Netherlands use this ex post method of funding.

Insurance systems also differ in the percentages of deposits they cover. Some provide unlimited coverage. Most, however, provide limited coverage, perhaps to encourage market discipline. A unique feature applied to commercial banks is found in the German system. To provide an incentive for depositor-imposed market discipline, insurance is limited to 30 percent of a bank's equity capital. Thus, depositors have an incentive to monitor bank capital and withdraw their deposits when capital reaches a dangerous level.

The most important similarity between the FDIC and the foreign insurance programs is the general unwillingness to permit a sudden and disorderly failure of a major banking institution, although, of course, exceptions may be found. A drastic difference between the U.S. system and other systems is the major role given to the FDIC, both as a supervising authority and, especially, as the key player in dissolving a failed institution. In all other countries the insurance entities have no supervisory authority and play only a supporting role in the resolution of a failed bank. In some countries, such as Japan, the central bank is the key player in handling insolvent banks, or even troubled nondepositories.

Under this form of aid the Federal Reserve may, for example, provide extended credit at the discount window or the FDIC may infuse capital. To see how this approach works, let's look at the celebrated case of Continental Illinois National Bank and Trust Company of Chicago, which was among the nation's ten largest banks in 1984 when it failed. Problems with energy loans at Continental Illinois first surfaced in 1982. Rumors of an impending collapse in 1984 led to a run on the bank, which had about $33 billion in deposits, of which $30 billion were uninsured. Foreigners held about half of these uninsured deposits. To prevent adverse repercussions at home and abroad, regulators put together an open bank assistance plan. As part of this assistance, the Fed made available $3.5 billion in extended credit at the discount window and later the FDIC infused $1 billion in additional capital in exchange for part ownership.

Massive extension of credit by the Fed had been used before the case of Continental Illinois. What was new and controversial was the infusion of capital into a commercial bank by a federal agency in exchange for part ownership. Nationalization of any company is frowned upon in our capitalist system. Since 1984 the FDIC has infused cash into other banks and bank holding companies and has retained part ownership. For example, in 1987 the FDIC contributed $150 million to assist the BancTexas Group, a bank holding company in Dallas, Texas, which was acquired by outside investors. These investors added $50 million of their own capital, which they lost in 1990 when the head bank in Dallas failed. In total, between 1971 and 1990 the FDIC used some form of open bank assistance in 5.5 percent of the bank failure cases it handled.

Another approach that regulatory agencies use to help banks stay open is **regulatory forbearance**, where the regulator refrains from enforcing the usual supervisory standards, especially the minimum capital-asset ratio. The FDIC employs capital forbearance when it considers a troubled financial institution to be viable. Forty-six banks, according to the chairman of the FDIC, that were granted capital forbearance since 1986 have eventually recovered. At the end of 1989, more than 200 banks were benefiting from forebearance programs. Critics of this approach argue that by closing their eyes to undercapitalized institutions, regulators have contributed to the large losses suffered by the FDIC and by taxpayers in the 1980s when a substantial number of thrifts and a smaller number of banks kept open by forbearance eventually failed.

Arguments for and against the Too-Big-to-Fail Policy

Regulators use the payoff method—by which banks are allowed to fail—mostly for small banks. On the other hand, they reserve open bank assistance and the P&A method primarily for large banks. This asymmetry in the way regulators handle large and small banks in trouble amounts to a **too-big-to-fail policy**.

Two major criticisms are leveled against this policy. First, it is unfair. Uninsured depositors and other creditors of large banks do not lose anything, while those of small banks lose part or all of their deposits and other holdings. A second criticism involves market discipline. Critics of open bank assistance and the P&A method argue that the payoff method is preferable because it enhances discipline by inflicting losses on uninsured depositors and other creditors. In other words, the payoff method teaches depositors a lesson. As a result, unprotected depositors are more likely to shop around and force banks to follow safer banking practices.

Regulators have justified the too-big-to-fail policy on the grounds that the policy promotes stability. The FDIC's unwillingness to inflict losses on uninsured depositors of a large bank or, especially, of a bank holding company is rooted in the fear of deleterious effects on the financial system and on the real sector of the economy. The health of the financial system and the economy is their goal. Support of large depositors is only incidental.

FDICIA of 1991 severely curtailed the too-big-to-fail policy by requiring that regulators use the *least-cost alternative* in resolving bank failures, which translates to *prompt resolution* of failed banks. The same requirement also means cutting back on the practice of forbearance. FDICIA allows for an exception, however. The least-cost requirement may be waived if the board of the FDIC, the Federal Reserve Board, and the secretary of the Treasury, in consultation with the president, agree that allowing a bank to fail will seriously harm the U.S. financial system and, hence, the U.S. economy. It is premature to announce the death of the too-big-to fail policy.

Pros and Cons of Deposit Insurance

FDICIA also mandated risk-based deposit insurance premiums. To understand why, we must examine the benefits and costs of deposit insurance. Deposit insurance was designed to protect small depositors from the loss of their savings in failing banks and to protect the economy from contagious *runs on banks* experienced periodically from the 1800s to 1933. Remember that a bank is a firm that transforms short-term liabilities (deposits) into long-term assets (loans). In the absence of deposit insurance, unprotected depositors will hasten—even run—to withdraw their deposits if they suspect a bank failure. The first depositors will be successful. However, to satisfy more depositors who want to withdraw their deposits, banks must liquidate their long-term assets and suffer losses on these sales. Soon the bank will run out of liquid assets to satisfy depositors. The bank fails, and the depositors who did not run will lose everything. Even rumors that a bank is in trouble can cause a run and certain failure.

If deposits are not insured, failure of one bank may trigger failure of many others, even healthy banks. The damage will not be restricted to individuals who lost their deposits. Because deposits are the key instrument in the payments system, the smooth functioning of the economy will be disrupted. Moreover, the accompanying reduction in the quantity of money will have contractionary effects on the real sector. Even failure of a single bank may have deleterious effects on the economy if the bank is large. The reduction in the quantity of money may be enough to affect significantly both the payments system and the real sector. And it may have contagious effects on other banks at home and abroad if they have investments with the failing bank.

On the negative side, perhaps the most detrimental aspect of deposit insurance is that it removes incentives for sound and prudent banking practices. Depositors, who are guaranteed repayment of their funds in case of bank failure, have no incentive to shop around for sound banks in which to deposit their funds. They shop only for the highest deposit rate. And after depositing their funds, they have no incentive to monitor the risk position of the banks and to withdraw their funds in order to pressure the bank into adopting safer practices.

Similarly, banks are not discouraged from investing the funds in high-yield, high-risk enterprises. The banks end up with high earnings if the high-risk investments succeed. If the investments fail because borrowers default in large numbers and the losses cause the bank to close, the owners of the bank lose their capital. Depositors, on the other hand, are paid by the insurer, which ultimately may be the public. The smaller a bank's capital-asset ratio, the greater its incentive to invest in risky, high-yield assets. In sum, there is a moral hazard because deposit insurance encourages higher risk taking by depositories and weakens or eliminates the incentives of depositors to monitor the risk taking of banks.

Reforming
Deposit
Insurance

Deposit insurance is a mixed blessing: On the one hand, it reduces the threat of bank runs and instability of the economy; on the other, it weakens market discipline exerted on banks by depositors. This trade-off between financial stability and market discipline has confronted regulators since the inception of the FDIC. Given that some insurance is needed to provide a safe medium of exchange, the key problem facing regulators is how to reach the appropriate balance: providing deposit insurance coverage that is sufficient to prevent instability and, at the same time, ensuring market discipline. In practical terms, the issue is how to guarantee that funds ultimately insured by taxpayers are not used by depositories in risky activities. Depositors and depositories must have adequate incentives to work toward this goal.

One of the ideas economists have suggested to deal with the problem of incentives is risk-based deposit insurance premiums, which were mandated by FDICIA. After examining this innovation, we consider two other proposals that have not been adopted: establishing "narrow banks" and privatizing deposit insurance.

Risk-Based Deposit Insurance Premiums   The insurance premiums assessed on insured depository institutions raise the funds for operating the insurance programs. At the end of 1987 the predecessor of the Bank Insurance Fund (BIF) had reserves of $18.3 billion. Subsequently, because of an increase in the number of bank failures, the reserves in the insurance fund declined considerably: to $13.2 billion in 1989 and to $8 billion at the end of 1990. The fund for thrifts was in even worse condition. It had $6.4 billion at the end of 1980, but by the end of 1988 was in the red by $75 billion.

The dire straits of the insurance fund for thrifts prompted the passage of FIRREA in 1989. Until the enactment of FIRREA, the premium for banks was a flat 8.3 cents per $100 of deposits; that is, all banks paid the same insurance rate regardless of the riskiness of their loans. The premium for thrifts was a flat 20.8 cents per $100 of deposits. In 1989 FIRREA phased in a higher rate of 23 cents for both banks and thrifts, but the rate was still a flat rate.

Two years later FDICIA mandated that the FDIC switch from flat rates to risk-based rates by 1994. The precise implementation was left to the FDIC. On December 15, 1992, the FDIC's board of directors introduced the risk-based premiums that went into effect on January 1, 1993, one year ahead of schedule. In assessing the premiums, the FDIC uses two criteria to measure risk: a bank's capital adequacy and its supervisory status, based on the noncapital components of its CAMEL rating. The less capitalized a bank, the riskier the bank, and the higher its insurance premium. Similarly, the lower a bank's supervisory status, the riskier the bank, and the higher its insurance premium.

Table 17–2 shows that as of January 1, 1993, well-capitalized banks with the best supervisory rating were assessed the lowest premium of 23 cents per $100 of deposits, while undercapitalized banks with the worst supervisory status were assessed the highest premium of 31 cents. Note that for the best rated banks the FDIC did not change the premium of 23 cents introduced by FIRREA. Because most banks fell in this category in 1993 according to the FDIC, the average premium turned out to be only 25.4 cents per $100 of deposits rather than the expected average of 28 cents. Critics argued that the average was too low and that the range of 8 cents between the highest and lowest

TABLE 17–2
Risk-Based
Insurance
Premiums:
*Premiums per $100
of Deposits (effective
January 1993)*

Capital Category	Supervisory Status		
	Best	Middle	Worst
Well capitalized	23¢	26¢	29¢
Adequately capitalized	26¢	29¢	30¢
Under capitalized	29¢	30¢	31¢

Source: FDIC.

premiums was too narrow to provide meaningful incentives to high-risk banks not to gamble with insured deposits.

Narrow Bank   An alternative approach to dealing with the moral hazard of deposit insurance is to give depositors two choices: insured deposits and uninsured deposits. Insured checkable deposits would be issued by a **narrow bank** that would invest the funds it attracted in a narrow range of high-grade, short-term money market instruments, such as Treasury bills and commercial paper.[1] The concept of a narrow bank is similar to a money market mutual fund, except the deposits of the narrow bank would be insured. The bank's deposit insurance premiums would be low because of the low credit risk of its assets. A separately capitalized institution on the same physical premises as the narrow bank would issue uninsured savings and time deposits and make loans to households and firms. These uninsured deposits, of course, would pay higher deposit rates to reflect the higher credit risk of the assets that back them. Depositors would have an incentive to monitor the bank's lending practices. One drawback of this proposal is that major runs on banks could still occur and intermediation could suffer. However, the medium of exchange issued by the insured narrow bank would be protected.

Privatizing Deposit Insurance   Another method of imposing market discipline is to transfer the function of insuring bank deposits to the private sector. One way would be for private insurance companies to offer deposit insurance. By putting their own capital at risk, these private companies would have a greater incentive than a federal agency to price risk appropriately and to take prompt corrective measures, such as canceling an insurance policy if a bank takes excessive risks. Another way is for the banking system to insure itself, in which case the net worth of the entire banking system would take the place of the reserve funds of the FDIC. This is the practice followed in several countries, as GlobalWatch 17.1 explains.

   For private insurance to be successful in preventing bank runs, as the FDIC has been since its inception, it must be accompanied by government guarantees that the federal government will intervene in extreme cases that threaten the health of the entire banking

---

[1] Among the economists who advocate narrow banks are James Tobin of Yale, James Pierce of Berkeley, and Robert Litan of the Brookings Institution. See, for example, James L. Pierce, *The Future of Banking* (New Haven: Yale University Press, 1991).

system. This guarantee can take the form of a lender of last resort, which is a function of the central bank. An additional reason why the government must have a role in a privately run system is to ensure that insurance companies, in their pursuit of higher profits, do not close or penalize viable banks. That is, private deposit insurance must itself be regulated.

THE STRUCTURE AND REGULATION OF THRIFTS

Banks, which have been the subject of our discussion until now, are the major type of depository institution. They provide more than twice the amount of credit to the U.S. economy as thrifts, which are the other type of depository. The thrift industry consists of savings and loan associations, savings banks, and credit unions. Savings and loan associations and savings banks made their first appearance in the early 1800s and credit unions in the early 1900s.

One common characteristic of all three institutions is that they collect the savings of households, which accounts for their name: **thrifts**. Thrifts were designed to use the funds collected from households to finance the borrowing needs of the household sector itself. Traditionally, S&Ls and savings banks have financed long-term mortgages, and credit unions have financed short-term consumer loans. To a large degree these thrifts still gear their activities toward satisfying the financial needs of households. However, with the liberalization of their lending practices, introduced by legislative changes in the 1980s, more and more thrift funds have been channeled toward commercial purposes, as Chapter 5 discusses. The remainder of this chapter examines the structure and regulation of thrifts.

Savings and Loan Associations (S&Ls)

As with commercial banks, savings and loans may be chartered at either the federal or the state level. State S&Ls are supervised and examined by their state S&L or banking authority. Today almost all S&Ls are federally insured and, thus, also come under the regulation and supervision of federal agencies.

Federally chartered S&Ls are members of the **Federal Home Loan Bank System**. This system, established by the Federal Home Loan Bank Act of 1932, consists of 12 district Federal Home Loan banks, the purpose of which is to provide liquidity to federally chartered S&Ls.[2] Each federally chartered S&L owns stock in the Federal Home Loan bank in its district. Thus, each Federal Home Loan bank is owned, technically, by the S&Ls in its district, just as each district Federal Reserve bank is owned by the member banks in that district. The Federal Home Loan Bank System sells notes and bonds of varying maturities in the open market to raise funds, which it lends to member S&Ls at cost. Because the cost of borrowing in the open market is lower for the Federal Home Loan Bank System than it would be for the S&Ls themselves, the long-term loans constitute a regular subsidy to the S&Ls. Of course, the Federal Home Loan Bank System is not the only federal agency that makes loans to depository institutions at below market rates. The discount rate charged by the Federal Reserve is often below market rates. But

---

[2] The 12 districts in the Federal Home Loan Bank System do not coincide with the 12 districts in the Federal Reserve System.

most loans at the discount window are only for a day or two. The Fed grants extended credit only in special cases (troubled banks) and levies a surcharge. Also, the Fed does not borrow in the open market to lend to depository institutions; it simply writes a check on itself, thus creating borrowed reserves.

The 1932 act that set up the Federal Home Loan Bank System also established the Federal Home Loan Bank Board, an independent agency headquartered in Washington, D.C., to charter and regulate federal S&Ls. Two years later FSLIC was established to provide deposit insurance to S&Ls and was placed under the Federal Home Loan Bank Board. This arrangement remained in place until 1989 when FIRREA overhauled the regulatory structure for S&Ls in the aftermath of the failure of hundreds of S&Ls.

Savings and Loan Failures   Chapter 5 introduced the thrift crisis that led to the passage of FIRREA in 1989. The reasons for failure range from bad luck (bad overall economic conditions) to insider abuse and fraud. A critical phase came in the early 1980s with the dramatic rise in interest rates paid on short-term deposits while most assets were long-term fixed-rate mortgages. The consequent capital loss put the entire S&L industry in the red and caused the official closure of nearly 500 S&Ls.

Many others were kept alive by artificial means. Edward Kane of Ohio State University coined the term *zombies* for S&Ls that regulators kept alive by regulatory changes and accounting gimmicks that exaggerated their capital.[3] On the one hand, regulators reduced minimum capital requirements from 5 percent of liabilities to 4 percent in 1980 and to 3 percent in 1982. On the other hand, they also liberalized the accounting methods for calculating the capital of an institution. As a result, many S&Ls were undercapitalized in 1982 when Congress passed the Garn–St Germain Act of 1982. Remember that this act enabled S&Ls to invest in far riskier assets than in previous years, while their deposits were insured at $100,000 per account.

Undercapitalization, deregulation, and a permissive system of deposit insurance created a fatal combination. From 1982 to 1989, when FIRREA became law, more than 1,000 S&Ls were declared insolvent and closed their doors or merged.

FIRREA of 1989   The **Financial Institutions Reform, Recovery and Enforcement Act (FIRREA) of 1989** addressed both short-run and long-run maladies of the thrift industry. In the short run, because the FSLIC was bankrupt, the act created the **Resolution Trust Corporation (RTC)**, a cleanup agency funded primarily by taxpayers to sell or liquidate failed thrifts. In 1993 Congress extended the mandate of the RTC to January 1995 and authorized additional funds for the cleanup, bringing the total to just under $200 billion. For longer-run reform, FIRREA dismantled the Federal Home Loan Bank Board and its insuring agency, the FSLIC. The Federal Home Loan Bank Board was replaced by the **Office of Thrift Supervision (OTS)**, a five-member board that is a bureau of the U.S. Treasury. (The Clinton administration's plan to streamline federal banking regulators would abolish the OTS and transfer its functions to the proposed new

---

[3] See Edward J. Kane, *The Gathering Crisis in Federal Deposit Insurance* (Cambridge, Mass: The MIT Press, 1985).

federal banking agency.) As discussed previously in this chapter, FIRREA also established two new insurance funds, the SAIF for thrifts and the BIF for banks, to be administered by the FDIC.

Addressing the capitalization problem, FIRREA required that by 1994 all thrifts maintain tangible capital of 3 percent on their assets. Tangible capital excludes "goodwill," which thrifts had previously been allowed to count as part of capital. Finally, the act imposed some restriction on the assets held by thrifts, such as requiring them to raise their housing and housing-related assets to 70 percent of their portfolio, from an estimated 60 percent at the time the law was passed. In addition, FIRREA prohibited thrifts from investing in junk bonds and placed restrictions on the amount of commercial real estate loans that they may make.

The history of the thrift crisis makes clear that prompt closure of failed S&Ls would have saved taxpayers tens of billions of dollars. That they were not promptly closed illustrates the **principal-agent problem**, in which the interests of parties to a decision diverge. In this case, the interest of the principal, the taxpaying public, was that insolvent S&Ls be promptly closed. However, the agents—the thrift regulators, Congress, and the administration—found it in their professional or political interests to postpone large-scale closures of S&Ls, resulting in additional losses that ultimately had to be borne by the public.

Aided by falling interest rates, the fortunes of the S&L industry turned in 1991. The rates S&Ls paid on their short-term deposits fell more than the rates they earned on their long-term assets. As a result, after five years of losses, the industry recorded a profit in 1991. By that time there were just over 2,000 S&Ls—down from 6,000 in the 1960s. At the end of 1993 the number of S&Ls stood at 1,667, with total assets of $780 billion.

Savings Banks   Savings banks came into existence soon after S&Ls, but their growth did not keep up with that of S&Ls. Savings banks are primarily a northeastern institution; only 16 are outside this region. Moreover, 95 percent of all assets held by savings banks are in eastern institutions.

Originally only state authorities chartered savings banks, but since 1978 federal charters have been available. Before the passage of FIRREA in 1989 all savings banks had the choice of being insured by the FDIC or the FSLIC. Since 1989 they may choose to be insured by either the Bank Insurance Fund or by the Savings Association Insurance Fund.

Like S&Ls, the portfolio of savings banks concentrates on mortgages. The Garn–St Germain Act of 1982, however, authorized a more liberal diversification for savings banks than for S&Ls. The same legislation also allowed S&Ls to readily convert to savings banks (and vice versa). The combination of federal charters and easy conversion of S&Ls to savings banks, as well as their ability to be insured by the FDIC, increased the prestige of savings banks. Their number and their size grew rapidly. They increased from about 400 in 1982 to nearly 900 before declining in the late 1980s. Savings banks as a group did not get involved in high-risk endeavors, as did their S&L counterparts. They were, however, hit by the decline in real estate values in the Northeast. In 1993 there were about 600 savings banks with total assets of about $225 billion.

Credit Unions

Credit unions are cooperatives that have some common bond, or association, such as occupation or place of residence. They are formed to promote thrift among members of the group and to provide credit and other financial services to them. A majority of the credit unions in the United States are based on occupation and are usually sponsored by employers. Originally, credit unions were restricted to providing mostly short-term unsecured loans to members. Since DID&MCA of 1980 and the Garn–St Germain Act of 1982, the list of permissible activities has been expanded to include real estate loans to members. Today credit unions even invest a small fraction of their deposits in U.S. Treasury and federal agency securities. More important, a combination of laws and technological progress has enabled credit unions to expand their activities to such new services as selling life insurance and offering investment advice. Thus, with the exception of providing credit to the U.S. government, all their activities are for their members. For this reason they are classified as nonprofit institutions, with associated tax benefits.

As with the other depository institutions we have examined, credit unions are chartered at either the federal or the state level. Federal credit unions are supervised and examined by their chartering agency, the **National Credit Union Administration (NCUA)**, and state credit unions by the state's banking authority. Credit unions may branch within a state or even across state lines without asking for approval.

In the United States the first credit unions appeared at the beginning of the twentieth century, and their number kept increasing (except during the Great Depression) until the late 1960s, when it approached 24,000. Since then, the number has been declining, to a total of about 12,000 at the end of 1993, with total assets of about $280 billion.

Deposits in credit unions, called *shares,* are insured either by the National Credit Union Share Insurance Fund, a fund of the National Credit Union Administration, or by a fund of a state banking authority. Since the passage of DID&MCA of 1980, credit unions can issue checkable deposits, called *share drafts,* as Chapter 5 discusses. The NCUA insures the deposits of all federal credit unions and a substantial fraction of state credit unions up to a maximum of $100,000 per account.

As was the case with S&Ls, credit unions failed in droves in the early 1980s; high interest rates (combined with stiff usury laws on consumer credit) caused capital losses and closures. The deep recession that followed wiped out not only thousands of businesses, but also the credit unions of their employees. Twelve hundred credit unions failed during the early 1980s. Although there are provisions for assistance from the U.S. Treasury in case of the insolvency of the National Credit Union Share Insurance Fund, the National Credit Union Administration handled the multitude of credit union failures by doubling insurance premiums in the early 1980s to replenish its rapidly depleting insurance fund.

SUMMARY

- Depository institutions are either commercial banks or thrifts. The Banking Act of 1933 separates the ownership and activities of depository institutions from those of commercial (industrial) firms. Since 1933 there has also been a separation between depositories and nondepositories, such as insurance companies, brokerage firms, and pension funds.

· A unique feature of the U.S. depository system is *dual banking*. U.S. depository institutions may be chartered either at the federal level, by the Office of the Comptroller of the Currency, or at the state level, by the state's banking commission.

· An outgrowth of the dual banking system was the restriction on interstate banking and branching. This is the major reason for the large number of U.S. banks compared with other countries. Prohibition of interstate banking reduces competition, fosters inefficiency, and contributes to bank failures because it prevents geographic diversification of bank assets. Legislation passed in 1994 permits nationwide banking in the United States.

· Another feature of the U.S. depository system is overlapping regulatory and supervisory jurisdiction over U.S. banks. The chartering authority is a regulator of the bank. Thus, national banks are regulated by the Office of the Comptroller of the Currency and state banks by the state's banking commission. The Federal Reserve also regulates banks that are members of the Federal Reserve System, and the FDIC regulates all depository institutions whose deposits it insures. Simplifying the regulatory environment of banks is a major aim of proposed bank reforms.

· Banks are regulated and supervised to ensure that they remain healthy by following prudent banking practices. Regulation of commercial banks entails administering laws and issuing regulations and decisions that affect the size of banks and permissible activities. Supervision is concerned with the soundness of banks and usually is exercised by on-site examination of banks.

· Bank examiners evaluate a bank on the basis of five characteristics: Capital adequacy, Asset quality, Management, Earnings, and Liquidity. The resulting CAMEL rating is a measure of the overall health and soundness of a bank's operations.

· A bank's capital is a good indicator of its health. The larger its capital (relative to deposits or assets), the more likely that a bank will survive inadvertent misfortune. The smaller its capital, the more likely it will fail. Moreover, the larger the stake of the bank's owners, the more likely that the bank will follow prudent, sound practices.

· The FDICIA of 1991 introduced risk-based capital requirements that signal the need for prompt corrective action by regulators. When a bank examination suggests that a bank is insolvent and nonviable, the supervisory agencies must dissolve it. Primary responsibility for deciding and carrying out the mechanics of bank closures falls on the FDIC.

· The FDIC insures bank deposits in commercial banks and, since FIRREA of 1989, the deposits in almost all thrifts. Deposit insurance guarantees that depositors will be able to withdraw their deposits in case of bank failures, thereby discouraging runs on banks that could force closure of even healthy banks and put the entire economy at risk.

· The 1980s and early 1990s witnessed bank failures of epidemic proportions. These massive failures were the consequence of increased risk taking by banks, encouraged in part by deposit insurance. On the one hand, banks have an incentive to invest insured funds in risky activities, especially if they have little capital of their own at stake. On the other hand, depositors lose the incentive to monitor the activities of the bank in which they deposited their funds. Thus, deposit insurance reduces market discipline.

· FDIC practices include regulatory forbearance and the too-big-to-fail policy. With forbearance, the FDIC postpones the closure of a bank in the hope that it can be brought back to good health. With the too-big-to-fail policy, if the closure of a failed bank threatens the stability of the monetary system, the FDIC, with the assistance of the Fed and other regulators, keeps the banks open. FDICIA mandated prompt resolution of failed banks, thereby curtailing forbearance and the too-big-to-fail policy.

· Three types of depository institutions comprise the thrift industry: savings and loans associations, savings banks, and credit unions. Thrift institutions may be chartered federally or by states. S&Ls and savings banks are supervised by the Office of Thrift Supervision (OTS), which is the successor to the Federal Home Loan Bank Board and is a bureau of the U.S. Treasury.

· All S&Ls and savings banks are insured by one of two funds within the FDIC. S&Ls are insured by SAIF, and savings banks either by SAIF or BIF, which also insures commercial banks.

· Credit unions are chartered and supervised either at the federal level, by the National Credit Union Administration, or at the state level, by a banking commission. Similarly, deposit (or share) insurance is either federal or state.

· The 1980s witnessed the failure of large numbers of S&Ls. The massive losses bankrupted the insurance fund, and eventually taxpayers had to bail out the S&L industry.

KEY TERMS AND CONCEPTS

charter

national banks

state banks

Office of the Comptroller of the
  Currency (OCC)

dual banking system

bank holding company

branching

McFadden Act

Riegle-Neal Interstate Banking and
  Branching Efficiency Act

bank supervision

bank regulation

Federal Deposit Insurance
  Corporation (FDIC)

CAMEL rating

capital adequacy

moral hazard

Basle Agreement

Federal Deposit Insurance
  Corporation Improvement Act
  (FDICIA) of 1991

Bank Insurance Fund (BIF)

Savings Association Insurance
  Fund (SAIF)

payoff method

purchase and assumption (P&A)
  method

bridge banks

open bank assistance

regulatory forbearance

too-big-to-fail policy

narrow bank

thrifts

Federal Home Loan Bank System

Financial Institutions Reform,
  Recovery, and Enforcement Act
  (FIRREA) of 1989

Resolution Trust Corporation
  (RTC)

Office of Thrift Supervision (OTS)

principal-agent problem

National Credit Union
  Administration (NCUA)

QUESTIONS AND PROBLEMS

1. What is the rationale for prohibiting industrial and commercial firms from owning banks in the United States? For prohibiting banks from owning stock of commercial and industrial firms?

2. Explain what is meant by *dual banking*. What are the pros and cons of a dual banking system?

3. What is the relation between bank holding companies and interstate banking in the United States?

4. In the United States there is a large number of small banks. Why?

5. Who will benefit from allowing national banks to branch nationwide and why? Who will lose and why?

6. Identify the agency that, as of January 1994, had primary responsibility for supervising: (*a*) bank holding companies, (*b*) national banks, (*c*) state member banks, and (*d*) state nonmember banks.

7. What are the pros and cons of streamlining regulatory agencies?

8. What is a CAMEL rating and how is it used?

9. "The size of a bank's capital-asset ratio is related to moral hazard." True, false or uncertain? Explain.

10. In September 1992, the FDIC, in consultation with the other federal regulators, announced four categories of capital adequacy for banks: well capitalized, adequately capitalized, undercapitalized, and critically undercapitalized.
  a. What is the relation between these categories and the risk-based capital ratios introduced as a result of the Basle Agreement?
  b. How do regulators use these four categories of capital adequacy?

11. If you were a large depositor, would you have an incentive to keep your funds with a small or a large bank?

12. How does the FDIC measure risk to levy its risk-based deposit insurance premiums?

13. How do risk-based deposit insurance premiums and narrow banks deal with the problem of the moral hazard of deposit insurance?

The Wall Street Journal

14. Do you agree or disagree with the following statement from James Tobin, "Deposit Insurance Must Go," *The Wall Street Journal*, November 22, 1989: "The 'savings and loan crisis' is in a deeper sense a crisis of federal deposit insurance"?

15. What is the Office of Thrift Supervision (OTS)? The Resolution Trust Corporation (RTC)? How did they come into existence and for what purpose?

SUGGESTED READINGS

Federal Deposit Insurance Corporation. *1992 Annual Report.* July 1993.

A report published at midyear on the previous year's activities of the FDIC.

Kane, Edward J. *The S&L Insurance Mess: How Did It Happen?* Washington, D.C.: The Urban Institute Press, 1989.

A comprehensive analysis of the thrift crisis.

Kaufman, George G., and Robert E. Litan, eds. *Assessing Bank Reform: FDICIA One Year Later.* Washington, D.C.: The Brookings Institution, 1993.

Papers and discussants' comments from a symposium held at the Brookings Institution on December 16, 1992, to assess the impact of the Federal Deposit Insurance Corporation Improvement Act of 1991.

Klausner, Michael, and Lawrence J. White, eds. *Structural Change in Banking.* Homewood, Ill.: Business One Irwin, 1993.

Papers presented at a conference on the structure of banking held at the New York University Salomon Center on November 21–22, 1991.

Pierce, James. *The Future of Banking.* New Haven: Yale University Press, 1991.

An analysis of current and future problems of the banking industry and suggestions for reform.

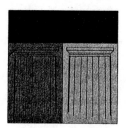

THE PROFIT-MAXIMIZING BANKING FIRM

CHAPTER PREVIEW

The interest banks earned on loans and securities fell in 1992, but the interest they paid on deposits fell even more. As a result, their net income rose. Moreover, fewer customers were defaulting on their loans as the economy slowly recovered from the recession of 1990–91. Hence, banks had to set aside less revenue to cover bad loans. Effective in April 1992, the Fed reduced the reserve requirement ratio on transactions deposits, which acts like a tax on banks. All of these factors boosted bank profits in 1992, which were at their highest level since the FDIC started keeping records in 1934. Bankers, however, were concerned that the future would not be as bright, because of higher costs stemming from the full implementation of FDICIA in December 1992. They predicted that capital-based regulation, risk-based deposit insurance, and additional paperwork would discourage banks from attracting deposits and making loans.

This chapter explains the rational, purposeful behavior of banks. It belongs in the first pillar of our two-pillar framework, alongside the behavior of the public (households and nonfinancial firms) and the Fed examined in previous chapters. Our analysis connects two financial statements: the bank's balance sheet and its income statement. An *income statement* is a record of a bank's revenues, costs, and profits.

The chapter brings the bank's balance sheet to life by considering each item to be the result of conscious decisions made by the banking firm. A bank, like any other firm, chooses the size of each item in its balance sheet at the level that maximizes its profits. Examining profit-maximizing strategies permits us to establish the determinants of a bank's supply of deposits, its demand for loans and securities, its borrowed reserves, and its excess reserves. We used these behavioral relations in previous chapters, where we explained them intuitively. Our purpose here is to derive them from rational decision making by banks. The chapter ends by connecting theory with practice to explain the credit crunch of the 1990s and the response of the Fed.

THE BALANCE SHEET OF U.S. BANKS

Before explaining the rational behavior of a bank by connecting its balance sheet and its income statement, it is necessary to examine the anatomy of these financial statements. We begin with the **balance sheet**, which is a statement of a bank's assets, its liabilities, and its net worth at a moment of time.

Table 18–1 presents the aggregate balance sheet of all U.S. banks at the end of 1992.[1] The items on the liability side of the balance sheet are the **sources of bank funds** and those on the asset side the **uses of bank funds**. We examine each of these items, beginning on the asset side.

_____1. Total cash assets consist of all the non-interest-bearing assets held by banks. These cash assets include reserve balances with the Fed, item 1a, and vault cash, item 1b, the sum of which is total reserves held by banks. Banks use these reserves as required reserves or excess reserves. Item 1c, **cash items in the process of collection (CIPC)**, consist mainly of checks deposited with banks but not yet collected. When the check collection process is completed, the reserve accounts of the receiving banks will be credited by the amount of these checks, as Chapter 12 explains. Some banks also hold non-interest-bearing deposit accounts, item 1d, with other banks. The deposit-holding banks are usually small banks that form a business relationship, called a **correspondent relationship**, with larger banks. The correspondent banks often use the accounts with larger banks for check clearing. The larger banks may also provide the correspondents with investment advice or may actually participate with them in making loans.

_____2. The next item is loans and securities, which consist of the bulk of earning assets held by banks. The holdings of open market debt securities, such as U.S. Treasury securities, agency securities, and municipal securities, are also referred to as investments, item 2a. Loans, item 2b, include funds lent to nonfinancial firms and to households, as well as to other banks and financial institutions in the federal funds market. Table 18–1 shows that total bank loans were almost three times as large as investments in 1992. The ratio of loans to investments in 1992 was low compared with the 1980s, when banks were aggressively making loans.

_____3. The final entry on the asset side is simply called *other assets*. They consist mainly of bank buildings and equipment.

---

[1] Every month the *Federal Reserve Bulletin* publishes the balance sheets for different categories of commercial banks.

TABLE 18–1
Aggregate Balance
Sheet of U.S.
Commercial Banks:
December 1992

	Billions of Dollars	Percent
Assets		
1. Total cash assets	210.2	6.70
a. Reserves with Federal Reserve banks	28.6	0.91
b. Cash in vault	36.4	1.16
c. Cash items in process of collection	91.1	2.90
d. Demand balances of U.S. depository institutions	34.0	1.08
e. Other cash items	20.1	0.64
2. Loans and securities	2,714.2	86.48
a. Investment securities	731.6	23.31
(1) U.S. government securities	591.3	18.84
(2) Other	140.3	4.47
b. Total loans	1,982.5	63.17
(1) Interbank loans	137.7	4.39
(2) Loans excluding interbank	1,844.8	58.78
(i) Commercial and industrial	438.7	13.98
(ii) Real estate	839.1	26.74
(iii) Individual	361.9	11.53
(iv) All other	205.1	6.53
3. Other assets	214.1	6.82
Total assets	3,138.4	100.00
Liabilities and Net Worth		
4. Deposits	2,381.4	75.88
a. Transactions deposits	789.0	25.14
b. Savings deposits	737.6	23.50
c. Time deposits	854.8	27.24
5. Borrowings and other liabilities	489.4	15.59
Total liabilities	2,870.8	91.47
6. Net worth	267.6	8.53
Total liabilities plus net worth	3,138.4	100.00

Source: *Federal Reserve Bulletin,* March 1993, A.20.

4. On the liability side, deposits are the largest source of funds. Transactions deposits consist of demand deposits, NOW accounts, and Super-NOW accounts that make up M1. Savings and time deposits are the other deposits, such as passbook savings accounts, money market deposit accounts, small time deposits, and large time deposits, included in M2 and M3.

5. The next item, borrowing and other liabilities, refers to nondeposit sources of funds. They include funds borrowed from other banks in the federal funds market, from foreign branches in the Eurodollar market, from nonfinancial firms through repurchase agreements, and from the Fed itself at the discount window.

6. The last entry in the balance sheet is the net worth of banks. Banks increase their net worth by selling shares or by retaining profits. In Table 18–1 net worth is about 8.5 percent of total assets. This means that at the end of 1992 equity capital provided 8.5 percent of the funds used by banks compared with only 7 percent in 1990. Deposits, on the other hand, provided 76 percent of the funds, and nondeposits the remaining 16 percent.

THE INCOME STATEMENT OF BANKS: REVENUE, COST, AND PROFIT

All of the items in a bank's balance sheet are stocks, which means they are measured at a moment of time. The items in the income statement, on the other hand, are flows. The **income statement** of a bank is a record of the bank's revenues, its costs, or operating expenses, and the resulting profit per period, say, per year. A bank earns revenues and incurs costs every year by providing intermediation services, that is, by channeling funds between savers and borrowers; by providing transactions services, mainly by issuing checkable deposits; and by providing other financial services by engaging in off-balance-sheet activities. Table 18–2 presents the income statement of all U.S. banks for 1992. Let us examine each of the entries in this statement.

TABLE 18–2
Consolidated
Income Statements
of U.S.
Commercial Banks:
1992

	Millions of Dollars	Percent
Revenue		
1. Interest income	256,356	78.32
a. Interest on loans	185,900	56.80
b. Interest on securities	51,818	15.83
c. Other interest	18,637	5.69
2. Noninterest sources of revenue	67,010	20.47
3. Capital gains on securities	3,951	1.21
Total revenue	327,317	100.0
Expenses		
4. Interest expense	122,426	43.48
a. Interest on deposits	98,690	35.05
b. Interest on other borrowed funds	23,736	8.43
5. Loan loss provisions	26,556	9.43
6. Noninterest expense	132,612	47.09
a. Salaries and employee benefits	55,449	19.69
b. Buildings, furniture, and other	18,137	6.44
c. Other operating expenses	59,026	20.96
Total Expenses	281,594	100.0
Net income (profit) before taxes	45,722	

Source: *Federal Reserve Bulletin,* July 1993, 663.

Revenue

1. The first item on the revenue side is interest income. At the end of 1992, 56.8 percent of bank revenue came from interest on loans. Although this percentage has been decreasing over the last 20 years, it still accounts for the largest portion of bank revenue. Income from direct finance, that is, interest on securities, at 15.8 percent of bank revenue, was about the average of the last two decades. Other interest income refers primarily to interest earned from lending to other banks.

2. Unlike interest income, noninterest income, or revenue, does not have its source in the balance sheet. This income consists of fees earned from off-balance-sheet activities, such as standby letters of credit, loan commitments, and interest rate swaps discussed in Chapter 5. Noninterest revenue, at 20.4 percent of total revenue, was substantially higher than in earlier years, reflecting the increased importance to banks of off-balance-sheet activities.

3. The last item on the revenue side is capital gains from the sale of securities in the portfolios of banks.

Expenses

4. On the expenses side, interest payments on deposits are the single most important expense of banks—35 percent of all expenses in 1992. Another 8.4 percent was interest paid to others, mainly for interbank loans but also for discount window loans.

5. The next category of expenses is **loan loss provisions**. These are funds that a bank must put aside because some borrowers have defaulted on their loans or are expected to default. SectorWatch 18.1 explains how banks account for nonperforming loans. The explanation ties together items in a bank's income statement and its balance sheet.

6. The rest of bank expenses are lumped together under the category of noninterest expenses. The most prominent among the noninterest expenses is salaries and employee benefits—almost 20 percent of total expenses in 1992. These expenses, along with the 6.4 percent for buildings, furniture, equipment, and office supplies, amounted to about 26 percent of total expenses in 1992. These noninterest out-of-pocket expenses of the banking industry arise because banks have to cope with information. Understanding the link between information and bank operations is necessary to understanding the business of banking.

BANKING AND INFORMATION

Both the balance sheet and the income statement of banks show that lending deposited funds is the main business of banks. Attracting funds and making loans require banks to collect, analyze, and transmit information. The major expense associated with information gathering consists of costs incurred for loan management. A bank needs information before making a loan, throughout the life of the loan, and in deciding whether to foreclose if the loan turns bad.

Assessing and Pricing Risk on Loans

Lending is a risky business. If the borrower is a firm, its prospects of success are always uncertain. Risk is endemic to entrepreneurship. Thus, the lender must evaluate the prospects of success or failure of the business for which the loan is contemplated. In other words, the bank must set a lending rate that includes the risk premium. If the borrower is a household, its sources of future income must be evaluated. For example, how secure is the loan applicant's job? How much does he or she earn? What other financial commitments has the applicant made that require periodic payments?

Sector*Watch* 18.1
Accounting for Troubled Loans

Charge-offs, loan loss provisions, loan loss reserves—these are concepts associated with accounting for non-performing loans, which involves a bank's balance sheet and its income statement. Loan loss reserves are like the level of water in a bathtub at a moment of time. Charge-offs drain water from the tub, while loan loss provisions add water.

When a customer stops paying the interest and principal on a loan, the lending bank writes off, or charges off, the loan by reducing the assets in its balance sheet by the amount of the nonperforming loan. On the liability side of the balance sheet, net worth, that is, bank capital, must be reduced by an equal amount. Loan loss reserves are an earmarked part of bank capital that regulators require banks to maintain at a sufficient level to absorb expected losses. This balance sheet item is not allowed to fall below zero.

Replenishing or increasing loan loss reserves involves a bank's income statement. Loan loss provisions are an expense item in a bank's income statement. Other things equal, when a bank increases its provision for loan losses, its profit falls because part of its revenue must be set aside to cover bad loans instead of being used to improve the bank's bottom line, its profit.

The accompanying graph shows the history of net charge-offs, loan loss provisions, and loan loss reserves for U.S. banks from 1977 to 1992. The increase in

charge offs after 1982 stemmed from losses on Latin American debt and on domestic agricultural and energy-related loans. Loan loss reserves did not fall, however, because provisions for loan losses rose faster than net charge-offs. The graph also shows that banks increased their loan loss provisions drastically in 1987 and then reduced them in 1988.

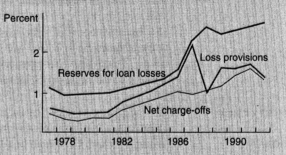

Reserves for loan losses, loss provisions, and net charge-offs as a percentage of loans, 1977–92.

Source: Allan D. Brunner and William B. English, "Profits and Balance Sheet Developments at U.S. Commercial Banks in 1992," *Federal Reserve Bulletin 79*, no. 7 (July 1993): 658.

From the late 1980s to 1991 charge-offs rose once again, mainly because of losses on commercial real estate loans. The situation improved in 1992, with a fall in both charge-offs and loan loss provisions. This helped to make 1992 a profitable year for U.S. banks because they didn't have to divert as much of their revenue to replenishing loan loss reserves.

Adverse Selection   Assessing the risk premium is complicated because the bank is faced with asymmetric information. As Chapter 2 discusses, **asymmetric information** means that one of the parties to a transaction has more information, or better information, than the other. In the case of loans, the prospective borrower has more information about the use of the loan than the lender (the bank), and the borrower has an incentive to underestimate the risk of the loan. The bank faces the danger that the borrower may not reveal all pertinent information about the risk of the project, the past history of the business, or the current health of the business. Thus, the bank runs the risk of approving a loan to a bad risk borrower, a "lemon." Approving a loan to a lemon is called **adverse selection**.

The concept of adverse selection can be seen vividly when a bank must raise the interest it charges borrowers. Higher interest rates will primarily drive away the good risks. The lemons will choose to stay and be selected. Similarly, suppose the bank cannot distinguish good risks from bad risks and, therefore, charges all borrowers the same risk premium. Obviously, the bad risks are undercharged while the good risks are overcharged and may be driven away. Thus, adverse selection may occur at any interest rate.

Moral Hazard   The bank also faces the danger that the borrower, after receiving the loan, may engage in riskier activities than those agreed upon. This problem, called **moral hazard**, arises because the borrower risks somebody else's money—the bank's. If the risky endeavor succeeds, the borrower will keep most of the spoils (and repay the bank.) If it fails, the bank will be the main loser. Moral hazard is related to asymmetric information because borrowers have an incentive not to reveal their intentions beforehand or to inform the bank that they are engaging in activities that are potentially harmful to the lender. Good loan management requires the bank to guard against the problems of adverse selection and moral hazard.

Preventing Adverse Selection: Screening

The screening of loan applicants is the major weapon against adverse selection. Before approving a loan, a bank screens the applicant to determine whether the applicant is a good risk or a lemon. For a loan to a household, the bank's loan officer gathers information about the household's income and expenditures, its assets and liabilities, and its credit history. A valuable tool to the loan officer is the information provided by the applicant in interviews and on application forms. For long-standing customers, the loan officer also examines the applicant's records with the bank to find out whether, for example, they repaid fully, and on time, any previous loans from the bank. Equally important, the loan officer has access to information contained in the applicant's checking account, from which the officer can develop a more complete profile of the applicant's creditworthiness.

Screening of business loans is even more extensive. Loan officers evaluate not only the viability of the project(s) for which the loan is intended, but also the overall economic strength of the business. They audit the company's books, that is, its balance sheet and income statement. Loan officers are experts in analyzing these financial statements to gather information that will help guide their decision to accept or reject the loan application and to set the risk premium if the loan is granted. This expertise is not exclusive to bank loan officers, however. Other lenders also have personnel that are as competent to examine and analyze these documents. Bank loan officers, however, have an advantage over other lenders because they have access to an applicant's checking account. The bank's loan officers can extract information from a firm's checking account to determine the economic health of the firm and its creditworthiness. The information in the checking account is especially useful in evaluating the creditworthiness of small business borrowers, which usually have only one checking account. It helps provide a more complete picture of the viability of the business than can be surmised from its balance sheet, income statement, and other information provided by the applicant.[2]

---

[2] For a detailed treatment of the informational advantage of banks, see Leonard I. Nakamura, "Commercial Bank Information: Implications for the Structure of Banking," in *Structural Change in Banking,* ed. Michael Klausner and Lawrence J. White (Homewood, Ill.: Business One Irwin, 1993), 131–60.

**Coping with
Moral Hazard**

Loan screening alone, no matter how competent, is not sufficient to eliminate the problems of adverse selection. Even if it could eliminate adverse selection, the bank would still have to cope with the moral hazard of lending. To prevent moral hazard, banks offer both legal and economic incentives to the borrower. The legal incentives simply prohibit certain risky practices by a binding agreement. The economic incentives go to the root of the problem. If borrowers are required to risk more of their own funds, then they have an economic incentive to be more prudent.

Restrictive Covenants   A bank usually requires a borrower to enter into a legal agreement, called a **covenant**, that restricts the use of the borrowed funds to certain specified activities or restricts the borrower to certain business practices. If the borrower is found to violate these restrictions, the covenant specifies the penalties, which usually include foreclosure of the loan. Covenants also include incentives for more prudent practices. For example, they specify the minimum net worth that a borrower must maintain. By requiring a sufficiently high net worth, banks create an incentive for borrowers to be prudent. Even if the borrowing firm engages in risky and unsuccessful activities, it will still be in a better position to survive and repay the loan. In the same spirit, some covenants require the borrower to pledge specific assets as collateral, which the bank may expropriate for repayment of the loan.

Monitoring   A restrictive covenant does not have any practical significance unless it can be enforced in a timely manner. This is why monitoring is important in lending. The bank's experts monitor the loan to ascertain whether the borrower adheres to the terms of the loan.

By discovering early that a borrower is engaging in unacceptable practices or that the borrower's financial condition is deteriorating, the bank may take corrective measures before it is too late. These corrective measures usually include the threat of foreclosure, which in some cases is sufficient to instill discipline in the borrower. Of course, foreclosure occasionally is inevitable in enforcing the covenants. The bank has a better chance of repayment if the decision to foreclose is made early.

Monitoring loans requires considerable information that is costly to collect and analyze. Banks, however, have an advantage over other lenders because they have access to information that is not available to others, namely, the information gleaned from the borrower's checking account. We have seen that this information is important at the approval stage of the loan. It is far more crucial, however, at the monitoring stage. By using information from the checking account, loan officers can follow the vital signs of their borrowers, especially small businesses. For example, they can have timely and nearly complete information about the trend of revenues and expenses of the firm, and, hence, early warning about an improvement or deterioration of its credit-worthiness.

SectorWatch 18.1 showed that provisions for losses from bank lending were high in the 1980s and early 1990s. These losses indicate that banks were not particularly successful in guarding against adverse selection and moral hazard in those years. In other words, banks underestimated and underpriced credit risk.

BRINGING THE BALANCE SHEET TO LIFE

The information gathered by a bank's loan officers is input in the deliberations of the **asset and liability management committee (ALCO)**, a key decision-making body of the bank. Every bank has a formal or informal ALCO that meets regularly to decide on the composition and even the size of the bank's balance sheet.

The Structure and Functions of the ALCO

The ALCO consists of three groups of officers: the asset managers, the liability managers, and the reserve managers. The asset managers are responsible for the size and composition of the bank's portfolio of assets. They are loan officers and specialists on securities who explore and rank the loan and investment opportunities open to the bank. They decide which loans to approve and what securities to hold. They also decide whether to restructure the bank's portfolio in favor of more securities than loans, as they did in the early 1990s, or vice versa.

The liability managers are responsible for exploring and ranking deposit and nondeposit sources of funds. They decide on the size and the composition of the bank's liabilities. For example, they may recommend that the bank intensify its efforts to attract more deposits when market lending rates rise or when the cost of attracting deposits falls.

Finally, the reserve managers have the responsibility of assessing the bank's needs for reserves and ensuring that it has enough reserves to satisfy reserve requirements. As Chapter 15 explains, when a bank loses deposits, it loses reserves. Therefore, it runs the risk of not meeting reserve requirements. To guard against a reserve deficiency, a bank's reserve officers continuously make decisions about alternative sources of reserves. One option is to borrow from the Fed's discount window. Reserve officers are experts in assessing the bank's reserve position with the Federal Reserve and the bank's standing with the Fed's discount window. They know, for example, whether they have overused or abused their privilege to borrow. Thus, they can decide whether it is safe for the bank to rely on the option of borrowing from the discount window. Other options are to borrow in the federal funds market or to hold highly liquid assets, such as Treasury bills, which can serve as "near reserves," or "secondary reserves," that the bank can easily convert to cash if needed. The most conservative option is for the bank to hold excess reserves that can be used to meet any unexpected need for reserves, such as when the bank unexpectedly loses deposits. Holding excess reserves eliminates uncertainty but also reduces income, because excess reserves do not earn interest. In sum, reserve officers have duties on both sides of the balance sheet.

The entire ALCO must meet to decide the exact content of the balance sheet. The loan and investment officers cannot make loans and investments based only on their knowledge of the soundness of these assets unless the liability experts tell them the cost and availability of funds. And the liability experts alone cannot decide the quantity of funds to attract as deposits unless they know there are enough good investment opportunities in which to place these funds. Furthermore, both the asset and the liability managers need the expertise of the reserve managers in assessing the availability of and need for reserves consistent with their decisions.

Cooperation of asset managers and liability managers is also crucial in coping with interest rate risk. Chapter 5 explains that this risk arises because of two imbalances in the balance sheet of banks: an imbalance in the maturities of assets and liabilities, and an imbalance between the quantities of assets and liabilities with variable (adjustable) rates. When the maturity of a bank's assets is longer than the maturity of its liabilities (which is the typical case), a rise in interest rates will inflict losses on the bank. In the second case, when assets primarily earn fixed rates while liabilities pay variable rates (which has been the traditional case), a rise in interest rates increases the cost of liabilities by more than the revenue from assets, again inflicting losses on the bank. Thus, asset managers and liability managers try to reduce these imbalances by making loans at adjustable rates or with shorter maturities. As Chapter 5 explains, banks have not been entirely successful in convincing borrowers to accept shorter maturities and adjustable rates. Therefore, they have resorted to other methods to deal with interest rate risk, such as shifting the risk to participants in futures and options markets. This method, however, creates off-balance-sheet obligations or risks.

We will show how the decisions made by the asset and liability management committee can be explained by examining profit-maximizing strategies available to banks. In this way we shall see how the entries in the balance sheet become behavioral relations.

The Simplified Balance Sheet

The twin functions of a bank are to attract deposits and to make loans. To concentrate on these functions, we begin by simplifying the form of the balance sheet. The simplified balance sheet is the one for depository institutions introduced in Chapter 4. On the asset side, there are two categories of assets: reserves are the first category, and loans and securities the other. The liability side lumps all deposits together and includes one nondeposit source of funds, borrowed reserves.

Table 18–3 presents our simplified version of a bank's balance sheet. This chapter uses this balance sheet to examine the banker's view. According to this view, a bank attracts deposits and makes loans and buys securities, as Chapter 15 explains. Therefore, we define *required reserves* as the product of the reserve requirement ratio, rr, and the **supply of deposits**, D^s, which is the quantity of deposits that banks want to attract, or provide. We denote by B^d the amount of loans and securities that banks want to hold, or demand. And ER and BR are, respectively, the excess reserves banks want to hold and the loans from the Fed that they want to assume. (For simplicity, we do not add the superscript d, for demand, to ER and BR.)

Profit Maximization

We now proceed to bring the bank's balance sheet to life, that is, finding the factors that determine, or influence, the composition of the balance sheet and, thus, the factors that determine the size of each of its components.

TABLE 18–3
The Simplified Balance Sheet of a Bank

Assets	Liabilities Plus Net Worth
Required reserves, rrD^s	Deposits, D^s
Excess reserves, ER	Borrowed reserves, BR
Loans and securities, B^d	Net worth, NW

A bank, as any other business, chooses the quantity of each item in its balance sheet at the level that maximizes its profit. Profit, which equals total revenue minus total cost, is the bottom line of the bank's income statement. Thus, profit maximization brings together a bank's balance sheet and its income statement. The **profit-maximizing condition** requires that a bank choose each item in its balance sheet at the level for which marginal revenue equals marginal cost.

Employing the marginal rule, we shall find the factors that determine the amount of deposits that a bank wants to issue, the amount of reserves it wants to borrow from the Fed, and the amount of excess reserves it wants to hold. Once we know these items, we can find the total amount of loans and investments the bank wants to make, and the factors that affect them from the *bank's balance sheet constraint*. This constraint requires that the sum of the bank's assets equals the sum of its liabilities plus net worth.

THE SUPPLY OF DEPOSITS

The analysis of the supply of deposits begins with the application of the marginal rule. A bank must supply (issue) deposits up to the point where the marginal revenue from one more dollar of deposits is equal to the marginal cost of that dollar's worth of deposits, which is the point at which the marginal revenue and the marginal cost curves intersect in Figure 18–1. Now let us see why we assume that the marginal revenue curve is horizontal and the marginal cost curve upward sloping and what factors shift the curves.

The Net Marginal Revenue from Supplying Deposits

Following the approach introduced in Chapter 7, on the revenue side we work with the net marginal revenue from issuing deposits, expressed as a percentage. When a bank takes in a dollar of deposits, it can lend $(1 - rr)$ of one dollar at the interest rate i. Thus, the marginal revenue equals $(1 - rr)i$. Subtracting the deposit rate, r_D, from the marginal revenue gives us the net marginal revenue that a bank earns by taking in a dollar of deposits:

**FIGURE 18–1
Determining the
Supply of Deposits**

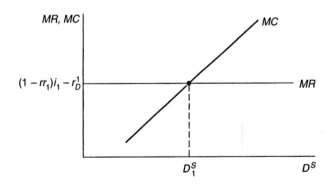

A profit-maximizing bank supplies deposits up to the point where the net marginal revenue from issuing deposits equals the marginal cost.

Net marginal revenue = $(1 - rr)i - r_D$

Figure 18–1 depicts the net marginal revenue curve from supplying deposits as a horizontal line, which means that we are assuming for simplicity that the (average) bank is a price taker: The bank takes the interest rate on loans and securities and the deposit rate as given. The reserve requirement ratio is also given. Thus, the position of the net marginal revenue curve depends on i, r_D, and rr. The marginal revenue curve shifts up when, other things equal, the interest rate rises, or the deposit rate falls, or the reserve requirement ratio falls.

The Marginal Cost of Supplying Deposits

The marginal cost of supplying deposits is also expressed as a percentage. It consists of the noninterest cost of acquiring and managing an additional dollar of deposits and the cost of placing a fraction of the dollar into loans and securities. As we know from examining the bank's income statement, this cost includes the cost of inputs such as labor and computers. It also includes the deposit insurance premium paid to the FDIC and loan loss provisions made by the bank. The positive slope of the curve in Figure 18–1 entails an assumption that the marginal cost of deposits (and banking) increases with the size of a bank's deposits.[3] We take the volume of deposits as a proxy for the bank's size.

Consider the position of the marginal cost curve. For the same level of deposits, marginal costs may increase or decrease. If a factor increases marginal costs, the curve shifts up and to the left; if a factor decreases marginal costs, the curve shifts down and to the right. We can lump all factors that shift the marginal cost curve into one all-inclusive variable, denoted by $\Im\mathcal{R}$. The state of technology is one of the factors included in $\Im\mathcal{R}$. The banking industry gathers, analyzes, and transmits information and funds. Technological progress that reduces the cost of processing information also reduces the (marginal) cost of banking. We refer to such reductions in costs as *cost-reducing financial innovations*, as in Chapter 5. Of course, these innovations shift the marginal cost curve down.

Changes in deposit insurance premiums and loan loss provisions will also shift the marginal cost curve. For example, an increase in deposit insurance premiums raises the marginal cost of issuing a given amount of deposits and, thus, shifts the marginal cost curve upward. A change in the perception by regulators or bankers of the risk of loan losses that results in an increase in loan loss provisions will also shift the marginal cost curve upward. More-intense scrutiny by regulators during periods of financial fragility may also increase the marginal labor costs of banks, as bank employees spend more time monitoring problem loans and preparing for meetings with bank examiners.

Following our conventions, all of these factors that shift the marginal cost curve are represented by $\Im\mathcal{R}$. Because technology and the regulatory structure are important components of $\Im\mathcal{R}$, we refer to $\Im\mathcal{R}$ as the *technology and regulatory index,* as in Chapter 7. In our definition of $\Im\mathcal{R}$ an increase in $\Im\mathcal{R}$ represents cost-increasing changes in technology and regulation, and a decrease in $\Im\mathcal{R}$ represents cost-reducing changes.

---

[3] For simplicity, Figure 18–1 depicts the entire supply curve as upward sloping. Empirical studies show that economies of scale are exhausted at levels well below the size of the average U.S. bank.

FIGURE 18–2
A Reduction in the
Deposit Rate

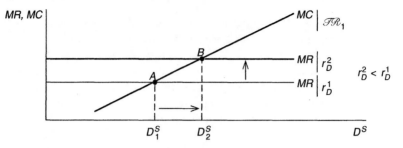

Other things equal, a reduction in the deposit rate raises the net marginal revenue from
issuing deposits, resulting in an increase in the quantity of deposits supplied shown by a
movement from point *A* to point *B*.

The Supply of Deposits Curve

Shifts of the marginal revenue and marginal cost curves affect the supply of deposits.
Figure 18–2 illustrates the effect on D^S of a reduction in the deposit rate. Point *A* is the
initial profit-maximizing level of deposits. Other things equal, a reduction in the deposit
rate raises the net marginal revenue from issuing deposits. As a result, the marginal
revenue curve shifts upward, and its intersection with the marginal cost curve occurs at a
higher level of deposits, shown by point *B*.

Thus, a reduction in the deposit rate increases the profit-maximizing level of deposits.
The economic reasoning is simple. An increase in the net marginal revenue increases a
bank's profit by making marginal revenue greater than marginal cost at the original level of
deposits. This difference between marginal revenue and marginal cost, in turn, induces the
bank to issue more deposits, until the higher marginal revenue equals the marginal cost
(which is higher because of increasing marginal costs). Schematically, the results are:

$$r_D \downarrow \rightarrow [(1 - rr)i - r_D] \uparrow \rightarrow D^S \uparrow$$

Connecting the endpoints of the schema, we have the negative relation between the
deposit rate and the quantity of deposits supplied: Other things equal, a fall in the deposit
rate increases the quantity of deposits that banks want to issue (supply), and an increase
in the deposit rate reduces the quantity of deposits that banks want to issue (supply):

$$r_D \downarrow \rightarrow D^S \uparrow \text{ (and } r_D \uparrow \rightarrow D^S \downarrow)$$

Figure 18–3 depicts this supply relation in a graph with the deposit rate on the vertical
axis and the quantity of deposits on the horizontal axis. A movement along the downward-sloping supply curve shows the inverse relation between the deposit rate and the
quantity of deposits supplied, other things equal. The curve's label displays the other
factors that affect the supply of deposits: *i*, *rr*, and $\mathscr{R}$.

Before examining how changes in these factors shift the supply of deposits curve, we
must explain why we choose to put the deposit rate on the vertical axis in Figure 18–3.
The answer is that we are building toward a theory of the determination of the deposit
rate. Chapter 21 combines the supply of deposits curve with a demand for deposits curve
to determine the deposit rate and the factors that affect it. Recall that Chapter 7 explains

FIGURE 18-3
The Supply of
Deposits

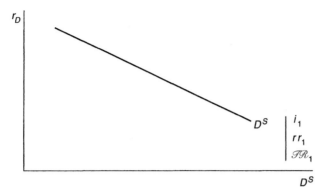

Other things equal, a fall in the deposit rate increases the quantity of
deposits that banks want to issue.

the deposit rate relation intuitively. The additional tools introduced here equip us to
explore this important relation in more detail in subsequent chapters.

Shifts in the
Supply of
Deposits Curve

Whenever a variable other than the deposit rate, r_D, changes to affect either marginal
revenue or marginal cost, the supply of deposits curve will shift. The two panels of
Figure 18-4 illustrate the case of an increase in the marginal revenue because of a rise in
the interest rate. Given r_D and given rr, an increase in i increases $[(1 - rr)i - r_D]$, which
shifts the marginal revenue curve upward. At the initial level of deposits, D^S_1, marginal
revenue exceeds marginal cost. Therefore, the bank wants to attract more deposits. The
increase in the quantity of deposits is shown by the movement from point A to point B in
the upper panel, and from point A' to point B' in the lower panel, where the D^S curve
shifts to the right.

A reduction in the reserve requirement ratio will also shift the marginal revenue curve
upward and shift the supply of deposits curve to the right. The graph looks the same as
the one in Figure 18-4, with the labels changed. On the other hand, a decrease in the
interest rate or an increase in the reserve requirement ratio reduces the net marginal
revenue and, therefore, reduces the supply of deposits, other things equal. Therefore, the
supply of deposits curve will shift to the left in these circumstances.

Consider the effects of a shift in the marginal cost of attracting deposits. An improvement in the technological and regulatory environment, $\mathcal{TR}$, reduces marginal cost in the
upper panel of Figure 18-5. At the existing level of deposits, marginal revenue from
deposits exceeds marginal cost. As a result, banks want to attract more deposits at each
level of marginal revenue and, hence, at each level of the deposit rate. The increase in the
quantity of deposits is shown by the movement from point A to point B in the upper panel
of the graph, and from point A' to point B' in the lower panel, where the D^S curve shifts to
the right.

Of course, an increase in marginal cost reverses the results depicted in Figure 18-5. The
marginal cost curve shifts upward, thereby reducing the quantity of deposits that profit-

FIGURE 18–4
The Interest Rate
and the Supply of
Deposits

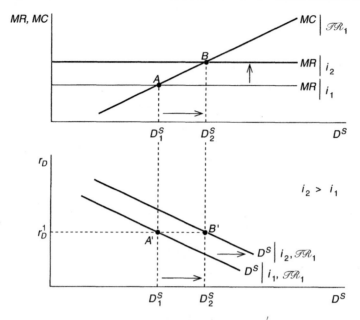

Other things equal, an increase in the interest rate increases the net marginal
revenue, which induces profit-maximizing banks to attract more deposits. The
supply of deposit curve shifts to the right.

maximizing banks want to supply, other things equal. Chapter 17 discusses the provisions
of the Federal Deposit Insurance Corporation Improvement Act of 1991, most of which
were implemented in December 1992. Many bankers objected to FDICIA, calling it a
"bank-bashing bill" that would increase the regulatory burden of banks and therefore
would increase the cost of doing business for banks and reduce the supply of deposits.

    Table 18–4 summarizes all the factors affecting the supply of deposits. Graphically,
the effect of a change in the deposit rate shown in the first row is depicted by a movement
along the downward-sloping D^S curve. A reduction in the deposit rate increases the
quantity of deposits banks want to attract because it increases marginal revenue, and an
increase in the deposit rate decreases the quantity of deposits desired because it decreases
marginal revenue. Changes in the factors in the other rows are depicted by a shift of the

TABLE 18–4
Factors Affecting
Deposit Supply, D^S

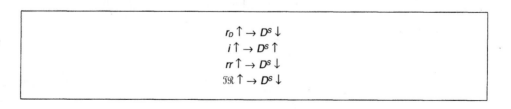

FIGURE 18–5
The Technology and Regulatory Index and the Supply of Deposits

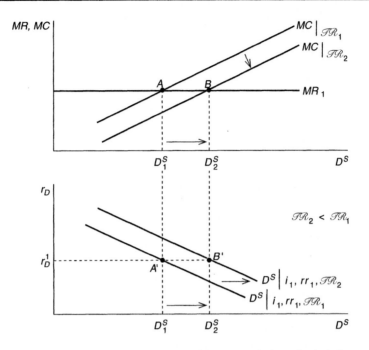

A reduction in marginal cost caused by an improvement in the technological and regulatory environment increases the supply of deposits.

supply of deposits curve. In the second row, other things equal, an increase in the interest rate (i.e., the interest rate banks charge) increases marginal revenue and the quantity of deposits banks want to attract. The D^S curve shifts up and to the right. In the third row, other things equal, an increase in the reserve requirement ratio, rr, reduces marginal revenue and profitability of deposits. Therefore, banks want to attract fewer deposits. Note that the reserve requirement ratio acts like a tax. An increase in the reserve requirement ratio reduces the net marginal revenue, $[(1-rr)i - r_D]$. Finally, in the fourth row, other things equal, an increase in the technology and regulatory index that increases the marginal cost of banking reduces the quantity of deposits banks want to attract.

The following statement succinctly summarizes our results: The supply of deposits is an increasing function of the net marginal revenue and a decreasing function of the index of financial technology and regulation. We represent this relation algebraically as follows:

$$D^S = D^S[\underbrace{(1-rr)i - r_D}_{+}, \underset{-}{\Im\Re}]$$

Note that an increase in the interest rate increases the net marginal revenue, while an increase in the reserve requirement ratio or the deposit rate decreases it.

TRY IT OUT 18.1

Suppose that deposit rates and interest rates on loans and securities both fall, but deposit rates fall more than interest rates. Use a marginal revenue–marginal cost diagram to show the effect on the supply of bank deposits.

RESERVE MANAGEMENT

Reserve management refers to how banks decide on the quantity of reserves they want to borrow from the Fed's discount window and the quantity of excess reserves they want to hold. In each case, the bank decides by applying the marginal rule.

Borrowed Reserves

A profit-maximizing bank decides to borrow from the discount window up to the point where the marginal cost of borrowing reserves equals the marginal revenue. This is the point at which the marginal revenue and the marginal cost curves intersect in Figure 18–6. To understand the shapes of these curves and why they shift, it is necessary to examine the behavior of banks and the Fed.

The Marginal Revenue from Borrowed Reserves   A bank borrows to satisfy reserve requirements, but it can also profit by borrowing from the Fed. When a bank borrows from the Fed to fund a reserve deficiency, it avoids having to liquidate securities or to borrow from other banks in the federal funds market. By borrowing from the Fed, the bank also earns a revenue, the spread between the interest rate on securities (or the federal funds rate) and the discount rate that it pays the Fed, $i - d$. This spread is usually positive because the discount rate is typically below short-term market rates of interest.

Admittedly, borrowing from the Fed is a privilege and not a right, and banks must show a need to borrow, as Chapter 12 explains. It is also true, however, that borrowing from the Fed makes additional funds available to a bank and to the banking system as a whole. By having more funds, the bank can lend more. Every additional dollar of funds, no matter how it is obtained, will earn the interest rate i when invested in loans or securities. Thus, the interest spread, $i - d$, is the net marginal revenue a bank earns by borrowing from the Fed.

In Figure 18–6, the horizontal line depicts the net marginal revenue of borrowing reserves. It is horizontal because of the assumption of a price-taking banking firm. The market rate of interest, i, is not affected by the size of funds borrowed from the Fed, and the discount rate, d, is a fixed number, irrespective of the size of borrowed reserves.

The Marginal Cost of Borrowing   Because we have subtracted the discount rate from the interest rate on the revenue side, the marginal cost of borrowing reserves consists entirely of nonpecuniary costs. These costs are implicit. First, borrowing from the Fed sends signals to its depositors and stockholders. Borrowing more from the Fed may taint a bank's reputation if depositors and stockholders worry that the bank is in financial trouble. Second, and more important, the Fed keeps track of the frequency and the amount of borrowing from the discount window. If the Fed determines that a bank has abused its borrowing privileges, the Fed may impose penalties, such as refusing access to the discount window. Thus, the greater a bank's quantity of borrowed reserves, the greater the likelihood that the Fed will impose penalties in the future. If the estimate of

FIGURE 18–6
Determining
Borrowed Reserves

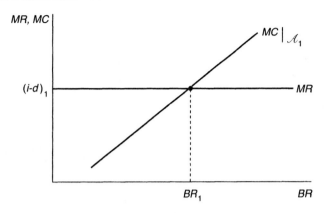

Profit-maximizing banks borrow from the Fed up to the point where
the marginal revenue from borrowing equals the marginal cost.

this cost of borrowing, called the *implicit marginal cost of borrowing,* increases with the
quantity of borrowed reserves, the marginal cost curve will be upward sloping, as shown
in Figure 18–6. (The vertical axis in Figure 18–6 measures the marginal cost in the same
units as the interest rate and the discount rate—as a percentage, for example, 3 percent on
borrowed funds.)

Any decision by the Fed to tighten or loosen the administration of the discount window affects the position of the *MC* curve. The Fed's administration of the discount
window, denoted by the symbol $\mathcal{A}$, generally includes not only the degree of looseness or
tightness in the Fed's administration of the discount window, but also the perception by
banks of the implicit cost of borrowing from the Fed, that is, the attitude of bankers about
borrowing from the discount window. In our definition of $\mathcal{A}$, called the *administrative
index* for brevity, an increase in the index raises the marginal cost of borrowing from the
Fed, and a reduction in the index lowers the marginal cost of borrowing.

The Determinants of Borrowed Reserves   How do shifts in the marginal revenue
or marginal cost curves change a bank's willingness to borrow from the Fed? Beginning
with a change in marginal revenue, suppose that the spread between the interest rate and
the discount rate rises because the Fed reduces the discount rate. Other things equal, the
net marginal revenue a bank earns by borrowing from the Fed rises. (The marginal
revenue curve shifts upward). At the existing level of borrowed reserves, marginal revenue will now be greater than marginal cost, inducing banks to borrow more until *MR*
equals *MC* once again. We leave the graphics as an exercise for the reader and simply
represent the results schematically:

$$d \downarrow \rightarrow (i - d) \uparrow \rightarrow MR \uparrow \rightarrow MR > MC \rightarrow BR \uparrow$$

Of course, net marginal revenue will also increase if the interest rate increases, other
things equal, that is, given the discount rate. As a result, the willingness of banks to
borrow from the Fed increases. Schematically,

FIGURE 18–7
Borrowing and the
Spread between the
Federal Funds
Rate and the
Discount Rate

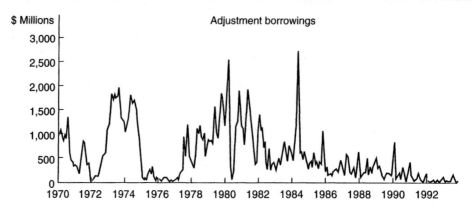

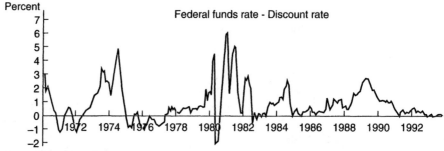

Source: Federal Reserve Board.

$$i \uparrow \rightarrow (i - d) \uparrow \rightarrow MR \uparrow \rightarrow MR > MC \rightarrow BR \uparrow$$

Putting these two results together establishes a positive relation between the spread and borrowed reserves:

$$(i - d) \uparrow \rightarrow BR \uparrow \text{ and } (i - d) \downarrow \rightarrow BR \downarrow$$

The actual data for borrowed reserves and the spread between the federal funds rate and the discount rate shown in Figure 18–7 are consistent with this analysis. The graph shows that borrowed reserves tend to rise when the spread rises, and fall when the spread falls.

If the Fed loosens the administration of the discount window, represented by a decrease in the administrative index $\mathscr{A}$, the implicit marginal cost is lowered at each level of borrowed reserves. (Graphically, the marginal cost curve would shift down and to the right.) As a result, at the existing level of borrowed reserves, marginal revenue will now be greater than marginal cost, inducing banks to borrow more. Schematically,

$$\mathscr{A} \downarrow \rightarrow MC \downarrow \rightarrow MR > MC \rightarrow BR \uparrow$$

If, on the other hand, the marginal cost of borrowing from the Fed rises, borrowed reserves will fall. For example, if banks perceive that borrowing from the Fed will reduce the public's confidence in the management of the bank, the implicit marginal cost of

FIGURE 18–8
Determining
Excess Reserves

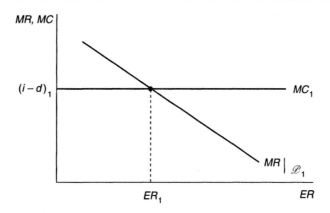

Profit-maximizing banks hold excess reserves up to the point where
the marginal revenue from excess reserves equals their marginal
cost.

borrowing from the Fed will increase even without a change in behavior of the Fed. As a result, for any given value of *i* and *d,* profit-maximizing banks will want to borrow less. Two upward shifts of the marginal cost curve in the 1980s were associated with well-publicized cases of financial distress, which means that some banks most likely were concerned that borrowing from the Fed would taint their reputations. Economists at the Federal Reserve Bank of New York have estimated that following the bailout of Continental Illinois Bank in 1984, the willingness of other banks to borrow at any given interest rate spread temporarily decreased by about $350 to $450 million. They also found that, other things equal, borrowing declined by about $100 to $125 million after the stock market crash of October 1987.[4]

Excess Reserves

Reserve management involves not only borrowed reserves but also excess reserves. Uncertainty is a major reason for holding excess reserves. A bank holds excess reserves because of uncertainty about its need for required reserves, uncertainty about future penalties imposed by the Fed in the case of a failure to meet reserve requirements, and uncertainty about future loan opportunities. A bank's ALCO determines the level of excess reserves that the bank will hold by applying the marginal rule. In this case, a bank decides to hold that level of excess reserves that balances marginal cost with marginal revenue, as shown in Figure 18–8.

The Marginal Cost of Excess Reserves   The marginal cost of excess reserves is not explicit; it must be inferred. By holding excess reserves rather than an earning asset, say, a security, a bank gives up the interest receipts that would accrue on the security.

4 See "Monetary Policy and Open Market Operations during 1988," *Quarterly Review,* Federal Reserve Bank of New York 13, no. 4 (Winter–Spring 1989): 98–99.

Thus, by not holding an additional dollar's worth of securities, a bank forgoes the interest rate, *i*. The bank, however, saves the interest payments to the Fed that would be required if the bank found itself with insufficient reserves and was forced to borrow at the discount window. What the bank saves by holding one more dollar in excess reserves is the discount rate, *d*. The discount rate is actually one component of marginal revenue. Subtracting it from the marginal cost, *i*, gives us the net marginal cost, $i - d$, of holding excess reserves. Because *d* is fixed and because we assume that the market interest rate cannot be influenced by the size of a single bank's holdings of securities, it follows that the net marginal cost is a given number that is independent of the size of the bank's excess reserves. Therefore, the marginal cost curve is a horizontal line in Figure 18–8.

The Marginal Revenue from Excess Reserves   The revenue from holding excess reserves is implicit. It consists of the benefit to a bank of better loan opportunities in the future and the benefit of avoiding potential penalties imposed by the Fed if the bank cannot satisfy its reserve requirements. It is natural to assume that this marginal benefit becomes smaller as excess reserves become larger. This is the reason that the marginal revenue curve in Figure 18–8 is downward sloping.

The symbol $\mathscr{P}$, representing the *index of prudence,* appears on the label of the marginal revenue curve in Figure 18–8. The more prudent a bank, the greater its estimate of the implicit marginal revenue from holding a given amount of excess reserves. Alternatively, the more prudent a bank, the more excess reserves it must hold to achieve a given marginal revenue. In graphical terms, the higher $\mathscr{P}$, the farther to the right the marginal revenue curve lies.

The Determinants of Excess Reserves   Shifts in the net marginal cost curve and the marginal revenue curve affect the amount of excess reserves that a bank wants to hold. Suppose the opportunity cost of holding reserves, $i - d$, increases because of an increase in *i* or a decrease in *d,* or both. The marginal cost curve would shift upward, making marginal revenue less than marginal cost at the original level of excess reserves. As a result, profit-maximizing banks will want to hold fewer excess reserves. We leave the graphics as an exercise for the reader and present the results schematically:

$$(i - d) \uparrow \rightarrow MC \uparrow \rightarrow MR < MC \rightarrow ER \downarrow$$

What happens if the index of prudence rises? An increase in $\mathscr{P}$ increases the (perceived) marginal revenue from holding excess reserves, which makes the marginal revenue greater than marginal cost at the original level of excess reserves. As a result, banks want to hold more excess reserves. Schematically,

$$\mathscr{P} \uparrow \rightarrow MR \uparrow \rightarrow MR > MC \rightarrow ER \uparrow$$

Chapter 8 notes that after the Fed switched from lagged (required) reserve accounting to contemporaneous reserve accounting in 1984, banks held more excess reserves. This rise in excess reserves can be explained as an increase in the index of prudence. Under lagged reserve accounting, a bank was certain of the required reserves it needed to hold in a given week because the requirements were based on deposits two weeks earlier. Under contemporaneous reserve accounting, the reserve maintenance period and the reserve computation period coincide. The increased uncertainty of banks in assessing their need to hold required reserves under contemporaneous reserve accounting raised the implicit marginal revenue of excess reserves and led banks to hold more excess reserves.

The extraordinary increase in excess reserves in the 1930s, from about $50 million at the beginning of 1930 to more than $6,000 million at the beginning of 1940, is a dramatic example of a shift in both the marginal cost and marginal revenue curves. The marginal cost of holding excess reserves fell because of declining market interest rates. Marginal revenue rose because of an economywide collapse in credit quality.

In sum, the quantity of excess reserves, *ER,* varies negatively with its opportunity cost and positively with the index of prudence. The following excess reserves function summarizes this relation:

$$ER = ER\ (\underset{-}{i - d}:\ \underset{+}{\mathscr{P}})$$

Schematically,

$$(i - d) \uparrow \rightarrow ER \downarrow$$
$$\mathscr{P} \uparrow \rightarrow ER \uparrow$$

THE DEMAND FOR LOANS AND SECURITIES

The final item in a bank's balance sheet is the amount of loans and securities that the bank wants to hold. There are two ways to explain how a bank decides on the total quantity of loans and securities in its balance sheet. One method is to equate the marginal revenue of attracting and managing loans and securities with the marginal cost. The other method is to use the balance sheet equation and the results derived from profit maximization for the other items in the equation. We prefer this second method because it links the two primary functions of a bank: making loans and buying securities, on the one hand, and attracting deposits, on the other.

The **bank's balance sheet equation** states that the sum of the bank's assets must equal the sum of its liabilities plus its net worth:

$$rrD^S + ER + B^d = D^S + BR + NW$$

Rearranging the balance sheet equation so that the demand for loans and securities is on the left side, we get:

$$B^d = (1 - rr)D^S + BR - ER + NW$$

This equation makes clear that the determinants of the demand for loans and securities must be the same as the determinants of the other items in the bank's balance sheet.

The Determinants of Demand for Loans and Securities

The factors that affect a bank's total demand for loans and securities are the reserve requirement ratio and the factors that affect the supply of deposits, borrowed reserves, excess reserves, and net worth. They are the interest rate, i; the deposit rate, r_D; the reserve requirement ratio, rr; the technology and regulatory index, $\mathfrak{R}$; the discount rate, d; the administrative index for discount window loans, $\mathscr{A}$; the index of bank prudence, $\mathscr{P}$; and net worth itself. Let us now examine the effect of a change in each of these factors. We begin by assuming that net worth is fixed.

First, other things equal, an increase in the interest rate increases the supply of deposits, increases borrowed reserves, and reduces excess reserves. In other words, an increase in i makes available a greater amount of funds that can be loaned out or invested in securities. Hence, other things equal, an increase in the interest rate raises the demand for loans and securities by a bank. Schematically, the linkages are:

$$i \uparrow \rightarrow \begin{cases} D^S \uparrow \\ BR \uparrow \\ ER \downarrow \end{cases} \rightarrow [(1-rr)D^S + BR - ER + NW] \uparrow \rightarrow B^d \uparrow$$

Of course, a reduction in the interest rate would reduce the demand for loans and securities. Thus, given the balance sheet constraint, there is a positive relation between the interest rate and the demand for loans and securities.

Second, other things equal, an increase in the deposit rate will reduce the quantity of deposits that a bank wants to issue and the quantity of loans and securities it wants to hold. Schematically, the linkages are:

$$r_D \uparrow \rightarrow D^S \downarrow \rightarrow [(1-rr)D^S + BR - ER + NW] \downarrow \rightarrow B^d \downarrow$$

Third, other things equal, an increase in rr increases the amount of required reserves that must be held against a given supply of deposits and reduces a bank's demand for loans and securities. Given D^S, the amount of disposable deposits, $(1-rr)D^S$, decreases when rr increases. Thus, a bank will have fewer funds to lend even if D^S remains unchanged. But D^S falls, because an increase in rr reduces the bank's net marginal revenue. In sum, the linkages by which an increase in rr reduces the demand for loans and securities are:

$$rr \uparrow \rightarrow \begin{cases} D^S \downarrow \\ (1-rr) \downarrow \end{cases} \rightarrow [(1-rr)D^S + BR - ER + NW] \downarrow \rightarrow B^d \downarrow$$

Of course, a reduction in rr would increase the demand for loans and securities. To stimulate bank lending in December 1990, the Fed reduced the average reserve requirement ratio by eliminating reserves on nonpersonal time deposits and net Eurodollar liabilities. In April 1992, the Fed reduced the reserve requirement ratio on transactions deposits from 12 percent to 10 percent. These unusual moves by the Fed were part of its response to the credit crunch of 1990, as we shall see.

Fourth, other things equal, an increase in the technology and regulatory index, $\Re$, raises the cost of issuing deposits, which reduces the quantity of deposits that a bank wants to attract, thereby decreasing the funds available to make loans or buy securities. Schematically

$$\Re \uparrow \rightarrow D^S \downarrow \rightarrow [(1-rr)D^S + BR - ER + NW] \downarrow \rightarrow B^d \downarrow$$

For example, marginal costs rise when deposit insurance premiums go up or when banks must make more provisions for loan losses. An increase in marginal costs reduces the quantity of deposits that a bank wants to attract and, thus, will decrease the funds available to invest in loans and securities, other things equal.

Fifth, other things equal, an increase in the discount rate reduces borrowed reserves and increases excess reserves, thereby reducing the demand for loans and securities.

TABLE 18–5
Factors Affecting
Demand for Loans
and Securities, B^d

$$i \uparrow \rightarrow B^d \uparrow$$
$$r_D \uparrow \rightarrow B^d \downarrow$$
$$rr \uparrow \rightarrow B^d \downarrow$$
$$\mathfrak{IR} \uparrow \rightarrow B^d \downarrow$$
$$d \uparrow \rightarrow B^d \downarrow$$
$$\mathcal{A} \uparrow \rightarrow B^d \downarrow$$
$$\mathscr{P} \uparrow \rightarrow B^d \downarrow$$
$$NW \uparrow \rightarrow B^d \uparrow$$

$$d \uparrow \rightarrow \begin{cases} ER \uparrow \\ BR \downarrow \end{cases} \rightarrow [(1 - rr)D^S + BR - ER + NW] \downarrow \rightarrow B^d \downarrow$$

Sixth, other things equal, a tightening in the administration of the discount window, represented by an increase in the administrative index, also reduces borrowed reserves, making fewer funds available for loans and securities.

$$\mathcal{A} \uparrow \rightarrow BR \downarrow \rightarrow [(1 - rr)D^S + BR - ER + NW] \downarrow \rightarrow B^d \downarrow$$

Seventh, other things equal, an increase in the index of prudence raises the quantity of excess reserves that banks want to hold and siphons off funds that would be used to make loans and purchase securities:

$$\mathscr{P} \uparrow \rightarrow ER \uparrow \rightarrow [(1 - rr)D^S + BR - ER + NW] \downarrow \rightarrow B^d \downarrow$$

Finally, a bank's capital, or net worth, can be increased either by issuing equity securities or by retaining profits. An increase in capital enables a bank to hold more assets that yield a return and to issue fewer liabilities that incur costs. In the simplest scenario, the entire increase in a bank's capital will be directed to making loans and buying securities, with no change in the other assets (excess reserves) or in liabilities (deposits and borrowed reserves). Similarly, a fall in net worth will reduce a bank's demand for assets by an equal amount. In this case, however, the capital-to-asset ratio may fall below required levels. A capital-deficient bank will have to reduce further its demand for assets or raise additional capital. As a summary, Table 18–5 shows all the factors that affect the demand for loans and securities.

The Credit
Crunch of
the 1990s:
Connecting
Theory with
Practice

The theory of profit maximization discussed in this chapter sheds light on the credit crunch of the early 1990s, when banks became less willing and able to lend, even to creditworthy customers. It can be used to explain the behavior of banks and the reaction of the Fed. The credit crunch began in the Southwest in the late 1980s and spread to other regions of the country, especially New England, in 1990.

Early in 1990 the financial press began to report anecdotal evidence of an increasing reluctance by banks in New England to lend. Banks in that region faced a weakening economy and a deteriorating real estate market. In the face of increasing risks, regulators were forcing banks to mark down (charge off) problem loans on their books sooner than in the past and to increase provisions for loan losses.

An increase in loan loss provisions, represented by a rise in $\mathfrak{IR}$ in our model, increases marginal costs and, thus, reduces the amount of deposits a bank wants to issue and the amount of total credit it wants to provide by making loans and purchasing securities. The story may not end there, however. If charge-offs are greater than provisions for loan losses, a bank's capital (its net worth) will fall. If the bank's capital-to-asset ratio falls below the legally required level (or the level considered healthy by regulators), the bank will be forced to cut back further on loans and securities. There are additional considerations, however. As Chapter 17 discusses, the risk-based capital requirements phased in after the Basle Agreement of 1988 assign lower risk weightings to securities, such as Treasury securities and federal agency securities, than to loans. Therefore, the agreement introduced a bias in favor of securities, which helps explain the restructuring of bank balance sheets in the 1990s, away from loans and toward securities.

On May 10, 1990, the nation's three top banking regulators—the comptroller of the currency, the chairman of the FDIC, and the chairman of the Federal Reserve Board— took the unusual step of meeting with directors of the American Bankers Association to urge bankers to lend to creditworthy customers. Nevertheless, the regulators continued to argue that market conditions and not regulatory overkill were the major cause of the credit crunch. For example, in testimony before the Committee on Banking, Housing, and Urban Affairs of the U.S. Senate on June 21, 1990, Alan Greenspan, the chairman of the Federal Reserve Board, made the following point: "Certain sectors or individual borrowers appear to be having trouble obtaining credit, but these specific difficulties are largely consistent with lenders' and regulators' reactions to shifting risks." [*Federal Reserve Bulletin* 76, no. 8 (August 1990): 632]

As the economy weakened and moved into recession in July 1990, the capital-to-asset ratios at many banks deteriorated further as problem loans continued to mount. The banks hardest hit by loan losses in the early 1990s found their capital depleted. In response, they cut back on their lending. Regulators also instructed banks nationwide to review their lending practices to highly leveraged corporate borrowers after the debacle in the junk bonds market in February 1990. Banks responded by cutting back on merger-related lending.

By year-end, banks nationwide were facing increased deposit insurance premiums and tighter capital requirements, which promised to erode further their lending. Thus, in December the Fed went beyond jawboning banks to lend. On December 5, 1990, the Fed reduced the reserve requirement ratio on nonpersonal time deposits and net Eurodollar liabilities from 3 percent to zero. This was the first change in reserve requirements since 1983. We know from our model that a reduction in the reserve requirement ratio increases the net marginal revenue from issuing deposits, thereby increasing the amount of deposits that a bank wants to issue and the amount of loans they want to make.

The reduction in reserve requirements was an attempt by the Fed to shore up bank profits and to signal banks to loosen up a notch in their lending. Fed officials estimated that the elimination of reserve requirements on nonpersonal time deposits would raise pretax profits in the banking system by $900 million, which is close to a 4 percent increase in profits for a typical year. On December 18, 1990, the Fed reinforced its signal to banks to lend by lowering the discount rate from 7 percent to 6 1/2 percent. Six weeks later, it lowered the discount rate another 50 basis points to 6 percent. As we have seen, a reduction in the discount rate induces banks to borrow more reserves and to make more loans or buy more securities. To add to the incentive for banks to borrow from the discount window, in February the chairman of the Federal Reserve Board signaled a loosening in its administration of the discount window—a reduction in the administrative index, $\mathscr{A}$, in our model. In written testimony prepared for his appearance before Congress on February 20, 1991, as part of the Fed's semiannual monetary policy report, chairman Alan Greenspan said:

> Despite bank reluctance, borrowing has been somewhat higher on occasion this year as banks were in the process of adapting to the lower reserve requirements. We would not be surprised to see somewhat higher adjustment borrowing persist. The Federal Reserve has no desire to circumscribe the legitimate use of the discount window, and market participants should not interpret such use as indicating underlying problems for the institutions involved.

The Fed continued to lower the discount rate, which it brought down to 3 percent by mid-1992. In addition, the Fed reduced the reserve requirement ratio on transactions deposits from 12 percent to 10 percent, effective April 1992. More important, between 1990 and 1992 the Fed aggressively used open market operations to bring down market rates of interest to reinvigorate the economy. The rates banks earned on their loans and securities fell, but their deposit rates fell even more, in part, because the maturity of bank loans and securities is longer than the maturity of bank deposits. As a result, the net interest income of banks rose. Moreover, the provisions banks had to make for loan losses fell drastically in 1992 because of the improving economy. The falling costs and higher revenues boosted bank profits, which were at record levels in 1992. Banks, however, were still restructuring their balance sheets, away from loans and toward securities. Signs of the easing of the credit crunch appeared in 1993, when there was a marked increase in the availability of loans to small business. In testimony before Congress in February 1994, Chairman Greenspan remarked that there was a drastic improvement in loan activity, although the credit crunch had not entirely been eliminated.

SUMMARY

- The balance sheet of a bank is a record of the bank's assets, liabilities, and net worth. The income statement is a record of the bank's revenues, costs, and profits.
- The twin functions of a bank are to attract deposits and make loans, which require banks to gather information.
- Loan managers must guard against moral hazard and adverse selection, which involve customers behaving in ways that are unprofitable for banks. Moral hazard and adverse selection stem from asymmetric information, which means

the borrower has more information about the use of the loan than the lender.
- The asset and liability management committee of a bank guides the bank's decisions about the composition and the size of its balance sheet. These decisions can be explained by profit-maximizing exercises, which connect a bank's balance sheet with its income statement.
- Profit equals total revenue minus total costs, which are items in a bank's income statement.

- To maximize profit, a bank must provide or hold each item in its balance sheet at the level that makes the marginal cost equal to the marginal revenue of that item.

- Applying the profit-maximizing rule to the supply of deposits gives the result that deposits supplied vary positively with the interest rate, i, and negatively with the deposit rate, r_D, and the reserve requirement ratio, rr.

- The shift parameter $\mathcal{TR}$, the *technology and regulatory index*, also affects the supply of deposits. An increase in $\mathcal{TR}$ represents all factors that shift the marginal cost curve for supplying deposits upward, such as cost-enhancing increases in deposit insurance premiums, in provisions for loan losses, or in other regulatory practices. A decrease in $\mathcal{TR}$ represents factors that shift the marginal cost curve downward, such as cost-reducing financial innovations or less stringent regulations. Profit maximization implies that the supply of deposits varies inversely with $\mathcal{TR}$.

- Applying the profit-maximizing rule to a bank's decision to borrow reserves from the Fed gives the result that borrowed reserves vary positively with the interest rate and inversely with the discount rate.

- The shift parameter $\mathcal{A}$, the *administrative index*, also affects borrowed reserves. An increase in $\mathcal{A}$ represents all factors that increase the implicit marginal cost of borrowing reserves, such as a tightening in the administration of the discount window. Profit maximization implies that borrowed reserves vary inversely with the shift parameter $\mathcal{A}$.

- Applying the profit-maximizing rule to the demand for excess reserves gives the result that this demand varies negatively with the interest rate and positively with the discount rate.

- The demand for excess reserves also depends on the shift parameter $\mathcal{P}$, the *index of prudence*. An increase in $\mathcal{P}$ represents the factors that shift the implicit marginal revenue curve for excess reserves upward, such as increased uncertainty about required reserves or the prospect of better loan opportunities in the future. Profit maximization implies that the demand for excess reserves varies positively with $\mathcal{P}$.

- The demand for loans and securities by a bank can be found from the balance sheet constraint and the results derived from profit maximization for the supply of deposits and for excess reserves and borrowed reserves.

- The demand for securities varies positively with the interest rate and inversely with the deposit rate. The demand for securities varies inversely with the reserve requirement ratio and the discount rate. And the demand for securities varies inversely with $\mathcal{TR}$, $\mathcal{A}$, and $\mathcal{P}$.

- In 1990 banks became increasingly unwilling or unable to lend. The banks hardest hit by loan losses from a deteriorating real estate market and a weakening economy not only could not make new loans but also had to call in existing loans as their capital-to-asset ratios fell below minimum requirements.

- Reacting to the credit crunch, the Fed moved to boost bank profits and, thereby, encourage banks to lend by reducing reserve requirements, lowering the discount rate, and signaling a loosening in the administration of the discount window.

KEY TERMS AND CONCEPTS

balance sheet

sources of bank funds

uses of bank funds

cash items in the process of collection

correspondent relationship

income statement

loan loss provisions

asymmetric information

adverse selection

moral hazard

covenant

asset and liability management committee (ALCO)

supply of deposits

profit-maximizing condition

bank's balance sheet equation

QUESTIONS AND PROBLEMS

1. What is the largest use of funds in the balance sheet of U.S. banks? The largest source of funds? Verify your answer by looking up the "Assets and Liabilities of Commercial Banks" in the financial and business statistics of a recent issue of the *Federal Reserve Bulletin*.

2. "A bank's balance sheet is a record of everything a bank does." True or false? Explain.

3. What is the largest source of revenue for U.S. banks? Of costs? In which financial statement do revenues and costs appear?

4. Explain the difference between loan loss provisions and loan loss reserves.

5. What is adverse selection and how does a bank cope with it?

6. How does a bank cope with the moral hazard it faces?

7. What role do reserve managers play on a bank's asset and liability management committee (ALCO)?

8. Suppose that deposit rates and market rates of interest both fall, but deposit rates fall more than market rates of interest. Use the appropriate profit-maximizing conditions and the bank's balance sheet constraint to explain the effect on a bank's total demand for loans and securities.

9. How would an increase in the ALCO's perception of the risk of lending affect a bank's supply of deposits?

10. Explain the difference between a movement along and a shift of the supply of deposits curve.

The Wall Street Journal

11. The accompanying table from "State of Siege: New Hampshire Firms Struggle as Bank Crisis Dries Up Their Credit; All 5 of the Biggest Lenders Are Ailing and Business Can't Finance Expansion," *The Wall Street Journal*, February 21, 1991, gives data on non-performing loans for the five largest New Hampshire banks as of September 30, 1990.

   Use the theory of profit maximization to explain how making provisions for nonperforming loans would "dry up credit."

The Wall Street Journal

12. Use a bank's balance sheet constraint combined with the appropriate profit-maximizing conditions to explain the following statement from "Fed Cuts Deposit-Reserve Requirements," *The Wall Street Journal*, February 19, 1992: "The Federal Reserve Board, in another attempt to shore up bank profits so bankers will be more willing to lend, reduced the fraction of deposits that must be held as reserves. The Fed cut from 12% to 10% the percentage of checking account deposits that banks are required to hold as reserves."

The Wall Street Journal

13. Provide the theoretical basis for the following statement from "Regulations Drive Lending to Non-Banks," *The Wall Street Journal*, July 30, 1993: "Caught in the grip of higher premiums, higher capital requirements, poor returns and regulatory pressure, it is not surprising the banking industry is rapidly losing its will to lend."

14. With the help of marginal revenue–marginal cost diagrams, show how the following changes would affect the amount of reserves a bank wants to borrow from the Fed and the amount of excess reserves it wants to hold: (*a*) a reduction in market rates of interest; (*b*) an increase in the discount rate.

15. Explain the logic behind the observed reductions in borrowed reserves following financial crises in the 1980s.

16. Use a bank's balance sheet constraint combined with the appropriate profit-maximizing condition to explain how the introduction of inexpensive software that reduces the cost of information gathering will affect the decision of banks to make loans and buy securities.

State of Unease

Major New Hampshire banks ranked by total assets, as of Sept. 30, 1990

	TOTAL ASSETS (in billions)	NON-PERFORMING ASSETS AS A PERCENT OF TOTAL ASSETS	CAPITAL LEVEL[1]
Amoskeag Bank Shares	$1.745	12.2%	2.92
New Hampshire Savings Bank	1.240	13.6	−0.37
Dartmouth Bancorp	1.024	15.6	1.79
Numerica Financial Corp.	0.990	8.0	2.75
BankEast Corp.	0.954	9.7	2.66

[1]Ratio of tangible equity to assets; 5% is considered healthy
Source: First Albany Corp.

SUGGESTED READINGS

Brunner, Allan D., and William B. English. "Profits and Balance Sheet Developments at U.S. Commercial Banks in 1992." *Federal Reserve Bulletin* 79, no. 7 (July 1993): 649–73.

An annual article, appearing around midyear, that analyzes developments in the income statement and balance sheet of U.S. commercial banks for the previous year.

Furlong, Frederick T. "Capital Regulation and Bank Lending," *Economic Review* (Federal Reserve Bank of San Francisco) 3(1992): 23–33.

An empirical analysis of the relation between bank lending and capital standards from 1985 to 1991.

Ikeo, Kazuto. "Information Technology and the Restructuring of Banking Services." *Monetary and Economic Studies* (Bank of Japan) 10, no. 1 (February 1992): 46–63.

An examination of the impact of new technology on banking.

Stigum, Marcia, and Rene O. Branch, Jr. *Managing Bank Assets and Liabilities: Strategies for Risk Control and Profit.* Homewood, Ill.: Dow Jones-Irwin, 1983.

A comprehensive, nonmathematical analysis of how banks can maximize profits subject to constraints imposed by risk and regulation.

NONDEPOSITORY FINANCIAL INSTITUTIONS

CHAPTER PREVIEW

In addition to depository institutions a wide variety of nondepository institutions provide financial services to households and firms. Consider the following scenarios:

- A person who has worked for 10 years in diners wants to open a diner of his own. He needs to borrow $25,000, but his loan application has been rejected by several banks because he has no established credit history. He turns to a finance company.

- A business with offices in several states wants to lease a small airplane. It too turns to a finance company.

- A recent graduate wants to start investing small amounts in the stock market each month but she also wants a diversified portfolio. She buys shares in a mutual fund.

- A person wants to provide for his young family in case of his premature death. He buys a policy from a life insurance company.

- A newly minted Ph.D. gets her first teaching job at a university. She enrolls in the nationwide pension plan for college teachers.

- A private company wants to go public by selling shares in the stock market. It approaches an investment bank.

This chapter examines the structure, regulation, and decision making of nondepository financial institutions: finance companies, mutual funds, life insurance companies, property/casualty insurance companies, pension funds, and securities firms.

FINANCE COMPANIES

Our discussion of nondepository institutions begins with **finance companies**, which are profit-seeking financial institutions that borrow and lend funds to households and businesses. In this way they are similar to banks and thrifts. Unlike banks and thrifts, however, finance companies do not issue checkable deposits or even savings and time deposits. Instead they raise funds in open markets and borrow from banks.

Early Finance Companies

Today's finance companies evolved from three types of finance companies, distinguished by the type of loans in which they specialized: sales finance companies, consumer finance companies, and business (or commercial) finance companies. Although contemporary finance companies provide loans for all three activities, this classification is a useful expository device.

Sales finance companies provide installment credit to buyers of big-ticket items such as automobiles and home appliances. These companies are typically subsidiaries or affiliates of manufacturers or distributors and thus are called *captive finance companies*. Three of the four largest finance companies in the United States are subsidiaries of the three major automobile manufacturers. The largest is the General Motors Acceptance Corporation (GMAC), whose assets in 1990 accounted for almost 20 percent of the total assets of all finance companies. In the same year captive finance companies owned 42 percent of the assets of the entire industry.

Consumer finance companies such as Household Financial and Beneficial Corp. specialize in consumer loans. These institutions make small loans to individuals—usually to persons with limited ability or no ability to borrow from banks and thrifts, because they have no established credit record or a poor record. To compensate for the high risk of default, the interest charged on these loans is higher than the interest charged on similar loans by banks and thrifts.

Commercial finance companies, also called *business finance companies*, are the business counterpart to consumer finance companies. They specialize in loans to small businesses that have difficulty securing loans from banks because they have no established credit record. Typically business loans extended by finance companies are asset-backed loans, which means they are secured by the borrowers' assets, such as accounts receivable, inventories, or equipment.

Anatomy of Today's Finance Companies

Table 19–1 presents the collective balance sheet of U.S. finance companies at the end of 1993. The liability side of the balance sheet shows that unlike banks and thrifts, finance companies do not issue deposits. Instead they borrow in the open market by issuing commercial paper and bonds and they even borrow from banks. Only large finance companies, however, have access to open markets. Smaller ones rely on banks. In recent years, however, bank loans have become a much smaller source of funds for finance companies.

The asset side of the balance sheet of finance companies is similar to that of banks and thrifts. Like depository institutions finance companies make loans to households and firms. These loans consist of consumer credit, mortgages, and business loans. Unlike depository institutions finance companies do not hold reserves with the Fed. They do, however, hold liquid assets in the form of currency and checking accounts.

TABLE 19–1
U.S. Finance
Companies*: *1993*
(billions of dollars)

Checking accounts and currency	13.3	Bank loans	25.3
Consumer credit	122.6	Commercial paper	159.2
Mortgages	68.6	Bonds	199.9
Business loans	290.1	Other liabilities	202.0
Other assets	163.6	Net worth	71.8
Total assets	658.2	Total liabilities	658.2

*Excludes mortgage companies.
Source: Federal Reserve Flow of Funds Accounts.

Consumer Credit   Consumer credit includes personal cash loans and installment credit for the purchase of consumer durables such as automobiles, appliances, and furniture. Personal cash loans are mostly unsecured, that is, without the backing of property as a collateral. Typically these are loans to individuals with a poor credit history or no credit history. Because these less creditworthy individuals would be turned down or have already been turned down by banks, banks do not compete with finance companies for this business. Installment credit provided by finance companies, however, is in direct competition with bank business. Moreover captive finance companies use installment credit as a marketing device for the parent's products. For example, GMAC may provide credit at below market rates to attract customers to new General Motors automobiles.

Mortgages: Home Equity Loans   Home equity loans are loans to homeowners, with the equity accumulated on the home serving as a collateral. A small portion of these loans are to households that have already paid off their mortgages. Most, however, are second mortgages, which means that the loan is not as secure and will be costlier to collect in case of default. Nevertheless for finance companies home equity loans provide more security than unsecured loans. For households home equity loans are desirable because interest payments are tax deductible. The volume of home equity loans has increased in recent years, with both depositories (banks and thrifts) and finance companies participating.

Business Loans   Loans to businesses accounted for nearly 50 percent of the total assets of finance companies in 1993. About one-third of business loans are asset-backed loans. One type of asset is the borrower's accounts receivable. For example, the borrowing firm may pledge as collateral the funds owed to it for goods and services delivered to customers. In other words the borrowing firm's accounts receivable are the assets that back up its loan. With a second type of loan, the finance company discounts credit that the firm has extended to others. This practice is called *factoring*. In this case, the finance company, in effect, buys from the firm the IOU that was in the firm's portfolio. Also captive finance companies, especially in the automobile industry, provide wholesale credit to their dealers.

Instead of making a loan to a business firm to buy equipment, the finance company may itself buy the equipment and lease (rent) it to the business firm for a specified period and specified future payments. Because finance companies have developed expertise in dealing with manufacturers, they can procure equipment at better terms than individual firms. They pass some of these savings to the leasing firm in the form of lower payments. Leasing equipment—from a fleet of company vehicles, to aircraft, to construction machinery, and even office equipment—has become commonplace because it is often cheaper than borrowing to buy the equipment outright. Finance companies, which initiated leasing, are reaping the fruits. Leasing accounted for nearly 50 percent of all assets of finance companies in 1993.

Operation of Finance Companies

Compared with banks and thrifts, finance companies are at a disadvantage on both sides of their balance sheet. On the asset side finance companies deal with more risk than depository institutions because their customers are usually less creditworthy. Even sales-related installment credit by captive finance companies has disadvantages. For example, repossessing an automobile is costly. On the liability side of their balance sheet, finance companies do not have the protection of deposit insurance because their source of funds is not deposits. Therefore they must pay higher rates than banks to attract funds, which they obtain by borrowing in the open market or by borrowing from banks.

With two strikes against them, how can finance companies be successful? As Chapters 2 and 18 explain, successful lending requires financial intermediaries to screen prospective borrowers carefully, to monitor compliance with the terms of the loan, and, if necessary, to foreclose on the loan. Finance companies charge a higher risk premium than banks because their clientele is less creditworthy. Finance companies are also at a disadvantage compared with banks in monitoring the health of borrowers, because banks have readily available information about a customer's checking account, which is one indicator of the customer's financial health. Thus monitoring is costlier per dollar at finance companies, the more so because the typical loan is smaller than at banks. The higher risk premium and the higher screening, monitoring, and enforcement costs account for the higher interest rates charged by finance companies on their loans.

To improve their chances of being repaid, finance companies prefer to make asset-backed loans to households and firms. Because of their early involvement with asset-backed loans, finance companies have more expertise in handling secured loans than banks and thrifts. This expertise has also helped finance companies enter new lines of business, such as equipment leasing, which is now a major source of revenue for them. Finally, with uncollaterized loans, such as personal cash loans, finance companies can diversify their loan portfolios because each loan is for a small amount. Small, personal, uncollaterized loans are the province of more than 1,500 small finance companies in the United States. These small finance companies compete with pawnshops, which make collaterized small loans. For high-risk borrowers, pawnshops are the last resort, short of loan sharks. To enforce the terms of the loans and to collect payments on delinquent loans, small finance companies typically rely on collection agencies. Only large finance companies can afford their own in-house collection force.

Regulation of Finance Companies

Because they lend to high-risk customers, finance companies charge high interest rates and aggressively pursue delinquent loans. The aim of laws, rules, and regulations governing finance companies is to protect borrowers from exorbitant interest rates and from strong-arm tactics to secure repayment of loans.

Most of the regulation of finance companies takes place at the state level. Finance companies are chartered (licensed) by states, whose regulators must also approve intrastate branching. State laws govern both the maximum level of the interest rate finance companies may charge and the methods they may use to collect delinquent and defaulted loans. Unfortunately state usury laws often have negative effects on those they seek to protect. Whenever market rates of interest exceed the legal ceiling, finance companies either leave the state or ration their loans to the least risky borrowers. Both methods deprive high-risk borrowers of credit. This result is the opposite of what the originators of consumer finance companies intended at the turn of the twentieth century. Finance companies owe their existence to a New York philanthropic organization, the Russell Sage Foundation, which campaigned for the creation of a financial intermediary that would provide credit to high-risk consumers who lacked property to mortgage or to pawn.

Federal truth-in-lending laws and laws that delineate the methods used to recover delinquent loans, such as seizing assets and garnishing wages, also apply to finance companies. Finance companies, however, have never been subject to interstate branching restrictions. Also, because their sources of funds are not deposits, they are not subject to reserve requirements or to deposit insurance premiums.

MUTUAL FUNDS

While finance companies cater to small and weak borrowers, mutual funds provide an outlet for small investors. **Mutual funds** pool the savings of small investors to buy securities. The investors in turn receive shares in the portfolio of securities in proportion to their invested funds. In essence mutual funds issue shares and buy securities with the proceeds. The shareholders are the owners of the portfolio of the fund, in much the same way that shareholders of IBM are owners of the plant, equipment, and other assets of IBM.

Table 19–2 presents the balance sheet of U.S. mutual funds at the end 1993. Total liabilities equal shares outstanding because mutual funds do not have a net worth of their own. Instead they are owned by the shareholders.

TABLE 19–2
U.S. Mutual Funds:* *1993*
(billions of dollars)

Checking accounts and currency	22.2	Total shares outstanding	1,426.9
Corporate equities	667.3	Net worth	0.0
U.S. government securities	289.0		
Tax-exempt securities	217.9		
Corporate and foreign bonds	186.0		
Open market paper	44.5		
Total financial assets	1,426.9	Total liabilities	1,426.9

*Excludes money market mutual funds and closed-end funds.
Source: Federal Reserve Flow of Funds Accounts.

Mutual funds are open-end funds, which means that the number of shares issued are not fixed. Instead investors can buy more shares or redeem shares any day at that day's price, called the *net asset value*. There are other funds organized as closed-end funds, in which the number of shares issued is fixed. Like ordinary stocks, existing shares of closed-end funds may be bought from other holders in the secondary market. The Federal Reserve's Flow of Funds Accounts classifies closed-end funds separately from mutual funds. At the end of 1993 there were 15 times as many mutual funds as closed-end funds. Mutual funds and closed-end funds, together with money-market mutual funds, are called *investment companies*, all of which pool the funds of a large number of small savers to invest in a diversified portfolio of market instruments.[1]

Types of Mutual Funds

The balance sheet of the mutual fund industry in Table 19–2 shows that at the end of 1993 nearly one-half (47 percent) of their assets were in corporate equities. Another 13 percent were in corporate bonds, while U.S. government securities accounted for 20 percent of the assets held by mutual funds. The collective balance sheet, however, masks the diversity of mutual funds.

There were nearly 4,000 individual mutual funds in the United States in 1993. They all, however, fit into some basic categories depending on the objective of the fund and, thus, the composition of the fund's portfolio. Some funds are dedicated to pursuing high growth. These funds invest in instruments that have the potential to appreciate substantially. Chapter 3 explains that the total return on an asset is the sum of periodic receipts (dividends or interest) plus capital gains. *Growth funds* invest primarily in assets that are expected to reap large capital gains. Because these assets are usually common stock, growth funds invest almost exclusively in equity securities. Of course expectations of high capital gains also mean expectations of high capital losses. Thus growth funds, by their nature, are risky.

In contrast *income funds* emphasize the periodic payment of dividends and interest. Thus income funds invest heavily in those stocks that regularly pay dividends and in notes and bonds. In recent years funds that combine both income and growth, naturally called *balanced funds*, have become popular.

There are also specialized funds, called *sector funds*, that invest in specific industries, such as health care, financial services, natural resources, precious metals, and utilities. These funds are designed to appeal to specific investor groups. The large families of funds, such as Fidelity, Vanguard, and Franklin, each offers funds in all categories.

The popularity of mutual funds stems from two attractive features. First, the transaction and management costs for the investor are small. Second, they provide asset diversification, a feature that is not available to the individual small investor. Two innovations in recent years have enhanced the ability to diversify with mutual funds. *Index funds* invest in a basket of securities that make up some market index, such as the S&P 500 index of stocks. *Global funds*, which invest in securities issued in many countries, allow investors to diversify across national boundaries.

---

[1] The Flow of Funds Accounts lists money market mutual funds separately from other mutual funds. Therefore, we examine them separately.

SectorWatch 19.1
Banks and Mutual Funds*

California-based Wells Fargo Bank sells a family of mutual funds called the *Stagecoach Funds*. They are sold exclusively through the bank and have a name selected by the bank. In addition to their own funds, banks also sell third-party funds, which are not sold exclusively through banks. About 93 percent of large banks offered mutual funds to retail customers in 1993.

The major involvement of banks in selling mutual funds is relatively new, dating back to the mid-1980s. The accompanying graph shows that since that time the share of household assets held in bank deposits has been falling, while the share of assets in mutual funds has been rising. By marketing mutual funds themselves, banks can recapture some of the business they have been losing because of the trend away from bank intermediation. The mutual fund activities of banks do not violate the Banking Act of 1933 (the Glass-Steagall Act) that separates commercial banking from investment banking because companies not affiliated with banks underwrite and distribute the shares.

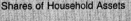

Shares of Household Assets

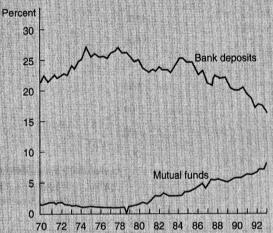

Source: Elizabeth Laderman, "Banks and Mutual Funds," Federal Reserve Bank of San Francisco *Weekly Letter*, 93-43, December 17, 1993.

Because mutual funds sold by banks are not deposits, they are not covered by deposit insurance. Federal banking regulators require banks to inform customers orally and in writing that mutual funds sold on their premises are not insured. They also recommend that the mutual funds be sold in an area that is physically demarcated from the area where retail deposits are taken.

---

* Adapted from Elizabeth Laderman, "Banks and Mutual Funds," Federal Reserve Bank of San Francisco *Weekly Letter*, 93-43, December 17, 1993.

Mutual funds are also classified according to whether they charge a sales commission, called a **load**. Load funds have traditionally been sold through brokers and financial planners, who actively solicit investors and provide investment advice. More recently they may also be purchased from banks, as SectorWatch 19.1 explains. No-load funds don't charge a sales commission and are typically purchased directly from the fund company. Both load and no-load funds, however, charge a fee for expenses, such as administrative, legal, and management costs.

Figure 19–1 shows that the size of the mutual fund industry, measured by total assets, increased from $51.8 billion in 1979 to $1,426.8 billion in 1993. The figure also shows that there was a dramatic increase between 1990 and 1993. What was the reason? Chapter 7 explains that rates on bank CDs fell substantially in this period. In search of higher yields investors flocked to stock and bond mutual funds. At the end of 1993 the total assets of mutual funds surpassed those of the entire thrift industry. Ranked by the size of

FIGURE 19–1
Total Financial
Assets of U.S.
Mutual Funds:
1979–1993

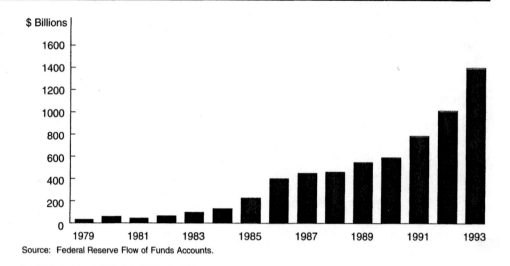

Source: Federal Reserve Flow of Funds Accounts.

their assets, mutual funds, including money market mutual funds, were a close second to pension funds and ahead of life insurance companies among nondepositories.

Regulation of Mutual Funds

Mutual funds, known by their broader name of investment companies, flourished in the 1920s. Following the stock market crash of 1929, however, a multitude of funds went bankrupt. To protect investors Congress enacted two major laws in 1940, the Investment Company Act and the Investment Advisers Act, which form the basis for the regulation and supervision of mutual funds to this day.

These laws prohibit investment companies from issuing debt and from engaging in speculation, two reasons for the many bankruptcies of investment companies in the 1930s. The laws also place investment companies under the oversight of the Securities and Exchange Commission (SEC), which is the regulator of primary and secondary markets and securities firms. Investment companies must register with the SEC and must also make periodic reports to it. The main aim of these reports is to protect retail investors by providing adequate information to them about the expense and the risk of investing in individual mutual funds. Investment companies must also satisfy other requirements if they are to be exempted from corporate taxes. These requirements include a diversified portfolio and mandatory distribution of at least 90 percent of the mutual fund's income to its shareholders. The Securities and Exchange Commission has recently expressed its intention to impose additional constraints concerning the choice and cost of management for further protection of investors in mutual funds.

Money Market Mutual Funds

Chapter 2 introduces money market mutual funds (MMMFs), and Chapter 5 examines the role they played in the evolution of the new financial environment. MMMFs are financial intermediaries that collect funds and place them in high-quality short-term securities. Because of their check-writing privileges, money market mutual funds compete with checking accounts as well as savings accounts issued by banks and thrifts.

TABLE 19–3
U.S. Money
Market Mutual
Funds 1993
(billions of dollars)

Checking accounts and currency	–1.2	Total shares outstanding	559.2
Time deposits (CDs)	24.7	Net worth	0.0
Repurchase agreements	66.9		
Foreign time deposits (CDs)	10.1		
U.S. government securities	147.7		
Tax-exempt securities	103.2		
Open market paper	164.9		
Miscellaneous	42.9		
Total financial assets	559.2	Total liabilities	559.2

Source: Federal Reserve Flow of Funds Accounts.

Unlike commercial banks and thrifts money market mutual funds are not always separate financial institutions. Often they are divisions within other traditional institutions, especially within investment banks and brokerage houses. They conduct their business mostly by mail and more recently by the electronic transfer of funds. The introduction of money market deposit accounts (MMDAs) in 1982 arrested the rampant growth of MMMFs, measured by the number of funds and by the assets held. Growth of MMMFs, however, resumed in the mid-1980s, as Chapter 5 shows. Table 19–3 presents the balance sheet of MMMFs at the end of 1993. The table shows that MMMFs held total assets of $559.1 billion, which were equal to 43 percent of the assets of the entire thrift industry.

The Fed includes MMMFs in its M2 measure of money. These funds, however, are not subject to reserve requirements and are not regulated or supervised by banking authorities. As a result they do not need permission for branching or merging with one another. Also, in contrast to funds placed in other depositories, funds in MMMFs are not insured by any agency. The major safety net for MMMFs comes from the short maturities of the investment instruments in which they place funds. None of the assets in Table 19–3 has a maturity longer than 13 months, while the (dollar-weighted) average maturity of assets held by MMMFs is no greater than 90 days. Securities with short maturities are essentially immune from interest-induced capital losses. The risk of default is present, however, as long as MMMFs invest in commercial securities such as commercial paper.

Although no bank or thrift regulators oversee MMMFs, they do have a regulator outside the depository environment. Because money market mutual funds are considered investment companies, they come under the jurisdiction of the SEC, which licenses new funds and ensures that they obey the securities laws, as mandated by the two 1940 acts.

INSURANCE COMPANIES

While mutual funds enable households to expand the mix of financial instruments in their portfolios, **insurance companies** sell contracts, called *insurance policies*, that provide protection against the economic consequences of some event, such as loss of life or loss of property. Before examining life insurance companies and property/casualty insurance companies, consider some basic principles that guide insurance management.

Some Fundamentals of Insurance

To price the risk of events such as the loss of life or the loss of property from an automobile accident or a fire, insurance companies rely on observed statistical regularities and the law of large numbers. For example, if a company insures a large enough number of drivers, the probability that a policyholder will have a major auto accident equals that of the population at large. Thus, by relying on the statistics of auto accidents, insurers may predict when the average driver will have an accident. Similarly, although it may be impossible to predict the timing of the death of a particular individual, statisticians can predict the timing of the death of the average person by relying on the life expectancy of the entire population. For example, if the life expectancy of nonsmoking Americans is 75 years, life insurers are reasonably confident that their average insured nonsmoker will live that long.

Insurance companies, however, cannot rely solely on the law of large numbers to estimate and price risk because, like banks, they face problems of asymmetric information, which gives rise to problems of adverse selection and moral hazard. Chapters 2 and 18 explain that applicants for bank loans have an incentive to hide information about the riskiness of their activities before they are granted a loan and to change their behavior after receiving the loan. Similarly, applicants for health insurance or auto insurance have an incentive not to reveal their health problems or their reckless driving habits when applying for insurance and to be less prudent after obtaining insurance. Thus insurance companies run the risk of insuring customers who are bad risks initially and who become even worse risks after receiving insurance. The risk of insuring "lemons" is adverse selection: Those who are anxious to obtain insurance are the ones with a higher risk than the population. The perverse incentives that insurance gives to insured parties to take excessive risk is moral hazard. Thus insurance companies run the danger of insuring people with higher risk than the population from which the statistical regularities were extracted.

The similarity with banks extends to the tools employed by insurance companies to cope with adverse selection and moral hazard. Like banks, insurance companies deal with adverse selection by screening applicants to ascertain the risk involved and to assess the appropriate risk-based premium. Sometimes the risks are so large that they refuse to insure the applicant. To cope with moral hazard, insurance companies use a mix of economic and legal incentives to induce the insured party to be more prudent. Economic incentives usually take the form of deductibles and coinsurance. A **deductible** is an initial fixed amount of a claim submitted to an insurance company that must be paid by the policyholder. **Coinsurance**, on the other hand, refers to a percentage of the amount of the claim (beyond the deductible) that is borne by the policyholder. For example, a policyholder may be reimbursed only 70 percent of his or her claim after subtracting the deductible. Legal incentives usually take the form of restrictive covenants combined with the penalties for noncompliance that include cancelation of the policy.

This introduction to the basic principles of insurance permits the examination of the operation of two types of insurance companies: life insurance companies and property/casualty insurance companies.

Life Insurance Companies

The simplest form of life insurance is pure risk insurance, called **term insurance**. For a fee, or premium, the life insurance company provides protection over a contracted period, or term, which may be a year, five years, or longer. If the insured person dies during the term of the policy, the company pays the beneficiaries the agreed-upon sum, called the *face value* of the insurance policy. If the insured person outlives the term, the policy expires and the company pays nothing. To determine the premium, the insurance company relies on mortality tables that predict the life expectancy of the average person in each age bracket. From the mortality rate and the face value of the insurance policy, the insurance company can predict fairly accurately its payments to policyholders as a group.

For most of the history of the life insurance industry, term insurance was not common. The first insurance companies interpreted broadly the meaning of the "economic consequences of the loss of life." Thus life insurance policies typically included savings to be left to the beneficiaries or to be used by the policyholders themselves at some future time.

Life insurance policies that combine pure risk insurance with contractual savings are called **whole life insurance**. Their premiums are high enough to include an amount beyond the pure risk premium. The additional amount is the policyholder's savings, which earns interest. The savings component accumulates over time and builds a *cash value*. The policyholder can withdraw part or all of this cash value or borrow against it. A cash value is what distinguishes term life from whole life. Term life does not have any cash value; at the end of the term there is nothing left for the surviving policyholder.

Assets and Liabilities of Life Insurance Companies   Like banks and thrifts, life insurance companies are financial intermediaries that transform liabilities into assets. A look at their balance sheet will help explain how they do this. Table 19–4 shows the balance sheet of U.S. life insurance companies at the end of 1993. The liability side describes their business and the asset side describes their investment policy.

The liability side is the sources of their funds. Life insurance companies receive funds by selling obligations to policyholders: obligations to the beneficiaries of term-life policyholders and obligations to policyholders or their beneficiaries for the cash value of the whole-life policy. The sum of these two obligations is called *life insurance reserves*. They are funds that are set aside, that is, invested, until needed to pay policyholders or their beneficiaries. Table 19–4 shows that at the end of 1993 U.S. life insurance companies

TABLE 19–4
U.S. Life Insurance Companies: *1993* (billions of dollars)

Checkable deposits and currency	6.3	Life insurance reserves	477.5
Money market funds	30.6	Pension fund reserves	1,043.5
Corporate equities	167.7	Miscellaneous liabilities	175.2
U.S. government securities	333.1	Net worth	95.8
Corporate and foreign bonds	723.9		
Mortgages	233.7		
Policy loans	77.4		
Other assets	219.3		
Total financial assets	1,792.0	Total liabilities	1,792.0

Source: Federal Reserve Flow of Funds Accounts.

held $477.5 billion of life insurance reserves. Obviously this amount is only an estimate. It is the present value of the companies' expected obligations.

Table 19–4 also shows that *pension fund reserves*, another reserve item on the liability side of the balance sheet of life insurance companies, were more than twice the size of life insurance reserves in 1993. Life insurance companies entered the business of selling pension contracts to households and institutions when their whole-life business began to decline in the 1970s. The reason for the decline was the low fixed interest rate they paid on the contractual-savings part of whole-life policies. By 1978 about two-thirds of the non-M1 component of M2 consisted of deposits that paid market-based interest rates. When the customers of life insurance companies realized that they could earn higher market rates of interest on their savings, they switched from whole life to term life insurance and placed their savings in other financial instruments, such as bank CDs. To compensate for this loss, life insurance companies explored alternative sources of revenues. An important new line of business was to provide pension services to households and institutions. By 1982 pension reserves overtook life insurance reserves, indicating that the main business of life insurance companies was no longer to provide life insurance policies.

The asset side of the balance sheet of life insurance companies reveals where they invest their reserve funds. Table 19–4 shows that life insurance companies invest heavily in long-term corporate bonds and mortgages, which accounted for more than 53 percent of their total assets in 1993. U.S. government securities, mostly bonds, were a distant second, followed by corporate equities.[2] Another important component of the portfolio of life insurance companies is loans to their own policyholders, which were $77.4 billion in 1993. The reason for the heavy concentration in long-term assets is simple: The revenues of life insurance companies are predictable, because life insurance policies are long-term contracts with known regular flows of premium receipts. On the other hand payments to policyholders are also predictable because of fairly accurate mortality tables and long-term obligations. Thus, as financial intermediaries, life insurance companies can plan their investment portfolios with little concern about liquidity. That does not make them immune, however, from balance sheet problems.

Life insurance companies responded to increased competition from depository institutions in the new financial environment not only by marketing pension contracts but also by introducing variable premiums and variable cash values to enable policyholders to switch from whole life to term life, and vice versa, depending on their current needs. They often combined life insurance with separate accounts that could be invested in riskier assets. Although these separate accounts increased the risk undertaken by policyholders, they did not, by themselves, necessarily increase the risk of providing life insurance. Nevertheless the risk undertaken by the life insurance industry has increased considerably because many insurers have been placing their regular funds—the ones based on the cash value of insurance policies—in riskier investments, such as junk bonds and commercial real estate. Moreover they have been operating with less capital. As a result in the early 1990s several life insurance companies, including the eighteenth largest, Mutual Benefit Life of Newark,

---

[2] The law does not prohibit life insurance companies, unlike banks, from investing in corporate stock.

New Jersey, failed, and an increasing number had their ratings downgraded by one or more of the agencies that rate life insurance companies.

Structure and Regulation of Life Insurance Companies   In 1993 there were about 2,000 life insurance companies in the United States. Most of them are organized as stock companies, which means they are owned by the stockholders. The rest are organized as mutuals, meaning they are owned (at least in name) by their policyholders. Most of the largest life insurance companies are mutuals.

Unlike depository institutions, life insurance companies are regulated exclusively by states. State insurance commissions issue charters and supervise the activities of life insurance companies, especially the setting of premiums and the holding of assets. In most states the state insurance commission must give prior approval for any increase in premiums.

In recent years life insurance companies have expanded their holdings into riskier assets with the approval of state commissions. Currently, however, insurance regulators are following the lead of bank regulators by designing capital requirements linked to the riskiness of an insurance company's portfolio. Finally, via subsidiaries, life insurance companies have been intruding on traditional banking territory, such as taking deposits or making loans. This intrusion is one of the reasons why banking reforms proposed in 1991 by the Bush administration would have allowed banks to sell insurance through a subsidiary. Congress, however, did not pass this proposal.

Property/ Casualty Insurance Companies

Property/casualty insurance companies offer protection against pure risk. For the appropriate risk-based premium, they insure against injury or property loss resulting from automobile accidents, fires, earthquakes, work-related accidents, malpractice, and even exotic activities, such as African safaris.

There were more than 3,000 property/casualty companies in the United States in 1993. Although the number of property/casualty insurance companies exceeds the number of life insurance companies, their total assets are much smaller. For example, at the end of 1993 property/casualty companies held total assets of $636.7 billion, about one-third the amount held by life insurance companies. Bonds and corporate stock form the bulk of these assets. Like life insurance companies, most property/casualty insurance companies are organized as mutuals. Also, like life insurance companies, property/casualty companies are chartered, regulated, and supervised by state commissions.

PENSION FUNDS

Measured by asset size, pension funds are the largest nondepository financial institution. **Pension funds** sell contracts to provide income to policyholders during their retirement years. Employees or their employers, or both, contribute to pension funds during the income-earning years of the employees. The contributions are made over the years of employment, and typically the disbursements are spread over the retirement years or given in a lump sum upon retirement. For the beneficiaries contributions are tax deferred while disbursements are taxed. For the employer contributions are a tax-deductible expense in the year they are made.

TABLE 19–5
Private U.S.
Pension Funds:
1993 (billions of
dollars)

Checking accounts and currency	4.5	Pension fund reserves	2.336.1
Time deposits	210.9		
Money market funds	19.9		
Open market paper	19.5		
Corporate equities	1,079.4		
U.S. government securities	400.4		
Corporate bonds	298.0		
Mortgages	39.0		
Mutual fund shares	77.7	Net worth	0.0
Miscellaneous assets	186.8		
Total financial assets	2,336.1	Total liabilities	2,336.1

Source: Federal Reserve Flow of Funds Accounts.

Types of Pension Funds

There are federal pension plans, state and local government plans, and private sector plans. The best known plan is Social Security, which is a general retirement benefit plan under the auspices of the federal government. Under this system, about 95 percent of the labor force have contributions deducted from their paychecks and invested in government securities. At retirement contributors begin receiving Social Security checks and other forms of benefits.

State, local, and federal governments also have their own employee pension plans, mostly administered by their own authorities. Private sector plans are usually sponsored by corporations and even by the employees themselves (the latter, typically, via their labor unions). Many smaller pension funds are administered either by trust departments of banks or by life insurance companies. Larger pension funds are usually administered by the sponsors themselves. The largest pension fund by far is the nationwide private pension program for college teachers, called the Teachers Insurance and Annuity Association, College Retirement Fund (TIAACREF).

Size and Assets of Pension Funds

Table 19–5 shows the cumulative balance sheet of private pension funds in the United States at the end of 1993. The source of their funds is the contractual obligations to policyholders, called *pension fund reserves*. The liability side of the balance sheet in Table 19–5 shows that at the end of 1993 private pension fund reserves were $2,366.1 billion. The asset side shows that pension funds held 76 percent of their funds in two instruments: long-term bonds, consisting of corporate bonds and U.S. government bonds, and corporate equities, including mutual funds. They held only a trivial amount of currency and deposits—less than one-fifth of one percent of their assets—and a small amount of short-term and other liquid assets—about 10 percent. Pension funds follow this investment policy because their liabilities to policyholders are long-term and predictable, while their regular disbursements are more than matched by their receipts, due to the strong growth of pension funds.

Regulation of Pension Funds

Two terms are crucial in understanding pension funds: *vesting* and *funding*. Vesting of benefits refers to the period of time that the employee must be on the job before his or her benefits are secured. Quick vesting means that an employee can retain part or all of the future retirement benefits even though he or she leaves the job or is fired after a short period of employment. Obviously employees prefer quick vesting, while employers prefer slow vesting of benefits. Typically there is a minimum number of years before any benefits are vested, with a gradual increase in the percentage of vested benefits as the number of years on the job increases. Vesting of benefits is one attribute of pension funds that has attracted legislative attention because of the potential for abuse. For example, workers sometimes claim that they were fired just before their pension benefits would become vested.

Funding of future obligations of pension funds is a more frequent source of potential trouble. In general a pension plan is fully funded if its contributions over the years have accumulated (or are expected to accumulate) to the point that they are adequate to cover the promised benefits.

To protect employees against abuse by underfunding, by excessive vesting requirements, or even by mismanagement, Congress enacted the Employee Retirement Income Security Act of 1974 (ERISA). This act imposed minimum standards on vesting and funding, and it mandated strict reporting requirements for sponsors and operators of private pension funds. ERISA mandates that pension funds be fully funded and that their investment practices be prudent.

ERISA provides the main vehicle for regulating pension funds, but the same law also created the Pension Benefit Guaranty Corporation (PBGC) to insure these funds. **Penny Benny**, as PBGC was nicknamed in the financial world, is to pension funds what the FDIC is to banks and thrift institutions. Like the FDIC, Penny Benny assesses insurance premiums on participating pension funds. The revenues are used to pay the commitments of failed pension funds, up to a maximum of $29,250 of annual pension benefits in 1993. Unlike the FDIC, Penny Benny does not have any regulatory or supervisory authority over participating pension funds.

Despite ERISA requirements for prudent investment practices, many private pension funds, succumbing to the pressures of sponsors and employees for high-yield investments, have followed unsafe practices and have failed. Penny Benny had to undertake payment of the retirement benefits of so many failed pension funds that its net worth turned negative in the mid-1980s. In response it tripled its insurance premiums. To deal with problems of moral hazard, Penny Benny, like the FDIC, now levies risk-based insurance premiums. In Penny Benny's case, it charges underfunded pension plans higher premiums.

Pension funds will continue to come under pressure because of changing demographics combined with the pay-as-you-go principle, which counts on incoming contributions to pay retirement benefits. The ability of funds to meet contractual obligations is squeezed as the ratio of working people over retirees falls, resulting in fewer contributions while benefits are increasing. These problems will become more acute in about 20 years when babyboomers begin to reach retirement age. Thus, despite ERISA, many funds, including Social Security, will come under increasing pressure.

INVESTMENT BANKS, BROKERS, AND DEALERS

The last group of nondepository financial institutions is investment bankers, security brokers, and security dealers, which Chapter 2 introduces. We mention them here to complete the list of nondepositories and to say a word about their regulation. *Investment banks* are financial firms whose function is to design and help sell new issues of securities. *Security dealers* are firms that stand ready to buy or sell existing securities for their own account. *Brokers* are firms that merely bring together buyers and sellers of securities; brokers buy or sell for their client's account—for a commission, of course. Most major firms perform all three functions and are referred to as **securities firms.** Most of the well-known names on Wall Street are investment banks, but most nationally known investment banks are also dealers and brokers.

The primary authority regulating the activities of investment banks, dealers, and brokers is the **Securities and Exchange Commission (SEC)**, a federal agency established by Congress in the 1930s in the aftermath of the crash of the stock market and in the midst of the Great Depression. A major objective of the SEC is to protect investors by providing adequate information about new and existing securities that are traded and by punishing trading based on inside information that affects the prices of securities.

The use of inside information is another consequence of asymmetric information and of the **principal-agent problem**, applied to corporations in this case. The management of a corporation, the agent, has more information about the company's health than the shareholders, the principal. Also the interests of management may differ from those of the shareholders. For example, management may want luxurious offices and modes of transportation or high salaries for friends and relatives. The SEC regulates all publicly traded corporations and brokers and dealers to ensure that management does not pursue policies or engage in actions that would benefit itself at the expense of the shareholders. Trading on insider information is a major abuse.

Until 1975 the SEC regulated commissions charged by brokers and dealers. With the passage of the Securities Amendments Act of 1975, these commissions have been deregulated. As a result discount brokerage houses such as Charles Schwab have proliferated and have drastically reduced the commissions charged by all types of brokers/dealers.

On the other hand the Banking Act of 1933 (the Glass-Steagall Act), which provides for the separation of investment banking from commercial banking, has not been repealed. Nevertheless, as Chapter 17 discusses, the wall between commercial banks and investment banks has been crumbling. Since the late 1980s the Federal Reserve has been using its authority to allow banks, on a case-by-case basis, to set up separately managed and capitalized subsidiaries within the bank holding company that can underwrite commercial paper, corporate bonds, and even corporate stock. J.P. Morgan, Bankers Trust, Chase Manhattan, and Citibank, which are all New York City banks, were among the first banks to receive this power from the Fed. This is a step in the direction of **universal banking**, practiced in a few other countries such as Germany where there is no legal separation between commercial banks and securities firms.

SUMMARY

- Nondepository financial institutions in the United States consist of finance companies, mutual funds, insurance companies, pension funds, and securities firms.

- Finance companies provide loans to consumers and small businesses with no established credit records. They also provide installment credit to purchasers of consumer durables. Recently, they have become experts in equipment leasing. Finance companies raise funds by borrowing in the open market and by borrowing from banks.

· Finance companies are experts in screening and monitoring risky borrowers. Finance companies are regulated almost exclusively at the state level.

· Mutual funds pool the savings of small investors and invest these funds in open market securities. Growth funds invest in securities expected to appreciate in the long run. Income funds invest in securities for their periodic payment of interests and dividends. Depending on whether or not mutual funds charge a sales commission, they are classified as load funds or no-load funds, respectively. The Investment Company Act and the Investment Advisers Act of 1940 placed mutual funds under the oversight of the Securities and Exchange Commission.

· Insurance companies issue contracts that provide protection against specific events. Whole-life policies also provide a thrift plan for policyholders. In recent years insurance companies also began offering pension plans. State commissions charter and regulate insurance companies, which, like banks and thrifts, have been suffering from excessive risk taking and low levels of capital.

· Pension funds issue contracts that provide income to retirees. Because of the failure of so many private funds, Penny Benny, the agency that insures pension funds, became insolvent in the mid-1980s and had to triple insurance premiums levied on participating pension funds.

· Because their liabilities are long term, insurance companies and pension funds invest primarily in long-term assets, that is, bonds and stocks.

· Investment banks are financial firms that design and sell new securities issued by corporations and governments. Dealers are firms that are ready to buy or sell existing securities for their own accounts. Brokers bring together buyers and sellers of securities. They all come under the jurisdiction of the Securities and Exchange Commission, which oversees and regulates primary and secondary financial markets.

KEY TERMS AND CONCEPTS

finance companies

mutual funds

load

insurance companies

deductible

coinsurance

term insurance

whole-life insurance

property/casualty insurance companies

pension funds

Penny Benny

securities firms

Securities and Exchange Commission (SEC)

principal-agent problem

universal banking

QUESTIONS AND PROBLEMS

1. "The liability side of the balance sheet of finance companies and banks have more in common than the asset side." True, false, or uncertain? Explain.

2. "State usury laws increase the business of loan sharks." Do you agree or disagree? Explain.

3. Some finance companies borrow from banks and lend to households and firms that have been turned down for bank loans. How can these finance companies survive?

4. Suppose that when you graduate you approach a finance company for a loan. Would you expect to pay a higher rate to borrow to finance a trip around the world or to finance a new car? Explain why.

5. In its Flow of Funds Accounts, the Federal Reserve classifies mutual funds and money market mutual funds separately. Use the asset side of their balance sheets to explain the difference between them.

6. Explain the difference between a mutual fund and a closed-end fund.

7. "A rate of return of 12 percent on a load mutual fund is superior to a rate of return of 7 percent on a no-load fund." True, false, or uncertain? Explain.

The Wall Street Journal

8. Refer to the mutual fund quotations in a recent issue of *The Wall Street Journal* (Section C) to find the following information for the "Index 500 Fund" in the Vanguard Group: the investment objective, the net asset value, and the percentage return year to date. Also determine whether this fund is a load or a no-load fund. (The explanatory notes that accompany the mutual fund quotations will help you extract this information.)

9. "Deposit rate deregulation adversely affected the business of providers of whole-life insurance." Do you agree or disagree? Explain why.

10. What is the purpose of deductibles in automobile collision insurance policies?

11. Finance companies and insurance companies both face problems of asymmetric information, adverse selection, and moral hazard. How do they cope with them?

12. What specific measures do providers of term-life insurance take to deal with adverse selection?

13. In the 1980s pension fund reserves overtook life insurance reserves in the collective balance sheet of life insurance companies. Explain why.

14. Why do pension funds and insurance companies hold primarily long-term assets?

15. *a.* Explain the similarities between Penny Benny and the FDIC.

    b. Why did they both introduce risk-based insurance premiums?

16. How does the Securities and Exchange Commission address the principal-agent problem?

SUGGESTED READINGS

Kopcke, Richard W. "The Capitalization and Portfolio Risk of Insurance Companies." *New England Economic Review* (Federal Reserve Bank of Boston), July/August 1992, 43–57

   Analyzes the financial health of insurance companies and remedies to reduce failures.

Remolona, Eli M., and Kurt C. Wulfekuhler. "Finance Companies, Bank Competition, and Niche Markets." *Quarterly Review* (Federal Reserve Bank of New York) 17, no. 2 (Summer 1992): 25–38.

Compares the performance of banks and finance companies since the advent of the new financial environment.

Sellon, Gordon H. "Changes in Financial Intermediation: The Role of Pension and Mutual Funds, *Economic Review* (Federal Reserve Bank of Kansas City) 77, no. 3 (Third Quarter 1992): 53–70.

   Examines the impact of pension funds and mutual funds on the financial system and the implications for regulation.

PART 6

FINANCIAL MARKETS, INTEREST RATES, AND THE CONDUCT OF MONETARY POLICY

20 The Theory of Money Demand
21 The Deposit Market and Money Demand
22 The Money Market
23 The Structure of Rates of Return

Part 6 belongs in both pillars. Chapter 20 examines the purposeful behavior of households and firms as demanders of money, which fits into the first pillar. Chapters 21, 22, and 23 examine the interaction of participants in financial markets, which is the subject of the second pillar. Chapters 21 and 22 provide a richer explanation of the determination of the deposit rate and the interest rate than in Part 3. Chapter 23 extends the framework to explain more rates of return.

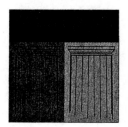

THE THEORY OF MONEY DEMAND

CHAPTER PREVIEW

Why do individuals hold money? Answering this question has attracted the interest of great economists, from Irving Fisher in the early 1900s; to John Maynard Keynes in the 1920s and 1930s; to William Baumol, James Tobin, Harry Markowitz, and Milton Friedman from the 1950s on. Keynes is the acknowledged father of modern theories of money demand. He introduced a conceptual framework that fostered the development of all modern theories.

Three motives examined by Keynes underlie the modern theory of money demand. They are the transactions motive, the precautionary motive, and the speculative motive. According to Keynes, the *transactions motive* for holding money arises from the *foreseen* need for cash payments; the *precautionary motive* from the *unforeseen* need for cash payments; and the *speculative motive* from the *uncertainty* of returns on securities.

This chapter derives the laws of money demand from these motives in a way that shows how the theory has evolved over the past 100 years. The chapter begins by examining the quantity theory approach to money demand. Classical quantity theorists, such as Irving Fisher, relying on the medium of exchange property of money, examined the transactions motive and argued that real income was the prime determinant of money demand. By using the store of value property of money, in the 1930s Keynes introduced the interest rate as one of the factors affecting money demand through the speculative motive. The original Keynesian approach, however, suffered from a shortcoming. It implied that individual investors do not diversify their portfolios. This shortcoming was remedied 20 years after Keynes by Harry Markowitz and James Tobin. In addition, William Baumol and James Tobin also provided the theory that explains why the transactions demand and even the precautionary demand depend on the interest rate. Friedman combined all three motives in his contribution to the theory of money demand.

After examining the early quantity theory and Keynes's innovations, this chapter focuses on modern treatments of the transactions motive and the speculative motive. The chapter fits into the first pillar of our framework because it explains the rational behavior of the public. It extends the analysis of the laws of asset demand introduced in Chapter 6 by delving further into the theoretical underpinnings of these laws as applied to money.

THE EARLY QUANTITY THEORY APPROACH

Modern theories of money demand trace their origins to the quantity theory of money introduced in the early 1900s. However, the primary aim of the early, or classical, quantity theorists was not to derive money demand. Instead, it was to derive velocity, V, or its inverse, the Cambridge k, for use in the quantity theory. The demand for money could be inferred from V and k.

Planned velocity is the number of times per year that individuals want money to turn over in buying final goods and services. As Chapter 16 discusses, planned velocity is the ratio of real income to real money demand:

$$V = Y/M^d \qquad\qquad (20\text{--}1)$$

Thus, planned velocity and money demand are related; knowing one amounts to knowing the other.

The **Cambridge k**, also introduced in Chapter 16, is the inverse of velocity. It follows that planned k is the fraction of annual income that the public wants to hold in the form of money: $k = M^d/Y$. By rearranging this relation, we find that the demand for real money balances is proportional to real income, Y:

$$M^d = kY \qquad\qquad (20\text{--}2)$$

Until the mid-1930s, the theory of money demand implied by the quantity theory recognized only the transactions motive for holding money. The payments habits of society were considered to be a key factor affecting V and k and, thus, the transactions demand for money. Other factors, such as the interest rate, were treated only parenthetically, if at all. In tracing the evolution of modern theories of money demand, we begin with these early theories.

Figure 20–1 illustrates the role of the payments habits in determining V and k. For simplicity, we assume that a year consists of 12 4-week months, that is, 48 weeks. We consider the case of an employee who is paid $2,800 once a month, or $33,600 a year, and who spends his income evenly—$100 a day—over the 28-day month. The horizontal axis in Figure 20–1 measures time, and the vertical axis measures money holdings. The moment the individual receives his monthly income, at time 0, he holds $2,800. The next

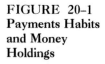

FIGURE 20-1
**Payments Habits
and Money
Holdings**

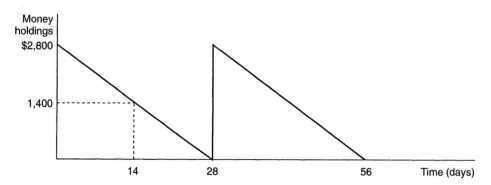

An employee who is paid $2,800 per month and spends $100 per day will hold, on average, $1,400 in cash.

day he holds $2,700 (having spent $100); the day after he holds $2,600, and so on, until the 28th, and last, day of the month when he spends his remaining $100. At that moment he is paid again, and the process continues indefinitely. As Figure 20–1 shows, on an average day, this individual holds $1,400.

To find monthly velocity, we divide the individual's monthly income (expenditures) of $2,800 by his average money holdings of $1,400. Thus, monthly velocity is 2. The average dollar turns over twice a month, or 24 times a year. On the other hand, dividing the individual's average money holdings of $1,400 by his income (expenditures) of $2,800, we find the Cambridge k, which is 1/2. The 1/2 means that this individual's average holdings of (demand for) money is 1/2 of his monthly income, which is equivalent to 1/24th of his annual income.

Let us now examine the effect of a change in the payments habits on V and k. In particular, suppose that employees are paid once a week instead of once a month. With the same annual income, our hypothetical employee will now receive $700 each week, which he spends, as before, at the rate of $100 per day. Figure 20–2 shows that this individual now holds, on average, $350. That is, he holds one-half his weekly income, or 1/96th of his annual income, in cash. Thus, the value of the *annualized* Cambridge k has fallen from 1/24th to 1/96th. Velocity is now 2 per week, or, 96 per year. This example demonstrates that, other things equal, the more frequently employees are paid, the higher the velocity and the lower the money demand.

Until the 1930s the accepted theory was that velocity and the Cambridge k depended only on the payments habits of society, which are usually included in the collective variable, $\mathcal{C}$, introduced in Chapter 6. Therefore, the money demand function was a simple one, depending only on Y and payments habits, $\mathcal{C}$:

$$M^d = M^d(Y, \mathcal{C}) \tag{20-3}$$

Because the payments habits change slowly over time, for practical purposes they were considered constant, that is, parameters. In sum, according to classical quantity theory,

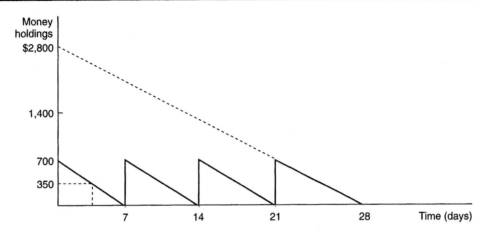

FIGURE 20–2
A Change in
Payments Habits

If employees are paid $700 once a week rather than $2,800 once a month, other things equal, average money holdings fall from $1,400 to $350.

individuals demanded money for transactions purposes, and this demand varied only with real income.

THE KEYNESIAN APPROACH

To understand Keynes's break from the classicists, we must explore two versions of the early quantity theory. The Fisher version, introduced by Irving Fisher of Yale in the early 1900s, is a *money-moving version*:[1]

$$MV = PY \qquad (20\text{–}4)$$

Money is moving because MV and PY in Equation 20–4 are both flows, measured in dollars per period. MV on the left side is planned expenditures per year, and PY on the right side is nominal income per year.

In contrast, the Cambridge version, introduced in the early 1900s by economists at Cambridge University in England, is a *money-sitting version*, represented by Equation 20–5:

$$M = kPY \qquad (20\text{–}5)$$

Money is sitting according to Equation 20–5 because M and kPY are both stocks, measured in dollars at a moment of time. On the left side of Equation 20–5, M is the supply of the nominal stock of money. On the right side, kPY is the nominal stock demand, where k is the fraction of a year's income individuals want to hold in the form of money

---

[1] Chapter 16 examines the modern treatment of this version of the quantity theory, called the *Fisher-Friedman version* in recognition of the extensions of Milton Friedman. Friedman's approach to money demand is considered later in this chapter.

and *PY* is income (dollars) per period. Therefore, *kPY* is the amount of money measured in current dollars that individuals want to hold, that is, demand. To transform the money-sitting equation from money measured in current dollars to money measured in dollars of a base year, divide both sides of Equation 20–5 by *P*. Equation 20–6 says that the real supply of money equals the real demand, or the supply of real balances equals the demand for real balances:

$$M/P = kY \tag{20--6}$$

The Cambridge version of the quantity theory, which emphasized the concept of real balances *held*, used the concept of money demand directly, as opposed to the Fisher version, which only implied it. It was natural, then, that John Maynard Keynes, a product of Cambridge, would further extend the concept of money demand. Today, Keynes is the acknowledged father of the modern theory of money demand.

Keynes himself used the Cambridge equation in two of his works on money, *A Tract on Monetary Reform* (1923) and *A Treatise on Money* (1930). By the time he finished writing the *Treatise*, he came to realize that the interest rate must also be an important determinant of money demand. Searching for reasons why money demand depends negatively on the interest rate, he embarked upon a detailed examination of the demand for real balances. His research culminated in the publication of the *General Theory of Employment, Interest, and Money* in 1936.

In the *General Theory* Keynes introduced three reasons, or motives, for holding money: the transactions motive, the precautionary motive, and the speculative (or portfolio) motive. Each of these motives is associated with one component of money demand examined by Keynes:

- The **transactions demand** arises from the need to hold cash for current personal and business expenditures.
- The **precautionary demand** arises from the need to provide for unforeseen events requiring sudden expenditures.
- The **speculative demand** arises from uncertainty about future interest rates.

The sum of the three components gives us the demand for money, or using the term that Keynes favored, the **liquidity preference**.

While Keynes explicitly recognized that both the transactions demand and the precautionary demand for money depend on the interest rate, he argued that the influence of the interest rate was minor compared with that of real income. Thus, he lumped the transactions demand and the precautionary demand together as one component of money demand that depended exclusively on *Y*. He denoted this functional relationship by $L_1(Y)$, where *L* stands for liquidity preference. In contrast, he specified that the speculative demand depends on the interest rate and denoted this functional relationship by $L_2(i)$.[2] The three motives examined by Keynes constitute the centerpiece of the theory of money demand today. However, his way of deriving money demand from these motives has been so refined and modified by subsequent economists as to have little semblance to the

---

[2] Keynes used the symbol r, not *i*, for the interest rate.

Keynesian original. Nevertheless, more than half a century after the publication of Keynes's *General Theory*, we distinguish the various measures of money along Keynesian lines: M1 corresponds to Keynes's transactions and precautionary balances, his L_1; M2 and M3 correspond to Keynes's speculative balances, his L_2.

MODERN TREATMENT OF THE TRANSACTIONS DEMAND

Keynes was willing to go along with the classical view that the transactions demand for money is independent of the interest rate. In the 1950s, William Baumol and James Tobin challenged that view. Independently of each other, Baumol and Tobin established that the transactions demand for money depends on the rate of interest.[3] We begin with Tobin's explanation of the relation between the interest rate and the transactions demand for money because it extends naturally the results from the classical quantity theory examined in the previous section. Then we consider Baumol's explanation, which introduced the now classic "square-root rule" for the transactions demand for money. Using this rule, we can easily establish four of the five laws of money demand, which in this case apply primarily to M1 because the transactions demand relies on the use of money as a medium of exchange.

Tobin's Explanation

This chapter has already shown that the more often employees are paid, the lower the demand for money. Tobin noted that the classical approach merely asserts that an individual must hold one-half of the period's receipts (and expenditures) as transactions balances. It does not specify the form in which these balances are held.

Consider the case of a person who is paid $3,000 once a month and who spends $100 a day until the 30th of the month. The classical quantity theory leads to the conclusion that this individual must hold, on average, $1,500 of transactions balances in cash, or one-half of her monthly income. But this conclusion is valid only if the individual holds the transactions balances in cash.

The issue can perhaps be illustrated best by an alternative scenario. Suppose that upon receiving her payroll check of $3,000, she deposits all of it in a bond account with her broker. Each day as she returns from work, she stops at her broker's office and converts $100 worth of bonds into cash, which she immediately spends at the shopping center where the broker's office is located. For all practical purposes, this individual does not hold any cash. She holds, on average, $1,500 worth of transactions balances, but in bonds, not in cash.

Now we have two polar cases. One case suggests that the individual holds one-half her monthly income in cash, the other that she holds no cash. The difference between the two cases lies in the number of times the individual is willing to move her transactions balances between cash and securities. In the first case, none; in the second, 30 times in 30 days.

---

[3] See William Baumol, "The Transactions Demand for Cash: An Inventory Theoretic Approach," *Quarterly Journal of Economics*, November 1952; and James Tobin, "The Interest Elasticity of Transactions Demand for Cash," *Review of Economics and Statistics*, August 1956.

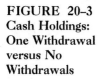

**FIGURE 20–3
Cash Holdings:
One Withdrawal
versus No
Withdrawals**

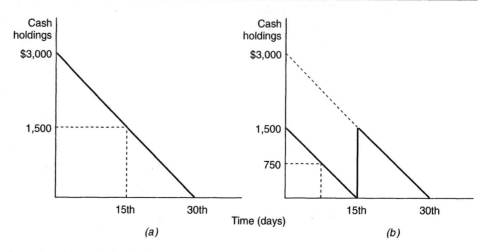

In panel *a*, with no withdrawals from a bond account during the month, an individual who earns $3,000 a month holds on average $1,500 in cash. In panel *b*, with one withdrawal, the individual holds on average $750 in cash.

From now on the terms *transfers* between money and bonds and *trips* to the broker to exchange bonds and cash are used synonymously. We shall also refer to the *withdrawal* of funds from bonds. Following Tobin, we can show that the demand for cash diminishes as the number of transfers between money and securities increases. Earlier discussion showed that with no trips to the broker after payday, an individual will hold one-half of her spendable income in cash. The left panel of Figure 20–3 illustrates this case.

Suppose instead this individual wants to make one transfer of funds from bonds to cash after payday. Therefore, on payday she deposits $1,500 in interest-bearing securities and keeps $1,500 in cash. The right panel of Figure 20–3 illustrates this case. She spends $100 per day until the 15th of the month, when she runs out of cash. For these 15 days she holds, on average, $750 in cash. Now, on the 15th of the month, she replenishes her cash by withdrawing from her bond account the remaining $1,500, which she spends again at the rate of $100 per day, until the funds are exhausted on the 30th of the month. Between the 15th and the 30th of the month, she holds, on average, $750 in cash. With one trip to the broker, this individual reduces her demand for cash from $1,500 to $750, as shown by the two panels of Figure 20–3. What did she accomplish by making one trip to the broker after payday? She earned interest on $1,500 for one-half of a month. If i denotes the monthly interest rate, she earned $1,500 \times (i/2) = $750i$. Of course, if the individual did not want to make any trips, she would earn no interest. Thus, the marginal revenue of one trip equals the total revenue of $750i$.

Continuing with our example, Figure 20–4 depicts the case of two equal withdrawals after payday, on the 10th and the 20th of the month. On payday, this individual deposits two-thirds of her income, or, $2,000, in her bond account and keeps one-third, or $1,000, in cash to spend in ten days. During the first ten days, she holds, on average, $500 in cash. On the 10th, she makes the first trip to the broker and withdraws from her bond

FIGURE 20–4
Cash Holdings:
Two Withdrawals
versus No
Withdrawals

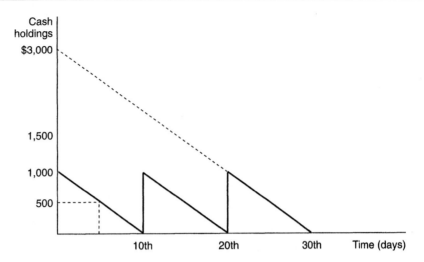

With two withdrawals from a bond account during the month, individuals hold $500 in cash, compared to $1,500 with no withdrawals.

account $1,000, which she spends between the 10th and the 20th. (These $1,000 earned interest for one-third of a month.) Therefore, on average, she holds $500 in cash between the 10th and the 20th. Finally, on the 20th she withdraws from her bond account the remaining $1,000, which she spends between the 20th and 30th. With two transfers, she earns total revenue of $1,000 \times (i/3) + ($1,000) \times (2i/3)$, because the $1,000 she withdrew on the 10th remained in interest-earning bonds for only one-third of a month, while the $1,000 she withdrew on the 20th was in bonds for two-thirds of a month. In total, with two withdrawals she earned $1,000i$ in interest. The marginal revenue of two transfers is $250i$, which is the difference between $1,000i$ and $750i$. Note that the marginal revenue of two transfers is lower than that of one transfer; that is, marginal revenue diminishes with the number of transfers.

The demand for money is determined, in part, by the number of transfers between money and securities. *The higher the number of transfers, the lower the demand for money.* Therefore, to establish the demand for money, it is necessary to determine the number of transfers. To do so, we assume that the individual is rational. A standard criterion of rationality is profit maximization, which requires equating the marginal revenue with the marginal cost of transfers to find the optimum number of transfers.

The marginal revenue from each transaction with the broker is the extra interest earned by holding more securities and fewer money balances. As the number of transfers increases, the marginal revenue from each transaction diminishes, as our numerical example illustrated. The downward-sloping marginal revenue curve in Figure 20–5 illustrates the general principle that the marginal revenue falls as the number of transfers (from securities to cash) rises. The marginal costs consist of the brokerage fees, or transactions costs, of transferring securities to money, and vice versa. These costs include the "time and trouble" of switching between securities and money. The marginal cost curve in

FIGURE 20–5
The Optimum
Number of
Transfers

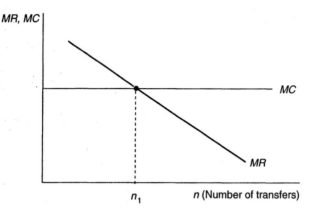

The optimum number of transfers is determined at the point where
marginal revenue equals marginal cost.

Figure 20–5 is horizontal, which indicates a constant marginal cost of each transfer. The optimum number of transfers is determined at the point of equality between marginal revenue and marginal cost. The number of transfers determines the demand for money.

How does the optimum number of transfers and, hence, money demand, change when the underlying factors of marginal revenue and marginal cost change? To answer, consider point A in Figure 20–6, where marginal revenue equals marginal cost. Other things equal, an increase in the interest rate, i, increases the marginal revenue. With marginal revenue now greater than marginal cost, profit can be increased by increasing the number of transfers, shown by the movement from point A to point B. More transfers, of course, means less money demand. Therefore, it follows that a higher interest rate reduces money demand, which is shown graphically in Figure 20–7.

TRY IT OUT 20.1

1. Suppose that a reduction in brokerage fees reduces the marginal cost of transfers between money and bonds. Use a marginal revenue–marginal cost diagram to show the effect on the optimum numbers of transfers.
2. What will be the effect on money demand? Depict this result graphically.

**Baumol's
Explanation**

In the title of his classic paper, Baumol called his approach the *inventory-theoretic approach*. To find the optimal quantity of transactions balances that an individual should hold, Baumol applied optimizing techniques previously used to find the optimal inventory of goods that a firm should hold. In Baumol's analysis, as in Tobin's, the demand for transactions balances depends on brokerage costs and the opportunity cost of deposits. Baumol assumes that every time an individual buys or sells a bond, he or she incurs a brokerage fee, denoted by b. Thus, with n transactions the brokerage costs equal bn. Brokerage costs are one of two components of the total cost of securing transactions

**FIGURE 20–6
An Increase in the
Interest Rate and
the Optimum
Number
of Transfers**

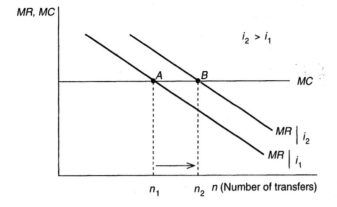

An increase in the interest rate on bonds raises the marginal revenue
of transfers, thereby increasing the optimum number of transfers.

**FIGURE 20–7
Money Demand**

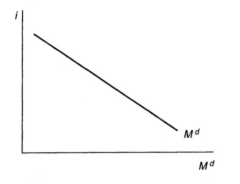

Other things equal, the quantity of
money demanded varies inversely with
the interest rate.

balances. The second component is interest forgone by holding wealth in money (deposits) rather than in securities. This opportunity cost of money equals $(i - r_D)M^d$.[4] Thus, total costs, TC, are:

Total costs = Brokerage costs + Opportunity costs

$$TC \quad = \quad bn \quad + \quad (i - r_D)\, M^d \qquad\qquad (20\text{–}7)$$

The amount of money an individual demands for transactions purposes is related to the amount of funds that he or she switches from securities to money during each transfer. Let T denote the amount of funds transferred from bonds to money at each withdrawal. Average cash balances, or individual money demand, equal $T/2$. For example, in our previous illustration, an individual who is paid $3,000 per month deposits $2,000 with a

---

[4] In the 1950s checking accounts did not pay interest. Therefore, the opportunity cost did not include r_D, which has been added here.

broker, makes two withdrawals of $1,000, and holds $500 of cash balances. In this illustration, T equals $1,000, and $T/2$ is therefore $500.

With M^d equal to $T/2$, the opportunity cost of deposits is $(i - r_D) \times (T/2)$. Brokerage costs are also related to T, because n depends on T. We can find n, the number of times that the individual will incur brokerage fees, if we know the individual's income, Y, which is the same as total transactions. In particular, n equals Y/T. For example, an individual with a monthly income of $3,000 who converts $1,000 of bonds to cash with every transfer at the broker must go to the broker three times per month: $n = 3 = (\$3,000/\$1,000)$. Thus, the brokerage costs are $b(Y/T)$, and the total costs, TC, are:

$$TC = b(Y/T) + (i - r_D) \times (T/2) \tag{20–8}$$

According to Equation 20–8, total costs depend on i, r_D, Y, b, and T. Given i, r_D, Y, and b, an individual is faced with the problem of deciding on the amount of funds to convert from bonds to cash at each withdrawal in order to minimize total costs. Determining the optimal size of T also gives us the size of money demand. It is simply one-half of T: $M^d = (1/2)T$. The investor's aim is to choose the level of T that minimizes total cost.

Performing elementary calculus and algebra on Equation 20–8 yields Equation 20–9:[5]

$$T = \sqrt{\frac{2bY}{i - r_D}} \tag{20–9}$$

Since $M^d = \dfrac{T}{2}$, it follows that

$$M^d = \frac{1}{2}\sqrt{\frac{2bY}{i - r_D}} \tag{20–10}$$

Equation 20–10 is the famous **square-root rule**. The transactions demand for money is proportional to (that is, one-half of) the square root of the quantity $[2bY/(i - r_D)]$. In other words, the transactions demand is directly proportional to the square root of the quantity of transactions and inversely proportional to the square root of the opportunity cost. Four of the five laws of money demand introduced in Chapter 7 follow directly from the square-root rule.

- *First law:* Other things equal, an increase in the deposit rate, r_D, reduces the opportunity cost of money, which increases the transactions demand for money.

---

[5] To minimize a function, we must find its derivative with respect to the decision variable and set this derivative equal to zero. The decision variable in our problem is T. Taking the derivative of total cost with respect to T and setting it equal to zero, we find that:

$$d(TC)/dT = -b(Y/T^2) + (i - r_D)/2 = 0$$

Solving for T^2, we have:

$$T^2 = [2bY/(i - r_D)]$$

To find T, we must take the square root of the right side.

Sector*Watch* 20.1
Illustrating Baumol's Money Demand Equation

To illustrate the laws of money demand using Baumol's approach, his square-root rule for the transactions demand for money serves as a starting point:

$$M^d = \frac{1}{2}\sqrt{\frac{2bY}{i - r_D}}$$

First, hypothetical values are assigned to the four factors that affect the transactions demand.

National income: Y = $8,000 billion per year
Interest rate (on bonds): i = 0.07
Deposit rate: r_D = 0.03
Brokerage fees (transactions costs): b = $8 per transaction

Substituting these values into the money demand equation, the initial level of money demand is:

$$M^d = \frac{1}{2}\sqrt{\frac{2\times8\times8,000}{0.07-0.03}} = \frac{1}{2}\sqrt{\frac{128,000}{0.04}} = \frac{1}{2}\sqrt{3,200,000}$$

$$= \frac{1}{2} \times 1,788.854$$

$$M^d = \$894.427 \text{ billion}$$

Second, beginning with national income, the effect of a change in each of the factors affecting money demand is determined.

An increase in Y. Suppose that national income (Y) rises (by 10 percent) from $8,000 billion to $8,800 billion per year. Substituting into the M^d equation,

$$M^d = \frac{1}{2}\sqrt{3,520,000} = \$938.083 \text{ billion}$$

As expected, the transactions demand increases when Y rises.

An increase in the interest rate, i. Now suppose that, starting from the initial position, the interest rate on securities, i, rises from 0.07 to 0.08, other things equal. Note that the opportunity cost of holding deposits rises from 0.04 to 0.05. Substituting this higher opportunity cost into the M^d equation,

$$M^d = \frac{1}{2}\sqrt{\frac{128,000}{0.05}} = \frac{1}{2}\sqrt{2,560,000} = \frac{1}{2} \times 1,600$$

$$M^d = \$800 \text{ billion}$$

As expected, the increase in the interest rate reduces money demand.

A fall in the deposit rate, r_D. Next, suppose that the deposit rate falls from 0.03 to 0.02, other things equal. The opportunity cost of money again rises from 0.04 to 0.05. Thus, the effect on M^d should be the same as in the previous case. Substituting r_D = 0.02 in the M^d equation,

$$M^d = \frac{1}{2}\sqrt{\frac{128,000}{0.05}} = \$800 \text{ billion}$$

As expected, the fall in the deposit rate reduces money demand.

A reduction in transactions costs, b. Suppose that the introduction of new technology reduces the cost of transferring funds from checking accounts to securities. In particular, suppose that b falls from $8 to $7 per transaction, other things equal. Substituting in the M^d equation,

$$M^d = \frac{1}{2}\sqrt{\frac{14\times8,000}{0.04}} = \frac{1}{2}\sqrt{2,800,000} = \frac{1}{2} \times 1,673.32$$

$$M^d = \$836.660 \text{ billion}$$

As expected, the lower the cost of transferring funds between money and securities, the greater the demand for securities and the smaller the demand for money.

- *Second law:* Other things equal, an increase in the interest rate, i, increases the opportunity cost of money, which reduces the transactions demand for money.
- *Third law:* Other things equal, an increase in income, Y, increases the transactions demand for money.
- *Fourth law:* Wealth is not an explicit factor in the transactions demand, but it is an important factor in the speculative demand, as we shall see.

· *Fifth law:* Other things equal, an increase in brokerage costs, *b*, increases money demand. Brokerage costs fall under the collective variable, $\mathcal{C}$; an increase in brokerage costs is represented by an increase in $\mathcal{C}$.

SectorWatch 20.1 illustrates these results arithmetically with a hypothetical example of Baumol's square-root rule.

A Word on the Precautionary Demand

Keynes defined the *precautionary demand* as cash held to provide for unforeseen expenditures and unforeseen opportunities of advantageous purchases. Building on this definition, subsequent economists elaborated on the meaning of unforeseen expenditures. A straightforward way to examine precautionary demand is by replacing the certainty in the timing of future expenditures, which is implied in the transactions motive, with uncertainty in the timing of cash inflows and outflows. Because of this uncertainty, households and firms set aside cash. The modern literature, by extending the Baumol-Tobin approach to include uncertainty, shows that the higher the opportunity cost of holding cash, the lower the precautionary demand for money. Instead of continuing with this approach to examine uncertainty, we examine uncertainty through the speculative motive.

MODERN TREATMENT OF SPECULATIVE DEMAND

Keynes emphasized risk and the uncertainty of expectations as the reasons behind the negative relation between the interest rate and the speculative demand for money. For example, in the *General Theory* he wrote that "*uncertainty* as to the future course of the rate of interest is the sole intelligible explanation" (p. 201) of this relation. His formal analysis, however, dealt with risk emanating from *certain*, but different, expectations among different groups of individuals. A major shortcoming of Keynes's derivation of the speculative demand is that his theory predicted that individuals would hold all their wealth in money or bonds. They would not diversify their portfolios. The subsequent work of Harry Markowitz and James Tobin remedied this deficiency.

In the 1950s Harry Markowitz and James Tobin provided a formal and definitive treatment of portfolio choice based on uncertainty. In 1952 Markowitz used probability theory to show that investors will maximize their expected return for a given amount of risk by holding a diversified portfolio. In 1958 Tobin extended the analysis of uncertainty, especially as it applies to the demand for money.[6]

The simplest way to explain the Tobin-Markowitz model is by considering an individual investor or group of investors who want to allocate their given wealth, *W*, between holding money, M^d, and holding bonds, B^d; that is,

$$M^d + B^d = W \tag{20–11}$$

Dividing both sides of this equation by *W* yields the fraction of wealth held in each asset. Of course, the sum of these fractions must equal 1, as the following equation shows:

$$(M^d/W) + (B^d/W) = 1 \tag{20–12}$$

---

[6] James Tobin, "Liquidity Preference as Behavior towards Risk," *Review of Economic Studies* 25, no. 67 (February 1958: 65–86).

If A_1 denotes the fraction of wealth held in money and A_2 the fraction held in bonds, Equation 20–12 becomes:

$$A_1 + A_2 = 1 \qquad\qquad (20\text{–}13)$$

Now we want to find the expected return per dollar on the portfolio, which we denote by R. It is the weighted average of the rates of return on the two assets, where the weights are the fraction of wealth held in each asset.

Chapter 3 shows that the expected rate of return on bonds, denoted by r_2, is the sum of the current yield and the capital gains rate:

$$r_2 = \text{Current yield} + \text{Capital gains rate} \qquad\qquad (20\text{–}14)$$

The rate of return on deposits is denoted by r_1:

$$r_1 = r_D \qquad\qquad (20\text{–}15)$$

Using these definitions, we can express the expected return per dollar on an investor's portfolio by:

$$R = A_1 r_1 + A_2 r_2 \qquad\qquad (20\text{–}16)$$

The rate of return on bonds is uncertain because the capital gains rate is uncertain. On the other hand, the rate of return on money is the deposit rate, which is certain and smaller than the rate on bonds. Thus, the uncertainty of R stems from the term $A_2 r_2$. The higher the portion of securities in an investor's portfolio, A_2, the more uncertain the return and the riskier the portfolio. Conversely, the higher the portion of money in the portfolio, A_1, the safer the portfolio. Also, based on Equation 20–16, the return, R, increases when the fraction of wealth held in bonds, A_2, increases. The higher A_2, the higher the weight of bonds, the high-yielding asset, and the lower the weight of money, the low-yielding asset. Hence, investors face a trade-off. To achieve a higher expected return, R, on their portfolio, investors must increase the portion of their wealth held in the riskier asset, bonds, and must assume more risk. Alternatively, to reduce risk, they must reduce their proportionate holdings of securities (and increase their holdings of money) and must therefore accept a lower return.

To decide exactly which combination of bonds and money to hold, investors must consider their preferences about return and risk. The typical investor is *risk averse*. This means that to undertake more risk, the investor wants a higher return. The average investor's taste for risk also decreases as the amount of risk increases. This property of preferences is referred to as *increasing risk aversion*. With increasing risk aversion, an investor will take on successive extra units of risk only if the additional return becomes increasingly greater.

In general, individual investors with increasing risk aversion will allocate their wealth between securities and money according to the following rule: *The return they have to give up to reduce risk by one additional unit must equal the return they are willing to give up to reduce risk by an additional unit.* Several results follow from this rule of investment. The most important is that individual investors diversify their portfolios. They hold both the high-yielding bond and the low-yielding money. This eliminates the shortcoming of the original Keynesian explanation of speculative demand for money that suggested that an investor holds either cash or money, but not both.

It follows from the decision rule that the higher the expected rate of return on bonds, the more bonds and the less money an investor would hold. Let us see why. The higher the rate of return on bonds, the greater the sacrifice an investor must make to reduce risk by one unit. That is, safety in cash becomes more expensive, or risk taking becomes cheaper. The rational investor will give up some safety and assume more risk by investing in securities.[7] In other words, the demand for securities rises and the demand for money falls. By using similar reasoning, we can see that the higher the deposit rate, the fewer bonds and the more money an investor would hold. In addition, the higher an individual's wealth, W, the higher both M^d and B^d. Several components of the collective variable are also determinants of the speculative demand for money. For example, when securities are considered riskier, the demand for money rises and the demand for bonds falls.

Finally, it is worth noting the recognition given to the work of Tobin and Markowitz. Harry Markowitz's work, as originally presented and as extended and applied by Tobin, provided the foundations for the modern theory of finance. For these contributions, Markowitz was one of three recipients of the Nobel Prize in economics in 1990.[8] Tobin received the Nobel Prize in 1981, in part, for his contributions to portfolio theory, as Chapter 6 notes.

MODERN TREATMENT OF THE QUANTITY THEORY

Another modern derivation of money demand is that of Nobel laureate Milton Friedman, whose principal aim was to show how to derive velocity for use in the quantity theory. Chapter 16 explains Friedman's contributions to the quantity theory of money in his restatement of money demand. That chapter, however, does not present all the properties of Friedman's money demand.

Friedman considers money one of four assets in which investors can hold their wealth: money, bonds, equity shares, and commodities. He relies on standard household choice-theoretic techniques to specify the demand for money as dependent upon the rates of return of the four assets and upon income (which is related to wealth). Assuming bonds and equity capital are perfect substitutes, with equal rates of return, Friedman's money demand is:

$$M^d = M^d(i, r_D, \Delta P/P, Y, W) \tag{20-17}$$

One advantage of Friedman's approach over other statements of money demand is that he explains how inflation affects the demand for money. Because holding commodities is an alternative to holding money in the Friedman model, the rate of price inflation is one of the factors affecting money demand. The current yield on commodities is, of course, zero. Thus, the rate of return on commodities is equal simply to the rate of appreciation in

---

[7] This effect of an increase in the expected rate of return is the substitution effect, which we assume dominates any income effect in the opposite direction.

[8] The other two recipients were William Sharpe and Merton Miller. The Nobel committee cited all three for their seminal contributions in finance.

the price of commodities, that is, the rate of inflation. Other things equal, an increase in the expected rate of inflation increases the demand for commodities and reduces the demand for money.[9] An additional advantage of the Friedman approach is that it does not examine separately the three motives and, hence, the three separate demands for money balances. The Keynesian distinction of the three motives is a good expository device, but, in practice, one cannot assert that each dollar demanded is held for specific functions; each dollar can satisfy all motives.

STABILITY OF MONEY DEMAND

Early empirical work on the demand for money naturally focused on the Keynesian novelty—the interest sensitivity of money demand. Since then a huge body of literature has been generated to quantify the relationship between interest rates and the demand for money. As early as 1947 James Tobin confirmed statistically the Keynesian view that the demand for money depends negatively on the interest rate (on securities). The Keynesian view was challenged 12 years later in a study by Milton Friedman.[10] And, in turn, the Friedman study was soon challenged by several economists, especially Allan Meltzer (1963) and David Laidler (1966).

By the late 1960s the interest sensitivity of money demand was an accepted fact. The debate then turned mostly to technical issues. For example, which measures of the interest rate should be used in empirical studies: the short-term rate or the long-term rate, the time deposit rate or the commercial paper rate? Similarly, researchers debated which measure of expenditures to use: current GNP or permanent income, income or consumption? They also debated whether to include income or wealth, or both, as arguments in the money demand function.

A study by Stephen M. Goldfeld, published in 1973, soon became the definitive treatment of the statistical estimation of demand for the M1 measure of money.[11] The Goldfeld study distinguished between the short-run and the long-run interest sensitivity of money demand, and between the short-run and the long-run income sensitivity of money demand. The study established that, in the long run (over five or six quarters), the interest sensitivity *and* the income sensitivity of money demand increase. But the long-run income sensitivity remains below 1—around 0.50.[12] The study relied on data for the period from 1952 to 1972. Hence, Goldfeld's study was heralded as establishing a stable money demand relation over the entire postwar period (two decades). A **stable demand function for money** means that the demand for money can be accurately predicted by a function that relates money demand to a few key variables, such as interest rates and income.

---

[9] The value of money equals $1/P$. The percentage change in the value of money equals the negative of the rate of inflation, that is, *minus* $\Delta P/P$. Thus, the rate of return on money vís-a-vís commodities is the loss of purchasing power that results from holding money when the rate of inflation increases.

[10] Milton Friedman, "The Demand for Money: Some Theoretical and Empirical Results," *Journal of Political Economy*, June 1963, 327–51.

[11] Stephen M. Goldfeld, "The Demand for Money Revisited," *Brookings Papers on Economic Activity* 3(1973): 577–638.

[12] Chapter 16 shows that velocity increases with income if the income elasticity is less than 1. Thus, the Goldfeld study also resolved that issue empirically.

In the early 1970s, soon after economists pronounced money demand stable, financial innovations and deregulation raised new puzzles and stirred old debates. The next chapter extends the theory of money demand by finding all the factors that affect the deposit rate in the new financial environment. It also surveys the empirical evidence since the mid-1970s.

SUMMARY

- The primary aim of classical quantity theorists was to derive velocity, V, or its inverse, the Cambridge k, for use in the quantity theory. The demand for money was a by-product.

- Until the 1930s the accepted theory was that V and k depended only on the payments habits of society. An example of a change in payments habits is an increase in the number of paydays per month, which will increase V and reduce k. Because the payments habits changed slowly over time, they were considered constant. According to the classical quantity theory, individuals demanded money only to carry out their transactions, and this demand varied positively with real income.

- In his *General Theory of Employment, Interest, and Money* (1936), Keynes divided money demand into three components: a transactions demand arising from the foreseen need for cash payments, a precautionary demand arising from the unforeseen need for cash payments, and a speculative demand arising from the uncertainty of returns on securities. The Keynesian innovation was to make the speculative demand vary negatively with the interest rate on securities.

- The inventory-theoretic approach of Baumol and Tobin, introduced in the 1950s, relates the transactions demand for money to the interest rate. The benefit of holding transactions balances in securities is the interest earned. The cost is the brokerage fees, which includes the time and trouble of transferring between securities and money. The optimal number of transfers is determined by a cost-minimizing exercise.

- The square-root formula derived by Baumol from cost minimization establishes that the transactions demand for money varies negatively with the opportunity cost of money, $i - r_D$, and positively with real income and with brokerage fees.

- A major shortcoming of Keynes's derivation of the speculative demand for money is that it predicted individuals will not diversify their portfolios. In the 1950s Markowitz and Tobin introduced uncertainty into the theory of portfolio choice. The Tobin-Markowitz model predicts that if individuals exhibit increasing risk aversion, individuals will hold both bonds (the high-yielding, high-risk asset) and money (the low-yielding, low-risk asset). Increasing risk aversion means that an investor will take on successive extra units of risk only if the additional return becomes increasingly greater.

- Milton Friedman's approach to money demand examines the transactions, precautionary, and speculative motives simultaneously. One important feature of the Friedman approach is that it establishes the inverse relation between the rate of inflation and money demand.

- A study by Stephen Goldfeld in 1973 showed that demand for the M1 measure of money could be accurately predicted by a function that relates money demand to a few key variables, such as the interest rate and income. In the mid-1970s, however, problems began to arise in estimating money demand.

KEY TERMS AND CONCEPTS

planned velocity

Cambridge k

transactions demand

precautionary demand

speculative demand

liquidity preference

square-root rule

stable demand function for money

QUESTIONS AND PROBLEMS

1. Suppose that Jessica Paar's annual income is $24,000 and that she is paid monthly. Also suppose that she spends her entire monthly income of $2,000 evenly over the month.
   a. What is the *annual* velocity of circulation (V) in this example? The *annual* Cambridge k? Explain what these numbers mean.
   b. Suppose that Jessica is paid twice a month instead of once. If Jessica's spending pattern is unchanged, how will the *annual* values of V and k change?

2. Consider the case of an employee who is paid $4,500 once a month and who makes two transfers per month between bonds and cash.
   a. Find the marginal revenue of two transfers if the annual interest rate is 12 percent.
   b. Find the marginal revenue of two transfers if the annual interest rate rises to 18 percent.

3. Use a Tobin-type marginal cost–marginal revenue graph to examine the effect of an increase in the deposit rate, r_D, on the transactions demand for money. Will it rise, fall, or remain unchanged? (Hint: First modify the concept of marginal revenue to include the deposit rate.)

4. Confirm your answer to question 3 by using Baumol's technique instead of Tobin's.

5. Suppose that the value of b in Baumol's money demand equation is zero. What will be the amount of the transactions demand for money? Provide an economic explanation for your answer.

6. Suppose money demand is given by $M^d = kY$, where k is the Cambridge k. Explain why:
   a. An increase in the interest rate reduces money demand.
   b. An increase in the deposit rate increases money demand.
   c. An improvement in cash management techniques reduces money demand.

7. "Baumol's square-root rule is most applicable to the M2 measure of money." True, false, or uncertain? Explain.

8. Use Baumol's square-root rule to answer the following questions:
   a. What will be the value of money demand if $Y =$ $6,400 billion, $b = 10 (per transaction), $i = .09$, and $r_D = .04$?
   b. Suppose that i falls to .075 and r_D falls to .03. Other things equal, calculate the new value of money demand and explain your result.

9. Why do investors hold both money and bonds according to the theory of the speculative demand for money?

10. "According to the theory of speculative demand for money, an increase in the riskiness of securities will increase the demand for securities." True or false? Explain your answer.

11. Explain why a reduction in the expected rate of return on bonds increases the demand for money.

12. Whose theory of money demand has the rate of inflation as a factor affecting money demand? According to this theory, how does a decrease in the expected rate of inflation affect the demand for money?

13. What do economists mean when they say that the demand function for money is stable?

SUGGESTED READINGS

Breit, William, and Roger W. Spencer, eds. *Lives of the Laureates: Seven Nobel Economists.* Cambridge, Mass.: The MIT Press, 1986.
   Contains autobiographical essays by Milton Friedman and James Tobin.

Keynes, John Maynard. *The General Theory of Employment, Interest, and Money.* New York: Harcourt Brace Jovanovich, 1936.
   The book that launched the modern theory of money demand.

Laidler, David. *The Demand for Money: Theories, Evidence, and Problems.* 4th ed. New York: Harper Collins College Publishers, 1993.
   An extensive survey of theories of money demand and the empirical evidence on the demand for money; also contains an extensive bibliography.

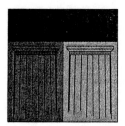

THE DEPOSIT MARKET AND MONEY DEMAND

CHAPTER PREVIEW

Empirical work in the early 1970s showed that money demand had been stable for the preceding two decades. It could be accurately predicted by a function relating money demand to a few key variables, such as interest rates and real income. Beginning in the mid-1970s, however, the stability of money demand began to erode.

In the late 1970s the actual quantity of M1 balances held by the public was less than the amount predicted using standard money demand functions. In the 1980s, on the other hand, the public held a larger quantity of M1 than predicted. Because of difficulties in predicting the demand for M1, the Fed stopped setting M1 targets in 1987, but it continued to set targets for M2. By the early 1990s, however, the demand for M2 began to misbehave. The public held a smaller amount of M2 balances than predicted, which caused the Fed to downgrade M2 as an intermediate target in 1993. In attempting to explain the instability of money demand since the mid-1970s, analysts have looked to financial innovations, deregulation of deposit rates, and special factors, such as the thrift crisis, as the culprits.

The preceding chapter established a positive relation between the demand for money and the deposit rate from the speculative motive and the transactions motive. In the old financial environment, regulators set the deposit rate. Thus, the deposit rate itself was an ultimate determinant of money demand. In contrast, in the new financial environment, the interaction of demand and supply in the deposit market determines the deposit rate. Therefore, in the new financial environment, the determinants of the deposit rate are also determinants of money demand.

This chapter explores the workings of the deposit market in which the interaction of the public and banks determines the deposit rate. It expands material in Chapter 7, which explains the factors affecting the deposit rate intuitively. The chapter also shows how the concept of deposits demanded introduced in Chapter 7 is the deposit-market-clearing quantity of deposits demanded. The last step to find all the factors affecting money demand is simply to combine the deposit-market-clearing quantity of deposits demanded with the demand for currency. Finally, this chapter sheds light on the instability of money demand since the 1970s.

THE DEPOSIT MARKET

The analysis of how markets work is the subject of the second pillar of economics. As with any market, the market for deposits has a demand side and a supply side. Deposits are an asset in the balance sheet of the public, who are the demanders. On the other hand, they are a liability in the balance sheet of banks, who are the issuers, or suppliers. Because our goal is to determine the deposit rate, it is natural to depict the demand and supply curves with the deposit rate on the vertical axis.

The Demand Curve for Deposits

The upward-sloping demand curve for deposits in Figure 21–1 depicts the first law of asset demand: Other things equal, the quantity of deposits demanded rises as the deposit rate increases.[1] The other factors affecting the demand for deposits are listed in the curve's label: the interest rate, i; real income, Y; and the collective variable, $\mathcal{C}$.[2]

The Supply Curve for Deposits

Figure 21–2 depicts the supply curve for deposits, which is downward sloping. Chapter 18 established that the supply of deposits increases when the net marginal revenue of issuing deposits, $[(1 - rr)i - r_D]$, rises. Therefore, other things equal, when the deposit rate falls, profit-maximizing banks want to issue more deposits because the net marginal revenue rises. The curve's label lists the other factors affecting the amount of deposits that banks want to issue: the interest rate, i; the reserve requirement ratio, rr; and the technology and regulatory index, $\mathcal{TR}$.

Equilibrium in the Deposit Market

The demanders and suppliers of deposits make their plans independently of each other. They interact in the market for deposits, in which the deposit rate moves to make their plans match. Figure 21–3 shows how the process works. At the deposit rate r_D^2, there is excess supply of deposits equal to CD: Banks want to issue a greater quantity of deposits than the public wants to hold. To induce the public to hold more deposits, banks increase the deposit rate, which increases the quantity demanded and reduces the quantity supplied, thereby reducing the excess supply of deposits. The deposit rate keeps rising until the plans

---

[1] Note that this is not the first time we encounter an upward-sloping demand curve. In Chapter 9, the demand curve for securities is also upward sloping, reflecting the first law of asset demand applied to securities: Other things equal, as the interest rate on securities rises, the demand for securities rises. Therefore, if the interest rate is depicted on the vertical axis, the demand curve for securities is upward sloping.

[2] For simplicity, we have omitted wealth as one of the factors affecting deposits demanded because we are not going to examine the effects of a change in wealth.

FIGURE 21–1
The Demand for
Deposits

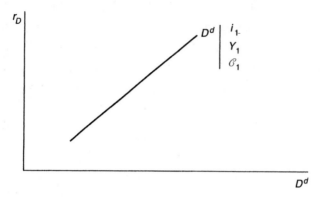

Other things equal, when the deposit rate rises, the quantity of
deposits demanded by the public increases.

FIGURE 21–2
The Supply of
Deposits

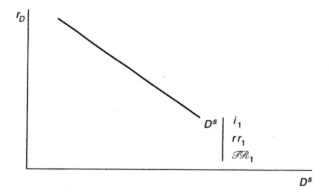

Other things equal, when the deposit rate falls, the quantity of
deposits supplied by banks increases.

of the demanders and suppliers match at point E, the equilibrium point. At this point the
deposit rate is r_D^1, and the quantity of deposits is D_1. On the other hand, at the deposit rate
r_D^3, which is above the equilibrium level, there is excess demand for deposits equal to AB:
At this deposit rate the public wants to hold more deposits than banks want to issue. Banks
lower the deposit rate until the quantity of deposits that the public wants to hold matches
the quantity that banks want to issue, at point E. Therefore, the deposit rate is determined at
the point where the demand for deposits equals the supply of deposits:

$$D^d = D^S \tag{21–1}$$

We have seen that, *other things equal*, the deposit rate and the quantity of deposits are
determined at the point where the quantity of deposits demanded equals the quantity of
deposits supplied. The other things that are kept equal are the values of the variables that

FIGURE 21–3
The Deposit
Market

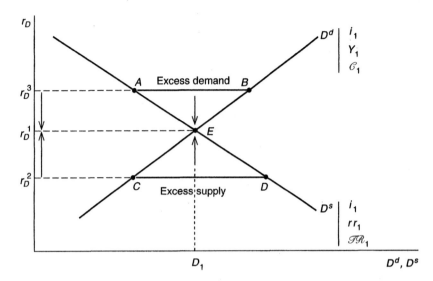

If $r_D < r_D{}^1$, there is excess supply of deposits $\Rightarrow r_D \uparrow$.
If $r_D = r_D{}^1$, the deposit market is in equilibrium and r_D does not change.
If $r_D > r_D{}^1$, there is excess demand for deposits $\Rightarrow r_D \downarrow$.

appear in the labels of the two curves: i, Y, C, $\Im R$, and rr. If one of these variables changes, the demand curve or supply curve will shift, and the equilibrium level of the deposit rate and the corresponding equilibrium quantity of deposits will change. Therefore, the **equilibrium deposit rate** and the **equilibrium quantity of deposits** depend on five variables: i, Y, C, $\Im R$, and rr.

Equation 21–2, which is the deposit rate relation introduced in Chapter 7, shows the ultimate determinants of the deposit rate:

$$r_D = r_D(i, Y, C, \Im R, rr) \tag{21–2}$$

Equation 21–3 represents the relation between the equilibrium quantity of deposits D, and the same set of ultimate determinants.

$$D = D(i, Y, C, \Im R, rr) \tag{21–3}$$

Because demand equals supply in equilibrium, D is both deposits demanded and deposits supplied. Equation 21–3 is in compact form. A more detailed version of the same information comes from substituting the deposit rate relation into the original demand function for deposits, as shown in Chapter 7:

$$\begin{aligned} D^d &= D^d(i - r_D, Y, C) \\ &= D^d[i - r_D(i, Y, C, \Im R, rr), Y, C] \end{aligned} \tag{21–4}$$

Equation 21–4 shows the different channels through which a change in each variable affects the **equilibrium quantity of deposits demanded**. Ultimately, however, we are interested in the net effects, as summarized by Equation 21–3.

FIGURE 21–4
An Increase in the
Interest Rate

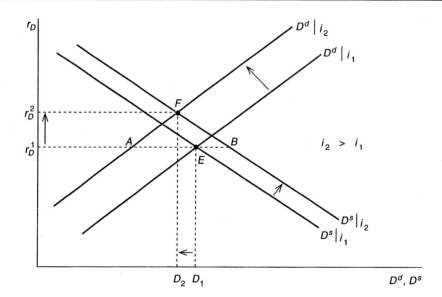

An increase in the interest rate shifts the demand curve to the left and the supply curve to the right. The equilibrium point moves from *E* to *F*, with the deposit rate rising and the quantity of deposits falling.

Next we inquire how a change in each of the ultimate determinants affects the equilibrium level of the deposit rate and the quantity of deposits. We begin with an increase in the interest rate.

THE INTEREST RATE AND THE DEPOSIT MARKET

The interest rate is the only factor that appears in the label of both the demand and supply curves. A change in *i* shifts the demand and supply curves, resulting in a change in the equilibrium values of the deposit rate and the quantity of deposits. We examine the case of an increase in *i*.

The Interest Rate, the Deposit Rate, and the Quantity of Deposits

To see how an increase in *i* affects the demand curve for deposits, recall from Chapter 7 that the demand for deposits depends negatively on the opportunity cost, $i - r_D$, of holding deposits. Given the deposit rate, an increase in the interest rate increases the opportunity cost, inducing the public to lower its demand. This is shown in Figure 21–4 by a leftward shift of the demand curve for deposits when the interest rises from i_1 to i_2.

The effect of an increase in *i* on the supply of deposits works through the net marginal revenue, $[(1 - rr)i - r_D]$. Given the deposit rate, the reserve requirement ratio, and the marginal cost of banking, an increase in the interest rate increases the net marginal revenue of issuing deposits, which induces banks to supply more. Thus, an increase in the interest rate from i_1 to i_2 increases D^s, shifting the supply curve to the right, as illustrated in Figure 21–4.

FIGURE 21–5
The Interest Rate
and the Deposit
Rate

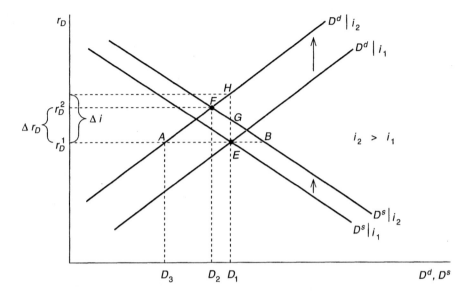

When the interest rate rises, the equilibrium deposit rate rises, but by a smaller amount than the increase in the interest rate.

As a result of the shifts of the demand and supply curves, at the initial equilibrium deposit rate, $r_D{}^1$, banks want to issue more deposits than the public wants to hold. There is excess supply of deposits equal to AB in Figure 21–4. To eliminate this excess supply and restore market clearance, the deposit rate must rise—to $r_D{}^2$ in our graph. This much is clear from Figure 21–4. What is not clear is whether the volume of deposits will decline, even though Figure 21–4 depicts this decline.

In Figure 21–4, the volume of deposits falls because the leftward shift of the demand curve is greater than the rightward shift of the supply curve. Equivalently, the reduced volume of deposits results from a greater *upward* shift of the demand curve than the supply curve. If it were possible for the supply curve to shift more than the demand curve, then the volume of deposits would rise rather than fall. However, we can show that this is impossible and that, therefore, the volume of deposits definitely falls when the interest rate rises. At the heart of the result lies the reserve requirement ratio, rr, which acts like a tax on the net marginal revenue of banks, the suppliers of deposits.

To establish that the upward shift of the demand curve is greater than that of the supply curve when the interest rate rises, see Figure 21–5, which adds more detail to Figure 21–4. First, examine the vertical shift of the demand curve. Suppose that the interest rate rises from i_1 to i_2, a change indicated by Δi on the vertical axis. Also suppose that the quantity of deposits demanded remains at its original volume, D_1. This can happen only if the opportunity cost of holding deposits remains at its original level, $i_1 - r_D{}^1$. For the opportunity cost to remain unchanged when the interest rate rises, the deposit rate must rise by the same amount, that is, $\Delta r_D = \Delta i$. This is the magnitude of the vertical shift in the demand curve at the original volume of deposits, D_1; it is equal to the distance EH in Figure 21–5. The same pattern holds at every level of deposits, not only at D_1. Therefore, the vertical shift of the demand curve equals the increase in the interest rate.

Now let us perform the same exercise for the supply curve and inquire about the conditions under which the quantity of deposits supplied will remain at its original level, D_1, when the interest rate rises from i_1 to i_2. The quantity of deposits supplied will remain at D_1 only if the net marginal revenue $[(1 - rr)i - r_D]$ remains at its original level when the interest rate rises from i_1 to i_2. This requires r_D to rise by $(1 - rr)\Delta i$, which is less than the change in i because $(1 - rr)$ is less than 1. Thus, the vertical shift of the supply curve is less than that of the demand curve. Figure 21–5 confirms this result. The shift of the supply curve equals EG, which is less than EH.

Because the shift of the supply curve is less than the shift of the demand curve, the new intersection of the demand and supply curves will be to the left of the original intersection, thereby resulting in a smaller volume of deposits. The smaller shift in the supply curve also establishes that the change in the deposit rate is less than the change in the interest rate, as seen in Figure 21–5: The change in the deposit rate equals the vertical distance between point E and point F, which is less than the vertical distance between the demand curves. Thus, $\Delta i > \Delta r_D$, meaning that the opportunity cost of holding deposits, $i - r_D$, has increased, which explains why the demand for demand deposits has fallen to D_2.

Figure 21–5 can also be used to compare the old and new financial environments. If the deposit rate were regulated and fixed at $r_D{}^1$, the final equilibrium would not be at point F. Instead, it would be at point A. When regulations prevent the deposit rate from rising, the quantity of deposits must do all the work. In this case, the rise in the opportunity cost of deposits would be equal to the rise in the interest rate, and the quantity of deposits would fall from D_1 to D_3. This fall is greater than the reduction from D_1 to D_2 when the deposit rate is market determined.

The Equilibrium Relations

Four results follow from our analysis of the effect of an increase in the interest rate on the deposit market:

1. The equilibrium level of the deposit rate rises when the interest rate rises, other things equal.
2. The deposit rate rises by less than the increase in the interest rate.
3. The equilibrium level of the opportunity cost, $i - r_D$, of holding deposits rises when the interest rate rises.
4. The equilibrium quantity of deposits demanded (and supplied) falls when the interest rate rises.

The first result confirms that the deposit rate curve introduced in Chapter 7 and depicted in Figure 21–6 is upward sloping. The second result indicates that the slope of the curve is less than 1. Therefore, when the interest rate rises from i_1 to i_2, the deposit rate rises by a smaller amount, shown by the distance between $r_D{}^1$ and $r_D{}^2$.

The third result—that the opportunity cost rises when the interest rate rises—follows from the first two. Because deposits demanded depend negatively on the opportunity cost, it follows that an increase in the interest rate reduces the deposit-market-clearing quantity of deposits demanded, which is the fourth result:

$$i\uparrow \; \rightarrow \; [i - r_D(i)]\uparrow \; \rightarrow \; D^d\downarrow \; \rightarrow \; D\downarrow$$

FIGURE 21–6
The Deposit Rate
Curve

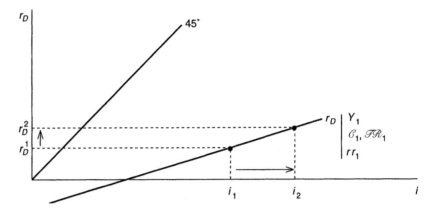

Other things equal, when the interest rate rises, the deposit rate rises, but by a smaller amount.

FIGURE 21–7
The Equilibrium
Demand Curve for
Deposits

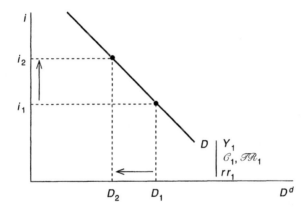

Other things equal, when the interest rate rises, the deposit-market-clearing quantity of deposits falls.

Figure 21–7 illustrates the negative relation between the interest rate and the equilibrium quantity of deposits. When the interest rate rises from i_1 to i_2, the quantity of deposits falls from D_1 to D_2.

We can represent these results concisely with a plus sign under the interest rate in the r_D relation and a minus sign under i in the D relation:

$$r_D = r_D \; (i, \; Y, \; \mathcal{C}, \; \mathcal{IR}, \; rr)$$
$$+$$
$$D = D(i, \; Y, \; \mathcal{C}, \; \mathcal{IR}, \; rr)$$
$$-$$

Finally, the three panels of Figure 21–8 shows at a glance how (*a*) the deposit market, (*b*) the deposit rate curve, and (*c*) the equilibrium curve for deposits demanded are related.

**FIGURE 21–8
The Interest Rate
and the Deposit
Market:** *Putting the
Pieces Together*

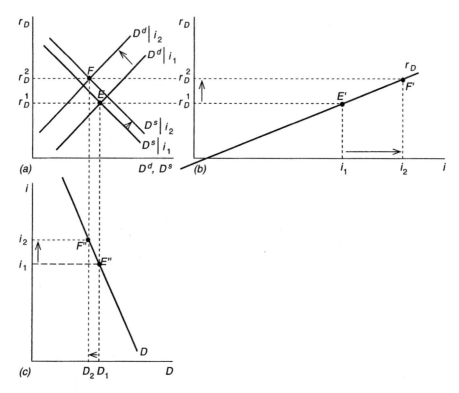

In panel *a*, an increase in *i* increases the equilibrium level of r_D and reduces the equilibrium level of *D*. Thus, in panel *b* there is a movement along the r_D curve and in panel *c* a movement along the *D* curve.

Panel *a* shows that when the interest rate rises, the equilibrium deposit rate rises and the equilibrium quantity of deposits falls; the equilibrium point moves from *E* to *F*. Panel *b* shows the positive relation between the deposit rate and the interest rate by a movement along the r_D curve, from point *E′* to point *F′*. Panel *c* shows the inverse relation between the equilibrium quantity of deposits demanded and the interest rate by a movement along the *D* curve from point *E″* to point *F″*.

**A Numerical
Illustration**

Next we illustrate our analysis of the deposit market with a hypothetical numerical example. We start with the demand for deposits, described by Equation 21–5:

$$D^d = 290 - 3(i - r_D) + 0.10Y + 0.2\mathcal{C} \qquad (21\text{–}5)$$

The minus sign in front of the $(i - r_D)$ means that deposits demanded vary inversely with the opportunity cost; the plus signs in front of *Y* and $\mathcal{C}$ mean deposits demanded vary positively with real income and the collective variable.

Equation 21–6 describes deposits supplied:

$$D^s = 800 + 20[(1 - rr)i - r_D] - 0.15\mathcal{IR} \qquad (21\text{–}6)$$

The plus sign in front of $[(1 - rr)i - r_D]$ means that deposits supplied vary positively with the net marginal revenue, while the minus sign in front of $\mathfrak{IR}$ means that they vary inversely with the technology and regulatory index. For simplicity, our calculations are based on a reserve requirement ratio, rr, of 0.10.

To find the deposit rate relation, first set deposits demanded equal to deposits supplied.

$$\underset{D^d}{290 - 3(i - r_D) + 0.10Y + 0.2\mathcal{C}} = \underset{D^s}{800 + 20[(1 - rr)i - r_D] - 0.15\mathfrak{IR}} \qquad (21\text{--}7)$$

Next solve Equation 21–7 for r_D. Of course r_D will be an equation that depends on all the factors that affect deposits demanded and deposits supplied:

$$r_D = (1/23) \times (510 + 21i - 0.10Y - 0.2\mathcal{C} - 0.15\mathfrak{IR})$$
$$r_D = 22.1739 + 0.913i - 0.004348Y - 0.0087\mathcal{C} - 0.006522\mathfrak{IR} \qquad (21\text{--}8)$$

Next, substitute the deposit rate relation for r_D in Equation 21–5 to find the equilibrium relation for deposits demanded:

$$D = 356.5217 - 0.261i + 0.08696Y + 0.1739\mathcal{C} - 0.0196\mathfrak{IR} \qquad (21\text{--}9)$$

Equations 21–8 and 21–9 show that the equilibrium deposit rate and the equilibrium quantity of deposits demanded depend on the values assigned to i, Y, $\mathcal{C}$ and $\mathfrak{IR}$. If the value of rr had not been specified, it also would appear on the right side of both equations.

Finally, suppose that the initial values of real income, the collective variable, and the technology and regulatory index are given by:

$Y = \$6,000$ billion per year
$\mathcal{C} = 100$
$\mathfrak{IR} = 100$

Substituting these values into Equations 21–8 and 21–9, it becomes clear that the deposit rate and the quantity of deposits demanded are a function solely of the interest rate:

$$r_D = -5.4363 + 0.913i \qquad (21\text{--}10)$$

$$D = 893.7117 - 0.261i \qquad (21\text{--}11)$$

The plus sign in front of i in Equation 21–10 means that, other things equal, when the interest rate rises the deposit rate rises. Moreover, a coefficient of 0.913 means that for every percentage point increase in the interest rate, the deposit rate rises by 0.9 of a percentage point. In other words, 0.913 is the slope of the r_D curve. Finally, the minus sign in front of i in Equation 21–11 means that the equilibrium quantity of deposits demanded varies inversely with the interest rate.

TRY IT OUT 21.1

Equation 21–5 and Equation 21–11 are both equations for deposits demanded. The coefficient of the interest rate is –3 in Equation 21–5 but only –0.261 in Equation 21–11. What is the economic explanation of this difference?

**FIGURE 21–9
Effects of an
Increase in Real
Income, Y**

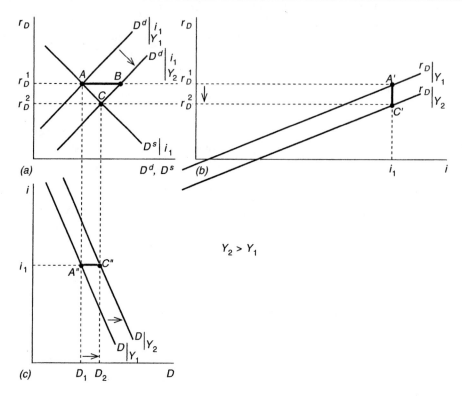

In panel *a*, an increase in Y reduces the equilibrium level of r_D and increases the equilibrium level of D. Thus, in panel *b*, the r_D curve shifts down, and in panel *c* the D curve shifts to the right.

OTHER FACTORS AFFECTING THE DEPOSIT MARKET

In addition to the interest rate, four factors affect the deposit market. Real income and all the factors lumped into the collective variable affect the demand side of the market. The technology and regulatory index and the reserve requirement ratio affect the supply side. When one of these factors changes, the equilibrium deposit rate and the equilibrium quantity of deposits change at each level of the interest rate. Thus, both the deposit rate curve and the equilibrium quantity of deposits demanded curve shift. This section examines in detail one factor on each side of the deposit market—a change in the real income on the demand side, and a change in the technology and regulatory index on the supply side. Because the mechanics of the graphs work the same, we explain the effects of the other factors intuitively.

**A Change in
Real Income**

The three-panel graph of Figure 21–9 shows the effects of an increase in Y, from Y_1 to Y_2. Points A, A', and A'' represent the initial situation, meaning that the interest rate, the deposit rate, and the quantity of deposits are equal to i_1, r_D^1, and D_1, respectively.

Next, suppose that the level of income rises to Y_2, while i, $\mathcal{C}$, $\mathfrak{IR}$, and rr remain at their initial levels. According to the third law of asset demand introduced in Chapter 6, the public increases its demand for deposits when real income rises. Thus, the increase in Y shifts the demand curve for deposits to the right in Figure 21–9a. At the initial equilibrium deposit rate, $r_D{}^1$, there is excess demand for deposits, equal to the horizontal distance AB. The public wants to hold more deposits than banks want to issue. To clear the deposit market, the deposit rate falls to $r_D{}^2$, depicted by point C. The fall in the deposit rate causes banks to increase the quantity of deposits supplied, shown by the movement from point A to point C along the supply curve. And the fall in the deposit rate induces the public to reduce the quantity of deposits demanded, shown by the movement from point B to point C along the new demand curve. At point C, the quantity of deposits demanded is less than at point B, but it is still greater than at point A. In sum, the increase in Y reduces the deposit rate and increases the quantity of deposits demanded (and supplied).

Figure 21–9b and Figure 21–9c show the effects of the increase in Y on the r_D curve and the D curve, respectively. Figure 21–9b illustrates that for the same level of the interest rate, i_1, the deposit rate is lower. This means that point A' shifts vertically down to point C'. And in Figure 21–9c, for the same level of the interest rate, i_1, the market-determined quantity of deposits increases to D_2, as shown by the displacement of point A'' to point C''.

Repeating the process for all levels of the interest rate and connecting all points such as C'', yield a D curve in the lower panel shifting to the right. Also connecting all points such as C' in the right top panel results in the deposit rate relation also shifting down and to the right. In sum, this exercise shows that the market-determined quantity of deposits, D, depends positively on the level of income and that the market-determined deposit rate depends negatively on the level of income.

A Change in the Collective Variable

An increase in the collective variable has the same qualitative effects as an increase in Y. An example of an increase in $\mathcal{C}$ is greater uncertainty, which makes individuals want to hold more deposits and fewer securities. The graph is identical to that of Figure 21–9 if we substitute $\mathcal{C}_1$ for Y_1, and $\mathcal{C}_2$ for Y_2. Thus, the quantity of deposits, D, depends positively on $\mathcal{C}$, and the deposit rate, r_D, depends negatively on $\mathcal{C}$. Of course, a reduction in $\mathcal{C}$ would have the opposite effects. It would increase the deposit rate and reduce the quantity of deposits, other things equal. An example is the **demand-reducing financial innovations** that made their appearance in the mid-1970s. The catalyst for these reductions in the demand for deposits and corresponding increase in the demand for securities was advances in computer technology that enabled households and firms to manage their money more effectively. They could carry out a given volume of transactions with fewer balances in their checking accounts.

A Change in the Technology and Regulatory Index

Financial innovations are not limited to the demand for deposits. As Chapter 18 discusses, **cost-reducing financial innovations** increase the supply of deposits, other things equal. At the existing interest rate and deposit rate, a reduction in marginal costs makes profit-maximizing banks want to supply more deposits and fund more loans.

FIGURE 21–10
Effects of a Fall in
the Technology and
Regulatory Index,
$\mathfrak{IR}$

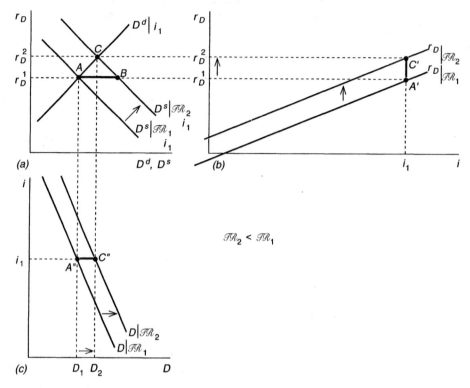

In panel *a* a fall in $\mathfrak{IR}$ increases the equilibrium levels of r_D and D. Thus, in panel *b* the r_D curve shifts up, and in panel *c* the D curve shifts to the right.

Figure 21–10*a* shows that a fall in $\mathfrak{IR}$ shifts the D^s curve to the right. As a result, at the original deposit rate, r_D^1, there is excess supply of deposits equal to AB. In response, the deposit rate rises to r_D^2, shown by point C in Figure 21–10*a*. And at point C the quantity of deposits demanded and supplied is larger than at point A.

Figure 21–10*b* shows the effect of this shock on the r_D curve. The curve shifts upward because for each level of the interest rate the market-clearing deposit rate is greater. For example, at the interest rate i_1 the increase in the deposit rate is shown by the movement from point A' to point C'.

Finally, Figure 21–10*c* shows the effect on the D curve. At the interest rate i_1 the quantity of deposits increases from D_1 to D_2, shown by the movement from point A'' to C''. The equilibrium quantity of deposits demanded increases because the improvement in financial technology raises the deposit rate, which reduces the opportunity cost of holding deposits, other things equal.

In sum, a cost-reducing improvement in financial technology induces banks to bid more aggressively for deposits at each interest rate. As a result, the deposit rate rises and the equilibrium quantity of deposits demanded and supplied also rises. On the other hand,

MarketWatch 21.1
Banks Bid Less Aggressively for Deposits

In its monetary policy reports to Congress in July 1990 and February 1991, the Fed argued that depository institutions bid less aggressively for deposits in 1990 because of the contraction of the thrift industry and the credit crunch in the banking industry. In particular, the report in July 1990 states:

Not only has the thrift industry contracted more rapidly than expected, but commercial banks have picked up little of the lending forgone by thrifts and, in fact, have curtailed their own lending in some sectors, thus further depressing depository credit. With little need to fund asset growth, banks and thrifts have pursued retail deposits less aggressively, leading to the opening of a sizable gap between yields available in the open market and those on deposits. Partly as a result, M2 also has slowed, moving down into the lower portion of its annual growth range. (Emphasis added)

An increase in nonperforming assets that required an increase in provisions for loan loss precipitated the

thrift crisis and the credit crunch. The increase in provisions for loan losses—represented by an increase in the technology and regulatory index, $\mathfrak{TR}$ in our model—increased the marginal cost of supplying deposits and acquiring securities. As a result, the demand for loan securities fell, the supply of deposits fell, and the deposit rate fell. In the case of the thrift crisis, the increased provisions for loan losses caused net losses that wiped out net worth and bankrupted hundreds of thrifts. In the case of the credit crunch in the banking industry, banks remained in business, but they made fewer loans and issued fewer deposits, especially time deposits.

The reduction in the rate on time deposits induced the public to shift funds into open market securities and into mutual funds. The public also moved out of time deposits into checkable deposits because of the rate-setting practices of banks in which banks lowered the rate on time deposits faster than the rate on checkable deposits. These patterns continued in 1992 and 1993, contributing to the sluggish growth of M2 and the more robust growth of M1.

an increase in marginal costs caused by higher expected or actual loan losses and increased provisions for loan losses causes banks to bid less aggressively for deposits, as MarketWatch 21.1 explains.

A Change in the Reserve Requirement Ratio

Finally, a change in the reserve requirement ratio also shifts the supply curve. The reserve requirement ratio acts like a tax on banks. Other things equal, when the Fed reduces the reserve requirement ratio, banks want to issue more deposits because the net marginal revenue from issuing deposits rises. Thus, a reduction in *rr* will increase the supply of deposits causing a rise in the deposit rate and an increase in the quantity of deposits demanded at each level of the interest rate. The deposit rate curve shifts up and the equilibrium deposits demanded curve shifts to the right.

Summary

Equations 21–12 and 21–13 summarize our results for the deposit rate and the quantity of deposits demanded, respectively. Their magnitudes depend on i, Y, $\mathcal{C}$, $\mathfrak{TR}$, and rr. The sign under each determinant indicates the direction of the relation. The positive sign under the symbol i in Equation 21–12 denotes the positive slope of the r_D curve. The signs under the remaining symbols denote the direction of the shift of the r_D curve when each of the four shift factors increases. For example, a minus sign under Y means that r_D falls when real income rises, so the r_D curve shifts down, and similarly for $\Im\mathcal{R}$ and *rr*. In the *D* relation, the negative sign under *i* denotes the negative slope of the curve depicting the equilibrium quantity of deposits demanded, and the signs under the remaining variables denote the direction of the shift in this curve. For example, the positive sign under *Y* means the *D* curve shifts to the right when *Y* increases, while the negative sign under $\Im\mathcal{R}$ means the curve shifts to the left when $\Im\mathcal{R}$ increases.

$$r_D = r_D(i, Y, \mathcal{C}, \Im\mathcal{R}, rr) \qquad (21\text{--}12)$$
$$+\ -\ -\ -\ -$$

$$D = D(i, Y, \mathcal{C}, \Im\mathcal{R}, rr) \qquad (21\text{--}13)$$
$$-\ +\ +\ -\ -$$

As an example of these two relations, consider again the r_D equation and the *D* equation derived in the numerical illustration of the deposit market earlier in the chapter.

$$r_D = 22.1739 + 0.913i - 0.004348Y - 0.0087\mathcal{C} - 0.006522\Im\mathcal{R} \qquad (21\text{--}10)$$

$$D = 356.5217 - 0.261i + 0.08696Y + 0.1739\mathcal{C} - 0.0196\Im\mathcal{R} \qquad (21\text{--}11)$$

The coefficients of the determinants of r_D and *D* in Equations 21–10 and 21–11 have the signs predicted by our theory. For example, there is a minus sign in front of *Y* in the r_D equation and a plus sign in front of *Y* in the *D* equation.

MONEY DEMAND

Money consists of deposits and currency. Money demand is the sum of deposits demanded and currency demanded. In the new financial environment, the demand for deposits is the deposit-market-clearing quantity of deposits demanded. Therefore, to find money demand, simply add the demand for currency to *D*:

$$M^d = Cur^d + D$$

Assume, as in Chapter 7, that currency is independent of the interest rate. It depends solely on real income and the payments habits of society, denoted by $\mathcal{H}$:

$$Cur^d = Cur^d(Y, \mathcal{H})$$

Therefore, in a graph with the interest rate on the vertical axis, the curve representing the demand for currency is vertical, as shown in Figure 21–11. Of course, the *D* curve, representing the deposit component of money demand, is downward sloping. Adding horizontally the two curves of panel *a* gives us the downward-sloping money demand curve in panel *b* of Figure 21–11.

The factors affecting money demand are the determinants of the demand for currency and the demand for deposits. Real income is common to both components. An increase in *Y* increases the demand for currency and the demand for deposits, thereby increasing money demand. On the other hand, the interest rate, the technology and regulatory index, and the reserve requirement ratio affect only the deposit component of money demand. But what about the payments habits? Suppose, for example, that an increase in the volume of illegal activities, such as drug dealing, increases the use of currency and

FIGURE 21–11
Money Demand
and Its
Components

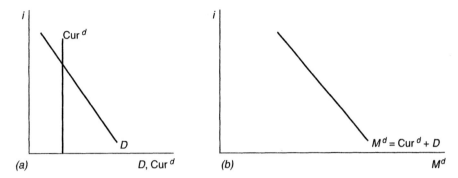

To find money demand in panel *b*, we add the currency demand curve to the equilibrium demand curve for deposits from panel *a*.

reduces the use of checks to make payments. There will be a change in the composition of the demand for money but not in its magnitude.[3] Therefore, payments habits are not included as one of the factors affecting money demand in Equation 21–14. This does not mean the payments habits have no effect on the money market. Chapter 15 shows that the amount of currency that the public wants to hold affects the money supply.

Equation 21–14 gives a compact view of the factors affecting money demand and the direction of the relationships:

$$M^d = M^d(i, Y, \mathcal{C}, \mathfrak{IR}, rr) \tag{21–14}$$
$$- \; + \; + \; - \; -$$

The minus sign under *i* means the money demand curve is downward sloping. The plus sign under *Y* means the M^d curves shifts to the right when *Y* increases. Similarly, when $\mathcal{C}$ rises the M^d curve also shifts to the right. On the other hand, the minus signs under $\mathfrak{IR}$ and *rr* indicate that the M^d curve shifts to the left if either of these factors increases.

THE OLD FINANCIAL ENVIRONMENT: A SPECIAL CASE

This chapter has concentrated on money demand in an environment of deregulated deposit rates—the new financial environment. The old financial environment, in which the deposit rate was regulated, is a special and simple case.[4]

The two panels of Figure 21–12 show the effect of an increase in the interest rate on the quantity of deposits in the old financial environment. Assume that $\bar{r}_D$ is the maximum

---

[3] With market-determined deposit rates, there actually will be a small net effect on money demand that we are ignoring here for simplicity. An increase in the demand for currency and a reduction in the demand for deposits create excess supply of deposits in the deposit market. The resulting increase in the deposit rate increases the quantity of deposits demanded by the public. Therefore, on net, the quantity of deposits will fall by less than the increase in the demand for currency.

[4] Because we assume that the demand for currency does not depend on interest rates, only the deposit component of money demand is different in the two financial environments.

FIGURE 21–12
A Regulated
Deposit Rate, The
Interest Rate, and
Deposits
Demanded

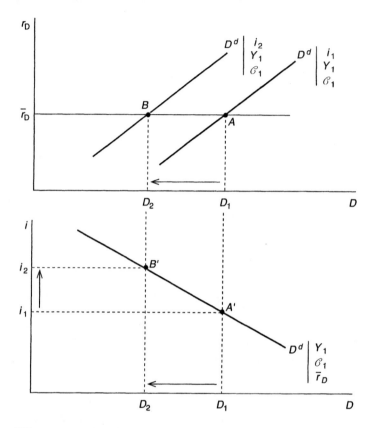

With a regulated deposit rate, an increase in the interest rate reduces the
quantity of deposits demanded.

deposit rate that the law allows banks to pay. Furthermore, assume that the maximum
level of the deposit rate is below the equilibrium level of the deposit rate. Then the
volume of deposits is demand determined: At $\bar{r}_D$, banks are willing to issue all the
deposits that the public wants to hold.

In the upper panel of Figure 21–12, when the interest rate is i_1, the quantity of deposits
that the public wants to hold is D_1, shown by point A. When the interest rate rises to i_2,
the demand curve shifts to the left, and the quantity of deposits demanded falls to D_2, as
shown by point B. In the lower panel of the graph, in which the interest rate is measured
on the vertical axis, the deposits demanded curve is downward sloping. When the interest
rate rises from i_1 to i_2, the decrease in the quantity of deposits demanded is shown by a
movement along the demand curve from point A' to point B'. Of course, the opportunity
cost of holding deposits at point B' is higher than at point A'. Moreover, with the deposit
rate fixed, the change in the opportunity cost equals the change in the interest rate, which
explains why the deposits demanded curve in the old financial environment must be

FIGURE 21–13
An Increase in the
Regulated Deposit
Rate

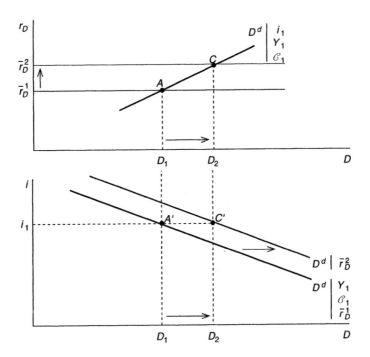

An increase in the regulated deposit rate increases the quantity of deposits
demanded.

flatter than the equilibrium deposits demanded curve in the new financial environment.
As Chapter 7 discusses, for the same change in the interest rate, there is a greater change
in the opportunity cost in the old financial environment and, hence, a greater change in
the quantity of deposits demanded.

The deposits demanded curve in the lower panel of Figure 21–12 shifts when the
factors in the label of the curve change. Real income and the collective variable are
common shift factors in the old and new financial environments. The deposit rate, however, is a shift factor only in the old financial environment. Let us see, then, what happens
if regulators increase the level of the deposit rate.

Figure 21–13 illustrates this case. In the upper panel of the graph, the horizontal line
depicting the regulated deposit rate shifts upward. Other things equal, including the
interest rate, an increase in the deposit rate reduces the opportunity cost of deposits,
which increases the quantity of deposits demanded, shown by a movement along the D^d
curve in the upper panel. In the lower panel, at each level of the interest rate, there is a
higher quantity of deposits demanded, which means the D^d curve shifts to the right. This
graph depicts the transition to the new financial environment that began in 1981 when for
the first time banks nationwide were allowed to pay interest on checking accounts, called
NOW accounts. As Chapter 5 discusses, originally the rates on NOW accounts were

regulated rates. The next section on the empirical evidence shows that there was an outward shift in money demand around the time of the nationwide introduction of NOW accounts.

EMPIRICAL STUDIES OF MONEY DEMAND

This chapter and the preceding chapter examine several theories capable of establishing the demand for money. Despite differences in emphasis, these theories indicate the existence of a relationship between the stock of money demanded and a few basic economic variables: the interest rate, income, wealth, and several potential shift variables. The overall body of empirical research confirms our theoretical treatment. This does not mean, however, that there has not been controversy. In the early 1970s, when the controversies seemed to be settled, financial innovations and deregulation raised new puzzles and stirred old debates.

Shifts in the Demand Curve for M1: The Case of "Missing Money"

In early 1976 three economists at the Federal Reserve Board, Jared Enzler, Lewis Johnson, and John Paulus, discovered that the money demand equation, estimated using pre-1974 data, was systematically overpredicting actual money demand after 1974: For a given level of the interest rate and a given level of income, the observed quantity of money was lower than the quantity predicted by the estimated equation.[5] In other words, the money demand curve had shifted inward. The Federal Reserve economists attributed this inward shift to the introduction of cash management techniques. (Remember that at the time the deposit rate on M1 deposits was regulated.) Using our terminology, the inward shift of money demand was caused by a reduction in the collective variable. Borrowing from the title of a 1976 paper on the topic by Stephen Goldfeld, economists began to refer to this episode as the case of **missing money**.[6] Explaining missing money occupied researchers for several years.

Another Federal Reserve study completed three years after the Enzler, Johnson, and Paulus study reported that money demand continued to shift inward throughout the rest of the 1970s. This second study examined in greater detail the role of new cash management techniques.[7] The empirical studies that identified new methods in cash management as the major contributor to the downward shifts in money demand in the 1970s naturally relied on the Baumol-Tobin models of cash management. Recall from Chapter 20 that these earlier studies showed that when there is a reduction in "brokerage fees" (which represent all the adjustment costs of moving between money and securities), the public holds less money, because the public can satisfy its liquidity needs with fewer money balances.

All of these studies examined the narrowest measure of money, M1, often referred to by the Fed as a measure of transactions balances. Beginning with the nationwide intro-

---

[5] Jared Enzler, Lewis Johnson, and John Paulus, "Some Problems of Money Demand," *Brookings Papers on Economic Activity* 1 (1976): 261–82.

[6] Stephen Goldfeld, "The Case of the Missing Money," *Brookings Papers on Economic Activity* 3 (1976): 683–730.

[7] Several of the factors included in $\mathscr{C}$ have their origin in the studies that attempted to explain the shifts in money demand.

duction of NOW accounts on December 31, 1980, interest-bearing checkable deposits became an important part of the M1 measure of money. Paying interest on checkable deposits was bound to create some portfolio adjustments, which leads us to the next problem.

Shifts in and Tilts of the Demand Curve for M1: The Case of "Too Much Money"

Monetary economists hardly became accustomed to attributing the inward shifts in M1 demand to the introduction of new cash management techniques when, in 1982, they discovered that the demand for M1 had shifted outward. Now the estimated demand equation for M1 was underpredicting the observed quantity of money. Of course, underpredicting money demand means overpredicting velocity, as Chapter 16 discusses.

A consensus has not yet been reached on the reasons behind the outward shift in M1 demand in 1982 and 1983. There is even a dispute over whether such a shift occurred. The most often-cited explanation for a shift focuses on the introduction of NOW accounts. The nationwide introduction of checkable deposits that paid a positive, but fixed, deposit rate marked the beginning of the transition to the new financial environment. The outward shift in money demand occurred during this period of transition. The simplest explanation is that the nationwide introduction of NOW accounts amounted to an increase in the deposit rate in a regime of regulated deposit rates. As a result, the M^d curve shifted outward.

Even economists who agree that a shift occurred in the demand for M1 argue that the shift itself is only part of the story. For example, in their 1989 study of money demand, Hetzel and Mehra, economists at the Federal Reserve Bank of Richmond, point out that NOW accounts were introduced in 1981, but the too-much-money puzzle did not appear until the middle of 1982, when market rates of interest fell.[8] Thus, Hetzel and Mehra argue that the complete story is that the money demand curve not only shifted but also tilted. Confirming earlier studies, Hetzel and Mehra found that the interest responsiveness of M1 increased in the 1980s. A recession accompanied by disinflation caused interest rates to fall in 1982. And as interest rates fell, households and nonfinancial firms increased their demand for M1 balances more than in previous decades. Let us see why.

The most common explanation relies on the rate-setting behavior of banks in the transition to the new financial environment. In 1982 the rate on NOW accounts was still fixed. On the other hand, by that time more than two-thirds of the non-M1 component of M2 consisted of deposits that paid market-related, or market-determined, rates. When market rates of interest fell in 1982, the spread between open market rates and the M1 deposit rate fell. As in the past, market participants shifted funds from open market debt instruments to checkable deposits. But the spread between the market-determined deposit rates on non-M1 deposits and the fixed rate on NOW accounts also fell. Thus, market participants also shifted funds from M2 deposits not included in M1 to checkable deposits, especially NOW accounts. As a result, the demand for M1 increased still more, thereby accounting for part of the too-much-money puzzle. Because of the sluggish adjustment of the M1 deposit rate, M1 still shows a substantial amount of interest responsiveness, even though all ceilings have been removed on NOW accounts.

---

[8] Robert L. Hetzel and Yash P. Mehra, "The Behavior of Money Demand in the 1980s," *Journal of Money, Credit, and Banking* 21, no. 4 (November 1989): 455–63.

Deregulation of the Deposit Rate and the Interest Sensitivity of the Demand for M2

The deregulation of deposit rates reopened the debate about the interest sensitivity of money demand. As our theoretical treatment in this chapter indicates, estimating the interest responsiveness of money demand in the new financial environment involves two steps: estimating the relationship between the deposit rate and the interest rate, and estimating the relationship between the demand for deposits (money) and the opportunity cost.[9] Intensive empirical research, especially by Fed economists, has shown that although the interest sensitivity of M1 increased in the 1980s, the interest sensitivity of the non-M1 component of M2 decreased.

The economic reasoning behind the decreased interest sensitivity of the non-M1 component of M2 is a straightforward application of our theoretical analysis of the new financial environment. A decrease in the interest rate reduces the opportunity cost of holding money less in the new financial environment than in the old financial environment because the deposit rate also falls. Hence, when the deposit rate is market determined, a decrease in the interest rate increases money demand by less than when the deposit rate is regulated.

Empirical investigations show not only that the long-run interest sensitivity of the non-M1 component of M2 has fallen in the 1980s, but also that the long-run interest sensitivity of the entire M2 measure of money has fallen. In other words, the reduction in the interest rate sensitivity of the non-M1 component of M2 has been large enough to negate the increased interest sensitivity of M1.

The Case of Missing M2

In the early 1990s the case of missing money reappeared. This time the quantity of M2 held was less than predicted. In other words, the demand curve for M2 shifted inward. A consensus seems to be emerging from ongoing research that shifts in both the demand curve and the supply curve for deposits are responsible. According to Bryon Higgins, an economist at the Federal Reserve Bank of Kansas City, the preponderance of evidence shows that "actions of both depository institutions and their customers have contributed to the recent M2 shortfall."[10] In terms of our model, this means that both the supply curve and the demand curve for deposits shifted.

On the supply side, stricter regulatory enforcement and increased provisions for loan losses, represented by an increase in $\Re$, shifted the supply curve for deposits inward. As a result, both the equilibrium quantity of deposits and money demand fell. On the demand side, an increased appetite for risk, represented by a decrease in the collective variable, $\mathcal{C}$, shifted the demand curve for deposits inward, as the public moved out of bank deposits and into bonds and stocks. Again, the equilibrium quantity of deposits and money demand fell. One reason the public was willing to take on more risk is because of large spreads between long-term and short-term market rates of interest. If we think of i as the short-term rate, then increases in the long-term rate that increase the spread and reduce the demand for deposits must be reflected in the collective variable. Recall from Chapter 16 that work done at the Federal Reserve Board shows that although the short-run oppor-

---

[9] For an example of this approach to estimating the demand for M2, see David H. Small and Richard D. Porter, "Understanding the Behavior of M2 and V2," *Federal Reserve Bulletin* 75, no. 4 (April 1989): 244–54.

[10] Bryon Higgins, "Policy Implications of Recent M2 Behavior," *Economic Review*, Federal Reserve Bank of Kansas City 77, no. 3 (Third Quarter 1992): 30.

tunity cost of deposits fell in the early 1990s, the long-run opportunity cost rose. In hindsight, the long-run opportunity cost was a better explanatory factor of the demand for M2. Because of the difficulty in predicting the demand for M2, in July 1993 the Fed downgraded monetary aggregates as intermediate targets, as Chapter 16 discusses.

SUMMARY

- The deposit rate and the quantity of deposits are determined in the deposit market at the point where deposits demanded equal deposits supplied.
- The equilibrium deposit rate and the equilibrium quantity of deposits depend on five factors: the interest rate, i; the level of real income, Y; the collective variable, $\mathcal{C}$, the technology and regulatory index, $\mathfrak{TR}$, and the reserve requirement ratio, rr.
- An increase in the interest rate increases the equilibrium deposit rate by less, thereby increasing the opportunity cost of holding deposits and reducing the quantity of deposits demanded.
- The r_D curve depicts the positive relation between the deposit rate and the interest rate. The D curve depicts the negative relation between the equilibrium quantity of deposits and the interest rate. In the new financial environment, the D curve is the deposit component of money demand.
- For a given interest rate, an increase in Y or $\mathcal{C}$ increases the demand for deposits, which causes the deposit rate to fall and the equilibrium quantity of deposits to rise. As a result, the r_D curve shifts down and the D curve shifts to the right.
- For a given interest rate, an increase in $\mathfrak{TR}$ or rr reduces the supply of deposits, which causes the deposit rate and the equilibrium quantity of deposits to fall. As a result, the r_D curve shifts down and the D curve shifts to the left.
- The demand for currency is the other component of money demand. An increase in Y raises the demand for currency as well as the demand for deposits. A change in the payments habits of society, on the other hand, changes the composition of money demand but not its size.
- The downward-sloping M^d curve depicts the negative relation between the interest rate and the demand for money. An increase in Y or $\mathcal{C}$ will shift the money demand curve to the right, while an increase in rr or $\mathfrak{TR}$ will shift the curve to the left.
- A rise in the interest rate reduces money demand by a smaller amount in the new financial environment than in the old. Thus, the money demand curve is steeper in the new financial environment.
- In the mid-1970s individuals held less money than predicted by the standard demand equation for M1, estimated using pre-1974 data. Analysts attributed the missing money to a downward shift in money demand caused by more intensive use of cash management techniques. In terms of our model, there was a reduction in the collective variable, $\mathcal{C}$.
- In 1982 money demand equations began to underpredict the demand for M1. The most common explanation is that the demand curve for M1 shifted to the right and became flatter during the transition to the new financial environment.
- Empirical work shows that deregulation of the deposit rate has reduced the long-run interest responsiveness of M2, as this chapter's theory predicts.
- In the early 1990s the demand curve for M2 shifted inward because of inward shifts of both the demand curve and the supply curve in the deposit market.

KEY TERMS AND CONCEPTS

equilibrium deposit rate

equilibrium quantity of deposits

equilibrium quantity of deposits demanded

demand-reducing financial innovations

cost-reducing financial innovations

missing money

QUESTIONS AND PROBLEMS

1. Who are the demanders for deposits? Why is the demand for deposits curve upward sloping in a graph with the deposit rate measured on the vertical axis?

2. Who are the suppliers of deposits? Why is the supply curve downward sloping?

3. "If there is excess demand for deposits, the deposit rate rises." True or false? Explain and illustrate graphically.

4. Suppose that the rate of interest falls from i_1 to i_2. Use a graph of the deposit market to show that the fall in the deposit rate will be less than the fall in the interest rate. Also explain the effect on the equilibrium quantity of deposits.

5. "If the interest rate falls and real income falls, the deposit rate will definitely fall." True or false? Explain and illustrate graphically with the deposit rate curve.

6. Assume that the demand and supply equations describing the deposit market are given by:

$$D^d = 920 - 3(i - r_D)$$
$$D^S = 785 + 20[(1 - rr)i - r_D]$$

Also assume that the reserve requirement ratio, rr, is set at 0.10. Derive the deposit rate relation and the equilibrium equation for deposits demanded. Is the form of these equations consistent with the predictions of economic theory?

7. Explain the difference between demand-reducing and cost-reducing financial innovations. With the help of a graph of the deposit market, compare their effects on the equilibrium deposit rate and the equilibrium quantity of deposits.

8. In 1992 the Fed reduced the reserve requirement ratio on transactions deposits from 12 percent to 10 percent. With the help of a graph of the deposit market, explain the effect on the deposit rate and the quantity of deposits, other things equal.

9. Assume that the demand and supply equations describing the deposit market are given by:

$$D^d = 300 - 3(i - r_D) + 0.10Y + 0.20\mathcal{C}$$
$$D^S = 800 + 20[(1 - rr)i - r_D] - 0.15\mathfrak{IR}$$

   a. Derive the deposit rate equation and the equilibrium equation for deposits demanded as functions of i, Y,

$\mathcal{C}$, and $\mathfrak{IR}$. Explain the economic meaning of the signs in front of these variables. In your calculations assume that $rr = 0.10$.

   b. Reduce these equations to functions solely of the interest rate by assuming the following values of Y, $\mathcal{C}$, and $\mathfrak{IR}$: $Y = \$6,000$ billion; $\mathcal{C} = 100$ points; and $\mathfrak{IR} = 100$ points.

   c. Compare your results to your answer in question 6.

10. Suppose the demand for currency is given by:

$$Cur = 150 + 0.01Y$$

   a. Use this information and your results from question 9a to find the money demand equation as a function of i, Y, $\mathcal{C}$, and $\mathfrak{IR}$.

   b. Use your results from question 9b to find the money demand equation as a function solely of the interest rate.

11. Suppose that deposit rates are market determined and that your answer to question 10b describes the initial situation. Next, suppose that the authorities reregulate the deposit rate and fix it at 3.26 percent.

   a. Find the money demand equation as a function solely of the interest rate and illustrate this equation graphically.

   b. On the same graph as your answer to (a), add the money demand curve that depicts your answer to 10b. Explain the difference between these two curves.

   c. Suppose that the interest rate is 10 percent. What would the value of money demand be in each case?

12. Suppose that the consolidation of regulatory agencies reduces the costs to banks of complying with regulations in the new financial environment. What will be the effect on money demand? Illustrate your result graphically.

13. "The factors that shift the money demand curve are identical in the old and new financial environments." True or false? Explain.

14. Explain the difference between the "cases of missing money" in the 1970s and 1990s.

SUGGESTED READINGS

Duca, John V. "Regulation, Bank Competitiveness, and Episodes of Missing Money." *Economic Review* (Federal Reserve Bank of Dallas), Second Quarter 1993, 1–23.

    Examines three episodes of missing money between 1973 and 1991.

Hadjimichalakis, Michael G. *The Federal Reserve, Money, and Interest Rates: The Volcker Years and Beyond.* New York: Praeger, 1984, Chapters 5–8.

Examines the theory and policy implications of the new financial environment.

Higgins, Bryon. "Policy Implications of Recent M2 Behavior." *Economic Review* (Federal Reserve Bank of Kansas City) 77, no. 3 (Third Quarter 1992): 21–36,

    Examines the erratic behavior of M2 in the 1990s and its implications for economic policy.

THE MONEY MARKET

CHAPTER PREVIEW

The early 1990s were interesting years for observing the workings of the money market. Between 1989 and mid-1992, the Fed used open market operations to reduce interest rates 23 times. It also lowered the discount rate to a 30-year low and even reduced reserve requirement ratios. Other participants in the money market were also on the move. Capital-constrained banks bid less aggressively for deposits, and the public moved massive amounts of funds out of bank deposits into bond and stock mutual funds.

This chapter examines the interaction of the Fed, banks, and the public in the money market. The chapter begins by reviewing all the factors that affect the position of the money demand and money supply curves. Then it groups these factors into three categories: variables controlled by the Fed, variables that describe the behavior of the public and banks, and variables that are determined in the real sector of the economy. The chapter examines how changes in the factors in each category affect the interest rate, the quantity of money, and the deposit rate. It expands on Chapter 9, which introduces the workings of the money market. The chapter ends by examining alternative practices of the Federal Reserve, under which the Fed targets either the quantity of money or the interest rate.

DETERMINANTS OF MONEY MARKET EQUILIBRIUM

Equilibrium in the money market means that money demand equals money supply. Money demand refers to the demand for *real* money balances, and money supply to the supply of *real* money balances. The intersection of the money demand and supply curves determines the interest rate and the real quantity of money, as shown in the left panel of Figure 22–1. The right panel shows the deposit rate curve, from which the deposit rate is determined given the interest rate. The equilibrium levels of the interest rate, the quantity of money, and the deposit rate depend on the position of the money demand and money supply curves and the deposit rate curve. Therefore, to find all the factors that affect the interest rate, the quantity of money, and the deposit rate, we must examine the factors that affect the positions of these curves.

Factors Affecting Money Demand

Chapter 7 introduces the factors affecting money demand and Chapters 20 and 21 extend that analysis. These chapters establish that the demand for money depends on the interest rate, the deposit rate, real income, and the collective variable (For simplicity we ignore wealth.):

$$M^d = M^d(i, r_D, Y, \mathcal{C}) \qquad (22\text{--}1)$$
$$\quad - \ + \ + \ +$$

In the new financial environment, the deposit rate itself depends on the interest rate, real income, the collective variable, the technology and regulatory index, and the reserve requirement ratio:

$$r_D = r_D(i, Y, \mathcal{C}, \mathfrak{TR}, rr) \qquad (22\text{--}2)$$
$$\quad + \ - \ - \ - \ -$$

**FIGURE 22–1
The Money Market
and the Deposit
Rate**

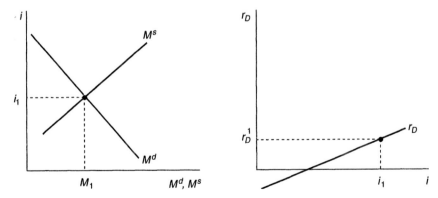

Equality between M^d and M^s determines the interest rate at i_1 in the left panel. The interest rate i_1 determines the deposit rate at r_D^1 in the right panel.

Therefore, five *ultimate factors* affect the demand for money, also called the *demand for real money balances:*

- Interest rate, i
- Real income, Y
- Collective variable, $\mathcal{C}$
- Technology and regulatory index, $\mathfrak{TR}$
- Reserve requirement ratio, rr

Equation 22–3 shows the money demand relation concisely. The sign under each variable indicates whether money demand varies positively or inversely with that variable. The negative sign under the interest rate denotes the negative slope of the money demand curve. Increases in the other factors shift the money demand curve to the right if the sign is positive and to the left if it is negative.

$$M^d = M^d(i, Y, \mathcal{C}, \mathfrak{TR}, rr) \tag{22-3}$$
$$\quad\quad\;\; - \;+\;+\; - \;-$$

Factors Affecting Money Supply

Chapters 8 and 15 establish the determinants of the money supply and summarize them in two equations, one for the supply of M1, the other for M2:

$$M1^s = Cur + (1/rr) \times (NBR/P + BR - ER) \tag{22-4}$$
$$M2^s = Cur + [(1+d2)/rr] \times (NBR/P + BR - ER) \tag{22-5}$$

Each measure of the money supply depends on the size of currency demanded by the public, *Cur*; the reserve requirement ratio, *rr*; and the quantity of effective reserves, which equals the sum of nonborrowed and borrowed reserves minus excess reserves, all expressed in real terms.[1] The M2 measure also depends on the ratio, $d2$, of nontransactions deposits, such as savings and time deposits, to transactions deposits, which are the checkable deposits that make up M1. Thus, both measures of the money supply depend on the determinants of nonborrowed reserves, borrowed reserves, and excess reserves, in addition to the reserve requirement ratio and the determinants of currency.

First, what are the determinants of nonborrowed reserves? Nominal nonborrowed reserves equal the Fed's holdings of U.S. Treasury securities, B_F, plus the reserves created by the net technical factors. The net technical factors equal the other sources of reserves (*OS*) minus the other uses of reserves (*OU*) and the nominal value of the quantity of currency held by the public (P $\times$ *Cur*); that is, the nominal value of the net technical factors is $OS - OU - P \times Cur$. In real terms, nonborrowed reserves are given by:

$$NBR/P = B_F/P + (OS - OU)/P - Cur$$

Borrowed reserves depend positively on the spread between the interest rate and the discount rate, $i - d$, and positively on the attitudes of the Fed and banks toward discount window loans, collectively represented by the index $\mathcal{A}$, called the *administrative index:*

---

[1] Because *NBR* is in nominal terms while *BR* and *ER* are in real terms, we must divide *NBR* by the price level, *P*, to express it in real terms so that all components of effective reserves are measured in the same units.

$$BR = BR(i - d, \mathcal{A})$$
$$\qquad\quad + \quad +$$

On the other hand, excess reserves depend negatively on the spread between the interest rate and the discount rate and positively on the index of prudence, $\mathcal{P}$, which represents the attitude of banks toward excess reserves:

$$ER = ER\ (i - d, \mathcal{P})$$
$$\qquad\quad - \quad +$$

Finally, currency in circulation depends positively on the level of real income, Y, and positively on the payments habits, $\mathcal{H}$, of the public:

$$Cur = Cur(Y, \mathcal{H})$$
$$\qquad\quad + \quad +$$

Thus, the following factors affect the money supply curve:

- Interest rate, i
- Fed's holdings of U.S. Treasury securities, B_F
- Technical factors OS and OU
- Price level, P
- Discount rate, d
- Administrative index, $\mathcal{A}$, affecting discount window loans
- Index of prudence, $\mathcal{P}$, affecting excess reserves
- Reserve requirement ratio, rr
- Real income, Y
- Payments habits, $\mathcal{H}$, of the public

Changes in the interest rate are depicted by a movement along the money supply curve. Other things equal, as the interest rate rises, the quantity of effective reserves rises because banks want to borrow more reserves from the Fed and to hold fewer excess reserves. As a result, the quantity of money supplied rises. Changes in the other factors shift the money supply curve. The factors listed above are common to the M1 and M2 measures of money. A change in the $d2$ ratio, on the other hand, affects only the M2 measure.

Grouping the Factors

To examine the effects of each of the shift factors on the interest rate, the quantity of real money balances, and the deposit rate, we group them according to whether they are policy variables controlled by the Fed, variables that describe the behavior of the public and banks, or variables that are determined in the real sector of the economy.

Four variables are policy instruments controlled by the Fed. They are the amount of Treasury securities held by the Fed, the discount rate, the reserve requirement ratio, and the administrative index for discount window loans.

Six variables are behavioral parameters that depend on the actions of the public or banks. They are the collective variable, which describes the portfolio decisions of the public; the technology and regulatory index, which describes the cost of funding deposits for banks and therefore affects money demand through the deposit rate; the index of prudence, which affects excess reserves; and the payments habits of the public, which affect currency. Even the administrative index belongs here when it refers to the attitude of banks about discount window loans. Finally, the other sources and other uses of reserves are also in this category, because they are factors not controlled by the Fed.

In the last category, *two variables are real-sector variables that describe conditions in the goods and services market*: the price level and real income.

CHANGES IN THE INSTRUMENTS OF MONETARY POLICY

The Fed influences the economy through changes in policy instruments that affect the availability or cost of reserves. Changes in the Fed's holding of Treasury securities, the discount rate, or the administrative control of the discount window shift only the money supply curve. On the other hand, changes in the reserve requirement ratio are more complex because, in the new financial environment, they shift both the money supply and the money demand curve. The Fed, however, changes the reserve requirement ratio infrequently.

Open market operations are the primary instrument of monetary policy. Therefore, our analysis of the effects of changes in the shift factors begins with an open market operation by the Fed that increases nominal nonborrowed reserves, *NBR*.

Open Market Operations

Suppose that, other things equal, the Fed purchases in the open market a quantity of Treasury securities equal to ΔB_F, increasing the Fed's holdings of Treasury securities from B_F^1 to B_F^2. The M^s curve will shift to right.

At the original interest rate, i_1, the Fed's open market purchase of securities will increase the money supply by $(1/rr)\Delta B_F$. Other things equal, this amount equals the size of the excess supply of money, represented by the horizontal distance between point 1 and point 1′ in the left panel of Figure 22–2. According to the principle of excess supply, the interest rate falls when there is excess supply of money (*ESM*). Schematically,

$$B_F\uparrow \rightarrow M^s\uparrow \rightarrow ESM \rightarrow i\downarrow$$

When the interest rate falls, the demanders of money want to hold a larger quantity of deposits because the opportunity cost of deposits falls (although by less than the fall in the interest rate, because the deposit rate also falls). Thus, the quantity of money demanded increases, as shown by a movement along the money demand curve from point 1 to point 2. On the other hand, a fall in the interest rate reduces effective reserves because banks want to hold more excess reserves and fewer borrowed reserves. Thus, the quantity of money supplied falls when the interest rate falls, as shown by a movement along the new money supply curve, from point 1′ to point 2.

At point 2 the excess supply of money has been eliminated. The equilibrium interest rate has fallen from i_1 to i_2, and the equilibrium quantity of money has risen from M_1 to M_2. Of course, the net increase in the quantity of money is less than $(1/rr)\Delta B_F$ because of the reduction in effective reserves induced by the fall in the interest rate.

The fall in the interest rate also causes a reduction in the deposit rate, but by less than the interest rate. This reduction is shown as a downward movement along the initial r_D

**FIGURE 22–2
An Open Market
Operation**

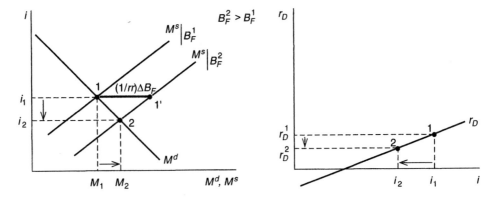

An open market purchase of securities by the Fed lowers the equilibrium interest rate and the equilibrium deposit rate, and increases the equilibrium quantity of money.

curve, from $r_D{}^1$ to $r_D{}^2$ in the right panel of Figure 22–2. To summarize schematically the final result of an increase in B_F:

$$B_F\!\uparrow \Rightarrow \begin{array}{c} i\!\downarrow \\ r_D\!\downarrow \\ M\!\uparrow \end{array}$$

Discount Window Operations	The Federal Reserve has two tools to influence the quantity of discount window loans: the discount rate, d, and the administrative index, $\mathscr{A}$. Each of these tools appears only in the money supply relation and, hence, affects only the M^s curve.

Discount Rate Policy   Consider first a change in the discount rate, in particular, an increase in d. Point 1 represents the initial equilibrium in the two panels of Figure 22–3. After the increase in the discount rate and at the original level of the interest rate, i_1, banks will reduce their borrowings from the Fed. They will also increase their holdings of excess reserves because the opportunity cost, $i - d$, of excess reserves falls. Other things equal, the reduction in borrowed reserves and the increase in excess reserves causes a reduction in effective reserves. As a result, the money supply falls, which means the M^s curve shifts inward in the left panel of Figure 22–3. At the interest rate i_1, there is now excess demand for money, shown by the horizontal distance between point 1 and point 1'. According to the principle of excess demand, the interest rate rises when there is excess demand for money (*EDM*). Schematically,

$$d\!\uparrow \rightarrow BR\!\downarrow \text{ and } ER\!\uparrow \rightarrow M^s\!\downarrow \rightarrow EDM \rightarrow i\!\uparrow$$

The increase in the interest rate leads to an indirect increase in effective reserves. At the higher interest rate, banks want to hold fewer excess reserves. They also will want to borrow more reserves from the Fed, partially offsetting the reduction in borrowed reserves and the increase in excess reserves from the higher discount rate. The increase in

FIGURE 22–3
An Increase in the
Discount Rate

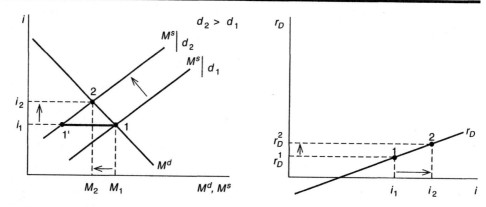

An increase in the discount rate raises the equilibrium interest rate and the equilibrium deposit rate, and reduces the equilibrium quantity of money.

the quantity of money supplied brought about by the rise in the interest rate is shown by the movement along the new money supply curve, from point $1'$ to point 2. In the end, the equilibrium quantity of money supply falls from M_1 to M_2. The public willingly holds this smaller quantity of money because the interest rate and the opportunity cost of deposits have risen. The left panel of Figure 22–3 shows the increase in the interest rate, from i_1 to i_2, and the right panel depicts the associated increase in the deposit rate. Schematically, the results of a discount rate increase are:

$$d\uparrow \Rightarrow \begin{matrix} i\uparrow \\ r_D\uparrow \\ M\downarrow \end{matrix}$$

Quantitative Administration of the Discount Window   A change in the discount rate by the Fed is very visible. On the other hand, because the discount rate is often below market rates of interest, the Fed also rations discount window loans directly, as Chapter 18 discusses. A tightening of the administration of the discount window, represented by an increase in the administrative index, $\mathcal{A}$, reduces borrowed reserves, other things equal. As a result, effective reserves fall and the money supply curve shifts to the left. At the original equilibrium interest rate, there will be excess demand for money, which causes the interest rate to rise. Schematically,

$$\mathcal{A}\uparrow \rightarrow BR\downarrow \rightarrow M^s\downarrow \rightarrow EDM \rightarrow i\uparrow$$

The higher interest rate leads to a higher deposit rate, while the quantity of money falls. Because the mechanics of the graphs are the same as those shown in Figure 22–3, only a schematic summary is given in this case:

$$\mathcal{A}\uparrow \Rightarrow \begin{matrix} i\uparrow \\ r_D\uparrow \\ M\downarrow \end{matrix}$$

Changes in the Reserve Requirement Ratio

A change in the reserve requirement ratio is more complicated to analyze because it shifts not only the money supply curve, but also the deposit rate curve and the money demand curve. An increase in the reserve requirement ratio shifts the money supply curve to the left because it reduces the simple money multiplier, $1/rr$, which has a drastic negative effect on the money supply.

The effects on money demand work through the deposit rate. An increase in rr acts like a tax on bank profits, reducing the quantity of deposits banks want to issue and, therefore, the deposit rate. As a result, the curve for the deposit rate shifts down: At the original equilibrium interest rate, the deposit rate is lower, as shown by the movement from point 1 to point 1' in the right panel of Figure 22–4. And the money demand curve shifts inward because, at the original interest rate, the lower deposit rate reduces the demand for money.

The effect on the quantity of money is unambiguous. The quantity of money definitely falls because of the inward shifts of the money supply and the money demand curves, as shown in the left panel of Figure 22–4. The effect on the interest rate is not clearcut, however, without further assumptions. Schematically,

$$rr\uparrow \rightarrow M^s\downarrow \rightarrow EDM \rightarrow i\uparrow$$
$$rr\uparrow \rightarrow r_D\downarrow \rightarrow M^d\downarrow \rightarrow ESM \rightarrow i\downarrow$$

Figure 22–4 shows the interest rate rising, which is the usual assumption, because of the large effect a reduction in the reserve requirement ratio has on the money supply curve. When the interest rate rises, however, two effects of an increase in rr pull the deposit rate in the opposite direction: There is a downward shift of the r_D curve from point 1 to point 1', and a movement upward along the new r_D curve from point 1' to point 2. Figure 22–4 shows the deposit rate rising on net, which is one possibility.

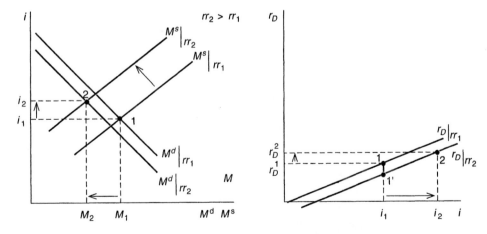

FIGURE 22–4
An Increase in the Reserve Requirement Ratio

An increase in rr reduces the equilibrium quantity of money. The equilibrium interest rate and deposit rate may rise, fall, or remain unchanged.

Schematically, the results of an increase in rr are:

$$rr\uparrow \Rightarrow \begin{matrix} i? \\ r_D? \\ M\downarrow \end{matrix}$$

CHANGES IN THE BEHAVIOR OF THE PUBLIC AND BANKS

The next category of factors affecting the financial sector is a host of shocks resulting from exogenous changes in the behavior of the public or banks. For example, the public may decide to hold more deposits and fewer securities, or to hold more currency and fewer deposits. And banks may try to issue more deposits and fund more loans, or to hold more excess reserves and to fund fewer loans. All of these changes in behavior will affect the interest rate, the deposit rate, and the quantity of money.

Money Demand Shocks

Consider first the two money demand shocks. One is a change in the portfolio decisions of the public, represented by a change in the collective variable. The other is a change in the technology and regulatory index that affects money demand only through the deposit rate.

Changes in the Portfolio Decisions of the Public   In the mid-1970s, improvements in cash management technology led the public to shift funds out of bank deposits into securities. In 1982, on the other hand, increased uncertainty about the state of the economy increased the demand for deposits and reduced the demand for securities. After the stock market crash of 1987, there was a flight to quality, in which the public again increased its demand for bank deposits and reduced its demand for securities. On the other hand, in the early 1990s, the public increased its appetite for risk, demonstrated by a movement from bank deposits to bond and stock mutual funds. All of these shifts are represented by a change in the collective variable in our model. According to our convention for the collective variable, shocks that increase the demand for deposits and reduce the demand for securities, other things equal, are represented by an increase in $\mathscr{C}$; those that reduce the demand for deposits and increase the demand for securities by an increase in $\mathscr{C}$.

The two panels of Figure 22–5 show the effects of an increase in $\mathscr{C}$. In the right panel, the deposit rate curve shifts downward because the increase in the demand for deposits results in a lower deposit rate, other things equal. The lower deposit rate mitigates, but does not offset, the original increase in the demand for deposits. As a result, the money demand curve shifts to the right. At the original interest rate, i_1, there is excess demand in the money market, as shown in the left panel of Figure 22–5. In response, the interest rate rises to i_2. Schematically,

$$\mathscr{C}\uparrow \rightarrow M^d\uparrow \rightarrow EDM \rightarrow i\uparrow$$

The higher interest rate is responsible for the greater quantity of money supplied, shown by a movement along the supply curve from point 1 to point 2. The net effect on the deposit rate, however, is ambiguous because the rise in the interest rate induces an increase in the deposit rate, depicted by a movement along the new lower deposit rate curve, from point 1′ to point 2 in the right panel. Whether the deposit rate rises sufficiently to negate the initial fall is an empirical matter.

FIGURE 22–5
An Increase in the
Collective Variable,
$\mathcal{C}$

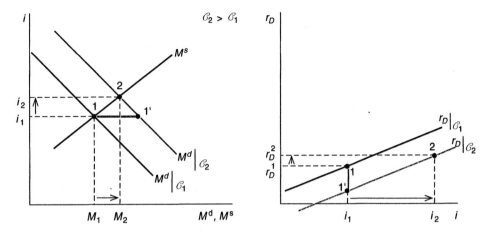

An exogenous increase in the demand for deposits by the public increases the equilibrium levels of the interest rate and the quantity of money. The equilibrium level of the deposit rate may rise, fall, or remain unchanged.

Schematically, the results of an increase in $\mathcal{C}$ are:

$$\mathcal{C}\uparrow \Rightarrow \begin{array}{l} i\uparrow \\ r_D? \\ M\uparrow \end{array}$$

Changes in the Technology and Regulatory Index   Changes in the portfolio behavior of the public are the most direct and obvious examples of shifts in money demand. In the new financial environment, however, the money demand curve will also shift if there is a change in the cost of banking brought about by changes in technology or regulation. For example, increases in provisions for loans losses and in deposit insurance premiums in the early 1990s, represented by a rise in $\mathfrak{IR}$, increased the marginal cost of issuing deposits, which lowered the deposit rate, as Chapters 7 and 21 discuss. Figure 22–6 illustrates this case. In the right panel, the deposit rate curve shifts down, and in the left panel, the money demand curve shifts to the left because of the lower deposit rate. As a result, at the interest rate i_1, there is excess supply in the money market and the interest rate falls. Schematically,

$$\mathfrak{IR}\uparrow \rightarrow r_D\downarrow \rightarrow M^d\downarrow \rightarrow ESM \rightarrow i\downarrow$$

The quantity of money supplied falls because of the lower interest rate. And the deposit rate falls even more, as shown by the movement from point 1′ to point 2 along the lower deposit rate curve. Schematically,

$$\mathfrak{IR}\uparrow \Rightarrow \begin{array}{l} i\downarrow \\ r_D\downarrow \\ M\downarrow \end{array}$$

FIGURE 22–6
An Increase in the
Technology and
Regulatory Index,
$\mathfrak{TR}$

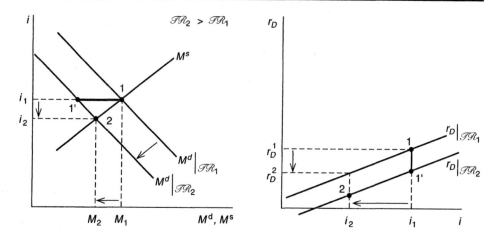

An increase in $\mathfrak{TR}$ caused by an increase in technological and regulatory cost reduces the interest rate, the deposit rate, and the quantity of money.

GlobalWatch 22.1 explains how a $\mathfrak{TR}$ shock was one of several disturbances to the money market in Japan in 1993.

Money Supply
Shocks

The remaining shocks affect the supply of money. The index of banking prudence, $\mathscr{P}$, affects the money supply through the quantity of excess reserves that banks want to hold. On the other hand, changes in the other sources and other uses of reserves affect nonborrowed reserves. Finally, a change in the payments habits of the public that alters the amount of currency demanded affects both the currency component of the money supply and the quantity of nonborrowed reserves, because currency is a technical factor affecting reserves.

Changes in the Reserve Management Decisions of Banks   An increase in the degree of prudence exercised by banks in their asset-management decisions, that is, an increase in $\mathscr{P}$, increases their demand for excess reserves and reduces their demand for loans. As Chapters 8 and 18 note, banks increased their demand for excess reserves following the introduction of contemporaneous reserve accounting by the Fed in 1984. A rise in excess reserves reduces effective reserves, thereby reducing the money supply, other things equal. (The money supply curve shifts to the left.) At the initial equilibrium level of the interest rate, there will be excess demand in the money market. As a consequence, the interest rate rises and the quantity of money falls. The higher level of the interest rate induces an increase in the deposit rate. Schematically, the results are:

$$\mathscr{P}{\uparrow} \Rightarrow \begin{matrix} i{\uparrow} \\ r_D{\uparrow} \\ M{\downarrow} \end{matrix}$$

GlobalWatch 22.1
Shocks to the Japanese Money Market in 1993

"In spite of continued monetary easing and the subsequent decline in the general level of interest rates, including lending rates, to an historical low, indicators such as the growth rates of monetary aggregates and bank lending have not rallied. This is a clear divergence from trends observed in previous periods of monetary easing."*

Governor Yasushi Mieno, governor of the Bank of Japan, made these comments on December 7, 1993, in a speech to the Capital Markets Research Institute in Tokyo. The divergence to which the governor refers came from tens of billions of dollars of bad real estate loans on the books of Japanese banks in the wake of

the bursting of the "bubble economy." Making provisions for bad loans increased the cost of issuing deposits for Japanese banks. This shock, represented by an increase in the technology and regulatory index in our model, led to lower deposit rates as banks bid less aggressively for deposits and made fewer loans. The lower deposit rates, in turn, reduced money demand. At the same time, a reduction of the discount rate to a record low of 1.75 percent in 1993 shifted the money supply curve outward. Both forces led to falling interest rates and deposit rates, as the accompanying graph shows.

The weak money growth referred to by the governor stemmed from reductions in money demand, which tempered the increase in money supply from the more stimulative monetary policy. Money demand was weak not only because of a rise in the technology and regulatory index, but also because there was no growth in real income in Japan in 1993. As a result, the broad measure of money (M2 + CDs) grew by a modest 1.1 percent, while the narrow measure of money (M1) grew at the slightly faster pace of 3.0 percent in 1993.

* Yasushi Mieno, "Roles of Financial and Capital Markets under Current Japanese Monetary and Economic Conditions," *Bank of Japan Quarterly Bulletin*, February 1994, 7.

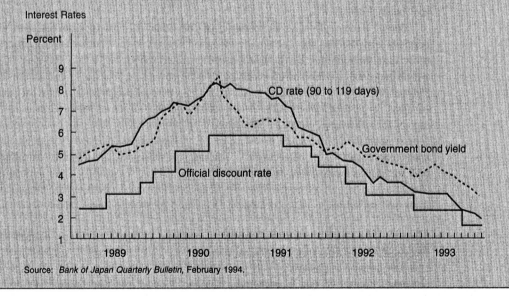

Source: *Bank of Japan Quarterly Bulletin*, February 1994.

The attitude of banks about borrowed reserves is also part of their reserve management decisions. Although the shift parameter $\mathcal{A}$ usually refers to the Fed's management of the discount window, it also represents how banks manage borrowed reserves. As Chapter 18 shows, an increased reluctance by banks to borrow reserves at any given spread between the interest rate and the discount rate is represented by an increase in $\mathscr{A}$. As a result, effective reserves fall and the money supply curve shifts to the left, which causes the interest rate and the deposit rate to rise and the quantity of money to fall. Chapter 18 notes two cases in the 1980s when banks increased their reluctance to borrow from the Fed. The first instance followed the collapse of Continental Illinois Bank in 1984, and the second followed the drop in the stock market in 1987.

TRY IT OUT 22.1

With the help of a graph of the money market, explain how the Fed can use open market operations to offset the effect on the interest rate of an increase in the demand for excess reserves by banks. What will be the effect on the quantity of money?

Changes in the Other Sources and Other Uses of Reserves   Changes in the other sources and other uses of reserves also affect the quantity of effective reserves and, thus, the money supply. The other sources and other uses of reserves, however, are technical factors that work through nonborrowed reserves. Chapter 8 introduces the technical factors and Chapter 14 discusses them in more detail. Most of the other sources of reserves are assets in the Fed's balance sheet and most of the other uses are liabilities in that balance sheet.

Federal Reserve float is an example of the other sources of reserves, and Treasury deposits with the Fed are an example of the other uses. If the check-clearing process takes more time than allotted by the Fed's predetermined schedule, Federal Reserve float rises, which increases nonborrowed reserves. Nonborrowed reserves also rise if the Treasury reduces its deposits with the Fed to make payments to the private sector for goods and services. In general, an increase in any of the other sources of reserves or a decrease in any of the other uses increases the quantity of nonborrowed reserves. The effects on the money market are the same as an increase in nonborrowed reserves brought about by open market purchases of securities: The interest rate falls, the quantity of money rises, and the deposit rate falls. If the Fed wants to offset these effects, it must engage in defensive open market operations. To keep nonborrowed reserves unchanged, the Fed must sell securities to offset the reserves created by the technical factors.

Changes in the Payments Habits of Society   Currency in circulation is also a technical factor affecting nonborrowed reserves. Unlike the other sources and uses of reserves, however, currency itself is a component of the money supply. A change in the payments habits, $\mathscr{H}$, that increases the demand for currency and reduces the demand for deposits does not affect the size of money demand, but it does affect the money supply. For example, suppose that an increase in the volume of illegal transactions increases the demand for currency and reduces the demand for deposits. The left panel of Figure 22–7 shows that the money supply curve shifts to the left. The reason, of course, is that every dollar increase in currency reduces nonborrowed reserves and, thus, effective reserves by a dollar. Deposits fall by a multiple of a dollar so that, on net, the money supply falls,

FIGURE 22–7
Change in
Payments Habits

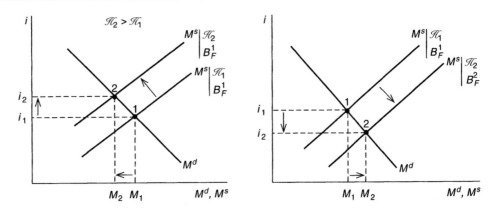

The left panel shows the effects of an increase in currency in circulation if the Fed does not react. The right panel shows the effects if the Fed uses defensive open market operations to offset the effect on nonborrowed reserves.

other things equal. The leftward shift of the M^s curve results in an increase in the interest rate and a decrease in the quantity of money. The deposit rate also rises. The schematic results are:

$$\mathscr{H}\uparrow \Rightarrow \begin{array}{c} i\uparrow \\ r_D\uparrow \\ M\downarrow \end{array}$$

The results will be different if the Fed engages in a defensive open market purchase of securities to offset the effect of the increase in currency on effective reserves, as it typically does. In this case, the supply of money will shift to the right by the amount of the increase in the demand for currency. The equilibrium level of the quantity of money will rise by the amount of the increase in the demand for currency, and the equilibrium levels of the interest rate and the deposit rate will fall. The right panel of Figure 22–7 shows this case.

CHANGES IN REAL-SECTOR VARIABLES

The price level and real income are the two factors denoting real-sector conditions. They are parameters when we consider the financial sector by itself. However, the price level and real income become market-determined variables when we add the goods and services market to the framework, as in Chapter 10.

Changes in the
Price Level

Consider first a change in the price level, which is easier to analyze. The price level, P, appears only in the money supply relation. Given the nominal quantity of nonborrowed reserves, NBR, an increase in the price level, from P_1 to P_2, reduces the real quantity of nonborrowed reserves, NBR/P. The fall in NBR/P reduces effective reserves, thereby reducing the money supply; the money supply curve shifts to the left. Other things equal, the fall in the money supply registers as an excess demand for money (that is, a shortfall of supply), which is eliminated by a rise in the equilibrium level of the interest rate. Schematically,

$$P\uparrow \rightarrow (NBR/P)\downarrow \rightarrow M^s\downarrow \rightarrow EDM \rightarrow i\uparrow$$

The leftward shift of the money supply curve reduces the quantity of money, while the increase in the interest rate raises the deposit rate. In sum,

$$P\uparrow \Rightarrow \begin{array}{c} i\uparrow \\ r_D\uparrow \\ M^s\downarrow \end{array}$$

Changes in Real Income

Examining the effects of an increase in the level of income is more complicated because a change in Y not only shifts the money demand curve but may also shift the money supply curve. An increase in real income increases both the currency component and the deposit component of money demand. Hence, the money demand curve shifts to the right, as shown in the left panel of Figure 22–8. Without a reaction by the Fed, an increase in currency will also shift the money supply curve to the left. Economists, however, usually work with a simple case in which an increase in Y shifts only the money demand curve. This simple case assumes that the Fed engages in defensive open market operations to offset the effect of any increase in currency on the supply of money. Therefore, the money supply curve does not shift.[2] As a result, at the initial equilibrium interest rate, i, there is excess demand for money equal to the horizontal distance between point 1 and point 1′, which causes the interest rate to rise. Schematically,

$$Y\uparrow \rightarrow M^d\uparrow \rightarrow EDM \rightarrow i\uparrow$$

Of course, the quantity of money supplied also increases when the interest rate rises. Finally, what about the deposit rate? The effect on the deposit rate is indeterminate. The rise in real income lowers the deposit rate, while the rise in the interest rate raises it, as the right panel of Figure 22–8 shows. Schematically,

$$Y\uparrow \Rightarrow \begin{array}{c} i\uparrow \\ r_D? \\ M\uparrow \end{array}$$

TARGETING MONEY VERSUS TARGETING THE INTEREST RATE OR DOING NOTHING

This chapter has examined the effects on the interest rate and the quantity of money of changes in the instruments of monetary policy and changes in the behavioral parameters separately. This section inquires how the Fed can use open market operations to keep the interest rate and the quantity of money unchanged in the face of expected or unexpected

---

[2] If the Fed used defensive open market operations to offset the effect of an increase in currency on nonborrowed reserves instead of on the quantity of money, the M^s curve would shift to the right by the amount of the increase in currency. Of course, this would be less than the amount by which the M^d curve shifts to the right.

FIGURE 22–8
Increase in Real
Income

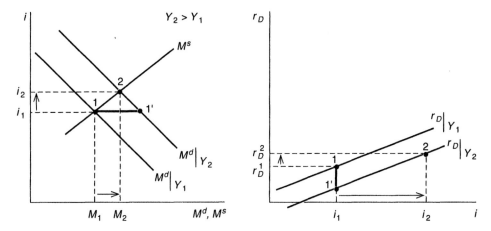

An increase in real income increases the equilibrium interest rate and the equilibrium quantity of money. The equilibrium deposit rate may rise, fall, or remain unchanged.

money demand shocks (due to changes in C and $\mathcal{IR}$). The short answer is that the Fed cannot do both. The Fed cannot keep both the quantity of money and the interest rate unchanged in the face of a shift in money demand. It is easy to see why. An increase, say, in C increases both the interest rate and the quantity of money. If the Fed sells securities, it will reduce the quantity of money, but it will also further increase the interest rate. On the other hand, if the Fed buys securities, it can restore the interest rate to its initial level, but it will further increase the quantity of money. Thus, the Fed must choose to keep either the interest rate or the quantity of money fixed. Of course, the Fed can also do nothing, in which case the interest rate and the quantity of money both rise.

Figure 22–9 illustrates these three scenarios. Point 1 is the initial equilibrium in the money market with the interest rate at i_1 and the quantity of money at M_1. If the Fed does not intervene, an increase in the collective factor from C_1 to C_2 will establish a new equilibrium at point 2, with an increase in the interest rate to i_2 and the quantity of money to M_2. Point 2 is the equilibrium if the Fed does nothing. If, instead, the Fed wants to restore the quantity of money to its original level, M_1, it must sell securities in the open market to reduce B_F to the level B_F^2. This open market operation shifts the money supply curve to the left, establishing equilibrium at point 3. At this point, the quantity of money is at its initial level, but the interest rate has risen to i_3. On the other hand, starting from equilibrium at point 2, if the Fed wants to reduce the interest rate to its initial level, i_1, the Fed must *buy* securities, increasing B_F to B_F^3. The consequent increase in the money supply establishes equilibrium at point 4. Restoring the interest rate to its original level, however, further increases the quantity of money, to M_3.

A Numerical Example

To gain a deeper understanding of the results in Figure 22–9, consider the following hypothetical numerical example. Suppose that Equation 22–6 represents the money supply equation after incorporating specific values for all factors except the interest rate and the quantity of nonborrowed reserves:

FIGURE 22–9
Targeting the
Quantity of Money
versus Targeting
Interest Rate

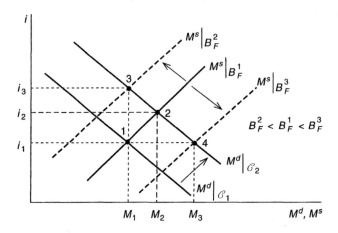

Point 1 is initial equilibrium in the money market. As a consequence of
a positive shift in money demand, the new equilibrium is at point 2 if
the Fed does not react, at point 3 if the Fed targets the quantity of
money, and at point 4 if the Fed targets the interest rate.

$$M^s = 300 + 4i + 10NBR \tag{22–6}$$

Also, suppose that Equation 22–7 represents money demand:

$$M^d = 933 - 0.25i + 0.2\mathcal{C} \tag{22–7}$$

Initial Equilibrium   To solve for the initial interest rate, we need the initial values of
nonborrowed reserves and the collective variable. Suppose they are:

NBR = $60 billion
$\mathcal{C}$ = 100 points

Substituting these values into Equations 22–6 and 22–7 yields the money supply and
money demand equations as functions solely of the interest rate:

$$M^s = 900 + 4i \tag{22–8}$$
$$M^d = 953 - 0.25i \tag{22–9}$$

Setting M^s equal to M^d, and solving for i, the initial equilibrium interest rate is:

i_1 = 12.47 percent

Substituting this value into either the money demand or money supply equation, the
equilibrium quantity of money is:

M_1 = $949.882 billion

Point 1 in Figure 22–9 depicts this equilibrium.

An Increase in $\mathcal{C}$ Now assume that $\mathcal{C}$ rises to 110 points. First examine what happens to the interest rate and the quantity of money if the Fed keeps nonborrowed reserves at their initial level of $60 billion. The money supply equation remains the same as Equation 22–8, but money demand changes because the value of $\mathcal{C}$ in Equation 22–7 is 110. The new equilibrium is described by the following equations:

$$M^s = 900 + 4i \tag{22–8}$$
$$M^d = 955 - 0.25i \tag{22–10}$$

Solving these two equations for i and M yields new equilibrium values of the interest rate and the quantity of money:

$i_2 = 12.94$ percent
$M_2 = \$951.764$ billion

As expected, the interest rate and the quantity of money rise, as depicted by point 2 in Figure 22–9. Point 2 is the equilibrium if the Fed does nothing in response to a money demand shock.

Targeting the Quantity of Money   Next, consider what happens if the Fed targets the quantity of money, with the initial quantity of $949.882 billion as the target. First, set the money demand Equation 22–10 equal to the money supply target to find the interest rate associated with keeping the quantity of money fixed when the collective variable rises to 110 points:

$955 - 0.25i = 949.882$
$i_3 = 20.47$ percent

This is the value of the interest rate at point 3 in Figure 22–9, which, as expected, is higher than at point 2.

Substituting 20.47 percent for the interest rate in Equation 22–6 and 949.882 for the quantity of money yields the level of nonborrowed reserves that can achieve the Fed's target for money.

$$M^s = 300 + 4i + 10NBR \tag{22–6}$$
$949.882 = 300 + (4 \times 20.47) + 10NBR$
$NBR_3 = \$56.800$ billion

Of course, the level of nonborrowed reserves at point 3 is less than at points 1 and 2. Subtracting $56.8 billion from the initial quantity of $60 billion gives the size of the open market sale of U.S. Treasury securities: The Fed must sell $3.2 billion worth of U.S. Treasury securities in the open market.

Targeting the Interest Rate   Finally, we illustrate point 4 in Figure 22–9 by finding how much the quantity of nonborrowed reserves and the quantity of money must increase if the Fed targets the interest rate instead of the quantity of money. The initial interest rate of 12.47 percent is the targeted rate. We know that when the collective variable rises to 110 points, the interest rate rises to 12.94 percent with nonborrowed reserves fixed. The

Fed must therefore purchase securities in the open market to bring the interest rate back to its original level. To find the size of the open market purchase, first use the money demand equation to find the quantity of money. With the collective variable at 110 points, money demand is:

$$M^d = 955 - 0.25i$$

Setting i equal to its targeted value of 12.47 percent gives the quantity of money at point 4:

$$M_3 = \$951.882 \text{ billion}$$

As expected, the quantity of money at point 4 is higher than at point 2.

To find the quantity of *NBR* that achieves this quantity of money, turn again to the money supply equation:

$$M^s = 300 + 4i + 10NBR$$

Substituting $951.882 for M^s and 12.47 percent for i, the quantity of nonborrowed reserves associated with the interest rate target is:

$$NBR = \$60.200$$

Because *NBR* was initially $60 billion, the Fed must purchase $0.2 billion worth of U.S. Treasury securities in the open market.

Uncertain Money Demand

Our example illustrated the effects of an increase in money demand. Analogous results follow from a reduction in the collective variable and a fall in money demand. If the Fed does not intervene, both the interest rate and the quantity of money fall. If the Fed targets the quantity of money, it must engage in an open market purchase of securities to increase the money supply. This open market purchase of securities, however, further reduces the interest rate. If the Fed targets the interest rate, it must sell securities in the open market and further reduce the money supply.

Given these results, we can extend our analysis to examine a commitment by the Fed to target the quantity of money or the interest rate *in the face of either an increase or a decrease in the collective variable*. Such examination shows that targeting the quantity of money effectively makes the money supply curve vertical. On the other hand, targeting the interest rate makes the money supply curve horizontal.

Figure 22–10 illustrates the case of monetary targeting. Suppose the money market is at equilibrium at point A with the interest rate at i_1 and the quantity of money at M_1. The current level of the collective variable is $\mathcal{C}_1$, and the Fed's holdings of U.S. Treasury securities equal $B_F{}^1$. Now suppose that there is uncertainty about the size of the collective variable and, hence, uncertainty about the position of the money demand curve. Let us assume that the collective variable can be as low as $\mathcal{C}_2$ and as high as $\mathcal{C}_3$. If the Fed's target for the quantity of money is M_1, the Fed must increase B_F when $\mathcal{C}$ falls and reduce B_F when $\mathcal{C}$ rises. As a result, the equilibrium in the money market can be as low as point B or as high as point C. In effect, the Fed's policy transforms the money supply curve from upward sloping to vertical. There is a price, however, to be paid for achieving the monetary target. The interest rate becomes volatile: It can be as low as i_2 and as high as i_3.

FIGURE 22–10
Targeting the
Quantity of Money

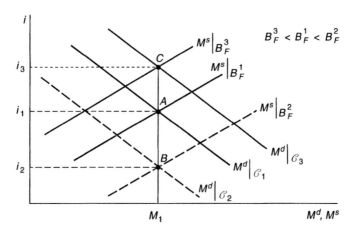

If the collective variable affecting money demand ranges from c_2 to c_3, the
interest rate will vary from i_2 to i_3 when the Fed targets the quantity of
money.

Figure 22–11 examines a money market prone to the same money demand shocks, but
with the Fed targeting the interest rate by fixing it at its initial equilibrium level of i_1.
Every time money demand rises, threatening an increase in the interest rate, the Fed buys
securities, which increases the money supply and restores the interest rate to its targeted
level. Similarly, every time money demand falls, threatening a decrease in the interest
rate, the Fed sells securities and reduces the quantity of money. With this policy, the
equilibrium points lie along a horizontal line passing through the initial equilibrium point
A, thereby effectively transforming the money supply to a horizontal curve.

In Figures 22–10 and 22–11, changes in the collective variable cause the shifts in the
money demand curve. The results are the same, however, if we change the labels of the
money demand curves so that changes in real income, instead of changes in the behavior
of the public, shift the money demand curve. An increase in Y increases the demand for
money, which leads to an increase in the quantity of money and the interest rate. If the
Fed targets the quantity of money, it must reduce the money supply, further increasing the
interest rate. A fall in Y reduces money demand, causing a fall in the interest rate and in
the quantity of money. If the Fed targets the quantity of money, it must increase the
money supply, which further reduces the interest rate.

Suppose, instead, that the Fed targets the interest rate. If real income rises, money demand
rises, causing an increase in the interest rate, requiring the Fed to intervene to increase the
money supply and lower the interest rate. If real income falls, money demand and the interest
rate fall, requiring the Fed to intervene to lower the money supply and raise the interest rate.

One Rule for All Reasons?

How should the Fed react to shifts in money demand? Is it better to target the interest rate
or the quantity of money if the ultimate goals of monetary policy are full employment
and price stability? There is no uniformly superior target. If the source of the change in

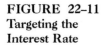

FIGURE 22–11
Targeting the
Interest Rate

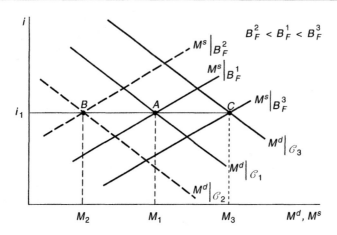

If the collective variable affecting money demand ranges from c_2 to c_3,
the quantity of money will range from M_2 to M_3 when the Fed targets
the interest rate.

money demand originates in the financial sector, the correct policy is to target the interest rate. If the source is in the real sector, however, targeting the quantity of money is the preferred policy. To see why, consider two reductions in money demand, one stemming from a fall in c because of behavioral changes, the other from a fall in real income. Assume that prior to the fall in money demand, real income (output) is at its full-employment level.

A fall in money demand caused by a reduction in c reduces both the interest rate and the quantity of money. The lower interest rate increases aggregate demand for goods and services, thereby overheating the economy. If the Fed targets the quantity of money, it must increase the money supply, causing a further fall in the interest rate and an additional increase in aggregate demand. Clearly, this is an inflationary policy. In contrast, if the Fed targets the interest rate when c falls, it must reduce the money supply to raise the interest rate, thereby reducing aggregate demand. This policy keeps output at its full-employment level without inflation. Thus, targeting the interest rate is the correct strategy in the face of a shock originating from changes in the portfolio preferences of the public. It insulates the real sector from money demand shocks originating in the financial sector.

In contrast, when the shock originates in the real sector, changes in the interest rate dampen the effect on aggregate demand. If the Fed targets the interest rate, it prevents these built-in stabilizing forces from working. For example, suppose that a reduction in consumer or business confidence lowers aggregate demand for goods and services, which causes output and income to fall. The fall in real income reduces money demand, causing a fall in the interest rate and in the quantity of money. The fall in the interest rate acts as a shock absorber by cushioning the original reduction in aggregate demand. If the Fed targets the interest rate, however, it must increase the interest rate (by reducing the money supply). An increase in the interest rate further reduces the demand for goods and services, which causes output to fall even more. Output moves away from, not toward, its potential level. If, instead, the Fed targets the quantity of money, it must increase the quantity of money. The increase in the quantity of money further reduces the interest rate, which stimulates aggregate demand and moves output back to its full-employment level.

In sum, there is no simple rule the Fed can follow to stabilize output in an economy subject to exogenous shocks. Interest rate targets are stabilizing when the shock originates in the money demand relationship, but destabilizing when the shock originates in the demand for goods and services. In contrast, monetary targets are destabilizing when the disturbance originates in the money demand relationship, but stabilizing when it originates in the demand for goods and services. Chapter 25 examines this issue in more detail with the help of a model of both the money market and the goods and services market.

SUMMARY

- Money market equilibrium, or financial-sector equilibrium, determines the interest rate, i; the quantity of money, M; and the deposit rate, r_D. The interest rate and the quantity of money are determined by the supply of and demand for money. The interest rate, in turn, determines the deposit rate by the deposit rate relation.

- Factors that shift the money demand and money supply curves affect the equilibrium values of i, M, and r_D. The factors that affect the deposit rate are accounted for because they are incorporated in the money demand relation.

- Among the shift factors affecting the equilibrium values of i, r_D, and M, are four policy parameters controlled by the Fed. They are the Fed's holdings of Treasury securities, B_F; the discount rate, d; the administrative control of the discount window, represented by the index $\mathcal{A}$; and the reserve requirement ratio, rr. (The index $\mathcal{A}$ does double duty because it also represents the attitude of banks about borrowed reserves.)

- Six shift factors are behavioral parameters that represent the decisions of the public or banks. First, the collective variable $\mathcal{C}$ is an index that represents the portfolio decisions of the public. An increase in $\mathcal{C}$ means that the public wants to hold more deposits and fewer securities. Second, the technology and regulatory index, $\mathfrak{R}$, affects the cost to banks of funding deposits and issuing loans. An increase in costs, represented by an increase in $\mathfrak{R}$, means that banks want to issue fewer deposits and fund fewer loans, which reduces the deposit rate and, hence, money demand. Third and fourth, the index of prudence, $\mathcal{P}$, and the administrative index, $\mathcal{A}$, represent the reserve man-

agement decisions of banks. An increase in $\mathcal{P}$ means that banks want to hold more excess reserves and acquire fewer securities. An increase in $\mathcal{A}$ means that banks are more reluctant to borrow from the Fed. Fifth, the index $\mathcal{H}$ represents the payments habits of society. An increase in $\mathcal{H}$ means that the public wants to hold more currency and fewer deposits. And sixth, the other sources (OS) and other uses (OU) of reserves are technical factors affecting nonborrowed reserves. An increase in OS or a decrease in OU increases nonborrowed reserves.

- The remaining two shift factors are real-sector variables. They are the price level, P, and the level of real GDP, Y.

- A change in the primary instrument of monetary policy, B_F, is a pure money supply shock. An open market purchase of securities by the Fed, which increases B_F, causes the interest rate and the deposit rate to fall and the quantity of money to rise. Other pure money supply shocks that have similar effects are a decrease in the discount rate, the administrative index, the index of prudence, or the price level.

- The shift factors $\mathcal{C}$ and $\mathfrak{R}$ are pure money demand shocks. An increase in $\mathcal{C}$ increases the interest rate and the quantity of money, but its effect on the deposit rate is an empirical matter. An increase in $\mathfrak{R}$, the technology and regulatory index, reduces the quantity of money, the interest rate, and the deposit rate.

- An increase in the price level, P, reduces the (real) quantity of money and increases the interest rate and the deposit rate.

- A rise in real income, Y, increases both the interest rate and the quantity of money, but the effect on the deposit rate is again an empirical matter.

- In the face of a money demand shock, the Fed loses control of the quantity of money if it targets (fixes) the interest rate. It loses control of the interest rate if it targets the quantity of money.

- Targeting the quantity of money, in effect, transforms the money supply curve to a vertical curve, while targeting the interest rate makes the money supply curve horizontal.

- Targeting the interest rate is a desirable policy if the Fed faces uncertain (volatile) money demand because of uncertainty about the portfolio preferences of the public or the technology and regulatory index.

- Targeting the quantity of money is a desirable policy if the Fed faces uncertain money demand because of uncertainty about the level of real income.

KEY TERMS AND CONCEPTS

This chapter applies concepts introduced in preceding chapters.

QUESTIONS AND PROBLEMS

1. "Sometimes we observe the interest rate and the quantity of money moving in the same direction and at other times in opposite directions." Explain and illustrate graphically.

The Wall Street Journal

2. The following statement is from "Fed Increases Interest Rates, Discloses Move," *The Wall Street Journal*, March 23, 1994: "Although the Fed wasn't explicit in its statement, its Open Market Committee decided to increase the benchmark federal-funds interest rate by ¼ percent point to 3½%. After holding rates steady for about a year and a half, the Fed raised the federal funds rate, at which banks lend to each other overnight, to 3¼% from 3% on February 4." Explain how the Fed implements an increase in the federal funds rate and what the effects are on the money market and the deposit rate relation.

3. Suppose that, other things equal, discount window loans fall because banks become more reluctant to borrow from the Fed. Explain and illustrate graphically the effects on the interest rate, the quantity of money, and the deposit rate.

4. "If the Fed reduces the reserve requirement ratio, the interest rate will definitely fall, but the effect on the quantity of money is uncertain." True or false? Explain and illustrate graphically.

5. Suppose that the demand for currency falls because of a reduction in illegal activities.
   a. What will happen to the money demand curve? The money supply curve?
   b. What will be the effects on the interest rate and the quantity of money if there is no reaction by the Fed?

6. Suppose that the U.S. Treasury's deposits with Federal Reserve banks increase because of an unexpected rush by Americans to pay their taxes early.
   a. If the Fed does not respond, what will happen to the interest rate, the deposit rate, and the quantity of money?
   b. Explain what will happen to the interest rate, the deposit rate, and the quantity of money if, instead, the Fed uses defensive open market operations to keep the quantity of nonborrowed reserves unchanged.

7. Suppose that the price level falls. What will be the effect on the interest rate and the deposit rate?

8. Suppose that the demand for securities rises because the public's appetite for risk increases.
   a. What will happen to the interest rate and the quantity of money if the Fed does not respond?
   b. What will happen to the interest rate and the quantity of money if the Fed targets the interest rate?

c. What will happen to the interest rate and the quantity of money if, instead, the Fed targets the quantity of money?

d. If the ultimate goal of monetary policy is to keep real output unchanged, what is the appropriate response by the Fed?

9. Suppose that banks must make increased provisions for loan losses. Also suppose that the Fed targets the quantity of money. What must the Fed do? Is this a good policy? Why?

10. Suppose that banks decide to hold fewer excess reserves because of a decrease in the prudence of bank managers. Given this, compare the effects if the Fed targets the interest rate with the effects if it targets the quantity of money.

11. Suppose that the following equations represent money demand and money supply (in billions of dollars):

$$M^d = 333 - 0.25i + 0.2\mathcal{C} + 0.10Y$$

$$M^s = 300 + 4i + 10NBR$$

a. If $\mathcal{C} = 100$, $Y = \$6,000$ billion per year, and $NBR = \$60$ billion, find the equilibrium levels of the interest rate, i, and the quantity of money M.

b. Suppose that Y falls to $5,980 billion per year. If the Fed does not react, what will happen to the interest rate and the quantity of money?

c. Suppose the Fed targets the interest rate and sets its target at the level you determined in *a*. Must the Fed buy or sell securities to achieve its target? Find the size of the open market operation needed to keep the interest rate fixed.

d. Suppose, instead, that the Fed targets the quantity of money and sets its target at the level you determined in *a*. Must the Fed buy or sell securities to achieve its target? Find the size of the open market operation needed to keep the quantity of money fixed.

e. If the full-employment level of output is $6,000 billion, which of the two policies is more desirable and why?

12. Suppose that the money demand and money supply equations are the same as in problem 11 and that the initial equilibrium is the one described in part *a* of that problem. Next, suppose that the collective factor falls to 90 points. If $6,000 billion is the full-employment level of real output, what should the Fed do and why?

SUGGESTED READINGS

Board of Governors of the Federal Reserve System, *Annual Report*. Each year's report has a section that explains developments in monetary policy and financial markets for the year.

Poole, William. "The Optimal Choice of Monetary Policy Instruments in a Simple Macro Model," *Quarterly Journal of Economics* 84 (May 1970): 192–216.

The classic paper on the issue of targeting interest rates versus targeting the quantity of money.

C H A P T E R   23

THE STRUCTURE OF RATES OF RETURN

CHAPTER PREVIEW

On the morning of April 18, 1994, the Federal Reserve announced that it would "increase slightly the degree of pressure on reserve positions." The Fed's action in the open market later that morning signaled that the Fed had raised its target for the federal funds rate from 3½ percent to 3¾ percent. In reaction interest rates on short- and long-term Treasury securities rose as their prices fell, and some large banks even raised their prime rate the same day. The tighter monetary policy also sent stock prices tumbling.

Previous chapters examine only two interest rates: the interest rate and the deposit rate. They show how the two rates are related and how they are affected by policy and other disturbances to the economy. Of course in the real world there are many assets and, hence, many rates of return; there is a spectrum of interest rates on debt securities and rates of return on equity securities. This chapter examines how these rates are related and how they are affected by policy and other shocks. Examining the interaction among financial markets belongs in the second pillar.

First this chapter examines the structure of interest rates by themselves. Chapter 6 shows that the demand for securities depends on their characteristics, such as length of time to maturity, credit risk, and liquidity. It is not surprising that interest rates on various debt securities are affected by these characteristics. The analysis of the structure of interest rates begins with an examination of the difference in interest rates that arises from differences in length of time to maturity, called the *term structure of interest rates*. Next the chapter examines the *default-risk structure of interest rates*, which refers to the differences arising from credit risk. It also shows how other factors, such as tax features, affect interest rates.

The chapter ends by reintroducing equity securities. Using a four-asset framework consisting of money, open-market debt securities, bank loans, and equity securities, it examines how the rate of return on equity securities moves with interest rates in response to changes in the instruments of monetary policy.

THE TERM STRUCTURE OF INTEREST RATES

The **term structure of interest rates** is the relation among interest rates on debt securities that differ only in the length of time to maturity. To isolate differences arising from the term to maturity, we must hold other characteristics, such as credit risk and special tax and redemption features, constant. Debt securities of different maturity issued by the same borrower usually possess the same credit risk. Because the only sizable borrower in all maturities is the federal government, analysis of the term structure usually focuses on U.S. government securities. These securities are free from default risk and usually not subject to early redemption.

The Yield Curve

The **yield curve** is a graphical depiction of the term structure of interest rates at a point in time. To construct a yield curve, we measure the length of time to maturity on the horizontal axis and the yield to maturity, or rate of interest, on the vertical axis, and then we plot the yields on comparable debt securities of different maturities. Thus, a yield curve depicts the yield to maturity.

Usually yield curves are upward sloping, as the curve in panel a of Figure 23–1 illustrates. An upward-sloping yield curve means that the longer the maturity of the security, the higher the interest rate. Occasionally, however, yield curves are horizontal, or flat, as the curve in panel b illustrates. And yield curves may even be downward

FIGURE 23–1
The Slope of Yield Curves

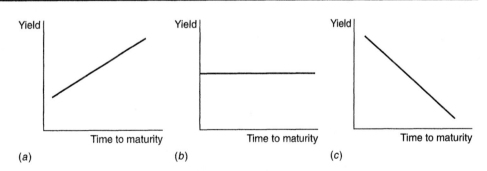

(a)   *(b)*   *(c)*

An upward-sloping yield curve, such as the one in panel *a*, means that long-term interest rates are higher than short-term rates. A flat yield curve, such as the one in panel *b*, indicates that interest rates are the same across the maturity spectrum. And an inverted yield curve, such as the one in panel *c*, indicates that short-term rates are higher than long-term rates.

MarketWatch 23.1

Tracking the Yield Curve in *The Wall Street Journal*

The daily "Credit Markets" column in *The Wall Street Journal* plots a graph of recent yield curves, as the accompanying graph from April 19, 1994, illustrates. The graph shows the yield curve for U.S. Treasury securities on April 18, 1994, one week earlier, and four weeks earlier. All three curves are upward sloping. The upward shift in the curves means that interest rates rose across the maturity spectrum between March and April. The catalysts for these upward shifts were two moves by the Fed to tighten monetary policy during this period, including one on April 18, as noted in the chapter preview.

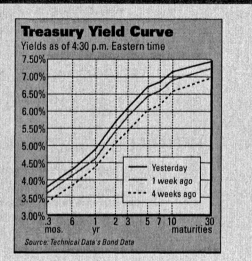

Source: Adapted from *The Wall Street Journal*, April 19, 1994, C21.

sloping, or *inverted*, as in panel c. An inverted yield curve means that short-term rates of interest are higher than long-term rates of interest. Historically yield curves have been inverted when interest rates have been high across the maturity spectrum. This section aims to find the reasons why the yield curve is usually upward sloping, why it is occasionally flat or inverted, and why it shifts over time. It shows that there are alternative explanations of the slope of the yield curve, depending on whether asset holders regard securities of different maturities as perfect substitutes for each other, as imperfect substitutes, or as no substitutes at all. MarketWatch 23.1 explains how to track yield curves in *The Wall Street Journal*.

Forward Rates and the Term Structure

The late Nobel laureate Sir John Hicks laid the foundations for modern investigations of the term structure of interest rates in his celebrated book, *Value and Capital*.[1] Hicks's treatment is remarkable for its clarity and its brevity. Key to understanding the term structure of interest rates is the distinction between spot rates and forward rates and the relation between them. Current interest rates, also called **spot interest rates**, apply to current loans of any duration. In contrast **forward interest rates** are for loans of any duration to be executed in the future. For example, the rate of interest on a one-year Treasury security to be sold three years from today is an example of a forward rate on a one-year loan.

Spot rates incorporate forward rates because any long-term loan can be broken into a series of renewable short-term loans. For example, a three-year loan can be considered as an immediate one-year loan and two subsequent, or forward, one-year loans, each renew-

---

[1] J. R. Hicks, *Value and Capital*, 2nd ed. (Oxford: Oxford University Press, 1946).

ing the principal and earned interest for a successive year. For the first year the interest rate is the current, or spot, one-year interest rate R_1; for the second year it is the forward one-year interest rate r_2; and for the third year it is the forward one-year rate r_3. Instead of agreeing to lend for the full three years at the current long-term rate, R_3, someone interested in investing for three years can lend for the first year at the one-year interest rate, R_1; for the second year at r_2; and for the third year at r_3. It can be shown that *any long-term interest rate is approximately the arithmetic average of its implied forward rates.*[2] Let us illustrate with a three-year loan.

Suppose that today's term structure of one-year, two-year, and three-year interest rates is $R_1 = 10\%$, $R_2 = 11\%$, $R_3 = 11.5\%$. For the first year the spot rate, R_1, and the forward rate, r_1, obviously coincide. To extract r_2 and r_3 from the current term structure of interest rates in this example, the rule that the long-term rate is the average of its implied forward rate applies:

$$R_1 = r_1 \tag{23-1}$$
$$R_2 = (r_1 + r_2)/2 \tag{23-2}$$
$$R_3 = (r_1 + r_2 + r_3)/3 \tag{23-3}$$

Substituting 10 percent for r_1, 11 percent for R_2, and 11.5 percent for R_3 in Equations 23–2 and 23–3 yields the forward rates implied by the given term structure of interest rates:

Current Term Structure of Interest Rates	Implied Forward Rates
$R_1 = 10\%$	$r_1 = 10\%$
$R_2 = 11\%$	$r_2 = 12\%$
$R_3 = 11.5\%$	$r_3 = 12.5\%$

This example, depicted graphically in Figure 23–2, illustrates that when the yield curve is upward sloping the implied forward rate (r_n) is greater than the spot rate (R_n) for the same year (except, of course, the first year). On the other hand, when the yield curve is downward sloping, the implied forward rates are below the spot rates, as the Try It Out exercise shows.

TRY IT OUT 23.1

Suppose you read in the financial press that the spot rates of interest on one-year, two-year, and three-year securities are $R_1 = 10\%$, $R_2 = 9\%$, $R_3 = 8.5\%$. Calculate the implied forward one-year rates and depict the spot and forward rates graphically.

The Pure Expectations Hypothesis of the Term Structure

Knowing how to extract forward rates from the term structure of interest rates is a prerequisite to understanding the expectations hypothesis of the term structure. The *pure expectations hypothesis* stipulates that, for the same holding period, investors should expect to earn the same return whether they invest in short-term or long-term securities. Because forward rates are calculated to give the same holding-period yield whether an investor buys a long-term security or a series of short-term securities, the hypothesis

---

[2] The exact relation is based on geometric means rather than arithmetic means.

FIGURE 23–2
Spot Rates and
Forward Rates

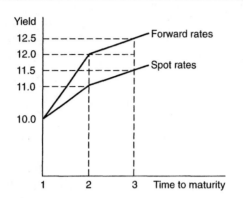

When spot rates are rising, the implied forward rates are greater than the spot rates.

amounts to requiring that expected future short-term interest rates equal the forward rates embedded in the term structure of current rates.

Using r_2^e for the one-year interest rate that is expected for the second year and r_3^e for the one-year interest rate expected for the third year assumes that

$$r_2^e = r_2 \tag{23–4}$$
$$r_3^e = r_3 \tag{23–5}$$

Incorporating these assumptions into Equations 23–2 and 23–3 yields the relation between the long-term interest rate in each holding period and the expected short-term rates:

$$R_2 = (R_1 + r_2^e)/2 \tag{23–6}$$
$$R_3 = (R_1 + r_2^e + r_3^e)/3 \tag{23–7}$$

Equations 23–6 and 23–7 describe the pure expectations hypothesis of the term structure of interest rates. According to Equation 23–6, the current rate of interest on a two-year bond is the average of the current one-year interest rate and the one-year interest rate expected to prevail in the second year. An alternative way of seeing this relation is that the current interest rate on a two-year bond is the expected return (yield) for the two-year holding period. Similarly, according to Equation 23–7, the current interest rate on a three-year bond is the average of the current one-year interest rate plus the one-year interest rates that are expected to prevail two and three years from now. This can also be seen as the expected yield for the three-year holding period. In general, according to the **pure expectations hypothesis** of the term structure, the rate of interest on a long-term loan of n years equals the average of the current short-term interest rate and the expected short-term interest rates over the life of the loan:

$$R_n = (R_1 + r_2^e + r_3^e + r_4^e + \ldots + r_n^e)/n \tag{23–8}$$

Forecasting Future Interest Rates   Using equations such as Equation 23–8, we can calculate long-term rates from knowledge of future short-term interest rates. We can do more, however, if we subscribe to the pure expectations theory. We can forecast future short-term interest rates from published daily data on the term structure of interest rates. For example, knowing the current interest rates on one-year, two year, and three year bonds, we can compute our forecast of the one-year interest rate for next year and the year after, that is, r_2^e and r_3^e. Using our earlier illustration in which $R_1 = 10\%$, $R_2 = 11\%$, and $R_3 = 11.5\%$, we solve for the implied future one-year interest rates. Obviously, they are identical to the implied forward interest rates we already determined: $r_2^e = 12\%$ and $r_3^e = 12.5\%$. How confident should we be about our forecast? As confident as we are about the pure expectations theory on which our forecasting method is based. Therefore, we must consider the relevance of this theory.

The Theoretical Basis of The Expectations Hypothesis   What is the basis for the restriction incorporated into the pure expectations hypothesis that the forward and expected interest rates be equal? In other words, what makes the expected return for the holding period the same whether one holds short-term or long-term securities, or any combination of shorts and longs? The answer lies in (1) competition, (2) the absence of transaction costs, and (3) the assumption that securities with different maturities are perfect substitutes for each other.

The last assumption simply means that investors in (and issuers of) securities are not wedded to any particular maturity. For them only the return on the portfolio matters. If the return they expect from a string of short-term securities were lower than the return of the long-term securities, investors would sell short-term securities and buy long-term securities, thereby raising short-term rates and lowering long-term rates. Investors would continue these transactions until expected returns were equalized. For example, if the yield from rolling over three one-year securities were lower than the yield from holding one three-year security, investors would switch to the three-year security, thereby bringing the three-year rate down.

Analogously, if the return expected from holding a string of short-term securities were greater than the return on the long-run security, a sufficient number of investors would quickly move out of long-term securities and into short-term securities, thereby raising long-term rates and lowering short-term rates. Note that this argument relies on the absence of transaction costs and on the presence of competition among investors, who, in their attempt to exploit profit opportunities, eliminate these opportunities; that is, they make the expected and actual returns equal.

A direct corollary to this result is that changes in the relative supplies of securities of different maturities will not matter, because any long-term loan can be broken into a series of short-term loans. For example, a 10-year loan can be broken into 10 1-year loans. Changing the relative quantities of securities of different maturities does not change the ultimate supply of short-term loans outstanding. According to the pure expectations hypothesis, changes in relative supplies will be absorbed by willing investors without any change in the expected yield for the holding period.

The Expectations Hypothesis and the Yield Curve   The result that a long-term, actual interest rate is the average of successive expected one-year interest rates provides the basis for an elegantly simple explanation of the shape of the yield curve. According to the pure expectations hypothesis, the current short-term interest rate and the expected future interest rates are the sole determinants of the shape of the yield curve. An upward-sloping yield curve is the consequence of higher expected future short-term interest rates. An inverted, or downward-sloping, yield curve signals that short-term interest rates are expected to fall. And a flat yield curve signals that short-term interest rates are not expected to change in the future.

Equation 23–9 illustrates the expectations hypothesis in its simplest form:

$$R_2 = (R_1 + r_2^e)/2 \qquad\qquad (23\text{--}9)$$

Suppose that r_2^e is greater than R_1, which means that the short-term interest rate is expected to rise next year. Then R_2 must be greater than R_1. The reason that the interest rate on a two-year loan is greater than the rate on a one-year loan is the expected increase in the one-year interest rate. In general, higher future short-term rates raise present long-term rates. This also means that the reason for an upward-sloping yield curve is the expected increase in the short-term interest rates. Or conversely, an upward-sloping yield curve indicates a future increase in the short-term rate. On the other hand, a downward-sloping yield curve means investors expect interest rates to fall in the future. For example, in 1981 the yield curve in the United States was inverted: Short-term interest rates were higher than long-term rates. As Chapters 10 and 16 discuss, in the early 1980s the Fed was reducing money growth to reduce inflation and thereby reduce the inflation premium embedded in interest rates. According to the expectations hypothesis, the downward-sloping yield curve indicates that investors expected the Fed's disinflationary monetary policy to work.

In sum, according to the pure expectations hypothesis, future short-term interest rates are the sole determinant of the shape of the yield curve. Because there is as much chance for short-term interest rates to fall as to rise, according to the expectations hypothesis there is an equal chance that the yield curve will be inverted. But we know that usually the yield curve is upward sloping. The expectations hypothesis by itself cannot explain this fact. However, when the pure expectations hypothesis is augmented to include risk premiums, the usual tendency of yield curves to be upward sloping can be explained.

The Liquidity Preference Hypothesis and the Liquidity Premium

In his analysis of the term structure, Hicks considered the pure expectations theory a stepping-stone to more realistic variants. He argued that demanders of securities (lenders) prefer to hold short-term bonds if the yield on both short and long bonds is the same; that is, lenders prefer liquidity. The primary reason for this preference is that bonds with longer maturities are more vulnerable to interest rate risk. A given change in the interest rate changes the price of long-term securities by more than it changes the price of short-term securities. The risk of capital losses creates a preference for bonds of shorter maturities, other things equal; therefore, short-term securities and long-term securities are *imperfect substitutes*. This preference for shorts over longs causes, in Hicks's words, a "constitutional weakness" of the demand for longs, which can be remedied only if investors (demanders) in long-term securities are compensated by a *liquidity premium*, which is a risk premium. According to this theory, a long-term interest rate is not simply the average of the present and future one-period interest rates. Instead, the long rate is this average plus a liquidity premium denoted by L_n. The liquidity premium increases with length of time to maturity because interest rate risk is greater on long-term securities than on short-term securities. Equation 23–10 represents the **liquidity preference hypothesis**, or liquidity-augmented expectations hypothesis:

$$R_n = (R_1 + r_2^e + r_3^e + \ldots r_n^e)/n + L_n \qquad\qquad (23\text{–}10)$$

Because of the increasing liquidity premium, the yield curve is upward sloping when expected short-term interest rates equal today's one-period interest rate. If interest rates are expected to rise in the future, the yield curve will have an even steeper slope. On the other hand, for the yield curve to be downward sloping, the future interest rate must be expected to fall sufficiently so that it offsets the liquidity premium. Historically yield curves have tended to be inverted when short-term interest rates have been unusually high, such as in the early 1980s in the United States.

Since Hicks's groundbreaking contribution in the 1930s, there has been extensive theoretical and empirical research on the liquidity premium. Although there is controversy in the empirical literature, some evidence—beyond the observation that upward-sloping yield curves are more common than inverted yield curves—has emerged to support the liquidity premium hypothesis.[3]

The notion that demanders have a preference for liquidity restores the role of the relative supplies of securities with different maturities to determine the prices of securities and, hence, the interest rates on different maturities. For example, an increase in the supply of short-term bonds at the expense of long-term bonds will raise the short-term rate and lower the long-term rate, other things equal. MarketWatch 23.2 explains how this theory was behind the decision to shorten the maturity structure of the debt in 1993.

The Preferred Habitat Hypothesis

The liquidity preference approach identifies the typical investor as a short-horizon investor who has a preference for liquidity and, hence, a preference for short-term securities. The preferred habitat approach introduced by Nobel laureate Franco Modigliani and Richard Sutch[4] generalizes the liquidity preference theory by assuming that investors have a preferred maturity, but that preference may be for longs over shorts. In both approaches, long-term securities and short-term securities are imperfect substitutes. Therefore, expectations of future interest rates and relative supplies of securities affect the shape of the yield curve according to both theories.

A natural strategy of investors is to attempt to match the maturity of their assets with those of their liabilities. On the basis of this strategy, **short-horizon investors**, such as commercial banks whose major liabilities consist of short-term deposits, would prefer securities with short-term maturities. On the other hand, **long-horizon investors**, such as insurance companies and pension funds whose liabilities have longer maturities, would prefer securities with long-term maturities.

According to the **preferred habitat hypothesis**, the long-term interest rate is the average of all expected interest rates plus a *habitat premium*, which is a risk premium

---

[3] For a compact discussion of the extensive empirical literature on the term structure, see James C. Van Horne, *Financial Market Rates and Flows*, 3rd ed. (Englewood Cliffs, N.J.: Prentice Hall, 1990), 118–24.

[4] Franco Modigliani and Richard C. Sutch, "Innovations in Interest Rate Policy," *American Economic Review* 56 (May 1966): 178–97.

Market*Watch* 23.2
Reducing the Supply of T-Bonds

"Can the government really save taxpayers money and at the same time stimulate business activity by curbing sales of 30-year Treasury bonds?"* The "Credit Markets" column in *The Wall Street Journal* on January 6, 1992, posed this question. The column noted that in the preceding 12 months, the Fed had lowered the federal funds rate 3 percentage points, from 7 percent to 4 percent, and the yield on 3-month T-bills had fallen 2.7 percentage points, to just under 4 percent. The yield on 30-year Treasury bonds, however, had fallen a mere three-quarters of a percentage point, to about 7.5 percent, resulting in a steep yield curve.

According to *The Wall Street Journal*:

Burton Malkiel, a Princeton University economist and a student of markets and interest rates, suggests that a substantial move by the Treasury to curb its sale of 30-year bonds could reduce long-term interest rates by as much as one-half of a percentage point. . . . Mr. Malkiel, like many others, believes that reducing sales of 30-year bonds might help stimulate economic activity, cutting long-term rates and thus allowing corporations and consumers to replace high-interest rate debt with lower-rate debt. With lower debt service, consumers and corporations would have more to spend on goods and services.

This prediction is consistent with the liquidity preference theory of the term structure, according to which relative supplies of securities as well as expectations affect the slope of the yield curve.

Arguing against the reduction of 30-year bonds was Robert Giordano, an economist on Wall Street. According to *The Wall Street Journal*: "Mr. Giordano of Goldman Sachs said that a shift away from long-term bonds is 'unlikely to lower long-term interest rates appreciably, save the government much, if any, money or help the private sector.'" This argument is based on the pure expectations hypothesis, according to which only expectations of future interest rates affect the shape of the yield curve.

In February 1992 and again in February 1993, the U.S. Treasury made a modest reduction in its supply of

30-year Treasury bonds. Beginning in May 1993, however, the Treasury took a bolder step. It shifted from quarterly to semiannual auctions of 30-year T-bonds in a move to reduce the supply of 30-year bonds by about 40 percent. The accompanying graph shows that the yield curve flattened significantly between May and August 1993, with long-term rates falling about 70 basis points.

Percent, weekly averages

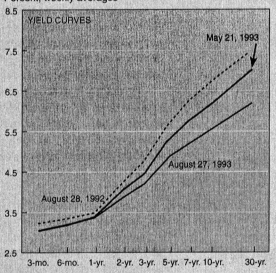

Source: *Economic Trends*, Federal Reserve Bank of Cleveland, September 1993, 3.

Even those economists who argued in favor of shortening the maturity structure of the debt did not attribute the entire fall in long-term rates to the scarcity of long-term bonds, especially because the flattening of the yield curve began in the fourth quarter of 1992. According to the liquidity preference theory, expectations are also an important explanatory factor of the yield curve. Why were investors expecting lower interest rates in the future? One reason is continuing

---

* Constance Mitchell and David Wessel, "Will 30-Year T-Bond Become Extinct Species?" *The Wall Street Journal*, January 6, 1992, C1.

continued

Market*Watch* 23.2

**Reducing the Supply
of T-Bonds** *(concluded)*

good news on inflation, which reduced expected inflation and the inflation premium embedded in interest rates. Another reason is prospective reductions in the deficit, which would reduce the government's need to borrow in the future and, hence, reduce future interest rates.

Finally, what about the argument that the government would save by shifting to short-term debt? Only time will answer this question. If short-term rates over the next 30 years average less than about 6.8 percent, which was the 30-year rate when the Treasury began to shorten the maturity of the debt, the Treasury will save not only in the short run but also in the long run.

necessary to lure investors to the maturity they do not prefer. Equation 23–11 describes this approach, where H_n represents the habitat premium.

$$R_n = (R_1 + r_2^e + r_3^e + \ldots + r_n^e)/n + H_n \qquad (23\text{–}11)$$

If the average investor is a short-horizon investor, the habitat premium, like the liquidity premium, is positive. Long-term bonds must pay a premium to lure investors concerned about liquidity and, hence, the risk of capital loss. Long-horizon investors, on the other hand, expect to hold the security for a long time. For these investors, the major risk of investing is not the risk of capital loss but the risk of income loss. If they buy short-term securities and interest rates fall, they lose interest income by having to reinvest at lower rates. Thus, for long-horizon investors the habitat premium is negative, because short-term securities are more risky than long-term securities. The long-term interest rate is less than the sum of expected short-term interest rates. If the average investor were a long-horizon investor, the yield curve would be downward sloping if expected future interest rates equal the current one-year rate. In this case, an upward-sloping yield curve means expectations of rising rates outweigh the habitat premium.

The Segmented-Markets Hypothesis

The pure expectations hypothesis states that bonds of different maturities are perfect substitutes and, hence, that only expectations matter in explaining the yield curve. At the opposite pole is the **segmented-markets hypothesis**, which states that securities of different maturities are not substitutes at all. If asset holders have an absolute preference for one maturity and never make substitutions, expectations do not matter, but relative supplies do. The prices of securities and, hence, the yields on securities are determined by supply and demand in each separate market.

According to this theory, an upward-sloping yield curve implies that investors have a preference for short-term securities. Demand for short-term securities is relatively higher than that for longs, resulting in a high price and an a low yield on short-term securities. On the other hand, a downward-sloping yield curve means that investors have a preference for long-term securities. Obviously a theory that assumes there is no shifting among securities of different maturities no matter how large the gap between long-term rates and expected future short-term rates is not realistic. It can only be an abstraction of the theory that assumes that bonds of different maturities are imperfect substitutes.

THE DEFAULT RISK STRUCTURE OF INTEREST RATES

So far this chapter has examined the influence of length of time to maturity on interest rates. Another important characteristic affecting rates is the quality of the security. Quality refers to the safety of the bond against *default risk*, that is, the risk that the issuer of the bond will default on the agreed-upon payments of interest or principal.

Chapter 3 shows that rating services such as Moody's and Standard and Poor's rank the credit risk on new and old bonds. The rating services draw a basic distinction between investment-grade bonds and below-investment-grade bonds. Within each category approximately five refinements provide additional information. This section investigates how default risk affects interest rates on debt securities, other things equal.

Default Risk, the Default Risk Premium, and Interest Rates

The default risk premium on a debt security is the difference between the yield on that security and the yield on a U.S. Treasury security of the same maturity. U.S. Treasury securities are default free because of the federal government's power to levy taxes and to issue reserves (via the Federal Reserve) to finance interest and principal payments on federal debt. At the other end of the spectrum, corporations have neither the power to tax nor the power to issue reserves. Municipalities are in between the two extremes—they can levy taxes but not issue reserves. Because of voter resistance to new taxes in recent years, however, municipalities can and do default on their bonds. Thus, the risk premium on municipals is positive and occasionally substantial.

The **default-risk structure of interest rates** refers to the relation between the yield on debt securities and the risk of default, assuming that all other characteristics of the security, especially the term to maturity, are kept constant. Figure 23–3 depicts the relation between yield and default risk, with yield on the vertical axis and default risk measured on the horizontal axis. The vertical intercept is the default-free rate of interest,

FIGURE 23–3
The Relationship between Yield and Default Risk

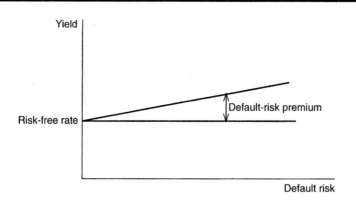

The interest rate on a Treasury security of a given maturity is the default-free rate for that maturity. The interest rate on other debt securities with the same maturity increases as the risk of default increases. The difference between the yield on a risky security and the yield on a Treasury security is the default-risk premium.

in particular, the interest rate on a U.S. Treasury security of a given maturity. The horizontal line at this level of the interest rate indicates that the interest rate on a U.S. Treasury bond of a given maturity is independent of the default risk on bonds of other issuers. The upward-sloping curve denotes the relation between the default risk and the interest rate on bonds of other issuers. And the distance between the horizontal curve and the default-risk yield curve measures the risk premium.

The default risk curve depicted in Figure 23–3 shows that the higher the default risk, the greater the interest rate investors demand and receive in the marketplace. Alternatively the higher the default risk, the greater the risk premium added to the risk-free rate. The economic process that increases the interest rate when the risk of default rises is a straightforward application of the laws of supply and demand applied to the workings of the market for bonds. Other things equal, an increase in the presumed risk of default on a bond reduces demand for the bond. At the original interest rate, there is excess supply, which is eliminated by a rise in the yield or the interest rate on the bond. MarketWatch 23.3 explains how to track default risk premiums in *The Wall Street Journal*.

The State of the Economy and Default Risk

The level of economic activity is a major determinant of default risk. In periods of economic prosperity, the perceived danger of default is small because cash flows of businesses are robust, thereby making it easier for firms to fulfill their contractual obligations to make payments of interest and principal. By contrast, in periods of economic recession or depression, the actual and the perceived dangers that corporations may not fulfill their contractual obligations are greater, and, hence, the risk of default is greater.

During downturns in the economy the demand for safe assets rises at the expense of risky bonds. The term *flight to quality* refers to selling risky bonds and replacing them with safer or even risk-free bonds. Economic downturns are also the time when the issuers of risky bonds must borrow more because of their diminished cash flows. The combination of reduced demand for risky bonds by investors and increased supply by businesses causes excess supply at the original level of the interest rate, thereby forcing the interest rate on risky business debt to rise. On the other hand, the markets for safe and risk-free bonds experience excess demand, which reduces their yield. This is the reason why during severe economic downturns we observe substantial increases in the risk premium, that is, the difference between the interest rates on risky bonds and risk-free bonds.

The facts support this prediction of the theory. During the Great Depression of the 1930s, the difference between the interest rate on corporate bonds and the interest rate on U.S. Treasury bonds of the same maturity was substantially greater than in other periods. Similarly the default risk premium rose during the "great recessions" of 1974–1975 and 1981–1982. Another measure of default risk is the rate of default itself. For example, the ratio of bonds in default over bonds not in default was very high during the Great Depression and the two great recessions.

Liquidity, Marketability, and Default Risk

Liquidity is another attribute of securities that is interrelated with default risk. The greater the default risk of a bond, the less marketable it is and, hence, the smaller its liquidity. As a consequence, the demand for the illiquid bond falls, thereby raising its yield.

Of course liquidity exerts an influence on interest rates independent of default risk. The easier and the less costly it is for one to convert a bond to cash, the more desirable

MarketWatch 23.3
Tracking Default Risk Premiums

MarketWatch 23.1 explains how to follow the yield curve in the "Credits Market" column in *The Wall Street Journal*. The yield curve depicts the effect of term to maturity on interest rates, other things equal. This discussion shows how other factors such as risk of default affect interest rates by examining a table of "Yield Comparisons" that appears with the yield curve in *The Wall Street Journal* each day. The accompanying table is from April 19, 1994.

The first column of the table shows that on April 18, 1994, the average interest rate on Treasury securities with maturities from 1 to 10 years was 6.18 percent, while the average interest rate on federal agency securities with the same maturity was 6.73 percent. The higher yield on agencies of the same maturity reflects the risk premium; agency securities do not have the same backing of the U.S. government as Treasury securities. Further down the first column, there is an even higher risk premium on corporate securities. High-quality corporate securities with maturities from 1 to 10 years paid an average interest rate of 7.14 percent, and medium-quality corporate securities with the same maturity paid an average interest rate of 7.47 percent. Finally, further down the column the average rate of

YIELD COMPARISONS

Based on Merrill Lynch Bond Indexes, priced as of midafternoon Eastern time.

	4/18	4/15	–52 Week– High	Low
Corp.-Govt. Master	6.90%	6.74%	6.90%	5.19%
Treasury 1-10yr	6.18	5.99	6.18	4.23
10+ yr	7.60	7.49	7.63	6.01
Agencies 1-10yr	6.73	6.60	6.73	5.03
10+ yr	7.77	7.71	7.77	6.40
Corporate				
1-10 yr High Qlty	7.14	6.99	7.14	5.32
Med Qlty	7.47	7.31	7.47	5.76
10+ yr High Qlty	8.04	7.95	8.04	6.93
Med Qlty	8.47	8.39	8.47	7.29
Yankee bonds(1)	7.70	7.57	7.70	6.27
Current-coupon mortgages (2)				
GNMA 8.00%	8.18	7.98	8.37	6.07
FNMA 8.00%	8.12	7.92	8.24	6.10
FHLMC 8.00%	8.14	7.93	8.25	6.10
High-yield corporates	10.49	10.39	10.49	9.25
New tax-exempts				
7-12-yr G.O. (AA)	5.81	5.76	5.97	4.56
12-22-yr G.O. (AA)	6.18	6.16	6.69	4.91
22+yr revenue (A)	6.52	6.47	6.71	5.30

Note: High quality rated AAA-AA; medium quality A-BBB/Baa; high yield, BB/Ba-C.
(1) Dollar-denominated, SEC-registered bonds of foreign issuers sold in the U.S. (2) Reflects the 52-week high and low of mortgage-backed securities indexes rather than the individual securities shown.

Source: *The Wall Street Journal,* April 19, 1994, C21.

return on high-yield corporate bonds (junk bonds) of all maturities was 10.49 percent, which was substantially higher than the yield of 8.47 percent on medium-quality corporate securities with maturities of 10+ years.

the bond. One way to increase the liquidity of an asset is to reduce its maturity. Another way is to increase the marketability of the asset. According to the laws of asset demand, the greater the liquidity of a bond, the stronger its demand and, hence, the lower the interest rate. Conversely the greater the liquidity of a bond, the smaller the liquidity premium added to the interest on the bond. Thus more-illiquid bonds command a higher interest rate.

Junk bonds provide an interesting example of a security that interweaves several attributes of bonds. Junk bonds do not command higher interest rates solely because of their higher default risk premium. They are also far less liquid than U.S. Treasury bonds. Because investors find it more difficult to convert junk bonds to cash, they demand and receive a liquidity premium to compensate for this inconvenience. The low liquidity of junk bonds, in turn, is explained by their limited marketability.

The investment firm of Drexel Burnham Lambert, Inc., was ingenious in creating a secondary market for high-yield, or junk, bonds. The collapse of Drexel in 1990 dealt a severe blow to this market. With reduced marketability, the liquidity premium and, hence, the yield on junk bonds increased further.

TAX FEATURES AND INTEREST RATES

Another factor influencing interest rates is the differential tax treatment of some debt securities. Interest payments on bonds issued by local and state governments, collectively called *munis*, are tax exempt, a property that makes them desirable to investors. Thus, other things equal, the demand for tax-exempt bonds is stronger than the demand for taxable bonds, thereby reducing the interest rate to make the tax-free yield comparable to the after-tax yield on taxable bonds. For example, an investor in the 25 percent bracket would consider a taxable bond with a before-tax interest rate of 8 percent inferior to a tax-free bond with an interest rate of 7 percent, because the after-tax return on the taxable bond is only 6 percent. In such circumstances the demand for the tax-free bond will rise and its yield will fall, while the demand for the taxed bond will fall and its yield will rise until the two tax-adjusted rates become equal.

It is interesting to combine the effect of tax incentives and default risk to compare the interest rates on municipal bonds and U.S. Treasury bonds. In the absence of default risk and hence of a default risk premium, the yield on municipals should be lower than on Treasuries of the same maturity. This is not always the case, however. In the aftermath of actual defaults by some important municipal issues—such as, in 1983, bonds of the Washington Power Supply System, aptly nicknamed Whoops—the risk premium on municipal bonds rose, which explains why nontaxed bonds occasionally earn higher yields.

EQUITY CAPITAL IN A FOUR-ASSET MODEL

So far this chapter has focused exclusively on debt securities. This section expands our analysis to include equity capital. It uses a four-asset framework that consists of money, open-market debt securities, bank loans, and equity securities.

Figure 23–4 shows how the four-asset model extends the two-asset model consisting of money and debt securities introduced in Chapter 9. First, debt securities are broken down into open-market debt securities and bank loans. Open-market securities are bills, notes, and bonds issued by the government and the private sector and sold in the open market. Bank loans, on the other hand, are IOUs issued and signed by the borrowing public and given to the lending bank. In addition to disaggregating debt securities into

FIGURE 23–4
From Two Assets to Four Assets

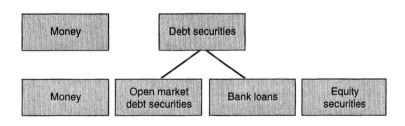

two components, the model also adds a fourth security to our framework: equity securities. A basic assumption is that these assets are imperfect substitutes for each other in the portfolios of market participants. Our primary aim is to see how the rates of return on these assets are determined and how they are influenced by policy. Lurking behind the scenes in both models is another asset: reserves issued by the Fed and held by banks. Because reserves are the raw material out of which money is created, they are incorporated in the money supply equation.

The Model

Consider the equations that describe equilibrium in the financial sector. First review the two-asset model, represented by Equations 23–12 to 23–14.

$$\left.\begin{array}{l} M^d = M^s \\ B^d = B^s \end{array}\right\} \quad i \tag{22–12}$$
$$\tag{22–13}$$
$$r_D = r_D(i) \qquad r_D \tag{22–14}$$

There are two rates to determine in this model: the interest rate, i, on debt securities and the deposit rate, r_D. Note that the interest rate appears between Equations 22–12 and 22–13, because there are two alternative ways of explaining interest rate determination. According to the *liquidity preference theory*, which is based on the money market, the interest rate on debt securities is determined by the equality of money demand and money supply. When there is excess demand for money the interest rate rises, and when there is excess supply it falls. According to the *loanable funds theory*, based on the debt securities market, the interest rate on debt securities is determined in the debt securities market. When there is excess demand for debt securities, the price of debt securities rises and the interest rate falls. And when there is excess supply of debt securities, the price of debt securities falls and the interest rate rises. Finally the equilibrium relation between the deposit rate and the interest rate determines the deposit rate.

Now consider the four-asset model in which B denotes open-market debt securities (bills, notes, bonds), L denotes banks loans, and K denotes equity capital. There are four rates to determine in this model: r_B, the rate on open-market securities, or simply bills for short; r_L, the bank loan rate; r_K, the rate of return on equity capital; and r_D, the deposit rate. Equations 23–15 through 23–19 represent equilibrium in the four-asset model.

$$\left.\begin{array}{l} M^d = M^s \\ B^d = B^s \end{array}\right\} \quad r_B \tag{23–15}$$
$$\tag{23–16}$$
$$L^d = L^s \qquad r_L \tag{23–17}$$
$$K^d = K^s \qquad r_K \tag{23–18}$$
$$r_D = r_D(r_B, \ldots) \qquad r_D \tag{23–19}$$

Note that the bill rate, r_B, appears between Equation 23–15 for the money market and Equation 23–16 for the bills market to denote that this rate is "determined" by either market. Actually all rates are affected by all markets. Determination of an interest rate in a particular market merely means that the interest rate changes by the principles of excess demand and excess supply applied to the identified market. We need to include only one of these two markets along with the remaining equations.

Bank loans refer to the piece of paper, the IOU, issued by the public and given to the lending bank. In the loans market, the bank, which is the lender, demands loan securities.

The public, which is the borrower, supplies loan securities. Excess demand means the banks want to hold more IOUs of the public than the public wants to issue. To entice the public to borrow more, banks lower the loan rate. Excess supply means the public wants to issue more IOUs than the bank wants to hold. As a result banks raise the loan rate. Equilibrium exists when loans demanded equal loans supplied, as Equation 23–17 shows.

Equation 23–18 represents equilibrium in the market for equity securities. The demanders of equity capital are the public. Banks are not allowed to hold equity securities, and the Fed does not conduct open market operations in them. At any moment in time the supply of equity capital is the existing shares in the companies. If there is excess demand for equity capital, the market valuation of equity capital rises, and the rate of return falls, other things equal. If there is excess supply, the market valuation falls, and the rate of return rises, other things equal.

Finally note that the deposit rate varies positively with the bill rate. This relationship is analogous to the deposit rate relation in the two-asset model, where r_D varies positively with i. In the four-asset model, r_D can also vary with the loan rate and the equity capital rate. For simplicity, these effects are ignored here. Because bills are the closest substitute for deposits in the portfolio of the public, we assume that the effect on the deposit rate of changes in other rates is captured by the bill rate.

Specifying the exogenous variables, or parameters, of the system and solving the four equations—$B^d = B^s$; $L^d = L^s$; $K^d = K^s$; and $r_D = r_D(r_B \ldots)$—we can determine the initial values of the four rates of return. Let us denote the initial equilibrium with the superscript 1. Thus the solution is $(r_B{}^1, r_L{}^1, r_K{}^1, r_D{}^1)$. Given the solution for these four rates, we can derive all other endogenous variables, such as the quantity of money.

Effects of Monetary Policy on Rates of Return

The equilibrium values of the rates of return can change because of changes in the instruments of monetary policy, in the behavior of banks or the public, or in real-sector variables. To illustrate the effects of disturbances to the financial sector on rates of return, this section considers changes in the instruments of monetary policy.

Open Market Operations   First, suppose the Fed makes an open market purchase of securities equal to ΔB_F. This purchase initially affects the demand for bills, the demand for loans, and the supply of money. The demand for bills increases by the amount of the open market operation. Depending on whether the Fed buys the bills from nonbank security dealers or bank dealers, most or all of the accompanying increase in reserves will show up on the balance sheet of banks as an increase in excess reserves. At the initial rates of return, however, banks do not want to hold additional excess reserves. Thus they increase their demand for loan securities. They may even want to buy more bills.[5] In the market for money there is an increase in the money supply because at the initial rates banks want to make more loans and investments and to create more deposits. As a result, at the initial rates—$r_B{}^1$, $r_L{}^1$, $r_K{}^1$, and $r_D{}^1$—the market for bills and the market for loans will register excess demand, while the market for money registers excess supply. In response the bill rate and the loan rate will fall.

---

[5] During the credit crunch of the early 1990s, banks increased their demand for U.S. Treasury securities.

At the initial rate of return on equity capital, the reduction in the bill rate will make equity capital more attractive. Therefore the public will want to invest more in the stock market and less in the bills market. The reduction in the loan rate will also make equity capital more attractive, because the lower loan rate reduces the cost of borrowing to finance the acquisition of equity capital. Thus there will be excess demand for equity capital, which reduces its rate. Of course, a reduction in the equity rate reflects itself as an increase in equity (stock) prices. Hence investors in the stock market as well as in the bills (bonds) market follow the conduct of monetary policy. Finally, according to the deposit rate relation, the lower bills rate will reduce the deposit rate.

To review and summarize the effects of an open market operation, the schematics below illustrate the linkages in the interdependent markets. The first schema is the initial equilibrium—position 1—represented by the rates of return that clear all markets, given specific values of the policy and other parameters. The next schema represents an open market operation that increases the Fed's holdings of Treasury securities, B_F. It shows how excess demand for bills and loans, and subsequently for equity capital, reduces all three rates in addition to the deposit rate. When the rates reach their new equilibrium value—denoted by the superscript 2 in the third schema—demand equals supply once again in each financial market.

Initial Equilibrium

$$\left. \begin{array}{l} B^d = B^s \\ L^d = L^s \\ K^d = K^s \\ r_D = r_D(r_B, \ldots) \end{array} \right\} \longrightarrow \left\{ \begin{array}{l} r_B{}^1 \\ r_L{}^1 \\ r_K{}^1 \\ r_D{}^1 \end{array} \right.$$

Open Market Operation

$$B_F\uparrow \begin{array}{l} \nearrow B^d\uparrow \quad \rightarrow \quad EDB \rightarrow r_B\downarrow \searrow \\ \searrow ER\uparrow \rightarrow \left[\begin{array}{l} L^d\uparrow \rightarrow EDL \rightarrow r_L\downarrow \\ B^d\uparrow \rightarrow EDB \rightarrow r_B\downarrow \end{array} \right. \nearrow \end{array} K^d\uparrow \xrightarrow{\rightarrow} EDK \xrightarrow{\substack{r_D\downarrow}} r_K\downarrow$$

New Equilibrium

$$\left. \begin{array}{l} B^d = B^s \\ L^d = L^s \\ K^d = K^s \\ r_D = r_D(r_B, \ldots) \end{array} \right\} \longrightarrow \left\{ \begin{array}{l} r_B{}^2 < r_B{}^1 \\ r_L{}^2 < r_L{}^1 \\ r_K{}^2 < r_K{}^1 \\ r_D{}^2 < r_D{}^1 \end{array} \right.$$

Results: $B_F\uparrow \Rightarrow \left\{ \begin{array}{l} r_B\downarrow \\ r_L\downarrow \\ r_K\downarrow \\ r_D\downarrow \end{array} \right.$

But what about the omitted market, the money market? After the open market operation, effective reserves and the money supply increase; hence there is excess supply in the money market. However, when the bill rate and the loan rate start to fall, the quantity of borrowed reserves falls and the quantity of excess reserves rises. Both these developments contribute to a reduction in effective reserves and, hence, in the quantity of money supplied. On the other side of the market, the falling bill and equity capital rates increase the quantity of money demanded. Thus the combination of the reduction in the quantity of money supplied and the increase in the quantity of money demanded will erase the initial excess supply of money, a process that will be completed when the other markets clear. In the new equilibrium the quantity of money is higher. Finally, if all of these repercussions happen too rapidly for the level of income to rise, the demand for currency will not change. Hence the entire increase in the quantity of money will result from an increase in the quantity of deposits.

In sum an open market purchase of Treasury bills by the Fed reduces all four rates of return. These results are consistent with the results derived from the two-asset model. They are the **generalized liquidity effect**, that is, the effect of a change in monetary policy on the structure of rates of return, other things equal. Of course the other variables being held equal are real income, the price level, and expectations of inflation.

TRY IT OUT 23.2

The Chapter Preview pointed out that on April 18, 1994, the Fed raised its target for the federal funds rate. First explain how the Fed must change B_F to implement this policy. Then use the four-asset model to explain the effects on the Treasury bill rate, the bank loan rate, the deposit rate, and the rate of return on equity capital.

A Change in the Discount Rate   This section applies the same technique to examine the effects of a change in the discount rate, the second most important instrument of monetary policy. Again starting from an initial equilibrium denoted by the superscript 1, suppose that the Fed reduces the discount rate, d. Other things equal, a reduction in the discount rate increases the spread between the bill rate and the discount rate, and the spread between the loan rate and the discount rate, that is, $(r_B - d)$ and $(r_L - d)$, rises. At these higher spreads banks will want to borrow more reserves from the Fed and to hold fewer excess reserves, thereby increasing effective reserves. And a greater quantity of effective reserves increases the money supply. In the markets for bills and loans, the increased spreads in turn increase the demand for bills and loans by banks. As a result there will be excess demand in the bills market and the loans market. By the principle of excess demand these excess demands will be eliminated only when the bill rate and the loan rate fall.

The public does not have access to the discount window. Hence a lower discount rate does not directly affect the demand for equity capital by the public. However, there is an indirect effect through a chain of substitution. As a result of the lower bill rate and the lower loan rate, investing in stocks becomes more attractive, thereby inducing the public to switch some funds away from bills and toward buying more stock in the stock market. The increase in the demand for equity capital will cause excess demand, which will lower the equity capital rate, r_K; that is, it will increase stock prices. Therefore the reduction in the discount rate lowers all three rates of return, which in turn will lower the fourth rate, the deposit rate.

The following schematics illustrate the results of a decrease in the discount rate:

$$d\downarrow \rightarrow \begin{cases} BR\uparrow \text{ and } ER\downarrow \rightarrow \text{Effective reserves}\uparrow \rightarrow M^s\uparrow \\ B^d\uparrow \rightarrow EDB \rightarrow r_B\downarrow \searrow \quad \rightarrow \quad\quad r_D\downarrow \\ K^d\uparrow \rightarrow EDK \rightarrow r_K\downarrow \\ L^d\uparrow \rightarrow EDL \rightarrow r_L\downarrow \nearrow \end{cases}$$

Therefore,

$$d\downarrow \Rightarrow \begin{cases} r_D\downarrow \\ r_B\downarrow \\ r_L\downarrow \\ r_K\downarrow \end{cases}$$

Monetary policy, therefore, affects the rate on equity capital in much the same way it affects interest rates. An open market purchase of securities reduces equity rates just as it reduces all interest rates. So does a reduction in the discount rate. The analysis in this section reminds us of the imperfectly segmented markets for debt securities of various maturities. Here, of course, more characteristics are involved than just length of time to maturity. Therefore more reasons exist for imperfect segmentation of markets and for differing rates.

The Q-Ratio, the Stock Market, and Investment Demand

In the two-asset model the connection between the real sector and the financial sector works through the interest rate. A fall in the interest rate reduces the cost of borrowing, which sparks an increase in investment by firms. In the four-asset model interest rates are not the only connection between the financial sector and the real sector. In addition to introducing the four-asset model that incorporates the stock market, James Tobin provides a simple, common-sense explanation of the linkage between the stock market and the real sector.[6] Two observations form the basis of Tobin's analysis.

First, the higher the market price of an existing business, relative to the cost of building an identical business from scratch, the more one is inclined to build a new business. For example, if it costs more to buy the titles to an existing business by purchasing shares in the stock market than it costs to start a business, entrepreneurs will build the new business. On the other hand, if it costs less to buy the shares to an existing business than to build one, entrepreneurs have an incentive to buy the existing one. The same principle can be applied to housing. If building a new house is less expensive than buying an identical existing house, prospective homeowners will build the new house. However, if buying an existing house costs less than building a new one, the prospective owners will buy the existing house rather than build a new one. Finally, if it costs more to buy a used durable good in the secondhand market than to buy an identical new one, shoppers will buy the new one. Of course this does not apply to collectors' items or items of sentimental value to the purchaser. These illustrations lead to the principle that *the higher the market value of existing capital items relative to their replacement cost, the higher the demand for newly produced capital items.*

---

[6]   See, for example, James Tobin, "A General Equilibrium Approach to Monetary Theory," *Journal of Money, Credit, and Banking* 1 (February 1969): 15–29.

Tobin called the ratio of the market value of an existing physical capital item over its replacement cost the **Q-ratio**. The profession has dubbed the ratio *Tobin's* Q. And it is now standard to see the relationship between investment in plant, equipment, and residential structures; market valuation of capital goods; and replacement costs stated in these words: *The demand for fixed investment is positively related to Tobin's* Q; *investment demand increases when Tobin's* Q *increases and falls when Tobin's* Q *falls.*

Tobin also expressed the *Q*-ratio in an alternative way, as the ratio of two rates of return. To derive this alternative expression of the *Q*-ratio, first note the fact that the total returns to equity capital equal the total returns to physical capital. Equivalently the total returns to the holders of the titles of ownership (that is, the stockholders) of a corporation equal total corporate profits. We can write this relationship as an accounting identity:

Total returns to equity capital = Total returns to physical capital
= Total corporate profits

If r_K denotes the rate of return on equity capital and *MVE* denotes the market value of equity capital, the total returns to equity capital equal, by definition, $r_K \times MVE$. On the other side of the equation, total profits equal the rate of profit times the quantity of physical capital. The accepted measure of the size of physical capital is its replacement cost. If the symbol r represents the rate of profit (in percentage terms) and the symbol *RC* replacement cost, total corporate profits equal $r \times RC$. Thus the basic identity is:

$r_K \times MVE = r \times RC$

We call this relationship *Tobin's identity*, which can be rewritten as:

$MVE/RC = r/r_K$

Note that the left side of this new equation is Tobin's *Q*, which means that:

$Q = r/r_K$

An increase in the rate of profit relative to the rate of return on equity capital increases *Q*. Since an increase in *Q* encourages more fixed investment, an increase in the rate of profit relative to the rate of return on equity capital increases fixed investment. On the other hand a decrease in the rate of profit relative to the rate of return on equity capital decreases *Q* and consequently decreases fixed investment.

Having established the relationship between the *Q*-ratio and fixed investment, we can now establish the connection among changes in the instruments of monetary policy, the stock market, and the entire economy by applying the results from our four-asset model. The discussion in the previous section shows than an expansionary monetary policy, such as an open market purchase of securities, reduces all rates of return, including the equity capital rate, r_K. Given the rate of profit, a reduction in the equity capital rate increases the *Q*-ratio. As a result the investment component of aggregate demand for goods and services increases, which increases output. On the other hand a contractionary monetary policy action, such as an increase in the discount rate, increases all rates of return, including r_K. And given the rate of profit, the *Q*-ratio falls, and thus investment falls. MarketWatch 23.4, excerpted from an op-ed piece in *The Wall Street Journal* by James Tobin, explains the behavior of the *Q*-ratio in 1993 and its implications for investment.

MarketWatch 23.4
Tobin on Q*

In principle, the par value of the q-ratio is 1. At that value, financial markets would simply be reflecting the current prices of the assets to which stocks and bonds are titles. Values above 1 would encourage, and values below 1 discourage, companies' acquisition of newly produced physical assets, especially assets similar to the existing ones the markets are evaluating.

A problem in interpreting observable q's is that, while low corporate q's signal obsolescence of existing installations and deter further investments of the same type, those overall ratios do not register the possible profitability of investment in new technologies and products. Thus in the 1970s, energy-using industries had low q's but were busy investing in energy-saving equipment and techniques.

In any case, the theoretical norm of q = 1 cannot be taken literally in practical applications, because of the vagaries of accounting and statistics. One reason is that corporations possessing monopoly power or other sources of intangible "good will" may enjoy exceptionally high values of q for years and decades. Q-ratios have been calculated world-wide, both for individual companies and for whole economies.

The chart shows year-end q-ratios for the U.S. non-financial corporate sector 1945–93, calculated mainly from Federal Reserve Flow of Funds data. The 1993 estimate assumes, among other things, that current market values will prevail on Dec. 31. If so, 1993 will set a mean-

ingful new record, the highest postwar value of q—70% above year-end 1987 and 7% above 1968.

There are signs that this incentive is working to lift business fixed investment from the doldrums. If the trend continues, the Clinton economic team will have something to cheer about. Despite the improvement, however, business fixed investment remains distressingly low relative to gross domestic product.

Will President Clinton's bull market continue? We can't rule out a December surprise. Movements of stock prices are always surprises, because if investors had anticipated them, they would already have occurred. The best that "experts" can do is to rationalize events after the fact.

What explains the contrast between the pessimism Americans express in polls and the apparent optimism with which they have been bidding up stock prices? Stocks have become popular with individual investors disappointed at the interest they can earn these days on bank certificates of deposit, money market funds and bonds. They have been flooding equity mutual funds with purchases. It's natural that as bond prices rise and bond yields fall the same thing happens to stocks but only within limits.

Danger of Stagnation

The bullishness of bond markets appears to reflect the satisfaction of bond-holding pension funds and insurance companies with the prospects of slow, weak, inflation-safe, high-unemployment "recovery." "Stagnation" would be a more accurate description. To bondholders, those prospects signal a tame future in which the Fed will never have a reason to raise interest rates, a future with little threat of capital losses on bonds and some chances of capital gains.

While low interest rates *per se* are good for stock prices, the environment bondholders count on to keep interest rates low is quite another story. Stagnation will not be good for corporate sales and profits, which are ultimately decisive for stock values and q. This is the main danger for Mr. Clinton's bull market, his economic program and his electoral success in 1994 and 1996.

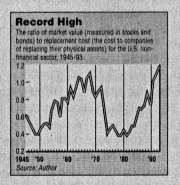

Record High
The ratio of market value (measured in stocks and bonds) to replacement cost (the cost to companies of replacing their physical assets) for the U.S. non-financial sector, 1945-93.

Source: Author

---

* Source: Excerpted from James Tobin, "Clinton's Bull Market," *The Wall Street Journal*, November 30, 1993, A14.

SUMMARY

- The term structure of interest rates is the relationship between interest rates and length of time to maturity on debt securities, other things equal.

- The yield curve is a graphical depiction of the term structure that relates yield to maturity and length of time to maturity on comparable debt securities, usually U.S. Treasury securities.

- The yield curve is usually upward sloping, indicating that the longer the term to maturity, the higher the interest rate on the debt security. Occasionally, however, the yield curve is flat or downward sloping.

- The expectations hypothesis explains the slope of the yield curve solely in terms of current and expected short-term interest rates. The pure expectations theory asserts that the rate of interest on a long-term security equals the average of the current short-term interest rate and expected short-term interest rates over the life of the security.

- According to the pure expectations theory, an upward-sloping yield curve means that the market expects short-term interest to rise, while a downward-sloping curve means the opposite.

- There is an equal chance for interest rates to rise or fall. Therefore, the pure expectations hypothesis suggests that there is an equal chance for the yield curve to be downward sloping or upward sloping. But this result does not agree with the facts, because yield curves are usually upward sloping.

- The pure expectations theory asserts that investors should not care about the maturities of their portfolios, because, for a given holding period, any combination of maturities will produce the same return. This theory also suggests that the relative supplies of debt with different maturities have no effect on the term structure.

- The pure expectations theory is a benchmark that depends on three key assumptions: (1) competition; (2) absence of transactions costs; and (3) perfect substitutability among debt securities of different maturities in the portfolios of market participants. When any one of these assumptions is dropped, other factors besides expectations, such as relative supplies, have an independent influence on interest rates.

- The liquidity preference theory, or liquidity-augmented expectations hypothesis, drops the assumption of perfect substitutability. This theory asserts that investors prefer short-term debt securities over long-term securities. This preference for liquidity prompts investors to demand a risk premium, called a *liquidity premium*, to invest in long-term securities.

- According to the liquidity preference theory, the long-term interest rate equals the average of the current short-term interest rate and the expected short-term interest rates plus a liquidity premium. The liquidity premium on long-term debt explains why long-term rates are usually higher than short-term rates.

- The preferred habitat theory generalizes the liquidity preference theory. According to the preferred habitat hypothesis, the long-term interest rate is the average of the current short-term interest rate and the expected short-term interest rates plus a habitat premium. For short-horizon investors, such as commercial banks, who have a preference for short-term securities, the habitat premium is positive. For long-horizon investors, such as insurance companies, who have a preference for long-term securities, the habitat premium is negative.

- According to the liquidity preference theory and the preferred habitat theory, both expectations and relative supplies of securities matter in explaining the term structure of interest rates.

- The segmented-markets theory of the term structure is the polar opposite of the pure expectations hypothesis. This theory asserts that only demand and supply in separate markets determine the term structure. This theory is not realistic because it assumes that investors never make substitutions among securities of different maturities no matter how great the opportunities for profit.

- The default risk structure of interest rates is the relationship between the yield on debt securities and the risk that the issuer may default on its obligations to pay interest or principal. The default risk premium is the difference between the interest on the debt of a specific issuer and the interest on a U.S. Treasury security with the same maturity.

- The default risk premium increases with the default risk of securities. Thus the default risk curve is an upward-sloping function of the default risk. The curve typically shifts upward when the economy weakens, because the risk of default usually increases during economic downturns.

- Other characteristics, such as special tax features, also affect interest rates.

- The four-asset model explains the structure of rates of return on U.S. Treasury securities (bills), bank loans, bank deposits, and equity capital (stocks). An open market purchase of Treasury securities by the Fed reduces all rates of return. The rate of return on equity capital falls along with the Treasury bill rate, the bank loan rate, and the deposit rate. A fall in the equity rate means a rise in the price of equities, that is, in stock prices. A reduction in the discount rate has similar effects.

- Tobin's Q is the ratio of the price in the stock market of the economy's capital and the replacement cost of this capital. This ratio also equals the ratio of the economy's rate of profit (marginal productivity of capital) and the equity capital rate. Investment in plant and equipment depends positively on Tobin's Q. It follows that an open market purchase of Treasury securities by the Fed increases investment because the open market operation reduces the equity capital rate and hence increases Q.

KEY TERMS AND CONCEPTS

term structure of interest rates

yield curve

spot interest rates

forward interest rates

pure expectations hypothesis

liquidity preference hypothesis

short-horizon investors

long-horizon investors

preferred habitat hypothesis

segmented-markets hypothesis

default-risk structure of interest rates

generalized liquidity effect

Q-ratio

QUESTIONS AND PROBLEMS

1. What is the relation between the term structure of interest rates and the yield curve?

2. What factors are assumed constant along a yield curve?

3. The term structure of interest rates contains information about the future course of interest rates. Why isn't this information useful as a guide for investment according to the expectations hypothesis?

4. Why are forward rates above spot rates when the yield curve has a positive slope? Why are they below spot rates when the yield curve is inverted?

5. Everybody agrees with the statement that forward rates exceed spot rates when the yield curve is upward sloping. Why is there disagreement about the statement that *expected rates* exceed spot rates when the yield curve is positively sloped?

6. "According to the preferred habitat theory, long-term rates will definitely be below short-term rates if short-term rates are expected to fall and if the average investor is a long-horizon investor." True, false, or uncertain? Explain.

7. Suppose that the structure of current interest rates on one-year, two-year, and three-year U.S. Treasury securities is 7 percent, 6.5 percent, and 6 percent, respectively. Use the pure expectations theory of term structure of interest rates to forecast the one-year interest rate two and three years from now.

8. The structure of current interest rates contains information about future short-term interest rates. Calculate expected short-term (one-year) interest rates from the following data: Current interest rates on one-year, two-year, and three-year U.S. Treasury securities are 7 percent, 8 percent, and 9 percent, respectively, and the liquidity premiums are zero for one-year securities, 0.5 percent for two-year securities, and 1 percent for three-year securities.

9. Suppose that the yield curve on U.S. Treasury securities has the shape shown in the accompanying graph:
   a. According to the pure expectations theory, what does this curve imply about the short-term interest rates expected to prevail from 1996 to 1998? From 1998 to 2000? After 2000?
   b. What economic factors could be responsible for this pattern of expected interest rates?

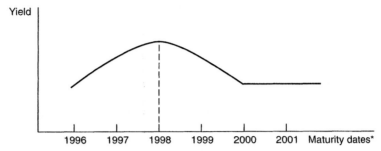

*The horizontal axis depicts the year in which the securities mature.

10. Why is an inverted yield curve often interpreted as forecasting a recession in the near future?

The Wall Street Journal

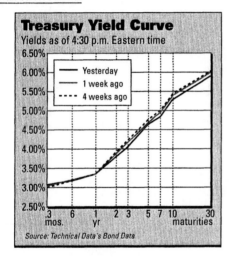

11. The above graph of yield curves is from the "Credit Markets" column in *The Wall Street Journal* on October 15, 1993. It shows that the yield curve became flatter between September and October 1993, as long-term rates fell, while short-term rates were unchanged. How could this change in the shape of the yield curve be explained by the pure expectations hypothesis? Could this explanation also be valid according to the liquidity preference hypothesis and the preferred habitat hypothesis?

12. What is meant by the default risk structure of interest rates?

13. In recessions, interest rates on debt of the same maturity rise for some corporations and fall for others. Explain why.

14. "In recessions, prices of 30-year U.S. Treasury bonds usually rise while prices of many corporate bonds fall." True or false? Explain.

15. "Open market purchases of U.S. Treasury securities increase the Q-ratio." True or false? Explain.

16. Suppose that, other things equal, banks decide to borrow less from the Fed's discount window and to make fewer loans to households and firms. What will happen to the interest rate on U.S. Treasury bonds, the loan rate, and the equity capital rate?

17. Suppose that business profits are expected to rise. What will happen to the Q-ratio?

SUGGESTED READINGS

Cogley, Timothy. "Interpreting the Term Structure of Interest Rates." *Federal Reserve Bank of San Francisco Weekly Letter* 93, no. 5 (April 16, 1993).

A short and lucid explanation of the term structure.

Nelson, Charles. *Term Structure of Interest Rates.* New York: Basic Books, 1972.

An early, influential work on the term structure.

Tobin, James. "Monetary Policies and the Economy: The Transmission Mechanism." *Southern Economic Journal* 44, no. 3 (January 1978): 421–31.

Tobin explains the relation between monetary policy, Q, and the real sector.

Van Horne, James C. *Financial Markets Rates & Flows,* 3rd ed. Englewood Cliffs, N.J.: Prentice Hall, 1990.

Chapters 5 and 8 summarize the theory and review the empirical evidence on the term structure and default structure of interest rates, respectively. They also contain a selected bibliography of the extensive literature.

P A R T 7

THE INTEGRATION OF THE FINANCIAL AND REAL SECTORS

24 Determining the Interest Rate and Real Income: *The* IS-LM *Model*

25 Monetary and Fiscal Policy in the *IS-LM* Model

26 The Price Level and Real Income: *The Aggregate Demand-Aggregate Supply Model*

27 Aggregate Supply, Expectations, and Policy

28 Inflation, Unemployment, and Economic Policy: *History and Theory*

Part 7 extends the discussion of the entire economic system introduced in Chapter 10. This part examines factors that affect interest rates, output, and the price level by analyzing the interconnections between financial-sector markets and real-sector markets. Therefore, it is the epitome of the second pillar of our two-pillar framework.

DETERMINING THE INTEREST RATE AND REAL INCOME
The IS-LM *Model*

CHAPTER PREVIEW

In our model of the financial sector, real income and the price level are given from outside the model. We analyze the effects on the financial sector if real income and the price level change, but we do not have an explanation of why they change. This chapter first examines the factors affecting real income by analyzing the goods and services market in isolation. The expenditure and taxation policies of the government and the attitudes of households, firms, and the foreign sector all affect the demand for goods and services and, ultimately, the level of real income. So does the interest rate, which is determined in the financial sector.

To determine simultaneously the interest rate and real income, the chapter next combines the goods and services market with the money market. This combined model of the real and financial sectors is called the **IS-LM model**. After a thorough treatment of the technique of simultaneously determining the interest rate and real income in this chapter, the next chapter connects theory with practice by applying the technique to analyze the effects of monetary and fiscal policies. Subsequent chapters further extend the analysis to include the price level.

GENESIS OF THE MODERN THEORY OF INCOME DETERMINATION

Before the publication of Keynes's *General Theory of Employment, Interest, and Money* in 1936, economists focused on the long run, when a free market economy gravitates toward capacity, or the full-employment level of output. Pre-Keynesian macro-economists, called *classical economists*, assumed full employment and proceeded to determine the two remaining unknowns: the price level, P; and the interest rate, i. They compartmentalized the two problems and their solutions: First they employed the quantity theory to determine the price level; and, separately, they employed the equality between the demand for investment (in plant and equipment) and the supply of savings to determine the interest rate.

Keynes, seeking to explain why the economy was operating considerably below capacity for the first half of the 1930s, stated that the supply and demand for goods and services determine real income (output). When, at a given level of output, there is excess supply of goods and services (*ESG*), the level of output falls. When there is excess demand for goods and services (*EDG*), output rises. Thus, other things equal, the level of output is determined at the point where aggregate demand for output equals supply. For a given period of time, say, for a year, supply is the output of that year. Aggregate demand consists of planned consumption expenditure, C; planned investment in plant and equipment, I; planned government expenditures, G; and planned net exports, NX, that is, exports minus imports:

$$AD = C + I + G + NX$$

Keynes's adjustment mechanism for the goods and services market can be summarized by the following schema:

When $AD > Y$, there is *EDG*, and Y rises.
When $AD < Y$, there is *ESG*, and Y falls.   (24–1)
When $AD = Y$, the goods and services market is in equilibrium, and Y remains unchanged.

Keynes also used an alternative statement of Schema 24–1 that relies on investment and savings. To derive this alternative statement of the adjustment mechanism for the goods and services market, recall first that national output is identical to national income, hence the use of the same symbol, Y. Further note that national income can be consumed, C; saved, S; or paid in net taxes, T, where net taxes equal total taxes, TA, minus transfer payments, TR. The relation between consumption, savings, net taxes, and national income is called the *disposition-of-income relation*: $C + S + T = Y$.

Substituting $C + I + G + NX$ for AD and $C + S + T$ for Y yields:

$$AD > Y \Rightarrow C + I + G + NX > C + S + T \Rightarrow I + G + NX > S + T$$
$$AD < Y \Rightarrow C + I + G + NX < C + S + T \Rightarrow I + G + NX < S + T$$
$$AD = Y \Rightarrow C + I + G + NX = C + S + T \Rightarrow I + G + NX = S + T$$

For simplicity, assume there is no government and no international trade, that is, G, T, and NX each equals zero. Given such an assumption, Keynes's adjustment mechanism for the goods and services market becomes:

When $I > S$, there is *EDG*, and Y rises.

When $I < S$, there is *ESG*, and Y falls.   (24–2)

When $I = S$, the goods and services market is in equilibrium and Y remains unchanged.

Having asserted that the equality between investment and savings determines (real) income and not the interest rate, Keynes had to face the question of where the interest rate is determined. Here he introduced another novelty. According to Keynes, the interest rate is determined in the money market at the level that makes the demand for money equal to the supply of money. Moreover, when there is excess demand for money (EDM), the interest rate rises, and when there is excess supply of money (ESM), the interest rate falls. Of course, this is the liquidity preference theory of interest rate determination introduced in Chapter 9. In schematic form:

When $M^d > M^S$, there is *EDM*, and i rises.

When $M^d < M^S$, there is *ESM*, and i falls;   (24–3)

When $M^d = M^S$, the money market is in equilibrium, and i remains unchanged.

The *General Theory* provided the blueprint for the simultaneous determination of the interest rate and output. A year after the publication of the *General Theory*, J. R. Hicks of Oxford University formalized that approach in a simple model that has since been popularized as the **IS-LM model**.[1] This model solves two equations for two unknowns, the interest rate and real income:

$$\left.\begin{array}{l}\text{Goods market equilibrium: } AD = Y \\ \text{Money market equilibrium: } M^d = M^s\end{array}\right\} \text{ determine } i \text{ and } Y$$

This chapter develops the *IS-LM* model. First the chapter examines the factors that affect the equilibrium level of income (and output), assuming that the interest rate is given. Then it explains how changes in the interest rate affect the equilibrium level of income. Finally it brings the money market into the model to determine simultaneously i and Y. The emphasis in this chapter is on building the *IS-LM* model. The next chapter applies the model.

DETERMINING NATIONAL INCOME: THE MARKET FOR GOODS AND SERVICES

The simplest way to introduce the Keynesian model of national income determination is to assume that of all the components of *AD* only consumption, C, depends on the level of real income, Y. The relation between consumption and its determinants is called the **consumption function**. The primary determinant of the level of consumption is the level of real income. According to the consumption function, the higher the level of real income, the higher the level of consumption demand. The consumption function is illustrated by the upward-sloping *CC* curve in Figure 24–1, where real income is measured on

---

[1] J. R. Hicks, "Mr. Keynes and the Classics," *Econometrica*, April 1937, 147–59. Hicks received the Nobel Prize for his contributions to both macroeconomics and microeconomics.

FIGURE 24–1
Components of
Aggregate Demand

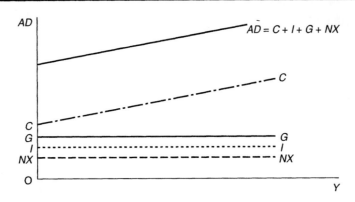

Aggregate demand for goods and services is the sum of consumption demand, investment demand, government demand, and demand for net exports. The vertical intercept of the *AD* curve measures that part of demand that is independent of income. The positive slope of the *AD* curve means that aggregate demand varies positively with income, because consumption varies positively with income.

the horizontal axis and aggregate demand and its components on the vertical axis. The vertical intercept measures that part of consumption, *OC*, that is independent of national income. And the slope of the curve is the **marginal propensity to consume out of national income**, $\Delta C/\Delta Y$, which measures the change in consumption induced by a given change in national income.

It is assumed that all the other components of aggregate demand are independent of income. The horizontal line *II* in Figure 24–1 indicates that planned investment in plant and equipment, inventories, and residential structures is a given quantity, *OI*, independent of the level of real income. The horizontal line *GG* indicates that the level of government expenditure on final goods and services, *0G*, is also independent of the level of real income. Finally, the level of net exports, *0NX*, is also independent of *Y* and illustrated by the horizontal line *(NX)(NX)*. Adding the four lines *CC*, *II*, *GG*, and *(NX)(NX)* derives an upward-sloping curve for aggregate demand, *AD*. The slope of the aggregate demand curve is the **marginal propensity to spend out of national income**, $\Delta(AD)/\Delta Y$, which is the amount by which aggregate demand changes in response to a given change in national income. Because only consumption depends on national income in Figure 24–1, the marginal propensity to spend out of national income equals the marginal propensity to consume out of national income; that is, the slope of the *AD* curve equals the slope of the *CC* curve.

Equilibrium in the goods and services market is determined at the level of output where *AD* = *Y*, that is, at the point where aggregate demand equals aggregate output. To depict this equilibrium graphically, Figure 24–2 uses the *AD* curve and the 45-degree line. The 45-degree line is the locus of points for which the horizontal distance equals the vertical distance. The 45-degree line can transform any given level of *Y* from a horizontal

FIGURE 24–2
Equilibrium in the
Market for Goods
and Services

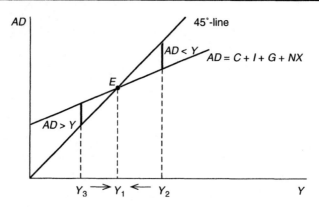

Equilibrium in the goods and services market occurs at the point
where the *AD* curve crosses the 45-degree line. For levels of
output greater than the equilibrium level, Y_1, there is excess supply
of goods and services, and *Y* falls. For levels of output less than
the equilibrium level, there is excess demand for goods and
services, and *Y* rises.

distance to an equivalent vertical distance. At the level of output Y_1, where the *AD* curve
crosses the 45-degree line, *AD* equals *Y*. Thus, at Y_1, the goods and services market is in
equilibrium. On the other hand, for levels of output greater than Y_1, such as Y_2, aggregate
demand is less than aggregate output, and there is excess supply of goods and services
equal to the vertical distance between the 45-degree line and the *AD* curve. In response,
the level of output falls. Finally, for levels of output less than Y_1, such as Y_3, there is
excess demand for goods and services equal to the vertical distance between the *AD*
curve and the 45-degree line. In response, the level of output rises. Only when *Y* equals Y_1
will there be no tendency for output to change, other things equal. Because output
(income) is determined at the point where the *AD* curve crosses the 45-degree line, the
graph in Figure 24–2 has been dubbed the *Keynesian cross*.

Endogenous
and Exogenous
Changes in
Aggregate
Demand

An **endogenous variable** is one determined in the model. In the Keynesian model of the
goods and services market by itself, we solve the equation $AD = Y$ for *Y*. Therefore, *Y* is
the ultimate endogenous variable. And changes in *AD* caused by changes in *Y* are endogenous, or induced, changes in *AD*. They are shown graphically by movements along the
AD curve. On the other hand, additional factors, such as tastes of consumers and government expenditure and taxation policy, also affect *AD*. These other factors are **exogenous
variables**, that is, parameters whose values are determined outside the model. The interest rate is also an exogenous variable in our model of the goods and services market by
itself. However, when the money market is part of the model, the interest rate becomes
endogenous.

Changes in *AD* caused by changes in exogenous factors will shift the *AD* curve. For
example, if the curve shifts upward, at each level of *Y* the demand for goods and services

FIGURE 24-3
An Exogenous
Increase in
Consumption

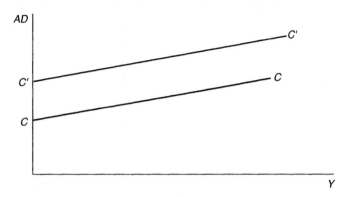

At each level of *Y*, households plan to consume more.

will be greater. If it shifts downward at each level of *Y*, demand will be smaller. The shift may be a parallel shift or a tilt of the *AD* curve that changes the slope. First consider parallel shifts.

An Exogenous Increase in Private Consumption   If the public decides to increase its consumption by a fixed amount at each level of its income, say because of an increase in consumer confidence about the economy, the *CC* curve will shift upward. The corresponding *CC* curve will be parallel to the original curve, but with a lengthier intercept as shown in Figure 24–3. The difference between the new and the old intercept measures the size of the exogenous increase in consumption. The *AD* curve (not shown in Figure 24–3) also shifts by the same vertical distance. The size of the exogenous increase in *AD* equals the increase in its intercept.

An Exogenous Increase in Investment Demand   Another reason why the *AD* curve shifts upward is an exogenous increase in investment demand. For example, if at each level of real income business firms want to undertake a greater investment in plant and equipment or in inventories, there will be an upward parallel shift in the II curve by the amount of the increase in investment, and an upward shift of the *AD* curve by the same amount.

The increase in investment may be caused by any factor other than an increase in real income. For example, it may result from an improvement in the attitude of firms—what Keynes called the *animal spirits of entrepreneurs*. Financial factors, such as the interest rate, also affect the position of the investment curve. The interest rate is the cost of borrowing. Other things equal, a fall in the (nominal) interest rate increases investment. The availability of bank credit and the *Q*-ratio are two other financial factors that affect investment.

Because of asymmetric information and adverse selection, banks ration credit, as Chapters 2 and 10 discussed. **Credit rationing** means that *at any given interest rate* there is a fringe group of unsatisfied customers who can't obtain loans, although they appear similar to other customers who do obtain them. When banks become less willing to lend at any given interest rate, there is a *credit crunch*. Borrowers, such as small firms that are dependent on banks for loans, have less access to credit. As a result, investment in plant and equipment falls, which means the investment curve shifts downward. The end of the credit crunch, on the other hand, shifts the curve upward.

The stock market also influences investment. The Q-ratio, introduced in Chapter 23, is the market valuation in the stock market of the existing capital stock compared with its replacement cost. When this ratio falls, it is cheaper to buy existing plant and equipment than to build new ones. Investment falls and the II curve shifts downward. For example, the falling Q-ratio in the 1970s helped spur the wave of mergers and acquisitions in the early 1980s. Since the mid-1980s the Q-ratio has been rising. More important, in 1993 the estimated value of Q was above the threshold value of 1.0, at which market valuation equals replacement cost. (See MarketWatch 23.4 in Chapter 23). The last time Q was above one, in the mid-to-late 1960s, there was an investment boom, which means the II curve shifted upward. In the first six months of 1994, an increasing number of U.S. companies were expanding plant capacity, at least in part because it was cheaper to build new plants than to buy existing ones.

An Exogenous Increase in Net Exports   An upward shift in the aggregate demand curve will also result from an increase in net exports, NX, again for reasons other than a change in domestic real income.[2] For example, a change in tastes that increases the demand for U.S. products by the rest of the world means U.S. exports rise. Such an increase will shift the (NX)(NX) curve to a higher position, which, in turn, will shift the AD curve by the same vertical distance.

An Exogenous Increase in Government Expenditure   Finally, the aggregate demand curve will shift upward because of a change in fiscal policy. In particular, an increase in government expenditure on final goods and services, G, will shift the AD curve upward.

The Effect on Real Income of Exogenous Changes in Aggregate Demand

This section examines the effect on the level of real income of an exogenous increase in aggregate demand. In Figure 24–4 the original equilibrium level of real income, Y_1, is determined by the intersection of the aggregate demand curve AD and the 45-degree line at point E. Suppose that an exogenous increase in any component of aggregate demand displaces the curve to position AD′. At the level of output Y_1, there is excess demand for goods and services equal to the distance ED, which is the distance between the AD′ curve and the 45-degree line. Excess demand for goods and services means that firms can sell more output than they are currently producing. Therefore, they hire more labor and produce more output.[3] The increase in Y induces further increases in aggregate demand,

---

[2] The net export curve is horizontal because of the simplifying assumption that net exports do not vary with income. If imports vary positively with income, however, the net export curve will be downward sloping, which will reduce the slope of the AD curve.

[3] We assume that the economy is operating below the full-employment level of output so there is room for expansion. This expansion may also result in an increase in the price level, as Chapter 10 shows. We assume prices are fixed at this point because our model consists of only one equation, $AD = Y$, which determines one unknown, Y. Chapter 26 expands the model to explain the determination of the price level.

FIGURE 24–4
The Effect of an
Exogenous
Increase in
Aggregate Demand

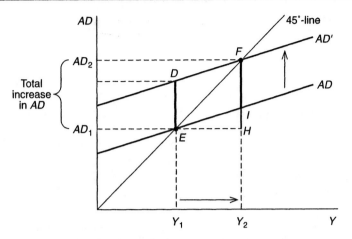

The initial equilibrium level of output is Y_1. An exogenous increase in
aggregate demand, equal to *ED*, creates excess demand for goods and
services. As a result the equilibrium level of output increases to Y_2.
Because the increase in *Y* induces further increases in aggregate demand,
the total increase in *AD* and, hence, in *Y* is a multiple of the initial
exogenous increase in *AD*.

as shown by the movement along the AD' curve from point D to point F. At point F,
aggregate demand equals aggregate output, with Y equal to Y_2. In sum, the equilibrium
level of Y has increased from Y_1 to Y_2, and the equilibrium level of aggregate demand
from AD_1 to AD_2, as shown on the vertical axis in Figure 24–4.

Now consider the magnitude of the increase in Y. The **income multiplier** is defined as
the ratio of the increase in real income, or real output, Y, to the exogenous increase in
aggregate demand that causes the increase in output. The income multiplier is a number
greater than 1 as long as the aggregate demand curve is upward sloping. Figure 24–4
shows the reason for the multiplier effect. The exogenous increase in AD increases
demand by the amount ED. Again, however, the subsequent increase in Y induces further
increases in aggregate demand, shown by the movement along the new aggregate demand
curve. These induced increases in aggregate demand are the source of the multiplier.
They make the total increase in aggregate demand and, hence, the increase in aggregate
output greater than the initial exogenous increase in aggregate demand.

In Figure 24–4 the income multiplier equals the ratio (HF/IF). Let us see why. Real
income increases by the horizontal distance EH. Using the 45-degree line, this increase in
income equals the vertical distance HF. The exogenous increase in aggregate demand in
the denominator of the multiplier equals the vertical distance ED, which equals the
vertical distance IF, where IF is less than HF. The multiplier equals (HF/IF), which is
greater than 1.

Given the magnitude of the exogenous increase in aggregate demand and the magnitude
of the income multiplier, it is possible to find the magnitude of the change in output, Y:

$$\Delta Y = \text{Income multiplier} \times \text{Exogenous } \Delta(AD)$$

To verify this relation, use the example in Figure 24–4:

$$\Delta Y = (HF/IF) \times IF$$
$$= HF$$
$$= EH$$
$$= Y_1Y_2$$

Figure 24–4 shows an increase in Y brought about by an increase in AD. Of course, downward shifts in the AD curve create economic slack and unemployment, causing Y to fall. A sustained period of falling real income is called a **recession**. In the United States, the Business Cycle Dating Committee of the National Bureau of Economic Research—a private, nonprofit research organization that pioneered work on the business cycle—dates the beginning and ending of recessions. SectorWatch 24.1 examines the factors that depressed aggregate demand in the recession of 1990–1991.

Changes in Fiscal Policy and Other Shocks: The Details

The instruments of fiscal policy are the tax, transfer, and government expenditure variables controlled by the government. We have seen that government purchases of final goods and services affect aggregate demand directly. Taxes and transfers, however, influence aggregate demand indirectly through their effect on disposable income. As Chapter 2 explains, transfers are payments by the government, such as social security payments and unemployment benefits, for which no currently produced good or service is received in exchange.

To examine the effects of changes in taxes and transfers, more specific discussion about the consumption function is needed. Consumption depends positively on the level of **disposable income**, not merely national income. Disposable income, Y_D, is determined by subtracting taxes from national income and adding transfer payments. Thus, disposable income is:

$$Y_D = Y - TA + TR \tag{24–4}$$

The consumption function relates the level of consumption demand positively to the level of disposable income:

$$C = C(Y_D, \ldots)$$
$$+$$

 The change in consumption with respect to the change in disposable income is the **marginal propensity to consume out of disposable income**, $\Delta C/\Delta Y_D$. In our Keynesian cross diagrams, the horizontal axis depicts Y, not Y_D, because Y is the variable for which we solve. With Y on the horizontal axis, the slope of the consumption curve is not the marginal propensity to consume out of disposable income. Instead, the slope is the marginal propensity to consume out of national income, which equals the marginal propensity to consume out of disposable income multiplied by the change in disposable income with respect to the change in national income. If taxes or transfers vary with Y, the two marginal propensities will not be the same.

To illustrate the difference between these two marginal propensities to consume, suppose that the consumption function is given by the simple linear equation:

$$C = \overline{C} + c \times Y_D \tag{24–5}$$

SectorWatch 24.1

Aggregate Demand and the Recession of 1990–1991

In July 1990 the U.S. economy entered a recession that lasted until March 1991. One factor dampening aggregate demand in 1990 was the lagged effect of a tighter monetary policy initiated in 1988. Concerned about the risk of an uptick in inflation in the late 1980s, the Fed pushed up short-term interest rates, which depressed demand.

A more immediate factor dampening demand in the summer of 1990, however, was a drastic fall in consumer confidence because of increased uncertainty after the Iraqi invasion of Kuwait in August. In the three months after the invasion, the University of Michigan's *Index of Consumer Sentiment* registered its biggest decline since its introduction in 1956. As a result of the decline in confidence, household expenditure on consumer durables fell at a 15 percent annual rate in the fourth quarter of 1990.* In addition, a reduction in business confidence depressed investment by firms.

The 3.9 percent fall in output (and income) in the fourth quarter of 1990 exposed the balance sheet distress of many households and firms, which had increased their debt burdens in the 1980s. Difficulties in servicing their existing debt made households and firms reluctant to borrow and spend in 1991 even though the Fed was pushing interest rates down. Moreover, tighter scrutiny by bank regulators and a need to strengthen capital positions made banks less willing and able to lend to households and firms. Instead, they increased their loans to the U.S. government by purchasing Treasury securities. As a result, although the recession ended in the spring of 1991, the ensuing recovery was weak by historical standards. The U.S. economy grew by a total of 6 percent in the 2½ years after the end of the 1990–1991 recession, compared with about 13 percent in the typical recovery since World War II.

---

* See Carl E. Walsh "What Caused the 1990–1991 Recession?" *Economic Review* (Federal Reserve Bank of San Francisco), no. 2 (1993): 33–48.

---

where $\overline{C}$ denotes the part of consumption that is independent of disposable income, and c denotes the marginal propensity to consume out of disposable income, a number between zero and one, usually between 0.6 and 0.9. Also suppose that tax revenue consists of a lump sum part, $\overline{TA}$, and a proportional part, tY, where t is the tax rate:

$$TA = \overline{TA} + tY \tag{24–6}$$

Finally, suppose that transfer payments are entirely independent of national income:

$$TR = \overline{TR} \tag{24–7}$$

Substituting Equations 24–6 and 24–7 into the definition of disposable income, Equation 24–4, and combining terms yield:

$$Y_D = (1 - t)Y + \overline{TR} - \overline{TA} \tag{24–8}$$

The coefficient of Y, that is, $(1 - t)$, equals the change in disposable income with respect to the change in national income. For example, if the tax rate is 0.20, disposable income increases by $0.8 billion when national income increases by $1 billion. Now that the change in disposable income with respect to the change in national income is known, merely multiplying that magnitude by the marginal propensity to consume out of disposable income, c, gives the marginal propensity to consume out of national income: $c(1 - t)$. For example, suppose $t = 0.2$ and $c = 0.8$. In this case, when national income increases by

$1 billion, disposable income increases by $0.8 billion, and consumption increases by $0.64 billion.

To confirm these relationships, substitute Equation 24–8 for disposable income into the consumption function, Equation 24–5:

$$C = \overline{C} + c(\overline{TR} - \overline{TA}) + c(1 - t)Y \qquad (24\text{–}9)$$

The coefficient of Y in the consumption function is the marginal propensity to consume out of national income, $c(1 - t)$: Every dollar increase in national income increases disposable income by $(1 - t)$ times a dollar, and consumption by $c(1 - t)$ times a dollar. Figure 24–5 depicts Equation 24–9 graphically. The vertical intercept equals $\overline{C} + c(\overline{TR} - \overline{TA})$, which is that part of consumption that is independent of national income; and the slope of the curve is the marginal propensity to consume out of national income, $c(1 - t)$.

A Decrease in Total Taxes, *TA*   How does a change in taxes influence aggregate demand and, ultimately, the equilibrium level of output? A reduction in lump sum taxes, $\overline{TA}$, increases disposable income by the amount of the tax cut. As a result, consumption rises. The increase in consumption equals the increase in disposable income multiplied by the marginal propensity to consume out of disposable income. Aggregate demand rises by the same amount. As a result, at the initial equilibrium level of output there will be excess demand for goods and services, which causes a rise in real output (real income). Schematically, the following linkages result:

$$\overline{TA}\downarrow \rightarrow Y_D\uparrow \rightarrow C\uparrow \rightarrow AD\uparrow \rightarrow AD > Y \rightarrow Y\uparrow$$

So far we have examined a cut in lump sum taxes. A more frequent form of tax cut is a reduction in the income tax rate(s). A cut in the tax rate, t, increases disposable income at each level of income by *minus Y* times the change in the tax rate: $\Delta Y_D = -Y \times \Delta t$. ($\Delta t$ is negative in our example). As a result, at each level of national income, consumption increases by the marginal propensity to consume out of disposable income *times* the change in disposable income: $\Delta C = -cY\Delta t$. Aggregate demand will exceed national output, thereby causing a rise in output and real income. Schematically, the result of a tax rate reduction is:

$$t\downarrow \rightarrow TA\downarrow \rightarrow Y_D\uparrow \rightarrow C\uparrow \rightarrow AD\uparrow \rightarrow AD > Y \rightarrow Y\uparrow$$

Figure 24–6 depicts this case graphically. The fall in the tax rate from t_1 to t_2 increases the slope of the consumption curve and, hence, the AD curve from $c(1 - t_1)$ to $c(1 - t_2)$. As a result, at the initial equilibrium level of output, Y_1, there is an exogenous increase in consumption and in aggregate demand equal to *minus* $cY_1\Delta t$. With aggregate demand now greater than aggregate output, Y rises, inducing further increases in aggregate demand. And equilibrium is reached at a higher level of output, Y_2.

An Increase in Transfer Payments, *TR*   Transfer payments also affect aggregate demand indirectly, via their impact on the size of disposable income. An increase in lump sum transfer payments has an effect similar to a cut in lump sum taxes. Other things equal, disposable income increases by the amount of the increase in transfer payments,

FIGURE 24–5
The Consumption
Function

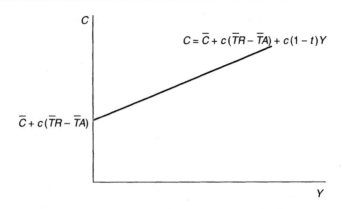

Consumption increases as national income increases. The slope of the
curve is the marginal propensity to consume out of national income,
$c(1 - t)$, and its intercept is the portion of consumption that is
independent of national income.

FIGURE 24–6
The Effect of a Cut
in the Tax Rate on
Real Income (and
Real Output)

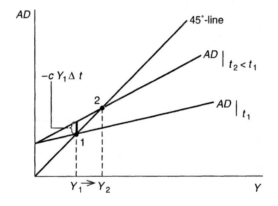

A fall in the tax rate increases the
slope of the consumption curve and,
hence, the AD curve. As a result, at
the initial equilibrium level of output,
Y_1, there is excess demand for goods
and services. In response, the
equilibrium level of output rises to Y_2.

and, hence, consumption and aggregate demand increase. As a result, national production
and national income rise. Schematically, the results are:

$$\overline{TR}\uparrow \rightarrow Y_D\uparrow \rightarrow C\uparrow \rightarrow AD\uparrow \rightarrow AD > Y \rightarrow Y\uparrow$$

An Increase in Government Expenditure, G   Unlike taxes and transfers, government expenditures on final goods and services affects aggregate demand directly. An
increase in government expenditures increases aggregate demand, which will stimulate
production and increase output. Schematically, the linkages are:

$$G\uparrow \rightarrow AD\uparrow \rightarrow AD > Y \rightarrow Y\uparrow$$

An Increase in Consumption, C The consumption curve will shift even without a change in fiscal policy, if the public changes its behavior. Suppose, for example, that a prediction of brighter prospects for the future leads to an increase in $\overline{C}$. The resulting increase in aggregate demand will cause an increase in production and real income:

$$\overline{C}\uparrow \rightarrow AD\uparrow \rightarrow AD > Y \rightarrow Y\uparrow$$

The equilibrium level of output also rises when the marginal propensity to consume out of disposable income, c, rises. Schematically, the linkages are:

$$c\uparrow \rightarrow AD\uparrow \rightarrow AD > Y \rightarrow Y\uparrow$$

In this case, the slope of the consumption curve and that of the AD curve increase. Although the graph resembles the one in Figure 24–6, the steeper slope now results from an increase in c rather than a decrease in t.

An Increase in Investment Demand, I An increase in investment—either in plant and equipment, inventories, or residential structures—increases AD directly, causing an increase in real income:

$$I\uparrow \rightarrow AD\uparrow \rightarrow AD > Y \rightarrow Y\uparrow$$

An Increase in Net Exports, NX Finally, the level of net exports, NX, affects aggregate demand directly. An increase in the trade surplus or a reduction in the trade deficit increases aggregate demand directly and, hence, increases national product and real income:

$$NX\uparrow \rightarrow AD\uparrow \rightarrow AD > Y \rightarrow Y\uparrow$$

In summary, Table 24–1 presents the schematics for changes in eight factors affecting aggregate demand. These factors are the fiscal policy parameters and the behavioral parameters examined in this chapter.

TABLE 24–1 **The Effects of** **Exogenous** **Changes in Eight** **Factors Affecting** **Aggregate Demand**	$\overline{C}\uparrow \rightarrow AD\uparrow \rightarrow AD > Y \rightarrow Y\uparrow$ $c\uparrow \rightarrow AD\uparrow \rightarrow AD > Y \rightarrow Y\uparrow$ $\overline{TA}\downarrow \rightarrow Y_D\uparrow \rightarrow C\uparrow \rightarrow AD\uparrow \rightarrow AD > Y \rightarrow Y\uparrow$ $t\downarrow \rightarrow tY\downarrow \rightarrow Y_D\uparrow \rightarrow C\uparrow \rightarrow AD\uparrow \rightarrow AD > Y \rightarrow Y\uparrow$ $\overline{TR}\uparrow \rightarrow Y_D\uparrow \rightarrow C\uparrow \rightarrow AD\uparrow \rightarrow AD > Y \rightarrow Y\uparrow$ $G\uparrow \rightarrow AD\uparrow \rightarrow AD > Y \rightarrow Y\uparrow$ $I\uparrow \rightarrow AD\uparrow \rightarrow AD > Y \rightarrow Y\uparrow$ $NX\uparrow \rightarrow AD\uparrow \rightarrow AD > Y \rightarrow Y\uparrow$

<table>
<tr><td>The Simple
Algebra of
Income
Determination</td><td>

Using simple algebra to illustrate all the preceding results can deepen our understanding of income determination. Consider first the (goods market) equilibrium relation:

</td></tr>
</table>

The Simple Algebra of Income Determination

Using simple algebra to illustrate all the preceding results can deepen our understanding of income determination. Consider first the (goods market) equilibrium relation:

$$AD = C + I + G + NX = Y \tag{24-10}$$

By substituting consumption function 24–9 for C and collecting terms, the equilibrium condition becomes:

$$AD = \overline{C} + c(\overline{TR} - \overline{TA}) + \overline{I} + \overline{G} + \overline{NX} + c(1 - t)Y = Y \tag{24-11}$$

where a bar over a variable denotes a given value of that variable. Equation 24–11 shows that aggregate demand consists of two components: a collective component that does not depend on national income; and a component that varies with national income. $\overline{A}$ denotes the collective component, called *autonomous demand*, that does not depend on national income:

$$\overline{A} = \overline{C} + c(\overline{TR} - \overline{TA}) + \overline{I} + \overline{G} + \overline{NX}$$

By using $\overline{A}$, the equilibrium condition becomes:

$$\overline{A} + c(1 - t)Y = Y \tag{24-12}$$

Finally, solving Equation 24–12 for Y determines the equilibrium level of real national income:

$$Y = \{1/[1 - c(1 - t)]\} \times \overline{A} \tag{24-13}$$

The term $1/[1 - c(1 - t)]$ is the income multiplier, where $c(1 - t)$ is the slope of the AD curve. The greater this slope, the greater the income multiplier, because a greater slope means greater induced increases in aggregate demand. To find the equilibrium level of Y, we must specify the level of each component of collective autonomous expenditure, $\overline{A}$, and multiply the resulting $\overline{A}$ by the income multiplier.

Equally important, use of Equation 24–13 can determine the effects on real national income of a change in one or more components of $\overline{A}$. A given increase in any of the autonomous components will result in an increase in Y by a multiple of that change, other things equal:

$$\Delta Y = \{1/[1 - c(1 - t)]\} \times \Delta\overline{A}$$

For example, suppose that the marginal propensity to consume out of disposable income, c, is 0.80 and that the tax rate is fixed at 0.20. The income multiplier will be 2.78. For every increase in $\overline{A}$ of \$1 billion, real income will rise by \$2.78 billion.

When the change in aggregate demand results form a change in c or t, the multiplier itself changes. The multiplier will increase if c rises or t falls. A higher c or a lower t will increase the slope of the AD curve, and any exogenous increase in aggregate demand will therefore lead to a greater induced increase in aggregate demand. Suppose, for example, that the tax rate falls from 0.20 to 0.10 as a result of a change in fiscal policy. In this case, with c still equal to 0.8, the multiplier will be 3.57.

Figure 24–6 depicts the case of a fall in the tax rate. To find the change in national income, we must multiply the income multiplier calculated at the new tax rate by the exogenous change in aggregate demand calculated at the initial equilibrium level of income. Figure 24–6 shows that the exogenous change in aggregate demand equals *minus* $cY\Delta t$. In our example, minus $\Delta t = 0.10$. Multiplying 0.10 by the initial equilibrium level of national income, Y_1, gives the change in disposable income at the initial level of Y. Finally, multiplying this magnitude by the marginal propensity to consume out of national income yields the exogenous change in consumption at the initial level of Y, to which we apply the multiplier. In general, the change in the equilibrium level of income equals the exogenous change in aggregate demand at the initial equilibrium level of income times the multiplier.

TRY IT OUT 24.1

Consider the following model of the goods and services market, in which C, I, and G are all expressed in billions of dollars:

Consumption function: $C = 400 + 0.80Y_D$
Disposable income: $Y_D = Y + TR - TA$
Investment: $I = 100$
Government purchases: $G = 100$
Taxes: $TA = 0.25Y$
Transfer payments: $TR = 0$
Net exports: $NX = 0$

a. Calculate the equilibrium value of real income, Y.
b. What is the size of the multiplier?
c. Suppose that the government reduces the tax rate, so that $TA = 0.20Y$. Find the new value of the multiplier. Find the change in the equilibrium level of real income.

GOODS MARKET EQUILIBRIUM: THE *IS* CURVE

So far the interest rate has been implicit in our discussion of the factors affecting aggregate demand. The interest rate is one of the factors included in $\bar{I}$, the exogenous factors affecting investment. Now we want to separate the interest rate from the other factors affecting investment, because when we add the money market to our model, i will become an endogenous variable.

Investment Demand

As Chapter 10 explains, investment in plant and equipment, inventories, and residential structures depends negatively on the cost of borrowing, that is, the interest rate. The lower the interest rate, the higher investment demand. In general functional form:

$$I = I(\underline{i}, \ldots) \qquad (24\text{–}14)$$

A simple linear example of the investment relation is:

$$I = \bar{I} - fi \qquad (24\text{–}15)$$

FIGURE 24-7
Investment
Demand

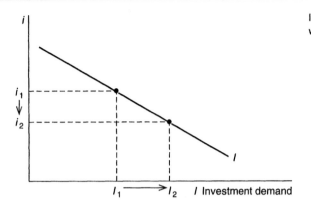

Investment demand varies inversely
with the interest rate.

where f is the interest sensitivity of investment, that is, the amount by which investment changes in response to a given change in the interest rate. On the other hand, $\bar{I}$ is that part of investment that is independent of the interest rate. Both $\bar{I}$ and f are positive in this equation.

Figure 24-7 depicts the inverse relation between the interest rate and investment in a graph with i measured on the vertical axis and I on the horizontal axis. At the interest rate i_1, investment demand is I_1. At the lower interest rate, i_2, investment demand increases to I_2.

The position of the investment demand curve is affected by the risk of doing business, or, in Keynes's words, by the "animal spirits" of entrepreneurs. The riskier the business, the smaller the investment demand at each level of the interest rate. Thus, an increase in the risk of doing business shifts the investment curve inward. The investment curve would also shift inward if a credit crunch made it more difficult for businesses to borrow from banks at each interest rate, or if a decrease in expected profits decreased the market valuation of the existing capital stock, thereby reducing the Q-ratio.

Derivation of the *IS* Curve

Because the level of the interest rate affects investment, which, in turn, affects aggregate demand, there is a relation between the interest rate and the equilibrium level of income, Y: A fall in the interest rate, i, increases investment demand, I, and aggregate demand, AD; the increase in aggregate demand causes excess demand for goods and services, stimulating production to meet this increased demand; and increased production is seen as a higher real income at the new equilibrium. Schematically, the results of a decrease in the interest rate are:

$$i \downarrow \Rightarrow I\uparrow \Rightarrow AD\uparrow \Rightarrow AD > Y \Rightarrow Y\uparrow$$

The two panels of Figure 24-8 depict the negative relation between the interest rate and the goods-market-clearing level of output, or, income, Y. In the upper panel of the graph, AD is measured on the vertical axis and Y on the horizontal axis. Therefore, a change in the interest rate shifts the AD curve. This shift results from a shift of the II curve (the investment

FIGURE 24–8
Derivation of the
IS **Curve**

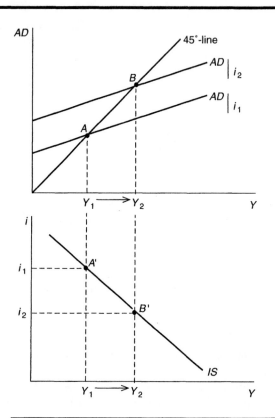

Other things equal, $i\downarrow \rightarrow I\uparrow \rightarrow AD\uparrow \rightarrow AD > Y \rightarrow Y\uparrow$.

demand curve) in Figure 24–1. There is one II curve for each level of the interest rate; the lower the interest rate, the higher the position of the II curve.[4] As a consequence, there is also one *AD* curve for each possible level of the interest rate. The lower the interest rate, the higher the *AD* curve, and the higher the equilibrium level of output.

The lower panel of Figure 24–8 depicts the negative relation between the interest rate, i, and the level of real income, Y, that has been dubbed the ***IS* curve**. Note that the interest rate is on the vertical axis and real income on the horizontal axis in this diagram. The *IS* curve is the locus of all combinations of the interest rate and real income that clear the market for goods and services: $AD = Y$.[5] The *IS* curve in the lower panel of Figure 24–8 shows that when the interest rate is i_1, the goods-market-clearing level of output is Y_1. And when the interest rate falls to i_2, the goods-market-clearing level of output rises to Y_2.

To derive the *IS* curve, go back to the upper panel of Figure 24–8. If the interest rate is i_1, the level of Y that clears the goods and services market, given by point A, is Y_1. Now transfer this result to the lower panel of Figure 24–8 as point A'. When the interest rate is

---

[4] For simplicity, we ignore the effects of the interest rate on consumption. Empirically they are not large.
[5] In the simple case when there is no government sector and no international sector, equilibrium in the goods market implies that investment (I) equals savings (S). Hence, the name, *IS curve*.

lower, say, i_2, the new equilibrium is at point B in the upper panel, indicating that the equilibrium level of Y rises to Y_2. Now transfer this result to the lower panel as point B'. Repeating this process for all levels of the interest rate and connecting the corresponding points in the lower panel yield the curve called the *IS curve*.

Adding the International Linkages

The negative relation between the interest rate and aggregate demand for goods and services causes the *IS* curve to slope downward. The investment component of aggregate demand depends directly on the interest rate. Net exports, on the other hand, depend indirectly on the interest rate. This linkage runs through the foreign exchange market.

A decrease in domestic interest rates (relative to foreign interest rates) makes foreign securities more attractive than domestic securities. As a result, the demand for foreign securities by Americans rises. To buy foreign securities, however, Americans need foreign currency. The increased demand for foreign exchange creates excess demand for foreign exchange, which causes the price of foreign currency, e, to rise. And when e rises, foreign goods become relatively more expensive for Americans, and American goods become relatively cheaper for foreigners. As a result, American exports rise and American imports fall, so that net exports, *NX*, rise.

When we incorporate the international linkages, a given fall in the interest rate results in a greater increase in *AD* and, hence, in Y. Graphically, the *IS* curve with the international linkages is flatter than the *IS* curve without the international linkages as shown in Figure 24–9. Schematically, the domestic and international linkages are:

$$i\downarrow \begin{matrix} \nearrow I\uparrow \quad \rightarrow \quad AD\uparrow \\ \searrow e\uparrow \rightarrow NX\uparrow \rightarrow AD\uparrow \end{matrix} \Bigg\} \rightarrow AD > Y \rightarrow Y\uparrow$$

**FIGURE 24–9
The *IS* Curve with and without the International Linkages**

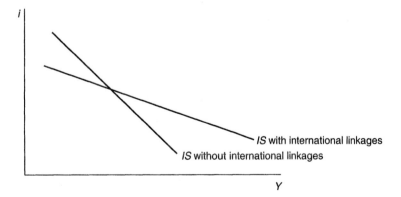

With the international linkages, a given reduction in the interest rate causes a greater increase in aggregate demand and, hence, in *Y*. Therefore, the *IS* curve with the international linkages is flatter than the *IS* curve without the international linkages.

MONEY MARKET EQUILIBRIUM: THE *LM* CURVE

Relying only on the equilibrium of the goods and services market to determine the level of income results in an indeterminancy. The *IS* curve makes clear that determining the level of income, Y, is not possible without knowing the level of the interest rate, i. Therefore, we need another relation between the interest rate and the level of income that will enable us to determine simultaneously the interest rate and real income.

The problem is similar to solving for two unknowns, say, x and y, in high school algebra. This requires two equations in x and y. Here the unknowns are i and Y. The *IS* relation amounts to one equation in two unknowns, hence, the need for another equation in these two unknowns. Graphically, there must be another curve in the (i, Y)-plane that will intersect the *IS* curve in order to determine not only the level of real income, Y, but also the interest rate, i. Here is where the *LM* curve enters the picture.

The **LM curve** is the locus of all combinations of the interest rate and income that clear the money market; that is, all the pairs of (i, Y) that make the demand for money, M^d, equal to the supply of money, M^s. The name of the curve comes from Keynes's notation of money demand, L, and money supply, M. Therefore, *LM* stands for the equality, $L = M$.

Chapters 9 and 21, using a graph of the money market in which i is on the vertical axis and the quantity of money on the horizontal axis, show that an increase in real income increases the demand for money, thereby creating excess demand for money. As a result, the interest rate rises. Schematically, an increase in real income has the following results:

$$Y\uparrow \rightarrow M^d\uparrow \rightarrow M^d > M^s \rightarrow i\uparrow$$

The right panel of Figure 24–10 depicts the upward-sloping *LM* curve. It shows that when the level of real income is Y_1, the money-market-clearing level of the interest rate is i_1. And when the level of real income rises to Y_2, the money-market-clearing level of the interest rate rises to i_2. To derive the *LM* curve, go back to the left panel of Figure 24–10, which depicts the money demand and money supply curves. When the level of income is equal to Y_1, the interest rate is determined by the intersection of the M^s curve and the M^d curve with the label Y_1. The intersection occurs at point A in the left panel. Now transfer this information to the right panel as point A'. When the level of real income rises to Y_2, the money demand curve shifts to the right. The increased money demand creates excess demand for money at the original level of the interest rate, which forces the money-market-clearing interest rate to rise. The intersection of M^d and M^s occurs at point B. Now transfer this to the right panel as point B'. Repeating this process for all levels of Y and connecting the resulting points in the right panel derive the upward-sloping *LM* curve.

THE *IS-LM* MODEL

We are now ready to determine all the unknowns except the price level, which we still assume is constant. From the *IS-LM* graph, we determine the equilibrium levels of the interest rate and real income. Knowing this pair, we can determine consumption and investment, which depend on them.

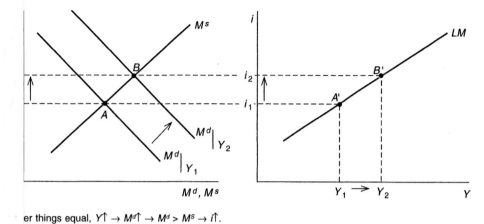

er things equal, $Y\uparrow \rightarrow M^d\uparrow \rightarrow M^d > M^s \rightarrow i\uparrow$.

the given price level and the assumed values of all exogenous variables, the equilib-
m levels of the interest rate and real income, i_1 and Y_1, respectively, are determined at
point of intersection between the *IS* and the *LM* curves—at point *E* in Figure 24–11.
:ause the intersection point lies on the *IS* curve, it has the property that the goods and
vices market is in equilibrium. And because the same point lies on the *LM* curve, the
ney market and, hence, the entire financial sector is in equilibrium. Thus, at (i_1, Y_1)
h markets are in equilibrium.

equilibrium values of i and Y will change if the *IS* curve or the *LM* curve shifts.
ure 24–12 depicts a shift of the *IS* curve to the right and up. Such a shift of the *IS*
ve means that at each level of i, the level of real income that clears the goods and
vices market is greater than it was before. The interest rate, i, however, does not

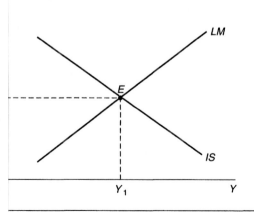

The intersection of the *IS* and *LM*
curves determines the values of i and
Y such that the goods and services
market and the money market are in
equilibrium, other things equal.

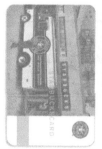

FIGURE 24–12
A Shift of the *IS*
Curve

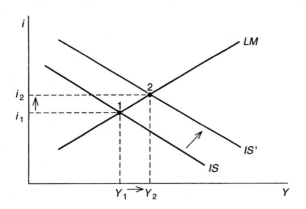

When the *IS* curve shifts to the right
and up, the equilibrium level of the
interest rate and that of real income
rise.

remain at its original level. At the new equilibrium, where the new *IS* curve intersects the original *LM* curve, both *i* and *Y* are higher than at the original equilibrium.

Figure 24–13 depicts a shift of the *LM* curve to the right and down. Such a shift of the *LM* curve means that at each level of real income, the level of the interest rate that clears the money market is less than it was before. Real income, *Y*, however, does not remain at its original level. The intersection of the new *LM* curve and the original *IS* curve occurs at a lower level of *i* and at a higher level of *Y*.

In sum, depending on whether the *IS* curve shifts or the *LM* curve shifts, an increase in real income will be accompanied by a rise or a fall in the interest rate. Chapter 25 examines shifts of these two curves and the interactions they trigger between the real and the financial sectors. In preparation for that analysis, consider the type of factors that shifts the *LM* and *IS* curves.

Factors Affecting the Position of the *LM* Curve   Movements along the *LM* curve show how the money-market-clearing interest rate changes as the level of real income changes. Any factor other than *Y* that shifts the M^d curve or the M^S curve will shift the *LM* curve. At each level of *Y*, the interest rate that clears the money market will be higher or lower, depending on the shock, and, will therefore lie on a different *LM* curve.

Among the factors that shift the *LM* curve are changes in the instruments of monetary policy, changes in the reserve management practices of banks, or changes in the price level. All of these factors work through the money supply curve. On the other hand, a change in the portfolio behavior of the public, which also shifts the *LM* curve, works through the money demand curve.

Factors Affecting the Position of the *IS* Curve   Movements along the *IS* curve show how the goods-market-clearing level of output changes as the interest rate changes. Any factor other than *i* that shifts the *AD* curve will shift the *IS* curve. At each level of the interest rate, the level of *Y* that clears the goods and services market will be higher or lower, depending on the shock, and will therefore lie on a different *IS* curve.

FIGURE 24–13
A Shift of the *LM*
Curve

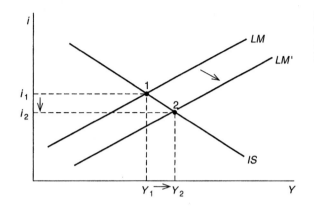

When the *LM* curve shifts down and to the right, the equilibrium level of the interest rate falls and the equilibrium level of real income rises.

Some of these factors that shift the *IS* curve are changes in fiscal policy instruments, such as the level of government expenditure on final goods and services, the tax rate, and transfer payments. In other cases, the shifts arise from changes in behavior and attitudes of households and nonfinancial firms, both domestic and foreign.

SUMMARY

- The *IS-LM* model is a two-equation model of the real and the financial sectors that simultaneously determines two variables: real income, or real output, Y; and the interest rate, i. One of the two equations represents equilibrium in the market for goods and services: $AD = Y$. And the other equation represents equilibrium in the market for money: $M^d = M^s$.

- Assuming the interest rate is given, we first examine equilibrium in the market for goods and services by itself. The key graphical tool is the Keynesian cross diagram in the (AD, Y)-plane. The upward-sloping AD curve means that aggregate demand for goods and services varies positively with real income. Equilibrium occurs at the point where the AD curve crosses the 45-degree line.

- In the model of the goods and services market by itself, any factor other than Y that affects AD is an exogenous variable, that is, a parameter determined outside the model. A change in an exogenous variable will result either in a parallel shift or a tilt of the AD curve.

- An exogenous increase in aggregate demand first leads to an equal increase in real output, or real income, which induces further increases in aggregate demand and real income. As a result, an exogenous increase in

aggregate demand causes a multiple increase in the equilibrium level of income (and output), where the income multiplier is a number greater than 1. The steeper the aggregate demand curve, the greater the induced increases in aggregate demand and, hence, the greater the multiplier.

- Table 24–1 sums up the effects on the goods and services market of changes in eight exogenous factors affecting aggregate demand, including the three instruments of fiscal policy: government expenditures on final goods and services, transfer payments, and tax rates. Government expenditures affect aggregate demand directly. But transfers and taxes affect aggregate demand indirectly through disposable income. Disposable income equals national income plus transfer payments minus taxes. The consumption component of aggregate demand varies positively with disposable income.

- In the (i, Y)-plane, the *IS* curve is the locus of combinations of i and Y for which $AD = Y$, other things equal. The curve is downward sloping because a reduction in the interest rate increases aggregate demand for goods and services and, therefore, increases the goods-market-clearing level of output.

- A lower interest rate affects aggregate demand through two channels: investment and net exports. A lower i directly increases investment. On the other hand, a lower i indirectly increases net exports: a reduction in i leads to an increase in demand for foreign securities, an increase in the foreign exchange rate and, thus, an increase in net exports. The *IS* curve with the international linkages is flatter than the *IS* curve without the international linkages.

- The *LM* curve represents equilibrium in the money market. It is the locus of combinations of i and Y for which money demand equals money supply, other things equal. The *LM* curve is upward sloping because an increase in real income increases the demand for money. As a result, there will be excess demand for money, which forces the interest rate to rise.

- The intersection of the *IS* and *LM* curves determines simultaneously the equilibrium level of real income and of the interest rate.

- When the *IS* curve shifts, the equilibrium level of the interest rate and of real income move in the same direction. When the *LM* curve shifts, the equilibrium level of the interest rate and that of real income move in the opposite direction.

KEY TERMS AND CONCEPTS

IS-LM model	endogenous variable	disposable income
consumption function	exogenous variables	marginal propensity to consume out of disposable income
marginal propensity to consume out of national income	credit rationing	*IS* curve
marginal propensity to spend out of national income	income multiplier	*LM* curve
	recession	

QUESTIONS AND PROBLEMS

1. Suppose that at each level of the interest rate the availability of credit for firms to finance investment in plant and equipment falls because of a credit crunch. With the help of a Keynesian cross diagram, explain the effect on the equilibrium level of real income, Y.

2. Suppose that because of a reduction in consumer confidence the marginal propensity to consume out of disposable income falls. With the help of a Keynesian cross diagram, explain the effect on the equilibrium level of real income.

3. Consider a simple economy with no international or government sectors, with investment, $\bar{I}$, equal to $100 billion, and a consumption function described by the following equation:

$$C = 400 + 0.80Y_D$$

where Y_D is disposable income.
   a. Calculate the equilibrium value of real income, Y.

   b. What is the size of the multiplier?

4. When is the marginal propensity to consume out of national income equal to the marginal propensity to consume out of disposable income?

5. A reduction in income tax rates:
   a. increases the multiplier.
   b. reduces the multiplier.
   c. leaves the multiplier unchanged.

6. "A $1 billion increase in government expenditure on goods and services has the same effect on the economy (national output) as a $1 billion increase in net exports." Explain why you agree or disagree with the statement.

7. "A $1 billion increase in government expenditure on goods and services has the same effect on the economy as a $1 billion increase in government expenditure on transfers." Explain why you agree or disagree.

8. Explain why an increase in government purchases of goods and services financed by an increase in lump sum taxes increases real GDP.

9. Suppose that because of a fall in their animal spirits, entrepreneurs reduce their planned investment in plant and equipment by $5 billion. Is a reduction of lump sum taxes of the general public by $5 billion sufficient to negate any adverse effect on real GDP? Why or why not?

10. Consider the following hypothetical model of the goods and services market, in which C, I, G, and NX are in billions of dollars:

Consumption function: $C = 800 + 0.80Y_D$

Taxes: $TA = 150 + 0.20Y$

Transfers: $TR = 700$

Investment: $I = 151.604$

Government purchases: $G = 800$

Net exports: $NX = -50$

a. Find the equilibrium value of real income, Y.
b. What is the size of the multiplier?
c. Starting from the initial position (that is, your answer to a), find the effect on Y when I changes to 231.604 because of an increase in the animal spirits of entrepreneurs.
d. Starting from the initial position, assume that, other things equal, G increases by 80. What will happen to Y? Illustrate your results graphically.
e. Again, starting from the initial position, assume, instead, that transfers change to $TR = 780$. What is the effect on Y? Explain why this result is different than your result in d.
f. Next, find the effect on Y if, instead, the tax equation changes to $TA = 70 + .20Y$.

11. What is wrong with the following statement: "The IS curve depicts in the (i, Y)-plane all the combinations of i and Y."

12. Explain in words why the IS curve is downward sloping.

13. Explain in words why the LM curve is upward sloping.

The Wall Street Journal

14. The following quotation is from "Firms to Boost Their Spending 8.3% This Year," *The Wall Street Journal*, June 10, 1994, A2: "The Commerce Department said businesses plan to boost capital spending 8.3% this year, compared with plans for an 8.0% rise expected in the April report. Business investment in capital equipment and buildings rose 7.1% in 1993 and 3.4% in 1992. . . . the report suggests higher interest rates haven't dampened business appetite for investment." Explain what factors could be offsetting the effects of higher interest rates on investment. Also explain how these factors affect the IS curve.

15. Consider the following real sector of an economy:

Consumption function: $C = 800 + 0.80Y_D$

Taxes: $T_A = 150 + 0.20Y$

Transfers: $TR = 700$

Investment: $I = 250 - 10i$

Government purchases: $G = 800$

Net exports: $NX = -50$

Derive the IS curve as an equation by solving for Y as a function of i. Verify that the equation has the economic properties of an IS curve. (Note that with the exception of investment, I, this is the same economy examined in question 10.)

16. Consider the following financial sector of an economy:

Money demand: $M^d = 450 - 0.261i + 0.097Y$

Money supply: $M^S = 155 + 10NBR/P + 4i$

where NBR is nominal nonborrowed reserves and P is the price level. Suppose

$NBR = \$78$ billion and $P = 1$

Derive the LM curve as an equation by solving for i as a function of Y. Verify that the equation has the economic properties of an LM curve.

17. Combine the IS equation you derived in 15 with the LM equation in 16 to determine the values of the interest rate, i, and income, Y. Illustrate your result with a diagram.

18. "Sometimes we observe the interest rate and real income moving in the same direction and other times in the opposite direction." Illustrate graphically and explain.

SUGGESTED READINGS

Bernanke, Ben and Alan Blinder, "Credit, Money, and Aggregate Demand," *American Economic Review*, May 1988, 435–39.

Incorporates credit into the IS-LM framework.

Hansen, Alvin H. *Guide to Keynes* (New York: McGraw-Hill, 1953).

A classic book that is a tutorial guide to the *General Theory*. It popularized the *ISLM* model, which is also referred to as the *Hicks-Hansen model*.

Kahn, George A. "The Changing Interest Sensitivity of the U.S. Economy." *Economic Review* (Federal Reserve Bank of Kansas City), November 1989, 13–34.

Examines how financial deregulation and the increasing importance of international trade have affected the interest sensitivity of the U.S. economy.

Throop, Adrian W. "Consumer Sentiment: Its Causes and Effects." *Economic Review* (Federal Reserve Bank of San Francisco), no. 1 (1992), 35–59.

Examines the effects of consumer attitudes, as measured by the University of Michigan index, on household purchases of goods and services.

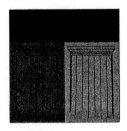

MONETARY AND FISCAL POLICY IN THE *IS-LM* MODEL

CHAPTER PREVIEW

Changes in monetary policy originate in the financial sector and, therefore, directly affect the interest rate. The story does not end there, however. Changes in the interest rate ricochet off the goods and services market, affecting real income, which feeds back on the interest rate. Analogously, changes in fiscal policy originate in the real sector and directly affect real income, which affects money demand and, hence, the interest rate. Changes in the interest rate, in turn, affect the aggregate demand for goods and services.

This chapter uses the *IS-LM* model developed in Chapter 24 to examine the effects of changes in monetary and fiscal policies on the interest rate and real income and on the variables that depend on them. By incorporating the international linkages, the chapter explains how tax cuts in the United States in the early 1980s created not only budget deficits but also trade deficits. The two deficits were dubbed the **twin deficits**.

Policy shocks are not the only factors that affect the interest rate and real income. Changes in the behavior of the public, nonfinancial firms, and financial intermediaries can also shift the *IS* curve or the *LM* curve. The analysis of behavioral shocks that change the interest rate and real income raises questions about the targets of monetary policy. This chapter revisits the issue of targeting monetary aggregates discussed in Chapter 16 to answer the following questions: If a goal of monetary policy is to minimize the volatility in real income, when is it preferable for the central bank to target the quantity of money? And when is it preferable to target the interest rate? The chapter connects theory with practice by using the *IS-LM* model to explain the actions of the Fed in the 1990s.

MONETARY POLICY

Figure 25–1 depicts the *IS-LM* model developed in Chapter 24. The *IS* curve represents equilibrium in the goods and services market, and the *LM* curve represents equilibrium in the money market. The position of the *LM* curve depends on the instruments of monetary policy. Changes in these instruments shift the curve. For example, an open market purchase of Treasury securities by the Fed, a reduction in the discount rate, or a loosening of the administration of the discount window by the Fed will all shift the *LM* curve down and to the right. Because open market operations are the primary instrument of monetary policy, this chapter concentrates on them.

Open Market Operations

An open market purchase of Treasury securities by the Fed increases nonborrowed reserves in the banking system, which increases the money supply. As a result, there is excess supply of money, which causes the interest rate to fall, other things equal. Among the other things held equal is the level of real income. As Chapter 10 explains, this fall in the interest rate, given real income, is called the **liquidity effect** of an increase in nonborrowed reserves, because the Fed adds more liquidity to the banking system. Figure 25–2, which depicts money demand and money supply, illustrates the liquidity effect by a movement of the intersection of the M^s and M^d curves from point A to point B in the left panel. The given level of real income, Y_1, is in the label of the M^d curve. The increase in nonborrowed reserves from NBR_1 to NBR_2 shifts the money supply curve to the right.

The right panel shows that at the original level of real income, Y_1, the money-market-clearing interest rate, i_2, is lower. This fall in the interest rate is shown by a shift from point A' to point B', the counterparts of points A and B in the left panel. Repeating this exercise for all levels of Y results in the new LM curve that lies to the right of (and under) the original position. Thus, an open market increase in nonborrowed reserves shifts the LM curve down and to the right.

To examine the reactions of the goods and services market to open market operations, the IS curve must be added to the graph. Figure 25–3 shows that point B' is on the LM

FIGURE 25–1
The *IS-LM* Graph

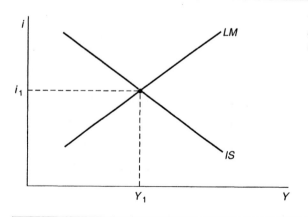

The intersection of the *IS* and *LM* curves determines the interest rate, *i*, and real income, *Y*.

FIGURE 25–2
An Increase in
Nonborrowed
Reserves and the
LM Curve

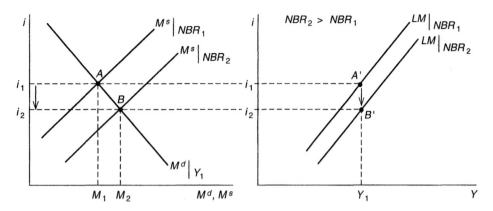

For a given level of *Y*, an increase in nonborrowed reserves, *NBR*, increases the money supply and lowers the money-market-clearing level of the interest rate—as shown by the movement from point *A* to point *B* in the left panel and from point *A′* to point *B′* in the right panel, when *Y* equals Y_1. If we repeat this exercise for each level of *Y*, we find that the *LM* curve shifts downward when *NBR* increases.

FIGURE 25–3
Increase in
Nonborrowed
Reserves: *Effects on
Real Income and the
Interest Rate*

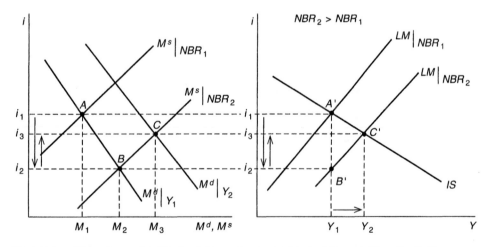

The initial equilibrium is at point *A′* in the right panel and point *A* in the left panel. When the Fed increases *NBR*, the new equilibrium in the goods and money markets together is at point *C′* in the right panel. Real income rises; and the interest rate falls, but not by as much as with *Y* fixed. The corresponding point in the left panel is point *C*.

curve but off the *IS* curve. This means that the goods and services market is out of equilibrium, because the lower interest rate increases the investment component of aggregate demand for goods and services. As a result, at point *B′*, aggregate demand is greater than aggregate supply. In response, *Y* increases. The increase in *Y* has repercussions in the money market.

The increase in real income increases money demand, creating excess demand for money. In response, the interest rate rises. The increase in the interest rate that results from an increase in real income is the **real-income effect on the interest rate** that Chapter 10 introduces. In the *IS-LM* graph in Figure 25–3, the increases in Y and i are shown by the movement along the *LM* curve from point B' to point C'. Point C' represents simultaneous equilibrium in the goods and services market and the money market. The right panel shows that the interest rate is lower than at point A' (but not as low as at point B') and that real income is higher than at point A'.

The left panel of the graph shows the effects on i and M. The increase in Y shifts the money demand curve to the right. The final equilibrium is at point C, the counterpart of point C'. At point C the interest rate is lower than at point A (but higher than at point B), and the quantity of money is greater than at point A.

The following schematic sums up the effects of an increase in nonborrowed reserves in the *IS-LM* model. The first row shows the direct effect on the interest rate. The second row shows the indirect effect of a lower interest rate on real income. And the third row shows the feedback effect of a higher level of real income on the interest rate. The last row shows that on net the interest rate falls and real income rises.

Money market: $NBR{\uparrow} \to M^s{\uparrow} \to M^d < M^s \to ESM \to i{\downarrow}$
Goods and services market: $i{\downarrow} \to I{\uparrow} \to AD{\uparrow} \to AD > Y \to EDG \to Y{\uparrow}$
Money market: $Y{\uparrow} \to M^d{\uparrow} \to M^d > M^s \to EDM \to i{\uparrow}$
Net effects: $i{\downarrow}, Y{\uparrow}$

Adding the International Linkages

We have shown that an increase in nominal nonborrowed reserves is expansionary: Real income rises. Adding the international linkages to the model results in an even higher equilibrium level of real income. As Chapter 24 explains, a given reduction in the interest rate increases not only investment but also net exports. Net exports rise because a reduction in domestic interest rates relative to foreign interest rates increases demand for foreign securities, which increases the exchange rate, e. As a result, the *IS* curve is flatter: A given change in i results in a greater change in AD and, hence, in Y. We can incorporate the international linkages into the schematic by adding the following chain of events to the goods and services market in the second row:

$$i{\downarrow} \to e{\uparrow} \to NX{\uparrow} \to AD{\uparrow} \to AD > Y \to Y{\uparrow}$$

Finally, a flatter *IS* curve means that a given shift in the *LM* curve will lead to a smaller change in the equilibrium level of the interest rate and a greater change in the equilibrium level of output, as shown in Figure 25–4.

Discount Window Operations

The second most common method of increasing the money supply is to increase borrowed reserves by reducing the discount rate, d. Chapters 9 and 22 explain that a reduction in the discount rate increases the money supply at each level of the interest rate because banks have an incentive to increase their borrowing from the discount window and to reduce their excess reserves. In other words, a reduction in the discount rate shifts the money supply curve to the right. As a result, the *LM* curve shifts down and to the right. The graph looks like the one in Figure 25–3. All that is needed is to change the labels of the money

FIGURE 25-4
The Effects of an
Increase in
Nonborrowed
Reserves with and
without the
International
Linkages

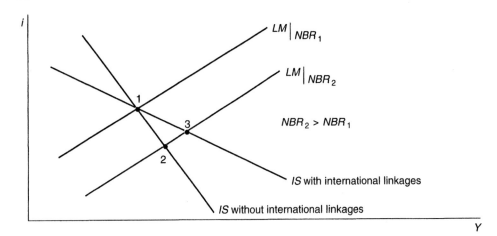

When the Fed increases *NBR*, the equilibrium moves from point 1 to point 2 when the international linkages are ignored. Incorporating the effect of a lower interest rate on the exchange rate and net exports places the final equilibrium at point 3: The fall in *i* is less and the rise in *Y* is greater.

supply curves and the *LM* curves from NBR_1 and NBR_2 to d_1 and d_2, respectively, where d_2 is less than d_1. It follows that a reduction in the discount rate lowers the equilibrium level of the interest rate and increases the equilibrium level of real income.

   The Fed can also increase the quantity of borrowed reserves in the banking system by loosening its administration of the discount window at any given discount rate. Chapter 18 introduces the symbol $\mathscr{A}$ to represent the Fed's administration of the discount window. Other things equal, a reduction in $\mathscr{A}$ means the marginal cost of borrowing reserves from the Fed is lower because the Fed is willing to lend more reserves to banks at any given discount rate. Therefore, banks will be less concerned about being turned down for future discount window loans if they approach the window today, for example. The resulting increase in borrowed reserves shifts the money supply curve to the right and the *LM* curve down (and to the right). Hence, a loosening of the administration of the discount window has the same qualitative effects as a reduction in the discount rate: The interest rate falls and real income rises.

FISCAL POLICY

While monetary policy is the province of the Federal Reserve, fiscal policy is the province of Congress and the president, who decide on changes in tax rates, transfer payments, and government purchases of goods and services. Changes in these policy instruments have their initial effect on the real sector. Applying the results of Chapter 24 shows how changes in various instruments of fiscal policy can shift the *IS* curve and, ultimately, affect not only the level of income but also the interest rate. Incorporating the repercussions in financial markets diffuses the effects of fiscal policy on real income and output. To begin, consider the effects of an increase in government spending, *G*.

Effects of an Increase in Government Spending

To see how the *IS* curve shifts when government spending on final goods and services increases, consider the following experiment. Starting from a point on the *IS* curve, with the interest rate given, suppose that G increases. The goal is to find the effect on Y of an increase in government spending.

Chapter 24 has spelled out this effect using the Keynesian cross graph. At a given interest rate, say, i_1, an increase in G shifts the *AD* curve upward in the top panel of Figure 25–5. The resulting excess demand for goods and services spurs an increase in output and real income. In the upper panel, the equilibrium moves from point F to point J, and the equilibrium level of output from Y_1 to Y_2. The bottom panel reflects this result as a shift from point F' to point J'. Repeating this exercise for all levels of the interest rate and connecting the resulting points such as J' lead to a new *IS* curve, one that lies to the

FIGURE 25–5
Increase in Government Expenditure, *G*, and the *IS* Curve

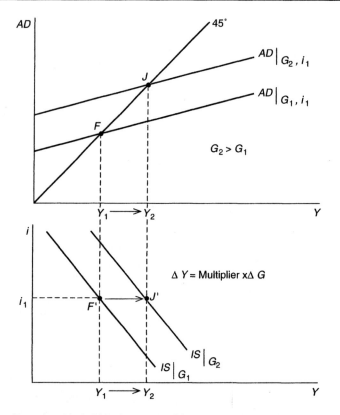

For a given level of i, an increase in G increases aggregate demand for goods and services and, thus, raises the goods-market-clearing level of output Y—as shown by the movement from point F to point J in the upper panel, and from point F' to point J' in the lower panel—when i equals i_1. Repeating this exercise for each level of the interest rate causes the *IS* curve to shift to the right.

right of the original: At each level of the interest rate, an increase in *G* increases the goods-market-clearing level of output. Moreover, the increase in output equals the change in *G* times the income multiplier, which is the amount by which the *IS* curve shifts to the right.

Adding the interactions with the financial sector tempers the multiplier effect as Figure 25–6 shows. In the bottom panel, point *J'* is on the new *IS* curve but off the *LM* curve. This means that the money market is not in equilibrium, because the increase in *Y* creates excess demand for money. As a result, the interest rate must rise. The increase in the interest rate feeds back on the goods and services market and reduces investment. This interest-induced reduction in investment demand, called the **crowding out of investment**, creates excess supply of goods and services, thereby reducing output. The increase in *i* and decrease in *Y* are shown by the movement along the new *IS* curve from

FIGURE 25–6
Increase in Government Expenditure: *Effects on Real Income and the Interest Rate*

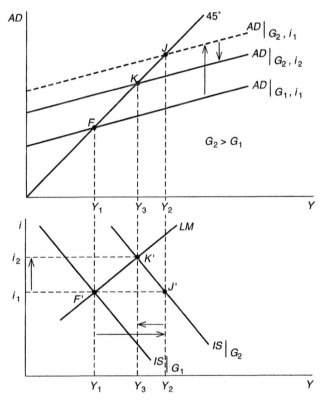

The initial equilibrium is at point *F'* in the lower panel and point *F* in the upper panel. When *G* increases, the new equilibrium in the goods and money markets together is at point *K'* in the lower panel. The interest rate rises, and real income also rises, but not by as much as with *i* fixed. The corresponding point in the upper panel is point *K*.

point J' to point K'. Point K' represents the new equilibrium in the goods and services and the money market. The interest rate has risen. And Y has risen, but not as much it rises with a fixed interest rate, because the increase in i crowds out investment.

The upper panel of the graph shows that the decrease in investment caused by the rise in the interest rate shifts the AD curve downward.[1] And the final equilibrium is at point K, the counterpart to point K' in the lower panel.

As with our discussion of monetary policy, a simple schematic sums up the effects of an increase in G. The first row shows the direct effect of an increase in government purchases on real income. The second row shows the effect of the increase in real income on the interest rate. And the third row shows the feedback effect of the increase in the interest rate that crowds out investment. The last row shows that on net the interest rate and real income both rise.

Goods and services market: $G\uparrow \rightarrow AD\uparrow \rightarrow AD > Y \rightarrow EDG \rightarrow Y\uparrow$
Money market: $Y\uparrow \rightarrow M^d\uparrow \rightarrow EDM \rightarrow i\uparrow$
Goods and services market: $i\uparrow \rightarrow I\downarrow \rightarrow AD\downarrow \rightarrow AD < Y \rightarrow ESG \rightarrow Y\downarrow$
Net effects: $i\uparrow$, $Y\uparrow$

The Crowding Out of Net Exports

When we incorporate the international linkages, there is a second type of crowding out: the **crowding out of net exports**, which Chapter 10 introduces briefly. This refers to the reduction in net exports that results from a fiscal stimulus. The connection comes from the decrease in the exchange rate induced by the increase in the interest rate. We can incorporate the international linkages into the schematic by adding the following chain of events to the third row:

$$i\uparrow \rightarrow e\downarrow \rightarrow NX\downarrow \rightarrow AD\downarrow \rightarrow AD < Y \rightarrow ESG \rightarrow Y\downarrow$$

As Chapter 24 shows, the IS curve with the international linkages is flatter than the IS curve without the international linkages. For a given increase in the interest rate, Y falls in response to a decrease in investment demand and a decrease in demand for net exports. Finally, a flatter IS curve means that the increase in G will result in a smaller increase in the equilibrium level of Y and i, as shown in Figure 25–7.

Effects of a Reduction in Taxes

What are the effects of a reduction in taxes? Suppose that, for simplicity, the government reduces the tax revenue in a lump-sum fashion, from $\overline{TA}_1$ to $\overline{TA}_2$. The reduction in total taxes increases disposable income, which, in turn, increases consumption demand by *plus* $c\Delta Y_D$ = *minus* $c\Delta TA$, where c is the marginal propensity to consume out of disposable income.[2] The increase in aggregate demand stimulates the economy, whose output increases. The top panel of Figure 25–8 shows that for the same interest rate, i_1, the reduction in taxes shifts the AD curve up to the position $AD|\overline{TA}_2 i_1$, which causes an increase in Y from Y_1 to Y_2. This result is shown in the lower panel of Figure 25–8 as a movement from point A' to point B'. The IS curve shifts to the right. Equilibrium in both markets is reestablished at point C', with a higher interest rate and a higher level of real

---

[1] Chapter 10 introduces the concept of *crowding out*. The Keynesian cross graph and the *IS-LM* graph enable us to give fuller accounts of this phenomenon.
[2] A reduction in taxes means ΔTA is negative, so *minus* ΔTA is positive; that is, disposable income rises.

FIGURE 25–7
The Effect of an
Increase in *G* with
and without the
International
Linkages

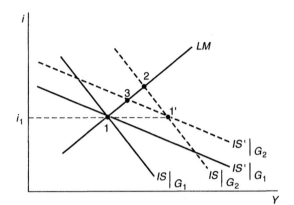

IS' denotes the *IS* curve with the
international linkages incorporated,
and *IS* denotes the curve without the
international linkages. At the initial
equilibrium interest rate, i_1, an increase
in *G* shifts the two *IS* curves to the
right by the same amount—from point
1 to point 1'. But the final equilibrium
is at point 2 without the international
linkages and point 3 with the
international linkages. At point 3, the
interest rate is lower than at point 2, so
the crowding out of investment is less.
But at point 3 the exchange rate has
fallen, resulting in the crowding out of
net exports.

income. Again, note that the increase in output is smaller than the amount that would
have resulted based on consideration of the goods and services market alone. Schematically, the effects on the goods and money markets of a lump sum decrease in taxes are as
follows:

Goods and services market: $\overline{TA}\downarrow \rightarrow Y_D\uparrow \rightarrow C\uparrow \rightarrow AD\uparrow \rightarrow AD > Y \rightarrow EDG \rightarrow Y\uparrow$

Money market: $Y\uparrow \rightarrow M^d\uparrow \rightarrow M^d > M^s \rightarrow EDM \rightarrow i\uparrow$

Goods and services market:
$$\left.\begin{array}{l} i\uparrow \quad \rightarrow I\downarrow \rightarrow AD\downarrow \\ \qquad\searrow \\ \qquad\qquad e\downarrow \rightarrow NX\downarrow \rightarrow AD\downarrow \end{array}\right\} \rightarrow AD < Y \rightarrow ESG \rightarrow Y\downarrow$$

Net effects: $i\uparrow$, $Y\uparrow$

Among the multiple interconnections shown in the schematic is that a policy-induced
reduction in taxes leads to a reduction in net exports, *NX*. GlobalWatch 25.1 applies the
theory of changes in fiscal policy to the U.S. economy in the 1980s and the German
economy in the 1990s.

Financing the Budget Deficit

The budget deficit equals the difference between government expenditure on final goods
and services, *G*, and net taxes, *T*. It increases when the government increases expenditures on final goods and services, reduces tax rates, or increases transfer payments. The
deficit, however, does not rise by as much as the increase in *G* itself or by as much as the
decrease in net tax revenue *at the initial level of income*. The reason is that the rise in the
equilibrium level of income increases tax revenues, thereby tempering the increase in the
deficit.

Bond Financing   The U.S. Treasury finances the excess of federal government expenditures over tax receipts by issuing Treasury securities. With a **bond-financed deficit**,
the Treasury securities are sold to the U.S. public or to foreign participants, but not to the
Federal Reserve. Thus, there is no permanent change in nonborrowed reserves, NBR.

FIGURE 25–8
Reduction in Taxes:
Effects on Real
Income and the
Interest Rate

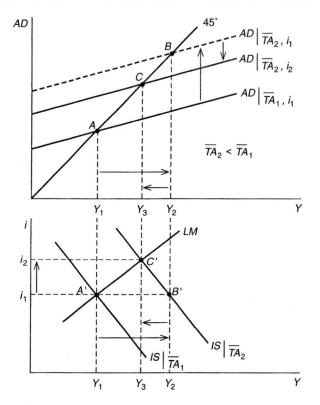

A lump sum reduction in taxes increases the equilibrium level of
the interest rate and the equilibrium level of output.

There may, however, be a transitory change in *NBR*. An examination of the mechanics of
bond financing shows the reason for this change.

Suppose that the public pays for the purchase of Treasury securities by writing checks
on its accounts with U.S. commercial banks. Check-clearing transfers the funds from the
reserve accounts that commercial banks have with the Fed to the account that the U.S.
Treasury has with the Fed. As Chapter 14 explains, Treasury balances with the Fed are a
technical factor affecting reserves. Increases in these balances drain reserves from the
banking system, other things equal. But other things do not remain equal. When the U.S.
Treasury pays for the excess of government expenditures over tax receipts by writing
checks on its account with the Fed, the reserves are put back into the system. Thus, there
is no permanent change in nonborrowed reserves and, thus, no shift in the *LM* curve.
With a bond-financed deficit, only the *IS* curve shifts. This is the case illustrated in Figure
25–6 for an increase in *G* and in Figure 25–8 for a decrease in $\overline{TA}$.

Monetizing the Deficit   When the securities issued by the U.S. Treasury are ultimately sold to the Federal Reserve, the deficit is monetized. With a **monetized deficit**,

GlobalWatch 25.1
The Twin Deficits: The United States and Germany

Martin Feldstein, a professor of economics at Harvard and chairman of President Reagan's Council of Economic Advisors from 1982 to 1984, coined the term *twin deficits* to refer to the increase in the budget deficit and the increase in the trade deficit that occurred in the United States in the 1980s. The following excerpt from the *Annual Report of the Council of Economic Advisors 1984** explains how tax cuts in the early 1980s contributed to the twin deficits:

The tax cuts in 1982 and 1983 raised after-tax incomes and therefore contributed to the rise in consumer spending that has been responsible for so much of the recovery. Similarly, the direct fiscal stimulus of the large 1984 deficit will do more to raise demand in 1984 than the increased real interest rates that result from the 1984 deficit will do to depress demand.

It is the continuing string of large deficits projected out through the end of the decade and beyond that is the serious threat to the health of the near-term recovery. The prospect of such prolonged deficits inevitably raises the real long-term interest rate above what it

otherwise would have been, reducing current activity in key interest-sensitive sectors and causing the recovery to be lopsided. The most conspicuous example of such current crowding out is the sharp decline in net exports. High interest rates in the United States attract funds from the rest of the world, causing the exchange value of the dollar to rise.[†] The strong dollar makes it difficult for U.S. products to compete in world markets and makes foreign products more attractive to American buyers. In addition, the high real interest rate is no doubt also causing the demand for housing, for some consumer durables, and for some plant and equipment investment to be lower now than it would otherwise have been. [Economic Report of the President 1984, 39]

The increase in budget deficits and trade deficits experienced by the United States in the 1980s were repeated in Germany in the 1990s.[‡] The dismantling of the Berlin Wall in 1989 and the subsequent reunification of East and West Germany brought with them huge government expenditures on infrastructure in rundown East Germany and large transfer payments to prop up the incomes of East Germans. As a result budget deficits rose, interest rates rose in Germany, the Deutsche mark rose in value (which means foreign currency fell in value), and the trade balance went from a surplus to a deficit beginning in 1991.

---

* Every February the United States Government Printing Office publishes the *Economic Report of the President* together with *The Annual Report Of The Council Of Economic Advisors*. The entire document is usually referred to as the *Economic Report of the President*.

† The exchange value of the dollar is 1/*e*; an increase in 1/*e* implies a decrease in *e*, the dollar value of foreign exchange.

‡ Figures 2–3 and 2–4 in Chapter 2 show the history of U.S. budget deficits and trade deficits, respectively.

---

the Federal Reserve supplies reserves to finance the excess of government expenditures over tax revenues. Because an increase in reserves increases the money supply, the deficit is said to be monetized. In this case, not only does the *IS* curve shift up and to the right, but also the *LM* curve shifts down and to the right (because nonborrowed reserves rise). Therefore, monetized deficits are more expansionary than bond-financed deficits.

Examining the mechanics of monetizing the deficit shows why nonborrowed reserves increase. We begin with a simplification that abstracts from institutional arrangements arising from an independent Fed. If the Treasury were to sell its securities directly to the Fed, the Fed would credit the account of the Treasury by the amount of the sale of securities. On the asset side of the Fed's balance sheet, Treasury securities held by the Fed would rise; and on the liability side, deposits of the U.S. government would rise by the same amount. At this point, there would be no change in reserves. However, when the

Treasury writes checks against its account with the Fed to pay for the excess of its expenditures over its receipts, nonborrowed reserves rise. As Chapter 14 explains, the recipients would deposit the checks in their banks, which would send the checks to the Fed for collection. The Fed, in turn, would credit the reserve accounts of the receiving banks.

In the United States, the central bank is independent from the Treasury, and the Treasury does not sell its securities directly to the central bank. Instead, the Treasury sells these securities to the public. Through open market operations, the Fed buys Treasury securities from the public. The Fed takes the debt of the U.S. Treasury out of the hands of the public and replaces it with the debt of the Fed, that is, reserves. The effect is the same as if the Treasury sold its securities directly to the Fed.

An important point, however, is that the Fed and not the Treasury determines the amount of the deficit to monetize. The Fed determines the size of open market operations, based on its goals of price stability, full employment, and maximum sustainable economic growth. If the Fed were to monetize large deficits, it would overheat the economy and cause large increases in prices. At this point in the model, the price level is fixed because the model does not have a theory of the determination of the price level. However, Chapter 10 shows that an increase in the price level reduces the real value of nonborrowed reserves and, thus, the real money supply. As a result, the *LM* curve shifts upward, the interest rate rises, and real income falls, moderating the effect on real income of an increase in nominal nonborrowed reserves.

OTHER SHOCKS: CHANGES IN THE BEHAVIOR OF THE PUBLIC AND BANKS

So far this chapter has examined deliberate shifts in the *IS* curve or the *LM* curve that have been engineered by policymakers. But the *IS* curve or *LM* curve may also shift when participants in the private sector change their behavior. Shocks that shift the *LM* curve originate in the financial sector. For example, changes in the portfolio decisions of the public begin by shifting the M^d curve, and changes in the reserve management decisions of banks begin by shifting the M^s curve. On the other hand, shocks that shift the *IS* curve originate in the real sector. For example, changes in consumer confidence or in the animal spirits of entrepreneurs begin by shifting the *AD* curve. This section examines the effects of these shocks on the equilibrium value of i and Y.

LM Sector Shocks

Consider first a change in the portfolio decisions of the public, represented by a change in the collective variable, c, introduced in Chapter 6. In Figure 25–9, point A' on the *LM* curve in the right panel is the starting point, which corresponds to point A in the left panel. As the labels of the original M^d and *LM* curves indicate, the initial value of c is c_1. Next, suppose a reduced appetite for risk, represented by an increase in c from c_1 to c_2, increases the demand for money: At each level of i and Y, individuals want to hold more money and fewer securities. The resulting excess demand for money causes the interest rate to rise. The money market clears at point B, where the interest rate is i_2. The corresponding point in the right panel is point B', which lies vertically above point A', indicating that at the level of income Y_1 the interest rate rises. Repeating the same process

FIGURE 25–9
Money Demand
Shocks: An
Increase in the
Collective Variable,
$\mathcal{C}$, and the *LM*
Curve

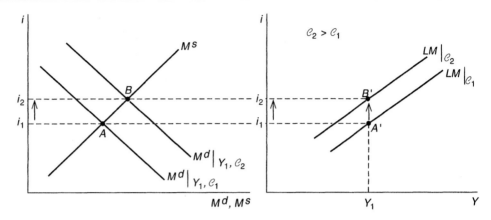

An increase in the collective variable $\mathcal{C}$ increases money demand, other things equal. As a result, the money-market-clearing interest rate rises at each level of Y, and the *LM* curve shifts upward and to the left.

for all levels of income results in a positive shift in money demand shifting the *LM* curve upward and to the left.

We can now assemble the pieces of the entire system. Schematically, the interactions in the money and goods markets are as follows:

Money market: $\mathcal{C}\uparrow \rightarrow M^d\uparrow \rightarrow M^d > M^s \rightarrow EDM \rightarrow i\uparrow$

Goods and services market: $i\uparrow \rightarrow I\downarrow \rightarrow AD\downarrow$

$\qquad\qquad\qquad\qquad\qquad\searrow e\downarrow \rightarrow NX\downarrow \rightarrow AD\downarrow$ $\Big\} \rightarrow AD < Y \rightarrow ESG \rightarrow Y\downarrow$

Money market: $Y\downarrow \rightarrow M^d\downarrow \rightarrow M^d < M^s \rightarrow ESM \rightarrow i\downarrow$

Net effect: $i\uparrow, Y\downarrow$

The net effect is shown in the right panel of Figure 25–10 by the movement from point A' to point C'. An increase in $\mathcal{C}$ increases the interest rate and reduces real income; that is, an increase in $\mathcal{C}$ is recessionary. The left panel shows that the quantity of money rises, on net, from M_1 to M_3. Therefore, *when the collective variable $\mathcal{C}$ increases, there is a rise in the quantity of money that is contractionary.* This result is not surprising in light of our earlier examination of the quantity theory of money in Chapter 16. According to that theory, increases in money demand brought about by increases in the collective variable are contractionary because they reduce the velocity of circulation of money.

The result of this example is general: Any shock that shifts the M^d curve to the right moves the *LM* curve upward and to the left. And the opposite is true: Any shock that shifts the money demand curve to the left moves the *LM* curve downward and to the right. In the new financial environment, a change in the portfolio decisions of the public is not the only exogenous factor that shifts the money demand curve. As Chapters 7, 21, and 22 discuss, changes in the cost of banking that affect the deposit rate will also shift the money demand curve. For example, an increase in the technology and regulatory

**FIGURE 25–10
An Increase in
Money Demand:
*Effects on Interest
Rate, Real Income,
and Quantity of
Money***

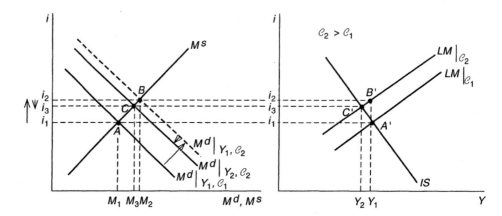

A change in the portfolio decisions of the public that increases money demand results in an increase in the equilibrium level of the interest rate, an increase in the quantity of money, and a decrease in the equilibrium level of real income.

index, $\mathfrak{IR}$, that increases the marginal cost of issuing deposits will reduce the deposit rate at each level of the interest rate. As a result, the public will reduce its demand for money, shifting the money demand curve to the left. Hence, at each level of real income, the demand for money falls, resulting in a lower interest rate, which means the *LM* curve shifts downwards. The results are the opposite of those in Figure 25–10: The interest rate falls, and real income rises, but the quantity of money falls. In this case, there is a reduction in the quantity of money that is expanionary: economic activity rises.

Money supply shocks also shift the *LM* curve. As an example of a money supply shock, consider an increase in the prudence of banks, manifested by their desire to hold more excess reserves and to make fewer loans and buy fewer securities, other things equal. An increase in the quantity of excess reserves banks want to hold reduces effective reserves in the banking system (that is, the reserves available to support deposits), thereby reducing the supply of money at each level of the interest rate. In the left panel of Figure 25–11, the money supply curve shifts to the left, to the one with $\mathscr{P}_2$ in its label, where $\mathscr{P}$ represents the index of prudence introduced in Chapter 18. At the original interest rate, i_1, there is excess demand for money, pushing the interest rate upward to i_2. This is shown as a movement of the equilibrium from point *A* to point *B*. In the right panel, this movement is represented by a shift from point A' to point B'. This shift shows that at the same level of real income, Y_1, an increase in $\mathscr{P}$ shifts the *LM* curve upward and to the left.

Again, putting the pieces together (without drawing the graph) gives the effect on the interest rate, real income, and the quantity of money: The upward shift in the *LM* curve will cause the interest rate to rise and the level of real income to fall. Thus, an increase in $\mathscr{P}$, like an increase in $\mathcal{C}$, is contractionary for the economy. With the money supply shock, however, the quantity of money also falls, whereas with the money demand shock, the quantity of money rises.

FIGURE 25–11
Money Supply
Shocks: *An Increase*
in Desired Excess
Reserves, 𝒫, and the
LM *Curve*

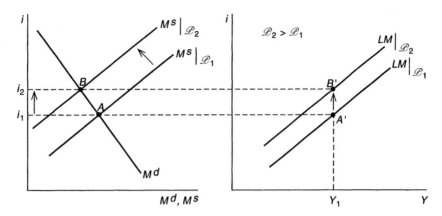

An increase in the index of prudence, 𝒫, which increases the quantity of desired excess reserves reduces the money supply, other things equal. As a result, the money-market-clearing interest rate rises at each level of Y, and the *LM* curve shifts upward and to the left.

IS **Sector**
Shocks

Moving from shocks that originate in the money market to shocks that originate in the goods and services market, we note that exogenous changes in the behavior of households, nonfinancial firms, or the rest of the world that increase aggregate demand for goods and services, other things equal, shift the *IS* curve to the right. Examples are an increase in consumer confidence that shifts the consumption function upward at each level of Y; an increase in the animal spirits of entrepreneurs that shifts the investment curve upward at each level of Y; and a change in the tastes of the rest of the world that increases demand for U.S. goods and services and shifts the *NX* curve upward at each level of Y. The effects on the equilibrium values of the interest rate and real income are qualitatively the same as the effects of an increase in government expenditure, as shown in Figures 25–6 and 25–7. On the other hand, exogenous shocks that reduce the aggregate demand for goods and services, such as reductions in consumer and business confidence or credit crunches, cause the interest rate and output to fall. FedWatch 25.2 examines the response of the Fed to contractionary *IS* sector shocks in the early 1990s.

THE CHOICE OF AN INTERMEDIATE TARGET FOR THE CONDUCT OF MONETARY POLICY

The *IS-LM* model provides a framework for reevaluating the use of monetary aggregates as intermediate targets in the conduct of monetary policy. Applying the quantity theory of money in Chapter 16, we saw that problems arise when actual velocity deviates from estimated velocity. If, for example, actual velocity falls short of predicted velocity, the Fed must raise the quantity of money above the targeted level to achieve its projection for nominal GDP.

The issue can also be analyzed in the *IS-LM* model. A fall in velocity means a rise in money demand, which shifts the *LM* curve upward and reduces the equilibrium level of

FedWatch 25.2
Headwinds

In numerous policy reports and official statements by the Fed chairman in the early 1990s, the term *headwinds* kept cropping up. For example, the *79th Annual Report 1992* of the Board of Governors of the Federal Reserve System began with the following assessment of the U.S. economy:

Economic activity accelerated over the course of 1992, and the rise in real gross domestic product during the year cumulated to more than 3 percent, the largest increase since 1988 . . .

Although the rise of real GDP in 1992 was far from robust by the standards of past cyclical upswings in activity, it was a much larger gain than many analysts— both inside and outside government—had thought likely, given the extraordinary headwinds *(emphasis added) with which the economy had to contend. Chief among the influences restraining growth were budgetary stresses at all levels of government, widespread structural changes in the business sector, both in defense-related industries and elsewhere, exceptional caution among financial intermediaries, and ongoing efforts by businesses and households to strengthen their finances by restricting the growth of their indebtedness. Adding still further to the drag on the economy in 1992 was the sluggish performance of foreign industrial economies, a number of which still were struggling at year-end to regain forward momentum.*

The force of the headwinds *(emphasis added) seemed greatest in the first half of the year. In the second half, their power appeared to abate somewhat. In addition, a number of important sectors—housing, consumer durables, and business fixed investment—continued to benefit in the second half from the substantial easing of money market conditions that had been implemented over time by the Federal Reserve.* [*Board of Governors of the Federal Reserve System,* 79th Annual Report 1992, *3*]

The accompanying graph shows the headwinds as a contractionary *IS* sector shock and the Fed's monetary policy as an expansionary *LM* sector shock. In the *IS* sector, spending on goods and services fell because of a reduction in defense spending and a downturn in foreign economies that reduced exports. Spending also fell because of an increasing inability and unwillingness by banks to lend to firms and households at any given interest rate and a reluctance by debt-burdened households and firms to borrow and spend. In response to these headwinds, the Fed added more reserves to the banking system through open market operations and discount window operations numerous times between 1989 and 1992. In implementing this more expansionary policy, the Fed reduced its operating target for the federal funds rate 23 times and it reduced the discount rate seven times.*

_____

* Chapter 13 discusses how the Fed uses the federal funds rate as an operating target to guide its open market operations.

continued

real income. To prevent real income from falling, the Fed must increase the money supply. The *IS-LM* model, however, does more than merely confirm results already derived from the quantity theory. The *IS-LM* model makes it possible to ask and answer questions that are difficult to frame in the quantity theory model.

This chapter has shown that the economy may be prone to *IS* sector shocks as well as to *LM* sector shocks. Examination of the choice of an intermediate target in the face of uncertainty about real sector shocks and financial sector shocks will focus on answering two questions. If the Fed wants to minimize volatility in real income, when is it preferable to target the quantity of money? And when is it preferable to target the interest rate?[3]

_____

[3] Two classic papers on the conduct of monetary policy under uncertainty are: William Poole, "Optimal Choice of Monetary Policy Instruments in a Simple Stochastic Macro Model," *Quarterly Journal of Eco-*

FedWatch 25.2

Headwinds (concluded)

Although economic growth picked up in 1992, it was weak again in the first quarter of 1993. By the fourth quarter of 1993, however, the economy gained considerable momentum. Convinced that the headwinds were abating and that the economy faced the danger of overheating, the Fed pushed up its target for the federal funds rate four times in the first half of 1994 and also raised the discount rate once.

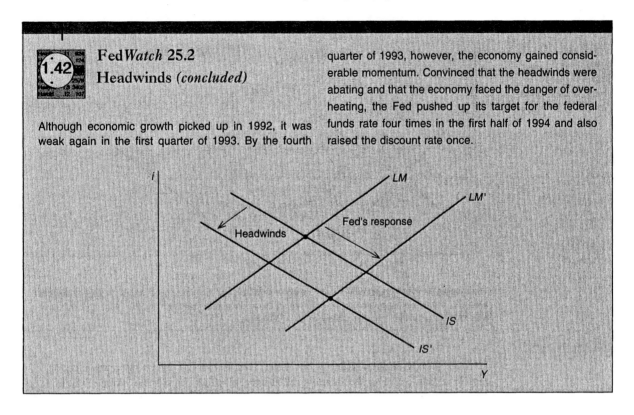

Targeting the Quantity of Money and the Slope of the LM Curve

We have drawn the *LM* curve for a given amount of the nonborrowed reserves, *NBR*. Before we can compare monetary aggregate targets to interest rate targets in the *IS-LM* model, we must derive the *LM* curve with *M* fixed.

In Figure 25–12, when the level of income is Y_1 and the level of nonborrowed reserves is NBR_1, the interest rate that clears the money market is i_1, shown by point 1 in the left panel and point 1' in the right panel. When the level of income rises to Y_2, the money demand curve shifts to the right. With NBR fixed, the money-market-clearing interest rate rises to i_2, at point 2 in the left panel, which becomes point 2' on the *LM* curve with *NBR* fixed in the right panel.

With *NBR* equal to NBR_1, the equilibrium quantity of money rises from M_1 to M_2 when the interest rate rises from i_1 to i_2. If the Fed targets the original level of *M*, that is, if the Fed is committed to achieving the quantity of money M_1, it must take measures to return the quantity of money to the targeted level. To return money to target, the Fed must reduce the quantity of nonborrowed reserves to NBR_2 enough to shift the M^s curve to the left so that it intersects the new M^d curve at point 3. Transferring this information to the right panel, we have point 3', which shows that if the Fed targets the (original) quantity of money, the interest rate must rise to i_3 when income rises to Y_2. Thus, the *LM* curve with

nomics, May 1970, and William C. Brainard, "Uncertainty and the Effectiveness of Monetary Control," *American Economic Review, Papers and Proceedings* 57 (May 1967).

FIGURE 25–12
Targeting Money and the Slope of the *LM* Curve: *A Steeper* LM *Curve*

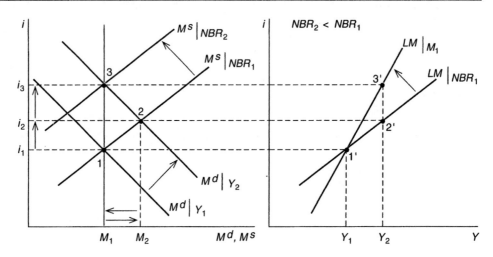

The quantity of money rises when Y increases and *NBR* is fixed. To return money to its original targeted level, M_1, the Fed must reduce *NBR*. As a result, the interest rate rises further. Therefore, the *LM* curve with *M* fixed is steeper than the *LM* curve with *NBR* fixed.

M fixed passes through point 3′; in other words, the *LM* curve becomes steeper. The reason is that targeting the quantity of money, in effect, makes the money supply curve vertical in the left panel.

Targeting the Quantity of Money versus Targeting the Interest Rate

Having derived the *LM* curve with *M* fixed, we use that curve to compare monetary aggregate targets to interest rate targets. This comparison will reveal that with *IS* sector shocks, targeting the quantity of money minimizes the volatility in real income. On the other hand, with *LM* sector shocks, targeting the interest rate minimizes the volatility in real income.

Real Sector Shocks   When the economy faces uncertainty about real sector shocks, aggregate demand for goods and services may rise or fall. In such cases, we say that the *IS* curve is unstable. Suppose that the Fed faces an uncertain, unstable *IS* curve that may lie anywhere between positions IS_2 and IS_3 in Figure 25–13. If the *IS* curve is at position IS_1, it is likely that it may shift to the right to a position such as IS_2, because the animal spirits of entrepreneurs are higher, for example. Or the *IS* curve may shift to the left, to a position such as IS_3, because the animal spirits of entrepreneurs are lower.

Targeting the Interest Rate   When the *IS* curve shifts to position IS_2, the level of income will rise to Y_2 if the Fed decides to keep the interest rate fixed at the original level, i_1. To achieve its interest rate target, the Fed must increase the money supply by increasing nonborrowed reserves. The increase in the money supply shifts the *LM* curve down and to the right, negating the upward pressure on the interest rate that results from an increase in Y and money demand. In equilibrium, curve IS_2 intersects the new *LM* curve at point 2.

FIGURE 25–13
IS Sector Shocks:
Targeting the
Interest Rate

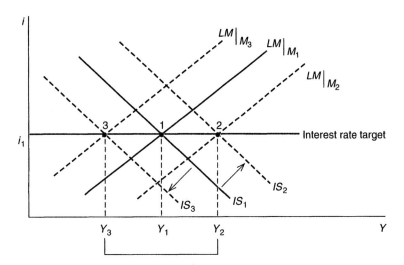

Suppose the economy is at point 1, but there is an uncertain, unstable *IS* curve that may lie between IS_2 and IS_3. If the Fed targets the interest rate, that is, if the Fed uses open market operations to keep the interest rate fixed at i_1, real income will be anywhere between Y_2 and Y_3.

On the other hand, when the *IS* curve shifts to position IS_3 (and the Fed keeps the interest rate fixed at i_1), the level of income will fall to Y_3. In this case, the curve IS_3 must intersect an *LM* curve at point 3. This requires the Fed to reduce nonborrowed reserves to reduce the money supply. The lower supply of money offsets the effect on the interest rate of the falling demand for money created by a decline in real income.

In sum, when the economy is under expansionary (inflationary) pressure from an *IS* shock, the interest rate rule requires the Fed to accommodate the expansion by increasing the money supply. And when the economy is under recessionary pressure from an *IS* shock, the interest rate rule requires the Fed to aggravate the recession by reducing the money supply. In Figure 25–13, if the Fed targets the interest rate, real income would be anywhere between Y_3 and Y_2. The difference between Y_2 and Y_3 is an absolute measure of the instability of income with an interest rate target. The Fed can do better if it targets the quantity of money.

Targeting the Quantity of Money   Suppose the Fed targets the quantity of money and seeks to keep the quantity of money equal to the amount implied by point 1 in Figure 25–14. With a target for the quantity of money, the *LM* curve will not shift. Therefore, when the *IS* curve shifts, the equilibrium will move along the given *LM* curve. In Figure 25–14, the intersection of the $LM|_{M_1}$ *curve with* IS_2 and IS_3 occurs at points 2′ and 3′, respectively. Thus, with a monetary target the volatility in income is the difference between $Y_{2'}$ and $Y_{3'}$, which is smaller than the difference between Y_2 and Y_3. Thus, *when the economy faces, or is prone to, real sector shocks, the Fed should target the quantity of money and not the interest rate.*

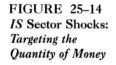

FIGURE 25–14
IS Sector Shocks:
*Targeting the
Quantity of Money*

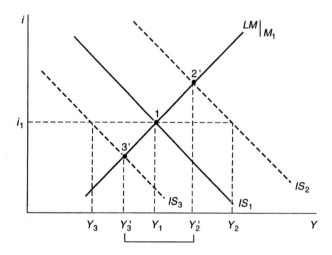

If the Fed uses open market operations to keep the quantity of money
fixed at M_1, real income will vary between $Y_{2'}$ and $Y_{3'}$. On the other
hand, with an interest rate target, real income varies between Y_2 and
Y_3. Therefore, targeting the quantity of money in the case of *IS* sector
shocks results in a smaller volatility in income than targeting the
interest rate.

LM Sector Shocks   With uncertainty about financial sector shocks, the results are
reversed. Targeting the interest rate produces less volatility in real income than targeting
the quantity of money. The importance of this result has increased since the advent of the
new financial environment. In addition to all those factors grouped into the index $\mathcal{C}$ that
shift the money demand curve and the *LM* curve, we must now add the technology and
regulatory index, $\mathfrak{TR}$. A change in $\mathfrak{TR}$, as well as a change in $\mathcal{C}$, may now shift the *LM*
curve.

Targeting the Quantity of Money   In Figure 25–15, suppose that the *LM* curve may shift
around the position LM_1, say, from LM_2 to LM_3. Uncertainty about shift factors that affect
money demand—such as $\mathcal{C}$ or $\mathfrak{TR}$—or uncertainty about shift factors that affect money
supply—such as $\mathcal{P}$—may be the cause of such volatility. Consider the case of a money
demand shock caused by a change in the collective variable.

   Suppose the *LM* curve is at position LM_1 and that there is a reduction in money
demand. If the Fed does not modify its target for the quantity of money, the interest rate
will fall to make the reduced money demand equal to the fixed money supply. Such a
shock will shift the *LM* curve to the right, say, to position LM_2, and the equilibrium level
of income will increase to Y_2. Similarly, when money demand increases, the *LM* curve
will shift to the left, say, to position LM_3. If, again, the Fed does not modify its target for
money, income will fall to Y_3. Thus, if the Fed targets the quantity of money, absolute
income volatility is equal to the difference between Y_2 and Y_3.

FIGURE 25–15
LM Sector Shocks:
*Targeting the
Quantity of Money*

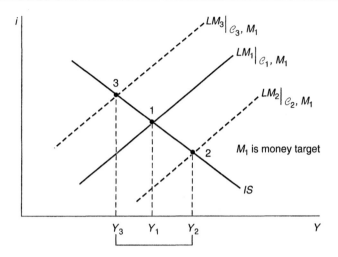

Targeting the quantity of money when the economy faces uncertainty
in the financial sector creates volatility in income, measured here by
the difference between Y_2 and Y_3.

Targeting the Interest Rate   With *LM* sector shocks, the Fed can eliminate the volatility in real income by targeting the interest rate. Figure 25–16 shows that a reduction in $\mathcal{C}$ and, hence, in money demand, increases income to Y_2 when the quantity of money is fixed; in this case, the interest rate falls to i_2. The Fed can bring the interest rate back to i_1 by reducing the quantity of money and shifting the *LM* curve to its original position. Not only is the interest rate returned to target, but also the level of income is restored to its original level. Of course, the quantity of money is lower.

Similarly, if the economy experiences a positive money demand shock and the quantity of money is fixed, income falls to Y_3 while the interest rate rises to i_3. The Fed can eliminate the volatility in real income by increasing the quantity of money in order to return the interest rate to its original level. Thus, *targeting the interest rate in the face of financial sector shocks is a better rule than targeting the quantity of money.*

**Variability in
Real Income
versus
Variability in
the Interest
Rate**

The comparison of targeting monetary aggregates versus targeting interest rates has been based on choosing the target that minimizes the volatility in real income. But why is this a desirable criterion for choosing a target? The argument is that real GDP is the single most important measure of economic welfare, and therefore the smaller the ups and downs of this magnitude, the more advantageous for society.[4]

But what about the volatility in interest rates? Figure 25–14 shows that when the economy is faced with real sector shocks, targeting the quantity of money makes

---

[4] Issues of quality of life or of depletion of natural resources can be considered by refining this measure of economic welfare.

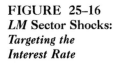

FIGURE 25–16
LM Sector Shocks:
Targeting the
Interest Rate

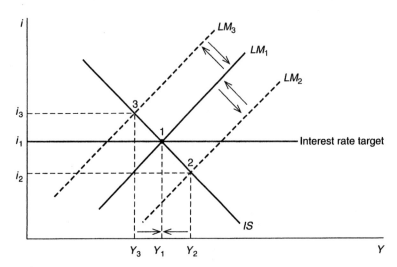

Targeting the interest rate is the preferred policy when the economy faces uncertainty
in the financial sector, because targeting the interest rate keeps *Y* fixed at Y_1.

the interest rate volatile. In this case, there is a clash between the interests of
financial investors and financial institutions and those of society as a whole. It is
natural for financial investors and financial institutions concerned about the risk of
capital losses to prefer interest rate targeting. With interest rate targeting, there is no
uncertainty about the level of the interest rate and, hence, no uncertainty about the
price of financial instruments. Thus, there are no risks of capital losses or of capital
gains. In case of financial sector shocks, targeting the interest rate is the most preferred policy for the economy as a whole, as well as for financiers and financial
institutions.

The problem, of course, is that the Fed cannot usually discern the source of the
shock. The Fed monitors interest rates continuously but can observe other conditions
only with some lag. If interest rates begin to change because of financial shocks, the
Fed should accommodate such shocks by keeping the interest rate constant so that the
shocks do not get transmitted to the real economy. If rates change because of spending
shocks, the Fed should not accommodate them because this would make monetary
policy procyclical; that is, policy would reduce demand during downturns and increase demand in periods of inflation. Keynesians believe that financial shocks are
common and large so that they tend to prefer targeting or at least smoothing interest
rates, while monetarists believe that real shocks are more common and, hence, should
be allowed to change interest rates, giving some built-in stabilization to the economy.
FedWatch 25.3 uses the *IS-LM* model to explain why the Fed downgraded money in
1993.

FedWatch 25.3
Downgrading Money in 1993

In recent years the Fed has become increasingly pragmatic, relying on a wide range of indicators to guide its conduct of monetary policy instead of using just one intermediate target. Beginning in the summer of 1993, the Fed further downgraded its targets for the monetary aggregates. Growth in M2 was extremely weak at the time, as Chapters 13 and 16 discussed. Our analysis in this chapter shows that in the presence of demand-side shocks, reductions in the quantity of money can be expansionary. For example, regulatory-induced increases in the cost of banking that lower the deposit rate cause a flight from low-yielding bank deposits to open-market securities. The result is a reduction in the quantity of money that is expansionary: The *LM* curve shifts down and to the right. This was the situation in the early 1990s. However, headwinds that were shifting the *IS* curve to the left were offsetting any expansionary impulse from shifts in money demand. When the headwinds began to abate in 1993, the Fed became less concerned about the weak growth of money.

SUMMARY

- Changes in the instruments of monetary policy will shift the *LM* curve. An increase in nonborrowed reserves, a reduction in the discount rate, or a loosening of the administration of the discount window shifts the *LM* curve down and to the right.

- When the *LM* curve shifts down, the interest rate that clears the money market at the initial level of real income falls. The lower interest rate increases investment. It also leads to an increase in the exchange rate and in net exports. As a result, aggregate demand rises, and real income rises. The increase in real income feeds back on the money market, raising the demand for money and the interest rate. In the end, real income rises and the interest rate falls, but the interest rate does not fall as much as when real income is fixed.

- Changes in the instruments of fiscal policy will shift the *IS* curve. An increase in government expenditures, a decrease in tax rates, or an increase in transfer payments shift the *IS* curve up and to the right.

- When the *IS* curve shifts to the right, the level of real income that clears the goods and services market at the initial interest rate is higher. The higher level of real income increases the demand for money, thereby raising the interest rate. And the increase in the interest rate feeds back on the demand for goods and services, thereby reducing, or crowding out, investment and net exports. The crowding out of net exports results from the interest rate–induced fall in the exchange rate. In the end, the interest rate increases and real income increases, but real income does not increase as much as when the interest rate is fixed.

- Changes in the instruments of monetary or fiscal policy are not the only factors that shift the *LM* or the *IS* curves. An increase in money demand brought about by a change in the portfolio decisions of the public—an increase in $\mathcal{C}$—shifts the *LM* curve upward. The *LM* curve also shifts upward when money demand increases because of a fall in the technology and regulatory index, $\mathfrak{IR}$. And an increase in the reserve management index, $\mathcal{P}$, that increases desired excess reserves, and, thus, reduces the supply of money, shifts the *LM* curve upward. In each case, the interest rate rises and real income falls.

- An increase in aggregate demand brought about by changes in the behavior of households, nonfinancial firms, or the rest of the world shifts the *IS* curve to the right. As a result, the interest rate and real income rise.

- To compare targeting the interest rate to targeting the quantity of money in the face of *IS* sector shocks and *LM* sector shocks, we must first derive the *LM* curve with the quantity of money fixed. This curve is steeper than when the Fed keeps nonborrowed reserves fixed.

* When the economy faces uncertainty about real sector shocks, targeting the quantity of money results in less variability in real income than targeting the interest rate.

* When the economy faces uncertainty about financial sector shocks, targeting the interest rate results in less variability in real income than targeting the quantity of money.

KEY TERMS AND CONCEPTS

twin deficits

liquidity effect

real income effect on the interest
   rate

crowding out of investment

crowding out of net exports

bond-financed deficit

monetized deficit

QUESTIONS AND PROBLEMS

The Wall Street Journal

1. The following quotation is from "Fed's Strong Moves Spark Rally," *The Wall Street Journal*, May 18, 1994, C1: "The central bank announced it increased the federal funds rate by a half point to 4.25%, and the discount rate also by a half point, to 3.5%." How does the Fed implement an increase in its operating target for the federal funds rate? With the help of an *IS-LM* diagram, explain the effects on the economy of the Fed's actions.

2. Suppose that the Japanese government lowers income tax rates in Japan. Other things equal, what will happen to the interest rate and real income in Japan? What will be the effect on Japan's trade surplus with the rest of the world?

3. Suppose that the U.S. government increases its purchases of goods and services, financing them with an equal increase in taxes. What will happen to the interest rate and real income?

4. "Bond-financed deficits are more expansionary than monetized deficits." True, false, or uncertain? Illustrate graphically.

5. Suppose that because of the introduction of new cash management techniques, money demand falls. What will happen to the interest rate, real income, and the quantity of money?

6. Suppose that because of a fall in animal spirits, entrepreneurs reduce their planned investment in plant and equipment.
   a. If the Fed does not intervene, what will happen to the interest rate and real income?

   b. Should the Fed buy or sell U.S. Treasury securities if it wants to restore real income to its original level?
   c. Should the Fed buy or sell securities if it wants to prevent the interest rate from changing?
   d. What should the Fed do if it wants to keep the quantity of money unchanged?

7. Suppose that, because of an increase in deposit insurance premiums paid by banks, the deposit rate falls and, thus, money demand falls.
   a. What will happen to real income if the Fed wants to keep the interest rate unchanged?
   b. How can the Fed achieve its goal?
   c. What should the Fed do if it wants to keep the quantity of money unchanged? What will happen to real income in this case?

8. Suppose that, other things equal, banks want to borrow $1 billion fewer reserves from the discount window. What should the Fed's response be if it wants to prevent any change in the interest rate and real income?

9. Suppose that banks want to hold $1 billion more excess reserves, other things equal. Design a response by the Fed that would prevent any adverse effects on the economy.

10. Assume that an economy is described by the following model of the real and financial sectors, where C, I, G, NX, NBR, and so on, are measured in billion of dollars:

Real Sector (IS Sector)

Consumption function: $C = 800 + 0.80Y_D$

Taxes: $TA = 150 + 0.20Y$

Transfers: $TR = 700$

Investment: $I = 250 - 10i$

Government purchases: $G = 800$

Net exports: $NX = -50$

(Note that this simple model does not incorporate effects of changes in the exchange rate on net exports; instead net exports are assumed constant.)

Financial Sector (*LM* Sector)

Money demand: $M^d = 400 - 0.261i + 0.097Y$

Money supply: $M^s = 155 + 10NBR/P + 4i$

Where:

$NBR = 78$

$P = 1$

Derive the *IS* equation and the *LM* equation. Next, solve the two equations for the equilibrium values of the interest rate, i, and real income, Y. (Note that i is a percentage, which means that if i were 8 percent, for example, it would be written $i = 8$.)

11. Assume that your answer to question 10 is the initial equilibrium. Examine, one at a time, the effects on i and Y of the following shocks to the real sector and illustrate your results graphically:

   a. Government expenditures, G, increase from 800 to 880.

   b. Net exports increase from -50 to $+30$.

   c. Because of an increase in the animal spirits of entrepreneurs, the investment equation changes to $I' = 260 - 10i$.

   d. Because of an increase in consumer confidence, the consumption function changes to $C' = 880 + 0.8Y_D$.

   e. Transfer payments increase from 700 to 780.

   f. The tax equation changes to $TA' = 70 + 0.2Y$.

12. Assume that your answer to question 10 is the initial equilibrium. Examine, one at a time, the effects on i and Y of the following shocks to the financial sector and illustrate your results graphically:

   a. NBR increases from 78 to 80.

   b. The money supply equation changes to $M^{s'} = 175 + 10NBR/P + 4i$.

   c. The money demand equation changes to $M^{d'} = 420 - 0.261i + 0.097Y$

13. Assume that your answer to question 10 is the initial equilibrium. Next, suppose the *IS* sector is unchanged, but the money demand and money supply equations change. The money demand equation changes to: $M^{d'} = 420 - 0.261i + 0.097Y$. And the money supply equation changes to: $M^{s'} = 955 + 4i$.

   a. Find the new equilibrium value of the quantity of money and compare it with the initial equilibrium value.

   b. Calculate the changes in i and Y

   c. Provide an economic and graphical explanation of these results.

SUGGESTED READINGS

Economic Report of the President, published annually in February.
   Each report contains a discussion of the previous year's conduct of monetary and fiscal policy as well as an analysis of other shocks to the economy.

Feldstein, Martin, ed., *The Risk of Economic Crisis* (University of Chicago Press, 1991).
   Papers presented at a conference on dealing with financial and economic crises. Academics and nonacademics with experience in the policy arena participated.

Kretzmer, Peter E., "Monetary vs. Fiscal Policy: New Evidence on an Old Debate," *Economic Review* (Federal Reserve Bank of Kansas City) 77, no. 2 (Second Quarter 1992): 21–30.
   Compares the effectiveness of monetary and fiscal policy.

Lindsey, David E. and Henry C. Wallich. "Monetary Policy." In *The New Palgrave: Money*, ed. John Eatwell, Murray Milgate, and Peter Newman. New York: W. W. Norton, 1989, 229–243.
   A Fed officer and a former Fed governor analyze alternative guides for the conduct of monetary policy and the role of discretion.

Mieno, Yasushi, "Current Monetary and Economic Situations in Japan and the Issue of External Imbalance," *Quarterly Bulletin* (Bank of Japan) 2, no. 2 (May 1994): 25–30.
   Speech by the governor of the Bank of Japan in which he uses the "headwinds analogy" introduced by the Fed to draw a parallel between economic conditions in the United States and Japan and the challenges for monetary policy.

THE PRICE LEVEL AND REAL INCOME

The Aggregate Demand–Aggregate Supply Model

CHAPTER PREVIEW

As with any market-determined variable, the price of the composite good called *real GDP*, or *output*, is determined by supply and demand. Therefore, the macroeconomic model for determining the price level is called the **aggregate demand–aggregate supply *(AD–AS)* model**. Chapter 10 introduces and applies the model. This chapter extends that discussion. The chapter begins with the derivation of the aggregate demand curve and the factors that shift the curve. Despite its name, the *AD* curve is not an ordinary demand curve; it is an equilibrium curve distilled from the entire *IS-LM* model.

After examining movements along and shifts of the AD curve, this chapter investigates the aggregate supply relationship. The analysis begins with two polar cases: the horizontal, fixed-price curve of Keynes and the vertical, long-run curve of the classicists. Next follow a derivation of the Keynesian version of the upward-sloping, short-run aggregate supply curve and an explanation of movements along and shifts of this curve. Finally, the chapter combines the Keynesian short run with the classical long run to explain why ultimately the aggregate supply curve is vertical at full employment. Having explained traditional Keynesian and classical versions of the aggregate supply relation, the chapter examines the effects of policy and other shocks on interest rates, real income (output), and the price level in the short run and the long run.

The chapter connects theory with practice by applying the model to explain how supply shocks as well as demand shocks brought the longest peacetime expansion in U.S. history—the expansion of 1982–1990—to an end. The addition of supply shocks to the model expands the story of the recession Chapters 24 and 25 tell. The chapter also introduces policy debates between traditional Keynesians and classicists by comparing the views of seven economists who received the Nobel prize for their research in macroeconomics.

LOOKING BACKWARD AND FORWARD

Before deriving the *AD–AS* model, it is instructive to review how our models of the financial sector and the real sector have unfolded up to this point. Part 6 examines the financial sector in isolation and determines the interest rate, *i*, and the factors affecting the interest rate. In models of the financial sector, real sector variables are parameters. Hence, the level of real income, *Y*, and the price level, *P*, are among the exogenous factors affecting the interest rate.

Part 7 deals with the determination of real income. Chapter 24 begins by determining the equilibrium level of real income from the goods and services market. It also finds the factors affecting the goods-market-clearing level of real income. The interest rate is one of these factors. The second half of Chapter 24 combines the financial sector and the real sector into one model—the *IS-LM* model. This model simultaneously determines the interest rate, *i*, and real income, *Y*, as well as the factors affecting the pair (*i*, *Y*).

The price level is a parameter in the *IS-LM* model. For each price level, there is a different *LM* curve and, hence, a different combination of *i* and *Y* that simultaneously clears the goods and money markets. With the additon of the aggregate supply relation to the framework, it is possible to also determine the price level. Figure 26–1 shows that once the equilibrium price level is known from the *AD–AS* graph, it is possible to pick out the relevant *LM* curve from the infinity of possible *LM* curves—one for each different level of *P*.

AGGREGATE DEMAND

Chapter 10 explains that the macroeconomic **aggregate demand curve** is an equilibrium curve. This means that for each value of the price level, *P*, the *AD* curve depicts the level of real output, *Y*, that can be supported by the market for goods and services and the market for money. When we add the international linkages, the *AD* curve also incorporates equilibrium in the foreign exchange market.

The Schematics of the *AD* Curve

The negative relation between the price level and aggregate demand for goods and services operates through the money market and through the goods and services market. An increase in the price level reduces real nonborrowed reserves, which reduces the quantity of real effective reserves. This reduction in real effective reserves decreases the (real) money supply, M^s, which raises the level of the interest rate that clears the money market. In turn, the rise in the interest rate reduces investment in plant and equipment and the demand for consumer durables. Thus, aggregate demand falls. Consequently, the level of output that can be supported by aggregate demand falls. Schematically, the linkages are:

$$P\uparrow \rightarrow (NBR/P)\downarrow \rightarrow M^s\downarrow \rightarrow i\uparrow \rightarrow (C+I)\downarrow \rightarrow AD\downarrow \rightarrow Y\downarrow$$

When the model includes the international linkages, an increase in *P* leads to an even greater reduction in aggregate demand because net exports fall. An increase in the price level increases the domestic interest rate, *i*. Other things equal, domestic interest rates rise relative to foreign interest rates, and the demand for U.S. securities by foreigners rises, while the demand for foreign securities by Americans falls. As a result, the international

FIGURE 26–1
The *IS-LM*,
AD–AS Graph

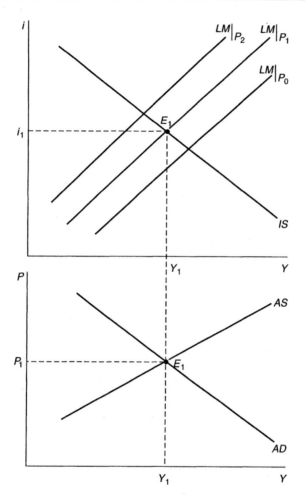

The bottom panel determines P and Y.
Once we know that the equilibrium
price level is P_1, we can pick out the
corresponding *LM* curve and, hence,
the equilibrium level of the interest rate
in the top panel.

price of the dollar, $1/e$, rises, and the dollar price of foreign exchange, e, falls, as preceding chapters show. This fall in e reduces net exports.[1]

The Graphics

To derive graphically the inverse relation between the price level and *AD*, the top panel of Figure 26–2 starts with P equal to P_1 on the label of the *LM* curve. The intersection of the *IS* and *LM* curves at point A determines the initial level of output at Y_1. In the (P, Y)-plane in the bottom panel of Figure 26–2, point A' represents the pair

---

[1] An increase in P also directly reduces net exports by making U.S. goods relatively more expensive and foreign goods relatively cheaper at each value of the nominal exchange rate, e. For simplicity, we ignore the direct effect of a change in P on net exports at this point. The effect is introduced in Chapter 29. An increase in the price level may also directly reduce consumption by reducing the real value of the wealth of households.

FIGURE 26–2
Derivation of the
Aggregate Demand
Curve

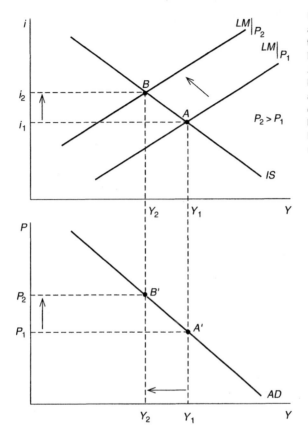

In the (i, Y)-plane in the upper panel, an increase in the price level from P_1 to P_2 shifts the *LM* curve up and to the left. The equilibrium moves from point *A* to point *B*. In the (P, Y)-plane in the lower panel, the corresponding points are *A'* and *B'*, which lie on the *AD* curve. The curve is downward sloping because an increase in *P* reduces the level of *Y* that clears the goods and money markets.

(P_1, Y_1). Note also that the top panel explicitly displays the interest rate, which has the value i_1 at point *A*. In the bottom panel, however, the interest rate is implicit, because there is no axis to measure it; instead the price level is measured on the vertical axis.

Next, suppose that the price level rises to P_2. The *LM* curve shifts up and to the left, to position $LM_{|P_2}$. This new *LM* curve intersects the original *IS* curve at point *B*. As a result, the level of output that clears the goods and money markets falls from Y_1 to Y_2. We record this result as point *B'* in the bottom panel. Repeating this process for several price levels and connecting all such points as *A'* and *B'* yields the *AD* curve.

The *AD* curve is downward sloping. The higher the price level, the smaller the quantity of output that can be supported by the goods and money markets.[2]

---

[2] Recall from Chapter 24 that the *IS* curve with the international linkages is flatter than the *IS* curve without the international linkages. The same result holds for the *AD* curves. A rise in *P* leads to a greater fall in *AD* and, hence, in *Y*, with the international linkages than without them.

Shifts of the Aggregate Demand Curve

Any factors that influence the position of the *IS* curve or the *LM* curve must also affect the position of the *AD* curve. Thus, ideally every *AD* curve should have a label identifying the values of all the shift factors. To avoid cluttering the graphs, however, we list the shift factors separately and specify on the *AD* curve only the individual factor that we intend to change or emphasize.

The list below identifies 13 factors that affect aggregate demand by shifting the *AD* curve. (Some of these factors may not only shift but also tilt the curve.) Changes in the instruments of fiscal or monetary policy that shift the *AD* curve are naturally called **demand management policies**.

Factors that Shift the *IS* Curve

1. Exogenous factors affecting consumption.
2. Exogenous factors affecting investment.
3. Government spending.
4. Transfer payments.
5. Tax rates.
6. Exogenous factors affecting net exports.

Factors that Shift the *LM* Curve

7. Nonborrowed reserves.
8. Discount rate.
9. Administrative index, $\mathscr{A}$, affecting borrowed reserves.
10. Reserve requirement ratio.
11. Index of prudence, $\mathscr{P}$, affecting excess reserves.
12. Collective variable, $\mathscr{C}$, affecting the demand for deposits.
13. Technology and regulatory index, $\mathscr{R}$, affecting the deposit rate and, thus, the demand for deposits.

Among the six factors that shift the *IS* curve, three are instruments of fiscal policy that change because of deliberate decisions by Congress and the president: government spending, tax rates, and transfer payments. On the other hand, changes in the other factors depend on the behavior of households, firms, or the rest of the world. Examples are a change in domestic tastes that results in an increase in consumption; a change in the animal spirits of entrepreneurs that results in an increase in investment; and a change in foreign tastes that results in an increase in exports. From the six *IS* shift factors, this chapter examines fully how a change in government spending, *G*, shifts the *AD* curve, but only briefly describes the other five shifts.

The remaining seven factors work through the *LM* curve. The quantity of nonborrowed reserves, the discount rate, the administration of the discount window ($\mathscr{A}$), and the reserve requirement ratio are policy parameters controlled by the Fed. The other parameters change with alterations of behavior by banks or the public. From the *LM* shift factors, this chapter examines fully how a change in nonborrowed reserves, *NBR*, shifts the *AD* curve, and briefly describes the other shifts.

FIGURE 26–3
An Increase in
Government
Expenditure, *G*,
Shifts the *AD*
Curve to the Right

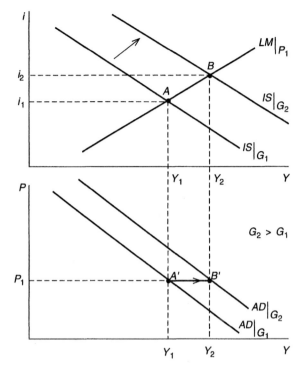

When *G* equals G_1, the economy is at point *A* in the top panel and at point *A'* in the bottom panel. An increase in *G* shifts the *IS* curve to the right. As a result, when the price level equals P_1, the level of output increases from Y_1 to Y_2, shown by the movement from point *A* to point *B* in the top panel and from point *A'* to point *B'* in the bottom panel. Point *B'* is one point on the new *AD* curve. Repeating this exercise for many price levels, we find the new *AD* curve, which lies to the right of the original curve.

Fiscal Policy: An Increase in Government Expenditure, *G*   To see how an increase in *G* affects the position of the *AD* curve, assume that the economy is initially at point *A'* on the *AD* curve in the bottom panel of Figure 26–3; point *A* is the corresponding point in the top panel. At these initial points, government expenditure equals G_1, while the interest rate, real income, and the price level are (i_1, Y_1, P_1). Next suppose that government expenditure increases from G_1 to G_2, while all other shift factors remain the same.

In the top panel the increase in government expenditure from G_1 to G_2 shifts the *IS* curve to the right. The new *IS* curve intersects the original *LM* curve at point *B*. The move from point *A* to point *B* shows that the increase in *G* increases the level of output that clears the goods and money markets from Y_1 to Y_2, *if the price level remains at P_1.* In the (*P, Y*)-plane in the bottom panel, this result appears as a horizontal displacement of point *A'* to point *B'*, which is one point on the new *AD* curve.

Repeating the same process for each level of *P* (and for the same new level of government expenditure, G_2) and connecting the resulting points such as *B'* yield the new *AD* curve, identified by G_2 in its label. In sum, the *AD* curve shifts to the right when government expenditure rises. On the other hand, a reduction in government expenditure would shift the *AD* curve to the left.

Changes in the Remaining Shift Factors for the *IS* Curve   Now it is easy to visualize how any one of the remaining factors that shift the *IS* curve will affect the *AD* curve. The result depends on whether the factor shifts the *IS* curve to the right or to the left. The corresponding shift of the *AD* curve will be in the same direction.

An increase in transfer payments or a reduction in tax rates will shift the *IS* curve to the right, because these factors increase consumption at each level of national income. As a result, the *AD* curve also shifts to the right.[3] The *IS* and *AD* curves also shift to the right when there are exogenous changes in the behavior of households, firms, or the rest of the world that increase consumption, investment, or net exports. Of course, the opposite is true: An exogenous decrease in consumption, investment, or net exports shifts the *IS* and *AD* curves to the left, as does a decrease in government expenditure, a decrease in transfer payments, or an increase in taxes.

Monetary Policy: An Increase in Nonborrowed Reserves   Now consider shift factors originating in the *LM* sector. We examine in detail the effects of a change in the quantity of nonborrowed reserves and then explain by analogy, the effects of the remaining *LM* shift factors.

Suppose that the economy is at point A' in the bottom panel of Figure 26–4, which corresponds to point A in the top panel. Next suppose that the Fed increases nonborrowed reserves from NBR_1 to NBR_2 and that all other shift factors remain constant. At the initial price level, P_1, does the level of real income rise or fall?

In the top panel, the increase in *NBR* shifts the *LM* curve down and to the right, from position $LM|_{NBR_1,P_1}$, to position $LM|_{NBR_2,P_1}$. The new *IS-LM* equilibrium is point C, corresponding to a higher level of real income, Y_2 (and a lower interest rate, i_2). This effect appears as a displacement of point A' to point C' in the bottom panel. Point C' is on the new *AD* curve, identified by the label $AD|_{NBR_2}$. Thus, an increase in nonborrowed reserves increases the level of output that clears the goods and money markets at each price level and shifts the *AD* curve to the right. Similarly, a reduction in nonborrowed reserves shifts the *AD* curve inward.

Changes in the Remaining Shift Factors for the *LM* Curve   As with the factors that shift the *IS* curve, it is easy to visualize how each factor that shifts the *LM* curve will affect the *AD* curve. Any factor that shifts the *LM* curve down and to the right will also shift the *AD* curve to the right.

LM shift factors either shift the money supply curve or the money demand curve. Changes in shift factors that increase the money supply will shift the *LM* and *AD* curves to the right, as the discussion of an increase in nonborrowed reserves shows. Among the remaining policy parameters, a reduction in the discount rate, a loosening in the administration of the discount window (represented by a decrease in $\mathcal{A}$), or a reduction in the reserve requirement ratio will also shift the *AD* curve to the right. Turning to the behavior of banks, we see that a reduction in their demand for excess reserves, represented by a decrease in $\mathcal{P}$, will increase the money supply and will shift the *AD* curve to the right.

---

[3] A reduction in lump-sum tax rates produces a parallel shift of the *IS* and *AD* curves, while a reduction in income tax rates would make the curves flatter.

FIGURE 26–4
An Increase in
Nonborrowed
Reserves, *NBR*,
Shifts the *AD*
Curve to the Right

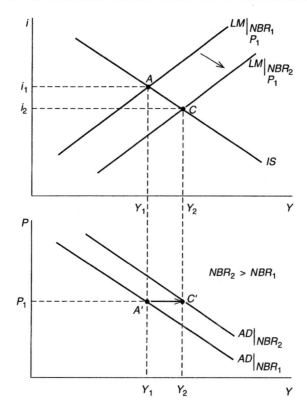

When *NBR* equals *NBR₁*, the economy is at point *A* in the top panel and at point *A'* in the bottom panel. An increase in *NBR* shifts the *LM* curve down and to the right. As a result, when the price level equals P_1, the level of output increases from Y_1 to Y_2, shown by the movement from point *A* to point *C* in the top panel and from point *A'* to point *C'* in the bottom panel. Point *C'* is on the new *AD* curve. Repeating this exercise for many price levels yields the new *AD* curve, which lies to the right of the original curve.

The remaining shift factors (the collective variable and the technology and regulatory index) affect the demand for money. Changes in these factors shift the *LM* curve down and to the right and the *AD* to the right when they reduce money demand, which causes the interest rate to fall. For example, a reduction in the demand for deposits by the public, represented by a decrease in $\mathscr{C}$, reduces money demand. The demand for deposits and, hence, the demand for money, also fall when there is an increase in the technology and regulatory index, $\mathscr{TR}$. An increase in $\mathscr{TR}$ increases the cost of banking, thereby inducing banks to lower the deposit rate, which reduces the demand for deposits. Conversely, when each of these shift factors changes in the opposite direction, the *LM* curve will shift up and to the left, and the *AD* curve to the left.

THE AGGREGATE SUPPLY

The introduction of the *AD* curve reveals that the *IS-LM* framework is incomplete: There are infinitely many pairs (*P*, *Y*) that clear the *IS-LM* market system. To determine the equilibrium values of *P* and *Y*, we need another curve, the aggregate supply, or *AS* curve.

The Keynesian Fixed-Price Aggregate Supply Curve

There is one special case in which the *IS-LM* model, by itself, is capable of determining the triplet (i, Y, P): the case of a fixed price level. In this case there is only one *LM* curve, and the intersection of the *LM* curve with the *IS* curve determines the full equilibrium level of Y. This result can be transferred to the (P, Y)-plane. Fixing the price level, say, at P_1, in Figure 26–5 determines income, the level of which is Y_1.

Suppose the price level is fixed and assume that the aggregate supply curve is horizontal at P_1, as Figure 26–6 shows. A horizontal aggregate supply curve means that firms can produce larger amounts of national output at the same per unit costs as smaller amounts. Therefore, they are willing to offer for sale at the same price any level of output that is demanded.

The *AD–AS* model with a horizontal supply curve is known as the **Keynesian fixed-price model**, or simply the fixed-price model. All the comparative statics results derived from the *IS-LM* model hold, without modification, in the fixed-price model. The major

FIGURE 26–5
The Case of a Fixed Price Level

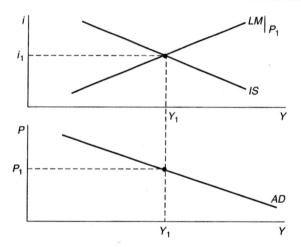

If the price level is fixed at P_1, the *IS-LM* model determines the equilibrium level of income: Y_1. Given P_1, we can find the point on the *AD* curve where the economy operates.

FIGURE 26–6
The Case of Perfectly Elastic Supply: *The Keynesian Fixed-Price Model*

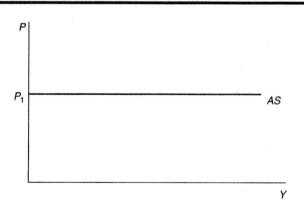

With a horizontal *AS* curve, firms are willing to supply any quantity of output at the same price.

FIGURE 26-7
Expansionary
Demand
Management
Policies in the
Keynesian Fixed-
Price Model

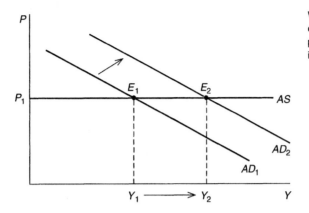

With a horizontal *AS* curve,
expansionary fiscal or monetary
policies increase output without
increasing the price level.

implication for macroeconomic policy is that monetary and fiscal policy have considerable effects on national output and no effect on the price level, as Figure 26–7 shows. An increase in either government expenditure or in nonborrowed reserves shifts the *AD* curve from position AD_1 to position AD_2. Real income increases to Y_2 without an accompanying increase in the price level.

How realistic is this fixed-price, or perfectly elastic aggregate supply, model? The model may be a reasonable approximation of reality during severe downturns in the economy, which are characterized by much unemployed labor and unused productive capacity. With extensive excess capacity in the economy, firms may increase output without having to incur higher marginal costs. Keynes designed his model for such a period. The fixed-price model grew out of Keynes's search for policy instruments to take the economy out of the Great Depression of the 1930s. Therefore, the model would need modification to be applicable to periods of nondepression.[4] Before examining modifications of the original Keynesian model, consider first the pre-Keynesian, classical model, which is the polar opposite of the Keynesian model.

The Classical Aggregate Supply Curve

In the **classical model**, the *AS* curve is vertical, as in Figure 26–8, because there is no excess capacity or involuntary unemployment. Any attempt to increase output raises wages and, hence, marginal costs, without achieving an increase in output. The key implication of the classical model is that expansionary demand management policies will fail to increase output; they will merely raise the price level, as Figure 26–9 shows. In contrast, with the Keynesian fixed-price model (Figure 26–7), the same policies increase output without any change in the price level.

How realistic is the classical, vertical aggregate supply curve? The answer depends on the length of the period being examined. In the long run, a vertical *AS* curve is reasonable. Natural causes, such as the size of the fully employed labor force and the size of the fully

---

[4]   Chapter 27 shows, however, that the fixed-price model has been partly rehabilitated in recent years. Serendipitously the fixed-price model may turn out to be realistic after all.

FIGURE 26–8
The Classical Case

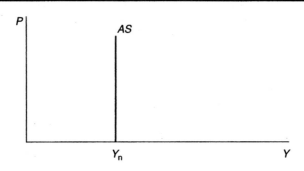

With a vertical *AS* curve, firms supply the full employment level of output, Y_n, which is independent of the price level.

FIGURE 26–9
Expansionary
Demand
Management
Policies in the
Classical Model

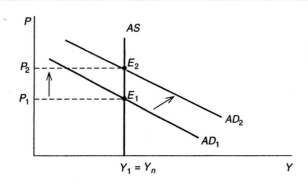

With a vertical *AS* curve, expansionary fiscal or monetary policies increase the price level but have no effect on output.

employed stock of plant and equipment, determine the full employment level of output, also called **potential output**, or the **natural level of output**, denoted by Y_n. Figure 26–9 shows that activist monetary or fiscal policy will not change Y_n; instead, only the price level rises. The full employment level of output grows at its natural rate, determined by the rate of growth of the population and the rate of improvement in productivity.

The Keynesian Short-Run Aggregate Supply Curve

Soon after Keynes introduced the fixed-price model, economists recognized that the model needed modification to be useful under general circumstances. Hence, the **short-run aggregate supply curve** depicted in Figure 26–10 was introduced. This supply curve shows a positive relation between the price level and output produced and supplied. If firms produce output under conditions of increasing marginal costs, they will be willing to offer more output for sale only at a higher price level. Consider then, how to establish increasing marginal costs to arrive at an upward-sloping short-run aggregate supply curve, *SAS*.

Profit Maximization and Movements Along the Supply Curve   Profit maximization implies two equivalent rules that guide firms in hiring labor (*N*) and producing

**FIGURE 26–10
Short-Run
Aggregate Supply
Curve**

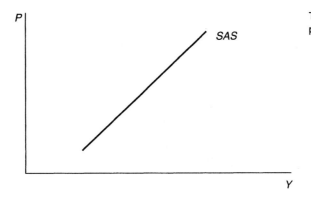

The supply of output increases with its price.

output (Y). *First, if firms operate in competitive markets for inputs and output, profit maximization implies that they hire labor up to the point where the marginal product of labor equals the real wage.* The marginal product of labor is the extra output produced by an extra unit of labor. If W represents the nominal, or money, wage, the real wage is W/P: The real wage equals the money wage multiplied by the purchasing power of money, $(1/P)$. Thus, the real wage is ultimately expressed in units of output per unit of labor, the same units as the marginal product. Denoting the marginal product of labor by MP_N, the decision rule is:

$$W/P = MP_N \tag{26–1}$$

Equation 26–1 says that firms hire labor up to the point where the real wage equals the marginal product of labor.

An equivalent rule is based upon the supply practices of firms: *Profit-maximizing firms operating in competitive markets supply output up to the point where price equals marginal cost (MC):*

$$P = MC \tag{26–2}$$

The rule for hiring labor implies the rule for supplying output, which is easily shown by rearranging Equation 26–1 so that the price level is on one side of the equation by itself:

$$P = W/MP_N \tag{26–3}$$

According to Equation 26–3, profit maximization implies that the price level (that is, the price of output) must equal the nominal money wage divided by the marginal product of labor. But W/MP_N is the marginal cost; that is,

$$MC = W/MP_N$$

To illustrate that W/MP_N is the marginal cost of output, suppose a firm hires one more hour of labor for $W = \$10$, and the marginal product of an additional hour of labor is five units of output. Then each of these five units costs two dollars.

We can derive an increasing relation between the price level, P, and output supplied, Y, if we can establish that marginal cost increases with output produced. We establish this result by using the **principle of diminishing marginal product of labor**, which means that the marginal product of labor falls as more labor is employed.

The argument is straightforward. To produce more output, firms must hire more labor. But each additional hour of work produces less. Therefore, for the same money wage, fewer additional units of output are produced. Hence, each additional unit of output costs more.

We can also explain increasing marginal cost schematically from the MC formula itself. An increase in Y supplied requires more labor, N. With more N, the marginal product, MP_N, falls. As a result, W/MP_N rises; that is, the right side of the MC equation rises. For example, if the marginal product of labor falls from five units of output to four units, the marginal cost will rise from $2 per unit of output to $2.50 per unit when the money wage is $10 per hour.

Thus, the marginal cost of output increases with the level of output produced. However, since profit maximization requires that marginal cost equal price, there is an increasing relation between the price of output and the level of output produced; the SAS curve is upward sloping.

The economy moves along the SAS curve in response to demand-side shocks. Figure 26–11 shows the effect of a rightward shift in the AD curve. An increase in aggregate demand caused by expansionary demand management policies or by changes in the behavior of the private sector shifts the AD curve to the right, thereby increasing the price level and output. It is important to understand the reasons for the increase in output. Output increases because the real wage falls when the price level rises and the money wage is fixed. The reduction in the real wage persuades (enables) firms to hire more labor and increase the production of goods and services.

Shifts of the SAS Curve   Nominal rewards to labor and to other variable factors of production are fixed along the Keynesian SAS curve. Exogenous factors that affect the marginal product of labor, such as the quality of education and of infrastructure, are also fixed. When any of these factors change, the SAS curve shifts.

Changes in the Money Wage   How does an increase in the money wage shift the SAS curve up and to the left? This result follows from the marginal cost formula:

$$MC = W/MP_N$$

For a given level of employment and output and, hence, for a given level of the marginal product of labor, marginal cost will rise if the money wage rises. Because marginal cost must equal the asking price, the price level must also rise (and it will increase by the same percentage as the money wage). The increase in price means that the same quantity of output is supplied at a higher price. For example, with a marginal product of labor equal to five units of output, an increase in wages from $10 to $12.50 an hour raises marginal cost from $2.00 to $2.50 per unit of output.

Figure 26–12 depicts the result of this conceptual exercise. Start at point A on the short-run supply curve $SAS|_{W_1}$, so denoted to indicate that the money wage is fixed at W_1

FIGURE 26–11
Expansionary
Demand Shocks
and the Short-Run
Aggregate Supply

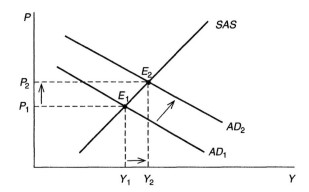

With an upward-sloping short-run aggregate supply curve, an increase in aggregate demand results in an increase in the price level and output.

FIGURE 26–12
The Effect of an
Increase in the
Money Wage, W,
on the SAS Curve

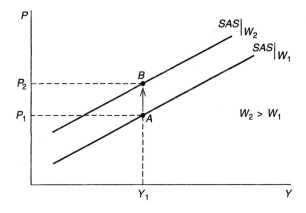

A rise in the money wage from W_1 to W_2 increases the marginal cost at each level of output. For price to equal marginal cost, P must rise at each level of output. Thus, the SAS curve shifts up and to the left.

along this curve. The higher money wage, W_2, increases the marginal cost by the distance AB, requiring a rise in the price level from P_1 to P_2 if firms are to supply the same quantity of output, Y_1. (As noted above, the percentage increase in the price level must equal the percentage increase in the money wage.) Repeating this exercise for all levels of Y and connecting the resulting points, such as B, yield the supply curve $SAS|_{W_2}$ that corresponds to the higher money wage, W_2. This curve lies above and to the left of the supply curve for W_1. Thus, an increase in the money wage shifts the short-run aggregate supply curve up by the same percentage. Alternatively, we can explain the shift of the SAS curve as a leftward shift: At each price level, there is a decrease in aggregate supply. Of course, a decrease in the money wage shifts the SAS curve down and to the right; at each price level, there is an increase in aggregate supply.

Changes in the Nominal Rewards to Other Variable Factors of Production   Thus far, the explanation of short-run aggregate supply has introduced only one variable factor of production, labor. In the real world, however, there are several variable factors of production, including raw materials and energy inputs such as oil. For the model to be a good representation of the real world, money wages and the symbol W must be considered a collective variable that represents the reward denominated in current dollars to all variable factors of production. (And the marginal product in the denominator of the MC formula is the marginal product of this collective factor of production.) It follows that when any one of these rewards decreases, the marginal cost of output falls; and the SAS curve will shift down and to the right. Similarly, an increase in any of the nominal rewards shifts the SAS curve up and to the left.

Exogenous Changes in the Marginal Product of Labor   Changes in the rewards to factors of production are not the only factors that shift the SAS curve. An exogenous increase in the marginal product of labor will shift the entire family of short-run supply curves down and to the right, because such improvements in the marginal product of labor reduce the marginal cost of producing output at each money wage.

One important determinant of the productivity of labor is the level of education and training of the labor force. The better educated and trained the labor force, the higher its productivity and, hence, the lower the cost of producing output. Thus, the higher the education level and the better the training of the labor force, the lower the position of each short-run aggregate supply curve.

A second important determinant of productivity is the size and the quality of the fixed factor, namely, the size and quality of plant, equipment, and infrastructure, such as roads, bridges, and airports. The newer and the more modern a country's plant and equipment and its infrastructure, the lower the marginal cost of output and, hence, the further to the right the location of the short-run curves.

Combining the Keynesian Short Run with the Classical Long Run

Keynesian economists also examined what will happen in the long run. With the prodding and participation of classical economists, the Keynesians showed—and conceded—that the long-run aggregate supply is vertical at the potential level of output,[5] Y_n. To prepare to show how the economy moves from a short-run, upward-sloping aggregate supply curve to the long-run vertical supply curve, we examine the market for labor and the assumption of rigid money wages.

The Market for Labor and Rigid Money Wages   Figure 26–13 depicts the demand curve for labor and the supply curve of labor in a graph with the real wage measured on the vertical axis and the quantity of labor on the horizontal axis. The demand curve is derived from the rule that firms hire labor up to the point where the marginal product of labor equals the real wage. Because the marginal product of labor diminishes with an increase in the amount of labor used, it follows that firms will want to hire, or demand, more labor as the real wage falls. Thus, the demand for labor curve, N^d, is downward sloping. The supply of labor comes from utility-maximizing households. The higher the real wage, the higher the labor supplied. In other words, the supply curve is an upward-sloping curve.

---

[5] A vertical long-run supply curve is consistent with Keynes's own explanation in Chapter 19 of the *General Theory of Employment, Interest, and Money.*

FIGURE 26–13
Fixed Money
Wages and
Involuntary
Unemployment

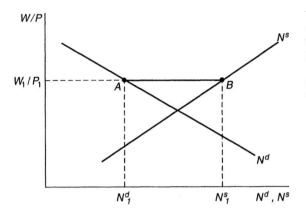

There will be involuntary
unemployment in the labor market if
the money wage is fixed at W_1 and the
price level is P_1. At the real wage
W_1/P_1, the quantity of labor supplied is
greater, by the amount AB, than the
quantity demanded.

The same graph also shows the original Keynesian stipulation that a rigid money wage, W_1, and a given price level, P_1, may result in **involuntary unemployment**, which means that more workers are willing to work than firms are willing to employ at the existing real wage. At the real wage W_1/P_1, the quantity of labor supplied is greater, by the amount AB, than the quantity demanded.

Although Keynes was willing to accept that sooner or later workers will accept cuts in money wages, he claimed that workers resist these cuts for some time. Until they acquiesce to a lower wage, there can be substantial unemployment. According to Keynes, the right remedy is for policymakers to use activist fiscal and monetary policies to stimulate aggregate demand rather than wait until workers are willing to accept sufficient cuts in money wages to restore full employment. Furthermore, he argued that cuts in money wages and consequent decreases in the price level may be counterproductive. If falling wages and prices create a depression psychology and, hence, reduce aggregate demand, the economy will slide into a deeper economic depression.

Many economists, notably classical economists, object to the idea of disequilibrium of the labor market. Continuous equilibrium is a hallmark of both pre-Keynesian and modern classical thought. Keynes, himself, did not give a reason why rational workers would resist cuts in money wages even though they may be forced to accept cuts in real wages when the price level rises. Several reasons for money-wage rigidity were introduced by James Tobin in 1947 and extended in his presidential address to the American Economic Association in 1972.[6]

One of the reasons given by Tobin is the price level expected by workers. For example, suppose workers are persuaded to accept a money-wage cut on the grounds that cuts in money wages will lead to falling prices. Further suppose that subsequently the price level rises and returns to its original level. Workers who agreed to accept lower money wages will be stuck with a lower real wage for the duration of their labor contract. Thus,

[6] James Tobin, "Money Wage Rates and Employment," reprinted in James Tobin, *Essays in Economics: Volume 1, Macroeconomics* (Chicago: Markham Publishing Co., 1971), 12–26; and "Inflation and Unemployment," *American Economic Review*, March 1972, 147–60.

workers are rational to refuse cuts in their money wage if they expect the price level to rise and return to its original level. Also, employers do not force the employed workers to accept lower wages merely because there are unemployed persons who are willing to work for less; employers fear loss of morale and the consequent loss of productivity that can accompany money-wage cuts. Tobin, however, did not provide a formal analysis of these reasons. Beginning in the 1980s, the new Keynesians examined formally these and other reasons why workers may refuse money-wage cuts and why firms may refrain from forcing such cuts. (Chapter 27 examines the arguments of the new Keynesians.)

Flexible Money Wages   Now consider what will happen when workers do accept money wage cuts (assuming that no depression psychology develops). Figure 26–14 shows how the economy moves from short-run equilibrium to long-run equilibrium, when output is initially below its potential level. In the process, the long-run aggregate supply curve (LAS) is also derived. Point A, where the AD curve intersects the AS curve, represents the initial short-run equilibrium. At this point the price level is P_1 and the level of output is Y_1, which is less than the natural, or potential, level of output, Y_n.

Suppose that after some time the involuntary unemployment induces workers to accept a lower money wage, so that W falls from W_1 to W_2. As a result, the short-run aggregate supply shifts down and to the right, to position $SAS|_{W_2}$ in Figure 26–14. The price level

FIGURE 26–14
Falling Money Wages and the Movement to Potential Output

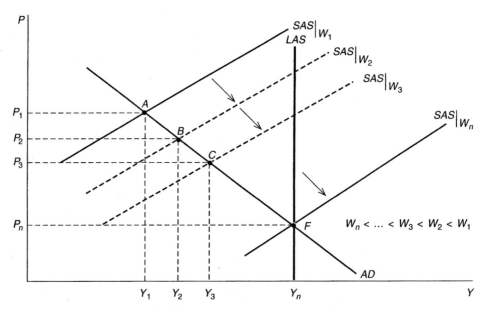

Suppose that the economy starts at point A, with actual output below potential output, Y_n. Also suppose that workers agree to accept cuts in their money wage. As the money wage falls from W_1 to W_2 to W_3, the SAS curve shifts down and to the right. As a result, the price level falls and output rises. Eventually, full employment is restored at point F, with Y equal to Y_n.

FIGURE 26–15
Rising Money
Wages and the
Movement to
Potential Output

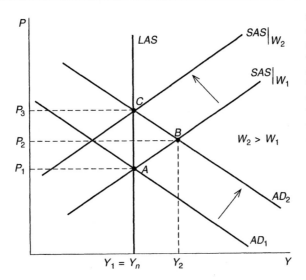

Suppose an expansionary demand
shock hits a fully employed economy,
represented by point *A*. If money
wages were to remain fixed, the
economy would move to point *B*. But
when money wages rise because of
excess demand in the labor market,
the economy moves to point *C*. In the
end, only the price level rises; the
percentage increase in the price level
equals the percentage increase in the
money wage, so the real wage
remains unchanged.

falls to P_2, and output rises to Y_2. As long as output is below its potential level, Y_n, there
will be unemployment, and the money wage will continue to fall. Furthermore, as the
money wage continues to fall, the price level will also fall and output will continue to
rise. Eventually, at point *F*, national output reaches its full employment potential.

Point *F* is a full equilibrium point because it is where all markets clear. Point *F* is on the
AD curve so that the goods and services market, the money market, and the foreign exchange market clear. It is also on the **long-run aggregate supply curve**, which is a vertical
line at the full-employment level of output. At this level of output the labor market clears.
At the real wage implied by point *F*, the demand for labor equals the supply of labor. There
is full employment of the labor force, meaning there is no involuntary unemployment.

The initial equilibrium in Figure 26–14 is point *A*, with output below the full employment level. But how did the economy get to point *A* in the first place? The movement from
Y_n to point *A* (not depicted in the graph) may have been the consequence of an inadvertent
recessionary shock originating on the *AD* side or the *AS* side. Now consider the case
where a fully employed economy is hit with an expansionary shock. This case shows how
the economy will revert back to its initial output, Y_n, and, hence, to the *LAS* curve.

Suppose that the economy starts from a position of full equilibrium with output at its
potential level, Y_n, the price level at P_1, and the money wage at W_1, as depicted by point *A*
in Figure 26–15. Next suppose that an expansionary shock shifts the *AD* curve to the
right. With given money wages, there is upward pressure on the price level and the
production of output that establishes a new short-run equilibrium at point *B*.[7] To attract
more labor from its workers, firms must pay overtime wages and, in general, increase the

---

[7] At this point there is excess demand for labor because the real wage falls below the equilibrium real wage
   when the price level rises and the money wage is fixed.

nominal wage, say, to W_2. This increase in the money wage shifts the short-run aggregate curve upward, to position $SAS|_{W_2}$. Full, or long-run, equilibrium is reestablished at point C; the price level rises by the same percentage as the nominal wage, so that the real wage reverts to its original value: $W_2/P_3 = W_1/P_1$. And output returns to its potential level, Y_n. The upshot of this exercise is that in a fully employed economy an increase in the price level does not increase the supply of output. The long-run aggregate supply curve is vertical at the potential level of output.

THE EFFECTS OF POLICY AND SHOCKS IN THE KEYNESIAN SHORT RUN AND THE CLASSICAL LONG RUN

Having explained movements along and shifts of the aggregate demand curve and the aggregate supply curves, we now consider the effects of demand-side and supply-side shocks on i, Y, and P. We employ the two-panel graph to account for all three variables.

The Keynesian Short Run

Following Keynesian analysis, assume that the short-run equilibrium level of output may be below the full employment level, Y_n, because of **sticky money wages**, which means the money wage falls very slowly in response to excess supply in the labor market. Figure 26–16 illustrates this case. In the lower panel of the graph, the AD curve intersects the SAS curve at point E_1, at this point output equals Y_1, which we assume is less than Y_n, and the price level equals P_1. Given this price level, it is possible to pick out the relevant LM curve in the upper panel, the one labeled P_1. This LM curve intersects the IS curve at point E_1, where Y, of course, equals Y_1, and the interest rate equals i_1. Thus, we have determined the triplet (i, Y, P).

FIGURE 26–16
The Initial Short-Run Equilibrium

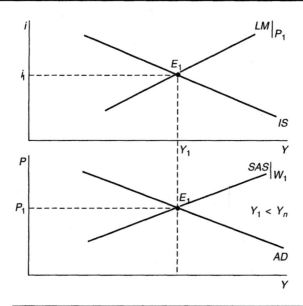

In the (P, Y)-plane, the AD curve intersects the SAS curve at point E_1; the short-run equilibrium values of P and Y are P_1 and Y_1, respectively. Once we know that P equals P_1, we can find the equilibrium value of i in the (i, Y)-plane by picking out the LM curve with label P_1. This LM curve intersects the IS curve at point E_1 where the equilibrium interest rate equals i_1.

Shifts in Aggregate Demand   Keynesian analysis asserts that money-wage (and other) rigidities will persist for some time and that the government can and should use demand management policies to shift the *AD* curve to the right and increase output. Such an increase can come about by manipulating a variety of shift factors. Congress and the president may increase expenditures, increase transfer payments, or reduce taxes. Alternatively, the Fed can inject the necessary stimulus by increasing nonborrowed reserves, reducing the discount rate, easing its administration of the discount window, or lowering the reserve requirement ratio.

While any positive shift of the *AD* curve will increase both the price level and output with an upward-sloping *SAS* curve, the effects on the interest rate depend on whether the shift originates in the *IS* sector or the *LM* sector. We already know from the *IS-LM* model that an increase in output precipitated by a positive shift in the *IS* curve will be accompanied by an increase in the interest rate. On the other hand, an increase in output caused by a positive shift of the *LM* curve will be accompanied by a fall in the interest rate. However, we also know that an increase in the price level increases the interest rate, because it shifts the *LM* curve up (and to the left):

$$P\!\uparrow \;\to\; (NBR/P)\!\downarrow \;\to\; M^s\!\downarrow \;\to\; EDM \;\to\; i\!\uparrow$$

This effect of a change in the price level on the interest rate is Milton Friedman's *price level effect* that Chapter 10 discusses. (The effect is also referred to as the *Keynesian real balance effect* because a change in *P* affects the interest rate through its effect on the supply of real balances, that is, the real money supply.) To find the overall effect of each policy on the interest rate, we must combine the price level effect with the other effects.

LM *Sector Shocks*   The two-panel graph in Figure 26–17 examines the case of an increase in nonborrowed reserves and, hence, an increase in the quantity of money. Point E_1 represents the initial equilibrium, with nonborrowed reserves equal to NBR_1.

When the Fed increases nonborrowed reserves to NBR_2, the *AD* curve in the lower panel shifts to the right. If the price level were to remain unchanged at P_1, the economy would move from point E_1 to point E_1', and the level of output would increase to Y_1'. The upper panel shows that the interest rate would fall from i_1 to i_1'. This is the result derived from the *IS-LM* model in Chapter 25, because that model keeps the price level fixed. Chapter 25 shows that the decrease in the interest rate between points E_1 and E_1' can itself be divided into two effects: the liquidity effect and the real income effect. The liquidity effect is the fall in *i* that results from an increase in *NBR*, when *Y* and *P* are unchanged. The real income effect is the rise in *i* that results from a rise in *Y*, given *P*. To avoid cluttering the graph, these two effects are not shown explicitly in the upper panel of Figure 26–17, but the reader should identify them. Given this information, it is possible to incorporate the price level effect.

With an upward-sloping *AS* curve, the price level rises from P_1 to P_2. The final equilibrium is at point E_2 and not E_1'. Incorporating this information into the *IS-LM* graph, we see that the *LM* curve shifts up (and to the left), establishing E_2 as the full equilibrium. The interest rate rises to i_2, which is still less than the initial interest rate, i_1. Because a rise in the interest rate reduces aggregate demand, output falls back from Y_1' to Y_2; that is, the rise in the interest rate by itself is contractionary. This exercise shows that

**FIGURE 26–17
Effects of an
Increase in *NBR*
on (*i*, *P*, *Y*)**

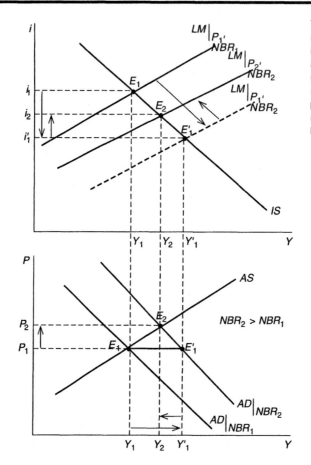

The effect of an increase in *NBR* with
a fixed price level is shown by the
movement from E_1 to E_1' in the upper
and lower panels. Incorporating the
rise in the price level from P_1 to P_2
results in the final equilibrium being at
point E_2 rather than at E_1'. The interest
rate falls by less, and output rises by
less, than when the price level is fixed.

*an assumption that the price level is fixed leads to overestimating the amount by which an
increase in nonborrowed reserves reduces the interest rate and increases output.*

TRY IT OUT 26.1

Suppose that because of reduced appetite for risk the public increases its demand for
money and reduces its demand for debt securities, other things equal. With the help of
an *IS-LM*, *AD–AS* diagram, explain the effects on the interest rate, the price level, and
real income.

IS *Sector Shocks*   Now consider the case when the positive shift of the *AD* curve results
from a shift of the *IS* curve. For example, suppose government expenditure rises from
G_1 to G_2. In Figure 26–18 the economy starts at the initial equilibrium point E_1 in both

FIGURE 26–18
Effects of an
Increase in *G* on
(*i*, *P*, *Y*)

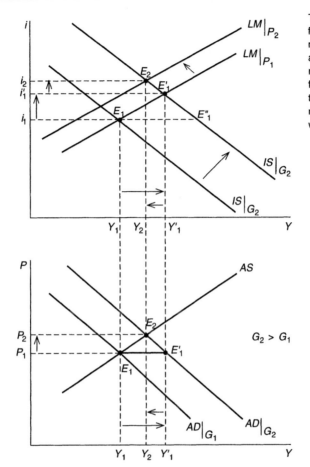

The effect of an increase in *G* with a
fixed price level is shown by the
movement from E_1 to E_1' in the upper
and lower panels. Incorporating the
rise in the price level from P_1 to P_2, the
final equilibrium is at point E_2 rather
than at E_1'. The interest rate rises by
more, and output rises by less, than
when the price level is fixed.

the upper and the lower panels. Thus, the initial values of the interest rate, output, and the
price level are (i_1, Y_1 P_1). The increase in *G* shifts the *IS* curve (in the top panel) to the
right. If the price level is assumed fixed at its initial level of P_1, the interest rate will
rise to i_1' and output to Y_1'. The bottom panel shows, however, that the increase in *G*
shifts the *AD* curve up and to the right and, as a consequence of the excess demand
(E_1E_1'), the price level rises to P_2. Incorporating this information into the top panel results
in the *LM* curve shifting up and to the left; the final equilibrium will be reached at E_2,
where the interest rate, i_2, is higher than at E_1. This extra increase in the interest rate, from
i_1' to i_2, is the price level effect on the interest rate. Thus, the interest rate will rise by
more than the earlier IS-LM analysis suggested. In other words, *ignoring the price level
effect of an increase in government expenditure leads to underestimating the consequent
increase in the interest rate and to overestimating the increase in output.*

The top panel of Figure 26–18 provides a concise summary of the effects of an increase in government expenditure. The distance E_1E_1'' measures the simplest multiplier effect of an increase in government expenditure: the increase in output that results from an increase in G if we ignore the effect on the interest rate and the price level. The horizontal distance between E_1'' and E_1' measures the decrease in output that results from the consequent increase in the interest rate, with the price level fixed. And the horizontal distance between E_1' and E_2 factors in the additional decrease in output that results from the price-induced increase in the interest rate. Of course, output falls when i rises because private sector demand is reduced, or crowded out. With an upward-sloping aggregate supply curve, the crowding out is incomplete. On net, AD and Y rise when G increases.

Summary of **AD** *Shocks*   The following schematics summarize the short-run effects on endogenous variables of shocks to the LM sector and the IS sector:

LM Sector Shocks

$$\text{Shocks that shift the } LM \text{ curve to the right (and down)} \rightarrow \begin{matrix} i\downarrow \\ Y\uparrow \\ P\uparrow \end{matrix}$$

IS Sector Shocks

$$\text{Shocks that shift the } IS \text{ curve to the right (and up)} \rightarrow \begin{matrix} i\uparrow \\ Y\uparrow \\ P\uparrow \end{matrix}$$

Shifts in Aggregate Supply   Now consider supply-side shocks. This section illustrates an adverse supply shock, which reduces aggregate supply and, hence, shifts the aggregate supply curve up and to left.

Point E_1 represents the initial equilibrium in Figure 26–19, where the AD–AS graph is in the upper panel and the IS-LM graph is in the lower panel. Now suppose there is a shock, say, an embargo, that results in a worldwide increase in the price of oil. An increase in the nominal reward to this variable factor of production (denoted by W) shifts the SAS curve up and to the left, as shown in the top panel of Figure 26–19. As a result, the price level rises to P_2 and output falls to Y_2.

In the bottom panel, the increased price level reduces the real value of nonborrowed reserves, NBR/P, and shifts the LM curve to the left. The consequent excess demand for real money balances raises the interest rate to i_2. (This is the price-level effect.) And the rise in the interest rate reduces aggregate demand and, hence, aggregate output. MarketWatch 26.1 explains that an oil price shock was one of the factors responsible for the recession of 1990–1991.

An increase in the cost of variable inputs is not the only factor that shifts the SAS upward. A reduction in the marginal product of labor, caused by a deterioration in the quality of education or in the quality of the fixed factor of production, will also shift the SAS curve upward. As a result, P rises, Y falls, and i rises.[8]

---

[8] Exogenous reductions in productivity also shift the demand for labor curve inward, which results in an inward shift in the long-run aggregate supply curve. In contrast, changes in the money wage or in the nominal

FIGURE 26–19
An Adverse Supply
Shock

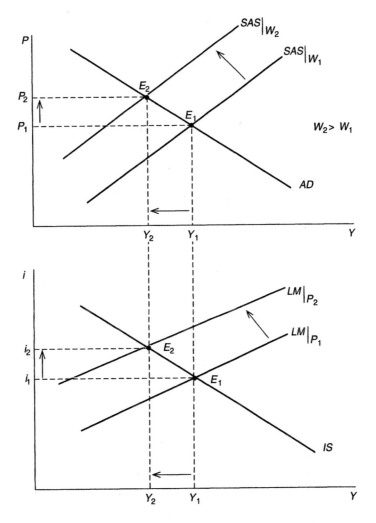

In the upper panel, an increase in the price of oil shifts the supply curve up
and to the left. The price level rises and real output falls, as shown by the
movement from E_1 to E_2. In the bottom panel, the increase in the price level
shifts the *LM* curve up and to the left because *NBR/P* falls. As a result, the
interest rate also rises.

Summary of Supply-Side Shocks   As with demand shocks, we can sum up the effects of
supply shocks schematically. For simplicity, *W* represents the collective nominal reward
to all variable factors of production.

---

rewards to other variable factors of production do not shift the demand for labor curve or the long-run
aggregate supply curve.

MarketWatch 26.1
The Oil Shock of 1990

"Economic expansions do not end on their own; they end as a result of external shocks to the economy, economic imbalances that must be worked off, or inappropriate economic policies." This is how the *Economic Report of the President 1992* (p. 42) introduced its explanation for the end of the 1982–1990 expansion. It then went on to describe the shocks, imbalances, and policies that caused the recession of 1990–1991:

Hopes that the expansion would continue were dashed in August 1990, when the economy was hit with an external shock—the rise in oil prices resulting from the Iraqi invasion of Kuwait. Oil prices rose sharply, from less than $19 a barrel in July to more than $30 in late August, and peaked at about $40 in early October. It is natural to point to the oil shock—coupled with the resulting declines in consumer and business confidence—as the event that pushed the economy into recession. However, a number of structural imbalances and the lagged effect of tight monetary policy in 1988 and 1989

also slowed the economy. While the oil shock significantly aggravated weakness in the economy, it is a matter of debate whether these other factors on their own eventually would have pushed the economy into recession, or, alternatively, whether the economy would have experienced a prolonged period of sluggish growth. [Economic Report of the President 1992, p. 42]

The structural imbalances referred to in the report are the headwinds discussed in Fed*Watch* 25.1, such as the balance sheet distress of households and firms and the cutbacks in defense spending. The accompanying graph shows that the headwinds shifted the aggregate demand curve to the left, while the oil shock shifted the aggregate supply curve to the left. Unlike the oil shocks of the 1970s, the oil shock of 1990 was short-lived, with prices falling back to their original levels after Operation Desert Storm in January 1991.* The headwinds, however, were more enduring. The Fed's expansionary monetary policies from 1990 to 1992 were designed to counter the headwinds by shifting the *AD* curve to the right.

_____

* Chapters 27 and 28 discuss the oil shocks of the 1970s.

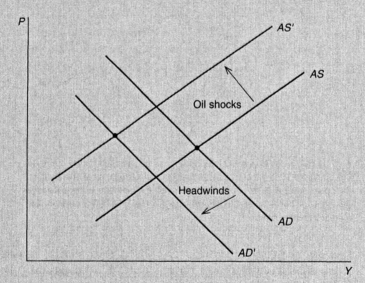

$$W\uparrow \rightarrow \begin{matrix} i\uparrow \\ Y\downarrow \\ P\uparrow \end{matrix}$$

An identical set of results will materialize in the short run if, instead, the economy experiences an exogenous reduction in the marginal product of labor.

$$MP_N\downarrow \rightarrow \begin{matrix} i\uparrow \\ Y\downarrow \\ P\uparrow \end{matrix}$$

The Classical Long Run

Finally, consider the long run. We know that in the long run, expansionary demand management policies increase the price level but not the level of real income. The next two sections look at the details of expansionary monetary and fiscal policies to establish two benchmark results that are the hallmark of classical macroeconomics: the neutrality of money and complete crowding out.

Neutrality of Money   As Chapter 10 explains, money is neutral when an increase in the quantity of nominal nonborrowed reserves, NBR, has no effect on the quantity of real nonborrowed reserves, NBR/P, or on the real money supply, M^S. Instead, the price level rises by the same percentage as nominal nonborrowed reserves: $\Delta P/P = \Delta NBR/NBR$. It is also true that the price level increases by the same percentage as the nominal money supply, M. The reason is simple. As Chapter 10 notes, the real money supply is equal to the nominal money supply divided by the price level; that is, $M^S = M/P$. For the real money supply to remain unchanged when the price level rises, the nominal money supply must rise by the same percentage. With the real money supply unchanged, the interest rate, i, remains unchanged. As a result, aggregate demand does not change, and neither does aggregate supply, because the nominal wage rises by the same percentage as the price level, thereby leaving the real wage unchanged. In sum, the **neutrality of money** means that the rate of wage inflation ($\Delta W/W$) equals the rate of price inflation, which, in turn, equals the rate of growth of the nominal money supply, which equals the rate of growth of nominal nonborrowed reserves:

$$\Delta W/W = \Delta P/P = \Delta M/M = \Delta NBR/NBR$$

The two panels of Figure 26–20 show that money is neutral in the long run. In the lower panel, the equilibrium moves along the long-run aggregate supply curve when the quantity of nominal nonborrowed reserves increases from NBR_1 to NBR_2. The price level increases from P_1 to P_2, and the money wage increases from W_1 to W_2. Of course, the increase in the money wage shifts the short-run aggregate supply curve upward. In the upper panel, only the label of the LM curve changes, from NBR_1/P_1 to NBR_2/P_2.

Figure 26–20 establishes the neutrality of money through all the linkages of the AD–AS model. This classical result can also be derived directly from the quantity theory of money. Recall from Chapter 16 that according to the quantity theory of money, velocity-adjusted growth of money equals the rate of growth of nominal *GDP*:

$$\Delta M/M + \Delta V/V = \Delta P/P + \Delta Y/Y$$

FIGURE 26–20
Neutrality of
Money

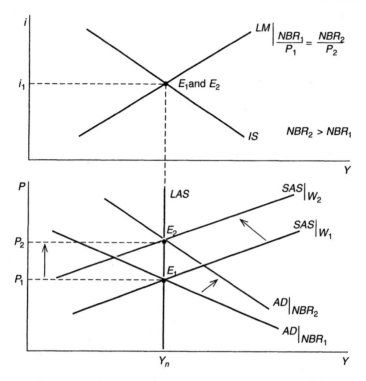

In the long run, money is neutral, which means that the rate of wage inflation
equals the rate of price inflation, which, in turn, equals the rate of growth of
the quantity of nominal nonborrowed reserves. Thus, an increase in *NBR* has
no effect on output, employment, or the interest rate.

In the long run, without growth, $\Delta Y/Y = 0$. Moreover, $\Delta V/V = 0$, because the factors
affecting velocity—the interest rate, real income, and exogenous factors—are unchanged.
Hence, according to the quantity theory of money, the percentage change in the nominal
money supply will equal the percentage change in the price level:

$$\Delta P/P = \Delta M/M$$

In practice, economists use a variety of models to explain the real world. The quantity
theory is a compact model that emphasizes the relation between money growth and
inflation. The *IS-LM*, AD–AS model is a more detailed framework that emphasizes the
numerous interconnections between the financial sector and the real sector.

Complete Crowding Out   Now consider fiscal policy. As Chapters 10 and 25 explains, crowding out means that an increase in government expenditure, G, is accompanied by a reduction in private sector demand. **Complete crowding out** occurs when the
decrease in private sector demand totally offsets the increase in government demand so

FIGURE 26–21
Complete
Crowding Out

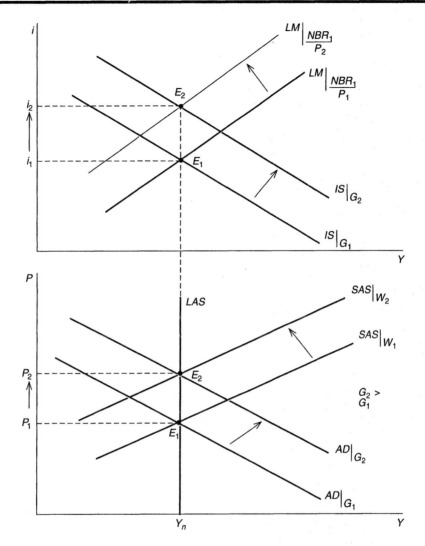

In the long run an increase in *G* reduces or, crowds out, private sector demand by an
equal amount. The increase in *G* causes the price level and the interest rate to rise until
aggregate demand and aggregate output return to their original level.

that aggregate demand and, hence, aggregate output, remain unchanged. Figure 26–21
shows that crowding out is complete in the long run. In response to an increase in *G*, the
price level and the interest rate rise until private sector demand falls by the amount
needed to keep aggregate demand unchanged. The distribution of the reduction in private
sector demand among consumption, investment, and net exports depends on the interest
sensitivity of each of these components. Remember that the interest sensitivity of net
exports runs through the foreign exchange market.

ECONOMIC POLICY AND SCHOOLS OF THOUGHT

Among the economists who laid the foundations of modern macroeconomics from the 1940s to the 1970s are several Nobel laureates. They are Paul Samuelson of the Massachusetts Institute of Technology, Milton Friedman of the University of Chicago and the Hoover Institution, the late Sir John Hicks of Oxford University, Lawrence Klein of the University of Pennsylvania, James Tobin of Yale University, Franco Modigliani of the Massachusetts Institute of Technology, and Robert Solow of the Massachusetts Institute of Technology.

Samuelson, Hicks, Klein, Tobin, Modigliani, and Solow are **Keynesians**, who built the **neoclassical synthesis** by combining the Keynesian short run with the classical long run. Recall that Keynesians acknowledge that the economy will eventually gravitate to full employment, but they believe that the process is painfully slow. Therefore, they advocate the use of demand management policies to stabilize output and employment.

On the other hand, Milton Friedman is a classicist. **Classicists** believe that the labor market clears rapidly and therefore do not advocate discretionary policies. Moreover, Friedman argues that discretionary policy is more likely to destabilize rather than to stabilize the economy, because of lags between the time a policy is implemented and the time it affects output and employment. Friedman is the founder of the modern doctrine of **monetarism**, which was explained in terms of the quantity theory of money in Chapter 16. In a keynote paper presented in 1983 at the Bank of Japan on the occasion of the centennial celebration of the bank, Friedman summed up his views about monetary policy and time lags as follows:

> An unanticipated increase or decrease in the quantity of money tends to affect total *nominal* (italics added) spending some six to nine months later in countries like the United States, Japan, and Great Britain. The initial effect is primarily on output rather than on prices. Prices tend to be affected only some 18 months to two years later. This does not mean that there is no further effect on real quantities. On the contrary, the delayed impact on prices means an overshooting of output—up or down depending on the initial stimulus—which will then require an overshooting in the opposite direction to allow the price level to reach its appropriate level. As a result the cyclical reaction pattern in both output and prices tends to last for a considerable period—years, not months. That is precisely why monetary instability is so destructive of economic stability. [Milton Friedman, "Monetarism in Rhetoric and Practice," *Monetary and Economic Studies* (Bank of Japan) 1, no. 2 (October 1983): 2.]

And describing monetarist policy in the same paper, Friedman said:

> The policy implication that monetarists like myself have drawn from this analysis is that the primary task of the monetary authorities should be to avoid introducing uncertainty in the economy, that their primary task should be to produce a predictable pattern of monetary growth, preferably a steady one. The idea that monetary growth should be steady and predictable is the core of the monetarist policy view. All monetarists, I believe, favor steadiness. However, they differ considerably with respect to what monetary aggregate or aggregates should be targeted, what the numerical rate of growth of the selected aggregate or aggregates should be, and how it should be

determined. [Milton Friedman, "Monetarism in Rhetoric and Practice," *Monetary and Economic Studies* (Bank of Japan) 1, no. 2 (October 1983): 3–4]

In most of his writings, Friedman has advocated that the Fed set a target for a measure of money that resembles the present M1. Other prominent monetarists, notably, Alan Meltzer of Carnegie-Mellon University and the late Karl Brunner of the University of Rochester, have advocated that the Fed target the monetary base (currency plus reserves), which is the raw material out of which money is created.

LOOKING AHEAD

The next chapter will show that seminal work on aggregate supply in the late 1960s by Milton Friedman and by Edmund Phelps was the forerunner of the new classical revolution that began in the mid-1970s. It will also show that Robert Solow's presidential address to the American Economic Association in 1979 provided a blueprint for the research agenda of the new Keynesians, who emerged in the 1980s.

Using an apt characterization introduced by Franco Modigliani, like their namesakes, new classicists maintain that the labor market clears at a gallop, while new Keynesians maintain that it does so at a crawl. Moreover, new classicists argue that discretionary policies that are expected and understood will be ineffective, while new Keynesians argue that demand management policies, even if expected, can be effective devices for stabilization.

SUMMARY

- The aggregate demand (*AD*) curve depicts the level of output that can be supported by the markets for goods and services, money, and foreign exchange at each price level.

- The *AD* curve is downward sloping in the (*P, Y*)-plane. There are two main channels through which an increase in *P* reduces aggregate demand. First, an increase in *P* reduces real nonborrowed reserves, which raises the interest rate and reduces the investment component of aggregate demand. Second, the price-induced rise in the domestic interest rate attracts capital from abroad, which leads to an appreciation of the home country currency, a depreciation of foreign currency, and a reduction in net exports.

- The position of the *AD* curve is influenced by policy parameters and behavioral parameters that affect the position of the *IS* curve and the *LM* curve.

- Any factor that shifts the *IS* curve up and to the right, such as an increase in government expenditures, shifts the *AD* curve to the right. Any factor that shifts the *LM* curve down and to the right, such as an increase in nonborrowed reserves, also shifts the *AD* curve to the right. A rightward

shift of the *AD* curve means an increase in the level of output that can be supported by the market system at each price level.

- The aggregate supply (*AS*) curve depicts the quantity of output that the nation can produce at each price level.

- One polar case is the horizontal fixed-price aggregate supply curve of Keynes. A horizontal supply curve means that output can be increased without any increase in the price level. This relation can hold only in the very short run and only if there is extensive unemployment of labor and unused productive capacity.

- The other polar case is the vertical supply curve of the classicists, which applies to the long run. A vertical curve at the potential level of output means that production is at the full employment level, independent of the price level.

- An upward-sloping short-run supply curve means that national output increases with the price level.

- According to the Keynesian explanation, the money wage is fixed along the short-run supply curve. This curve is upward sloping because of the diminishing marginal product of labor. To produce more output, firms must hire more labor; diminishing marginal product of labor leads to an increase in marginal costs and, hence, in price.

- An increase in the money wage or in the nominal reward to other variable factors of production reduces aggregate supply and shifts the short-run supply curve inward. Exogenous decreases in the marginal product of labor also reduce aggregate supply and shift the *SAS* curve inward.

- The Keynesian short run can be combined with the classical long run. In the short run output is determined by aggregate demand and the Keynesian short-run aggregate supply curve. Output may be below its potential, or full employment, level. Given sufficient time, however, money wages will begin to fall, and the short-run aggregate supply curve will shift down and to the right. The process will continue until involuntary unemployment is eliminated and output settles at its potential level.

- Changes in policy or shocks that shift the *LM* curve down and to the right lower the interest rate and increase the price level and real income in the short run.

- Changes in policy or shocks that shift the *IS* curve up and to the right raise the interest rate, the price level, and real income in the short run.

- Adverse supply shocks that shift the *SAS* curve up and to the left increase the interest rate and the price level, and they reduce the level of real income.

- In the long run, money is neutral. An increase in the quantity of nominal nonborrowed reserves, *NBR*, increases the nominal money supply, the money wage, and the price level by the same percentage as *NBR*. Real income, employment, and the interest rate remain unchanged.

- In the long run, an increase in government expenditure raises the interest rate, the price level, and the money wage. The real wage, employment, and output, however, remain unchanged. The crowding out of private sector demand is complete, which means that demand of the private sector falls by the amount that government demand rises.

KEY TERMS AND CONCEPTS

aggregate demand–aggregate
  supply *(AD–AS)* model

aggregate demand curve

demand management policies

Keynesian fixed-price model

classical model

potential output, or natural level of
  output

short-run aggregate supply curve

principle of diminishing marginal
  product of labor

involuntary unemployment

long-run aggregate supply curve

sticky money wages

neutrality of money

complete crowding out

Keynesians

neoclassical synthesis

classicists

monetarism

QUESTIONS AND PROBLEMS

1. Choose the correct explanation of the aggregate demand *(AD)* curve:
   a. The *AD* curve is derived from the money market alone.
   b. The *AD* curve is derived from the goods market alone.
   c. The *AD* curve is derived from both the money market and the goods market.

2. Explain why the *AD* curve is downward sloping in a graph with *P* on the vertical axis and *Y* on the horizontal axis.

3. Explain why the short-run aggregate supply curve is upward sloping.

4. Why is the long-run aggregate supply curve vertical?

5. When is the *IS-LM* model a good representation of the real world?

The Wall Street Journal

6. Use an *IS-LM*, AD–AS graph to explain the following quotation from "Economy Is Already Feeling the Impact of Federal Government's Spending Cuts," *The*

Wall Street Journal, August 18, 1993, A2: "Kurt Karl of the WEFA Group, economic consultants based in suburban Philadelphia, estimates that cuts in purchases by the federal government knocked as much as 0.5 percentage point off the gross domestic product last year, costing roughly 400,000 jobs, and will probably do the same in 1993. . . . To be sure, government spending cuts are hardly the only culprit in the sluggish recovery that has gripped the nation for more than two years. The commercial real-estate sector is still coming back from overbuilding and high vacancy rates. The housing sector is erratic. U.S. exporters are having trouble selling goods to struggling economies overseas."

7. Use an *IS-LM*, AD–AS graph to identify the following effects of an increase in nonborrowed reserves on the interest rate in the short-run: the liquidity effect, the real income effect, the price-level effect.

8. Suppose that the animal spirits of the entrepreneurs fall.
   a. What will happen to output and prices in the short run in the absence of government intervention?
   b. What can the Federal Reserve do to prevent the change in output?

9. Suppose that while the economy is operating at potential output, consumer confidence rises.
   a. What will happen to output, the price level, and the interest rate?
   b. Can the Fed design a policy to prevent a change in all three?

10. Suppose that the deposit rate rises because of a decrease in bank regulation that decreases the cost of issuing deposits.
    a. What will be the effect on the demand for money? On the *AD* curve? On the price level and output in the short run?

    b. What should the Fed do to prevent a change in the price level and output in the short run?

11. Suppose that because of increased prudence, banks decide to hold more excess reserves and to borrow less from the Federal Reserve.
    a. If the instruments of monetary policy are unchanged, what will happen to output and prices?
    b. What can the Fed do to prevent that outcome?

12. Suppose that oil prices rise because of newly acquired market power on the part of the owners of factors of production.
    a. What can the Fed do prevent a change in the price level?
    b. What can the Fed do to prevent a change in output?

13. Suppose that the marginal productivity of labor falls, other things equal.
    a. What will happen to national output in the short run?
    b. What will happen to national output in the long run?
    c. What, if anything, can the government do to prevent each outcome?

14. Suppose that the marginal product of labor rises, other things equal. Explain what will happen to the interest rate.

15. When will an increase in the quantity of money increase both the price level and output?

16. When will an increase in the quantity of money cause an equiproportionate increase in prices? In that case, by how much will output change?

17. Explain why and under what circumstances an increase in transfer payments will leave output unchanged.

SUGGESTED READINGS

De Long, Bradford J., and Lawrence H. Summers, "Macroeconomic Policy and Long-Run Growth," *Economic Review* (Federal Reserve Bank of Kansas City) 77, no. 4 (Fourth Quarter 1992), 5–30.
   Addresses the role of macroeconomic policies in determining rates of productivity growth.

Kuttner, Kenneth, "Monetary Policy with Uncertain Estimates of Potential Output," *Economic Perspectives* (Federal Reserve Bank of Chicago) 16, issue 1 (January–February 1992), 2–15.

Describes a method for estimating potential output.

Perry, George L., and Charles L. Schultze, "Was This Recession Different? Are They All Different?" *Brookings Papers on Economic Activity* 1 (Washington, D.C.: Brookings Institution, 1993), 145–211.
   Analyzes actual output compared with potential output during the eight recessions since the mid-1950s.

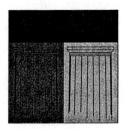

AGGREGATE SUPPLY, EXPECTATIONS, AND POLICY

CHAPTER PREVIEW

Is it possible for the central bank to reduce inflation without any pain, that is, without creating a recession? New classicists answer yes. According to this school of thought, if contractionary monetary policy is expected and understood, disinflation will be painless because aggregate supply will rise rapidly. Keynesians and new Keynesians, on the other hand, answer no to this question. They argue that money wages are sticky so that a recession cannot be avoided even if contractionary monetary policy is expected and understood because aggregate supply will rise gradually. Some classicists also answer no, but not because they believe wages are sticky. Instead they base their argument of a slow increase in supply on sticky price expectations in the form of a misperceived price level.

This chapter examines the aggregate supply relation under alternative assumptions about expectations and market clearance and looks at the policy implications of the different approaches. Because the theory is controversial and difficult, the chapter begins with an overview of the development of the aggregate supply relation.

EVOLUTION OF THE THEORY

Chapter 26 examines the neoclassical synthesis in which the short-run aggregate supply curve is positively sloped while the long-run curve is vertical. The reason for the positive slope of the short-run curve is the assumption that in the short-run money wages are sticky and the labor market does not clear. Because wages are sticky, it takes time for a sufficient fall in money wages to erase excess supply of labor (unemployment) and for the supply curve to become vertical.

Modern classical economists, like their pre-Keynesian counterparts, object to the assumption of sticky wages. Instead, they assume that prices and wages are flexible. As a result, the labor market and other markets always clear. In the 1960s, Milton Friedman and Edmund Phelps, independently of each other, introduced an approach that derives an upward-sloping aggregate supply curve while assuming that money wages are flexible and the labor market always clears. The reason behind the upward slope is worker misperception of the true real wage. For example, an increase in the money wage fools workers into wanting to supply more labor even though the price level rises by the same percentage and, hence, the real wage is unchanged. Workers confuse nominal and real wages because they revise their expectations of prices gradually, or adaptively. Eventually, their expected price level is the actual price level and the supply curve becomes vertical.

In 1973, Robert Lucas challenged the assumption of **adaptive expectations**, according to which the expected price level is a weighted average of past prices. Adaptive expectations are backward looking because they are formed on the basis of past experience, which may not be relevant. Lucas introduced rational expectations into macroeconomics. **Rational expectations** mean that workers and firms are forward looking and use all available information in forming their expectations of future prices. Relying on wage flexibility and labor market clearance as well as rational expectations, Lucas derived an upward-sloping short-run aggregate supply curve by introducing an additional assumption: the assumption of *imperfect information*. Forward-looking market participants use all available information but the information is incomplete, or imperfect. Thus, the reason for the upward-sloping short-run aggregate supply curve, now referred to as the **Lucas supply curve**, is the disparity between the true price level and the perceived, or expected, price level. When the disparity disappears, the aggregate supply curve becomes vertical.

By combining continuous market clearance, rational expectations, and imperfect information, Lucas provided an alternative to the Keynesian explanation of why the short-run aggregate supply curve is upward sloping and why it shifts. Several other new classical economists used the Lucas supply curve to show that anticipated changes in the money supply have no effect on output. Only unanticipated changes can affect it. As soon as the public learns about the change in the money supply, output reverts to its original natural level. This statement, that anticipated monetary policy has no effect on real output, is known as the **policy ineffectiveness proposition**. Policy ineffectiveness means that money is neutral, which is a key tenet of all versions of classical macroeconomics.

The Lucas supply curve and policy ineffectiveness are the cornerstones of the **new classical school** of macroeconomics, which is built on rational expectations and continuous market clearance. In the 1980s, a **new Keynesian school** of thought emerged to challenge the policy ineffectiveness proposition. Like new classicists, new Keynesians assume that expectations are rational. But they do not assume that the labor market clears continuously. A key part of the research agenda of new Keynesians is to explain why rational workers may refuse money wage cuts and why rational firms may refrain from raising prices. New Keynesians argue that if expectations are rational but markets do not clear continuously, even anticipated changes in the money supply will affect output.

This chapter derives the Lucas supply curve and relates it to the earlier work of Friedman and Phelps. After using the Lucas supply curve to establish the ineffectiveness proposition, it looks at how criticisms of policy ineffectiveness gave rise to the new Keynesian school of macroeconomics. Finally, it compares the policy prescriptions of Keynesians, classicists, new classicists, and new Keynesians and examines the legacy of rational expectations.

THE LUCAS AGGREGATE SUPPLY CURVE

The investigation of the Lucas supply curve begins with an examination of the theoretical underpinnings in the labor market. This demonstrates how Lucas's work builds on the earlier work of Friedman and Phelps.

Continuous Clearance of the Labor Market

We have seen that the supply of labor depends on the real wage, because rational, utility-maximizing households care about the purchasing power of their earnings. Analogously, rational, profit-maximizing firms also care about the real wage they pay to their employees. The left panel of Figure 27–1 shows the downward-sloping demand curve for labor and the upward-sloping supply curve for labor in a graph with the real wage on the vertical axis and the quantity of labor on the horizontal axis. At the real wage W_1/P_1, the labor market clears; at this real wage, firms are willing to hire N_1 units of labor, and workers are willing to supply that amount.

The information in the left panel of Figure 27–1 can be represented on a graph where the vertical axis measures the money wage, W, as the right panel shows. Because the price level is not accounted for on the axis, it must affect the position of the N^d and N^s curves, as the labels indicate: There is one pair of demand and supply curves for each price level. The graph shows the demand and supply curves when P equals P_1. At this price level, the money wage that clears the labor market is W_1, and the equilibrium quantity of labor is N_1. Of course, the real wage is W_1/P_1.

The relevant price level that enters the calculations of firms and workers is the price level that is expected, or perceived, over the duration of the contract. Thus, the perceived, or expected, price level, P_e,[1] is the relevant price level that must be identified on the N^d and N^s curves in the (W, P)-plane. There is one pair of N^d and N^s curves for each perceived price level, P_e, as Figure 27–2 shows.

Changes in the Perceived Price Level   Now consider how a higher perceived price level shifts each curve. For a given money wage, W, an increase in the expected price level depreciates the real wage, W/P. Because a reduction in the real wage reduces the

---

[1] We use the terms *perceived price level* and *expected price level* synonymously.

FIGURE 27–1
Two Alternative
Graphs of the
Labor Market

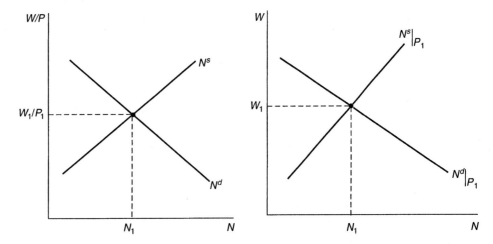

The demand and supply of labor depend on the real wage. In the left panel, W/P is measured on the vertical axis. Thus the market-clearing real wage, W_1/P_1, is shown on this axis. In the right panel, the money wage, W, is measured on the vertical axis. The price level affects the position of the curves, as the labels of the curves indicate. When the price level is P_1, the money wage that clears the labor market is W_1, and the real wage is therefore W_1/P_1.

FIGURE 27–2
An Increase in the
Expected Price
Level: *Symmetric*
Information

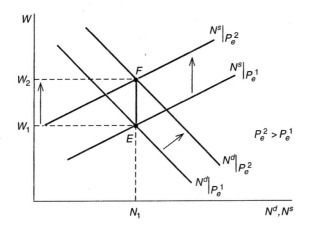

There is one demand curve and one supply curve for each expected price level. If the price level expected by households and firms rises from P_e^1 to P_e^2, the demand and supply curves shift upward by an amount equal to the increase in the price level. The equilibrium value of the money wage rises by the same percentage as the expected price level. The (expected) real wage and employment remain unchanged.

supply of labor, the increase in the price level shifts the N^s curve to the left and up. *The size of the upward shift equals the percentage increase in the (perceived) price level.* The reasoning is straightforward. If the price level rises, workers will supply the same amount of labor only if the money wage rises by the same percentage, so that the real wage would remain unchanged.

On the demand side, the N^d curve shifts to the right and up when the (perceived) price level rises. Firms will want to hire more labor at each money wage when an increase in the price level reduces the real wage. *The upward shift of the labor demand curve will be equal to the percentage increase in the perceived price level.* The reasoning is analogous to that for an upward shift in the supply of labor. A given increase in the price level will keep the real wage the same, and, hence, the demand for labor unchanged, only when the money wage rises by the same percentage.

Figure 27–2 illustrates the case when the expected increase in the price level is symmetric, or uniform, which means that workers and employers expect the price level to rise by the same amount. In this case, the expected increase in the price level leaves the equilibrium quantity of labor unchanged. The quantity of real GDP will also be unchanged because labor is the only variable factor of production.

On the other hand, if employers and employees have different expectations about the price level, aggregate supply, *AS*, will be affected. Assume that employers predict correctly the actual price level, but employees underpredict it. In particular, suppose that employees do not realize that the price level rises. (The reason for this assumption of asymmetry is discussed later in this chapter.) The demand curve for labor will shift upward by a vertical distance equal to the correctly perceived change in the price level, but the labor supply will not shift at all. The result is an increase in the quantity of labor employed and used in production, as Figure 27–3 shows. Of course, an increase in the quantity of labor employed results in an increase in real GDP (aggregate supply).

Compare point *F* with point *E* in Figure 27–3, and note that as the price level rises, the quantity of labor employed rises from N_1 to N_2 because the real wage falls. We confirm this result by observing that the increase in the money wage between point *E* and point *F* is equal to *EG*, whereas, by construction of the graph, the increase in the price level is equal to *EE'*. Thus, the ratio *W/P* falls. However, workers don't realize that the real wage has fallen, because the price level expected by workers is unchanged. Workers incorrectly assume that the increase in the money wage means an increase in their real wage. Thus, they are "fooled" into accepting jobs. (The reader may want to depict these results in a graph of the labor market with the real wage, *W/P*, on the vertical axis. This exercise would show that workers are on their supply curve, supplying N_2 units of labor, and firms are on their demand curve, hiring N_2 units of labor. The demand and supply curves, however, do not intersect when *N* equals N_2, because the real wage expected by workers is higher than the real wage expected by firms.)

Relation to the Friedman-Phelps Fooling Model   The discussion thus far has assumed that firms possess perfect information and workers do not in order to relate the contribution of Lucas to earlier work by Friedman and Phelps, who introduced the idea of fooling workers.[2] Lucas, however, made a different assumption about "fooling" in his paper.[3] He assumed that firms do not recognize that a rise in the price of their own

---

[2]   Milton Friedman, "The Role of Monetary Policy," *American Economic Review* 58 (March 1968): 1–17; and Edmund Phelps, "Money Wage Dynamics and Labor Market Equilibrium," *Journal of Political Economy*, July–August 1967, 678–711.

[3]   Robert E. Lucas, Jr., "Some International Evidence on Output-Inflation Tradeoffs," *American Economic Review* 63 (June 1973): 326–34.

FIGURE 27–3
An Increase in the
Expected Price
Level: *Asymmetric
Information*

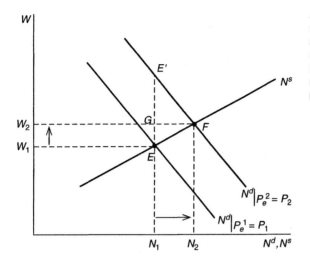

An increase in the price level that is
recognized by firms but not by workers
shifts the demand for labor but not the
supply of labor. As a result, employed
labor rises from N_1 to N_2 because the
money wage rises by less than the
price level.

product is accompanied by a rise in the general price level. Thus, firms mistakenly
believe that the price of their product has risen *relative* to the general price level, which
induces them to raise their production and supply. Had they recognized that the rise in the
price of their product was accompanied by a rise in all prices, they would not have
increased their supply. In this sense they are fooled. And they are fooled because they
have imperfect information.

Friedman and Phelps introduced the idea of fooling workers in order to overcome the
classical objection to the Keynesian approach that suggests that with rigid money wages
workers are forced off their supply curve of labor when the price level changes. (Figure
26–13 in the preceding chapter depicts this result.) In the **fooling model** in Figure 27–3,
both workers and firms are on their supply and demand curves. And the labor market
clears in the sense that the demand for labor equals the supply at the existing money wage
and at the price level expected by households and firms.

A shortcoming of the fooling model of Friedman and Phelps is that it does not provide
a satisfactory explanation of why rational workers underperceive the actual price level.
Friedman's explanation is that workers, learning from the past, modify their expectations
of the price level (and changes in the price level) only gradually, or adaptively. Adaptive
expectations are backward looking, and they may not be rational in the sense of making
use of all available economic information.

**Rational
Expectations**

Lucas provided a reason why rational workers are fooled: It is because they do not have
access to correct information. They use all available information but it is not the correct
information. Thus, Lucas adopted the market equilibrium approach of Friedman and
Phelps while introducing and relying on rational expectations. Lucas's introduction of
this new element inspired a generation of economists to pay more attention to information and its influence on economic dynamics.

As with most major discoveries in the history of thought, the concept of rational expectations starts with a simple, unassailable proposition, or axiom: Expectations held by a participant are rational if they are based on all available information. In other words, workers and firms must use all available information in forming their expectations. This axiom of rationality was introduced in 1961 by John F. Muth,[4] who stated the original axiom in these words:

> I should like to suggest that expectations, since they are informed predictions of future events, are essentially the same as the predictions of the relevant economic theory.

Muth, almost apologetic for the wording, added the qualifying sentence:

> At the risk of confusing this purely descriptive hypothesis with a pronouncement as what firms ought to do, we call such expectations "rational."

Muth applied rational expectations to microeconomic problems. It was Robert Lucas who first applied the axiom of rational expectations to macroeconomics—12 years after Muth introduced the concept. Lucas assumed that in making forecasts of the price level workers and firms are rational: They use all the information available to them. However, they may not have the correct information. Lucas introduced the concept of *imperfect information* to describe the situation in which market participants lack the correct information on which to base their decisions. *Asymmetric information* refers to a particular type of imperfect information. With asymmetric information, workers and firms have different information.[5]

Two Approaches to the Lucas Supply Curve

Now combine continuous clearance of the labor market with asymmetric information to derive the upward-sloping Lucas supply curve. Begin at point E in the left panel of Figure 27–4, where the labor market clears at the money wage W_1 and the quantity of labor N_1. At point E, the price level expected by workers equals the actual price level, P_1. The output produced by the labor-market-clearing quantity of labor, when workers correctly predict the price level, is the natural level of output, Y_n. The right panel plots, as point E', the pair (P_1, Y_n), which is one point on the Lucas supply curve.

To find the other points on the curve, how does output change when the actual price level changes, but the price level expected by households remains unchanged at P_e[1]? In the left panel, when the price level rises to P_2, the equilibrium moves from point E to point F; the labor-market-clearing quantity of labor rises from N_1 to N_2. Firms are willing to hire more labor (at higher nominal wage, W_2) because they know that the real wage has fallen. And households are willing to supply more labor because they mistakenly believe that the rise in their money wage represents a rise in their real wage. In the right panel, the quantity of output rises to Y_2, as shown by the movement from point E' to point F'. On the other hand, when the price level falls from P_1 to P_3, the levels of employment and output fall, as shown by the movement from point E to point G in the left panel, and E' to

---

[4] John F. Muth, "Rational Expectations and the Theory of Price Movements," *Econometrica* 29 (July 1961): 315–35.

[5] Chapters 2, 10, and 24 apply asymmetric information to credit markets. Here we use the concept to explain the labor market.

FIGURE 27–4
Deriving the Lucas Supply Curve from Continuous Clearance of the Labor Market and Asymmetric Expectations

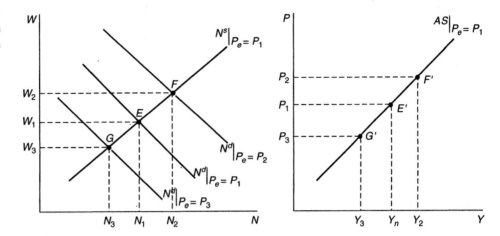

When the expected price level equals the actual price level, P_1, firms hire N_1 units of labor and produce Y_n units of output, as shown by points E and E'. When the price level expected by workers remains at P_1, but the actual price level rises to P_2, firms hire N_2 units of labor and produce Y_2 units of output, as shown by point F and F'. On the other hand, when the price level expected by workers remains at P_1, but the actual price level falls to P_3, firms hire N_3 units of labor and produce Y_3 units of output, as shown by points G and G'. Connecting points E', F', and G' in the right panel yields the upward-sloping Lucas supply curve.

G' in the right panel. In this case, households are fooled into reducing their supply of labor because they believe their real wage has fallen.

Connecting points E', F' and G' yields an upward-sloping Lucas supply curve. Equation 27–1 represents the Lucas supply curve algebraically:

$$AS = Y_n + h(P - P_e) \tag{27–1}$$

where h is a positive constant that indicates the amount by which the supply of output changes when the actual price level deviates from the expected price level.

According to Equation 27–1, *the aggregate supply of goods and services equals the potential, or natural, level of output plus or minus some amount, depending on whether the actual price level is above the expected price level or below it.* When $P - P_e > 0$, the actual price level is greater than the expected price level, and output supplied is greater than the natural level of output. When $P - P_e < 0$, the actual price level is less than the expected price level, and output supplied is less than the natural level. And when $P = P_e$, the actual price level equals the expected price level, and output supplied equals the natural level of output.

Equation 27–1 assumes asymmetric information between workers and firms. Lucas himself derived an upward-sloping supply curve from the assumption of imperfect information on the part of firms. Lucas starts with the observation that the ith firm's supply of its product depends on the perceived relative price of that product, P_i/P_e. The higher the relative price, the higher the supply, Y_i, by the ith firm. Schematically,

$$P_i\uparrow \rightarrow (P_i/P_e)\uparrow \rightarrow Y_i\uparrow$$

For the economy as a whole, this linkage is described algebraically by the following equation:

$$AS = Y_n \times (P/P_e) \tag{27-2}$$

Equation 27–2 is an alternative version of the Lucas supply relation. According to this equation, if the perceived price level is below the actual price level, the ratio P/P_e is greater than 1. Hence, aggregate supply is greater than the natural level of output, Y_n. If, on the other hand, the perceived price level is above the actual price level, the ratio is smaller than 1, and aggregate supply is below the natural level. The following numerical example illustrates this relation.

Suppose that the price level rises by 10 percent, from 1.00 to 1.10. If firms do not realize that the price level has risen and they keep their forecast of the expected price level at $P_e = 1.00$, the ratio P/P_e will be 1.10. As a result, $AS = 1.10 \times Y_n$, which means that actual output is above potential output. On the other hand, if the price level falls to 0.90 while P_e remains at 1.00, $AS = 0.90 \times Y_n$, which means that output is below the natural level.

Regardless of the method used to derive the Lucas supply curve, the driving force is the difference between actual and perceived price level. And this divergence is the consequence of imperfect information. The graph in Figure 27–5 represents both versions of the Lucas supply curve.

Shifts of the Lucas Supply Curve   Unlike the Keynesian short-run supply curve that relies on a given money wage, the Lucas short-run curve relies on incomplete and temporarily incorrect perceptions, or expectations, of the price level by workers. Thus, there is one AS curve for each perceived, or expected, price level. As the expected price level changes, the Lucas supply curve shifts. Methodologically the two approaches are similar. The Keynesian short-run curve moves as the money wage changes, driven by excess demand for or excess supply of labor. The Lucas short-run curve moves not because of excess demand for or excess supply of labor, but because of changes in the expected price level, driven by new information gained by workers.

Figure 27–6 shows that when the expected price level rises from P_e^1 to P_e^2, the curve shifts to the left, which means that aggregate supply falls. At each price level, the economy produces and supplies less. For example, at the price level P_1, output falls below the natural level. This result is supported by applying Equations 27–1 or 27–2. According to Equation 27–1, the divergence between the actual price level and the expected price level becomes negative, so aggregate supply is less than Y_n. According to Equation 27–2, the ratio of P to P_e becomes less than 1, and aggregate supply is again less than Y_n. Alternatively, the shift of the AS curve can be viewed as an upward movement: Each level of output is supplied at a higher price. For example, when the expected price rises from P_e^1 to P_e^2, firms will be willing to supply the natural level of output only at a higher price, namely, at price P_2.

The Vertical Curve   The divergence between the actual and the perceived price level is the reason that the Lucas supply curve is upward sloping rather than vertical. When the

FIGURE 27–5
The Lucas Supply
Curve

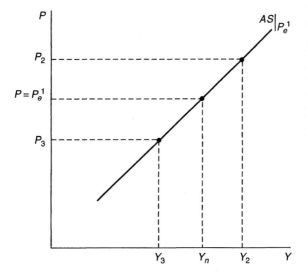

The expected price level is fixed along the curve. When the actual price level equals the expected price level, output is at the natural level, Y_n. Output rises above the natural level when the actual price level is greater than the expected price level; output falls below the natural level when the actual price level is less than the expected price level.

FIGURE 27–6
A Shift of the
Lucas Supply
Curve

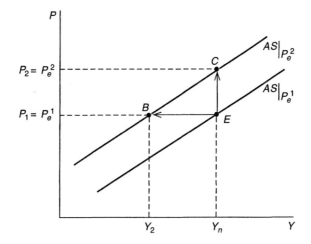

When the expected price level rises, the *AS* curve shifts up and to the left. For example, at the price level P_1, output will fall from Y_n to Y_2. Alternatively, firms will be willing to supply the output Y_n only if the price level rises from P_1 to P_2.

correct information becomes available, the divergence disappears. The "long-run" supply curve is vertical at the natural level of output, which is shown by setting $P = P_e$ in Equation 27–1 or 27–2. [The reader can derive this result graphically by using a graph like Figure 27–4. Show that in the labor market the locus of equilibrium points at which the expected price equals the actual price lie on a vertical line through point E. The corresponding points in the (P, Y)-plane lie on a vertical line through Y_n.] Note that with the Lucas supply curve the money wage changes when the economy moves along the curve. It also changes when the curves shift. In the Lucas scenario the movement to full employment is rapid and virtually painless. In the Phelps-Friedman scenario, the movement to full employment is slow and painful because expectations are adaptive, or sluggish.

THE POLICY INEFFECTIVENESS PROPOSITION OF THE NEW CLASSICISTS

Having derived the Lucas supply curve, we turn to establishing the policy ineffectiveness proposition, which Thomas Sargent and Neil Wallace put forth in 1975.[6] Applying the Lucas supply curve to monetary policy, Sargent and Wallace showed that expected changes in monetary policy have no effect on real output.

Figure 27–7 starts from the equilibrium position at point A, with the price level at P_1 and output at its natural level, Y_n. Next assume that the money supply increases because the Fed increases the quantity of nonborrowed reserves, from NBR_1 to NBR_2. This expansionary monetary policy will shift the AD curve to the right. If nothing happens to the AS curve, equilibrium will occur at point B: Both the price level and output will increase. However, point B may not be consistent with rational expectations, unless it is assumed that the public is unaware of the increase in the money supply or ignorant of the theory that changes in the money supply affect the price level.

Rational expectations require that market participants use all available information, or, according to Muth, *rational expectations are the predictions of the relevant economic theory*. If the public knows the *IS-LM* model, it knows by how much the AD curve will shift, that is, by how much the price level will rise at the original equilibrium level of output. As soon as the public learns of the increase in the money supply, it will incorporate the consequent increase in the price level into its plans. Thus, point B is only a

FIGURE 27–7
The Effectiveness
of Monetary Policy
in the New
Classical Model

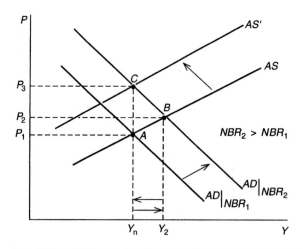

An unanticipated increase in the money supply moves the economy from point A to point B. As soon as the public learns that the money supply has increased, it expects the price level to rise. As a result, the Lucas supply curve shifts upward, and output reverts to its natural level at point C. If the increase in the money supply were anticipated, the economy would move from point A to point C, without any effect on output.

---

[6] Thomas J. Sargent and Neil Wallace, "Rational Expectations, The Optimal Monetary Instrument, and the Optimal Money Supply Rule, *Journal of Political Economy* 83 (April 1975): 241–54.

temporary point. Workers will increase their money wage demands by the same percentage that they expect the price level to rise. As a result, the *AS* curve will shift up by this percentage, which is the amount by which the *AD* curve shifts upward. The intersection of the *AD* curve with the ultimate *AS* curve will occur at point *C*, which establishes the classical case.

The assumption that workers know as much about the *IS-LM* model as students of macroeconomics is not as farfetched as some may think. Individual workers may not know the theory, but the economists employed by labor unions do. And if they cannot afford a full-time economist, labor unions subscribe to consulting services that employ economists. Hence, the assumption is a reasonable approximation.

It is interesting to note the similarities between Figure 27–7 and Figure 26–15. Figure 26–15 shows that with sticky money wages an anticipated or unanticipated increase in the money supply has a temporary affect on output. As soon as the money wage rises, however, the aggregate supply also shifts up, and eventually the level of output reverts back to its potential level. The trip from *A* to *B* to *C* in Figure 26–15 corresponds to the trip from *A* to *B* to *C* in Figure 27–7. Methodologically, the two theories are similar. In the Keynesian model, the driving force is the level of money wages. At first, the money wage is rigid; eventually it becomes flexible and gradually negates the gains in output. In the new classical model, the misperceived monetary policy and, hence, the misperceived price level permit monetary policy to have a temporary effect on output; this effect, however, is negated as information about monetary and price statistics becomes available.

**Painless
Disinflation**

So far, the discussion has concentrated on the negative aspect of the impotence of anticipated monetary policy. But there is a positive, desirable side when the Fed wants to reduce the price level. According to new classical theory, disinflation can be achieved painlessly—without any loss in output—if monetary policy is *credible*. Figure 27–8 illustrates this result.

**FIGURE 27–8
Painless
Disinflation**

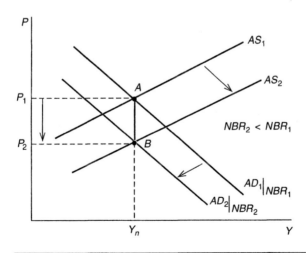

To reduce the price level from P_1 to P_2, the Fed must reduce the money supply so that the *AD* curve shifts from AD_1 to AD_2. Suppose that the Fed announces its intention to reduce the money supply by the required amount. If the Fed is credible, the public will expect the price level to fall from P_1 to P_2. As a result, the Lucas supply curve will shift downward; and the economy will move from point *A* to point *B* without a loss in output.

Assume that the economy is at point *A* and that the Fed wants to reduce the price level from P_1 to P_2. First, the Fed must calculate the reduction in the quantity of money that is consistent with the targeted reduction in the price level. In particular, the Fed must determine what reduction in the money supply will shift the *AD* curve inward to position AD_2. Second, the Fed must announce its intention to reduce the quantity of money by the required amount. As soon as firms and workers are convinced that the Fed is serious, the *AS* curve will shift down by the same distance to position AS_2, intersecting the AD_2 curve at point *B*. The price level will fall by the desired amount without any reduction in output (and employment).

Empirical Investigations of the Policy Ineffectiveness Proposition

Because of its striking implications, the policy ineffectiveness proposition attracted immediate attention and scrutiny. Empirical studies ranged from direct tests of the proposition itself to tests of the underpinnings of the Lucas supply relation, including the specific assumptions about information available to firms and workers.

Empirical investigation of the Lucas supply curve began with Lucas himself in his famous 1973 article. Lucas compared the response of output to changes in aggregate demand and confirmed the rapid shifting of the short-run supply curve only in extreme cases. He found that in countries such as Argentina with great variability in aggregate demand, the variability of output was small, which is consistent with a rapidly shifting short-run supply curve. In countries such as the United States with low variability of aggregate demand, the variability of output was great. This result can mean that activist policy, say, monetary policy, has an effect on output if it is used less frequently. It is also more likely to be a surprise.

The publication of the Sargent and Wallace paper stimulated empirical investigation of the policy ineffectiveness proposition itself. Early research by Sargent (1976) found inconclusive evidence. However, Robert Barro (1977 and 1978) found strong support for the thesis that unanticipated changes in money have strong effects on output and unemployment, while anticipated changes have little effect for the U.S. economy. Later work by Sargent (1982) showed that in countries with a history of inflationary monetary policies, increases in the money supply have little effect on output. Sargent also showed that in these countries drastic reductions in monetary growth succeed in reducing inflation without a major decline in output. That is, disinflation is relatively painless.[7]

Several economists, for example, David Small (1979), Robert Gordon (1982), and Frederic Mishkin (1982), challenged Barro's results. Today there are still disagreements, especially about statistical techniques employed by various researchers. However, the majority opinion seems to be that anticipated, as well as unanticipated, changes in the money supply affect output and employment.

Other New Classical Results

Recall that the neutrality of money is a key principle of classical economics. Neutrality means that changes in the money supply affect only nominal variables, such as the price level and nominal interest rates, but not real variables, such as real output. The neutrality

---

[7] See Thomas J. Sargent, "The Ends of Four Big Inflations," in *Inflation: Causes and Effects*, ed. Robert Hall (Chicago: University of Chicago Press, 1982).

of money is also referred to as the *classical dichotomy*, which means that the monetary sector is separated from the real sector: Money affects nominal variables, while real forces affect the real sector.

Traditional classicists, represented by Milton Friedman and, earlier, Irving Fisher, established the neutrality of money as a long-run proposition. New classicists, represented by Robert Lucas, went a step further by establishing neutrality of money as a short-run proposition. With a Lucas supply curve, only unanticipated changes in the money supply affect real variables. Thus, money affects real variables in the shortest of short runs.

Another school of new classical economists, the **real business cycle school**, dispenses with even the short-run effects of money supply changes. Real business cycle theorists start with the assumption that money is neutral. Thus, by construction of the model, only real forces cause a business cycle, which is the upward and downward movement of real output. In the real business cycle model, all changes in output are changes in potential output caused by such factors as changes in the economy's productivity or in the taste of workers for supplying labor and consuming leisure. For example, an increase in the country's marginal productivity increases aggregate supply and, thus, output.

The real business cycle theory is new and, hence, controversial.[8] Several economists take issue with the assumption that money is always neutral. More important, they question whether there are sufficient ups and downs in a country's productivity to explain the short-run ups and downs of the economy.

Disagreements about the effectiveness of macroeconomic policy have not been confined to monetary policy. Using rational expectations, Robert Barro argued that tax cuts are ineffective; his work preceded that of Sargent and Wallace on the ineffectiveness proposition for monetary policy. MarketWatch 27.1 examines the proposition, called the **Ricardian equivalence theorem**, that tax cuts have no effect on output.

THEORETICAL CHALLENGES TO POLICY INEFFECTIVENESS AND THE EMERGENCE OF THE NEW KEYNESIANS

In addition to extensive empirical scrutiny, the policy ineffectiveness proposition has undergone considerable theoretical scrutiny. The three mainstays of the Lucas supply curve and policy ineffectiveness are rational expectations, imperfect information, and continuous market clearance. Most economists accept rational expectations as a working hypothesis. Thus, theoretical critiques have concentrated on imperfect information and continuous market clearance.

Imperfect Information

Examination of the assumption of imperfect information has focused on two questions. First, what information are workers and firms supposed to have, and how timely and accurate is the information? Second, what can firms and workers do when they discover they have erred?

---

[8] For a survey of the literature on real business cycles, see Charles Plosser, "Understanding Real Business Cycles," *Journal of Economic Perspectives* 3 (Summer 1989): 51–77.

MarketWatch 27.1
Are Tax Cuts Effective?

The conventional view of income tax cuts is that they increase consumption and, thus, real output. The increase in output, however, is mitigated by the crowding out of investment and net exports that result from higher interest rates, as GlobalWatch 25.1 explains. In 1974, Robert Barro challenged the conventional view of tax cuts.* Using rational expectations, Barro argued that a reduction in taxes will not succeed in increasing consumption and, hence, will not increase aggregate demand and output.

A reduction in taxes without a reduction in government expenditures increases the budget deficit, which is financed by issuing new debt (assuming the deficit is not monetized). Barro argues that rational households will recognize that taxes must be raised in the future to meet the interest and principal payments on the new debt, and they will take these higher future payments into consideration when making their decisions about current consumption and savings. In other words, they will discount their future tax liabilities. The gist of Barro's argument is that forward-looking, rational individuals will increase their private savings by the amount of the tax cut to meet future tax liabilities. The proposition that changes in taxes have no effect on aggregate demand and aggregate output is known as the *Ricardian equivalence theorem*, in honor of the classical economist David Ricardo.†

Until the 1980s, most large deficits in the United States were cyclical, arising from recessions, or they occurred during wartime and were monetized. The Reagan tax cuts that were phased in from 1981 to 1984 provided an opportunity to test the alternative views, because large deficits remained even after the economy recovered from the recession of 1981–82. Many econo-

mists consider the Reagan tax cut as "nearly a controlled experiment." Contrary to the predictions of Ricardian equivalence, private savings did not rise in the 1980s. Instead, gross private savings remained unchanged. Average annual gross private savings, measured as a percentage of GNP, were 16.8 percent between 1950 and 1979, and 16.7 percent between 1980 and 1988. As a result, gross national savings (i.e., private savings minus government dissavings) fell by the amount of the increase in government dissavings.

Barro argues that the results depend on how we measure savings. He points out that rates of private savings in the United States in the 1980s would be larger if expenditure on consumer durables is considered investment rather than current consumption. (Recall from Chapter 2 that the flow of funds accounts of the Federal Reserve classify expenditure on durable consumer goods as investment, while the national income and product accounts of the Department of Commerce treat these expenditures as current consumption.) Moreover, he cites the rates of savings in other countries to support Ricardian equivalence. For example, Barro refers to the case of Israel in the 1980s, when changes in government savings were offset by changes in private savings in the opposite direction, so that rates of national savings were "relatively stable."

Today, the majority of economists accept the conventional view that a cut in taxes will decrease national savings. Also, in an open economy with flexible exchange rates, investment will not fall by an equal amount, because savings will flow in from abroad in response to higher (risk-adjusted) domestic interest rates. As a result, the domestic currency will appreciate and net exports will be partially crowded out—as they were in the 1980s in the United States. Although the Ricardian equivalence theory represents a minority opinion, it is an influential one in the profession.‡

---

* Robert Barro, "Are Government Bonds Net Wealth?" *Journal of Political Economy*, November/December 1974, 1095–117.

† In 1821 Ricardo noted that it makes no difference whether the government finances its expenditures by issuing bonds or by raising taxes. The effects will be equivalent.

‡ In 1987, Barro estimated that 22 percent of the membership of the American Economic Association found that the Ricardian equivalence theorem was the most convincing explanation of the effect of tax cuts on the economy. See Robert Barro, "Budget Deficits: Only a Minor Crisis," *The Wall Street Journal*, January 16, 1987, 22.

Research on the first question has focused mostly on monetary and price statistics, although some economists have also examined information about fiscal policy. Money supply data provided by the Federal Reserve are published in *The Wall Street Journal* every Friday. These figures are normally very accurate; the frequent revisions are usually minor. The price statistics, published monthly by the Department of Commerce, are also, on average, very accurate, even though, by their nature, not as accurate as the monetary statistics. Information about fiscal policy is also available from the budget itself and from other announcements. These observations cast doubt on the realism of the assumption that firms or workers know the prices of the goods or services they are selling but not the general price level.

If information becomes available quickly, surprises will not last long. But if surprises are short-lived, they cannot explain persistent departures of output from its potential level. For example, surprises cannot explain why output remained below capacity for several years in the 1930s. Nor can they explain why recessions often last for several quarters, as has been the case in most of the recessions since World War II.

Rigidity in Nominal Wages

If surprises are short-lived, the primary reason for the persistence of below-potential levels of output must lie elsewhere. This observation leads us to the second question: What can firms (and workers) do when they discover that they have erred in their guesses about the actual money supply and the price level? If workers are prevented from renegotiating their money wages or if firms refrain from changing the price of the goods they sell, the labor market or the goods market will not clear. And if these markets do not clear, unemployment or over full employment will result in and will be accompanied by a level of output below or above potential output.

Two papers published in 1977 gave reasons for wage and price rigidities. One, by Stanley Fischer, emphasized long-term contracts that prevent workers from renegotiating their money wages even when they learn of actual change in the money supply.[9] The other paper, by Edmund Phelps and John Taylor, emphasized the price-setting and wage-setting practices of firms, such as using catalogs to announce the price of their products ahead of time.[10] According to Phelps and Taylor, rational firms preset prices and wages because they "find it advantageous as a device for attracting and keeping customers and employees to save them the trouble of direct inquiry into the firm's price and wage scale, thus removing or reducing their cost of learning the firm's offer and reducing their incentive to inquire elsewhere," and because "there are disadvantages from too-frequent or too-precipitate revisions of price lists and wage schedules."

Both papers assumed and relied on rational expectations. And yet both papers established wage or price rigidity and the consequent failure of markets to clear. Thus, they proved that it is not the assumption of rational expectations that causes policy ineffectiveness but, rather, the assumption of perfect wage and price flexibility, which results in continuous market clearing. Because wage-price rigidity and market failure are consistent

[9] Stanley Fischer, "Long-Term Contracts, Rational Expectations, and the Optimal Money Supply Rule," *Journal of Political Economy* 85 (February 1977): 191–205.

[10] Edmund S. Phelps and John B. Taylor, "Stabilizing Powers of Monetary Policy under Rational Expectations," *Journal of Political Economy* 85 (February 1977): 163–90.

with the facts and with rational expectations, these economists rehabilitated the Keynesian model of involuntary unemployment and the *AD–AS* rendition of it. In the words of Phelps and Taylor, they "have produced not a new wine but an old wine in a new and more secure bottle."

Rigidity in Real Wages

The Keynesian explanation of involuntary unemployment that is based on rigid money wages has a shortcoming that it shares with the Lucas supply approach. Both approaches imply that real wages are *countercyclical*, which means they fall when employment and output rise, and they rise when employment and output fall. But the data do not reveal such countercyclical behavior of real wages, which are either constant or mildly procyclical; that is, real wages rise with economic activity.

Implicit Contract for Real Wages   Several new Keynesian theories have examined the reasons for real-wage rigidity. One approach was introduced by Martin Neil Baily in 1974 and by Costas Azariades, in 1975. These economists introduced the idea of *implicit contracts*, which are informal, long-run arrangements between employers and employees. In particular, Baily and Azariades argued that workers are risk averse and are willing to accept real wages that are below their market-clearing level in exchange for security of real income. Firms agree to the practice because it is in the nature of firms to take risks.

Efficiency Wages to Promote Loyalty   The papers by Baily and Azariades were the forerunners of a variety of ideas that establish Keynesian involuntary unemployment and relative stability of real wages. A paper by George Akerlof was the first of a new breed that looks to sociology to discover facts that can be useful in explaining involuntary unemployment.[11] In commenting on the work of Akerlof, Nobel laureate Robert Solow has said that Akerlof "takes seriously the elementary social facts of life."[12]

Akerlof's paper identifies loyalty between employees and employers as the reason for real wages above their market-clearing level. Workers are so committed to their firm that they are prepared to work harder than would be consistent with the market-clearing level of the real wage. That is, their marginal productivity (MP_N) is higher than the market-clearing value of W/P. Firms, in turn, reward the loyalty of their employees by paying them a higher real wage. The higher wages paid to these productive, or efficient, workers, have been called **efficiency wages**.

Efficiency Wages to Prevent Shirking   Another version of the efficiency-wages paradigm is that of punishing shirking by workers. In this model, firms pay higher real wages not to reward loyalty but to prevent shirking. If workers are paid real wages higher than the market-clearing real wage, they will refrain from shirking because they do not want to risk being fired and ending up with a lower real wage—the one that clears the

---

[11] George Akerlof, "Labor Contracts as a Partial Gift Exchange," *Quarterly Journal of Economics* 97 (November 1982): 543–69.

[12] Solow's own presidential address to the American Economic Association provides a blueprint for the new Keynesian agenda of the 1980s. See Robert Solow, "On Theories of Unemployment," *American Economic Review* 70 (March 1980): 1–11.

market. In other words, the firm "bribes" workers with a higher real wage to prevent shirking.

Efficiency Wages to Prevent Adverse Selection   Still another model explains higher real wages by stipulating that the workers who are willing to accept the going real wages are those with lower productivity. Thus, it pays the firm to hire workers who demand higher wages. This is called the *adverse selection model.*

The role of adverse selection is easiest to see by examining the case of a reduction in aggregate demand. If a firm responds by reducing real wages, the firm will induce the most productive workers to leave because they can find jobs elsewhere. The least productive workers will remain; hence the term *adverse selection.* Thus, the firm prefers to keep real wages at the original level and to fire the least productive workers.

There are more theories that can explain real wages above their market-clearing level, and, no doubt, even more will appear in the future as economists test the sociological waters and discover facts that can be useful in explaining involuntary unemployment. Already economists are looking to different social environments to explain differences in rates of unemployment between countries, such as the United States and Japan. All of these theories have two common characteristics. First, they explain involuntary unemployment; and second, they explain why real wages are relatively stable.

Rigidity in Prices

So far, discussion has concentrated on wage rigidities. But the literature on price rigidities has also proliferated; it has rehabilitated the *IS-LM* model. In the (P, Y)-plane, all we have to do is draw a horizontal *AS* curve at the price level that is assumed given in the *IS-LM* graph. If there is a contractionary shock in this model, the *AD* curve will shift inward, with a reduction in output and no fall in the price level. As long as firms resist price cuts when they are faced with a reduction in the demand for their products, the reduction in output below its potential level will persist and so will the involuntary unemployment.

But why would rational firms not reduce their prices when they are faced with reduced demand for their products? One reason comes from the Phelps-Taylor paper. It costs firms to reduce their prices; these reductions entail reprinting price lists and catalogs and informing customers, who then have an incentive to inquire elsewhere. Borrowing an analogy from the restaurant industry, economists call the costs of adjusting prices **menu costs.** Restaurant keepers do not change their menus often because it is costly to print a new menu; also, frequent changes in prices may cause uncertainty.

One group of models with menu costs shows that even in a purely competitive environment firms may find it profitable to behave noncompetitively and, thus, to refrain from lowering their prices in the face of a reduction in demand. Another group departs from the assumption of purely competitive markets and, instead, explains price rigidities by relying on models of imperfect competition. Yet other models rely on markups to supplement fixed prices for another variant of the fixed-price model. New Keynesian economics is an active area of research in macroeconomics today.[13]

---

[13] A wide variety of articles on new Keynesian economics are reprinted in N. Gregory Mankiw and David Romer, eds., *New Keynesian Economics* (Cambridge, Mass.: MIT Press, 1991).

THE ROLE OF POLICY: KEYNESIANS, CLASSICISTS, NEW CLASSICISTS, AND NEW KEYNESIANS

Given the examination of the theories of classicists, new classicists, Keynesians, and new Keynesians, this section compares the policy prescriptions of these four schools of macroeconomic thought. First, it examines the existence of below-capacity output (and, hence, involuntary unemployment) caused by an exogenous shock, say, a reduction in consumer confidence. Next, it examines the pursuit of an anti-inflationary policy in a fully employed economy with high (or rising) prices.

An Inward Shift in Aggregate Demand

Suppose that an adverse demand shock, say, a reduction in consumer confidence, hits an economy that is operating at full capacity. As a result, the *IS* curve and the *AD* curve will shift inward. Figure 27–9 shows the inward shift in aggregate demand as a movement from position AD_1 to position AD_2. It shows that both the price level and output will fall—to P_2 and Y_2, respectively. Suppose the federal government, because of budget problems, leaves the job of stabilizing the economy to the Federal Reserve, as it has in recent years. What should the Fed do?

Before answering this question, we depict schematically and explain briefly the reason why output will fall below the natural level according to the different schools of thought.

Classicists and New Classicists:

$$\overline{C}\downarrow \rightarrow AD\downarrow \rightarrow ESG \rightarrow \begin{Bmatrix} P\downarrow \text{ to } P_2 \\ \text{But } P_e \text{ unchanged} \end{Bmatrix} \rightarrow (P/P_e)\downarrow \rightarrow Y_n \times (P/P_e)\downarrow \rightarrow Y_2 < Y_n$$

In the schematic, aggregate demand falls because of a reduction in autonomous consumption, represented by $\overline{C}$. As a result, there is excess supply of goods and services and the price level falls. With the expected price level unchanged, the ratio of actual to expected price level falls, and output falls below its potential level. In Figure 27–9, the economy moves along the short-run supply curve to a lower price level and a lower level of output.

FIGURE 27–9 An Adverse Shock in *AD*

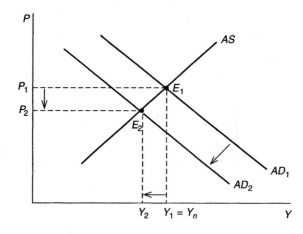

The expected price level is constant along this curve, but the money wage is not. The money wage falls, but not by as much as the price level, because firms but not workers realize that the price level has fallen. Hence the real wage is higher, which is the reason that firms hire fewer workers and produce less output.

Next, consider traditional Keynesians and new Keynesians separately to highlight a slight difference between the two.

Traditional Keynesians:

$$\overline{C}\downarrow \;\rightarrow\; AD\downarrow \;\rightarrow\; \begin{Bmatrix} P\downarrow \text{ to } P_2 \\ W \text{ unchanged} \end{Bmatrix} \;\rightarrow\; (\overline{W}/P_2)\uparrow \;\rightarrow\; N^d\downarrow \;\rightarrow\; Y_2 < Y_n$$

Again, a reduction in consumption results in excess supply of goods and services, and the price level falls. In the Keynesian model, the money wage is fixed along the short-run supply curve. A lower price level results in a higher real wage, which induces firms to hire less labor and supply less output.

New Keynesians:

$$\overline{C}\downarrow \;\rightarrow\; AD\downarrow \;\rightarrow\; \begin{Bmatrix} P\downarrow \text{ to } P_2 \\ W\downarrow \text{ to } W_2 \end{Bmatrix} \text{ But } (W_2/P_2)\uparrow \;\rightarrow\; N^d\downarrow \;\rightarrow\; Y\downarrow \;\rightarrow\; Y_2 < Y_n$$

In the new Keynesian explanation, the money wage falls, but not by the same percentage as the price level because the adjustment of the money wage is sluggish. As a result, the real wage rises, which again induces firms to reduce their demand for labor and their production. (Because the money wage is fixed along the Keynesian aggregate supply curve, the fall in the money wage will shift the short-run aggregate supply curve downward. For simplicity, Figure 27–9 ignores this complication.)

Now we are ready to explain the policy prescriptions of the four schools. Keynesians, both the old and the new, will say: "Be an activist; shift the *AD* curve to the right." Although they agree that there are forces that will eventually shift the *AS* curve to the right and erase the shortfall of output, they argue that it will take time. Besides, some negative psychology may develop in the meantime, which will further shift the *AD* curve to the left.

Classicists and new classicists, on the other hand, will say: "Do not intervene." Both classicists and new classicists attribute the involuntary unemployment to the discrepancy between the actual and the perceived price level. (We identify the classical position with the work of Friedman in the 1960s.) New classicists believe that the discrepancy will disappear almost immediately, as soon as firms and workers learn the actual price level. In contrast, classicists believe that this discrepancy will take time to disappear, because firms and workers revise their expectations of the price level gradually, or adaptively. In the meantime, output will fall and unemployment will rise. In this respect, classicists agree with Keynesians. In contrast to Keynesians, however, classicists argue that the Fed should not intervene, because the Fed will make matters worse. Neither should the government.

Because of time lags, demand management policies may start to affect the real sector after the problem of unemployment disappears. The policy will then be inflationary. In this view, the *AS* curve will already have shifted to the right, intersecting the *AD* curve at the potential GDP level. Thus, when the expansionary policy begins to work, the economy will already be at capacity output; any expansionary effect will be inflationary.

The Consequences of an Anti-Inflationary Policy

This section applies the various theories to the issue of anti-inflationary policies. Assume that the economy is in long-run equilibrium, but the price level is at a higher level than desired.

Recall that the policy ineffectiveness proposition can be applied in this case. New classicists argue that a credible contractionary monetary policy will not only shift the *AD* curve inward but will also shift the *AS* curve to the right (and by the same vertical distance). Hence, the Fed can achieve the desired reduction of the price level without any negative effect on output. Output will remain at its potential level, Y_n. The movement from point E_1 to point E_2 in Figure 27–10 describes this policy. The economy will stay at the intermediate point, E_1', only for a fleeting moment, reflecting the ignorance of firms and workers about the fall in the actual price level, to P_2. As soon as they discover the new price level, they will revise their expectations to P_e^2, which reduces real wages and increases the supply of output.

Classicists also argue that in the short run output will fall to Y_2. Like the new classicists, they attribute the reduction in output to an expected price level that is above the actual price level, P_2. Unlike the new classicists, however, classicists believe that actual output may remain below the natural level for some time, because the public is sluggish in revising its expectations toward a lower price level. As expectations are being revised, the *AS* curve will be moving gradually to the right, thereby keeping the level of output below Y_n for some time. Disinflation will not be painless, although it is desirable. Keynesians and new Keynesians agree with the classicists that recession is unavoidable. Their explanation relies on the sluggishness in the adjustment of money wages and in the prices of other variable inputs rather than on a misperceived price level.

In our explanation we have assumed that a high price level is undesirable. Actually, a high price level is not considered a problem by any of the four schools of thought. Rather,

FIGURE 27–10
A Disinflationary
Monetary Policy

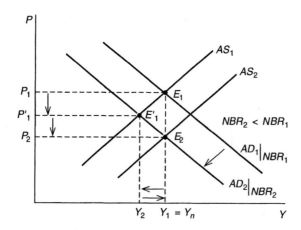

the problem arises from prices rising continuously at a high rate, that is, high rates of inflation. The *AD–AS* model is not perfectly suited for examining anti-inflationary policies. The next chapter examines the issue of inflation in greater detail and with greater precision.

THE LEGACY OF RATIONAL EXPECTATIONS

The introduction of rational expectations has been a major contribution to the fields of money, finance, and macroeconomics. Moreover, rational expectations continue to influence the agenda for research in these fields. Therefore, in conclusion this section elaborates on and takes stock of this contribution.

First, in an early application of rational expectations, Robert Lucas severely criticized the use of macroeconomic models that are constructed from past experience (data) to judge the effectiveness of policy.[14] Lucas pointed out that these models, the coefficients of which are estimated from past experience, may be useless for evaluating policy. The reason is that the relevant coefficients reflect the behavior of market participants, but this behavior will change when the economic environment changes, including the targets and goals of monetary policy.

For example, the coefficient that depicts the interest responsiveness of money demand may change when the policy regime changes. If, in order to decide on its target for the money supply, the Fed uses a money demand relation derived from data that were generated when the Fed targeted interest rates, for example, the Fed will miss its target for money. If, furthermore, the response of aggregate demand for goods and services to a change in the quantity of money also changes with the policy regime, there will be yet another problem in judging the effectiveness of the adopted policy. Lucas's argument, known as the *Lucas critique*, that econometric models must incorporate the effects of prospective policy on estimated coefficients is widely accepted. The difficult task of implementing this approach is being investigated.

Second, although the extreme claims of the new classical school of the total ineffectiveness of anticipated policy have been challenged on theoretical and empirical grounds, milder versions of the proposition are now the norm. (Recall that the ineffectiveness proposition was the consequence of the assumption of market clearing, not of rational expectations.) Anticipated policy may not be totally ineffective, but it is less effective than unanticipated policy. For example, negotiations of labor contracts reveal that workers seek protection from the erosion of their real wages when they expect that policymakers will pursue an inflationary policy. Or they demand protection from layoffs if they expect a disinflationary monetary and fiscal policy.

Third, discussions of the credibility of policy have spread from academic journals to government reports and to the financial press. The credibility of policy is an important ingredient in forming expectations, as explained in GlobalWatch 27.2.

Fourth, the acceptance of the principle of rational expectations is almost universal. So much so that in constructing macroeconomic models, economists routinely incorporate

---

[14] Robert E. Lucas, Jr., "Econometric Policy Evaluation: A Critique," in *The Phillips Curve and Labor Markets*, Supplement to the *Journal of Monetary Economics* 1 (April 1976): 19–46.

GlobalWatch 27.2
Credibility of Monetary Policy: The United States and Japan

The oil shock of 1990–91 prompted the economic advisers to President Bush to look back at lessons from the 1970s. In the *Economic Report of the President 1991* they wrote that: "The experiences of the United States and other large industrialized countries during the previous oil price shocks show the crucial role that maintaining *credible* [emphasis added] and systematic long-run fiscal and monetary policies play in allowing the economy to respond relatively smoothly." (p. 94)

The *Economic Report* compares the case of the United States and Japan. Inflation was high and rising in both countries before the first oil shock in 1973. The oil shock, by reducing aggregate supply, aggravated price pressures. The *Economic Report* argues that when the first oil shock hit monetary policy was not credible in either country. Therefore, neither the Fed nor the Bank of Japan could temporarily ease monetary policy, shifting the aggregate demand curve to the right, to permit a one-time increase in the price level from the oil shock, "without giving firms and households the impression of continued accommodation and tolerance of higher inflation. An increase in money growth could not credibly be viewed as temporary." (p. 95) Instead, monetary policies were tightened, which caused a recession in both countries.

In the aftermath of the first shock, the Bank of Japan moved systematically to reduce money growth to re-

duce inflation, so that the rate of inflation was less than 5 percent when the second oil shock struck in 1979–80. In contrast, the U.S. money supply grew by double digits between 1975 and 1977, and inflation was approaching 10 percent when the oil shock of 1979–80 hit. To prevent inflation from accelerating, the U.S. tightened monetary policy. Japan, however, weathered the second oil shock better than other industrialized countries. According to the *Economic Report*: "The more credible systematic stance of monetary policy followed in Japan between the two oil price shocks made it possible for Japan to avoid much of the negative economic impact that other industrialized economies experienced during the second oil shock without generating fears that inflation and expectations of inflation would spiral upward. As a result, inflation was not permanently raised, and output remained close to its longer run path." (pp. 96–97)

In other words, credibility gives a central bank the flexibility to increase the money supply in response to an adverse supply shock without triggering inflationary expectations. When the 1990 oil shock hit, inflation was low in the United States and monetary policy could be described as credible. The 1990 shock, however, was shorter lived and less severe than the shocks in the 1970s. Expansionary monetary policy in the early 1990s was aimed, instead, at offsetting the headwinds that were shifting the *IS* curve and, hence, the *AD* curve, inward.

assumptions about forward-looking expectations. Although the issue of how market participants form these expectations is still unresolved, it is high on the agenda of current research.

Fifth, the revolution created by rational expectations forced the new Keynesians to come up with better explanations of why wages and prices are sticky and why labor and goods markets do not clear instantaneously. Promising work that combines utility-maximizing or profit-maximizing behavior and rational expectations to explain wage stickiness began to appear in the literature in the 1980s.

Finally, combining rational expectations with continuous market clearance has been applied to financial markets, such as the stock market, the bond market, and the foreign market. Financial markets, unlike labor and goods markets, deal with more homogeneous instruments; are better organized; and, hence, are more likely to exhibit continuous market clearing. The application of rational expectations and continuous market clearance to financial markets is called the **efficient markets theory**. According to this theory, financial markets incorporate new information quickly. Therefore, actual prices represent equilibrium prices, or fundamental values, so that there are no unexploited opportunities for profits. The efficient markets hypothesis is widely accepted in the finance literature. Recently, however, it has been challenged by Robert Shiller whose empirical work on the stock market rejects the efficient markets hypothesis.[15] Since financial markets clear quickly, if Shiller's results stand the test of time, they will also be a challenge to the rational expectations hypothesis itself.

---

[15] Robert Shiller, *Market Volatility* (Cambridge, Mass.: MIT Press, 1990).

SUMMARY

- The modern, or new, classical version of the upward-sloping aggregate supply curve is called the *Lucas supply curve*. Lucas assumes that the labor market clears continuously and that expectations are rational, which means that market participants make use of all available information. He attributes the positive slope of the short-run curve to imperfect information about the price level. The expected, or perceived, price level is fixed along a Lucas supply curve. Output is greater than, equal to, or less than the natural level, depending on whether the actual price level is greater than, equal to, or less than the perceived price level.

- There is an array of Lucas supply curves, one for each expected price level. An increase in the expected price level shifts the curve up and to the left.

- When the correct information becomes available, the basis for any divergence between the actual and the perceived price level disappears, and the economy reverts to the natural level of output.

- The Lucas supply curve is an extension of the Friedman-Phelps fooling model. However, with the Friedman-Phelps approach, expectations are backward looking, or adaptive, so that the approach to full employment may be slow or painful. With the Lucas approach, expectations are forward looking, or rational, so that the movement to full employment may be rapid and painless.

- Lucas's introduction of information into the system launched the rational expectations revolution of the last 25 years. Expectations are rational if they are the predictions of the relevant economic theory. A model is rational if it assumes that participants make use of all available information, that is, they use all information efficiently.

- The combination of rational expectations with continuous market clearance gave rise to the policy ineffectiveness proposition. According to this proposition, only an unexpected change in the money supply will affect output or employment. An anticipated increase in the money supply will merely raise the price level. The other side of the coin is painless disinflation; that is, an expected reduction in the money supply will reduce the price level without any reduction in employment and output.

- The requirement that a model should satisfy rational expectations is widely accepted; the assumption of continuous market clearance is not. Neither is the argument that business cycles are caused by imperfect information.

- In the 1980s, a new Keynesian school emerged that argued that rigidities in money wages and in prices exist in the real world and that labor and product markets do not clear continuously. In this case, both expected and unexpected changes in the money supply will affect output and employment, and disinflation will not be painless.

- Reasons given by new Keynesians for rigidities in nominal and real wages range from explicit and implicit contracts, to rewards for loyalty and punishments for shirking, to adverse selection. Other reasons for wage and price rigidities include the costs of adjusting wages and prices, called *menu costs*.

- The rational expectations revolution also led to debates about the effectiveness of tax cuts. The Ricardian equivalence theorem maintains that a reduction in taxes will not increase output, because households will increase their savings. That is, households recognize that in the future they or their offspring will have to repay the government debt issued to finance the deficit arising from tax cuts. The tax cuts of the 1980s in the United States did not confirm Ricardian equivalence.

· The real business cycle school, another branch of new classical macroeconomics, assumes that money is always neutral and explains changes in output primarily by technological factors.

· There is agreement in the profession that the aggregate supply curve is upward sloping in the short run and verti-

cal, at the natural rate of output, in the long run. However, disagreement exists about why the short-run supply curve is upward sloping and, hence, about the process that leads the economy to full employment. As a corollary, disagreement exists about the speed at which the economy moves to the natural, or full-employment, level of output. Disagreement also exists about whether monetary and fiscal policies should be used to bring the economy back to full employment, or whether the economy should be left to gravitate to full employment on its own.

KEY TERMS AND CONCEPTS

adaptive expectations

rational expectations

Lucas supply curve

policy ineffectiveness proposition

new classical school

new Keynesian school

fooling model

real business cycle school

Ricardian equivalence theorem

efficiency wages

menu costs

efficient markets theory

QUESTIONS AND PROBLEMS

1. Suppose that in its monetary policy report to Congress in July of this year the Federal Reserve announces that it will reduce its targets for money growth next year. Will this affect your expectations of inflation if you have adaptive expectations? Rational expectations?

2. What distinguishes classical economists from Keynesian economists?

3. What distinguishes traditional classical economists, such as Milton Friedman, from new classicists, such as Robert Lucas?

4. What distinguishes Keynesian economists of the 1960s from new Keynesian economists?

5. In the fooling model of Friedman and Phelps why do workers supply more labor when nominal wages rise even though prices may rise by a greater percentage?

6. "A reduction in the expected price level shifts the Lucas aggregate supply curve to the right just as a reduction in the nominal wages shifts the Keynesian aggregate supply curve to the right." True, false, or uncertain? Explain.

7. What is the practical difference between Friedman's fooling model and Lucas's imperfect information model?

8. "Continuous clearance of the labor market in the classical and new classical models means that the economy will always be producing the natural level of output." True, false, or uncertain? Explain.

9. Suppose the Lucas supply relation is described by the following equation: $Y = Y_n \times (P/P_e)$.
   a. Find the value of Y (in terms of Y_n) for each of the following values of P and P_e:

   $P_e = 1, P = 1, Y = ?$
   $P_e = 1, P = 1.10, Y = ?$
   $P_e = 1.10, P = 1, Y = ?$

   b. Which of these points lie on the same upward-sloping supply curve? Explain.

10. Suppose that the central bank's move to permanently reduce nonborrowed reserves by 10 percent is fully anticipated.

a. What happens to output and the price level according to the new classical school?

b. What happens to output and the price level according to the new Keynesian school?

11. "According to the Ricardian equivalence theorem, a reduction in the tax rate will crowd out investment." True, false, or uncertain? Explain.

12. "According to the real business cycle school, monetary policy has no effect on inflation." True, false, or uncertain. Explain.

13. Combine the concept of efficiency wages with adverse selection to explain involuntary unemployment.

14. Combine the concept of efficiency wages with worker loyalty to explain involuntary unemployment.

15. Combine the concept of efficiency wages with shirking to explain involuntary unemployment.

16. Suppose that a credit crunch reduces the availability of funds to finance investment.

a. What will be the effect on output in the new classical model? The new Keynesian model?

b What policy would each of these schools recommend to the Federal Reserve to offset the effects of the credit crunch on the economy?

17. Why might the cost of reducing inflation be lower if the central bank's credibility as an inflation fighter is enhanced?

SUGGESTED READINGS

Akerlof, George A., and Janet L. Yellen, ed., *Efficiency Wage Models of the Labor Market* (Cambridge, England: Cambridge University Press, 1986).

A collection of articles on involuntary unemployment and efficiency wage theory, with an integrative introduction by the editors.

Klamer, Arjo. *Conversations with Economists* (Lanham, Md.: Rowman and Allanheld, 1984).

An assessment of different schools of macroeconomic thought through a series of interviews with eleven prominent economists.

Rock, James M., ed., *Debt and the Twin Deficits Debate* (Mountainview, Calif.: Mayfield Publishing Company, 1991).

A collection of articles that explore the different views about the effects of deficits on the economy.

Sheffrin, Steven M., *Rational Expectations* (New York: Cambridge University Press, 1983).

An accessible survey of the literature on rational expectations that integrates empirical evidence with theoretical discussions.

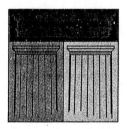

INFLATION, UNEMPLOYMENT, AND ECONOMIC POLICY

History and Theory

CHAPTER PREVIEW

Inflation is the rate of change in the price level. This chapter begins by employing the *AD–AS* model to introduce the concepts of demand-pull inflation and cost-push inflation. The chapter connects theory with practice by applying the model to explain and interpret the effects on inflation, output, unemployment, and interest rates of four wars in the twentieth century; supply-side shocks in the 1970s; deliberate and inadvertent shocks to the monetary sector in the early 1980s; two crashes in the stock market, one in 1929 and the other in 1987; and the headwinds and policies of the late 1980s and early 1990s. Next, the chapter examines two revolutions in economic policymaking: the Kennedy revolution of the 1960s and the Reagan revolution of the 1980s.

The relation between inflation and unemployment, represented graphically by the Phillips curve, is considered next. The differences and controversies about the impact of policy and shocks presented in the *AD–AS* framework resurface in the examination of the possible trade-off between inflation and unemployment. The chapter concludes with a discussion of the costs of inflation.

DEMAND-PULL VERSUS COST-PUSH INFLATION

The early modern literature on inflation distinguished between two types of inflation. One, called **demand-pull inflation**, is the result of an increase in aggregate demand. The other, called **cost-push inflation**, results from a reduction in aggregate supply. An increase in marginal cost will push up the price level. Hence, the term *cost-push inflation*.

Demand-Pull Inflation

The concept of demand-pull inflation was introduced in the 1940s as the United States and other countries moved out of the depression of the 1930s and into the inflationary period that began with World War II. Figure 28–1 illustrates demand-pull inflation.

Suppose the economy is initially at point E_1 with the price level equal to P_1 and output equal to Y_1. Next, suppose the AD curve shifts to the right because of a change in either a policy parameter or a behavioral parameter. As the economy moves to the new equilibrium point, E_2, the price level rises. Until the new equilibrium is reached, the economy experiences inflation. This is *transitory inflation*.

When the economy reaches the new equilibrium, inflation ceases. In Figure 28–1, point E_2 is the point of full equilibrium if Y_2 equals the natural level of output, Y_n. The associated level of unemployment is called the **natural rate of unemployment**.

Of course, if Y_1 is the natural level of output, E_2 will be above the full level of output. Unemployment will be below the natural rate, and inflation will continue. Money wages will rise, the short-run aggregate supply curve will shift upward, and the price level will rise until equilibrium is reached at a point vertically above point E_1. After that, the price will continue to rise only if there are repeated positive shocks to aggregate demand.

This exercise shows that positive demand-side shocks raise the price level, but inflation persists only if these shocks continue. The result applies to any shift factor on the demand side, including policy parameters. With fiscal policy, there may be social or

FIGURE 28–1
Demand-Pull Inflation

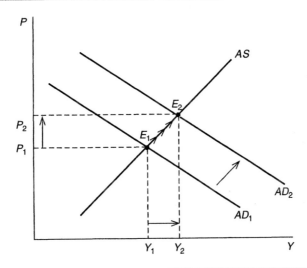

A rightward shift of the *AD* curve leads to a rising price level between points E_1 and E_2. A demand-induced rise in the price level is called *demand-pull inflation*. When the new equilibrium is reached, the price level is higher, but inflation ceases.

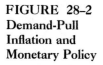

FIGURE 28–2
Demand-Pull
Inflation and
Monetary Policy

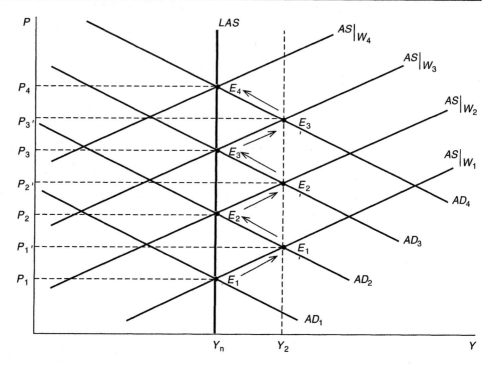

Inflation results when the central bank attempts to peg the level of output above the natural rate. To keep
Y at Y_2, the Fed must keep increasing nonborrowed reserves, which results in continuous increases in the
price level.

political reasons why government expenditures continuously increase without corresponding increases in taxes. Other things equal, such a policy can account for a price level that is continuously rising. But what about monetary policy? Why would the Fed want to increase the money supply if the economy is operating at its capacity level of output?

One explanation may be that the Fed wants the economy to operate above capacity. This explanation is not convincing, however, because central banks in major industrial countries are known to be inflation fighters during peacetime. A more plausible explanation is that there may be uncertainty about the potential level of output itself, leading the Fed to overestimate it. The uncertainty in estimates of potential output arises because its magnitude varies over time for a variety of reasons, including the demographic structure and the level of training of the population. Another explanation is that in the face of uncertainty the Fed may decide to err on the side of fighting a possible recession, especially if it suspects the economy is prone to adverse demand or supply shocks.

Figure 28–2 depicts the case where the Fed is determined to keep output at Y_2, which is above potential output. Assume full long-run equilibrium at point E_1. Next, suppose the Fed increases the quantity of money, via an increase in the quantity of nonborrowed reserves, to achieve the higher level of output, Y_2. The price level starts rising and continues to rise until it reaches P_1'. As a result, at the original level of the money wage, the real wage falls, and firms hire more workers to produce the higher level of output. The pressure in the labor market increases the money wage to W_2 and shifts the supply curve to the left and up by the percentage increase in the price level. The equilibrium is achieved at point E_2, where the price level and money wages rise by the same percentage as nonborrowed reserves. Continuing the process, the Fed again increases nonborrowed reserves by the same percentage, which shifts the AD curve so that it intersects the $AS|W_2$ curve at point E_2', raising the price level to P_2'. Next, the money wage catches up, rising to W_3, and the AS curve shifts to the left to intersect the AD curve at E_3, reducing output to its potential level. And the story goes on. The result of this exercise is that the rate of inflation equals the rate of growth of nonborrowed reserves, which equals the rate of growth of nominal money supply. Money is neutral.

The discussion above uses the traditional Keynesian model to tell the story behind Figure 28–2. The story remains essentially the same under new classical theory. One difference is that changes in the perceived price level, rather than changes in the money wage, shift the AS curve up in the new classical framework. Another is that the process will be substantially faster in the new classical framework.

Cost-Push Inflation

Chapters 26 and 27 show that an exogenous increase in costs increases the price level and reduces output. Figure 28–3 depicts that result again, where the AS curve shifts from position AS_1 to position AS_2. As a result, the price level rises from P_1 to P_2, and output falls from Y_1 to Y_2. During the process of moving from the initial equilibrium, E_1, to the new short-run equilibrium, E_2, the price level must be rising. This rising price level has been called *cost-push inflation*, or, in recent years, *stagflation*, because inflation is accompanied by stagnation of output.

FIGURE 28–3
Cost-Push Inflation

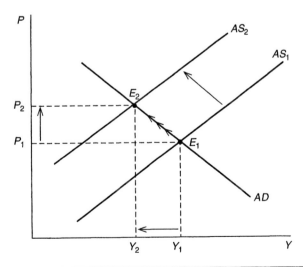

A leftward shift of the AS curve leads to a rising price level between points E_1 and E_2. A cost-induced rise in the price level is called *cost-push inflation*. When the new equilibrium is reached, the price level is higher, but inflation ceases.

FIGURE 28–4
An Adverse Supply
Shock and
Alternative
Monetary Policies

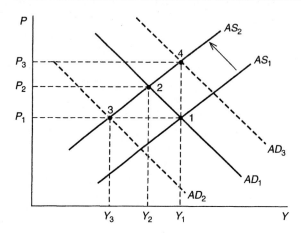

An adverse supply shock, by itself,
moves the economy from point 1 to
point 2. To keep the price fixed, the
Fed must reduce the money supply,
which reduces output further, as
shown by point 3. To keep output
fixed, the Fed must increase the
money supply, as shown by point 4.

Cost-push inflation figured prominently in the economic literature of the 1950s, which concentrated exclusively on the market power of businesses and labor unions as the reason for the rise in the cost of national output and, hence, for the inward shift of aggregate supply. In addition, another popular term in the literature on inflation was coined at the time: the *cruel dilemma*. It was argued that cost-push inflation confronts the policymaker with a dilemma, because such inflation can be eliminated only by a reduction in aggregate demand and, hence, by a (further) reduction in output. Thus, the dilemma is whether to accept higher prices or lower output.

If the central bank aims at keeping the price level at its original level, P_1, it must reduce aggregate demand to AD_2 by following a restrictive monetary policy. This policy will further reduce output to Y_3, as point 3 in Figure 28–4 shows. On the other hand, if the central bank aims at keeping output at its original level, Y_1, expansionary monetary policy is needed to increase aggregate demand to AD_3. This policy will further increase the price level to P_3, as point 4 in Figure 28–4 shows.

Of course, the inflation caused by the Fed in accommodating a one-time adverse supply shock is transitory. In the absence of expected inflation, the economy settles down at a higher price level. As GlobalWatch 27.2 in Chapter 27 explains, if monetary policy is credible, inflationary expectations will not be aggravated because market participants will believe that the looser monetary policy is temporary.

Persistent adverse supply shocks, however, are more of a problem. If the Fed accommodates persistent supply shocks, the price level will rise continuously. By pursuing an accommodative monetary policy, the Fed becomes a partner in cost-push inflation. If the accommodative policy triggers inflationary expectations, there will be further effects. As Chapter 10 explains, an increase in expected inflation decreases the expected real interest rate, which increases the demand for goods and services. As a result, the AD curve shifts to the right and the price level rises more. On the supply side, the upward-sloping aggregate supply curve shifts upward, further increasing the price level.[1]

OF WARS, PEACE, STOCK MARKET CRASHES, AND OTHER ECONOMIC SHOCKS

Next, based on the historical experience of the U.S. economy in the twentieth century, use of the *AD–AS* model shows how the economy reacted to changes in policy and to external shocks. This historical review analyzes episodes of demand-pull inflation and cost-push inflation, as well as periods of disinflation, that is, falling inflation. It examines four major wars in the 1900s and the aftermath of each; the supply-side shocks of the 1970s; selected deliberate and inadvertent shocks to the monetary sector in the 1980s; the stock market crashes of 1929 and 1987; and the headwinds and economic policy in the 1990s.

Economic Performance during Wars

Two phases are common in war economies. The first is the mobilization and the conduct of the war. During this phase, aggregate demand increases and economic activity rises. Eventually demand-pull inflation appears. In the second phase, during the transition from war to peace, aggregate demand falls as the economy readjusts to a diminished level of economic activity. In the aftermath of long wars, aggregate supply usually falls as well, because the skills acquired by the labor force during wars do not coincide with those needed for production in peacetime. Structural, or natural, unemployment increases, and economic activity diminishes. Both phases were present in the four lengthy wars of this century: World War I, World War II, the Korean War, and the Vietnam War.

World War I   Output and prices rose as the United States entered this war. During the three years following the war, 1919 to 1922, the economy contracted; real output fell below potential output. The reduction in output was a natural consequence of inward shifts of aggregate demand and, perhaps, of inward shifts of aggregate supply. The economy rebounded from 1923 onward. By 1926, output reached its potential level and stayed at or above that level for three years, until 1929.

World War II   The "roaring twenties" came to a close with the crash in the stock market in October 1929. The ensuing economic downturn, called the *Great Depression* because of its severity, lasted more than 10 years. By 1941, when the United States entered World War II, the level of economic activity was returning to its 1929 level, with output equal to potential GNP. By 1942, mobilization for the war increased aggregate demand and raised output above its potential level. Throughout the war years, output was substantially above its potential, and unemployment was well below its natural level. The government administered price controls and rationing, but monetary policy was not restrictive during this period. Instead, monetary policy was mildly accommodating, and inflation persisted.

---

[1] For more on supply shocks and economic policy, see Robert J. Gordon, "Alternative Responses of Policy to External Supply Shocks," *Brookings Papers on Economic Activity* 6, no. 1 (1975): 183–206.

FIGURE 28–5
U.S. Rate of
Inflation: *1960–1993*

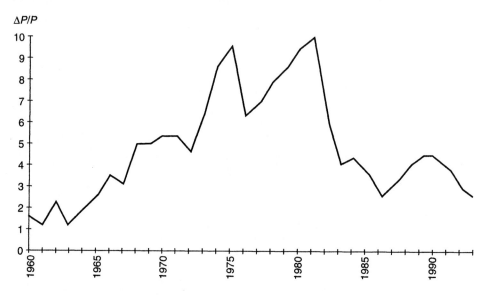

Source: *Economic Report of the President, 1994*, Table B-3.

With the conclusion of the war, the economy entered a phase of reduced aggregate demand, falling output, and increased unemployment. By 1949, when the decompression of the war economy was completed, output was below its potential.

The Korean War   In 1950 the United States entered the Korean War, and the process repeated itself, albeit on a smaller scale, until the war ended in 1953. This time the transition to a peacetime economy was fast. Within a year, output climbed above the potential level.

The Vietnam War   The Vietnam War was the longest of the four wars. Substantial U.S. participation began in 1964. As U.S. involvement in the war increased, the economy was approaching full employment, with output close to its potential level. During the preceding three years, the advisers to Kennedy and Johnson had recommended expansionary demand management policies to guide the economy toward full employment. As the war escalated, however, the Council of Economic Advisers recommended to then President Johnson that he propose a tax increase to prevent the economy from overheating. But politics collided with economics. Concerned about the growing political resistance to the war, President Johnson rejected the advice of his Council of Economic Advisers. When he finally agreed to a tax surcharge in 1968, the remedy was too little and too late. Figure 28–5 shows the rise in inflation after the mid-1960s. By 1969 the inflation rate was 5 percent and the unemployment rate was 3.5 percent, which was below the then-estimated natural rate of 4 percent.

The Vietnam War ended in 1973, at the beginning of President Nixon's second term. Before that, in 1971, President Nixon imposed wage-price controls in an attempt to keep inflation low prior to the 1972 presidential election. As expected, the controls caused shortages. By the time the controls were fully phased out in 1974, "catch-up effects" combined with other adverse supply shocks to send the inflation rate higher, as the next section explains.

Supply-Side Shocks of the 1970s

The supply shocks began in 1972 and 1973 when crop failures led to a rise in the price of grains, which are factors of production for several other products. This shock shifted the aggregate supply curve to the left, as Figure 28–6 illustrates. This adverse shift in aggregate supply increased the price level and also reduced output, as point 2 shows. The Fed reacted by reducing money growth by more than one percent. This contractionary policy moved the economy to point 3, resulting in a further decrease in output, while moderating the increase in the price level.

The Fed's reaction can be interpreted as an effort to stem the inflation that was created as the *AS* curve fell and the price level was moving up and to the left on the *AD* curve— from its initial equilibrium at point 1 toward the new equilibrium at point 2. At the time, the Fed was criticized for confusing a higher price level with higher inflation. Critics argued that inflation induced by the shift of the supply curve would stop when the new

**FIGURE 28–6
Supply-Side Shocks
and Contractionary
Monetary Policy:
*1972–1975***

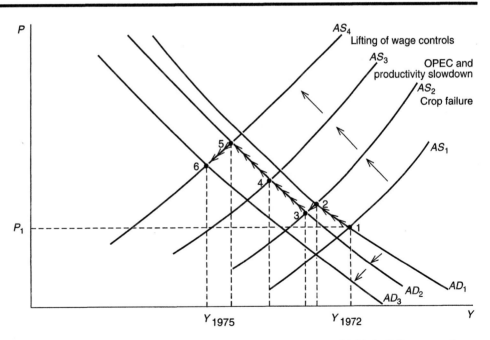

A series of adverse supply shocks coupled with contractionary monetary policy hit the U.S. economy from 1972 through 1975.

equilibrium was reached at point 2. The Fed, however, might have been concerned that even transitory inflation would exacerbate inflationary expectations by workers and firms.

In 1973 and 1974, a more devastating supply-side shock hit the U.S. economy. The Organization of Petroleum Exporting Countries (OPEC) began to raise the price of oil, quadrupling it within a short period of time. This shock further shifted the aggregate supply to the left, again increasing the price level and reducing output. About this time, the wage-price controls were lifted. Wages had a lot of catching up to do. They rose by 9 percent, up from 6 percent in 1972. This one-time adjustment of wages again shifted the aggregate supply curve to the left, reducing output and exerting upward cost-push pressure on the price level. There was also a substantial slowdown in the growth of productivity in 1973.[2] By the end of 1975, unemployment had reached 8.5 percent, which, at the time, was the highest rate of unemployment since the Great Depression. And the rate of inflation was 9.6 percent.

The economy was recovering when Jimmy Carter became president in 1977. Unemployment, at 7.4 percent, was still above the natural rate, considered at the time to be about 5 percent.[3] High rates of money growth in 1977, 1978, and 1979 brought unemployment down to 5.8 percent in 1979. As expected, inflation rose, as Figure 28–5 shows. To complicate the picture, another major increase in oil prices, first by OPEC and then by domestic suppliers, hit the economy beginning in 1979. In addition to these exogenous supply shocks, the Carter administration created two supply shocks: increases in social security and other payroll taxes, as well as increases in the minimum wage.

Another shock of Carter's own making was the reintroduction of wage-price "controls." Unlike Nixon's 1971 mandatory controls, the Carter controls were voluntary. But they were equally ineffective and, in fact, backfired. Instead of reducing inflation, they fueled it. The guidelines created expectations of mandatory controls that were quickly translated into further inflationary expectations, as both unions and businesses tried to avoid getting caught with lower wages and prices. This was another adverse supply-side shock, perhaps the most severe. Prices kept rising, as Figure 28–5 shows.

The reaction of the Carter administration was similar to that of the Ford administration: tighter demand management policies. In 1979 President Carter appointed Paul Volcker as chairman of the Federal Reserve Board. With the blessing of Carter, in October 1979 the newly appointed chairman embarked on a contractionary monetary policy to reduce inflation, as Chapter 16 discusses. Contractionary demand management policies led to a short recession, called the *Carter-Volcker recession*, in the first half of 1980. The steepness of the decline in GNP was exacerbated by credit controls imposed in March

---

[2] At the time, analysts attributed the slowdown in productivity growth to the oil shock. However, the slowdown turned out to be too persistent for that to be a convincing explanation. From World War II to 1973, the average rate of growth of productivity was just under 3 percent in the United States. For almost the next 20 years, it averaged just over 1 percent. Many factors can explain the slowdown. Economists do not really know which of them are the most important.

[3] A change in the age-sex composition of the labor force is one factor that contributed to the higher natural rate of unemployment in the 1970s. At the time, the rate was estimated to be about 5 percent, compared with 4 percent in the 1960s. The natural rate is difficult to estimate. Some recent empirical work has revised each of those estimates upward by 1 to 1½ percentage points.

1980. The Carter administration invoked the Credit Control Act of 1969 to impose constraints on the growth of credit. In the second quarter of 1980, the economy experienced the steepest one-quarter drop in real GNP since World War II. The controls were lifted in July 1980, and growth in real GNP turned positive. Nevertheless, unemployment rose from 5.8 percent in 1979 to 7.1 percent in 1980. (A graphical summary of all these shocks would be similar to that of Figure 28–6.)

Deliberate and Inadvertent Shocks to the Monetary Sector: 1981–1982

With the encouragement of the Reagan administration, the restrictive monetary policy continued unabated after President Reagan took office in 1981. The Reagan-Volcker strategy was to wring high inflation out of the economy, which resulted in the Reagan-Volcker recession of 1981–82. In its "Monetary Policy Report to Congress" in February 1981, the Fed predicted that the rate of inflation would fall within a range of 9 to 10.5 percent and that the rate of growth of real GNP would be between *minus* 1.5 percent and *plus* 1.5 percent. Actual inflation did fall within the forecasted range, at 9.7 percent, as did the actual growth of real GNP, at 0.9 percent. In its 1982 report, the Fed predicted that the rate of inflation in 1982 would be between 6.5 and 7.75 percent. At 6.4 percent, actual inflation was slightly less than forecasted inflation. Growth in real GNP, however, was less than expected in 1982. The Fed predicted that the growth of real GNP would be between 0.5 and 3 percent. Instead, the actual rate of growth of real GNP was *minus* 2.5 percent. Thus, monetary policy was more contractionary than predicted.

At the time neither the Volcker-led Fed nor the Reagan administration realized the magnitude by which deregulation was increasing money demand and making monetary policy more contractionary than intended. The increase in money demand, coupled with the contractionary monetary policy, shifted the *LM* curve and, thus, the *AD* curve, to the left more than the Fed intended, measured by the unemployment rate, and caused the most severe recession since the Great Depression. In 1982 unemployment climbed to 9.7 percent, where it stayed through 1983.

With inflation falling and high unemployment, the Fed retreated from its disinflationary policy in October 1982. For the remainder of the decade, the Fed essentially targeted velocity-indexed money growth, which equals growth in nominal GDP. As Chapter 16 explains, the Fed adjusted its targets for money growth to accommodate shifts in velocity, which varies inversely with money demand. With a more expansionary monetary policy, unemployment fell from 1984 through 1986. Unemployment was 6.2 percent when the stock market crash of October 1987 hit the economy.

Two Stock Market Crashes: 1929 and 1987

The two major stock market crashes in this century provide an opportunity for us to compare the economic knowledge available at each decline. The 1929 crash was followed by a prolonged and painful economic downturn—the Great Depression. The 1987 crash did not produce even a recession. Consider how policymakers reacted in these two cases.

The Stock Market Crash of 1929 and the Great Depression   The stock market crash of 1929 reduced consumer demand for two reasons. The drastic reduction in wealth, by itself, reduced consumption. The unprecedented decimation of the financial markets further reduced consumer confidence and consumer demand. The consequent reduction in aggregate demand, prices, and output also diminished producer confidence, causing a reduction of investment in plant and equipment. Another reason that investment may have declined is that there were massive bank failures in the early 1930s. These bank failures reduced the availability of credit to firms to finance investment.[4] In terms of the *IS-LM* model, these factors shifted the *IS* curve inward. Bad fiscal policy also shifted the *IS* curve inward. In 1931 and 1932, in the midst of this downturn, the Hoover administration, with the concurrence of Congress, engineered a steep increase in taxes to balance the budget. Of course, at the time, Keynesian theory was not available to steer policy-makers away from such a disastrous policy.

On the monetary side, in a deteriorating economy many borrowers were unable to repay their bank loans. Banks hard hit by defaults failed. In the absence of deposit insurance, bank failures made the public fearful about the safety of their deposits, which led to runs on banks and more bank failures. The flight from bank deposits to currency drained reserves from the banking system. To try to meet the deposit withdrawals and thereby avoid failing, banks increased their demand for excess reserves. As a result of the increase in the demand for currency and the demand for excess reserves, reserves available to support deposits fell, and the money supply fell.

The classic work on the role of monetary factors in the Great Depression is that of Milton Friedman and Anna Schwartz.[5] Friedman and Schwartz show that although the monetary base increased by about 20 percent between 1929 and 1933, the monetary base multiplier fell because of the rise in currency and in excess reserves.[6] As a result, the money supply fell by 28 percent, producing a severe negative shock to the *LM* sector that further shifted the *AD* curve inward. Friedman and Schwartz argue that the Fed, by allowing the money supply to fall, was chiefly responsible for the Depression. Others argue that even if the Fed had aggressively added more reserves to the banking system, the money supply would not have increased. With Treasury bill rates below 1 percent by 1931 and with banks concerned about runs by their depositors, these skeptics argue that banks would simply have held more idle excess reserves. Nevertheless, by its passive reaction to the early bank runs, the Fed failed to fulfill its function as lender of last resort and, thus, did not try to keep the situation from deteriorating.

A debate about the importance of monetary (*LM* sector) and nonmonetary (*IS* sector) factors in causing the Great Depression continues to this day. A statistical study by Robert Gordon and James Wilcox found that monetary and nonmonetary factors both played a role, with monetary factors playing a larger role after 1931.[7] Figure 28–7 depicts the major shocks to the *AD* curve from 1929 to 1941. The inward shift of the curve from position AD_{1929} to AD_{1931} resulted from the stock market crash that reduced wealth and

---

[4] This view has been put forth by Ben Bernanke, "Non-Monetary Effects of the Financial Crisis in the Propagation of the Great Depression," *American Economic Review* 73 (June 1983): 257–76.

[5] Milton Friedman and Anna Schwartz, *A Monetary History of the United States, 1867–1960* (Princeton: Princeton University Press, 1963).

[6] The appendix to Chapter 8 discusses the monetary base multiplier and explains the relation between our money supply equation that is expressed in terms of reserves and the equation that relates the quantity of money supplied to the monetary base.

[7] Robert J. Gordon and James A. Wilcox, "Monetarist Interpretations of the Great Depression: An Evaluation and Critique," in *Contemporary Views of the Great Depression*, ed. Karl Brunner (Hingham, Mass.: Martinus Nijhoff, 1981), 49–107.

FIGURE 28–7
The U.S. Economy
from 1929 to 1941

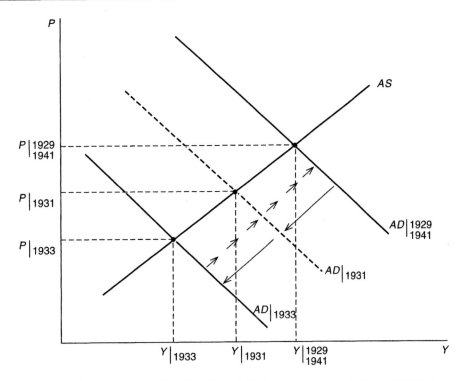

The inward shift of the *AD* curve from 1929 through 1931 resulted from a reduction in consumer and producer confidence precipitated by the stock market crash of 1929 that dramatically reduced wealth. Contractionary fiscal and monetary policies led to further inward shifts from 1931 to 1933. The journey back to the 1929 level of GNP, resulting from unstructured expansionary policies, took until 1941.

lowered consumer and producer confidence, thereby reducing consumption and investment. This shift may have contributed to about half of the reduction in real GDP during the Great Depression. The remainder came from contractionary fiscal policy, a reduction in the availability of credit to finance investment, and the reduction in the money supply. The inward shift of the *IS* curve (because of the increased taxes and reduced availability of credit) and the inward shift of the *LM* curve (because of the reduced money supply) appear as an additional inward shift of the *AD* curve from AD_{1931} to AD_{1933}.

The combination of these adverse shocks dramatically reduced output and employment. By 1933, unemployment rose to 25 percent of the labor force, and real GNP fell by a total of nearly 30 percent. Money wages, however, did not fall until 1931. They continued to fall in 1932, after which they stabilized. GNP did not return to its 1929 level until 1941. During the intervening years, expansionary monetary and fiscal policies were used as antirecession tools. But these policies, especially fiscal policy, were not based on a well-thought-out analysis and, thus, were not methodical. With preparation for the coming war, aggregate demand picked up considerably and by 1941 output reached its 1929 level. When output bottomed out in 1933 and unemployment peaked at 25 percent, money wages stabilized; after 1933 they started rising slightly, despite the persistently high unemployment. The data show that the economy behaved as if the short-run aggregate supply curve remained unchanged from 1929 to 1941, as in Figure 28–7.

The Stock Market Crash of 1987   The "roaring eighties" were punctuated by the stock market crash on Monday, October 19, 1987, referred to as *Black Monday* to draw a parallel with its ancestor, the crash on Thursday, October 24, 1929, called *Black Thursday*. In a five-day period in 1987, the stock market fell 23 percent, which was slightly more than the fall in 1929. In 1987, however, the economy did not fall into a recession, let alone, an economic depression. What went right this time?

The answer lies in the handling of the crisis by the Federal Reserve System, led by Chairman Alan Greenspan. While the crash was unfolding, the Federal Reserve replenished the lost liquidity by injecting massive amounts of nonborrowed and borrowed reserves into the financial system. These measures stemmed further deterioration in the financial markets and prevented insolvencies of securities firms and of supporting commercial banks. When the dangers of a collapse in the financial system faded, the Fed began methodically to withdraw reserves from the system to avoid overstimulating the economy. At the same time, the Fed widened its target ranges for money growth to help counter swiftly and massively any possible deterioration of the economy. The integrity of the financial system was preserved along with the health of the economy. Economists praised the Fed for its masterly handling of the crisis.

Headwinds and Economic Policy in the 1990s

After the stock market crash of 1987, the Fed attempted to engineer a *soft landing at full employment*, that is, to achieve full employment with moderate inflation. In 1988 the inflation rate was 3.9 percent, growth in real GDP was 3.9 percent, and the rate of unemployment was 5.5 percent, considered to be at or slightly below the natural rate.

Hopes for maintaining full employment were dashed in the summer of 1990. The economic expansion that began in 1983 came to an end because of the lagged effects of tighter monetary policy, the adverse oil shock from the Iraqi invasion of Kuwait, and a collection of factors grouped together under the title of "headwinds"—the credit crunch induced by loan failures and inadequate bank capital, a reduction in consumer and producer confidence, a reduction in defense spending because of the end of the Cold War, a reduction in commercial construction because of an excess supply of commercial real estate, and a surge in corporate downsizings. Between 1989 and 1992, the Fed responded with 23 reductions in its operating target for the federal funds rate and 7 reductions in the discount rate. The recovery that began in March 1991, however, was weak compared with the typical recovery since World War II. In the 30 months following March 1991, real GDP grew by about 6 percent compared with 13 percent in the typical recovery. In that same period, job growth was 1.7 percent, compared with 7.4 percent in the typical recovery.[8] Citing the weak recovery, the Fed's critics argued that the policy actions of the Fed during this period were always too little, too late, The Fed's policy did, however, reduce inflation. In this environment of weak demand, inflation fell to 2.9 percent in 1992, as Figure 28–6 shows.

Fiscal Policy in the Bush Administration   The stance of monetary policy was important because unlike previous recoveries, the 1991 recovery did not get a boost from fiscal policy. Emphasis on long-term deficit reduction and the downsizing of defense limited the role of fiscal policy. Moreover, a political stalemate between the Bush administration and the Congress doomed any chance of a fiscal initiative in 1992.

To put the economy on a path of long-run deficit reduction, the Budget Enforcement Act of 1990 included a pay-as-you-go provision. This provision requires new spending programs to be offset by tax increases. Similarly, it requires tax cuts (that are projected to decrease revenue) to be offset by spending cuts. The pay-as-you-go provision can be waived, however, in a low-growth economy—two consecutive quarters of less than 1 percent growth or a forecast of two or more consecutive quarters of no growth. It can also be waived in a weak economy that doesn't fit the low-growth stipulations, if the president declares an emergency.

At the start of 1992, the Bush administration proposed some fiscal stimulus initiatives, including a temporary investment tax allowance, a temporary tax credit for first-time homebuyers, and a reduction in the tax rate on capital gains. The administration argued that this package would increase capital formation and the potential for long-term growth without increasing the deficit. Congress and the administration, however, could not agree on a stimulus package. The Bush administration did unilaterally accelerate some expenditures already in the pipeline and reduce tax withholding. In the fourth quarter of 1992, real GDP grew by 5.9 percent annual rate—the fastest growth rate since 1987. In the first quarter of 1993, however, the growth rate dipped to less than 1 percent.

Fiscal Policy in the Clinton Administration   When President Clinton took office in 1993, he proposed a very modest fiscal stimulus program ($13 billion) to boost the economy in the short run, to be followed by a deficit reduction program to increase national savings and, hence, investment, in the long run. When Congress failed to pass the stimulus package, the administration focused exclusively on deficit reduction. In August 1993, Congress passed a package of tax increases and spending cuts forecasted to lower the deficit by about $500 billion over five years.

According to the *IS-LM*, *AD–AS* model, tax increases and spending cuts lower demand for goods and services, which reduces output. The lower level of output and real income, in turn, reduces interest rates, which increases interest-sensitive spending. In the short-

---

[8] In previous recoveries, a 6 percent increase in output led to a 2.2 percent increase in employment. Therefore, the productivity of labor rose in the 1991–92 recovery. Productivity optimists argue that the long-awaited payoff from the use of computers was at hand. In contrast, productivity pessimists argue that this was merely the usual pickup in productivity that accompanies a recovery, and that productivity growth will fall again. It is too soon to know which view is correct.

run, however, the lower interest rates do not offset the contractionary impulse from deficit reduction.

The administration, however, argued that *credible* deficit reduction could provide short-run stimulus *if sufficient declines in long-term interest rates preceded the actual tax increases and spending cuts*. Federal Reserve Board Chairman Alan Greenspan shared this view. In Humphrey-Hawkins testimony in July 1993, Greenspan said: "To be sure, the conventional wisdom is that budget deficit reduction restrains economic growth for a time and I suspect that probably is correct. However, over the long run, such wisdom points in the opposite direction. *In fact, one can infer that recent declines in long-term interest rates are bringing forward some of these anticipated long-term gains* (italics added). As a consequence, the timing and magnitude of any net restraint from deficit reduction is uncertain."

Figure 28–8 shows that the nominal long-term interest rates fell through most of 1993. By the last quarter of 1993, the lower rates triggered a boom in residential construction, on top of increases in expenditures on consumer and producer durables that began earlier in the year. As a result, real GDP grew by 7.0 percent in the fourth quarter of 1993.

The 1994 *Economic Report of the President* attributes the fall in rates that boosted the economy to credible deficit reduction. According to the term structure of interest rates, explained in Chapter 23, expectations of future short-term rates are an important factor affecting current long-term rates. If the government needs to borrow less in the

FIGURE 28–8
Long-Term U.S.
Interest Rates:
1990–1994 (June)

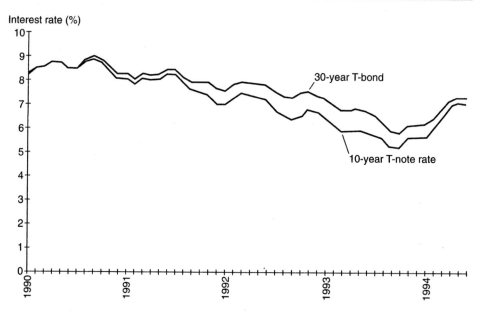

Source: Federal Reserve Board.

future, there will be a lower demand for credit, and, thus, lower interest rates in the future. The 1994 *Economic Report* argues that credible deficit reduction caused market participants to anticipate lower rates in the future, so that long-term rates fell immediately. Other factors, however, also contributed to lower long-term rates. Among these factors are: low actual and expected inflation resulting from a credible monetary policy; weak economies in Europe and Japan; and the Clinton administration's policy to shorten the maturity of the government debt, which Chapter 23 discusses. There is no consensus among economists about the relative importance of these factors in 1993.

Of course, the economy could not sustain a 7.0 percent increase in real GDP. In the first quarter of 1994, growth fell to 3.4 percent. Convinced that a recovery was firmly underway and that the economy was in danger of overheating, the Fed pushed up short-term rates between February and May of 1994. Figure 28–8 shows that long-term rates also rose, giving up the entire decline in 1993. At the time of the Fed's first move in February, the unemployment rate was 6.4 percent. Critics argued that the Fed's action was premature because there still was slack in the economy. By May, however, the unemployment rate fell to 6 percent, which is near most estimates of the natural rate. In its midyear policy review, the Clinton administration forecasted that GDP growth would slow in the second half of 1994 because of a reduction in excess capacity. For the year as a whole, the administration predicted a 3 percent growth rate, which is about the rate of growth of potential GDP.

REVOLUTIONS IN ECONOMIC POLICY: KENNEDY AND REAGAN

The design and implementation of policy in the Kennedy years (1961–1963) and the Reagan years (1981–1988) have been heralded as revolutions. We conclude our review of the historical record by explaining and comparing these policies.

The Kennedy administration took over while the economy was emerging from the recession of 1960. This was the second recession in three years and the third recession during the eight-year presidency of Dwight Eisenhower. The Reagan administration took over in the midst of the Carter-Volcker recession. However, the 9.3 percent rate of inflation (1980) inherited by Reagan was substantially higher than the 1.6 percent rate of inflation (1960) that Kennedy inherited. But the excess of unemployment over its natural rate was comparable at the outset of each administration. The actual unemployment rate of 1960 was 5.4 percent, while the natural rate was estimated at 4 percent. In 1980 the actual unemployment rate was 7 percent, but estimates of the natural rate had risen to 6 percent, in part because of changes in demographics and in the training of the labor force. With this background in mind, consider first the policies designed by the economic advisers to President Kennedy.

The Kennedy Years

The Full Employment Act of 1946, which created the Council of Economic Advisers (CEA) as an advisory body to the president, also directed the administration to pursue policies to achieve full employment. Before 1960 the accepted norm was for policy-makers to try to stem a falling output, that is, to prevent or reverse a recession. In 1962, in their first full-fledged economic report, Kennedy's advisers parted with this norm.[9] They interpreted the 1946 act to mean that policymakers should apply stimulus even when GNP is rising, as long as actual output is below potential output. In developing this argument, the CEA employed the concept of the *GNP gap*, which is the difference between potential GNP and actual GNP. They recommended demand management policies to close the GNP gap in the short run. Even more revolutionary was their remedy for stimulating aggregate demand. They recommended tax reductions even though there was a budget deficit. These two revolutionary aspects of their recommendations had to overcome the misgivings of President Kennedy, as well as those of a skeptical Congress and the financial community.

In arguing for tax cuts in spite of a budget deficit, they used the concept of the **full-employment budget deficit** (or surplus). This concept, introduced in the mid-1950s, makes a distinction between deficits in a fully employed economy and deficits (or surpluses) at other levels of income. That is, if tax and expenditure policies are set so that the budget is balanced at full employment, the deficits or surpluses that arise at other levels of output will be **automatic stabilizers**. In particular, the budget will go into deficit when the economy weakens, because tax payments will fall and transfer payments will rise. As a result, the fall in disposable income and the fall in aggregate demand will be tempered. On the other hand, the budget will go into surplus when the economy overheats, because tax payments will rise and transfer payments will fall. As a result, the increase in disposable income and aggregate demand will be moderated. In making a case for tax cuts, Kennedy's CEA argued that the budget would be balanced *if the economy were at full employment*, because incomes would be higher, tax receipts would be higher, and transfer payments would be lower. Congress passed the Revenue Act of 1964 after Kennedy's assassination.

In sum, Kennedy's advisers relied on fiscal policy for (aggregate) demand management.[10] The aim of these policies was to stabilize GNP at its potential level in the short run. To promote long-run growth in potential GNP, they introduced supply-side policies for the first time. Congress enacted two supply-side measures in 1962. To reduce the frictional, or natural, rate of unemployment, the Manpower and Development Act of 1962 initiated a training program to transform unemployed persons into trained workers whose skills matched those of unfilled vacancies. An investment tax credit that enabled firms to deduct a portion of their expenditure on investment was also introduced. The investment tax credit was a subsidy designed to stimulate investment in new plant and equipment. The ultimate goal was to increase the productive capacity of the economy and, hence, shift the long-run aggregate supply curve to the right.

The Reagan Years

The first full-fledged economic report of President Reagan's Council of Economic Advisers appeared in 1982.[11] On the microeconomic side, the primary goals were deregulating and privatizing the U.S. economy. On the macroeconomic side, the emphasis was on reducing inflation and promoting economic growth.

---

[9] Walter Heller was the chairman of the Council of Economic Advisers and James Tobin and Kermit Gordon were the other members.

[10] We shall see why they did not rely on monetary policy after we examine the Reagan revolution.

[11] Murray L. Weidenbaum was the chairman of the CEA, and Jerry L. Jordan and William A. Niskanen were the other members.

To further its macroeconomic goals in a manner consistent with its microeconomic goals, Reagan's advisers employed new economic concepts and theories. Supply-side remedies were applied as instruments of short-run fiscal policy. Rational expectations in the form of Ricardian equivalence and credibility of monetary (and fiscal) policy were also important ingredients.

On the tax side, the report recommended substantial reductions in the rates for individual and business taxes. According to Keynesian theory, a reduction in tax rates on personal income increases disposable income, thereby increasing consumption and, hence, aggregate demand. The Reagan report, however, downplayed the demand-enhancing effects of tax cuts. It took into consideration the Ricardian equivalence theorem. According to this theory (see MarketWatch 27.1 in Chapter 27), forward-looking individuals, who discount their tax liabilities, will increase savings instead of consumption when their taxes are cut. More important, the report concentrated on the incentive, or supply-side, effects of tax cuts on savings, investment, and work effort. For example, one argument was that the reduction in marginal tax rates would increase after-tax returns to savings, which would induce individuals to save more and consume less. Another argument was that an increase in after-tax real wages would be an incentive for individuals—especially married women—to increase their participation in the labor force, thereby shifting the aggregate supply curve to the right. Such a shift would have the advantage of increasing output and lowering the price level. Finally, by encouraging capital formation in the long run, the reduction in business taxes—like Kennedy's investment tax credit—would also shift the supply curve to the right.

In sum, the Reagan revolution was based on the argument that a reduction in personal and business taxes would enhance economic growth by increasing inputs of labor and capital. While the goal of fiscal policy was to promote growth, the aim of monetary policy was to reduce and eventually to eliminate inflation. The 1982 report argues strongly in favor of a monetarist rule for a fixed rate of money growth. To deal with the immediate problem of disinflating the economy, the report recommended setting a target for money growth and gradually reducing the target until inflation was eventually eliminated. Finally, the high rate of inflation at the time of the preparation of the 1982 report received priority treatment.

Comparison of Revolutions

On the issue of output and prices, the 1962 report and the 1982 report are similar in exaggerating the effectiveness of their policies. In retrospect, the Kennedy report exaggerates the stability of the relation between prices and output (or unemployment). After the initial success of expansionary policies in reducing unemployment and increasing output from 1961 through 1964, further stimulus to the economy from the Vietnam War and the war against poverty increased real output only marginally but increased prices considerably. Also, in retrospect, the Reagan report exaggerates the speed at which the inverse relationship between inflation and unemployment disappears and, therefore, underestimates the pain of reducing inflation. And it was this fight against inflation that created a deep and prolonged recession.

It seems that nothing of importance can be achieved easily. The eventual inflationary outcome of the expansionary policies of the middle to late 1960s confirms the Friedman-Phelps view, introduced in Chapter 27, that as soon as inflation is expected, expansionary policy has little or no effect on employment and output. This is also the theme of the

Lucas critique of policy effectiveness, which Chapter 27 also discusses. But the speed at which ineffectiveness ensues is another matter. As it took time for inflation to accelerate in the 1960s, it also took time to reduce inflation in the 1980s; in the meantime there was substantial unemployment.

On the issue of the supply-side effects of a reduction in business taxes, the two reports are similar. On the effects of tax reduction for individuals, however, they are diametrically opposite. The Kennedy report predicts an increase in consumption; the Reagan report an increase in savings. Thus, the Kennedy report predicts an increase in aggregate demand and aggregate output; the Reagan report predicts an increase in savings and a fall in the interest rate. Events proved the Kennedy advisers right in the 1960s and the Reagan advisers wrong in the 1980s. National savings fell in the 1980s, and, although nominal interest rates fell, real interest rates remained high.

This raises an interesting question. Since the reduction in personal income tax rates raised consumption in the 1960s and the 1980s, were the Reagan policies and the Kennedy policies the same? The answer is yes and no. The Economic Recovery Tax Act of 1981 mandated that the tax cuts be phased in gradually in 1982 and 1983. Thus, the tax cuts provided a stimulus while the economy was in recession and needed it most. In this respect, tax cuts were demand enhancing in 1982 and 1983, just as in 1964 and 1965. However, the similarity ends there.

Kennedy's advisers recommended tax cuts to stimulate the economy because monetary policy was needed for another goal. In the 1960s the United States was bound by international agreement to maintain a fixed exchange rate between the dollar and foreign currencies. Theoretical work in the early 1960s showed that in a regime of fixed exchange rates only fiscal policy is effective in changing output and employment, because monetary policy must support the external value of the dollar.[12] In 1988 James Tobin and Robert Solow, two architects of the Kennedy policy, explained this as the reason for their heavy emphasis on fiscal policy.[13] The circumstances were the opposite in 1982. The exchange rate was not fixed but market determined. And the same theoretical work in the early 1960s had shown that in a flexible-exchange-rate regime, monetary policy is more effective than fiscal policy in stabilizing output and employment because expansionary fiscal policy partially crowds out net exports. The 1984 *Economic Report of the President*, prepared under the leadership of Martin Feldstein, of Harvard University, who was the chairman of President Reagan's Council of Economic Advisers at the time, concluded that tax cuts in 1981 and 1982 increased consumption, raised real interest rates in the United States, attracted capital inflows from abroad, and crowded out net exports. On net, however, they increased aggregate demand and, thus, contributed to the recovery. (See GlobalWatch 26.1 in Chapter 26.)

INFLATION AND UNEMPLOYMENT: THE PHILLIPS CURVE

The preceding discussion of the historical record employs the *AD–AS* graph, which depicts the price level on the vertical axis and the quantity of real GDP on the horizontal axis. This section uses a graph that depicts the inflation rate, $\Delta P/P$, on the vertical axis

---

[12] Chapter 30 examines the theory behind this result.
[13] See James Tobin and Murray Weidenbaum, ed., *Two Revolutions in Economic Policy: The First Economic Reports of Presidents Kennedy and Reagan*, (Cambridge, Mass.: MIT Press, 1988), 11–13.

FIGURE 28–9
A Phillips Curve

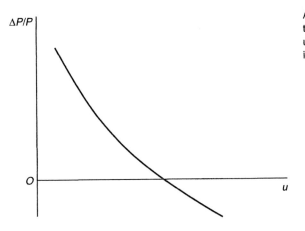

A movement from left to right along
this curve shows that as the level of
unemployment rises, the rate of
inflation falls.

and the unemployment rate, u, on the horizontal axis. The relation between inflation and unemployment is called the **Phillips curve**, in recognition of the work of the British economist A. W. Phillips. The Phillips curve in Figure 28–9 shows an inverse relationship between price inflation and unemployment: The higher the level of unemployment, the lower the rate of inflation.

In 1958 Phillips published an empirical study establishing a negative relation between wage inflation and unemployment. Economists soon noted, however, that the same negative relation exists between price inflation and unemployment. The price of goods and services is equal to marginal cost, which equals the ratio between the money wage and the marginal productivity of labor. In percentage terms, the rate of change in prices equals the rate of change in money wages minus the rate of change in productivity. Usually the growth of productivity is constant over the long run. Thus, subtracting a constant number from money-wage inflation yields price inflation.

If a Phillips curve exists, the implication is clear: To reduce inflation, society must absorb an increase in unemployment and a loss of national product; and to reduce unemployment, society must accept a higher rate of inflation. The choice is not good, but it could be worse. And it turned out to be worse as soon as policymakers began exploiting this relation by attempting to buy a lower level of unemployment with a higher rate of inflation. In the beginning, they were able to reduce unemployment with relatively small increases in the rate of inflation. But as they continued their attempts to reduce unemployment, they found it more difficult. Higher and higher inflation was needed to accomplish the same reduction in unemployment.

**A Simple
Derivation of
the Phillips
Curve**

One of the simplest ways to derive the Phillips curve is from the Lucas aggregate supply relation introduced in Chapter 27 and another relation, called *Okun's Law*. In examining the slope of the Phillips curve, we should not be surprised to see a resurfacing of the same controversies encountered when examining the slope of the aggregate supply curve in Chapter 27. The basic issues are the same.

Equation 28–1 is the Lucas supply relation, according to which output supplied equals the natural rate of output, multiplied by the ratio of the actual price level to the expected price level:

$$Y = Y_n \times (P/P_e) \tag{28-1}$$

The result of rewriting Equation 28–1 in percentage terms is that the rate of growth of output equals the rate of growth of natural, or potential, output plus the actual inflation rate minus the expected inflation rate:

$$(\Delta Y/Y) = (\Delta Y_n/Y_n) + (\Delta P/P) - (\Delta P_e/P_e) \tag{28-2}$$

Solving Equation 28–2 for the actual rate of inflation yields Equation 28–3:

$$(\Delta P/P) = (\Delta P/P)^e + (\Delta Y/Y - \Delta Y_n/Y_n) \tag{28-3}$$

The difference between the rate of growth of actual output and the rate of growth of potential output is the **GDP gap**:

$$\text{GDP gap} = \Delta Y/Y - \Delta Y_n/Y_n$$

Thus, Equation 28–3 says that *the actual rate of inflation equals the expected rate of inflation plus the GDP gap.*

In 1962 Arthur Okun formulated an empirical relation between the GDP gap and the unemployment rate gap, which is the difference between the natural rate of unemployment, u_n, and the actual rate of unemployment. The relation, called *Okun's Law*, can be stated succinctly as an equation:[14]

$$\Delta Y/Y - \Delta Y_n/Y_n = 2.5(u_n - u) \tag{28-4}$$

Okun's Law says that for every percentage point that the actual unemployment rate, u, is above the natural rate, u_n, there is a GDP gap of 2.5 percent, which means that the growth of output is 2.5 percent below its potential rate.

The final step to find the equation of the Phillips curve is to combine the Lucas supply equation and Okun's Law. Substituting Equation 28–4 into Equation 28–3 yields:

$$(\Delta P/P) = (\Delta P/P)^e + 2.5(u_n - u) \tag{28-5}$$

According to Equation 28–5, *actual inflation depends positively on expected inflation and on the difference between the natural and actual rate of unemployment.*

Movements Along a Phillips Curve   Applying Equation 28–5 shows that when expected inflation is held constant and the natural rate of unemployment is given, there is an inverse relation between actual inflation and the unemployment rate. For example, an increase in the actual rate of unemployment reduces the spread between the natural and the actual rate of unemployment, (and increases output) which results in lower inflation:

Other things equal, $u \uparrow \rightarrow (u_n - u) \downarrow \rightarrow \Delta P/P \downarrow$

---

[14] Okun's original work estimated that for every percentage point that actual unemployment is above the natural rate, the growth of output is 3 percentage points below its potential. Recent estimates put the coefficient closer to 2.5.

FIGURE 28–10

Three Points on a
Phillips Curve

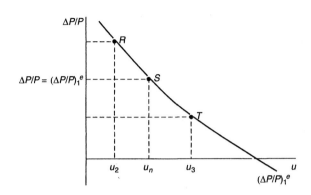

The expected rate of inflation is fixed along the Phillips curve, as indicated by the label of the curve. At point S, the actual rate of inflation equals the expected rate, and unemployment is at the natural rate. At point R, the actual rate of inflation is greater than the expected rate, and unemployment is less than the natural rate. At point T, the actual rate of inflation is less than the expected rate, and unemployment is above the natural rate.

It is important to recognize that the expected rate of inflation is fixed along a downward-sloping Phillips curve (just as the expected price level is given along a Lucas supply curve). For example, the label of the curve in Figure 28–10 indicates that expected inflation equals $(\Delta P/P)^e_1$. Consider three points on this curve. According to Equation 28–5, when actual inflation equals expected inflation, as at point S, actual unemployment equals the natural rate. Unemployment differs from the natural rate only if actual inflation is misperceived, that is, if expected inflation differs from actual inflation. For example, at point R, actual inflation is greater than expected inflation: $(\Delta P/P) > (\Delta P/P)^e_1$. In other words, workers underperceive inflation. Thus, at point R, unemployment will be below the natural rate, because the underperception of inflation fools workers into accepting jobs. On the other hand, if actual inflation is less than expected inflation, workers are fooled into not accepting jobs because they overperceive inflation. Hence, the actual unemployment rate is greater than the natural rate.

Shifts of the Curve   A higher expected rate of inflation shifts the Phillips curve up and to the right, which means that any given level of the unemployment rate can be achieved only at a higher actual rate of inflation. (The reasoning is analogous to the explanation of why the Lucas supply curve shifts up and to the left when the expected price level rises.) The reason is that a higher expected rate of inflation will erode some of the workers' money-wage increases; they will attempt to restore them by demanding higher wages. On the other hand, employers who expect to enjoy higher prices for their products are willing to pay the extra costs.

Figure 28–11 shows that when u equals u_n, an increase in expected inflation, from $(\Delta P/P)^e_1$ to $(\Delta P/P)^e_2$, increases actual inflation from $(\Delta P/P)_1$ to $(\Delta P/P)_2$, as shown by the movement from point S to point S'. Repeating the process for all possible levels of unemployment yields all the points of the Phillips curve designated $(\Delta P/P)^e_2$. It also follows that there is an infinity of Phillips curves, one for each expected rate of inflation. We can visualize a graph filled with many Phillips curves, each with a label to identify its assumed expected rate of inflation. The higher the expected rate of inflation, the further

**FIGURE 28–11
A Shift of the
Phillips Curve**

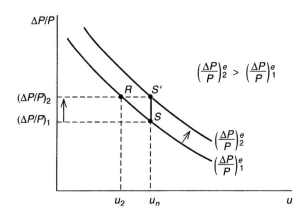

There is a different Phillips curve for each expected rate of inflation. An increase in expected inflation shifts the curve up and to the right.

to the right the corresponding Phillips curve lies. To avoid cluttering the graph, Figure 28–11 shows only two curves.

The existence of many Phillips curves rather than a single curve poses problems for policymakers. How does a policymaker select a curve on which to operate? The apparent answer is that the policymaker should first determine the rate of inflation that the economy expects and then operate on the Phillips curve that bears that label. This procedure, however, turns out to be more complicated; it is applicable only when expectations do not change. But expectations do change, and this is why policymakers face difficulties.

Suppose the economy has operated for some time at point S in Figure 28–11. At this point, the actual rate of inflation equals the expected rate of inflation, and the unemployment rate equals the natural rate, u_n. If the Fed decides to exploit the trade-off indicated by this curve to reduce unemployment, say, to u_2, it must conduct expansionary open market operations.

As long as expectations of inflation by firms and workers do not change, the Fed will achieve its aim of reducing unemployment to u_2. The economy will move along the curve with the label $(\Delta P/P)^e_1$, from point S to point R. As a result, actual inflation will increase to $(\Delta P/P)_2$. When firms and workers learn the correct rate of inflation and revise their expectations accordingly, however, the relevant Phillips curve will shift to the right. In Figure 28–11, the relevant (new) Phillips curve is the one with the label $(\Delta P/P)^e_2$. When the expected rate of inflation becomes equal to the actual rate of inflation, $(\Delta P/P)_2$, the economy will be operating on the new Phillips curve at point S', located directly above point S. The Fed will have created a higher rate of inflation without a lasting reduction in unemployment. Unemployment will have reverted back to its original rate—the natural rate.

**The Vertical
Long-Run
Phillips Curve**

The experiment that Figure 28–11 illustrates suggests the method of deriving the long-run Phillips curve—employing the property that in the long run actual inflation must equal expected inflation: $(\Delta P/P) = (\Delta P/P)^e$. Figure 28–12 depicts seven Phillips curves, one for each of seven assumed levels of expected inflation.

FIGURE 28–12
The Long-Run
Phillips Curve

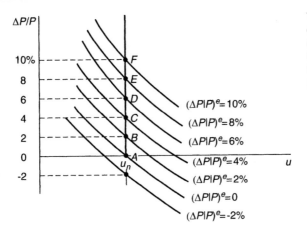

The long-run Phillips curve is the locus of points for which the actual rate of inflation equals the expected rate of inflation. The points lie along a vertical line through the natural rate of unemployment.

When actual inflation equals 0 percent, the economy must operate on the Phillips curve with a label of 0 percent for expected inflation. Thus, when actual inflation is 0 percent, the unemployment rate is the one at point *A*. At this point, actual inflation equals expected inflation; according to Equation 28–5, the actual unemployment rate must equal the natural rate. When actual inflation equals 2 percent, the economy operates on the Phillips curve with a 2 percent expected inflation on its label. Thus, the long-run point is *B*, which lies vertically above point *A*, at the natural rate of unemployment. Repeating the process for inflation rates of 4 percent, 6 percent, 8 percent, 10 percent, and higher, and connecting the points yield the long-run Phillips curve. The curve is vertical, which means that in the long run there is no trade-off between inflation and unemployment.

Policy Implications The architects of the theory of a vertical Phillips curve are Edmund Phelps (1967) and Milton Friedman (1968). The significance of a vertical long-run curve lies in the acceleration of inflation that results when policymakers attempt to peg the actual rate of unemployment below the natural rate. Figure 28–13 illustrates this result.

Consider starting point *B*, with the actual rate of inflation equal to the expected rate of 2 percent, and with the actual rate of unemployment equal to the natural rate. Suppose the Fed wants to lower the unemployment rate to u_2. It can exploit the short-run Phillips curve that passes through the natural rate. The Fed must increase nonborrowed reserves so that the money supply will increase sufficiently to reduce unemployment to u_2, which will raise inflation to 4 percent, at point *L* in Figure 28–12. Unemployment will remain at u_2 as long as market participants do not revise upward their expectations of inflation, say, because they are unaware of the increase in inflation. When they do revise their expectations of inflation to 4 percent, the Phillips curve will shift to the right by the appropriate distance so that unemployment reverts to its natural rate. Now the economy is at point *C*, which is directly above the initial point, *B*. In pursuit of lower unemployment, the Fed must again increase the growth of nonborrowed reserves and the money supply, raising

FIGURE 28–13
Pegging
Unemployment
below the Natural
Rate

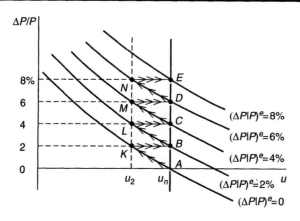

If the central bank attempts to peg the actual rate of unemployment below the natural rate, it will create accelerating inflation. Expansionary monetary policy will temporarily move the economy from right to left along a given Phillips curve, such as from point *B* to point *L*. As a result, inflation will rise. When the higher rate of inflation comes to be expected, the economy will revert to point *C*. In the pursuit of lower unemployment, the process will continue with the economy moving from point *C* to point *M*, and back to point *D*; from point *D* to point *N*, and back to point *E*; and so on.

the rate of inflation, say, to 6 percent. Riding on the Phillips curve with a label of 4 percent expected inflation, the economy will reach point *M*. But, again, when market participants become aware of the new rate of inflation of 6 percent, the Phillips curve will shift to the right, and the economy will revert to point *D*. Repeating the process reveals that inflation will keep rising at an ever-increasing, or at an accelerating, pace to try, in vain, to keep unemployment below its natural rate. For this reason, economists call the natural rate of unemployment the *nonaccelerating inflation rate of unemployment*, or **NAIRU** for short.

Because unemployment gravitates to the natural rate in the long run, Friedman argues that the Fed should not intervene whenever unemployment deviates from this rate. Instead, the Fed should follow a policy of targeting a fixed rate of money growth. By choosing a sufficiently low target for money growth, the Fed will achieve a low rate of inflation, in addition to the natural rate of unemployment.

The exercise in Figure 28–13 examines the consequences of the attempt to peg the unemployment rate below its natural rate. But how can such an attempt be justified? There can be two reasons—one political, the other economic. The political explanation is exemplified by the economic policy of the middle to late 1960s. Recall that President Johnson did not heed the recommendations of his economic advisers to reduce aggregate demand by raising taxes because he was concerned that opposition to the Vietnam War would increase. Another reason is that the natural rate of unemployment itself may rise because of demographic and other structural changes in the labor force. If policymakers are unaware of the change, they may inadvertently inflate the economy by trying to push unemployment below the new natural rate.

A more interesting case arises when the economy is at a point such as *Q* in Figure 28–14, with the actual rate of unemployment *above* the natural rate. (Note that at point *Q* not only is the unemployment rate above its natural rate, but also the actual rate of inflation, at 2 percent, is below the expected rate of inflation of 4 percent, indicated on the label.)

FIGURE 28–14
Unemployment above the Natural Rate

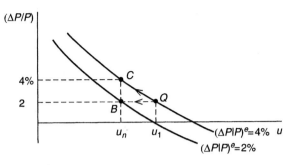

At point Q, the actual rate of inflation (2%) is less than the expected rate (4%), and the actual rate of unemployment is above the natural rate. If expected inflation quickly falls to equal actual inflation, unemployment will quickly revert to the natural rate, and actual inflation will remain at 2 percent, as shown by point B. If the process is slow, policymakers can use expansionary monetary policy to reduce unemployment to the natural rate, but the rate of inflation will also rise, as shown by the movement from point Q to point C. The other alternative is to do nothing and wait for unemployment to revert to the natural rate at point B.

If the economy were at point Q, Keynesians would favor an activist monetary policy to reduce unemployment to its natural rate, u_n. Of course, the rate of inflation would increase to 4 percent. Keynesians would consider the reduction of unemployment, from u_1 to u_n, at the cost of a higher inflation (from 2 percent to 4 percent, in our illustration) a good bargain.

On the other side, new classicists would argue that policymakers should not intervene, because expected inflation will quickly fall from 4 percent to 2 percent. Equally quickly, unemployment will fall to the natural rate. Graphically, the new classical view means that the Phillips curve will shift inward to the one with a label of 2 percent expected inflation, which passes through point B. According to this scenario, the excessive unemployment $(u_1 - u_n)$ will be erased without any increase in inflation, *if policymakers do not intervene*.

In between the two views is the position of Milton Friedman, who argues that it will take time to achieve the lower expected rate of inflation of 2 percent and the lower unemployment rate. According to Friedman, lingering excessive unemployment, above the natural rate, is the price society must pay to reduce inflation.

There are some similarities between the classical (Friedman) and the new classical positions: no intervention by policymakers and achievement of the natural rate of unemployment without an increase in inflation. The difference lies in the speed and the cost of reaching the natural rate: costlessly and quickly according to new classicists; slowly and painfully according to classicists. In contrast, Keynesians are willing to accept a permanently higher (but not accelerating) rate of inflation in order to achieve a faster return to the natural unemployment rate by the use of activist expansionary policy.[15] Because

---

[15] Note that as the economy moves from point Q to point C, inflation rises from 2 percent to 4 percent, but it is still below the expected level of 4 percent. When actual inflation becomes equal to the expected rate of 4 percent, inflation stops rising.

Keynesians are willing to accept more inflation to eliminate excessive unemployment, they are considered soft on inflation. Classicists, on the other hand, are considered soft on unemployment, because they are willing to accept lingering unemployment above the natural rate to erase unwanted inflation.

The 1960s and 1980s Revisited

The Kennedy and early Johnson years can be explained by Figure 28–14, and the late Johnson years by Figure 28–13. In the former period, the economy started at a point similar to Q in Figure 28–14, with unemployment above the natural rate. (This also means that output was below its potential level.) The stated policy was to bring unemployment down to its natural rate, or, in the language of the Kennedy advisers, to increase output to its potential level. The successive reductions in unemployment at the cost of some increase in inflation proceeded smoothly until the mid-1960s. Soon after, with the escalation of the Vietnam war and no increase in taxes, the economy entered the phase of over-full employment as unemployment fell below the natural rate. For the next few years, further reductions in unemployment became smaller and smaller, while inflation was accelerating, as predicted by the Friedman-Phelps analysis underlying Figure 28–13.

Now consider the 1980s. The Reagan years began at a point between C and Q in Figure 28–14, but on a much higher Phillips curve to reflect the higher rate of inflation inherited by the Reagan administration. The stated aim was to reduce inflation without increasing unemployment. Contractionary monetary policy was designed to move the economy in the southwest direction, toward point B, and to do it quickly. Of course, it was not easy. The economy detoured through a point similar to Q and took more than two years to reach its destination.

In sum, the positions of the three schools of thought on the significance of the Phillips curve are the same as their positions on the significance of the aggregate supply curve. All three agree that the short-run Phillips curve is downward sloping but that the long-run Phillips curve is vertical, as they agree that the short-run aggregate supply curve is upward sloping and the long-run aggregate supply is vertical. Keynesians and new Keynesians are willing to exploit the short-run trade-off between inflation and unemployment, if unemployment is above the natural rate. New classicists object to expansionary policies, because they believe that the trade-off will disappear quickly by itself. Classicists are also against expansionary policies, because they believe that the economy will end up with higher inflation.

That these positions are the ones encountered while examining aggregate supply is not surprising, because the issue under examination is the same, under a different guise. Instead of the price *level* and the output *level*, the focus is on the *rate of change* in prices and output (and, by Okun's law, unemployment).

TRY IT OUT 28.1

The accompanying graph shows inflation rates and unemployment rates in the United States from 1961 to 1993. Consider four sets of points on the graph: from 1961 to 1969; from 1976 to 1979; from 1981 to 1983; from 1986 to 1989. Use the theory of short-run

Phillips curves and the economic history examined in this chapter to explain each of these sets of points and the movement from one set to the other.

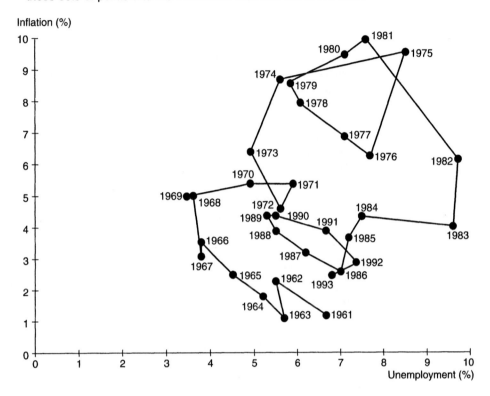

Source: *Economic Report of the President, 1994.*

COSTS OF INFLATION

The costs of unemployment are tangible. If we are out of work involuntarily, we forgo producing goods and services and earning income. Society as a whole suffers because actual output is below potential output. But what are the losses from inflation? The debate among economists about a *trade-off* between inflation and unemployment suggests that inflation also has detrimental effects. To examine the issue, it is necessary to distinguish between costs of unexpected inflation and costs of fully expected inflation and between overall costs and redistributive costs. The overall costs, called the **welfare costs of inflation**, are losses to the economy as a whole. Even when society as a whole does not lose, inflation redistributes wealth among participants. The **redistributive costs of inflation** refer to who gains and who loses from inflation.

Unexpected Inflation

Unexpected inflation is the part of actual inflation that exceeds anticipated inflation. For example, if market participants anticipate a 7 percent rate of inflation when making their decisions, but actual inflation turns out to be 10 percent, unexpected inflation is 3 percent.

The costs of unanticipated inflation are primarily redistributive. Some participants gain and some lose. Borrowers are typically the gainers and lenders the losers from unexpected inflation.

In negotiating long-term loan contracts, lenders and borrowers estimate future inflation. When inflation turns out to be higher than anticipated, lenders will be repaid in cheaper dollars than each side anticipated. Thus, borrowers gain and lenders lose from unanticipated inflation. Lenders are the surplus units. In the United States, the household sector is the major surplus unit, as Chapter 2 discusses. Thus, the household sector as a whole loses from unexpected inflation.

Although the entire household sector is a net loser, there are gainers and losers within the sector. The ones hardest hit by inflation are the very poor and the very rich. The poor are not debtors, because they cannot easily obtain loans. They hold their wealth primarily in money. The rich, especially the elderly rich, do not need to borrow. They hold their wealth, including retirement accounts, primarily in bonds or in bank CDs, which pay fixed nominal returns. On the other hand, the middle and upper middle classes borrow, primarily to buy houses, and they hold their net worth mainly in home equity and durable goods.

There are also redistributive effects of unexpected inflation by age groups. Unexpected inflation redistributes wealth from the elderly to the young. Like the middle and upper middle classes, the young are net debtors and their wealth is primarily invested in durable goods and houses.

The redistributive effects of unexpected inflation are large, which explains the public's dislike of inflation. The public on average is risk averse, which means that individuals fear losses more than they like gains. This risk aversion not only explains the public's vocal objection to inflation, but also induces the public to take measures to protect itself from unexpected inflation. One measure is to devote resources to predict inflation more accurately. This is an overall cost to the economy, not merely a redistributive cost.

There are other welfare costs from unexpected (and high) inflation. An unanticipated change in the price level distorts the relative price of a firm's product. Because relative prices are the signal to firms to allocate resources efficiently, the distortion of relative prices caused by unanticipated inflation imparts a welfare loss to the entire economy. (We saw this misperception effect while examining both the Friedman and the Lucas aggregate supply in Chapter 27.)

Welfare costs caused by wrong signals from relative prices can result even with fully anticipated inflation. The culprit is menu costs, which Chapter 27 discusses. When prices change frequently, firms must frequently change price lists and advertisements for their products. These changes, however, are costly, which induces firms to change their prices less frequently than is necessary to preserve the appropriate relative prices of their products. The result is a misallocation of resources and a welfare loss.

Another overall cost of unexpected inflation, especially *high* unexpected inflation, can be seen by observing countries with high inflation rates. Experience suggests that variable inflation usually accompanies high inflation. Variability causes uncertainty and risk. Uncertainty about inflation hampers decision making by firms, households, and depository institutions that imparts a welfare loss to society.

Fully Expected Inflation

It is easy to see why there are no redistributive effects when inflation is fully anticipated. If everybody expects that prices will be rising by 6 percent, a 6 percent rate of inflation will be built into every contract. For example, lenders will demand it, and borrowers will gladly accept it; workers will demand it, and firms will offer it.

Although there are no redistributive effects from fully anticipated inflation, there are welfare costs. In addition to menu costs, there are costs of more frequent trips to the bank, called *shoe-leather costs*. An increase in expected inflation increases the nominal interest rate, causing the public to hold fewer real money balances. Holding fewer real balances causes inconvenience because money is a medium of exchange. The public can make the same volume of transactions with less money only if it switches from other investments to cash more frequently. Doing so, however, takes time and effort. The cost of more frequent switching from other assets to cash is called the *shoe-leather cost of inflation* because, at least in earlier times, one had to make more frequent trips to the bank, resulting in worn-out shoes more frequently. Effort spent to make frequent trips to the bank is effort not spent in producing goods and services, resulting in a loss of real GDP.

The increase in the interest rate resulting from expected inflation affects only the currency component of money. Deposits pay market-determined rates of return, which increase when interest rates on open-market securities rise. Thus, a rise in fully expected inflation affects only holdings of currency. Therefore, only currency accounts for the shoe-leather cost of inflation.

Research published in 1981 estimates the shoe-leather cost from a fully expected inflation rate of 10 percent in the United States to be 0.3 percent of GDP.[16] In 1993 this would have been $19 billion, in current dollars. The study, however, used data from a period when checkable deposits did not pay explicit interest. Accounting for the payment of deposit rates reduces the estimated loss to 0.25 percent of GDP, or $16 billion in 1993.

Another cost of fully anticipated inflation arises from the tax system. Until the 1980s, the U.S. government levied taxes on nominal income, with no provision for its erosion from inflation. Thus, the same real income was taxed more in the presence of inflation, which increases nominal income. This loss is greater with progressive income taxation, which pushes taxpayers into higher brackets even though their real income has not risen. Reforms of the tax code beginning in 1985 have reduced the burden from each of these features. In addition to reducing the progressivity of the tax system, these reforms require income tax brackets to be adjusted for inflation. The tax code, however, still taxes nominal—not real—returns on assets such as common stock, which distorts the incentives to save.

Our analysis to this point applies to the costs of moderate rates of inflation. The costs change drastically in cases of **hyperinflation**, in which money ceases to perform the functions of a store of value and a medium-of-exchange. One rule of thumb is that hyperinflation exists when a country's annual inflation rate reaches 1,000 percent. At these rates of inflation, the medium of exchange property of money breaks down. In such circumstances, workers are paid daily and rush to buy goods and services in order to

---

[16] Stanley Fischer, "Toward an Understanding of the Cost of Inflation: II," in Karl Brunner and Alan Meltzer. ed., *Carnegie-Rochester Conference Series on Public Policy* 15 (Autumn 1981).

spend their money before it becomes worthless. Many transactions involve barter or the use of foreign currencies.

One major cost of hyperinflation is the loss of output resulting from barter, which wastes time and effort for transactions. Another major cost is the loss of economic efficiency, because prices change so fast that they stop emitting the right signals for the efficient allocation of resources.

An often-cited example of hyperinflation is the German hyperinflation from 1922 to 1923. During that period, prices rose so rapidly that people carried their money in boxes and wheelbarrows and rushed to spend it before it became worthless. Hyperinflations are not a historical curiosity. GlobalWatch 1.2 in Chapter 1 recounts the hyperinflation in Russia following the collapse of communism. Another recent example is the Bolivian hyperinflation of the first half of 1985, when prices were rising at an annual rate in excess of 40,000 percent. As with the German hyperinflation, the welfare costs of the Bolivian hyperinflation were massive.

SUMMARY

- Demand-pull inflation is a continuous rise in the price level brought about by positive shifts in the *AD* curve. Rising prices will materialize as the economy moves toward the new *AD-AS* equilibrium and will stop thereafter, unless there are persistent shocks to the *AD* curve. Demand-pull inflation is accompanied by output above its natural level.

- Cost-push inflation arises from inadvertent supply-side shocks, that is, inward shifts of the *AS* curve. Cost-push inflation appears only during the move toward the new *AD-AS* equilibrium, unless there are continuous adverse supply-side shocks or the Fed validates the inflation by pursuing antirecession policies. Cost-push inflation is accompanied by output below its natural level; hence, the Fed faces a cruel dilemma.

- Demand-pull inflations usually occur during wars because the war effort increases aggregate demand or because politicians often hesitate to ask for the sacrifices inherent in higher taxes or lower expenditures for social programs. World War II and the Vietnam War are classic examples of wartime demand-pull inflation.

- Adverse supply-side shocks beset the U.S. economy in the 1970s. They included oil-price shocks caused by OPEC, rises in money wages after the abolition of wage-price controls, and a slowdown in productivity.

- Demand-side deflations and disinflations arise from deliberate contractionary monetary policies and from inadvertent adverse shocks to the financial and real sectors. The Great Depression combined inadvertent financial-sector shocks, such as the widespread collapse of banks; inadvertent real-sector shocks, such as a drastic fall in consumer and producer confidence; and faulty monetary policy. The recession of 1981–1982 was caused by inadvertent financial-sector shocks and deliberate contractionary (anti-inflationary) monetary policy.

- Two revolutions in economic policy stand out since the end of World War II: the Kennedy and the Reagan revolutions. Similarities between the two include reliance on fiscal policy and on supply-side remedies. The Kennedy advisers saw supply-side policies as long-run policies, while the Reagan advisers saw them as short-run policies, as well as long-run remedies. The two revolutions enabled economists to test several theories and aspects of macroeconomic policy.

- The Phillips curve depicts the graphical relation between inflation and unemployment. In the short run, there is a trade-off between inflation and unemployment, that is, the Phillips curve is downward sloping. In the long run, there is no trade-off; the Phillips curve is vertical.

- Expected inflation links the downward-sloping short-run Phillips curve and the long-run vertical Phillips curve. As a particular rate of inflation becomes expected by the public, the trade-off worsens. It becomes more difficult to reduce unemployment with an increase in inflation, and as time passes it becomes essentially impossible.

- All schools of economic thought agree that the short-run Phillips curve is downward sloping and that the long-run curve is vertical. Disagreement exists about the speed at which the trade-off disappears. Keynesians, new Keynesians, and classicists agree that it takes time. New classicists believe that the trade-off disappears almost immediately, to the point where it cannot be exploited by policymakers. Keynesians and new Keynesians believe that activist policy is possible and desirable. Classicists argue that even though possible, activist policy is not desirable; it merely leads to higher inflation.

- Unanticipated inflation redistributes wealth among participants in the economy. By distorting the signals given by prices, unanticipated inflation also reduces economic efficiency, which is a net loss to society.

- Even with fully anticipated inflation, there are losses of output because of shoe-leather costs and menu costs.

KEY TERMS AND CONCEPTS

demand-pull inflation	automatic stabilizers	NAIRU
cost-push inflation	Phillips curve	welfare costs of inflation
natural rate of unemployment	GDP gap	redistributive costs of inflation
full-employment budget deficit	Okun's Law	hyperinflation

QUESTIONS AND PROBLEMS

1. Explain the difference between demand-pull inflation and cost-push inflation, and give a historical example of each type.

2. "Persistent inflation arises if the central bank uses monetary policy to offset the effect on output of a one-time adverse supply shock." True, false, or uncertain? Explain and illustrate graphically.

The Wall Street Journal

3. Use an *AD-AS* diagram to explain the following quotation from "Regional Fed Bank Official Sees Further Rate Rise," *The Wall Street Journal*, April 20, 1994, A2: "In remarks prepared for delivery to an audience in Santa Barbara, Calif., Robert Parry [president of the Federal Reserve Bank of San Francisco], said: 'Slack in labor and product markets has all but evaporated. This means that we have little or no leeway to give extra stimulus to the economy without sowing the seeds of inflation in the future.'"

4. Why are wars often associated with high inflation?

5. Explain why bank failures during the Great Depression resulted in inward shifts in both the *IS* and *LM* curves. What was the effect on the *AD* curve?

6. Explain why the 1929 stock market crash was followed by an economic depression, while the 1987 stock market crash did not even cause a recession.

7. "The diminished influence of the labor union movement in the 1980s and 1990s has reduced the danger of cost-push inflation." Do you agree or disagree?

8. Explain how the economic advisers to President Clinton used the theory of the term structure of interest rates and the concept of credible deficit reduction to explain the fall in nominal long-term interest rates in 1993. What other factors might have caused interest rates to decline?

9. What factors might have caused nominal long-term interest rates to rise in the first half of 1994?

10. Explain Okun's Law both algebraically and verbally.

11. Explain how to derive the Phillips curve equation from the Lucas supply relation and Okun's Law.

12. "According to the Phillips curve equation, actual inflation varies positively with the growth rate of actual output and the growth rate of potential output." True or false? Explain.

13. "Perhaps actual inflation is high because it *is* expected to be high." Explain why you agree or disagree with the statement and illustrate your explanation graphically.

14. Use a Phillips curve diagram to explain the quotation in Question 2.

15. Distinguish between movements along and shifts of a short-run Phillips curve.

16. Explain the similarities and differences between the long-run aggregate supply and the long-run Phillips curves.

17. Suppose that the Fed tries to keep the unemployment rate permanently below its natural rate.
    a. What monetary policy should the Fed pursue?
    b. What will happen to inflation?

18. Suppose that the annual rate of money growth is 7 percent and that the actual rate of unemployment equals the natural rate. If the central bank announces and achieves a reduction in money growth from 7 percent to 4 percent, what will happen to unemployment according to:

    a. New classical economists?
    b. Traditional classical economists (Friedman)?
    c. Keynesian and new Keynesian economists?

19. Suppose that unemployment is above the natural rate.
    a. How could this happen?
    b. What should the central bank do according to: new classicists; traditional classicists; Keynesians and new Keynesians?

20. "Unlike their grandparents, college students generally benefit from inflation." True, false, or uncertain? Explain.

21. "Deposit rate deregulation has reduced the shoe-leather costs of inflation." True, false, or uncertain? Explain.

SUGGESTED READINGS

Krugman, Paul, *The Age of Diminished Expectations: U.S. Economic Policy in the 1990s* (Cambridge, Mass.: The MIT Press, 1992).

A short, lucid briefing book on the U.S. economy in the 1990s.

Stein, Herbert, *Presidential Economics: The Making of Economic Policy from Roosevelt to Reagan and Beyond*, 2nd ed. (Washington, D.C.: American Enterprise Institute for Public Policy Research, 1988).

An enjoyable book on economic policy and policymakers by an economist who has been analyzing economic policy for more than 50 years and who was chairman of the Council of Economic Advisers in the Nixon administration and an adviser to the Reagan administration.

Tobin, James, and Murray Weidenbaum, eds., *Two Revolutions in Economic Policy: The First Economic Reports of President Kennedy and Reagan* (Cambridge, Mass.: The MIT Press, 1988).

Members of the Council of Economic Advisers in the Kennedy and Reagan administrations use the first economic report of each administration as a vehicle for discussing their economic strategies.

P A R T   8

INTERNATIONAL FINANCE

29   International Payments and the Foreign Exchange Market

30   Economic Policy in an Open Economy

Part 8 extends the discussion of international topics that has been incorporated throughout the book, beginning in Chapter 2, which introduces the foreign sector. The chapters in this part explain the connections between the domestic economy and foreign economies that run through the foreign exchange market. Therefore, they fit into the second pillar of our two-pillar framework.

INTERNATIONAL PAYMENTS AND THE FOREIGN EXCHANGE MARKET

CHAPTER PREVIEW

Every day Americans buy foreign goods, travel to foreign lands, purchase foreign stocks and bonds, and even purchase foreign factories. And foreigners buy American goods and services, and American financial and tangible assets. The record of a country's international transactions is called its **balance of payments accounts**. This chapter begins by looking at the 1993 U.S. accounts. Familiarity with these accounts helps us understand the size and scope of the country's international transactions and the role of the Fed and foreign central banks in settling international accounts.

The chapter brings the balance of payments accounts to life by connecting them to the market for foreign exchange in which participants buy and sell foreign currencies. After explaining the difference between floating and fixed exchange rate systems, it examines the factors that affect the *nominal exchange rate,* which is the dollar price of foreign currencies. These factors fall into four broad categories: domestic and international interest rates; the expected rate of change in the exchange rate; domestic and international income; and domestic and international price levels.

Next, the chapter introduces the concept of the *real exchange rate,* which is a measure of the amount of domestic goods that must be given up to obtain foreign goods. This concept is used to establish two benchmark conditions in international trade and finance, called *purchasing power parity* and *real interest parity.* The chapter connects theory with practice by using real interest rate parity to explain the rise and fall of the international value of the dollar in nominal and real terms in the 1980s.

The chapter concludes by explaining the evolution of the existing international payments system, which is a mix of floating and fixed exchange rates. For example, the United states has floating exchange rates with Germany and France, but Germany and France have semifixed rates with each other. The floating rate system is not pure, however, because central banks sometimes intervene to affect exchange rates. Hence the term *dirty float.*

BALANCE OF PAYMENTS ACCOUNTS

The Bureau of Economic Analysis of the Department of Commerce publishes the U.S. balance of payments accounts in its *Survey of Current Business,* a monthly publication. Table 29–1 shows the accounts for 1993. The table follows the accounting practice of denoting receipts, or surplus items, with a plus sign (+) and payments, or deficit items, with a minus sign (–).

The two major components of the balance of payments accounts are the **current account** and the **capital account**. The current account consists of lines (1) to (12) in Table 29–1. It records receipts from and payments to the rest of the world arising from the export and import of goods and services, from investment income, and from unilateral transfers. The capital account, consisting of lines (13) to (16) and (18) to (20), records payments and receipts from the purchase or sale of assets. Lines (17) and (21) refer to the overall balance of payments, as we shall see.

Anatomy of the Current Account

Lines (1) through (3) deal with trade in goods, called *merchandise trade.* This much-watched balance has recorded deficits since the mid-1970s. For 1993, receipts from exports fell short of payments on imports by $132.6 billion.

Lines (4) to (6) record receipts and payments from the trade of services, such as travel and royalty fees. Typical of the last three decades, the balance of services showed a healthy surplus of $56.9 billion in 1993.

Next, lines (7) to (9) record payments and receipts from *investment income.* Line (7) refers to income paid to U.S. nationals from foreign assets, such as an American-owned factory in Germany, stocks issued in Japan, or bonds issued in Australia. Because of large investments abroad and relatively small foreign investments in the United States prior to the 1980s, this account has been consistently in surplus. This surplus is becoming smaller, however, mainly because the United States became a net debtor nation in the mid-1980s, as Chapter 2 explains. In 1993, the surplus from investment income was $3.9 billion.

Adding the balance on merchandise trade (line 3), the balance on services (line 6), and the balance on investment income (line 9) gives the *balance on goods, services, and income,* recorded in line (10). Finally, adding net unilateral transfers, such as U.S. government grants to other countries, pensions, and other transfers to U.S. citizens retiring abroad yields the current account balance of –$103.9 billion. The minus sign means payments exceeded receipts: the United States had a current account deficit in 1993. By comparison, the United States ran current account surpluses in most years prior to 1976.

TABLE 29–1
U.S. Balance of Payments Accounts: *1993 (Billions of Dollars)*

	Payments, Receipts	Balance
Current account		
(1) Merchandise Exports	+456.8	
(2) Merchandise Imports	−589.4	
(3) Balance on Merchandise Trade		−132.6
(4) Services Sold	+184.8	
(5) Services Bought	−128.0	
(6) Balance on Services		+56.9
(7) Income Received on U.S. Assets Abroad	+113.9	
(8) Income Paid on Foreign Assets in United States	−109.9	
(9) Balance on Investment Income		+3.9
(10) Balance on Goods, Services, and Income (3) + (6) + (9)		−71.8
(11) Net Unilateral Transfers		−32.1
(12) Balance on Current Account (10) + (11)		**−103.9**
Capital account		
(13) Private Capital Inflow	+159.0	
(14) Private Capital Outflow	−146.2	
(15) Statistical Discrepancy	+21.1	
(16) Net Private Capital Flows (13) + (14) + (15)		**+33.9**
(17) Balance of Payments (12) + (16)		**−70.0**
(18) Net Official Capital Inflow	+71.4	
(19) Change in U.S. Reserve Assets, Net	−1.4	
(20) Official Settlements Balance (18) + (19)		**+70.0**
(21) Final Balance (17) + (20)		**0.0**

Memo: Plus sign (+) denotes receipts (surplus item); minus sign (−) denotes payments (deficit item).
Source: Adapted from *Survey of Current Business*, April 1994, 67.

Since then, the account has been in deficit every year except 1980 and 1981, when there were small surpluses, as Figure 2–4 in Chapter 2 shows.

Anatomy of the Capital Account

Now consider the capital account, which records the international purchases and sales of assets. This account consists of both private and official capital flows. When Americans sell assets to the rest of the world, funds flow into the United States. Hence the term **capital inflows**. On the other hand, **capital outflows** refers to the purchase of foreign assets by Americans, in which cash funds flow out of the United States.[1]

---

[1] Capital inflows and capital outflows are marked in the table as *changes* in assets. The amount of an asset is a *stock* concept, while the change in an asset is a *flow*.

Private capital inflows recorded in line (13) include the purchase by foreign individuals and businesses of U.S. Treasury securities, business sector securities (debt or stock), bank deposits, and direct foreign investment in the United States. The balance of payments accounts consider as direct foreign investment the creation of a new business, such as the construction of a new Honda factory in the United States, and the acquisition of the controlling interest in an existing business. The purchase of property by foreigners is also direct investment. Line (14) records the capital outflows, which are purchases by the U.S. private sector of foreign financial and tangible assets.

Adding lines (13) and (14), we calculate the reported net private capital inflows. The sum of these two components is +$12.8 billion. The usual assumption is that the unreported items captured by the statistical discrepancy in line (15) are all private capital account items. In reality, some of the errors and omissions can be attributed to components of the current account, such as unrecorded remittances or even unrecorded exports and imports. Line (16) records net private capital flows, including the statistical discrepancy of $21.1 billion. The +$33.9 billion means that receipts exceeded payments by that amount. In other words, there was a surplus in the private capital accounts.

The sum of the current account (line 12) and net private capital flows (line 16) is the balance of payments (line 17).[2] In 1993, the United States ran a balance of payments deficit of $70 billion: −103.9 + 33.9 = −70.

Lines (18) and (19) show how the United States financed its deficit. Line (18) indicates that foreign governments poured into the United States a net amount of $71.4 billion, primarily by purchasing U.S. Treasury securities. This official net capital inflow exceeded the $70 billion deficit in the Balance of Payments by $1.4 billion. Therefore, to settle the U.S. balance of payments deficit, the Fed did not have to run down its inventory of **international reserve assets**, which consists of foreign currencies, foreign government securities, and other assets that central banks use to settle international accounts. Instead, the Fed added $1.4 billion to its inventory of reserve assets, as shown in line (19). The minus sign in front of the $1.4 billion in line (19) follows the accounting practice of recording the acquisition of foreign assets with a minus sign. The official settlements balance in line (20) is the sum of the net capital inflows and the change in reserve assets. Finally, adding the official settlements balance of +$70 billion in line (20) to the −$70 billion balance of payments deficit yields a final balance of zero. The balance of payments balances.

What do the 1993 accounts illustrate? That a U.S. balance of payments deficit may be financed by selling U.S. Treasury securities to foreign governments (central banks). Of course, if the United States has a balance of payments deficit, foreign countries, as a group, have a balance of payments surplus, which means their international receipts exceed their international payments. When the central banks of these surplus countries buy Treasury securities, they acquire dollar-denominated assets, which become part of their inventory of international reserve assets.

---

[2] To focus attention on the individual components of the accounts, in 1976 the U.S. Treasury stopped publishing a number that signifies the overall balance of payments position of the United States. The sum of the balance on current account (line 12) and net private capital flows (line 16) is what economists outside government usually consider the balance of payments.

The following is a summary of the lesson about deficits and surpluses from the balance of payments accounts:

· To finance a balance of payments deficit, the central bank of the deficit country must run down its inventory of international reserve assets or the central bank of the surplus country must buy foreign securities. The latter action increases the international reserve assets of the surplus country.

· To absorb a balance of payments surplus, the central bank of the surplus country must increase its inventory of reserve assets or the central bank of the deficit country must sell foreign currencies. The latter action depletes the international reserve assets of the deficit country.

In general, then, deficit countries lose international reserve assets and surplus countries gain them.

THE FOREIGN EXCHANGE MARKET

So far this chapter has examined the particulars of the balance of payments accounts and highlighted important characteristics. Before connecting the accounts with the foreign exchange market, we explain the mechanics of exchange rates.

The Mechanics of Exchange Rates

Chapter 10 introduces the nominal exchange rate, *e,* which we called simply the exchange rate. The **nominal exchange rate** is the dollar price of foreign currency. Therefore, $1/e$, the inverse of the exchange rate, is the international price of the dollar. There is a different bilateral nominal exchange rate for each foreign currency. Market Watch 29.1 explains how to track these bilateral exchange rates in *The Wall Street Journal.*

To understand the mechanics of exchange rates, consider the United States the home country and Great Britain as the foreign country. Thus, the exchange rate, *e,* denotes dollars per British pound. Of course, the inverse of *e* is the international value of the dollar, measured as British pounds per dollar.

$$e = \text{Dollars/pound} \tag{29–1}$$
$$1/e = \text{Pounds/dollar}$$

An increase in *e* means the amount of dollars paid to buy a British pound increases. The pound becomes more expensive, or appreciates. Of course, the dollar falls in value because the pounds received from selling a dollar falls. In other words, the dollar depreciates. In general, **appreciation** of a currency means its international value rises, and **depreciation** of a currency means its international value falls.[3]

The exchange rate can be used to translate prices from dollars ($) to pounds (£), and vice versa. Multiplying the pound price of foreign goods, P_f, by the exchange rate, *e,* gives the dollar price of British goods. Similarly, multiplying the dollar price of Ameri-

---

[3] The terms *appreciation* and *depreciation* refer to a flexible exchange rate system, in which exchange rates change in response to supply and demand in the foreign exchange markets. The terms *revaluation* and *devaluation* are used when the government of the country changes the exchange rate of its currency.

Market*Watch* 29.1

Tracking Exchange Rates in *The Wall Street Journal*

A table of exchange rates appears every day in section C of *The Wall Street Journal*. Let's see how we can track exchange rates by looking at an excerpt from the table that appeared in the July 14, 1994, issue.

We'll use the French franc (FF) as our illustration. The first row of quotes for the franc gives prices in the *spot market,* which is the market for immediate delivery of the franc. The first column shows that on Wednesday, July 13, the spot exchange rate of the French franc was .18966. This means it took almost 19 cents to buy one franc: $e = \$.18966/FF1$. The third column gives the same day's price of the dollar, which is the inverse of e: $1/e = FF5.2725/\$1$. In other words, the price of a dollar was about 5.3 francs.

The next three rows of numbers for the franc are quotes in the *forward market,* which is the market for delivery of foreign currency at a future specified date. For example, on Wednesday, July 13, the exchange rate for francs to be delivered in 180 days was $\$.18913/FF1$. Thus, the 180-day forward rate was about 5/100ths of one cent lower than the spot rate on July 13. This must mean that the 180-day forward exchange rate of the dollar was higher than the spot rate. Check the third column to verify this relationship.

EXCHANGE RATES

Wednesday, July 13, 1994

The New York foreign exchange selling rates below apply to trading among banks in amounts of $1 million and more, as quoted at 3 p.m. Eastern time by Bankers Trust Co., Dow Jones Telerate Inc. and other sources. Retail transactions provide fewer units of foreign currency per dollar.

Country	U.S. $ equiv. Wed.	Tues.	Currency per U.S. $ Wed.	Tues.
Argentina (Peso)	1.01	1.01	.99	.99
Australia (Dollar)	.7383	.7365	1.3545	1.3578
Austria (Schilling)	.09237	.09303	10.83	10.75
Bahrain (Dinar)	2.6522	2.6522	.3771	.3771
Belgium (Franc)	.03156	.03175	31.69	31.50
Brazil (Real)	1.0989011	1.0905125	.91	.92
Britain (Pound)	1.5665	1.5700	.6384	.6369
30-Day Forward	1.5659	1.5694	.6386	.6372
90-Day Forward	1.5655	1.5690	.6388	.6373
180-Day Forward	1.5653	1.5688	.6389	.6374
Canada (Dollar)	.7245	.7223	1.3803	1.3845
30-Day Forward	.7236	.7214	1.3820	1.3862
90-Day Forward	.7216	.7194	1.3858	1.3900
180-Day Forward	.7177	.7155	1.3934	1.3976
Czech. Rep. (Koruna)				
Commercial rate	.0360244	.0361246	27.7590	27.6820
Chile (Peso)	.002430	.002430	411.56	411.56
China (Renminbi)	.115221	.115221	8.6790	8.6790
Colombia (Peso)	.001217	.001217	821.90	821.90
Denmark (Krone)	.1657	.1664	6.0355	6.0081
Ecuador (Sucre)				
Floating rate	.000462	.000462	2164.03	2164.03
Finland (Markka)	.19652	.19787	5.0886	5.0539
France (Franc)	.18966	.19066	5.2725	5.2450
30-Day Forward	.18947	.19046	5.2780	5.2505
90-Day Forward	.18926	.19025	5.2837	5.2562
180-Day Forward	.18913	.19011	5.2875	5.2600
Germany (Mark)	.6500	.6545	1.5385	1.5280
30-Day Forward	.6483	.6527	1.5425	1.5320
90-Day Forward	.6501	.6546	1.5382	1.5277
180-Day Forward	.6514	.6559	1.5351	1.5246
Greece (Drachma)	.004301	.004331	232.50	230.90
Hong Kong (Dollar)	.12943	.12943	7.7260	7.7260
Hungary (Forint)	.0100715	.0100857	99.2900	99.1500
India (Rupee)	.03212	.03212	31.13	31.13
Indonesia (Rupiah)	.0004610	.0004610	2169.01	2169.01
Ireland (Punt)	1.5502	1.5527	.6451	.6440

can goods, P, by the pound price of the dollar, $1/e$, yields the pound price of American goods. In symbols, we have:

$$
\left.
\begin{aligned}
eP_f &= (\$/\pounds) \times (\pounds/\text{British goods}) \\
&= \$ \text{ price of British goods} \\
(1/e)P &= (\pounds/\$) \times (\$/\text{American goods}) \\
&= \pounds \text{ price of American goods}
\end{aligned}
\right\}
\tag{29--2}
$$

When e rises, other things equal, the dollar price of British goods rises. Trips to Britain, British woolens, and British cars become more expensive for Americans in dollars. Of course, an increase in e means that $1/e$ falls, so that the pound price of American goods falls. For the British, American goods get cheaper.

TRY IT OUT 29.1

1. Suppose that it costs $1.60 to buy one British pound; £100,000 to buy a Rolls Royce; and $40,000 to buy a Cadillac. Find the dollar price of a Rolls Royce and the pound price of a Cadillac.

2. Suppose the dollar price of a pound falls from $1.60 per pound to $1.50 per pound, other things equal. Find the new dollar price of a Rolls Royce and the new pound price of a Cadillac.

To gain a broader picture of the exchange rate, the government constructs a multilateral exchange rate, called the **effective exchange rate**, which is a trade-weighted index of the bilateral exchange rates of several currencies. Figure 29–1 depicts the history of an index of the exchange value of the dollar, $1/e$, constructed from the currencies of nine major industrial countries. The graph shows a stunning rise and fall in the value of the dollar in the 1980s. After examining the factors that affect exchange rates, we shall connect theory with practice to explain why the curve in Figure 29–1 looks like a mountain.

The Demand for Foreign Exchange

To determine the exchange rate in the market for foreign exchange, it is necessary to determine the demand for and the supply of foreign exchange. The private demand for foreign exchange comes from two sources:

· The first is imports of goods and services, Q, which correspond to the sum of items (2), (5), (8), and (11) in Table 29–1.

FIGURE 29–1
Nominal Exchange Value of the Dollar

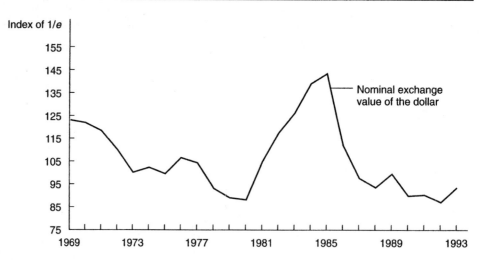

The nominal exchange value of the dollar is a trade-weighted index of the foreign exchange price of the dollar, $1/e$.

Source: *Economic Report of the President, 1994,* Table B-110.

FIGURE 29-2
The Demand for
Foreign Exchange

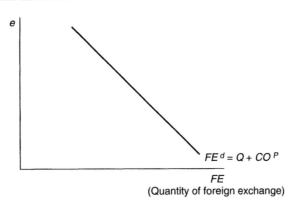

The demand for foreign exchange comes from the demand for imports and from private capital outflows. The demand curve is downward sloping because the quantity of imports demanded varies inversely with the exchange rate. Private capital outflows affect the position of the demand curve but not its slope because they are independent of the current level of the exchange rate.

· The second source is purchases of foreign assets by U.S. citizens; these private capital outflows, denoted by CO^P, correspond to item (14) in Table 29–1.

Because there are no official capital flows in a pure system of flexible exchange rates, we ignore them temporarily. Therefore, total demand for foreign exchange, denoted by FE^d, equals the private demand:

$$FE^d = Q + CO^P \qquad\qquad (29\text{--}3)$$

The downward-sloping demand curve in Figure 29–2 illustrates the inverse relationship between the quantity of foreign exchange demanded and the foreign exchange rate. The curve is downward sloping because the demand for imports varies inversely with the exchange rate. The reason is that, other things equal, a fall in the dollar price of a pound, e, reduces the dollar price of British goods, thereby inducing Americans to buy more British goods. Thus, a fall in the exchange rate increases the quantity of imports demanded and, hence, the quantity of foreign exchange demanded. We can represent this relation schematically as follows:

$$e\downarrow \ \rightarrow eP_f\downarrow \text{ (i.e., the dollar price of foreign goods falls)} \rightarrow Q\uparrow \rightarrow FE^d\uparrow$$

Private capital outflows affect the position but not the slope of the demand curve, because they do not depend on the current level of the exchange rate.[4]

The Supply of Foreign Exchange

The private supply of foreign exchange is also the sum of two components:

· The first is receipts from exports, X, which corresponds to the sum of lines (1), (4), and (7) in Table 29–1.

· The second is receipts from private sales of U.S. assets to foreigners, which are private capital inflows, CI^P (line 13).

---

[4] We shall see that private capital flows depend on the expected rate of change in the exchange rate.

FIGURE 29–3
The Supply of
Foreign Exchange

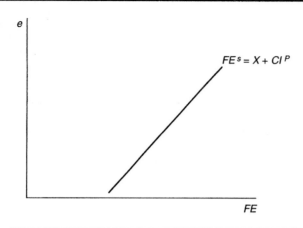

The supply of foreign exchange comes from exports and from private capital inflows. The supply curve is upward sloping because the quantity of exports demanded varies positively with the exchange rate. The quantity of private capital inflows affects the position but not the slope of the curve.

Consistent with the treatment of the demand side, this analysis temporarily ignores official capital inflows, which would be zero in a pure system of flexible exchange rates. Therefore, the total supply of foreign exchange, denoted by FE^s, equals the private supply:

$$FE^s = X + CI^P \tag{29–4}$$

In our example, exports are American goods demanded by the British. In making decisions whether to buy American goods, the British care about the price of those goods in pounds, which equals $(1/e)P$. An increase in e means the international value of the dollar, $1/e$, falls. As a result, the pound price of American goods falls, which induces the British to buy more American goods. Hence, the quantity of exports demanded rises, which means the quantity of foreign exchange supplied rises. Schematically:

$$e \uparrow \rightarrow (1/e) \downarrow \rightarrow (1/e)P \downarrow \text{ (i.e., the pound price of American goods falls)} \rightarrow X \uparrow \rightarrow FE^s \uparrow$$

The upward-sloping curve in Figure 29–3 illustrates the positive relationship between the exchange rate and the quantity of exports demanded. The quantity of private capital flows affects the position but not the slope of the supply curve.

Flexible Exchange Rates

In a **flexible exchange rate system**, also called a **floating exchange rate system**, supply and demand determine the exchange rate. In Figure 29–4, the equilibrium value of the exchange rate is e_1. At this value of e, demand for foreign exchange equals supply. If the exchange rate is lower, say, at e_2, demand is greater than supply because the lower exchange rate increases the quantity demanded of foreign exchange and reduces the quantity supplied. According to the principle of excess demand, the exchange rate rises. If the exchange rate is higher, say, at e_3, the excess supply brings it down.

Shifts of the demand curve or the supply curve change the equilibrium level of the exchange rate. An increase in demand, depicted by a rightward shift of the demand curve

FIGURE 29–4
The Foreign
Exchange Market:
*The Principle of
Excess Demand and
Excess Supply*

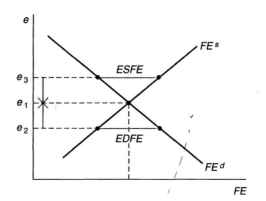

At the exchange rate e_3, $FE^d < FE^s$
$\rightarrow ESFE \rightarrow e \downarrow$

At the exchange rate e_1, $FE^d = FE^s$
$\rightarrow$ the market is in equilibrium

At the exchange rate e_2, $FE^d > FE^s$
$\rightarrow EDFE \rightarrow e \uparrow$

FIGURE 29–5
The Effect of
Increases in
Demand and
Supply on the
Exchange Rate

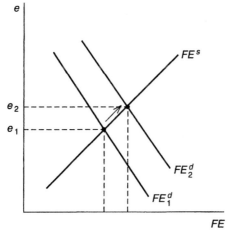 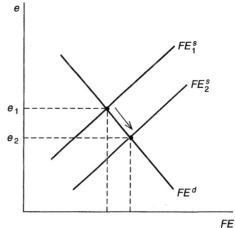

The left panel shows that an increase in demand, depicted by a rightward shift of the demand curve, causes the exchange rate to rise. The right panel shows that an increase in supply, depicted by a rightward shift of the supply curve, causes the exchange rate to fall.

in the left panel of Figure 29–5, increases the exchange rate. The demand curve will shift to the right if a change in some factor other than the exchange rate, such as a rise in domestic income, causes imports to rise. It will also shift to the right if private capital outflows rise.

On the other hand, an increase in the supply of foreign exchange, depicted by a rightward shift of the supply curve in the right panel, reduces the exchange rate. The supply curve will shift to the right if a change in some factor other than the exchange rate, such as a rise in foreign income, causes exports to rise. It will also shift to the right if private capital inflows rise.

Fixed Exchange Rates

In a system of pure floating exchange rates, any potential excess demand disappears by an appropriate rise of the exchange rate, and any potential excess supply by a fall in the exchange rate. Thus, there are no official capital flows or changes in reserve assets to equilibrate the foreign exchange market. A **fixed exchange rate system** is the polar opposite. When governments agree to peg the exchange rate and, hence, the international value of the dollar, the market for foreign exchange will usually register either excess demand or excess supply. Only by coincidence will the exchange rate be at the level that corresponds to market clearance. Moreover, because the underlying determinants of demand and supply—such as interest rates, incomes, and prices—continuously change, the market-clearing level of the exchange rate will also change. If international agreements peg the exchange rate, the price of foreign exchange cannot adjust to clear the market. As with any system of price controls, the quantity must adjust. In this case, the central banks are the "adjustors."

When the fixed level of the exchange rate is below its market-clearing level, the market registers excess demand for foreign exchange. For example, at the exchange rate $\bar{e}$ in Figure 29–6, there is excess demand equal to the distance CD. Excess demand means that American payments for imports and private capital outflows exceed receipts from exports and private capital inflows. In other words, there is a deficit in the U.S. balance of payments.

Because the international value of the dollar is the inverse of the foreign exchange rate, an undervalued foreign exchange rate means an overvalued dollar. In the international market for dollars, there will be excess supply of dollars, which means that foreign countries are surplus countries. Their receipts from selling goods and selling assets to the United States exceed their payments for buying goods and buying assets from the United States.

Without some action by the Fed or foreign central banks, market forces will push up the exchange rate and, therefore, push down the value of the dollar. Suppose that to keep the exchange rate at $\bar{e}$, the Fed sells foreign currencies or foreign securities from its inventory of international reserve assets. This action by the Fed increases the supply of

FIGURE 29–6
A Balance of Payments Deficit

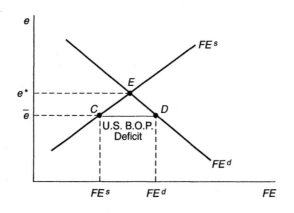

If the government fixes the exchange rate at $\bar{e}$, there will be excess demand for foreign exchange equal to the distance CD, and an equal deficit in the U.S. balance of payments.

foreign exchange. The FE^s curve in Figure 29–6 will shift to the right to intersect the demand curve at point D.

The Fed's foreign exchange market operation will also affect the U.S. money supply. The Fed's inventory of foreign assets is a technical factor affecting reserves in the U.S. banking system, as Chapters 8 and 14 discuss. A sale of foreign securities by the Fed reduces reserves in the U.S. banking system and, thus, reduces the U.S. money supply.[5]

Suppose, instead, that the central bank of the foreign country does the adjusting. In this case, the foreign central bank will buy U.S. Treasury securities in the open market. This official capital inflow into the United States increases the supply of foreign exchange. Again, the supply curve of foreign exchange in Figure 29–6 shifts to the right, to keep the exchange rate fixed at e. The purchase of U.S. Treasury securities by foreign central banks has implications for the foreign money supply. By acquiring more dollar-denominated assets, foreign central banks inject reserves into their banking systems. As a result, the foreign money supply rises.

In principle, either the central bank of the deficit country can reduce its money supply to keep the exchange rate fixed or the central bank of the surplus country can increase its money supply. In practice, during the fixed exchange rate regime that prevailed from 1944 to 1971, foreign central banks usually undertook the interventions. However, in 1971 the United States abandoned the fixed exchange rate system rather than pursue contractionary monetary policy, as the last section explains.

A Hybrid System

In a pure system of flexible, or floating, exchange rates, there are no changes in the international reserve assets of central banks because movements in exchange rates eliminate any excess demand or excess supply. A **managed, or dirty, float** combines adjustments in price with adjustments in quantity. Exchange rates fluctuate, but not by as much as when there are no official settlements. This describes the arrangement between the United States and the rest of the world since the 1970s.

With a managed float, central banks sometimes intervene in the foreign exchange market by buying or selling foreign exchange. In some cases, the intervention is temporary, to counter disorderly conditions in the foreign exchange market. The goal of intervention in these cases is to smooth short-term fluctuations of the exchange rate. In other cases, the intervention is undertaken as a means of influencing the exchange rate for longer periods, or even to affect the relative prices of imported and exported goods.

Intervention by a central bank in the foreign exchange market may be either a sterilized or a nonsterilized operation. With a **nonsterilized intervention**, reserves in the banking system and the money supply change. With a **sterilized intervention**, the central bank undertakes an offsetting domestic open market operation, called a *defensive open market operation,* to counter any effect on reserves and the money supply.

To illustrate the two types of intervention, assume that there is excess demand for foreign exchange and that the Fed wants to prevent a rise in the exchange rate and, hence, a fall in the dollar. To keep the exchange rate from rising, the Federal Reserve Bank of

---

[5] Foreign exchange market operations are conceptually similar to domestic open market operations: Sales of securities reduce reserves in the banking system and purchases increase reserves.

Market*Watch* 29.2

An Ineffective Intervention in 1994

Describing a foreign exchange market intervention that took place in June 1994, Thomas Friedman, a reporter for *The New York Times,* wrote: "The global currency markets trade about $1 trillion worth of dollars each day. When the world's 17 largest central banks, led by the Federal Reserve, intervened last month to try to prop up the dollar, they dug deep into their pockets and came up with about $5 billion and change, which they threw into the market in an effort to bid up the value of the American currency. No wonder they had little effect on the dollar. The central banks were like a zoo keeper

trying to calm a starved gorilla by offering it a raisin for lunch."*

To be effective, the raisin must be accompanied by a main dish, such as a change in monetary policy that alters the economic fundamentals. The Fed could have pushed up interest rates in July 1994 to halt the flight from the dollar, but it didn't. The reason is that the Fed had already pushed up interest rates four times in 1994 to keep the U.S. economy from overheating. Because of the lagged effect of interest rates on the economy, the Fed was waiting to see by how much U.S. economic activity would slow. From the U.S. perspective, the intervention of 1994 was a small, ineffective, sterilized operation.

---

* Thomas Friedman, "When Money Talks, Governments Listen," *The New York Times,* July 24, 1994. E3.

New York must sell foreign exchange in the open market. A sale of foreign exchange reduces reserves in the banking system. If this is the extent of the Fed's involvement, the intervention is not sterilized. As a result, the money supply falls and interest rates rise. With a sterilized intervention, the Fed would combine a sale of foreign exchange with an offsetting open market purchase of U.S. Treasury securities of equal value. Thus, there is no change in reserves, no change in the money supply, and, hence, no change in interest rates. Sterilized interventions, however, are less effective than nonsterilized interventions. With sterilized interventions, there are no changes in the economic fundamentals, such as interest rates. MarketWatch 29.2 examines a coordinated intervention by several central banks in June 1994.

FACTORS AFFECTING EXCHANGE RATES

Having examined how the foreign exchange market reacts to shifts of the demand and supply curves under alternative systems, now consider four types of factors that cause the curves to shift. In a system of flexible exchange rates, these factors induce changes in the exchange rate. The four factors are interest rates, the expected rate of change in the foreign exchange rate, incomes, and price levels.

Foreign and Domestic Interest Rates

Interest rates affect capital inflows and outflows. These capital flows result from changes in asset demand. Chapter 6 explains that the demand for an asset depends positively on its own rate of return and negatively on the rates of return on competing assets. Alternatively, the higher the rate of return on an asset relative to the return on competing assets, the higher its demand.

These laws of demand also apply to the decision about whether to hold foreign or domestic assets. The basic principle is the same: Other things equal, the higher the level

FIGURE 29–7
An Increase in
U.S. Interest Rates

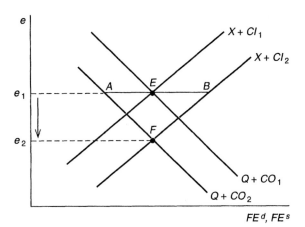

Point E denotes the initial equilibrium. Other things equal, an increase in the U.S. interest rate increases the spread between U.S. and foreign interest rates. The demand curve shifts to the left and the supply curve to the right because capital outflows fall and capital inflows rise. As a result, at the original equilibrium exchange rate, e_1, there is excess supply of foreign exchange equal to AB, and the equilibrium value of the exchange rate falls to e_2.

of interest rates in the United States, the greater the amount of funds that flow into the United States, and the smaller the amount of funds that flow out. In other words, a rise in U.S. interest rates increases capital inflows and reduces capital outflows. On the other hand, a rise in interest rates in the rest of the world reduces capital inflows and increases capital outflows.

Using relative rates, we can say that capital flows depend on the spread between U.S. interest rates and foreign interest rates: The higher this difference, the greater the amount of capital inflows and the smaller the amount of capital outflows. Thus, the spread ($i_{US} - i_f$) is a major determinant of supply and demand in the foreign exchange market.

An increase in the spread between domestic and foreign interest rates increases the supply of foreign exchange, as foreigners move more capital into the United States. At the same time, the demand for foreign exchange falls, as Americans reduce their holdings of foreign securities. Thus, an increase in the spread between the domestic and foreign interest rates shifts the demand curve for foreign exchange inward and the supply curve outward, creating excess supply of foreign exchange. As a result, the exchange rate falls:

$$(i_{US} - i_f)\uparrow \rightarrow CO\downarrow \rightarrow FE^d\downarrow \text{ and } CI\uparrow \rightarrow FE^s\uparrow \rightarrow ESFE \rightarrow e\downarrow$$

Figure 29–7 depicts this case graphically. In a system of flexible exchange rates, the graph shows that the exchange rate falls from e_1 to e_2. Looked at from the other side, an increase in U.S. interest rates relative to foreign interest rates increases the international value of the dollar.

Expectations
of Currency
Appreciation
or Depreciation

For an investor to be persuaded to buy American securities, it is not sufficient to know that the difference between the nominal interest rate in the United States and Japan is +3 percent, say, because the nominal interest rate is 9 percent in the United States and 6 percent in Japan. The spread between the U.S. interest rate and the foreign interest rate must be adjusted for anticipated changes in the exchange rate. Why?

An American investor in a Japanese security yielding 6 percent must convert the yen to dollars. If the yen appreciates by 4 percent, the dollar return from investing in Japan will be 6 percent plus 4 percent, for a total of 10 percent. Thus, the true spread between the return on American and Japanese securities is *minus* 1 percent, (9 percent − 10 percent), instead of the +3 percent that was calculated based on ignoring the expected appreciation of the yen.

The general formula for the difference between U.S. and foreign interest rates is easy to establish. To find the expected foreign rate of return, add the expected percentage change in the exchange rate, $(\Delta e/e)^{exp}$, to the foreign interest rate, i_f to get the risk-adjusted foreign rate: $i_f + (\Delta e/e)^{exp}$. This entire term must be subtracted from the American interest rate, i_{US}, to find the expected spread:

$$\text{Spread} = i_{US} - [i_f + (\Delta e/e)^{exp}]$$
$$= i_{US} - i_f - (\Delta e/e)^{exp}$$

(29–5)

Capital inflows vary positively with the spread and capital outflows vary inversely with the spread. Suppose that the spread falls because, other things equal, investors increase their expectations of the rate of change in the exchange rate, say, from $(\Delta e/e)^{exp}_1$ to $(\Delta e/e)^{exp}_2$. The lower spread encourages capital outflows, which increases the demand for foreign exchange. On the other hand, the supply of foreign exchange falls because the lower spread reduces capital inflows. As a result, there is excess demand for foreign exchange and the exchange rate rises:

$$(\Delta e/e)^{exp}\uparrow \rightarrow [i_{US} - i_f - (\Delta e/e)^{exp}]\downarrow \rightarrow CO\uparrow \rightarrow FE^d\uparrow \rightarrow \text{and } CI\downarrow \rightarrow FE^s\downarrow \rightarrow EDFE \rightarrow e\uparrow$$

Hence, an increase in the expected rate of change in the exchange rate causes the current level of the exchange rate to rise. This is also evident from the perspective of the dollar. An increase in the expected rate of appreciation of foreign currencies means an increase in the expected rate of dollar depreciation. This change in expectations causes a flight away from the dollar and into foreign currencies. For example, in the spring and summer of 1994, market participants may have been fleeing from the dollar because they expected that foreign currencies, especially the yen, would have to rise more against the dollar to reduce Japan's trade surplus with the United States.

Such a flight from or to a currency because of expectations can cause upheaval in foreign exchange markets. The Fed refers to such changes as *disorderly conditions*. Because of such disorderly conditions, the Fed, in cooperation with central banks of major industrial countries, intervened in support of the dollar in the summer of 1994. As Market*Watch* 29.2 explains, that intervention was not successful.

Interest Rate Parity

The case in which the risk-adjusted interest rate spread is zero is an important benchmark in international finance. A zero spread means that the domestic interest rate equals the foreign interest rate plus the expected rate of change in the foreign exchange rate.:

$$i_{US} = i_f + (\Delta e/e)^{exp}$$

(29–6)

This equality is called **interest rate parity**. Parity is brought about by arbitrageurs whose specialty is to exploit any profit opportunity that arises from a positive or a negative spread. In the contemporary financial environment, capital moves quickly across national boundaries. For example, if the risk-adjusted foreign interest rate is lower than the domestic interest rate, arbitrageurs move funds into the United States. The increased demand for U.S. securities lowers the domestic interest rate until it equals the risk-adjusted foreign interest rate. On the other hand, if the domestic interest rate is below the adjusted foreign rate, arbitrageurs reduce their demand for U.S. securities and invest the funds in foreign securities. The excess supply of U.S. securities raises the U.S. interest rate until it equals the adjusted foreign rate.

Equation 29–6 adjusts only for exchange rate risk. Behind this equation is the assumption that domestic and foreign securities are perfect substitutes. Perfect substitutability means that domestic and foreign securities are equally appealing to investors because these securities have the same characteristics, such as the same degree of credit risk and liquidity. Suppose, instead, that investors have a preference for American securities. One reason might be that investors consider the United States more stable than other countries. Another might be that information about U.S. financial markets is easier and less costly to obtain. To be lured from their preferred habitat in the United States to more risky habitats abroad, investors must be compensated. Equation 29–7 modifies the interest rate parity condition to include a habitat premium denoted by H:[6]

$$i = i_f + (\Delta e/e)^{\text{exp}} + H \tag{29–7}$$

When the United States is the preferred habitat, H is negative. This means that the interest rate in the United States will be lower than the foreign interest rate adjusted for exchange rate risk alone. For example, suppose that i is 6 percent, i_f is 5 percent, and $(\Delta e/e)^{\text{exp}}$ is 2 percent. Applying Equation 29–7, we find that H is −1 percent. In this example, interest rates are 1 percent lower in the United States than in the rest of the world because investors consider the United States a safe haven. In general, H is a wedge that accounts for all other factors, such as capital controls and taxes, that affect the spread between domestic interest rates and foreign interest rates.[7]

Foreign and Domestic Incomes

Domestic and foreign incomes also affect the position of the demand and supply curves in the foreign exchange market. Unlike changes in interest rates, however, changes in income affect the current account of the balance of payments.

Like the demand for any good, the demand for foreign goods depends on income. Imports, which are the demand for foreign goods by Americans, vary positively with American income, Y. When Y increases, imports rise and the demand for foreign exchange rises, creating excess demand for foreign exchange. As a result, the exchange rate rises.

$$Y\uparrow \rightarrow Q\uparrow \rightarrow FE^d\uparrow \rightarrow EDFE \rightarrow e\uparrow$$

Exports are the demand for American goods by foreigners. When foreign income, Y_f, rises, exports rise. As a result, the supply of foreign exchange rises, creating excess supply in the foreign exchange market, which pulls down the exchange rate:

$$Y_f\uparrow \rightarrow X\uparrow \rightarrow FE^s\uparrow \rightarrow ESFE \rightarrow e\downarrow$$

---

[6] This habitat premium is conceptually similar to the habitat premium Chapter 23 introduces in the discussion of the term structure of interest rates.

[7] The next chapter shows that the size of the country is one of these factors.

These results show that the ups and downs of the business cycle affect exchange rates. For example, in the first quarter of 1994, real GDP rose 3.4 percent in the United States, while output in Germany and Japan was stagnant. This difference in economic conditions helped to push the dollar down and foreign exchange up.

Foreign and Domestic Prices

The demand for any good depends not only on income but also on the price of that good and the price of competing goods. Therefore, domestic and foreign prices also affect the current account balance and, ultimately, the exchange rate. Equation 29–8 summarizes all factors that affect imports.

$$Q = Q(eP_f, P, Y,) \qquad (29\text{–}8)$$
$$\quad\;\; -\;\; +\;\; +$$

Consider a simple case where there are two goods, called *domestic goods* and *foreign goods*. Imports are foreign goods demanded by Americans. The demand for imported goods depends on the price of foreign goods expressed in dollars, eP_f; the price of American goods, P, also expressed in dollars; and American income, Y.

The sign under each factor in Equation 29–8 denotes a law of demand. The plus sign under Y indicates the already examined positive relation between domestic income and demand for imports. The negative sign under eP_f indicates an inverse relation between the dollar price of imported goods and the quantity demanded of imported goods. For a given value e, the higher the foreign price level, P_f, the higher the dollar price of imports, and the smaller the demand for imported goods. On the other hand, the positive sign under P in Equation 29–8 means that the higher the price of goods produced at home, the higher the demand for imported goods. The reason is that the higher the price of American goods, the greater the incentive for Americans to switch to foreign goods. In other words, the goods are substitutes.

Now consider exports, and note that exports are American goods demanded by foreigners (the British, in our example). This demand depends on the price of American goods expressed in pounds, $(1/e)P$; on the price of competing goods, that is, of British goods, expressed in pounds, P_f; and on foreign (i.e., British) income, Y_f. Equation 29–9 summarizes these relations.

$$X = X[(1/e)P, P_f, Y_f] \qquad (29\text{–}9)$$
$$\qquad\;\; -\;\; +\;\; +$$

The negative sign under the first factor in Equation 29–9 captures the inverse relation between the quantity demanded of a good and the price of that good. For a given international value of the dollar, $1/e$, the higher the price level in the United States, the higher the pound price of American goods, and the lower their demand by the British. Hence, the higher the U.S. price level, the lower the level of American exports. On the other hand, the positive sign under the price of foreign of goods indicates that the higher the price of their own goods, the greater the incentive for foreigners to switch to American exports. Finally, the positive sign under Y_f summarizes the positive relation between foreign income and American exports.

Given how changes in prices affect imports and exports, consider how they affect the exchange rate. Other things equal, an increase in foreign prices induces Americans to switch from foreign goods to domestic goods. At each level of the exchange rate, the demand for imported goods, Q, falls, which shifts the demand curve for foreign exchange to the left. Foreigners, on the other hand, find American goods less expensive and increase their demand for them. Thus, the demand for U.S. exports, X, rises, which shifts the supply curve for foreign exchange to the right. The increased demand for U.S. exports and reduced demand for imports cause an excess supply of foreign exchange, which lowers the exchange rate, as the following schematic verifies:

$$P_f\uparrow \;\rightarrow\; Q\downarrow \;\rightarrow FE^d\downarrow \text{ and } X\uparrow\rightarrow FE^s\uparrow \;\rightarrow\; ESFE \;\rightarrow\; e\downarrow$$

Finally, what is the effect of changes in domestic prices on the exchange rate? An increase in the U.S. price level, P, increases the demand for foreign exchange because imports rise. On the other hand, the supply of foreign exchange falls because exports fall. As a result, there is excess demand for foreign exchange and the exchange rate rises:

$$P\uparrow \;\rightarrow\; Q\uparrow \;\rightarrow\; FE^d\uparrow \text{ and } X\downarrow \;\rightarrow\; FE^s\downarrow \;\rightarrow\; EDFE \;\rightarrow\; \rightarrow e\uparrow$$

This result can be seen in a more revealing way. An increase in the domestic (U.S.) price level is a fall in the domestic purchasing power of the dollar, $(1/P)$, and an increase in the exchange rate is a fall in the international purchasing power of the dollar, $(1/e)$. *Thus, a fall in the domestic purchasing power of a currency leads to a fall in its international purchasing power.*

$$\left(\frac{1}{P}\right)\downarrow \;\rightarrow\; \left(\frac{1}{e}\right)\downarrow$$

To summarize this section, Table 29–2 gathers the factors that affect the exchange rate: domestic and foreign nominal interest rates; the expected rate of change in the exchange rate; domestic and foreign incomes; and domestic and foreign prices. The next section explores the relation between prices and the nominal exchange rate further. It also relates expectations of currency appreciation or depreciation to expectations of inflation or deflation.

TABLE 29–2
Factors Affecting
the Exchange Rate

Change in Factor	Effect on Demand or Supply	Change in Exchange Rate, e
$i_{US}\uparrow \rightarrow$	$CO\downarrow$ and $CI\uparrow \rightarrow ESFE \rightarrow$	$e\downarrow$
$i_f\uparrow \rightarrow$	$CO\uparrow$ and $CI\downarrow \rightarrow EDFE \rightarrow$	$e\uparrow$
$(\Delta e/e)^{exp}\uparrow \rightarrow$	$CO\uparrow$ and $CI\downarrow \rightarrow EDFE \rightarrow$	$e\uparrow$
$Y\uparrow \rightarrow$	$Q\uparrow \rightarrow EDFE \rightarrow$	$e\uparrow$
$Y_f\uparrow \rightarrow$	$X\uparrow \rightarrow ESFE \rightarrow$	$e\downarrow$
$P\uparrow \rightarrow$	$Q\uparrow$ and $X\downarrow \rightarrow EDFE \rightarrow$	$e\uparrow$
$P_f\uparrow \rightarrow$	$Q\downarrow$ and $X\uparrow \rightarrow ESFE \rightarrow$	$e\downarrow$

THE REAL EXCHANGE RATE

So far this chapter has examined only the *nominal exchange rate,* which is the number of dollars per unit of foreign exchange. The *real exchange rate* focuses on what the dollar can buy in real terms. This section begins by explaining the mechanics of the real exchange rate. Then it uses the concept of the real exchange rate in two ways: to put together the effects of changes in domestic and foreign prices on the nominal exchange rate; and to establish and apply a condition for real interest rate parity that is the real counterpart to the nominal condition introduced earlier in this chapter.

The Mechanics of the Real Exchange Rate

The **real exchange rate**, E, is defined as the ratio of foreign prices to domestic prices, each expressed in units of the same currency, for example, in dollars:

$$E = \frac{eP_f}{P} \tag{29-10}$$

We can find the dimensions of E from the dimensions of the components that make up E:

$$E = \frac{\dfrac{\$}{\cancel{P_f}} \times \dfrac{\cancel{P_f}}{\text{Foreign goods}}}{\dfrac{\$}{\text{American goods}}}$$

$$= \frac{\cancel{\$}}{\text{Foreign goods}} \times \frac{\text{American goods}}{\cancel{\$}}$$

$$= \frac{\text{American goods}}{\text{Foreign goods}}$$

Our calculations show that the real exchange rate, E, measures the number of units of American goods that must be given up to import one more unit of foreign goods. Other names for E are the *terms of trade,* or the *relative price of imports.* An increase in E means that foreign goods become relatively more expensive, so that Americans must give up more domestic goods to buy one unit of foreign goods. The definition of E shows that the real exchange rate rises when e rises, P_f rises, or P falls.

TRY IT OUT 29.2

1. Suppose that it costs $1.60 to buy one British pound, £100,000 to buy a Rolls Royce, and $40,000 to buy a Cadillac. Calculate the value of E. Be specific about the units.
2. Suppose that the price of a British pound falls from $1.60 to $1.50. Calculate the new value of E.

It is helpful for the upcoming discussion of purchasing power parity to find the expression for the rate of change in the real exchange rate. Applying to Equation 29–10 the rules for finding the rate of change in a variable, we determine that:[8]

---

[8] The rules for finding rates of change are: The rate of change in the product of variables equals the sum of the rate of change in each of the variables; the rate of change in the quotient equals the rate of change in the numerator minus the rate of change in the denominator.

$$\frac{\Delta E}{E} = \frac{\Delta e}{e} + \frac{\Delta P_f}{P_f} - \frac{\Delta P}{P} \qquad (29\text{--}11)$$

Equation 29–11 says that the rate of change in the real exchange rate equals the rate of change in the nominal exchange rate plus the difference between foreign and domestic inflation rates.

Purchasing Power Parity

The concept of the real exchange rate leads directly to the theory of **purchasing power parity**, which involves the long-run determinants of nominal exchange rates. According to this theory, the nominal exchange rate, e, moves to offset changes in foreign prices relative to domestic prices, so that the real exchange rate remains constant. Thus, if P_f/P rises, the theory of purchasing power parity predicts that e will fall by an equal amount.

A constant real exchange rate means that $\Delta E/E = 0$. Setting $\Delta E/E$ equal to zero in Equation 29–11 and solving for $\Delta e/e$ yield a simple algebraic statement of purchasing power parity:

$$\frac{\Delta e}{e} = \frac{\Delta P}{P} - \frac{\Delta P_f}{P_f} \qquad (29\text{--}12)$$

According to Equation 29–12, the magnitude of appreciation or depreciation of a country's currency depends only on relative inflation rates. If, for example, the American rate of inflation is 7 percent and the foreign rate of inflation is 4 percent, there will be a 3 percent appreciation of foreign currency and an equal depreciation of the dollar, according to the theory of purchasing power parity.

The words *purchasing power* in the term *purchasing power parity* are meant to indicate that the theory links changes in external prices of currencies to relative changes in internal purchasing power, as measured by inflation rates. In our example, an inflation rate of 7 percent in the United States means that the purchasing power of the dollar in the United States is falling by 7 percent per year. Similarly, an inflation rate of 4 percent in England means that the purchasing power of the pound is falling by 4 percent annually in England. Purchasing power parity predicts that the dollar will depreciate internationally by the differences of 3 percent.

To find the economic rationale behind purchasing power parity, it is necessary to ask why the real exchange rate should remain constant when P_f/P changes. Consider first the special case in which E is not only constant, but also equal to one. If $E = 1$, the dollar price of foreign goods equals the dollar price of domestic goods: $eP_f = P$. Ignoring transportation costs, this will happen only if the export goods and the import goods are identical.

Consider, for example, soybeans. Suppose the dollar price of soybeans in England, eP_f, is less than the dollar price of soybeans in the United States, P. Profit seekers will buy soybeans in England, ship them to the United States, and sell them. They will continue buying and selling soybeans until all profits from arbitrage are eliminated, which occurs when the dollar price of soybeans is the same at home and abroad (assuming no transportation costs). Thus, international arbitrage ensures that identical goods that can be traded will sell for the same dollar price around the world. Thus, the theory of purchasing power parity is also called the *law of one price*. The same good must have the same price when expressed in the same currency.

Usually, however, the export good and the import good are not the same, because countries export the goods in which they have a comparative advantage. And even when exports and imports are goods of the same name, say, automobiles, they are not identical and, hence, are not perceived as perfect substitutes. A Mazda is not the same as a Chevy. The theory of purchasing power parity, however, can hold even if E is not equal to one. Deriving Equation 29–12 required only that E remain constant when P_f and P change.

Other factors, however, violate the condition that E is constant. Purchasing power parity asserts more than simply the law of one price for individual goods, because P and P_f are the price indexes at home and abroad. These price indexes represent all goods and services consumed in each country. Even if the baskets of goods consumed are the same, the weights used to derive the indexes usually are not the same because of differences in tastes. Moreover, because several goods and services are not traded between countries, changes in their prices do not influence directly the nominal exchange rate. Figure 29–8 depicts trade-weighted indexes of the nominal and real exchange values of the dollar over the past 20 years; that is, it depicts indexes of $1/e$ and $1/E$. The graph shows that the value of $1/E$ has not been constant. Instead, it has followed closely the ups and downs of $1/e$.

Thus, both logic and empirical evidence tend to reject the strict version of purchasing power parity in Equation 29–12. Facts and reason, however, do confirm a weaker version of the theory: A country that experiences a higher rate of inflation than another country will eventually see its currency devalued against the currency of the other country, even though the devaluation may not be the same percentage predicted by the strict version of the theory.

FIGURE 29–8
Nominal and Real Exchange Values of the Dollar

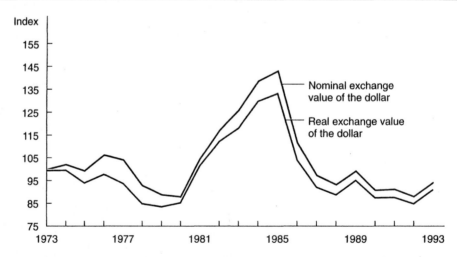

The nominal exchange value of the dollar is a trade-weighted index of the foreign exchange price of the dollar, $1/e$. The real exchange value of the dollar is a price-adjusted, trade-weighted index of the foreign exchange price of the dollar, $1/E$.

Source: *Economic Report of the President, 1994*, Table B-110.

**Real Interest
Rate Parity**

The concept of the real exchange rate also leads to a distinction between *nominal interest rate parity* and *real interest rate parity*. After establishing the condition for real interest parity, we connect theory with practice to explain why the curves depicting the nominal and real exchange values of the dollar in Figure 29–8 look like mountains.

The interest rate parity condition introduced earlier in this chapter was the nominal condition, according to which the nominal domestic interest rate equals the nominal foreign interest rate plus the expected rate of change in the nominal exchange rate:

$$i_{US} = i_f + (\Delta e/e)^{\exp} \tag{29–6}$$

Real interest rate parity, on the other hand, says that the expected real domestic interest rate, i^r_{US}, equals the expected real foreign interest rate, i^r_f, plus the expected rate of change in the real exchange rate, $(\Delta E/E)^{\exp}$.

$$i^r_{US} = i^r_f + (\Delta E/E)^{\exp} \tag{29–13}$$

Deriving the real interest rate parity condition from the nominal condition requires considering how participants form their expectations of changes in the nominal exchange rate. Rearranging Equation 29–11 gives a rate of change in the nominal exchange rate that equals the rate of change in the real exchange rate plus the difference between the domestic and foreign inflation rates:

$$\frac{\Delta e}{e} = \frac{\Delta E}{E} + \left(\frac{\Delta P}{P} - \frac{\Delta P_f}{P_f}\right) \tag{29–14}$$

Suppose that market participants form their expectations of changes in the nominal exchange rate on the basis of Equation 29–14. That is, the expected rate of change in the nominal exchange rate equals the expected rate of change in the real exchange rate plus the difference between the expected domestic and foreign inflation rates:

$$\left(\frac{\Delta e}{e}\right)^{\exp} = \left(\frac{\Delta E}{E}\right)^{\exp} + \left(\frac{\Delta P}{P}\right)^{\exp} - \left(\frac{\Delta P_f}{P_f}\right)^{\exp} \tag{29–15}$$

Substituting Equation 29–15 into the nominal interest rate parity condition, Equation 29–6, yields:

$$i_{US} = i_f + \left[\left(\frac{\Delta E}{E}\right)^{\exp} + \left(\frac{\Delta P}{P}\right)^{\exp} - \left(\frac{\Delta P_f}{P_f}\right)^{\exp}\right] \tag{29–16}$$

Rearranging terms in Equation 29–16 gives:

$$i_{US} - \left(\frac{\Delta P}{P}\right)^{\exp} = \left[i_f - \left(\frac{\Delta P_f}{P_f}\right)^{\exp}\right] + \left(\frac{\Delta E}{E}\right)^{\exp} \tag{29–17}$$

By definition, the expected real interest rate in each country equals the difference between the country's nominal interest rate and its expected rate of inflation. Making this substitution in Equation 29–17 gives Equation 29–18, which is the condition for real interest rate parity (that is, Equation 29–13):

$$i^r_{US} = i^r_f + \left(\frac{\Delta E}{E}\right)^{\exp} \tag{29–18}$$

FIGURE 29–9
Exchange Value
of the Dollar and
Interest Rate
Differential

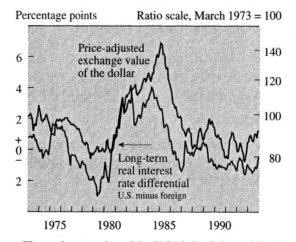

The exchange value of the U.S. dollar is its weighted average exchange value in terms of the currencies of the other Group of 10 (G-10) countries using 1972–76 total trade weights. Price adjustments are made using relative consumer prices.

The interest rate differential is the rate on long-term U.S. government bonds minus the rate on comparable foreign securities, both adjusted for expected inflation estimated by a thirty-six-month moving average of actual consumer price inflation or by staff forecasts where needed.

The data are monthly.

Source: Board of Governors of the Federal Reserve System, *80th Annual Report, 1993*, 29.

Suppose that initially Equation 29–18 holds. Next, suppose that a rise in the real U.S. interest rate makes the real U.S. interest rate greater than the risk-adjusted real foreign rate. As a result, funds will flow into the United States, where securities have become relatively more attractive. Capital will continue flowing in the direction of the United States until the risk-adjusted real interest rates are equalized.[9] This increase in the demand for U.S. securities will increase the current nominal and real values of the dollar. On the other hand, if expected real U.S. interest rates fall, other things equal, capital will flow out of the United States, thereby depressing the current nominal and real values of the dollar.

---

[9] As we modified the condition for nominal interest rate parity to include risk factors other than exchange rate risk, we can modify the condition for real interest rate parity.

The Exchange Rate Mountains of the 1980s

Real interest rate parity explains why the international value of the dollar rose in nominal and real terms in the early 1980s and fell beginning in 1985. The culprit was real interest rates. Real U.S. interest rates rose in the early 1980s because U.S. monetary policy was contractionary while fiscal policy was expansionary, as Chapter 28 discussed. As a result, the spread between the U.S. and foreign real interest rate rose, and the dollar increased in value, as Figure 29–9 shows. When real interest rates fell after the mid-1980s, the dollar fell in value, as the theory predicts. Figure 29–9 shows the close relation between the real interest rate spread and the real exchange value of the dollar.

Real interest rate parity also predicts that if the expected real interest rate is greater in the United States than the rest of the world, market participants expect the real exchange rate to rise in the future. This means they expect the real exchange value of the dollar to fall in the future, which it did beginning in 1985. In sum, the experience of the 1980s shows that international differences in real interest rates are an important factor affecting nominal and real exchange rates.

A BRIEF HISTORY OF THE INTERNATIONAL SYSTEM OF PAYMENTS

Having analyzed the workings of the foreign exchange market, we conclude by explaining the evolution of the current international payments system. Until 1971, gold played an important role in the international payments system. The current system is a mix of flexible and fixed exchange rates in which gold is no longer an anchor.

The Gold Standard

The use of gold and other precious metals as a medium of international trade goes back to ancient times, when importers paid exporters in gold coins. In modern times, countries found it advantageous to standardize their media of exchange so that traders would not have to ship gold for each international transaction. With the modern **gold standard**, each trading nation agreed to tie its currency to gold. This amounted to a fixed exchange rate system in which the exchange rate between each pair of currencies was fixed. For example, suppose a British pound could be redeemed for five times as much gold as one dollar. Then the exchange rate between the dollar and the British pound would be five dollars per pound, because five dollars could buy the same amount of gold as one pound.

With the modern gold standard, which lasted until the 1930s, international transactions in goods, services, and assets were conducted in convertible currencies. Currencies are convertible if they can be exchanged without impediments for other currencies. A currency is convertible to gold if it can be exchanged for a specified amount of gold. Gold was used only for settlements, which means that only the balance required a final settlement by transferring gold. To keep exchange rate fixed, deficit countries lost gold and surplus countries gained gold.

Because gold is a factor affecting reserves in the banking system, reserves fell in deficit countries and rose in surplus countries. As a result, the money supply fell in deficit countries and rose in surplus countries. Thus, the gold standard automatically forced contractionary monetary policies on deficit countries and expansionary monetary policies on surplus countries. When internal and external needs clashed, the external needs dominated. For example, by losing gold, a country with a depressed economy and a balance of payments deficit automatically reduced its money supply, thereby further depressing its economy. On the other hand, a country with an overheated economy would be forced to inflate its economy by increasing its money supply. In addition, liquidity in the international payments system fluctuated with gold discoveries, which added to the supply of international reserves.

The system based on the gold standard and fixed exchange rates began to collapse around World War I and broke down during the Great Depression. In an attempt to boost domestic output by making their export goods more competitive, some countries devalued their currencies, which invited retaliation by other countries. These competitive devaluations contributed to a large reduction in international trade in the 1930s.

The Bretton Woods System

In July 1944, 10 months before the end of World War II, representatives of 44 countries met in Bretton Woods, New Hampshire, to design a new international monetary and financial system that would provide a stable environment to foster prosperity and world trade. Concerned that the movements in exchange rates in the 1930s had caused instability, the participants created a fixed exchange rate system that was another version of the gold standard. Instead of linking the currency of every nation to specific quantities of gold, only the dollar was given a direct link. The connection of the remaining currencies was indirect, via their link to the dollar. This new payments system, called the **Bretton Woods system**, established the dollar as the reserve currency for the international payments system.

The agreement created the *International Monetary Fund* to be the official accountant, enforcer, and banker of the payments system. It committed the United States, which possessed most of the existing gold, to provide IMF-member countries with gold at a fixed price of $35 per ounce. At the same time, each foreign currency was fixed at so many dollars per unit of that currency. For example, the British pound was fixed at 2.80 dollars per pound. By selling a pound for 2.80 dollars, a central bank could buy with the proceeds 2.8/35ths of an ounce of gold. In this way the system effectively established the gold content of the British pound at 2.8/35ths of an ounce of gold.

To settle their balance of payments accounts, central banks held dollars or dollar-denominated government securities as foreign reserves. A country with a balance of payments surplus would be adding to its dollar reserves, and a country with a deficit would be losing dollars. Because the Bretton Woods system was a fixed exchange rate system, it had the same disadvantages as the traditional gold standard. The system tied the hands of central banks by committing them to buy or sell currencies to maintain a fixed exchange rate. Thus, policymakers lost considerable freedom in conducting monetary policy for domestic objectives. The agreement, however, did make provisions for changes in exchange rates by allowing a country with a "fundamental disequilibrium" to devalue or revalue its currency to a different fixed exchange rate with the dollar. The IMF interpreted fundamental disequilibrium to mean persistent deficits or surpluses.

As an example, consider the choices of a country that ran persistent deficits. Suppose this country financed its deficit by running down its inventory of dollars or dollar-denominated assets. Also, suppose it sterilized the effect on the domestic money supply. Eventually the central bank would exhaust its inventory of dollar assets. As a stopgap measure, it might borrow temporarily from the IMF or from other countries. Ultimately, however, it was left with two choices to eliminate its deficit: pursue contractionary monetary policy, say, contractionary open market operations, to raise domestic interest rates sufficiently to attract capital inflows and discourage outflows; or devalue the domestic currency. Sometimes countries would raise interest rates and contract their domestic economies. Other times, however, governments were unwilling to inflict a recession at home to solve a balance of payments deficit. Sensing an impending devaluation, speculators, whose business it is to profit from changes in prices, would often move a massive amount of funds out of the currency of the deficit nation. These speculative attacks frequently caused a crisis that was resolved by devaluation.

For the United States, the situation was more complicated because the Bretton Woods agreement tied the dollar to gold. Thus, the dollar could be devalued only if all other countries revalued *their* currencies with respect to the dollar. Other countries, however, were not always willing to revalue their currencies sufficiently. Thus, in the case of persistent balance of payments deficits, the only option for the United States was to pursue contractionary policies.

The United States found itself in this situation in 1971, a year before the presidential elections. At the time, the U.S. economy was faced with rising inflation and massive capital outflows. Contractionary monetary policy, by raising interest rates, would have tackled both problems. The Nixon administration, however, did not want interest rates to rise in the election season. To deal with inflation, the administration imposed wage and price controls, as Chapter 28 discusses. On the international front, the Nixon administration saw an opportunity to dismantle the fixed exchange rate system and move to a system in which the exchange rate would change to absorb shocks. Thus, in August 1971 it suspended the convertibility of dollars to gold. Foreign central banks could no longer exchange their dollars for gold at $35 per ounce. This action sent a clear message to world markets that the United States would not attempt to keep exchange rates fixed. The floating exchange rate system that gradually emerged was better suited to handle the supply-side shocks that beset the United States and other economies in the 1970s.

Managed, or Dirty, Float

It took IMF members several years to agree to the current system of floating exchange rates. In 1973, the major industrial countries agreed to float their currencies. Eventually, the current system of a managed float was legitimized by an agreement at an IMF conference in Kingston, Jamaica, in 1976.

The wording of this agreement is such that it grants member countries substantial discretion to intervene in foreign exchange markets. The agreement mandates that no country should intervene in foreign exchange markets to gain unfair competitive advantage. It empowers member countries, however, to intervene to counter disorderly conditions in the exchange markets.

When it suits their collective interests, the United States and other major industrial countries coordinate their actions in the foreign exchange market. For example, in a meeting at the Plaza Hotel in New York City in September 1985, finance ministers from the United States, Japan, Germany, France, and the United Kingdom agreed to a coordinated intervention to try to bring down the value of the dollar.[10] The dollar had skyrocketed in the first half of the 1980s, as Figure 29–8 shows. As a result, U.S. goods became

---

[10] This group, known as the *Group of Five (G-5)*, began meeting in the late 1970s. The group became the *Group of Seven (G-7)* when Canada and Italy joined in 1986.

less competitive in world markets and the U.S. trade deficit soared. Mounting concern that trade deficits would give rise to protectionist policies in the United States provided an incentive for the G-5 countries to cooperate to push the dollar down.

After the announcement of the agreement, called the *Plaza Accord,* for coordinated intervention to bring down the value of the dollar, the dollar fell on its own. This initial fall, combined with subsequent declines in response to heavy intervention, brought the nominal value of the dollar down by about 12 percent against the yen and 9 percent against European currencies by the end of October. The intervention was successful, in large part because economic fundamentals were consistent with a falling dollar, as the preceding section explained.[11] The G-5 countries were not trying to change the direction of a moving train. They simply were trying to accelerate the train's movement in the direction that it was already headed. Without much additional intervention, by January 1986 the dollar was about 25 percent lower than its 1985 peak.

The Fiftieth Anniversary of Bretton Woods

Since the introduction of floating exchange rates in the 1970s, there has been more volatility in exchange rates than can be explained by economic fundamentals, such as interest rates, income, and prices. The usual explanation is that speculative trading for very short-term profits is the source of this volatility. Excessive volatility hampers global trade by increasing uncertainty for businesses and households operating in the international arena.

Volatility in exchange rates was on the minds of a private group of economists, bankers, and diplomats who met in Washington, D.C., in July 1994, the fiftieth anniversary of the Bretton Woods conference. Headed by former Federal Reserve Board chairman Paul Volcker and called the *Bretton Woods Commission,* this group recommended a two-step approach to more stable exchange rates:

- The first step would be for IMF members to coordinate monetary and fiscal policies to reduce the pressure for movements in exchange rates.
- The second step would be for countries to set adjustable target ranges within which governments would allow exchange rates to fluctuate.

Real interest rate parity explains the first part of the proposal to coordinate monetary and fiscal policies. When policy is pushing up real interest rates in one country and pushing them down in another, exchange rates change as capital flows out of the low interest rate country into the high interest rate country. Coordination, however, is not easy to achieve when countries are at different stages of the business cycle.

The second part of the proposal to set semirigid target ranges for currencies resembles the European Monetary System introduced in 1979. That system, however, has not been without problems. In a floating rate system, exchange rates automatically adjust when

[11] Paul Volcker was chairman of the Federal Reserve Board in 1985. In a 1992 book, Volcker wrote: "I was pretty well convinced by then as a matter of market judgment that the basic direction of the dollar was lower. Certainly, the growth of the U.S. economy seemed to be losing momentum, and if there was to be any change in monetary policy it would likely be toward greater ease and lower interest rates." Paul Volcker and Toyoo Gyohten, *Changing Fortunes: The World's Money and the Threat to American Leadership* (New York: Times Books, 1992): 242–43.

there are major disturbances. Although in principle the governments can adjust the target ranges to mimic market forces, in practice they may not budge, even in the face of a major shock, as the next section explains.

The European Monetary System

In 1979 the members of the European Community created the *European Monetary System (EMS)* to limit the variability of exchange rates among member countries. The majority of members of the EMS agreed to be a party to the **Exchange Rate Mechanism** *(ERM)*, which ties participating countries together in a system of semirigid exchange rates. Until 1992 the exchange rates of most of the countries in the mechanism were allowed to fluctuate within a band of 2.25 percent on either side of a central value.

The deutsche mark emerged as the anchor for the ERM not only because the German economy is the largest in the system but also because Germany has a history of low and stable inflation rates. The Netherlands, a much smaller economy, also has a history of using monetary policy to keep inflation low, whereas France, Belgium, and especially Italy have had much higher inflation rates. As expected, in the early years there were numerous realignments because of these vast differences in inflation rates and economic policies among the member countries. Between 1987 and 1992, however, there were no realignments. The reason is that the high-inflation countries used the Exchange Rate Mechanism as a political weapon in their quest to disinflate their economies through contractionary monetary policies. When their constituents complained about rising unemployment, governments committed to disinflation pointed to their international commitment to keep exchange rates fixed.

The creators of the European Monetary System envisaged the Exchange Rate Mechanism as the first step toward monetary union, with a single currency and a single central bank. By eliminating uncertainty about exchange rates, a single currency would reduce the risk to businesses of operating across national boundaries. Meeting in the Dutch city of Maastricht in 1991, the members took the next step toward monetary union. The Maastricht Treaty set forth conditions for monetary union by the end of the decade. Currency crises in 1992 and 1993, however, cast doubt on this timetable.

The seeds for the crisis were sown in 1990 when the reunification of East and West Germany changed the economic circumstances confronting policymakers in Germany. As Chapter 25 discusses, large government expenditures on infrastructure to rebuild East Germany and on transfer payments to East Germans increased budget deficits in Germany. When inflation rates began to rise, Germany combined its expansionary fiscal policy with a tight monetary policy, thereby pushing up real interest rates in Germany. With a flexible exchange rate regime, the deutsche mark would have risen against the French franc and other currencies in the mechanism, as it did against the dollar, which is not part of the ERM. Of course, the countries in the ERM could have imitated market forces by revaluing the mark against all other currencies in the mechanism. But they didn't. Instead they tried to stick with the status quo. This forced the other countries to follow the monetary policy of Germany. That is, they had to use contractionary monetary policy to push up domestic interest rates to try to keep their currencies within the established bands. The economic slowdowns that resulted became politically intolerable in England and Italy, which both left the ERM in September 1992.

Another crisis in July 1993 threatened to dissolve the ERM. Market participants were anticipating that the Bundesbank would lower the German discount rate at the end of July. The Bundesbank's decision to keep the discount rate unchanged set off speculative attacks against the French franc and other currencies in the ERM. As a last ditch effort to save the mechanism, the participants increased the bands within which exchange rates could fluctuate from 2.25 percent on either side of a central value to 15 percent on either side. This return to a nearly floating exchange rate system pushed monetary union further into the future.

SUMMARY

- The balance of payments is a record of a country's international transactions. The current account records the flow of funds from the purchase or sale of goods and services, from the repatriation of investment income, and from unilateral transfers. The capital account records the flow of funds from the purchase and sale of assets.

- When a country's international payments exceed its receipts, it has a balance of payments deficit. To finance the excess of its payments over its receipts, the central bank of the deficit country must deplete its inventory of international reserve assets or the central bank of the surplus country must buy securities from the deficit country. The latter action increases the international reserve assets of the surplus country.

- The nominal exchange rate is the number of dollars needed to buy one unit of a foreign currency. Its inverse, the nominal international value of the dollar, is the number of units of a foreign currency that one dollar can buy.

- Demand for foreign exchange arises from imports, which depend inversely on the exchange rate, and from capital outflows. The supply of foreign exchange arises from exports, which depend positively on the exchange rate, and from capital inflows.

- Under a pure system of flexible, or floating, exchange rates, changes in the exchange rate eliminate any deficit or surplus in the balance of payments. The polar opposite case is a system of fixed exchange rates, in which changes in the international reserve assets of central banks replace movements in the exchange rate.

- The current system of international payments between the United States and its major trading partners is called a *managed float* or a *dirty float* because it is a mixture of flexible and fixed exchange rates. The Fed and other central banks intervene in the foreign exchange market to prevent disorderly movements of the exchange rate. The Fed can sterilize its foreign exchange operations by combining them with offsetting open market operations. Sterilized interventions do not affect reserves in the banking system or the domestic money supply, but they are also less likely to be effective.

- In a system of flexible exchange rates, four types of factors affect the nominal exchange rate: domestic and foreign interest rates, expectations of currency appreciation or depreciation, domestic and foreign income levels, and domestic and foreign price levels.

- Nominal interest rate parity is an important benchmark condition in international finance, according to which the domestic nominal interest rate equals the foreign nominal interest rate plus the expected rate of change in the nominal exchange rate.

- The real exchange rate, also called the *terms of trade,* is the nominal exchange rate multiplied by the foreign price level and divided by the domestic price level. Thus, the real exchange rate is the number of units of domestic goods a country gives up to import one more unit of foreign goods. The percentage change in the real exchange rate equals the percentage change of the nominal exchange rate plus the difference between foreign and domestic inflation rates.

- According to the doctrine of purchasing power parity, international arbitrage in goods and services keeps the real exchange rate constant in the long run. A constant real exchange rate implies that the percentage change in the nominal exchange rate equals the difference between domestic and foreign inflation rates. In a looser and empirically more relevant form, the theory of purchasing power parity states that in the long run the currencies of countries with relatively high inflation rates will depreciate.

- The concept of the real exchange rate also provides a bridge from nominal interest rate parity to real interest rate parity. Real interest rate parity means that the domestic real interest rate equals the foreign real interest rate adjusted for the expected change in the real exchange rate.

- Real interest rate parity predicts that, other things equal, if the spread between domestic and foreign real interest rate rises, the current level of the international value of the dollar will rise in nominal and real terms. Real interest rate parity provides a good explanation for the rise and fall of the dollar in nominal and real terms in the 1980s.

- The gold standard refers to an international payments system in which the value of each country's currency is fixed in terms of gold. Under the Bretton Woods system established in 1944, only the dollar was linked directly to gold.

The exchange rate of all other currencies was fixed vis-à-vis the dollar, thereby establishing an indirect connection between other currencies and gold.

- Both systems—the gold standard and the Bretton Woods standard—were based on fixed exchange rates. The Bretton Woods system collapsed in 1971 when the U.S. severed the link between the dollar and gold. This eventually led to the current system of a dirty float.

- In 1979, the members of the European Community created the Exchange Rate Mechanism, which ties participating countries together in a system of semirigid rates. After crises in 1992 and 1993, the ERM increased the bands within which the exchange rates of participating countries could fluctuate, resulting in a near float.

KEY TERMS AND CONCEPTS

balance of payments accounts
current account
capital account
capital inflows
capital outflows
international reserve assets
nominal exchange rate
appreciation

depreciation
effective exchange rate
flexible exchange rate system
floating exchange rate system
fixed exchange rate system
managed, or dirty, float
nonsterilized intervention

sterilized intervention
interest rate parity
real exchange rate
purchasing power parity
gold standard
Bretton Woods system
Exchange Rate Mechanism

QUESTIONS AND PROBLEMS

1. "Receipts from exports are recorded in the current account of the balance of payments whereas interest income on foreign bonds is recorded in the capital account." True or false? Explain.

2. "Purchases of U.S. Treasury securities by the Japanese government are recorded in the capital account of the balance of payments." True or false? Explain.

3. "A deficit in the U.S. balance of payments means that in the rest of the world receipts from transactions with the United States exceed payments." True or false? Explain.

4. "The Fed can settle a surplus in the U.S. balance of payments either by purchasing foreign securities or by running down its inventory of international reserve assets." True or false? Explain.

The Wall Street Journal

5. Find the following information in *The Wall Street Journal*: A recent value of the dollar price of the yen in the spot market. The yen price of the dollar in the spot market on the same day. What is the relation between these two prices?

6. Suppose that a store on the Canadian side of the U.S. border with Canada sells a T-shirt for 20 Canadian dollars. Also suppose the store sells the same T-shirt for 18 U.S. dollars in its branch 200 yards down the road on the U.S. side. What is the exchange rate between the U.S. and the Canadian dollar?

7. "Other things equal, a depreciation of the U.S. dollar is bad news for U.S. consumers and good news for U.S. exporters." Explain why you agree or disagree with the statement.

8. Suppose a financial commentator on the evening news says that the U.S. current account worsened last quarter because the U.S economy came out of its recession while its major trading partners were still mired in recessions. Does this statement make economic sense? Explain.

9. Suppose that the Fed increases the U.S discount rate while the central banks of other major industrial countries reduce their discount rates. With the help of a graph of the foreign exchange market, explain the effect on the international value of the dollar.

10. Suppose that the dollar price, P, of U.S goods falls because of an improvement in productivity in the United States. With the help of a graph of the foreign exchange market, explain the effect on the foreign exchange rate.

11. Suppose that the nominal interest rate is 3 percent in Japan and 5 percent in the United States.
    a. According to interest rate parity, what is the expected rate of change in the yen?
    b. How will your answer to a be affected if U.S securities and Japanese securities are not perfect substitutes?

12. Suppose that starting from a situation of nominal interest rate parity, the nominal interest rate in the United States rises. Explain what will be the effect on the current level of the nominal exchange rate.

13. Suppose that a change in tastes by Americans increases the demand for foreign goods.
    a. Describe the actions the Fed must undertake to keep the exchange rate fixed. Will there be any effect on the U.S. money supply? Explain.
    b. Suppose that foreign central banks, rather than the Fed, undertake to keep the exchange rate fixed. What must they do? Will there be any effect on the U.S. money supply?

14. Suppose that the dollar/mark exchange rate is $0.25 per deutsche mark, that the mark price of a Volkswagen is DM100,000, and the dollar price of a Ford Taurus is $15,000. What is the real exchange rate? Be specific about the units.

15. Explain the relation between the following concepts:
    a. The nominal exchange rate and the real exchange rate.
    b. Nominal interest rate parity and real interest rate parity.

16. Describe the relation between the law of one price and purchasing power parity.

17. Suppose the dollar price of a haircut in Tokyo is $40 while in New York it is only $20. Why doesn't the law of one price hold?

18. Is purchasing power parity a requirement for real interest rate parity?

19. Suppose the Fed pursues a credible policy of reducing inflation by 2 percentage points, while foreign inflation remains unchanged. Explain whether the dollar will appreciate or depreciate and by how much, according to the strict version of the purchasing power parity theory.

The Wall Street Journal

20. The accompanying statement is from "Treasury Official Plays Down Pull of Inflation Fear," *The Wall Street Journal*, July 22, 1994, A2: The Treasury's top international official tried to quell the idea that fears of future price increases are behind the dollar's unwelcome weakness. . . . Mr. Summers told the Senate Banking Committee: 'Of the various factors that have been relevant to currency fluctuations, I would not assign a high weight to inflation expectations.' Appearing before the same committee on Wednesday, Mr. Greenspan described the weak dollar as a sign that inflation expectations in financial markets are rising. Mr. Summers blamed the drop in the dollar on improved prospects of recovery in Europe, which have strengthened the German mark, and the concern that the new government in Japan may not be able to deal with its current-account surplus." Use a model of the foreign exchange market to explain how the factors mentioned by Summers and Greenspan affect the demand and supply of foreign exchange. (Hint: In your answer, consider how a recovery in Germany affects German interest rates.)

21. In what way is the Exchange Rate Mechanism of the European Monetary System similar to the old Bretton Woods system? In what way is it different?

22. What are the benefits of fixed exchange rates? The costs?

23. In 1994, the private Bretton Woods Commission recommended that IMF-member countries should coordinate their monetary and fiscal policies. Explain the economic rationale for this recommendation.

SUGGESTED READINGS

Cooper, Richard N., "The Gold Standard: Historical Facts and Future Prospects," *Brookings Papers on Economic Activity* 1 (1982): 1–56.

A thorough review of the history of the gold standard.

Feldstein, Martin, ed., *International Economic Cooperation* (Chicago: The University of Chicago Press, 1988).

Proceedings of a National Bureau of Economic Research conference on international economic cooperation, with an introduction by the editor.

"Treasury and Federal Reserve Foreign Exchange Operations," *Federal Reserve Bulletin* 80, no. 7 (July 1994): 584–88.

Quarterly report on foreign exchange operations.

Volcker, Paul, and Toyoo Gyohten, *Changing Fortunes: The World's Money and the Threat to American Leadership* (New York: Times Books, 1992).

Former leading policymakers in the United States and Japan explore the past, present, and future international monetary systems.

ECONOMIC POLICY IN AN OPEN ECONOMY

CHAPTER PREVIEW

Consider the following events in the history of economic policymaking:

- The conference at Bretton Woods, New Hampshire, in 1944 established a system of fixed exchange rates in which the dollar was tied to gold and other currencies were tied to the dollar.

- In 1961, economic advisers to President Kennedy recommended tax cuts to stimulate the sluggish U.S. economy because monetary policy was needed to maintain the commitment to a fixed exchange rate.

- In 1971, President Nixon severed the link between the dollar and gold rather than have the Fed pursue contractionary monetary policies to keep the exchange rate fixed.

- In 1984, some economic advisers to President Reagan argued that tax cuts in the early 1980s had contributed both to the recovery of the U.S. economy and to the rise in the international value of the dollar that induced a trade deficit.

- In 1992, Great Britain left the Exchange Rate Mechanism rather than pursue contractionary monetary policy to keep the value of the pound fixed against the currencies of other countries in the European Monetary System.

- In June 1994, when the dollar fell to its post–World War II low against the yen, the Fed pondered whether to tighten monetary policy to keep the dollar from falling further.

These events, discussed in previous chapters, illustrate the international dimensions of economic policy. By comparing the conduct of monetary and fiscal policies under fixed and flexible exchange rates, this chapter provides a richer understanding of the international linkages that policymakers confront.

Chapters 24 and 25 build and apply the *IS-LM* model, in which the *IS* curve represents goods market equilibrium and the *LM* curve represents money market equilibrium. The intersection of these two curves determines the interest rate and real income. This chapter extends the model by adding a third curve, called the *balance of payments, or BP, curve* which represents equilibrium in the foreign exchange market. The expanded model, called the *IS-LM–BP model*, is well suited for comparing the conduct of monetary and fiscal policies under fixed and flexible exchange rates and for examining shocks, such as an increase in foreign interest rates or an increase in the expected rate of appreciation of foreign currencies, that enter the domestic economy through the foreign exchange market.

A MODEL OF THE OPEN ECONOMY

Chapter 29 examines the workings of the foreign exchange market in isolation. This chapter connects that market with the goods and services market and the money market.

The *IS-LM–BP* Graph

The **IS-LM–BP model** is described compactly by the simultaneous clearance of three markets:

$$
\left.
\begin{array}{l}
\text{Clearance of the goods and services market:} \\
\text{Clearance of the money market:} \\
\text{Clearance of the foreign exchange market:}
\end{array}
\right\}
\Rightarrow
\left\{
\begin{array}{l}
AD = Y \\
M^d = M^s \\
FE^d = FE^s
\end{array}
\right.
\qquad (30\text{–}1)
$$

Each equation in (30–1) represents an equilibrium curve in Figure 30–1: $AD = Y$ is the *IS* curve; $M^d = M^s$ is the *LM* curve; and $FE^d = FE^s$ is the *BP* curve. The intersection of the three curves determines the interest rate, real income, and the nominal exchange rate. The vertical axis displays the value of the interest rate and the horizontal axis the value of real income. There is no axis, however, for the exchange rate. Its equilibrium value can be read off the labels of the *IS* curve and the *BP* curve. Before explaining the slope of the *BP* curve, we consider how international factors affect the *IS* and *LM* curves.

The *IS* Curve in the Open Economy

The demand for goods and services consists of consumption expenditure, C; investment in plant and equipment, I; government expenditure, G; and net exports of goods and services, NX. The supply is the national output, Y. The market for goods and services clears when aggregate demand equals aggregate supply:

$$
AD = C + I + G + NX = Y \qquad (30\text{–}2)
$$

Equation 30–2 is a familiar one. The only extension in this chapter is to incorporate all the determinants of NX that Chapter 29 introduces. Any factor other than Y that increases

FIGURE 30–1
The *IS-LM–BP*
Model

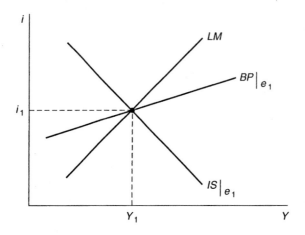

The *IS-LM–BP* model consists of three equilibrium curves: The *IS* curve represents equilibrium in the goods and services market; the *LM* curve represents equilibrium in the money market; and the *BP* curve represents equilibrium in the foreign exchange market.

NX will shift the *IS* curve to the right; any factor other than *Y* that decreases *NX* will shift the *IS* curve to the left. Of particular importance is the nominal exchange rate, *e*. Other things equal, an increase in *e* increases the dollar price of foreign goods, which makes American goods more competitive. As a result, *NX* rises, and the *IS* curve shifts to the right.

A word of caution must be added here. Recall that there is an indirect link between a change in the domestic interest rate and a change in net exports that runs through the foreign exchange market. For example, a decrease in *i* increases the exchange rate, *e*, which increases exports and reduces imports. In Chapters 24 and 25, movements along the *IS* curve incorporated the effect on *Y* of the change in net exports by adding the increase in net exports to the increase in investment, which resulted from a lower interest rate. As a result, the *IS* curve became flatter. This chapter divorces movements along the *IS* curve from the extra baggage of the exchange rate by drawing the curve for a given *e*. Hence, any change in *e* will shift the *IS* curve. This approach makes it easier to compare the effects of policy and shocks in a fixed and flexible exchange rate system and in a closed and open economy.

The *LM* Curve in the Open Economy

International factors also influence the position of the *LM* curve. The effects appear in the money supply, but originate in the quantity of nonborrowed reserves, which itself is derived from the balance sheet of the Fed. Chapter 8 explains that the quantity of nonborrowed reserves equals the Fed's portfolio of Treasury securities, B_F; plus the other assets, *OA*, in the Fed's balance sheet; minus the other liabilities, *OL*, and currency in circulation, *Cur*:

$$NBR = B_F + (OA - OL - Cur) \qquad (30\text{–}3)$$

One of the components of the term *other assets, OA,* is the Fed's inventory of foreign currencies and other foreign reserve assets, which is denoted by *FR*. When the Fed intervenes in the foreign exchange market, it influences the quantity of nonborrowed reserves, the money supply, and ultimately the position of the *LM* curve. If the Fed buys foreign currencies, nonborrowed reserves and the money supply increase, thereby shifting the *LM* curve down and to the right. A sale of foreign currencies has the opposite effect. The effects of purchases and sales are shown schematically as follows:

Fed Purchase of $FE \rightarrow FR \uparrow \rightarrow OA \uparrow \rightarrow NBR \uparrow \rightarrow M^s \uparrow \rightarrow LM \uparrow$ (shifts right)
Fed Sale of $FE \rightarrow FR \downarrow \rightarrow OA \downarrow \rightarrow NBR \downarrow \rightarrow M^s \downarrow \rightarrow LM \downarrow$ (shifts left)

The *BP* Curve

The final curve in the model, the *BP* curve, must be built from the ground up. This curve describes equilibrium in the foreign exchange market, which is identical to equilibrium in the balance of payments.

The *balance of payments* is the difference between the supply of foreign exchange, FE^s, and the demand for foreign exchange, FE^d:

$$BP = FE^s - FE^d \tag{30–4}$$

Chapter 29 explains that the supply of foreign exchange equals the sum of exports (X) and capital inflows (CI), and the demand equals the sum of imports (Q) and capital outflows (CO). Making these substitutions in Equation 30–4 and rearranging terms yield Equation 30–5:

$$BP = (X - Q) + (CI - CO) \tag{30–5}$$

Finally, substituting net exports, *NX,* for the difference between exports and imports in Equation 30–5, and net capital flows, *CF,* for the difference between capital inflows and capital outflows gives the balance of payments as the sum of net exports plus net capital flows:

$$BP = NX + CF \tag{30–6}$$

When the foreign exchange market clears, the balance of payments is in equilibrium: $BP = 0$. In this case, foreign exchange supplied from exports and capital inflows equals foreign exchange demanded for imports and capital outflows. Of course, equilibrium in the balance of payments does not require the current and capital account to each balance.[1] For example, a country may run a trade deficit of $60 billion that is financed by net capital inflows of $60 billion; in Equation 30–6, $-60 + 60 = 0$.

On the other hand, when the supply of foreign exchange is greater than demand, there is a balance of payments surplus: $BP > 0$. Alternatively, a balance of payments surplus means that the sum of net exports and net capital inflows is positive.

Finally, when the supply of foreign exchange is less than the demand, there is balance of payments deficit: $BP < 0$. A balance of payments deficit also means that the sum of net exports and net capital inflows is negative.

Now it is possible to derive the *BP* curve, or more precisely, the $BP = 0$ curve. The **balance of payments**, or, **BP curve** is the locus of all combinations of i and Y that guarantee equilibrium of the foreign exchange market. To derive this curve, we use the

---

[1] By identifying *NX* with the current account, we ignore unilateral transfers.

FIGURE 30–2
The Upward-
Sloping *BP* Curve

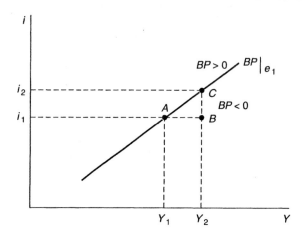

Starting from point *A* on the *BP* = 0 curve, an increase in *Y* increases imports and lowers net exports. Thus, at point *B* there will be a balance of payments deficit: *BP* < 0. For *BP* to equal zero, net capital inflows must rise, which means a higher *i* is required, as shown by point *C*. Therefore, the *BP* = 0 curve is upward sloping.

fact that *i* and *Y* affect the demand for foreign exchange and the supply of foreign exchange, as Chapter 29 explains. In particular, an increase in the domestic interest rate, *i*, increases the supply of foreign exchange and reduces the demand, because this increase in the interest rate encourages capital inflows and discourages capital outflows. On the other hand, an increase in the domestic level of income, *Y*, increases the demand for foreign exchange, because it encourages more imports.

Now, consider as a starting point a pair of *i* and *Y* such that $FE^s = FE^d$, which means $BP = 0$. For example, in Figure 30–2, starting point *A* has $i = i_1$ and $Y = Y_1$. Other things equal, an increase in *Y* from Y_1 to Y_2 moves the economy to point *B*. At this point, there will be a deficit in the balance of payments because the increase in *Y* increases the demand for imports, thereby creating excess demand in the foreign exchange market. Therefore, point *B* is off the $BP = 0$ curve. To remain on the $BP = 0$ curve, the domestic interest rate will have to change to eliminate the balance of payments deficit caused by the increase in *Y*. In Figure 30–2, an increase in *i* to i_2 will attract foreign capital and discourage capital from fleeing the country, thus creating a sufficient capital account surplus to match the current account deficit. As a result, the foreign exchange market and the balance of payments will be in equilibrium at point *C*.

It is clear, therefore, that an increase in *Y* necessitates an increase in *i* if the market for foreign exchange is to remain in equilibrium, *other things equal*. Thus, the *BP* curve is upward sloping. Schematically, the linkages behind the upward-sloping *BP* curve are:

$$Y{\uparrow} \rightarrow Q{\uparrow} \rightarrow FE^d {\uparrow} \qquad \rightarrow FE^d > FE^s \rightarrow BP < 0$$

which requires that

$$i{\uparrow} \rightarrow \begin{Bmatrix} CI\ {\uparrow} \\ CO\ {\downarrow} \end{Bmatrix} \rightarrow \begin{Bmatrix} FE^s\ {\uparrow} \\ FE^d\ {\downarrow} \end{Bmatrix} \rightarrow FE^d < FE^s \rightarrow BP > 0$$

such that $BP = 0$.

Finally, note that the exchange rate, *e,* is fixed along the upward-sloping *BP* curve. Hence, a change in *e* will shift the curve.

Perfect and Imperfect Capital Mobility

The derivation of the *BP* curve suggests that its positive slope is the result of the interest sensitivity of capital flows. To see the importance of the effect of a change in the interest rate on capital flows, consider two polar cases. In the extreme case of no interest sensitivity, the curve would be vertical. For example, if regulations prohibited capital flows between countries, no capital would flow into or out of the home country at any interest rate. In this case, capital would be *perfectly immobile,* and the *BP* curve would be vertical.

A vertical *BP* curve does not describe the contemporary environment in which large amounts of capital flow across national boundaries. The polar opposite case of a horizontal *BP* curve depicted in Figure 30–3 is much more realistic. A horizontal *BP* curve means there is nominal interest rate parity: The domestic interest rate equals the risk-adjusted foreign interest rate, which determines the position of the *BP* curve. A horizontal *BP* curve requires **perfect capital mobility**, which depends on two conditions: first, capital must flow freely between countries; second, investment in financial assets at home and abroad must be considered equivalent, which means that domestic and foreign assets are *perfect substitutes.* In addition to perfect capital mobility, a horizontal *BP* curve requires the home country to be small in the economic sense that it cannot affect the world interest rate by its own actions. In other words, the **small-country case** means the home country is an "interest rate taker" in global financial markets.

To illustrate the role of these assumptions, suppose that the economy is initially at point *A* in Figure 30–3. Now suppose that the home country tries to increase its interest rate to i_2, shown by point *B*. If capital is perfectly mobile, funds will come pouring into

FIGURE 30–3
The Horizontal *BP* Curve

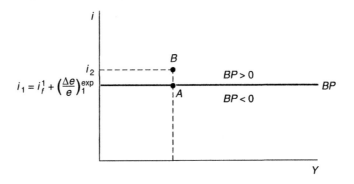

The assumptions of perfect capital mobility and a small country mean that the domestic interest rate must equal the expectations-adjusted foreign rate, which determines the position of the *BP* curve. Any attempt to push the domestic rate above the risk-adjusted foreign rate, such as at point *B*, would result in massive capital inflows that would push the domestic interest rate back to its original level.

the home country. If the market for domestic securities is a small part of the world market, this massive inflow of foreign funds will drive the domestic interest rate back down to the risk-adjusted foreign rate.

In contrast, the *BP* curve will be upward sloping if capital is imperfectly mobile or the home country is large. **Imperfect capital mobility** means domestic and foreign assets are imperfect substitutes or capital flows are restricted. The **large-country case** means the home country is too big to borrow an unlimited amount at the going international rate of interest. For example, the United States, Japan, and Germany are all large countries by this criterion.

In the real world, domestic and foreign assets are not perfect substitutes. There are differences among countries in taxes on returns and even differences in political stability and, hence, in the safety of foreign assets. Moreover, outright restrictions on capital flows may also be imposed, a practice common until the 1980s. However, international agreements among the major industrial countries for free capital flows and for relative equalization of taxes on foreign capital, combined with recent financial innovations, have contributed to globalization of the financial environment, as Chapter 5 points out.

Empirical evidence shows that in recent years the spread between domestic and foreign interest rates, adjusted for expected appreciation or depreciation of currencies, has been small. For this reason, this formal analysis continues with the case of perfect capital mobility. Moreover, even though not all countries are small, the analysis assumes a horizontal *BP* curve because of its simplicity. The effects on *i* and *Y* of changes in policy and of shocks in the small-country case give us an important benchmark that can be compared with the effects in a closed economy. Armed with these two benchmarks, it will become clear that the large-country case is an intermediate case, in which the effects of policy and of shocks usually lie between the two extremes.

**FIGURE 30–4
Equilibrium in a
Small Open
Economy**

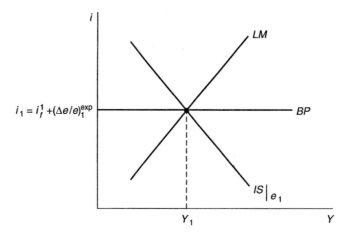

The intersection of the *IS*, *LM*, and *BP* curves determines the equilibrium values of *i*, *Y*, and *e*. The value of *e*, not measured on either axis, is read off the label of the *IS* curve.

Equilibrium in
the *IS-LM–BP*
Model

Now we are ready to describe the equilibrium of the extended model, called the *IS-LM–BP model,* or the *Mundell-Fleming model,* in recognition of the ground-breaking contributions of Robert Mundell and Arthur Fleming in the 1960s.[2] In Figure 30–4, the *IS* curve, the *LM* curve, and the horizontal *BP* curve intersect at point *E.* Because *E* is a point common to all curves, all three markets clear. The coordinates of point *E* give the equilibrium levels of income and the interest rate. Notice that there is no label denoting a given level of *e* attached to the *BP* curve. The reason is the current level of the exchange rate is not fixed along a horizontal *BP* curve. The equilibrium value of *e* can, however, still be read off the label of the *IS* curve.

MONETARY POLICY UNDER FIXED AND FLEXIBLE EXCHANGE RATES

The historical events in the Chapter Preview indicate that the actual conduct of economic policy depends on whether exchange rates are fixed or flexible. This section uses the *IS-LM–BP* apparatus to examine monetary policy under fixed and flexible exchange rates.

Flexible
Exchange Rates

Figure 30–5 depicts the effects of expansionary monetary policy under flexible exchange rates. Point 1 represents the initial equilibrium. Suppose that the central bank uses open market operations to increase its holdings of domestic securities from $B_F{}^1$ to $B_F{}^2$. This expansionary monetary policy increases nonborrowed reserves and the money supply, thereby shifting the *LM* curve down and to the right. In a closed economy, the equilibrium would settle at point 2, with a lower interest rate and a higher output.

In an open economy, point 2 is not a full equilibrium point, because it lies below the *BP* curve. Thus, the foreign exchange market is not cleared. The domestic interest rate, *i,* is lower than the expectations-adjusted foreign interest rate. Therefore, capital outflows rise and capital inflows fall. Thus, at point 2, there is excess demand for foreign exchange and a deficit in the balance of payments. A rise in the nominal exchange rate eliminates the excess demand for foreign exchange. At the given domestic and foreign price levels, the real exchange rate also rises, thereby making exports more attractive and imports less attractive. Net exports rise, shifting the *IS* curve to the right until it passes through point 3, where all markets clear.

At point 3, the interest rate is the same as at point 1. Thus, a small country cannot affect the domestic interest rate through expansionary monetary policy. It can, however, affect the level of domestic output, *Y,* which presumably is the purpose of expansionary monetary policy. Moreover, the equilibrium level of output rises by more than in the closed economy. Although there is no fall in the interest rate to induce an increase in investment, there is a rise in the exchange rate, which leads to an increase in net exports.[3]

---

[2] See Robert A. Mundell, "Capital Mobility and Stabilization Policy under Fixed and Flexible Exchange Rates," *Canadian Journal of Economics,* November 1963; and Marcus Fleming, "Domestic Financial Policies under Fixed and under Floating Exchange Rates," International Monetary Fund *Staff Papers* 9, (1962).

[3] The domestic price level will rise, but this is not shown on the graph. The ultimate equilibrium position will be to the left of point 3, with both the *IS* and *LM* curves moving to the left as the price level and the exchange rate increase from P_1 and e_2, respectively. Permitting the price level to rise, as we must, dampens the increase in output and the increase in net exports.

FIGURE 30–5
Monetary
Expansion under
Flexible Exchange
Rates

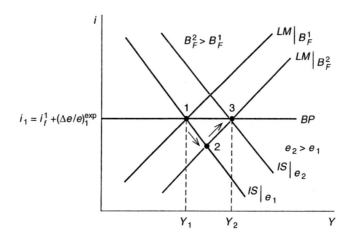

In a closed economy, an open market purchase of domestic securities by
the central bank moves the economy from point 1 to point 2. In a small
open economy, the equilibrium will be at point 3 because capital flows
move the domestic interest rate back to the risk-adjusted foreign rate and
the accompanying increase in the exchange rate increases net exports
and shifts the *IS* curve to the right. At point 3, the interest rate is the same
as at point 1, but *e* and *Y* are higher. In a large open economy, the
equilibrium would lie on the new *LM* curve between point 2 and point 3.

In a large open economy like the United States, the equilibrium would lie between
points 2 and 3, with *Y* increasing more than in a closed economy but not as much as in a
small open economy. The interest rate would not fully revert to its original level because
the United States is large enough to push down world interest rates through a change in
domestic monetary policy. Of course, the lower interest rate means that the exchange rate
and net exports would not rise as much as in a small open economy.

**Fixed Exchange
Rates**

Now consider what happens if the central bank engages in an open market purchase of
domestic securities, while committed to a fixed exchange rate. In Figure 30–6, with the
economy again starting at point 1, the central bank increases nonborrowed reserves by
increasing its holdings of securities from B_F^1 to B_F^2, thereby shifting the *LM* curve to
the right. As before, the equilibrium moves from point 1 to point 2 in a closed
economy.

In an open economy, at point 2 the domestic interest rate is below the risk-adjusted
foreign rate. The resulting net capital outflows cause a deficit in the balance of payments
and exert pressure on the foreign exchange market. The exchange rate, however, is not
allowed to respond to this pressure. How, then, can the central bank prevent a rise in the
exchange rate? As Chapter 29 explains, the central bank of the deficit country satisfies the
excess demand for foreign exchange by selling foreign currencies in the open market,
which reduces nonborrowed reserves and the money supply. Consequently, the *LM* curve
shifts inward. The central bank must sell enough foreign exchange to shift the *LM* curve

FIGURE 30–6
Monetary
Expansion in a
Small Country
under Fixed
Exchange Rates

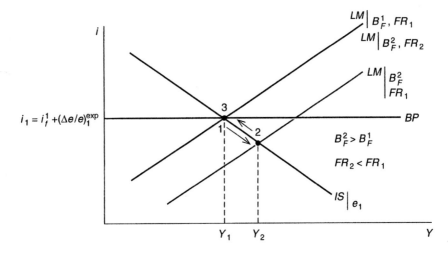

An open market purchase of domestic securities by the central bank raises nonborrowed reserves. If we ignore the international linkages, the economy would move from point 1 to point 2. At point 2, there is pressure for e to rise. To keep e from rising, the central bank must sell foreign exchange, reducing its foreign reserves, FR. The sale offsets the effect on NBR of the increase in B_F and pushes the LM curve back to its original position. In the end, there is no change in i, Y, or e in a small economy.

back to its initial position, again intersecting the other two curves at point 1, now identified as point 3.

What does the central bank accomplish with this exercise? The answer is that it sends the *LM* curve on a trip out and back again. When the trip is over, there is no effect on output if the home country is a small country. Monetary policy is impotent under a fixed exchange rate system in a small country.

What about a large country like the United States? Figure 30–7 shows that monetary policy is also impotent in a large country with fixed exchange rates. With e fixed and with fiscal policy given, the equilibrium must lie on the original *IS* and *BP* curves, which intersect at point 1. Hence, the *LM* curve must also intersect at this point. As in a small open economy, the central bank must offset any open market purchase of domestic securities with a sale of international reserve assets.

FISCAL POLICY UNDER FIXED AND FLEXIBLE EXCHANGE RATES

The historical review in Chapter 28 points out that the advisers to President Kennedy recommended tax cuts rather than expansionary monetary policy to stimulate the economy, because exchange rates were fixed in the 1960s. That review also compared the effects of tax cuts in the 1960s with those in the 1980s, when exchange rates were free to respond to market forces. This section provides the analytical foundations for those comparisons by using the *IS-LM–BP* model to examine how fiscal policy fares under fixed and flexible exchange rates.

FIGURE 30–7
Monetary
Expansion in a
Large Country
under Fixed
Exchange Rates

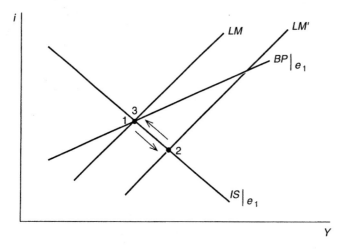

In a large open economy with fixed exchange rates, monetary policy
cannot affect output because the equilibrium must lie on the initial *IS* and
BP curves.

Flexible
Exchange Rates

Figure 30–8 depicts the case of a flexible exchange rate. The story begins at the original
equilibrium, point 1, with output at Y_1. The domestic interest rate, i_1, equals the expectations-adjusted foreign interest rate. Suppose that the government embarks on an expansionary fiscal policy, raising government purchases from G_1 to G_2 and, hence, shifting the
IS curve to the right. The economy reaches point 2, with a higher level of output, Y_2, and
a higher level of the interest rate, i_2. (A decrease in taxes will also shift the *IS* curve to the
right because lower taxes raise disposable income and, hence, consumption.)

By assumption, the foreign interest rate and the expected rate of appreciation or
depreciation of currencies remain at their original levels. Therefore, the increase in i
creates a positive spread between the domestic interest rate and the adjusted foreign
interest rate: $i_2 > i_f^1 + (\Delta e/e)_1^{exp}$. This spread attracts capital inflows and discourages
capital outflows, causing excess supply of foreign exchange and a surplus in the balance
of payments. The foreign exchange rate, e, falls and the international value of the home
currency appreciates. This development reduces the home currency price of imports and
increases the foreign currency price of exports, thereby discouraging exports and encouraging imports; net exports, *NX*, fall. The higher trade deficit or lower trade surplus
reduces aggregate demand and shifts the *IS* curve inward, back to its original position.
Equilibrium is reestablished at point 1, now renamed point 3.

Thus, under flexible exchange rates, the *IS* curve takes a seemingly inconsequential
trip. The trip is not entirely inconsequential, however, because the mix of aggregate
demand changes. The lower exchange rate and higher international value of domestic
currency makes domestic goods less competitive internationally and reduces *NX*. Government purchases *completely crowd out* net exports, which means that government purchases reduce net exports by an equal amount. This can be contrasted to the results in a

FIGURE 30–8
Fiscal Expansion
under Flexible
Exchange Rates

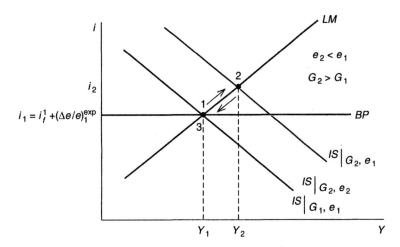

In a closed economy, an increase in G (or a reduction in t) moves the economy from point 1 to point 2. In an open economy, at point 2, the domestic interest rate is greater than the adjusted foreign rate. The resulting increase in net capital inflows causes an excess supply of foreign exchange and a reduction in e. The lower e reduces net exports and shifts the *IS* curve back to its original position in a small open economy. At point 3, the levels of i and Y are the same as at point 1, but the level of e is lower. In a large open economy, the equilibrium would be between point 1 and point 2.

closed economy, captured by point 2. Because the domestic interest rate is higher at point 2, government purchases partly crowd out domestic demand, primarily, investment in plant and equipment.

Complete crowding out is the result of the small country assumption. With a large country, the crowding out would be incomplete. Some net exports would be crowded out, along with some investment in plant and equipment, but their sum would not be enough to crowd out completely the increased aggregate demand. In Figure 30–8, the equilibrium would lie on the *LM* curve between point 1 and point 2. This, of course, is the case of the U.S. *twin deficits* in the 1980s. Increases in defense expenditures and tax cuts increased the international value of the dollar, which induced trade deficits. The higher trade deficits did not, however, completely offset the expansionary effects of the fiscal stimulus. Thus, output rose.

Investment,
National
Savings, and
Capital Inflows

When a country runs a trade deficit, it spends more than it produces. That is, the sum of consumption, investment, and government purchases outstrips domestic production, Y, by the amount of the excess of imports over exports. The country finances the excess of its spending over its domestic production by borrowing from abroad. Another way of stating this same relationship is to say that domestic investment is greater than national savings by the amount of the funds borrowed from abroad.

To derive the relationship among investment, national savings, and net capital inflows, start with the condition for clearance of the goods market:

$$AD = C + I + G + NX = Y \tag{30-7}$$

Next, recall the national income identity, according to which the sum of consumption (C), private savings (S), and net taxes (T) must equal national income (Y):

$$C + S + T \equiv Y$$

Substituting $C + S + T$ for Y in Equation 30–7 and canceling C from both sides of the equation yield:

$$I + G + NX = S + T$$

Rearranging terms gives:

$$I = S - (G - T) - NX \tag{30-8}$$

National savings is the difference between private savings, S, and government dissavings, $G - T$: national savings = $S - (G - T)$. With a budget deficit, $G - T$ is positive, and national savings is less than private savings. On the other hand, with a budget surplus, $G - T$ is negative. In other words, a surplus means the government is a net saver. Therefore, national savings exceed private savings.

According to Equation 30–8, investment equals national savings minus net exports. If net exports are zero, domestic investment must equal national savings. On the other hand, if net exports are negative, domestic investment will exceed national savings.

According to Equation 30–6, equilibrium in the balance of payments requires that net capital inflows be equal in value but opposite in sign to net exports: $CF = -NX$. Making this substitution yields:

$$I \quad = \quad S - (G - T) \quad + \quad CF \tag{30-9}$$

Investment = National savings + Net capital inflows

Equation 30–9 shows that the opportunity to borrow from or lend to other countries permits investment to differ from national savings. A country with low national savings, such as the United States, may invest more than it saves by borrowing from abroad. On the other hand, a country with high national savings, such as Japan, may invest less than it saves by lending to other countries.[4]

Table 30–1 illustrates the relationship among investment, national savings, and foreign borrowing with data for the United States; all numbers are percentages of GDP. The first row of the table shows that between 1977 and 1979, the government budget was practically balanced, which means that national savings was only slightly less than private savings. Investment exceeded national savings by the amount of the net capital inflows of 0.8 percent of GDP, which means the United States ran a trade deficit (current account deficit) of that magnitude.

---

[4] Measured as a percent of GDP, national savings in Japan has persistently been almost double that of the United States, which has a lower national savings rate than most major industrial countries.

TABLE 30–1
U.S. Investment,
Savings, and
Foreign Borrowing:
*1977–1993 (percent
of GDP)*

		I	=	S	–	$(G - T)$	+	CF
		Investment	=	Private savings	–	Government dissavings	+	Net capital inflows
					National savings			
1977 to 1979		19.0	=	18.3	–	0.1	+	0.8
					18.2			
1983 to 1989		16.9	=	17.9	–	2.8	+	1.8
					15.1			
1992 to 1993		13.6	=	16.1	–	4.0	+	1.5
					12.1			

Source: *Economic Report of the President* and *Survey of Current Business*.

The next row shows the twin deficits of the 1980s.[5] Budget deficits ran 2.8 percent of GDP and trade deficits 1.8 percent. As a result of borrowing from abroad that accompanies a trade deficit, investment did not fall as much as national savings. Also note that not only did government dissavings rise but also private savings fell in the 1980s.

Finally, the third row shows the United States also ran trade and budget deficits in 1992 and 1993. The trade deficits and accompanying foreign borrowing were slightly less than the 1980s, but the budget deficits rose. National savings fell by a greater amount than the rise in the budget deficits because private savings also fell. The lower national savings is reflected in lower investment on the left side of the equation.

In sum, the U.S. experience since the late 1970s shows that foreign borrowing permits a country to invest more than it saves.

Fixed Exchange Rates

Finally, to complete the analysis of economic policy, consider how fiscal policy fares in a regime of fixed exchange rates. Starting from equilibrium at point 1 in Figure 30–9, government expenditure is increased from G_1 to G_2. Point 2 denotes the new equilibrium in a closed economy. Output and the interest rate rise, the latter to the level i_2. In an open economy, the increased domestic interest rate attracts capital inflows and discourages outflows, causing a surplus in the balance of payments (excess supply of foreign exchange).

This surplus, unless absorbed, will appreciate the home currency and depreciate foreign currencies. The central bank, committed to a fixed exchange rate, buys the excess

---

[5] The table excludes the recessionary years 1980 to 1982 and 1990 to 1991, because budget deficits automatically rise in depressed economies.

FIGURE 30–9
Fiscal Expansion
under Fixed
Exchange Rates

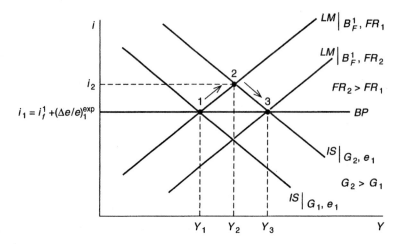

With a regime of fixed exchange rates, the central bank must intervene to keep
e from changing after an increase in G. Therefore, the central bank buys foreign
exchange, which increases nonborrowed reserves and shifts the LM curve to the
right. In a small economy, the final equilibrium is at point 3, with a higher Y than at
point 1. In a large economy, the equilibrium is between point 1 and point 2 on the
IS curve labeled G_2, e_1.

supply of foreign exchange. Its inventory of foreign currencies increases from FR_1 to
FR_2, nonborrowed reserves rise, and the money supply increases by a multiple of this
amount. As a result, the LM curves shifts to the right until it intersects both the IS curve
and the BP curve at point 3. Thus, with a fixed exchange rate, the government does not
have a pure fiscal policy. Instead, expansionary fiscal policy is combined with expansionary monetary policy. Output increases to Y_3, and the interest rate returns to its original
level, at i_1. Because the interest rate has not increased, no crowding out of investment
occurs. The current account will deteriorate only because the increase in domestic income
encourages more imports.

Of course, point 3 is the equilibrium in a small open economy. In a large open
economy, the equilibrium would lie between point 2 and point 3, on the IS curve labeled
G_2, e_1. The domestic interest rate would be higher than the risk-adjusted foreign rate. The
exchange rate, however, would not change because the higher level of income and the
higher interest rate would offset each other in the foreign exchange market.[6]

SUMMARY OF THE EFFECTS OF POLICY

Table 30–2 collects the results from our analysis of the effects of monetary and fiscal
policies with perfect capital mobility. Two results stand out:

- In a system of universal fixed exchange rates, monetary policy is impotent in both
  large and small countries, because it has no effect on interest rates or output.

---

[6] The equilibrium would be on the same upward-sloping BP curve that goes through point 1.

TABLE 30–2
The Effects of
Monetary and
Fiscal Expansions

	Expansionary Monetary Policy	Expansionary Fiscal Policy
Flexible exchange rates		
Small country	Output rises Interest rate unchanged Exchange rate rises	Output unchanged Interest rate unchanged Exchange rate falls
Large country	Output rises Interest rate falls Exchange rate rises	Output rises Interest rate rises Exchange rate falls
Fixed exchange rates		
Small country	Output unchanged Interest rate unchanged Exchange rate fixed	Output rises Interest rate unchanged Exchange rate fixed
Large country	Output unchanged Interest rate unchanged Exchange rate fixed	Output rises Interest rate rises Exchange rate fixed

· In a small country, the actions of domestic policymakers do not affect the domestic interest rate under fixed or flexible exchange rates. The results are even stronger. No shift of the *IS* curve or the *LM* curve changes the domestic interest rate.

SHOCKS FROM THE FOREIGN EXCHANGE MARKET

If shifts of the *IS* curve or the *LM* curve do not change the interest rate in a small country with perfect capital mobility, what does? The answer is shocks from outside the country that shift the *BP* curve. There are two possibilities: a change in foreign interest rates or a change in the expected rate of appreciation or depreciation of foreign currencies.

A Rise in
Foreign Interest
Rates

Suppose that the balance of payments curve shifts upward because the foreign interest rate rises. Figure 30–10 shows the two possible outcomes for a small country, depending on whether it maintains fixed or flexible exchange rates with the large country.

Initially, the economy of the small country, called the *home country,* is at point 1, with income at Y_1 and the interest rate at i_1. Moreover, i_1 equals the adjusted foreign interest rate, $i_f^1 + (\Delta e/e)^{\exp}_1$. Therefore, point 1 is on all three curves: *IS, LM,* and *BP.*

When the foreign interest rate rises to i_f^2, the position of the *BP* curve changes. In Figure 30–10, the *BP* curve shifts upward from BP_1 to BP_2. (We assume that the expected rate of appreciation or depreciation of foreign currencies remains the same.) Now point 1 lies under the *BP* curve. At the interest rate i_1 in the home country, there will be a balance of payments deficit, because capital will flow out of the home country. In other words, at the initial exchange rate, e_1, there will be excess demand for foreign exchange and excess supply of the home country's currency.

If the home country is committed to a fixed exchange rate, it must supply foreign exchange by reducing its inventory of international reserve assets, which reduces the domestic money supply and shifts the *LM* curve up and to the left. On the other hand, with a fixed exchange rate, there is no reason for the *IS* curve to move. Therefore, the

FIGURE 30–10
Effects of an
Increase in Foreign
Interest Rates
under Fixed and
Flexible Exchange
Rates

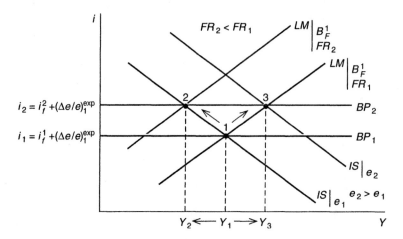

With a fixed exchange rate, an increase in the foreign interest rate raises the
domestic interest rate but lowers the level of output. The economy moves from point
1 to point 2, because the *LM* curve shifts to the left when the central bank sells
foreign exchange to keep *e* fixed. In contrast with a flexible exchange rate, *e* rises,
the *IS* curve shifts to the right, the economy moves from point 1 to point 3, and the
interest rate and output rise.

central bank of the home country must supply enough foreign exchange so that the new
LM curve intersects the original *IS* curve and the higher *BP* curve at point 2, which is the
new equilibrium point. At point 2, the domestic interest rate is higher and output is lower
than at point 1.

In sum, when foreign interest rates rise, the central bank of a small country must slow
down the domestic economy to keep the exchange rate from rising. If economic conditions are already sluggish, further contraction will be undesirable. Of course, in the
opposite case of a fall in foreign interest rates and a flight *to* the home currency, the
policy of the central bank will produce an expansion of output and, perhaps, unwanted
inflation to keep the exchange rate fixed. In other words, under a system of fixed exchange rates, the economy is deprived of the use of monetary policy as an instrument for
affecting the domestic economy. Instead, monetary policy must be used to keep the
exchange rate fixed.

Under a flexible exchange regime, a rise in foreign interest rates will actually lead to
expansion in the home country, as shown by point 3. The reason is that the flight from the
home currency raises the foreign exchange rate, say, to e_2 (and depreciates the home
currency to $1/e_2$). As a consequence, the home country's exports are more attractive and
imports less attractive, leading to an increase in the exports surplus, *NX*. This increase
shifts the *IS* curve up and to the right until it passes through the intersection of the other
two curves at point 3. Once again, the domestic interest rate equals the risk-adjusted
foreign interest rate. At point 3, however, the higher interest rate is the outcome of an
expanding economy rather than the route through which monetary policy contracts the
economy.

Crises in the European Monetary System

The graph in Figure 30–10 is well suited for analyzing the crises in the Exchange Rate Mechanism (ERM) of the European Monetary System in 1992 and 1993. As Chapter 29 explains, the exchange rates of countries in the mechanism are fixed in the sense that they are not allowed to move outside of preset bands. On the other hand, the currencies of these countries float against the currencies of countries outside the mechanism. When Germany, the largest country in the ERM, pursued an expansionary fiscal policy and a contractionary monetary policy following reunification in 1990, German interest rates rose. For the other countries in the ERM, such as France and Great Britain, the rise in German interest rates was an external shock that pushed up their balance of payments curves. To keep their currencies fixed against the deutsche mark, the Bank of England and the Banque de France (the British and French central banks) had to pursue contractionary monetary policies, which resulted in rising unemployment and falling output in France and Britain, as illustrated by the movement from point 1 to point 2 in Figure 30–10.

In September 1992, after the political and economic costs of keeping the pound within the preset bands became unacceptable, Britain withdrew from the ERM and allowed the pound to float. The withdrawal allowed the Bank of England to pursue an expansionary monetary policy, thereby pushing British interest rates down. In Figure 30–10, we can imaging the British *LM* curve shifting down and to the right, toward point 1. The resulting lower domestic interest rates helped jump-start the British economy. The falling pound also made British goods more competitive, thereby pushing the *IS* curve rightward. Of course, we know that without any further action by Germany, the final equilibrium would be at point 3, with British interest rates back to the level they were at point 2. The higher rates in Britain, however, would be the symptom of expansion rather than the result of contractionary monetary policies.

Germany, however, did act. In 1992 the Bundesbank began slowly to push down German interest rates. The actions of the Bundesbank were not large enough or fast enough, however, to prevent another crisis in the ERM in 1993. As Chapter 29 points out, at the end of July 1993, market participants were expecting the Bundesbank to lower the German discount rate. When the Bundesbank failed to act, speculators, sensing impending devaluations of the franc and of other currencies tied to the mark, fled from these currencies. The crisis was resolved by moving to a near floating system in which the currencies within the ERM were allowed to fluctuate by 15 percent above and below a central value. This new arrangement set the central banks of the participating countries free to use monetary policy for domestic purposes. Any narrowing of the bands and revival of the goal of a single European currency will require convergence in economic conditions and economic policies among countries in the European Monetary System.

Expected Currency Appreciation or Depreciation

Changes in the expected rate of appreciation or depreciation of foreign currencies will also shift the *BP* curve. For example, if the expected rate of appreciation of foreign currencies rises, say from 2 percent to 5 percent, the *BP* curve shifts upward by 3 percentage points. As a result, the risk-adjusted spread between domestic interest rates and foreign interest rates falls, which triggers a flight from domestic securities to foreign securities and an increase in the current level of the exchange rate (e). The resulting fall in the international value ($1/e$) of the home currency makes domestic goods more competitive in international markets. Thus, net exports rise and the *IS* curve shifts to the right.

FedWatch 30.1

How to Respond to a Falling Dollar

In a preemptive strike against inflation, the Federal Reserve pushed up short-term U.S. interest rates a total of 125 basis points between February and May 1994. Nevertheless, in June 1994 the dollar fell to a post–World War II low against the yen by dipping below the level of 100 yen to a dollar. What was the reason?

One explanation is a rise in the expected rate of appreciation of the yen may have sent investors fleeing from U.S. financial markets. That explanation, however, leads to another question. Why were investors revising upward their expectations of the rate of appreciation in the yen? They may have been concerned about future inflation in the United States. Or they may have become convinced that greater increases in the yen would be needed in the future to reduce the large and persistent Japanese trade surplus with the United States.

The Clinton administration itself had helped to foster the latter view. In 1993, at the beginning of the adminis-

tration, Treasury Secretary Bentsen, in an attempt to pressure Japan to reduce its trade surplus, had stated that the administration would like to see a stronger yen. By the summer of 1994, however, he had changed his view, declaring that the administration favored a stronger dollar. Despite the secretary's comments, with trade talks between the United States and Japan at an impasse, investors may have come to the conclusion that there was no alternative to a falling dollar to alter the trade imbalance between the two countries.

A falling dollar, of course, makes U.S. goods more competitive in Japan and Japanese goods less competitive in the United States, thereby boosting domestic production in the United States. It also feeds U.S. inflation by making imports more expensive and by reducing price discipline in import-competing industries. Thus, in July 1994, the Federal Reserve was waiting to see if its preemptive strike against inflation earlier in the year had slowed the U.S. economy enough to reduce the threat of inflation. If it had, the falling dollar would not be a problem. If it hadn't, the Fed would respond by pushing up U.S. interest rates another notch or two.

The graph looks like the one in Figure 30–10, with the equilibrium moving from point 1 to point 3. FedWatch 30.1 explains why an increase in the expected rate of appreciation of the yen with respect to the dollar may have triggered the rise in yen and the fall in the dollar in 1994.

SUMMARY

· The *IS-LM–BP* model of the economy consists of three markets: the goods and services market, depicted by the *IS* curve; the money market, depicted by the *LM* curve; and the foreign exchange market, depicted by the *BP* curve.

· International factors affect not only the *BP* curve but also the *IS* and *LM* curves. An increase in the exchange rate, *e*, shifts the *IS* curve to the right. Also, the *LM* curve shifts to the right when the Fed purchases foreign exchange in the open market.

· The *BP* curve is the locus of all pairs of *i* and *Y* such that the balance of payments is zero, which means that the foreign exchange market clears. The intersection of the *IS*, *LM*, and *BP* curves represents equilibrium in the three-market model of the open economy. The level of the exchange rate, which is not measured on either axis, is read off the label of the *IS* curve.

· The upward-sloping *BP* curve depicts the extent to which the domestic interest rate must rise when domestic income rises if the foreign exchange market is to remain in equilibrium. The *BP* curve is upward sloping if capital is imperfectly mobile or the home country is large.

- With perfect capital mobility and a small country, the domestic interest rate must equal the foreign interest rate adjusted for exchange rate risk. Hence, the *BP* curve is horizontal at the intercept where the domestic interest rate equals the expectations-adjusted foreign interest rate. If the domestic interest rate is below that rate, there will be massive capital outflows; if the domestic rate is above the adjusted foreign rate, there will be massive capital inflows.

- In a regime of flexible interest rates and perfect capital mobility, expansionary monetary policy will increase real income. An open market purchase of domestic securities reduces the domestic interest rate and encourages investment in plant and equipment, thereby raising output. The reduction in the interest rate also increases the exchange rate, *e*, further stimulating aggregate demand by increasing net exports. When capital is perfectly mobile and the home country is small, the end result is an increase in domestic output and a return of the interest rate to its initial value. When the home country is large, the domestic interest rate falls but the exchange rate does not rise as much. Therefore, output does not increase as much.

- In a regime of fixed exchange rates and perfect capital mobility, monetary policy is ineffective in small and large countries. An open market purchase of domestic securities by the central bank initially lowers the interest rate and increases output. The lower interest rate induces net capital outflows, which put upward pressure on the exchange rate. To prevent appreciation of foreign currencies and depreciation of the home country's currency, the central bank of the home country must sell foreign exchange. The sale reduces nonborrowed reserves and, hence, the money supply. As a result, domestic real output and the domestic interest rate revert to their initial levels.

- In a regime of flexible exchange rates and perfect capital mobility, an increase in government expenditure or a reduction in taxes will initially increase aggregate demand and output. But the domestic interest rate will also rise, which will encourage net capital inflows and appreciate the home country's currency. As a consequence, net exports will fall, reducing aggregate demand and output to their original levels in a small country. The interest rate will also revert to its original level in a small country but not in a large country. Also, in a large country, real output rises because net exports don't fall as much as in a small country.

- With fixed exchange rates and perfect capital mobility, an increase in government expenditure or a reduction in taxes will initially increase domestic output and the interest rate. The increased interest rate will attract foreign capital, producing a surplus in the balance of payments, which exerts a downward pressure on the foreign exchange rate. To prevent a fall in the foreign exchange rate, the central bank must buy the excess supply of foreign exchange, thereby increasing nonborrowed reserves and the supply of money. In a small country, this increase in the money supply will lower the interest rate to its initial level and further increase output. In a large country, the interest rate rises. Output also rises, but not as much as in a small country.

- In a small country, the domestic interest rate changes only when the balance of payments curve shifts. Changes in foreign interest rates or in the expected rate of appreciation or depreciation of foreign currencies shift the balance of payments curve.

- An increase in foreign interest rates will have expansionary effects in a regime of flexible exchange rates and contractionary effects in a regime of fixed exchange rates. The increase in foreign interest rates produces a deficit in the home country's balance of payments. If the foreign exchange rate is allowed to rise, aggregate demand and real income increase. If the foreign exchange rate must remain fixed, the home country's central bank must sell the necessary quantity of foreign currencies, thereby reducing nonborrowed reserves and the money supply. As a consequence, output will fall.

KEY TERMS AND CONCEPTS

IS-LM–BP model

balance of payments, or *BP*, curve

perfect capital mobility

small country case

imperfect capital mobility

large country case

national savings

QUESTIONS AND PROBLEMS

1. What is the difference between the *IS* curve of the *IS-LM* model and the *IS* curve of the *IS-LM–BP* model?

2. How do international factors affect the position of the *LM* curve?

3. Under what conditions will the *BP* curve be upward sloping?

4. What is the relation between interest rate parity and a horizontal *BP* curve?

5. "The current level of the exchange rate and the expected rate of change of the exchange rate are fixed along a horizontal BP curve." True, false, or uncertain? Explain.

6. Suppose that the introduction of new financial technology reduces the demand for money in the home country, which is a small country. With the help of an *IS-LM–BP* curve, explain the effect on the domestic interest rate and domestic output if the exchange rate is fixed. On the same graph, show how your results will change if the exchange rate is flexible.

7. "An open market purchase of domestic securities by the central bank will lead to an improvement in the country's current account balance." True, false, or uncertain? Explain.

8. Suppose that, because of an improvement in the quality of U.S. automobiles, both foreign and U.S. consumers buy more U.S. cars and fewer foreign cars. With the help of an *IS-LM–BP* graph, explain the effects on the interest rate and output in the United States. What will be the effect on the U.S. current account balance?

9. "In a small country with perfect capital mobility, a change in fiscal policy will affect the domestic interest rate, but a change in monetary policy will not." True, false, or uncertain? Explain.

10. "Investment is less than national savings in a country that runs a trade deficit." True, false, or uncertain? Explain.

11. If you were the economic adviser to the president of a large country, what change in the mix of monetary and fiscal policy would you recommend to reduce the current account deficit while avoiding a change in real GDP?

12. If you were the CEO of an export-oriented company, would you favor fiscal or monetary policy to expand the U.S. economy? Would you favor fiscal or monetary policy to disinflate the U.S. economy?

13. When U.S. and Japanese trade negotiators meet to discuss the trade imbalance between the two countries, the Japanese tell the Americans: "Your country should save more." And the Americans tell the Japanese: "Your country should spend more." Who is right? Why?

The Wall Street Journal

14. Explain the economic rationale for the following statement from "Europe's Money Move May Pave Way to Rise in the Global Economy," *The Wall Street Journal,* August 3, 1993, A1: "Europe's near abandonment of its system of fixed currencies is a humiliating defeat for its political leaders and throws into doubt visions of greater unity. But it just may be the tonic the world economy needs."

15. "An increase in the expected rate of appreciation of the yen is bad for the United States economy." True, false, or uncertain? Explain.

SUGGESTED READINGS

Klitgard, Thomas, "In Brief: Understanding the Rising Japanese Trade Surplus," Federal Reserve Bank of New York *Quarterly Review* 19, no. 1 (Spring 1994): 34–37.
    An examination of the relation between the international value of the yen and the Japanese trade surplus.
Krugman, Paul, *Peddling Prosperity: Economic Sense and Nonsense in the Age of Diminished Expectations* (New York: W.W. Norton & Co., 1994).

A lively and provocative book on the connection between economic theory, economic policy, and economic policymakers.
"The United States in the World Economy," Chapter 6, *Economic Report of the President, 1994,* 205–48.
    Discussion of the international aspects of economic policy in the 1990s.

actual real interest rate Nominal interest rate minus actual rate of inflation

actual velocity-indexed money growth The sum of actual money growth and actual velocity growth

adaptive expectations Expectations formed on the basis of past experience, according to which the expected value of a variable equals a weighted average of its past values

adjustment borrowings Very short term loans provided by the Fed to meet a temporary need for reserves that cannot reasonably be funded in other ways

adverse selection Problem arising from uncertainty in which the least desirable party is selected for an activity

aggregate demand (*AD*) curve A curve that depicts an inverse relation between the demand for economywide output and the price of output

aggregate demand–aggregate supply model Economic model that explains the determination of the price level and real income and the variables that depend on them

aggregate demand for goods and services The sum of planned consumption, investment, government purchases, and net exports

aggregate supply (*AS*) curve A curve that shows how much output firms are willing to produce at each price level

appreciation Increase in the international value of a currency

approximation of the annual rate of return The current yield plus the average annual capital gains rate

asked price The price at which dealers are willing to sell a security

asset and liability management committee (ALCO) Decision-making unit of a bank that decides on the composition of the bank's balance sheet

assets The property of households, firms, and other participants in the economy

asymmetric information Condition in which one party to a transaction has more information than the other party

automatic stabilizers Mechanisms that increase demand in a downturn and reduce demand in an overheated economy without a change in policy

average annual capital gains rate Total capital gains divided by the purchase price times the number of years the asset is held

balance of payments accounts Record of a country's international transactions

balance of payments, or *BP*, curve Graphical depiction of all the combinations of *i* and *Y* such that the balance of payments is in equilibrium, which means the foreign exchange market clears

balance sheet A statement of the financial condition of a participant that shows the participant's financial and tangible assets; its obligations, or liabilities; and the difference, called *net worth*

banker's acceptance A bank-backed marketable financial instrument issued by a firm and commonly used to finance international trade

bank holding company Corporation that owns stock in one or more banks

Banking Act of 1933, or Glass-Steagall Act Financial legislation that prohibited banks from paying interest on demand deposits, that gave the Fed the authority to impose ceilings on member bank savings and time deposits, and that separated commercial banking from investment banking

Banking Act of 1935 Banking legislation that extended ceilings on savings and time deposits to banks that were not members of the Federal Reserve System

Bank Insurance Fund (BIF) Fund run by the FDIC since 1989 to insure banks

bank loans A variety of obligations of households and firms that are held by banks, such as home mortgages and commercial and industrial loans

bank regulation Issuing rules about what banks may or may not do

bank's balance sheet equation Requirement that the sum of a bank's assets equals the sum of its liabilities plus its net worth

bank supervision Overseeing and examining banks for safety and soundness

basis point One one-hundredth of a percentage point

Basle Agreement International accord signed by 12 industrial countries agreeing to adopt risk-based capital requirements as of December 1992

Beige Book Report, prepared for FOMC meetings, on economic conditions in the 12 reserve districts

bid price The price at which dealers are willing to buy a security

Board of Governors of the Federal Reserve System Refers both to the seven members appointed by the president and to the agency, located in Washington, D.C., that they head

bond-financed deficit Budget deficit financed by issuing Treasury securities

borrowed reserves Reserves that originate in loans provided by the Fed to banks

branching Operation of a bank in more than one office

Bretton Woods System International payments system from 1944 to 1971, in which foreign currencies were tied to the dollar, which was fixed in terms of gold

bridge bank Temporary bank created by the FDIC to assist it in handling a failed bank

brokers   Market specialists that do not buy securities for their own accounts but instead earn commissions by bringing together buyers and sellers of marketable securities

bubble economy   Characterization of an economy in which speculation feeds on speculation, causing asset prices to rise above their long-run equilibrium values

budget deficit   The excess of government expenditures over tax receipts

budget surplus   The excess of tax revenues over government expenditures

buyout   The purchase of controlling interest in a company either by another company or by a group of investors

call provision   A feature of a bond that gives the issuer the right to repay borrowed funds before the maturity date

Cambridge equation   The identity stating that the product of the Cambridge k and nominal GDP equals the nominal money supply

Cambridge k   The inverse of velocity, calculated by dividing the nominal quantity of money by nominal GDP

CAMEL rating   Evaluation of the health of a bank based on capital adequacy, asset quality, management, earnings, and liquidity

capital account   Part of the balance of payments that records payments and receipts from the international purchase and sale of financial and tangible assets

capital adequacy   Whether a bank's net worth is sufficient for a safe and sound operation

capital goods   Lasting physical objects consisting of consumer durables, producer durables, and residential structures

capital inflows   The flow of funds into a country as a result of the sale to foreigners of financial and tangible assets

capital market securities   Long-term securities, which are debt securities with maturities of more than a year and equity securities

capital outflows   Flow of funds out of a country as a result of the purchase of foreign financial and tangible assets

capital stock   The quantity of a nation's plant and equipment at a moment in time

cash concentration system   Mechanism used by a firm to economize on funds that it holds in its demand deposits nationwide by wiring funds from a central account to regional deposit accounts that have a minimum balance until a check is presented for collection

cash items in the process of collection   Primarily checks deposited with banks but not yet collected

cash management account (CMA)   An account with a broker that combines a money market mutual fund, a securities account, and a credit line

central bank   A national institution that controls monetary policy and oversees the banking system

charter   License to set up a bank or thrift

check collecting and clearing   The process of moving a check between the depositor's bank and the recipient's bank and moving funds in the opposite direction

circumstances of the investor   Factors that constrain an investor's behavior, such as income, wealth, and the state of financial technology

classical model   Aggregate demand–aggregate supply model in which the supply curve is vertical

classicists   Economics who believe that the labor market clears rapidly and that discretionary polices are not useful in stabilizing output and employment

clean float   A floating exchange rate regime with no intervention by central banks to influence the exchange rate

coinsurance   The percentage of an insurance claim, net of the deductible, that the policyholder must pay

collective factor   A catchall variable that includes all the factors affecting asset demand other than the own rate of return, the rate of return on competing assets, income, and wealth

commercial banks   Depository institutions that were traditionally the only intermediaries allowed to issue checkable deposits and make business loans

commercial paper   Short-term marketable IOUs issued by creditworthy corporations; sold at a discount

complete crowding out   Situation in which an increase in government expenditures is totally offset by a decrease in private expenditures so that aggregate demand is unchanged

consumer price index   A measure of the price level constructed from a basket of goods that represent the consumption of a typical urban family

consumption   Expenditures by households on final goods and services, which in the national income and product accounts includes consumer nondurables and durables

consumption function   The relation between consumption and its underlying determining variables such as income

consumption goods   Goods that are used up in the year of purchase by households

corporate bonds   Long-term marketable, interest-bearing IOUs issued by corporations

corporate stock   Marketable certificates of ownership in a company

correspondent relationship   Arrangement in which a small bank receives banking services from a large bank

cost-push inflation   Increases in the price level caused by supply-side shocks

cost-reducing financial innovations   Improvements in financial technology that reduce the cost of banking

coupon   Fixed periodic dollar payments on debt securities

coupon equivalent yield   Yield on a zero coupon security that is equivalent to the yield on a coupon-bearing security

coupon rate   Ratio of annual coupon to face value

covenant   Restriction placed on a borrower

credit crunch   Situation in which banks become less willing and able to lend at any given interest rate

credit rationing   Situation in which there is a fringe of borrowers who cannot obtain loans although they appear similar to those who do

crowding out An effect of fiscal policy on private expenditures where a rise in government expenditure financed by borrowing raises the interest rate, which reduces private expenditures

crowding out of investment The interest-induced reduction in investment that results from a fiscal stimulus

crowding out of net exports The exchange rate–induced reduction in net exports that results from a fiscal stimulus

currency in circulation Paper notes and coins held by the public

current account Part of the balance of payments that records payments and receipts from trade in goods and services, from investment income, and from unilateral transfers

current account deficit The excess of payments to the rest of the world for imports of goods and services and for international transfers over receipts from the rest of the world from exports of goods and services and from international transfers

current account surplus The excess of receipts from imports and international transfers over payments for exports and international transfers

current yield Annual receipts on an asset divided by the current purchase price

debt security An IOU that is a promise to make fixed payments at specified future dates

deductible Fixed initial amount of an insurance claim that the policyholder must pay

default risk The risk that the issuer of a debt security may not make all the interest payments or repay the principal at maturity

default risk premium The component of the interest rate on a debt security that compensates the holder for default risk

default risk structure of interest rates Relation between the risk of default and the interest rate on debt securities, other things equal

defensive open market operations The purchase or sale of securities in the open market by the Fed in order to offset the technical factors affecting reserves

deficit unit A participant whose current gross savings is less than current expenditure on capital goods

degree of reserve pressure The amount of reserves in the banking system relative to the needs of banks

demand deposit Non-interest-bearing checking account issued by depository institutions

demand for real money balances The demand for money measured in terms of the prices of a base year

demand for securities The sum of the amount of securities that the public, the banks, and the Fed want to hold at each level of the interest rate

demand for total reserves Sum of required reserves and excess reserves

demand management policies Policies that shift the aggregate demand curve

demand-pull inflation Increases in the price level caused by demand-side shocks

demand-reducing financial innovations Improvements in financial technology and other innovations that reduce the demand for deposits and increase the demand for securities

deposit insurance A guarantee to pay depositors in legal tender if the depository institution goes bankrupt

deposit multiplier for M2 The inverse of the reserve requirement ratio multiplied by one plus the ratio of nontransactions deposits to transactions deposits

deposit rate curve The graphical depiction of the deposit rate relation

deposit rate relation The positive relation between the interest rate and the deposit rate, other things equal

depository institutions Financial institutions whose obligations are deposit accounts, such as checking deposits and savings and time deposits

Depository Institutions Deregulation and Monetary Control Act of 1980 (DID&MCA) Banking and financial legislation that ushered in the new financial environment by authorizing the nationwide introduction of interest-bearing checking accounts and providing for the gradual phase out of all interest ceilings on deposits by 1986

depreciation Decrease in the international value of a currency

direct finance A method of finance where funds flow from surplus units to deficit units without the services of a financial intermediary

direct security A security issued by a surplus unit and sold to a deficit unit

discount rate The interest rate that the Fed charges depository institutions to borrow at the discount window

discount window loans Credit extended by the Fed to depository institutions

discounting A technique that reduces the value of a future receipt to today's dollars

disintermediation The outflow of funds from deposit accounts issued by banks and thrifts

disposable income National income minus taxes plus transfer payments

District Federal Reserve banks Twelve regional banks located throughout the United States that serve as the operating arm of the Federal Reserve System

diversifiable risk Risk that can be reduced through diversification

diversifying Holding assets with different possibilities of losses so that gains from assets that do well offset losses from assets that do poorly

divisibility A characteristic of securities that describes the smallest unit in which a security is available

domestic policy directive Written instructions about open market operations from the FOMC to the Federal Reserve Bank of New York

dual banking system Coexistence of federally chartered and state-chartered banks

durable consumer goods Goods that are purchased by households and that have a useful life of more than three years

dynamic open market operations   The purchase or sale of government securities in the open market by the Fed in order to increase or decrease reserves in the banking system

effective exchange rate   A trade-weighted average of the bilateral exchange rates of several countries

effective reserves   The amount of reserves available to be used as required reserves to support deposits; nonborrowed reserves plus borrowed reserves minus excess reserves

efficiency wages   Real wages that are above the market-clearing level and that are paid to productive workers to maintain their loyalty

efficient markets theory   Theory that there are no unexploited opportunities for profits in financial markets because expectations are rational and markets clear quickly

endogenous variable   A variable whose value is determined within an economic model

equation of exchange   The identity stating that the product of the quantity of money and velocity equals nominal GDP

equilibrium   A market condition in which quantity demanded equals quantity supplied

equilibrium deposit rate   The deposit rate at which the quantity of deposits demanded equals the quantity supplied

equilibrium quantity of deposits   The quantity of deposits demanded and supplied when the deposit market is in equilibrium

equilibrium quantity of deposits demanded   The quantity of deposits demanded when the deposit market is in equilibrium

equilibrium real interest rate   The rate that, if maintained, would keep the economy at full employment

equity security   A certificate of ownership in a business enterprise

Eurodollar deposits   Dollar-denominated deposits in banks outside of the United States

excess demand   A market condition in which quantity demanded exceeds quantity supplied

excess reserves   Discretionary reserves held by depository institutions

excess supply   A market condition in which quantity demanded falls short of quantity supplied

exchange rate   The dollar price of a unit of foreign currency

Exchange Rate Mechanism   System of semirigid exchange rates maintained by some countries in the European Community

exogenous variables   Variables whose values are determined outside the model

expected inflation effect   The positive relation between a change in expected inflation and a change in the nominal interest rate

expected real interest rate   Nominal interest rate minus expected rate of inflation

extended credit   Long-term loans made by the Fed to banks in trouble

face value   The amount that will be paid by an issuer of a debt security at maturity; also called the *principal*

federal agency securities   Marketable, interest-bearing IOUs issued by federal agencies and federally sponsored agencies to channel funds to targeted sectors of the economy

Federal Deposit Insurance Corporation (FDIC)   Federal agency that insures deposits issued by banks and thrifts

Federal Deposit Insurance Corporation Improvement Act of 1991 (FDICIA)   Banking legislation that mandated risk-based deposit insurance, early regulatory intervention, and prompt closure of failed banks

federal funds market   The interbank loan market, which consists primarily of overnight loans

federal funds rate   The interest rate charged on overnight interbank loans

Federal Home Loan Bank System   Network of 12 banks created in 1932 to provide liquidity to savings and loan associations

Federal Open Market Committee (FOMC)   The policymaking committee within the Federal Reserve that decides on short-term and long-term open market operations; the committee consists of the seven governors, the president of the Federal Reserve Bank of New York, and four reserve bank presidents, who serve on a rotating basis

Federal Reserve repurchase agreement   An arrangement where the Fed buys securities in the open market and agrees to sell them back at a specified price and date, usually within a week

Federal Reserve System, or Fed   The U.S. central bank that consists of a seven-member Board of Governors, 12 regional reserve banks, and member commercial banks

Federal Savings and Loans Insurance Corporation (FSLIC)   Agency that insured the deposits of S&Ls between 1934 and 1989

Fedwire   The computer network connecting the Fed and banks

fiat money   Money created by government order

finance companies   Nondepository financial intermediaries that make loans to households and firms and raise funds by borrowing in the open market and from banks

financial assets   Claims to immediate or future cash payments

financial indicators   Financial gauges of the stance of monetary policy

financial innovations   Novelties incorporated into the financial system as a result of changes in laws, regulations, institutional arrangements, and the state of financial technology

Financial Institutions Reform, Recovery, and Enforcement Act of 1989 (FIRREA)   Legislation that overhauled the regulatory authority and deposit insurance system for savings and loan associations

financial instruments or securities   Other terms for financial assets

financial intermediaries   Financial go-betweens that channel funds among other participants and issue their own financial instruments

financial system   Consists of participants, financial instruments, and the markets in which the instruments are traded

firms   The sector that produces goods and services for households and for other businesses

fiscal policy   Government expenditure and taxation policy

Fisher effect   A relation between expected inflation and the interest rate where a change in the nominal interest rate equals the change in expected inflation, which equals the change in actual inflation, which equals the change in money growth

Fisher equation   A relation among the nominal interest rate, the real interest rate, and expected inflation according to which the nominal interest rate equals the real interest rate plus expected inflation

fixed exchange rate system   A system where the government sets the exchange rate and buys or sells foreign exchange to keep the rate at its predetermined level

flexible exchange rate system   A system in which demand and supply in the foreign exchange market determine the exchange rate

float   A transitory source of reserves that arises when the check collection process takes longer than a preset schedule

floating exchange rate system   A synonym for a flexible exchange rate system

flow   A variable that is expressed as a quantity per period of time

fooling model   An approach to aggregate supply based on continuous market clearance and workers' misperceptions

foreign currency directive   Written instructions by the FOMC to the Federal Reserve Bank of New York about buying and selling foreign currencies

foreign participants   The sector that comprises all the participants from the rest of the world

forward interest rates   Rates on loans of any duration to be executed in the future

full equilibrium   The point at which the demand for goods and services equals supply, money demand equals money supply, and foreign exchange demanded equals foreign exchange supplied

full-employment budget deficit   Magnitude of the deficit at a benchmark, high level, of employment

full-employment level of output   The level of output at which there is no idle capacity in the economy

futures market   The market for exchange of an item at a specified date in the future for a specified price

Garn–St Germain Depository Institutions Act of 1982   Financial legislation designed mainly to aid the thrift industry by extending the permissible menu of assets held and liabilities issued; perhaps best known for authorizing the introduction of the money market deposit account

GDP gap   Difference between the rate of growth of actual output and potential output

GDP price deflator   A measure of the price level calculated by dividing nominal GDP by real GDP

generalized liquidity effect   The effect of a change in monetary policy on the structure of rates of return, other things equal

gold certificates   Warehouse receipts for the U.S. gold stock that are issued by the U.S. Treasury and given to the Fed, which credits the Treasury's deposits by an equal amount

gold standard   The payments system that used gold as the unit of account, store of value, and earlier as the medium of exchange; also the international payments system in which exchange rates are fixed in terms of gold

government   The federal, state, and local bodies that have the power to levy taxes and make expenditures on behalf of the public

government purchases   Government expenditures on final goods and services

gross domestic product (GDP)   The value of final goods and services produced in a country in a year

gross national product (GNP)   The quantity of final goods and services produced per year by a nation's labor and capital, whether located at home or abroad

gross retained profits   The business sector's gross savings

gross savings   The difference between current income and current expenditures

hedge   To take an action to reduce exposure to risk of losses

holding-period yield   Rate of return for length of time security is held

households   The sector that provides labor and other inputs and receives income, which it spends or saves

hyperinflation   Annual rates of inflation of 1,000 percent or more

imperfect capital mobility   Situation in which domestic and foreign assets are imperfect substitutes or international capital flows are restricted

income elasticity of money demand   Measures the responsiveness of money demand to changes in real income

income multiplier   The amount by which real income changes in response to an exogenous change in aggregate demand

income statement   Financial statement of a firm's revenues, costs, and profits per period

indirect finance   Method of finance where funds flow from surplus units to financial intermediaries to deficit units

indirect securities   A security issued by a financial intermediary

inflation rate   Annual rate of change in the price level

inflation risk   The risk that repayment of debt may be in cheaper dollars than originally anticipated

innovations in cash management practices   Improvements in techniques that allow households and firms to economize on their money holdings and, hence, to carry out their transactions with a smaller volume of money balances

insurance companies   Nondepository financial intermediaries that issue contracts that provide protection against the economic consequences of some event and that invest primarily in long-term debt securities and equity securities

interest rate   Yield to maturity

interest rate parity   Benchmark condition in international finance according to which the domestic interest rate equals the foreign interest rate plus the expected rate of change in the exchange rate

interest rate risk   The likelihood that the interest rate of a security will rise or fall resulting in capital losses or capital gains

interest rate swap   An arrangement between two parties to swap the interest payments on their liabilities or the interest receipts on their assets

intermediate targets   Objectives the Fed sets for financial variables that are linked to its ultimate goals

international reserve assets   Inventories of foreign currencies, foreign securities, and other assets held by central banks for use in the settlement of international accounts

investment   Expenditures by firms on plant, equipment, and inventories and expenditures by households on new houses

investment banks   Market specialists that originate, underwrite, and distribute new issues of marketable securities

involuntary unemployment   Situation in which there is excess supply of labor at the existing real wage

IS curve   All the combinations of the interest rate and real income such that the goods and services market is in equilibrium, other things equal

IS-LM–BP model   Model of the goods and services, money, and foreign exchange markets

IS-LM model   A model of goods market equilibrium and money market equilibrium, which explains the determination of the interest rate and real income

junk bonds   Securities that pay high yields because of high risk of default

Keynesian fixed-price model   Aggregate demand-aggregate supply model in which the supply curve is horizontal

Keynesians   Economists who believe that the labor market clears slowly and that discretionary policies are useful in stabilizing output and employment

L   A broad concept of liquidity that consists of M3 plus some obligations of the U.S. government and of firms

large country case   Situation in which the home country is big enough to affect world interest rates by its own actions

law of asset demand   A relation between the amount of an asset that the public wants to hold and an underlying determining factor, other things equal

legal tender   Money that by law must be accepted in payment for goods and services and taxes and in repayment of debt

lender of last resort   Role of the Fed as lender of funds to banks with a temporary or a more lasting need for funds after they have explored reasonable alternatives

liabilities   A claim on a participant

liquidity   A characteristic of an asset that describes the ease and convenience with which the asset can be converted to cash

liquidity effect   The inverse relation between a change in the money supply and a change in the interest rate when the price level, real income, and expected inflation are given

liquidity preference   Demand for money

liquidity preference hypothesis   Theory of the term structure of interest rates according to which the long-term rate equals the average of the present and expected future one-period rates plus a liquidity premium

liquidity preference theory of interest rate determination   The theory that the interest rate is determined in the money market by the interaction of money demand and money supply

LM curve   All the combinations of the interest rate and real income such that the money market is in equilibrium, other things equal

load   Sales commission charged on a mutual fund

loanable funds theory of interest rate determination   The theory that the interest rate is determined in the market for debt securities by the interaction of demand and supply

loan-generated deposits   The deposits a bank creates when it makes a loan or buys a security

loan loss provisions   Funds a bank must put aside to cover bad loans

lockbox   Post office box operated by banks to speed up the collection of checks for their customers

long-horizon investors   Investors who have a preference for long-term securities

long-run aggregate supply curve   Vertical aggregate supply curve, according to which the quantity of output supplied is independent of the price level

Lucas supply curve   Aggregate supply relation derived from rational expectations, market clearance, and imperfect information

M1   The narrow measure of money, consisting of currency, traveler's checks, and non-interest-bearing and interest-bearing checking accounts.

M2   A broad measure of money, consisting of M1 plus savings deposits, small time deposits, privately held money market mutual funds, money market deposit accounts, overnight repurchase agreements, and Eurodollars

M3   The broadest measure of money, consisting of M2 plus large time deposits, money market mutual funds held by institutions, term Eurodollars, and repurchase agreements

managed, or dirty, float   A system where demand and supply determine the exchange rate but where the government sometimes enters the market as a demander or supplier to influence the rate

marginal propensity to consume out of disposable income   The amount by which consumption changes in response to a given change in disposable income

marginal propensity to consume out of national income   The amount by which consumption changes in response to a given change in national income

marginal propensity to spend out of national income   The amount by which aggregate demand for goods and services changes in response to a given change in national income

market clearance   A synonym for equilibrium

market risk   The likelihood that the price of a security will rise or fall resulting in capital gains or losses

market specialists   Financial institutions that move funds through the system but do not issue their own financial instruments

marketability   A characteristic that describes whether a security can be sold before maturity to another party

matched sale-purchase transaction A reverse repurchase agreement, where the Fed sells securities in the open market and agrees to buy them back at a specified date and price

maturity The date at which the issuer of a debt security must repay borrowed funds

McFadden Act 1927 legislation prohibiting interstate branching by national banks

medium of exchange Anything generally acceptable as a means of payment

member banks Banks that are members of the Federal Reserve System; all national banks must be members; eligible state banks may be members

menu costs The costs of adjusting prices

missing money Term coined by Stephen Goldfeld to refer to the inward shifts in the demand for M1 beginning in the mid-1970s

monetarism A school of thought that argues that to control inflation money should grow at a constant rate

monetary aggregates M1, M2, and M3

monetary base The sum of currency in circulation and total reserves

monetary base constraint The requirement that the demand for the monetary base equal the supply of the monetary base

monetary policy The methods and actions of the Federal Reserve designed to influence the quantity of money and interest rates and ultimately inflation and growth

monetary policy instruments The tools of monetary policy: open market operations, the discount rate, and reserve requirement ratios

monetized deficit Budget deficit financed by the central bank issuing reserves

money demand The sum of the demand for deposits and the demand for currency

money growth The rate of change in the quantity of money

money market deposit account (MMDA) An interest bearing deposit instrument of banks and thrifts that has limited checking privileges; introduced in 1982 to allow depository institutions to issue a financial instrument that could compete with money market mutual fund shares

money market mutual funds (MMMFs) Mutual funds that invest in short-term money market instruments, thereby earning market-determined rates; MMMFs permit redemption of shares by check

money market securities Debt securities with maturities of a year or less

money multiplier The amount by which the monetary base is multiplied to find the money supply

money supply The sum of currency in circulation and the amount of deposits that can be supported by reserves

Monthly Money Market Model The Federal Reserve's econometric model of the financial sector by itself

moral hazard Perverse incentives that insurance gives to insured parties to take excessive risks

multiple deposit creation The process by which banks increase deposits by a multiple of unwanted excess reserves in the banking system

municipal securities, or munis IOUs issued by state and local governments; interest payments are exempt from federal income taxes

mutual funds Nondepository financial intermediaries that pool the funds of small savers and invest in a diversified portfolio of securities

NAIRU The inflation-safe, or nonaccelerating inflation, rate of unemployment; synonym for the natural rate of unemployment

narrow bank A bank that issues checkable deposits and invests in a narrow range of safe assets, such as Treasury bills

national banks Banks chartered by the federal government

National Credit Union Administration (NCUA) Federal agency that charters and supervises credit unions

national income The sum of the payments to the inputs that produce the nation's output

national product identity An accounting relation according to which the sum of the actual values of consumption, investment, government purchases, and net exports equals a nation's gross domestic product

national savings Private savings reduced by government dissavings or augmented by government savings

natural rate of unemployment Inflation-safe unemployment rate

negotiable CDs Marketable time deposits of $100,000 or more

neoclassical synthesis Economic model that combines the Keynesian short run, in which money wages are sticky, with the classical long run, in which money wages are flexible

net creditor nation A country whose stock of assets in other countries exceeds the stock of foreign-owned assets at home; a net lender to the rest of the world

net debtor nation A country whose stock of assets in other countries is less than the stock of foreign-owned assets at home; a net borrower from the rest of the world

net domestic product (NDP) Gross domestic product minus depreciation

net exports Exports minus imports of goods and services

net marginal revenue of deposits The net pecuniary return per additional dollar of deposits, which equals the reserve-adjusted interest rate minus the deposit rate

net technical factors affecting reserves A net measure of the noncontrolled factors affecting reserves; the other sources of reserves, minus currency in circulation, minus the other uses of reserves

net technical factors affecting the monetary base The "other assets" in the Fed's balance sheet minus the "other liabilities"

net worth The difference between a participant's assets and liabilities

neutrality of money A characteristic of a fully employed economy where changes in growth of the nominal money supply do not affect real variables

new classical school Economists whose models of the economy are built on continuous market clearance and rational expectations

new financial environment (NFE) The financial system that emerged in the 1980s and that is characterized by market-determined rates on assets and liabilities of depository institutions and by greater homogeneity among these institutions

new Keynesian school Economists whose models of the economy incorporate wage or price stickiness so that markets do not clear continuously

nominal exchange rate Dollar price of a unit of foreign exchange

nominal GDP Output measured at current prices

nominal interest rate Observed rate of interest; the amount received by the lender and paid by the borrower

nonborrowed reserves Total reserves supplied by the Fed minus borrowed reserves; also equals the amount of Treasury securities held by the Fed plus net technical factors

nondepository institutions Financial intermediaries, such as pension funds and insurance companies, whose obligations are not deposit accounts

nondiversifiable risk Risk that is endemic to the market and cannot be reduced through diversification

nondurable consumer goods Goods that are used up in the year in which they are acquired by households

nonsterilized intervention A foreign exchange market operation that changes the domestic money supply because it is not offset by a domestic open market operation

nontransactions balances A term that describes all the non-M1 components of M2 and M3, which are restricted in their use for making payments

NOW accounts and Super-NOW accounts Interest-bearing checking accounts issued by depository institutions

off-balance-sheet activities Specialized lines of a bank's business that do not show up on the bank's balance sheet

Office of the Comptroller of the Currency (OCC) Federal agency within the U.S. Treasury that charters national banks

Office of Thrift Supervision Bureau of the U.S. Treasury established by FIRREA of 1989 to charter and regulate S&Ls

Okun's Law Empirical relation between output and unemployment according to which output falls by 2.5 percent for every percentage increase in the unemployment rate

old financial environment (OFE) The financial system in the United States from 1933 to 1980; this system placed ceilings on deposit rates and imposed restrictions on the portfolios of depository institutions, especially thrifts

open bank assistance Variety of practices used by regulators to help banks remain open

open market debt of firms All IOUs issued by nonfinancial firms and sold in the open market

open market operations Purchases and sales of government securities in the open market by the central bank

open market securities Securities sold in the open market through market specialists

operating targets Objectives the Fed sets for financial variables that are linked to its intermediate targets

opportunity cost of deposits The difference between the interest rate on debt securities and the deposit rate

opportunity cost of money The interest forgone by holding money instead of an alternative asset

options market A market where contracts that give the right but not the obligation to buy or sell a financial instrument within a given time period at a specified price are traded

other checkable deposits A catchall category that refers to all the interest-bearing accounts that comprise M1

payoff method Arrangement for handling an insolvent bank by allowing the bank to fail and paying off insured depositors

Penny Benny Nickname for the Pension Benefit Guaranty Corporation, the agency that insures pension funds

pension funds Nondepository financial intermediaries that issue contracts to provide income payments to retirees and that invest primarily in long-term debt securities and equity securities

perfect capital mobility Situation in which domestic and foreign assets are perfect substitutes and international capital flows are unrestricted

Phillips curve Graphical relation between inflation and unemployment

planned, or estimated, velocity The number of times per year the public wants money to turn over in buying final goods and services; calculated by dividing real GDP by real money demand

planned velocity-indexed money growth The sum of targeted money growth and estimated velocity growth

policy ineffectiveness proposition New classical version of the neutrality of money according to which expected changes in monetary policy have no effect on real output

potential output, or, natural level of output Level of output at which all factors of production are fully employed

pragmatic monetary targeters Economists who are in favor of revising monetary targets if actual velocity deviates from estimated velocity

precautionary demand Demand for money arising from uncertainty about future payments

precise rate of return The rate on an asset that makes the present value of a stream of receipts accruing to the asset holder equal to the purchase price of the asset

preferred habitat hypothesis Theory of the term structure of interest rates according to which expectations of future interest rates and the preferences of investors for short-term or long-term securities determine the shape of the yield curve

present value The value in today's dollars of a stream of future receipts

price level The collective price of goods and services

price-level effect on the interest rate The positive relation between a change in the price level and a change in the interest rate

primary dealers Thirty-nine investment banks and commercial banks through which the Fed carries out open market operations

primary market The market for new issues of securities, called primary securities

prime rate A base rate on bank loans mostly to small and medium-sized businesses

principal-agent problem A divergence of interests between principal parties, such as owners or taxpayers, and their agents, such as managers or politicians, because of a difference in incentives

principle of diminishing marginal product of labor Economic relation according to which the extra output produced by an additional unit of labor falls as more labor is employed

principles of excess demand and excess supply Explanations of movements in prices or rates of return that restore equilibrium in a market

producer durable goods Goods used in production by firms over many years

profit-maximizing condition Stipulation that a bank choose each item in its balance sheet at the level for which marginal revenue equals marginal cost

profits The remuneration of capital

property/casualty insurance companies Nondepository financial intermediaries that sell protection from losses resulting from property damage and injuries

purchase and assumption (P & A) method Arrangement for handling an insolvent bank by closing the bank and allowing new owners to purchase it

purchasing power of money, or value of money The amount of goods and services that a dollar can purchase

purchasing power parity Theory that the rate of change in the nominal exchange rate equals the difference between the domestic and foreign inflation rates

pure expectations hypothesis Theory of the term structure of interest rates according to which the long-term interest rate equals the average of the current short-term rate and expected future short-term rates

Q-ratio The ratio of the market value of an existing physical asset to its replacement cost

quantity theory of money The theory that planned velocity is the link between money and nominal GDP and that changes in the quantity of money lead to changes in nominal GDP

Quarterly Model The Federal Reserve's econometric model of the real and financial sectors of the economy

rate of inflation The rate of change in the price level

rate of return Annual reward to an asset holder

rational expectations Forward-looking expectations formed on the basis of all available information and knowledge of economic models

real assets Property that has physical characteristics

real business cycle school Economists who assume that money is always neutral and explain changes in output by changes in real factors such as productivity

real exchange rate The amount of domestic goods that must be given up to buy a unit of foreign goods; calculated by multiplying

the nominal exchange rate by the foreign price level and dividing by the domestic price level

real GDP A nation's annual output measured in the prices of a base year, currently 1987

real income National income measured in terms of the prices of a base year

real income effect on the interest rate The positive relation between a change in real income and a change in the interest rate

recession A sustained period of economic weakness in which real income (and output) is falling

redistributive costs of inflation Inflation-induced transfers of wealth among participants in the economy

Regulation A The Federal Reserve regulation that sets guidelines for the operation of the discount window

Regulation Q The defunct Federal Reserve regulation governing the maximum interest rate payable on savings and time deposits issued by member banks

regulatory forbearance Practice in which regulators keep unhealthy banks and thrifts open by not enforcing usual supervisory standards

repurchase agreements (RPs) Sales of securities by depository institutions in order to acquire funds with the understanding that the securities will be repurchased for a specified price and at a specified time (e.g., the next day for overnight RPs)

required reserves Reserves that the law and the Fed require depository institutions to hold

reserve balances with the Fed Accounts that banks and other depository institutions have with the Fed

reserve requirement ratio The fraction of deposits that must be held in the form of reserves

reserves Vault cash and reserve balances with the Fed, which are obligations of the Fed to banks and other depository institutions

reserves constraint Requirement that total reserves demanded equal total reserves supplied

Resolution Trust Corporation (RTC) Agency established by FIRREA of 1989 to dispose of failed thrifts

Ricardian equivalence theorem Proposition that tax cuts have no effect on output because forward-looking individuals discount their future tax liabilities

Riegle-Neal Interstate Banking and Branching Efficiency Act Legislation passed in 1994 that permits nationwide branching by banks

rigid monetary targeters Economists who advocate setting targets for money growth and sticking with the targets regardless of the behavior of velocity

risk Predictability of the return on an asset

risk averse Description of investors who dislike capital losses more than they appreciate capital gains and therefore are willing to give up some return to reduce risk

Savings Association Insurance Fund (SAIF) Fund run by the FDIC since 1989 to insure S&Ls

seasonal credit   Loans provided by the Fed to banks, often in agricultural areas, to meet a periodic, seasonal need for funds

secondary market   The market for existing securities, called *secondary securities*

sector   A group of participants who share the same characteristics and exhibit similar behavior

Securities and Exchange Commission (SEC)   The federal agency that oversees and regulates primary and secondary markets and securities firms

securities firms   A collective term for investment banks, security dealers, and brokers

securitization   The process of transforming bank loans into marketable assets by packaging them and selling them to investors

segmented-markets hypothesis   Theory of the term structure of interest rates according to which only the preferences of investors matter in determining the shape of the yield curve

sell at a discount   Purchase price is less than face value

Shadow Open Market Committee   Formed in 1973, this group of private economists meets twice a year to analyze and comment on economic conditions and the conduct of U.S. monetary policy

short-horizon investors   Investors who have a preference for short-term securities

short-run aggregate supply curve   Curve depicting a positive relation between the quantity of output supplied and the price level

short-term securities/intermediate securities/long-term securities   Securities on which the length of time to maturity ranges from overnight to 1 year/from more than 1 year to 10 years/from more than 10 years upward

simple deposits multiplier   Inverse of the reserve requirement ratio

small-country case   Situation in which the home country is too small to affect world interest rates by its own actions

sources and uses of reserves statement   An accounting statement of the factors supplying reserves and absorbing reserves; the balance sheet of the Fed augmented by the monetary accounts of the U.S. Treasury

sources of bank funds   A bank's liabilities and its net worth

special drawing rights (SDRs)   International reserves that are an obligation of the International Monetary Fund and that can be used in settling debt among nations

speculative demand   Demand for money arising from uncertainty about future interest rates

spot interest rates   Rates on current loans of any duration

spot market   The market for immediate delivery of an item

square-root rule   Stipulation that the transactions demand for money is directly proportional to the square root of the volume of transactions and inversely proportional to the square of the opportunity cost of money

stable demand function for money   Property that the demand for money can be accurately predicted by a function that relates money demand to a few key variables

state banks   Banks chartered by states

sterilized intervention   A foreign exchange market operation that does not change the domestic money supply because it is offset by an open market operation

sticky money wages   Situation in which money wages fall slowly in response to excess supply in the labor market

stock   A variable that is expressed as the quantity existing at a point in time

store of value   A reservoir of future purchasing power

stripped securities   Coupon-bearing securities from which the coupon payments have been removed, thereby transforming them into zero coupon securities

supply of deposits   Quantity of deposits a bank wants to provide

supply of real money balances   The supply of money measured in terms of the prices of a base year

supply of securities   The sum of the amount of securities the public and the Treasury want to issue at each level of the interest rate

supply of total reserves   Total amount of reserves issued by the Fed, which equals Treasury securities held by the Fed, plus discount window loans, plus "other assets," minus currency in circulation and "other liabilities"

surplus unit   A participant whose current gross savings is greater than current expenditure on capital goods

technical factors affecting reserves, or noncontrolled factors   The "other assets" and "other liabilities" in the Fed's balance sheet and currency in circulation; these items affect the supply of total reserves but are outside the Fed's control

technology and regulatory index   A measure of the technological and regulatory factors that affect the marginal cost of issuing deposits

term insurance   Life insurance that pays a fixed amount upon the death of the insured party

term structure of interest rates   Relation between short-term and long-term rates on comparable debt securities

theory of asset choice or portfolio choice   The theory that explains how the public decides to allocate its wealth among alternative assets

thrift crisis   Widespread failure of savings and loan associations in the 1980s

thrifts   Depository institutions that traditionally specialized in issuing savings and time deposits and in making loans to households. Since the early 1980s, thrifts have been permitted to issue checking accounts and to make a limited amount of business loans

time deposits   Interest-bearing accounts that are issued by depository institutions and that do not have immediate maturity

too-big-to-fail policy   Practice in which regulators refrain from allowing large banks to fail because of the side effects on the health of the financial system

total capital gains   The difference between the redemption price of an asset and its current purchase price

total domestic nonfinancial debt A broad measure of debt that includes the borrowing of households, firms, and federal, state, and local governments

total monetary base demanded The sum of currency in circulation and total reserves demanded by banks

total monetary base supplied The sum of currency in circulation and total reserves supplied by the Fed

Trading Desk, or Desk The unit of the Federal Reserve Bank of New York that implements the FOMC's domestic policy directive by overseeing and undertaking open market operations

transactions balances All components of M1

transactions demand Demand for money arising from the need to hold cash for current personal and business expenditures

transfer payments Expenditures by the government for which no currently produced goods or services are received in exchange

Treasury bills, or T-bills Marketable short-term Treasury securities; sold at a discount

Treasury bonds, or T-bonds Marketable long-term Treasury securities with semiannual coupon payments

Treasury notes, or T-notes Marketable intermediate-term Treasury securities with semiannual coupon payments

Treasury securities Marketable and nonmarketable interest-bearing debt issued by the U.S. Treasury to finance the excess of government expenditures over tax receipts

twin deficits Concurrent budget deficits and trade deficits

U.S. Treasury Department of the federal government that collects federal tax revenues, makes expenditures authorized by Congress and the president, and issues financial instruments to finance the excess of government expenditures over tax receipts

ultimate goals The final objectives of monetary policy, usually expressed as price stability, full employment, and maximum sustainable economic growth

unit of account A yardstick for measuring prices and values

universal banking The practice of not legally separating the activities of commercial banks and securities firm

unwanted excess reserves Excess reserves above the level desired by banks

uses of bank funds A bank's assets

variable-rate asset or liability A financial instrument whose rate of return moves up or down with market rates of interest

vault cash The paper notes and coins that banks and other depository institutions have on hand

velocity of circulation, V The number of times each dollar turns over in buying final goods and services

velocity-indexed money growth The sum of money growth and velocity growth

velocity-indexed supply of money The product of the nominal money supply and velocity

wages The remuneration of labor

welfare costs of inflation Net losses to society from inflation

whole-life insurance Life insurance that combines term insurance with savings

yield curve Graphical depiction of the relation between the yield to maturity on a debt security and the length of time to maturity

yield on a discount basis A traditional method of calculating the yield on short-term zero coupon securities that understates the true, or coupon equivalent, yield

yield to maturity Rate of return to maturity, at which time the final payment is the face value of the debt security

zero coupon securities Securities that make no interest payments; they have only face value

Try It Out 3.1

1. *a.* Coupon rate = (1,000/10,000) = 0.10, or 10%
   Current yield = (1,000/9,800) = 0.1020, or 10.2%
   Yield to maturity = current yield plus capital
   gains rate
   = (1,000/9,800) + [(10,000 −
   9,800)/9,800]/10
   = 0.1020 + 0.002
   = 0.104, or 10.4%

   b. Holding period yield = (1,000/9,800) + [(4,000 −
   9,800)/9,800]/5
   = 0.102 − 0.118
   = −0.016 or −1.6%

   c. Yield to maturity = (1,000/4,000) + [(10,000 −
   4,000)/4,000]/5
   = 0.25 + 0.30
   = 0.55 or 55%

2. Because the two securities have the same maturity
   and are identical in all other characteristics, they must
   have the same yield to maturity. We can employ this
   requirement to find the price of the old security.

New security: yield to maturity = (100/1,000) = 0.10

Old security: yield to maturity = $(90/P_a)$ + [(1,000 −
$P_a)/P_a$]/10

Setting the old-security yield equal to 0.10 and solving for
P_a, we find:

$0.10 = (90/P_a) + [(1,000 − P_a)/P_a]/10$

$0.10P_a = 90 + 100 − 0.10P_a$

$0.20P_a = 190$

$P_a = \$950$

Try It Out 4.1: Characteristics of U.S. Financial Instruments

Treasury bills

1. U.S. Treasury
2. All other participants—households, firms, depository
   institutions, Federal Reserve, foreign sector

3. 1 year or less (13, 26, or 52 weeks)
4. active secondary market
5. sold at a discount
6. low
7. zero

Treasury notes

1. U.S. Treasury
2. all other participants
3. more than 1 year to 10 years
4. active secondary market
5. interest payments plus capital gain/loss
6. moderate
7. zero

Treasury bonds

1. U.S. Treasury
2. all other participants
3. more than 10 years
4. active secondary market
5. interest payments plus capital gain/loss
6. high
7. zero

Federal agency securities

1. federal agencies and federally sponsored agencies
2. all other participants
3. varies
4. active secondary market
5. interest payments plus capital gain/loss
6. varies
7. very low

Municipal securities

1. state/local governments
2. households, firms, financial institutions
3. varies
4. secondary market exists

5. interest payments plus capital gain/loss
6. varies
7. varies, typically low

Reserve balances with Fed and vault cash

1. Fed
2. depository institutions
3. immediate maturity
4. not applicable
5. none
6. zero
7. zero

Currency in circulation

1. Fed and U.S. Treasury
2. households and firms
3. immediate maturity
4. not applicable
5. none
6. zero
7. zero

Federal funds

1. depository institutions
2. depository institutions
3. overnight
4. no secondary market
5. interest payments
6. very low
7. low

Commercial paper

1. firms
2. nonbank financial institutions, firms, foreign sector
3. 1 month to 9 months
4. secondary market exists, although somewhat limited for some issuers
5. sold at a discount
6. low
7. varies

Bankers' acceptances

1. created by banks on behalf of firms engaged in trade

2. financial institutions, firms, foreign sector
3. less than one year
4. secondary market exists
5. sold at a discount
6. low
7. varies

Corporate bonds

1. firms
2. households, nonbank financial institutions, foreign sector
3. 10 to 40 years
4. active secondary market
5. interest payments plus capital gain/loss
6. high
7. varies

Corporate stocks

1. firms
2. households, nonbank financial institutions, foreign sector
3. never matures
4. active secondary market
5. dividend payments plus capital gain/loss
6. high
7. not applicable

Bank loans

1. households and firms
2. banks
3. varies
4. secondary market exists for some types of loans, especially home mortgages
5. interest payments
6. varies
7. varies

Demand deposits

1. depository institutions
2. households and firms
3. immediate maturity
4. not applicable

5. no explicit interest (implicit interest in the form of free services)

6. zero

7. very low

NOW and Super-NOW accounts

1. depository institutions

2. households and nonprofit organizations

3. immediate maturity

4. not applicable

5. interest payments

6. zero

7. very low

Negotiable CDs

1. depository institutions

2. nonbank financial institutions, firms, foreign sector

3. less than 1 year

4. secondary market exists

5. interest payments plus capital gain/loss

6. low

7. varies

Try It Out 6.1

1. Adding the same items on each side of the two balance sheets, we find:

Public

Assets		Liabilities plus Net Worth	
Currency	150	Bank loans	500
Bank deposits	350	Open market debt	
U.S. Treasury		of firms	200
securities	600	Net worth	1,450
Real assets	650		
Open market debt			
of firms	200		
Corporate stock	200		
Total	2,150	Total	2,150

2. $1,450 + 500 + 200 = 150 + 350 + 600 + 200 + 200 + 650$

3. Net worth = Money + Securities + Real assets
$$1,450 = 500 + 300 + 650$$

Try It Out 7.1

1. $i\downarrow \Rightarrow D^d\uparrow \Rightarrow M^d\uparrow$: movement along the money demand curve

2. $Y\downarrow \Rightarrow D^d\downarrow \Rightarrow M^d\downarrow$: inward shift of money demand curve

3. $rr\downarrow \Rightarrow [(1-rr)i - r_D]\uparrow \Rightarrow$ the net marginal revenue from issuing deposits rises $\Rightarrow$ net marginal revenue from issuing deposits is greater than the marginal cost $\Rightarrow$ banks want to issue more deposits $\Rightarrow r_D\uparrow \Rightarrow D^d\uparrow \Rightarrow M^d\uparrow$: outward shift of money demand curve

4. $\mathfrak{IR}\uparrow \Rightarrow$ the marginal cost of issuing deposits rises $\Rightarrow$ the marginal revenue from issuing deposits is less than the marginal cost $\Rightarrow$ banks want to issue fewer deposits $\Rightarrow r_D\downarrow \Rightarrow D^d\downarrow \Rightarrow M^d\downarrow$: inward shift of money demand curve

5. No effect on money demand in the United States

Try It Out 8.1

1. $NBR = B_F + (OA - OL - Cur)$
$$= 202 + (20 - 14 - 150)$$
$$= \$58 \text{ billion.}$$

2. $BR \equiv DWL = \$5$ billion

3. Effective reserves $= NBR + BR - ER$
$$= 58 + 5 - 5$$
$$= \$58 \text{ billion}$$

4. Simple deposits multiplier $= (1/rr) = 10$

5. $D_R = (1/rr) \times$ Effective reserves $= \$580$ billion.

Try It Out 8.2

1. $\Delta NBR = \Delta B_F + (\Delta OA - \Delta OL - \Delta Cur)$
$$= 0 + (0 - 0 - 2)$$
$$= -\$2 \text{ billion}$$

2. ΔEffective reserves $= \Delta NBR + \Delta BR - \Delta ER$
$$= -2 + 0 - 0$$
$$= -\$2 \text{ billion}$$

3. $\Delta D_R = (1/rr) \times \Delta$Effective reserves
$$= 10 \times (-2)$$
$$= -\$20 \text{ billion}$$

4. $\Delta M^s = \Delta Cur + \Delta D_R$
$$= 2 + (-20)$$
$$= -\$18 \text{ billion}$$

Try It Out 9.1

M^s falls by \$1,000 million, other things equal, that is, *at the original interest rate* i_1:

$$\Delta M^s = (1/rr) \times \Delta B_F$$
$$= 10 \times (-100)$$
$$= -\$1,000 \text{ million}$$

Hence, the money supply curve shifts inward by 1,000. This is shown by a movement from point 1 to point 2 in the accompanying graph. The excess demand for money increases the interest rate to i_2. At the higher interest rate, banks supply more money because borrowed reserves rise and excess reserves fall. This increase in the quantity of money supplied is shown by a movement along the money supply curve from point 2 to point 3, which is the new equilibrium point. Thus, the rise in the interest rate makes the fall in the quantity of money less than \$1,000 million, as shown by the horizontal distance between point 1 and point 3.

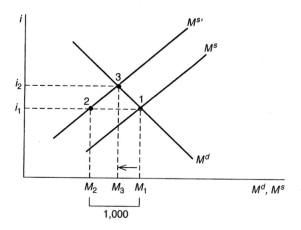

Try It Out 9.2

1. In the accompanying graph depicting the loanable funds theory, the B^d curve shifts to the left when the demand for securities falls. In the absence of Fed intervention, the market would settle at point 2, at a higher interest rate.

2. The Fed's open-market purchase of securities shifts the B^d curve to the right, restoring the initial equilibrium—point 1.

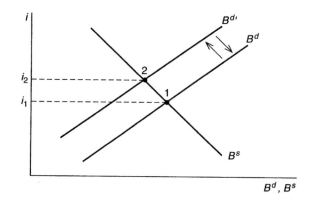

Try It Out 10.1

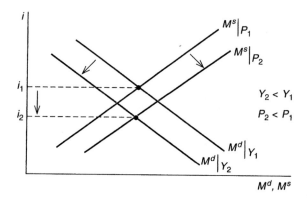

The fall in real income, Y, shifts the money demand curve to the left. The fall in the price level, by increasing real nonborrowed reserves, increases the money supply and shifts the money supply curve to the right. Each shift creates excess supply of money, which reduces the interest rate. Schematically, we have:

$$\left.\begin{array}{l} Y\downarrow \Rightarrow M^d\downarrow \\[2mm] P\downarrow \Rightarrow M^s\uparrow \end{array}\right\} \Rightarrow ESM \Rightarrow i\downarrow$$

Try It Out 10.2

$$P\downarrow \Rightarrow \left.\begin{array}{l} (NBR/P)\uparrow \Rightarrow M^s\uparrow \Rightarrow ESM \Rightarrow i\downarrow \Rightarrow (C+I)\uparrow \\[2mm] (NBR/P)\uparrow \Rightarrow M^s\uparrow \Rightarrow ESM \Rightarrow i\downarrow \Rightarrow e\uparrow \Rightarrow NX\uparrow \end{array}\right\} \Rightarrow AD\uparrow$$

A fall in the price level increases the real value of nonborrowed reserves, which increases the money supply, creating excess supply of money. As a result, the interest rate falls. The lower interest rate directly increases consumption and investment. The lower interest rate also leads to an increase in demand for foreign securities, which increases the demand for foreign exchange. As a result, the foreign exchange rate rises, making foreign goods more expensive at home and domestic goods cheaper internationally. In response, net exports rise. The increase in consumption, investment, and net exports increases the aggregate demand for goods and services.

Try It Out 12.1

Ann		George	
Deposits	Net Worth	Deposits	Net Worth
with Bufbank	−100	with Seabank	+100
−100		+100	

Bufbank		Seabank	
Reserves	Deposits	Reserves	Deposits
with Fed	−100	with Fed	+100
−100		+100	

Fed	
	Reserve Account of
	Bufbank −100
	Reserve Account of
	Seabank +100

Try It Out 14.1

1.

Sources of Reserves
1. Federal Reserve portfolio of securities 350,821
2. Discount window loans 178
3. Other sources of reserves 72,987

Uses of Reserves
4. Currency in circulation + Other uses of reserves
   374,016 + 22,663 = 396,679
5. Total reserve balances with the Fed 27,308

2. Net technical factors:
$$OS - OU - Cur = 72,987 - 22,663 - 374,016$$
$$= -\$323,692 \text{ million}$$

The net technical factors, at −$323,692 million, are opposite in sign and smaller in size than the Fed's portfolio of securities of $350,821 million.

3.
$$\begin{array}{ccccc} \text{Nonborrowed} & = & \text{Fed's portfolio} & + & \text{Net technical} \\ \text{reserves} & & \text{of securities} & & \text{factors} \\ \$27,129 & = & \$350,821 & + & (-\$323,692 \\ \text{million} & & \text{million} & & \text{million}) \end{array}$$

Try It Out 15.1

A single bank does not undertake a multiple expansion of deposits by making $9,000 million of loans because it will almost immediately lose those deposits and an equal amount of reserves in check clearing with other banks. As a result, the bank will be reserve deficient and will have to liquidate (call in) the loans.

Try It Out 18.1

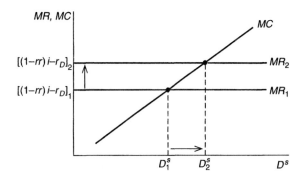

If the deposit rate falls by more than the interest rate, the net marginal revenue from issuing deposits, which equals the reserve-adjusted spread, $(1 - rr)i - r_D$, rises. The marginal revenue curve moves up, inducing banks to attract more deposits. For example, if $rr = 0.10$ and if the deposit rate falls from 5 percent to 3 percent and the interest rate falls from 10 percent to 9 percent, the net marginal revenue rises from 4 percent to 5.1 percent.

Try It Out 20.1

1.

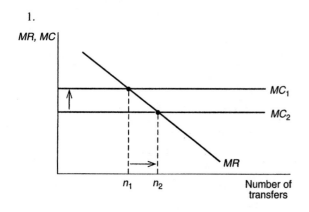

A fall in the marginal cost of transfers between money and bonds increases the number of transfers from n_1 to n_2. As a consequence, fewer cash balances are needed and money demand falls as the graph in part 2 illustrates.

2.

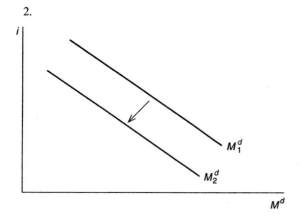

Try It Out 21.1

$$D^d = 290 - 3i + 3r_D + 0.10Y + 0.20\ell \qquad (21–5)$$
$$D = 893.7117 - 0.261i \qquad (21–11)$$

The smaller coefficient of the interest rate in (21–11) indicates the property that deposit demand (and money demand) is less interest sensitive when the deposit rate is market determined than when it is fixed. The reason for this is that with a market determined deposit rate a rise in the interest rate increases the deposit rate and, thus, the opportunity cost of holding deposits rises by less than the increase in the interest rate. In contrast, with the deposit rate fixed, the opportunity cost increases by the full increase in the interest rate.

Try It Out 22.1

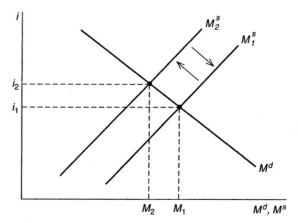

Other things equal, an increase in excess reserves reduces the money supply, that is, the M^s curve shifts to the left to position M^s_2. As a result, the interest rate rises to i_2 and the quantity of money falls to M_2. The Fed can purchase in the open market an amount of securities equal to the initial increase in excess reserves, thereby increasing the money supply and shifting the M^s curve back to its initial position, which restores both the interest rate and the quantity of money to their original values.

Try It Out 23.1

For the first year, the spot rate and forward rate coincide. Thus, $r_1 = R_1 = 10\%$.

To determine r_2, we use the formula that $R_2 = (r_1 + r_2)/2$. Substituting the known values for R_2 and r_1 into this formula, we find that $9 = (10 + r_2)/2$, from which we find that $r_2 = 8\%$.

To determine r_3, we use the formula that $R_3 = (r_1 + r_2 + r_3)/3$. Substituting $R_3 = 8.5$, $r_1 = 10$, and $r_2 = 8$ into this formula and solving for r_3, we find that $r_3 = 7.5\%$.

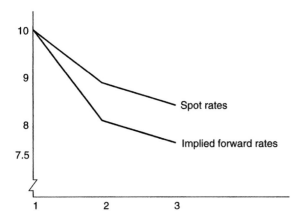

Try It Out 23.2

1. To achieve the higher federal funds rate, the Fed must conduct open market sales of Treasury bills, that is, the Fed must reduce B_F. The sales of T-bills reduces reserves in the system and increases the degree of reserve pressure in the federal funds market, which increases the federal funds rate as well as the bills rate.

2. Schematically, we have:

$$B_F\downarrow \Rightarrow B^d\downarrow \Rightarrow B^d < B^s \Rightarrow r_B\uparrow$$
$$r_B\uparrow \Rightarrow L^d\downarrow \Rightarrow ESL \Rightarrow r_L\uparrow$$
$$\left.\begin{array}{c} r_B\uparrow \\ r_L\uparrow \end{array}\right\} \Rightarrow K^d\downarrow \Rightarrow ESK \Rightarrow r_K\uparrow$$

In words, the sale of T-bills by the Fed reduces the demand for T-bills, which causes excess supply and raises the bill rate. In turn, the increase in the bill rate reduces the demand by banks for the asset loans, causing excess supply of loan securities and raising the loan rate. Finally, with both the bill rate and the loan rate higher, the public switches funds to bills, borrows less from the banks, and reduces its demand for equities (capital.) The consequent excess supply of equities raises the equity capital rate. Thus, all three rates rise. The deposit rate also rises.

Try It Out 24.1

Substituting TA into Y_D, we get:

$$Y_D = Y - 0.25Y = 0.75Y$$

Substituting Y_D into C, we get:

$$C = 400 + 0.6Y$$

Next, we use the equilibrium relation:

$$C + I + G + NX = Y$$

After substituting C and the values of I, G, and NX into this equation, we solve for Y:

$$400 + 0.6Y + 100 + 100 = Y$$
$$(1 - 0.6)Y = 600$$
$$Y = (1/0.4)600$$

a. $Y = \$1,500$ billion

b. The multiplier is $(1/0.4) = 2.5$

c. $(1/[1 - (1 - t)c] = [(1/(1 - 0.64)] = (1/0.36) = 2.78$

That is, the multiplier rises to 2.78.

The new level of output, $Y = 1,668$, is found by multiplying 600 by 2.78. The change in Y is: $\Delta Y = 1,668 - 1,500 = 168$. The same effect is found by using the formula:

$$\Delta Y = -(cY_1\Delta t) \times (1/0.36) = -[0.8 \times 1,500 \times (-0.05)] \times$$
$$(1/0.36) = 60 \times 2.78 = 167$$

(The slight difference is due to rounding.)

Try It Out 26.1

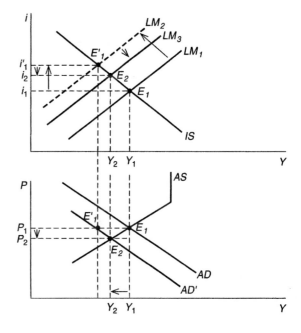

Point E_1 represents the initial equilibrium in the upper and lower panels of the graph. The exogenous increase in money demand causes excess demand in the money market and raises the interest rate, which causes the *LM* curve to shift upward from LM_1 to LM_2 in the upper panel. The higher interest rate reduces aggregate demand, so that given the initial value of the price level, the equilibrium moves from point E_1 to Point E_1' in the upper panel. In the lower panel, the reduction in aggregate demand at each price level shifts the *AD* curve to the left. If the price level were to remain unchanged, the economy would move from point E_1 to point E_1' in the lower panel. However, the reduction in aggregate demand creates an excess supply of goods and services, which lowers the price level. The final equilibrium is at point E_2 in both panels of the graph. In the upper panel, the lower price level shifts the *LM* curve down to LM_3, because the lower price level increases the real money supply, which reduces the interest rate. In the end, the price level and output fall while the interest rate rises.

Try It Out 28.1

From 1961 to 1969 there was a stable Phillips curve. Reducing unemployment from 7 percent to about 3.5 percent raised inflation from 1 percent to 5 percent. Inflationary expectations and a series of adverse supply-side shocks shifted the curve upward, where it stayed in the mid to late 1970s. Inflationary expectations shifted the curve further up where it stayed in the early 1980s. The severe contractionary policies of that period reduced inflationary expectations and shifted the curve down considerably where it stayed in the late 1980s.

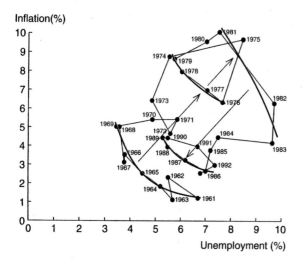

Try It Out 29.1

1. $e = \$1.60/£$, $P_f = £100,000/\text{Rolls Royce}$
    $eP_f = (\$1.60/£) \times (£100,000/\text{Rolls Royce}) = \$160,000$ per Rolls Royce
    $(1/e) = (£0.625/\$) \times (\$40,000/\text{Cadillac}) = £25,000$ per Cadillac
2. $e = \$1.50/£$, $P_f = £100,000/\text{Rolls Royce}$
    $eP_f = (\$1.50/£) \times (£100,000/\text{Rolls Royce}) = \$150,000$ per Rolls Royce
    $(1/e)P = (£0.6667/\$) \times (\$40,000/\text{Cadillac}) = £26,668$ per Cadillac

Try It Out 29.2

1. $E = (eP_f)/P = [(\$1.60/£) \times (£100,000/\text{Rolls Royce})]/$
    $[\$40,000/\text{Cadillac}]$
    $= (\$160,000/\text{Rolls Royce})/(\$40,000)/$
    Cadillac)
    $= (160,000/\text{Rolls Royce}) \times (\text{Cadillac}/$
    $40,000)$
    $= 4$ Cadillacs per Rolls Royce
2. $E = (eP_f)/P = [(\$1.50/£) \times (£100,000/\text{Rolls Royce})]/$
    $[\$40,000/\text{Cadillac}]$
    $= (\$150,000/\text{Rolls Royce})/(\$40,000/$
    Cadillac)
    $= (150,000/\text{Rolls Royce}) \times (\text{Cadillac}/$
    $40,000)$
    $= 3.75$ Cadillacs per Rolls Royce

The depreciation of the nominal exchange rate, that is, a fall in the dollar price of the British pound, leads to a depreciation of the real exchange rate, which makes the Rolls Royce cheaper for Americans in terms of the number of Cadillacs that must be given up to buy one Rolls Royce.

INDEX

A

Actual real rate of interest, 58
Actual velocity-indexed money growth, 340–41
Adaptive expectations assumption, 605
Adjustable-rate mortgages, 106
Adjustment borrowings, 149
Adjustment credit, 255–57
Administration of the discount window, 228, 399
  and money supply, 322
  quantitative, 478
Administrative index, 399, 474–75
Adverse selection, 387–88
  and bank credit, 200
  efficiency wages to prevent, 621
  in insurance, 420
Adverse selection model, 621
After-tax rate of return, 47–48
Aggregate demand, 574–79
  effect on real income of exogenous changes in, 528–30
  endogenous and exogenous changes, 526–28
  and fiscal policy changes, 530–34
  and recession of 1990–91, 531
Aggregate demand-aggregate supply model, 572
Aggregate demand curve, 204–5
  in Great Depression, 640–41
  impact of changes on Keynesian short-run model, 591–94
  inward shift, 622–24
  schematic, 574–75
  shifts in IS and LM curves, 576–79
Aggregate demand for goods and services, 198–200
Aggregate supply, evolution of theory, 605–6
Aggregate supply curve, 205–6; see also Lucas aggregate supply curve
  classical model, 581–82
  impact of shifts in Keynesian short-run model, 594–97
  ISLM model, 579–80
  Keynesian fixed-price model, 580–81
  Keynesian short-run model, 582–86
Akerlof, George A., 35, 620, 629
Alesina, Alberto, 243
American Bankers Association, 406
American Stock Exchange, 77
Ando, Albert, 220

Angell, Wayne, 227
Animal spirits of entrepreneurs, 527, 537
Annual Report of the Board of Governors, 247, 562
Annual Report of the Council of Economic Advisers, 557
Anti-inflationary policy, 624–25
Apple Computer, 123
Appreciation of currency, 668, 713–14
  expectations about, 677–78
Approximation of the annual rate of return, 47–48
Asked price, 54, 59
Asset and liability management committee, 390–92
Asset-backed loans, 413, 414
Asset choice theory, 121–23
Asset demand, laws of, 123–29
Asset quality, 366–67
Assets, 12
  bank financial innovations, 103–11
  of banks, 383
  of life insurance companies, 421–23
  liquidity, 58–60
  minimum denomination, 60
  net worth, 89
  of pension funds, 424
  of property/casualty companies, 423
  rate of return, 122
  relative liquidity, 128–29
  relative marketability, 128
  relative maturity, 128
  relative risk, 128
Asymmetric information, 35–36, 387
  and bank credit, 200
  compared to imperfect information, 610
  and insider trading, 426
  overcoming disadvantages of, 36
Austro-Hungarian Bank, 224
Automatic stabilizers, 646
Automatic teller machines, 110
Automatic transfer services account, 101
Autonomous demand, 535
Average annual capital gains rate, 47
Axilrod, Stephen H., 167
Azariades, Costas, 620

B

Bailey, Martin Neil, 620
Balanced funds, 416
Balance of payments; *see also* BP curve *and* ISLM-BP model
  definition, 699
  financing deficit, 667–68
Balance of payments accounts
  in Bretton Woods system, 688–89
  capital account, 666–68
  components, 665
  current account, 665–66
  definition, 664
Balance sheet
  and asset and liquidity management committee, 390–92
  of banks, 86–87, 383–85
  components, 84–85
  demand for loans and securities, 403–7
  external, 88
  federal government, 87
  Federal Reserve, 87–88
  of firms, 85–6
  households, 85
  mutual fund industry, 416
  national, 87
  of pension funds, 424
  reserve management, 397–403
  simplified, 391
Balance sheet constraint, 392
Balance sheet equation, 119–21
Banca d'Italia, 224
BancTexas Group, 371
Bank credit
  linkage of economic sectors, 200
  seasonal versus extended, 149
Bankers' acceptances, 75–76
Bankers Trust, 426
Bank failures, 38, 93, 354
  during Great Depression, 368, 640
  least-cost alternative, 372
  methods of resolving, 369
  prevention of, 365–68
Bank funds, sources and uses items, 383
Bank holding companies, 357
  regulation of, 361
Bank Holding Company Act, 357, 362
  Douglas Amendment, 359
Banking Act of 1913, 260–61
Banking Act of 1933, 93, 109, 223, 355, 356, 359, 361, 369, 417, 426; *see also* Glass-Steagall Act

Banking Act of 1935, 93, 223, 262, 369
Bank Insurance Fund, 369, 373
Bank loans, 510–11; *see also* Loans
Bank of Credit and Commerce
    International, 365
Bank of England, 224, 370, 713
Bank of Japan, 217, 224, 370, 483
Bank regulation, 8, 261
    branching, 359–60
    definition, 360
    Depression-era, 93–94
    geographical restrictions, 358–60
    government agencies, 38
    multiple and overlapping jurisdictions,
        361–63
    in nineteen-eighties, 95
    reasons for, 360–61
    reform proposals, 362–63
    too-big-to-fail policy, 371–72
    views on centralization of, 364
Banks; *see also* Commercial banks *and*
    Investment banks
    asset and liability management
        committee, 390–92
    balance sheet, 86–87, 383–85
    benefit to economy, 37–39
    bidding for deposits, 461
    changes in money demand behavior,
        480–85
    changes in reserve management
        decisions, 482–84
    circumvention of deposit rate rules,
        100–101
    compared to thrifts, 357
    competition for, 108–10
    correspondent relationship, 383
    cost innovations, 111
    credit crunch of 1990s, 113–14, 405–7
    credit rationing, 527–28
    debt of, 80–82
    demand for loans and securities, 403–7
    deposit contraction, 319
    deposit creation, 310–12
    deposit rate determination, 134–39
    deposits and loans, 310
    financial innovation in liabilities, 98–103
    financial innovations for assets, 103–11
    as financial intermediaries, 22
    floating rates, 106–7
    fractionally backed deposits, 8–9
    history of deregulation, 99
    impact of globalization, 109
    income statement, 385
    increased profits, 382
    IS sector shocks, 561
    lending policies, 36
    LM sector shocks, 558–61
    loan policies, 386–89
    loans to firms and households, 78–80
    management of interest rate risk, 105–8

Banks—*Cont.*
    members of Federal Reserve, 235
    and money supply, 322–23
    moral hazard, 366
    and mutual funds, 417
    national and state, 357
    number of, 354
    off-balance-sheet activities, 109
    portfolio imbalances, 103–5
    profit maximization, 391–92
    reserve accounts, 82
    reserve balances, 8–9
    reserve management, 397–403
    revenues and expenses, 386
    risk-based deposit insurance premium,
        373–74
    supply of deposits, 391, 392–97
    3-6-3 rule, 92
    too-big-to-fail policy, 371–72
    types of deposits, 9–11
    types of hedging, 107–8
    vault cash, 8
Bank's balance sheet constraint, 392
Bank's balance sheet equation, 403
Bank supervision, 261, 363
    by Board of Governors, 228
    CAMEL rating, 364–65, 366, 368
    capital adequacy, 365–68
    definition, 360
    by FDIC, 368–75
    prompt corrective action, 368
Banque de France, 224, 713
Barro, Robert, 616, 617, 618
Barter, 4
Barth, James R., 116
Basis point, 50
Basle Agreement, 113–14, 367–68, 406
Bauman, Laurence, 296
Baumol, William, 430, 435, 447
    on transactions demand, 428–42
Becketti, Sean, 66
Beige Book, 263
Beneficial Corporation, 412
Bentsen, Lloyd, 714
Bernanke, Ben S., 41, 546, 640 n
Bid price, 54, 59
Black Monday, 128, 286, 642
Black Thursday, 642
Blinder, Allan, 227, 242, 546
Blue Book, 233
Board of Governors of the Federal
    Reserve, 24, 222, 309, 362, 495 328
    Annual Report, 247, 562
    background of members, 227
    description, 225–26
    Division of Monetary Affairs, 229
    Division of Research and Statistics,
        229
    econometric models, 229
    financing activities, 229

Board of Governors of the Federal
    Reserve—*Cont.*
    overview of functions, 226–29
    Regulation A, 253
    tension with Federal Reserve banks, 262
Boeing Company, 72
Bond-financed deficit, 555–56
Bond market, 198
Bond ratings, 57
Bonds, 72–74
    call provision, 43
    held by foreigners, 73
Bond stripping, 61
Bookkeeping services, 253
Boorman, John T., 318
Borrowed reserves, 149, 151
    bank attitude, 322
    determinants of, 399–401
    marginal cost of, 398–99
    marginal revenue from, 398
    and money supply, 158
    operating target, 282–85
Borrowers, benefits of financial
    intermediaries, 37
BP curve, 699–701; *see also* ISLM-BP
    model
Brainard, William C., 563 n
Branch, Rene O., Jr., 410
Branch banking, 359–60
Breit, William, 122, 447
Bretton Woods Commission, 690
Bretton Woods system, 68–89, 696
    50th anniversary of, 690–91
Bridge banks, 369
Broaddus, Alfred, 116
Brokerage services of Federal Reserve
    banks, 259
Brokers, 34, 426
Brunner, Allan D., 387, 410
Brunner, Karl, 18, 167, 240, 601
Bubble economy, 217
Budget deficit, 29–30, 709; *see also* Twin
    deficits
    bond financing, 555–56
    financed by foreign borrowing, 32
    monetizing, 556–58
Budget Enforcement Act of 1990, 643
Budget surplus, 29
Bundesbank, 224, 243, 364, 692, 713
    on interest rates, 180
Bureau of Economic Analysis, 665
Bureau of Engraving and Printing, 257
Bureau of Labor Statistics, 193
Bureau of the Mint, 257
Burns, Arthur F., 116, 242
Bush, George, 69, 227, 242
Bush administration, 261, 354, 355
    fiscal policy, 643
Business cycle, political, 242 n; *see also*
    Recession

Business Cycle Dating Committee, 530
Business finance companies, 412
Business loans, 413–14
Buyouts, 77–78

C

Callable bond, 73
Call provision, 43
Cambridge equation, 332
Cambridge k, 330–31, 431–32
CAMEL rating, 365–68
Cantor, Richard, 116
Capital account
    anatomy of, 666–68
    definition, 665
Capital adequacy, 365–68
Capital-asset ratio, 114, 366
    Basle Agreement, 367–68
    determination, 406
    risk-based, 366–68
Capital gains and losses
    corporate stock, 77
    on gold, 48
Capital gains or losses, calculation, 47
Capital goods, 22
Capital inflows, 666–67
    impact of interest rates, 676–77
    national savings and investment, 707–9
Capital markets, 45
Capital market securities, 45
Capital mobility, perfect and imperfect,
    701–2
Capital outflows, 666
    impact of exchange rates, 676–77
Captive finance companies, 412
Carter, Jimmy, 227, 242, 638–39
Carter-Volcker recession, 638–39, 645
Cash concentration system, 96
Cash items in the process of collection,
    383
Cash management
    by firms, 95–97
    by households, 97–98
Cash management accounts, 97–98
Cash management techniques
    and interest rates, 187–88
    and shifts in money supply, 180–81
Cash management technology, 127
CATS, 61
Central banks, 8; see also Federal Reserve
    System
    comparative performance of, 243–44
    discount rate, 254
    functions, 224
    increase and decrease of reserves, 8–9
    ineffective intervention in exchange
        market, 676
    intervention in exchange market, 675–76
    price stability goal, 241

Certificate of deposit, 81
    origin of, 102
Chandross, Robert, 189
Change in Bank Control Act, 362
Charge-off, 387
Charles Schwab, 426
Chase Manhattan, 426
Checkable deposits, innovations in,
    100–101
Check collecting and clearing, 249–52
Checks, 7
Chicago Board of Trade, 45
Circumstances of the investor, 124
Citibank, 426
Classical dichotomy, 617
Classical long-run model, impact of policy
    shocks, 597–99
Classical model of aggregate supply curve,
    581–82
Classicists, 523, 600
    assumptions about wages, 605
    policy prescriptions, 622–25
Clean float, 197
Clinton, Bill, 216, 227, 238, 242–45, 516,
    661
Clinton administration, 30, 38, 69, 71, 261,
    355, 376–77, 714
    fiscal policy, 643–45
Closed-end funds, 416
Coca-Cola Company, 73
Cogley, Timothy, 519
Coin and currency distribution, 257–58; see
    also Currency
Coin and currency outstanding, 306–7
Coinsurance, 420
Collective factor, 125
    and asset demand, 127–29
Commerce Department, 193, 229, 618, 619
    Bureau of Economic Analysis, 665
Commercial and industrial loans, 78–80
Commercial banks, 22; see also Banks
    compared to thrifts, 357
    number of, 358
    structure and regulation of, 358–75
Commercial finance companies, 412
Commercial paper, 74–75, 80
Commercial paper rate, 75
Commodities trading, 45
Commodity, medium of exchange, 4–5
Commodity Exchange, 48
Commodity money, 6
Compaq Computer, 123
Complete crowding out, 598–99, 707
Comptroller of the Currency, 261, 360
    bank regulation, 361–63, 364
    bank supervision, 366–68
    establishment of, 357
Conference of Chairmen, 262
Conference of Governors, 262
Conference of Presidents, 262

Congress
    accountability of Fed to, 236–37
    creation of Federal Reserve, 223
Conrail, 72
Consolidated balance sheet
    of Federal Reserve banks, 263–65
    sources and uses of reserves statement,
        292, 297–307
Consultation range, 286–87
Consumer credit, 413
Consumer finance companies, 412
Consumer goods, 21
Consumer loans, 78
Consumer price index, 193
Consumers, 21
Consumption, 195
    aggregate demand and increase in, 534
    exogenous increase in, 527
Consumption function, 524–25
Consumption goods, 22
Continental Illinois Bank, 150, 257,
    370–71, 401, 484
Contractionary demand management
    policies, 207
Convertible bonds, 73
    in Japan, 74
Cooper, Richard N., 695
Corporate bond rate, 73
Corporate bonds; see Bonds
Corporate stock, 76–78
    buyouts, 77–78
Correspondent relationship, 383
Cost-push inflation, 633–35
Cost-reducing financial innovations, 111,
    393, 459–61
Council of Economic Advisers, 636
    under Kennedy, 645–46
    under Reagan, 646–47
Coupon, definition, 51
Coupon equivalent yield, 61
    Treasury securities, 62–63
    zero coupon notes and bonds, 61
Coupon rate, 51
Covenants, 389; see also Restrictive
    covenants
Credit
    access to, 37
    adjustment, 257
    extended, 257
    seasonal, 257
Credit cards, 98
Credit Control Act, 639
Credit crunch, 113–14, 405–7, 461, 528
Credit provision, 37–38
Credit rationing, 527–28
Credit risk, 56
Credit unions, 378
Credit union share drafts, 100–101
Crowding out, 207–8, 598–99, 707
    of investment, 553

Crowding out—*Cont.*
  of net exports, 554
Currency
  appreciation or depreciation, 668
  crisis in Europe, 691–92
  demand for, 142–43
  expectations of appreciation or
    depreciation, 677–78
  expected appreciation/depreciation,
    713–14
  public demand for, 323
Currency in circulation, 8, 82, 147,
    152–53, 303
  in money supply, 159
  and nonborrowed reserves, 484–85
Currency outstanding, 306–7
Current account
  anatomy of, 665–66
  definition, 665
Current account deficit, 30–32
Current account surplus, 31–32
Current expenditures, 125–26
Current income, 125–26
Current yield
  calculation, 46–47
  definition, 51

D

Danish National Bank, 224
Debit cards, 110
Debt
  bank deposits as, 80–82
  of Federal Reserve, 82–83
  of firms and households, 78–80
Debt hangover, 79, 86
Debt securities, 26
  bankers' acceptances, 75–76
  commercial paper, 74–75
  corporate bonds, 72–74
  default risk structure of interest rates,
    506–9
  differential tax treatment, 509
  federal agency securities, 70–72
  interest rate determination, 172–73
  terminology, 50–53
  and term structure of interest rates,
    497–505
  Treasury securities, 68–70
  types, 509–10
Decision rule, 443–44
Deductibles, 420
Default risk, 56–57
  definition, 506
  liquidity and marketability, 507–9
  and state of the economy, 507
Default risk premium, 57, 506–7
  tracking, 508
Default risk structure of interest rates,
    506–9

Defensive open market operations, 269,
    294–95
Deficit reduction, 643–45
Deficit reduction act of 1993, 47–48,
    216–17
Deficit units, 25–26
  direct finance for, 33–34
  firms, 27–28
  foreign participants, 30–32
  funding gap financing, 26
  government, 29–30
  households, 26–27
Degree of reserve pressure, 292
De Long, Bradford J., 603
Demand
  for loans and securities, 403–7
  for real money balances, 201
  for reserves, 153–54
  for securities, 182–84
  for total reserves, 153–54
Demand, and quantity of money, 15
Demand curve
  for deposits, 449, 452–54
  for M1, 466–67
Demand deposit, 9, 80–81
Demand management policies
  definition, 206–7
  fiscal policy, 207–8
  monetary policy, 208
Demand-pull inflation, 631–33
Demand-reducing financial innovations,
    459
Demand-side shocks, 206–8
Department of Education, 71
Deposit contraction, 319
Deposit creation, 310–12
  and open market operations, 312–19
Deposit demand
  factors affecting, 139–42
  laws of, 132–34
Deposit insurance, 8, 358
  international comparisons, 370
  moral hazard, 366
  narrow bank solution, 374
  origin of, 368–69
  privatization proposal, 374–75
  pros and cons, 372
  reform proposals, 373–75
  risk-based premium, 373–74
Deposit market
  change in collective variable, 459
  and change in technology and regulatory
    index, 459–61
  and changes in income, 458–59
  and changes in reserve requirement, 461
  demand curve, 449
  equilibrium, 449–52
  equilibrium relations, 454–58
  and interest rate, 452–58
  and money demand, 462–63

Deposit market—*Cont.*
  in regulated environment, 463–66
  supply curve, 449
Deposit multiplier, for M2, 163–64
Depository institutions, 22, 93
  deposit insurance, 7–8
  disintermediation, 95
  versus nondepositories, 355–56
  reserve requirement ratio, 39
Depository Institutions Deregulation and
    Monetary Control Act, 95, 100–101,
    106, 112–13, 223, 228, 235, 249, 257,
    378
Depository Institutions Deregulation
    Committee, 100, 102
Deposit rate curve, 135–39
Deposit rate deregulation, 468
Deposit rate relation, 135
Deposit rates, 82
  changes in, 175–81
  circumvention of, 99–101
  deregulation, 99
  falling during 1990s, 140
  theory of determination, 134–39
Deposits
  bank bidding for, 461
  demand and supply curves, 449
  demand curve, 452–54
  nontransaction, 324
  opportunity cost of, 132–34
  supply curve, 454
  supported by reserves, 155–57, 320
  transactions and nontransactions, 162
Deposits other than reserve balances,
    304–5
Depreciation of currency, 668, 713–14
  expectations about, 677–78
Deregulation
  of banking, 22
  of deposit rates, 99
  globalization of, 109
  and thrift crisis of 1980s, 112–13
Desert Storm, 32, 596
Deutsche mark, 691
DID&MCA; *see* Depository Institutions
    Deregulation and Monetary Control
    Act
Direct finance, 33–34
Direct security, 33
Dirty float; *see* Managed float
Discount, 52
  zero coupon securities at, 61
Discount brokerage houses, 426
Discount Corporation of New York, 102
Discounting, 254
Discount rate, 82, 226–28, 254
  and money supply curve, 161–62
  as policy instrument, 269
  rates of return and changes in, 513–14
Discount rate policy, 477–78

Discount rate policy—*Cont.*
  and interest rates, 187
  and shifts in money supply, 177–79
Discount window, 322
Discount window loans, 82, 226–28,
    253–57, 300
  administrative index, 474–75
  borrowed reserves, 151
  types of, 149
Discount window operations
  discount rate policy, 477–78
  in ISLM model, 550–51
  quantitative administration, 478
Disinflation, 615–16
Disintermediation, 95, 102
Disposable income, 530
Disposition-of-income relation, 523
Diversifiable risk, 122–23
Diversifying, 122
Dividends, 77
Divisibility, 60
Division of Monetary Affairs of the
    Federal Reserve Board, 229
Division of Research of the Federal
    Reserve Board, 229
Dollar
  under Bretton Woods system, 688–89
  decline against yen, 696
  end of gold convertibility, 689
  under managed float, 689–90
  and real interest rate parity, 687
  response to decline in, 714
Domestic goods, 680–81
Domestic policy directives, 234
  interpreting, 285–86
Dorgan, Byron, 238
Double coincidence of wants, 4
Douglas Amendment to the Bank Holding
    Company Act, 359
Dow Jones Industrial Average, 182
Drexel Burnham Lambert, 58, 508–9
Dual banking, 235, 357
Duca, John V., 471
Durable goods
  consumer, 21, 21
  producer, 22
Dykes, Sayre Ellen, 262
Dynamic open market operations, 269,
    294–95

              E
Eatwell, John, 167, 190, 351
Econometric models, 229
  Lucas critique, 625
Economic activity, 13–15
  measures of, 21
Economic independence, 241
Economic policy; *see also* Fiscal policy
    and Monetary policy

Economic policy—*Cont.*
  comparison of Kennedy and Reagan
      years, 647–48, 656
  Japan, 217–18
  Kennedy years, 645–46
  in 1990s, 642–43
  and Phillips curve, 653–56
  Reagan years, 646–48
  schools of thought, 600–601
  summary of effects, 710–11
  United States, 215–17
Economic Recovery Tax Act, 648
Economic Report of the President, 225,
    268, 571, 596, 644–45, 648, 716
Economic research, 263
Economy; *see also* Open economy
  aggregate demand-aggregate supply
      model, 204–8
  automatic stabilizers, 646
  benefit of banks to, 37–39
  and default risk, 507
  demand-side shocks, 206–8
  financial sector, 191, 198–204
  full equilibrium, 206
  under gold standard, 687–88
  real sector, 191, 192–98
  supply shocks of 1970s, 637–39
  two pillars of, 15–16
  wartime performance, 635–37
Effective exchange rate, 670
Effective reserves, 15–57
Efficiency wages
  to prevent adverse selection, 621
  to prevent shirking, 620–21
  to promote loyalty, 620
Efficient markets theory, 627
Eguchi, Hideakazu, 220
*Eightieth Annual Report of the Board of
    Governors,* 232
Eisenhower, Dwight D., 242, 645
Eisenhower administration, 241
Elastic currency, 260
Electronic funds transfer, 8, 252
  Fedwire, 96
Employee Retirement Income Security Act,
    425
Employment, and asset demand, 127–28
Endogenous variables, 526
English, William B., 387
Enzler, Jared, 466
Equation of exchange, 330–31
Equilibrium, 173
  in deposit markets, 449–52
  in goods and services market, 525–26
  in ISLM-BP model, 703
  money market, 473–76
  securities market, 185
Equilibrium deposit rate, 451
Equilibrium quantity of deposits, 451

Equilibrium quantity of deposits demanded,
    451
Equilibrium real interest rate, 276
Equity capital, four-asset model, 509–16
Equity securities, 26
  corporate stock, 76–77
ERM; *see* Exchange Rate Mechanism
Eurodollar deposits, 102
European Community, 691
European Monetary System, 713
  origin and operation, 691–92
  problems in, 690–91
Ex ante real interest rate, 274–76
Ex ante real long-term interest rate, 271
Excess demand, 173
  for securities, 185
Excess demand for money, 174
  and interest rate, 524
Excess reserves, 82, 158, 475
  bank attitude, 323
  determinants of, 402–3
  marginal cost, 401–2
  marginal revenue from, 402
  and money supply, 159
  unwanted, 311–12
Excess supply, 173
  of securities, 186
Excess supply of money, 174–75
  and interest rate, 524
Exchange process, 4
Exchange Rate Mechanism, 691–92
  British withdrawal, 696
  crisis in, 713
Exchange rates, 197; *see also* Fixed
    exchange rates, Flexible exchange
    rates, *and* Real exchange rate
  Bretton Woods system, 688–89
  crisis in ERM, 713
  European Monetary System, 691–92
  expectations of appreciation and
      depreciation, 677–78
  factors affecting, 676–81
  and foreign and domestic prices, 680–81
  under gold standard, 687–88
  impact of foreign and domestic incomes,
      679–80
  and interest rate parity, 678–79
  and interest rates, 676–77
  managed float, 675, 689–90
  mechanics of, 668–70
  nominal versus real, 682
  reform proposals, 690–91
  volatility, 690
Exogenous variables, 526–28
Expansionary demand management
    policies, 206–7
Expected inflation effect, 211–14
Expected real interest rate, 57–58
Expenditures, timing of, 48–49
Expenses, of banks, 386

Exporters, bankers' acceptances, 75–6
Exports, 195
Extended credit, 149, 257
External balance sheet, 88

F

Fabozzi, Frank J., 91, 130
Face value, 47
    definition, 51
    of insurance policy, 421
    zero coupon securities, 60
Factoring, 413–14
*Factors Affecting Reserves of Depository
    Institutions and Condition Statement
    of Federal Reserve Banks,* 300
Factors of production, changes in rewards
    to, 585–86
Farmer, Roger, 220
Federal agency securities, 70–72
Federal Banking Agency, 362–63
Federal Deposit Insurance Corporation,
    261, 364
    authority of, 93
    bank regulation, 361–63
    bank supervision, 366–68
    creation of, 38
    and deposit insurance, 368–75
    deposit insurance reform, 373–75
    keeping banks open, 369–71
    resolving bank failures, 369
    too-big-to-fail policy, 371–72
Federal Deposit Insurance Corporation
    Improvements Act, 113, 355, 368,
    372, 373, 382
Federal funds market, 82–83
Federal funds rate, 83
    operating target, 276–78, 286–87
Federal Guaranteed Student Loan Program,
    71
Federal Home Loan Bank Act of 1932, 375
Federal Home Loan Bank Board, 376
Federal Home Loan Bank system, 375–76
Federal Home Loan Mortgage Corporation,
    71
Federal National Mortgage Association, 71
Federal Open Market Committee, 24, 226,
    229, 288; *see also* Open market
    operations
    Beige Book, 263
    Blue Book, 233
    composition of, 232–33
    creation of, 223
    in currency markets, 260
    meetings and deliberations, 233
    and monetary policy, 262–63
    policy directives, 233–34
    policy signals, 291
    reform proposals, 237–40
    secrecy issue, 238–40

Federal Open Market Committee—*Cont.*
    Trading Desk, 292–97
Federal Reserve, MIT, Research Council,
    Pennsylvania model, 229
Federal Reserve Act, 223, 236, 254, 260,
    361
    bank regulation requirement, 358
Federal Reserve Bank of Kansas City, 468
Federal Reserve Bank of New York, 260,
    263, 290, 294
    domestic policy directives, 285–86
    in foreign exchange market, 675–76
    policy directives, 233–34
    Quarterly Review, 266
    Trading Desk, 292–97
Federal Reserve Bank of Richmond, 467
Federal Reserve Bank of St. Louis, 168,
    263
Federal Reserve Bank of Washington, D.C.,
    294
Federal Reserve banks, 24
    as bankers to federal government,
        258–60
    bookkeeping services, 253
    brokerage services, 259
    check collecting and clearing, 249–52
    coin and currency distribution, 257–58
    consolidated balance sheet, 263–65
    description, 229–30
    discount window loans, 253–57
    earnings, 231–32
    economic research, 263
    and foreign organizations, 260
    management of foreign exchange
        reserves, 259–60
    and monetary policy, 261–63
    organization and control, 230–31
    overview of functions, 231
    primary functions, 249
    selection of presidents, 237–38
    sources and uses of reserves statement,
        292, 297–307
    supervision by Board of Governors,
        228–29
    supervision of member banks, 260–61
    tension with Board of Governors, 262
Federal Reserve Bulletin, 229, 234, 238,
    247
Federal Reserve float, 305
    other sources of reserves, 484
Federal Reserve repurchase agreement, 294
Federal Reserve System; *see also* Open
    market operations
    accountability to Congress, 236–37
    balance sheet, 87–88
    bank regulation, 361–63, 364
    bank supervision, 366–68
    basic components, 24
    borrowed reserves from, 398–401

Federal Reserve System—*Cont.*
    changes in monetary policy tools,
        476–80
    control of money supply, 8–9
    creation of, 38
    currency in circulation, 82
    and decline of dollar, 714
    disinflationary policy of 1980s, 639
    disinflation policy, 213–14
    downgrading money in 1993, 569
    and economic policy, 215–17
    federal funds market, 82–83
    Fedwire, 96
    financial independence, 236
    and financial innovations, 111–12
    Flow of Funds Account, 22 n, 84, 416
    foreign exchange market operation,
        674–75
    goals, 202
    government role, 222
    history of, 223–25
    holder of US securities, 72
    and Humphrey-Hawkins Act, 329–30
    independence of, 241–42
    inflation and interest rates, 214
    from instruments to ultimate goals,
        268–70
    Interdistrict Settlement Fund, 252
    interest rates in 1990s, 140
    intermediate targets, 268
    from intermediate targets to ultimate
        goals, 270–76
    lender of last resort, 253
    liabilities and capital accounts, 305
    loan rationing, 256
    measures of money, 9–11
    member banks, 235
    miscellaneous assets, 307
    monetary policymaker, 39
    monetary policy tools, 267–68
    objections to reform, 362–63
    operating targets, 267
    from operating targets to intermediate
        targets, 276–87
    policies in early 1990s, 642–43
    policy change of 1993, 287
    policy compared to Bundesbank, 180
    policy instruments, 322
    policy stance in 1994, 288
    political pressures on, 242–45
    portfolio of securities, 299–300
    reform versus status quo, 237–40
    regulation of banks, 357
    Regulation Q, 93
    reliance on financial indicators, 270
    reserve requirement ratio, 137
    response to crash of 1987, 642
    role in financial system, 23–24
    secrecy issue, 238–40
    and stock market crash of 1987, 182

Federal Reserve System—*Cont.*
  supply of reserves, 148–53
  total reserves, 82
  targeting interest rates or money, 486–93
  tracking monetary aggregates, 12
  ultimate goals, 267
Federal Reserve System: Purposes and Functions, 247
Federal Savings and Loan Insurance Corporation, 376
  origin of, 369
Fedwatching, 294–97
Fedwire, 96, 252
Feinman, Joshua N., 167, 290, 351, 468
Feldstein, Martin, 86 n, 290, 557, 571, 648, 695
Fiat money, 7–8
Final goods, 193
Finance
  direct, 33–34
  indirect, 34–35
Finance companies
  purpose and operation of, 412–14
  regulation of, 415
Financial assets, 12; *see also* Assets
Financial environment, old versus new, 92
Financial futures contract, 45
Financial go-between, 25, 33–39
Financial indicators, 270
  real interest rate, 274–76
Financial innovation, 92–93
  in liabilities, 98
  by public, 95–98
Financial innovations
  bank assets, 103–11
  cost-reducing, 111
  and Federal Reserve, 111–12
  technological progress and, 109–11
Financial institutions; *see also* Nondepository financial institutions
  versus industrial firms, 355
  overview, 355–57
Financial Institutions Reform, Recovery, and Enforcement Act, 113, 354, 361, 369, 373
  provisions, 376–77
Financial instruments, 12; *see also* Securities
  classifying, 68
  federal agency securities, 70–72
  of firms, 72–78
  issued by government, 30
  municipal securities, 72
  sale to foreign participants, 30–32
  Treasury securities, 68–70
Financial intermediaries; *see also* Banks *and* Thrifts
  benefits to borrowers, 37
  benefits to economy, 37–39
  benefits to lenders, 37

Financial intermediaries—*Cont.*
  federal agencies, 70–71
  in financial system, 22–23
  functions, 36
  indirect finance, 34–35
  new financial environment, 92
Financial markets, 12
Financial sector of economy, 191
  linkage to real sector, 198–204
Financial system
  definition, 20
  and Federal Reserve, 23–24
  financial intermediaries in, 22–23
  foreign participants, 24
  foreign presence in, 73
  and government, 23
  households in, 21
  nonfinancial firms in, 22
  role of financial go-betweens, 25, 33–39
  role of monetary policymakers, 25, 39
  role of surplus/deficit units, 25–32
  sectors, 21
  stocks and flow of money, 24–25
Firms, 22
  balance sheets, 85–86
  bank loans, 78–80
  buyouts of 1980s, 77–78
  cash management innovations, 95–97
  corporate stock, 76–78
  debt accumulation, 79
  debt securities, 72–76
  as surplus/deficit units, 27–28
FIRREA; *see* Financial Institutions Reform, Recovery, and Enforcement Act
First Fidelity Bancorp, 360
First National City Bank of New York, 102
Fiscal policy
  Bush administration, 643
  changes and national income, 530–34
  Clinton administration, 643–45
  for demand management, 207–8
  under fixed exchange rates, 709–10
  under flexible exchange rates, 706–7
  in ISLM model, 551–57
  Japan, 218
  and national savings, 707–9
  shift in aggregate demand and, 577
  United States, 216–17
Fischer, Stanley, 619, 659 n
Fisher, Irving, 212, 335–36, 430, 433, 617
Fisher effect, 212–13
Fisher equation, 213
Fixed exchange rates, 197, 665, 674–75
  Bretton Woods system, 688–89
  European Monetary System, 691–92
  fiscal policy under, 709–10
Fixed interest rates, 106–7
Fleming, Marcus, 703 n
Flexible exchange rates, 197, 672–73
  fiscal policy under, 706–7

Flexible exchange rates—*Cont.*
  monetary policy under, 703–5
Flight to equality, 507
Flight to quality, 128
Float, 305
Floating exchange rates, 665, 672–73; *see also* Flexible exchange rates
Floating interest rates, 80, 106–7
Flow of Funds Account, 22 n, 84, 416
Flow of money, 24–25
FOMC; *see* Federal Open Market Committee
Ford, Gerald, 227
Ford administration, 638
Foreign and domestic incomes, 679–80
Foreign and domestic prices, 680–81
Foreign borrowing, pros and cons, 32
Foreign currency directive of FOMC, 234–35
Foreign exchange, 197–98
  demand for, 670–71
  supply of, 671–72
Foreign exchange market
  BP curve, 699–703
  and crisis in European Monetary System, 713
  demand for foreign exchange, 670–71
  and expected appreciation/depreciation of currency, 713–14
  factors affecting rates, 676–81
  fixed exchange rates, 674–75
  flexible exchange rates, 672–73
  hybrid exchange system, 675–76
  intervention in, 234–35, 259–60
  mechanics of exchange rates, 668–70
  and open economy, 697–703
  and rise in foreign interest rates, 711–12
  sterilized/nonsterilized intervention, 675–76
  supply of foreign exchange, 671–72
Foreign exchange reserves, 259–60
Foreign goods, 680–81
Foreign interest rates, 711–12
Foreign official accounts, 304
Foreign participants, 24
  in financial system, 73
  surplus or deficit units, 30–32
Forward rates, 498–99
Foss, Murray, 220
Four-asset model of equity capital, 509–16
Fractionally backed deposits, 8–9
Fractionally backed paper money, 6–7
France, deposit insurance, 370
Fraser, Donald R., 116
Friedman, Benjamin, 200 n, 290, 351
Friedman, Benjamin M., 86 n
Friedman, Milton, 3 n, 18, 93 n, 208–9, 213, 220, 240, 247, 271, 282, 334 n, 336, 337 n, 338, 351, 430–31, 433 n,

Friedman—*Cont.*
　447, 605–6, 608–9, 617, 623, 628,
　　640, 653, 654–55
　on monetary policy, 600–601
　on quantity theory, 444–45
Friedman, Thomas, 676
Friedman-Phelps analysis of Phillips curve,
　653–56
Friedman-Phelps fooling model, 608–9
Frydll, Edward J., 79, 86, 91
Full employment
　and inflation, 212
　level of output, 206, 582
Full Employment Act of 1946, 223, 236,
　270, 645–46
Full Employment and Balanced Growth
　Act, 223, 236, 271; *see also*
　Humphrey-Hawkins Act
Full employment budget deficit, 646
Full employment policy, 236–37, 271–73,
　642–43
Full equilibrium, 206
Funding gap, 25–26
　current account deficit, 30–31
Funding of pension plans, 424–25
Furlong, Frederick T., 410
Future income, and asset demand, 127–28
Futures contract, 45
Futures market, 45, 107–8
Future value
　calculating, 49–50
　of the stream of receipts, 49

G

Garn-St. Germain Depository Institutions
　Act of 1982, 95, 100, 106, 112, 376,
　377
GDP; *see* Gross domestic product
GDP price deflator, 193
General accounts of Treasury Department,
　304
Generalized liquidity effect, 513
General Motors Acceptance Corporation,
　412–13
*General Theory of Employment, Interest,
　and Money* (Keynes), 434–35, 442,
　523, 524, 586 n
Geographic restrictions on banking, 358–60
Germany, 243–44
　budget deficit, 557
　deposit insurance, 370
　hyperinflation, 660
　interest rates, 713
　role in European Monetary System,
　　691–92
Giordano, Robert, 504
Glass-Steagall Act, 93, 101, 355, 361, 369,
　417, 426; *see also* Banking Act of
　1933

Globalization, impact on banking, 109
Gold, 5
　as investment, 48
　severed from paper money, 7
Gold certificates, 305
Goldfeld, Stephen M., 445, 466
Gold standard, 6–7
　end of, 689
　and exchange rates, 687–88
Gold stock, 305–6
Gonzalez, Henry, 238, 239
Goodhart, Charles, 224
Goods, foreign and domestic, 680–81
Goods and services
　aggregate demand for, 198–200
　in national income, 524–36
　in national product and income, 196–97
　output, 193
Goods market equilibrium, IS curve,
　536–37
Gordon, Robert J., 616, 635 n, 640
Government
　balance sheet, 87
　and financial system, 23
　issuer of fiat money, 7
　as surplus or deficit unit, 29–30
Government debt, 30
　financial instruments for, 68–72
Government expenditure
　aggregate demand and increase in, 533
　and complete crowding out, 598–99
　exogenous increase in, 528
　financing by borrowing, 707
　in ISLM model, 552–54
Government National Mortgage
　Association, 70–71
Government purchases, 195
Governors Conference, 262
Gramley, Lyle, 227
Great Britain, deposit insurance, 370
Great Depression, 38, 93, 635, 639–42
　Federal Reserve legislation, 223
　interest rates, 507
Greenspan, Alan, 86, 227, 246, 247,
　274–76, 288, 349, 364, 406, 407, 642,
　644, 694
Greider, William, 247
Gross domestic product
　definition, 13, 192–93
　and quantity of money, 14
　real and nominal, 193
　switch from GNP, 193
Gross investment, 195
Gross National Product
　during Great Depression, 641–42
　during 1980s, 86
Gross National Product gap, 646
Gross retained profits, 27
Gross savings, 21
　definition, 25

Gross savings—*Cont.*
　of firms, 27
　of households, 26
Group of Five, 689 n
Group of Seven, 689 n
Growth funds, 416
Gyohten, Toyoo, 690 n, 695

H

Habitat premium, 503–5, 679; *see also*
　Preferred habitat hypothesis
Hadjimichalakis, Michael G., 116, 290, 471
Hall, Robert, 616 n
Hamilton, Lee, 238
Hansen, Alvin H., 546
Havrilesky, Thomas M., 227, 242, 247, 318
Hawkins, Augustus, 223
Headwinds, 562–63
　and economy policy in 1990s, 642–45
Hedging
　futures and options, 107
　interest rate risk, 105
　interest rate swaps, 107–8
Heller, H. Robert, 227
Heller, Walter, 646 n
Hetzel, Robert L., 467
Hicks, John R., 498, 502–3, 524, 600
Hicks-Hansen model, 546; *see also* ISLM
　model
Higgins, Byron, 468, 471
Holding-period yield, 53
Home banking, 111
Home country, 711–12
Home equity loans, 413
Home mortgages, 78
House Committee on Banking, Housing,
　and Urban Affairs, 236, 360
Household Financial, 412
Households
　balance sheet, 85
　balance sheet equation, 119–21
　bank loans, 78–80
　cash management by, 97–98
　debt accumulation, 79
　in financial system, 21
　as surplus or deficit units, 26–27
Humphrey, Hubert H., 223
Humphrey-Hawkins Act, 223–25, 236,
　271–72, 329
Humphrey-Hawkins report, 274
Hybrid accounts, 103
Hyperinflation, 659–60

I

IBM, stock decline, 122–23
Identities, 330
Ikeo, Kazuto, 410
Imperfect capital mobility, 702
Imperfect information

Imperfect information—*Cont.*
  compared to asymmetric information,
    610
  and policy ineffectiveness proposition,
    617–19
Implicit marginal cost of borrowing,
    398–99
Implicit (wage) contracts, 620
Income
  changes and deposit market, 458–59
  and consumption function, 524–25
  foreign and domestic, 679–80
Income determination
  algebra of, 535–36
  modern theory of, 523–24
Income effect, and interest rate, 209–10
Income elasticity of demand, 335
Income funds, 416
Income multiplier, 529, 535–36
Income statement, of banks, 385
Index of Consumer Sentiment, 531
Index of prudence, 402
Indirect finance, 34–35
  and asymmetric information, 35–36
Indirect securities, 35
Inflation; *see also* Purchasing power
  control by reserves operating target,
    278–85
  cost-push, 633–35
  costs of, 657–60
  decline under Reagan, 639
  demand-pull, 631–33
  equation guidelines, 338
  expected, 211–14
  Fisher effect, 212–13
  fully expected, 659–60
  impact on banks, 94
  and long-term interest rate, 271
  and monetarism, 271
  supply shocks of 1970s, 637–39
  and unemployment, 223–25
  unexpected, 657–58
Inflation rate, 15
Inflation risk, 57–58
Inflation-unemployment tradeoff, 648–57;
    see also Phillips curve
Information, impact on economics, 609–10
Innovations in cash management practices,
    95
Insider trading, 426
Installment credit, 413
Insurance companies, 22–23
  life insurance, 420–23
  property/casualty, 423
Insurance fundamentals, 420
Insurance policies, 419
  face value, 421
Interdistrict Settlement Fund, 252
Interest, on bank deposits, 81

Interest rate, 50; *see also* Term structure of
    interest rates
  and cash management techniques,
    187–88
  default risk structure, 506–9
  definition, 52
  and deposit market, 452–58
  and discount rate policy, 187
  effects of money supply, 208–14
  and equilibrium level of income, 537–39
  expected inflation effect, 211–14
  fall in 1993, 644–45
  falling during 1990s, 140
  Federal Reserve versus Bundesbank, 180
  from fixed to floating, 106–7
  floating, 80
  forecasting, 500–501
  impact on exchange rates, 676–77
  income and price level effects, 209–10
  increase under inflation, 659
  inflationary increase, 94–95
  inverse relation to price, 52–53
  ISLM graph, 541
  Keynes on, 524
  linkage of economic sectors, 198–200
  liquidity effect, 208–9
  liquidity preference theory, 173–81
  loanable funds theory, 172–73
  and money demand, 445
  and money market, 472
  and money supply, 321–22
  and neutrality of money, 210–11
  nominal and real, 57–58
  and open market operations, 186–87
  price-level effect, 203–4
  prime rate, 80
  and quantity of money, 12, 13–14
  real income effect, 201
  real-income effect on, 550
  rise in foreign, 711–12
  and sectors of the economy, 191
  shift factors influencing, 475–76
  tax features, 509
  term structure, 56
  variability versus real income variability,
    567–68
  volatility, 105
Interest rate ceilings, 415
  phase-out, 95
Interest rate determination, 510
  liquidity preference theory, 173–81
  loanable funds theory, 182–88
  theory, 134–39
Interest rate parity, 678–79; *see also* Real
    interest rate parity
Interest rate risk; *see also* Market risk
  management of, 105–8
  portfolio imbalances, 103–5
Interest rate swaps, 105–6, 107
  essence of, 108

Interest rate targeting, 564–67
  versus money targeting, 486–93
Interest sensibilities, of money supply, 160
Intermediate targets, 268
  criteria, 270
  long-term interest rate, 271
  and operating targets, 276–87
  quantity of money, 271–76
  and ultimate goals, 270–76
Intermediate-term securities, 44
International Monetary Fund
  managed float authorization, 689
  origin and function, 688
  reserves created by, 306
International reserve assets, 667
International system of payments
  since Bretton Woods, 690–91
  Bretton Woods system, 688–89
  European Monetary System, 691–92
  gold standard, 687–88
  managed float, 689–90
Interstate banking, 359–60
Inventories, 195–96
Inventory-theoretic approach to transactions
    demand, 438
Investment, 195
  decision rule, 443–44
  national savings and capital flows, 707–9
Investment Advisers Act, 418
Investment banks, 34, 355–56, 417, 425–26
Investment companies, 416
Investment Company Act, 418
Investment demand
  aggregate demand and increase in, 34
  exogenous increase in, 527–28
  in IS curve, 536–37
  and Q-ratio, 514–16
Investment income, 665
Investors
  circumstances of, 124
  default risk structure of interest rates,
    506–9
  flight to quality, 507
  law of asset demand, 124–25
  risk averse, 122
  short or long horizon, 503–5
  and term structure of interest rates,
    497–505
Involuntary unemployment, 587, 620
Iraq, 215–16, 596, 642
IS curve
  in aggregate demand, 574–79
  definition, 537
  derivation, 537–39
  factors that shift, 576–79
  in Great Depression, 640–41
  in open economy, 697–98
  shifts in, 541–43
ISLM-BP graph, 697
ISLM-BP model

ISLM-BP model—*Cont.*
  equilibrium in, 703
  fiscal policy, 705–10
  monetary policy, 703–5
  and shocks to foreign exchange market, 71–14
ISLM model, 540–43
  aggregate supply curve, 579–90
  and choice of monetary policy tools, 561–68
  fiscal policy, 551–58
  and Keynesian short-run model, 590–94
  monetary policy, 548–51
  price level parameter, 574
  and price rigidities, 621
  worker knowledge of, 614–15
IS sector shocks, 561
  impact on Keynesian short-run model, 592–94

J
J. P. Morgan, 426
Japan, 244
  bubble economy, 191, 217
  convertible bonds, 74
  economic policy, 217–18
  money market shocks, 483
  national savings, 708 n
Johnson, Lewis, 466
Johnson, Lyndon B., 636, 654, 656
Johnson, Manuel, 227
Jones, David M., 247, 309
Jones, Frank J., 66
Jordan, Jerry L., 646 n
Junk bonds, 57
  liquidity, 508–9
  rise and fall of, 58

K
Kahn, George A., 546
Kane, Edward J., 376, 381
Karl, Kurt, 603
Kaufman, George C., 381
Kelley, Edward, 227
Kennedy, John F., 636, 645–46, 696, 705
Kennedy administration
  economic policy, 645–46
  and Phillips curve, 656
  policies compared to Reagan administration, 647–48
Keynes, John Maynard, 15, 175, 190, 330 n, 430–31, 445, 537, 540, 587
  on income determination, 523–24
  on interest rate determination, 524
  on involuntary unemployment, 620
  on money demand, 433–35
  on speculative demand, 442, 444
Keynesian cross, 526

Keynesian fixed-price aggregate supply curve, 580–81
Keynesian long-run and short-run supply curves, 586–90
Keyensian model of income determination, 524–36
Keynesians, 600
  on policy prescriptions, 622–25
Keynesian short-run aggregate supply curve, 582–86
Keynesian short-run model
  compared to Lucas supply curve, 612
  effect of policy shocks, 590–97
  Lucas alternative to, 605–6
Kimball, Ralph C., 95 n
Klamer, Arjo, 629
Klausner, Michael, 381, 388 n
Klein, Lawrence, 600
Klitgard, Thomas, 716
Kopcke, Richard W., 428
Korean War, 636
Kretzmer, Peter E., 571
Krugman, Paul, 78 n, 662, 714
Kuttner, Kenneth, 603
Kuwait, 215–16, 596, 642

L
Labor market
  clearance, 605–9
  equilibrium, 587
Labor supply, and real wage, 606–8
Lademan, Elizabeth, 417
Laidler, David, 445, 447
Large country case, 702
LaWare, John, 227
Law of asset demand, 124–25, 344
Law of deposit demand, 132–34
Law of one price, 683
Least-cost alternative in bank failures, 372
Legal tender, 11
Lehman, Michael, 66
Lemons problem, 35–36
Lender of last resort, 253
Lenders, benefits of financial intermediaries, 37
Liabilities
  on balance sheet, 84
  bank financial innovations, 98–103
  of banks, 384
  of life insurance companies, 421–23
Liability swap, 108
Life insurance companies, 420–23
Life insurance reserves, 421–22
Lindsey, Lawrence, 227, 246
Liquidity, 9
  bank deposits, 81
  default risk and marketability, 507–9
  from financial intermediaries, 37
  L measure, 11

Liquidity—*Cont.*
  relative, 128–29
  of securities, 58–60
Liquidity effect, 208–9, 548
Liquidity preference, 434
Liquidity preference theory
  of interest rate determination, 172–73
  of money market, 173–81
  and term structure of interest rates, 502–3
Liquidity premium, 502–3
Litan, Robert E., 374 n, 381
LM curve
  in aggregate demand, 574–79
  derivation, 540
  factors that shift, 576–79
  in Great Depression, 640–41
  in open economy, 698–99
  shifts in, 541–43
  and targeting quantity of money, 563–64
LM sector shocks, 558–61
  impact on Keynesian short-run model, 591–92
  and monetary policy, 566–67
Load funds, 417
Loanable funds theory, 510
  essence of, 185–86
  of interest rate determination and securities markets, 182–88
Loan-backed securities, 108–9
Loan commitments, 109
Loan-generated deposits, 314
Loan losses, 113–14
Loan-loss provisions, 386
  increase in, 406
Loan loss reserves, 387
Loan rationing, 256
Loans
  adverse selection, 387–88
  assessing and pricing risk, 386–88
  finance company, 413–14
  from fixed to floating, 106–7
  home equity, 413
  interbank, 82–83
  lemons problem, 35–36
  monitoring, 389
  moral hazard, 388–89
  restrictive covenants, 389
  screening applicants, 388
  securitization, 80
  troubled, 387
  types, 78–80
Loans and securities, demand for, 403–7
Lockboxes, 96
Long-horizon investor, 503–5
Long-run monetary aggregates targeting, 337–38
Long-run rate of inflation, 338
Long-term interest rate, as intermediate target, 271

Long-term securities, 44
Loyalty, of workers, 620
Lucas, Robert E., Jr., 605–6, 608, 617, 625, 628
Lucas aggregate supply curve
  continuous clearance of labor market, 606–9
  definition, 605–6
  empirical investigations, 616
  and Friedman-Phelps fooling model, 608–9
  and Phillips curve, 649–51
  rational expectations, 609–10
  shifts of, 612
  two approaches to, 610–14
  and vertical curve, 612–14
Lucas critique, 625

M

M1, 9–10, 101
  difficulty of predicting, 448
  estimation of demand, 445
  growth in 1980s, 341–44
  narrow measure of money, 321–23
  target range, 272–73, 274, 285–86
  velocity of circulation, 332
M1 equation, 162–63, 164
M2, 9–11
  broad measure of money, 323–26
  demand curve shifts, 468–69
  difficulty of predicting, 448
  growth in 1980s, 344–46
  growth in 1990s, 324–26, 346–49
  interest sensitivity of demand for, 468
  money market mutual funds, 419
  target range, 272–73, 274, 275–76, 285–86, 330
  velocity of circulation, 332
M2 deposit rate, 136–37
M2 equation, 163–64
M3, 11
  target range, 272–73, 274, 276, 285–86
Maastricht Treaty, 691
Macroeconomics
  Lucas critique, 625
  New classicists, 605–6
  schools of thought, 600–601, 622–25
Malkiel, Burton, 504
Managed float, 197–98, 675
  since Nixon administration, 689–90
Mankiw, N. Gregory, 621 n
Manpower and Development Act, 646
Marginal cost, 135
  of borrowing, 398–99
  of excess reserves, 401–2
  of supplying deposits, 393
Marginal product of labor
  diminishing, 584
  exogenous changes in, 586

Marginal propensity to consume
  out of disposable income, 530
  out of national income, 525
Marginal revenue, 135
  from borrowed reserves, 398
  from excess reserves, 402
Marginal rule
  application of, 392–97
  and reserve management, 397
Marketability, 44–45
  and liquidity, 59
  liquidity and default risk, 507–9
  relative, 128
Marketable debt
  Treasury securities, 68–69
  US savings bonds and notes, 70
Market clearance, 173
Market for labor, 588–90
  and rigidity in wages, 586–88
Market interest rates, 349
Market risk, 55–56
  corporate stock, 77
Markets, function of, 173
Market specialists, 22, 33
Markowitz, Harry, 130, 430, 442, 444
Marshall, Alfred, 330 n
Martin, Preston, 227
Matched sale-purchase transaction, 294
Maturity
  and liquidity, 59, 508
  shorter versus longer, 128
  Treasury securities, 69
Mayer, Thomas, 284 n
McCarthy, F. Ward, Jr., 296
McCracken, Paul, 291
McFadden Act, 359, 360
Measures of money, 11
Medium of exchange, 3–5
  provided by banks, 37
Mehra, Yash P., 467
Melloan, George, 220
Melton, William C., 247, 284 n
Meltzer, Allan H., 18, 240, 445, 601
Member banks, 235
  number of, 358
  supervision by Federal Reserve banks, 260–61
Menu costs, 621
Merchandise trade, 665
Merger Act of 1960, 362
Merrill Lynch, 34, 61, 97
Meulendyke, Anne-Marie, 91, 293, 309
Microsoft Corporation, 123
Mieno, Yasushi, 217, 483, 571
Milgate, Murray, 167, 190
Milken, Michael R., 58
Miller, G. William, 227
Miller, Merton, 444 n
Minimum denomination, 60
Ministry of Finance, Japan, 218

Misery index, 244
Mishkin, Frederic, 616
Mitchell, Constance, 296
Modified payout method, 369
Modigliani, Franco, 130, 503, 600
Monetarism, 271, 600
Monetary aggregates, 11
  downgrading, 274
  tracking, 12
Monetary aggregates targeting
  experience in 1980s, 341–46, 341–46
  experience in 1990s, 346–49
  long-run, 337–38
  pragmatic versus rigid, 339–41
  and quantity theory of money, 336–41
  short-run, 338–39
Monetary base, 39
Monetary base constraint, 169
Monetary base multiplier, 168–71
Monetary Control Act of 1980, 24
Monetary policy, 9
  changes in instruments, 476–80
  consequences of anti-inflationary policy, 624–25
  as demand management, 208
  discount window operations, 477–78
  effect on rates of return, 511–14
  experience in 1980s, 341–46
  under fixed exchange rates, 704–5
  under flexible exchange rates, 703–4
  Friedman on, 600–601
  generalized liquidity effect, 513
  in ISLM model, 548–51
  ISLM model and tools of, 561–68
  Japan, 217–18
  open market operations, 292–97, 476–77
  painless disinflation, 615–16
  in Reagan administration, 639, 647
  reform proposals, 240
  reserve requirement ratio changes, 479–80
  response to crash of 1987, 642
  role in Great Depression, 640–41
  role of Federal Reserve banks, 261–63
  schools of thought, 622–25
  sources and uses of reserves statement, 292, 297–307
  targeting money or interest rate, 486–93, 564–67
  targeting quantity of money and LM curve, 563–64
  tools of, 226–28, 268–87
  United States, 215–16
  variabilities in real income and interest rate, 567–68
Monetary policy instruments, 267–68
  and ultimate goals, 268–70
Monetary policy makers, 25, 39
Monetary Policy Report to the Congress, 272, 292, 346, 348, 461

Monetized deficit, 556–58
Money
    Cambridge equation, 332
    currency in circulation, 8
    current measures of, 9–11
    equation of exchange, 330–31
    excess supply or demand, 174–75
    fiat money, 7–8
    financial markets and rate of return, 12
    fractionally backed paper, 6–7
    gold standard, 6
    M1 as narrow measure of, 321–23
    M2 as broad measure of, 323–26
    medium of exchange, 3–5
    misconceptions about, 3
    neutrality of, 210–11, 597–98, 616–17
    opportunity cost, 95
    prices and economic activity, 12–15
    purchasing power, 15
    quantity theory, 273–74
    role in economy, 11–15
    stocks and flows, 24–25
    store of value, 5–6
    unit of account, 5
    velocity of circulation, 330–31
    velocity theories, 332–36
Money demand, 131, 323
    and behavior of public and banks,
        480–85
    components, 434
    definition, 473
    and deposit market, 462–63
    early quantity theory, 431–33
    economists and, 430–31
    empirical studies, 466–69
    erosion of stability, 448
    factors affecting, 142–43, 473–74
    and federal funds rate, 277–78
    income elasticity of, 335
    interest sensitivity of, 468
    Keynesian approach, 433–35
    modern quantity theory, 444–45
    and price level, 201–2
    and regulated environment, 463–66
    shifts in, 179–81
    shifts in demand curve for M1, 466–67
    speculative demand, 442–44
    stability of, 445–46
    transactions demand, 435–42
    uncertain, 490–91
Money demand shocks, 480–82
Money market
    and interest rates, 472
    Japan, 483
    liquidity preference theory, 173–81
Money market certificates, 102–3
Money market deposit accounts, 103
Money market equilibrium, 174, 201
    determinants, 473–76
    LM curve, 540

Money market mutual funds, 23, 97, 356,
    418–19
Money market securities, 45
Money-moving version of quantity theory,
    433
Money multiplier, 168
Money-sitting version of quantity theory,
    433
Money supply, 6
    borrowed reserves, 158
    and changes in real-sector variables,
        485–86
    currency in circulation, 159
    definition, 473
    determinants, 319–26
    downgrading in 1993, 569
    excess reserves, 159
    and expected inflation effect, 211–14
    factors affecting, 158–62, 474–75
    under gold standard, 687–88
    income and price-level effects, 209–10
    interest sensitivity, 160
    liquidity effect, 208–9
    M1 and M2 equations, 162–64
    and monetary base multiplier, 168–71
    nonborrowed reserves, 158
    and price level, 202–3
    and reserve requirement ratio, 159–60
    shifts in, 176–79
    steps for deriving, 148
    and supply of reserves, 148–53
    targeting money or interest rate, 486–93
Money supply curve, 160–62, 321–22
    factors affecting, 475
Money supply equation, 157, 168
Money supply notation, 203
Money supply shocks, 482–85
Money wages; see also Wages
    changes in, 584–85
    flexible, 588–90
    rigidity in, 586–88
Monitoring loans, 389
Monthly Money Market Model, 229
Moody's Investors Service, 57, 58, 73, 506
Moral hazard, 366, 388–89
    and insurance, 420
    narrow bank solution, 374
Mortgage-backed securities, 109
Mortgages, 26, 413
    adjustable-rate, 106
    variable-rate, 107
Mullins, David, 227, 246
Multiple deposit creation, 312–19
Mundell, Robert A., 703 n
Mundell-Fleming model, 703
Municipal bonds, 509
Municipal securities, 72
Muth, John F., 610, 614
Mutual Benefit of Newark, 422–23

Mutual funds, 22–23
    and banks, 417
    definition, 415–16
    divisibility, 60
    money market, 418–19
    regulation of, 418
    types of, 416–18

                    N

Nakamura, Leonard I., 388 n
Napoleon, 224
Narrow bank, 374
National Association of Securities Dealers,
    77
National Bank Act of 1863, 357, 361
    and branch banking, 359
National Bank of Belgium, 224
National banks
    compared to state banks, 357
    number of, 358
    regulation of, 361–63
National Bureau of Economic Research,
    Business Cycle Dating Committee,
    530
National Credit Union Administration, 261,
    378
National Credit Union Share Insurance
    Fund, 378
National Housing Act of 1934, 369
National income, 196–97
    and changes in fiscal policy, 530–34
    collective and variable, 138
    Keynesian model, 524–36
    market for goods and services, 524–36
    theory of determinants, 523–24
National Income and Product Accounts,
    195, 618
National Monetary Commission, 224
National product, 196–9–7
National product identity, 194–96
National savings, 707–9
Nationwide branch banking, 359–60
Natural rate of output, 582
Natural rate of unemployment, 631
Neal, Stephen L., 240
Negotiable CDs, 81, 102
Nelson, Charles, 519
Neoclassical synthesis, 600
Net creditor nation, 32
Net debtor nation, 32
Net debtor position, 88
Net domestic product, 195
Net exports, 195
    exogenous increase in, 528
    increase in aggregate demand, 534
Net marginal revenue curve, 392–93
Net marginal revenue of deposits, 135
Net technical factors affecting monetary
    base, 168

Net technical factors affecting reserves, 149, 300
Net worth
  on balance sheet, 84
  of banks, 385
Neutrality of money, 210–11, 597–98, 616–17
New classicists, 605–6
  policy ineffectiveness proposition, 614–17
  policy prescriptions, 622–25
New financial environment, 92
  credit crunch, 113–14
  deposit rate regulation, 133–34
  thrift crisis, 112–13
New Keynesians, 605–6
  policy prescriptions, 622–25
  on wage rigidities, 620–21
Newman, Peter, 167, 190, 351
New York Stock Exchange, 77
New York Times, 242
New Zealand, 243
Nichols, Dorothy, 328
Nikkei stock average, 74, 217
Niskanen, William A., 646 n
Nixon, Richard M., 637, 638, 696
Nixon administration
  end of gold standard, 689
  managed float since, 689–90
No-load funds, 417
Nominal GDP, 13, 193
  equal to velocity-indexed money supply, 274, 329, 336–41
  and equation of exchange, 331–32
  experience in 1990s, 346–49
  and velocity of circulation, 331
Nominal Gross Domestic Product, and quantity of money, 14
Nominal interest rate, 57–58
  and expected inflation, 213
  and inflation, 271
Nominal interest rate parity, 685
Nominal wage, 197
  versus real wage, 605
  rigidities, 619–20
Nomura Securities Company, 34
Nonaccelerating inflation rate of unemployment, 654
Nonborrowed reserves, 149–50, 151–53, 269, 474
  and aggregate demand shifts, 578
  and currency in circulation, 484–85
  Fed actions to increase, 476–77
  and money supply, 158
  operating target, 277, 281–82
Noncontrolled factors affecting reserves, 149
Nondepository financial institutions, 22–23, 355–56
  finance companies, 412–13

Nondepository financial institutions—*Cont.*
  insurance companies, 419–23
  investment banks, brokers, and dealers, 425–26
  mutual funds, 415–19
  pension funds, 423–25
Nondeposit transactions, 324
Nondiversifiable risk, 123
Nondurable consumer goods, 21
Nonpersonal time deposits, 81
Nonsterilized intervention, 675–76
Nontransactions balances, 9–11
Nontransactions deposits, 162
Norway, 244
Notation, 203
NOW accounts, 81
  origin of, 100–101

O

Off-balance-sheet activities, 109
Office of Business Economics of the Commerce Department, 193
Office of the Comptroller of the Currency, 38
Office of Thrift Supervision, 261, 376
Oil price increases, 215–16, 596, 638
Okun, Arthur, 244, 650
Okun's law, 649, 650
Old financial environment, 92
  deposit rates, 133–34
  rise and fall of, 93–95
Open bank assistance, 369–71
Open economy
  BP curve, 699–701
  equilibrium in ISLM-BP model, 703
  IS curve, 697–98
  ISLM-BP graph, 697
  LM curve, 698–99
  perfect and imperfect capital mobility, 701–2
Open-end funds, 416
Open market debt, 72–76
Open market operations, 9, 151–52, 226
  defensive/dynamic, 269, 294–95
  and deposit contraction, 319
  and interest rates, 186–87
  in ISLM model, 548–50
  monetary policy and, 269
  and money supply, 322, 476–77
  and money supply curve, 161
  multiple deposit creation, 312–19
  policy shifts, 297
  processes, 292–97
  and rates of return, 510–14
  and shifts in money supply, 176–77
Open market securities, 34
Operating expenses, 27–28
Operating targets, 268
  federal funds rate, 276–78, 286–87
  and intermediate targets, 276–87

Operating targets—*Cont.*
  reserves, 278–85
Opportunity cost
  of deposits, 132–34
  of money, 95
Options market, 107–8
Organization of Petroleum Exporting Countries, 638
Other assets, 87–88, 149, 383, 698–99
Other checkable deposits, 9, 100–101
Other liabilities, 149
Other liabilities plus net worth, 87–88
Other sources and uses of reserves, Federal Reserve float, 484
Output
  during Great Depression, 641–42
  impact of tax cuts, 618
  natural rate of, 582
Output of goods and services, 193
Overnight repurchase agreements, 103
Over-the-counter securities, 77
Own rate of return, 125

P

Painless disinflation, 615–16
Paper gold, 306
Paper money
  fiat money, 7–8
  fractionally backed, 6–7
  unit of account, 5
Parry, Robert, 661
Partlan, John, 352
Paulus, John, 466
Payoff method, 369
Pension Benefit Guaranty Corporation, 425
Pension fund reserves, 422, 424
Pension funds, 22–23, 423
  regulation of, 424–25
  size and assets, 424
  types, 424
Perceived price level, 606–8
Perfect capital mobility, 701–2
Perry, George L., 603
Persian Gulf War, 596
Personal cash loans, 413
Phelps, Edmund S., 543, 601, 605–6, 608–9, 618–20, 621
Phillips, A. W., 649
Phillips, Susan, 227, 246
Phillips curve
  Kennedy and Reagan administrations, 656
  movements along, 650–51
  origin of, 648–49
  policy implications, 653–56
  shifts of, 651–52
  simple derivation of, 649–52
  vertical long-run, 652–56
Pierce, James, 374 n, 381
Pigou, A. C., 205 n, 330 n

Pigou effect, 205 n
Plain-vanilla bonds, 74
Planned (or estimated) velocity, 333–34, 431
Planned velocity-indexed money supply, 340–41
Plant and equipment, 28 n, 196
Plaza Accord, 698–90
Plosser, Charles, 617 n
Point-of-sale terminals, 110
Policy directives, 233–35
    interpreting, 285–86
Policy ineffectiveness proposition, 605–6, 614–15
    empirical investigations, 616
    and imperfect information, 617–19
    legacy of rational expectations, 625–27
    painless disinflation, 615–16
    and price rigidities, 621
    and wage rigidities, 619–21
Political business cycle, 242 n
Political independence of the Fed, 241–42
Poole, William, 351, 495, 562 n
Porter, Richard D., 130, 137, 146, 351, 468
Portfolio choice, 121–23, 442–43
    and inflation, 212
Portfolio imbalances, 103–5
Portfolio management
    decision changes, 480–82
    by Federal Reserve banks, 232
Portfolio theory, 122
Potential level of production, 276 n
Potential output, 582
Pragmatic monetary targeters, 339–41
Precautionary demand, 430
    definition, 434
    Keynes on, 442
Preferred habitat hypothesis, 503–5
Premium, 52
Present value
    calculating, 49–50
    definition, 49
Price deflator, 194
Price-level effect, 203–4, 209–10
Price levels, 13, 193–94
    and aggregate demand curve, 574–79
    changes in, 485–86
    demand-pull inflation, 631–33
    Friedman-Phelps fooling model, 608–9
    in ISLM model, 574
    linkage of economic sectors, 201–4
    and quantity of money, 15
    and real wage, 606–8
    in Russia, 15
Price rigidities, 619, 621
Prices
    foreign and domestic, 680–81
    inverse relation to interest rate, 52–53
    law of one price, 683
    money and economic activity, 13–15

Price stability, 241
Primary dealers, 151, 292
Primary market, 44–45
Primary securities, 44–45
Prime rate, 80
Principal-agent problem, 377, 426
Principle of diminishing marginal product of labor, 584
Principles of excess supply/demand, 173
Problem bank, 365
Problem loans, 406
Producer durable goods, 22
Profit, 197
    gross, 27–28
    retained, 27
Profit maximization, 391–92
    and credit crunch of 1990s, 405–7
    movement along supply curve, 582–84
Property/casualty insurance companies, 423
Public
    balance sheet equation, 119–21
    changes in money demand behavior, 480–85
    changes in payment habits, 484–85
    and financial innovation, 95–98
    IS sector shocks, 561
    LM sector shocks, 558–61
    portfolio decision changes, 480–82
Public demand for money, 323
Purchase and assumption method, 369
Purchasing power, 5–6, 15
    international, 681
    in Russia, 15
Purchasing power parity, 664, 683–84
Pure expectations hypothesis, 499–502

Q

Q-ratio
    and investment, 528
    and stock market, 514–16
Quantity of money
    controlling, 8–9
    and interest rates, 12, 13–14, 174–75
    as intermediate target, 271–76
    purchasing power, 15
    and reserves operating target, 279–85
    stocks and flow, 24–25
Quantity theory equation, 336–39, 341
    experience in 1980s, 341–46
    experience in 1990s, 346–49
Quantity theory of money, 273–74
    early approach, 431–33
    market forces behind, 335–36
    modern treatment, 444–45
    and monetary aggregates targeting, 336–41
    money-moving/money-sitting versions, 433
Quarterly Model, 229

R

Ramirez, Maria Fionni, 296
Rate of profit, 197
Rate of return, 12
    approximating, 46–48
    asset choice theory, 121–23
    on competing assets, 125
    formula, 50
    open market operations and, 510–14
    present and future value, 49–50
    sources, 45–46
    timing of receipts and expenditures, 48–49
Rational expectations
    definition, 605
    legacy of, 625–27
    in Lucas supply curve, 609–10
    and policy ineffectiveness proposition, 614–15
Reagan, Ronald W., 227, 242, 557, 618, 639, 648, 696
Reagan administration
    economic policies, 645, 646–47
    and Phillips curve, 656
Reagan-Volcker recession, 639
Real assets, 12
Real business cycle school, 617
Real exchange rate, 664
    definition, 682
    mechanics of, 682–83
    during nineteen-eighties, 687
    and purchasing power parity, 683–84
    and real interest rate parity, 685–86
Real GDP, 13, 193
Real income
    aggregate demand and changes in, 528–30
    changes in money supply, 486
    ISLM graph, 541
    linkage of economic sectors, 201
    variability versus interest rate variability, 567–68
Real-income effect on interest rates, 201, 550
Real interest rate, 57–58
    and expected inflation, 213
    financial indicator, 274–76
Real interest rate parity, 664
    impact during 1980s, 687
    and real exchange rate, 685–86
Real money balances, factors affecting demand for, 474
Real sector of economy, 191
    definition, 192–93
    foreign exchange, 197–98
    linkages to financial sector, 198–204
    national product and income, 196–97
    national product identity, 194–96
    output of goods and services, 193
    price level, 193–94

Real sector of economy—*Cont.*
  shocks and monetary policy, 564
Real wages, 197
  countercyclical, 620
  implicit contract for, 620
  and labor supply, 606–8
  versus nominal wages, 605
  rigidities, 620–21
Receipts, timing of, 48–49
Recession
  and aggregate demand, 531
  and budget deficit, 30
  Carter-Volcker, 638–39
  default risk, 507
  definition, 530
  of 1982, 329–30
  of 1990–91, 216
Record of Policy Actions of the FOMC,
  234
Rediscounting, 254
Redistributive effects of inflation, 658
Regan, Donald, 234
Regulation A, 253
Regulation Q, 93, 98, 103, 113, 137
Regulatory climate, 137–38
Regulatory forbearance, 371
Reichsbank, 224
Reischauer, Robert, 288
Relative price of imports, 682
Remolona, Eli M., 428
Repurchase agreements, 96–97, 103
Required reserves, 82
Reserve balances with the Federal Reserve,
  8–9
Reserve management
  borrowed reserves, 398–401
  decision changes, 482–84
  definition, 397
  excess reserves, 401–3
Reserve pressure, 292
Reserve requirement, deposit market and
  changes in, 461
Reserve requirement ratio, 39, 136–37, 228
  changes in, 479–80
  and money supply, 159–60, 322
  as policy tool, 269
Reserves
  borrowed and nonborrowed, 151–53
  demand for, 153–54
  deposits supported by, 155–57, 320–21
  fractionally backed, 8–9
  individual technical factors affecting,
    303–7
  other sources and uses, 323
  sources and uses of reserves statement,
    292, 297–307
  supply of, 148–53, 299–300
  technical factors affecting, 149
Reserves constraint, 154–55
  tracking, 156

Reserves maintenance period, 293 n
Reserves operating target, 278–85
Resolution Trust Corporation, 376
Restrictive covenants, 389
  in insurance, 420
Revenue, of banks, 386
Revenue Act of 1964, 646
Ricardian equivalence theorem, 617, 618,
  647
Ricardo, David, 618
Rice, Emmett, 227
Rigid monetary targeters, 339–41
Riksbank, Sweden, 224
Risk; *see also* Interest rate risk
  adverse selection, 387–88
  default, 56–57
  diversifiable, 122–23
  of inflation, 57–58
  and insurance, 419
  and liquidity, 69
  market, 55–56
  moral hazard, 388–89
  nondiversifiable, 123
  relative, 128
Risk averse investors, 122, 443
Risk-based capital asset ratios, 36–68
Risk-based deposit insurance premiums,
  372, 373–74
Risk premium, 503–5
Risk reduction, with financial
  intermediaries, 37
Rock, James M., 629
Role of financial go-betweens, 25, 33–39
Role of monetary policy makers, 25, 39
Role of surplus or deficit units, 25–32
Roley, V. Vance, 284 n
Romer, David, 621 n
Roosa, Robert V., 294 n
Roosevelt, Franklin D., 368–69
Rose, Peter S., 116
Russia, 5
  hyperinflation, 660
Russian ruble, 6
  decline in purchasing power, 15

S
Sachs, Jeffrey, 15
SAFER index, 242
SAIF; *see* Savings Association Insurance
  Fund
Sales finance companies, 412
Sallie Mae; *see* Student Loan Marketing
  Association
Salomon Brothers, 61
Samuelson, Paul A., 290, 600
Sarbanes, Paul, 238, 289
Sargent, Thomas J., 614, 616, 617
SAS; *see* Short-run aggregate supply curve
Savings, national versus private, 708

Savings accounts, substitutes for traditional,
  101–3
Savings and loan associations, 22; *see also*
  Thrifts
  crisis, 112–13
  failures, 376
  and FIRREA, 376–77
  principal-agent problem, 377
  structure and regulation, 374–77
Savings Association Insurance Fund, 369,
  377
Savings banks, 377
Schultz, Frederick, 227
Schultze, Charles L., 220, 603
Schwartz, Anna J., 18, 93 n, 209, 213, 247,
  337 n, 640
Screening, 388
SDRs; *see* Special drawing rights
Seasonal credit, 149, 257
Secondary market, 44–45
  for capital stock, 77
  negotiable CDs, 102
  for student loans, 71
Secondary securities, 44–45
Sector funds, 416
Securities, 12; *see also* Bonds *and* Debt
  securities
  debt versus equity, 26
  default risk, 56–57
  default risk structure of interest rates,
    506–9
  demand for, 182–84
  differential tax treatment, 509
  direct, 33
  divisibility, 60
  face value, 47
  held by banks, 383
  indirect, 35
  inflation risk, 57–58
  intermediate-term, 44
  junk bonds, 57
  liquidity, 58–60
  long-term, 44
  marketability, 44–45
  market risk, 55–56
  maturity, 43–44
  open market, 34
  rate of return, 45–54
  short-term, 44
  supply of, 184–85
  terminology, 51–53 .
  and term structure of interest rates,
    497–505
  zero coupon, 60–63
Securities Amendments Act of 1975, 426
Securities and Exchange Commission
  function, 426
  and mutual funds, 418
Securities firms, 426

Securities market, loanable funds theory, 182–83
Securitization, 80
  globalization of, 109
  loan-backed securities, 108–9
Security dealers, 426
  primary market, 151
Seger, Martha, 227
Segmented market hypothesis, 505
Seidman, William, 364
Sellon, Gordon H., 428
Senate Committee on Banking, Housing, and Urban Affairs, 236, 360, 406
Shadow Open Market Committee, 240; see also Federal Open Market Committee
Share drafts, 378
Shares, 378
Sharpe, William, 130, 444 n
Sheffrin, Steven M., 629
Shiller, Robert, 627
Shirking, 620–21
Shoe-leather costs of inflation, 659
Short-horizon investor, 503–5
Short-run aggregate supply curve, 582–86
  combined with long-run curve, 586–90
  shifts in, 584–86
Short-run monetary aggregates targeting, 338–49
Short-term interest rates, 271
  Fed increase in, 242–45
Short-term securities, 44
Simple deposits multiplier, 157
Simpson, Thomas D., 18, 95 n
Small, David H., 130, 137, 146, 468, 616
Small country case, 701
Small-saver certificates, 102–3
Social Security, 424
Solow, Robert, 600, 601, 620, 648
Sources and uses of bank funds, 383
Sources and uses of reserves, changes in, 484
Sources and uses of reserves statement, 292, 297–307
Spain, 243
Special drawing rights, 306
Speculation demand
  definition, 434
  modern treatment of, 442–44
Spencer, Roger W., 122, 447
Spot interest rates, 498–99
Spot market, 45
Spread
  between bid and asked price, 54
  in exchange rates, 677–78
Square-root rule, 440–42
Stable demand function for money, 445
Stagecoach Funds, 417
Stagflation, 633
Standard and Poor's, 57, 58, 73, 506
Standby letters of credit, 109

State banks
  compared to national banks, 357
  number of, 358
  regulation of, 361–63
States
  banking commissions, 38, 361–62
  regulation of finance companies, 415
Stein, Herbert, 220, 662
Sterilized intervention, 675–76
Sticky wages, 605
Stiglitz, Joseph E., 200 n
Stigum, Marcia, 91, 410
Stock market
  impact on investment, 528
  Q-ratio, 514–16
Stock market crash of 1929, 639–42
Stock market crash of 1987, 286, 642
  Federal Reserve response, 182
Stock of money, 24–25
Store of value, 5–6
STRIPS, 61
Strong, Benjamin, 262
Student Loan Marketing Association, 71
Summers, Lawrence H., 243
Sun Microsystems, 123
Super-NOW accounts, 81, 100–101
Supply
  of foreign exchange, 671–72
  of securities, 184–85
Supply and demand
  excess, 173
  foreign and domestic goods, 680–81
Supply curve
  for deposits, 449, 454
Supply of deposits
  definition, 391
  marginal cost, 393
  marginal rule, 392
  net marginal revenue, 392–93
Supply of deposits curve, 394–95
  shifts in, 395–97
Supply of real money balances, 202–3
Supply of total reserves, 149
  changes in, 150–53
Supply shocks
  and inflation, 634–35
  during 1970s, 637–38
  oil price increases, 215–16
Surplus unit
  definition, 25
  firms, 27–28
  government, 29–30
  households, 26–27
Surplus units, foreign participants, 30–32
Survey of Current Business, 665
Sutch, Richard C., 503
Suzuki, Yoshio, 220
Sweden, 244
Swiss National Bank, 224, 243

T
T-account, 84
Tangible assets, 12
Tax cuts
  and aggregate demand, 532
  effect of, 554–55
  impact on output, 618
  Kennedy years, 646
  under Reagan, 647
Taxes
  impact of inflation, 659
  and interest rates, 509
Tax-exempt securities, municipals, 72
Tax increases, impact on output, 643–44
Tax Reform Act of 1986, 47
Taylor, John B., 619–20, 621
Teachers Insurance and Annuity Association College Retirement Fund, 424
Technical factors affecting reserves, 149
Technological progress, 109–11
Technology, and regulatory climate, 137–38
Technology and regulatory index, 393
  changes in, 482–83
  deposit market and change in, 459–61
  Japan, 483
Teeters, Nancy, 227
Term insurance, 420–21
Term repurchase agreements, 103
Terms of trade, 682
Term structure of interest rates, 56
  definition, 497
  and forward rates, 498–99
  liquidity preference hypothesis, 502–3
  preferred habitat hypothesis, 503–5
  pure expectations hypothesis, 499–502
  segmented market hypothesis, 505
  yield curve, 497–98
Texaco, 73
Theories, 330
3-6-3 rule, 92
Thrifts, 22
  bail-out, 30
  compared to commercial banks, 357
  crisis of 1980s, 112–13
  disintermediation, 102
  failures, 354
  old financial environment, 92
  purpose of, 375
  structure and regulation, 375–78
Throop, Adrian W., 546
TIGRS, 61
Time deposits, 81
  innovations in, 101–3
Time drafts, 76
Tobin, James, 18, 69, 116, 122, 123 n, 130, 200 n, 220, 290, 332 n, 351, 374 n, 380, 430, 442, 444, 445, 447, 514–16, 519, 587, 600, 648, 662
  on transactions demand, 435–38

Tobin's identity, 515
Too-big-to-fail policy, 371–72
Tootell, Geoffrey M. B., 266
Total capital gains, 47
Total domestic nonfinancial debt, 272
Total monetary base
   demanded, 168–69
   supplied, 168
Total reserves, 149
   changes in supply, 150–53
Tract on Monetary Reform (Keynes), 434
Trade deficits, 665, 707–9
Trading Desk
   currency outstanding, 306–7
   multiple deposit creation, 313–19
   operations, 292–97
Transaction costs, 59
   and divisibility, 60
Transactions balances, 9
Transactions demand
   Baumol's explanation, 438–42
   definition, 434
   Tobin's explanation, 435–38
Transactions deposits, 101, 162
Transaction services, innovations in,
   110–11
Transactions medium; *see* Medium of
   exchange
Transactions motive, 430
Transfer payments, 29
   aggregate demand and increase in,
   532–33
Transfers, 436–38
Transitory inflation, 631
Travelers checks, 9 n
Treasury bills, 69
Treasury bonds, 69
   reducing supply of, 504
Treasury Department, 23
   bond stripping, 61
   cash holdings, 303–4
   checking account, 258–59
   gold stock, 305–6
   intervention in currency markets, 234
   proposal to centralize regulation, 364
Treasury notes, 69
Treasury securities
   coupon equivalent yield, 62–63
   held by foreigners, 73
   open market operations, 151–52
   tracking rates, 54, 64
   types, 68–70
Treatise on Money (Keynes), 434
Trips, 436
Truth-in-lending laws, 415
Tsiang, S. C., 190
Twin deficits, 707, 709; *see also* Budget
   deficit *and* Trade deficits
Tyson, Laura, 288

U

Ultimate goals, 267
   intermediate targets and, 270–76
   from policy instruments to, 268–70
Uncertainty, and speculation demand,
   442–44
Underground economy, 143
Unemployment
   during Carter administration, 638
   costs of, 657
   in Great Depression, 641–42
   and inflation, 223–25, 648–57
   involuntary, 587, 620
   natural rate of, 631
Uniform capital requirements, 113–14
United States
   debt binge, 79
   economic policy, 215–17
   net debtor position, 32, 88
   transactions with foreign countries,
   30–32
United States savings bonds and notes, 70
Unit of account, 5
University of Michigan, 531
Unwanted excess reserves, 311–12
Uses of bank funds, 383
Usury laws, 415

V

Value and Capital (Hicks), 498
Value of money, 15
Van Horne, James C., 41, 503 n, 519
Variable-rate asset or liability, 104
Variable-rate mortgages, 107
Variables, influencing interest rates, 475–76
Vault cash, 8
Velocity-indexed money supply, 273–74,
   332, 349
   experience of 1980s, 341–46
   and nominal GDP, 329, 336–41
Velocity of circulation, 273
   Cambridge k, 330–31
   equation for, 335
   factors affecting, 334–35
   planned or estimated, 333–34
   recent history, 332
Vertical long-run Phillips curve, 652–56
Vesting, 424–25
Vietnam War, economic performance
   during, 636–37
Volcker, Paul A., 213, 220, 227, 234, 241,
   242, 638–39, 690, 695

W

Wage and price controls, 638
Wage rigidities, 619–21
Wages, 197
   efficiency, 620–21
   increases during 1970s, 638
   real versus nominal, 605

Wallace, Neil, 614, 616, 617
Wallich, Henry C., 167
Wall Street Journal, 12, 48, 54, 64, 69, 74,
   149, 155, 156, 242, 288, 296, 301,
   308, 364, 515–16, 619
   tracking default risk premiums, 508
   tracking exchange rates, 668, 669
   tracking yield curve, 498
Walsh, Carl E., 531
Walt Disney Company, 73
Wartime economic performance, 635–37
Washington Power Supply System, 509
Wealth
   and asset demand, 126–27
   asset types, 12
   and deposit demand, 138–39
Weidenbaum, Murray L., 646 n, 648 n, 662
Weiner, Stuart E., 66
Weiss, Andrew, 200 n
Welfare costs of inflation, 658–59
Wells Fargo Bank, 417
Wenninger, John, 116, 130, 146, 352
Wessel, David, 288, 504
White, Lawrence J., 381, 388 n
Whitehouse, Michael A., 262
Whole life insurance, 421
Wilcox, James A., 640
Wire transfer of funds, 252
Workers
   efficiency wages, 620–21
   Friedman-Phelps fooling model, 608–9
   imperfect information, 617–19
   implicit contracts, 620
   knowledge of ISLM model, 614–15
   and policy ineffectiveness proposition,
   614–15
   rational expectations, 609–10
   real wage and price level, 606–8
   rigidity in nominal wages, 619–20
World War I, economic performance
   during, 635
World War II, economic performance
   during, 635–36
Wulfeskuhler, Kurt C., 428

Y–Z

Yellen, Janet, 227
Yellen, Janet L., 629
Yield curve, 497–98
   and expectations hypothesis, 501–2
Yield on a discount basis, 61
   calculation, 63
Yield to maturity, 50
   definition, 51
   zero coupon bonds, 61–63
Zero coupon securities, 60–61
Zombies, 376